W9-AEX-691

The Modern American College

Responding to the New Realities of Diverse Students and a Changing Society

Arthur W. Chickering and Associates

Foreword by
Nevitt Sanford

The Modern American College

 Jossey-Bass Publishers

San Francisco • Washington • London • 1981

THE MODERN AMERICAN COLLEGE
Responding to the New Realities
of Diverse Students and a Changing Society
by Arthur W. Chickering and Associates

Copyright © 1981 by: Jossey-Bass Inc., Publishers
433 California Street
San Francisco, California 94104
&
Jossey-Bass Limited
28 Banner Street
London EC1Y 8QE

Library of Congress Cataloging in Publication Data

Main entry under title:

The modern American college.

      Includes bibliographical references and indexes.
      1. Universities and colleges—United States.
2. College students—United States. 3. Continuing
education—United States. I. Chickering,
Arthur W., 1927-
LA227.3.M63   378.73   80-8010
ISBN 0-87589-466-6

Manufactured in the United States of America

JACKET DESIGN BY WILLI BAUM

FIRST EDITION

Code 8026

The Jossey-Bass
Series in Higher Education

Contents

Contents

Foreword

Nevitt Sanford

In 1962, twenty-nine of my colleagues and I published *The American College,* a set of studies organized around the idea that the development of the student as a person is the central aim of education and that all the resources of our colleges should be put into the service of that aim. Just a few years earlier, however, Sputnik had been launched. In response, America was accenting science and technology and "national strength," and the traditional liberal idea of education that we sought to support was already being put to one side.

Today, that idea is seldom discussed. But this, it seems, is not so much because of national needs as because of students' personal insecurity about employment in an economy oversupplied with graduates. Most freshmen arrive at college with vocational aims clearly in mind. We educators, responsive to the market, hardly ever bring the idea of liberal education to the attention of the general public. We give the impression that vocational or professional training is the only purpose of college education. For example, the only discussion of higher education that I have seen on television was a talk show in which two authorities on college questioned Carolyn Bird about her best-seller, *The Case Against College* (1975). Neither of them pointed out that education has values over and above the economic one; nobody mentioned what these values are. The only question was whether it is really true that graduation from college no longer assures one a high income.

Nonetheless, in the following pages, Arthur Chickering boldly states that "the overarching purpose of our colleges and universities should be to encourage and enable intentional developmental change throughout the life cycle." I heartily agree. I am delighted with the way he and his coauthors marshall the arguments in favor of this proposition, and I hope this book promotes the proposition even more successfully than did *The American College.*

Changes Since *The American College*

The American College was well received, on the whole, by part of the higher education community—researchers in the behavioral sciences, professors of higher education, student service professionals, and administrators—and the same was true of its much more manageable and briefer version, *College and Character,* published in 1964. It has been my impression, however, that these volumes received little attention from professors in disciplines other than education. For example, during the 1960s I spoke, lectured, and conducted workshops at many colleges and universities on education for human development. At each place, I met a few kindred spirits, but for the most part I encountered indifference and some resistance in the Freudian sense of the word. The worst trouble was that very few people would discuss the developmental uses of the curriculum. Everyone agreed that it was important to do more for students than to stuff their heads with facts and principles, but few cared to hear anything that, if accepted, might threaten their interest in research, in advancing their disciplines, or in teaching graduate students.

Today there is evidence that professors in general are more open to discussing the approach to higher education set forth in *The American College* (1962) and advocated here by Arthur Chickering and his colleagues; this book offers an example. For *The American College,* Joseph Katz and I wrote a chapter, "The Curriculum in the Perspective of the Theory of Personality Development," in which we discussed, among other things, ways in which the study of history, literature and the arts, philosophy and religion, mathematics, and natural science could assist students in their self-development. We did not anticipate that professors in the arts and sciences would familiarize themselves with our theory and research and then be willing to write about the interconnections of this material and their own work as teachers. But this is exactly what Arthur Chickering's associates have done in this volume. Here professors from a wide variety of disciplines have collaborated with social scientists and educators in producing a book about personality development in colleges and universities. Their collaboration has been genuine and thoroughgoing; they read one another's draft chapters and discussed them as a group in a two-day workshop before completing them. As a result, this book contains thirteen authoritative chapters by professors in the arts, sciences, and professions, in which these authors not only discuss the implications for their disciplines of knowledge about human development but also show how the study of their disciplines can contribute to human development. In fourteen other chapters, academic administrators and student personnel professionals perform the same service for their own specialties. This feat of interdisciplinary collaboration is the most impressive feature of an impressive book.

Probably this feature owes something to changing times as well as to Arthur Chickering's resourcefulness as a recruiter. It seems clear that there is greater receptivity to the human development idea among academic people now than there was in the 1950s and 1960s. Apparently, this is due in considerable part to the spread of faculty development programs in the intervening years. A new perspective on faculty renewal and professional growth, in which faculty development was seen as a special case of human development, grew out of work at the Wright Institute in Berkeley beginning in 1968, when graduate students under my direction began obtaining comprehensive life history interviews from professors. Beginning around 1970, several large foundations, recognizing that continuing retrenchment in higher education would require institutions to make do for a long time with the faculty they now have, began making substantial grants to colleges and universities for programs designed to help their faculty become more effective. There ensued a steady flow of books and articles by specialists on the topic (Sanford,

1971-1972; Brown and Shukraft, 1971; Freedman and others, 1979). *Change* magazine played a significant role in making this material available to a large audience of administrators and professors (Group for Human Development in Higher Education, 1974). Today, most colleges and universities are actively involved in programs of faculty development, and it is clear that sophisticated programs based on adequate theory of adult development can enable faculty members to see themselves and their students in a new perspective and thus change their approaches to education.

Further, it is evident that the "human potential movement" has touched more than a few faculty members. Even the faddish aspects of this movement have helped spread the word that we, too, can develop ourselves more fully. There is no question but that professors who think and talk about their own lives and about possible changes of direction in them will be increasingly open to the idea of student development.

Most important, surely, in accounting for this change has been the expanding body of knowledge about adult development in educational settings. Faculty tend to be skeptical about new ideas, and arrogance among them is not uncommon, but they can almost always be persuaded by facts. Unfortunately, perhaps, *The American College* contained far more ideas than demonstrated propositions. I can recall, when I try hard enough, that when talking with faculty in the 1950s and 1960s there were times when I could not successfully back up one or another of my plausible propositions with research data. Of course, *The American College* did contain more than a few reports of research, much of it by the authors themselves. But its primary aim was to establish higher education as a field of inquiry and to underline its importance. It mapped a territory and set up outposts of evidence. Now, the map is being filled in; the outposts are growing towns, quickly becoming interconnected; and the knowledge that has been rapidly accumulating in recent years has outdated much of our earlier work. Thus last year, when Joseph Axelrod and I were preparing a revised edition of *College and Character* (1979), we were happy to find that several chapters, all reporting research, had to be completely rewritten. Higher education has become established as a field of inquiry. Any doubt about that will be dispelled by the appearance of this present volume.

Perhaps nothing illustrates the growth of knowledge within the field so much as Arthur Chickering's organization of this book around the concept of life cycle development, in contrast to the focus of *The American College* on students aged seventeen to twenty-one. Today it seems obvious that if people can develop at age twenty, there is no reason why they cannot develop at thirty or fifty, but dealing with educational issues involving the middle-aged and the elderly has required a major shift in the thinking of personality theorists and the research of other psychologists. When my colleagues and I began our studies that led to *The American College,* it was generally assumed by theorists in the tradition of Freud and Henry Murray that the personality was formed in childhood and largely set by adolescence. Thus, in *The Authoritarian Personality* (1950), T. W. Adorno, Else Frenkel-Brunswik, Daniel Levinson, and I marshalled much evidence in support of the hypothesis that enthnocentrism and susceptibility to fascist propaganda were based in a largely unconscious pattern of personality that had its roots in childhood. Accordingly—and, in retrospect, unfortunately—we made no mention of education at the college level as a possible countermeasure. In 1951, a group of us at the Institute of Personality Assessment and Research of the University of California, Berkeley, carried on a comprehensive study in which we sought to predict levels of creativity, professional promise, and personal soundness in graduate students on the basis of personality and background factors. Yet it never occurred to us to ask what was the impact on these students' creativity, promise, and personality of their experience in graduate school. Only when, in our subsequent studies of students at Vassar, we began to observe that not just attitudes and values but personality itself changed in college, did we realize we had a problem: how to account for these changes without abandoning the traditional psychodynamic orientation toward childhood. Other theorists such as Erikson (1950) and White (1952) were beginning to question the traditional outlook as well, and I found that, without neglecting the theory of unconscious processes or my psychodynamic preferences, I also needed to get away from psychoanalytic reductionism. I have now come to conceive of personality as an open system, and I believe there are no dispositions of personality that cannot be changed through education, provided we know enough about these dispositions and the conditions and processes of their change. For example, although authoritarianism in personality still seems to me to be largely determined before a young person enters college, I now believe, in contrast to what I thought in 1950, that it can be reduced in college through educational procedures. The tack that Arthur Chickering and his associates take here in *The Modern American College* by defining the responsibility of college as adult development throughout the life cycle illustrates this considerable advance in our thinking about education. I endorse their concern for faculty and administrative development as well as student development as part of this responsibility.

Neglected Opportunities for Reform

This current volume may have better prospects for impact than did *The American College* for other reasons than the maturation of higher education research. The hardest thing about educational reform is finding, or arousing, the motivation for it. From my point of view, the 1960s were in this regard a time of missed opportunities.

Not everyone knows or recalls that the student protest movement of the 1960s and early 1970s, which had the potential for effecting reform, began as a protest against academic structures and procedures rather than government policies. During the summer of 1964, a group of liberal and radical students at Berkeley led by Bradford Cleveland met repeatedly with me to talk about educational reform. As members of a student organization called "Slate," they sought to stimulate alternatives to the "course-unit-credit system" and to the impersonality of Berkeley campus life. They had prepared literature for a mass rally on the opening day of school in order to persuade hundreds of students to call on professors with a view to enlisting their support for educational reform.

The day before the rally was scheduled to take place, a member of the group arrived at my door to say "All hell's busted loose." Berkeley's dean of students had issued a statement saying that the university regulation prohibiting on-campus recruitment for off-campus organizations was going to be enforced and that, hence, the signs and posters at Sather Gate had to be removed. What was to have been a rally for educational reform quickly became a demonstration for "free speech." The rest is history. Bradford Cleveland, whose activities accounted in large part for the extraordinary organization of the protesting students at Berkeley that fall, was soon replaced by Mario Savio. Then, after the vast expansion of United States forces in Viet Nam in 1965, the Free Speech movement was largely displaced by the movement of protest against the Viet Nam war and other ill-considered government actions.

As the protest movement spread to institutions all around the country and abroad, it came to be dominated by the political left. The educational left continued to be active, but it faced self-inflicted difficulties. Some willing and able leaders were available for assistance, but the rebelling students found it difficult to accept adult initiative of any kind. "Don't trust anyone over thirty" was the rallying cry. (Leo Lowenthal, then professor of sociology at Berkeley and now retired, said, "I can understand why they can't trust anyone over thirty, but I can't understand why they don't trust me!" I felt much the same way, especially after the Graduate School of the Wright Institute was started in 1969.) But a greater problem was the lack of educational leadership on the part of administrators and faculty. A student from another institution told me in 1965, "All you have to do is go to the dean's office and mumble something about Berkeley, and you get what you want." Many institutions found it expedient just to give students what they said they wanted. On very few campuses was there enough unity with respect to the purposes of education, or enough knowledge about how particular purposes might be achieved, so that those in power could use the free energy abundant among the students to good effect. What most students—apart from those of the extreme left politically— wanted was some attention to what they needed as developing human beings. But educational philosophy and the theory of human development was so foreign to those in charge that they too often found themselves at a loss as to what to do.

Looking back, one can see that both bad and good came out of student activism. On the negative side, there seems to be no doubt that standards were lowered, grading became easier, and curriculums became thinner as they proliferated. Inevitably, reaction set in. The public disenchantment with higher education, provoked not only by the students' political activities but also by their new life styles and counterculture attitudes, impaired the fund-raising activities of many institutions; together with the economic recession of 1974-75 this led to painful budget tightening throughout higher education. As usually happens in such circumstances, the arts and the humanities were the first to suffer.

Nevertheless, some constructive things were done. Students gained more freedom to shape their education—a blessing at least in places where they could find adult guidance regarding what to do with their lives. They also gained a larger voice in governance and a more secure role as students, most visible in provisions for due process and adjudication of grievances. Professors found themselves more willing to discuss educational issues and to say where they stood on them, having been forced to do so during crises on their campuses. Although some of the wounds they suffered then have not yet healed, many of them found they could speak with passion about education, and they got to know each other better in doing so. Now, questions of value seem to be more squarely faced than before, inside the classroom as well as at the faculty club.

In addition, institutions expressed greater openness to ethnic and other minorities. It is startling, even embarrassing, to think that just a little over ten years ago we in higher education were officially color-blind. Not only were there no Black Studies, there were no studies of blacks. Indeed, the word *black* was just beginning to supercede the word *negro.* And there was an almost universal tendency for professors to soften their criticism of the work of some students because they were black—a form of prejudice that they themselves recognized, as did their students. Once the way had been opened by black student activists, it became easier for Spanish-surnamed people, Asians, Native Americans, women, and homosexuals to get their fair share of what higher education had to offer. At times, it seemed that the campus was being divided into competing factions, with Black Studies, Chicano Studies, Asian Studies, and Women's Studies, and many have suggested that the intellectual content of these programs left much to be desired. But we must admit, I think, that because of them we know much more about these cultures and subcultures than we did before. It seems to me that this cultural factionalism is receding as ethnic prejudice diminishes and as more members of minority groups find places in the sun, and I hope that the awareness of cultural diversity that they have brought into our predominantly Anglo-Saxon institutions will remain. For it to do so, however, does not mean that courses or programs of study in all cultures represented by students and faculty must be offered. Instead, all professors should pay attention to the cultural backgrounds of their students and themselves, using examples and course content that show awareness of these backgrounds. They would find, I think, that many more than minority students would see these examples and content as relevant to their needs.

Besides these new programs, other curricular reforms occurred, including whole new institutions started both within and without existing colleges and universities. At Berkeley, a faculty committee under the chairmanship of Charles Muscatine (1968) issued a report that contained both a fine analysis of the conditions and needs of students and a series of well-conceived recommendations for academic reform, many of which were carried out and some of which are still in effect. Stanford instituted an excellent program of freshman seminars taught by scholars other than the regular undergraduate teaching faculty. Curricular changes were made at institutions all around the country, and I think it is fair to say that both *The American College* and *College and Character* played a role in more than a few of them, for each of these books contained many suggestions for reformers.

So, on balance, I believe the upheavals of the 1960s and 1970s did more good than harm. While many of the reforms instituted then have been eroded, some have endured and become part of the academic world. Today, Arthur Chickering and his colleagues have more likelihood of seeing the idea of human development become a unifying ideal for higher education than we did twenty years ago. But they unfortunately have a long way to go before colleges implement this ideal in all their activities.

Problems for the Future

One great trouble is that the idea of basing educational procedures on what we know about human development has hardly touched institutions in the forefront of the academic procession. Thus the 1978 Harvard report on its "Core Curriculum" is a major step backward in this regard from its "Redbook" of 1945. I have read various Harvard professors' comments on the "core" and have talked with some of them, and the only one who has shown any inclination to view the curriculum in the perspective of students' development has been David Riesman.

Similarly, in the Fall 1974 and Winter 1975 issues of *Daedalus,* eighty-five distinguished contributors representing the top of the academic pecking order—sixty-six of them from the Northeast and ten of the remaining nineteen from Stanford and Berkeley—addressed the topic, "American Higher Education: Toward an Uncertain Future." The group analyzed the troubles of the 1960s and the problems of the mid 1970s with intelligence and thoroughness, but nowhere in the seven hundred pages of the two issues was there mention of the notion of development as my colleagues and I had presented it in *The American College.* The only contributors whose essays suggested familiarity with work on human development were Donald Light, a former student of mine at Stanford, and, again, David Riesman, who contributed to *The American College.* One essayist, an assistant professor of economics at Harvard, seemed to epitomize the provinciality of the others by the major conclusion of her paper: "systematic high-quality investigation of educational questions is almost nonexistent" (*Daedalus,* 1974, p. 195).

Elite institutions were noticeably absent from Project Change in Liberal Education, a three-year effort sponsored by the Commission on Liberal Learning of the Association of American Colleges in cooperation with four other national associations, devoted to developing and evaluating alternatives to traditional patterns of teaching and learning in undergraduate liberal education. In fact, of the thirty institutions that participated, twelve were very obscure if not "invisible" colleges, eleven were among the already experimenting colleges, and the remaining seven were quite far back in the academic procession. Just as the idea of faculty development has spread throughout most of higher education but will only eventually penetrate the elite institutions—and then probably only under a different name—so is it the case that elite institutions seldom lead in implementing the ideas about student development generated by their own scholars.

Arthur Chickering and his colleagues have a problem of communication. It is not only that they face the intellectual snobbery of the elite institutions, but they must also get the attention of professors who are much too busy to read or think about educational issues: professors who feel that they must attend curriculum committee meetings largely to make sure that their disciplines and specialties are protected. Addressing the role of faculty in curriculum making in *The American College,* I stated that "when we have sufficient knowledge of the processes of higher education and sufficient conviction about purpose, it will be possible to find and to apply the incentives necessary to induce faculties to do what they know they ought to do" (Sanford, 1962, p. 20). The authors of this present volume have gone a long way toward synthesizing this needed knowledge, and they offer convincing evidence of purpose, but I must confess I am not as sanguine as I once was about inducing faculties to do what they know they ought to do.

Perhaps we really should not expect college faculties, acting as decision-making bodies, to be able to make a curriculum—as Beardsley Ruml suggested some years ago (1959). Indeed, my colleagues on *The American College* and I did not fully believe that colleges could be reformed from within. We thought that the best hope lay in informing the parents of college-bound youths and these youths themselves about what went on in our institutions of higher learning and impressing on them the values of general education. This still seems a good idea. Offering courses to high school students about what colleges are like, as the Carnegie Council has recommended in *Giving Youth a Better Chance* (1980), may in the long run lead to wider adoption of the ideas in this book than will efforts to persuade college curriculum committees to read it. Parents and prospective college students should know that if information about human development were applied to the curriculum, the costs of college could be made much less than they are now. Curricular offerings could be pruned, learning increased, and teaching made more effective.

The large foundations are likely to be less imaginative than one would hope in supporting programs or institutions that seek to implement the ideas of this book. Innovative and experimental programs have to rely mainly on "soft money," and most foundations have been willing to support new ventures only until they could prove their worth sufficiently to be included in an institution's regular budget, rather than as ongoing models of what should be undertaken elsewhere. In few instances have these ventures found regular funding. Faculty members can tolerate and even show interest in their colleagues' educational adventures—until they become threats to departmental budgets; most departments are not enthusiastic about interdisciplinary general education, hoping to pick up bright students early for concentration in their fields and specialties. With economic cutbacks, experimentation soon suffers. A shameful case in point was the Collegiate Seminar Program ("Strawberry Creek College") at Berkeley. This excellent program was kept going for five years, owing to the resourcefulness of its founders and the imaginativeness of some funding agencies, especially the federal Fund for the Improvement of Postsecondary Education, but finally had to fold up. I once asked the president of one of the large foundations why such obviously good programs could not be kept going until economic times improved. He said that he and his staff had thought about doing so, but it was clear that if they did the staff would soon be out of work.

Finally, a new wave of authoritarianism seems to be sweeping across America—one set in motion, in part, by the genuine liberations and the excesses of the 1960s and early 1970s. One result is likely to be increased government regulation of higher education, designed to emphasize "accountability" and standardization under the guise of "quality control," and reduced encouragement for experimentation. The authoritarian frame of mind is evident in the items contained in a recent, nationally distributed political document that is anti-abortion, anti-ERA, anti-gun control, and anti-Panama Canal Treaty, and pro-capital punishment, pro-jingoism in foreign affairs, and pro-family in a way that protests too much. We have far too many people in positions of national power or influence whose view of cultures radically different from our own is ethnocentric and whose thinking about the Soviet Union is essentially paranoid—both common features of authoritarianism. And a recent study (Gieser, 1980) suggests that authoritarianism in college freshmen is no less pronounced today than it was in the 1940s.

In this book, Arthur Chickering lists as goals of higher education intellectual competence, moral and ethical development, interpersonal competence, humanitarian concern, and other desirable individual characteristics. These are certainly high goals toward which we should continue to strive. But there are also states and conditions lower down on the developmental scale that very many people need to get over—indeed, must get over if these high goals are to be approached—and authoritarianism is one such condition. To reduce it among college students, let alone throughout American society, requires a full understanding of the nature of the phenomenon, including why such social and political attitudes as those just listed go together statistically and how the attitudes behind them are related dynamically. This in turn requires a theory that comes to grips with unconscious processes. Unconscious processes are obviously at work in faculty members and administrators as well as students, and I have been working on the problem of dealing with these processes through educational procedures since the 1950s (Sanford, 1956, 1980). From my perspective, the next great advance in our understanding of development will come from further effort to understand these unconscious processes. Thus I agree wholeheartedly with Arthur Chickering that our nation needs people who can think well of other peoples, particularly those in the Third World nations and in the other superpowers. But we need further theory-based study of the unconscious processes behind authoritarianism before we will be able to meet this need.

Arthur Chickering has been wise in choosing to be eclectic in regard to theory in this volume, for research, which he and his associates accent here, is usually tied to particular concepts and theories—and theorists. But among the various theorists given prominence here are some strange bedfellows—for example, Erikson and Kohlberg. Such theorists may be induced to lie down together for a time, on the ground that they all believe that adults can develop. Sooner or later, however, the differences among them will have to be further analyzed and dealt with. We will need to clarify what, if anything, each of the theories is good for, and we will need to deal with the perplexities, such as the unconscious, which each of them fudges over. What higher education needs most is a unified field theory of personality development in social systems. This will come in time. Until then, because of the excellence of its overall conception, the scope and richness of its content, and the distinction of its authors, this book will be a landmark in the field of educational inquiry.

References

Adorno, T. W., and others. *The Authoritarian Personality.* New York: Harper & Row, 1950.

Bird, C. *The Case Against College.* New York: Bantam, 1975.

Brown, J. W., and Shukraft, R. C. "Personality Development and Professional Practice in College and University Professors." Unpublished doctoral dissertation, Graduate Theological Union, Berkeley, Calif., 1971.

Carnegie Council on Policy Studies in Higher Education. *Giving Youth a Better Chance: Options for Education, Work, and Service.* San Francisco: Jossey-Bass, 1980.

Daedalus. Fall 1974, *103* (4) and Winter 1975, *104* (1).

Erikson, E. H. *Childhood and Society.* New York: Norton, 1950.

Freedman, M. B., and others. *Academic Culture and Faculty Development.* Berkeley, Calif.: Montaigne, 1979.

Gieser, M. "The Authoritarian Personality Revisited." Unpublished doctoral dissertation, the Wright Institute, Berkeley, Calif., 1980.

Group for Human Development in Higher Education. *Faculty Development in a Time of Retrenchment.* New Rochelle, N.Y.: Change Magazine Press, 1974.

Muscatine, C., and others. *Education at Berkeley: Report of the Select Committee on Education, Berkeley Division, Academic Senate.* Berkeley and Los Angeles: University of California Press, 1968.

Ruml, B. *Memo to a College Trustee: a Report on Financial and Structural Problems of the Liberal College.* New York: McGraw-Hill, 1959.

Sanford, N. "Personality Development During the College Years." *Personnel and Guidance Journal,* 1956, *35,* 74-80.

Sanford, N. (Ed.). *The American College: A Psychological and Social Interpretation of the Higher Learning.* New York: Wiley, 1962.

Sanford, N. (Ed.). *College and Character: A Briefer Version of "The American College."* New York: Wiley, 1964.

Sanford, N. "Academic Culture and the Teacher's Development." *Soundings,* Winter 1971-1972, pp. 357-371.

Sanford, N. *Learning After College.* Berkeley, Calif.: Montaigne, 1980.

Sanford, N., and Axelrod, J. (Eds.). *College and Character.* Berkeley, Calif.: Montaigne, 1979.

White, R. W. *Lives in Progress.* New York: Holt, 1952.

To Alan, Susan, Peri, and Nancy Chickering,
who have taught me so much about living and learning

Preface

This volume on *The Modern American College* stems from the fact that colleges and universities of the 1980s will have to deal with an increasingly diverse range of students—diverse in age, educational purposes, background and preparation, socioeconomic status, and ethnicity. If these institutions are to play a significant role in meeting the nation's educational needs in the future, they cannot limit their concern to students who are between the ages of 18 and 25, white, middle-class, and academically skilled. That group will continue to be a major focus of attention for some institutions, but major pressures for change will come from nontraditional groups of students new to higher education: those over 25 (who already outnumber students under 25), women with families, minority students, and students from nonacademic backgrounds.

To respond effectively to these new students, undergraduate education in the upcoming decades must be anchored in a sound understanding of them: their motives; their orientations toward family, work, and citizenship; the challenges they face; the competence and knowledge they require; and the ways they learn. We need conceptual handles to help us grasp the major dimensions of this diversity. Research concerning adult development and learning provides a rich source of concepts that can help us increase our working knowledge of the wide range of new students—and thus our capacity to meet their educational needs. The growing sophistication in research and theory concerning adult development opens the opportunity to apply new findings to the educational process. Organized presentation of key conceptual frameworks and their implications is needed to help narrow the gap between the ideals of education and the realities of its results. By understanding how students from 18 to 80 meet life cycle challenges and grow in terms of intellectual competence, ego development, moral and ethical development, humanitarian concern, interpersonal competence, capacity for intimacy, and professional development, educators can examine the potential contributions of various disciplines, areas of professional preparation, and educational practices. Program changes and professional development activities can be undertaken to address dimensions of adult development and at the same time respond to the more immediate educational needs of diverse students. Thus *The Modern American College* suggests a conceptual framework and a unifying purpose that can be the basis for needed change. Moreover, it goes well beyond theory by suggesting concrete modifications across a wide range of areas.

This perspective, as well as the specific suggestions that make clear its workability and significance, is pertinent to every policy maker, faculty member, administrator and student personnel professional throughout higher education. The implications reach into all aspects of college life and educational practice; they can be powerfully addressed by all disciplines and areas of professional preparation; they are influenced by institutional practices concerning administration, governance, professional development, and research. Since every college or university is a tight system of interacting parts, broad-based understanding is necessary if significant institutional development is to occur. All major segments of the educational community need to understand better how this knowledge can be translated, not only into long-range institutional goals, but also into day-to-day programs and practices. Whether one is concerned with curricular and course content, teaching practices, extracurricular activities, residential settings, advising and career planning, off-campus experiential learning, administration, or governance, understanding better the major elements of the life cycle and adult development can provide a basis for more effective performance.

The various sections of this book can be used for a variety of purposes. The chapters in Part One can be used for general in-service training and professional development activities designed to increase sophistication about adult development and learning. The chapters in Part Two, addressing specific disciplines and professions, can be used by departmental committees as a basis for rethinking curricular content, course sequences, teaching practices, and educational resources. The chapters in Part Three, concerning diverse educational practices and learning environments, can be used by faculty members and administrators to examine more generally the appropriateness of current institutional environments and activities for the particular students being served. Thus the chapters on instructional methods, individualized education, field experience education, assessing experiential learning, distance learning and student-faculty relationships present sophisticated thinking concerning educational approaches useful across a wide range of disciplines and professions and pertinent to the concerns of many teachers and faculty committees. The chapters on out-of-class activities, residential learning, and educational advising and career planning are pertinent to the diverse responsibilities of student-personnel professionals and provide specific suggestions about useful adaptations for diverse adults. The final chapters on administration, governance, professional development, and research will be useful to administrators concerned with creating institutional environments where there is internal consistency among institutional goals, educational practices, administrative organization and behavior, professional development, and research programs examining institutional effectiveness.

This logic has led to the underlying structure of this book. Part One offers a synthesis of basic information about the development and learning of adults, including traditional college students aged 18 to 25. Its fourteen chapters contain key information and concepts regarding the life cycle of adults, including the typical challenges and concerns of each life stage, intellectual and ego development, and the learning problems that adult students face.

Part Two develops the implications of the research and theory from Part One for the curriculum—in particular, for a variety of academic disciplines and professional programs, including anthropology, business administration, engineering, English, history, human services, and philosophy. For each of thirteen areas of knowledge or competence, its chapters address two general questions: "How can the ideas from Part One regarding student development and learning help achieve the objectives of this discipline or professional program more effectively?" And, turning this question around, "How can this particular area of knowledge or practice help students cope more effectively with the developmental and life cycle challenges described in Part One?"

Part Three applies this new knowledge about adults to college and university operations, including instructional methods, student-faculty relationships, out-of-class activities, administration, governance, and faculty development programs. The fourteen chapters in this concluding part of the book show how these practices can be managed in ways that respond to the developmental needs and life cycle concerns not only of students but also of staff.

In designing this book, we decided that chapters focusing on a wide variety of concrete topics would be more helpful to readers than more general rhetoric about larger issues. We wanted teachers, program directors, administrators, and nonteaching professionals to be able to see implications for their own activities and get specific ideas about what they might do in the future. This is why we examine several different facets of development in Part One, examples of specific disciplines rather than larger divisions of knowledge such as the "humanities" or the "behavioral sciences" in Part Two, and particular kinds of educational activities and practices rather than the more abstract topics of "teaching effectiveness" or "the learning environment" in Part Three. Our assumption is that readers will be able to apply these ideas from allied fields or areas in their own work —that a political scientist, for example, will find close analogues to his or her own teaching in Paul Ward's chapter on history, that James Gibbs' chapter on anthropology will be provocative for social psychologists and sociologists, and that Jane Shipton's and Elizabeth Steltenpohl's ideas on career planning will be helpful to administrators and nonteaching professionals concerned with other student services.

We also wanted to demystify human development and "the affective domain." Many think that these terms imply some esoteric topic understood only by psychologists or psychoanalysts. But as the chapters in Parts Two and Three demonstrate, professors and administrators from a wide range of backgrounds beyond psychology can understand and apply these ideas creatively and wisely. It is this same logic that has led us to encourage our authors to express their personal views, based on their own experiences and knowledge of pertinent research. In this book, professionals state what they think and believe in order to stimulate thought and action on the part of the reader, rather than present an impersonal summary of received opinion or definitive answers. The topic of individual development during adulthood is too young and complex for such a posture.

The result is a book that can be examined on two general levels. At the more immediate level, it can be perused for specific suggestions about adapting a particular discipline, professional preparation area, or educational practice to meet the requirements of adult motivation, learning, and development. Thus, a faculty member will be able to find some useful ideas for teaching in Part Two, and an administrator will be able to find helpful suggestions about particular institutional policies and practices in Part Three. We have cross-referenced these ideas among the chapters as well as in the index so that readers can identify other concepts and applications pertinent to their particular concerns.

But the larger problem this book addresses extends substantially beyond the particular modifications it may suggest for specific courses, curriculums, educational practices, or learning environments. This larger problem is that of the overall purpose or goal of American higher education. At this level, the book will be useful to institutional planners, curriculum specialists, policy analysts, and everyone else concerned with the mission of colleges and universities in the future—including students and trustees who are serving with faculty members and administrators on institutional task forces and planning groups. As stated in the Introduction, this book tests the argument that the idea of human development can supply a unifying purpose for higher education. We propose that questions about institutional policies—about instruction and evaluation; about appropriate student-faculty relationships; about the priorities among teaching, research, and services; about faculty qualifications and the reward systems that shape them—can best be answered by focusing on what we now know from research about the psychological and social development of adults. Our initial soundings indicate that this argument stands up well: The concept of human development can meet the modern American college's need for a unifying purpose, and knowledge of adult development can lead to substantive improvements in curricular areas and educational practices.

Acknowledgments

My introduction to the study of higher education began in 1959 at Goddard College, an institution that was then, and still is, strongly committed to helping students achieve significant learning and personal development. Thus, I wish to recognize Tim Pitkin, George Beecher, Tom Yakhub, Robert Mattuck, and Forest Davis—Goddard colleagues, mentors, and lasting friends. Some theorists hold that the human organism learns more during the first six years of life than in all the years that follow. Though I hope some learning still goes on, certainly my six years at Goddard, with its stimulating faculty and students, created both a solid foundation and lasting motivation for more complex understanding and for application of research and theory in the service of change in higher education.

My thinking has profited greatly from a substantial accumulation of research and theory pertinent to educational effectiveness and the impact of higher education on human development. *The American College,* edited by Nevitt Sanford and published in 1962, served as a cornerstone reference for many years. The work of Sanford during the late 1960s and the more recent contributions of his associates at the Wright Institute have been continued sources of stimulation and insight. Joseph Katz's persistent study and penetrating perceptions have been similarly sustaining, carrying forward the kind of detailed analyses he presented in *No Time For Youth.* Theodore Newcomb's twenty-five-year follow-up of his 1938 study of Bennington College, *Persistence and Change,* remains for me the best longitudinal study and soundest theory of educational outcomes available. And Feldman and Newcomb's 1969 synthesis of research on *The Impact of College on Students* remains a major reference.

Student Development During the College Years by Lois Murphy and Esther Raushenbush, reporting detailed studies of Sarah Lawrence, and Douglas Heath's continued studies of Haverford remain the most sophisticated studies of the educational power of small liberal arts colleges. And that gem by Esther Raushenbush, *The Student and His Studies,* remains unique in its outstanding analysis of the relationships between various disciplinary studies and developmental concerns. At a more general level, Robert Pace's continued attempts to study college and university environments in ways that yield practically useful information have contributed valuable instruments and insights. Then, of course, Alexander Astin's multivariate analyses of multi-institutional data provide a continuing flow of fundamental contributions that speak powerfully to general policy issues. Finally, I should recognize the wide-ranging synthesis and pointed observations supplied by Patricia Cross. Her unfailing ability to cut to the heart of things seldom fails to provide a new perspective. These are only a few among many who, as scholars of higher education and as individuals, have contributed to my education and personal development and, I believe, to that of many of my colleagues in this volume.

A substantial number of persons and organizations made major direct contributions to this book. They should not, however, be held accountable for the particular views expressed by me as editor and author or by other contributors. This has been a collaborative effort from the beginning, but it has aimed to encourage clear expression of individual views. Among the sources of personal encouragement and financial support, the contributions of Empire State College in the early stages of this work, from 1974 to 1976, were invaluable. The College made possible the allocation of substantial time and energy by myself and others to reading, writing, and discussion of these emerging ideas. Some more adventurous faculty members tested the ideas in their work with students, developing learning contracts and degree programs that gave explicit attention to life cycle issues or particular dimensions of development. I hesitate to mention names. Given the passage of time, I may omit someone who was most helpful. But I take the risk in order to credit several whose support and critical advice stand out in my mind: Mary Ann Biller, William Dodge, Jay Gilbert, James Hall, William Laidlaw, Lois Lamdin, Timothy Lehmann, Pearl Mindell, Fredrick Mayo, Robert Morrison, Jane Shipton, Elizabeth Steltenpohl, and Rhoada Wald. If there are any seminal contributions here, it is because these persons and others at Empire State responded warmly to what was then only a gleam in the editor's eye.

During the formative stages of this work several other persons offered timely encouragement. At a delightful lunch in the summer of 1976, William Perry, director of the Bureau of Study Counsel at Harvard, said, "It's an absolutely crazy idea [long pause] but I'd be delighted to help." Chris Argyris, at the Harvard Graduate School of Education, gave the initial prospectus and outline a good going over and thought it was worth tackling. Harry Lasker, also at the Harvard Graduate School of Education and actively thinking about the implications of ego development for varied kinds of interventions in industry and education, helped reveal some of the powerful possibilities here. Harold Hodgkinson, both while director of the National Institute of Education and subsequently, emphasized the significance of research and theory concerning the life cycle. Jack Lindquist, while executive director of the Strategies for Change Project and a colleague at Empire State, saw the applicability to planned change, institutional development, and professional development in colleges and universities, and reinforced the notion of trying to help institutions move systematically in these directions. So as early ideas were taking shape, these persons strengthened the notion that a major effort to address their implications would be worthwhile.

During 1976-77, the Danforth Foundation, through the good offices of Vice-President Warren B. Martin, supplied sufficient support so that a half-year sabbatical from Empire State could be extended to a full year, and so that secretarial assistance during this period could be made available. This support came through Empire State's Center for Individualized Education, directed and brought to national prominence by Thomas Clark, who was, and continues to be, one of the most thoughtful critics of the ideas set forth in this volume. More important, perhaps, he has been, to my knowledge, the most sophisticated translator of these ideas into action.

Since September of 1977, Memphis State University has been most supportive of my work on this book. That support has included not only recognition that the undertaking may be important but also budgetary allocations to the Center for the Study of Higher Education at a level that provided significant resources in secretarial time, telephone costs, correspondence, xeroxing, and the like so that the enterprise could go forward. Furthermore, since my arrival at Memphis State, Virginia Bland, my secretary, has masterfully managed the logistics of multiple drafts from diverse authors. She has kept straight which manuscripts were at what stage, coped with copious correspondence, and supplied major amounts of emergency typing when authors' local resources were short-handed. So I owe her also a strong thank you.

The culmination of Memphis State's strong backing occurred when President Billy Mac Jones authorized an expenditure of $8,000 to help support a workshop that brought contributors and expert critics together for three days to examine chapter drafts. These monies made it possible for each chapter to receive a thorough critical review by two other persons and for the contributors themselves to receive small stipends. The workshop, which took place in July 1978, was really sparked by Winton Manning, vice-president for research at Educational Testing Service. Several of us had realized the value of such a meeting, but attempts to raise sufficient funds had failed. In January 1978, Manning offered to defray housing and food costs at the Henry Chauncey Center up to $7,000. With that start, we were encouraged to look further. Alden Dunham, of the Carnegie Corporation, agreed to add another $7,000 to cover travel costs. Suddenly our workshop had become a reality. Thus, the combined support of Memphis State University, Educational Testing Service, and the Carnegie Corporation made it possible to take a giant step toward finishing the project that had begun four years earlier with help from Empire State and the Danforth Foundation. That workshop contributed substantially to our understanding of what we were about and to the level of integration among the various parts of the volume. Finally, I must mention the invaluable editorial assistance rendered by JB Hefferlin at Jossey-Bass. His expert judgment and wide-ranging perspectives continually strengthened the content, and his sharp sense of our audience led to more effective sequence and organization. And Joan Westcott did a most thoughtful and comprehensive job in copy editing the entire manuscript.

Of course, much more remains to be achieved in both understanding and applying research and theory to higher education. This volume is only one more brick added to those already set. We think it is sound and solid, but we recognize its many limitations. Someone has said that a work of art is never really finished—it is simply abandoned. Judgments will differ as to how much art there is in this volume; most persons will agree that it is unfinished. But although the coordinated effort to put out this volume has come to a halt, exploration of the ideas and action on them continue. We invite your thoughtful examination, your consideration of their implications for your own concerns about higher education, and your careful application to the extent you judge it appropriate.

Memphis, Tennessee   Arthur W. Chickering
October 1980

The Authors

Arthur W. Chickering is Distinguished Professor of Higher Education and director of the Center for the Study of Higher Education at Memphis State University. After receiving a B.A. degree in modern comparative literature from Wesleyan University (1950) and a M.A. in teaching English from the Graduate School of Education, Harvard University (1951), Chickering completed a Ph.D. degree in school psychology at Teachers College, Columbia University (1958).

Chickering began his career in higher education as psychology teacher and coordinator of evaluation for the experiment in college curriculum organization at Goddard College from 1959-1965, after working as a secondary school teacher and chairman of the Department of Education at Monmouth College. Chickering then directed the "Project on Student Development in Small Colleges," a four-year study of college influences on student development in thirteen diverse private colleges. During 1970-71, he was a visiting scholar at the Office of Research at the American Council on Education. From 1971 to 1977, he played a major role in creating Empire State College as vice-president for academic affairs.

Chickering is the recipient of the Outstanding Service Award from the National Association of Student Personnel Administrators, a Distinguished Service Citation from the Sex Information and Education Council of the United States, and the Distinguished Contribution to Knowledge Award of the American College Personnel Association. He is a member of the board of trustees of the Council for the Advancement of Experiential Learning, the board of scholars of the Higher Education Research Institute, the editorial board of the *Journal of Higher Education,* and the panel of advice of the Institute for Higher Education, University of New England, Australia.

Chickering's major publications include *Education and Identity,* which received the 1969 American Council on Education Book Award for its "outstanding contribution to higher education," *Commuting Versus Resident Students* (1974), *Experience and Learning* (1977), and *Developing the College Curriculum* (with W. Bergquist, D. Halliburton, and J. Lindquist, 1977). In addition, he is the author of numerous journal articles concerning relationships among educational practices, college environments, and student development.

Louis T. Benezet is professor in the Research Group for Human Development and Educational Policy at the State University of New York at Stony Brook. Previous to 1975, he served for twenty-seven years as president successively at Allegheny College, Colorado College, Claremont University Center, and the State University of New York at Albany. He earned his A.B. degree (1936) from Dartmouth College and his M.A. degree (1939) in psychology from Reed College and his Ph.D. degree in higher education (1942) from Columbia University.

He has written several articles and monographs on educational impact in collegiate organizations and has served as guest editor of *Building Bridges to the Public* (with Frances W. Magnusson, 1979) in the Jossey-Bass series, *New Directions for Higher Education.* Benezet's research interests center on the mission and principal characteristics of the liberal arts college of middle resources and following the current developments in the leadership role of the American college and university president.

Jessie Bernard is research scholar honoris causa at Pennsylvania State University. At the University of Minnesota she received her B.A. degree in 1923 in sociology and economics and her M.A. degree in 1924 in sociology and psychology; she earned her Ph.D. degree in sociology and psychology in 1935 at Washington University.

For several years she was research assistant to L. L. Bernard and later spent several years on the Consumer Expenditures project at the Department of Labor in Washington. In 1940 she began teaching at Lindenwood College, where she remained until 1947, when she moved to Pennsylvania State University. She left teaching in 1965 to devote all her time to independent research, especially in the areas of marriage, family, community, and women. Bernard was a Visiting Fellow at the National Institute of Education in 1974-75 and Visiting Scholar at the U.S. Civil Rights Commission in 1975. Among her awards are four honorary degrees from Washington University, Northwestern University, Radcliffe College, and Hood College. An award has been named for her by the American Sociological Association.

Bernard is the author of numerous articles and books, including *Academic Women* (1964), *Remarriage, A Study of Marriage* (1957), *Women and the Public Interest* (1971), *The Future of Marriage* (1972), *Self-Portrait of a Family* (1978), and *The Female World* (1980).

Donald H. Blocher is professor of counseling psychology at the State University of New York at Albany. He received his B.A. degree in history (1950) and his M.A. degree in political science (1954) from Ball State University and his Ph.D. degree in educational psychology (1959) from the University of Minnesota. He was on the faculty of the University of Minnesota from 1960 to 1975 and was professor of education and psychology at the University of Western Ontario from 1975 to 1977.

Blocher has held visiting professorships at the University of Keele in England, the University of British Columbia, the University of Colorado, and Utah State University.

Currently, he is president-elect of the Division of Counseling Psychology of the American Psychological Association. He is the author of *Developmental Counseling* (2nd ed., 1974), *Guidance Systems* (with W. E. Dugan and R. Dustin, 1971), and numerous articles and monographs about counseling psychology.

William B. Bondeson is professor of philosophy and medicine at the University of Missouri in Columbia and co-director of the Program in Health Care and Human Values. He was awarded the B.A. degree in philosophy, German, and Greek from Augustana College (1958), M.A. degree in Greek from the University of Illinois (1962), and a Ph.D. degree in philosophy from the University of Chicago (1964). He has been at the University of Missouri since 1964 and has served as chairman of the Department of Philosophy, director of the Honors College, and director of the College of General Studies.

Bondeson has published articles on the history of ancient philosophy, especially on Plato and Aristotle, and on open learning and higher education. He is the editor of *The Moral Uses of New Knowledge in the Bio-Medical Sciences* (vol. 9, 1979) and *The Concept of Person and Its Implication for the Use of the Fetus in Bio-Medicine* (forthcoming). Bondeson has won several awards for teaching and has received fellowships and other kinds of support from the University of Chicago, the Danforth Foundation, the American Philosophical Association, the National Endowment for the Humanities, the American Council in Education, the Harvard Institute for Educational Management, and the American Council of Learned Societies.

Elof Axel Carlson is Distinguished Teaching Professor of Biology at the State University of New York at Stony Brook. He received his B.A. degree in biology from New York University (1953) and his Ph.D. degree in genetics at Indiana University (1958). Carlson has been a lecturer at Queen's University, Ontario (1958-1960), assistant and associate professor at the University of California at Los Angeles (1960-1968), and a professor at Stony Brook since 1968. He was a Distinguished Visiting Professor at San Diego State University (1969) and at the University of Minnesota (1974).

For his successful development of a biology course for nonmajors, Carlson received the E. Harris Harbison Award for Gifted Teaching from the Danforth Foundation in 1972 and in 1974 was named a Distinguished Teaching Professor at Stony Brook.

Carlson's publications include *The Gene: A Critical History* (1966) and *Gene Theory* (1967). He has published seventy-five technical articles in professional journals and edited two volumes of H. J. Muller's essays (1972). Recently he completed a biography of H. J. Muller and a text for his nonmajors course. Carlson's research includes mutation studies (chemicals and radiation), gene structure, and developmental genetics, which he has applied to basic human genetics and genetic counseling.

Thomas F. Clark is vice-president for instructional services at Rockland Community College, Suffern, New York, and adjunct professor at Memphis State University, where he teaches and consults with the Center for the Study of Higher Education and the Institute for Academic Improvement. He was awarded the A.B. degree in history and government (1962) from Allegheny College and the M.A. degree in philosophy (1964) and the Ed.D. degree with work in literature, psychology, sociology, and education (1968) from Cornell University.

Clark was assistant dean of students (counseling services) at Cornell University (1966-1968) and associate dean of students at Claremont Men's College (1968-69). At the University of Massachusetts at Amherst (1969-1973), he was director of the Higher

Education Center, director of the University Without Walls Program, and assistant professor of education. He joined Empire State College in 1973 as dean of the Northeast Regional Center and in 1975 became director of the Center for Individualized Education. In 1978-79, he served as associate director of the Institute for Academic Improvement at Memphis State University.

Clark has published numerous articles on individualized education, contract learning, and faculty development. He has been a consultant in these areas as well as in evaluating experiential learning and race relations.

Audrey C. Cohen is founder and president of the College for Human Services in New York, California, and Florida, an experimental urban college dedicated to social justice and improved service delivery. She received a B.A. degree in political science from the University of Pittsburgh (1953) and did graduate work at George Washington University. In 1976, Cohen was Visiting Professor in the doctoral program of the Graduate School of Education at the University of Massachusetts.

Cohen is one of the chief architects of the new profession of human services. Under her guidance, the College for Human Services (established as the Women's Talent Corps in 1964) developed a transdisciplinary model of professional education based on a synthesis of field work and theory through performance assessment.

In 1958, she founded Part Time Research Associates in Washington, D.C., the first consultant corporation exclusively employing college-educated women to do social science research for government and business. She served as chairperson of the Task Force on Women, Education, and Work for the Department of Health, Education, and Welfare in 1976 and was a member of the Newman Committee.

Cohen's writings about human services have appeared in a variety of journals and books. As president of the College for Human Services, Cohen has accepted many awards for the college's pioneering work in education, social service, and feminism, including the Academy for Educational Development's 1979 Certificate of Achievement.

George G. Dawson is professor of economics and director of the Center for Business and Economic Education at Empire State College in New York. He was awarded the B.S. degree in social studies from New York University in 1956 and the A.M. degree in social studies in 1957. He received his Ph.D. degree in labor and economic history from New York University in 1959.

From 1957 to 1970, Dawson was a member of the New York University faculty. He served as director of the Peace Corps project in Somalia from 1962 to 1964. From 1970 to 1975, he was director of research and publications for the Joint Council on Economic Education. He is presently managing editor of *The Journal of Economic Education* and a member of the board of directors of the New York State Council on Economic Education.

Among the books authored or coauthored by Dawson are *Introductory Economics* (with S. Gordon, 4th ed., 1980), *Guide to Economics* (two vols., 1965), *Economics* (with R. McClain, 1963), *Our Nation's Wealth* (1968), *Teaching Economics in American History* (with E. Prehn, 1973), and *Social Science Theory, Structure and Application* (with H. London, 1975). A pioneer in economic education research who continues to be active in the field, Dawson received the Certificate of Leadership in Education from the Long Island Association of Commerce and Industry in 1978, first place in the Kazanjian Foundation's Awards Program for the Teaching of College Economics in 1967, and the Certificate of Merit from the New York State Council on Economic Education in 1969.

Elizabeth Douvan is Catherine Neaffie Kellogg Professor of Psychology at the University of Michigan. She received her A.B. degree in history (1946) from Vassar College and her M.A. and Ph.D. degrees in social psychology (1951) from the University of Michigan.

Douvan is a member of the Society of Fellows at the University of Michigan. She has held offices in the Division on the Psychology of Women and the Society for the Psychological Study of Social Issues of the American Psychological Association. She is coauthor of *The Adolescent Experience* (with J. Adelson, 1966) and co-editor of *Adolescent Development* (with M. Gold, 1970). She is currently involved in a national study of adult adaptation and well-being in marriage, work, and parenthood, *Culture and Comfort* (with J. Vernoff and R. Kulka, forthcoming). Her professional interests have centered on adolescence, the family, and the psychology of women.

John S. Duley is instructional development consultant and associate professor in the Office of Learning and Evaluation Service at Michigan State University (MSU). He was awarded, with distinction, a B.S. degree in social work from Ohio State University (1943) and a M. Div. degree from Union Theological Seminary, New York (1949).

For twenty years, Duley served as a Presbyterian university pastor at Western Michigan University, Kalamazoo College, Pennsylvania State University, and Michigan State University. At Michigan State he served as a lecturer in religion and from 1965 through 1968 directed the MSU-Rust College Student Tutorial Education Project (STEP), helping Rust College, Holly Springs, Mississippi, attain full accreditation and organizing and offering, with MSU faculty and students, a study skills improvement program for entering freshmen. Duley studied with the Cambridge University Divinity Faculty (1956-57) and served as a consultant to the Presbyterian Church of Formosa (1967). He joined the faculty of Justin Morrill College in 1968 as director of the field study program. In 1977, he was a Visiting Fellow at the Institute for Research and Development in Post Compulsory Education at the University of Lancaster, England.

Duley is on the board of trustees of the National Society for Internships and Experiential Education and of the Council for the Advancement of Experiential Learning (CAEL); he is also a consultant and workshop leader for CAEL. He edited *New Directions in Higher Education: Implementing Field Experience Education* (1974) and coauthored *College-Sponsored Experiential Learning—A CAEL Handbook* (with S. Gordon, 1977). He has contributed several articles and chapters to other books on instructional development in experiential learning.

Martin Esslin is professor of drama at Stanford University, where he teaches during the winter and spring quarters of each year; he resides in England during the remainder of the year. Esslin attended Vienna University and the Reinhardt Seminar of Dramatic Art at Vienna from 1936 to 1938. He graduated from the Reinhardt Seminar in 1938, shortly before he left Austria as a refugee from Hitler.

Esslin joined the British Broadcasting Corporation (BBC) in 1940 and worked for that organization until 1977; from 1963 to 1977 he was head of BBC radio drama. In 1972, Esslin was awarded the Order of the British Empire for his services to broadcasting. He was visiting professor of drama at Florida State University, 1969-1975.

Esslin is the author of *Brecht* (1959), *The Theatre of the Absurd* (1961), *Reflections* (1969), *The Peopled Wound: The Plays of Harold Pinter* (1970), *An Anatomy of Drama* (1977), *Artaud* (1977), and *Mediations* (1980); he is the editor of *Samuel Beckett: A Collection of Critical Essays* (1965) and *The Genius of the German Theatre* (1968).

Jacqueline Fleming is consulting psychologist for the United Negro College Fund in New York City, where she also directs the Carnegie Corporation-funded research project, "The Impact of Predominantly White and Predominantly Black College Environments on the Functioning of Black Students." As a current adjunct professor of Barnard College, she teaches the psychology of racism. Fleming received the B.A. degree in psychology from Barnard College in 1969 and the Ph.D. degree in personality and development from Harvard University in 1974.

While a Fellow of the Radcliffe Institute from 1974 to 1976, she conducted research into the behavioral correlates and developmental antecedents of achievement-related motives in black adolescents. Fleming has authored a number of articles on motivational phenomena, including women's attitudes toward success and differences in the educational and occupational goals of black women. Her forthcoming book is *The Impact of College Environments on Black Students.*

Lois J. Fowler is associate professor of English at Carnegie-Mellon University. She was awarded the B.S. degree (1948) in English and natural sciences from Carnegie Institute of Technology and the M.A. (1955) and Ph.D. (1960) degrees in English from the University of Pittsburgh.

With grants from the U.S. Office of Education, the Ford Foundation, and the Carnegie Corporation of New York, she has studied the teaching of English. Her publications range from traditional work on the British novel and American drama to extensive work in English education and communications. She is co-editor of the *Insight* textbook series (with E. Steinberg, R. Slack, and B. Cottrell, 1966-1975), *English Education Today* (with E. Steinberg, 1970), coauthor of *Four Films on Women's Studies: A Curriculum Guide* (with P. McCorduck, 1978), and editor of *English for the Academically Talented* (1970). She has also written numerous articles on literature and five biographical entries for *American Women Writers* (1979-1980). Currently, Fowler is at work (with D. H. Fowler) on a biography of Jane G. Swisshelm, nineteenth-century reformer, abolitionist, and journalist, and has received grants from the Heinz and Bittner foundations to complete that biography.

Fowler has served on the President's Panel for Teacher Education (1961-1967) and the Executive Committee of the Conference on English Education; she was program chair for the 1977 Conference on English Education, sponsored by the National Council of Teachers of English.

Larry Friedlander is adjunct professor of literature at Stanford University. He was awarded the B.A. degree in English from Yeshiva University (1958) and the M.A. degree in English from Harvard University (1960).

Friedlander has taught drama and literature at Harvard, Wellesley, and the State University of New York. He has worked extensively abroad and was visiting professor of theater at the London Academy of Music and Dramatic Arts (1973-74).

In addition to teaching, Friedlander helped set up drama groups at Harvard and at Stanford, where he founded The Company, Stanford's largest undergraduate theatrical company. As an actor and as a director, he has appeared in all the major Shakespearean festivals on the West Coast. He will be acting with the Ashland Shakespeare Festival in the 1981 season and then goes to Berlin to teach in 1982.

Jerry G. Gaff is director of the Project on General Education Models, an activity of the Society for Values in Higher Education. He obtained a B.A. degree from DePauw University in 1958 after studying psychology and philosophy. He received his Ph.D. degree in psychology from Syracuse University in 1965.

He taught at Raymond College, an experimental cluster college at the University of the Pacific, and subsequently wrote *The Cluster College* (1970). After joining the staff of the Center for Research and Development in Higher Education at the University of California, Berkeley, Gaff conducted research on faculty, especially their teaching roles and relationships with students. *College Professors and Their Impact on Students* was published with his colleagues in 1975, the same year he published *Toward Faculty Renewal*.

Gaff is active in directing projects to establish teaching improvement programs and in designing appropriate curriculums for the great diversity of students today. He consults with colleges and universities and serves on advisory committees and editorial boards.

Sally Shake Gaff is an independent consultant based in Washington, D.C., where she is involved in educational research, policy analysis, resource development, and writing. After first attending DePauw University, she was awarded the B.A. degree in psychology by Syracuse University (1960) and pursued doctoral work there in psychology, sociology, and higher education at the Maxwell School of Citizenship and Public Affairs.

Currently she serves as a consultant to the National Association of State Boards of Education and is a staff member of the Project on Adult Education Opportunities in Industrialized Countries. Gaff is interested in the policy implications and practical applications of education over the lifespan. She has taught adults in several postsecondary settings and served as a public school system administrator in compensatory education, training teachers and parents. She worked on a feasibility study for the California legislature on postsecondary alternatives to meet the needs of adults in that state. Gaff is senior author of *Professional Development: A Guide to Resources* (with C. Festa and J. Gaff, 1978), and coauthor of *Community Needs for Postsecondary Alternatives* (with R. E. Peterson and others, 1975), a study for the California legislature.

James Lowell Gibbs, Jr., is professor of anthropology at Stanford University, where he has taught since 1966. He received the B.A. degree in sociology and anthropology from Cornell University in 1952 and the Ph.D. degree in social anthropology from Harvard University in 1961. At Harvard he was a teaching fellow and resident tutor; Gibbs also studied anthropology in 1953-54 at the University of Cambridge as a Rotary Foundation Fellow.

At the University of Minnesota, he received the Distinguished Teacher Award of the College of Science, Literature, and the Arts. At Stanford he served as the first dean of undergraduate studies (1970-1976) and was a recipient of the Danforth Foundation's E. Harris Harbison Award for Gifted Teaching. Gibbs has been a visiting professor at Cornell University, where he serves as alumni trustee, and a visiting scholar for Phi Beta Kappa. He has been a member of the board of trustees of Mills College, Harvard's Visiting Committee on General Education, the Executive Board of the American Anthropological Association, and the Board of Directors of the African Studies Association. He also has been a fellow of the Center for Advanced Study in the Behavioral Sciences and the Woodrow Wilson International Center for Scholars.

Gibbs is the editor of and a contributor to *Peoples of Africa* (1965). He is co-producer and co-director (with M. Silverman) of the prize-winning documentary film, *The Cows of Dolo Ken Paye,* which portrays conflict resolution among the Kpelle of Liberia, the group among which he has done his anthropological fieldwork.

Carol Gilligan is associate professor of education at Harvard University, where she is a member of the Laboratory of Human Development and the faculty of the Graduate School of Education. She received the A.B. degree in English literature, psychology and history from Swarthmore College in 1958 and was elected to Phi Beta Kappa. Gilligan was awarded the A.M. degree in clinical psychology from Radcliffe College in 1961 and the Ph.D. degree in social psychology from Harvard University in 1964. As a graduate student, she was an Ann Radcliffe Scholar and a Woodrow Wilson Fellow.

Gilligan has taught psychology at the University of Chicago and at Harvard University, and in 1978-79 she was a Mellon Fellow at the Wellesley College Center for Research on Women.

Her publications include articles on adolescent and moral development, the relationship between moral judgment and action in a naturalistic study of abortion decisions, and women's development. Currently, she is working on a research project supported by the National Institute of Education on the development of thinking about self and morality among males and females aged five to seventy-five and is completing a book of essays on psychological theory and women's development.

Paul V. Grambsch is professor of management in the College and Graduate School of Business Administration at the University of Minnesota. He was awarded the B.A. degree in sociology from North Central College (1941), the M.A. degree in economics from the University of Mississippi (1947), and the Ph.D. degree in management at the Graduate School of Business, Indiana University (1955).

Prior to his present position, Grambsch served as dean of the School of Business at the University of Minnesota (1960-1970) and at Tulane University (1952-1960). He was acting chairman of economics and assistant professor at the University of Mississippi from 1948 to 1950.

He is coauthor (with E. Gross) of *University Goals and Academic Power* (1968) and *Changes in University Organization* (1974). Grambsch is a Fellow of the Academy of Management; a member of the Dean's Advisory Council, Graduate School of Business, Indiana University; and a consultant to the American Management Associations and the U.S. General Accounting Office. He is a past president of the American Assembly of Collegiate Schools of Business and a former trustee of North Central College.

Thomas F. Green is professor of education and philosophy, School of Education, Syracuse University, where he is also director of the Division of Educational Foundations. Green received the B.A. degree in 1948 in philosophy and English and the M.A. degree in 1949 in philosophy and political science from the University of Nebraska and, in 1953, the Ph.D. degree in philosophy from Cornell University.

He previously taught at Michigan State University. Green is a Guggenheim Fellow and a member of the National Academy of Education. He was a Whitehead Fellow at Harvard University, is past president of the Philosophy of Education Society, and served for one year as a Fellow within the National Institute of Education. He is the author of *Work, Leisure, and The American Schools* (1968), *The Activities of Teaching* (1972), *Perspectives on Planning* (1971), and *Predicting the Behavior of the Educational System* (forthcoming). Green is now engaged in efforts to develop an adequate philosophy of moral development relevant to education and public policy.

Dean E. Griffith is director of the extension, Division of Engineering, Technology, and Architecture, at Oklahoma State University in Stillwater. Griffith attended the University of Omaha before transferring to Iowa State University, where he received his B.S. degree and M.S. degree in chemical engineering in 1953 and 1957, respectively.

He taught at Rice University and the University of Houston before joining Dow Chemical Company as an engineering consultant. At the University of Texas at Austin, Griffith was engineering program director (1965-1968) and director of continuing engineering studies and engineering institutes (1968-1977). Griffith was Clemson University Alumni Visiting Professor (1977-78) before joining Oklahoma State University in 1978.

Griffith is chairman, Continuing Professional Development Division, American Society for Engineering Education (1979-80), and has been very active in that society since 1961. Griffith was editor of the *Professional Engineering Career Development Series* published during the early 1970s and has written many articles on continuing engineering studies and continuing professional development in engineering.

David Halliburton, founder of the Center for Teaching and Learning and the Program for Faculty Renewal, teaches in Stanford University's Department of English and the interdisciplinary programs in American studies, comparative literature, humanities, international relations, and modern thought and literature. He is the first chairman of the committee for faculty seminars and was recently appointed chairman of the modern thought and literature program. Halliburton received a B.A. degree in 1958 and a Ph.D. degree in English in 1966 from the University of California at Riverside, where he was named the outstanding National Defense Education Act Fellow in the history of the school. Other honors include fellowships from the American Council of Learned Society and the American Philosophical Society, in addition to news-reporting awards.

A member of the National Humanities Faculty, Halliburton participated in the first national workshop on the evaluation of teaching-improvement programs. He has held regional or national workshops on a variety of topics, including educational management, professional development, quality control and evaluation, interdisciplinary studies, medical ethics, women's studies, the bicameral mind, and mathematics. A vice-president of the Academy for Professional Development, he is currently active in projects concerning evaluation, the organization of knowledge, and the development of conceptual models.

Halliburton is the author of *Edgar Allan Poe: A Phenomenological View* (1973), the coauthor of *Developing the College Curriculum* (with A. W. Chickering, W. H. Bergquist, and J. Lindquist, 1977), the editor of *How to Succeed as a New Teacher* (1977), and a contributor to *The Monday Morning Imagination: The Workshop on State Higher Education Systems* (1976). He is an editor for *The Structuralist Review* and Urizen Press.

Robert J. Havighurst is professor emeritus of human development and education at the University of Chicago, where he maintains his office and continues research and writing. He earned the B.A. degree at Ohio Wesleyan University (1921) and the Ph.D. degree at Ohio State University in chemistry (1924).

Havighurst held a National Research Council postdoctoral fellowship in physics at Harvard University (1924-1926). After a year as assistant professor of chemistry at Miami University, Havighurst joined the faculty of the University of Wisconsin as assistant professor of physics in the Experimental College (1928-1932). Havighurst next served as assistant director (1934-1937) and then director (1937-1940) of the general education board of the Rockefeller Foundation's program to support experimental work at the senior high school and college levels. This experience led him into the field of sociological and psychological foundations of education; he became professor of education and coordinator of the interdepartmental Committee on Human Development at the University of Chicago in 1941. In 1945 Havighurst collaborated with Ernest Burgess to set up a program of life-span developmental social psychology at the University of Chicago.

Havighurst has been president of the Gerontological Society (1957) and of the Division on Adulthood and Aging of the American Psychological Association (1959). He has received the Kleemeier Award for Research on Gerontology (Gerontological Society, 1967); Thorndike Award for Research, Division of Educational Psychology (American Psychological Association, 1969); American Educational Research Association-Phi Delta Kappa Award for Educational Research (1973); and the Brookdale Award for Social Science Research in Gerontology (Gerontological Society, 1979). Among his books are *Human Development and Education* (1953), *Developmental Tasks and Education* (3rd ed., 1972), *Comparative Perspectives on Education* (1968), *American Higher Education in the 1960s* (1960), *Society and Education* (with D. U. Levine, 5th ed., 1979), *Adolescent Character and Personality* (with H. Taba, 1949), *The Meaning of Work and Retirement* (with E. Friedmann, 1954), and *Older People* (with R. Albrecht, 1953).

Harold L. Hodgkinson is president of the National Training Laboratories Institute for Applied Behavioral Sciences. Hodgkinson was awarded a B.A. degree in literature and philosophy from the University of Minnesota (1953), an M.A.T. degree from Wesleyan University (1955), and an Ed.D. degree in education and sociology from Harvard University (1959).

From 1977 to 1979 he was executive director of the Professional Institute of the American Management Associations. An adjunct professor of education at the University of Michigan, Hodgkinson is also a trustee of Ottawa University and Hartwick College and vice-president of the Council for Applied Social Research.

Hodgkinson has served Simmons College as dean of the School of Education (1958-1961) and Bard College as dean (1962-1968); at the University of California at Berkeley, he was research director of the Center for Research and Development in Higher Education (1968-1975). For the Department of Health, Education, and Welfare, he served as director of the National Institute of Education from 1975 to 1977; he received a special citation from the Secretary of Health, Education, and Welfare and the Distinguished Service Award. Hodgkinson has directed several research projects, including the Institutions in Transition study for the Carnegie Commission from 1968 to 1970. He has held a variety of editorial posts, including editor of the *Harvard Education Review*; currently he is a member of the editorial boards of the *Journal of Higher Education* and *The Review of Education*.

Among the books he has authored are *Education in Social and Cultural Perspectives* (1962), *Educational Decisions: A Casebook* (1963), *Education, Interaction and Social Change* (1967), which received the Pi Lambda Theta Award for Best Book in Education in 1967; *Institutions in Transition: Change in American Higher Education* (1970); *Implementing the Learning Society: Alternatives for the Finance of Higher Education* (1974); and *How Much Change for a Dollar? A Review of the Developing Institutions Program* (1974). Hodgkinson is co-editor of *Power and Authority: Transformation of Campus Governance* (with L. R. Meeth, 1971) and *Identity Crisis in Higher Education* (with M. B. Bloy, 1971).

John D. Jones is vice-president for student affairs at the University of Alabama in Birmingham, where he is also a professor of education and a member of the graduate faculty in the Department of Human Services Education. He was awarded the B.S.E. degree (1949) and the M.Ed. degree (1959) from the University of Arkansas and the Ed.D. degree from the University of Mississippi (1969).

Jones entered professional education in 1949 as a high school science teacher, later becoming a high school administrator. His first assignment in higher education was at the University of Arkansas in Monticello (1960-1970), where he was dean of students and associate professor of education. From 1970 to 1978, Jones was vice-president for student affairs and professor of education at Memphis State University.

Jones' professional involvements include serving as vice-president of the National Association of Student Personnel Administrators and executive director of the Southwest Association of Student Personnel Administrators. He has been a member of the editorial board of the *National Association of Student Personnel Administrators Journal* and the executive committees of the National Association of Student Personnel Administrators and the Committee of the Southern College Personnel Association. His articles have appeared in such journals as the *Journal of College Student Personnel, Journal of Drug Education,* and *National Association of Student Personnel Administrators Journal.*

Morris Keeton is president of the Council for the Advancement of Experiential Learning (CAEL). Keeton received degrees in philosophy from Southern Methodist University (B.A., 1935; M.A., 1936) and Harvard University (M.A., 1937; Ph.D., 1938).

He has taught at Southern Methodist University (1938-1941) and Antioch College (1947-1977), where he also served as dean of faculty, academic vice-president, and provost and vice-president. For the American Friends Service Committee, Keeton has served as dean or director of eight international student seminars (1947-1958) and one for younger diplomats (1961); chief administrator for operations in Germany (1953-1955); head of an eight-member delegation to East and West Germany (1963), reported in *Journey Through a Wall;* and chair of the International Seminars and Conferences Committee (1959-1963). With the American Association for Higher Education, Keeton directed the Campus Governance Program (1966-1969), was twice elected to the executive committee, and served as president (1972-1973). Keeton has been a member of the American Philosophical Association since 1938. He was an institutional evaluator for the North Central Association of Colleges and Secondary Schools from 1959-1977.

Keeton is coauthor of *Ethics for Today* (with H. Titus, 5th ed., 1973), *Struggle and Promise, A Future for Colleges* (with C. Hilberry and others, 1969), *Experiential Learning: Rationale, Characteristics, Assessment* (1976) and *Learning by Experience: What, Why, How* (with P. Tate and others, 1978). He is also one of the editors-in-chief of CAEL publications and the author of *Models and Mavericks* (1969). He is currently preparing for the Ford Foundation an evaluation of its Private Black Colleges Program of 1972-1979 and working with S. Wright on a book on the functions and the prospects of predominantly black institutions of higher education.

Francis Keppel is director of the Aspen Institute Program in Education for a Changing Society and senior lecturer on education at Harvard University. He joined the Aspen Institute in 1974 after a career in education, government, and business. Keppel received his A.B. degree from Harvard in 1938, studied sculpture for a year at the American Academy in Rome, and resumed academic studies while serving as an assistant dean at Harvard College from 1939-1941.

In 1948, he was appointed dean of the Graduate School of Education. Keppel was a U.S. Commissioner of Education and later Assistant Secretary of Health, Education, and Welfare (for education) during 1962-1966. He served as chairman of the board of the General Learning Corporation, the educational affiliate of General Electric Company and Time Incorporated, from 1966-1974 and was vice-chairman of the board of higher education of the City University of New York (1967-1970). In 1979, Keppel received the

James B. Conant Award for distinguished service to American education; he has also received several honorary degrees.

David A. Kolb is professor of organizational behavior and management at Case Western Reserve University. He received his A.B. degree from Knox College in 1961 and his M.A. degree in psychology from Harvard University in 1965. In 1967 he received his Ph.D. degree in social psychology from Harvard.

Prior to coming to Case Western Reserve University, Kolb taught at the Massachusetts Institute of Technology. Since 1965, when he worked with the Peace Corps on the development of a self-assessment process based on experiential learning, Kolb has been interested in experiential learning theory and its applications. Currently, he is engaged in two major research projects on experiential learning and adult development that focus on the impact of mid-career changes on adults and the role of professional education in career development. He has worked with a variety of national and international businesses and governments, including IBM, Sun Oil Company, the Australian Institute of Management, and the Indonesian Ministry of Industries. He is the coauthor of *Organizational Psychology: An Experiential Approach* (with I. Rubin and J. McIntyre, 3rd ed., 1979), *Organizational Psychology: A Book of Readings* (also with Rubin and McIntyre, 3rd ed., 1979), and *Changing Human Behavior: Principles of Planned Intervention* (with R. Schwitzgebal, 1974).

Lois Lamdin is currently an associate dean at Empire State College of the State University of New York. She holds a Ph.D. degree in English (1967) from the University of Pittsburgh, where she also received her B.A. (1948) and M.A. (1960) degrees in English.

From 1965 to 1969, Lamdin taught English at Carnegie-Mellon University. During the next four years at Hostos Community College, she encountered, as head of the English department, the upheaval in higher education that accompanied the City University of New York's open admissions policy. Her interest in innovative education stimulated by that experience, she moved in 1974 to Empire State College, where she has been involved in curriculum design, the assessment of experientially gained learning, and the identification and encouragement of independent learning skills.

A National Endowment for the Humanities grant in 1974 enabled Lamdin to study contemporary European critical theories at Yale University. She is active in the Modern Language Association, serves on the advisory board of *Alternative Higher Education,* and is a frequent consultant in individualized education; she has been a member of the task force for the Center for Individualized Education. Her publications include *The Ghetto Reader* (with D. Demarest, 1970), a monograph on *Interpersonal Competencies in an Institutional Setting* (with M. Tatzel, 1975), and a number of journal articles on Victorian literature, the Jewish-American novelists, modern poetry, and individualized education. She is currently planning a book on the Jewish-American novel.

Timothy Lehmann is director of program evaluation in the Office of Research and Evaluation at Empire State College of the State University of New York. He was awarded a B.S. degree in industrial management (1959) and an M.A. degree in sociology (1963) from Ohio State University and a Ph.D. degree in sociology from the University of California, Berkeley (1971).

Lehmann has taught at Ohio State University, Chabot Community College, University of California, Berkeley, Colorado State University, and Empire State College. His publications include *Higher Education by Design: A Sociology of Planning* (with E. Palola and W. Blischke, 1970), *Success After Graduation: A Study of the Baccalaureate Gradu- ates of Empire State College* (1974), *Program Effectiveness and Related Costs (PERC) Handbook* (with E. Palola and others, 1977), and *Adult Learning in the Context of Adult Development* (with V. Lester, 1978). Lehmann is currently engaged in studying adult learners.

Jack Lindquist is director of the Institute for Academic Improvement in the Center for the Study of Higher Education at Memphis State University, where he is also associate professor of educational foundations. His degrees are from the University of Michigan: B.A. (1963) and M.S. (1964) in English and Ph.D. (1972) in higher education.

Lindquist has taught English literature, speech, and education and has been a stu- dent counselor and dean. Recently he has directed three national projects regarding the improvement of undergraduate curriculum and teaching: Strategies for Change and Knowledge Utilization, Kellogg Use of Innovations, and the Institute for Academic Im- provement. He also served as research associate for policy analysis and planning at Empire State College. Among his publications are *Strategies for Change* (1978) and *Designing Teaching Improvement Programs* (1978); he is the editor of *Increasing the Impact* (1980).

Richard D. Mann is professor of psychology at the University of Michigan. He received the B.A. degree in social relations from Harvard College (1954) and the Ph.D. degree in psychology from the University of Michigan (1958).

After a year of teaching at the University of Michigan, he was an assistant pro- fessor of social psychology at Harvard for five years. In 1964 he returned to the Univer- sity of Michigan as associate professor of psychology. He received the Distinguished Teaching Award from the University of Michigan in 1968 and the E. Harris Harbison Award for Gifted Teaching from the Danforth Foundation in 1970. His research on class- room groups was reported in *Interpersonal Styles and Group Development* (1967), in *The College Classroom: Conflict, Change, and Learning* (with S. Arnold and others, 1970), and in *Analysis of Groups* (with G. S. Gibbard and J. J. Hartman, 1974). His current scholarly and teaching interests are in the area of spiritual development and comparative religion.

Robert J. Menges is professor and program director at the Center for the Teaching Profes- sions, Northwestern University, where he teaches in the instructional psychology graduate programs. He received his B.A. degree in psychology (1960) from Gettysburg College, his M.A. degree in general psychology (1963) from Boston University, and his Ed.D. in the college teaching of psychology (1967) from Columbia University. He has taught courses in psychology and educational psychology at Columbia, University of Illinois at Urbana- Champaign, and, since 1972, Northwestern University. Menges' publications include studies of prediction of academic achievement, alternative instructional strategies, and instructional evaluation. He is the author of *The Intentional Teacher* (1977); his most recent review of research on student evaluation of teaching appeared in *Liberal Education* (1979). Menges lectures and consults widely on topics related to instructional planning and evaluation in colleges and professional schools; his series of discussion stimulus video- tapes, "College Classroom Vignettes," have received international distribution.

Rhoda Miller is an assistant professor at the Lower Hudson Regional Learning Center of Empire State College. She was awarded a B.S. degree in elementary education from Tren- ton State College (1957) and an M.S.W. degree from Columbia University (1968).

Miller has served as a Peace Corps volunteer in Liberia and has been a practitioner in health, welfare, and educational programs and agencies. Before coming to Empire State College, she was the director of Social Services at Planned Parenthood, New York City. At Empire State College, she coauthored *Community and Human Services Manual, A Guide for Mentors and Students* (with E. Wells and P. Mindell, 1966), designed to look at the human services from a variety of perspectives; she is currently revising this manual.

Theodore K. Miller is professor of counseling and human development services at the University of Georgia, where he is coordinator of the Student Development in Higher Education Preparation Program and director of the Student Development Laboratory. He was awarded the B.S. degree in business and English (1954) and the M.A. degree in counseling and guidance (1957) from Ball State University and the Ed.D. degree in counseling and student personnel services (1962) from the University of Florida.

Miller was a counselor and a teaching-research assistant at the University of Florida (1957-1962) and a counseling psychologist (1962-1964) and assistant professor of counselor education (1962-1967) at the State University of New York in Buffalo. Miller is coauthor of *The Future of Student Affairs: A Guide to Student Development for Tomorrow's Higher Education* (with J. Prince, 1976), *Students Helping Students* (with S. Ender and S. McCaffrey, 1979), and the *Student Developmental Task Inventory–Revised* (with R. Winston and J. Prince, 1979). He was president of the American College Personnel Association (1975-76) and chairperson of that association's Tomorrow's Higher Education Project (1974-75). Currently, he is a member of the board of directors of the American Personnel and Guidance Association. In 1976, Miller received the first annual Mel Hardee Award for Outstanding Achievement and Contribution to the College Student Personnel Profession from the Southern College Personnel Association.

Joyce Parr is executive director of the Foundation for Aging Research in Clearwater, Florida, and adjunct associate research scholar/scientist at the University of South Florida in Tampa. Parr was awarded the B.A. degree in psychology from William Jewell College (1958) and the Ph.D. degree in psychology from the Ohio State University (1962).

While teaching at Alderson-Broaddus College (1962-1974), she was active in the development of community mental health services and in professional training and ethical issues affecting the quality of those services. In 1974, she received a three-year National Institute on Aging Postdoctoral Research Fellowship at the University of California, Los Angeles. Her research involved the study of various psychophysiological and psychometric measures of competence in elderly persons.

She has written a number of chapters and papers on clinical issues and the elderly. Currently, she is engaged in a longitudinal study of persons living in retirement centers in Florida. She recently received an award from the Administration of Aging to develop a training program for managers of retirement housing at the University of South Florida.

William G. Perry, Jr., is professor emeritus of education at Harvard University, where he consulted with students as director of the Bureau of Study Counsel for over thirty years. He received his B.A. degree in English and Greek in 1935 and his M.A. degree in English in 1940 from Harvard University. From ten years of teaching various subjects in school and college he developed a fateful curiosity about the ways students succeed in learning and in not learning.

While the hours of counseling with young men and women about the meaning of learning in their lives provided a self-renewing source for varied articles and essays, the analysis of their tape recordings nourished twenty-five years of teaching the psychology of counseling. In turn the discipline forced by teaching increased the prospect that each counseling hour would be informative.

Perry is a translator of Homer's *Iliad* (with A. H. Chase, 1950) and the author of *Forms of Intellectual and Ethical Development* (1970). He is currently curious about the origins and uses of irony in the embrace of life's contradictions.

Richard E. Peterson is senior research scientist at the Educational Testing Service (ETS) in Berkeley, California. He was awarded B.A. degrees in political science (1953) and psychology (1957) and the M.A. and Ph.D. degrees in education (1959, 1962) from the University of California, Berkeley.

Between 1962 and 1969, when he worked at the main office of ETS in Princeton, New Jersey, Peterson directed development of several instruments used for college self-study. In the late 1960s, he conducted several surveys of the student protest movement nationally; his book *May 1970* (with J. Bilorusky, 1971) for the Carnegie Commission on Higher Education dealt with campus reactions to the Kent State shootings and the Cambodia invasion.

Peterson's current interest in lifelong learning as public policy began in 1972, when he worked on a national survey of adult learning for the Commission on Non-Traditional Study, funded by the Carnegie Foundation. He later directed a feasibility study for the California legislature, which was published as *Postsecondary Alternatives to Meet the Needs of California's Adults* (with J. L. Hefferlin, 1975). During 1977 and 1978 he directed an Exxon-funded review of education, which resulted in *Lifelong Learning in America: An Overview of Current Practices, Available Resources, and Future Prospects* (1979). Most recently, Peterson headed a study of adult education opportunities in nine industrialized countries.

Rita S. Rapoza is research associate and instructor at Wilson Learning Corporation, Eden Prairie, Minnesota. She was awarded her B.A. degree in history from Chaminade College of Honolulu (1966), her M.L.S. degree from the University of Hawaii (1968), and her Ph.D. degree in counseling psychology from the University of Minnesota (1974).

Rapoza has taught at Mankato State University (1968-1972), Mounds View School District (1972-1975), and the University of Western Ontario. Her publications include a variety of articles and *Career Development and Counseling of Women* (co-edited with L. S. Hansen, 1978). Rapoza is currently studying women and their career choices at the managerial levels; her work involves testing, designing, and developing training materials for corporations and banks.

Harold C. Riker is professor of education at the University of Florida, Gainesville, where he is a faculty member of the Counselor Education Department, an adviser for housing programs of the Division of Housing, and a faculty associate of the Center for Gerontological Programs and Studies. Riker received his B.A. and M.A. degrees in English literature and history from the University of Florida (1936, 1938) and the Ed.D. degree in student personnel administration from Columbia University (1955).

At the University of Florida, he has served as assistant director of the Florida Student Union and director of housing. Active in regional and national professional associations, Riker has been president of the Association of College and University Housing Officers, a member of its journal's editorial board, and head of its research committee. He has chaired the Commission on Residential Programs of the American College Personnel

Association and served as a member of its Commission on Professional Development, the editorial board of its journal, and its media board. He is a member of the American Personnel and Guidance Association's Committee on Adult Development and Aging and edits the committee's quarterly newsletter. Riker received the Southern College Personnel Association's 1977 award for outstanding contributions to student personnel work. Among his publications are *College Students Live Here* (1961) and *College Housing as Learning Centers* (1965).

Dorcas S. Saunders is director of transfer studies and professional development at Shelby State Community College, Memphis, Tennessee. She was awarded the B.S., M.Ed., and Ed.S. degrees in education from Auburn University (1956, 1961, 1970) and the Ed.D. degree in higher education from the University of Mississippi (1977). Between 1944 and 1965, she taught in the public schools of Alabama and was supervisor of instruction in the Auburn, Alabama, City Schools during 1965-1970. In 1973, she joined the then new community college in Memphis to develop a reading instruction program.

Saunders is a member of the International Reading Association, Phi Delta Kappa, and the National Council for Staff, Professional, and Organizational Development. She is presently engaged in an academic improvement project concerned with instructional programs for a diverse adult student population.

Robert L. Saunders is dean of the College of Education and professor of educational administration and supervision at Memphis State University. Prior to that appointment in 1970, he was associate dean of education at Auburn University, Auburn, Alabama, coming to that position from several years' service in the public schools of Alabama as teacher and administrator. He earned his B.S. (1947) and M.S. (1950) degrees in science education and his Ed.D. degree (1957) in educational administration at Auburn University.

Saunders has served as president of the Alabama Education Association, Southern Regional Council on Educational Administration, Southern Council for Teacher Education, and the Teacher Education Council of State Colleges and Universities; he was executive secretary of the Southern States Work Conference and chairman of three professional evaluation teams for the National Council for the Accreditation of Teacher Education. For six years he served as consultant to the Tennessee Superintendents' Study Council.

In addition to several monographs and various articles in professional journals, Saunders has coauthored *A Theory of Educational Leadership* (with R. Phillips and H. Johnson, 1966) and *The Educational Manager: Artist and Practitioner* (with E. G. Bogue, 1976).

K. Warner Schaie is professor of psychology at the University of Southern California, where he directs the Gerontology Research Institute of the Ethel Percy Andrus Gerontology Center. Schaie was awarded the B.A. degree in psychology from the University of California at Berkeley (1952) and the M.S. and Ph.D. degrees in psychology from the University of Washington (1953, 1956).

After a year as a postdoctoral fellow in medical psychology at Washington University, he taught at the University of Nebraska (1957-1964) and at West Virginia University (1964-1973). He has been a visiting professor at the University of Missouri, University of the Saar, University of Washington, University of Bern, Macquarrie University, and University of Trier.

Books that Schaie has authored, coauthored, or edited include *Color and Personality* (with R. Heiss, 1964), *Theory and Methods of Research in Aging* (1968), *Life-Span*

Developmental Psychology: Personality and Socialization (with P. B. Baltes, 1973), *Developmental Human Behavior Genetics* (with V. E. Anderson, G. E. McClearn, and J. Money, 1975), and *Handbook of the Psychology of Aging* (with J. E. Birren, 1977). Schaie is currently preparing an undergraduate text for students of adult development and aging and a monograph that integrates the findings of a twenty-one-year longitudinal study of adult intelligence.

Jane Shipton is associate professor of community and human services at Empire State College. She received the B.A. degree in speech from the State University of Iowa (1944) and the M.A. degree in student personnel from New York University (1958).

Following a career in broadcasting, advertising, and publishing, Shipton held positions in student affairs at Barnard College and New York University. During 1954-1958 she was assistant director of the Career-Changing Clinic and produced a series of vocational information booklets for a nationally syndicated newspaper column. Since joining the Empire State College faculty in 1973, Shipton has had major responsibility at the Long Island Center for the assessment of prior learning; she has designed and implemented workshops in career development and educational planning for adults. Shipton is the coauthor of a *Guide to Resources for Life/Career/Educational Planning for Adults* (with E. Steltenpohl, 1976). She is presently extending the scope of the planning guide with special emphasis on the self-assessment of academic skills and materials for adults' use in educational planning.

Elizabeth H. Steltenpohl is professor of educational studies at the Long Island Regional Center of Empire State College. She was awarded the B.A. degree in English (1952) and the M.A. degree in education (1954) from the University of Detroit and the Ed.D. degree in teacher education (1965) from Columbia University.

Following initial teaching experience in the Detroit Public Schools, Steltenpohl taught education courses and supervised student teachers at the University of Detroit, Manhattanville College, and Queens College of the City University of New York. Between 1970 and 1973, Steltenpohl served as director of education for Catalyst, a nonprofit organization in New York City concerned with educational and career opportunities for women. At Empire State College, Steltenpohl has further pursued her special interest in the education of adults. She serves as a mentor in educational studies to a largely adult student population in the nontraditional mode of the college. She is the coauthor of the *Guide to Resources for Life/Career/Educational Planning for Adults* (with J. Shipton, 1976). Currently, Steltenpohl is working on compilations of self-assessment and educational planning materials for adults.

William R. Torbert is associate dean for the graduate division of the Boston College School of Management and associate professor of organizational studies. He is also president of the Theatre of Inquiry, Inc. Torbert received his B.A. degree in political science and economics in 1965 and his Ph.D. degree in administrative sciences in 1971, both from Yale University.

He served as associate director of the Yale Summer High School and director of Yale Upward Bound before joining the faculty of the Southern Methodist University School of Business in 1970 and then the Harvard Graduate School of Education in 1972 for four years. Torbert is a member of the Academy of Management, the National Training Laboratories, Phi Beta Kappa, and the Society for Values in Higher Education. He was awarded a Danforth Graduate Fellowship (1966-1970), was named Outstanding Professor at

Southern Methodist University in 1971, and was a Distinguished Visiting Professor at Oregon State University in 1976. In addition to numerous articles, Torbert has authored *Being for the Most Part Puppets: Interactions Among Men's Labor, Leisure and Politics* (with M. P. Rogers, 1972), *Learning from Experience: Toward Consciousness* (1973), *Creating a Community of Inquiry* (1976), and *A Collaborative Inquiry into Voluntary Metropolitan Desegregation* (with L. Berry, W. Bickley, and P. Wohlstetter, 1976). He is currently working on a book that describes the epistemology, the politics, and the psychology of effective, self-correcting action.

Allen Tough is an associate professor of adult education at the Ontario Institute for Studies in Education and at the University of Toronto. He holds a B.A. degree (1958) in psychology and a M.A. degree (1962) in education and psychology from the University of Toronto and a Ph.D. degree (1965) in adult education from the University of Chicago.

For several years, Tough's central interest has been the major efforts of men and women to learn and change, particularly self-guided efforts, and those that rely on help from peers, as well as professionally guided methods. He is the author of *Learning Without a Teacher* (1967), *The Adult's Learning Projects* (1971), and *Expand Your Life* (in press). He is active internationally as a consultant and speaker.

Paul Ward is executive secretary emeritus of the American Historical Association, which he served from 1965 to 1974. He combines retirement with research and occasional consultantships. Ward received his B.A. degree (1933) in history from Amherst College and his M.A. (1934) and Ph.D. (1940) degrees in history from Harvard University, where he was Junior Fellow (1935-1938) in the Society of Fellows.

He taught briefly at Harvard and at Russell Sage College and then served in Washington during World War II in the Office of Strategic Services. Ward next taught at Huachung University in Wuchang, China, during 1947-1949. After two years at Colby College, he served from 1953-1960 as head of the history department at the Carnegie Institute of Technology in Pittsburgh and 1960-1965 as president of Sarah Lawrence College.

His academic interests have focused on constitutional history and on the nature of historical work. He is the editor of William Lambarde's *Archeion* (1957), the first constitutional history of England, and *Notes on the House of Commons of 1584* (1977). His writings on historical learning have been chiefly review articles in *History and Theory*. One of Ward's principal concerns while with the American Historical Association was to promote attention to the teaching of history; he wrote the association's pamphlet, *Elements of Historical Thinking* (1959, 1971).

Rita Preszler Weathersby is an assistant professor of organizational behavior at the University of New Hampshire's Whittemore School of Business and Economics. She was awarded the B.A. degree in English from the University of California at Berkeley (1965) and received her M.A.T. and Ed.D. degrees from the Harvard Graduate School of Education (1968, 1977).

She has held a variety of teaching, administrative, and professional positions, including affiliations with the Vallejo, California, Public Schools, the Far West Laboratory for Educational Research and Development, Wheelock College, and the Boston Center for Religion and Psychotherapy. In 1972-73, she was selected as an Educational Policy Fellow with the George Washington University Institute for Educational Leadership and the U.S. Department of Health, Education, and Welfare. She is the coauthor of *New Roles for Educators* (with A. Blackmer and P. R. Allen, 1970). At the Far West Laboratory, she collaborated on developing training materials for secondary teachers, *Minicourse 9: Higher Cognitive Questioning* (1971) and *Discussing Controversial Issues* (1972). A member of the Gestalt Institute of Cleveland, Weathersby is a trainer and consultant for organizations.

Robert W. White is professor emeritus of clinical psychology at Harvard University, where he served on the faculty from 1937 to 1969. He is now self-employed as a writer and lives in Marlborough, New Hampshire.

White received his three degrees from Harvard: A.B. (1925) and A.M. in history (1926), and Ph.D. in psychology (1937). He taught history at the University of Maine and psychology at Rutgers, 1930-1933. During his Harvard appointment, he was director of the Psychological Clinic (1946-1950) and chairman of the Department of Social Relations (1957-1962).

White's first book was *The Abnormal Personality* (1948, 5th ed., with N. F. Watt, forthcoming), followed by *Lives in Progress* (1952), *The Enterprise of Living* (1972), *Opinions and Personality* (with M. B. Smith and J. S. Bruner, 1956), and *A Case Workbook in Personality* (with M. M. Riggs and D. C. Gilbert, 1976).

Carol Wolff is coordinator of the undergraduate core curriculum in human services at Antioch University. She was awarded the B.A. degree in community development from Rutgers University, Livingston College (1973) and the M.A. degree in counseling from Kean College (1975).

She has worked with a number of colleges, agencies, and community organizations to create educational opportunities for paraprofessionals, women, and minorities. While working with the New Jersey State Department of Education, Wolff helped to develop the Urban Education Corps, a national recruitment and training program to place minority teacher interns in urban school districts. Wolff designed and later directed the Perth-Amboy Storefront College, a community-based educational center that provided external degree study opportunities primarily for Hispanic adults. She worked with a statewide education consortium in New Jersey to develop field-based human services curriculum for experienced practitioners seeking to combine career and educational interests. She has also conducted numerous workshops for union leaders, inmates, and hospital workers on developing individualized programs of study, assessment of prior learning, and approaches to actively exploring or creating options in higher education.

The Modern American College

Responding to the New Realities of Diverse Students and a Changing Society

Introduction

"The supreme need of American education is for a unifying purpose or idea," wrote the authors (Committee on the Objectives . . . , 1945, p. 36) of the Harvard "redbook," *General Education in a Free Society,* at the end of World War II. Most educators feel that need keenly today. Their feeling is evidenced by the widespread concern about core curriculums, general education, and the integration of professional preparation with liberal arts. It is documented by the articles and reports coming from institutional committees and national commissions.

Unfortunately, the recent Harvard core curriculum plan, adopted in 1978, did not seem to do the trick. It has been faintly praised at best. Certainly, course content and curricular requirements need periodic analysis and revision. Yet how can we hope to effect significant changes if the underlying assumptions about student motives and learning styles, effective teaching, appropriate student-faculty relationships, priorities among teaching, research, and service, and reward systems all remain unexamined? Stephen K. Bailey's (1977) observations bring us up sharp against reality:

> Required general education courses, whatever good they did the first generation of teachers and students who participated, have a long history of progressive disaffection, increased deputization to lower academic ranks, and general faculty antagonism. . . . Furthermore, distribution requirements across academic divisions—at least in a large university—all too frequently prompt a mindless student search for convenient hours and easy grades [p. 253].

Harvard's action did trigger, and serve to validate, analogous curricular reviews at a number of colleges and universities throughout the country. But few persons are optimistic that simply reshuffling content and reintroducing distribution requirements will be a sufficient response to the need for a unifying purpose or idea for American higher education in the 1980s and beyond.

This book addresses that problem of purpose. It offers a consistent line of attack based on the unifying idea of *adult development*. Its basic argument is that the overarching educational purpose of our colleges and universities should be to encourage and enable intentional developmental change in students throughout the life cycle.

"But what is new or startling about taking human development as a unifying purpose?" you may ask. "We have been concerned about educating 'the whole person'—about effective character development and effective citizenship—all along." At one level of abstraction, it is true: there is nothing new. Such formulations of purpose have been in our rhetoric at least since Cardinal Newman expressed his idea of a university in 1852. His ringing words sound as pertinent today as then:

> University training is the great ordinary means to a great but ordinary end; it aims at raising the intellectual tone of society, at cultivating the public mind, at purifying the national taste, at supplying true principles to popular enthusiasm and fixed aimes to popular aspiration, at giving enlargement and sobriety to the ideas of the age, at facilitating the exercise of political power, and refining the intercourse of private life. It is the education which gives a man a clear conscious view of his own opinions and judgments, a truth in developing them, an eloquence in expressing them, and a force in urging them. It teaches him to see things as they are, to go right to the point, to disentangle a skein of thought, to detect what is sophisticated, and to discard what is irrelevant. It prepares him to fill any post with credit, and to master any subject with facility. It shows him how to accommodate himself to others, how to throw himself into their state of mind, how to bring before them his own, how to influence them, how to come to an understanding with them, how to bear with them. He is at home in any society, he has common ground with every class; he knows when to speak and when to be silent; he is able to converse; he is able to listen; he can ask a question pertinently, and gain a lesson seasonably, when he has nothing to impart himself; he is ever ready, yet never in the way; he is a pleasant companion and a comrade you can depend upon; he knows when to be serious and when to trifle; and he has a sure tact which enables him to trifle with gracefulness and to be serious with effect. He has the repose of a mind which lives in itself, while it lives in the world, and which has resources for its happiness when it cannot go abroad. He has a gift which services him in public, and supports him in retirement, without which good fortune is but vulgar, and with which failure and disappointment have a charm [1973 (1852), pp. 177-178].

Now that paragraph is hard to match for eloquence. Few latter-day formulations come close in power and specificity. It encompasses and improves upon the stated objectives found in most college and university bulletins. Take it apart and you have a full statement of mission and a detailed curriculum outline to boot. The words "a clear conscious view of his own opinions and judgments, a truth in developing them, an eloquence in expressing them, and a force in urging them" suggest clear values, integrity, and communication skills—those basic goals of the liberal arts. The words "to see things as they are, to go right to the point, to disentangle a skein of thought, to detect what is sophisticated, and to discard what is irrelevant" imply critical thinking skills, analysis, synthesis, and evaluation—those high levels of Bloom's (1956) *Taxonomy of Educational Objectives* in the cognitive domain. "To fill any post with credit and to master any subject with facility" calls to mind professional or vocational preparation and learning how to learn. "He is at home in any society, he has common ground with every class" evokes that sense of tolerance and interdependence so critical to our times. "How to accommodate himself to others, how to throw himself into their state of mind, how to bring before them his own, how to influence them, how to come to an understanding with them, how to bear with them" summarizes the major elements of interpersonal competence—empathy, understanding, and cooperation with others. "A pleasant companion and a comrade you can depend upon" proposes a capacity for intimacy that goes beyond mere competence and tolerance. And "a repose of a mind which lives in itself, while it lives in the world" refers to our basic sense of identity.

Thus, the dimensions of human development that are described in Part One of this book—intellectual competence, ego development, moral and ethical development, humanitarian concern, interpersonal competence, capacity for intimacy, vocational development—express the same values and objectives for education as those extolled by Newman and many other educators before and after. So there really is nothing new here at the level of general purposes.

Then what is new? What is new is our growing knowledge from the social sciences about the factors that contribute to the development of these human characteristics. What is new is our awareness of the discontinuities between this knowledge and the reality of our social systems, of the gap between our educational purposes and the actual outcomes, of the gap between our aspirations for our graduates and what they really achieve as they function as workers, citizens, family members, and friends. What is new and sobering is our growing recognition that our success in achieving our educational objectives may be critical to our individual and collective health and well-being, with personal, social, and worldwide problems challenging the best we can muster in just these human characteristics we seek to encourage in college.

Challenges of the Eighties

In the "underdeveloped" countries of the world, with a few exceptions, the poor are getting poorer, the hungry, hungrier. The number of countries with known nuclear capability has increased from six to thirty. It seems likely that before long plutonium generated as a by-product of nuclear power will put nuclear weapons in the hands of any country or terrorist group willing to risk a life or two. Nonrenewable resources are gradually running out. The known supplies of these resources, particularly oil and other key minerals, the use rates, and patterns of worldwide distribution spell out potential for conflict on a scale completely unknown fifty years ago. Complex international cooperation and trade-offs will be required. And if those days of severe resource shortages arrive, national autonomy will have to be compromised as it never has been before. In addition, for the first time in human history self-sacrifice by the "haves" will need to go beyond token contributions by a benevolent Santa Claus, to levels of sharing which will affect the living standards of each person in the "developed" world.

But we do not need to think globally to see how important developmental dimensions concerning intellectual competence, moral and ethical development, interpersonal competence, integrity, and sense of interdependence have become. Consider simply the basics of population density, technological complexity, and human interaction. In Colonial America the population density averaged one person per square mile: 314 persons inside a circle 20 miles in diameter—a good day's walk—with the chance of human contact 313 to 1. The opportunities for interpersonal encounter and exchange of information were limited. Today, Chicago has a population density of more than 10,000 persons per square mile. Modern demographic and social forces have brought more different kinds of people into contact with each other: blacks, whites, rich, poor, intellectuals, rednecks, and hippies. The fight for the five-o'clock subway, where the conductor crams two more persons into the car so the door can close, or the battle for the first lane on the "freeway" at eight in the morning are only part of our daily rounds.

These rounds are supported by complex arrangements for housing, transportation, heat, light, food, waste collection, and other basic necessities. Such conditions put power for disruption in the hands of each person and each special interest group. A five-day railroad or truck strike slows the nation to a walk. A monkey wrench or human error in the electrical power system blacks out five states. These and other complex interdependencies require entirely new levels of tolerance, sensitivity, understanding, perspective, social responsibility for all of us.

The complexity of the problems that confront us makes it difficult for any of us to have confidence in the rightness of our views and behavior. We may have strong feelings about mandatory proficiency testing or local zoning ordinances, nuclear power, wilderness conservation, or foreign aid. But we are aware of the gap between our strong feelings and our limited information on these complex questions. And we shudder at the work required to become informed and keep up to date. Throughout the world, more than 100,000 journals are published in more than sixty languages. Much of the research published in these journals rests on broad-based scientific and technological advances, which have been growing exponentially. Graphs plotting such things as the discovery of natural resources and the isolation of natural elements, the time lag between successive discoveries, the speed of transportation, and the growth of computerization look like rocket trajectories. Most trend lines are fast approaching the vertical. Of course, exponential curves only grow to infinity in mathematics. In the real world they turn around, often with a catastrophic drop caused by the forces they themselves set in motion.

The social implications of these changes are immense, as are their implications for higher education. We know by now how much these developments and the social problems accompanying them magnify the need for perspective, judgment, and other critical human qualities. And we know that we cannot depend on just a select few, who, by controlling the production and distribution of information, and by controlling the resources and energy we live by, control our daily lives and the destinies of our children. To meet these problems certainly we need competent and knowledgeable persons who can manage the machinery and the bureaucracies. But more than that we need persons who have breadth of perspective and personal characteristics such that they can participate effectively in the processes of social self-determination.

As Stephen Bailey (1977) puts it:

> This nation is in woefully short supply of people equipped to look at problems as a whole, at life as a whole, at the earth as a whole. Without a sense of the whole we have no way of evaluating the parts, no ways of appraising the importance of the expert, no way of seeing that the fragmentation and violence we lament in the world around us is but the mirror image of our own cluttered and frenetic psyches.
>
> Liberal learning at its best is not designed to relieve life of its pain and uncertainty. It is designed to help people have creative engagements with adversity, to discover and draw upon the wellsprings of existential joy, to recognize our common plight and need for one another [pp. 257-258].

One of the things that is strikingly new since Newman delivered his discourses, and even since the Harvard redbook, is a sharp sense of urgency. It does not matter a great deal whether we credit the doomsday books that give us twenty years or the more generous projections that give us fifty or a hundred. Any objective analysis, based on the record of history, would no doubt predict that we would let other nations suffer starvation and chaos before voluntarily taking a serious cut in our standard of living; that we would use up the last drop of available resources before cutting consumption sufficiently; that we would suffer nuclear war before surrendering significant national autonomy. And we in the United States are not much better or worse than any other peoples in the world in this regard. But our human resources, economic power, and armed might give us a capacity for influence still unequalled throughout the world. Thus, our own orientations and actions can be fateful. By changing ourselves we can exert influence far beyond our numbers.

We recognize that closing the gap between our rhetoric and the reality of our institutional practices has become a critical matter for ourselves and our spaceship Earth companions. This sense of urgency has led us to recognize the need for more intentional attacks on these issues. We no longer feel complacent in assuming that those outcomes will occur as a natural by-product of institutional business as usual. The need to be more explicit, more directly concerned, more concretely devoted to such ends has become apparent.

The need for a more direct concern with human development in education has been recognized by increasing numbers of persons across the country—by those in positions of established leadership as well as by many others less well known, working daily with students and pushing as best they can for institutional changes and professional development activities that will advance the broader goals of human development. Certainly, these persons do not constitute a majority. That is not the way change occurs. There will be no massive conversion. Change will occur incrementally as increasing numbers of teachers, departments, schools, and colleges tackle self-consciously and directly one or a combination of the general education objectives or one or more major dimensions of development.

But we have had waves of concern for general education, "character development," and the like before. They have rolled over us and passed on with little apparent legacy. What reason is there to believe that these current concerns will last and actually make a difference?

There is room for increased hope because our understanding of human development, of the conditions that encourage and retard it, and of the impacts of varied institutional arrangements and human interactions, has increased dramatically in the last forty years. Research and theory concerning such things as motive acquisition, value change, influence processes, organizational behavior, group dynamics, intellectual development, moral and ethical development, career patterns, and humanitarian concern have become increasingly sophisticated. Do not misunderstand. No one is claiming a level of sophistication that permits anything approaching accurate predictions or clear programming for particular individuals. But at the statistical level, substantial strides have been made. Given the right kind of information about institutional environments and student characteristics, we can predict completion rates, attrition patterns, and certain kinds of educational outcomes at a level far beyond chance. If we hold certain institutional characteristics constant, we can predict differential outcome frequencies for different types of students. If we hold certain student characteristics constant, we can predict different outcome rates as a function of institutional differences. For details and documentation, see, for example, Feldman and Newcomb (1969), Chickering (1969, 1974), Trent and Medsker (1968), Astin (1977), and Bowen (1977). In addition, there are numerous supporting references supplied by authors of Part One chapters for their particular areas of expertise. So one reason for increased optimism is our increased knowledge about how to create environments for learning and personal development that are sufficiently differentiated and rich to be helpful to many different types of students.

Another major ground for hope lies in our increased understanding of how persons can more effectively take charge of their own lives. Howard Bowen (1977) has pointed out that perhaps one of the most important benefits of higher education is the increased capacity to cope with bureaucracies, fend off social pressures, recognize false claims and misleading advertising, distinguish sound evidence from emotional appeal, and resist manipulation. No less important is the ability to continue learning on one's own. In recent years, we have come to understand a good deal about self-directed learning, about how to help persons clarify objectives, identify appropriate learning activities and resources, and evaluate their own progress. Tough's chapter reveals that adult students in our learning society undertake 80 percent of their learning on their own, outside formal educational structures and without help from specially trained teachers. Self-initiated, self-directed learning is going on all around us every day. There is every reason to believe that with the appropriate use of educational resources these same energies could be channeled toward the types of development discussed in Part One of this book. "The students are alive," said Whitehead, "and the purpose of education is to stimulate and guide their self-development" (1966, p. 21). We need to accent our concern for "self-development." In proposing that we address more intentionally life cycle issues and developmental dimensions, we are not arguing for a piecemeal approach. What we need is a more nutritious soil in which many kinds of life can flourish and grow.

But perhaps the major reason for hope lies in what is also our most difficult problem—the dramatic increase in student diversity resulting from the inexorable trend toward mass education. Mass higher education is here, and it is fast developing in other countries around the world. Cerych and Furth (1972, pp. 15-18), who have thoroughly studied the phenomenon for the Organization for Economic Cooperation and Development (OECD), describe what is happening:

> The educational policies of most of the industrialized countries are based predominantly on the principle of satisfying social demand for higher education and opening its gates not only to those qualified by traditional criteria (that is, all applicants who have successfully completed general secondary education), but also to students who up to now have been excluded, either formally or in practice, because of their social origin, educational background, or age.
>
> This social demand for higher education will most probably continue to grow; no major constraints or ceilings can be identified which would lead to its decline in the foreseeable future.
>
> It must also be born in mind that of the various factors correlated with the rate of participation in higher education of different social groups, by far the most significant is the educational level of parents. An increase in the number of fathers and mothers with university degrees (or merely secondary school diplomas) inevitably implies more children demanding entry into higher education a generation later.

The combined trends toward mass education and lifelong learning will bring the full range of citizens into our colleges and universities for a multitude of purposes. As the Carnegie Commission summarized in its report, *Reform on Campus* (1972):

> Higher education in America has been marked by greater diversity than that in any other system in the world. Its amazing variety reflects both the historical origins of colleges in many divergent public and private endeavors, and also the

continuing pluralism of American society. This diversity has been one of the greatest strengths of higher education; a major source of much of its dynamism.

The need for more diversity, rather than less, flows from the more varied backgrounds of the students now entering college and their more varied interests once in college, from the new occupations constantly being created and the new training necessary for them, from the new or at least newly visible problems of society, and from the new emphasis on quality of life and on independent choice of life-styles. . . . The trend toward homogenization can lead to dull conformity, to the meanest kind of petty competition, and to less meaningful service to students and society as each institution tries to climb higher up a single greasy pole of success.

The main direction of development we see ahead is an effort at the creation of a more diverse series of optimal learning environments to meet more precisely the needs of each college-age person—diverse as these needs are and hard to accomplish as this goal will be—so that each young person will have an equality of opportunity, through one form of education or another, to maximize the quality of his or her life. This is our basic vision of where higher education should be moving. This is our view of the proximate end goal for the American campus. We want to see the opportunity structure of higher education greatly expanded—first, to make it available to more people, and second, to make it more responsive to the varied individual needs of the participants. A century ago the direction of development was toward greater compatibility between higher education and an American society responding to industrialization and to populism; now the development should be toward a more humane system of higher education as part of the further humanization of American society [pp. 35, 68].

The words of Newman in 1852 and of the Carnegie Commission in 1972, one hundred twenty years later, make good bookends for this volume on the mission of higher education. For we cannot pursue the objectives set forth by Newman without recognizing "more precisely the needs of each college-age person." The growing diversity among students requires that we pay more attention to the developmental needs of each. When higher education served an aristocratic few, and later when it filtered large collections of applicants through a narrowly defined meritocratic sieve, it could afford to treat students in more or less the same way. It could establish a limited set of options for learning, a restricted range of educational practices, and an isolated set of institutional environments, and expect all students to adapt themselves to those conditions.

But now institutions must devise alternatives to meet the needs of diverse students. This means that each teacher, administrator, and student personnel professional will have to give much more thought to the persons being educated than in the past. We will thus need an increased working knowledge about the human characteristics that influence learning. Such knowledge can help us better understand the kinds of heterogeneity that will maximize learning through peer interaction in our classes and our campuses. It also will help us tailor curriculums and educational practices to particular individual needs. The Part One chapters concerning the life cycle, adult development, and adult learning supply a range of conceptual frameworks within which to examine these needs.

So the overarching purpose of this book is to suggest that explicit concern for adult development can provide the "unifying purpose or idea" for higher education—that direct attention to life cycle concerns and aspects of personal growth can restore a sense of coherence and direction to our efforts. We do not pretend that the necessary know-how for any grand design is at hand. We have much to learn. Change will be incremental.

It will involve risk and aborted efforts. It will require collaboration and generate conflicts. But when the Harvard redbook addressed the problem of "general education in a free society," going to the moon seemed a far-fetched dream. If that dream can be realized, surely our educational goals are not beyond reach.

Achieving Immediate Ends

Our limited knowledge and experience argue against creating any grand design—organizing major policy debates, national commissions, task forces on long-range planning, and the like. In most cases, the objectives set forth here have already been adopted at the general level of institutional policy. We need only the will, the courage, and the competence to realize them.

At the level of a single course, discipline, or area of professional preparation, it is possible to think through in fairly concrete terms what modifications of course content and learning environments might be appropriate. At the level of particular educational processes, teaching practices, extracurricular activities, residential settings, and arrangements for advising and career planning, it is possible to envision the implications of one or another life cycle concern or aspect of personal development. Thus, no great magic is required. A thoughtful professional can examine conceptual frameworks such as those presented in Part One and make intelligent use of them. We believe the chapters in Parts Two and Three demonstrate just that.

But those examples demonstrate another critical point: *Recognizing and responding to life cycle concerns and helping students address developmental needs can be synergistic with achieving more immediate instrumental ends.* The two need not detract from each other. It is possible to select content and to manage teaching, learning, and evaluation in ways that promote achievement of particular objectives important to a discipline or profession and at the same time promote those larger developmental values and purposes. Take any Part Two chapter and ask whether that synergy indeed seems likely. Ask, for example, whether students who tackle the study of history in ways consistent with Paul Ward's suggestions will make more or less progress toward objectives important to historians than others whose approach does not recognize the concerns he speaks to. Ask of Audrey Cohen's chapter on human services whether those graduates will be more or less competent, after a program that explicitly confronts key issues of individual development, than graduates of more traditional programs. Pick that discipline or professional area closest to your own and consider seriously the question of synergy. Then consider whether the same might be possible for your particular area.

It seems unlikely that all our chapters will pass the tests posed by diverse readers. But the general proposition seems sound. Living and learning in any discipline or profession provides ample challenge and opportunity for significant growth in at least one or more of the major dimensions of development described in Part One. Just look around at colleagues—setting aside for a moment our jaundiced views of some antagonistic departments or divisions. In all areas we see persons who continue to grow in significant ways through their work and study.

The important point is that achieving these larger institutional purposes will not depend solely on our activities in the name of general or liberal education. With thoughtful application, those objectives can be served and intentionally addressed as part of "majors," particular areas of professional preparation, or graduate study, as well as through social issues or personal problems. Thus, we can tackle these objectives at all levels of our curriculum and through a wide range of educational processes and conditions. We need not settle for simple rearrangements of general education requirements and course content, for isolated and compartmentalized efforts that leave the rest of the system untouched. We can instead carry these concerns throughout the full curriculum. We can examine our extracurricular activities, student-faculty relationships, residential arrangements, and the like for their potential contributions. And in so doing we can achieve immediate ends while also working consistently to serve the more general objectives of adult development.

In proposing human development as a unifying purpose, our aim is not to narrow or restrict the mission of any college or university. We do not suggest that every student should major in human development. Nor do we suggest that the developmental needs of a particular student should be the sole basis for determining his or her educational program. Those needs must be addressed in the light of the requirements for knowledge, competence, and human capacities set by particular disciplines or professions. We are not espousing a self-centered, narcissistic, glorification of individual needs and desires over the hard realistic requirements for effective social contribution. On the contrary. Our view is that by giving proper attention to life cycle challenges and developmental needs we can design coherent programs that better prepare persons for the kind of praxis, for the kind of service as workers and citizens, required by the social changes rushing toward us.

Furthermore, by recovering a unifying purpose meaningful to faculty, administrators, and students alike, we may also recover a sense of community. We may regain a measure of internal coherence, which has broken apart under the onslaught of the knowledge explosion, with its attendant proliferation of disciplines, departments, and professional specializations. Such a change might help our institutions recover a sense of shared commitment and shared cultural values, which can give added weight to each individual effort.

Human Manipulation and Social Control

Let us put it boldly. We propose that colleges and universities concern themselves more deliberately and explicitly with human development. We go further. We propose that the values and aims of human development be taken as unifying purposes, as organizing frameworks for all institutional efforts—from initial orientation and advising, through general education programs and core requirements, to concentrations, majors, and areas of professional specialization. We suggest that teaching practices and activities, residential arrangements, and other institutional environments can be organized in ways that promote various aspects of development. To some, this may sound like 1984. The question is not whether higher education should be in the business of human engineering and social control? It already is in that business. Listen to Veysey (1974) as he comes to the end of his detailed study, *The Emergence of the American University*:

> The university in the United States had become largely an agency for social control. . . . The custodianship of popular values comprised the primary responsibility of the American university. It was to teach its students to think constructively rather than with an imprudent and disintegrative independence. It was to make its degrees into syndicated emblems of social and economic arrival. It was to promise, with repetitive care, that the investigations of its learned men were dedicated to the practical furtherance of the common welfare. It was to organize its own affairs to such a businesslike fashion as to reassure any stray industrialist or legislator who chanced onto its campus. It was to become a place prominently devoted to non-abstractive good fun: to singing and cheering, to the

rituals of club life and 'appropriate' oratory; it was to be the place where the easy, infectious harmonies of brass band and stamping feet found few toes unwilling at least faintly to tap in time [pp. 440-441].

Every college and university, public or private, church-related or not, is in the business of shaping human lives. They will continue to be. It is one of the fundamental reasons for their existence. It is the bedrock basis for state support, federal incentives, and tax-exempt status.

Given this fact, what consequences can we expect from taking human development as the unifying purpose of higher education? What consequences for the individual and society will follow from greater awareness of interactions between self and system? Will a greater awareness of life cycle trajectories help persons understand their own and others' problems better and take a more active part in creating their own futures? If men and women throughout the life cycle become more aware of the opportunistic, conformist, conscientious, and autonomous stages of ego development and of the dominant structures organizing their existence; if they can understand their dualistic thinking, or unfettered relativism, in the context of large systems of moral and ethical development, how will their frameworks for judgment and action change? If they understand better the experiences that work for and against their own humanitarian concern, how will this affect their views and their actions? If they see more clearly the forces steering their own professional or vocational development, recognize more fully the path on which they are set, and contemplate the pros and cons of alternative directions, will they be better able to take charge of their own lives? If they develop increased interpersonal competence and capacity for intimacy will they be able to avoid manipulation and exploitation of others? If they acquire a more sophisticated understanding of their own learning styles and the constraints and pressures of various disciplinary inquiry norms, will they have a better idea of what and how to study? If they acquire clearer purposes, through better grasping the complex interactions among individual goals, institutional objectives, and social values, what form will those purposes take?

Our own answers to those questions are optimistic. The evidence to date does indeed indicate that the direction of change in ego development is toward integrity, not toward opportunism, and that the direction of moral and ethical development is toward contextual relativism, which assigns human welfare the highest value. The evidence does indicate change toward increased intellectual competence and complexity, toward increased concern for collaborative inquiry modes and for intimate, caring relationships. Individual purposes and identities do become clearer and stronger; with age they are put in the larger perspectives of institutional objectives and social values. Persons do learn how to learn and how to take charge of their own development.

Given the social forces and cultural contexts to which we are subject, we seldom reach those developmental goals we value. Our becoming typically falls short of what we would become. But the striving is there in most of us. And the directions of our strivings are documented by the conceptual frameworks presented in Part One. Thus it is that we argue for increased attention to those strivings, increased opportunities for each person to define more clearly those developmental issues and dimensions significant for him or her, and increased investment of institutional resources and expertise in the service of those purposes.

André Malraux describes a crisis of civilization in which the gods are dead and the image of man has disappeared. The belief in the hereafter is replaced by the valley of the shadow of death. There is little optimism about walking through and reaching the other side. Boundless forces seem too complex to manage, too powerful to control. The rods and staffs available, religious or secular, may offer comfort but not hope. Whether or not a crisis of civilization is indeed upon us, the problems before us require that we regain a clear image of the human personality. The social science research reported in Part One helps to outline such an image and suggests that new levels of human complexity, of self-understanding and social perspective can be achieved, given the appropriate conditions. Whether or not those research findings will stand the test of time and action remains to be seen. And whether or not the appropriate conditions can be created remains an open question. But can educators turn their backs on the challenge, just as the means are becoming available to meet it? It is the view of this volume that we cannot. We should instead tackle those challenges straightforwardly, systematically, and with the best judgment and competence we can muster. We should take adult development as our unifying purpose and by directly addressing the problem attempt to help individuals and society reach those as yet unrealized potentialities of caring and complexity, interdependence and integrity.

References

Astin, A. W. *Four Critical Years: Effects of College on Beliefs, Attitudes, and Knowledge.* San Francisco: Jossey-Bass, 1977.

Bailey, S. K. "Needed Changes in Liberal Education." *Educational Record,* 1977, pp. 250-258.

Bloom, B. S., and others. *Taxonomy of Educational Objectives.* New York: McKay, 1956.

Bowen, H. R. *Investment in Learning: The Individual and Social Value of American Higher Education.* San Francisco: Jossey-Bass, 1977.

Carnegie Commission on Higher Education. *Reform on Campus: Changing Students, Changing Academic Programs.* New York: McGraw-Hill, 1972.

Cerych, L., and Furth, D. E. "On the Threshold of Mass Education." In W. R. Niblett and R. F. Butts (Eds.), *Universities Facing the Future: An International Perspective.* San Francisco: Jossey-Bass, 1972.

Chickering, A. W. *Education and Identity.* San Francisco: Jossey-Bass, 1969.

Chickering, A. W. *Commuting Versus Resident Students: Overcoming Educational Inequities of Living Off Campus.* San Francisco: Jossey-Bass, 1974.

Committee on the Objectives of General Education in a Free Society, Harvard University. *General Education in a Free Society: Report of the Harvard Committee.* Cambridge, Mass.: Harvard University Press, 1945.

Feldman, K. A., and Newcomb, T. M. *The Impact of College on Students.* San Francisco: Jossey-Bass, 1969.

Newman, J. H. *The Idea of a University.* Westminster, Md.: Christian Classics, 1973. (Originally published 1852.)

Niblett, W. R., and Butts, R. F. *Universities Facing the Future: An International Perspective.* San Francisco: Jossey-Bass, 1972.

Trent, J. W., and Medsker, L. L. *Beyond High School: A Psychosociological Study of 10,000 High School Graduates.* San Francisco: Jossey-Bass, 1968.

Veysey, L. R. *The Emergence of the American University.* Chicago: University of Chicago Press, 1974.

Whitehead, A. N. *The Aims of Education and Other Essays.* London: Benn, 1966.

Part One

Today's Students and Their Needs

We open the first part of this book with a chapter that synthesizes research and theory concerning the life cycle. This chapter briefly outlines the major conceptions of the adult life cycle advanced by Erikson, Gould, Levinson, Neugarten, Lowenthal, and others, and then presents a summary formulation of the cycle using Havighurst's developmental task approach. It describes the shifting challenges, tasks, and orientations associated with each of six periods from late adolescence and youth through early adulthood, midlife transition, middle adulthood, late-adult transition, and late adulthood. And it addresses the key educational implications of these changes over the adult years for curricular content, educational practice, and institutional administration.

Chapters Two through Nine then present separate conceptual frameworks for understanding the major dimensions of development over the life cycle. Chapter Two opens this series with a broad look at ego development. As its author, Rita Weathersby, explains, *ego* is a general term for that part of each of us which strives for coherence in our lives and assigns meaning to our experience. The concept of ego development unites patterns of cognitive, affective, and interpersonal development in successive, hierarchically ordered world views, which themselves become organizers for beliefs and behavior. Chapter Two, therefore, introduces us to specific dimensions of development discussed more thoroughly in later chapters dealing with intellectual, moral, and ethical development, interpersonal competence, and the capacity for intimacy. It suggests relationships between various aspects of ego development and traditional educational objectives, and it develops the implications for colleges of taking ego development itself as an intentional objective for higher education.

12

The next two chapters focus on the primary concern of most faculty members: cognitive development. In Chapter Three, William Perry uses actual statements of students to show how they move from one stage to the next of intellectual and ethical development—from "dualism" and "multiplicity" through "relativism" to "evolving commitments." He also illustrates the strategies of escape, retreat, and temporizing that students use when developmental challenges get too tough to handle. Perry's ideas have bedrock significance not only for teachers, whose teaching will be construed by students according to their level of intellectual development, but also for administrators and student personnel professionals concerned with arranging institutional environments and resources for maximum educational effectiveness.

In Chapter Four, Warner Schaie and Joyce Parr bring us the good news that intellectual development continues throughout the life cycle and that most of us get smarter as we get older—in contrast to the message drawn from earlier research that intellectual ability peaks in young adulthood and declines thereafter. Schaie and Parr describe an intellectually "acquisitive" stage during childhood and adolescence, an "achieving" stage during young adulthood, "executive" and "responsible" stages during middle age, and a "reintegrative" period in old age. They show that particular areas of intellectual competence associated with each of these stages can be modified, and they consider how curriculums and educational practices may be adapted to encourage further intellectual development.

Perry's studies of intellectual and ethical development document clearly the important interrelationship between intellect and morality—between cognitive processes and the ways in which values and belief systems are acquired. In Chapter Five, Carol Gilligan introduces us to new findings from studies of the development of moral judgment and its cognitive components, including the work of Lawrence Kohlberg and his colleagues. She examines Kohlberg's work in light of Perry's concepts and emphasizes the significance of students' attaining "contextual relativism" for their full moral development and its consequences for intellectual development. She argues that contextual relativism must be integrated with experiences of moral responsibility for the development of moral understanding, and shows how the study of history and literature can contribute to moral education and cognitive development by extending students' understanding of other lives, both past and present.

Robert White then expands on this theme in Chapter Six, dealing with the development of humanitarian concern. In view of our increasing urban, regional, national, and international interdependencies, this chapter addresses what for many educators seems the single most significant but currently neglected aspect of student development: altruism. Tapping a personal reservoir of more than thirty years of research, scholarship, and teaching on human development, White identifies the basic principles underlying humanitarian concern, including the root requirement of empathy, and describes the conditions that lead to the expansion or extinction of empathy. His conception of "principled humanitarian concern" is consistent with the higher stages of moral and ethical development postulated by Kohlberg and Perry, and his description of how social relationships develop and maintain this concern leads to suggestions of how colleges and universities can encourage its development both in undergraduate programs and in professional training.

Chapters Seven and Eight take us to two distinct but interrelated areas of interpersonal relations: interpersonal competence and intimacy. Students' problems in these areas of development can block their achievement and success in other areas; conversely, success in both these areas can greatly enhance their energies and capabilities for more instrumental activities on the job, at home, or in the community. In Chapter Seven, William Torbert focuses on competence in making one's way in the interpersonal world—the ability to work cooperatively with others, to compete effectively, to seek and offer help, to influence others, and to create a network of honest communication with colleagues and associates. Building on his own research and that of Chris Argyris and Donald Schön, he offers concrete illustrations of how teachers can foster such competence and thereby increase their own, their students', and their institution's effectiveness.

In Chapter Eight, Elizabeth Douvan examines the capacity for intimacy—the willingness and ability to commit oneself to close affective relationships. She takes intimate adult friendship as her model of this capacity for intimacy, discusses the ways in which the elements of this ability shift throughout the life cycle from young adulthood to middle age to older adulthood, illustrates the role of peers and faculty members in developing this capacity in college, and explains the implications of this evidence for curriculum, educational practice, and student learning.

Chapter Nine turns to the last major facet of adult development discussed in Part One: professional development. Most students say that getting a better job—better in terms of pay, responsibility, challenge, and consistency with their talents and aspirations—is their main reason for attending college. But professional development is not achieved once and for all. It is a recurrent process of vertical and lateral movement, of training and retraining, certification and recertification, learning and then learning some more. In Chapter Nine, Donald Blocher and Rita Rapoza bring us up to date on this process, referring to a sequence of life cycle stages similar to that in Chapter One and pointing out the special vocational needs and characteristics of adolescents and young adults, college women, minority students, and older students. They share research evidence concerning the ways in which college can—but often does not—assist students' vocational development, and they foresee the need for sweeping changes in the nature, organization, and delivery of career planning services in order to facilitate this development.

With Chapter Ten, we shift from a focus on specific areas of adult development to an analysis of problems facing various groups of students. In this chapter, David Kolb examines the differences among students in their cognitive and learning styles. On the basis of concrete versus abstract and active versus reflective orientations, he identifies four major types of learners: "convergers," "divergers," "assimilators," and "accommodators." He then explores the relationship between students' learning styles and the requirements of different disciplines and professions. It turns out that each of these learning styles tends to predominate in particular fields—for example, "divergers" tend to major in English and political science, while "assimilators" congregate in the natural sciences—which may help explain the dynamics of attraction or alienation between particular students and different disciplines. Kolb describes the different knowledge structures and inquiry processes that characterize the major areas of knowledge and professional practice; he identifies the reward systems that currently drive teaching and learning in these areas; and he points to the implications of these differences for disciplinary and professional preparation.

The next two chapters discuss the special problems of women and minority students. Since academic culture has traditionally been dominated by white males, academic policies and even behavioral research have tended to reflect white, male biases. Now that a much broader range of students is pursuing higher education, it is critical that colleges reexamine those policies and assumptions that may fit white, male students but not others.

In Chapter Eleven, Jessie Bernard points out how women's life cycles and developmental stages differ from those of men—a fact ignored by much of the earlier research. She cites various "contingency schedules" for women that lay out different sequences for them of marriage, childbearing, professional training, career initiation, and career resumption. Bernard's subsequent discussion of the implications for curriculum, professional development, and administrative style suggest important ways in which colleges and universities can respond more effectively to the educational needs of their women students.

In Chapter Twelve, Jacqueline Fleming calls attention to the problems of minority students, focusing particularly on blacks in predominantly white colleges. After suggesting the kinds of development these colleges might facilitate in minority students, in terms of the facets of development examined by the authors of earlier chapters, she goes on to describe what actually tends to happen to these students. Not only are their social relationships and extracurricular participation limited but their intellectual development may also suffer, in part because of their preoccupation with social problems. Faculty members could play a key role in easing these social and academic problems, but Fleming finds that black students experience overt and covert racism in their interaction with many faculty. This evidence for blacks has obvious implications for other minority groups—among them, Chicanos, native Americans, and foreign students.

In Chapter Thirteen, Allen Tough synthesizes what we now know from his and other researchers' work about adults' interest in continuing learning—and the problems they face in having colleges assist them in their learning. He reports that nine out of ten American adults now undertake a major learning effort—involving an average of a hundred hours of activity—at least once a year; but most of them learn on their own. They are seldom interested in mastering an entire body of subject matter as offered in most college courses; instead they are motivated by fairly immediate problems that require particular knowledge and skill. Tough identifies ways that educators can better facilitate these learning efforts, beyond offering more problem-oriented courses. His suggestions range from direct teaching to acting as "brokers" in putting prospective learners in touch with appropriate teachers and like-minded students outside of higher education.

Finally, Richard Peterson brings Part One to a close and provides a transition to Part Two by summarizing the wealth of opportunities that now exist for lifelong learning in American society. He points out that only 11 million out of the estimated 65 million participants in postcompulsory education are enrolled in colleges and universities. Showing how colleges' present educational practices inhibit greater participation by adults, he proposes additional services by means of which colleges could promote learning throughout the adult life cycle.

In short, the chapters in Part One offer a basic research-based introduction to what we know about the students who will be coming to the American college of the future, about their psychological development and the learning problems they are likely to encounter. On the basis of these chapters, Parts Two and Three then offer specific examples and suggestions for institutional change.

1

Arthur W. Chickering
Robert J. Havighurst

The Life Cycle

As educators, we have devoted most of our attention to providing a good education for college-age youth, whose numbers have grown rapidly over the recent decades—the number of college students climbed from 2.3 million to 7.42 million between 1955 and 1975, and the percentage of 18- to 21-year-olds in the population, from 28 to 46 percent. Now college enrollment has stabilized and may even decrease as a consequence of the decreasing numbers of births since 1970. Froomkin and Dresch (1974) have predicted a decline of 25 percent in college enrollment from the 1975 level to that of 1985.

At the same time, however, participation in college programs by adults beyond the traditional college age is expected to increase significantly—for a variety of reasons. In the first place, statistics show that people who have completed high school enroll more frequently in continuing education than people with less formal education—and the proportion of people over 25 who have graduated from high school is increasing, as is the proportion who have graduated from college. No one doubts that the colleges will have more adult students, though estimates vary widely.

What we are calling the *postindustrial society,* following Daniel Bell (1973), has shifted the occupational distribution of workers from goods-producing to service-providing jobs. Thus, in 1950 a good 50 percent of American workers were producing goods, whereas it is estimated that 70 percent will be providing services in 1980. Since the service occupations require more formal education than do the goods-producing occupations, education will more and more be the means of access to status, income, and further opportunities.

Since 1900 the work-life span has more than doubled. The average life expectancy for men age 50 is 78; for women it is 83. Two twenty-year careers are now possible for most healthy persons. Thus, increasing numbers of people in their forties and fifties are looking for educational courses that will train them for new jobs.

In this context, research and theory concerning the life cycle from eighteen to eighty becomes increasingly important for educational planning and program development in our colleges and universities. The challenges at different stages of the life cycle create recurrent needs for lifelong learning; these are the dynamics behind the decisions of increasing numbers of older students to invest their time, money, and energy in education. The research on the life cycle reveals some of the underlying purposes that power degree aspirations, pursuit of a promotion or career change, or desire to meet new persons, read more widely, or explore new ideas and interests. These studies also remind us that existential questions about meaning, purpose, vocation, social responsibility, dependence, and human relationships, which so many adolescents face with difficulty, are confronted again by many 40-, 60-, and 80-year-olds. There is much grist here for curricular content, educational practice, administration, and professional development in higher education. Increased working knowledge of this research and theory holds promise for increasing our educational effectiveness for students throughout the life cycle.

The recurrent formulations of the life cycle suggest some cross-cultural and historical consistency. But we should recognize that many of the findings reported by recent social science research would undoubtedly differ in significant particulars from results which would be obtained in Latin America, Africa, or the Middle or Far East. We should also recognize that these findings, with some important exceptions, come from studies of white, middle- and upper-class men. The patterns identified are probably off-target in some significant ways for farmers, factory and construction workers, truck drivers, and other blue-collar workers. No doubt they are also significantly off-target for many blacks, Orientals, native Americans, Chicanos, and other minorities. These findings would also be different for women, as the growing research identified in Chapter Eleven makes clear.

Literature on the Life Cycle

Philosophers, poets, and playwrights supply ancient as well as modern descriptions of the human life cycle. It was not until the present century, however, that social scientists began to put together the facts and concepts needed for a life-span description of personal and social development.

Adult Life Stages. Charlotte Buehler (1962), working in Vienna, collected life histories from elderly persons and, on the basis of these data, postulated five basic life tendencies: (1) need-satisfaction, (2) adaptive self-limitation, (3) creative expansion, (4) establishment of inner order, and (5) self-fulfillment. These tendencies are acting to some extent at all ages but have periods of dominance at various points in the life cycle. For instance, Buehler saw the age period from 18 to 25 dominated by the young person's tentative self-determination of an adult occupational role, in response to the need for *adaptive self-limitation.* This is followed in the twenty years between ages 25 and 45 by self-realization in occupation, marriage, and family development, in response to the need for *creative expansion.* The drive for *establishment of inner order* takes the form of critical self-assessment in the mature years from 45 to 65, and the need for *self-fulfillment* is normally fairly well met in the period of well-earned rest and retirement after about age 65.

The next great step was taken by Erik Erikson (1950, 1959), who conceived of growth through the life span as a process of meeting and achieving a series of eight *psychosocial tasks,* each of which dominates the development of the individual at a certain stage of life. These eight major developmental issues are given below, with their approximate modal age periods:

Basic Trust versus Mistrust	Infancy
Autonomy versus Shame and Doubt	Early Childhood
Initiative versus Guilt	Prepuberty
Industry versus Inferiority	Puberty
Identity versus Role Confusion	Adolescence
Intimacy versus Isolation	Early Adulthood
Generativity versus Stagnation	Middle Adulthood
Integrity versus Despair	Later Adulthood

In Erikson's view, if one or another of these tasks was not successfully resolved, it created persistent problems. Moreover, final resolution was seldom achieved because new circumstances and experiences could unsettle a previously satisfactory level of trust, autonomy, initiative, industry, identity, or intimacy.

The years since 1950 have seen a great deal of path-breaking research on adult roles, needs, and performance, which has laid a base for the extension of education through the adult range of the life cycle, beyond the usual ages of attendance at college and university. The following are some of the major research groups and their principal activities:

- The Kansas City Study of Adult Life, conducted by the Committee on Human Development of the University of Chicago between 1951 and 1964, with repeated interviewing and testing of men and women between the ages of 40 and 75.
- The Duke University social and medical studies of a group of adults in the North Carolina area, focusing mainly on middle-aged people and following them into the period of retirement during the seventies.
- The continuing studies of adults at various age levels made by the Andrus Institute of Gerontology at the University of Southern California.
- The Normative Aging Study of a sample of men from early adult to late adult age in Boston, carried out under the auspices of the Veterans' Administration.
- The research by Marjorie Fiske Lowenthal and her colleagues (1975) at the University of California at San Francisco, studying men and women from early adulthood to old age.
- The study of men from their mid thirties to their mid forties by Daniel Levinson and his colleagues (1978) at Yale University.
- The study of men and women from early adulthood to middle age made by Roger Gould (1972) in Los Angeles.
- The Harvard Grant Study, directed for the last ten years by George E. Vaillant, which follows ninety-five graduates from the classes of 1942, 1943, and 1944.

Bernice L. Neugarten of the University of Chicago, in a summary chapter called "Personality and Aging" (1977), gives an overview of personality development during the adult years. She, more than any other theorist, has elaborated the role of functional events and timing in adult development. Her studies place special emphasis on functional events happening "on time," such as reaching a peak of occupational achievement, seeing children grow up and leave home, reaching the menopause, retiring from one's principal occupation, losing a spouse, and even facing one's own death. These events are not experienced as crises if they are "on time." Loss of loved ones causes grief, as does the prospect of one's own death, but when these events occur at times and in ways consistent with the normal expected life course, most persons manage without major upset.

The psychologist interested in the study of adult personality asks whether there are orderly, sequential personality changes related to age, and if so, whether these personality changes cause changes in behavior. Research studies of adults aged 18 to 80 confirm the broad hypothesis that human personality does change perceptibly as people grow older. These changes in personality are caused, not by the passage of time, but by the various biological and social events that occur with the passage of time. Adult development from youth to old age can be seen as a process of adaptation in which personality is the key element.

Life stages are often defined by society. The appropriate age period to bear and rear children is socially as well as biologically defined. So, too, is the appropriate age period to encourage grown children to leave the parental home, as well as the appropriate age to retire. The timing for many changes is determined by the prevailing career and family development patterns in our postindustrial society. And this timing still tends to be determined by male career patterns—a fact that frequently puts women at a disadvantage in the working world. The age expectations based on male careers may be unreasonable and even impossible for some women, given earlier decisions about marriage and child rearing. Medical schools do not accept people over age 35, sometimes not over age 30. Businesses do not want to train people for top managerial positions after the mid twenties. One young black woman who graduated as an accounting major at age 26 was told by a firm that interviewed her that she was too old for their training program by two years. During the decade from ages 30 to 40, even some males find breaking into a new career difficult, especially if the career requires some investment by the employer. For women with less direct experience, whose timing differs from the standard pattern, education may offer only broken promises of access to new careers.

Figure 1 gives an overview of typical changes in personality and social adjustment during the adult part of the life cycle. It draws on the work of Neugarten, and especially her report on research conducted with adults in Kansas City by members of the Committee on Human Development at the University of Chicago. It is clear that there are significant differences for men and women.

The development of young men and women under age 45 has recently been studied by three separate researchers: Levinson (1978), Gould (1972), and Sheehy (1976). They describe a general pattern that begins with the transition from adolescence to adulthood during the late teens and early twenties (see Figure 2). During the mid twenties—a period of *provisional adulthood*—first commitments to work, marriage, and family, and to other adult responsibilities are explored. Then another transitional period occurs during the late twenties and early thirties, when these initial commitments are reexamined and their meanings questioned. The long-range implications of continuing with the current work, spouse, community, or life-style have become apparent; one or more of these may look less challenging or satisfying than at 22. In some cases, changes must be made. In others, reaffirmation and renewed commitment occur, sometimes after flirtations with one or more alternatives.

The thirties are a time for settling down, for achievement, for becoming one's own person. But as the forties approach, time becomes more finite. Responsibility for parents

Figure 1. Typical Life Changes

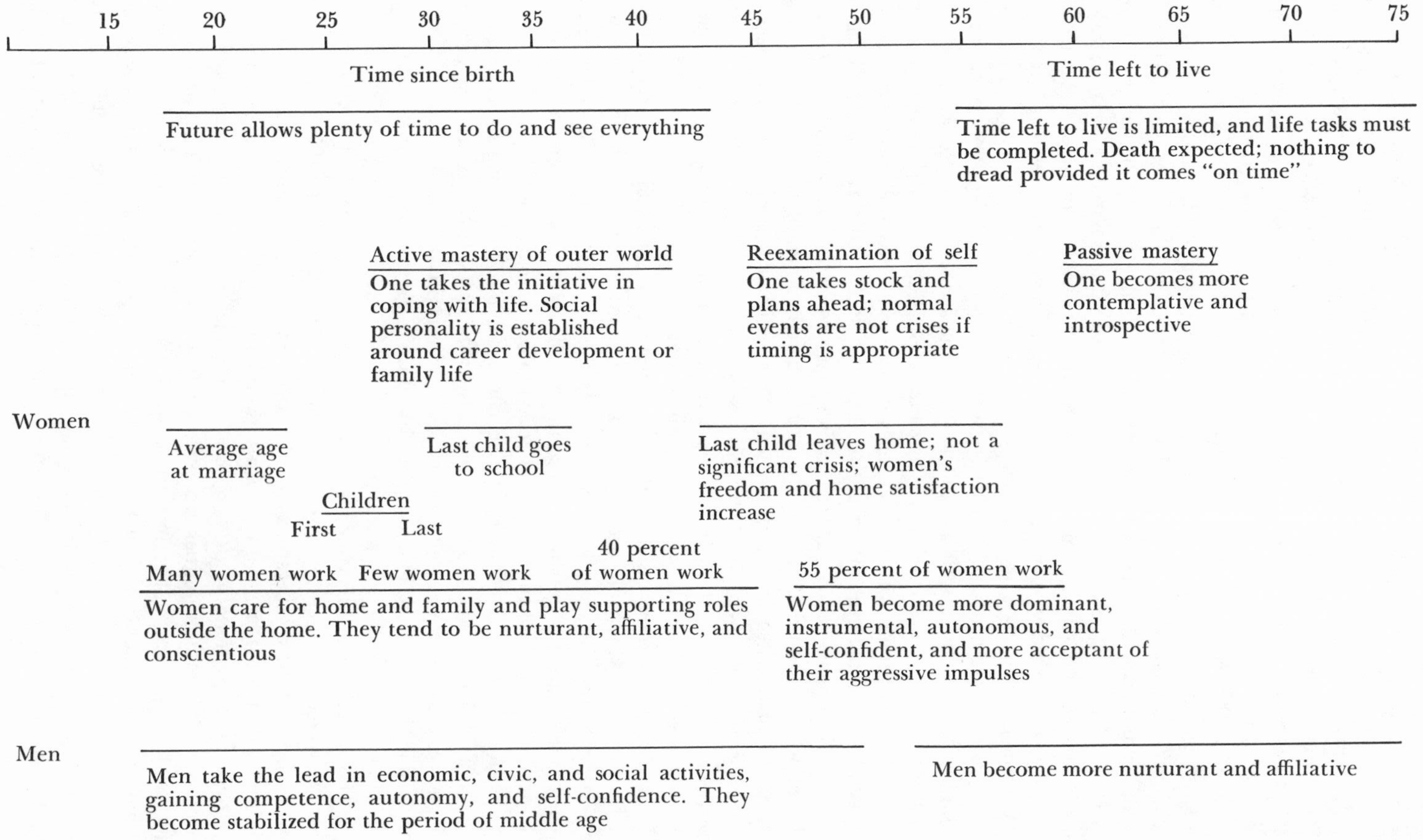

Time since birth

15	20	25	30	35	40	45	50	55	60	65	70	75

Future allows plenty of time to do and see everything

Active mastery of outer world
One takes the initiative in coping with life. Social personality is established around career development or family life

Reexamination of self
One takes stock and plans ahead; normal events are not crises if timing is appropriate

Time left to live
Time left to live is limited, and life tasks must be completed. Death expected; nothing to dread provided it comes "on time"

Passive mastery
One becomes more contemplative and introspective

Women

Average age at marriage

Children
First   Last

Last child goes to school

Last child leaves home; not a significant crisis; women's freedom and home satisfaction increase

Many women work   Few women work   40 percent of women work   55 percent of women work

Women care for home and family and play supporting roles outside the home. They tend to be nurturant, affiliative, and conscientious

Women become more dominant, instrumental, autonomous, and self-confident, and more acceptant of their aggressive impulses

Men

Men take the lead in economic, civic, and social activities, gaining competence, autonomy, and self-confidence. They become stabilized for the period of middle age

Men become more nurturant and affiliative

Sources: Based on Neugarten, 1968a, 1968b, 1970, 1977.

Figure 2. Three Views of the Life Cycle

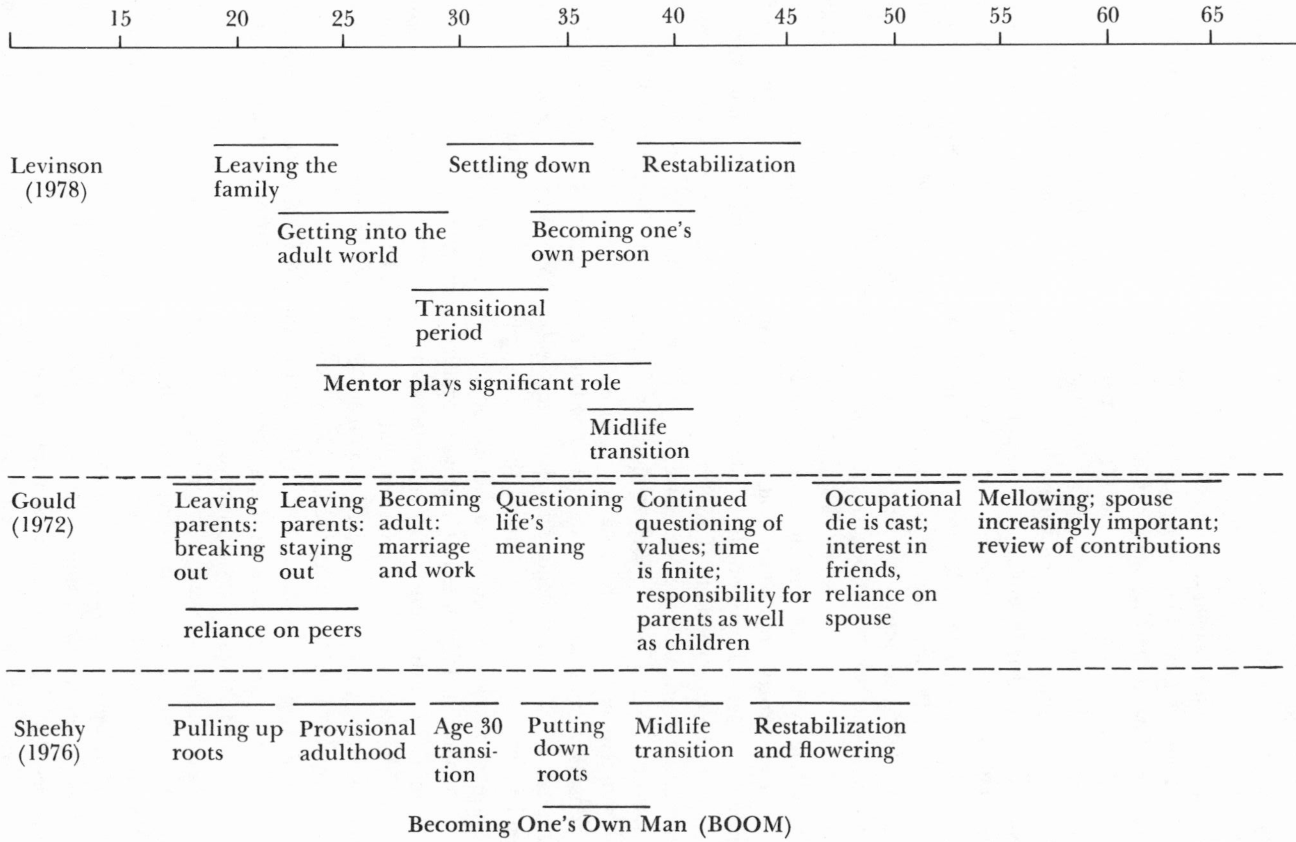

15   20   25   30   35   40   45   50   55   60   65   70   75

Levinson (1978)

Leaving the family

Settling down   Restabilization

Getting into the adult world

Becoming one's own person

Transitional period

Mentor plays significant role

Midlife transition

Gould (1972)

Leaving parents: breaking out

Leaving parents: staying out

reliance on peers

Becoming adult: marriage and work

Questioning life's meaning

Continued questioning of values; time is finite; responsibility for parents as well as children

Occupational die is cast; interest in friends, reliance on spouse

Mellowing; spouse increasingly important; review of contributions

Sheehy (1976)

Pulling up roots

Provisional adulthood

Age 30 transition

Putting down roots

Midlife transition

Restabilization and flowering

Becoming One's Own Man (BOOM)

begins to be assumed, while responsibilities for adolescent or college-age children continue. The likely limits of success and achievement become apparent, and the *midlife transition* is at hand. Major questions concerning priorities and values are examined. Unless a change in work is made now, the die is cast. Affirmation of the earlier career most frequently occurs, but with moderated expectations and drive. A long-standing marriage may be temporarily or permanently upset. Friends, relatives, and spouse become increasingly important as *restabilization* occurs during the late forties or fifties. Interests forgone in the service of work receive more attention. Mellowing and increasing investment in personal relationships characterize the fifties.

Women's Lives Versus Men's. Levinson's (1978) findings for men provide a useful framework for contrasting women's life experiences with men's. His first stage, *leaving the family,* may often be aborted for women; they typically leave parental constraints only to enter the family constraints of husband and children. Levinson found that leaving one's parents and establishing a new home base can be a time to discover and stretch one's newly found independence, to experiment with a career, and to develop one's individual talents. But independence, experimentation, and self-development are *not* congruent with the expected roles of mothers; they are not even consistent with the expected roles of wives. In fact, there is substantial evidence that most women leave a dependent status with their parents for a dependent status with their husbands. This may appeal to the woman who wants to dodge responsibility for directing her own life. But when these persons have major responsibility for directing the lives of our youth, an unfortunate self-perpetuating dynamic of role diffusion, dependence and constraint is created.

The reports from women pursuing continuing education tell us that they are encountering a decade or more later the experiences that Levinson's male subjects went through in the early periods of adulthood. Establishing identity is bound up closely with choosing a career. What are the consequences for a woman who first opts for the role of mother or wife and later in life searches for a new career? There seems little doubt that most women view a return to school as an initial investment in a new career. Large proportions of women explicitly state that they have come back to school to get a better job; others report that they begin school to meet various achievement needs but definitely intend to work after graduation. Is this strong impetus toward work really an effort to establish, or recover, an identity distinct from husband and children?

Women in the United States have for a long time been programmed to keep their ego boundaries diffuse until they find a husband. Then their decisions about doing and being can be shaped to conform to husband and family. Parents have sent clear messages: "Find someone who will take care of you." "A man likes a woman to be dependent on him; it makes him feel important." "Play dumb, even if you know. No one likes a smartie." But women reaching for further education and employment outside the home are turning away from those messages, reaching for a broader basis of self-definition. (See Chapter Eleven, in which Jessie Bernard develops some of these ideas more fully.)

Levinson also describes a long period of investment in career, of developing options, and of a growing confidence, which culminates in a new stage for men in the early thirties. Women who begin a career and then leave it for childrearing, and who return to a career later, appear to reach that stage of confidence and options much later. Epstein's (1974, p. 7) observations support this view: "Both men and women are probably afraid of the heights of ambition, achievement and accomplishments; all these have their costs. But men are forced to face these fears. For those men who are successful in conquering them, the lives they chart may be rich and meaningful. Women are not challenged to face their fears and thus never lose them and remain self-doubting. Without the support to do their best, to be their best, and to enjoy doing well, most of those who could 'make it' don't." These fears occur even though many women develop important skills through homemaking, community responsibilities, volunteer activities, and part-time employment. Educational institutions should help these women recognize the competence and knowledge they have and thus build confidence more quickly.

For generations, the education of women was thought to be useful only as it prepared young women to perform better as wives and mothers. For all but the wealthiest families, college was a luxury reserved for sons, who would head households. Within the past two decades, another theory gained favor with those who counseled women—a life cycle theory based on the biological role women play as child-bearers and child-rearers. It hypothesized that since a woman would need to omit education during an extended period of childrearing, she should choose some form of postsecondary training that would prepare her for work before and after childrearing, that had flexible hours so she could be home with children, and that would be available on a drop-in, drop-out basis. Thus teaching, nursing, and office work gained favor as feminine occupations.

Over the last ten years, a few persons have criticized such counsel. Alice Rossi, as early as the mid sixties, claimed that encouraging women to think of their educational experience as something they could develop gradually over a period of years, and creating special access features for women returning to college, only increased women's chances of *not* having a significant career. She pointed out that continued and uninterrupted investment of self in education and its outcomes, especially in the early adult period of life, was required for outstanding achievement and recognition. Studies of women highly successful in their fields have revealed a pattern of uninterrupted devotion to their careers. These women often married but seldom had children, or had them later in life (Rossi, 1975).

Lowenthal (1975) recently reported a study of 216 urban men and women from blue-collar, white-collar, managerial, lower middle- and middle-class backgrounds that provides somewhat different perspectives on the life cycle. There is much here that is consistent with the other work reported above. But one of her most important contributions lies in the significant differences documented for men and women. Figure 3 signals some of those differences as they occur among high school seniors, newlyweds, persons at "middle age" (now defined as age 50!) and preretirement. (She did not study 25- to 45-year-olds.)

In general, self-assertion and achievement seem to be valued less by women than by men. There is also the suggestion that women may be more willing to recognize shortcomings and men more compelled to deny them. Note that both men and women experience a general increase in effectiveness, efficiency, overall self-reliance, and self-control. Feelings of vulnerability decline, as does the need to misrepresent oneself and manipulate others, or to evoke conflict. Older persons develop more rewarding lives through selective disengagement from nonrewarding involvements.

Lowenthal's *Four Stages of Life* shows that the mother whose children have left home feels discontented, at a time when her spouse is most job-focused. The mother who finds reward in work and education enriches her own life and that of her spouse. She becomes stronger, more able to make decisions. She tunes in to her masculine components at a time in life when it is more acceptable. Her husband is driving less for achievement and control and is glad to have her take increased responsibility. Many women feel that the most important thing they gain in postsecondary education is the discovery that learning gives them not only factual information but a new relationship to things, to people, and to self. The reward comes in discovering that one can do something as well as or better than anyone else, young or old, male or female. The women who come back want that. They often demand it and will not settle for less.

But the women who take the step toward education and a career are bucking

Figure 3. Lowenthal's Four Stages of Life

15	20	25	30	35	40	45	50	55	60

High School Seniors (Age 16–18)	Newlyweds (Average age 24)	Middle-aged (Average age 50)	Preretirement (Average age 60)
Women	*Women*	*Women*	*Women*
Diffuse life-style Negative self-concept Helpless, dependent	More complex life-style than men Warm; lacking energy Jealous of activities that separate them from husbands	Last child leaves home Negative self-concept Unhappy; absent-minded Simplistic life-style Men seen as dominant Increased marital problems Critical of husband	More positive self-image Competent; less dependent Frank; more assertive
Men	*Men*	*Men*	*Men*
Insecure Discontented Limited perseverance	Expansive Buoyant Risk-taking	Life-style narrowed and focused Heightened sense of orderliness Seen as boss of family Reject ideas of self-pity Plateau re job advancement Strain and boredom potential problems	More simplistic life-style Concern for companionship, nurturance Self-protective; avoiding stress
	Men and Women		*Men and Women*
	84 percent work Shared interests Critical of parents		Renewed interest in spouse

Across All Stages

Women—Concerned with affect and reciprocity; self-ratings higher on charming, cooperative, easily embarrassed and hurt, friendly, helpless, sincere, sympathetic, timid, undecided

Men—Concerned with interests and activities; self-ratings higher on ambitious, assertive, competitive, confident, guileful, calm, hostile, reasonable, self-controlled, shrewd, sophisticated, unconventional, versatile

Both Men and Women—16 negative attributes declined: absent-minded, dependent, disorderly, dissatisfied, easily embarrassed, guileful, helpless, lazy, restless, sarcastic, self-pitying, stubborn, suspicious, timid, undecided, unhappy

3 positive attributes increased: frank, reserved, self-controlled

some deeply embedded attitudes. Matina Horner's (1972) research on why bright women fail found that graduating at the top of the class was seen as the beginning of tragic stories for women. Both men and women saw the "successful" woman as a tragic figure, often penalized for being aggressive intellectuals. A study by Broverman and others (1970) gives a different, more comprehensive, and more distressing slant on the same dynamic. Professional men and women were asked to describe the characteristics of a "healthy man," a "healthy woman," and a "healthy person." The characteristics given for the "healthy man" and the "healthy person" were very similar, but the characteristics given for the "healthy woman" were quite different. Apparently it was not possible to be both a "healthy woman" and a "healthy person." If the woman began to assume the characteristics of a "healthy person," she was becoming too aggressive, assertive, and dominating to be a "healthy woman." But if she retained the passive characteristics assigned to her, she was not really a very healthy person.

Freud asked, "What do women want?" They are now answering, "We want to function as insiders." When society asks, "Why do you want to crash a man's world?" they answer, "We are not trying to crash a man's world. We only want to re-enter the world in which we live. There is no other." As this re-entry occurs, it is inevitable that women will help men redefine their roles. Women have refused to let men play certain roles. They often have forbidden men entrée to the rituals of the home, forbidden men close access to their children's affections, forbidden men life-style options outside middle-class values. If education provides a means for women to establish, at least for themselves, an identity dimension related to *doing*, perhaps it will help men to establish an identity dimension related to *being*.

Developmental Tasks of the Adult Years

According to Havighurst (1972), the developmental tasks of life are those required for healthy and satisfactory growth in our society. They are the physiological, psychological, and social demands a person must satisfy in order to be judged by others and to judge himself or herself to be a reasonably happy and successful person. A given developmental task typically arises during a certain period of an individual's life. Successful achievement contributes to happiness and success in later tasks; failure contributes to unhappiness, social disapproval, or later difficulties.

Developmental tasks are imposed by both internal and external forces. The internal forces are primarily biological and operate most prominently during the early and late years of human development. The infant's legs grow longer and stronger, crawling and walking soon follow. The child's nervous system becomes more complex, permitting more precise eye-hand coordination, more discriminating perception, more sophisticated thought. The pubertal youth experiences rapidly developing secondary sex characteristics, new urges, and new interests as sex glands pour hormones into the bloodstream. The older person's decreasing stamina, speed, and sensory loss require changing life-styles and responsibilities.

Other developmental tasks arise primarily from social roles and from pressures and opportunities in the social environment. For instance, a young woman marries at 23 years of age and soon finds that she has two new tasks—becoming a competent homemaker and becoming a competent parent. A typical college freshman enters a student culture with several alternative subcultures. Clark and Trow (1966) described four types of campus subcultures: academic, collegiate, vocational, and nonconformist—each new student must somehow create a fit between the characteristics brought to college and one or another college subculture.

Developmental tasks may also arise out of personal values and aspirations. As each self evolves, it becomes increasingly a force in its own right; it has its own momentum, its own particular shape and constituents. A concern for civil rights or interest in local politics may influence choice of work and friends and lead to a particular life style and set of social commitments. Special talent in music or athletics may create rewards and contributions leading in a very different direction. With increasing age and experience, the developmental trajectories and barriers, the human potentialities and limits to growth, tend to become more sharply etched for each of us. But as the life cycle research touched on earlier indicates, trajectories can be deflected, barriers are not immutable, new potentialities may become apparent, and limits may turn out to be largely contextual and personal.

Thus, developmental tasks may arise from physical maturation or change; from social roles, pressures, or opportunities; or from aspirations and values of a constantly emerging personality. In many cases they arise from combinations of these three major forces acting together. During early and middle adulthood, social demands and personal aspirations dominate in setting and defining major developmental tasks. With later middle age and beyond, biological changes become an increasingly significant consideration.

It is worth noting also that a chosen activity can be either *instrumental* or *expressive,* and often both. An instrumental task is undertaken in order to achieve a goal that lies beyond the particular task itself. For example, descriptive and inferential statistics are learned in order to understand and carry out quantitative research. Accounting, sales, and management skills are learned in order to run a business. An expressive task is undertaken to reach a goal that lies within the act itself. Learning how to create a novel, poem, symphony, or sonata may be pursued for the pleasures derived from such creation. Studies in history, literature, psychology, anthropology, biology, physics, mathematics—any area that offers increasingly complex and satisfying challenges—may be pursued for the intrinsic satisfactions involved, for the increased perspective, sensitivity, or self-understanding that may follow.

But this distinction should not be pushed too far. Many of our most satisfying activities turn out to be both instrumental and expressive; they serve ends larger than themselves while expressing and satisfying needs and values close to our hearts. The skillful athlete or performer achieves status and income while doing what he or she enjoys most. The accomplished administrator, organizing human and material resources to accomplish ends important to his or her colleagues, is expressing significant values while serving instrumental objectives. Ideally, work should be both instrumental and expressive. Thus, many developmental tasks serve both ends.

Other students of the life cycle have found Havighurst's (1972) developmental task approach useful. Blocher and Rapoza, in their chapter on professional development, posit some relationships among life stages, social roles, developmental tasks, and coping capacities from infancy through retirement. There are echoes of Erik Erikson in some of the terminology they use for various developmental tasks they propose. The tasks are global, suggesting broad dimensions of development and learning. The age periods used do not precisely fit those posited by Levinson, Gould, and Sheehy, for example, but they do coincide at some major transitional points. More important, the roles, tasks, and coping behaviors proposed jibe very well with the formulations set forth by those researchers as well as by Neugarten and Lowenthal.

Vivian Rogers McCoy (1977) has taken a much more detailed approach to developmental tasks (see Figure 4). Keying them explicitly to age periods identified by Levinson and Sheehy, she posits both life cycle tasks and outcomes sought. Although there is a certain redundancy and obviousness about those two complementary columns, in many

Figure 4. Adult Life Cycle Tasks and Educational Program Responses

Developmental Stages	Tasks	Program Responses	Outcomes Sought
Leaving home 18-22	1. Break psychological ties 2. Choose careers 3. Enter work 4. Handle peer relationships 5. Manage home 6. Manage time 7. Adjust to life on own 8. Problem-solve 9. Manage stress accompanying change	1. Personal development, assertive training workshops 2. Career workshops; values clarification; occupational information 3. Education/career preparation 4. Human relations groups 5. Consumer education/homemaking skills 6. Time/leisure use workshop 7. Living alone; successful singles workshops 8. Creative problem solving workshops 9. Stress management, biofeedback, relaxation, TM workshops	1. Strengthened autonomy 2. Appropriate career decisions 3. Successful education/career entry 4. Effective social interaction 5. Informed consumer, healthy homelife 6. Wise use of time 7. Fulfilled single state, autonomy 8. Successful problem solving 9. Successful stress management, personal growth
Becoming Adult 23-28	1. Select mate 2. Settle in work, begin career ladder 3. Parent 4. Become involved in community 5. Consume wisely 6. Home-own 7. Socially interact 8. Achieve autonomy 9. Problem-solve 10. Manage stress accompanying change	1. Marriage workshops 2. Management, advancement training 3. Parenting workshops 4. Civic education; volunteer training 5. Consumer education; financial management training 6. Home-owning, maintenance workshops 7. Human relations groups, TA 8. Living alone, divorce workshops 9. Creative problem solving workshops 10. Stress management, biofeedback, relaxation, TM workshops	1. Successful marriage 2. Career satisfaction and advancement 3. Effective parents; healthy offspring 4. Informed, participating citizen 5. Sound consumer behavior 6. Satisfying home environment 7. Social skills 8. Fulfilled single state, autonomy 9. Successful problem solving 10. Successful stress management, personal growth

(continued on next page)

Figure 4 *(Continued)*

Developmental stages	Tasks	Program Responses	Outcomes Sought
Catch-30 29-34	1. Search for personal values 2. Reappraise relationships 3. Progress in career 4. Accept growing children 5. Put down roots, achieve "permanent" home 6. Problem-solve 7. Manage stress accompanying change	1. Values clarification 2. Marriage counseling and communication workshops; human relations groups; creative divorce workshops 3. Career advancement training, job re-design workshops 4. Parent-child relationship workshops 5. Consumer education 6. Creative problem solving workshops 7. Stress management, biofeedback, relaxation, TM workshops	1. Examined and owned values 2. Authentic personal relationships 3. Career satisfaction, economic reward, a sense of competence and achievement 4. Growth producing parent-child relationship 5. Sound consumer behavior 6. Successful problem solving 7. Successful stress management, personal growth
Midlife reexamination 35-43	1. Search for meaning 2. Reassess marriage 3. Reexamine work 4. Relate to teenage children 5. Relate to aging parents 6. Reassess personal priorities and values 7. Adjust to single life 8. Problem-solve 9. Manage stress accompanying change	1. Search for meaning workshops 2. Marriage workshops 3. Mid career workshops 4. Parenting: focus on raising teenage children 5. Relating to aging parents workshops 6. Value clarification; goal setting workshops 7. Living alone, divorce workshops 8. Creative problem solving workshops 9. Stress management, biofeedback, relaxation, TM workshops	1. Coping with existential anxiety 2. Satisfying marriages 3. Appropriate career decisions 4. Improved parent-child relations 5. Improved child-parent relations 6. Autonomous behavior 7. Fulfilled single state 8. Successful problem solving 9. Successful stress management, personal growth
Restabilization 44-55	1. Adjust to realities of work 2. Launch children 3. Adjust to empty nest 4. Become more deeply involved in social life 5. Participate actively in community concerns 6. Handle increased demands of older parents	1. Personal, vocational counseling, career workshops 2. Parenting education 3. Marriage, personal counseling workshops 4. Human relations groups 5. Civic and social issues education 6. Gerontology workshops 7. Leisure use workshops	1. Job adjustment 2. Civil letting go parental authority 3. Exploring new sources of satisfaction 4. Effective social relations 5. Effective citizenship 6. Better personal and social adjustment of elderly 7. Creative use of leisure 8. Sound consumer behavior

	Tasks	Program Response	Outcomes
	7. Manage leisure time	8. Financial management workshops	9. Fulfilled single state
	8. Manage budget to support college-age children and ailing parents	9. Workshops on loneliness and aloneness	10. Successful problem solving
	9. Adjust to single state	10. Creative problem solving workshops	11. Successful stress management, personal growth
	10. Problem-solve	11. Stress management, biofeedback, relaxation, TM workshops	
	11. Manage stress accompanying change		
Preparation for retirement 56-64	1. Adjust to health problems	1. Programs about nutrition, health	1. Healthier individuals
	2. Deepen personal relations	2. Human relations groups	2. Effective social skills
	3. Prepare for retirement	3. Preretirement workshops	3. Wise retirement planning
	4. Expand avocational interests	4. Art, writing, music courses in performing and appreciation; sponsored educational travel	4. Satisfaction of aesthetic urge; broadening of knowledge; enjoyment of travel
	5. Finance new leisure	5. Money management training	5. Sound consumer behavior
	6. Adjust to loss of mate	6. Workshops on aloneness and loneliness, death and dying	6. Adjustment to loss, fulfilled single state
	7. Problem-solve	7. Creative problem solving workshops	7. Successful problem solving
	8. Manage stress accompanying change	8. Stress management, biofeedback, relaxation, TM workshops	8. Successful stress management, personal growth
Retirement 65+	1. Disengage from paid work	1, 4, 5, 6. Workshops on retirement, volunteering, aging; conferences on public issues affecting aged	1, 4, 5, 6. Creative, active retirement; successful coping with life disengagement; public policies responsive to needs of aged
	2. Reassess finances	2. Financial management training	2. Freedom from financial fears
	3. Be concerned with personal health care	3. Health care programs	3. Appropriate health care
	4. Search for new achievement outlets	7. Religious exploration	7. Help in search for life's meaning, values of past life
	5. Manage leisure time	8. Workshops on aloneness and loneliness	8. Fulfilled single state
	6. Adjust to more constant marriage companion	9. Death and dying workshops	9. Philosophic acceptance of death, help in caring for dying and handling of grief
	7. Search for meaning	10. Creative problem solving workshops	10. Successful problem solving
	8. Adjust to single state	11. Stress management, biofeedback, relaxation, TM workshops	11. Successful stress management, personal growth
	9. Be reconciled to death		
	10. Problem-solve		
	11. Manage stress accompanying change		

Source: McCoy, 1977.

instances the two taken together suggest different aspects of the challenges to be met during the particular age period cited. Especially thought-provoking is her proposal of diverse educational program responses that might be made by a Division of Continuing Education. Note that many of these responses fall quite legitimately within the purview of the regular curriculum or areas of concern typically served by various college student personnel services. Consider, for example, "education/career preparation," "human relations," "parent-child relationships," "civic and social issues education," "programs about nutrition and health," and "art, writing, and music courses in performing and appreciation." All these areas can be well served within the frameworks of our traditional disciplines and professional preparation areas. Student personnel services often offer responses like "career workshops; values clarification; occupational information," "career advancement training," "value clarification; goal setting workshops," "human relations groups," "marriage, personal counseling workshops," "health care programs," and "religious explorations."

The remainder of this chapter describes major developmental tasks to be achieved from late adolescence through the adult years. Of course, we must bear in mind that substantial individual variability exists within and around the age periods specified. We must also recognize that most complex developmental tasks are never achieved once and for all. Shifting circumstances and new challenges may require tackling them again at other levels of complexity and sophistication.

Figure 5 summarizes our major dimensions, which rest heavily on the research cited earlier in this chapter. The following sections touch briefly on each period and on the tasks within it, with some reference to the assistance that education, formal or informal, is able to give.

Late Adolescence and Youth: 16-23

Achieving Emotional Independence. During childhood, parents and other adults are typically seen as omniscient and omnipotent. With adolescence, parents are seen more clearly for what they are—middle-aged persons with fancies and foibles, strengths and weaknesses. Enter doubt, anxiety, disillusionment, anger. As the fallibility of these previously strong and reliable guides becomes more clear, reliance shifts to peers, to other adults, and to occupational, institutional, or social reference groups. In time there is less need to lean so heavily on such supports. Totalistic absorption or commitment gives way to increased willingness to risk loss of friends, approval, or status to "be oneself," to pursue a strong interest, or to stand by an important belief.

This task is pursued by both young men and young women. In many ways their relationships with peers and with older persons of the opposite sex carry the same freight and serve the same purposes. But, as we suggested earlier, traditional sex role expectations make the task more complicated for women. The expectation of dependency on, and service to, a husband may make it seem necessary to maintain a "diffuse ego," which permits ready adjustment to his needs and life-style. But although this may well be expedient and less painful in the short run, it may create problems later.

Preparing for Marriage and Family Life. Increasing options and rising expectations have made decisions about marriage and family life more and more complex. The issue is no longer whether to be single or married. Contractual partnerships, trial marriages, short-term relationships to achieve economy, efficiency, and mutual support in matters ranging from room and board through shared interests, affection, and sex—all these options are more or less legitimate alternatives to the either-or conditions that prevailed before World

Figure 5. Developmental Tasks of the Adult Years

16–23 Late Adolescence and Youth	23–35 Early Adulthood	35–45 Midlife Transition	45–57 Middle Adulthood	57–65 Late-Adult Transition	65 + Late-Adulthood
Achieving emotional independence					
Preparing for marriage and family life					
Choosing and preparing for a career					
Developing an ethical system					
	Deciding on a partner				
	Starting a family				
	Managing a home				
	Starting in an occupation				
	Assuming civic responsibilities				
		Adapting to a changing time perspective			
		Revising career plans			
		Redefining family relationships			
			Maintaining a career or developing a new one		
			Restabilizing family relationships		
			Making mature civic contributions		
			Adjusting to biological change		
				Preparing for retirement	
					Adjusting to retirement
					Adjusting to declining health and strength
					Becoming affiliated with late-adult age groups
					Establishing satisfactory living arrangements
					Adjusting to the death of a spouse
					Maintaining integrity

War II. These complexities are compounded by more open exploration of sex role alternatives that deviate from the traditional masculine and feminine mystiques.

Although most young persons do see marriage and family in their futures, timing, employment arrangements, and family roles are becoming more flexible. Traditional expectations concerning solid employment and financial stability on the part of the husband and full-time homemaking by the wife now give way to assumptions concerning mutual employment, shared homemaking, and joint responsibility for childrearing. The ideal of many is continued personal, vocational, and avocational development for both parties. Of course, most young men and women still seek happiness and fulfillment in traditional marriages and traditional roles. But the high divorce rate testifies to the difficulty of achieving arrangements that respond to current complexities and rising expectations.

Choosing and Preparing for a Career. Perhaps choosing and preparing for a career is the most challenging developmental task of all for the late adolescent and young adult. It is essential for achieving emotional independence and for making decisions concerning marriage and family. It is the organizing center for the lives of most men and women.

A young person can no longer expect that a few months or even a few years of explicit training for a career will carry him or her through the next forty or fifty years of life work. Owing to advancing technology, employment may decline in some fields, as it has in farming. Even the professions, which once appeared to provide a lifetime of stimulating challenges and opportunities for service, no longer hold their appeal for many, as demonstrated in Sarason's research (Sarason, Sarason, and Cowden, 1975), which shows a surprising number of middle-aged doctors, lawyers, and business executives feeling frustrated and desiring a change.

Underneath it all there is a major shift in attitudes that is sending tremors throughout the world of work. For the generation born during the early years of this century, who were in their twenties and thirties during the Depression years, the major purpose of work was to supply the wherewithal for food, shelter, and clothing. The next generation, born during the 1920s and 1930s and brought up during the Depression, had that attitude impressed upon mind and belly by the daily experiences of tight living. But children born, raised, and educated in relative affluence during the post-World War II boom, accustomed to plenty of food, clothes, ample allowances, cars, and television sets, think and feel quite differently about the role of work in their future existence. The most important thing about work for them is that it be fulfilling, that it conform to their present interests and offer opportunities for further challenges and satisfactions. Adequate food, clothing, shelter, and material possessions are viewed more as a by-product than as a primary objective.

Thus the very meaning of the words *work* and *career* has changed. The relationships among alternative careers, with consequent implications for alternative strategies of education, training, and on-the-job preparation, to maximize self realization, income, and social contribution, have become a tapestry of knots, interwoven through time. The difficult task, as Blocher and Rapoza explain in their chapter, is to understand those knots and their interrelationships, and then to unravel them so as to recreate one's own tapestry —esthetically appealing, well-constructed, and at least minimally functional.

For women the tapestry is especially complex and the knots, soaked in the seas of social expectations, especially hard to untie. As Jessie Bernard points out in her chapter, women face different *contingency schedules.* First, there is the typical sequence of school, marriage, family, and work. Then, there is the modified version for college-bound, career-oriented young women: school, college, marriage, family, further education, work. It is clear that this sequence leaves such women starting their careers from the bottom in their forties, trying to compete for status, income, and advancement with men who have a ten- to twenty-year head start. So there are other schedules to consider: (a) college, further education, full-time professional employment, marriage, family, re-employment; (b) college, further education, full- or part-time professional employment with concurrent marriage and family; (c) college, concurrent marriage and further education, professional employment, family, re-employment. And so on. These scheduling issues are much more difficult for women than for men, and the choices made during this period, whether deliberately, by chance, or by default, can be fateful for the future.

Despite these difficulties, most young men and women do take a job or choose an occupation, start work in it or begin formal preparation for it. Studies undertaken with the Strong Vocational Interest Inventory show that occupational interests for many persons do stabilize, at least in terms of general occupational families, by age 16. The problem is that the knowledge and competence called for today go quickly out of date. Retraining and recertification are called for across increasing numbers of occupations and professions. And changing job requirements periodically raise questions for many of us about continuation or change. So this developmental task is confronted at different points throughout the life cycle.

Developing an Ethical System. Erik Erikson (1959) makes ideology the central element in achieving identity. He defines it as "a coherent body of shared images, ideas, and ideals which, whether based on a formulated dogma, an implicit *Weltanschauung,* or a highly structured world image, a political creed or a way of life, provides for the participants a coherent if systematically simplified overall orientation in space and time, in means and ends" (p. 159). During childhood, parental values are internalized, and behavior consistent with them is gradually shaped. Contrary behavior produces either diffuse anxiety, specific fear of discovery and punishment, guilt, or all three. Most of these values are inexplicit and unconsciously held. Most are not readily subject to conscious control or modification.

During late adolescence and young adulthood, we become more conscious of this baggage. We begin to examine its contents, to decide which items to keep, which to throw out, which to retailor to suit the careers, life-styles, and larger social contexts that are emerging for us. More important, as the later chapters by Gilligan and Perry consider in some detail, the ways in which we acquire and hold our values may undergo significant change. The glue that holds our ethical system together, formerly laid on by authorities, peers, or social reference groups, begins to be supplied from our own cognitions and developing convictions. Instead of wearing our rubbers and combing our hair just so, taking Adam, Eve, and the Garden of Eden as literal truth, assuming the inferiority of minority groups, according to the dictates of our parents, their surrogates, or our peers, we respond to the pluralistic alternatives encountered as we range through larger life spaces, by selecting and fashioning our own styles and trademarks. Thus, gradually we create the best system of beliefs and behaviors we can, given the complex contexts in which we find ourselves.

Some Implications. There is, of course, a substantial literature pertinent to these developmental tasks of Late Adolescence and Youth: achieving emotional independence, preparing for marriage and family life, choosing and preparing for a career, developing an ethical system, and other key areas of development. The works of Astin (1977) and Astin and others (1969), Bowen (1977), Chickering (1969, 1974), Feldman and Newcomb (1969), Heath (1968), Katz and associates (1968), Murphy and Raushenbush (1960), Newcomb and others (1967), Raushenbush (1964), Sanford (1966), Stern (1970), and others detail ways in which college environments, academic experiences, and extracurricular activities influence typical college age students in these areas. Later chapters in Part

One give us up-to-date perspectives: Weathersby's discussion of ego development is pertinent to achieving emotional independence, and Douvan's chapter on intimacy is pertinent to preparing for marriage and family. Blocher and Rapoza's chapter concerning professional/vocational development and Green's concerning the acquisition of purpose, in Part Three, both speak to choosing and preparing for a career. The chapters by Gilligan and Perry concerning moral and ethical development, and by White concerning humanitarian concern, spell out some of the complexities and educational implications of helping students develop an ethical system.

In Part Two, many of the chapters concerning particular disciplines and professions suggest ways in which content and process can be managed to both strengthen achievement of objectives in those areas and help students address their major developmental tasks. And finally, the chapters in Part Three concerning varied approaches to advising, teaching, evaluation, out-of-class activities, residential experiences, and student-faculty relationships suggest ways in which current practices can be modified to give more explicit attention to these developmental tasks.

The value of these chapters lies in their specific suggestions for the particular content areas or educational activities under consideration. But a survey of these contributions, and the more detailed literature that they cite, reveals several general implications for education.

Many of the objectives and much of the content of various disciplines and professions can be addressed in ways that strengthen a student's capacity to achieve the key developmental tasks of late adolescence and youth. English literature and composition, drama, history, philosophy, economics, anthropology, psychology, biology, and interdisciplinary studies can include reading, research, and writing pertinent to these developmental tasks which also communicates the concepts and insights important to the course or area of study. Many of our typical teaching practices—lectures, group discussions, field studies, term papers, evaluation activities, and other projects—can be managed in ways that not only communicate the inquiry methods and scholarly approaches of the field but also enhance students' individual development through direct learning experiences and exchanges with other students and faculty. The same complementary approach seems equally valid for professional preparation in human services, education, engineering, and business administration. The trick is to design the appropriate combinations of content and process with the developmental tasks in mind while maintaining a clear focus on the important disciplinary objectives. If this approach produces a synergistic effect in the disciplines and professions considered in Part Two, and the educational activities addressed in Part Three, it seems likely that it will also do so for a substantial portion of other disciplines and educational activities.

Educational practices designed primarily to serve diverse adults also turn out to be useful alternatives for traditional college-age students. Contract learning and other approaches to individualized education, the assessment of learning from work and life experience, improved integration of work and education through more sophisticated management of field experience education, more varied and flexible approaches to residential experiences, educational advising and career planning that takes a larger perspective on values clarification and the life cycle—all these strengthen our services to those below the age of 23 as well as those beyond that age.

Early Adulthood: 23-35

Early adulthood is a period of special sensitivity, readiness to learn, and multiple challenges.

Deciding on a Partner. The exploratory intimacies of late adolescence and young adulthood, coping with the tensions between intimacy and isolation characteristic of that age period, typically evolve into marriage or into a sustained relationship on some alternative basis. For a few persons the problem of isolation persists, sometimes in the form of serial engagements: intense brief encounters, alternating fire and ice, recurrent cycles of ecstacy, anguish, and renewed hope. Developing the capacity to sustain intimate relationships through time, hardships, and tempting new possibilities requires sensitivity and self-understanding far beyond those necessary for managing the more transient friendships of the preceding period. Elizabeth Douvan tells us much more about this in Chapter Eight concerning the capacity for intimacy.

But it is worth noting here that the world of marriage and family, like the world of work, also is suffering from escalating expectations. Until recently, and still throughout most of the world, both men and women recognized that marriage involved trade-offs for both parties. Roles became more narrow, responsibilities more heavy, relationships with others more limited, satisfactions more constrained. These were assumed to be the necessary consequences of linking two lives closely together—a union that added significantly to one's security, comfort, and emotional well-being, and a commitment necessary for raising a family. Couples could once wholeheartedly sing "Blest be the tie that binds/ Our hearts in Christian love. The fellowship of kindred minds/ Is like to that above."

Now the tie that binds, chafes. Marriage or a lasting partnership is now expected to lead to increased *self*-realization, *individual* fulfillment, and *personal* growth and expansion. Earlier marriage contracts were satisfied by general vows to love, honor, cherish, and obey, in sickness and in health. Today's centripetal and individualistic expectations seem to require marriage contracts that are legalistic documents, painfully negotiated, spelling out rights, privileges, and responsibilities, establishing dates and conditions for renegotiation, and setting consequences for violations. Thus, that relationship which earlier aimed to epitomize faith, trust, mutual concern, and caring, seasoned with large doses of hope, now is to be planned and managed so as to maximize individual self-satisfaction and self-development *and* provide all the other blessings formerly enjoyed. Small wonder increasing numbers of persons judge themselves to have failed this task, throw in the towel, leave the ring, and search for a better match.

Starting a Family. With the development and widespread use of more effective contraception, starting a family has become more often intentional and less often accidental. Conception less frequently precedes or immediately follows marriage; more frequently it is targeted to suit other significant plans and aspirations. Sometimes starting a family becomes the reason to shift from a sustained partnership to a marriage. Often the decision is strongly influenced by the career plans and preparatory activities of husband and wife, and timed so that sacrifices in professional development and occupational advancement do not fall disproportionately to the wife.

This increased intentionality is accompanied by increased sensitivity to the conditions that seem necessary for the healthy development and socialization of children. This sensitivity in turn generates needs for information and sound judgments about a host of decisions. The first complex of decisions concerns prenatal care and preparation for birth, with diverse options across the range from "natural childbirth" at home through various hospital options. Assuming successful delivery of a healthy child, there are then choices among diverse approaches to feeding schedules, toilet training, disciplinary styles, and parent-child relationships.

If the question of schooling was not anticipated in the choice of community and neighborhood, then that issue arises as time for nursery school, kindergarten, or first grade approaches. The increased importance attached to schooling and increased parental awareness of variability in quality from school to school mean that choice of community and school remains an issue for at least twelve to fourteen years. And the advent of busing, with its consequent shifts in classmates and school assignments, means that even the best-made plans may be disrupted. Moreover, as various forms of postsecondary education become the *sine qua non* for occupational access and achievement, parental judgment, support, and participation often continue through the late teens and early twenties. So raising a family has taken on problematic aspects that did not exist when a nearby job and continued involvement with the extended family were more the rule.

Managing a Home. Family life is built in and around a physical center, the home. Home management can interact powerfully with marital relationships and childrearing practices. Good home management is only partly a matter of working out agreements concerning how neat and clean things will be, or whether disciplined protection of paint, plaster, and furnishings will predominate over more casual use. It also involves decisions concerning who does what chores in the house and around the yard, what the children have to do to help, who is accountable for what and to whom.

It goes beyond simply buying food and getting it on the table, to questions of diet, health foods, gourmet meals, and other combinations aimed to satisfy diverse tastes and needs. Mass media and the supermarkets have put good old meat and potatoes, with a chicken in the pot on Sunday, in the shade. Time was when corn flakes, shredded wheat, or rice crispies, and oatmeal, ralston, or cream of wheat exhausted the summer and winter alternatives. Now we can spend an hour checking nutrients, weights, and comparative prices.

As we move from spacious and forgiving rural and small town turf to fenced-in urban and suburban islands, who controls what space becomes increasingly important. Does the wife have "a room of her own" for pursuing her own interests? Or is any such space reserved for the husband's study or the children's playroom? How many TV sets are required, where are they located, who gets to watch what when?

All these decisions concerning possessions, food, space, and shared responsibilities are faced in a climate where authoritarian and authoritative styles are questioned, where discussion, debate, and compromises through family councils or other less formal means are more expected. Wife, children, and husband no longer routinely accept the conventions that laid out clear roles and responsibilities. These former givens are increasingly subject to negotiation and then to renegotiation as shifting circumstances for different family members call former arrangements into question.

Starting in an Occupation. During late adolescence and youth most persons will have held various part-time jobs. Some of these may have been used to explore various occupational alternatives or career plans. By early adulthood a more long-range choice usually has been made. For some persons the choice has involved conscious decisions, job-seeking strategies, and deliberate compromises when doors to first choices are closed. For other persons the decisions occur by chance or default: a tolerable job becomes available and is accepted; it turns out to be manageable; and inertia takes over, helped by the preoccupations with starting a family and managing a home.

When the choice is the result of conscious plans and aspirations, heavy investments of time and energy typically follow. Spouse, children, and the home are taken along for the ride, but often in the back seat. Nights out with the boys, coffee klatches or cocktails with the girls, give way to new combinations of professional associates and social relationships. Sports activities and other avocational interests may fall by the wayside as spare time is used to develop career-related knowledge, competence, and contacts.

If the career-oriented woman has not already faced and resolved, at least tentatively, Jessie Bernard's contingency schedules, she will begin to now. Of course, by the time the contingencies are driven home it may be too late to do much without some very tough choices. Marriage and family roles and responsibilities may have crystallized; expectations, living arrangements, community responsibilities, and the like may have become so well established that change would cause major disruption. So inertia or indecision may prevail. Making the best of things for a while may seem to be the best strategy.

Decisions made by chance or default may also turn out to be challenging and absorbing. Most of us are much more adaptable than we think. We can find satisfaction and success through a wide array of interests and activities. But the brute fact remains that the marketplace contains many more dull, repetitive, muscle-taxing, and mind-numbing jobs than stimulating ones. And those are the ones most of us land in when our choices fail. In those cases the notion of career is typically absent. Instead of identifying with our work, we are frustrated by it. Consequently, we give it as little time, energy, and emotion as possible and look elsewhere for status, pleasure, and personal growth.

Assuming Civic Responsibilities. If there is any time and energy left after the demands of marriage, family, and occupation have been satisfied, then early levels of civic participation and responsibility may be added. Usually this step awaits some settling in the other areas. Often the responsibilities are part of an occupational life-style, a community climate, or a church expectation. Community organizations, professional associations, and fraternal orders may provide handy contexts. Rotary, Kiwanis, Masons, Lions, Elks, and their ilk, PTA, League of Women Voters, Junior League, bowling and softball leagues, and other volunteer activities all provide opportunities to do good, get out of the house, make new friends, and achieve a certain measure of social status and recognition.

Some Implications. This period of Early Adulthood and its major developmental tasks challenge many of our traditional educational structures and practices. Students in this age group have heavy demands on their time, energy, and emotions. Deciding on a partner, starting a family, managing a home, starting an occupation, and assuming civic responsibilities all require heavy personal investments. These students must study part-time, and their study arrangements must be flexible enough to allow for unanticipated emergencies at home, on the job, or in the community. Their educational orientation is more likely to be instrumental than expressive. They want curricular content directly relevant to the new range of responsibilities they are learning to manage. They need educational activities that integrate academic study with the heavy round of new experiences they are encountering. They need teaching practices that recognize their individual needs and constraints.

These students usually will have little interest in establishing new relationships with fellow students because they already have an expanding range of friendships. They will have little interest in extracurricular activities, special interest groups, and the like because they already are overcommitted to various school, church, or community groups and projects.

Thus, for these students curricular content in the social and behavioral sciences pertinent to child development and childrearing, family dynamics, interpersonal competence, group processes, organizational behavior, leadership, community power structures, and the like will probably be of most interest. These studies may be complemented by professional, paraprofessional, and vocational studies, oriented frequently toward diverse human services occupations or toward business and less frequently toward various applied technologies, engineering, and teaching. We would predict least interest in the arts, humanities, and foreign languages because the leisure for intellectual and cultural pursuits simply is not there, even though the interest may be. There will be similarly limited interest in the natural sciences because few of these persons will be oriented toward the graduate studies or professions that call for such undergraduate majors.

Institutional arrangements and educational processes that recognize the commitments and constraints of this period can make education accessible when typical on-campus course schedules are not. Weekend colleges, short-term intensive residential courses, as well as lunch-break, late afternoon, and evening classes can be offered at work sites, local libraries, churches, shopping centers, and various other convenient community locations. Such arrangements cut travel time and costs, putting instructional services, faculty members, and educational resources close to students' daily rounds. Various strategies for distance learning using home study supplemented by radio or television, and backed by tutorial assistance at local learning centers, can serve those who cannot meet regularly scheduled classes even when they are held next door. Contract learning, personalized instruction, and diverse arrangements for recognizing individual differences within regular class groups can respond more effectively to particular backgrounds and concerns. Experiential learning activities that help students use ongoing work, family, and community responsibilities as the basis for field studies, observation, reflection, and analysis can strengthen understanding of the abstract concepts and terminology of special fields of study and bring life to key principles. Procedures for assessing the learning accrued from work and life experiences allow these more mature students to avoid courses that duplicate what they already have learned and help them create educational programs that build on the knowledge and competence they already have.

Midlife Transition: 35-45

Folklore has long recognized the midlife transition, dubbed "middlescence" by Harold Hodgkinson, as a turbulent period. Sure enough, social scientists have found the same thing. In the process, they have identified some of the key issues that comprise this great divide. And it is a great divide. The long climb up through the valleys and foothills of youth and early adulthood, with their numerous ups and downs, receding peaks, and impasses, reaches a kind of culmination, or high ground, in midlife. The watershed of the past recedes behind us, and the watershed of the future is dimly outlined ahead.

For some the summit is a gentle broad plateau. There is plenty of time to ramble around sampling wild berries, admiring alpine flowers, basking in the warm sunshine of successful careers, satisfying relationships with family and friends, and solid respect of fellow workers and community associates. But even they eventually must begin the long ramble toward the setting sun.

For others the summit is like *A Night on Bald Mountain,* negotiated through dark and stormy weather, punctuated by lightning strikes and rolling thunder, stung by hail and drenched by downpours. There is no time or disposition to look back nor little chance to take a bearing on the future. The main thing is to find a route toward less exposure; a ledge, cranny or cave, out of the elements, to catch one's breath.

Adapting to a Changing Time Perspective. Perhaps it is the shift from a sense of time since birth to time left to live, together with the shift from a sense of self-determination to a sense of life cycle inevitability, that most marks this great divide. Until this point the future has stretched limitlessly outward. There was time to do everything, to see the whole wide world. Gains in altitude revealed ever larger perspectives. Energy was plentiful—sufficient to meet any challenges and opportunities—self-confidence grew with successive achievements making us ready to tackle whatever came up. But gradually, or sometimes suddenly, we come to see that we have gone about as far as we can go. The height and shape of our particular peak become apparent, the route to be taken up and over becomes clear. Time is running out, with much still undone, unseen, unexperienced.

We shall not spend the precious second half of our life that way, despite the successes and satisfactions we may have had. But how shall we use it better? What are our new priorities? How can we manage the inexorable realities and ponderous momentum created through forty years of living, loving, and work? Shall we stick to the well-trodden routes or take that road less traveled? Maybe we should strip to bare essentials and go bushwhacking instead. If we start rappelling down this sharp face, will we find a manageable route before we run out of rope? Should we take the long way around instead? In the course of time, decisions get made. Like those of adolescence and youth, they may be made more or less by design, by chance, or by default. But in some fashion we cross this divide and trudge on toward our fates.

Revising Career Plans. After fifteen or twenty years in a particular vocation or profession most of us arrive close to wherever we will end up. By this time we have mastered most of the challenges, learned whatever is there to be learned, sucked the juices from whatever plums are to be had. Whether we are plumber, nurse, electrician, teacher, shop foreman, secretary, business executive, banker, doctor, lawyer, or Indian chief, we know most of the ropes and can run off most of the routines. The question is, do we want twenty more years, a thousand more weeks, five thousand more days of the same— the same faces, the same paper, the same noise and dirt, the same walls and washroom, memos and meetings? Or can we make a change? Is there a lateral arabesque that might propel us to a different place on the stage, with different perspectives and partners? Might we jump over to an entirely different stage, calling for a different type of performance? Could we handle the switch from Balanchine to Martha Graham, where some of our weaknesses might be strengths, or where new types of knowledge or competence might be mastered?

Or must we be stuck with the "one life, one career" model so reinforced by social expectations, stereotypes, and discriminatory employment practices. As each year takes us toward the fifties and sixties, the choice becomes tougher. If we do not change soon, we will probably ride it out to retirement. And most of us do just that, sometimes with quiet resignation, finding challenge, satisfaction, and new experiences elsewhere.

For women who have followed the typical route from school or college through marriage and childrearing, the questions are different: Now what shall I do? Shall I go back to school or to work? How capable am I anyway? What level of aspiration will my abilities permit? What levels are realistic, entering the market at this late date? What kinds of knowledge and competence have I achieved through the past twenty years of home-making, childrearing, and community activities? Am I still a quick study—the sharp, perceptive person I was back in college and graduate school days? Or has all that atrophied and gone to pot along with some of my other parts?

For husband and wife to find some kind of coordinated response as both parties face these questions is difficult indeed. And of course the decisions concerning career revision create consequences for other developmental tasks.

Redefining Family Relationships. Often these career decisions are in the air about the time children are leaving home. To some degree the career questions are triggered by those anticipated departures, which not only free the wife but also free the couple to pick up and go elsewhere, to start a new chapter in a different location. Even if they remain in the same location, departure of the children ushers in the possibility of a new chapter in the relationship between husband and wife. Without the children to think about, the time is their own, for doing things together and rediscovering each other, for recapturing some of the carefree spontaneity that was possible before the first child. But there is also the possibility that there is not much there to enjoy, that one or both finds the other dull, unadventurous, stagnant. There may turn out to be no shared interests beyond the children; when they leave, the cement that has held the relationship together may crumble.

So here we are with thirty good years ahead. Is this the person, warts and all, with whom I want to spend those years—the only ones I have left? Or would it be better in the long run if we each made a change now? Perhaps someone younger would help me stay alive and fit. Or perhaps I need a more mature and sophisticated companion whose interests and energy complement mine.

Of course, the children are still alive and kicking. We may not hear from them much or see them often, but we miss them after they move out to establish their own identities, their emotional independence and self-sufficiency. That transition they are making drives home, more than anything else perhaps, the inevitability of the life cycle. But they are not yet settled and fully on their own. Some are in and out of college, others in and out of jobs. We hear obliquely, or after the fact, about the ups and downs of their relationships with various partners, their trial balloons, and impending marriages. We want to supply a crash pad until they manage those developmental tasks of late adolescence and youth, until they become fairly well established in a marriage and occupation. So, although we feel more free to change locations, take a new job, and even branch out into new relationships, considerations concerning the kids are still there to be reckoned with.

Some Implications. Students in this Midlife Transition face many of the demands from family, work, and community that characterize students in Early Adulthood. Thus, many of the institutional arrangements that increase accessibility will be useful here as well. Because these persons bring more wide-ranging knowledge and competence growing out of their more extensive experience, educational practices that assess and build on that prior learning become even more important. The processes of self-examination, self-assessment, planning, and institutional validation that accompany the assessment of prior learning are especially important for persons who are adapting to a changing time perspective, revising career plans, and redefining family relationships. Reviewing the experiences, activities, and academic studies completed and articulating the range of knowledge and competence acquired can provide a solid footing for a new start. Looking forward, with the help of counseling, instructional exercises, and resource materials that help clarify values and life-style aspirations, as well as sharpen career and educational plans, helps students come to grips with the existential issues that have surfaced again during this period. Research studies find that students who have undertaken a thorough process of assessing prior learning and program planning report the experience to be the most significant of their educational career up to that time. The Shipton and Steltenpohl chapter on educational advising and career planning, in Part Three, gives us some good suggestions for this area.

For many of these persons, opportunities for substantial exchanges with fellow students and faculty members may be more important than for students in Early Adulthood. Often the balance has shifted from an instrumental to an expressive educational orientation. The kinds of adaptations and redefinitions under way call for sharing, reaction, hearing from others about their own hopes and fears, trial balloons, and tentative solutions. The term "middlescence" reminds us of the intense, extended personal conversations that characterize so many late-adolescent freshmen and sophomores. Older persons in transition may bring more perspective to the discussion, both bitter and sweet, but the need for such discussions, and the special relationships that make them possible, may be equally great. They also need to stand back from their current conditions and appraise them with greater objectivity. Thus, these students are apt to make better use of counseling and advising services—providing the services are supplied by persons with sufficient maturity to understand their particular situation. They are more likely participants in varied workshops and special interest groups that speak to their needs and let them step outside their daily rounds. The range of alternatives given in Figure 4 earlier in this chapter illustrates some of the possibilities here.

Because of the emotional and personalized nature of the concerns that bring these students back to college, instructional processes that recognize their individual needs also become more important. Many faculty members accustomed to younger students are astonished at the amount of drive and work that results when an individual learning contract provides insights, conceptual handles, or vicarious experiences pertinent to these needs; they are startled at the perceptivity and complexity shown in field studies, interviews, original research, and self-reflective activities. So contract learning can be an especially powerful educational tool, along with other forms of personalized instruction and distance learning that respond to individual interests and backgrounds. But, as noted above, these students also thrive on opportunities to discuss emerging understandings and academic concepts, so group meetings that permit these changes are also important. Thus, perhaps the most effective process is one that provides a combination of group sessions under a broadly defined course title with opportunities for individual or subgroup contracts within that larger framework. Clark's chapter on individualized education in Part Three discusses some of these possibilities in very helpful fashion.

The curricular interests of these Midlife Transition students will range more widely than those in Early Adulthood. Literature, art, history, philosophy, and studies of other cultures all can provide rich perspectives on the students' own situations. They can suggest alternative life-styles and personal relationships, as well as different value hierarchies and modalities for integrity and generativity. Anthropology, sociology, economics, and more broadly oriented studies in the social and behavioral sciences can help improve understanding of the local, national, and international contexts within which these persons will have to create their own futures. Thus, these students are apt to show more interest in general education and the liberal arts than many younger classmates. The Part Two chapters on literature and writing, drama, history, philosophy, anthropology, economics, and interdisciplinary studies show how such areas can respond to particular needs emerging from life cycle differences and at the same time maintain academic integrity concerning disciplinary objectives and standards.

Middle Adulthood: 45-57

After successfully negotiating the great divide of the Midlife Transition, many persons find Middle Adulthood to be the most full, satisfying, and creative time of their lives. They are most sure of themselves, where they stand, what they want, what they can and cannot do, and are at peace with that knowledge. Neugarten (1968a), for example, reports, "Despite the new realization of the finiteness of time, one of the most prevailing themes expressed by the middle-aged respondents is that middle adulthood is the period of maximum capacity and ability to handle a highly complex environment and a highly differentiated self. Very few express a wish to be young again" (p. 142). At this age, having experienced the vicissitudes of fifty years, we have a substantial repertoire of coping strategies. We pretty much know what will work in most situations and what will not. We are beyond the trial-and-error stages of youth and early adulthood. We are practiced.

Maintaining a Career or Developing a New One. Middle Adulthood is the period

during which many persons attain their highest status and income. If they resolve to continue in the same occupation, they usually know it thoroughly enough to make the most
of whatever possibilities there are. As Neugarten observes: "In pondering the data on
these men and women, we have been impressed by the central importance of what might
be called the executive processes of personality in middle age: self-awareness, selectivity,
manipulation and control of the environment, mastery, competence, the wide array of
cognitive strategies.... These people feel that they effectively manipulate their social
environments on the basis of prestige and expertise; and that they create many of their
own rules and norms. The successful middle-aged person often describes himself as no
longer 'driven' but now as the 'driver'—in short, 'in command' " (p. 143).

These successful, well-established persons, less driven by their own needs for
achievement and success, can now give more attention to human relationships on the job.
They can let concern for the development and achievement of others replace the concern
for their own development, which consumed them during Early Adulthood and the Midlife Transition. This "sponsorship" and "mentoring" also becomes a way of pursuing
valued long-range goals, of trying to ensure that the flag will be grasped by energetic,
competent hands, that the investments and achievements of the past twenty years will
not wither and die. So, as with most significant and complex tasks, both instrumental and
expressive ends are served.

Of course, a number of men may change jobs during this period and start on a
new career back near the beginning. This is particularly true of persons whose earlier
work has required levels of physical skill and stamina that cannot be maintained into the
fifties: athletes, policemen, firemen, and heavy laborers, for example. There are also those
who simply decide to break away from the routines of their past work. About 10 percent
of the men between 40 and 60 fall into this category of career-changers. For those persons, the developmental task is not maintaining effective performance, status, and income
but learning new roles, new skills, and new systems. Additional training may be required
through two- or four-year colleges, graduate schools, professional training programs on
the job, or self-study. Women moving from twenty years of homemaking and childrearing
into part-time and full-time employment may find themselves similarly challenged to update earlier knowledge and competence, develop new skills, and undertake other kinds of
personal changes, through assertiveness training and the like, to prepare themselves for
new roles and responsibilities.

For these men and women, moving into occupations or developing new careers
can be a high-risk, high-gain period. It can be full of excitement, self-validation, growing
self-esteem, and sense of competence. When challenging new employment is found and
managed well, career trajectories for these mature persons can be steep indeed as they and
their employers discover sophistication and know-how unrecognized before. But this can
also be a period of frustration, anxiety, trial, and self-doubt. The marketplace may offer
only positions well below our competence and knowledge. When we take such positions
rather than do nothing, and find ourselves at a dead end, with no way up or good way
out, we may look back with regret on the "contingency schedule" we wittingly or unwittingly chose, frustrated at our inability to turn the clock back and create a personal history more pertinent to our current condition.

So for some the rose garden promised by Middle Adulthood is more like a briar
patch. Getting through it may require reconfrontation of those earlier psychosocial conflicts: autonomy versus shame and doubt, initiative versus guilt, industry versus inferiority, identity versus role confusion, generativity versus stagnation. Our experiences of this
reconfrontation drive home Erikson's caution: "The assumption that on each stage a

goodness is achieved which is impervious to new inner conflicts and to changing conditions is, I believe, a projection on child development of that success ideology which can so dangerously pervade our private and public daydreams and can make us inept to a heightened struggle for a meaningful existence in a new industrial era of history. The personality is engaged with the hazards of existence continuously, even as the body's metabolism copes with decay" (1950, p. 274).

Restabilizing Family Relationships. Persons in Middle Adulthood typically become the functional heads of three-generation families. Relationships between husband and wife are stabilized for better or worse during these years. Couples learn to make the most of their long history together, to value the positive and overlook the negative. Usually there is increased affection, sharing, and respect. Adjustments necessary to accommodate career changes or new occupations are made to maximize shared objectives and compensate for past inequities. Personal sacrifices may be made to enhance the other's well-being. This same climate obtains as well when people have remarried. The perspectives brought to the new relationships, whether with a younger person or a peer, make for easier and more open negotiation.

One key to this increased flexibility and generosity lies in changed priorities. Relationships with spouse, friends, and family tend to assume priority over achievement motives. With this shift in priorities, time, energy, and emotion become more available. Satisfaction and self-esteem now rest more on helping and enjoying others than on satisfying marketplace demands.

This shift is reflected in the gradual development of easier relationships with aging parents. Their needs can now be more readily heard and addressed. They are coping with retirement, reduced income, declining vigor, and failing health. Relationships with aging parents require gradual redefinition as their needs for time, attention, and various forms of direct assistance grow. Those who just a few short years ago were strong, energetic, and respected on the job and in the community may now be weak, querulous, and frightened. Their demands may try our love and patience. Unconscious dynamics and latent hostilities built in when we were the dependent ones may get their innings now, or at least cause ambivalence and irritation. But usually there develops greater openness in confronting the consequences of death, coping with shifting requirements for housing and care, their financial needs, and their adjustment to a spouse's death. However, these easier relationships do not occur spontaneously, without some trials and tribulations. Achieving them is a major developmental task of this period.

The same kind of shift occurs in relationships with children as they start their own families and careers. It takes a while to let go, to learn to let them make their own mistakes and create their own answers to the world as they find it—quite different from the world we experienced at their age. But most of us move into the roles of grandparents and sounding boards without serious disruption or upset. Gradually, we define the limits of our own contributions and availability, and learn how to temper our own expectations and demands. So working out these varied *modi vivendi* presents another set of developmental challenges for this period.

Making Mature Civic Contributions. With a more deliberate orientation toward work and with restabilization of family relationships well under way, more time and energy are released for civic contributions. The broad knowledge, competence, and personal and professional contacts of the middle adult, combined with reasonably solid health and vigor make these men and women ideal candidates for civic leadership. They provide not only the backbone but strong arms and legs to define and carry out major social contributions. Learning how to assume those roles and carry them effectively provides opportunities for new challenges, settings, and personal relationships. These new opportunities can compensate for the boredom and routine at work. Indeed, the ability to maintain those work routines fairly automatically with one hand leaves the other hand and much of the mind and heart free for these new investments.

Adjusting to Biological Change. At this age, when you sit down to breakfast you hear the snap, crackle, and pop before you pour milk on your cereal. Even the most fit of us experience decreased stamina, speed, and flexibility during these middle adult years. If we have been physically active, staying in shape seems harder and harder. The dues paid in morning-after stiffness, aches, and pains seem to rise like runaway inflation. If we lay off for a week, it takes a month to recover, and even then we may not make it all the way back. Somehow the balls come faster, and the court seems longer. Bouncing down moguls leads to disaster, beautifully carved turns get out of control. Any aspirations toward further improvement go down the drain: now we struggle to stay even. Activities that have supplied twenty years of release and recreation now more often yield frustration and defeat.

Physical changes also require adjustments on the job, whether or not we are among those for whom vigorous physical activity has been important. Marathon meetings, late-night sessions, and emotional battles take more out of us than they used to. Those sixty- to eighty-hour weeks responding to some crisis or opportunity do not come so easily any more. Two late nights in a row may finish us off for a week. Try as we may, we cannot keep the wheels turning.

For women there is the additional adjustment to menopause. Neugarten's research indicates that for most persons, although there may be occasional discomfort, this adjustment is managed with relative ease and equanimity.

Then there is that sneaky metabolic shift that occurs during the late thirties and forties and starts to hit us hard during middle adulthood. Suddenly a piece of cake equals a pound. Those three squares a day, which were a minimum required to keep us well fueled for our energetic rounds of work and love, suddenly create jowls and flab. We struggle to cut back. The pattern on the weight chart looks like a yo-yo. Five days of self-discipline go down the drain with a five-pound surge over a party weekend. In these days of gourmet foods and free-flowing liquor, readjusting eating habits is one of the most frustrating developmental tasks many of us face.

Some Implications. The demands of family, work, and community for persons in Middle Adulthood have slackened somewhat. Children are out of the house, off at college, working, and becoming increasingly self-sufficient, at least in terms of daily requirements. Most jobs have been pretty well mastered; skills of sizing up a new job and managing its requirements have matured so that a promotion or lateral move does not create quite the overload of earlier days. Community contacts and relationships have become better established, so those activities can also be handled more easily. Most important, perhaps, the increased competence and self-assurance are often accompanied by a gradual change in orientation that gives greater priority to personal satisfaction and development as against satisfying external demands for performance or social norms for achievement. Thus, these persons who for better or worse have come to terms with the Midlife Transition attend college more prepared to concentrate on educational activities. Of course, they still face real constraints. They are still working, and many hold positions of substantial responsibility. Often they are in administrative or supervisory positions where others depend on them and where emergencies cannot go unattended. But they also have a larger measure of self-determination and the capacity to exercise it than younger subordinates still driving hard for achievement, status, and income.

For these persons, therefore, institutional arrangements that increase accessibility will still be useful, but not quite so critical. Flexible arrangements for study and distance learning may not be quite so necessary because these persons can control their own schedules to conform to more regularly scheduled class activities. These students will represent the full range of individual differences that characterize the younger groups, but in the aggregate they will display more balanced emphasis on instrumental and expressive educational orientations. Some will be developing new careers and assuming positions of significant community leadership; these persons will want particular kinds of professional or vocational education or solid studies pertinent to particular community responsibilities such as schooling, transportation, town planning, resource management, urban development, political organization, and arts and humanities councils. Others may be renewing avocational or intellectual interests pushed aside by the demands of work and family.

For these mature persons, recognition of prior learning and the integration of academic studies with ongoing experiential learning will be important. Collegial relationships with faculty members will also be important. Faculty members will want to capitalize on the accumulated experience such students have to offer. Courses that bring late adolescents and youth together with these more mature students in discussions, team projects, and field studies can be stimulating and valuable for both. The younger learn from sharing and testing the insights of the older; the older get new perspectives on social changes. And these new perspectives on the attitudes, behaviors, and beliefs of the young in turn contribute to the restabilization of family relationships, which is one of the key developmental tasks of this period.

Late-Adult Transition: 57-65

Probably most observers see the transition from middle to late adulthood as an accelerating downhill slide. But shifting life expectancies, with increasingly flexible and delayed retirement options, mean that there is plenty of life left. The average life expectancy for men who reach age 50 is 78, of women, 83. There is time enough to put together a very solid final chapter, if only the right combination of living arrangements, vocational and recreational interests, and family and social relationships can be created. There is no need to give up the ghost just yet.

The possibility of early, regular, or late retirement raises issues concerning future life-styles, income requirements, and alternative locations. How can we simplify our lives and cut our expenses? What interests and activities do we really want to continue? What possessions are we ready to give up? How will it feel if we leave this house and community, which have shared so many of our joys and supported us through the bad times? Will we find others elsewhere who can equal our good friends here? Can we establish ourselves in similar comfort and respect with the church, clubs, and community organizations of some distant town or city? How will it feel to be spending all our time with "old folks"? Is there some way we can keep alive relationships with our children, grandchildren, and other younger friends?

With these new options comes copious time. What shall we do with it all? Will regenerating those atrophied interests really suffice? Or will they quickly go stale when we really throw ourselves into them? Will we be able to move beyond the superficial skills we have had as a dabbler or dilettante? Are there new interests, emerging social concerns, or other community activities that might be fertile soil for seeding new investments of time, emotion, money, and energy?

Late Adulthood: 65+

The developmental tasks of Late Adulthood differ in one fundamental way from those of earlier ages: they require reduced activity and involvement. Although this shift has begun with the Late-Adult Transition, it becomes central in this final period. In the physical, mental, and economic spheres, the older person must work hard to hold on to what he or she already has. In the social sphere, there is a fair chance of offsetting the demise of certain friendships and interests by developing new ones. In the spiritual sphere, boundaries may expand rather than shrink.

Adjusting to Retirement. In American society a job is the axis of life for most men and for many women. Without a job, a person feels that he or she does not count, is not a worthy member of society, is a burden, a leech. The central role of work is simply an extension of our emphasis on "doing." "What are you going to do?" probably bugs the adolescent more than any other question. And it is an unusual youth indeed who can answer, "I'm not going to *do,* I'm going to *be!*" The same question plagues the adult on the verge of retirement. Although it may not carry such a heavy freight of social expectation, it is still a tough problem for one who has spent fifty years oriented toward doing—toward constructive, valued, socially useful, paid work and civic contributions. Familiar responses are "We're going to travel." "We're going to just sit back and relax for awhile, then we'll see." "I'm going to sharpen up my golf game, fix up my shop and get back to woodworking, pick up my painting or music, write that book." But often these responses have the same hollow ring we hear behind the adolescent answer created to fend off further probing.

Of course, most older persons learn to *do* less and *be* more. They learn to relax and take it easy, to develop new interests. They find part-time employment or volunteer activities that sustain a sense of social contribution with reduced commitment of energy and emotion. And changing practices concerning retirement age and age-related discrimination will gradually make employment alternatives increasingly available.

Adjusting to Declining Health and Strength. The human body does age in almost every cell and cellular system. Poisonous materials gradually accumulate that cannot be expelled. Nutritional processes slow down and cells gradually lose their self-repairing capacity. Current health practices and nutrition in the United States enable most persons to remain fairly active and vigorous into the mid seventies and often well beyond. But all of us face continual readjustment in pace as well as load. We tend to shy away from noisy environments and stressful situations. Discos have hardly any appeal at all. A book by the fire serves much better. Cruises and car camping replace rock climbing and back packing; flat water canoeing replaces whitewater kayaking.

Becoming Affiliated with Late-Adult Age Groups. Many persons fight acknowledging they have become "senior citizens." They hold on tenaciously to middle-adulthood associations. But gradually they come to feel more comfortable with others of their own age. They find positions in organizations of older persons in which the issues and tempos match their own. For thirty or forty years, position and status have been determined by power, talent, income, and personal contacts. Now age frequently becomes a determining factor. Finding oneself sorted into any kind of box is never easy. Fortunately, as the proportions of people over 65 in the total population increase, we have more and more compatriots to fight that sorting, to increase our freedom of choice in affiliations. Of course, those increased options may increase the complexity of this developmental task, but we expect the price will be worth the candle.

Establishing Satisfactory Living Arrangements. Commonly, persons have to change their living arrangements after the age of 65. A smaller house or apartment may be called for. A shift to warmer, less-demanding climes may look appealing or be necessary for health reasons. Finding some location where others handle residential maintenance and upkeep, where health facilities and medical treatment are readily available, and where one can find a caring network of friends and associates may be important. Perhaps some congregate living arrangement or retirement community will be the answer.

These issues, raised initially during the Late-Adult Transition, now need to be met directly. When initial decisions have been made, negotiations with children, real estate agents, bankers, lawyers, salesmen, and the like become necessary. For those of us who have lived fairly settled lives, this move can present a substantial challenge.

And even then, new arrangements may not work out nearly as well as we anticipated. Sun City may not measure up to the old home town; all that social engineering and managed recreation may leave us cold. Tearing up our roots may be more than we can manage. We find ourselves starved and withering without that friendly soil. So first decisions may be only the beginning of a painful process of working out acceptable compromises.

Adjusting to the Death of a Spouse. After a long-standing marriage, or even one of less duration, living alone is difficult. Although with advancing years death becomes a normal expectation, we still contend with grief and remorse. In addition, concrete adjustments may be required: living on a reduced income, moving to smaller living quarters, or learning to manage business affairs or housekeeping chores formerly handled by one's spouse. Above all, there is the loneliness. Friends and groups we enjoyed as couples may not feel the same when we are alone. And if our spouse has become a central source of satisfaction and support during these last years, there may not seem to be much reason left to live.

Maintaining Integrity. While we are caught up meeting marketplace demands and doing the myriad tasks required for raising a family and participating in the community, we may not have much time to think about whether it all makes sense. Questions about the larger meaning of things and our relation to them, settled somehow during Adolescence and Youth, and resolved again during the Midlife Transition, now are once again substance for reflection. It is time to create or find a larger rationale that provides some justification for our existence. Religious roots may be strengthened or rediscovered. Reassurance, affection, validation, and support from children and friends may be sought tentatively, unobtrusively, indirectly. And this may be complicated by long-standing interpersonal dynamics that rule out certain kinds of sharing, feelings, or actions. So we do the best we can to achieve this life's final restructuring, to create that rod and staff for our journey into the valley of the shadow of death.

Some Implications. Persons in this age period may be testing new areas to provide stimulation and enrichment for the more leisurely years ahead. Arts, crafts, and humanities may be of special interest to many of these persons, as well as studies pertinent to social problems to which they could apply their wisdom and experience. Other persons may call for studies that are both practical and philosophical—some studies that will help them cope with immediate problems and others that will provide perspectives on life's meaning and their own place within it. Concerns about strength, stamina, and health often call for new knowledge about nutrition, exercise, and disease. The need to establish new living arrangements, often as a result of death of a spouse, call for thoughtful judgments about location, community, and friendships, as well as concrete information about managing shrinking resources and the pros and cons of owning or renting condominiums, or congregate living arrangements. At the same time, religious and philosophical studies that provide perspectives on the life that has passed, on death and dying, mortality and immortality may help create and sustain integrity, or help stave off despair at potentials unrealized, relationships unfulfilled, affections unexpressed, help ungiven, love untendered.

For these persons, less pressed for time by heavy demands, access to education depends more on ease of transportation than on flexible schedules. Studies need not necessarily be available close to home if there are adequate means for travel to and fro. But even so, there are real advantages to arrangements that locate learning opportunities where people live. Working and learning with others is apt to be much more satisfying than solitary study. Sharing past experiences and debating interpretations that grow out of varied backgrounds make group studies that are part of a larger sense of community especially appealing. And when these can be provided in ways that permit intergenerational exchange as well, the learning of all seems to be enlivened. Riker's discussion in Part Three of various kinds of on-campus intergenerational living arrangements, elder hostels for short-term residencies, and the like, notes the apparent value of such alternatives. But colleges and universities have hardly scratched the surface of possibilities for this growing age group. The numbers will continue to grow and become a major proportion of the total population. As this occurs, political and economic power will likewise increase. Higher education has much to offer these older persons. More important, it has much to gain from their accumulated experience. It is a fairly safe bet that during the 1980s and 1990s creative efforts will sharply increase services to such persons and at the same time elicit contributions by active "retirees" to our institutions themselves.

Conclusion

This book on the future American college takes as a major premise the need for educators to become more knowledgeable about individual differences among the increasing numbers of diverse adults seeking higher education. Life cycle differences seem to be one of the most significant dimensions of that diversity. There is certainly much to be known beyond the brief synopses supplied by this chapter. The references that follow suggest some of the pertinent literature. There are educational implications that go well beyond those briefly signaled here. Many of these implications are explored in greater depth by the authors of chapters in Parts Two and Three. But there are surely many other implications as yet unnoted and unanticipated. These new constituencies for higher education create exciting challenges and opportunities. Significantly, they may also serve as a catalyst for changes beneficial to typical college-age students, who will continue to be the largest single age group to be served, at least for the next decade or two. If we can create alternatives responsive to wide-ranging life cycle differences, we can at the same time improve the effectiveness of higher education for all.

References

Astin, A. W. *Four Critical Years: Effects of College on Beliefs, Attitudes, and Knowledge.* San Francisco: Jossey-Bass, 1977.

Astin, A. W., and others. *National Norms for Entering Freshmen.* Washington, D.C.: American Council on Education, Fall 1969.

Bell, D. *The Coming of Post-Industrial Society.* New York: Basic Books, 1973.

Bowen, H. R. *Investment in Learning: The Individual and Social Value of American Higher Education.* San Francisco: Jossey-Bass, 1977.

Broverman, D., and others. "Sex-Role Stereotypes and Clinical Judgments of Mental Health." *Journal of Consulting and Clinical Psychology,* 1970, *34* (1), 1-7.

Buehler, C. "Genetic Aspects of the Self." *Annals of the New York Academy of Sciences,* 1962, *96,* 730-764.

Chickering, A. W. *Education and Identity.* San Francisco: Jossey-Bass, 1969.

Chickering, A. W. *Commuting Versus Resident Students: Overcoming Educational Inequities of Living Off Campus.* San Francisco: Jossey-Bass, 1974.

Clark, R., and Trow, M. "The Organizational Context." In T. M. Newcomb and E. K. Wilson (Eds.), *College Peer Groups: Problems and Prospects for Research.* Chicago: Aldine, 1966.

Epstein, C. F. "Bringing Women In." In R. B. Knudson (Ed.), *Women and Success: The Anatomy of Achievement.* New York: Morrow, 1974.

Erikson, E. H. *Childhood and Society.* New York: Norton, 1963. (Originally published 1950.)

Erikson, E. H. *Identity and the Life Cycle.* Psychological Issues Monograph 1. New York: International Universities Press, 1959.

Feldman, K. A., and Newcomb, T. M. *The Impact of College on Students.* San Francisco: Jossey-Bass, 1969.

Froomkin, J., and Dresch, S. P. *The College, the University, and the State: A Critical Examination for Institutional Support in the Context of Historical Development.* New Haven, Conn.: Yale University Institute for Social and Policy Studies, 1974.

Gould, R. L. "The Phases of Adult Life: A Study in Developmental Psychology." *American Journal of Psychiatry,* 1972, *129,* 521-531.

Havighurst, R. J. *Developmental Tasks and Education.* (3rd ed.) New York: McKay, 1972.

Heath, D. H. *Growing up in College: Liberal Education and Maturity.* San Francisco: Jossey-Bass, 1968.

Horner, M. "Toward an Understanding of Achievement-Related Conflicts in Women." *Journal of Social Issues,* 1972, *28,* 157-175.

Katz, J., and Associates. *No Time for Youth: Growth and Constraint in College Students.* San Francisco: Jossey-Bass, 1968.

Levinson, D. J., and others. *The Seasons of a Man's Life.* New York: Knopf, 1978.

Loevinger, J. *Ego Development: Conceptions and Theories.* San Francisco: Jossey-Bass, 1976.

Loevinger, J., Wessler, R., and Redmore, C. *Measuring Ego Development.* 2 vols. San Francisco: Jossey-Bass, 1970.

Lowenthal, M. F., Thurnher, M., Chiriboga, D., and Associates. *Four Stages of Life: A Comparative Study of Women and Men Facing Transitions.* San Francisco: Jossey-Bass, 1975.

McCoy, V. R. *Lifelong Learning: The Adult Years.* Washington, D.C.: Adult Education Association, 1977.

Murphy, L. B., and Raushenbush, E. *Achievement in the College Years.* New York: Harper & Row, 1960.

Neugarten, B. L. "Adult Personality: Toward a Psychology of the Life Cycle." In B. L. Neugarten (Ed.), *Middle Age and Aging.* Chicago: University of Chicago Press, 1968a.

Neugarten, B. L. "The Awareness of Middle Age." In B. L. Neugarten (Ed.), *Middle Age and Aging.* Chicago: University of Chicago Press, 1968b.

Neugarten, B. L. "Adaptation and the Life Cycle." *Journal of Geriatric Psychology,* 1970, *4* (1), 71-87.

Neugarten, B. L. "Personality and Aging." In J. E. Birren and K. W. Schaie (Eds.), *Handbook of the Psychology of Aging.* New York: Van Nostrand Reinhold, 1977.

Newcomb, T. M., and others. *Persistence and Change: A College and Its Students after Twenty-five Years.* Huntington, N.Y.: Krieger, 1967.

Raushenbush, E. *The Student and His Studies.* Middletown, Conn.: Wesleyan University Press, 1964.

Rossi, A. S. "Women in Science: Why so Few?" *Science,* 1975, *148.*

Sanford, N. *Self and Society: Social Change and Individual Development.* Chicago: Aldine, 1966.

Sarason, S. B., Sarason, E. K., and Cowden, P. "Aging and the Nature of Work." *American Psychologist,* 1975, pp. 584-592.

Sheehy, G. *Passages: Predictable Crises in Adult Life.* New York: Dutton, 1976.

Stern, G. G. *People in Context: Measuring Person-Environment Congruence In Education and Industry.* New York: Wiley, 1970.

2

Rita Preszler Weathersby

Ego Development

Ego development is an implicit aim of higher education and can be one of its most significant results. Stages of ego development constitute qualitatively different frames of reference for perceiving and responding to experience. Each successive stage represents a major reorganization of ways of understanding and reacting to situations, people, and ideas—a watershed change in patterns of thinking and feeling about oneself, others, authority, ethics, knowledge, and the central concerns that hold a life together. As a corollary, these stages reflect distinct views of the meaning and value of education, as well as characteristic styles of coping with the tasks of lifelong learning. Development through these stages parallels many other goals of higher education and tacitly informs our judgments about "what's good" and "what's next" for students in their intellectual journeys.

Higher education has a great deal to gain from recognizing these patterns of ego development as the framework of consciousness within which learning occurs. Educators are traditionally present at turning points in students' lives, whether the students are 18 or 80 and whether the curriculum is undergraduate, graduate, traditional, nontraditional, liberal arts, or vocational. A knowledge of ego development provides a "map for growth," which can help us find the best ways to reach our students. Equally important, our own stage of ego development is the frame of reference out of which we learn and teach. To be aware of the biases underlying our pedagogy, we need to know our own inner maps. The root word of *education* means to elicit or lead forth. This chapter offers ego development as a guide to understanding the personal and transformative meaning of education and explores its validity as an explicit aim for higher education.

Definition of Ego Development

By *ego,* students of ego development do not mean what is popularly called to mind by the term *ego,* such as one's self-concept or self-esteem, nor Freud's familiar idea of the ego in unconscious conflict with superego and id. Instead, they mean that aspect of personality that "keeps things together" by striving for coherence and assigning meaning to experience. The term *ego development* thus refers to a sequence, cutting across chronological time, of interrelated patterns of cognitive, interpersonal, and ethical development that form unified, successive, and hierarchical world views. Each stage or world view is a qualitatively different way of responding to life experience, which can be illustrated by representative types of individuals from Archie Bunker to Mahatma Gandhi.

Many psychologists have studied aspects of ego development as independent phenomena. Jane Loevinger and her associates (1970, 1976) have articulated a synthesis of their findings by linking insights from philosophical and humanistic psychology with psychoanalytic ego psychology and with contemporary stage-type notions of personality. She draws upon the conceptualizations of such diverse researchers as Alfred Adler, David Ausubel, Erik Erikson, Erik Fromm, Kenneth Isaacs, Lawrence Kohlberg, Abraham Maslow, George Herbert Mead, Jean Piaget, Carl Rogers, and Harry Stack Sullivan. At present, her scheme of ego development is the most inclusive of all developmental stage theories applicable to adolescents and adults. It has the added advantage of a measuring instrument (a projective test calling for sentence completions) and a scoring manual that makes explicit the experiential worlds of each stage.

Loevinger (1970, p. 7) traces her use of the term *ego development* to Adler's concept of "style of life," which at various times he equated with self, or ego, unity of personality, one's method of facing problems, and one's whole attitude toward life. Harry Stack Sullivan called this the *self-system* and advanced a theory of selective inattention to explain why an individual's ego stage is stable, or changes only slowly. According to this theory, a person tends to pay attention only to what is in accord with his or her already-existing perceptual framework. Discordant observations cause anxiety and give rise to the ego's major task: searching for coherent meanings in experience. The important point here is that one's ego stage is a pervasive, self-reinforcing frame of reference for experiencing. Additionally, it is the personality framework in which learning of any kind is embedded. What is learned is selectively assimilated to one's current patterns of cognition, introspection, interpersonal relations, and motivation. However, some learning is of such magnitude that it changes these patterns unalterably, giving rise to the next stage of development.

Piaget (in Tanner and Inhelder, 1960; see also Kohlberg, 1973) has identified the fundamental features of a concept of developmental stages. Stages are usually thought of as having an invariant sequence (no stages can be skipped), with each stage building on, incorporating, and transforming the elements of the previous one. Each stage has an inner logic that accounts for equilibrium and stability. Loevinger's conceptualization does not necessarily entail so strict a notion of a stage; it is possible to see progressions of ego development as gradations along a qualitative continuum. If one sees discrete stages, the focus is on broad character orientations. If one sees a continuum, the focus is on the dynamics of transition from one stage to the next.

In either case, ego development is considered by Loevinger to be not just *a* personality trait: it is a *master trait* second only to intelligence in determining an individual's pattern of responses to situations. Ego development is marked by a succession of turning points called *milestone sequences,* which represent broad patterns of change involving many aspects of personality. Thus, the presence, absence, or intensity of a single personality trait is best interpreted in the context of how that characteristic fits into an interrelated sequence of development. For example, concern for achievement is most pronounced at a stage of ego development midway in the sequence. A woman with little apparent urgency about achieving may be at lower stages—or may have gone beyond to higher stages in which concern for individual fulfillment transcends conventional notions of achievement. Loevinger's concept of milestone sequences (a trait develops, peaks in importance, and then reappears in a new context) allows us to place this woman's "lack of achievement motivation" in perspective.

Stages of Ego Development

Table 1 presents in summary form Loevinger's (1976) description of the milestone sequences of ego development. The descriptive phrases in the table identify milestones in character development, interpersonal relations, conscious concerns, and cognitive style associated with general stages of ego development. Reading down the columns, one sees successive levels of complexity in each facet of development; reading across, one sees the broad character patterns of each stage. Granted that this is only one way to label complex phenomena, there is substantial empirical evidence to support this formulation (Loevinger, 1970, 1976). Moreover, to most people the progressions make intuitive sense. It is obvious that change in one aspect of ego development is likely to stimulate change in another. Conversely, if there is little change in one facet, further development is necessarily restricted. Consider, for example, how difficult it would be to have a deeply held respect for the individuality and autonomy of others—a salient concern at the Autonomous Stage—if appearance and social acceptability were predominant life themes and one thought in stereotypes and clichés—characteristics of the Conformist Stage, which is earlier in the sequence.

It is helpful to have a more solid sense of these stages before considering their relevance to education (for a more complete description, see Loevinger, 1976, pp. 18-28). The earliest stages are usually thought of as childhood stages. Adults who remain in them are often marginal to society and usually the targets of other's efforts at socialization. A student at the *Self-Protective Stage,* for example, would be concerned with control and advantage in relationships; would follow rules opportunistically; would reason illogically and think in stereotypes; would tend to see life as a zero-sum game; and would externalize blame to other people or to circumstances.

A major step in ego development is the transition from the Self-Protective Stage to the series of essentially conventional stages in which individuals with increasing self-awareness identify with social rules and society. Kohlberg (1969) divides his stages of moral reasoning into preconventional, conventional, and postconventional world views; although the parallel with ego development stages is not exact, this distinction is useful in identifying the major differences in perspective across stages. A student at the *Conformist Stage* would be concerned with appearances and social acceptability; would tend to think in stereotypes and clichés, particularly moralistic ones; would be concerned about conforming to external rules; and would behave with superficial niceness. Emotions would be described in undifferentiated terms that betray little introspection. Group differences would be perceived in terms of obvious external characteristics such as age, race, marital status, and nationality. There would be almost no sensitivity to individual differences.

At the *Conscientious-Conformist Transition,* or *Self-Aware Stage,* an individual develops an increasing self-awareness and the ability to think in terms of alternatives,

Table 1. Some Milestones of Ego Development

Stage	Impulse Control, Character Development	Interpersonal Style	Conscious Preoccupations	Cognitive Style
Impulsive	Impulsiveness, fear of retaliation	Receiving, dependent, exploitative	Bodily feelings, especially sexual and aggressive	Stereotyping, conceptual confusion
Self-Protective	Fear of being caught, externalization of blame, opportunism	Wary, manipulative, exploitative	Self-protection, trouble, wishes, things, advantage, control	
Conformist	Conformity to external rules, shame, guilt for breaking rules	Concerned with belonging, superficially nice	Appearance, social acceptability, banal feelings, behavior	Conceptual simplicity, stereotypes, clichés
Conscientious-Conformist (Self-Aware)	Differentiation of norms, goals	Aware of self in relation to group, helping	Adjustment, problems, reasons, opportunities (vague)	Multiplicity
Conscientious	Self-evaluated standards, self-criticism, guilt for consequences, long-term goals and ideals	Intensive, responsible, mutual, concerned with communication	Differentiated feelings, motives for behavior, self-respect, achievements, traits, expression	Conceptual complexity, idea of patterning
Individualistic	*Add:* Respect for individuality	*Add:* Dependence as an emotional problem	*Add:* Development, social problems, differentiation of inner life from outer	*Add:* Distinction of process and outcome
Autonomous	*Add:* Coping with conflicting inner needs, toleration	*Add:* Respect for autonomy, interdependence	*Add:* Vividly conveyed feelings, integration of physiological and psychological, psychological causation of behavior, role conception, self-fulfillment, self in social context	Increased conceptual complexity, complex patterns, toleration for ambiguity, broad scope, objectivity
Integrated	*Add:* Reconciling of inner conflicts, renunciation of unattainable	*Add:* Cherishing of individuality	*Add:* Identity	

Note: "*Add*" means in addition to the description applying to the previous level.

Source: Adapted from Loevinger, 1976, pp. 24-25.

exceptions, and multiple possibilities in situations. Students at this stage are sometimes painfully aware of their separateness in relation to social groups; they are concerned primarily with taking advantage of opportunities, solving problems, finding reasons for the way life works, and adjusting to situations and roles.

At the *Conscientious Stage,* an individual lives according to self-evaluated standards. Rules are not absolute; exceptions and contingencies are recognized, and reasoning is more complex and based on analytical patterns. A student at this stage would be concerned about responsibility and mutuality in relationships; would see individuals as having real choices in life; would value achievement highly and be concerned with self-respect; would have long-term goals and ideals, and a tendency to look at events in societal terms, or in a broad social context. Individuals at the Conscientious Stage understand psychological causation and development over time; they also have a deeper and more differentiated self-understanding.

The *Autonomous Stage* represents yet another restructuring of personality. This world view is postconventional; one can analyze one's own social group and other social systems, and make choices and commitments despite an awareness of the complexity and social forces at work. An ability to acknowledge inner conflict is the hallmark of this stage. The autonomous individual also respects others' autonomy (for example, being willing and able to let one's children make their own mistakes) while valuing interdependence. The *Individualistic Stage* is a transition to this stage, characterized by a heightened respect for individuality and a concern for development, social problems, and differentiating one's inner and outer life. A student at the Autonomous Stage would take an expanded view of life as a whole; would tend to be realistic and objective about himself and others; would respond to abstract ideals such as social justice; would be able to unite and integrate ideas that appear as incompatible opposites to those at lower stages; and would have a cognitive style characterized by complexity and a high tolerance for ambiguity. Self-fulfillment would become an important concern, partly supplanting the importance of achievement at earlier stages. Feelings would be expressed vividly and convincingly, including sensual experiences and the kind of existential humor that shows a recognition of life's paradoxes.

The highest stage, the *Integrated Stage,* intensifies the characteristics of the Autonomous Stage and adds reconciliation of inner conflicts in a more consolidated sense of identity. Identity is a conscious preoccupation, and interpersonal relations reflect a cherishing of individuality within the broadest possible context of human life. Loevinger finds this stage rare and therefore difficult to study. Maslow's (1971) description of self-actualizing persons is an approximation of these higher stages.

Education's Role in Promoting Ego Development

From this brief review it should be clear that ego development is not a trivial, easily accomplished personality change. What conditions are propitious for ego development? Erikson (1968) says, "Ego identity gains real strength only from wholehearted achievement that has meaning in our culture" (p. 135). Sanford (1962) goes into more detail: "Anything that increases the likelihood that the sense of self will be based on personal experience rather than on outside judgment favors the stabilization of ego identity. Being placed in social roles that require new responses, having to make decisions concerning what roles one is going to take, learning from experience that some roles are suited and others not suited to one's interests and needs—any situation that brings awareness to one's real preferences and inner continuities helps to establish sound ego identity.

So, too, does the condition of being relatively free from circumstances, whether unconscious drives or external pressures, that force one to cling to an earlier inadequate identity" (p. 281). In short, there seem to be three basic conditions that foster ego development: (1) varied direct experiences and roles, (2) meaningful achievement, and (3) relative freedom from anxiety and pressure.

It is instructive to examine the progressions of cognitive style embedded in ego development. At the earliest stages, thinking is stereotyped and characterized by conceptual confusion. At the Conformist Stage, thinking is simplistic, and stereotypes and clichés abound. With the Conscientious Stage come conceptual complexity and the idea of patterns among causal relationships, along with awareness of alternatives, exceptions, and contingencies and a broader time perspective based on long-term goals and ideals. Next is added the crucial ability to distinguish between process and outcome—between a sequence of events and the results that follow. The highest stages are distinguished by increased conceptual complexity, complex patterns of thought and feelings, objectivity, an ability to tolerate ambiguity, and a broad perspective.

These progressions lie at the heart of a liberal arts education and reflect some of the central aims of higher education. They are highly relevant to increased capacity to function effectively in multiple and sometimes conflicting adult roles, and as citizens in a complex world community. They are also central to an individual's ability to learn from experience, in that each person's ego stage places constraints on understanding and action that ultimately determine how much he or she can gain from an education environment. Although higher ego stages do not necessarily mean greater personal goodness or happiness, they do enable individuals to respond more adequately to progressively deeper and more complex issues and problems, both intellectual and personal.

William Perry (1970, see Chapter Three), working independently from Loevinger, derived a compatible progression from longitudinal interviews with Harvard undergraduates. As students advanced from freshmen to seniors, they were asked, "What stood out in your experience?" Students' answers showed a progression along a series of intellectual and ethical positions from simple dualistic thinking, in which the sources of knowledge and authority are viewed in polar terms of "we-right-good" and "other-wrong-bad," through various positions in which multiple views and diversity of opinion are considered legitimate, to a contextual and relativistic view of knowledge in which personal commitment is required in assuming responsibility for the framework within which one's opinions and actions are taken. This research, having started with students and not statements of the purpose of education, lends credence to the claim that colleges are unwittingly engaged in the creation of settings that promote basic personality change. This is not to say that colleges are primarily in the business of psychological education but only to note unequivocally that the experience of being a college student can alter fundamentally the *structures* in which an individual thinks, feels, and acts.

Here, we must discard the outworn rhetorical dichotomies between intellect and emotion and between personal growth and academic achievement, for these very dichotomies embody a thought process characteristic of middle levels of development. There is a unity postulated among all facets of ego development. If higher education induces major changes in students' cognitive style, it is likely to induce change in other aspects of personality as well. According to Piaget's notion of *horizontal décalage,* a change in one dimension requires assimilation and "filling in" across other aspects of functioning. If the changes are significantly widespread and irreversible, a new stage of development may be reached. This potential impact of learning on personality may be one reason why the process of education and its intended result, learning, are almost inevitably accompanied by anxiety. It is also the reason that most educational institutions can be said to be in the business of promoting ego development, even if they merely conceive of themselves as providing students with opportunities to gain intellectual skills and mastery of a discipline or profession.

Ego Development Research in Higher Education

At what stages of ego development are we likely to find our students—and, for that matter, faculty and administrators? Loevinger's research (1970) puts the majority of late adolescents and adults at the Conformist or Conscientious Stages, or squarely between them. (See her sentence completion test, 1970.) Loevinger estimates that this transition (the Self-Aware Level) is the modal stopping place for adults in our society. This also appears to be a transition made by many traditional-age students in their first two years of college. A longitudinal study still in progress (Loevinger, at Worcester Polytechnic Institute) shows that traditional-age students go from about the Self-Aware Stage to about the Conscientious Stage between the beginning of their freshman and the end of their sophomore year. At the end of their senior year they test the same as at the end of their sophomore year.

Data for faculty and administrators are more scarce than for students; my data (Weathersby, 1977) for a very small sample suggest that scores of faculty and administrators are slightly higher than students' scores but, interestingly, cover the same range, omitting the preconventional stages.

Nancy Goldberger, at Simon's Rock Early College (enrolling students 16 to 20 years old), has compiled comparative data on college freshmen from Simon's Rock, an Ivy League college, an urban university, an engineering school, and a teacher's college and juxtaposed them with ego development scores from a national survey of college and noncollege youth conducted by Daniel Yankelovich. The data show that most, but clearly not all, college freshmen are at the Conformist Stage or beyond, and that the proportionate mix of stages in any student group varies with age and with type of institution. Table 2 reproduces Goldberger's data (Goldberger, 1977), adding data from adult undergraduates at Goddard College (Weathersby, 1977) and unpublished data from students enrolled in an external degree program of the Vermont State College System.

The data in Table 2 suggest provocative differences by age and institution. For example, the proportion of traditional-age freshmen at the Ivy League college scoring beyond conformist stages of ego development is more than double that of their general peers. One possible hypothesis is that ego development accounts for their presence at an elite institution—that this is an implicit basis upon which they were admitted. Other hypotheses are possible—for example, social class or alumni bias in recruiting. However, one has only to recall the folklore in higher education about the different kinds of students who attend different types of institutions to gain an appreciation of the validity of these figures as both descriptors of students and of educational milieus.

In Table 2, it is instructive to examine the proportion of students who score at the Conscientious Stage and higher, across age and institutions. Again, for traditional-age students, the Ivy League school and the urban university have the larger proportions. In general, 18-year-olds score higher than 16-year-olds, and undergraduate adults score still higher. Thus, age makes a global difference, at least up to middle levels of development. Additionally, the two adult programs sampled had substantial proportions of students (38 to 49 percent) who scored at the Individualistic, Autonomous, and Integrated Stages. These scores are rare for students of traditional college age. These data are suggestive

Table 2. Ego-Stage Scores of College Students of Varying Ages
at Different Types of Institutions

Traditional-Age High School Students (16 years old)	Preconformist Stages (2)[a]	Conformist Stages (3, 4)	Conscientious Stage and Above (5, 6, 7, 8)
National Survey	32%	61%	7%
Simon's Rock Early College	14%	60%	20%
Selective Prep School	3%	78%	19%
Traditional-Age College Freshmen (18 years old)			
National Survey	16%	52%	31%
Ivy League College	7%	25%	68%
Urban University	8%	45%	47%
Engineering School	13%	48%	39%
Teacher's College	10%	56%	34%
Adult Undergraduates (21-81 years old)			
Goddard College Adult Degree Program	3%	16%	81%
Vermont State Colleges External Degree	—	30%	70%

[a]These codes refer to the stages listed in Table 1. In this formulation, the Self-Protective Stage (2) is preconventional, the Conformist (3) and Self-Aware (4) Stages are conventional, and the Conscientious Stage (5) is above conformity but still conventional in the terms described in this chapter. The Individualistic (6), Autonomous (7), and Integrated (8) Stages are postconventional stages.

Sources: Data for the upper portions of this table were compiled by Nancy Goldberger at Simon's Rock Early College (Goldberger, 1977). The national survey data were supplied by Daniel Yankelovich and Robert Holt and drawn from a 1975 Yankelovich survey of college and noncollege youth. The figures here represent college youth only. Data on adult undergraduates are drawn from Weathersby, 1977, and from an ongoing study of adult learners in the Vermont State Colleges External Degree Program, sponsored by the Fund for the Improvement of Postsecondary Education/DHEW.

rather than conclusive because of differences in sampling and scoring methods among the studies cited. Nonetheless, they raise questions concerning appropriate institutional responses to students' diversity or homogeneity, and also the differential impact of different kinds of college environments upon students' development.

To summarize, we can expect most traditional-age college students to start out at the Conformist or Self-Aware Stage and then move beyond, although probably not past the Conscientious Stage. Some students will still be at preconventional stages; they can be expected to have serious trouble making their way in any college environment. Those at the Conscientious Stage and beyond should tend to perform better academically and function better socially, although this relationship may not necessarily be apparent in individual grade-point averages.

An extraordinarily interesting question is how far beyond conventional stages adult students have ventured. Data from adult students in nontraditional undergraduate programs suggest that they have moved far beyond indeed, much farther than is believed representative of the general adult population. Although the proportion of students at each stage will vary across programs and institutions, most groups of students will exhibit a wide range of individual differences in ego levels. Adult students, taken as a group, probably exhibit both the highest stages and the greatest range of diversity.

We can hypothesize that adults who return to school have progressed along these dimensions as a result of life choices and nonformal learning. Furthermore, many adults "go back to school" in response to deeply felt inner imperatives. That is, their decision to enroll is dictated less by convention than that of traditional-age students. Hence this decision may in itself bespeak a radical personal transformation, or readiness to undergo such a transformation.

Data are scarce for a further and potentially promising use of these statistics: that is, to compare the range and mix of scores across age, sex, and institutions. For example, Goldberger has found sex differences in ego development scores among students at Simon's Rock. The girls who enroll tend to score higher than the boys. In Goddard's Adult Degree Program, women in their twenties tended to score higher than males in the same age group, and also higher than women in other age groups. Women in their forties, many of whom were making the transition from a career in the home to work roles in the larger society, tended to score lower than women in other age groups. Assuming these differences are generalizable past small groups at single institutions, we can account for them by hypothesizing different trajectories of development influenced by sex-related structures of opportunity.

Informally, we acknowledge that different "types" of students appear in different "types" of institutions, giving each its unique character and potential social mission. The findings reported earlier suggest individual differences in ego development may be related to choice of college and to educational outcomes. If this is so, we can employ the concept of ego development to gain a greater understanding of students' reasons for enrolling, and the meaning for them of their educational experiences. There are implications here for admission and attrition, and for brokering services that will help students of all ages find settings in which they can succeed.

Conceptions of Education at Different Ego Levels

Individuals at different stages of ego development have different conceptions of what education is, why it is valuable, and how closely tied education is to what is taught or required by a college faculty. College faculty and administrators exhibit the same diversity of views as students. Our conceptions of education are crucial because they guide our objectives and actions. Nearly everyone says education is valuable; however, across stages the source of value shifts from concern with the practical benefit of getting a job, or a more desirable job, to a means of developing one's skills and capacities for advancement and personal growth, to help in coping with life and involvement in a lifelong learning process that has intrinsic value for self-fulfillment. Table 3 illustrates these differences in one-sentence responses characteristically given to the sentence stem "Education," which appears on most forms of Loevinger's sentence-completion test.

People at the lowest stages tend to view education as external to the self, something that one gets in school and then has. At the Conformist Stage, education is equated with school attendance and the socially defined number of necessary years of schooling. This view is both practical and idealized. Education is "an essential requirement in acquiring a good job" and "the greatest thing on earth." At the Self-Aware Stage, education becomes important as an investment in one's life or future. There is a shift away from thinking of education as a concrete entity toward thinking of it as a goal and an asset. Education becomes "a very important step in life" and "is the best investment anyone can make."

At the Conscientious Stage, education is usually seen as an experience that affects a person's inner life. It is no longer merely a number of years of useful schooling. Its importance lies in intellectual challenge and in potential enrichment for the individual. It

Table 3. Perceptions of Education by Ego Stages

Ego Stage	Characteristic Responses to Sentence-Completion Stem "Education"
Impulsive and Self-Protective Stages Education is viewed as a *thing* that you get in school and then have. Positive remarks are undifferentiated. There are also expressions of distaste for education, or of not getting along in school.	Education . . . . . . *is fun and hard.* . . . *is a very good thing.* . . . *is OK.* . . . *is very nice to have if you ain't got it you can't get a job.* . . . *and me don't get along too good.* . . . *is useless and a lot of bother.* . . . *is good for finding a job.* . . . *is a drag but important.* . . . *is good, although I hate it, because where would the world be without it?*
Conformist Stage Education is generally interpreted as school attendance, which has practical usefulness; one can get a better job with it than without it. An uncritical, idealized view of education is expressed, in which the current number of years of schooling is considered necessary for everyone.	. . . *is of the utmost importance.* . . . *is a very important and useful thing today.* . . . *is a necessity for all U.S. citizens.* . . . *is very important for children.* . . . *I think everyone should graduate high school.* . . . *is an essential requirement in acquiring a good job.* . . . *helps everyone.* . . . *is the greatest thing on earth.* . . . *I had ten and one half years of schooling and someday I will get that last year. Because that's important.*
Self-Aware Stage Education's importance is viewed in terms of one's life or future. There is a shift away from thinking of education as a concrete entity toward thinking of it as a goal and an asset.	. . . *is a very important step in life.* . . . *is a preparation for life.* . . . *is very important and invaluable to one's future.* . . . *should be a prized possession.* . . . *is very desirable and a goal for all members of my family.*
Conscientious Stage Education is viewed as an experience that affects a person's inner life. It is no longer merely a prescribed number of years of useful schooling. Its importance lies in intellectual stimulation and enrichment. It influences a person's whole life, making it more worthwhile and enjoyable. Education is an opportunity that should be available to everyone. It is seen as being a significant force in improving society, though the educational system may be seen as needing improvement as well.	. . . *is the standard for a strong America.* . . . *seldon lives up to its goals.* . . . *will get quite poor if the type and quality of teachers does not improve.* . . . *is not just what they teach at school.* . . . *is very important, and worth working for.* . . . *is a privilege and not a right.* . . . *should be provided with equal opportunity for all.* . . . *is a challenge but also a necessity.* . . . *is a constant process not limited to a classroom.*

Table 3 *(Continued)*

Ego Stage	Characteristic Responses to Sentence-Completion Stem "Education"
Conscientious Stage (Continued)	Education ... ... is a source of satisfaction in the present and for the future. ... is essential in gaining maturity. ... helps one acquire insight into problems. ... is the most important thing along with being able to love. ... is the foundation for a socially and secure life.
Individualistic Stage This view has an element of both the conscientious and autonomous perspectives; conscientious themes are more fully elaborated, and the focus is shifting to education as a lifelong process essential for a full life.	... is a lifelong process. ... you can never have enough of it. Life should be a process of learning as much as you can about anything at all. ... opens new avenues of thought and produces more joy in living. ... is a must because the more I learn, the more I enjoy life. ... is necessary now but the general trend of education should be training for life not a profession. ... is necessary. What we learn is not as important as the fact that we are learning to think for ourselves.
Autonomous and Integrated Stages Education is seen as leading to a deeper understanding of oneself and others, as helping to cope with life, as leading to creativity, self-fulfillment, and deeper values; hence, education is intrinsically valuable. It is not a thing one has or gets, once and for all, nor is it identified solely with school and intellectual achievement apart from interpersonal relations and emotional involvements.	... seems valuable in itself. ... will help me through life. I am not being educated because I have to, but education is a wonderful thing. ... can be a means or an end depending on other characteristics of those who pursue it. ... is learning to solve problems in a better way—to know what needs doing and when and how to do it. ... means a lot to me, I'll stagnate if I never do anything creative. ... is a necessary part of my development as a unique individual. ... is the development of the entire man, mental, physical and spiritual. ... is rewarding only if you learn to see things in a variety of ways and can have feelings for other people's beliefs.

(continued on next page)

Table 3 *(Continued)*

Ego Stage	*Characteristic Responses to Sentence-Completion Stem "Education"*
Autonomous and Integrated Stages (Continued)	Education . . . . . . *is both a stimulation to growth and method for accumulating knowledge for future use.* . . . *is a many splendored thing. It is also a necessity, a responsibility and at times a trouble, a sadness.*

Note: The left column gives scoring guidelines; the right column gives characteristic responses to the sentence stem "Education . . . ," which appears on the standard form of the sentence-completion test for ego development.

Source: Material in this table is abstracted from the scoring manual for *Measuring Ego Development* (Loevinger, Wessler, and Redmore, 1970, Vol. 2), pp. 97-107.

influences a person's entire life, making it more worthwhile and enjoyable. Education "broadens and enlightens the view," and "helps one acquire insight into problems." Education is seen in social terms as a privilege or opportunity that should be available to everyone. Education is also seen as a significant force in improving society, and individuals at this level often express definite opinions about ways in which the educational system needs improvement. At the Individualistic Transition, these themes are more fully elaborated as the time horizon stretches to a view of education as a lifelong process essential for full life. Education is "a lifetime pursuit," "an ongoing experience," and "a never-ending process." Some responses are slightly clichéd, as if overemphasizing the discovery of one's own role in this process. For example, one enthusiastic student at this stage commented that education is "a never-ending daily life growth experience."

At the Autonomous and Integrated Stages, education has intrinsic value apart from the goal-orientation of earlier stages. It is not a thing one has or gets, nor is it identified with schooling or intellectual achievement apart from interpersonal relationships and emotional involvements. Education is seen primarily as leading to a deeper understanding of oneself and others, as helping to cope with life, and as leading to creativity and deeper values. It is part of an individual process of growth and development seen in broad social perspective. Education is "the means of new ideas and knowledge that can be tools of change and growth in the context of any life-style." It is "a many-splendored thing: it is also a necessity, a responsibility, and at times a trouble, a sadness."

These statements are not isolated responses: they represent pervasive assumptions that influence how students respond to educational settings. Consider, for example, two students in Goddard's individualized, external Adult Degree Program (ADP) who are within two years of the same age and at opposite ends of the continuum of ego development. Philip (age 24), an entering student whose sentence-completion test is scored at the Self-Protective Stage, explains his reasons for enrolling in concrete terms. His view of education is seemingly external to his inner life; a degree is necessary for job security and fulfilling family obligations. "I enrolled so that I can get a degree in Art, since I have been involved in Art most of my life." Philip explains that his father has died recently and that, as the oldest son, he "gets the responsibilities with the family." The major issue in his work right now is "to be able to work in the U.S. and in Canada"; the major issue in his personal life is to "get my degree and help my family get an education." In response to the "Education" sentence-completion stem, he writes that education "is a necessity."

In contrast, Mark (age 26), whose ego development score falls between the Autonomous and Integrated Stages, describes his reasons for enrolling in the abstract terms of personal integration. He writes that "education is traditionally a matter of knowing but is much more powerful when it includes understanding and using." He describes being frustrated in a conventional undergraduate program, where he took shelter from what he described as "bone-chilling mediocrity" by taking advantage of opportunities to study in unconventional ways. Mark chose Goddard as a positive alternative "because it seemed to emphasize skills I thought were important, but which I was not confident in, and do so within a structure which I thought I would find challenging but not impossible." The major issue in his work is to define a career after eight years of many different jobs—"I am using my time in the ADP not to prepare myself for a career but to help me get the intellectual background to choose a field. I am preparing to prepare for a career, if you wish. I see an appropriate career as being an outgrowth of my personal concerns." Like Philip, Mark notes that Goddard's individualized instructional mode matches his style of learning reasonably well. However, the reasons are different. Mark comments on the quality of the instructional system: "One of the important aspects of the ADP is that the style of instruction and modes of learning are open to wide variation and considerable negotiation as long as sufficient rigor is maintained."

The patterned differences in perspective between these two men illustrate the wide range of individual differences within a single sex and age group, as well as different concerns at the extremes of ego development. Philip thinks of frustration as external to himself, whereas Mark is explicit about his responsibility for making use of what he describes as "an incoherent environment characterized by the tremendous amounts of energy which individuals invest in finishing and evaluating their six months' studies and planning the next." When each was asked what was frustrating or missing in the learning environment, Philip replied, "a basketball court" (which, in fact, would be a useful addition). Mark spoke of inner frustration—"The greatest frustrations are the ones I bring on myself when my self-discipline fails, and I get bogged down by my own confusion." The difference in individualizing education for these two students is obvious. Loevinger's scheme permits these differences to be viewed as positions on a continuum describing interrelated patterns and not merely as individual idiosyncrasies.

Students' Motives and Values

The important point is that individuals at different stages of ego development have very different capacities for framing educational goals, for using the structure of a college program (whether teaching is individualized or in lecture format), and for developing relationships with faculty and peers. For some students, the intellectual task is to develop mastery of logical and contextual reasoning; others need help in choosing among authorities and commitments. One use of ego development as a map is to clarify the themes and central issues around which students' struggles take place. This requires paying close attention to what students are doing and thinking while learning and how they are reacting. The next two sections of this chapter illustrate differences in students' inner structuring of experience. The examples are from a participant-observation study of adult undergraduates at Goddard College (Weathersby, 1977). Students' reasons for enrolling and the outcomes of study they value most become multidimensional when superimposed upon the matrix of ego development.

I asked adult students in the Goddard study, "Why did you enroll?" Then I asked whether there was a critical incident or realization leading to this decision. Seven basic reasons emerged: (1) a degree was necessary for work or career goals, either current or anticipated (22 percent); (2) it was important to continue or finish one's education, in many cases to pursue career plans but also to complete "unfinished business" with respect to one's education (16 percent); (3) enrollment came at a time when outside resources were sought for a reorientation or redirection of both work and personal concerns (16 percent); (4) enrollment made it possible to study valued interests in depth and in an individualized manner not permitted by other modes of study (14 percent); (5) studying was a means of seeking personal growth and fulfilling one's potential (12 percent); (6) studying provided an enjoyable challenge and intellectual stimulation (10 percent); and (7) this seemed to be the appropriate time in one's life to enroll (10 percent). Many people, particularly those at higher ego levels, mentioned several reasons.

The content of these "basic reasons for enrolling" changed somewhat systematically by ego level. Even generalized statements of individuals' reasons for enrolling, robbed of their nuances of wording and experiential contexts, seem to cluster at particular ego levels, forming "milestone sequences" similar to those outlined in the theory of ego development. Reorientation and redirection are most salient at the Conscientious Stage and below; the importance of getting a degree or finishing one's education peaks at the Conscientious Stage (which is noted for its focus on achievement), as does the importance of intellectual challenge and stimulation. No one at the Self-Aware Stage or below gave in-depth study or wanting to pursue one's own pressing interests as a reason for enrolling. The importance of being able to study valued interests in depth becomes salient at postconventional stages, as do personal growth and fulfillment. Responses at the lower ego levels are often flat and one-dimensional; beginning at the Individualistic Stage people give multifaceted reasons that reflect their personal goals and life experience. Thus, in the reasons given for enrollment there is a clear progression of themes, which peak in salience and then become transformed. At successively higher ego levels the "same" motives may assume significantly different meanings.

I have observed a similar phenomenon in reviewing application forms and evaluation questionnaires for other adult programs. Lasker (1978), in a study of achievement motives across ego levels, found that at lower ego levels the motivation to achieve often seems linked to a sense of correcting deficiencies or fixing something that is wrong. At middle levels, achieving seems related to the sense of crossing a self-set goal line. At higher levels, goals for achievement are related to an ongoing process of personal growth and social concern. Several examples will illustrate these points. For one man (age 29) at the Self-Aware Stage, getting a degree was clearly related to tangible benefits now denied him. Being laid off at work as the result of not having the B.A. degree was a critical incident that led to enrollment.

> I felt that time was running out. I wanted the benefits of a B.A. while I still had time to use it.

A woman at the Conscientious Stage described her desire for a degree as a means to meet specific, personal goals within a long-term time perspective. This woman (age 44) says:

> I enrolled in the ADP because my last child is about ready to leave home, and I wanted to prepare myself for some satisfying work. My goal is to go into library science, and in that you need a degree. Also, I liked the way ADP functions. . . . There was also the added thought that I need some mind stimulation now.

In contrast, a man (24) at the Individualistic Stage experiences his need for credentials in terms of the undesirable emotional dependency this lack creates in his work.

> I want to finish my undergrad work so that I can get my graduate degrees. I'm presently doing the work I would do after earning graduate degrees, but without proper academic credentials I'm dependent on others. . . . So, even though I'm left with not much time to do ADP work, I'm feeling almost urgent about finishing college so that I can be more independent in my work.

These responses illustrate Lasker's observations that at lower stages there is often a sense of compensating for a lack ("time is running out") and at middle levels a sense of crossing a goal line ("My goal is to go into library science"). At higher ego levels, there is a clear recognition that motives and goals for education are interconnected with the ongoing process of learning how to live one's life. The degree is important but is often mentioned as an afterthought, or as a natural outgrowth of other concerns. A woman (age 26) at the Individualistic Stage says:

> I am a seeker—in this case, seeking knowledge with enough discipline and supervision as well as personal contact to keep me on course, and enough freedom and self-direction to keep me interested. ADP was the only place I could find allowing both. I'm also career-oriented, and I find that the jobs I'm interested in require degrees.

Another woman at this level, an artist with a strong sense of what she wants to study to improve work already in progress, says:

> I have a very strongly developed learning program of my own, and it is extremely important to me that this not be truncated by any outside force. . . . [However,] having a college degree will help me to make my program of study into a career.

Personal growth is understood differently at different ego levels. One man at the Self-Aware Stage gives as his reason for enrolling:

> I need to have some organization in my growth. I also need to get credit (reinforcement) for the work I do.

Here the source of organization and reinforcement is external. By contrast, an internal orientation is displayed by a woman at the Autonomous Stage, who explains:

> For a long time now I have been searching for integration—growth—"profession"—calling in life. Here I am.

She experiences the program structure as a catalyst, a sequence of experiences, compressed in time, in which she can work out the personal integration she is seeking.

There are implications here for education. Some of these students have concrete goals for which training and skill development are important. Others have more general concerns regarding professional or vocational development and the clarification of work and values. Still others seek greater independence, self-definition, recognition, and validation. How the institution responds to these motivational differences deriving from variances in ego development will significantly affect the educational and developmental outcomes for each student. Students who are seeking personal growth at different ego levels need something else than the traditional educational setting, with its predominant focus on cognitive training and skills.

Implicit in ego development is an increasing ability to understand and articulate one's own motivation. Adults at higher ego levels make more conscious use of educational settings for clearly articulated ends. Those at lower ego levels may desire some of the same results as those at higher levels but be unable to articulate them. At postconventional stages there is greater apparent congruency between one's personal motives and one's articulated reasons for study (see Tarule, 1978).

Most Valued Outcomes of Study

Goddard students were also asked to identify the most valued outcomes of study and to comment on any changes in their lives, perspective, or sense of self that they would attribute wholly or in part to their experience of being a student. From the diverse responses given, many of which reflected individual differences that could not be attributed to ego development, there emerged, nevertheless, a clear patterning by ego stage of the perceived benefits of college. At the Self-Aware Stage, the orientation was to interpersonal relationships; this shifted to achievement themes at the Conscientious Stage, and to a series of more individually expressed concerns and realizations at the Individualistic Stage and beyond. Often the outcomes reported as most valued are changes that characterize the next steps in ego development. The differences lie in both the *content* of what an individual values and the *context* in which he or she experiences the impact of education. For example, almost everyone in the program wanted and expected some kind of certification of competency for valued social roles as a result of "getting a degree." Similarly, almost everyone at some point referred to the importance of supportive interpersonal relationships in easing the anxieties of study. However, these same themes have differential saliency as *the* most valued outcomes at different ego stages, and these shifts in emphasis describe a milestone sequence from validation by others to self-validation. This is central to the learning process, as the locus of authority is first seen as external, and then internalized, in conjunction with increasingly differentiated cognitive capacities. Perry describes this, as does Gilligan.

Table 4 summarizes characteristic responses concerning the most valued outcomes of study. Responses at the Self-Protective Stage deal with externalities, tangible results hoped for as an outcome of study—a "job possibility" and "my learning and the degree." The only response at the Conformist Stage is focused on interpersonal relationships— "Having met people in my field through the ADP, and the resulting interactions."

A common quality in answers at the Self-Aware Stage is, appropriately enough, a

Table 4. Most Valued Outcomes of Study by Ego Stage

Self-Protective Stage
. . . My learning and the degree
. . . Job possibility

Conformist Stage
. . . Having met people in my field through ADP, and the resulting interactions.

Conscientious-Conformist or Self-Aware Stage
. . . Exposure to new people and new ideas
. . . Focusing of goals, guidance and supervision as I work on them.
. . . I have had a place to take risks personally-professionally-academically. I have come to majority . . . As an individual I am more open and trusting. My self-worth has increased. I like myself.
. . . ADP has provided me with the confidence in myself to believe in myself and my abilities. I find that I am a "challenger" and a leader.
. . . Validation by others

Table 4 *(Continued)*

Conscientious Stage

... That my life does not stay limited to a few areas. That I'm experiencing or at least mulling over new interests which keep me rolling. My main objective of getting my B.A. and eventually M.A. in psych. has not changed, though.

... 1. sense of achievement, 2. B.A. (closer all the time), 3. New relationships, 4. more knowledge.

... The most important result is the ADP has helped me learn to try new areas, follow through on commitments and discover myself.

... Probably the rise in my self-concept as I see myself doing work that is recognized by others as well as myself, that what I do is not "magic" but the result of real and chosen effort.

Individualistic Stage

... The educational experience, itself. The options it will create for me.

... A wish to continue to read and to study and grow and learn and share: a wish to be in and of life.

... The increase in my ability to learn, to know I can approach many different topics and problems ... it has greatly broadened my style of learning ... and helped me appreciate my abilities more. .... Changes in confidence, ability to relate to others, pleasure in intellectual pursuits.

... I have become more inquisitive, questioning, observant and have learned that I am a creative person.

Autonomous and Integrated Stages

... Feeling more complete and whole as a person; Getting in touch with how, what I *really* think I want; Optimistic view towards others' realities, personal and worldly; Helping other people emotionally and intellectually; Integrating past confusements, decisions, reflections and feelings.

... Re-excitement in the learning process and new respect for concentrated effort in a field or endeavor.

... Continued growth re philosophy and science—personal satisfaction. Additionally, I find it gratifying working in a setting with such varying ages, ideas, backgrounds, and so on.

... For the first time in my life I am learning how to study something. I am particularly pleased about this as 2½ years of traditional University study failed to even start the process.

Note: These are answers to a questionnaire (Weathersby, 1977) that asked, "What is the most important result or outcome for you of your participation in the Goddard Adult Degree Program" and "In addition to what you said previously, have you experienced any other changes in your life, your perspective, or your sense of yourself which you attribute wholly or in part to your experience in the program?"

freshly experienced self-awareness. This is conceptualized as "exposure to new people and new ideas," better skills in relationships, and greater self-confidence. There is a poignancy to the answers of some women at midlife who are experiencing this self-awareness simultaneously with difficult life periods. For example, one woman (age 49), who entered the program after a long series of life changes and as a "last chance effort to pull myself together," reports upon graduating:

> I feel that I have grown to be a better person. ... My daily life is more exciting and interesting. I'm happier now. I am more conscious of my own actions. I am growing more aware of how I see the world around me and the people in it. My sense of confidence has returned. I am happy to see each new day begin.

Another woman (age 56), attending her first residency, reports that the outcome of the two weeks was "validation by others" and "experiencing myself as valuable." The outcome here may not be change from one stage of ego development to another; it may be restabilization and revitalization within one's current personality structure.

As mentioned previously, there is a negative cast to the responses of many subjects near or below the Conformist Stage, as if the subjective purpose of education were to make up for a serious lack in one's life. One man (age 30) at the Self-Aware Stage identified the most important result of study for him as "my getting a teaching certification and my pursuing and persevering in my desires without regard to others' expectations." He explains:

> Throughout my previous education, force was applied externally. I hated school. The ADP was (is) an opportunity to do it myself, to prove that I didn't need to be pushed, to prove that in fact it was the pushing itself that caused my intellect to atrophy.

A woman near the same age and also at the Self-Aware Stage of ego development says "I don't feel right now, as I usually do, that I'm working in isolation or that my goals are futile." The coauthor of a successful book, she explains her reasons for enrolling in terms of making up for a lacking sense of herself as a successful student.

> I think it's important now because I seem to be going through a period of rapid growth. I finally have some work I'm proud of. I'm earning a good salary at work I can respect, if not love. . . . One of the two things still missing for me is a sense of myself as a successful student. It frustrates me very much that I don't have my degree. It frustrates me very much that I don't have *several* degrees. So, I'm here to prove to myself that I can be a successful student.

This sense of lack also appears at higher stages, but there is a greater sense of ease with oneself.

At the Conscientious Stage, the most valued outcomes mentioned are the degree itself, a sense of achievement, new ideas, increased self-esteem, and learning to follow through on commitments. Goals are personally set, and time is seen in long-term perspective in relation to goals. Responses tend to be more abstract—for example, "concretization of certain ideas" and "greater awareness of potential" (man, 22). One woman (age 41) speaks for a noticeable group whose goal is to find meaningful work. In response to the question about the result she most valued, she joked, "I don't know what it will be. One might be having to take gainful employment (as opposed to wife, mother, and maid) in order to pay back money borrowed!" Then she explains:

> I am ready to run the risk now. I have heard such glowing accounts of the ADP program that I am convinced I have to try it. My perspective of the world and my place in it is changing. I understood Goddard was quite selective in its students, so my acceptance indicated they thought I could do their work. Perhaps there is other work in the world for me to do and this will prepare me to accept the challenge.

Here the emphasis is on direction toward a goal, on crossing the finish line in a race set according to the individual's internalized standards.

At the Individualistic Stage, the most valued outcomes of study are often described as differentiated, personally relevant learning: an increased sense of competence, learning how to learn as well as mastering a body of knowledge, commitment to a personal and career-oriented learning process, the assumption of responsibility for one's perceptions and actions, and the integration of past experience with present and future agendas for growth. Responses tend to be elaborated and to describe a critical insight that has ramifications for other areas of life. For example, a woman of 25 observed:

> It took me the best part of a cycle [a six-month academic term] to fully realize that it was really up to me to determine what I wanted and needed and what would and would not be worth the effort. . . . That piece of learning added a major new feature to my perspective on my whole life.

The word *growth* appears more frequently, along with expressions of the intrinsic pleasure of study. One woman (age 56) whose most valued outcome was the opportunity to study and "enjoy it while doing so" reported realizing that "an interesting study can be done just for the joy of doing it—and it does not have to be 'justified.' Next time I'd like to try a totally different study—say, in the interrelated arts just to see what I might create."

Overall, many people at this level report a richly articulated sense of discovery about their own learning processes, and make a point of identifying their own responsibility in those processes. For example:

> My experience in the ADP has cultured my willingness to assume full responsibility for my perceptions and my actions. Having developed a greater "sense of self" and a greater self-confidence, I have also developed my capacity to honestly try to accept self-responsibility.

This same woman (age 27) also talked of developing her capacities to give others "the space and support they need for their own growth and development." There is a clear difference in perspective between this response and that of the man (age 30) at the Self-Aware Stage, quoted earlier, who sees the program as "an opportunity to do it myself, to prove that I didn't need to be pushed," as well as that of the woman (age 56) at the same stage who sought "validation by others." The link point in this progression is the discipline and goal-orientation of the Conscientious Stage—"I hope to learn how to do a better job learning more" (woman, age 52)—and the concomitant sense of control over one's destiny—"the result being an alive sense of discovery that what I do is not 'magic' but the result of real and chosen effort" (woman, 41).

A more explicit appropriation of the learning process appears at the Individualistic Stage. One man (age 25) views his increasing resourcefulness in solving problems and increased assertiveness in all aspects of his life as the result, in part, of Goddard's instructional process:

> It has helped me to grow a great deal, both intellectually and personally. Even more important than the sizable body of knowledge I have acquired is the increase in my ability to learn, to know I can approach many different topics or problems and understand or appreciate them. It has greatly broadened my style of learning and approach to learning. It has also helped me appreciate my abilities more.

This implies a kind of mastery of the process of "learning how to learn" that is probably the hallmark of self-directed learners. This self-conscious awareness of one's own *process* of learning is undoubtedly heightened by the program's instructional mode. However, a differentiated knowledge of one's own learning process and an increasing sense of personal agency and effectiveness in learning are characteristic of this stage of ego development.

At the Autonomous and Integrated Stages, the valued outcomes of study are expressed in terms of pleasure in the process of studying. No one at this level mentioned a degree as the most valued outcome, neither did anyone mention increased self-confidence or self-esteem. Instead, respondents mentioned valued pursuits or personal learning—for example, "feeling more complete and whole as a person, getting in touch with how, what I *really* think or want" (woman, 24) and "re-excitement in the learning process or new respect for concentrated effort in a field or endeavor" (woman, 26). Also noted were increased commitment to one's self and one's chosen work—"I am beginning to take myself and my work much more seriously. I am less quick to judge other people's lives and more willing to accept my own responsibilities" (woman, 27), and increased satisfaction from pursuing valued interests in a setting with people of different backgrounds. A businessman (40) reports as outcomes "continued growth re philosophy (and) science—personal satisfaction. Additionally, I find it gratifying working in a setting with such varying ages, ideas, and backgrounds."

Increases in self-confidence are often cited as a valued outcome of study, and there is a progression across ego levels in the manner in which this concept is understood. Mentions of increased self-confidence are proportionately more frequent at the Self-Aware and Conscientious Stages; at the Individualistic Stage the concept seems to disappear and become reworded as an increased sense of competence or an increase in self-esteem. Often at this level it appears as one of a series of items rather than the major and most valued outcome. At the Self-Aware Stage, the source of self-confidence appears to be experienced as external to oneself. For example, "ADP has provided me with the confidence in myself to believe in myself and my abilities." One woman reports that her self-confidence has returned, and another values the validation by others that she has received. Adults at the Conscientious Stage tend to see their increased capacities and ability to meet their goals as the source of their self-confidence. For example, one observes, "I feel very good about myself; where I am, how I am getting there. I feel like all the parts of myself are working together." Self-evaluated standards are important as well as recognition by others. A student reports, for example, a "rise in my self-concept as I see myself doing work that is recognized by others as well as myself as being well done." At the Individualistic Stage, the source of self-confidence is related to greater awareness, a greater sense of self, and acknowledged responsibility for one's choices, as this statement by a 34-year-old woman reveals:

> My anticipated results of the ADP are an increase in knowledge, but even more important, an increase in self-esteem as the result of completing something I want very much to do. Fourteen years as a housewife have left me with a lack of confidence in my abilities.

Ego Development as an Outcome of Study

In the Goddard Adult Degree Program, awareness of students' ego development provided a background against which to understand their aspirations and dilemmas. The most convincing evidence of the relevance of ego development appeared in students' accounts of their exciting experiences and their frustrations. They reported critical incidents, realizations, and changes in perspective that were consistent with the direction of ego development. For example, "validation from others" as one moves away from the Conformist Stage is a necessary foundation for the self-confidence in internalized standards and goals inherent in the achievement-orientation of the Conscientious Stage. This, in turn, is a necessary foundation for exploring one's learning preferences and personal patterns of achievement at the Individualistic Stage, and for exploring possible conflicts between achievement and self-fulfillment at the Autonomous and Integrated Stages.

One respondent at the Self-Protective Stage volunteered that "It is a new experience for me to be in such a program with so many different kinds of adults." For a student at this stage, being in the program means exposure not only to people of different backgrounds but also to people further along in ego development; if he feels accepted and supported, the effect may be to facilitate movement to the Conformist Stage. A businessman (age 42) who is probably at the Self-Aware Stage commented with surprise that he never would have expected to have anything in common with a roommate who labels himself a Communist. However, his much younger roommate in the residency did call himself a Communist, and the businessman found they had some common interests in history and politics. This man said that his ability to relate to people beyond stereotyped group labels had increased as a result of his Goddard experience. This is at least a move beyond conformist thinking into the realm of multiplicity. Similarly, a 43-year-old woman who described herself as "a traditional mother of six children" and felt she did not want to apologize for believing in the institution of marriage, being chairperson of her local school board, or belonging to a formal religion said:

> The Goddard experience has helped me to understand my own children better. It has also given me the opportunity to identify with many people of different life-styles that I would not have had the opportunity to meet. It has given me more tolerance to meet problems head on and a better discipline to my life. I see the absolute need for the two-week residency. It is mind-boggling at times but does provide for intensive situations, which I found I can cope with.

Her sentence-completion score placed her at the Individualistic Stage. Her ability to identify with diverse life-styles and increased tolerance for the ambiguities of an intensive group residency are characteristics that distinguish the Individualistic Stage from the Conscientious Stage. She reports them as new; this is perhaps a reflection of ego development over the two years of her experience in the program.

Implications for Instruction

I have shown how ego development forms the framework in which learning and teaching take place, and have traced qualitative differences across stages in individuals' experience of educational settings. Now the question of application arises. Now that we can label the progressions and classify, approximately, students and groups of students, what do we do differently? This is a tough question for any psychological theory, especially one that describes sequences of development. I do not propose that we use measures of ego development like intelligence tests, as sorters of students or indicators of program effectiveness. Nor do I believe we should try to force ego development. After all, it represents a major personality change and, as such, takes time. An assignment, a semester, or even four years of college may not substantially alter an individual's frame of reference, although clearly some students do move rapidly and sometimes explosively along these progressions. Every student will not move along these progressions, and our institutions per se may have relatively little influence in this regard. We do not yet have enough knowledge of the dynamics of transition, or the conditions that promote development, or the impact of college, to establish highly structured programs geared toward ego development. However, exposure to higher-level reasoning, opportunities to take others' roles and perspectives, discomfiting discrepancies between one's actual experiences in a situation and one's current explanations and beliefs—these are basic elements of the transition process. It is possible, therefore, to open doors and to help students open doors for themselves. But it is their choice to walk through.

Thus, the major use of this body of theory is, as suggested in this chapter, as a map or matrix that can help us identify the next steps in development. It can also heighten our appreciation for shared patterns of differences among students. If we tune our ears so that we can hear students across different frameworks of meaning, we are more likely to communicate effectively and to respond with an appropriate form of support or challenge. Familiarity with the patterns of ego development can create simple and profound differences in our perceptions, attitudes, and behavior as we approach teaching, administration, and counseling. For example, we are more likely to be humbled by the task of facilitating learning, and less likely to be judgmental of students who do not fit our molds or our institutions. We are more likely to listen to students' frames of references, to *ask* for their reasons and feelings about a situation, to expect patterns of diversity, and to value responses that represent advances in development regardless of our norms of expected levels of achievement. We are likely also to have some humility about grading, realizing that for some students what is asked for may not yet be comprehensible, and that what is being graded may not be simply gains in knowledge or competence, seriousness of purpose or effort expended, but, at least in part, responses made more or less difficult by a student's stage of development. We will be more aware that faculty play different roles with different students, and that these roles become more complex as the range of developmental stages broadens. Corresponding to the major stage-related orientations, faculty roles can range from authoritative transmitters of knowledge and agents of socialization, to role models helping develop cognitive skills and mastery, to facilitators of personally relevant, transformative learning. Goal setting and evaluation are present whatever the role, but in different degrees of colleagueship with students. Finally, we are more likely to recognize causes of soul searching and confusion inherent in the material we teach, or the methods we use, and to offer support.

It is possible to design assignments and curriculums that more directly facilitate development, although other schemes such as Perry's lend themselves more easily to direct application. The basic principle is to create a course structure in which the assignments and interpersonal interactions foster ego development. Often diversity of perspectives is involved. For example, in the introductory behavioral science course at the University of New Hampshire's School of Business and Economics, students work in groups to analyze cases, develop arguments for and against managerial decisions, study group dynamics, and participate in experiential exercises designed to simulate the effects of divergent leadership styles. Each work group is responsible for evaluating its own members. The students are mostly traditional-age undergraduates; many are at the Self-Aware Stage in ego development, while some are above and some are below this stage. The course structure employs a group setting—especially suitable for students at the Self-Aware Stage—to encourage complex and contingent thinking, to support the validity of diverse viewpoints, and to avoid group thinking and conformity. Many students report learning that there is no right or wrong way of thinking about a management problem and that others' viewpoints, although different, deserve consideration. Although this course was not designed to promote ego development (the intent was to create an effective teaching environment), it is a developmental intervention in students' lives, aimed intellectually and emotionally at higher-stage thinking and action.

Arthur Chickering (1976), adapting materials developed by Harry Lasker primarily from studies of ego development, has sketched out broad correspondences between stages of ego development and various conceptualizations of faculty and student roles, institutional functions, and teaching practices such as lectures, discussions, programmed instruction, and contract learning. Generally speaking, an instructional system based on lectures and exams fits the orientation of a Conformist Stage or lower, in which the teacher is the transmitter of knowledge and functions as a judge and certifier of the students' mastery. This is teaching to the lowest common denominator. Instructional methods that involve discussion and other forms of active participation, and require individuals to make decisions around goals, activities, and standards or methods of evaluation are more suited to students at the middle and higher stages; they are also more likely to create the interpersonal interactions and self-questioning that facilitate development. This accounts for the sometimes powerful unleashing of energy associated with these teaching practices. The issue at hand is not a narrow argument about teaching methods. A skilled teacher can use almost any method with success and find ways to create an environment that fosters development for some students. Correspondingly, no curriculum or method will suit every student. Miller (1978) describes some adults as dependent learners for whom the individualized learning contracts employed in most external degree programs are as highly frustrating as they are rewarding to other adult students seeking the opportunity for self-direction.

The central issue is that of creating teaching practices that are congruent with the developmental orientations of students. Knowledge of ego development suggests teaching practices that honor students' multiple frames of references and allow multiple levels of progress. Ego development theory also provides a framework for examining the curriculum for intended or unintended emphases. For example, very little of our current formal education is designed to help students reorganize past conceptions on the basis of new experience and develop personally generated insights and paradigms, although these are learning processes that reflect higher stages of ego development. Any methodology conveys underlying messages; if the message is that education consists only of providing individuals with access to certification, information, and increased cognitive skill, this is far too narrow a conceptualization.

Education as a Support for Lifelong Development

Chickering and Havighurst's perspective on the adaptive tasks of the life cycle (Chapter One) adds dimensions of lifelong learning to the picture. Reasons for enrolling in educational programs and outcomes of study may vary not only according to one's ego development but also according to one's place in the life cycle and the developmental tasks associated with each life period. Both perspectives help explain the amount and nature of developmental change that can accompany higher education—the intrapsychic work necessitated or stimulated by the academic process. Traditional-age college students are certainly in a major life cycle transition. Many adults also enroll in academic programs, or other programs in higher education, at transition points in their lives, or as a help in coping with new adaptive tasks. If the combination of new life tasks and education stimulates ego development as well, the amount of inner stress and disequilibrium can be considerable. Expanding Erikson's (1968) idea of a "developmental crisis" to include simultaneous changes in one's life structure *and* one's framework of coping, we can predict that some students will be "at risk" in the face of life transitions. They may experience heightened anxiety in the course of their studies but will also have the opportunity to emerge with new personality strengths forged in the educational process.

We must not forget that educational institutions serve a certifying and credentialing function in society. Traditional-age students are more or less required to attend college by virtue of the opportunity structure in society. Adults choose to attend, at varying life periods and for varying reasons, but the social functions of accrediting learning and providing access to opportunity remain. In a society in which lockstep patterns of schooling and careers are being broken and education is becoming an intrinsic as well as a practical good, educational institutions can be a support structure, encouraging ego development for individuals of all ages. This outcome can be enhanced while the certifying and accrediting function is also maintained. To do so creates implications for program design, curriculum planning, teaching effectiveness, and counseling and support services—for designing higher education in ways that legitimize and facilitate our continuing need to grow.

The possibility of developmental change as an outcome of study raises the all-important question of the purposes of education. One's stage of ego development is a framework for experiencing education and assigning to it both value and meaning. Ego development is quite probably an unintended consequence for many students as well as a good many teachers. Should it be an intentional goal? On the one hand, it is doubtful that students enrolling in college to "better their opportunities" or "get an education" have in mind learning tolerance for ambiguity, relativism, and greater acceptance of responsibility for creating their perceptual worlds. And in the end, students are the final arbiters of educational purposes and results. But on the other hand, institutions can unwittingly put ceilings on development. For those students whose aim is a greater ability to deal with complex problems—a greater mastery of the learning process, by means that constantly push the limits of their current ways of thinking and living—colleges can and ought to support ego development. Society needs individuals who can cope with a world of uncertainty, rapid change, and global interrelationships, which means people at the higher stages of ego development. These same people, of course, are apt to view society's rules with a critical eye—including the cherished values and procedures of academic institutions. Discussions of educational policies and procedures can perhaps be approached with greater humility if we recognize that everyone involved—students, faculty, administrators, and legislators—understands educational goals and outcomes within the legitimate context of his or her own stage of development.

For my own part, I believe that ego development is an inextricable goal of higher education. The very process of education invites and enforces developmental change. Acknowledging ego development as a conscious purpose gives us a multidimensional map that unites intellect and emotion, helps us interpret students' difficulty with subject matter and self-esteem, highlights the need for courage and community, and points to the necessity of providing support and challenge with teaching practices that take students beyond their current ways of constructing useful knowledge.

References

Chickering, A. W. "Developmental Change as a Major Outcome." In M. T. Keeton and Associates, *Experiential Learning: Rationale, Characteristics, and Assessment.* San Francisco: Jossey-Bass, 1976.

Erikson, E. *Identity: Youth and Crisis.* New York: Norton, 1968.

Goldberger, N. "Breaking the Educational Lockstep: The Simon's Rock Experience." Great Barrington, Mass.: Simon's Rock Early College, 1977.

Kohlberg, L. "Stage and Sequence: The Cognitive-Developmental Approach to Socialization." In D. A. Goslin (Ed.), *Handbook of Socialization Theory and Research.* Chicago: Rand McNally, 1969.

Kohlberg, L. "Continuities in Childhood and Adult Moral Developmental Revisited." In P. B. Baltes and K. W. Schaie (Eds.), *Life-Span Developmental Psychology: Personality and Socialization.* New York: Academic Press, 1973.

Kohlberg, L., and Mayer, R. "Development as the Aim of Education." *Harvard Education Review,* November 1972, *42* (4), 449-496.

Landa, A., and others. "Towards a Developmental Curriculum: Principles and Applications." Plainfield, Vt.: Goddard College, 1977.

Lasker, H. "Ego Development and Motivation: A Cross-Cultural Cognitive-Developmental Analysis of Achievement." Unpublished doctoral dissertation, University of Chicago, 1978.

Loevinger, J. *Ego Development: Conceptions and Theories.* San Francisco: Jossey-Bass, 1976.

Loevinger, J., Wessler, R., and Redmore, C. *Measuring Ego Development.* 2 vols. San Francisco: Jossey-Bass, 1970.

Maslow, A. H. *The Farther Reaches of Human Nature.* New York: Viking, 1971.

Miller, M. R. "Retaining Adults: New Educational Designs for a New Clientele." In L. Noel (Ed.), *New Directions for Student Services: Reducing the Dropout Rate,* no. 3. San Francisco: Jossey-Bass, 1978.

Perry, W. G., Jr. *Forms of Intellectual and Ethical Development in the College Years.* New York: Holt, Rinehart and Winston, 1970.

Piaget, J. "The General Problem of the Psychobiological Development of the Child." In J. M. Tanner and B. Inhelder (Eds.), *Discussions on Child Development.* Vol. 4. New York: International Universities Press, 1960.

Sanford, N. "The Developmental Status of the Entering Freshman." In N. Sanford (Ed.), *The American College.* New York: Wiley, 1962.

Tarule, J. "Patterns of Developmental Transition in Adulthood: An Examination of the Relationship Between Ego Development Stage Variation and Gendlin's Experiencing Levels." Unpublished doctoral dissertation, Graduate School of Education, Harvard University, 1978.

Weathersby, R. "A Synthesis of Research and Theory on Adult Development: Its Implications for Adult Learning and Postsecondary Education." Special Qualifying Paper, Graduate School of Education, Harvard University, 1976.

Weathersby, R. "A Developmental Perspective on Adults' Uses of Formal Education." Unpublished doctoral dissertation, Graduate School of Education, Harvard University, 1977.

3

William G. Perry, Jr.

Cognitive and Ethical Growth:
The Making of Meaning

Have you received the latest "printout" of your students' evaluation of your teaching from the computer? If so, I trust you are properly encouraged. But my intent is to raise the possibility that those comfortable "means" and "standard deviations" may conceal unexamined educational riches. In the usual form of such evaluations, the shortness of the scale (commonly five or seven points, from superb to awful), the neatness of the standard deviations, and the comfort of the mean inspire in us all a confidence that further analysis would tell us little. Indeed, our friends assure us that even those vagaries in our students' opinions that prevent the mean ratings from being as high as we had hoped can be chalked up to our credit under the rubric, "The best teacher never pleases *everybody*."

Surely it seems reasonable enough to average check marks on items like

	1	2	3	4	5
Organization of assignments:	Excellent	Good	Fair	Poor	Very Bad

and to print 1.9 as the mean. But if you have ever given your students an opportunity to be more expansive, you can never again be wholly comforted. What can you do with such unaverageable judgments as "This course has changed my whole outlook on education *and life*! Superbly taught! Should be required of all students!" and "This course is falsely advertised and dishonest. You have cheated me of my tuition!"

Over the years I have received just such comments at the end of a noncredit course on Strategies of Reading, when I asked, "What did you expect of this course?" (big space) and "What did you find?" (big space). I do not ask the students for their names, just for their scores on pre- and post-tests. Twenty years ago I reported on the course in a faculty meeting (Perry, 1959) and read one student's comment as my punch line. Since the student had scored 20 percent comprehension at 120 words per minute on pre-test and 90 percent comprehension at 600 words per minute on post-test, I had looked forward to some flattery. What I found was, "I expected *an organized effort to improve my reading,*" followed by, "This has been the most sloppy, disorganized course I've never taken. Of course I *have* made some improvement (arrow to the scores), but this has been due *entirely to my own efforts.*" This got a good laugh from the faculty, largely, I suspect, owing to the realization that "evaluations" threaten not only the vanity of teachers but their very sanity as well.

At the time, no one, myself included, stopped to inquire whether this student's outrage bespoke more than some comical aberration. It took my colleagues and me twenty years to discover that such comments reflect coherent interpretive frameworks through which students give meaning to their educational experience. These structurings of meaning, which students revise in an orderly sequence from the relatively simple to the more complex, determine more than your students' perception of you as teacher; they shape the students' ways of learning and color their motives for engagement and disengagement in the whole educational enterprise. Teachers have, of course, always sensed this and have tried to teach accordingly.

This chapter illustrates, in students' own words, the typical course of development of students' patterns of thought. Twenty years ago, a small group of us, counselors and teachers, were so puzzled by students' varied and contradictory perceptions of ourselves and their other teachers that we set out to document their experience. We invited volunteers to tell us, at the end of their freshman year, what had "stood out" for them. We encouraged them to talk freely in the interview without preformed questions from us, and the diversity of their reports exceeded even our own expectations. After the manner of the time, we supposed the differences arose from differences in "personality types." However, as the same students returned to report their experience year by year, we were startled by their reinterpretations of their lives. Then these reinterpretations seemed to fall into a logical progression. Each step represented a challenge to the student's current view of the world. Different students might respond differently, with courage or defeat, but all faced the same basic challenges to making meaning in a complex world (Perry, 1970).[1]

We found that we could describe the logic or "structure" of each of these successive reinterpretations of the world and identify the challenges that precipitated them. We made a map of these challenges—a "Pilgrim's Progress" of ways of knowing, complete with Sloughs of Despond—giving each of the successive interpretations a numbered "Posi-

---

[1] *Forms of Intellectual and Ethical Development in the College Years: A Scheme* (New York: Holt, Rinehart and Winston, 1970; first published Cambridge, Mass.: Bureau of Study Counsel, Harvard University, 1968). It embarrasses me that in the argot of the field this ponderous title has been shortened, inevitably, to "The Perry Scheme"; the evolution of the scheme required teamwork involving more than thirty people over a span of fifteen years—six to eight counselors at any one time, working in a small office without formal provisions for research.

tion." We then put the map to a test by giving raters a number of interviews and asking them to state for each interview that Position which seemed most congruent with the pattern of the student's thought. Since the raters agreed strongly with one another, we knew that the developments that we had seen were there for others to see. This map of sequential interpretations of meaning, or *scheme of development,* has since been found to be characteristic of the development of students' thinking throughout a variety of educational settings (see this chapter's reference section). This chapter makes this developing sequence of interpretations explicit. Along the way, I shall suggest what I see to be the general implications of this sequence for educational practice. Readers interested in the ways these implications have found particular expression in various educational contexts can then consult the work of those researchers and practitioners whom I cite.

Scheme of Development

One naturally thinks of any scheme of development in terms of its "stages"—or "Positions," as we called them in our own scheme. In summarizing our students' journey for the reader of this chapter, I therefore first excised from all our students had told us a quotation or two to illustrate each Position. To my dismay, the drama died under the knife.

Then I realized that Positions are by definition static, and development is by definition movement. It was therefore the Transitions that were so fresh and intriguing. Each of the Positions was obvious and familiar in its delineation of a meaningful way of construing the world of knowledge, value, and education. The drama lived in the variety and ingenuity of the ways students found to move from a familiar pattern of meanings that had failed them to a new vision that promised to make sense of their broadening experience, while it also threatened them with unanticipated implications for their selfhood and their lives. I thus decided to select quotations illustrating for each step the breakup of the old and the intimations of the new. (Perhaps development is all transition and "stages" only resting points along the way.)

But this expansion of the summary puts severe strains on the boundaries of this chapter and on the reader. I can surely trust the reader to remember that each simple quotation stands for many intriguing variants in the ways students gave meaning to the unfolding landscapes of the journey. But we have more to do than trace the journey. I have promised to note some further thoughts on these developmental progressions— thoughts that have arisen in a decade of dialogue with others who have used our scheme as a starting point for explorations of their own. Had my briefest summary of the scheme sufficed, I could have moved on directly to commentary on other researchers' work and on our own recent thinking about particular passages or issues in the scheme. After the more expanded summary, however, the reader and I would find ourselves too far away from the data relevant to such commentary. It has seemed best, therefore, to digress occasionally as relevant points emerge.

If the reader is to tolerate lengthy digressions at dramatic moments—as happens in early Victorian novels—I should at least give evidence in advance that I know where I am going. Figure 1 gives a synopsis, in bare bones, of our scheme of cognitive and ethical development—the evolving ways of seeing the world, knowledge and education, values, and oneself. Notice that each Position both includes and transcends the earlier ones, as the earlier ones cannot do with the later. This fact defines the movement as *development* rather than mere changes or "phases." Figure 2 gives a map of this development. Following are definitions of the key terms, abstractions to which the students' words will subsequently give life:

Figure 1. Scheme of Cognitive and Ethical Development

Dualism modified⸺

Relativism discovered⸺

Commitments in Relativism developed⸺

Position 1	Authorities know, and if we work hard, read every word, and learn Right Answers, all will be well.
Transition	But what about those Others I hear about? And different opinions? And Uncertainties? Some of our own Authorities disagree with each other or don't seem to know, and some give us problems instead of Answers.
Position 2	True Authorities must be Right, the others are frauds. We remain Right. Others must be different and Wrong. Good Authorities give us problems so we can learn to find the Right Answer by our own independent thought.
Transition	But even Good Authorities admit they don't know all the answers *yet*!
Position 3	Then some uncertainties and different opinions are real and legitimate *temporarily*, even for Authorities. They're working on them to get to the Truth.
Transition	But there are *so many* things they don't know the Answers to! And they won't for a long time.
Position 4a	Where Authorities don't know the Right Answers, everyone has a right to his own opinion; no one is wrong!
Transition *(and/or)*	But some of my friends ask me to support my opinions with facts and reasons.
Transition	Then what right have They to grade us? About what?
Position 4b	In certain courses Authorities are not asking for the Right Answer; They want us to *think* about things in a certain way, *supporting* opinion with data. That's what they grade us on.
Transition	But this "way" seems to *work* in most courses, and even outside them.
Position 5	Then *all* thinking must be like this, even for Them. Everything is relative but not equally valid. You have to understand how each context works. Theories are not Truth but metaphors to interpret data with. You have to think about your thinking.
Transition	But if everything is relative, am I relative too? How can I know I'm making the Right Choice?
Position 6	I see I'm going to have to make my own decisions in an uncertain world with no one to tell me I'm Right.
Transition	I'm lost if I don't. When I decide on my career (or marriage or values) everything will straighten out.
Position 7	Well, I've made my first Commitment!
Transition	Why didn't that settle everything?
Position 8	I've made several commitments. I've got to balance them—how many, how deep? How certain, how tentative?
Transition	Things are getting contradictory. I can't make logical sense out of life's dilemmas.
Position 9	This is how life will be. I must be wholehearted while tentative, fight for my values yet respect others, believe my deepest values right yet be ready to learn. I see that I shall be retracing this whole journey over and over—but, I hope, more wisely.

Dualism. Division of meaning into two realms—Good versus Bad, Right versus Wrong, We versus They, All that is not Success is Failure, and the like. Right Answers exist *somewhere* for every problem, and authorities know them. Right Answers are to be memorized by hard work. Knowledge is quantitative. Agency is experienced as "out there" in Authority, test scores, the Right job.

Multiplicity. Diversity of opinion and values is recognized as legitimate in areas where right answers are not yet known. Opinions remain atomistic without pattern or

Figure 2. A Map of Development

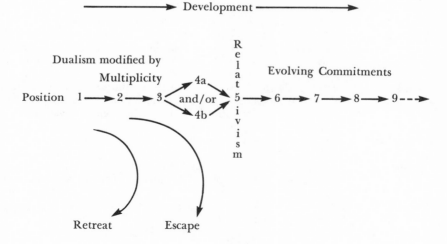

system. No judgments can be made among them so "everyone has a right to his own opinion; none can be called wrong."

Relativism. Diversity of opinion, values, and judgment derived from coherent sources, evidence, logics, systems, and patterns allowing for analysis and comparison. Some opinions may be found worthless, while there will remain matters about which reasonable people will reasonably disagree. Knowledge is qualitative, dependent on contexts.

Commitment (uppercase *C*). An affirmation, choice, or decision (career, values, politics, personal relationship) made in the awareness of Relativism (distinct from lowercase *c* of commitments never questioned). Agency is experienced as within the individual.

Temporizing. Postponement of movement for a year or more.

Escape. Alienation, abandonment of responsibility. Exploitation of Multiplicity and Relativism for avoidance of Commitment.

Retreat. Avoidance of complexity and ambivalence by regression to Dualism colored by hatred of otherness.

I shall now let the students speak for themselves as they spoke in interviews in which we asked unstructured questions (such as "what stands out for you as you review the year?") in order to allow the students freedom to structure their own meanings. I shall report our sense of the import of their words for the development we trace, and I shall digress on occasion to consider implications for teaching and educational policy.

Positions 1 Through 5

Position 1: Basic Duality. This is the Garden of Eden, with the same rules. Here the student is embedded in a world of We-Right-Good (Other-Wrong-Bad is "out there"). We called this Basic Duality. Right Answers for everything exist in the Absolute, and these are known to Authorities, whose role is to mediate (teach) them. Knowledge and goodness are perceived as quantitative accretions of discrete rightnesses to be collected by hard work and *obedience* (including the requirement to read *all* assigned books word by word from the beginning). We held our interviews in May and June, and no freshman still spoke from this Position in its purest form. A few, however, saw themselves in retrospect as having come to college with this view intact. This student's words show how hard it is to articulate an embeddedness so complete that it offered no place from which to observe it:

> Student: I certainly couldn't—before I was, you know, I wouldn't ask. /Yeah/ I wouldn't have—I wouldn't be able to *talk* on this subject at *all* . . . that what I had just—well, was *there* you know.

Only a dim sense that there is a boundary somewhere beyond which lies Otherness provides Eden with shape:

> Student: Well I come, I came here from a small town. Midwest, where, well, ah, everyone believed the same things. Everyone's Methodist and everyone's Republican. So, ah, there just wasn't any . . . well that's not quite true . . . there are some Catholics, two families, and I guess they, I heard they were Democrats, but they weren't really, didn't seem to be in town really, I guess. They live over the railroad there and they go to church in the next town.

But obedience is the Way:

> Student: Well the only thing I could say to a prospective student is just say, "If you come here and do everything you're supposed to do, you'll be all right," that's just about all.

But such innocence is short-lived:

Transition from Position 1 to Position 2. The first challenge often comes from peers:

> Student: When I went to my first lecture, what the man said was just like God's word, you know. I believe everything he said, because he was a professor, and he's a Harvard professor, and this was, this was a respected position. And, ah, ah, people said, "Well, so what?" . . . and I began to, ah, realize.

And especially in the dorm:

> Student: So in my dorm I, we've been, ah, [in] a number of discussions, where there'll be, well, there's quite a variety in our dorm, Catholic, Protestant, and the rest of them, and a Chinese boy whose parents, ah, follow the teachings of Confucianism. He isn't, but his folks are . . . And a couple of guys are complete, ah, agnostics, agnostics. Of course, some people are quite disturbing, they say they're atheists. But they don't go very far, they say they're atheists, but they're not. And then there are, one fellow, who is a deist. And by discussing it, ah, it's the, the sort of thing that, that really, ah, awakens you to the fact that, ah . . .

Diversity, experienced among peers and again in the classroom, must now be accounted for. Difference of opinion surely cannot exist in the Absolute. If earthly Authorities disagree, perhaps some are mere pretenders? Or do They put all the complexities in there just to exercise our minds? Such interpretations of diversity deny it a full legitimacy and preserve the simplicity of Truth:

Position 2: Multiplicity Prelegitimate. True authority may perform its proper role of direct mediation while complexities confuse pretenders:

> Student: For one thing, Professor Black who taught us [in First Term] . . . Christmas! you couldn't lose him on one point. Man, he wouldn't, you couldn't, you couldn't *find* a question *he* couldn't answer. I doubt. And you respected him for it. Not that you're trying to trick the, the section man, but you, when you come up with any kind of a reasonable question, he [Prof. Black] can answer it

for you, and he can answer it *well*. Whereas the section men dwiddle around and, and talk a lot of nonsense.

Or if True Authorities offer complexities, they enable us to learn the way to truth:

> Student: I found that you've got to find out for yourself. You get to a point where you, ah, see this guy go through this rigamarole and everything and you've got to find out for yourself what he's talking about and think it out for yourself. Then try to get to think on your own. And that's something I never had to do, think things out by myself, I mean. In high school two and two was four; there's nothing to think out there. In here they try to make your mind work, and I didn't realize that until the end of the year.
>
> Interviewer: You kept looking for the answer and they wouldn't give it to you?
>
> Student: Yeah, it wasn't in the *book*. And that's what confused me a lot. *Now* I know it isn't in the book for a purpose. We're supposed to think about it and come *up* with the answer!

So in Position 2, the student has given meaning to diversity, uncertainty, and complexity in Authority's realm by accounting for them as unwarranted confusion in poorly qualified Authorities or as mere exercises set by Authority "so we can learn to find The Answer for ourselves."

Transition from Position 2 to Position 3. This last concession—that answers sometimes must be *searched for* by students—can lead directly to a generalization that fatefully includes Authority itself. The issue may be avoided temporarily by dividing disciplines into the definite and the vague:

> Student: I'll tell you the best thing about science courses: Their lectures are all right. They sort of say the facts. But when you get to a humanities course, especially—oh, they're awful—the lecturer is just reading things into the book that were never meant to be there.

But in the end even Science fails:

> Student: That seems to be the, the excuse that natural science people give for these courses: They're supposed to teach you to arrive at more logical conclusions and look at things in a more scientific manner. Actually, what you get out of that course is that science is a terrifically confused thing in which nobody knows what's coming off anyway.

Position 3: Multiplicity Legitimate but Subordinate. If even Scientific Authority does not yet know all Truths in its own domain, one must, presumably, settle for less, at least for now:

> Student: I'd feel [laughs] rather insecure thinking about these philosophical things all the time and not coming up with any definite answers. And definite answers are, well, they, they're sort of my foundation point. In physics you get definite answers to a point. Beyond that point you know there *are* definite answers, but you can't reach them.

That is, as many students said, "you can't reach them *yet*." Uncertainty is temporary. The Truth is still there to be found in the Laplacean Universe. Some diversity of opinion, therefore, is legitimate, but temporary.

Transition from Position 3 to Position 4. The concession, "but you can't reach them [yet]," contains the seeds of destruction for the major structural assumptions of Positions 1 through 3. Human uncertainty has been accorded a legitimacy that has the potential of spreading from a temporary case to the whole of human knowledge. The tie between Authority and the Absolute has been loosened. Uncertainty is now unavoidable, even in physics.

> Student: Here was this great [physics] professor and *he* was groping *too*!

This realization can raise a severe procedural problem. How, in an educational institution where the student's every answer is evaluated, are answers judged? Where Authority does not know *the* answer yet, is not any answer as good as another?

So far, Authority has been perceived as grading on amount of rightness, achieved by honest hard work, and as adding an occasional bonus for neatness and "good expression." But in the uncertainty of a legitimized Multiplicity, coupled with a freedom that leaves "amount" of work "up to you" and Authority ignorant of how much you do, rightness and hard work vanish as standards. Nothing seems to be left but "good expression," and Authorities are suspected of different or obscure standards for that:

> Student: If I present it in the right manner it is well received. Or it is received . . . I don't know, I still haven't exactly caught onto what, what they want.

Authority's maintenance of the old morality of reward for hard work is called into serious question, and disillusion is imminent:

> Student: A lot of people noticed this throughout the year, that the mark isn't proportional to the work. 'Cause on a previous paper I'd done a lot of work and gotten the same mark, and on this one I wasn't expecting it . . . I just know that you can't, ah, expect your mark in proportion to the amount of work you put in . . . In prep school it was more of a, more, the relationship was more personal and the teacher could tell whether you were working hard, and he would give you breaks if he knew you were working. It wasn't grading a student on his aptitude, it was grading somewhat on the amount of work he put in.

This uncertain relationship between work and rewards can lead to bitterness:

> Student: This place is all full of bull. They don't want anything really honest from you. If you turn in something, a speech that's well written, whether it's got one single fact in it or not is beside the point. That's sort of annoying at times, too. You can put things over on people around here; you're almost given to try somehow to sit down and write a paper in an hour, just because you know that whatever it is isn't going to make any difference to anybody.

> Hence, an intellectual question has led to a precarious ethical dilemma:
> Student: It looks to me like it's [laughs] kind of not very good, you know? I mean you can't help but take advantage of these things.

Here, as in every transitional phase, the issues of development hang in the balance. The students have not yet distinguished between legitimate abstract thought and its counterpart, "bull."[2] They see the "bullster" winning honors while they themselves work hard and receive C's. They feel tempted. Their dilemma may appear false, looked at from the vantage point of later Positions, which transcend it, but at the moment it is bitter and poignant. In their disillusion they find cynicism and opportunism inviting indeed. The students are struggling in a moral battle, blind to the possibility that its resolution is intellectual.

[2]For a discussion of the relation of "bull" and "cow" in academia see Perry, 1969.

In this moment, then, the students are confronting two closely related perceptions incongruent with their construal of the world from Position 3: (a) the spread of uncertainty and diversity into Authority's domain of the known and (b) Authority's insistence on grading even in the domain of uncertainty. Our interviews reveal that a student's attitude toward Authority is crucial at this point. If the student is intensely resentful (Oppositional, as we called it), the temptation may be strong to take refuge in alienation (which we called Escape) or in the simplistic dualism of Position 2 (which we called Retreat), from which otherness, differentness, and complexity can be righteously hated.

In contrast, students whose opposition to Authority was less intense, and those whose trust in Authority we called Adherence, moved forward, but along a different path. The structure of the meaningful world constructed by the moderately Oppositional students requires attention first:

Position 4a: Multiplicity (Diversity and Uncertainty) Coordinate with the "known."

> Student: I mean if you read them [critics], that's the great thing about a book like *Moby Dick.* [Laughs] *Nobody* understands it!

Students such as this seize on the notion of legitimate uncertainty as a means of creating, out of personalistic diversity of opinion, an epistemological realm equal to and over against the world of Authority in which certain Right Answers are known. In this new realm, freedom is, or should be, complete: "Everyone has a right to his own opinion; they have no right to say we're wrong!"

This new structure, by dividing the world into two domains, preserves the fundamentally dualistic nature of earlier structures. To replace the simple dualism of the right-wrong world of Authority, these students create the double dualism of a world in which the Authority's right-wrong world is one element and personalistic diversity (which we labeled Multiplicity) is the other. The students have thus succeeded in preserving a dualistic structure for their worlds and at the same time have carved out for themselves a domain promising absolute freedom. In saying in this domain, "Everyone has a right to his own opinion," students are also saying, "Where Authorities do not know the Answer, any opinion is as good as any other."

> Interviewer: Can you say that one point of view is better and another worse?
> Student: No, I really can't on this issue [creation versus evolution of man]. It depends on your beliefs. Since there's no way of proving either one.
> Interviewer: Can you say that one is more accurate than the other?
> Student: No, I can't, I believe they're both the same as far as accuracy.
> Interviewer: Would you go so far as to say your opinion is the right one?
> Student: No.
> Interviewer: But yet you believe so strongly in it; that's why I'm asking . . .
> Student: I'm the type of person who would never tell someone that their idea is wrong—even if they have searched, well, even if they haven't searched, even if they just believe it—that's cool for them.
> Interviewer: Can you say that one opinion is better and one opinion is worse?
> Student: No, not at all. It's better for them and like their opinion would probably be worse for me.

I am indebted to King (1977a) for this vivid excerpt from her interviews. We have found few students who would defend this personalism so nobly against an interviewer's probes; under pressure most students move ahead into concessions, albeit still epistemologically quantitative: "Well, maybe some opinions might have more facts." The pure statement that, in the domain of uncertainty, to "have" an opinion makes it as "right" as any other expresses an egocentric personalism that we called *Multiplicity*. The students, as they moved on, were emphatic about the distinction between this outlook and that of disciplined Relativism (discussed later).

This personalism that we called Multiplicity Coordinate serves many purposes besides that of a hoped-for freedom from the tyranny of Authority. It makes sense in the midst of a diversity which can only appear chaotic until some reasoned qualitative distinctions can be discerned. Moreover, its egalitarian spirit provides a haven of ultimate peace at the end of dormitory bull sessions. At a deeper level, it expresses a respect for others through a respect for their views. (Others as persons are not yet differentiated from the opinions they *hold*; they *are* their opinions, as I am mine). As a stepping stone, then, Multiplicity is not to be dismissed as mere license or as a simple misapplication of religious tolerance to epistemological and ethical realms.

Yet in this structure all debatable propositions remain atomistic. An opinion is related to nothing whatever—evidence, reason, experience, expert judgment, context, principle, or purpose—except to the person who holds it. Even the relation of the opinion to the person is limited to the fact that the person "has" it. All that Authority cannot prove to be Wrong is Right. This structuring of meaning is therefore still dualistic; the world so construed is not yet open to Relativism's analysis, rules of evidence, disciplines of inference, and concern for the integrity of interpretations and systems of thought.

Unfortunately, the unconsidered statement, "Anyone has a right to his own opinion," is popularly thought to be the heart of Relativism, and its implication of moral license has given Relativism a bad name. King herself labels the excerpt quoted above as an illustration of "relativism," and such a veteran as Kohlberg has been perilously slow to acknowledge the distinction. I shall remark later in this chapter (see also Gilligan in her chapter) on the difficulties that have followed on such conflation in such crucial matters as evaluation of the moral development of women. Perhaps some simpler-sounding word than Multiplicity (Personalism, for example) would have helped distinguish this more simplistic structure.

In any case, the students, having construed diversity of opinion as a realm for personalistic rightness, are poised at the edge of a fateful moment in their destinies. Major incongruities face them. In their academic work, teachers insist on continuing to grade the students' opinions in such debatable areas as sociology and literature. On what grounds? What teacher has not experienced despair in trying to explain to a student at this level of development that grades depend, not on the *quantity* of work and "facts" and, especially, unsupported "opinions," but on the quality of the relationships between data and interpretations? Such a freshman, winner of a national prize in history in senior year of high school, once complained to me: "They told me here to 'Describe the theory of monarchy assumed in Queen Elizabeth's speech to the Commons in 1601.' I said what her main points were, but my section man says to look between the lines for her theory of monarchy! And I look between the lines and I can't see anything there!"

The capacity for *meta*-thought, for comparing the assumptions and processes of different ways of thinking, has not yet emerged. This is perhaps the most critical moment in the whole adventure for both student and teacher.

Transition from Position 4a (Multiplicity) to Position 5 (Relativism). Before taking up the smoother movement of the more Adherent students through Position 4b, I wish to note the special difficulty of transition into Relativistic thought experienced by the students who have embraced Multiplicity with greatest enthusiasm. I have suffered too many defeats by the ingenuity of Multiplistic Libertarians to offer any handy-dandy pedagogical devices for helping students in this transition. Together with the teacher-researchers, mentioned later in the chapter, who have focused their experimentation on this problem, I have found all solutions to be relative to the subject matter. The work of these researchers contains rich ore for any prospector. Here I wish to report our students' experience of first discovery, so vital and usually so explicit, of qualitative epistemological structures and complex relations.

Sad to say, the very spunk with which our most Oppositional students invented the realm of Multiplicity (to set against the Right-Wrong world they attributed to Authority) seemed to lead them into a stalemate. Entrenched in this Position, they found it difficult to abandon the slogan, "Every opinion is right," for the qualitative analyses and appraisals of Relativism to which the best of their instructors would try to introduce them. Most did find ways, as I shall suggest shortly in discussing the general mechanisms of transition, but some were cornered into a choice between leaving the field and outright capitulation. Most fortunate were those for whom the demand to substantiate opinion came from more advanced peers.

Those less entrenched in opposition moved more easily:

> Student: [Reading written statement handed him by interviewer] "In areas where experts disagree, everyone has a right to his own opinion"—Yeh, sure. I mean, if the answers aren't in, like in lots of things, then sure, anyone's opinion.
> Interviewer: So really you're saying that here, anyway, no opinion can be *wrong*, sort of, so one opinion is really as good as any other?
> Student: Yeh, ah, well—no, not really—I, well I hadn't thought of that before. No—I mean you've got to have some facts *under* the opinion, I guess.

"Some facts" is still a quantitative criterion, but it opens the door to the qualitative notion of "better" (rather than right-wrong) opinions. Though the student may still have much to learn about the relations of "facts" and "opinions," that learning has now a real potential. Here, the transition seems initiated by the interview itself. It is easy to imagine, however, a variety of experiences other than the interviewer's question that would have set the same process in motion.

Position 4b: Relativism Subordinate. The more trusting Adherent students seemed to find a smoother path. Their integrity seemed less entrenched in Multiplicity's fortress: "They have No Right to Call Me Wrong." Trusting in Authority to have valid grounds for grading even in areas of uncertainty, they set themselves to discover those grounds. Laurence Copes recently pointed out to me that some students may sensibly find their way out of the impass of Position 4a via the discovery of Position 4b as described later. A review of the data supports this proposition, namely that a path through Position 4a and 4b can be sequential. In some one course or another—or in some other particular context —they perceived relativistic thinking as a special case of "what They want":

> Student: Another thing I've noted about this more concrete and complex approach—you can get away without . . . trying to think about what they want— ah, think about things the *way* they want you to think about them. But if you try to use the approach the course outlines, then you find yourself thinking in *complex terms*: weighing more than one factor in trying to develop your own opinion. Somehow what I think about things seems to be more—oh—it's hard to say right or wrong—but it seems [pause] more *sensible*.

Here the correction from *"what* they want" to "the *way* they want you to think" signals the discovery of the articulation of the "concrete" with the "complex" in "weighing" relationships—a mode of thought that is the structural foundation of Relativism. The weighing of "more than one factor," or, as this student later explained, "more than one *approach* to a problem," forces a comparison of patterns of thought—that is, a thinking about thinking. The person, previously a *holder* of meaning, has become a *maker* of meaning. For most students, as for this student, the event seems to be conscious and explicit; that is, the *initial* discovery of meta-thought occurs vividly in foreground, as figure, against the background of previous ways of thinking, and usually as an assimilation to the old paradigm—that is, as an item in the *context of* "what They want."

Now, the capacity to compare different approaches to a problem in "developing one's own opinion" is presumably the ordinary meaning of *independent thought*. The paradox for liberal education lies in the fact that so many of our students learned to think this way because it was "the way They want you to think"—that is, out of a readiness to conform. The challenge of a more genuine independence then confronted these students later in the revolutionary perception of the general relativism of *all* knowledge, *including* the knowledge possessed by Authority itself (Position 5).

Transition from Position 4b (Relativism Subordinate) to Position 5 (Relativism). The first steps in the direction of Relativism are articulated by the same student just quoted:

> Student: I don't know if complexity itself [he has been speaking of relativistic analysis] is always necessary. I'm not sure. But if complexity is *not* necessary, at least you have to find that it *is* not necessary before you can decide, "Well, this particular problem needs only the simple approach."

Although this transitional statement implies that relativistic thinking will be required more *frequently* than "simple" (dualistic) solutions, the student does not yet recognize that even the "simple" case owes its simplicity to a complex context of assumptions, rules, and contingencies. That is, this same student, quoted in the illustration of Position 4b, first saw relativistic thought as a special case in the context of "what They want." This present statement catches him halfway to the perception of relativistic thought as general *context* and "what They want" as a special case. I shall refer to this transformation of a special case into a context later in considering the forms of transitions in general.

We found it rare to catch this momentous revolution in the act. By the next year this student simply took the whole matter for granted, with a kind of amnesia for the deep reorganization involved. Indeed, in senior year he had this to say on hearing himself as sophomore:

> Student: [scornfully] You can't even *talk* about taking a simple approach to something. I mean it's just a way of looking at things that is complex—it's not a conscious policy, it's just something that's been absorbed into you.

I recall, without the precise reference, that Piaget once remarked on this curiosity of cognitive growth: *assimilations*—the attributions of meaning to objects or events that reduce their dissonance with the person's extant structures of meaning—tend to be remembered; *accommodations*—the subsequent reorganizations of basic structures to achieve congruence with dissonant assimilations—tend to be forgotten (perhaps because memory's own filing system is, in the very process, in flux). Could it be that we teachers require special exercise in the recall of our own accommodations in order to understand some students' apparent density?

In any case, an understanding of the forms that such transitions take would seem fundamental to curriculum design and teaching strategies. The transitions we have noted so far appear to start with assimilation of some incongruity to an extant paradigm. In the transition just traced, for instance, the student first perceived relativistic thinking simply as a special case in the general dualistic frame of "what They want." But this assimilation turned out to be a Trojan Horse, its inner forms emerging to overwhelm its simplistic host and force an accommodation of fundamental assumptions. Education has thus changed from collecting "what They want" to developing a way of thinking shared by both teacher and student.

Here, then, the accommodation takes the form of a radical reversal of part and whole, detail and context: the task of generating and comparing several interpretations of a poem, for example, may first be assimilated as a special case into the larger context of "what They want." In short, contextual relativism is perceived as if it were similar to "right answers." And yet it is also perceived as not quite similar: "As soon as I saw what they wanted . . . well, no, not *what* they wanted but the *way* they wanted you to think. . . ." The shift from "what" (content) to "way" (generalized process), being a move to a higher level of abstraction, frees the "way" to become context, displacing the "what" and relegating it to the status of a particular. In other instances, accommodation appears to be brought about by the sheer weight of quantitative expansion of the assimilated incongruity: uncertainties or diversities multiply until they tip the balance against certainty and homogeneity, precipitating a crisis that forces the construction of a new vision of the world, be it one marked by cynicism, anxiety, or a new sense of freedom.

The use of analogy—what Piaget called *décalage*—is doubtless involved in these processes and will become more evident in the remaining steps of the journey. *Vertical décalage* manifests itself in the "lifting" of a pattern of meaning from a concrete experience and using it as an analogue for meaning at a level of greater abstraction. For example, one student, terrified after making an error on his job, was astounded by the calmness of his employer's quiet suggestion that he plan things more carefully next time. He reported that the experience freed him to think more creatively in his studies and to affirm his opinions more confidently, relieved of irrational anxiety about impending judgment. Likewise, there are many areas of life in which students have learned at early ages patterns of qualitative and contextual judgment, as opposed to all-or-none quantitative and absolutistic judgment. For example, they have moved in early years from "What's your *favorite* color, ice cream, friend, sport, and so on" to considerations of what color with what other colors, what ice cream with what other foods, what friend in what activity or sharing. These contextual schema provide ready analogies in concrete experience that the student may "lift" to provide patterns for abstract thought itself. Ideas can then be conceived as contextual, relativistic, and better or worse, rather than right or wrong.

This comparison of interpretations and thought systems with one another introduces *meta-thinking,* the capacity to examine thought, including one's own. Theories become, not "truth," but metaphors or "models," approximating the order of observed data or experience. Comparison, involving systems of logic, assumptions, and inferences, all relative to context, will show some interpretations to be "better," others "worse," many worthless. Yet even after extensive analysis there will remain areas of great concern in which reasonable people will reasonably disagree. It is in this sense that relativism is inescapable and forms the epistemological context of all further developments.

Position 5: Relativism. Let us now examine the reactions of students to the simultaneous discovery of disciplined meta-thought and irreducible uncertainty.

Student: It's a method that you're dealing with, not, not a substance. It's a method, a purpose—ah, "procedure" would be the best word, I should imagine, that you're looking for. And once you've developed this procedure in one field, I think the important part is to be able to transfer it to another field, and the example that I brought up about working with this, this crew of men. It's probably, ah, the most outstanding, at least one of the achievements that I feel that I've been able to make as far as transferring my academic experience to the field of everyday life.

This process of drawing an analogy between different areas of experience *(horizontal décalage)* highlights the fact that individuals mature their cognitive structures at different rates in different areas of their lives. They can thus transfer the more advanced patterns of thought learned in one area to areas in which they have been thinking more simplistically. The student just quoted has used relativism learned in academic work to broaden his understanding of others and expand his social skills. No doubt this has increased his potential for empathy. However, the salient initial experience is usually one of expanded competence:

Student: Besides your meeting people, it's—it's the way of thinking—I mean just by the process of going through school, the courses are lined up so they make you think, especially when you come to, say, hour exams and you have to take them. This rubs off—when you meet people and have to talk to them, the process is in your mind and then you can think about things and be able to come up on your feet.

Relativistic consideration has already grown somewhat beyond its value as a practical tool, and its epistemological implications soon become explicit.

Student: So here were all these theorists and theories and stuff in [economics] and psychology and historiography—I didn't even take any straight philosophy—and hell, I said, "These are *games,* just *games* and everybody makes up their own rules! So it's gotta be bullshit." But then I realized "What else have we got?" and now every time I go into a thing I set out to learn all its rules cold—'cause that's the only way I can tell whether I'm talking bullshit.

In this powerful statement, the responsibility and initiative that used to be the domain of Authority (leaving that of obedience to the student), have been internalized. This sense of agency as a learner is expressed first, appropriately enough, in a care for precision of thought within given contexts. Indeed, the student's redefinition of "bullshit" encapsulates his momentous revision of his epistemology and his self-definition in it. It is hardly surprising that there is still no hint in the protocol of a further responsibility to choose among contexts or "games." In Position 5 students seem much taken up with expansion of their new skills, exploring alternative perspectives in many disciplines and areas of life. Their explorations may occupy them for more than a year before they sense a necessity to orient themselves in a relativistic sea through their own Commitments (see the discussion of Positions 6-9). It is not really fair to describe the typical suspension of development at this point as Temporizing, since there is evidence of "lateral growth" (Perry, 1970, p. 175). This factor may help explain the findings of recent experiments (Knefelkamp, 1978c) that "developmental instruction" is more successful in facilitating students' movements from Dualism into Relativism than from Relativism into Commitments, at least within the limits of a semester.

Needless to say, many students react to the discovery of relativistic thinking with profound anxiety.

Student: You know, in the past months, it's been a matter of having really . . . having reduced to the level where I really wasn't sure there was anything in particular to follow. I, you do begin to wonder on what basis you'd judge *any* decision at all, 'cause there really isn't, ah . . . too much of an absolute you can rely on as to . . . and even as to whether . . . there are a lot of levels that you can tear it apart, or you can base an ethical system that's a, presupposes that there are men who . . . or you can get one that doesn't presuppose that anything exists . . . and try and figure out of what principles you're going to decide any issue. Well, it's just that right now I'm not sure that . . . of what the, ah, what those de-, how to make any decision at all. When you're here and are having the issues sort of thrust in your face at times . . . that is, just seeing the thinking of these men who have pushed their thought to the absolute limit to try and find out what was their personal salvation, and just seeing how that fell short of an all-encompassing answer to, for everyone. That those ideas really are individualized. And you begin to have respect for how great their thought could be, without its being absolute.

I picture this student standing beside Sisyphus (Camus' embodiment of the human predicament in the *Myth of Sisyphus*) and gazing in dismay at the rock of reason, which has turned on itself and rolled once again to the foot of the mountain. He sees, in wonder and terror, Sisyphus' wry smile bespeaking his awareness that he must again resume the quest for certainty of meaning, a labor that forever ends in the same defeat. Is this vision tolerable?

Deflections from Growth

We shall leave our students poised in their journey at this realization that even the most careful analytical thought and logical reasoning will not, in many areas vital to their lives, restore the hope of ultimate rightness and certainty promised by Authority in the Eden they have left behind. "I'm not sure how to make any decision at all." At this moment, the potential for apathy, anxiety, and depression may appear alarming clinically, and the potential for cynicism equally alarming educationally.

Looking back to the dualistic worlds of Positions 1-3, we can observe that the students and much of the environment were conspiring to maintain the illusion that meaning existed "out there," along with rightness, power, and sound advice. One should, of course, try to "think for oneself," but when such efforts end in uncertainty and confusion, one naturally appeals to external authority, secure in the expectation of an answer. Students in this frame of mind present themselves to "career counselors" expecting to be told "the right job" or even to be "placed" in it. "What do the tests say my interests are?"

When all knowledge is revealed to be relativistic, probabilistic, and contingent, Authority appears as limited authority, uncertain even in its specialties, and ignorant beyond them. In this collapse, the agency for making sense, originally supposed to exist "out there," may vanish entirely. We should note here, therefore, the reactions of those students (happily a small minority of our informants) who reacted with postponement, apathy, or rage. Against the background of their experience we can then better appreciate the transcendence of those who found a more positive resolution.

Temporizing. Some students simply waited, reconsigning the agency for decision to some event that might turn up:

Student: I'll wait and see what time brings, see if I pass the foreign service exam. Let that decide.

Or even more passively:

Student: It, ah . . . Well, I really, I don't know, I just, I don't get particularly worked up over things. I don't react too strongly. So that I can't think. I'm still waiting for the event, you know, everyone goes through life thinking that something's gonna happen, and I don't think it happened this year. So we'll just leave that for the future. Mainly you're, you're waiting for yourself to change, see after you get a good idea, continued trial and effort, exactly how you're going to act in any period of time, once you get this idea, then you're constantly waiting for the big chance in your life. And, it certainly didn't happen this year.

Students speaking this way often expressed a sense of guilt or shame—an uneasiness about a failure of responsibility with which they felt helpless to cope.

Retreat. In the late sixties and early seventies, some students found in the far extremes of political positions, both of the right and of the left, a way of preempting the absolutism that "wishy-washy" authorities had abandoned. The structure of thought to which they returned was that of Position 2, but with an added moralistic righteousness and righteous hatred of Otherness: "The others are so wrong they should have *no rights,* even to speak." Academically, however, this Retreat to the all-or-none of Position 2 often took the form of childlike complaints and demands:

Student: I mean, when I talk, as I say, I like to be out in the open. I mean I like to just, just come out with the facts and have them say, "Here's the information I want you to learn. This is the way I want you, this is what I want you to get out of the course when you come out." If I know what I want . . . I'm expected from a teacher . . . and what kind of questions he might ask, how thoroughly he wants you to read this material. . . . The big things are to get the basic principles. But he doesn't give you these! He ought to line them up right at the beginning; right at the first lecture he ought to tell you exactly what you're going to go over and what he wants us to basically get out of that course.

Escape. More complex reactions of alienation we labeled Escape. I shall not attempt to categorize or analyze their variants here; a few samples will speak for themselves —perhaps all too well:

Student: But, ah, I just, I don't, don't, don't have any, ah, consuming interest or burning desire or anything. And I just, just drift along, I guess you might say.

On the one hand, I, I—am, um, having an, an, ah . . . ah, an extremely comfortable life here. But, ah, perhaps later, I'm, I may find out that I'm ah . . . drifting and, and that I'm not happy in my drift.

And I was wondering if I might not be headed in that direction and, and it might turn out that when I get older I, I'll find that . . . umn . . . I am living a, a hollow life.

Is Relativism the road to Escape or the precondition of Commitment?

Student: I know that I had trouble, ah, first of all in just listening to the lectures, trying to make out what they meant . . . These, ah, ah, the pursuit of the absolute first of all . . . And then I . . . [laughs] sort of lost the absolute, and stuff like that. I think that gradually it sunk in, and, I don't know, maybe it's just . . . Well, it came to me the other night: if relativity is true on most things, it's an easy way out. But I don't think that's . . . maybe that's just the way I think now . . . Well, in, in a sense I mean that you don't have to commit yourself. And maybe that's just the push button I use on myself . . . right now, because I am uncommitted.

Does the purity of detachment preclude meaningful involvement?

Student: I've thought quite a bit about this: I've never really identified myself with anything. I hadn't permitted myself to so far as grades were concerned or as far as friends—particularly in a few isolated cases. I had just a sort of "I'm me, and I just like to stand out there and look things over" attitude, and I don't know whether this is good or bad.

But there's always impulse:

Student: So the best thing I have to do is just forget about deciding, and try to . . . I mean, not give up on any scheming or any basic set of ideas . . . that'll give myself, they'll give me a direction. Just give up completely, and when it comes down to individual choices, make them on what I feel like doing emotionally at the moment.

Not all the students who spoke this way left such statements with us as their final words. Many reported a resurgence of vitality and involvement:

Student: Emotionally I think I was trying to find some sort of rationalization for my feeling that I wasn't going to achieve anything. These are certainly not the values I have now. They're not the goals I want now. I don't think I'm going to be happy unless I can feel I'm doing something in my work.

Student: I think I've, to some extent, not perhaps as well as I like, have risen up to be able to accept it [academic work], and the responsibility that goes with it, but it's one little change.

Student: I was sort of worried when I came back, wondering if, "Well, shucks, am I just going to lie down on the job or am I going to do it because it has to be done?" I found out that I wasn't doing it because it *had* to be, but because things interested me. Some things didn't interest me so much, but I felt I couldn't let them slide and I took them as best I could, in what order I could.

We know from everyday observations and from studies of adults (Keniston, 1960; Vaillant, 1977; Salyard, in progress) that the alienation we called Escape can become a settled condition. For the students reporting their recovery of care, however, their period of alienation appears as a time of transition. In this time the self is lost through the very effort to hold onto it in the face of inexorable change in the world's appearance. It is a space of meaninglessness between received belief and creative faith. In their rebirth *they experience in themselves the origin of meanings, which they had previously expected to come to them from outside.*

Development Resumed

Position 6: Commitment Foreseen. Students who were able to come more directly to grips with the implications of Relativism frequently referred to their forward movement in terms of commitments.

Student: It took me quite a while to figure out that if I was going for something to believe in, it had to come from within me.

Many students foresaw the challenge:

Student: I would venture a guess that this problem bothers everybody except for, ah, a very, very small few, this, this constant worry about whether you can face up to it, and, and I think the earlier you find out that you can . . . I think the more important it is . . . A sense of responsibility is something which, I don't think . . . you're necessarily are born with, it's, ah . . . something that you're aware of . . . but . . . it's never very pronounced until you're on your own and until you're making your own decisions, more or less, and then you realize how very important it really is.

As a generalized realization, lacking as yet a focus in some specific content, the vision seems to derive from the felt exigency of "action":

Student: Once you get to be past twenty-one or twenty-two, if you haven't begun to get control of yourself, you can't, if you haven't begun to get a certain amount of direction, you can't expect these internal evolutions to just develop and then suddenly bloom, you've got to work at it, I think.

You've got to do something, you've got to act. You've got to act these things . . . if you have these thoughts, and you don't act on them . . . nothing happens.

But how to begin? The same student goes on to imagine that the first steps may require an almost arbitrary faith, or even a willing suspension of disbelief:

Student: You just have to jump into it, that's all, before it can have any effect on you. And the farther in you force yourself to get in the first place, the more possibilities there are, the more ideas and concepts there are that can impinge on you and so the more likely you are to get involved in it. Actually you have to make some kind of an assumption in the first place that it's worthwhile to get into it, but . . . and that you're capable of doing something once you get into it.

Commitments and choices are apprehended as "narrowing"—there are so many potentialities and alternatives to let go of. Yet the sustaining energy is the awareness of some sort of internal spiritual strength. Such an explicit affirmation as this one is rare:

Student: I wasn't *deploring* the fact that my interests were narrowing, I was just simply *observing* it. I don't see how I could get by without it. You know what Keats says in one of his letters, he says when he's sitting in a room and everybody is talking brilliantly and he's sitting in the corner and he's sulking and everybody is whispering to each other, "Oh that poet Keats is sitting over there like a wallflower," he says in moments like that, he doesn't care about that because he's aware of the, the resource in his breast. I think that's the expression he uses. And what goes along with this narrowing of the purpose is the greater and greater sense of, that resource in my breast which is, I don't suppose that everybody needs it, but I need it. You know, it just, it just puts a center and a focus into your life, into what you're doing. And it hasn't really anything to do with where you would like to think that it would go on, this "inner life" (which I think is really bad to call it) that will go on no matter what you're doing, whether you're traveling around the world or whether you're sitting in your stack in Widener. So I know that it must seem like a disparity, but I don't feel it that way.

More usually:

Student: There are all kinds of pulls, pressures and so forth . . . parents . . . this thing and that thing . . . but there comes a time when you've just got to say, "Well, . . . I've got a life to live . . . I want to live it this way, I welcome suggestions. I'll listen to them. But when I make up my mind, it's going to be me. I'll take the consequences."

So far I have chosen statements that are "contentless" in the sense that no specific value or activity is named as the investment of commitment. My object has been to allow the students to convey the sense and "feel" of commitment as an internal disposition through which one apprehends the possibility of orienting oneself and investing one's care in an uncertain and relativistic world. The next step, of course, is one of choice and action (see Positions 7, 8, and 9), as for example in one's academic work:

> Student: This year I'm beginning to see that you don't ever get anywhere unless you do work. You, you just can't sort of lie back and expect everything to come to you. That's the way I was trying to let it work, but that doesn't work.

That these emerging Commitments call upon a *new kind* of investment from within (as compared with unquestioned commitments—lowercase *c*—of the past) is evident in this student's report of her new sense of her religion. She has just reported that she had always "taken it for granted" that she would join the ministry:

> Student: The thing is, when you have a bunch of beliefs sort of handed to you, you don't really do that much thinking. I mean I was never even concerned with philosophy. I never read a single thing. I didn't have to. I mean, I accepted the Christian faith because my parents were Christians and I believed that, well, you know I never even thought, well, maybe there isn't any God. I mean it doesn't enter your mind. You just think, well, there's a God, you know, and he has a purpose for everybody's life. . . . But the thing is, I didn't know what I was really gonna do with my life. My life just sort of seemed, well, the main purpose was just telling everybody else that they had to believe in Jesus or they weren't going to go to heaven. . . . It's just that I was always going to be . . . working with the church, you know, but, I, I never really thought about what is my, you know, place in the universe, or anything. And, but the thing is, it really hasn't been unsettling, because . . . ahh . . . well, I don't know, now I'm more . . . somehow now I feel . . . I don't know, just more honest about, about my beliefs, now that I'm sort of getting them on my own.

Positions 7-9: Evolving Commitments. Our students, at sea in Relativism, now realized that they must choose, at their own risk, among disparate systems of navigation. What star to steer by? Many felt that once "I know what I'm going to do," all other problems would be solved—or at least fall in line. Then they made their first Commitment (Position 7), whether to a set of values ("This may sound sort of silly, but I've developed a sense of, ah, a set of morals") or to a person ("I started dating this girl"), or, most usually, to a career ("Right now I'd like to go into pediatrics; I'm really set on this deal"). In any case, the sense of "claiming" is vivid:

> Student: Then, by a few months or a few weeks ago, feeling new kinds of resolve, you know, just grabbing hold of myself and saying, "This I want, that I don't want, this I am, that I'm not, and I'll be solid about it."
> I'd never believed I could do things, that I had any power, I mean power over myself, and over effecting any change that I thought was right. I'd artificially try to commit myself to something, intellectually understand that I was this way, and then a few months later, the realization would come that yes, I really *am* that way. They're two different things. One's intellectual and comes fairly easily; one is emotional and is a process of absorbing something—the things inside just sort of slowly shifting around and there's a lot of inertia there.

The difference between such Commitments, made after doubt, and those unquestioned childhood beliefs that Erikson calls "foreclosed identity" was dramatized for us by a doctor-to-be who, after years of struggle, received notice of his admission to medical school. He reacted with panic: "But I've never *decided* to be a *doctor!*" He decided, and then had to decide if his decision was real or simply a way of justifying his investment. Such is the nature of Commitments.

Yet one Commitment does not, after all, order all one's life:

> Student: I don't think it reduces the number of problems that I face or uncertainties, it just was something that troubled me that I thought was—I always thought it was an unnecessary problem and based on my limited experience with a broadened world . . . [Now] I don't see it as something that is passed; it is something that I have to decide continually.

So when further Commitments are affirmed (Positions 8 and 9) it becomes necessary to balance them—to establish priorities among Commitments with respect to energy, action, and time. These orderings, which are often painful to make, can lead to periodic experiences of serenity and well-being in the midst of complexity—moments of "getting it all together":

> Student: Well, ah . . . I don't know exactly if there's any one thing that's central . . . this is the whole point that, ah . . . there are factors in the whole . . . you group all these facts . . . I don't know that there's one thing about which everything revolves . . . but it's rather just a circle.
> Interviewer: It's the constellation that, ah . . . you try to maintain?
> Student: Yeah. Right. Yeah, you think of the old, ah . . . the balance of powers, you know . . . you know it's not . . . north and south or black and white . . . it's . . . it's not a simple thing. It comes in any given occasion . . . and . . . it's different . . . This is what makes things exciting—it offers a challenge.

Another senior has been groping to describe the new sense of living with trust even in the midst of a heightened awareness of risk:

> Interviewer: And I take it, part of this mellowness that you speak of is being able to live in peace with this complexity . . . if it isn't so simple . . .
> Student: It's not as frightening as it may have been. . . . If you feel that, ah, whatever you do there's going, there's going to be much more to do, more to understand, you're going to make mistakes . . . but you have a certain sense of being able to cope with a specific, or rather, a small fragment of the general picture and, ah, doing a job, getting the most out of it, but never, never giving up, always looking for something.

Order and disorder may be seen as fluctuations in experience:

> Student: I sort of see this now as a natural thing—that you constantly have times of doubt and tension—a natural thing in existing and being open, trying to understand the world around you, the people around you.

In the loneliness or separateness implicit in these integrations and reintegrations, students seek among their elders for models not only of knowledgeability but of courage to affirm commitment in full awareness of uncertainty.

> Student: That was just about what it was. Somehow I wanted to emulate [such people] because they seemed in some way noble people, and what they were doing seemed somehow noble and lofty—a very moral and superior type of thing. I think I fastened on this.

Yet the same student must come to see that it is the nobility of their care that he wishes to emulate, not the content of their Commitments. At the level of "what they were doing," even the model must be transcended:

Student: One thing I have found *since* is that it's not really *right* to make decisions on this basis, because you may come out doing something you don't find yourself suited for. It's really strange.

Dialectical Logic of Commitments

If one knows one's Commitments are to flow and fluctuate and conflict and reform, is one committed at all? This is the first of the many paradoxes the students encountered in working out their Commitments. Allport (Allport, 1955) observed the paradoxical necessity to be both wholehearted and tentative—attitudes that one cannot "compromise" but must hold together, with all their tensions. The students wrestled with logic to express this paradox:

Student: Well, "tentative" implies . . . perhaps uncertainty and, and, I mean readiness to change to anything, and, ah, it's not that. It's openness to change, but, but not looking for change, you know, ah . . . At the same time, ah, believing pretty strongly in what you do believe, and so it's not, you know, it's not tentative.

In reporting the original study, I pointed to an array of such polarities in the account of a single student in his senior year (Perry, 1970, pp. 167-176). They included certainty versus doubt, focus versus breadth, idealism versus realism, tolerance versus contempt, internal choice versus external influence, action versus contemplation, stability versus flexibility, and own values versus others' values. Because a polarity of this kind does not represent the poles of a continuum, it cannot be resolved simply by finding some balance point or compromise. Instead, our most mature students saw that the tension must be embraced and somehow transcended. To do so, they appealed to dialectical logic, without actually calling it by name.

[Speaking of the necessity of trusting in a professional healer even when evidence contradicts] : See, this is the way you get educated [laughs] . . . that's the big surprise. See I'm still sort of ironical about it, 'cause that's about the only way you can be—'cause ironic—being ironic handles both values at once.

At the time of the original study, I sensed that the term *dialectical thought* meant many things to many people, and I was troubled by the absence of a sense of its limits in the works of Hegel, Nietzsche, and Marx. Various recent writers (Riegel, 1973; Fowler, 1978; Basseches, 1978) have delimited more clearly the reference of the term and write convincingly of the central role of dialectical processes in thought characteristic of the higher ranges of human development.

Basseches (1978) has recently delineated twenty-four characteristics of dialectical thought. He proposes that these analytical tools will distinguish, in the present scheme, between those persons whose Commitments involve forward transcendent movement and those whose Commitments represent more a regression into dualism. By way of analogy, he points to Fowler's Paradoxical-Consolidative stage in the development of faith:

[This stage] affirms and incorporates existential or logical polarities, acting on a felt need to hold them in tension in the interest of truth. It maintains its vision of meaning, coherence, and value while being conscious of the fact that it is partial, limited, and contradicted by the visions and claims of others.

It holds its vision with a kind of provisional ultimacy: remembering its inadequacy and open to new truth but also committed to the absoluteness of the truth which it inadequately comprehends and expresses.

Symbols are understood as symbols. They are seen through in a double sense: (1) their time-place relativity is acknowledged and (2) their character as relative representations of something more nearly absolute is affirmed [Fowler, 1978, p. 22].

Again, Basseches quotes Fowler regarding the *costs* of this "identification beyond tribal, racial, class, or ideological boundaries. To be genuine, it must know the cost of such community and be prepared to pay the cost" (Fowler, 1978, pp. 6-7). Basseches' distinction regarding this cost is trenchant: "The cost of this openness to universal community of identification surely includes having to embrace viewpoints in conflict with and contradictory to one's own, rather than avoiding those conflicts with 'separate but equal' or 'live and let live' attitude." In short, it is in one's way of affirming Commitments that one finds at last the elusive sense of "identity" one has searched for elsewhere, fearful lest Commitments might narrow and compromise the very self that only the investment of care can create. It is in the affirmation of Commitments that the themes of epistemology, intellectual development, ethics, and identity merge. Knowing that "such and such is true" is an act of personal commitment (Polanyi, 1958) from which all else follows. Commitments structure the relativistic world by providing focus in it and affirming the inseparable relation of the knower and the known.

In the poignant realization of our separateness and aloneness in these affirmations, we are sorely in need of community. Our mentors can, if they are wise and humble, welcome us into a community paradoxically welded by this shared realization of aloneness. Among our peers we can be nourished with the strength and joy of intimacy, through the perilous sharing of vulnerability.

A graduating senior, shaken by the questioning of values he thought he had so firmly established, said to his interviewer, "Now I know I'll never know how many times I'm going to be confronted." Indeed, the development we have traced in college students reveals itself now as "age-free."

Development as Recursive

Fowler's words, which speak of the paradoxical dialectic of holding absolutes in symbols acknowledged to be relativistic, reveal also the limits of the linear structure embedded in the metaphor of our journey. We have followed our students in their cumulative expansion of the meanings of their worlds. Our map of their adventure has required only two dimensions, for in the time at the students' disposal they could traverse this "Pilgrim's Progress" only once. But any adults who have perused the diaries of their teens know well that growth and discoveries are recursive. We are shocked at finding we "knew" at sixteen what we just discovered yesterday. Have we just been going around in circles? Yet the "same" issues, faced over and over again, may not really be the same.

Perhaps the best model for growth is neither the straight line nor the circle, but a helix, perhaps with an expanding radius to show that when we face the "same" old issues we do so from a different and broader perspective (Perry, 1977b). I have before me a letter from a professor:

I thought you might be interested in a small example of passing through your series of stages more than once. Two years ago I spent three months working on a Danforth Faculty Fellowship Grant on a topic in faculty development, which was a new area for me. For many years I have been confident about skimming, picking and choosing within, and even abandoning books in my own discipline. When reading in faculty development materials, however, I found it necessary to struggle constantly against the impulse to dutifully examine and finish anything that was recommended to me whether it seemed fruitful or even bore on my problem or not.

The old "impulse" was there, but the new person was not "subject" to it.

Further Explorations with the Scheme

After the graduation of our last sample of volunteers in the original study, eight years passed before our small office found the energies to follow another class through its experience of college. Even then, since our daily work of counseling had doubled, we were unable to afford the systematic rating of the interviews necessary to formal research and had to rely on the informal consensus of our impressions. The average Harvard-Radcliffe freshman of 1970-71 seemed a full Position in advance of his or her predecessor in 1959-60—in fact, beyond the developmental crisis of Position 5. We wondered if this accounted in part for the relative "flatness" we felt characterized most of these students' four-year reports (Perry, 1974). Their concerns with Commitments, too, seemed to focus more narrowly on careers, usually with less sense of permanence of investment (reflecting the slackening in economic growth? post-Vietnam depression?). The overall progression, however, appeared congruent with that traced in the original study. We would say the same of our present sample of the class of '79. The course of cognitive and ethical development outlined in our scheme appears to be a constant phenomenon of a pluralistic culture.

However, we could not subject our impressions to objective testing. Furthermore, the data, as in the original study, are provided by students in a single institution. It has therefore remained for other researchers to show that the scheme provides a useful description of students' development of meaning in other settings, to refine the scheme further, to design more economical measurements, and to illustrate its power for the improvement of teaching and counseling in higher education. James Heffernan was the first to use the scheme for research in his study of the outcomes of the Residential College at Michigan (Heffernan, 1971). Heffernan subsequently developed a cumulative bibliography of research and commentary relating to the scheme, a task currently under the direction of Laurence Copes.[3] This bibliography of over 100 entries (as of April 1980) is included in the references for this chapter.

Here I shall mention briefly the work of those researchers and practitioners most familiar to me, hoping only to show the direction of their explorations. Readers interested in more detailed reviews should start with Heffernan, 1975. Until September of 1975, I was unaware that anyone had taken up the study of our scheme—other than Heffernan and also Joanne Kurfiss (1975), to whose work I shall refer later. To be sure, I had received many requests for a quick pencil-and-paper rating scale to be used for all purposes from admissions to the evaluation of faculty. In the face of my doubts about the reliability of a quick checklist, my friend Eugene Hartley, of the University of Wisconsin at Green Bay, made one from brief illustrative quotations from the original study, which students were to check "acceptable" or "unacceptable" (Hartley, 1973). This prodded

---

[3] In compiling this bibliography, Laurence Copes has received assistance from L. Lee Knefelkamp, Katherine Mason, John Griffith, and others. Clyde Parker at the University of Minnesota has contributed library facilities and supported the distributions of a newsletter of which Copes is editor. Interested persons may address Copes at the Institute for Studies in Educational Mathematics, 1483 Hewitt Ave., St. Paul, Minn. 55104.

me into making an "improved" version myself to demonstrate that no such things would work. In this exercise I was so successful that my null hypothesis was unequivocally confirmed (unpublished study).

Then, at the Annual Conference of the American Psychological Association (APA) in 1975, Clyde Parker's students came forward with the fruits of three years' research on our developmental scheme. Carol Widick examined the scheme's theoretical structure. L. Lee Knefelkamp and Widick reported on college-level courses taught through "Developmental Instruction" based on the scheme. They adjusted four instructional variables to their students' Positions on the scheme: (1) diversity, (2) learning activity, (3) degree of structuring of assignments, and (4) personalism. Pre-post measures demonstrated superior substantive mastery and developmental progress in students in this special program, compared with those in a comparable course taught traditionally. A measuring instrument developed by Knefelkamp and Widick included sentence-completion and paragraphs susceptible of reliable rating. At the same meeting, Pierre Meyer reported on the uses of the scheme in a study of religious development (Meyer, 1977); Ron Slepitza and Knefelkamp demonstrated its contribution to a model of career counseling making salient the shift from external to internal locus of control (Slepitza and Knefelkamp, 1976); and Stephenson and Hunt confirmed Knefelkamp and Widick's pedagogical methods for furthering college students' movements from dualism to relativistic thinking (Stephenson and Hunt, 1977).

The outlines of this symposium delineated the types of studies that other researchers and teachers were already conducting with reference to our scheme and that later workers would also pursue: (1) elaborations and extensions, (2) use of the scheme to illuminate particular aspects of development, (3) validations in various settings, (4) design of curriculums, instruction, and advising in the light of the scheme, and (5) instrumentation.

Elaborations and Extensions. Blythe Clinchy and Claire Zimmerman at Wellesley College have been engaged in a longitudinal study (1975) in which they first assumed the general validity of the original scheme in order to explore it in greater depth. Their interviews are therefore more focused than those of the original study, with interviewers offering the students groups of statements from which to start their thinking, and following with probes. In 1978-79 they will have thirty complete four-year sequences of rich data. Movement along the scale is already evident, regression rare. They have elaborated on several Positions, especially 3-5, in which they find substages. They are especially interested in exploring the process and contents of Commitment in women. In this regard, they found differential development of girls in a "traditional" and a "progressive" high school (Clinchy, Lief, and Young, 1977) and plan follow-up studies with alumnae. In exploring linguistic and other differences in the "voices" of women and men, they are presently collaborating with Ann Henderson of our office and with Carol Gilligan.

Referring to this scheme as an initial framework, Patricia King (1977a) analyzed the forms of "Reflective Probabilistic Judgment" evident in various levels of development, especially the later ones. Her labeling of Multiplistic thought as "Relativistic" (see the distinction made earlier between these modes of thought) led her to refer to the reasoning she examined as "beyond relativism" (King, 1977b, pp. 12, 17), whereas it would seem in the terms of this scheme to articulate relativistic processes themselves. However, her analysis and scoring procedures, together with those of her colleague Karen Kitchener (1977), provide an invaluable contribution to the understanding of the development of disciplined relativistic thought.

I have already mentioned Basseches' contribution to the identification and analysis of dialectical logic in the upper stages of development.[4] King (1977a) documents a decline in strictly Piagetian formal operations from high school through graduate school, remarking that such logic, so necessary to solutions of "puzzles" in physics, is inadequate for addressing "problems" in life. I would add that a premise common to most formal logic, namely that nothing can be A and not-A at the same time, is too humorless to live by. As one of our students said, "Irony gets both sides."

Joanne Kurfiss, in her early study (Kurfiss, 1975), examined in depth the conceptual properties of the developmental scheme and individuals' comparative rates of development in different areas. She compared five areas—(1) Moral Values, (2) Counseling and Advice, (3) Evaluation of Essays, (4) Responsibility of the Professor, and (5) the Nature of Knowledge—using as a measure the person's capacity to paraphrase statements characterizing various Positions of development in each area. She found considerable disparity in levels of development within individuals. Correlations were found between the areas of Moral Values and The Nature of Knowledge, and also among the other three areas, but not across these two groups. She surmised that the former pair are each relatively abstract and the later trio more concrete.

Use of the Scheme to Illuminate Particular Areas of Education. Confirming the usefulness of our scheme in respect to development of women, Carol Gilligan reports in the present volume on the consequence of rescoring Kohlberg ratings on the basis of the distinction we made between Multiplicity (anything-goes personalism) and contextual Relativism. The rescoring reverses Kohlberg's previously reported differences in rates and achievements of moral development between men and women at the upper levels (see also Gilligan and Murphy, 1979; Murphy and Gilligan, in press). Women appear less interested than men in the issues of conflict of rights presented in Kohlberg's dilemmas; rather, they develop contextually relativistic thinking in their search for the loci of care and responsibility in human relationships. Where this concern has been rated as personalistic "relativism" (Multiplicity), it has been devalued developmentally. The findings of Murphy and Gilligan (1980) are therefore of first-order import in the study of moral development. Their work also rescues sophomores from the condition of anomalous regression to which the earlier scoring had consigned them.

I have mentioned the work of Knefelkamp and Slepitza in career development and of Pierre Meyer in religion. Nowakowski and Laughney (1978) are working with Knefelkamp on the uses of the scheme in the design of training in health careers.

Clyde Parker initiated a Faculty Consultation Project with the College of Agriculture at Minnesota (Parker, 1978b). Interviews revealed the faculty's purposes to be couched in terms proper to our Positions 5 to 9:

> *Professor C:* One criticism I've had is that I ask questions that don't have absolute answers . . . I give them these kinds of questions because that's what life is. There aren't nice clean answers. They must come up with alternatives, weigh things, and make a decision.

Students were responding with plaints characteristic of Positions 2 to 3:

> *Student A:* In biology, there's really not two ways you can look at it. A bird has two feet. That's pretty conclusive.

These are brief samples of findings that are proving seminal in many undertakings in fac-

---

[4]For a study of the whole developmental progression itself in dialectical terms, see Heffernan and Griffith, 1979.

ulty development throughout the country in which the present scheme forms a point of reference (Chickering, 1976).

Design and Evaluation of Curriculums, Instruction, and Advising. In May of 1976, researchers and teachers interested in the uses of our scheme for improvement of instruction met at Ithaca College on the initiative of Laurence Copes (Copes, 1974) and Frances Rosamond, both assistant professors of mathematics. (I shall remark near the end of this chapter on an incident in this conference linking students' growth in sophistication in mathematics with their experience of loss—a connection I had never imagined.) The patterning provided an opportunity to share the validations and expansions under review and to derive a sense of their momentum.

Heffernan (1975) has this to say of the work of Laurence Copes and also Jack K. Johnson:

> The process in teaching college-level mathematics and their relationships to students' concepts of knowledge, per the Perry framework, have recently been examined by Laurence C. Copes, in a Ph.D. dissertation at Syracuse University. Copes' contention is that the presentation of the relativistic nature of mathematics is conducive to students' developing concepts of knowledge, and that certain teaching methods may be employed which reveal the creative and transcendent aspects of mathematics. He also has examined the theoretical potential of a number of teaching models for creating environments supportive of such conceptual development. His work and a dissertation by Jack K. Johnson relating Positions to open versus closed learning styles and a proposed study on teaching effectiveness in terms of the Perry scheme at the University of Wisconsin-Whitewater represent promising new directions in the improvement of teaching practices by conceptual rather than experiential guidelines [p. 497].

At the conference in Ithaca and subsequently, Knefelkamp and Widick have reported on continued elaboration of their model of Developmental Instruction (Widick and Simpson, 1978; Knefelkamp and Cornfeld, 1977). Others have extended its implications into peer training (Clement, 1977), career education (Touchton, 1978), graduate curriculum in counseling (Knefelkamp and Cornfeld, 1978), and the teaching of history (Widick and Simpson, 1978) and English drama (Sorum, 1976).

Most promising, too, is Knefelkamp's cross-cutting of this developmental scheme with the personality typology of John Holland. Given their choice among six approaches to an assignment centering on the same content, students regularly choose the style designed for their type and level of development (Knefelkamp, personal communication, 1978).

The uses of the scheme in the design of curriculums (Kovacs, 1977) and individual advising of adult learners, as at Empire State (Chickering, 1976), have been elaborated beyond my ability to document here.

Instrumentation. Some economical way of estimating the levels of students' thinking in given areas is central to the scheme's usefulness. Knefelkamp has carried this work furthest in company with Widick in 1975, and Slepitza in 1976. She is presently establishing the reliability of two instruments, both consisting of sentence-completions and short essays. The measure centering on students' thinking about their careers correlates .78 with expensive full-length interviews. Knefelkamp has a rating manual in manuscript.

The probing procedures of Clinchy and Zimmerman (1975) and the paraphrase method used by Kurfiss (1975) need further investigation. The former is economical in assuming the scheme's validity, thus bypassing the diffuseness of our original open interviews. The latter assumes that students can adequately paraphrase short paragraphs where the complexity is not more than a step beyond the forms in which they characteristically think but will misperceive the meaning of paragraphs in which the structure of thought is more advanced.

Two standards apply to all such instrumentations. Experimenters will naturally require quite precise assessments.[5] For ordinary teaching purposes, however, rough-hewn groupings of students evidencing dualistic thinking, multiplistic thinking, and relativistic thinking will provide ample base for such differential instruction as is economically possible in most classes. For ourselves, we use two estimates. In one we ask for a short essay on "How I learn best." In the other we ask students to grade, with reasons, two students' answers to an essay question on familiar material. One essay, full of facts, is chosen as superior by students honoring memorization but blind to relevance; the other is designed to be chosen as superior by students alert to the issue of interpretation of data in reference to the issue posed in the question. For such rough purposes as selecting those who most stand to benefit from our course in strategies of learning, these measures suffice.

Pending the further development of measurements, it is encouraging to note that in classes with up to forty students, teachers who have simply tuned their ears to the distinctions among modes of thought outlined in this chapter have found themselves able to distinguish students in the major levels of development *in vivo*. Following Knefelkamp's model, they have then been able to create two or three combinations of different supports and challenges appropriate to the major groupings in the class.

Cognitive Styles, Learning Strategies, and Development

The attempts to gear strategies of teaching to students' modes of learning raise the issue of the mutability or immutability of cognitive and learning styles. (See Johnson, 1975; Messick, 1976; Witkin, 1967; Kagan and Kogan, 1970; Whitla, 1978; Santostefano, 1969; and Kolb, in this volume. For a review of contradictory findings see Danserau, 1974, and also Letteri, 1978.)

Hardly any of the studies dealing with this issue (except Johnson's) seem to relate observations and measurements of cognitive or learning styles to a student's development of perceived meaning of learning tasks. Yet when students radically revise their notions of knowledge, would they not be likely to change their ways of going about getting it?

Here, for example, a student recounts the radical change in his ways of learning:

> Student: *Then* it was just the weight of the thing. *Now* it's, it's not so much how many pages there are on the reading list, it's more what the books are worth. What sort of ideas do they have. I mean, I can read a book now, without regard for the pages. And read it pretty rapidly and get the ideas. That is, I'm looking for the ideas rather than plodding over the words and, . . . well, the ideas

---

[5]There is a problem inherent in making finer measurements with such an ordinal scale. The Positions are coherent *gestalten* in a hierarchical sequence. The scheme says nothing about the "distance" between Positions. If a student is rated as structuring the world from Position 5 three times out of four and from Position 4 once in four, is the rating 4.75 meaningful? The difficulty is compounded in averaging such ratings for groups of students and finding the "modal student" to be at, say, Position 3.83. We ourselves are among those who have committed this sin against parametric statistics. Whether the ends justify the means is a nice problem in contextual ethics, but the act should be deliberate and explicit. The use of parenthetical notation of secondary and tertiary patterns evident in a student's thought—for example, 4(5) or 3(2)(4)—is now a popular and effective way to express location on such ordinal schemes.

are what count, and unless it's a particularly well-written book, you're not going to get that much pleasure out of how the words are put together. And after all, I've finally decided that you don't read a book just to say you've read it, just to say that you've gone through it. But you read the book for what it's worth, for what it has in it. And this, this doesn't count on any, for exam purposes, that is, it's a broad outlook really. I mean, before maybe I was reading, whereas *now* I tend to generalize the things and get the main ideas and concepts, and then pick up a few illustrations here and there, and amplifications when it seems worthwhile. But it's the broader picture. It's just not reading to have read, but reading to learn something, perhaps.

Since this student has perceived anew the nature of knowledge and of Authority's relation to it, he has discarded obedience in favor of his own agency as a maker of meaning. He dares to select, to judge, to build. As he studies, his intent is now not simply to conciliate Authority, external or internalized, but to learn on his own initiative.

In keeping with this revolution, he tells us that his entire manner of studying has undergone profound change. Judging from what he says, this change should be evident in his observable behavior, all the way from his manner of searching library shelves to his eye movements in scanning a page. These surface changes will, of course, express changes in his altered modes of learning and cognition.

Let us suppose that we had the opportunity to observe this student at work before his restructuring of the meaning of his world and that we had set out to draw inferences about his cognitive and learning styles, selecting our categories from such sources as the glossary of cognitive styles provided by Messick (1976) and the related array explored by Whitla (1977). From the student's literal interpretation of his assignments and his undifferentiated word-by-word reading, we might guess that he would be rated as stylistically *field-dependent* rather than *field-independent.* The probable flatness of his notes and the inevitable confusion among cumulative details in his memory would be congruent with a *leveling* rather than *sharpening* manner of cognition. We would rate him more *cautious* than *risk-taking,* more *constricted* than *flexible* in control, more *receptive* than *perceptive,* more *narrow* than *broad* in scanning, more *data-minded* than *strategy minded,* and more *descriptive* than *analytical* conceptually.

Were we then to observe him again after his conversion, we would of course be led to the opposite inference in every case. Even at the perceptual level, he might report that those words that developmental reading teachers are fond of calling *signposts*—words like *however, moreover, first of all, in sum,* and the like—are beginning to "jump off the page" at him, just as faces hidden in pictures of trees emerge for *field-independent* people.

Granted, this hypothetical observation contradicts the impressive research demonstrating that an individual's "cognitive styles" are remarkably stable over time. Yet it speaks to the present-day concern about the "matching" and "mismatching" of learning styles with teaching styles and the structures of various academic disciplines. Are students' learning or cognitive styles enduring characteristics of the person, subject only to minor and uncomfortable adjustment to uncongenial teaching or subject matter? Kolb's suggestion, in this book, that higher education tends to increase specialization of styles rather than to broaden them has recently been supported by Whitla's findings (Whitla, 1977).

Stability and Mutability of Learning Styles. As a person whose daily work is directed toward increasing the range of students' learning styles to enable them to construct strategies appropriate to different contexts, I have reason to question whether learning styles are as stabile as some measures have made them seem. Allow me to introduce my "evidence."

Over the past thirty years we have in our office counseled over 15,000 students. If I estimate that only one in three of these consulted us explicitly and directly about ways of learning, the sample is still 5,000. In addition, we have provided direct instruction in strategies of learning to another 15,000 students in classes enrolling 80 to 200 at a time. Of this combined sample of 20,000 students (mostly bright undergraduates and graduate students with a scattering of advanced high school students, middle-aged students, and professors) I would say that a minimum of 40 percent reported to us, and demonstrated for us, the same kind of revolution in purpose and strategies of learning reported by the student just quoted; another 30 percent, who seemed already to have attained such a vision of meaning and purpose, used the time with us simply to extend and refine their range of strategies and skills; another 10 percent left us with inconclusive evidence; and 15 percent had a very hard time indeed.

Will the reader be content with that 40 percent figure—800 vivid instances of workaday observation as a substitute for some laboratory-type hard data? I am bargaining; the reader may make a much smaller concession and still share in the dilemma I wish to present. What I feel should concern all educators is the kind of contrast illustrated by the gap between those who experienced this "revolution" and those 15 percent who had a very hard time indeed. What can account for this difference in their response, at a given moment in their lives, to an invitation to alter certain strategies of learning?

Allow me to back up a moment and describe the nature of our instructional effort. Thirty years ago we inherited a conventional "developmental speed-reading" program, including instruction in preliminary scanning of reading material, asking oneself questions, watching for signposts, and all the rest, together with instructional films for pacing and increasing "eye-span." We had not a clue as to how "developmental" such instruction was going to turn out to be, but we did learn in our one-to-one counseling that ways of reading were often integrally embedded in assumptions about purpose, authority, and morals. Students who read word by word often told us that our recommendation to "look ahead" was commending to them a form of "cheating" in which they refused to participate. We found that these students had invested their courage in "concentrating" (that is, *not thinking* of other things) for long hours, and we could not help them to concentrate *on* thinking about what an author was saying until they could reinvest their courage in the risks of judgment.

Such findings led us to dramatize for the students in our large "reading course" the contrasting constellations of meaning, feeling, ethics, and risk that surround the more passive and more active strategies of reading. We created illustrative dramatic monologues of what it felt like to be studying in one's room and then asked the students to engage in reading exercises based on such contrasting assumptions. At the same time, we learned how necessary it was to continue daily the conventional exercises and visual aids as a "support."

Nowadays we regularly provide on the students' work sheets for each day a space for comment, and the next day we may read two or three to the class, anonymously. Recently, in about the middle of the eighteen-day program, I read this comment among others:

> Why does the instructor waste so much time *ranting*? We should be doing more exercises and films. All that ranting takes up time that could be *used.*

This provoked some laughter and many "comments" on the next day's sheets. These comments fell into four types, of which the following are representative:

Type 1. The "ranting" fellow is *right*! You're very funny *sometimes,* but when are you going to teach us to *read faster*?

Type 2. I don't think you're "ranting." I understand what you're saying, but I can't seem to *do* it, damn it.

Type 3. Hey! Rant away! I'm *getting* it! I've *got* it! Last week I did a research paper in half the time and got an A! More! More!

Type 4. Well, it isn't "ranting," but why do you go on repeating yourself? All you've been saying all along is, "think while you read," and I knew that in high school. (But it's still a good course! Courage!)

In the early 1950s, in keeping with much thinking of the time, we would have seen these comments as emanating from different "types" of students. Indeed, when we started out on the study I am summarizing in this chapter, we intended to document the experience of these different types—the "authoritarian," the "dogmatic," the "intolerant of ambiguity," and their opposites. Then, as we listened year by year, it was the students who turned us into developmentalists.

We now see comments of Types 4, 3, and 1 as follows:

- Type 4: Students commenting in this way have come to college construing the academic world in meanings characteristic of at least Position 5 in our scheme. Their capacity to sense the instructor's predicament ("Courage!") suggests that they perceive at these levels in their social worlds as well.
- Type 3: Students making such comments have just discovered (constructed?) the meanings we locate at Position 5 and beyond and have begun to use new strategies of learning and communicating appropriate to these meanings.
- Type 1: Students making such comments are construing the academic world through meanings we characterize as Position 2 or 3. Since I am offering alternatives at Position 5+, two Positions beyond their level of development, the students cannot hear me. Instead, they assimilate my behavior to their own structures by seeing it as "ranting," in which Authority is failing in its duties.

I shall return to the plight of students making comments of Type 2 in a moment. First, I wish to consider students of Types 4 and 1. Apparently, I was boring the former and had so far failed to "reach" the latter. The tone of the former is one of mild frustration, while the latter convey a sense of mounting anxiety and anger. In an early experiment in "matching and mismatching" of teaching-learning styles, Gordon Allport and Lauren Wispe gave instruction congruent and incongruent with students' preferred styles (Wispe, 1951). The experimenters assigned students judged to "want more direction" to one pair of sections and students judged to "want more permissiveness" to another pair of sections. In each of these pairs of sections, one section received its preferred style of teaching and the other received the opposite. The results in terms of students' satisfaction and frustration were as predicted. What startled the experimenters was the intensity of anxiety and hostility expressed by the students who desired precise directions and failed to receive them. In contrast, those who were disappointed of their desired freedom simply reported feeling frustrated.

If we consider "want more direction" and "want more permissiveness" in terms of our scheme, the parallel to our comment sheets is striking. Students thinking in the forms of advanced Positions can understand earlier meanings and procedures and be impatient; students thinking in earlier forms cannot understand the assumptions of advanced Positions. The fear of abandonment evident in Type 1 comments is understandable.

Toward the end of our course there are always some Type 1 comments still coming to us, ever more urgent, and we redouble our efforts to reach these students, mainly through individual counseling. This context makes these results possible: (a) Some students, encouraged to speak freely about their experience and concerns, will suddenly hit upon the very approach they missed in class and exclaim, "Oh, is that what you've been saying in class?" (b) Other students will respond to the counseling session as they did to the course; they give the impression that their emotional controls are so bound up with an internalization of the all-or-none, authority-oriented structures of Positions 2 and 3 that they cannot contemplate change without overwhelming anxiety. Whether their stylistic predispositions could allow them to act on new meanings if they could generate them cannot be determined. (c) The remaining students will make the same discoveries as the first group but not be able to make use of their discoveries. They will then report back with comments of Type 2 ("I understand you, but I can't do it").

We take it that students speaking to us through Type 2 comments have come to construe their educational worlds in ways that make the strategies we offer meaningful and desirable, especially for their approach to reading and research in expository materials characteristic of so much of higher education. Granted the academic performance they have demonstrated in their primary and secondary schooling, their measured "aptitude," and their evident emotional resilience, their sense of incapacity to "do" these strategies suggests strongly that their particular "styles" of cognition, information processing, or learning may be relatively resistant to change and of a kind that do not support the skills required by the strategies we invite them to learn.

Cognitive "Styles" Versus "Strategies." The questions with which I began this digression had to do with the stability and mutability of learning "strategies" and cognitive "styles." I have tried to indicate how this question is embedded in a fabric patterned by developmental status, emotional readiness to develop new interpretations of the world, "dynamics" and traits of personality, and the contexts of teaching and counseling. It should be clear why the researches on "strategies" and "styles" often appear contradictory. Despite the importance of all these threads to higher education, not even the terms of the question are stable; what for one writer is "style" is "strategy" for another.

Educators would be greatly aided in their efforts to make use of these vital researches if the investigators could come to some rough consensus about terms. I would propose that cognitive *style* be used to refer to the relatively stable, preferred configuration of tactics that a person tends to employ somewhat inflexibly in a wide range of environmental negotiations. The word *strategy* could then be used to refer to a configuration of tactics chosen or constructed from an array of available alternatives to address a *particular kind* of environmental negotiation. In short, a strategy would be dominant over "style."

Against this background, I can now say that cognitive styles have been demonstrated to be in many instances highly stable generalized traits often ill-fitted to the cognitive task at hand. However, I can also say that many people demonstrate (both rapid and gradual) acquisition of alternative styles, which then become available to strategies adaptable to the character of different tasks. The stability and mutability of styles are therefore both characteristics in need of explication. The apparently contradictory findings reported by Danserau (1974), for example, may reflect the interests and methods of the researchers. Such is the present state of the art. As practitioners in higher education, meanwhile, we must keep the stability of styles in mind while we also design instruction to maximize the probability that students will develop appropriate strategies.

Kolb, in this book, brilliantly summarizes the development of styles of "experiential learning," positing stages (phases) of *acquisition, specialization,* and *integration.* Acquisition is complete in adolescence. Specialization, the strengthening of one's preferred style, continues through higher education and into midlife. Integration, "the reassertion and expression of the nondominant adaptive modes or learning styles," which makes possible the exercise of what I call strategies, emerges in later life. Kolb's study at M.I.T. documenting the specialization process is paralleled by Whitla's (1977) contemporaneous study at three colleges: students with certain styles who major in subjects with structures congruent with these styles tend to be happy in their work and to become even more specialized in their styles.

These findings concern tendencies or differences statistically significant but "small" (Whitla, 1978). In order to obtain these differences, also, many measurements of "style" must be made under conditions in which the student is put under such stringent time limits that the possibility to exercise choice among procedures is virtually eliminated (Whitla, 1978). These studies, then, have documented the existence of individual differences in styles at certain levels, using large samples under limiting conditions. As educators, however, we stand to learn as much from the minority in the sample as from the majority. What would those students have to tell us who *have* developed a wider range of strategies, instead of specializing?

I suggest that further researches into cognitive and learning styles must include a consideration of the different meanings and purposes that the learners ascribe to learning in different contexts and at different times in their lives. This consideration remains primary to the whole problem of relating strategies and styles of teaching to strategies and styles of learning.

Values and Costs

From all that has been published, written but unpublished, in process of being written, and "personally communicated," I conclude that our scheme of development can be of more practical use to educators than I first supposed (Perry, 1970). Not only did I assume a substantial gap to exist between the scheme and the actual curriculum or classroom but also I felt a deep aversion to "application" in the sense of transforming a purely descriptive formulation of students' experience into a prescriptive program intended to "get" students to develop (Perry, 1974). Lee Knefelkamp took the initiative in challenging me on both these matters, and I joined in a battle that I have found edifying to lose.

Confronting the issues of values and ethics first, Knefelkamp pointed to my agreement that the values inherent in the scheme itself were indeed congruent with the commonly stated objectives of liberal education; there was a sense, then, in which progression toward these general values was inherently prescriptive. But in what sense? Surely educators cannot coerce students into intellectual and ethical development, even if it were ethical to do so. What was prescriptive was that the teaching and curriculums be optimally designed to invite, encourage, challenge, and support students in such development. Our scheme, therefore, is helpful to the extent that it contributes to the ability of planners and teachers to *communicate* with students who make meaning in different ways and to provide differential opportunities for their progress. Within the limits of institutional resources and teachers' energies, a better understanding of where different students are "coming from" can save wasted effort and maximize the effort expended. Knefelkamp has convinced me not only by this logic but by her demonstrations (see, for example, Knefelkamp, 1975).

At the same time, I am impressed by the extent of the revolution in our own thinking—a change that has been forced upon all of us who have become involved over time in what might be called *developmental phenomenology*. We seem so unconsciously immersed in the dregs of the Lockean tradition that we still suppose that there is at least some space in students' heads where a *tabula rasa* awaits the imprint of our wisdom. We observe in ourselves that there seems to be a developmental process involved in coming to understand development. We begin to feel strange and lonely.

I want to burst out to you, my reader, "Look! Do I sound crazy in saying that the *students* are the source of the meanings they will make of you? All right, so you feel that you are making meaning for them; you know your subject, they do not. But it is the meanings they make of your meanings that matter!" Obviously. Why am I shouting? After all, it is the meanings you make of my meanings that matter, and shouting will not help. It is not simply that I have forgotten the long trail of my own accommodations. Our common enemy is that Lockean heritage:

I find hope in the confluence of developmental studies. I do not mean parallelism in their "stages," which would be a dubious virtue in theories that should be complementary. I mean that whether the investigator starts from empirical observations made largely from outside (as did Loevinger with observations of sequential integrations of concerns; or Kohlberg with observations of sequential criteria in moral reasoning) or starts with empathic participation in the phenomenal experience of individuals (as we did in this study) the end products tend to converge. Weathersby, in the second chapter of this book, extends the rating cues of Loevinger's scale to reveal the patterning of individuals' construction of meaning in their lives and learning. Gilligan, in her chapter, does the same with the cues for Kohlberg's scoring, as Kegan (1977, 1979) has also done in an extraordinary reinterpretation of acute depression as a concomitant of transition. This confluence suggests that the centrality of the individual learner as a maker of meaning may be a radical notion but quite likely congruent with the facts.

I have spoken of development of meaning-making as a good thing, at least in our complex world. I have implied, too, in tracing the transitions of the scheme, that development has its costs. I want to end, therefore, with the educator's responsibility to hear and honor, by simple acknowledgment, the students' losses.

I have remarked elsewhere (Perry, 1978) on the importance we have come to ascribe to a student's "allowing for grief" in the process of growth, especially in the rapid movement from the limitless potentials of youth to the particular realities of adulthood. Each of the upheavals of cognitive growth threatens the balance between vitality and depression, hope and despair. It may be a great joy to discover a new and more complex way of thinking and seeing; but yesterday one thought in simpler ways, and hope and aspiration were embedded in those ways. Now that those ways are to be left behind, must hope be abandoned too?

It appears that it takes a little time for the guts to catch up with such leaps of the mind. The untangling of hope from innocence, for example, when innocence is "lost," may require more than a few moments in which to move from despair through sadness to a wry nostalgia. Like all mourning, it is less costly when "known" by another. When a sense of loss is accorded the honor of acknowledgment, movement is more rapid and the risk of getting stuck in apathy, alienation, or depression is reduced. One thing seemed clear: Students who have just taken a major step will be unlikely to take another until they have come to terms with the losses attendant on the first.

"Hearing" a student at such a moment may be best expressed simply by a nod or a respectful silence. We have been accustomed to these suspended moments in our counseling hours. But now we ask ourselves more broadly, "What is the responsibility of teachers, including ourselves, as we help our students to transcend their simpler ways of knowing?" Jesse Taft, a follower of Otto Rank, once wrote that "the therapist becomes the repository of the outworn self" (Taft, 1933). Perhaps the metaphor is too passive. Perhaps, in moments of major growth, the instructor can serve as a bridge linking the old self with the new: "He knew me when, and he knows me now."

There may be no subject matter in which teachers are wholly immune to the responsibilities of such moments. I was told of an extreme instance by a professor of mathematics who remarked to me after a meeting that he now understood the breakdown of a freshman to whom he insisted that there were indeed three equally good ways of finding the answer to a given problem. "I didn't even tell him there were other answers—just three ways of finding *the* answer—and he went all to pieces." The story made poignant for me a moment in the conference at Ithaca: I was attending the last minutes of a workshop "On Relativism in the Teaching of Mathematics," and on the board was an algebraic proof such as a student might find in an advanced junior class in high school. Under it was another proof, as offered in senior year in calculus, which revealed the false assumptions of the first. Discussion was lively and highly philosophical. The moderator was smiling and saying over and over, "Yes, ladies and gentlemen, but you haven't told me what *happened* to that *first* proof? It was a certainty, wasn't it? I want to know: where did it *go*?" The participants were sobered by their evident reluctance to address this question and finally remarked that it was after all, the same question Gödel has invited us to ask ourselves of all proofs. They wondered, since the question is painfully devoid of an answer, if we are refusing to hear the students ask it.

It is now clear to me that a teacher's confirmatory offering of community is necessary even in the highest reaches of development. Here, where both formal logic and even "reflective probabilistic judgment" fail to support the tensions of life's paradoxes, the students' development is at risk. Even if students do achieve a sense of irony, it may drift into a bitter alienation. Many institutions of higher learning have succeeded, sometimes through careful planning, sometimes through the sheer accident of their internal diversity, in providing for students' growth beyond dualistic thought into the discovery of disciplined contextual relativism. Many would hope to encourage in their students the values of Commitment, and to provide in their faculties the requisite models. To meet this promise, we must all learn how to validate for our students a dialectical mode of thought, which at first seems "irrational," and then to assist them in honoring its limits. To do this, we need to teach dialectically—that is, to introduce our students, as our greatest teachers have introduced us, not only to the orderly certainties of our subject matter but to its unresolved dilemmas. This is an art that requires timing, learned only by paying close attention to students' ways of making meaning.

I have before me the senior thesis of a student who survived an accident in his freshman year that led to the medical prediction that he could never read again or return to academic work. His defiance of the prediction, in the midst of his acceptance of it, led five years later to this honors thesis on the subject of Hope. His preface ends:

> I would define hope as a human self-transcending movement. Hope rests on a foundation of antithesis, particularly the dialectic of possibility and limitation. It serves a centering function within this dialectic; the hoping person at once acknowledges finitude and limitation, and with and within these limitations affirms the power to move forward in time and to create. With the affirmation of this power, hope is not just a mode of being in the world, but brings a world into being. The dialectical character of hope creates the possibility that, in acknowledging limitation and affirming creative possibility, the centered self may transcend its elements [Holmes, 1974].

References

Adams, H. B. *The Education of Henry Adams.* New York: Modern Library, 1931. (Originally published 1907.)

Allport, G. W. *Becoming.* New Haven, Conn.: Yale University Press, 1955.

Baron, J. "Some Theories of College Instruction." *Higher Education,* 1975, *4,* 149-172.

Basseches, M. "Beyond Closed-System Problem-Solving: A Study of Meta-Systematic Aspects of Mature Thought." Unpublished doctoral dissertation, Harvard University, 1978.

Blake, L. "A Measure of Developmental Change: A Cross-Sectional Study." Paper presented at 84th annual meeting of the American Psychological Association, Washington, D.C., September 1976.

Boyd, D. "Some Thoughts on a Comparison of Perry and Kohlberg." Unpublished manuscript, Harvard University, 1972.

Broughton, J. M. "The Development of Natural Epistemology in Adolescence and Early Childhood." Unpublished doctoral dissertation, Harvard University, 1975.

Buerk, D. "Women and Math Anxiety/Avoidance: A Developmental Approach." Doctoral dissertation proposal, State University of New York at Buffalo, 1979.

Camus, A. *The Myth of Sisyphus.* New York: Knopf, 1955.

Chandler, M. J. "Relativism and the Problem of Epistemological Loneliness." *Human Development,* 1975, *18,* 171-180.

Chickering, A. W. "Developmental Change as a Major Outcome." In M. T. Keeton and Associates, *Experiential Learning: Rationale, Characteristics, and Assessment.* San Francisco: Jossey-Bass, 1976.

Chickering, A. W. "A Conceptual Framework for College Development." Unpublished manuscript, Empire State College.

Chickering, A. W. "The Developmental and Educational Needs of Adults." Unpublished manuscript, Empire State College.

Clement, L., and others. "Paraprofessionals—Development of Our Systems and Our Human Resources—a Model for Training." Paper presented at the Maryland Student Affairs Conference, University of Maryland, March 1977.

Clinchy, B., Lief, J., and Young, P. "Epistemological and Moral Development in Girls from a Traditional and a Progressive High School." *Journal of Educational Psychology,* 1977, *69* (4), 337-343.

Clinchy, B., and Zimmerman, C. "Cognitive Development in College." Unpublished paper, Wellesley College, June 1975.

Connell, C. W. "Attitude and Development as Factors in the Learning of History: The Work of William Perry." Paper presented to the annual meeting of the American Historical Association, San Francisco, 1978.

Copes, J. "Forms and Patterns: A Book Review." *The Herald.* Geneva, New York: Hobart and William Smith Colleges, 1979.

Copes, L. "Teaching Models for College Mathematics." Unpublished doctoral dissertation, Syracuse University, 1974.

Copes, L. "Mathematics Education—or Vice Versa?" Paper presented at meeting of Seaway Section, Mathematical Association of America, 1976a.

Copes, L. "Musings on Growing." Unpublished manuscript presented to the Ithaca College faculty as an invitation to the Ithaca Perry Conference, 1976b.

Copes, L. "Mathematics and the Perry Development Scheme." Paper presented at 3rd International Conference on Educational Mathematics, 1978.

Copes, L. "College Teaching, Mathematics, and the Perry Development Scheme." Unpublished paper, Institute for Studies in Educational Mathematics, St. Paul, Minn., 1980.

Copes, L. "The Perry Development Scheme and the Teaching of Mathematics." In D. Tall (Ed.), *Proceedings of the Third International Conference for Psychology in Mathematics Education.* Warwick, England: University of Warwick, in press.

Cornfeld, J., and Knefelkamp, L. "Application of Student Development Theory to Graduate Education Sequence. The Developmental Instruction Design of a Year-Long Counselor Education Curriculum." In *Integrating Student Development Services and Professional Educations. The Maryland Approach.* A Commission XII sponsored presentation at the American College Personnel Association National Convention, Denver, 1977.

Danserau, D. *Learning Strategies: A Review and Synthesis of the Current Literature.* US AFHRL Technical Report 74-70, December 1974.

Entwistle, N., and Hounsell, D. "How Students Learn: Implications for Teaching in Higher Education." In N. Entwistle and D. Hounsell (Eds.), *How Students Learn.* Lancaster, England: Institute for Research and Development in Post-Compulsory Education, University of Lancaster, 1975.

Fowler, J. W. "Mapping Faith's Structures: A Developmental Overview." In J. W. Fowler, S. Keen, and J. Berryman (Eds.), *Life-Maps: The Human Journey of Faith.* Waco, Tex.: Word Books, 1978.

Froberg, B., and Parker, C. A. "Progress Report on the Developmental Instruction Project." Minneapolis: College of Agriculture, University of Minnesota, 1976.

Gilligan, C. "In a Different Voice: Women's Conceptions of Self and of Morality." *Harvard Education Review,* 1977, *47,* 481-517.

Gilligan, C., and Murphy, J. M. "The Philosopher and the 'Dilemma of Fact': Evidence for Continuing Development from Adolescence to Adulthood." In D. Kuhn (Ed.), *New Directions for Child Development: Intellectual Development Beyond Childhood,* no. 5. San Francisco: Jossey-Bass, 1979.

Goldberger, N. "Developmental Assumptions Underlying Models of General Education." Paper presented at Conference on General Education, William Patterson College, 1979a.

Goldberger, N. "Meeting the Developmental Needs of the Early College Student: The Simon's Rock Experience." Unpublished manuscript, Simon's Rock Early College, 1979b.

Goldberger, N., Marwine, A., and Paskus, J. "The Relationship Between Intellectual Stage and the Behavior of College Freshmen in the Classroom." Unpublished manuscript, Simon's Rock Early College, 1978.

Goldsmith, S. "Application of the Perry Schema in a College Course on Human Identity." *Pupil Personnel Services Journal,* Minnesota Department of Education, 1977, *6* (1), 185-196.

Hartley, A. "Contexts for Learning." *Bulletin* of the Office of Educational Development, University of Wisconsin at Green Bay, September 1974.

Hartley, A. "Contexts for Academic Achievement." *Bulletin* of the Office of Educational Development, University of Wisconsin at Green Bay, August 1973.

Heffernan, J. "Identity Formation, Identity Orientations, and Sex Differences Related to College Environment Features: A Comparative Study of Conventional and Innovative Undergraduate Programs." Unpublished doctoral dissertation, University of Michigan, 1971.

Heffernan, J. "An Analytical Framework for Planning and Research in Higher Education." *Liberal Education,* 1975, *61,* 493-503.

Heffernan, J., and Griffith, J. "Implications of a Dialectical Model for Extending the Perry Scheme of Development." Paper presented at the Association for the Study of Higher Education, Syracuse University, 1979.

Holden, J. C. "Structures of Ego Development in the College Student: An Interdisciplinary Approach." Unpublished doctoral dissertation, University of Wisconsin at Madison, 1978.

Holmes, L. "The Nature of Hope." Senior honors thesis, Harvard College, 1974.

Hursh, B. A., and Barzak, L. "Toward Cognitive Development Through Field Studies." *Journal of Higher Education,* 1979, *50,* 63-78.

Johnson, J. "Freshman Responses to Autonomous Learning: A Study of Intrinsic Versus Extrinsic Dispositions to Learn." Unpublished doctoral dissertation, University of Minnesota, 1975.

Kagan, J., and Kogan, N. "Individual Variation in Cognitive Processes." In P. H. Mussen (Ed.), *Carmichael's Manual of Child Psychology.* Vol. 1. New York: Wiley, 1970.

Kaul, T. J. "Students' Schemes and Harvard Dreams." *Contemporary Psychology,* 1971, *16,* 657-658.

Kegan, R. G. "Ego and Truth: Personality and the Piaget Paradigm." Unpublished doctoral dissertation, Harvard University, 1977.

Kegan, R. G. "The Evolving Self: A Process Conception for Ego Psychology." *The Counseling Psychologist,* 1979, *8* (2), 5-34.

Keniston, K. *The Uncommitted.* New York: Harcourt Brace Jovanovich, 1960.

King, P. M. "Perry's Scheme of Intellectual and Ethical Development: A Look at Assessment." Unpublished manuscript, University of Minnesota, 1975.

King, P. M. "The Study of Commitment: Pursuing an Ambiguous Construct." Paper presented at 84th annual meeting of the American Psychological Association, Washington, D.C., September 1976.

King, P. M. "The Development of Reflective Judgment and Formal Operational Thinking in Adolescents and Young Adults." Unpublished doctoral dissertation, University of Minnesota, 1977a.

King, P. M. "Taking a Stand with Yourself: Making Commitments in a Relativistic World." Unpublished manuscript, University of Minnesota, 1977b.

King, P. M. "William Perry's Theory of Intellectual and Ethical Development." In L. Knefelkamp, C. Widick, and C. A. Parker (Eds.), *New Directions for Student Services: Applying New Developmental Findings,* no. 4. San Francisco: Jossey-Bass, 1978.

King, P. M., and Parker, C. A. "Assessing Intellectual Development in the College Years." A report from the Instructional Improvement Project, University of Minnesota, 1978.

Kitchener, K. S. "Intellect and Identity: Measuring Parallel Processes in the Perry Scheme." Unpublished manuscript, University of Minnesota, 1976a.

Kitchener, K. S. "The Perry Scheme: A Review and Critique." Paper presented at 84th annual meeting of the American Psychological Association, Washington, D.C., 1976b.

Kitchener, K. S. "Intellectual Development in Late Adolescents and Young Adults: Reflective Judgment and Verbal Reasoning." Unpublished doctoral dissertation, University of Minnesota, 1977.

Kitchener, K. S. "Reflective Judgment: Concepts in Justification and Their Relationship to Age and Education." Unpublished manuscript, University of Minnesota, 1979.

Kitchener, K. S., and King, P. M. "Intellectual Development Beyond Adolescence: Reflective Judgment, Formal Operations, and Verbal Reasoning." Unpublished manuscript, University of Minnesota, 1978.

Knefelkamp, L. L. "Developmental Instruction: Fostering Intellectual and Personal Growth in College Students." Unpublished doctoral dissertation, University of Minnesota, 1974.

Knefelkamp, L. L. "Developmental Instruction: Fostering Intellectual and Personal Growth of College Students." Paper presented at 83rd annual meeting of the American Psychological Association, Chicago, August 1975.

Knefelkamp, L. L. "Training Manual for Perry Raters and Rater Training Cue Sheets." Unpublished mimeograph, University of Maryland, 1978.

Knefelkamp, L. L., and Cornfeld, J. L. "Counselor Education Basic Survey." Unpublished mimeograph, University of Maryland, 1975.

Knefelkamp, L. L., and Cornfeld, J. L. "Application of Student Development Theory to Graduate Education: The Developmental Instruction Design of a Year-Long Counselor Education Curriculum." Paper presented at the American College Personnel Association National Convention, Denver, 1977.

Knefelkamp, L. L., and Cornfeld, J. L. "The Developmental Issues of Graduate Students: A Model of Assessment and a Model of Response." Paper presented at the American Personnel and Guidance Association National Convention, Washington, D.C., 1978.

Knefelkamp, L. L., and Cornfeld, J. L. "Combining Student Stages and Style in the Design of Learning Environments: Using Holland Typologies and Perry Stages." Paper presented to the American College Personnel Association, Los Angeles, March 1979.

Knefelkamp, L. L., and Slepitza, R. "A Cognitive-Developmental Model of Career Development: An Adaptation of the Perry Scheme." *The Counseling Psychologist,* 1976, *6* (3), 53-58. Reprinted in C. Parker (Ed.), *Encouraging Development in College Students.* Minneapolis: University of Minnesota Press, 1978a.

Knefelkamp, L. L., and Slepitza, R. A. Comments made in Perry Rater Training Seminar, University of Maryland, 1978b.

Knefelkamp, L. L., Widick, C., and Parker, C. A. (Eds.). *New Directions for Student Services: Applying New Developmental Findings,* no. 4. San Francisco: Jossey-Bass, 1978.

Knefelkamp, L. L., Widick, C., and Stroad, B. "Cognitive-Developmental Theory: A Guide to Counseling Women." *The Counseling Psychologist,* 1976, *6* (2), 15-19.

Kohlberg, L. "The Concepts of Developmental Psychology as the Central Guide to Education: Examples from Cognitive, Moral, and Psychological Education." In M. C. Reynolds (Ed.), *Proceedings of the Conference on Psychology and the Process of Schooling in the Next Decade: Alternative Conceptions.* Washington, D.C., 1975.

Kohlberg, L., and Kramer, R. "Continuities and Discontinuities in Childhood and Adult Moral Development." *Human Development,* 1969, *12,* 93-120.

Kovacs, I. D. "Development of Cognitive, Coping, and Relational Abilities Through the Study of Participation in the University." Paper presented at 3rd International Conference on Improving University Teaching, Newcastle-on-Tyne, England, 1977.

Kroll, M., and Associates. *Career Development: Growth and Crisis.* New York: Wiley, 1970.

Kurfiss, J. "A Neo-Piagetian Analysis of Erikson's 'Identity' Formulation of Late Adolescent Development." In S. Modgil and C. Modgil (Eds.), *Piagetian Research: Compilation and Commentary.* New York: Humanities Press, 1974.

Kurfiss, J. "Late Adolescent Development: A Structural Epistemological Perspective." Unpublished doctoral dissertation, University of Washington, 1975.

Kurfiss, J. "What Makes Students Grow? A Survey and Theoretical Integration of Literature on College Student Development." Unpublished manuscript, Eastern Oregon State College, 1976.

Kurfiss, J. "Sequentiality and Structure in a Cognitive Model of College Student Development." *Developmental Psychology,* 1977, *13,* 565-571.

Lawson, J. M. "Review of the Literature on Perry Research." Unpublished manuscript, University of Minnesota, 1978.

Letteri, C. A. *Research Report of the Center for Cognitive Studies.* University of Vermont, 1978.

Mason, K. E. "Effects of Developmental Instruction on the Development of Cognitive Complexity, Locus of Control, and Empathy in Beginning Counseling Graduate Students." Unpublished master's thesis, University of Maryland, 1978.

Messick, S., and Associates. *Individuality in Learning: Implications of Cognitive Styles and Creativity for Human Development.* San Francisco: Jossey-Bass, 1976.

Meyer, P. "Intellectual Development: Analysis of Religious Content." *The Counseling Psychologist,* 1977, *6* (4), 47-50.

Meyerson, L. "Conception of Knowledge in Mathematics: Interaction with and Applications to a Teaching Methods Course." Unpublished doctoral dissertation, State University of New York at Buffalo, 1977.

Murphy, J. M. "Intellectual and Moral Development from Adolescence to Adulthood." Unpublished manuscript, Harvard University, 1979a.

Murphy, J. M. "Moral Judgment Coding Based on Perry's Scheme." Unpublished manuscript, Harvard University, 1979b.

Murphy, J. M., and Gilligan, C. "Moral Development in Late Adolescence and Adulthood: A Critique and Reconstruction of Kohlberg's Theory." *Human Development,* in press.

Nowakowski, L., and Laughney, J. "Health Education: Theory of Curriculum Design—Developmental Implementation." Unpublished manuscript, School of Nursing, Georgetown University, 1978.

Orr, C. J. "Communication, Relativism, and Student Development." *Communications Education,* 1978, *27* (2), 80-98.

Parker, C. A. (Ed.). *Encouraging Development in College Students.* Minneapolis: University of Minnesota Press, 1978a.

Parker, C. A. "Individualized Approach to Improving Instruction." *National Association of Colleges and Teachers of Agriculture Journal,* 1978b, *22,* 14-28.

Parker, C. A. "Teaching Students to Cope with Complexity and Uncertainty." Unpublished manuscript, University of Minnesota, 1979.

Parker, C. A., and Lawson, J. M. "From Theory to Practice to Theory: Consulting with College Faculty." *Personnel and Guidance Journal,* 1978, *56,* 424-427.

Perry, W. G., Jr. "Students' Use and Misuse of Reading Skills: A Report to the Faculty." *Harvard Educational Review,* 1959, *29* (3), 193-200.

Perry, W. G., Jr. "Examsmanship and the Liberal Arts: An Epistemological Inquiry." In M. Eastman and others (Eds.), *The Norton Reader.* New York: Norton, 1969.

Perry, W. G., Jr. *Forms of Intellectual and Ethical Development in the College Years: A Scheme.* New York: Holt, Rinehart and Winston, 1970.

Perry, W. G., Jr. "Counseling." In *Annual Report of the Bureau of Study Counsel, Harvard University, 1973-74.* Cambridge, Mass.: Harvard University Press, 1974.

Perry, W. G., Jr. "On Advising and Counseling." In *Annual Report of the Bureau of Study Counsel, Harvard University, 1974-75.* Cambridge, Mass.: Harvard University Press, 1975.

Perry, W. G., Jr. "A Study of Learning." In *Annual Report of the Bureau of Study Counsel, Harvard University, 1975-76.* Cambridge, Mass.: Harvard University Press, 1976.

Perry, W. G., Jr. "Comments, Appreciative and Cautionary." *The Counseling Psychologist,* 1977a, *6* (4), 51-52.

Perry, W. G., Jr. "Intellectual and Ethical Forms of Development." In *Pupil Personnel Services Journal,* Minnesota Department of Education, 1977b, *6* (1), 61-68.

Perry, W. G., Jr. "Sharing in the Costs of Growth, and Comments on Chapters 2, 3, 5, and 6." In C. A. Parker (Ed.), *Encouraging Development in College Students.* Minneapolis: University of Minnesota, 1978.

Perry, W. G., Jr., and Whitlock, C. P. "Of Study and the Man." In *Harvard Alumni Bulletin,* 1958.

Perry, W. G., Jr., and others. *Patterns of Development in Thought and Values of Students in a Liberal Arts College: A Validation of a Scheme.* United States Department of Health, Education, and Welfare, Office of Education, Bureau of Research, Final Report, Project No. 5-0825, Contract No. SAE-8973, April 1968.

Polanyi, M. *Personal Knowledge: Towards a Post-Critical Philosophy.* Chicago: University of Chicago Press, 1958.

Riegel, K. F. "Dialectic Operations: The Final Period of Cognitive Development." *Human Development,* 1973, *16,* 346-370.

Rust, V. "Review of *Forms of Intellectual and Ethical Development in the College Years: A Scheme,* by William G. Perry, Jr." *Teachers College Record,* December 1970, *72,* 305-307.

Salyard, A. "The Educated American: A Study of Intellectual Development in Adulthood." Doctoral dissertation in progress, University of California at Los Angeles.

Santostefano, S. "Cognitive Controls v. Cognitive Styles: Diagnosing and Treating Cognitive Disabilities in Children." *Seminars in Psychiatry,* 1969, *1,* 291-317.

Slepitza, R. A., and Knefelkamp, L. L. "Perry's Scheme of Intellectual Development: An Adaptation to Career Counseling." Paper presented at 83rd annual meeting of the American Psychological Association, Chicago, August 1975.

Slepitza, R. A. "The Validation of Stage Model for Career Counseling." Unpublished master's thesis, University of Maryland, 1976.

Slepitza, R. A., and Knefelkamp, L. L. "A Cognitive Developmental Model of Career Development: An Adaptation of the Perry Scheme." *The Counseling Psychologist,* 1976, *6* (3), 53-58.

Solt, L. F. "Comments about Connell and Rosenzweig Papers Concerning Perry and Kohlberg Schemes, Respectively." Presented to annual meeting of the American Historical Association, San Francisco, 1978.

Sorum, J., and Knefelkamp, L. L. "Developmental Instruction in the Liberal Arts: A Dialogue." Presentation at the Bureau of Study Counsel, Harvard University, 1976.

Stephenson, B. W., and Hunt, C. "Intellectual and Ethical Development: A Dualistic Curriculum Intervention for College Students." *The Counseling Psychologist,* 1977, *6* (4), 39-42.

Strange, C. C. "Intellectual Development, a Motive for Education and Learning During the College Years: A Comparison of Adult and Traditional-Age Students." Unpublished doctoral dissertation, University of Iowa, 1978.

Syracuse Rating Group. "Rater's Manual: Guide to Assessing 'Position.'" (Working draft.) Syracuse University, 1978.

Taft, J. *The Dynamics of Therapy in a Controlled Relationship.* New York: Macmillan, 1933.

Touchton, J. G. "Developmental Programming at a University Career Center—the Maryland Experience." A Commission XII sponsored presentation at the American College Personnel Association National Convention, 1977.

Touchton, J. G., and others. "Career Planning and Decision Making: A Developmental

Approach to the Classroom." In C. A. Parker (Ed.), *Encouraging Development in College Students.* Minneapolis: University of Minnesota, 1978.

Trabin, T., and Parker, C. A. "Evaluation Report for the Instructional Development Consultation Project." Unpublished manuscript, University of Minnesota, 1978.

Vaillant, G. E. *Adaptation to Life.* Boston: Little, Brown, 1977.

Valiga, T. M. "The Cognitive Development and Views about Nursing as a Profession of Baccalaureate Nursing Students." Doctoral dissertation proposal, Columbia University, 1979.

Welfel, E. R. "The Development of Reflective Judgment: Its Relationship to Year in College, Major Field, Academic Performance, and Satisfaction with Major among College Students." Unpublished doctoral dissertation, University of Minnesota, 1979.

Wertheimer, L. "A New Model and Measure for Career Counseling: Incorporating Both Content and Processing Aspects of Career Concerns." Unpublished master's thesis, University of Maryland, 1976.

Whitla, D. K. *Value Added: Measuring the Outcome of Undergraduate Education.* Cambridge, Mass.: Office of Instructional Research and Evaluation, Harvard University, 1977.

Whitla, D. K. Personal communication, 1978.

Widick, C. "An Evaluation of Developmental Instruction in a University Setting." Unpublished doctoral dissertation, University of Minnesota, 1975.

Widick, C. "The Perry Scheme: A Foundation for Developmental Practice." *The Counseling Psychologist,* 1977, *6* (4), 35-38.

Widick, C., Knefelkamp, L. L., and Parker, C. "The Counselor as a Developmental Instructor." *Journal of Counselor Education and Supervision,* 1975, *14,* 286-296.

Widick, C., and Simpson, D. "Developmental Concepts in College Instruction." In C. A. Parker (Ed.), *Encouraging Development in College Students.* Minneapolis: University of Minnesota, 1978.

Wispe, L. G. "Evaluating Section Teaching Methods in the Introductory Course." *Journal of Educational Research,* 1951, *45,* 161-186.

Witkin, H. A., Goodenough, D. R., and Karp, S. A. "Stability of Cognitive Style from Childhood to Young Adulthood." *Journal of Personality and Social Psychology,* 1967, *7* (3), 291-300.

4

K. Warner Schaie
Joyce Parr

Intelligence

If it is assumed that one of the major purposes of college education is to challenge students to think through issues affecting themselves and society in increasingly sophisticated and complex ways, then it is important to know to what extent the intellectual skills required are likely to change over the adult life course. As in other areas of human development, early studies of intelligence focused on acquisition of functions and skills in childhood. But even some of the pioneer theoretical writers (Hall, 1922; Pressey, Janney, and Kuhlen, 1939) became interested in issues such as age of peak performance level, transformation of structures of intellect (ways of thinking), and the decremental changes assumed to occur in late midlife and old age.

Interest in intellectual development was whetted, for example, by Yerkes' finding, in his 1921 study of World War I soldiers, that the mental function of young adults was only at about an age-13 level. Indeed, Terman's original standardization of the Binet intelligence test for American use had assumed that intellectual development peaked at age 16 and then remained constant (Terman, 1916). Such assumptions were soon questioned, however, by data from other empirical work. Jones and Conrad (1933), on the basis of cross-sectional studies in a New England community, showed significant age differences across adulthood on some, though not other, subtests of the Army Alpha intelligence test. Similar findings from the standardization studies conducted during the development of the Wechsler-Bellevue intelligence test indicated that intellectual development does not end in early adolescence, that peak ages apparently differ for different aspects of intel-

117

lectual functioning, and that age differences are not uniform across the full spectrum of abilities tapped by most of the major batteries measuring intellectual development (Wechsler, 1939; Schaie, 1970).

All these matters might be of purely historical interest if it were not for the fact that omnibus measures of intelligence have generally been found quite useful in predicting a person's competence in dealing with our society's educational system and later on succeeding in vocational pursuits in which educationally based knowledge and skills are required. Moreover, specific measures of ability, although less successful, have had some use in predicting ability to meet specific situational demands. The analysis of patterns of intellectual performance has also been found to be of help to clinicians in the diagnostic appraisal of psychopathology. In dealings with the mature adult, some determination of intellectual competence may be highly relevant to such questions as preparation for a second career, selection in and out of occupations requiring specific abilities, mandatory retirement, maintenance of individual living arrangements, and ability to conserve and dispose property (Matarazzo, 1972; Schaie and Schaie, 1977).

The plan of this chapter is, first, to consider the intellectual needs of students of different ages and the related problem of developing appropriate criteria for assessing adult intelligence and competence. Next we will consider how well different theoretical models of intelligence fit adults. From there we will go on to the practical problems of assessing intellectual competence across a large portion of the human life span—the kind of intellectual assessment that will be required for students in the future American college. Then we will review what is known about changes in intellectual ability and competence through adulthood. And finally, we will note some implications of adult intellectual development for higher education. It should become apparent that the intellectual needs of adults do differ by age, that measures of intellectual ability are useful only if their criteria have some meaning in themselves, and, perhaps most important, that old dogs can learn new tricks, given the right circumstances.

Intellectual Needs of Different Age Groups

Chickering and Havighurst, in Chapter One, suggested as a goal for college education the skills necessary to manage one's own occupation and family while maintaining sensitivity to community and world needs. Designing programs to further such ends requires comparing the background and current abilities of students with the situations and demands they are likely to face. Discrepancies between existing skills and those that are likely to be needed should be considered as a function of the time perspectives of the various age groups who will make up the future college.

Traditional 18- to 22-year-old students, on the average, can be expected to live fifty years or so beyond their initial college experience. They therefore need not only skills that will give them economic viability but also preparation for dealing with "future shock." Most projections suggest that they will have to function in a society that is moving toward greater cultural diversity, changing from an achievement orientation to a greater leisure orientation, and shifting its economy emphasis from the production of goods to the provision of services. Many older learners face the more immediate and critical challenge of overcoming obsolescence suffered from the vast technological changes that have occurred since their early educational experience. For this group, instruction should serve to update knowledge and also facilitate an active involvement with and use of systems and services available in present-day society. The most adaptive learning for many older adults will therefore focus on the here and now and the proximate rather than distant future.

Discussions such as that presented by Schaie (1977/78) regarding stages of adult cognitive development also suggest that different kinds of intellectual processes may be needed to accomplish the goals of different age groups. Schaie describes a stage in young adulthood characterized by a goal-directed, entrepreneurial style of achievement, which requires an efficient task-related, competitive cognitive style. A middle-adulthood stage characterized by the need to integrate long-range goals with the solution of current real-life problems calls for organizational, integrative, and interpretive intellectual skills. A later-adulthood stage characterized by the need to attain a sense of meaning in experience requires the ability to retrieve and attend selectively to information from the overload of material accumulated over the life span.

Thus, what students of different ages may want or need to learn by way of content and intellectual skills in order to enhance their functioning may differ markedly. This would not necessarily mean that completely separate academic programs would be required, though some courses in cognitive skill training might well be developed to meet the needs of different age groups. A careful consideration of the various contributions that persons in different phases of life experience and with different styles of cognitive function could make to discussions should be fruitful in designing multigenerational courses.

Intelligence and Competence Differentiated

Measures of intellectual function are useful only insofar as they predict abilities of interest. The early intelligence tests were designed to predict children's success in classical school subjects. The appropriateness of using the same measures across the life span and for a variety of situations has been called into question many times. Further, it has not always been clear whether observed deficiencies in prediction were a function of the methodologies of assessing intellectual function or the appropriateness of the criteria measures or both. In any case, for the young college student, performance as measured by grade-point average (GPA) may well be an important criterion for predicting relative standing in the competitive graduate school and job market, and general tests of intelligence have been helpful in predicting GPA. Even for the younger student, however, projections of future societal needs suggest that creative problem solving and behavioral flexibility may be equally important, and different sorts of tests will be needed to predict these variables.

For the older student, of diverse ages, much work remains to be done in developing criterion variables relevant to the life roles and societal requirements for competent functioning (see Schaie, 1977/78, for further discussion). The decision as to what kinds of tests are appropriate to use as predictors of success necessarily depends on what accomplishments or skills are seen as important. It may be, for example, that certain motor skills are important for younger students but much less important for older students. However, specific problem-solving skills may be important for both.

A recent distinction between intelligence and competence may be quite useful in confronting the questions of what to measure in assessing the abilities of adults. Connolly and Bruner (1974) distinguish between intelligence as passive and competence as active. Schaie (1978) describes *intelligence* as an inference of underlying traits, based on observations in many situations, and *competence* as a more situation-specific combination of intellectual traits, which with adequate motivation, will permit adaptive behavior. He also argues that traditional measures of intelligence are not likely to be very useful for predicting many of the more situation-specific skills of the older learner.

Another factor that must be taken into account when using tests with older students is the greater diversity of their skills and interests. This is only reasonable when one considers their wide range of experience over many years compared with the more uniform educational experience of students who have recently completed their secondary education. Thus, tests must be used that allow expression of abilities of many sorts.

Available information regarding scores on tests of intellectual abilities of younger and older persons can be quite useful in suggesting what learning goals might be appropriate for various age groups. Further, once learning goals have been outlined, such scores can also be used in designing the kinds of learning experiences that will be most successful in reaching these goals. In other words, what we are suggesting is that educational programs can be designed on the basis of currently available information to maximize older students' cognitive assets. What is also suggested by the literature is that a greater variety of educational programs will be required in order to optimize the learning of older students. The availability of such programs might have the effect of meeting more individual needs of younger students as well.

Intelligence and Plasticity of Behavior

Our whole educational system is based on the well-documented notion that there is a great deal of plasticity in the behavior of young persons. An increasing body of data regarding what and how older persons learn is also becoming available. This literature ranges from the study of how much practice improves performance in various tasks, to the effectiveness of teaching new strategies of problem solving, to an evaluation of various ways of presenting material to be learned. There are two kinds of issues that seem paramount in addressing the degree of plasticity in older students. The first concerns the effects of changing nervous system characteristics on tasks that involve, for example, speed of perceptual and information processing and storage in memory of newly learned material. The second seems to involve motivational and experiential factors, though changing physiology may also play a role. Whereas novelty seems to provide an adequate stimulus for information processing in younger persons, meaning and some degree of familiarity are required for material to be assimilated by older learners. The question is not, however, whether older persons can learn but how and what they can learn most efficiently. Obviously, the matching up of abilities, styles of learning, and reasons for learning will be a continuing and potentially fruitful task for educational designers. The remainder of this chapter will discuss issues and data that we hope will contribute to this design process.

Models of Intelligence

Any discussion of intellectual development must begin by specifying the nature of the construct whose development we wish to understand. We have already distinguished between the concepts of intelligence and competence. It will now be helpful to engage in a brief historical analysis of four different models of intelligence: (1) the notion of intelligence as a general construct, (2) multifactor theories of intelligence, (3) the distinction between fluid and crystallized intelligence, and (4) stage theories of adult intellectual development.

Intelligence as a General Construct. Spearman (1927) believed that all intellectual activities reflected some common factor, which he labeled the g factor. He observed that studies of the intercorrelations among test items show high agreement among the items that appear to be measures of intellectual functions. Indeed, omnibus tests of intelligence (such as the Binet test and its successors) have tended to be quite successful in predicting performance in certain educational situations. But a variety of *g* factors might be found if one were to examine test items predictive of performance in noneducational situations or, for that matter, in nontraditional educational situations.

Multifactor Theories of Intelligence. To test these theories, items are selected so that scores vary on significant aspects of intellectual performance in addition to correlating with a general factor. Resulting test batteries (of which the Wechsler tests are a prominent example) have only moderate correlations between their parts, although their sums (as expressed in total IQ) will measure competence for situations for which the particular combinations of component parts are important.

Thurstone (1938) studied the correlations among approximately sixty different measures of intelligence and concluded that one can identify a number of factors that have little or no relationship with one another. Thurstone's factors (as well as the even further explicated structure-of-intellect model of Guilford, 1967) represent latent variables, which can be measured only indirectly. Such factors may indeed be the building blocks of intelligence, but, unfortunately, knowledge of an individual's standing on any one of them will not help us predict competence either in a specific situation or across classes of situations, except in the unusual case where one and only one factor accounts for most of the differences among individuals in an observable behavior.

It is not likely that even the most rigorous search will turn up new factors accounting for individual differences in intelligence late in life; nevertheless, we still must be alert to the fact that some intellectual abilities may account for differences early in life but not later on and vice versa. Assessment strategies that have proven successful for the selection and counseling of young adults for particular educational programs may therefore be quite useless and misleading when applied to older students.

Crystallized and Fluid Intelligence. Abilities that depend primarily on sociocultural influences, such as number facility, verbal comprehension, and general information, form one class of intellectual abilities, which have been called the *crystallized* abilities. These skills are not innate but must be learned, usually as part of a person's formal education. Their level and maintenance will therefore depend heavily upon the content of the individual's educational experience during the formative years and upon vocational contexts during adulthood. Other abilities may be quite independent of acculturation; their function depends more upon genetic endowment, the neurophysiological state of the individual, and perhaps also incidental learning. These latter abilities, such as memory span, inductive reasoning, and figural relations, are called *fluid* abilities (see Cattell, 1963). It has been contended that crystallized abilities reach an optimal level in early adulthood and remain stable thereafter, while the fluid abilities show early decline in adulthood (Horn, 1970). Note, however, that the education to which older adults are currently exposed encourages learning facts (crystallized abilities), whereas younger students are more often involved in integrative learning (akin to fluid abilities).

Stage Theories and Adult Development. The Piagetian model of intelligence (Flavell, 1963) places emphasis on the development of biologically based cognitive structures that produce qualitative changes in the way cognitive operations are conducted as the individual matures. In principle, by the time adulthood is reached, Piaget's stage of *formal operations* should have been attained (Flavell, 1970). "Formal operations" involve identification of logical rules applicable to whole classes or types of problems—in other words, the application of abstract and integrative rules to problem-solving activities. But Piaget (1972) has recently admitted that not all adults attain the stage of formal operations, and that formal operations are not applied uniformly to all substantive areas of cognitive behavior (see also Schaie and Marquette, 1975).

A recent extension of this theory (Schaie, 1977/78) suggests the possibility of three adult stages: (1) an *achieving* stage, during which the young adult strives toward goal orientation and role independence, (2) a *responsible* stage, involving long-term goal integration and increased problem-solving skills, and (3) a *reintegrative* stage, during which there is relinquishment of occupational and familial responsibilities accompanied by the simplification of cognitive structures through selective attention to meaningful environmental demands. This kind of conceptualization is quite compatible with theories of adult moral development and of ego development (Erikson, 1964), and for that matter with Chickering and Havighurst's developmental task approach (see Chapter One of this volume).

Problems in Assessing Adult Intelligence. Studies of omnibus measures of intelligence in common use suggest that such measures are ill-suited for assessing the intellectual competence of middle-aged or elderly adults, in most situations. Furthermore, although studies of functional unities of intelligence, such as Thurstone's Primary Mental Abilities, may indeed explain most variance in individuals' abilities in early adulthood, other abilities—those relatively unimportant in youth—may require more detailed assessment in later adulthood. What then is to be done?

First, we must learn more about situations in which adults are required to display competence, and this requires a taxonomy of adult situations. Next, we must construct new measures of intelligence, based upon what we now know about adult intellect. Such measures must not rely upon novelty to be the impetus for the subject's response; instead, the tasks used must be meaningful and embedded in the life experience of the adult. Moreover, they must be attuned to the particular historical contexts of different age groups as well as to life cycle differences. Third, we must examine the mediating role of motivational variables and especially the effect on individuals over two or more points in time.

Research on adult intelligence requires sophisticated methods. Cross-sectional studies confound ontogenetic change with generational differences; longitudinal studies confound ontogenetic change with the effects of sociocultural change occurring between times of measurement (or what the sociologists call *period effects*). For most behavioral variables these confounding effects are substantial. It is therefore unlikely that findings of cross-sectional age differences will agree with findings obtained from longitudinal studies (see Schaie, 1967). In fact, many age differences reported in the research literature might be more parsimoniously interpreted as generational differences, and results from single-cohort longitudinal studies of human behavior may be no more than historical accounts of the life history of that particular generation (Schaie and Gribbin, 1975a).

Several alternative strategies, called *sequential methods,* have been proposed, in which two or more cross-sectional or longitudinal sequences are compared to determine the stability of observed findings. If one assumes that either age, cohort, or period effects are trivial, one can then estimate the specific magnitude of the two remaining effects. The interested reader will want to consult the references cited above for more detail. The important point is that results of studies that do not use the appropriate sequential method have only limited generalizability.

A further limitation on what we know about adult intellectual development is imposed by the problem of nonrandom drop-out of subjects from the panel studies upon which most of our better research findings are based. Two types of attrition occur. The first is attributable to psychological and sociological reasons, such as lack of interest, active refusal, change of residence, or disappearance. This type of attrition may be related to the investigator's skill in maintaining the original subjects in the study. The second type of attrition, over which investigator has no control, is the result of biological factors such as physical disease and individual differences.

Measurement of Intelligence

Although the statement "Intelligence is what intelligence tests measure" is quite simplistic, our assessments of intelligence do depend on our methods of measurement. So it is important to know in what manner we evaluate a person's intellectual function. In this section we will discuss the norms that should be used in measuring adult intelligence, the role of speed versus power tests, the difference between performance and potential, the developmental course of sex differences in intelligence, and the measures that seem to predict various types of educational abilities.

Age-Corrected Versus Absolute Norms. Most intelligence tests published commercially, such as the Wechsler Adult Intelligence Scale (Matarazzo, 1972), use age-corrected norms—that is, norms calculated by age group. There are several problems with this approach, if such tests are to be used as estimates of intellectual competence in educational situations. The most important problem is that if we are to predict abilities of any social consequence or utility, it is not sufficient to say that an individual can perform at average level for his or her age. What we must know is whether the test performance is at a level appropriate to some criterion of social or educational performance. Thus, if a given educational activity is programmed to the needs and abilities of younger students (such as career entry skills), then the test norms designed for younger students should be used to assess the abilities of the older students as well. However, it does not make sense to compare younger and older adults on the same norms for tests that do not have the same importance at different life stages.

A further problem is the fact that all such age-based norms found in the literature have been developed from cross-sectional studies and are thus cohort-specific. That is, as the norms age, they will overestimate level of performance on tests where there are unfavorable trends over time. It is to be hoped that manuals developed in the future will begin to provide adult norms in terms of the birth years for which specific norms were developed, rather than the age range, in order to overcome this problem (see Schaie and Parham, 1975, for an example of cohort-specific norms).

Speeded Versus Power Tests. Traditionally, tests of intelligence have used two different approaches, "power" and "speed." Power tests contain a series of items scaled in increasing order of difficulty, and items are presented to the examinee until a prescribed number of successive items are failed. For practical purposes, however, and particularly in group-administered tests, some time limit is also imposed. In this case we speak of a slightly speeded power test. Speeded tests, by contrast, present the examinee with a larger number of items of approximately equal difficulty, all within the scope of performance of the examinee. The examinee's performance then is the number of items completed within a specified period of time.

As we have already noted, one of the well-documented facts of adult development is the slowing of response speed (see Welford, 1977). This phenomenon should not have any effect upon pure power tests, and some have argued, therefore, that older adults should only be examined by means of power tests. Nevertheless, one aspect of competent intellectual performance is the ability to make an organized response within a reasonable length of time. Educators must thus decide whether or not speed of response—and how much speed—is required for performance in a particular situation. Obviously, speeded tests should be used with older individuals only if the problems to be dealt with require rapid responses. Such judgments are critical in planning educational technology—for example, programming Computer Assisted Instruction (CAI) modules—but are less useful in predicting whether older persons can profit from college instruction.

Matters become more complex with the slightly speeded power tests. For example, some of the factor-analytic work with the Wechsler Adult Intelligence Scale has shown that where a given subtest is a good measure of the intended construct for young adults, it may become a measure of response speed for older adults (Reinert, 1970). In the testing of older adults, the time limits must be sufficiently relaxed to permit the examinee to reveal whether or not he or she can solve the problem. Thus, tasks must be developed in which speed of response is not a critical element of successful performance. And while we are at it, we ought to consider removing also those constraints that tend to decrease speed of response, such as inappropriately small type size or anxiety-inducing instructions.

Performance Versus Potential. Existing tools for assessing intellectual competence, as well as new techniques specifically designed for older adult learners, will, of course, do no more than provide us with estimates of current performance. But a more important question may often be whether or not a potential older college student is likely to develop new abilities as a consequence of participation in a college program. While determining a minimally acceptable level of current performance may be essential, we also want to know what we can expect in terms of future intellectual development. In principle, such determination requires longitudinal data about individuals, but inferences from other sources may be possible. Some work, for example, has been done to predict stability or change in intellectual function from knowledge of individuals' life-styles (Schaie and Gribbin, 1975b). Another promising approach is the assessment of individuals' responses to brief experimental paradigms involving cognitive training—that is, instruction in problem-solving strategies for dealing with novel material of various types, such as figural relations (see, for example, Labouvie-Vief and Gonda, 1976; Plemons, Willis, and Baltes, 1978).

Again, work in this area will depend on a good understanding of what it is that we wish to determine. We suspect that clear performance criteria will be most useful in defining levels required for culturally valued aspects of education. However, measures of learning ability, such as those involving training paradigms, may be required to predict the individual student's potential for acquiring new skills. A combination of such measures, together with a better understanding of declines in performance due primarily to disuse of skills, may enable us to program more effective compensatory education programs for adults.

Sex Differences in Intellectual Development. Whether because of genetic differences or early socialization practices, men and women differ in their relative performance on tests of various intellectual abilities. In general, women seem to show superior performance in verbal skills and inductive reasoning, while men do better on tasks involving numerical and spatial abilities. But, although the differential between men and women remains fairly constant over the adult life span, within each sex the relative abilities tend to vary with age, owing to a different pattern of maintenance and decline.

This problem has received scant attention in the research literature but may be of considerable importance both for selecting adult college students and for developing programs designed to maximize successful performance of older students. Data from the Seattle longitudinal-sequential study of age changes in cognitive behavior illustrates this issue for men and women on two crystallized and two fluid abilities with differential age trends (see Schaie, 1978). When we examine the relationship of verbal to number skills, we find that at age 25 both men and women do better on number skills. By the fifties, however, women on average perform equally well on verbal and number skills, and men, by the sixties, do significantly better on number than on verbal skills. Turning to measures of fluid abilities, we find that at 25 men do about equally well on spatial and reasoning abilities, while women clearly do better on reasoning. But by the fifties this pattern is reversed; men do better on spatial orientation than on reasoning, while women do equally well on both abilities.

The reader must be cautioned once again that data such as these are based on cross-sectional studies reflecting age differences for today's adults. Shifting patterns in sex roles and occupational involvement for women may well change those age-related ability differences that are not of biological origin.

Predicting Educational Aptitude. What measures predict adults' educational aptitude? Any response to this question must of necessity be speculative, inasmuch as relevant predictive studies for older learners do not yet exist. What we have been saying regarding the needs and goals of older learners, however, suggests that educational aptitude may depend primarily on such skills as verbal meaning (recognizing words on vocabulary lists) and inductive reasoning. The peak of educational aptitude measured in this manner occurred around age 60, and at age 81 mean performance was still at 70 percent of the level of the 25-year-olds (Schaie and Willis, 1978).

Other variables, including personality, also correlate with measures of intellectual functioning. A composite flexibility score from the Test of Behavioral Rigidity (Schaie and Parham, 1975) has correlated around .60 with the composite IQ from the Primary Mental Abilities test until age 70. The motor-cognitive component of the flexibility score has shown a stable pattern across ages and across cohorts and a strong relationship with the IQ measure. The personality-perceptual component of the flexibility score, however, has shown positive cohort differences with increasing age but considerable intraperson stability even into the eighties. Thus, we can expect that successive groups of older learners will show greater personality flexibility.

A review of the educational implications of the experimental literature on behavior of older adults provided by Schaie and Willis (1978) indicates that on the average older learners are less likely than younger learners to be able to process and sort large amounts of new information efficiently. However, the ability to consider the meaning and implications of focused problem areas in light of experience should be strong into advanced age.

Adult Intellectual Development

Three distinct phases of intellectual development can be described (see Figure 1). The first phase emphasizes from the attainment of intellectual skills in the late teens and early twenties (the traditional college period) and their application to personal and societal goals as individuals establish family units and enter the world of work. The second period, from middle age to early old age, is one of relative stability and integration accompanied by some trade-offs, as response speed and perceptual processes begin to decline. During this phase environmental supports and the fruit of experience provide adequate compensation. In the final stage, although there is narrowing of interests and more focused attention, such compensation no longer offsets accumulating deficits.

From Young Adulthood to Middle Age. When we discussed the issue of adult stages earlier in this chapter, we mentioned that one of the characteristics of the transition into adulthood is a shift from the acquisition of skills to the application of those skills to goal-oriented achievements. We may therefore expect that in this *achieving* stage more efficient and effective cognitive behavior will be found in activities that have role-related achievement potential. Even in early middle age, though, peak performance may already have passed for problem-solving abilities and educational activities that are task-

Figure 1. Stages of Adult Cognitive Development

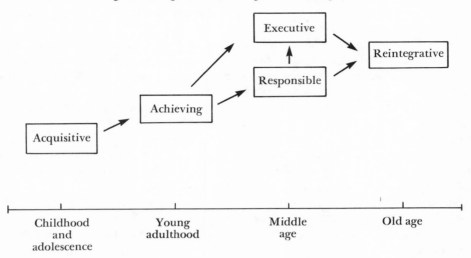

limited and not clearly related to broader personal and social goals. However, goal relevance is strongly influenced by environmental factors, within biologically determined limits. We would therefore expect that adult peak performance may shift in chronological age, as the average age at which a task becomes most goal-relevant may be modified by environmental demands.

Some work from our longitudinal study of the Primary Mental Abilities may be illustrative (Schaie, 1979). Take the example of Verbal Meaning, a recognition vocabulary task. Here we find gains throughout early adulthood, but for three successive samples, born seven years apart, the peak ages shifted from 32 to 46 years of age. Gains have also been reported for scores on the Stanford-Binet until age 30 by Bradway, Thompson, and Cravens (1958) and until age 42 by Kangas and Bradway (1971). The latter study also reported gains on both verbal and performance parts of the Wechsler Adult Intelligence Scale, confirming results earlier reported by Bayley and Oden (1955) and by Green (1969).

From Middle Age to Old Age. Middle age brings with it further transformations in the cognitive realm. When the individual has mastered cognitive skills to the point of attaining role independence—satisfactory identity and self-sufficiency—he must then move on, motivated both by biological and societal pressures, to assume responsibility for others. Whether one assumes full responsibility for one's mate, offspring, or elderly parents or whether one becomes the leader of an educational, vocational, or other social unit, transition must now occur to a *responsible* stage, which for most individuals extends from the late thirties to the early sixties.[1]

[1] Figure 1 indicates in addition an *executive* stage. This stage is reached by some during middle age under the pressure of assuming responsibilities for whole societal systems rather than simple units. Such individuals would be expected to show further increment on laboratory tasks such as pattern recognition, complex problem solving, and inductive reasoning.

The goal-directed but often egocentric style of the achieving stage will now be replaced by cognitive patterns that facilitate the solution of practical problems in the context of long-range goals and perceived consequences for the social units for which the individual has assumed responsibility. Translated into the formal measurement of intellectual ability, this means that we would expect further growth of problem-solving skills when measured by meaningful tasks, as well as maintenance and even slight growth of the crystallized abilities. At the same time we would expect, as individuals reach the sixties, decreased skill in task-specific situations, particularly when assessed by fluid ability measures or by speeded tasks, and perhaps more difficulty also in dealing with new items of information—as contrasted with the retrieval and integration of previously learned information.

Empirical studies reflecting behavior change over this period suggest that there is a maintenance of function for many abilities not involving speed of response (see Botwinick, 1977). And again, as over any long time period, sociocultural change leads to apparent differences between individuals decades apart in age, reminding us of the importance of understanding the level of earlier education when programming for the older learner. Our own studies suggest that until the late sixties differences in ability level between successive generations are most strongly implicated in any findings of cross-sectional age differences, with intraindividual change occurring primarily on highly speeded tests (Schaie and Parham, 1977).

Intellectual Changes in Old Age. The characteristic concern in old age with intellectual and emotional reintegration appears to shift the focus of intellectual performance from content to context. The transition to the *reintegrative* stage implies a shift from "What should I know?" through "How should I know?" to "Why should I know?" As a consequence, we would assume that motivational and attitudinal variables are much more involved in moderating intellectual competence at this stage than at other life stages.

For us, the successful older person is one who rather than having disengaged from society has become reengaged in a meaningful fashion. But such reengagement at the cognitive level is achieved by much more selective attention to those intellectual skills and activities that have either remained meaningful or have attained new meaning. This is why we have to be very careful not to overinterpret the empirical findings of intellectual deficits in old age, and in particular the observation that greater decrements have been found on the fluid than on the crystallized abilities (Horn and Donaldson, 1976). Such findings may reflect a selective interpretation of existing data (Baltes and Schaie, 1976; Schaie and Parham, 1977).

Part of the difficulty in interpreting the evidence of intellectual deficits in old age is that most measures of abstract intellectual functions involve techniques that put older people at a disadvantage. For example, they are apt to use personally meaningless material and testing paradigms that stress response systems which are no longer relevant over those used in daily living situations. More situationally relevant measures may help deal with this issue in the future, but their construction is still in an initial stage (Schaie, 1978).

We would like to suggest that the apparent intellectual deficits shown by the elderly reflect a combination of obsolescence and the consequences of progressive decrements in the efficiency of the peripheral sense organs and of the timing mechanisms involved in transmitting impulses to the brain and alerting the organism to the availability of stimuli to which it should respond. But how serious are these deficits? The statistics reported in the scientific literature tell us simply that a phenomenon has been reliably demonstrated. The practitioner in addition must know the magnitude of the phenomenon in order to decide whether it requires specific professional action.

The author has tried to attack this problem by measuring the performance of individuals at various ages as a proportion of the performance of young adults (at age 25). Figures 2 and 3 present data from longitudinal-sequential studies on psychometric tests

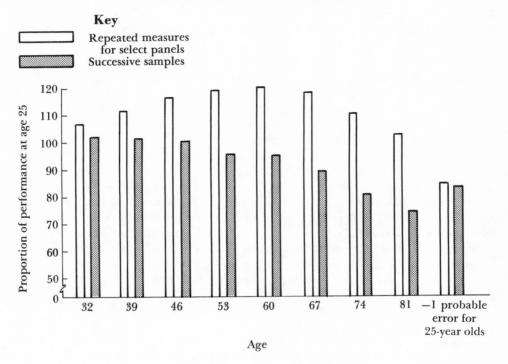

Figure 2. Performance on Recognition Vocabulary at Various Ages as a Proportion of Performance at Age 25

(designed for the young) for recognition vocabulary and numerical skills. Note that the solid bars in the graphs represent estimates from change data involving repeated measurement of panels, while the broken bars represent estimates from successive random samples. The latter data provide a good estimate of proportionate age change in the general population; the former represent a highly selected panel.

An objective appraisal of the practical significance of cumulative age changes involves assumptions familiar to most educators. That is, we note that 1 Probable Error about the mean defines the middle 50 percent (average) range of performance if mental abilities are normally distributed (see Matarazzo, 1972, pp. 124-126). Hence, performance decrements are assumed to have practical significance in those cases where the cumulative loss for the older sample reduces its performance below the performance level at 1 Probable Error below the mean of young adults. Inspection of Figure 2 (Recognition Vocabulary) shows that such decrement is reached for the general population sample only at age 74, while the select sample remains at or above the young adult level into the eighties. Figure 3 (Number skills), while showing evidence of some age decrement, also tells us that the decrement for this ability does not reach practical significance at any age.

**Figure 3. Performance on Number Skills at Various Ages
as a Proportion of Performance at Age 25**

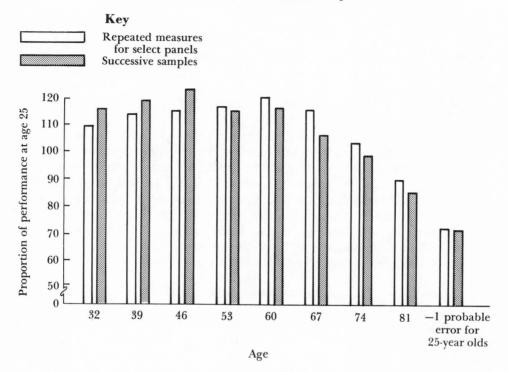

Modifiability of Adult Intelligence

To what extent can intellectual performance be modified in later life? This is a basic issue in the education of adults. Here we will address the issue in light of the limited training literature and studies of educational motivation.

Training Studies. As we noted earlier, a significant portion of the apparent decrement in older people's intellectual performance can be attributed to lack of training and experience in the skills measured by available tests of intelligence. To what extent, then, can this deficit be overcome by learning? Some intellectual traits, set down early in life, may be relatively difficult to change. Other behaviors may be much more amenable to change at later stages of life. For firm conclusions to be reached, each cognitive function of interest must be studied using several different training techniques. Would-be researchers in this area must also consider the criterion question carefully in choosing measures of cognitive function to train for. That is, the information obtained should predict behavior of interest. If speed is of questionable importance to an older person's interactions with his environment, then time might be better spent trying to train for improvement on another measure of intelligence.

A small but growing literature has reported successful modification of apparent low-level function on intellectual variables such as figure relations and perceptual speed (for example, Hoyer, Labouvie-Vief, and Baltes, 1973; Labouvie-Vief and Gonda, 1976; Plemons, Willis, and Baltes, 1978). Further evidence for the importance of even simple changes in instructional or reinforcement conditions has been demonstrated (Birkhill and

Schaie, 1975). Labouvie-Vief and others (1974), provide a review of assumptions related to the use of behavior modification techniques with older adults and discuss alternative designs for such studies.

Role of Motivational Factors. An age-related increase in cautiousness has been reported in a number of studies of performance (Birkhill and Schaie, 1975; Okun and DiVesta, 1976; Reese and Botwinick, 1971). Botwinick (1973) has suggested that some age-related decline in ability may be attributable to an increase in cautiousness. Sensitivity to the way instructions create sets for responding as well as studies that encourage the use of different response strategies may be helpful in clarifying how much the performance of older persons can be improved.

The role of arousal or anxiety in the performance of older learners has been studied by Eisdorfer, Nowlin, and Wilkie (1970). However, conflicting results have led to differing interpretations as to whether, and under what circumstances, older persons may be over- or underaroused for optimal performance (Marsh and Thompson, 1977). Further studies are needed to help clarify this issue. Sensitivity to conditions that affect the motivational levels of learners of all ages is critical but may be of particular importance where other factors related to efficient performance become marginal. The goal of educational designers and teachers should be to provide the combination of instructional set and training techniques that can optimize the conditions for learning.

Sensory and Perceptual Changes

Of major concern to the college teacher with older students are those performance decrements related not so much to basic ability as to the decreasing efficiency of the peripheral nervous systems. Specifically worthy of note here are common changes in auditory and visual acuity as well as in perceptual speed.

Visual Acuity. Changes in the transmission ability and accommodation power of the eye begin at age 35 to 45 years. Progressive thickening of the crystalline lens interferes with transmitting and refracting light and decreases accommodative power. Yellowing of the lens reduces the amount of light entering the retina. Reduced sensitivity to the shorter wavelengths of the visible spectrum leads to greater difficulty discriminating between blue, blue-green, and violet colors (Weale, 1965). Circulatory and metabolic changes in the retina around age 55 to 65 years also result in reduction of the size of the visual field, along with decreased sensitivity to flicker and to low quantities of light. The brightness gradient of the image on the retina appears to be critical in determining visual acuity. Corrective lenses can improve visual acuity by increasing retinal illumination, but acuity can also be sharpened by increasing the contrast between the object and its surrounding field, or by increasing overall illumination (Fozard and others, 1977).

Auditory Acuity. The most common auditory deficiency with advancing age is presbycusis, a loss of auditory acuity for the high frequency tones (Corso, 1977). Functional decrement occurs in the auditory thresholds for pure tones, speech and pitch discriminations, and information for processing of dichotic stimuli. Some degree of hearing loss is found from about 32 years of age for men and 37 years for women (Lebo and Redell, 1972). The hearing level of men is higher than that of women at or above 2000 Hz but below that of women for frequencies of 1000 Hz and below. Impairment in pitch discrimination has been noted as early as the fourth decade (Konig, 1957). However, Corso (1971) has suggested that age-related performance decrements may reflect different criteria of judgments (such as cautiousness) rather than functional losses in the auditory sensory modality.

Substantial associations have been found between hearing loss and intellectual functioning as measured by subtests of the Wechsler Adult Intelligence Scale, the Primary Mental Abilities, and the Raven Progressive Matrices (Granick, Kleban, and Weiss, 1976; Schaie, Baltes, and Strother, 1964).

Perceptual Speed. Age-related slowness in behavior has been attributed to a slower mediation process in the central nervous system (Birren, 1965). No qualitative differences in central perceptual processes have been found between young and older adults; however, beyond 60 years of age the peripheral perceptual system operates more slowly (Walsh, 1976). Older persons thus appear to require a slower rate of presentation and increased task duration (Talland, 1966). The slower processing mechanism for incoming stimuli with advancing age suggests a need for self-paced or reduced presentation rate of materials as well as varying complexity levels.

It is important to distinguish clearly between those aspects of the older learner's intellectual competence that are related to perceptual speed and those that are related to sensory acuity. For the former, we need to consider alteration of pace and timing of programs. For the latter, we need to make sure that visual and auditory difficulties are corrected when possible, either by individual prosthetic devices or by means of carefully designed educational settings. Once again, we need to note the vast range of individual differences. While some sensory-perceptual decrement will occur for all of us if we live long enough, such decrement for many will be relatively insignificant or its onset will be quite late in life.

Implications for Higher Education

In the final section of this chapter we would like to speculate a bit about the implications of adult intellectual development for education. To do so, we will summarize what we perceive to be the goals and needs of older learners and ask whether or not it is realistic to assume that many older learners indeed have the intellectual skills required to meet their educational goals. We will then consider what changes might be required in educational technology to serve the older learner better and, finally, what we now know about such issues as age mix in college classes, characteristics and preparation of teachers of older learners, and the like. For a more extensive discussion of these issues the reader may wish to refer to Schaie and Quayhagen (1978) and Schaie and Willis (1978).

Goals of Adult Learners. A major objective of education in youth is the development of intellectual and social skills required for adequate functioning in a particular society. By contrast, adult education is directed toward maintenance and renewal of skills. Five distinct needs of adult learners can readily be identified: (1) help in understanding the changes in one's own body and behavior produced by maturation and aging, (2) help in understanding the rapid technological and cultural changes of contemporary society, (3) skills for coping with the personal consequences of technological and sociocultural change, (4) new vocational skills required for a career change or pursuit of other new goals, and (5) guidance in finding meaningful and satisfying retirement roles.

From late middle age on there is a substantial need for information about the biological changes related to aging, and in particular those changes that affect memory, learning ability, and the ability to engage in successful interpersonal behavior (see Schaie and Gribbin, 1975a). The kinds of needs discussed by Douvan in her chapter on intimacy are also pertinent here.

Maintaining some comprehension of one's environment and thus exercising at least a modicum of control over one's life are made difficult by the rapid technological and sociocultural changes described by Toffler (1970) in his popular analysis of "future shock." The traditional objective of lifelong learning has in fact been to interpret to adults past the stage of formal education those new technologies and social transitions that are likely to affect both personal behavior and the course of societies.

Comprehending sociocultural change is an important educational goal in its own right, but even more pressing is the need to overcome personal obsolescence. The education acquired in one's youth may no longer suffice for coping with the environment decades later. Updating one's education is not just a matter of acquiring additional information but also of developing new learning skills and techniques. Generational differences in level of function have been described by sociologists (Riley, Johnson, and Foner, 1972) as well as psychologists (Schaie, 1975). These discussions and the results of related empirical studies (see Schaie and Gribbin, 1975a) make it clear now that much of the apparent intellectual deficit shown by older people is not deficit at all but rather can be attributed to the relative obsolescence of older people's intellectual skills.

Adult education can be instrumental in overcoming the generational differences in information and skills that have resulted in the obsolescence just mentioned. Whether there is need for another period of "compulsory" education in late middle age or not may be of concern to future social policy planners. At present, however, we do see an increase in what has been called the "graying of the universities," as more individuals try to overcome their perceived disadvantage in dealing with social change by reentering the educational process.

From our discussion in this chapter we conclude that all the aforementioned educational goals are within reach of the average older adult, certainly until the early seventies, and for many even beyond. But because of the wide range of individual differences, careful assessment of specific abilities in relation to educational goals becomes essential. The dictum should be that, as far as intellectual competence is concerned, some older learners can accomplish any educational objective, most older learners can accomplish some carefully selected objective, and some, as at any age, will receive little or no benefit from education.

Educational Technology. Efforts to bring older learners into the educational system will succeed only if they are preceded by efforts to make educators aware of how the older learner differs from the younger, and to educate the older learners themselves on these matters so that they can enter the educational process with better understanding of their own needs, capabilities, and limitations.

The human aging process is frequently taken for granted as something that one learns to live with and that does not require special attention until there is a physiological or psychological breakdown. However, most adults are conscious of physiological and psychological changes, as well as of the social stereotypes assigned by an age-graded society (Maas and Kuypers, 1975; Neugarten and Datan, 1973). It is the stereotypes, and their consequences, that are particularly amenable to educational intervention. Recent work in the psychology of aging (see Birren and Schaie, 1977, for an extensive review) indicates that, although there is undoubtedly a decline in the peripheral functions with age, there is much compensation, and that the perceived behavioral deficit may be largely a consequence of deleterious role assignment to the old by the middle-aged (Schaie, 1973b).

The possibility that intelligent behavior may be a function of cognitive abilities plus performance-related, noncognitive factors has been discussed in the child development literature in relation to the performance-competence distinction (Flavell and Wohlwill, 1969). There is evidence that noncognitive factors, such as sensory deficits, motivation, and response speed, play an increasingly important role in intellectual performance with age. A current research thrust in adult psychology, therefore, is to determine whether various learning changes in later adulthood are due to cognitive or noncognitive factors (Woodruff and Walsh, 1975).

Some observed learning differences between age groups have been related to the increasing time required for the aging adult to acquire information and to retrieve new information from memory. Providing a longer acquisition and response period has been shown to improve the older adult's learning performance. Furthermore, the amount of material and the number of task demands presented at a given point in instruction have been shown to influence learning in later adulthood (Craik, 1977). Such findings would suggest the utility of a self-pacing approach, in which the number of task demands and the amount of information presented are carefully regulated. A programmed instruction approach, for example, can be effective with the older adult. The mastery learning approach developed by Bloom (1968) and the competency-based method in general also provide accommodation for variations in learning pace.

The incentives governing adult learning must be heeded more closely. Educators accustomed to working with the young may assume that novelty or change has an intrinsic appeal for students. However, novelty has much less value for older students. Acquiring new habits and taking risks may therefore have low incentive value. New material must have some personal meaning if it is to be learned well (see Schaie, 1978).

Programming of Higher Education. The educational system must adapt itself to an increasing number of students who return with a wealth of experience and a far better understanding than younger students of what they expect from education. These older students do not necessarily want a liberal education. Certainly, they do not need to be kept around the university to mature sufficiently to enter a vocational role. What they need is not a theoretical foundation for learning but new skills and information geared to their specific needs. It is quite reasonable to expect that far more intensive and specialized counseling activities will be required. More individualized courses of study may also be required since preparation is generally sought for work and leisure roles rather than for degrees (although degrees may be important if their lack prevents the mature student from entering new roles).

Although, as we have already noted, novelty per se has less incentive value for older students than for younger ones, older students may be better able to appreciate new sociocultural developments. For it requires experience and perspective to recognize true innovation. Thus, for the young everything is new, even if a skill or idea traces back to the dawn of humanity. It is the older students who can distinguish between traditional cultural values and skills and the technological or sociocultural changes that represent true innovation.[2] This means that teaching practices and resource materials that encourage a critical approach and active application of prior experiences are to be preferred over those that call for passive acceptance of authoritative views.

Individual variability in almost every type of intellectual capacity increases across the life span. The greater range of individual differences in adulthood should be of primary concern to the educator. Extreme individual differences in any student population (for example, exceptional children or disadvantaged children) has usually required an individualized instructional approach. Such an individualized orientation would seem

---

[2]The distinction between novelty as an ontogenetic and as a phylogenetic concept was called to the authors' attention by the eminent French philosopher Michel Philibert, whose thoughtful comments on this issue are gratefully acknowledged.

imperative for adults. Over the life span, the role of the teacher appears to change from director of learning to facilitator or resource person (Houle, 1974; Huberman, 1974). Whereas society and the educator direct the education of the young, the content and method of learning in adulthood are largely determined by the adult himself. The developmental changes in the learner across the life span suggest the need for qualitatively different types of teacher training for educators working with different age groups. The techniques of the typical college instructor may be inappropriate in teaching middle-aged or older persons. Teacher training institutions must take an active part in translating the available information concerning adult intellectual competence and adult learning into a delineation of the skills required of the adult educator.

The quality of life in any society can be measured by how successfully cultural continuity is maintained in a rapidly changing world. In our modern society, cultural obsolescence is a constant threat. It is a challenge even to decipher the service manuals accompanying new equipment, to say nothing of keeping up with the new developments in one's field. A great deal of attention has been focused on compensatory education for children coming from culturally or educationally deprived backgrounds. Much less attention has been paid to the fact that society is full of adults who need compensatory education to cope with sociocultural change. If we, as educators, recognize that the problems of older students are more often those of obsolescence than decrement, we will do a better job of educational programming.

References

Baltes, P. B., Reese, H. W., and Nesselroade, J. R. *Life-Span Developmental Psychology: An Introduction to Research Methods.* Monterey, Calif.: Brooks/Cole, 1977.

Baltes, P. B., and Schaie, K. W. "On the Plasticity of Intelligence in Adulthood and Old Age: Where Horn and Donaldson Fail." *American Psychologist,* 1976, *31,* 720-725.

Bayley, N., and Oden, M. H. "The Maintenance of Intellectual Ability in Gifted Adults." *Journal of Gerontology,* 1955, *10,* 91-107.

Birkhill, W. R., and Schaie, K. W. "The Effect of Differential Reinforcement of Cautiousness in the Intellectual Performance of the Elderly." *Journal of Gerontology,* 1975, *30,* 578-583.

Birren, J. E. "Age Changes in Speed of Behavior: Its Central Nature and Psychological Correlates." In A. T. Welford and J. E. Birren (Eds.), *Behavior, Aging, and the Nervous System.* Springfield, Ill.: Thomas, 1965.

Birren, J. E., and Schaie, K. W. (Eds.). *Handbook of the Psychology of Aging.* New York: Van Nostrand Reinhold, 1977.

Bloom, B. S. *Learning for Mastery: Evaluation Comment.* Los Angeles: Center for the Study of Evaluation of Instructional Programs, University of California, May 1968.

Botwinick, J. *Aging and Behavior.* New York: Springer-Verlag, 1973.

Botwinick, J. "Intellectual Abilities." In J. E. Birren and K. W. Schaie (Eds.), *Handbook of the Psychology of Aging.* New York: Van Nostrand Reinhold, 1977.

Bradway, K. P., Thompson, C. W., and Cravens, H. B. "Preschool IQs After Twenty-five Years." *Journal of Educational Psychology,* 1958, *49,* 278-281.

Cattell, R. B. "Theory of Fluid and Crystallized Intelligence: A Critical Experiment." *Journal of Educational Psychology,* 1963, *54,* 1-22.

Connolly, K. J., and Bruner, J. C. *The Growth of Competence.* New York: Academic Press, 1974.

Corso, J. F. "Sensory Processes and Age Effects in Normal Adults." *Journal of Gerontology,* 1971, *26,* 90-105.

Corso, J. F. "Auditory Perception and Communication." In J. E. Birren and K. W. Schaie (Eds.), *Handbook of the Psychology of Aging.* New York: Van Nostrand Reinhold, 1977.

Craik, F. I. M. "Age Differences in Human Memory." In J. E. Birren and K. W. Schaie (Eds.), *Handbook of the Psychology of Aging.* New York: Van Nostrand Reinhold, 1977.

Eisdorfer, C., Nowlin, J. B., and Wilkie, F. "Improvement of Learning in the Aged by Modification of Autonomic Nervous System Activity." *Science,* 1970, *170,* 1327-1329.

Erikson, E. H. *Insight and Responsibility.* New York: Norton, 1964.

Flavell, J. H. *The Developmental Psychology of Jean Piaget.* New York: Van Nostrand, 1963.

Flavell, J. H. "Cognitive Changes in Adulthood." In L. R. Goulet and P. B. Baltes (Eds.), *Life-Span Developmental Psychology: Research and Theory.* New York: Academic Press, 1970.

Flavell, J., and Wohlwill, J. "Formal and Functional Aspects of Cognitive Development." In D. Elkind and J. Flavell (Eds.), *Studies in Cognitive Development: Essays in Honor of Jean Piaget.* New York: Oxford University Press, 1969.

Fozard, J. L., and others. "Visual Perception and Communication." In J. E. Birren and K. W. Schaie (Eds.), *Handbook of the Psychology of Aging.* New York: Van Nostrand Reinhold, 1977.

Friedrich, D. K., and Van Horn, K. R. *Developmental Methodology: A Revised Primer.* Minneapolis, Minn.: Burgess, 1976.

Granick, S., Kleban, M. H., and Weiss, A. D. "Relationships Between Hearing Loss and Cognition in Normally Hearing Aged Persons." *Journal of Gerontology,* 1976, *31,* 434-440.

Green, R. F. "Age-Intelligence Relationship Between Ages Sixteen and Sixty-four: A Rising Trend." *Developmental Psychology,* 1969, *1,* 618-627.

Guilford, J. P. *The Nature of Human Intelligence.* New York: McGraw-Hill, 1967.

Hall, G. S. *Senescence: The Last Half of Life.* New York: Appleton-Century-Crofts, 1922.

Havighurst, R. J. *Developmental Tasks and Education.* (3rd ed.) New York: McKay, 1972.

Hertzog, C., Schaie, K. W., and Gribbin, K. "Cardiovascular Disease and Changes in Intellectual Functioning from Middle to Old Age." *Journal of Gerontology,* 1978, *33,* 872-883.

Horn, J. L. "Organization of Data on Life-Span Development of Human Abilities." In L. R. Goulet and P. B. Baltes (Eds.), *Life-Span Developmental Psychology: Research and Theory.* New York: Academic Press, 1970.

Horn, J. L., and Donaldson, G. "On the Myth of Intellectual Decline in Adulthood." *American Psychologist,* 1976, *31,* 701-719.

Houle, C. O. "The Changing Goals of Education in the Perspective of Lifelong Learning." *International Review of Education,* 1974, *20,* 430-445.

Hoyer, W. J., Labouvie-Vief, G. V., and Baltes, P. B. "Modification of Response Speed and Intellectual Performance in the Elderly." *Human Development,* 1973, *16,* 233-242.

Huberman, M. "Looking at Adult Education from the Perspective of the Adult Life Cycle." *International Review of Education,* 1974, *20,* 117-137.

Johnstone, J. W. C., and Rivera, R. J. *Volunteers for Learning: A Study of the Educational Pursuits of American Adults.* Chicago: Aldine, 1965.

Jones, H. E., and Conrad, H. S. "The Growth and Decline of Intelligence: A Study of a Homogenous Group Between the Ages of Ten and Sixty." *Genetic Psychology Monographs,* 1933, *13,* 223-298.

Kangas, J., and Bradway, K. "Intelligence at Middle Age: A Thirty-Eight Year Followup." *Developmental Psychology,* 1971, *5,* 333-337.

Kohlberg, L. "Continuities in Childhood and Adult Moral Development Revisited." In P. B. Baltes and K. W. Schaie (Eds.), *Life-Span Developmental Psychology: Personality and Socialization.* New York: Academic Press, 1973.

Konig, E. "Pitch Discrimination and Age." *Acta Otolarygologica,* 1957, *48,* 475-489.

Labouvie-Vief, G., and Gonda, J. N. "Cognitive Strategy Training and Intellectual Performance in the Elderly." *Journal of Gerontology,* 1976, *31,* 327-332.

Labouvie-Vief, G., and others. "Operant Analysis of Intellectual Behavior in Old Age." *Human Development,* 1974, *17,* 259-272.

Lebo, C. P., and Redell, R. C. "The Presbycusis Component in Occupational Hearing Loss." *Laryngoscope,* 1972, *82,* 1399-1409.

Maas, H. S., and Kuypers, J. A. *From Thirty to Seventy: A Forty-year Longitudinal Study of Adult Life Styles and Personality.* San Francisco: Jossey-Bass, 1975.

Marsh, G. R., and Thompson, L. W. "Psychophysiology of Aging." In J. E. Birren and K. W. Schaie (Eds.), *Handbook of the Psychology of Aging.* New York: Van Nostrand Reinhold, 1977.

Matarazzo, J. D. *Wechsler's Measurement and Appraisal of Adult Intelligence.* Baltimore: Williams & Wilkins, 1972.

Neugarten, B. L., and Datan, N. "Sociological Perspectives on the Life Cycle." In P. B. Baltes and K. W. Schaie (Eds.), *Life-Span Developmental Psychology: Personality and Socialization.* New York: Academic Press, 1973.

Okun, M. A., and DiVesta, F. J. "Cautiousness in Adulthood as a Function of Age and Instructions." *Journal of Gerontology,* 1976, *31,* 571-578.

Piaget, J. "Intellectual Evolution from Adolescence to Adulthood." *Human Development,* 1972, *15,* 1-12.

Plemons, J. K., Willis, S. L., and Baltes, P. B. "Modifiability of Fluid Intelligence in Aging: A Short-Term Training Approach." *Journal of Gerontology,* 1978, *33,* 224-231.

Pressey, S. L., Janney, J. E., and Kuhlen, R. G. *Life: A Psychological Survey.* New York: Harper & Row, 1939.

Reese, J. N., and Botwinick, J. "Detection and Decision Factors in Auditory Behavior of the Elderly." *Journal of Gerontology,* 1971, *26,* 133-138.

Reinert, G. "Comparative Factor Analytic Studies of Intelligence Throughout the Human Life-Span." In L. R. Goulet and P. B. Baltes (Eds.), *Life-Span Developmental Psychology: Research and Theory.* New York: Academic Press, 1970.

Riley, M. W., Johnson, M., and Foner, A. *Aging and Society: A Sociology of Age Stratification.* New York: Russell Sage Foundation, 1972.

Schaie, K. W. "Age Changes and Age Differences." *Gerontologist,* 1967, *7,* 128-132.

Schaie, K. W. "A Reinterpretation of Age-Related Changes in Cognitive Structure and Functioning." In L. R. Goulet and P. B. Baltes (Eds.), *Life-Span Developmental Psychology: Research and Theory.* New York: Academic Press, 1970.

Schaie, K. W. "Methodological Problems in Descriptive Developmental Research on

Adulthood and Aging." In J. R. Nesselroade and H. W. Reese (Eds.), *Life-Span Developmental Psychology: Methodological Issues.* New York: Academic Press, 1973a.

Schaie, K. W. "Intervention Toward an Ageless Society?" *Gerontologist,* 1973b, *13,* 31-58.

Schaie, K. W. "Age Changes in Adult Intelligence." In D. S. Woodruff and J. E. Birren (Eds.), *Aging: Scientific Perspectives and Social Issues.* New York: Van Nostrand, 1975.

Schaie, K. W. "Quasi-Experimental Designs in the Psychology of Aging." In J. E. Birren and K. W. Schaie (Eds.), *Handbook of the Psychology of Aging.* New York: Van Nostrand Reinhold, 1977.

Schaie, K. W. "Toward a Stage Theory of Adult Cognitive Development." *Journal of Aging and Human Development,* 1977/78, *8,* 129-138.

Schaie, K. W. "External Validity in the Assessment of Intellectual Development in Adulthood." *Journal of Gerontology,* 1978, *33,* 695-701.

Schaie, K. W. "The Primary Mental Abilities in Adulthood: An Exploration in the Development of Psychometric Intelligence." In P. B. Baltes and O. G. Brim, Jr. (Eds.), *Life-Span Development and Behavior.* Vol. 2. New York: Academic Press, 1979.

Schaie, K. W., Baltes, P. B., and Strother, C. R. "A Study of Auditory Sensitivity in Advanced Age." *Journal of Gerontology,* 1964, *19,* 453-457.

Schaie, K. W., and Gribbin, K. "Adult Development and Aging." *Annual Review of Psychology,* 1975a, *26,* 65-96.

Schaie, K. W., and Gribbin, K. "Impact of Environmental Complexity on Cognitive Development." Paper presented at the meeting of the International Society for the Study of Behavioral Development, Guildford, England, 1975b.

Schaie, K. W., and Marquette, B. W. "Stages in Transition: A Bio-Social Analysis of Adult Behavior." Paper presented at the Satellite Meeting of the International Society for the Study of Human Development, Kiryat Anavim, Israel, 1975.

Schaie, K. W., and Parham, L. A. *Examiner Manual for the Test of Behavioral Rigidity.* Palo Alto, Calif.: Consulting Psychologists Press, 1975.

Schaie, K. W., and Parham, L. A. "Cohort-Sequential Analyses of Adult Intellectual Development." *Developmental Psychology,* 1977, *13,* 649-653.

Schaie, K. W., and Quayhagen, M. "Life-Span Educational Psychology: Adulthood and Old Age." In J. Brandstaetter, G. Reinert, and K. A. Schneewind (Eds.), *Probleme und Perspektiven der Paedagogischen Psychologie.* Stuttgart: Klett, 1978.

Schaie, K. W., and Schaie, J. P. "Clinical Assessment and Aging." In J. E. Birren and K. W. Schaie (Eds.), *Handbook of the Psychology of Aging.* New York: Van Nostrand Reinhold, 1977.

Schaie, K. W., and Willis, S. L. "Life Span Development: Implications for Education." *Review of Research in Education,* 1978, *6,* 120-156.

Spearman, C. E. *The Nature of Intelligence and the Principles of Cognition.* London: Macmillan, 1927.

Talland, G. A. "Visual Signal Detection as a Function of Age, Input Rate, and Signal Frequency." *Journal of Psychology,* 1966, *63,* 105-115.

Terman, L. M. *The Measurement of Intelligence.* Boston: Houghton Mifflin, 1916.

Thurstone, L. L. *Primary Mental Abilities.* Chicago: University of Chicago Press, 1938.

Toffler, A. *Future Shock.* New York: Random House, 1970.

Walsh, D. A. "Age Differences in Central Perceptual Processing: A Dichoptic Backward Masking Investigation." *Journal of Gerontology,* 1976, *31,* 178-185.

Weale, R. A. "On the Eye." In A. T. Welford and J. E. Birren (Eds.), *Behavior, Aging, and the Nervous System.* Springfield, Ill.: Thomas, 1965.

Wechsler, D. *The Measurement of Adult Intelligence.* Baltimore: Williams & Wilkins, 1939.

Welford, A. T. "Motor Performance." In J. E. Birren and K. W. Schaie (Eds.), *Handbook of the Psychology of Aging.* New York: Van Nostrand Reinhold, 1977.

Woodruff, D., and Walsh, D. "Research in Adult Learning: The Individual." *Gerontologist,* 1975, *15,* 424-430.

Yerkes, R. M. "Psychological Examining in the United States Army." *Memoirs of the National Academy of Sciences,* 1921, *15,* 1-890.

5

Carol Gilligan

Moral Development

When Hannah Arendt begins her consideration of *The Life of the Mind* (1978), she returns to the subject of Adolf Eichmann, whose trial in Jerusalem was the impetus for her "preoccupation with mental activities." Having sought at the trial for evidence, in Eichmann, of the demonic or the depraved, she had found instead the "banality of evil," an absence of thought so profound and pervasive as to render his mind lifeless. The "mindlessness" of Eichmann's adherence to standardized codes of expression and conduct was so striking to Arendt that it changed the moral question for her from one of character to one of thought. Eichmann's moral failure seemed, above all, a failure to think.

The connection between morality and thought is central to this chapter's discussion of moral development in the college years. This discussion brings together the separate strands of moral and intellectual development whose confluence in adolescence has been, throughout Western history, a subject of recurrent fascination. I will describe this convergence as it has again appeared in recent research on moral development, discussing the findings of that research and the interpretive disputes to which they have given rise. It is important, however, to establish at the outset that while moral and intellectual development are necessarily conjoined, they do not inevitably proceed hand in hand. The educated and cultured nation of "good Germans" stands as a reminder that moral development is not, in any simple sense, a natural outcome of higher education.

Beginning in childhood, moral judgments signify efforts to find an order in the chaos of social experience. These judgments are tied, on the one hand, to the structures of thinking that the child brings to bear on his experience and, on the other, to the experiences themselves of which he strives to make sense. Through the ongoing interaction of thought and experience, moral development acquires a history of its own, which, while tied to the development of thinking, is not solely a reflection of that development and, in any event, does not necessarily coincide with the timing or sequence of formal education.

Conversely, the development of thought, which at its higher levels constitutes the domain of college education, does not in any simple way facilitate moral development. In fact, at a critical juncture, thinking threatens rather to derail moral judgment altogether. The notable achievement of the adolescent mind is the capacity for reflective thought—the ability to include, among the facts of experience, the activity of thinking itself. When thought thus turns inward and begins to examine its own constructions, it calls into question knowledge formerly taken for granted, including the knowledge of good and evil. To think about morality is to confront the problem of judgment and thereby to discover the inevitable limitations of knowledge itself. This is the point in cognitive development where thought loses its innocence and knowledge its naive objectivity. That moral knowledge is the temptation that precipitates this event is both a part of the Biblical story and of our present narrative as well. The reconstruction of moral judgment in light of a reflective awareness of the limitations of moral knowledge will emerge as the focus of this chapter's discussion.

In beginning with Arendt's discovery of the moral problem as a problem of thought, I wished to call the reader's attention at the start to my central theme. Arendt's recognition that the capacity for moral response depends on the ability to discern the moral problem and thus that "the activity of thought as such . . . [could] be among the conditions that make men abstain from evil-doing" (1978, p. 5) led her then to inquire into the nature of thought and to rediscover, in its constructive activity, the contextually relative nature of human understanding. Once morality is recognized as a construction of human thought rather than as an objective fact of experience, then the whole nature of moral judgment undergoes a radical transformation. This discovery brings to a halt the endless search for objective justification and points instead to the realization that since actions have consequence, and commitment of one sort or another is embedded in the very fabric of life, responsibility is in the end unavoidable. The ethical responsibility that can grow out of this awareness is the culmination of the developmental process I trace. In this process, however, the understanding of relativism itself changes from the pejorative connotation of moral abandonment, which it seems to be from a conventional perspective, to a critical event in the development of moral understanding, where it appears instead as the prelude to the discovery of ethical responsibility.

When higher education stimulates the activity of the mind and develops its capacity for reflection and judgment, it inevitably becomes entangled with the process of moral development. The moral reflection to which it gives rise, however, occurs not only within the framework of a particular stage in cognitive and moral development but also within the context of a particular historical period and of a particular phase in the history of the individual life. The research on moral development has taken place within a limited span of time, which makes it impossible to separate its findings from the history of the period in which they arose. However, this research has been carried out in the setting of the traditional residential college, where the themes of late adolescent development are interwoven with moral and intellectual development and lend a distinctively familiar hue.

To the reflective adolescent, morality has always been a central concern. Whether one begins with Aristotle's description of the preference of youth for noble rather than youthful deeds or with the preoccupation with virtue and sin that runs through adolescent diaries and autobiographies, moral questions stand with questions of identity in the forefront of adolescent thought. Inhelder and Piaget's (1958) description of the ideological mind of the adolescent, with its penchant for metaphysical and utopian constructions, is closely tied to Erikson's (1958) observation that ideology is the other side of identity in adolescent psychosocial development. The changes of puberty and the incest taboo, which impel the sexually mature adolescent to leave the familial world of childhood and find his place within a wider societal arena, initiate a search for verification and justification, for an identity that confirms the self, and for a system of belief that supports that identity. Whether this search is resolved through the adoption of a conventional identity and ideology or whether conventional solutions are rejected and new ones forged, the search itself takes on a moral fervor that reveals its underlying function of delineating and justifying life choices. Identity and ideology impart meaning to commitments that might otherwise seem impossible to make and pointless to sustain.

The convergence of developmental themes in late adolescence around questions of morality, together with the intellectual capacity of the adolescent mind to think about moral questions in a new way, thus points to adolescence as a critical time for moral development in the human life cycle. The substance of adolescent moral concern and the reflexive nature of adolescent thought indicate, more specifically, that the crisis of this time is that of moral relativism—the crisis of Hamlet and Raskolnikov, of Stephen Dedalus, as well as more recent inhabitants of the university world. In seeking to understand the tie between moral relativism and university education, whose concurrence has been marked in the observations of Erikson (1963), Perry (1968), and Kohlberg and Kramer (1969), I begin with the literature on moral development, which provides the necessary background to this crisis and shapes as well one conception of its likely course and resolution.

Stages of Moral Development

The empirical study of moral development as a part of cognitive development began with Piaget (1965 [1932]), whose interest in the different logic of children's thinking led him to observe the moral judgments that they made. Employing his method of the interrogatory, he sought to determine the nature of children's practice and consciousness of rules. Focusing on the game of marbles, with its elaborate system of rules, and on the ways in which children resolved dilemmas arising from the violation of socially accepted rules, Piaget identified and described two distinct moralities in childhood thought, which followed one another in a developmental sequence. These were the moralities of *constraint* and *cooperation*—the first, heteronomous, harboring "an almost mystical respect for rules" (p. 61) and a "tendency to regard duty and the value attaching to it as self-subsistent and independent of the mind" (p. 111), the second, autonomous, considering rules as the product of mutual agreement, the natural outcome of free decision and mutual respect. The idea of justice, confused at first with obedience to authority and conceived initially in terms of moral realism and immanent retribution, develops with the achievement of individual autonomy into concepts of equality and reciprocity, which emerge spontaneously through children's cooperative play. The establishment of democratic social relationships among children and the concurrent development of their capacity for logical thought form the basis for a morality of cooperation, which centers on the concept of justice as fairness. The realization that "there is no end to revenge" becomes the triumphant recognition of maturing logical operations and of moral judgments, confirming the social experience of the child that "you have to stop quarreling in order to play properly" (Piaget, 1965 [1932], pp. 71, 323).

While Piaget traced the development of children's moral judgments from the preschool years through middle childhood, he left off at the beginning of adolescence, when the transition from concrete to formal operational thought sets the stage for a new kind of judgment. His research, however, was taken up by Lawrence Kohlberg, who focused specifically on adolescent moral judgment, choosing a sample of eighty-four boys aged 10 to 16 and following their development at three-year intervals (Kohlberg and Kramer, 1969). Since Piaget had found that abstract thinking—the capacity for hypothetical deductive logic—began usually between the ages of 11 and 13, and since this cognitive development coincided with the onset of puberty and the concomitant expansion in social experience, adolescence seemed a time when both the experiential and cognitive preconditions for moral development were present. The description of that development in terms of an extended sequence of stages was the discovery of Kohlberg's research.

Drawing on the works of medieval casuistry, Kohlberg constructed moral dilemmas that placed socially accepted values in conflict—for example, the value of life versus the value of property, the value of obedience versus that of keeping promises, respect for the individual versus concern for group welfare. He then set out to determine how these conflicts would be understood and resolved by his sample of boys. From the boys' various conceptions of life, law, property, authority, punishment, conscience, and so forth, Kohlberg was able to identify six different stages in the conception of justice, which appeared to form an invariant sequence. Each successive stage represented a hierarchical reorganization of the moral concepts of the preceding stage, leading to a more differentiated and complex understanding of the dilemma itself and hence a more just resolution. Each stage reflected a development in the moral capacity to take the point of view of the other—an expanded perspective conducive to a fairer resolution of the dilemma. Conceiving of justice as fairness, as an equilibration of natural rights, Kohlberg traced moral development through various stages in the understanding of the concept of rights and through the systematic expansion of the universe of persons whose rights were included in moral consideration. Thus, at each stage in Kohlberg's sequence, development was signified by an expansion in the social unit to which moral judgments applied, and a corresponding refinement in the concept of justice to maintain the balance of individual claims within an enlarged and more intricately perceived social world. Clearly, the adolescent capacity to conceive an abstract moral universe and the extension of adolescent experience beyond the particular boundaries of a childhood world set the stage for a concomitant expansion of moral judgment beyond the limits of conventional morality toward a postconventional or more universal ethical conception. This is precisely the progression that Kohlberg's data began to trace.

Kohlberg's description of his six stages of moral judgment thus centers around the concept of conventional morality, the equation of justice with the preservation of existing social systems through the maintenance of respect for their norms and values. Kohlberg groups his stages into three general levels, which he calls *preconventional, conventional,* and *postconventional,* reflecting the expansion in moral perspective from an individual, to a societal, to a universal point of view, but always with conventional morality as the point of departure. Whereas preconventional moral judgment denotes an inability to construct a societal viewpoint, postconventional judgment transcends that vision. *Preconventional judgment* is egocentric and derives moral constructs from individual needs; *conventional judgment* is based on the shared moral values that sustain relationships, groups, communities, and societies, while *postconventional judgment* adopts a prior-to-society perspective and constructs moral principles that are universal in application.

Deriving his stages from data that were largely—and, after the first interviews, exclusively—gathered from adolescents, Kohlberg discovered, within each of his three levels, two distinct stages of moral judgment. At the preconventional level, Stage 1 indicated the continuation into adolescence of the heteronomous morality of constraint, which Piaget had described as arising naturally in early childhood. The moral judgments of this stage reflect, even in adolescence, the perspective of an individual who feels vulnerable to the retribution of remote and powerful authorities and who tries to survive by staying out of trouble. At Stage 2, judgment remains egocentric—that is, tied to the needs of the self—but the authorities no longer seem so monolithic or so powerful. Instead, the recognition through experience that rules often conflict, that justice is not always immanent, that goodness is not always rewarded or evil punished, creates some room for individual enterprise. The emergent autonomy that accompanies this recognition is reflected in moral judgments based on a concept of justice as fairness, understood first in terms of simple reciprocity or even exchange.

At the conventional level of moral judgment, the incipient cooperation of individual exchange becomes transformed into a new moral perspective that fuses individual needs with those of the group and articulates, out of that fusion, a morality of shared norms and values. At Stage 3, judgment proceeds from stereotypic and conventional conceptions of goodness, which, whatever their specific content, reflect concern about others and an ability to see their perspective as different from one's own. The relationship or the group takes precedence over the individual needs of its component members in the articulation of moral decisions. Such decisions are now based on the shared assumptions that underlie mutual trust. At Stage 4, the group or relational perspective is extended to include society as a whole, conceived as a system that defines roles and rules, to which its members must adhere if the social order is to be preserved. The welfare of the individual seems at this stage inextricably tied to the preservation of the society, whose rules are binding and whose roles prescribe the nature and extent of moral obligation.

With the development of postconventional moral judgment, however, the limits of societal morality are transcended through the discovery of ethical principles that form the basis for the final reconstruction of morality at Stages 5 and 6. The principles of equality and reciprocity, generated at Stage 5 through an understanding of social contract and individual conscience, become at Stage 6 the foundation for a universal conception of justice as respect for persons. The Golden Rule is now understood in its fullest implication as Kant's categorical imperative—to act on that maxim which you can at the same time will to be a universal law. The social unit expands to the universe of all human beings as the moral capacity to take the role of the other reaches its fullest extension. Moral judgment, freed from both individual and societal constraints and anchored instead in principles of justice, becomes autonomous in its function and universal in its impartial application.

These six stages were found by Kohlberg to order and discriminate between the various responses of his sample of adolescent boys to hypothetical dilemmas of moral conflict and choice. Kohlberg's highest stages of moral judgment clearly relied on the adolescent capacity for formal operational thought. That is, they represented a reconstruction of social and moral understanding that manifested, in the social realm, the evolution in adolescent thought from concrete to formal logic described by Inhelder and Piaget (1958). By placing observed reality within the larger framework of logical possibilities and thus allowing the construction of contrary-to-fact hypotheses, principled moral judgment—like all formal logic—enabled the individual to judge independently of existing social and moral conventions.

Moral Relativism

The principles of Kohlberg's higher stages of moral development were rationally derived, reflecting a utopian, "prior-to-society perspective" and resting their claim to validity on the universality and objectivity of their underlying conception of justice. Therefore, they seemed to offer, both logically and psychologically, the perfect basis for adolescent social criticism. By using the logical capabilities of thought to escape the bounds of conventional morality and formulate the good in terms of a universal ethic, the adolescent could meet his psychological need to free initiative from guilt and justify choice independently of parental or societal values. It would seem that the expansion of intellectual capability associated with higher education should eventuate in the development of principled moral judgment as the solution to a multitude of adolescent concerns.

It thus came as something of a surprise to discover, among the college students in Kohlberg's longitudinal sample, a form of moral judgment that defied the compelling logic of his developmental sequence and posed for his theory the thorny problem of apparent regression. The phenomenon was that of *moral relativism*—the claim that in the face of individual difference and cultural heterogeneity, nonarbitrary or objective moral judgment was impossible and that therefore one "should" do whatever one thinks is right. Kohlberg's standard dilemma depicts the conflict of a man named Heinz who could save the life of his dying wife only by stealing an outrageously overpriced drug. Students who had, during high school, readily indicated what Heinz should do and why now disclaimed the validity of such knowledge and argued instead that there were a million ways to look at such a dilemma and no way of judging that any particular resolution was right or wrong. Heinz, they said, should do what he wants. Taken by themselves, these judgments sounded identical to those of a naive instrumental hedonist at Stage 2, who, without any notion of a societal moral perspective, had simply equated *would* and *should* and assumed that others would do the same. When such judgments reappeared in late adolescence after a societal perspective had been articulated, conventional morality appeared to unravel, giving way to a cynical pragmatism.

Thus, we arrive at the college years to find moral development out of joint and the problem of relativism the subject of continuing interpretive debate among developmental psychologists. When Kohlberg and Kramer, writing in 1969, published the results of Kohlberg's longitudinal study from the period when the subjects were between the ages of 16 and 25, they reported two dramatic findings. The first was a correlation of .89 between moral maturity scores at ages 16 and 25, which they interpreted to indicate that moral development ended in adolescence—a conclusion supported by Kramer's additional finding of no higher stages of judgment among the fathers of the boys in the sample. This stability of development, however, seemed to be interrupted during the college years. The second finding Kohlberg and Kramer reported was that the college sophomore stood as the sole exception to the "generalization that developmental change is forward and sequential" and therefore could be considered "the oddest and most interesting moral fish of all" (1969, p. 109).

The college sophomores were of interest because between late high school and the second or third year of college 20 percent of Kohlberg's middle-class sample dropped, or regressed, in moral maturity scores. Although these regressors were among the most advanced in their moral judgments at the end of high school, showing a mixture of conventional (Stage 4) and principled (Stage 5) thought, they had, in college, abandoned such judgments in favor of "good old Stage 2 hedonistic relativism, jazzed up with some philosophic and sociopolitical jargon" (p. 109). In addition, such judgments were accom-

panied, for at least half of the students, by "anti-conventional acts of a more or less delin-
quent sort" (p. 111). Noting ideologies ranging from the New Left to the New Right and
identifying a Nietzschean racist and a modern-day Raskolnikov determined to prove "that
the strong need not be moral and the good were good only out of stupidity and weakness," Kohlberg puzzled over the interpretation of this phenomenon and its significance
for his theory of moral stage progression.

Returning to the clear relationship between moral judgments at ages 16 and 25
and observing, as well, that all the regressors had returned, by age 25, to the mixture of
Stage 4 and 5 moral judgments they had shown at the end of high school, with somewhat
more principled and less conventional thinking, Kohlberg concluded that the relativism of
the college years was a transient aberration in moral development. The 20 percent of his
sample who were relativistic in college were among the highest in moral judgment at age
25, as they had been in high school, and their behavior, as far as Kohlberg could observe,
once again conformed to the conventional and principled moral standards reflected in
their judgments.

Thus, the same "mysterious forces of development [that] led our 20 percent from
upstanding conventional morality to Raskolnikov moral defiance ... set them all to
right" (Kohlberg and Kramer, 1969, p. 111). These forces themselves seemed to have less
to do with moral development in the structural sense of Kohlberg's theory than with the
Sturm und Drang of the adolescent identity crisis and the confrontation with relativism
that arose from the intellectual challenge of higher education. Conceived as a functional
rather than a structural regression in moral judgment, relativism seemed to serve two purposes in late adolescent moral development. The first was to free initiative from guilt and
allow the psychosocial moratorium that Erikson saw as essential to the search for a postconventional or "neo-humanist" identity (Erikson, 1968, p. 38). The second was to integrate the adolescent's awareness of the limitations and hypocrisy of conventional moral
thought and thus to set the stage for its replacement by the ethical principles whose discovery, in Kohlberg's eyes, would solve the problem posed by relativism.

Thus, relativism embodied adolescent protest not only against "the authoritarian
morality of parental figures" but also against "the immorality of the world itself" (Kohlberg and Kramer, 1969). Seen in this light, relativism appeared not as an impediment to
moral development but rather as a necessary transitional step in the progression from a
conventional moral ideology to a principled humanistic ethic. Relativism freed judgmental
initiative from childhood guilt and addressed the sins of the world, which otherwise were
obscured in conventional rationalization. In this sense, relativism was a manifestation of
the life of the mind as it engaged the reality of human suffering and conflict. The ability
to free moral judgment from the clichés and stock phrases of conventional interpretation
depends initially on the capacity to call that interpretation into question. The sweeping
and highly moralistic rejection of morality that characterized the responses of these transitional relativists appeared as part of the process of stabilizing and integrating the principled morality that, though nascent at the end of high school, had not yet been put to
the adult test of commitment.

Whatever its developmental role, however, this process was not without dangers of
its own. Erikson (1958) had pointed to the risks inherent in the adolescent's search for a
self-wrought identity, indicating how the search for "allness" could end in the "nothing-
ness" of an identity so diffuse as to obliterate any coherent sense of self. So, too, could
the struggle to find a morality beyond convention eventuate instead in an amoral hedonism or, more dangerously, in a cynical moral nihilism. When the injustices of conventional
morality were apparent and there seemed no alternative way to judge—when, as Hamlet

said, "there is nothing either good or bad but thinking makes it so"—then the flexibility of adolescent thought made anything seem possible. Given a morality that appeared both absurd and hypocritical, a matter more of rationalization than of reason, hedonism returned as at least an "authentic" basis for choice.

Kohlberg's Experiment in Moral Education

When the counter-culture of the late 1960s adopted moral relativism as its convention, proclaiming that the "right" thing to do was "to do your own thing," the possibility of transitional relativism hardening into a permanent condition of thought seemed underlined. Remembering, in Raskolnikov and Nietzsche, the destructiveness of a stance of moral defiance and nihilism, Kohlberg set out to apply his knowledge of development to shore up morality against the swelling relativistic tide. As he considered principled morality the naturally occurring solution to the problem of relativism, he sought to foster its development by teaching a course on moral and political choice to the Harvard freshmen of 1970. The course was conceived as an experiment in "education for justice," with development as the aim of education and justice the end of moral development. Kohlberg's course differed from previous efforts in moral instruction in that its approach was not doctrinaire but rather developmental. Having identified relativism as the classical moral problem of the college sophomore, he would "save the sophomores from relativism" by leading them as freshmen, in Socratic fashion, toward the discovery of its solution in moral principles upon which "all rational men could agree." Such principles, in transcending relativism, made it possible, once again, to take a stand, to judge, and to choose. Since, in Kohlberg's (1971) conception, the "is" of psychological development led to the "ought" of justice in its principled formulation, his efforts were directed toward facilitating a natural process, which the historical moment of the late sixties might otherwise have impeded.

He was encouraged, in this effort, by Turiel's (1972) reinterpretation of adolescent relativism, which identified it unequivocally as a transitional rather than a regressive phenomenon in moral development. While Kohlberg had focused on the potential for evil in the relativistic abandonment of moral judgment, Turiel saw, in all its moral confusion, a potential for good—that is, for development. He pointed out the contradictions in the highly moralistic adolescent rejection of morality ("It is *wrong* to make moral judgments." "Everyone *should* do what he wants.") and saw in this confusion a failure to differentiate between societal conventions whose limitations were apparent and moral principles, only dimly understood. While conventional morality constituted an unjustifiable impediment to the adolescent, who feared, above all, the constriction of his own initiative by "the morality of the great mass of people being imposed on me," morality itself might be separable from societal constraint. For the young person who was "casting around for my own, what is moral, in all these matters," relativism offered a protection that guaranteed this search, legitimizing it on intellectual grounds and disarming those whose interference otherwise might precipitate a mature commitment to values that could not yet be endorsed as one's own.

Relying on the capacity of the formally operational adolescent mind to understand and construct a morality based on principles rather than conventions of justice, Kohlberg taught, in conjunction, the philosophy of ethics and the psychology of moral development. Since the research of Rest (1973) had indicated that people prefer the highest stage of moral judgment that they can understand (generally one stage above the one they use) and Turiel (1966) had, in addition, shown that exposure to thinking one stage above one's own tends to facilitate development to that stage, the pedagogy of the course was empirically grounded. The expectation was that relativism would disappear as principles came to replace social conventions and provide a basis for an intellectually respectable, postconventional moral philosophy.

Since Kohlberg and Kramer (1969) had reported that "principled thought of the Stage 5 variety is [born in adolescence and] pretty completely developed by the end of high school" (p. 106), that "little development occurs after the early twenties" (p. 106), and that "there was no way of thinking about our moral situations found in adulthood and not found in adolescence" (p. 105), the adolescent years were a critical period for the establishment of principled moral thought. The final transformation in cognitive development, identified by Piaget as the development of formal thought, made possible the final transformation in moral development, which, if it did not occur at this time, was unlikely to occur at all. This was the development that seemed threatened by the counter-culture, which challenged both moral judgments and the adult commitments they supported and made adolescent relativism the justification for an alternative "life-style." In addition, however, Kohlberg's effort to solve the problem of relativism by fostering through education the development of principled moral judgment gained impetus from the startling and much-debated results of the Milgram study, which were reported at that time.

Milgram (1974) had conducted a series of studies on obedience to authority, which were conceived as an analogue to Nazi Germany. Milgram's legitimate authority, the scientific experimenter, ordered college students to administer apparently dangerous shocks to a seemingly innocent victim under the guise of studying the effects of punishment on learning. The willingness of the vast majority of students to ignore the cries of the victim and comply with the demands of the experimenter took everyone by surprise and seemed indicative of the same lifelessness of mind and absence of judgment that Arendt had found so alarming in Eichmann. When Kohlberg subsequently interviewed some of Milgram's subjects and found that 80 percent of those few who had disobeyed the unethical commands were principled in their moral judgments, while those who had complied were predominantly conventional, the social importance of efforts to facilitate undergraduate moral development seemed clear and pressing. Furthermore, the increasing involvement of the United States in Vietnam and the examples of Martin Luther King and the antiwar movement indicated how a principled morality could inform and support political action against injustice.

Despite this compelling conjunction of historical and psychological supports, the course on moral and political choice did not lead, in any consistent way, to the development and stabilization of principled moral judgment. Instead, relativism appeared both more tenacious and complex than had originally been assumed. The relationship between relativistic and principled thinking resisted the simple logic of Kohlberg's stage sequence and instead complicated the understanding of moral development at its higher stages. While some students progressed as Kohlberg had predicted, these students seemed often to have avoided rather than confronted relativism, while the relativists conversely resisted the solution that principles offered to the problem of moral judgment. Conventional, relativistic, and principled moral judgments swirled through the interviews that preceded and followed the course discussions in a complication of orderings which could not be embraced by Kohlberg's stage theory (Murphy and Gilligan, in press).

When Boyd, who as a graduate student had been involved in teaching the Harvard course, went on to conduct a similar experiment in moral education at Oregon, he reported similar findings (Boyd, 1976). While Kohlberg's stage sequence described the moral development of some of the students, there were others whose judgments it could not explain. Prominent among those who repeatedly fell outside the scale of Kohlberg's stages were women and relativists, both of whose judgments, in their reliance on context for interpretation, resisted assimilation to the categories of the coding scheme. Once again the problematic nature of moral development in the college years had been discovered, and once again relativism appeared central to the problem. Rather than being dispelled by an understanding of moral principles, relativism instead generated questions about the adequacy or the applicability of the principles themselves.

The capacity for formal thought and postconventional moral speculation was evident in the questions raised repeatedly by the students in the course, but these questions pertained often to problems of conflicting responsibilities to which Kohlberg's principles of justice offered no clear resolution. What were the limits of moral obligation, the students wanted to know, as they extended the consideration of hypothetical moral dilemmas to include the real moral problems of starvation in Biafra, of the continuation of an unjust war, of conflicts between commitments to friends and lovers, of competing obligations to self and others. How could a concept of equality be applied in a world where inequity was not only a lamentable product of social injustice but a condition of life itself? How could such inequities be reconciled with the claims of justice? As the assumptions underlying a concept of blind justice impartially enforced were challenged by experiences that opened the students' eyes to the reality of human pain and suffering, the critical tenets of formal thought came into conflict with the actuality of moral experience. The reversibility of logical operations came up against the irreversibility of history—the impossibility of return once choice had irrevocably transformed the conditions under which it had been made—and the assumption of "all other things being equal" tangled with the awareness that in reality they never were. Instead, the moral problem came to be seen as indissolubly tied to the conditions in which it arose and to the contingencies that would determine the actual consequences of its various possible resolutions.

Such questions were not easily amenable to solution within the framework of Kohlberg's theory since his principled conception of justice arose from a concept of natural rights that took for granted the objectivity of judgment that the students saw as open to question. While Kohlberg attributed these problems to the persistent encroachment of an intellectual relativism, Fishkin (1975) compounded the problem by demonstrating its capacity to undo even the most principled moral understanding. Studying honor students in philosophy at Oxford whose capacity for moral judgments at Stages 5 and 6 was readily apparent, he found among such students a total repudiation of the validity of all moral judgments. To these students, moral questions were unanswerable because there was, in their judgment, no way of knowing the "right" thing to do. While it was possible to ascertain the right (that is, successful or effective) way to save a life, it was impossible to say whether it was right (that is, good) to do so. Reason had outstripped morality, as Kant and Dostoevski had seen, and, in the absence of knowledge, moral judgment became a matter not of logic but of faith. Moral questions thus defied any possibility for objective agreement. While questions of fact could be answered within the context of scientific knowledge, it was impossible to know that which it was necessary to know to answer moral questions (Gilligan, 1976). Science could not provide answers to moral questions, and scientific or formal thinking could not support moral judgments, as Max Weber had seen (Weber, 1946). Quoting Tolstoi's conclusion that science was meaningless because it provided no answers to the questions of how to live or what to do, Weber depicted the dilemma of the modern adolescent, attempting, like Ivan Karamazov, to derive from a scientific understanding, answers to problems of moral judgment and choice.

In light of this dilemma, it is easy to see the appeal of Kohlberg's principled stages for the adolescent in search of an objective basis for justification, which would resurrect the orthodoxy of conventional thought on a new postconventional base of certainty. If all rational men could agree on what was the right thing to do, then responsibility for choice could be shared rather than borne alone. In any event, the principles of respect for persons and of equality and reciprocity in social interaction seemed worthy of universal endorsement and a basis for such rational agreement. The problem, however, lay not in their utopian conception but rather in their practical construction—in their application to the reality of the actual moral dilemma, to what one student called "the dilemma of the fact" (Gilligan and Murphy, 1979).

Reconstruction of Moral Judgment

The adolescent mind has an affinity for formal constructions and principled solutions to hypothetical problems. Thus, the developmental issue in late adolescence, when the constraints of choice impinge on the limitless world of hypothetical possibility, comes to center on the relationship between the ideal and the real. From the structural perspective of cognitive developmental theory, the question becomes, How can a formal construction of principled morality, with its claims to universalizability and reversibility, be accommodated to the particular and irreversible reality of social experience without undergoing the structural transformation of cognitive stage change? This question centers on the role of experience in late adolescent moral development and identifies the relationship between experience and judgment as an issue of critical importance, as both Piaget (1972) and Kohlberg (1973) saw. However, the understanding of the relationship between experience and judgment hinges on the way in which relativism is conceived within the framework of a cognitive-developmental theory.

Two papers that appeared in 1973 addressed this issue by considering the place of late adolescent moral relations within an expanded conception of moral development. These papers, written respectively by Gilligan and Kohlberg and by Kohlberg alone, provide different perspectives on the nature of moral development within the college years.

Gilligan and Kohlberg reaffirmed the relationship between formal operational thought and postconventional moral judgment by citing the results of a study by Colby (1972) that confirmed the dependence of principled morality on the presence of underlying formal logical operations. Colby demonstrated that an intervention designed to foster the development of principled moral judgment in students who were at the conventional stages was successful only with those whose thinking was predominantly formal operational. However, since formal operations give rise also to moral relativism, this finding led to a discussion of the relationship between relativism and principled morality, which appeared at the center of undergraduate moral concern. A pattern recurred in which the construction of a grandly principled scheme for moral judgment informed by a utopian conception of how things ought to be was subsequently brought into question by a discrepancy between that ideal conception and experiences in actual situations of moral conflict and choice. This discrepancy was resolved in a number of ways by different students. The solutions involved varying degrees of *assimilation* (the interpretation of experience in accordance with pre-existing categories of thought) and *accommodation* (the modification of thought to account for discrepant experience). Where accommodation prevailed, however, the resulting moral judgments were much changed from those of the grand scheme and reflected principles of a very different tenor.

A second-year law student, who had been a participant in moral judgment interviews while an undergraduate at Harvard, articulated the changes that had occurred in his own moral thinking during the college years. He recalled his construction, as a college freshman, of a "paradigm of abstract moral values," in which he "worked out in [his] mind what [he] personally considered to be the most important aspects of life and sort of ranked them one to ten." This paradigm, a subject of endless dormitory discussion, then guided his moral judgment; by fitting the problem into the correct category, he then could logically work out the answer. ("I would sort of try to apply that paradigm to any particular situation that I saw, try to figure out how I thought morally it should come out.") Kohlberg's Heinz dilemma, depicting a conflict between life and property, fit perfectly into this hierarchical scheme and was easily resolved in terms of the logical priority of life over property.

However, these "huge theoretical moral constructs and systems" fell prey at the end of his sophomore year (after the Harvard strike of 1970) to a period of extreme relativism in which he came to "the conclusion, not very much based on reason, that morality was, by and large, a lot of bunk, that there were no right or wrong answers whatsoever." Although the logical integrity of his principled construction had seemed to make it impregnable, his experience as a participant in the strike had been its undoing. This experience led him to reject the "reason" of his previous judgment and to conclude that "people did things that were givens of experience, and it was beyond anyone's judgment power not only to determine whether any person's acts were right or wrong but to determine whether there was a right or wrong. I read a lot of Kant, obviously, so he really got to me in those days." As a result, he said, "I stopped thinking in moral terms, or stopped thinking in abstract moral terms as I had been thinking" and instead, read a lot of Marx during his junior year.

Summarizing the course of his own development, he said: "During the first couple of years [of college], I went from a position of very abstract, sort of univeralistic moral concepts to a sort of nihilistic rejection, to sort of worrying about more immediate problems." He characterized his current approach to moral judgment as being more particular and more closely tied to the specific "facts" of the situation itself: "I look at each situation and now I try to extract the moral problems involved in a given situation, and rather than trying to pigeonhole a certain situation, I try to find out what those problems are." While he said, "To tell the truth, I don't think about those problems as much as I did four years ago," it was clear from his response to the Heinz dilemma that his judgment fundamentally had changed. When asked if it would be right for Heinz, the desperate husband, to steal the drug that would save his wife's life when he could get it no other way, he replied: "I almost find it impossible to speak to this particular fact situation in terms of should or ought." This impossibility stemmed from his realization that these concepts themselves were "indigenous to a Western culture and more particularly to the Judeo-Christian culture" and that people who have grown up within that culture necessarily have come to construe moral problems and moral concepts in a particular way. While affirming his belief that "there is a concept of should or ought," he indicated that this moral conception does not lead automatically to a solution of the moral problem, as a "paradigmatic view" might imply. Such a view, rather, contains "an element of deception," which stems from the failure to recognize the extent to which the moral structures that determine "what conclusions one is going to draw later on in life" are embedded in the structures of one's thinking, which themselves arise in early childhood. Thus, there is, inevitably, a self-deception in concluding that "in confronting moral problems there is an answer" independent of the moral construction in which the problem initially is framed.

Heinz's problem is thus at once "both moral and nonmoral." The moral problem focuses on "one thing and that is that Heinz's wife is dying," but this problem is inseparable from the emotional problem, which has to do with Heinz's feelings for his wife and the lack of feeling manifest in the druggist's refusal to compromise his profit. These problems are, in turn, connected with "a system of political values [that] borders on a system of moral values," which is responsible for the situation that gave rise to the dilemma in the first place. Thus, while formerly this student had considered the preservation of human life to be the paramount value in all situations—a view, he said, that guided his participation in antiwar activities—he now believed that "what we think is very much a part of how we live" and that in detaching thought from life he had been "building a castle in the air."

Still, the moral problem remains, not in terms of a "Platonic system which says a certain thing may be wrong in itself," but because "human beings come in contact with each other's lives." Moral values are human constructions, conventions of thought that inevitably are tied to the conditions in which people live and in which they must act. "A truly moral existence, if there is such a thing, [would be] relating to any person one comes across, not as a means, but as an end in himself and essentially as a human being and nothing more and nothing less, not as my client, not as my waiter." When people relate to one another in this way, they transcend the categories of moral judgment but, in doing so, resolve the problem of relativism as well. "When one is 'beyond good and evil,' you talk about human beings vis-à-vis other human beings rather than talking about right or wrong. I think that people who relate to each other that way don't think of each other as right or wrong. . . . You have to judge that person's acts in the context of everybody else's acts, and maybe you do attach moral judgments, but what I am trying to say is maybe that does not clash with my relativism. Maybe it does, but I guess to me the ideal societal situation is where everybody related to everybody like that and did not worry about right or wrong, because then moral dilemmas might not exist or might not arise. Maybe if Heinz comes into the druggist and the druggist looks at this guy and says this is not some guy who may or may not be able to pay me $2,000, this is a man and his wife is dying, maybe that is the ideal way for the druggist to perceive this problem, and then he gives him the drug."

Thus, the construction and resolution of the moral problem invariably go hand in hand. While relativism is recognized as a permanent condition of judgment, the problem of action nevertheless remains. The shift in focus from justification to response, however, turns the initial question from "Should Heinz steal the drug?"—a question of right and wrong—to "Shouldn't Heinz steal the drug?"—a question of whether the predicament of the wife calls for response. The dilemma itself, conceived to arise from a failure of response, is resolved with its occurrence, rendering the issues of judgment and blame ancillary if not an impediment to that solution. In this reconstructed moral understanding, the hierarchy of values and the nihilism that followed it are both replaced by a moral commitment to relate to others in a way that is not exploitative—the ultimate expression of the concept of respect for persons. In this sense, an ethic of intimacy, similar to that described in Douvan's chapter, which derives from knowledge and understanding of people, replaces the moral abstraction of justice and the judgments that stemmed from an ideology of right and wrong. This student thus described in his thinking the progression that Erikson characterized as the transformation of the ideological morality of adolescence into the adult ethic of taking care (Erikson, 1964).

Beyond Moral Principles

The experience of Kohlberg's subjects on reaching adulthood spurred Kohlberg's reconsideration in 1973 of the question of adult moral development. In the 1969 paper by Kohlberg and Kramer, the possibility of continued moral development in adulthood had been dismissed in the absence of empirical data and of any cognitive basis for moral stage change beyond adolescence. Now, Kohlberg considered the experiences of adulthood—of "irreversible choice and sustained responsibility for the welfare of others"—to constitute in themselves a sufficient base for moral development (Kohlberg, 1973). The adult experience of irreversible commitment would finally dispel the relativism that had eluded the ideological solution of his earlier conception and rescue moral judgment from the intellectual sea of adolescent relativism.

The puzzle of Kohlberg's 1973 paper, however, lay in the fact that while he now considered moral judgment to be radically transformed by adult experience, his description of the stages themselves remained unchanged. The same principled judgments that earlier had been considered the logical extension of adolescent thought were now seen instead as the developmental outcome of adult experience. Something seemed to be amiss in the new conjunction Kohlberg proposed between the rights conception of his principled stages, which articulated a logic of moral justification, and the experiences of responsibility, which pertained to the consequences rather than to the logic of choice.

This was precisely the shift in concern from justification to responsibility that Perry had described in his study of intellectual and ethical development in the college years (1968). Retelling the story of the Garden of Eden, he recounted the college student's epistemological development as a journey from the innocence of objective truth and moral justification to the knowledge of contextual relativism and the discovery of ethical responsibility. Relativism stands in the center of undergraduate moral development, as the serpent in the garden of a dualistic epistemology but also as the tree of a postmoralistic life. When the awareness of multiplicity, initially conceived as a special case within an absolute universe of moral right and wrong, explodes into a contextual relativism from which no knowledge is free, the search for "*the* right answer" comes to an end. Realizing that such an answer can never be found outside the context in which the question is asked, the student relinquishes the notion of objective moral truth and becomes, at once, more accountable and more free in his choice. These observations led Perry to suggest the need for "adding an advanced period to Piaget's outline for cognitive development," a period in which thinking was transformed "from the moral environment to the ethical, from the formal to the existential." By adding a new stage to the sequence of cognitive development, Perry thus formulated a basis for a corresponding change in moral judgment, which would meet the full requirements for developmental stage change.

Perry's suggested extension of cognitive development looked backward to Baldwin (1906), who considered adult cognition to be "postlogical," and forward to Riegel (1973), White and Basseches (1978), who argued the need for a dialectical cognitive psychology that could overcome the limitations inherent in Piaget's formal conception of mental operations. A similar notion of an advanced stage appeared in the subsequent work of Arlin (1975), who claimed to have found a "fifth Piagetian cognitive stage," which she called *problem finding* to distinguish it from the *problem-solving* orientation of formal thought. Arlin's interest lay in the creative capacity of adult intelligence, and her research therefore was focused on the kinds of questions people generated when shown an array of disparate items. She distinguished questions concerning the operation of variables within a formal system from questions of implication and transformation pertaining to the operation and the system itself. Her results suggested that formal operations were a necessary though not sufficient condition from the problem-finding capacity to raise generic or higher-order questions—a precondition for creative intelligence. Arlin's focus on questions rather than solutions distinguished her work from that of Piaget and

Kohlberg and tied in to Perry's interest in the students' discovery of the contextual limitations of formal systems of knowledge. Although Arlin's work itself is problematic, her approach is pertinent to the problem of moral relativism, since relativism appears in moral judgment data as a substitution of meta-ethical questions for normative answers to moral problems.

This substitution led Kohlberg to place relativistic judgments outside the stages of his developmental sequence, assigning them scores of 4½ or 4-5 and regarding them as the hallmark of the transition from a conventional to a principled conception of justice. In this regard, his interpretation of relativism differs radically from that of Perry, who saw, in the "radical reperception of all knowledge as contextual and relative," an end to the dualistic distinction between right and wrong. While, for Kohlberg, principled moral judgment *solved* the problem of moral relativism, for Perry, relativism *found* the problem in principled moral judgment. Since both Kohlberg and Perry considered these developments to occur during the college years, the study of undergraduate moral development would seem to provide an empirical basis for resolving this dispute.

With these questions in mind, Gilligan and Murphy (1979) turned to the longitudinal interviews conducted in 1973 with the students who had, as college freshmen, taken Kohlberg's course on moral and political choice. These interviews took place toward the end of the students' senior year, when questions of commitment and choice were particularly salient. Since these questions pertain both to ego and moral development—to the resolution of identity as well as moral problems—a close relationship between these issues could be expected at this time. This relationship guided the design of the interview, which asked students to discuss their experience of moral conflict and choice, their thinking about commitments, made and forseen, and their sense of themselves. They were also asked to resolve Kohlberg's hypothetical moral problems.

From the analysis of these intensive interviews, it became clear that the conception of relativism as a transitional problem in the developmental shift from Kohlberg's fourth to fifth stage did not fit the data. The transitional 4-5 score appeared regularly to follow as well as precede the attainment of principled (Stage 5 or 6) thinking. Kohlberg's scoring system did not impart a clear developmental ordering to the changes in moral judgment that occurred between freshman and senior year. In addition, on the senior-year interview, there was increasing evidence in the responses of some students to the Kohlberg dilemmas of a disparity between their conception of the moral problem and that which informed Kohlberg's structuring of his dilemmas and interview questions. These students, rather than answering the questions as asked, instead questioned the questions, indicating either that the wrong questions were being asked about the dilemma or that the information given was insufficient for answering such questions. Two themes recurred in these responses. The first was that the moral problem in the Heinz dilemma pertained not to the rightness or wrongness of Heinz's decision to steal the drug (an issue of justification) but rather to the inability of the druggist to respond to the predicament of the dying woman. This inability was attributed to a combination of psychological and social causes, which then became the subject of the students' consideration. Secondly, in order to answer Kohlberg's question as to whether or not Heinz should steal the drug, some students believed that they would have to know more about who these people were and where they lived—that is, about the contingencies of their particular lives and social circumstances, which would determine the actual consequences of Heinz's decision. Both patterns indicated a shift in the students' thinking from a concern with the logic of moral choice to an interest in the causes and consequences of such choices.

In these responses, Gilligan and Murphy saw evidence of "problem finding."

Specifically, the problem found was that of contextual relativism, identified by Perry as the critical transformation of undergraduate thought. However, rather than considering these epistemological or meta-ethical developments to lie outside the stage sequence of normative moral judgment, Gilligan and Murphy saw them as leading regularly to a distinct transformation in moral judgment. This transformation signified a development from the formal mode of Kohlberg's principled solutions to a contextual mode wherein the moral problem was seen, in Perry's terms, to be one of commitment in relativism. On the basis of this distinction, Gilligan and Murphy proposed the existence of two distinct types of postconventional moral judgment, each of which had recognizable stage properties (structured wholeness, invariant sequence, and so forth). To test this proposition, they modified Perry's coding distinctions to fit the moral judgment data and scored the students' responses to Kohlberg dilemmas in accordance with this expanded scheme.

This analysis resulted in the restoration of order and regularity to the sequence of undergraduate moral development. Problem finding followed problem solving in the moral as in the cognitive domain. Students who had been able unequivocally to assert on the basis of principles of equity and reciprocity that Heinz's theft was "*the just thing* to do" or that "it was fair to expect someone else to do something that is *the right thing* to do," came subsequently to believe that, while moral principles provide "simple resolutions [that] in the abstract sense will be fair, when you bring it down to reality again, it might not be fair." The epistemological recognition that "somehow there is a sense in which truth is relative" regularly was followed by a change in moral judgment whereby such judgments became "much less absolute and more relativistic," in Perry's sense.

This change in moral judgment was regularly attributed by the students to their own experience in actual situations of moral conflict and choice, specifically to the experiences of irreversible choice and of sustained responsibility for the welfare of others upon which Kohlberg subsequently predicated the attainment of his principled stages. During their college years several of the students had encountered such choices, particularly in their relationships with others, and some emerged from such encounters with a new perspective on moral problems. This new perspective more frequently entailed the modification than the attainment of Kohlberg's stages of principled moral judgment since the formal logic of these stages came to be seen specifically as an impediment to the kind of moral understanding that respect for persons entailed. The critical discovery made in these relationships was the discovery of difference, the recognition of the validity "not just of a different set of rules but of a whole other way of looking at things"—the distinction Perry makes (in this volume) between multiplicity and relativism. This discovery led students to consider their former mode of judgment as "high-handed" in its presumption of objectivity. Their rethinking of their moral position accompanied the recognition that, "Maybe I am not Mr. Hot-shit, and maybe there is no such thing as a hierarchy [of moral values] and you should really do all you can to tear it down if it is going to build those kinds of barriers [to understanding] between you and other people." With this recognition, the formal moral judgments whose operations followed the logic of hypothetico-deductive thought gave way to a more inductive approach to moral problem solving. This approach discovered the contextual relativism that invariably shaped the interpretation of what formerly were considered to be objective moral "facts," and even the facts of moral thought; it discovered that principles of justice were themselves irreducibly tied to a contextual—that is, to a psychological and historical—interpretation.

Thus, as toward the end of adolescence, issues of identity increasingly became entangled with or gave way to those of intimacy, the moral concerns of the students correspondingly shifted from a self-centered interest in justification, which found its utmost expression in a principled moral ideology, to a renewed concern with the fundamental moral question—the relationship between self and other. The end of the moratorium brought an end to the illusion that action, however justified, could be divorced from consequence. A new interest in understanding and predicting the actual consequences of choice in a historical world increasingly preoccupied those students whose senior-year moral judgments were moving beyond a formal principled model. To these students, the systems of moral principles that formerly had provided a fortress for identity now appeared as a barrier to intimacy. In relinquishing such systems, they spoke of "tearing down a wall" between themselves and others, a wall whose presence had "blinded" them to the validity of other points of view. The moral belief that "in interpersonal situations that dealt with psychological realities and psychological feelings, *truth should win out*" was complicated by the realization that such situations contained multiple truths, which could not be assimilated to a single, absolute, or objective moral perspective. Such a perspective, instead, came to be seen as arrogant and immoral in its disrespect for the validity of other points of view.

Conclusion

Moral development in the college years thus centers on the shift from moral ideology to ethical responsibility. This shift follows from the epistemological discovery of contextual relativism and is accompanied by a change in concern from issues of identity to those of intimacy. The ideological moral constructions made possible by the adolescent capacity for formal thought are realized in the moral systems and abstract principles of Kohlberg's highest stages. The disillusion with these systems, however, is followed by the reconstruction of morality, which centers on a new understanding of the moral concept of respect for persons. Such respect is now seen to depend not on a "veil of ignorance" (Rawls, 1971) but on an immediacy of knowing that dissolves the distinction between good and evil as it transcends the boundary between self and other. Then "you talk about human beings vis-à-vis other human beings rather than talking about right or wrong."

Moral development thus ultimately transcends the formal categories of moral thought only to rediscover the moral problem in the recognition that "human beings come in contact with each other's lives." The moral problem, which ultimately is insoluble in formal terms, thus reappears in everyday life as the adolescent illusion of the separate self gives way to a new awareness of the interdependence of self and other. The abstraction of justice, the keystone of moral ideology, fades as the concept of fairness is replaced by an ethic of responsibility, whose focus lies, as Erikson saw, on the activity of taking care. This shift could be seen in the interviews of seniors whose concept of morality as respect for persons entailed an "obligation to relieve human misery and suffering if possible." The exploration of moral possibility then led directly to the world of activity.

If the aim of higher education is to develop the life of the mind, then such education, in its entirety, bears a clear relationship to the pattern of moral development described in this chapter. The study of moral development in college students and the incipient research on adult moral judgment indicate the need for extending the sequence of moral development described by Kohlberg and for revising the conception of its highest stage. Such a revision, however, alters the conception of the preceding stages and thus of the entire sequence and changes as well the consideration of what experiences would foster its progression. The integration of contextual relativism with experiences of moral responsibility now appears as the precondition for the development of a moral understanding that goes beyond the balancing of individual claims within a formal conception of justice. When relating to others as ends rather than means depends not only on the logic of equality and reciprocity but also on a contextual understanding of actual differences in points of view, then the educational experiences that foster moral development will be those that enhance the capacity to shift perspectives. The study of history and literature thus take on central importance in moral education, not by virtue of the moral dilemmas that can be extracted from their texts, but because of their potential for extending experience through the study of other lives, both past and present. The chapters by Ward and by Lamdin and those in Part Two make this point vividly clear.

Since moral development depends on a continuing interplay of thought and experience, the vast extension of knowledge inherent in college education can provide a powerful stimulus to development. The active nature of knowledge, described so well by Piaget, indicates once again that the process of education begins in the discovery of ignorance. The success of education then depends on its leading students to question that which formerly was taken for granted. It was the absence of such questioning in the testimony of Eichmann that had led Arendt to see, in his thoughtless obedience, the evil of our time and to wonder if the activity of thought might stand as an impediment to its recurrence. If the architects of the future American college are attentive to this evil, they will design a college that keeps alive "the claim on our thinking attention that all facts and events make by virtue of their existence" (Arendt, 1978, p. 4), while supporting and developing the student's capacity to respond actively to that claim. Since the moral capacity to remain responsive to the reality of social experience vies with the tenacity of conventional interpretation that offers a simplification of that reality, moral education in the college years begins with calling into question the conventions of moral judgment and thought. To sustain that questioning through the pivotal discovery of the contextual relativism of moral knowledge and the consequent recognition of ethical responsibility constitutes the challenge of undergraduate education.

References

Arendt, H. *The Life of the Mind.* Vol. 1: *Thinking.* New York: Harcourt Brace Jovanovich, 1978.

Arlin, P. "Cognitive Development in Adulthood: A Fifth Stage?" *Developmental Psychology,* 1975, *11,* 602-606.

Baldwin, J. M. *Social and Ethical Interpretations in Mental Development.* New York: Macmillan, 1906.

Basseches, M. A. "Beyond Closed-System Problem Solving: A Study of Meta-Systematic Aspects of Matter Thought." Unpublished doctoral dissertation, Harvard University, 1978.

Boyd, D. "Education Toward Principled Moral Judgment: An Analysis of an Experimental Course in Undergraduate Moral Education Applying Lawrence Kohlberg's Theory of Moral Development." Unpublished doctoral dissertation, Harvard University, 1976.

Colby, A. "Logical Operational Limitations on the Development of Moral Judgment." Unpublished doctoral dissertation, Columbia University, 1972.

Erikson, E. *Young Man Luther.* New York: Norton, 1958.

Erikson, E. "Youth: Fidelity and Diversity." In E. Erikson (Ed.), *Youth: Change and Challenge.* New York: Doubleday, 1963.

Erikson, E. *Insight and Responsibility.* New York: Norton, 1964.

Erikson, E. *Identity: Youth and Crisis.* New York: Norton, 1968.

Erikson, E. "Reflections on the Dissent of Contemporary Youth." *Daedalus,* Winter, 1973.

Fishkin, J. "Meta-Ethical Reasoning, Ideology, and Political Commitment: Empirical Applications of a Proposed Theory." Unpublished doctoral dissertation, Yale University, 1975.

Gilligan, C., and Kohlberg, L. "From Adolescence to Adulthood: The Recovery of Reality in a Postconventional World." Proceedings of the Piaget Society, 1973. In M. Appel and B. Preseissen (Eds.), *Topics in Cognitive Development.* New York: Plenum Press, 1977.

Gilligan, C., and Murphy, J. M. "The Philosopher and the Dilemma of the Fact: Evidence for Continuing Development from Adolescence to Adulthood." In D. Kuhn (Ed.), *New Directions for Child Development: Intellectual Development Beyond Childhood,* no. 5. San Francisco: Jossey-Bass, 1979.

Gilligan, J. "Beyond Morality: Psychoanalytic Reflections on Shame, Guilt, and Love." In T. L. Lickona (Ed.), *Moral Development and Behavior.* New York: Holt, Rinehart and Winston, 1976.

Inhelder, B., and Piaget, J. *The Growth of Logical Thinking from Childhood to Adolescence.* New York: Basic Books, 1958.

Kohlberg, L. "From Is to Ought: How to Commit the Naturalistic Fallacy and Get Away with It in the Study of Moral Development." In T. Mischel (Ed.), *Cognitive Development and Epistemology.* New York: Academic Press, 1971.

Kohlberg, L. "Continuities in Childhood and Adult Moral Development Revisited." In P. B. Baltes and K. W. Schaie (Eds.), *Life-Span Developmental Psychology: Personality and Socialization.* New York: Academic Press, 1973.

Kohlberg, L., and Kramer, R. "Continuities and Discontinuities in Childhood and Adult Moral Development." *Human Development,* 1969, *12,* 93-120.

Kohlberg, L., and Scharf, P. "Bureaucratic Violence and Conventional Moral Thinking." Paper presented at Annual Conference of the American Orthopsychiatric Association, Detroit, April 1972.

Milgram, S. *Obedience to Authority.* New York: Harper & Row, 1974.

Murphy, J. M., and Gilligan, C. "Moral Development in Adolescence and Adulthood: A Critique and Reconstruction of Kohlberg's Theory." *Human Development,* in press.

Perry, W. G. *Forms of Intellectual and Ethical Development in the College Years.* Boston: Holt, Rinehart and Winston, 1968.

Piaget, J. *The Moral Judgment of the Child.* New York: Free Press, 1965. (Originally published 1932.)

Piaget, J. "Intellectual Evolution from Adolescence to Adulthood." *Human Development,* 1972, *15* (1), 1-12.

Rawls, J. *A Theory of Justice.* Cambridge, Mass.: Harvard University Press, 1971.

Rest, J. "Patterns of Preference and Comprehension in Moral Judgment." *Journal of Personality,* 1973, *41,* 86-109.

Riegel, K. "Dialectical Operations: The Final Period of Cognitive Development." *Human Development,* 1973, *16,* 346-370.

Turiel, E. "An Experimental Test of the Sequentiality of Developmental Stages in the Child's Moral Judgments." *Journal of Personality and Social Psychology,* 1966, *3,* 611-618.

Turiel, E. "State Transition in Moral Development." In R. M. Travers (Ed.), *Second Handbook of Research on Teaching.* Chicago: Rand McNally, 1972.

Weber, M. "Science as a Vocation." In H. H. Garth and C. W. Mills (Eds.), *From Max Weber.* New York: Oxford University Press, 1946.

6

Robert W. White

Humanitarian Concern

That human behavior can be scandalously self-seeking is brought to our attention every day in the news. That it can be directed toward the common good seems to be rated less newsworthy, yet it is implicit in much that goes on around us. When we read of minority group tenants evicted from their home by a heartless landlord, we shake our heads over this fresh example of human cupidity. Reading further, however, we find that civil rights workers are seeking a court injunction on behalf of the tenants. What leads these people to put out so much effort in a situation in which they can expect no personal gain? Some human behavior seems to be shaped entirely by self-interest, and especially by the incentive of financial reward. In other instances, the intention and the implicit reward include accomplishing something for the benefit of others.

This paradox has a long history in human thought. It is the subject of everything that has been written about altruism. Some fifty years ago, Alfred Adler brought the possibility of altruism back into psychological discourse, giving it the name of *Gemeinschaftsgefühl*. He used this term to describe a natural tendency that he believed flowered in all of us to the extent that we outgrew egotism and the urge to be superior. What is the English equivalent of this large German noun? The Ansbachers, in their valuable compendium of Adler's writings (1956), remark that his term "presented no mean difficulty to the translators." When discussing his idea, Adler (1927) used phrases that have been translated "sense of human solidarity" and "fellowship in the human community." The Ansbachers mention also these proposed equivalents: "social feeling, community feeling, fellow feeling, sense of solidarity, communal intuition, community interest, social sense, and social interest." The last term is now generally accepted as the best, even though imperfect, English translation. It is clear that Adler referred to something more profound than ordinary sociability. Like John Donne, he seems to have had in mind the experience of being "involved in *Mankinde*."

In order to point our discussion toward this larger meaning, we shall adopt for this chapter the expression *humanitarian concern*. This term preserves not only the *fact* of behavior directed toward the good of others but also the *feelings* that prompt such behavior. The extent to which, in any given generation, humanitarian concern is developed is obviously of vast importance for that generation's present and future. But we must be aware from the start that our expression covers a variety of processes and possibilities. Humanitarian concern develops in many different ways; it is encouraged and discouraged by many different influences. We cannot aim for a formula or a simple hypothesis. We can, however, start to unravel the many strands and perceive the alternative routes that lead to an interest in the common good.

Background in Recent Psychology

A conception of humanitarian concern similar to Adler's was put forward by Andras Angyal (1941). Like Adler, Angyal was trying to establish a basic and simple conceptual scheme for understanding personality. He acknowledged a *trend toward autonomy,* or self-aggrandizing tendency, akin to Adler's concepts of *egotism* and *superiority*. But Angyal, too, found this trend insufficient to account for human behavior. The individual longs, he wrote, "to become an organic part of something that he conceives as greater than himself . . . to be in harmony with super-individual units, the social world, nature, God, ethical world order, or whatever the person's formulation of it may be" (1941, p. 172). This tendency he called the *trend toward homonomy*. There is more to our experience than getting to be bigger, smarter, and more influential. We seek some larger form of membership.

Speaking in language more strictly developmental, Gordon Allport (1961, pp. 283-285) introduced the idea of *extension of the sense of self*. He considered that the sense of self was extended when the interests of another person became as important as one's own interests; "better said, the welfare of another is *identical* with one's own." Toward this we could advance "in proportion as lives are decentered from the clamorous immediacy of the body and of egocenteredness." Allport regarded self-love as an inescapable part of our nature, but "only self-extension is the earmark of maturity."

Similar language was used by Harry Stack Sullivan (1953) in his account of the first emergence of mature friendship in preadolescence. Novel in the relation between chums is "a real sensitivity to what matters to another person." This is not, Sullivan wrote, "in the sense of 'what should I do to get what I want,' but instead 'what should I do to contribute to the happiness or to support the prestige and feeling of worthwhileness of my chum.' " We are drawn here toward the roots in individual development of feelings that transcend self-interest.

The feeling aspect is prominent in the idea of *generativity* described by Erik Erikson (1950) as the seventh in his eight stages of ego development. "Generativity," he writes (1968), "is primarily the concern in establishing and guiding the next generation." Having its roots in caring for one's young, it can become extended to caring for the young in general, to education, to the building and maintaining of cultural institutions, and to creating, as Browning (1973) has put it, "a total environment ecologically supportive of the general health—not only of family and tribe, but of the entire human species" (p. 138). When generativity fails to develop, Erikson sees the growth of personality as coming to a halt in "a pervading sense of stagnation, boredom," and "self-concern."

These several contributions call attention to a range of possibilities in the development of humanitarian concern. It seems a long way from caring for children and chums to caring about the ecological future. Yet there is the common characteristic of concern for something beyond one's self, and we certainly should not assume that there are no connections among the different forms of caring.

A Paradigm: Student Volunteers in Mental Hospitals

There is a wide difference between how we like to think and how we ought to think about a subject such as humanitarian concern. We like to think that behavior can be classified as either selfish or altruistic, so that we can study the altruistic variety in pure form and isolate what brings it into being. The traditional path of science is to bring objects of study under experimental control so that the effects of single influences can be measured. However worthy this goal, we should be wary about assuming that we have reached it. Humanitarian feeling develops amidst the welter of motives typical of our ordinary behavior. So we need to start with a naturalistic description that shows the phenomenon in its frustrating complexity.

An appropriate paradigm is provided by student volunteering in mental hospitals (Umbarger and others, 1962). About twenty-five years ago, as part of the cultural revolution whereby mental health emerged from neglect to become a popular cause, college students began volunteering to serve as aides in mental hospitals. In its first form, this service consisted of being a friendly visitor to a patient, providing social interaction and practical help, possibly even assisting in a return to the community. The altruism in this behavior was heartening to those of us who were close to it, but nothing is gained by viewing it as a pure emanation of unselfishness.

The students' motives were typically complex. For some, there was great satisfaction in showing up the shortcomings of the older generation in its care of mental patients. If a patient could eventually go home, it was a triumph over the blundering Establishment, which without this prodding might have left the patient incarcerated for life. Other students were more preoccupied with testing their own personal worth. Did they have the stability and fortitude to deal with disturbing psychotic behavior; did they have the warmth and love to draw out a person sunk deep in self-concern? For some, volunteering was part of the search for a congenial vocation. The experience might serve to steer them into, or away from, one or another of the mental health professions. Then there were students who found their greatest rewards in participation with the other volunteers. Dealing with patients might be taxing, but they reveled in the weekly group conferences where reports were given and ideas exchanged. For still others, volunteering expressed a concern for those less fortunate, which still sounded more like a parental expectation than a true impulse from within.

Mixed motives, surely, and all the more mixed because any one volunteer might have several of them at once. But these were not mixed-up adolescents; they were just like all of us. Such is human motivation when operating in a natural setting. The altruistic element, in greater or smaller degree, was present in all the volunteers. The task required trying to do something for someone else. In quite a few cases the outcome was a strengthening of humanitarian concern. We shall not go far wrong, I think, if we take this as typical of the way in which altruistic motivation emerges and grows in a matrix of other motives. Humanitarian feeling does not have to be pure in order to become strong.

The Affective Root: Empathy

Psychology has long been in possession of a concept that points to the affective root of humanitarian concern. In its broadest sense, *empathy* means feeling the feelings that another person appears to be feeling. The definition includes any kind of feeling. We can share, with a joy of our own, the joy of someone blessed by sudden good fortune. We can participate in the elation of a victor or in the happiness of someone whose life and work are prospering. We can be angry when a friend is angry at an injustice, and surely, as every child so painfully knows, we can be anxious when we sense that those around us are anxious. Very obvious is the distress we experience when another person gives evidence of acute distress. Cries of pain have an almost primitive power to upset us.

Response to another's distress was chosen by Lois Murphy (1937) to illustrate the possible origins of empathy. Studying nursery school children, Murphy noticed that when one child was crying, another child, witnessing the scene, might look sad, begin to pucker, and finally break out in echoing lamentation. According to conditioning theory, the sounds of distress, which we make during bouts of pain, become conditioned stimuli capable of eliciting distress in us even when emitted by someone else. This somewhat mechanical account should not be taken to imply that on such occasions we shed merely crocodile tears. Feeling is part of the response. Anyone who has watched helplessly over a suffering child can testify to the almost unbearable quality of empathic distress.

It follows from this conception that empathy is related to our own history of feelings. We can come closer to experiencing another person's feelings when we have had like feelings of our own. Murphy's observations at nursery school tend to support this deduction. If a child arrives with an arm in a sling, the first to respond with expressions of concern is the child who has lately broken a collar bone and worn a similar bandage. This principle is important in understanding both empathy and the lack of it. When mourning the death of a parent, we expect the most comforting responses to come from people who have lost their parents. In contrast, if we are the victims of economic or ethnic injustice, we do not have much hope of being understood by those who have experienced neither handicap. Empathic feeling arises most directly out of what we have already experienced in ourselves.

Pertinent to this chapter is another of the points made in Murphy's early study. Responses to the empathic arousal of feeling, she pointed out, may take many different forms. One child merely cries and stands helpless when another cries. Another child may try actively to give comfort and to offer help. One of the more robust nursery school boys observed by Murphy responded to another child's grief by knocking down the tormenter who was causing the grief. We should not be surprised if this child, grown older, were someday found seeking to enjoin a heartless landlord from evicting his tenants. Though rooted in empathic distress, helping behavior can branch out in many directions according to circumstances, enlisting along the way other feelings like anger.

Responding to the distress of others is certainly a prominent aspect of humanitarian concern. But our feeling will be much richer if it includes responding to the joys as well as the sorrows, the prides as well as the humiliations, and the hopes as well as the frustrations of other people, near and far.

Expansion of Empathy

Studies of development show that empathy occurs very early in life. There has even been speculation, backed by a certain amount of observation, that empathy plays a significant part in the interactions between nursing mother and infant. If the mother is not at ease, if she is tense and anxious, the infant responds with unpleasant tension, which diminishes the satisfaction of feeding. By nursery school age, empathy and helping are easily observed, but they typically occur in specific episodes rather than as lasting attitudes. This limitation is overcome as a child's experience enlarges and becomes more organized. To be able to "support the prestige and feeling of worthwhileness" of a preadolescent chum implies experience of prestige, worthwhileness, and their vicissitudes in oneself—a far from elementary stage in self-understanding. Before adolescence the empathic feelings that support altruistic behavior are likely to be reserved for the immediate environment: for friends, relatives, and other people with whom there is active acquaintance. Humanitarian feeling stays within a local life space.

During adolescence, however, there is often an abrupt expansion of empathy. The growth spurt in abstract thinking and generalization makes it possible at this point to project one's sympathies onto a global canvas. Parents may be startled to hear their children suddenly espousing, often with considerable information, the cause of an emerging third world nation or the rights of an oppressed minority. Empathy has begun to fan out; altruism has begun to move from local to larger objects. Parents may wonder what ideas the teachers are putting into their children's heads, but this underestimates what the children's heads are now able to do for themselves. Allowing that the generalizations may be hasty, we must still see them as a phase in the growth of humanitarian concern.

When these transformations can be properly observed, as in detailed life history studies, a clear relation is often evident between personal problems and the larger cause. Empathy with a group of people occurs most readily when the group's problems are similar to those in one's personal sphere. We may find, for instance, that a young person, perhaps the eldest child, who has been cast in the family role described by Adler as "parents' foreman," and who has been having trouble maintaining authority over the younger siblings, suddenly develops a great interest in problems of government, showing strong fellow feeling for the police and the judiciary and for those who work to strengthen the rule of international law. A little later, one of the bossed younger siblings, reaching adolescence, experiences a similar outreach of sympathies, but the fellow feeling falls on victims of police brutality and judicial unfairness and on those who are engaged in protest and revolution. Many such examples could be cited to show that when empathy expands it often follows lines suggested by troublesome personal experience. In an intensive study of political opinions, Smith, Bruner, and White (1956) showed that, among the other influences that shaped and colored a person's opinions, a significant part was sometimes played by the externalizing of unresolved inner problems.

When empathy with another person is strong, it may expand along lines suggested by the other person's problems. Thus, we may find a youth advocating the cause of a disadvantaged ethnic group of which not he but his best friend is a member. Lovers are especially likely to take on one another's causes. Such examples are well captured in Allport's idea of extension of the sense of self, in which the interests of another become "identical with one's own." Sympathies developed from such roots are not necessarily transient. Life history studies provide examples of lasting and important influence. A young man called Chatwell, for example (White, 1976), knew that his father, an inventor, had been repeatedly fleeced out of the financial benefits of his work by sharp business operators. Early in adolescence Chatwell imagined a career in patent law, and when the time came he actually entered this specialty wherein he could constantly defend inventors against commercial exploitation.

The expansion of empathy is aided by variety of social experience. The adventurous wanderings of many contemporary young folk, during which they encounter a wide variety of people, often result in a marked increase of empathic understanding. Studies of college students show that empathic side effects can arise out of summer employment. A young man from a comfortable, vehemently Republican home, for instance, surprises us with a highly sympathetic description of laborers, white and black, in the construction industry. To make himself financially less dependent, he had taken a summer job on a construction project. Through sharing experience with his fellow workers he found new channels for the outflow of empathy.

The expansion of empathy to more distant objects may tend to dilute the intensity of the feelings. The frustrations of an oppressed minority on another continent may well be experienced with less force than one's own frustrations by parents and preferred siblings. To an extent, this fading of pure empathic feeling is counteracted if actions and attitudes prompted by it are progressively woven into the habits and principles that guide everyday life. As concerned behavior becomes better organized, we do not need constant sharp stabs of empathic feeling to keep us on course.

Circumstances that Block Humanitarian Concern

Before we go on to consider other routes of humanitarian concern, we need to remind ourselves of two points about empathy.

The first point is that distress is not the only kind of feeling capable of evoking an empathic response. Although it is correct to call empathy the affective root of humanitarian concern, in the sense that such concern can be strongly nourished by it, the very same process can produce results that are far from altruistic. A bystander at a scene of bullying may empathize with the bully's savage elation and join in hitting the victim. Feeling the feelings of another person applies to all feelings. The process itself contains no guarantee that what follows will be for the good of another person.

The second point is that even with respect to another's distress empathy is not an automatic process. Mere exposure to the hardships and sorrows of others does not ensure a sympathetic response. It simply creates the possibility of such response if nothing else gets in the way. But there is much that can get in the way. Humanitarian empathy can be blocked and killed by less kindly influences in our natures and in our training.

The idea of motivational conflict is helpful in understanding this blocking. Forwarding the interests and supporting the ego of another person will often be in conflict with satisfying other needs. No example is more telling than the conflict between needing to give help and needing to receive it. The latter motive can provide ready empathy for another's distress, but if the need to be helped is strong this may interfere with a continuing output of sympathy. The situation is described with remarkable candor by a young woman called Portia (White, Riggs, and Gilbert, 1976). During her sophomore year at college, her roommate's brother was killed in an accident. When the roommate returned to college, she continued for some time to be upset, sleepless, and depressed. Portia gave such consolation and encouragement as she could, but as the need continued she became increasingly impatient. Eventually she became aware of resentment at having to give so much when she herself craved guidance and help with her own problems. In ideal friendships the partners can help each other as occasion demands, but dependent tendencies and needs to be the object of sympathy can easily come in conflict with feeling for the good of others.

More directly blocking are those needs that center on aggression, competition, and self-aggrandizement. For pursuing these "selfish" purposes, empathy for others' woes is not adaptive; it is an interference. A child's effort to be the parents' favorite through good behavior would be weakened by fellow feeling for a sibling's naughtiness. A football team's drive down the field would lose power if the players imagined the sorrow of the other side at losing the game. To the extent that we want to dominate others, prove superiority, and win individual distinction, sympathy is a plain handicap. We cannot afford to be soft on rivals.

This principle is important in view of the large amount of rivalry that is built into our social system. Students of economic behavior have often expressed surprise at the callous way in which business decisions are made. Laying off workers seems done with scant regard for the personal consequences of unemployment. Seeking a larger share of the market is not impaired by sympathy for rivals who must accept a smaller share, and if a competing firm is put out of business it is occasion for self-congratulation. Legislation has proved necessary to prevent firms from discharging older employees just before they qualify for the company's pension. Yet these lacks of human sympathy can be perceived as adaptive in an economic system based on competition for profits, in which the measure of success is a favorable balance sheet. Company officers may be highly sympathetic when one of their number becomes incapacitated. The victim may be kept in office, made a consultant, or otherwise shielded from his misfortune. But the balance sheet would soon be adversely affected if such sympathy were extended to all ranks.

Humanitarian feeling can be blocked also by the striving for upward social mobility. An interest in higher social status seems to be associated with contempt, rather than sympathy, for those in lower status (Davis, Gardner, and Gardner, 1941). No doubt it is again the competitive spirit in upward mobility that encourages a view of those in lower status as a lazy, shiftless, mediocre lot who deserve to be losers. No adaptive purpose would be served by perceiving hardships and extenuating circumstances among those who have been outdistanced.

Empathic responses that lead in a humanitarian direction are thus always exposed to competition and the possibility of suppression by self-centered strivings. How much they will be blocked depends a good deal on the surrounding social system.

Principled Humanitarian Concern

Thus far we have described the growth of humanitarian concern largely in terms of its empathic roots. The sympathetic response to distress, observable in young children, becomes extended through widening experience to include more and more people—individuals and groups—the ideal end point being concern for all humankind. It is important to recognize this internal source even though we acknowledge the complexities of social learning. In an older vocabulary it might have been called the inherent goodness that stands at least a chance of prevailing over the evil in our nature. But altruistic motivation has usually been perceived as needing help in this struggle. Such help is provided by parental training and by educational and religious teachings. Pressure toward unselfishness thus enters a child's experience in the form of promptings and precepts that may not immediately connect with sympathetic feelings. Altruistic behavior looms as a duty before it has time to blossom as an expression of intrinsic concern. Even in adults, principled concern may stand at some distance from warm-hearted involvement with other people.

To illustrate principled humanitarian concern we turn again to Portia. She reported being surprised to discover that her boyfriend had none of "the feelings that I have of obligation to other people." Because she, like her friend, had been born into an advantaged social and economic position, she had "an obligation feeling, a debt feeling, that I ought to make some contribution to society." Thus, as an undergraduate she took part in various political activities, including ringing doorbells to enlist citizen interest, and she planned later to work professionally for "civil rights or some other cause that I believe in." Her father worked actively in civil rights and other causes in which he believed, often at cost to himself. Portia was thus drawn to good causes without, as far as her interviewers could tell, having vivid empathic feelings for the disadvantaged people she hoped to benefit.

Real sympathy in this instance has not caught up with sense of duty, but we cannot on that account dismiss Portia's principled altruism as merely conformist and immature. Intellectually, she is sophisticated and has placed her sense of duty under the principle of fairness: having received so much from society, she owes something to those who have received less. Her equally favored boyfriend is a stranger to such feelings of obligation; he views the world as a field for exploitation wherein he intends to make money. Current fashions in values, including psychological values, produce a curious uncertainty about the relative worth of these two attitudes. Influenced as we have been by Freud and psychotherapy, we tend to view guilt and a sense of duty as if they were necessarily neurotic, and we place a high value on authentic impulse expression. We may be put off by a touch of self-righteousness in Portia; we may question the purity and depth of her altruism; we may see her boyfriend as healthily uninhibited, even though the impulses that are not inhibited lead to exploitation. But Portia's is the common historic route to humanitarian concern, and it leaves the way open, as her boyfriend's attitude does not, to true sympathetic involvement. The idea of duty to humankind, picked up from parents and other educational sources, leads to action that benefits others; sympathetic feeling follows, in varying degree, as a consequence of actual acquaintance with these others.

We cannot expect to find a simple formula for the kinds of training that lead to principled concern or the lack of it. As shown in a review by Rushton (1976), there has been a lot of recent research on altruism in children. While the resulting picture is not clear-cut, there is reason to believe that altruistic behavior is more frequent in children from families that favor the expression of affect, including sympathy, and that provide models of helping behavior; it is less frequent in children whose families stress status and competition (Bryan and London, 1970). Being open to one's own feelings seems plausibly related to responding to another person's feelings, a relation for which experiments by Lenrow (1965) with young adult subjects provide further evidence. The influence of parental models seems clear in findings by Keniston (1968), who showed in a study of committed young radicals that a certain number, far from being rebels against conservative parents, came from homes in which working for radical causes was part of the accepted pattern of life. In another study Rosenhan (1970) compared fully committed with half-heartedly committed civil rights volunteers. With much greater frequency, the fully committed reported themselves to have positive relationships with their parents, and they saw their parents as having practiced the principles they preached. There is thus reason to suppose that it is easier to develop humanitarian concern in an environment containing parental models, and we can assume that models in school and community would have a similar influence.

Social Membership and Humanitarian Concern

Early students of social class, such as Warner (1949), Hollingshead (1949), and Kahl (1957), brought out the information that in the so-called upper and upper-middle classes there was a high level of community action expressing social concern. This was at odds with stereotypes of the selfish rich and of self-serving social climbers. It appeared that at these favored social levels there was some of the sense of social obligation described by Portia, but an important further value evidently lay in the sense of participation with others in community service. Beneficent action in the community calls for meetings, committees, and other forms of contact. However much people complain about meetings, these yield experiences of membership and fellowship that are highly valued. Newcomers to a neighborhood may find in organized community service a welcome channel to social acceptance. Strangeness and loneliness dissolve in shared activity.

Further rewards that can be gained in this way were described by a subject in the research of Smith, Bruner, and White (1956). The subject first encountered these rewards in his real estate business, where people to whom he had sold houses often called for his advice and help if something went wrong. "I don't think there's anything quite as pleasant," he said, "as to have people thank you ever so much and send their friends to you." The satisfaction obtained from this trouble-shooting was much magnified when he began to work in community service organizations. Presently he was on so many boards that scarcely an evening was left free, yet it was then that he said, "I'd like to devote my life to helping others." There were many satisfactions. He met and worked with his neighbors, he attained positions of some honor and power, he discharged a sense of obligation, and he received the thanks that are deserved by those who work in voluntary community service. Initially shaky about his worth, he had ceased to have doubts about it.

Described in these ways, the rewards of social participation sound more selfish than altruistic. And so they may be: they can be secured by devoting oneself to the local golf club or some other organization that benefits only oneself and one's immediate circle. The real estate man's interviewers did not hear much that suggested strongly aroused sympathy for the hospital patients, the handicapped children, the puzzled families, and the other beneficiaries of his charitable activity. Perhaps some spark of humanitarian obligation makes the difference in choosing a charity rather than a country club. But working to alleviate human distress is likely to bring about exposure to instances of distress and to a widening knowledge of human troubles. This at least invites empathy, and it can become an important route to deeper humanitarian concern.

Community service with charitable intent is merely an example of the way a sense of participation may strengthen humanitarian concern. Many activities in the political sphere, aimed at producing beneficent effects such as civil rights or responsive government, yield rewards to the participants even during periods when the cause does not seem to be prospering. Taking part in a serious endeavor, working with like-minded others, enjoying the warmth of membership in a group, all contribute to personal well-being while at the same time tending to expand the horizons of sympathy.

The Cognitive Aspect of Humanitarian Concern

Of special interest to higher education is the cognitive aspect of concern for human welfare. Concrete information about the living conditions of those less fortunate than we provides an important basis for action. What difficulties are occasioned by ignorance of the realities of the surrounding world? What changes occur as knowledge becomes wider and deeper? Although in some respects a person's humanitarian concern, or lack of it, is already established at the outset of young adulthood, there is room for substantial further development through learning more about the material well being and the social realities of others.

The interplay between empathic feeling and cognitive maturing in children has been clearly formulated by Hoffman (1975). This kind of analysis could be extended to adult years, but psychologists have been slow to direct their research toward cognitive development after adolescence. In a sense, cognitive maturity is reached when an adolescent attains those powers of abstraction that make it possible to talk and think on a global scale, seeing beyond the conditions of one's immediate community or class. The formal attainment of these powers, however, does not imply any great store of information; indeed, adolescent theorizing flourishes best when not tripped up by too much knowledge. Many young adults, even well-educated ones, are still extraordinarily ignorant of what goes on around them. Doubtless more than one young couple, venturing for the first time into local affairs, has advocated with equal zeal better schools for its children and lower taxes on its home, only to discover that school budget and tax rate are closely interlocked. Rough times may be ahead for humanitarian concern as people discover how complexly the world is put together, how strong are the competing interests, and how long it takes to get anything done.

To dramatize this point, we can again pick up the theme of mental health care and use it to contrast what can be called adolescent conscience with mature humanitarian concern. In a burst of empathy and moral indignation, an adolescent may decide that hospitalized mental patients are victims of bad management, medical ineptitude, Establishment neglect, and a callous disregard for human rights. This young person's heart, we must admit, is in the right place. The best professional opinion favors reducing the populations of mental hospitals; in recent years many have been emptied and closed. To adolescent conscience, however, reform should be instant: hospital doors should be flung open at once so that patients can walk out to freedom. If our youthful idealist can be persuaded that such liberality is hardly in the best interests of the patients unless strong community mental health centers are ready to guide and assist them, the next demand will be to start such centers at once. Only the seasoned advocate of community mental health will know about the long preliminary labor of organizing a program, educating the community, raising money, finding quarters, and hiring staff that is required to give the venture any hope of success. The transfer of mental health care from hospitals to the community is necessarily a complicated operation spread out over years. If instant results are sought, they are likely to be bad.

Knowledge of such toilsome realities can put severe strain on the humanitarian impulse. Experience with the slow pace of progress, the irritating disagreements among fellow workers, the forceful opposition of self-interested opponents, the unavoidable setbacks and compromises that go with any social movement—all these frustrations can kill the original urge to do something for the good of others. Sad to observe in life history studies is the occasional fading out of youthful idealism as the person concludes that the little that can be accomplished is not worth the requisite time and strength. Others, however, persist even while they scale down their ideas of what one person or one group can achieve. Knowledge of reality makes them sadder but also wiser—more ready to deal effectively with real human problems. And when we think of lives such as those of Mohandas Gandhi or Eleanor Roosevelt, we realize that such persistence, combined with favorable opportunity, can produce significant results.

There is another way in which knowledge of reality affects the humanitarian impulse. In the contemporary world, we are severely overloaded with information. We are told about droughts and famines, floods and earthquakes all over the world. We hear about poverty and violations of human rights in parts of the globe that few educated Americans a generation ago could locate on the map. We receive news about the aspirations and problems of people far away from us, both in terms of geography and cultural background. Potentially, this influx can be an asset. At its best, humanitarian concern should not be provincial. But overexposure to descriptions and scenes of need is not conducive to a successful transition from empathy to helpful behavior. Our feelings are constantly aroused, our sympathies and perhaps indignation are activated, yet the situations are so numerous and so remote that we see no possible way of doing anything about them. In a sense, it is easier to become involved in humanitarian enterprises if one is familiar with only a handful of local problems that appear more or less solvable. The information media flood us with impressions but help us little to discover channels for effective action. Our sympathies may be aroused, but so is our sense of helplessness.

Obviously, it is no easy matter to steer a steady course through these diverse influences. Increased knowledge, however it is gained, may put a blight on youthful idealism and discourage thinking beyond the bounds of immediate self-interest. The complexity and intransigence of social problems may seem overwhelming. Increased experience with beneficent change may similarly take the glow off hopes of making a significant contribution. Adverse and unanticipated consequences of well-intended intervention may forestall further effort. Against this is the solid satisfaction of actual accomplishment, however small, yielding a sense of competence to make at least something happen. And there is the further satisfaction that goes with increased knowledge: a sense of cognitive mastery, of understanding what is happening in one's world. Humanitarian concern need not be ground out by discouraging realities. It can remain strong while being tuned and shaped to realistically limited goals. And it can inspire a cognitive search that can transform what seemed impossible into effective beneficent action.

Implications for Higher Education

If we had to crowd into a nutshell the developmental implications of this chapter, we would find ourselves uttering a truism: Humanitarian concern is more likely to grow in a humanitarian environment. Such an environment might include a tradition of community service, a religious or other form of ethical orientation, concerned parents providing models of sympathy and involvement, an educational climate favorable to a broad understanding of human affairs, and a general playing down of competitive and acquisitive tendencies. This suggests a society more serious-minded than the hedonistic audience implied in commercial advertising. It suggests that endless fun and entertainment, brought about by the gratifying products of technology, are not enough for a good life. If there is to be concern for humankind, surroundings are required in which it is encouraged, modeled, nourished, and valued.

Higher education does not exist solely to promote humanitarian concern in the sense of this chapter. But we may well examine colleges and universities as humanitarian environments, asking how well they meet these particular specifications and how they might do so better. How do they look with respect to community service, ethical orientation, modeling of sympathy and involvement, broad understanding, and playing down of competitive and acquisitive tendencies?

Institutions of higher education come out of such scrutiny moderately well. Most graduates will have felt something of the stern ethic that governs scholarship and scientific research, an ethic of faithfully discovering and telling the truth. Most will remember courses that gave them a broad view and teachers who gave time and interest to their students. Most will have been aware of opportunities to broaden their social experience and take some part in services to others. Unfortunately, however, these may not be the predominant impressions. Recollection may be that no one really cared about the students, that teachers were absorbed in narrow specialties, that the atmosphere was that of an ivory tower devoid of human feeling. By many, higher education is experienced hardly at all as a move toward Adler's social interest, Allport's extension of the self, or Erikson's generativity.

What stands chiefly in the way of such movement is a form of self-definition that is common among college and university teachers. At the start of graduate school, future teachers, whatever their prior humanitarian concerns, learn that the present task is to become specialized scholars, with skills and techniques focused upon making additions to knowledge. They must become members of the profession, and "profession" is defined by the departments into which human knowledge has become divided. Thus, entering the profession means becoming a sociologist or a historian or a chemist or a Greek scholar. It means acquiring the special abilities that make for good research in that field. The candidate in sociology will eventually write a thesis to be judged for technical excellence, will get a position, if fortune smiles, in a sociology department, and will join the American Sociological Association. The reply to questions about occupation will be "sociologist," not "college teacher," and this indeed will be the basis for the sense of identity. In some cases, involvement in profession becomes so preemptive that teaching is regarded as a bore, and interest in students is confined to those who seem likely to become fellow specialists.

Large-minded people with strong social concerns enter graduate schools and there acquire the skills that support large-minded careers with powerful potentials for social contributions. But the atmosphere of technical specialization may hold a deadly attraction for those who are relatively unformed or burdened with personal insecurity and self-distrust. The profession, narrowly conceived, offers a refuge in which technical competence is the central virtue and from which the less definite, more worrisome aspects of life can be legitimately excluded. One need not risk unsupported judgments, intuitive guesses, indeed anything that would imply confidence in one's own experience; one can pretend to accept as real only what has been demonstrated by research. The sentence that ends so many scholarly reports—"the problem needs further research"—becomes a comfortable ritual that justifies never making up one's mind. Criticisms from other fields, even from some of one's colleagues, can be brushed off as technically incompetent. Teachers who have been overtrained in this direction, and who lack the personal resources to recognize the constriction, present to students the model of a narrow, spiteful technician, a small-minded scholar who cares nothing about the larger world.

These considerations suggest changes in graduate education. Without sacrificing technical training, the future specialist should not be drawn out of contact with the rest of the world. The first change might come at the point of admission to graduate work. A new college graduate with top grades but not much evidence of broader life experience should not be considered a prime candidate. Greater favor should be bestowed on those who have tried their hand at something besides school and formed a more realistic idea of themselves before applying for advanced education. Once admitted, the candidate should be encouraged to have contact with other fields, to engage in interdisciplinary research, and to participate in the discussion of larger ideas. In fields where it is appropriate, methods modeled on clinical teaching should be prominent, in which the teacher is seen working directly with people and helping the students to do likewise. Furthermore, there should be every encouragement to develop skill and interest in teaching. Assisting in courses, often in the past a routine way of earning money, should have status as an important part of the graduate program, to which senior professors give time and thought. Such changes should counteract the constrictive aspects of specialized training and replace the image of scholar by that of scholar-teacher-citizen.

This leavening of graduate training should have a good effect on undergraduate teaching and on continuing education. Such a change is especially important as people of more years and maturity become clients of higher education. Older students are more likely to be impatient with research they judge to be trivial and with conceptual schemes that sound like verbal games. They are likely, moreover, to be frustrated by the provincialism of academic departments. Wanting to pursue, for example, an interest in the Middle East, they will find it annoying if the history, politics, economics, religions, and arts are taught by five different departments that rarely speak to one another. The limitations of departmental organization are becoming better recognized and to some extent overcome, even though this threatens the conservative habits of many scholars. It should become increasingly possible to study the problems of the world and to pursue personal interests without bumping into departmental walls. Old molds need breaking, so that the problems of the particular discipline can shrink to their true proportions and the problems of humankind can grow to theirs.

As they change in these several ways, institutions of higher education will improve their standing as humanitarian environments. Especially will they gain in the modeling of sympathy and involvement, in a broad understanding of human affairs, and in playing down competitive tendencies. In such an environment we can expect an increase in the growth of humanitarian concern.

References

Adler, A. *Understanding Human Nature.* New York: Greenberg, 1927.

Allport, G. W. *Pattern and Growth in Personality.* New York: Holt, Rinehart and Winston, 1961.

Angyal, A. *Foundations for a Science of Personality.* New York: Commonwealth Fund, 1941.

Ansbacher, H. L., and Ansbacher, R. R. *The Individual Psychology of Alfred Adler.* New York: Basic Books, 1956.

Browning, D. S. *Generative Man: Psychoanalytic Perspectives.* Philadelphia: Westminster Press, 1973.

Bryan, J. H., and London, P. "Altruistic Behavior by Children." *Psychological Bulletin,* 1970, *73,* 200-211.

Davis, A., Gardner, B. B., and Gardner, M. R. *Deep South: A Social and Anthropological Study of Caste and Class.* Chicago: University of Chicago Press, 1941.

Erikson, E. H. *Childhood and Society.* New York: Norton, 1950.

Erikson, E. H. *Identity: Youth and Crisis.* New York: Norton, 1968.

Hoffman, M. L. "The Development of Altruistic Motivation." In D. J. DePalma and J. M. Foley (Eds.), *Moral Development: Current Theory and Research.* Hillsdale, N.J.: Erlbaum, 1975.

Hollingshead, A. B. *Elmtown's Youth: The Impact of Social Classes on Adolescents.* New York: Wiley, 1949.

Kahl, J. A. *The American Class Structure.* New York: Holt, Rinehart and Winston, 1957.

Keniston, K. *Young Radicals: Notes on Committed Youth.* New York: Harcourt Brace Jovanovich, 1968.

Lenrow, P. B. "Studies of Sympathy." In S. S. Tomkins and C. E. Izard (Eds.), *Affect, Cognition, and Personality: Empirical Studies.* New York: Springer-Verlag, 1965.

Murphy, L. B. *Social Behavior and Child Personality.* New York: Columbia University Press, 1937.

Rosenhan, D. "The Natural Socialization of Altruistic Autonomy." In J. R. Macauley and J. Berkowitz (Eds.), *Altruism and Helping Behavior.* New York: Academic Press, 1970.

Rushton, J. P. "Socialization and the Altruistic Behavior of Children." *Psychological Bulletin,* 1976, *83,* 898-913.

Smith, M. B., Bruner, J. S., and White, R. W. *Opinions and Personality.* New York: Wiley, 1956.

Sullivan, H. S. *The Interpersonal Theory of Psychiatry.* New York: Norton, 1953.

Umbarger, C. C., and others. *College Students in a Mental Hospital.* New York: Grune & Stratton, 1962.

Warner, W. L. *Democracy in Jonesville: A Study in Quality and Inequality.* New York: Harper & Row, 1949.

White, R. W. *The Enterprise of Living: A View of Personal Growth.* (2d ed.) New York: Holt, Rinehart and Winston, 1976.

White, R. W., Riggs, M. M., and Gilbert, D. C. *A Case Workbook in Personality.* New York: Holt, Rinehart and Winston, 1976.

7

William R. Torbert

Interpersonal
Competence

Academic involvement in learning that relates directly to students' everyday interpersonal experience—that develops not just their analytical, intellectual competence but also their interpersonal competence—has gained increasing currency over the past twenty years. At the same time, the notion of interpersonal competence arouses the suspicion of many members of the university community.

Interest in learning interpersonal competence is growing for several reasons:

One reason, which emerges as a repeated theme in this book, is that the population seeking postsecondary education is growing older, and older students are more motivated to learn when learning is related to practical interactional problems (see Schaie and Parr's chapter on intellectual development).

A second, related reason is that the "practical" divisions of higher education—the professional schools and continuing education departments—are growing most rapidly.

A third, more macroscopic and historical, reason may be that, with the increasing turbulence of change and the destruction of unquestioned sources and patterns of authority, people are finding their interpersonal relationships less regulated by habit or tradition and increasingly fragile—forming and dissolving in ways that seem difficult to control. They may thus be painfully aware that there is something about human relationships they do not understand and need to learn.

A fourth reason relates to ego development research (see Weathersby's chapter in this book), which indicates that the developmental level of people seeking higher education is rising. Since people at higher ego levels increasingly assume personal responsibility for the social dilemmas in which they find themselves, rather than externalizing blame onto others, this change may also be contributing to an increasing interest in learning how one's own actions affect interpersonal situations.

Finally, academics in general and social scientists in particular have been focusing more sharply on the gaps between intellectual analysis and interactional realities in an attempt to explain the failures of social policies, institutional reforms, and leadership strategies (Argyris and Schön, 1974; Cohen and Lindblom, 1979). They are asking whether there is a mode of knowing, qualitatively different from analytical knowledge, that can help to bridge these gaps between policy and practice in personal and social life.

Through examples of classroom, faculty, and administrative interactions, this chapter moves toward the conclusion that there really is a qualitatively more sophisticated mode of knowing than the ideal of formal academic inquiry, which has guided academic life for the past several centuries, and that the primary challenge to the academy during the next generation will be to explicate and to enact this "living inquiry." But before considering the evidence for this conclusion and before defining interpersonal competence as such, we should examine some of the reasons why the notion of interpersonal competence arouses the suspicion of many members of the university community.

The idea of interpersonal competence probably arouses suspicion because we generally think of competence as the ability to accomplish some *predetermined end* through the *manipulation of materials at hand.* At least some of us, however, feel a moral revulsion at the thought of treating other people as materials or means rather than as ends in themselves. And even if others are treated as ends in themselves, the notion of applying general, predetermined rules of "interpersonal competence" appears at once absurd and dangerous.

From another angle, interpersonal competence suggests a practical ability and perhaps even an anti-intellectual orientation, which, if given a chance, might displace rigorous intellectual education by a much more limited "charm school" kind of training. This anti-intellectual connotation may be reinforced by such historical facts as the name "T-Group" or "Training-Group" for the original process invented to cultivate interpersonal competence; the preeminence of business sponsorship in early research and education relating to interpersonal competence (see, for example, Argyris, 1962); and the tendency for a concern with interpersonal competence to enter academia through "applied" professional programs and adult extension programs rather than through the core liberal arts disciplines (Torbert, 1978).

In addition, interpersonal competence may be suspect, particularly among academics, because it implies explicit treatment of personal and ethical issues rather than the impersonal treatment of ethical dilemmas such as those described in Gilligan's chapter. Formal academic inquiry tends deliberately to avoid these personal and ethical issues in order not to invade people's privacy and in order to develop students' capacity for universalistic, rational inquiry pursued for its own sake.

There can be no doubt that the development of interpersonal competence as an aim of higher education courts the dangers just described—those of *training students narrowly* in some *form of manipulation,* rather than educating them to a widening inquiry, and *invading their privacy* in the course of doing so. Indeed, a series of studies of people's interactional patterns in academia, industry, and government indicate that a narrowly goal-oriented, manipulative interpersonal strategy is virtually universal among adults in their actual practice, whatever their espoused values may be (Argyris, 1969, 1971; Argyris

and Schön, 1974). Paradoxically, however, the very studies that demonstrate the prevalence of this narrow and manipulative strategy also argue strongly that this strategy results in interpersonal *in*competence. Let us examine more closely what these studies
show—and what they imply for the development of interpersonal competence as a goal of
college.

Two Interpersonal Strategies

The most common interpersonal strategy attempts to maximize one's *manipula-*
tive control over others, while keeping one's own motives and strategies secret so that
others cannot easily control one. This interpersonal strategy can be called the *mystery-*
mastery strategy (Bakan, 1967; Torbert, 1973), since one seeks to put a veil of mystery
over one's own intentions and to master others.

Argyris and Schön (1974) have found that this mystery-mastery strategy is characteristic of virtually all the professionals in their graduate courses, whatever their fields.
These professionals often espouse strategies of openness and collaboration, but their descriptions of their actual behavior in job settings (as well as tape recordings and instructors' observations of their behavior in the classroom) reveal a mystery-mastery pattern.
The incongruity between what the professionals say they do and what they actually do is
usually a complete (and unpleasant) surprise to them. Argyris and Schön (1974) identify
four governing variables of this mystery-mastery interpersonal strategy:

> 1. *Define goals and try to achieve them.* Participants rarely tried to de-
> velop with others a mutual definition of purposes; nor did they seem open to
> being influenced to alter their perception of the task.
> 2. *Maximize winning and minimize losing.* Participants felt that once they
> had decided on their goals, changing them would be a sign of weakness.
> 3. *Minimize generating or expressing negative feelings.* Participants were
> almost unanimous that generating negative feelings showed ineptness, incompe-
> tence, or lack of diplomacy. Permitting or helping others to express their feelings
> tended to be seen as a poor strategy.
> 4. *Be rational.* Be objective, intellectual, suppress your feelings, and do
> not become emotional [pp. 66-67].

Ironically, the very effort at unilateral control, winning, and being rational results,
in the long run, in lack of control over one's own time and in feeling emotional about,
and victimized by, external pressures. Admittedly, the more institutional and charismatic
power represented by the individual, the longer it will appear that his unilateral strategy
works—with Hitler perhaps the extreme example both of the possible scope of unilateral
control and of the resistance it ultimately crystallizes.

But why, in educational settings, should attempts at unilateral control ultimately
result in loss of control? Here is what happens: First, the mystery-mastery strategy en-
genders strong competition among all participants at an administrative, faculty, or class
meeting to control the limited air time, with the result that most people most of the time
will feel that they do not have the kind of control they want. Second, the "mystery" part
of the strategy prevents participants from clarifying purposes and discovering to what
degree they can work cooperatively toward shared purposes, to what degree they can
work separately toward different but nonhostile purposes, and to what degree they can
resolve conflicts among purposes. The result is an increasing sense of isolation and mutual
distrust. Third, both the "mystery" and the "mastery" parts of the strategy keep partici-

pants from publicly noting or personally acknowledging incongruities among purposes, strategies, practices, and effects, thus preventing any valid learning from experience (Torbert, 1973).

As Argyris and Schön argue and demonstrate, the effect of the mystery-mastery strategy on individual and organizational patterns of action is to create a self-sealing, or defensive, rather than a self-correcting interpersonal system of behavior. The very premises upon which the system is built are defensive, in that they effectively exclude the very data that could challenge them. If nobody is willing to take the risk of sharing how he or she really feels and thinks about others, about problems, issues, or the system, the result will be decreasing levels of trust, less risk-taking, less interactive learning, increasing interpersonal incompetence, and increasing sense of victimization by external pressures.

That these problems are not merely hypothetical but rather widely characterize higher education today is suggested by two studies of college presidents. One study reports that college presidents themselves testify that they are unable to direct their major efforts toward the area they perceive as their greatest responsibility—providing a sense of purpose for their institutions (Perkins, 1967). Another study of college presidents gives a concrete sense of why this should be so:

> The president's time is clearly rationed, but very few presidents with whom we talked had a serious sense that *they* were doing the rationing or that there was any particular logic to the resultant distribution of attention. . . . They felt themselves to be the victims of the pressures upon them and the limitations of time and their own energies. . . . Too many "trivial" activities that had to be engaged in. No time for thinking or reading or initiating action [Cohen and March, 1974, p. 134].

But how can a person achieve freedom, control, and fulfillment in the social world without attempting to control situations unilaterally and rationally? Argyris and Schön suggest an alternative interpersonal strategy, the inquiring strategy, which encourages learning from experience and increasing interpersonal competence and which helps to generate a community of inquiry in a given situation. They find that virtually none of their students initially uses this strategy and that learning it is very difficult for them. Argyris and Schön attempt to model this second interpersonal strategy in their own teaching and consulting. They outline the three governing variables of this strategy as follows:

> *Maximize valid information.* The actor provides others with directly observable data about their behavior and correct reports [about his or her own experiencing] so they may make valid attributions about the actor. It also means creating conditions that will lead others to provide directly observable data and correct reports that will enable one to make valid attributions about them.
> *Maximize free and informed choice.* A choice is informed if it is based on relevant information. The more an individual is aware of the values of the variables relevant to his decision, the more likely he is to make an informed choice.
> *Maximize internal commitment to decisions made.* Internal commitment means that the individual feels that he, himself, is responsible for his choices. The individual is committed to an action because it is intrinsically satisfying—not . . . because someone is rewarding or penalizing him to be committed [Argyris and Schön, 1974, pp. 86-89].

This inquiring interpersonal strategy makes designing and managing the environment, as well as protecting each person's freedom and privacy, shared tasks. Argyris and

Schön argue that this inquiring strategy creates the conditions for oneself and others to learn not only specific new ways of behaving that fit one's existing interpersonal strategy but also, and more important, entirely new strategies. In other words, the inquiring interpersonal strategy is actually a kind of meta-strategy, which permits a continuing interactional inquiry, a continuing clarification of purposes, and a continuing reformulation of strategies, as well as a continuing adjustment of specific behaviors to accomplish specific goals.

Problems in Learning a New Interpersonal Strategy

It is important to note that Argyris and Schön's work represents an early, exploratory probe into the unknown territory of interactional inquiry and that many fundamental issues remain unresolved. For example, their concept of valid information focuses heavily on behavioral descriptions of persons' actual practice. This emphasis on actual practice is extremely valuable, since most persons speak and think about action in sloppy, prematurely evaluative terms (for example, "brilliant" or "weak") from which it is difficult to learn how to improve one's practice. At the same time, however, the focus on behavior and the very precept "maximize valid information" cloak the difficulty of determining what aspects of experience (including memories, anticipations, and other texts) deserve to stand out from a given spatial-temporal context as information in the first place. Put differently, the governing variables Argyris and Schön propose for the inquiring interpersonal strategy are offered in universalistic analytical language that provides no clues about timing, about when and how to focus one's attention as they suggest.

Another set of unresolved issues concerns the difficulty of unlearning the mystery-mastery interpersonal strategy and learning the inquiring interpersonal strategy. Argyris and Schön carefully describe the difficulties their professional students have in their one-term course: first, in recognizing the incongruities in their behavior and their general interpersonal incompetence; second, in inventing genuinely alternative kinds of behavioral experiments rather than other variants of the mystery-mastery strategy; and third, in learning to produce these new behaviors fluently in everyday life.

The difficulty of learning a fundamentally new interpersonal strategy becomes more comprehensible if one compares it to the task of learning a new musical instrument or learning an entirely new approach to formal scientific research after one has mastered one methodology and used it for years. One can easily imagine that it may take years of intensive practice to become fluent in the playing of the new instrument or the implementation of the new methodology. In India, one studies the sitar twenty-one years before one can be considered a master. Learning a new interpersonal strategy is more difficult because the old strategy is even more intimately a part of one's sense of identity than an instrument. Furthermore, one is constantly reinforcing one's old strategy in every passing encounter with others, whereas, at least initially, one is likely to set aside only occasional times to practice the new strategy. Moreover, since the inquiring interpersonal strategy is really a meta-strategy, one is called upon to learn not one new strategy but many.

The task of learning the inquiring interpersonal strategy requires more than just a course or two, though courses can certainly help to initiate such learning. What is needed is a community of inquiry—a lifetime circle of friends who can help clarify, and when necessary challenge, each other's purposes and actions. Teachers of interpersonal competence must encourage dedicated students to cultivate such lifetime friendships in inquiry.

Granted, this is a difficult task in an age of mobility, dispersonal, and short-term relationships.

The foregoing comments bring to the surface still another issue—the power and ethical responsibility of a teacher of interpersonal competence. Argyris and Schön discuss the importance of openly acknowledging that the teacher is likely to be more competent interpersonally than the students and is therefore likely to be treated as a model. At the same time, they discuss the importance of the teacher's acting in ways that minimize students' continuing dependence. Argyris and Schön also make the general point that the more teachers use their power to encourage an inquiring interpersonal strategy in others, the more their class learning systems become self-correcting rather than self-sealing, and therefore the more likely is any abuse of power to be confronted. Yet they also appreciate the fact that to use power in a way that forces students to adopt the inquiring strategy is to contradict the governing variables of the inquiring strategy itself. How to maintain the paradoxical balances implied by these dilemmas of power requires continuing study by anyone who takes leadership responsibility in an organizing process that includes among its aims the development of interpersonal competence.

One way of approaching the question of what kinds of inquiry are relevant when is to think of human interaction as occurring across three "layers" of reality: (1) task, (2) process, and (3) purpose. Ordinarily, discussion focuses on the particular task at hand, taking for granted the process, or norms and structures of appropriate behavior, and the purpose, or general definition of the situation (Torbert, 1976b). Indeed, in general, the mystery-mastery interpersonal strategy treats the doing of a given task as the only layer of reality appropriate for public discussion. (Certain theories of family therapy are based on the "tangles" among layers that can result from this interpersonal strategy [Bateson, 1972; Laing, 1962; Watzlawick, Beavin, and Jackson, 1967]). Strategies to change the norms or the definition of a situation are pursued privately and covertly. But one can well imagine that different persons in a given situation in fact take different norms for granted, or that a situation in fact has no clear, shared definition. In such cases, the whole group might benefit by temporarily turning its attention from the *task* itself to the *process* of the group (for example, the norms one can infer from members' patterns of behavior), or to the *purpose* of the group (for example, the personal, political, or epistemological presuppositions that frame members' sense of purpose and define the situation for them).

Thus, an inquiring interpersonal strategy requires developing skills of observation, formulation, and expression at all three "layers" of interpersonal life. It also requires a sense of timing, to be able to gauge when it may be beneficial to the group to refocus discussion on another "layer." (The literature on group dynamics offers many insights into process issues likely to require attention at different periods of a group's history. See Bennis, 1964; Bion, 1961; Culbert, 1968; Dunphy, 1968; Mann, 1966; Mills, 1964.)

In general, most ongoing groups can best learn how to manage the "process" and "purpose" layers of their interaction by beginning with the "process" layer. For, as Argyris and Schön (1974) point out, the patterns of behavior inferred at the process level are based on evidence directly available to other members of the immediate group, so that conflicting interpretations can, to some extent, be resolved through closer inspection of the behavior in question. (Argyris, 1971, presents the most systematic discussion of process intervention strategies currently available. See also Beckhart, 1969, and Schein, 1969.) By contrast, discussion of the "purpose" layer often requires reference to longer-term, more abstract personal career patterns and institutional histories, and the evidence tends to be less accessible both to individuals themselves and to the group as a whole. A fruitful exploration of this layer requires the ability to shift focus between layers as necessary, and a high level of trust in a group.

Obviously, narrow training in a few interpersonal skills can become the basis for "one-upping" others rather than seeking a genuine collaborative inquiry. Erving Goffman (1974) sees this danger in *all* academic efforts to develop interpersonal competence:

> In several of the social sciences, instructors have come to occasionally turn their classes into arenas for the display of "group processes," the understanding being that live demonstrations are better than organized lecturing on related topics. In the manner of group psychotherapy, various roles (or "games") can be defined, the instructor directing attention to actual illustrations. The social organization of classroom activity can thus be uncovered, as well, perhaps, as features of discussion groups in general; the trouble is, of course, that that is *all* that can be done. Every topic becomes reduced to one. And incidentally, a lecture does not have to be prepared, nor need criticism of what occurs be treated at face value, since it becomes a topic of consideration, too [p. 411].

Goffman's fascinating analysis of how persons frame situations, from which the foregoing quotation is taken, reinforces the thesis advanced here that the socially prevalent mystery-mastery interpersonal strategy leaves the norms and frames of situations publicly undiscussed. Under these conditions, the norms and frames are susceptible to accidental breaks and private manipulations, but not to collaborative control. Interestingly enough, Goffman himself evidently does not recognize the possibility of collaborative control over purpose, process, and task, with appropriate shifting of attention among these layers in order to enhance *whatever* is at stake. Instead, he proposes that once group process becomes a legitimate topic, that is *all* that can be discussed. Clearly, the conclusion of this proposition does not necessarily follow from the premise. Nevertheless, it is certainly true that focusing on group process *may* be used as a way to avoid more serious inquiry and criticism.

Definition and Illustrations of Interpersonal Competence

The foregoing discussion of two interpersonal strategies—the prevailing mystery-mastery strategy and the alternative inquiring strategy—sets the stage for a formal definition of interpersonal competence. This definition strives to avoid the dangers of confusing interpersonal competence with a narrow manipulative skill.

Interpersonal competence can be defined as the capacity in one's work and play with others:

- To clarify, to formulate, and to do what one wishes
- To test for and correct incongruities among wish (purpose), formulation (theory or strategy), action (interactive process), and effect
- To help others do the same, given the limits of mutual commitment

Several implications are crowded into this short definition. First, the phrase "in one's work and play with others" suggests that interpersonal competence is an interactive social competence and not merely a kind of intellectual competence. Second, the phrase "to clarify, to formulate, and to do what one wishes" suggests that interpersonal competence is not merely skill in accomplishing predefined tasks but rather includes the practices of discovering what one wishes and defining (formulating) the tasks to be done.

Third, the phrase "to test for and correct incongruities among wish, formulation, action, and effect; and to help others do the same" suggests that interpersonal competence depends not so much on wielding social influence over others as on creating a social climate of inquiry, a social climate in which one can increasingly count on receiving truthful information from others about one's effects on them, as well as exploratory criticisms about possible ambiguities or incongruities among one's purpose, strategy, and action. Fourth, the phrase "given the limits of mutual commitment" suggests that no one particular kind of interpersonal behavior is always better than some other. Rather, one's choice of behavior must be guided by a concern for the boundaries and rhythms of the particular relationship in question—as well as by the foregoing principles. In short, interpersonal competence, by this definition, is not at all a matter of manipulating others successfully in order to achieve one's unexamined ends. Rather, interpersonal competence is a matter of creating a social climate of inquiry, which aids in clarifying both personal and communal purposes and relationships as well as in accomplishing specific tasks.

That the inquiring interpersonal strategy can result in the shared control of a situation and the clarification of purpose is illustrated by a classroom situation in which faculty members confronted one another, rather than "one-upping" students, and initiated first a "process-focusing intervention" and then a "purpose-focusing intervention," while not excluding further work on predetermined tasks. This classroom situation was the first meeting of an introductory undergraduate business course dedicated to preparing students to become self-directed, quality-conscious entrepreneurs. The challenge to the four-member course faculty and the twelve undergraduate teaching assistants was heightened by the scale of the course: 360 students. (How does one "batch process" 360 students toward self-direction?) As the course proceeded, students broke into small work groups and eventually contracted to do collaboratively determined projects as they gained sufficient skills in self-management. The introductory meetings were held in a large auditorium, with all 376 course members. The following description of the first meeting is offered by one of the four course faculty members:

> The staff had organized a multimedia "show" in an initial attempt to convey the special qualities of the course. This show included not only the usual media—such as music, movies, and slide-tapes—which render the "audience" passive, but also such additional media as conversation and decision making, which render everyone participant. At some point in the sequence—after the laughter at the Frankenstein slides that accompanied the interviewed student's description of the previous term's course as monstrous, after the groaning that greeted the announcement of an exam on the assigned reading next week, and after applause for the Alleluia chorus accompanying a movie about the raising of a plastic, student-built coffee house the previous spring—one of the faculty members, using an overhead projector, introduced a series of statistical tables as part of his explanation that active, experimenting students enjoyed and learned more from the course than passive students.
>
> Perhaps the incongruity between the message and the medium was too great in this case, although I seriously doubt that any of the students consciously analyzed the discrepancy. In any event, the previous balance of tension and excitement quickly began to dissipate into irate confusion, inattention, and side conversations as the faculty member talked. After questioning what was appropriate for what felt like an eon, I interrupted my colleague, causing an immediate, shocked stillness among all 380 persons in the auditorium. But the other faculty member said he would finish briefly and continued, to growing grumbles of discontent. I interrupted again, more forcefully, and this time he actually listened to

what was going on and stopped. One of the teaching assistants began to introduce the film of the steel foundry research team of which he had been a member the previous spring, but this time a third member of the faculty interrupted to suggest we discuss the previous incident for a few moments, since he saw it as symbolic of the courage, skill, and mutual trust required to learn in action.

While the rest of the evening was entertaining and informative, a skeptical person might dismiss it as slick public relations. This incident, by contrast, could alert students to the possibility that they were encountering a rare sort of social system dedicated to something beyond short-term goals, easily definable objectives, and saving face. In their first learning paper two weeks later, more students spontaneously referred to this incident than to any other event in the course [Torbert, 1978, pp. 122-123].

In the foregoing classroom scenario, the narrator's first two interventions seek to shift the focus of attention from the content of the statistical tables to the process of the class (on the grounds that most persons' attention has already shifted from the content). Then, the next intervention by the third faculty member seeks to shift the focus of attention from the ongoing agenda to the way in which the previous incident symbolizes the overall purposes of the course. In both cases, the comments are qualitatively different from the presentations they interrupt in that they tie the issues being discussed into what is actually happening in the discussion itself. Thus, to the degree that these comments are accurate and timely, they represent not so much interruptions in accomplishing the evening's task as shortcuts to accomplishing it. In both cases, also, these comments move, not in the direction of accomplishing a predefined external task in a particular way, but rather in the direction of encouraging a shared awareness and responsibility for what is actually at stake in the first place. Such comments, although they are primarily educational rather than visibly productive, may well lead to profound changes in visible patterns of accomplishment.

In the case of the foregoing scenario, the story seems to end happily: the two interventions do seem to increase the effectiveness of the occasion—that is, the degree of congruity between purpose and outcome, if only by gaining the students' attention. Of course, the narration is not detailed enough to allow us to make any conclusive judgments about the effectiveness of the interventions. Nevertheless, it is just such partial perspectives with which the person acting in any ongoing situation must work. Thus, the first intervenor in the foregoing scenario could not know what the response would be to the intervention, nor that another intervention would shortly influence the meaning of the first.

In the absence of the kind of public discussion here exemplified—discussion that can move back and forth dialectically, testing for and increasing congruity among original purposes, present practices, and future task goals, particular tasks will tend to become dissociated from ultimate purposes. Such dissociation between purposes and tasks confuses, lowers, and externalizes participants' motivation to perform (see Argyris, 1973; Bowles and Gintis, 1975; Torbert, 1972) and eventually generates institutional results that contradict the original purposes (Warner and Havens, 1968).

For example, in the following classroom scenario a seminar is studying one of Plato's dialogues. The teacher would almost certainly say that one of the purposes of the class session itself is to generate an educational dialogue among the class members; yet the teacher's mystery-mastery interpersonal strategy precludes such dialogue.

The Chairman lays his coat down carefully, takes a chair on the opposite side of the large round table, sits, and then brings out an old pipe and stuffs it for what must be nearly half a minute. One can see he has done this many times before.

In a moment of attention to the class he studies faces with a smiling hypnotic gaze, sensing the mood, but feeling it is not just right. He stuffs the pipe some more, but without hurry.

Soon the moment arrives, he lights the pipe, and before long there is in the classroom an odor of smoke.

At last he speaks:

"It is my understanding," he says, "that today we are to begin discussion of the immortal *Phaedrus.*" He looks at each student separately. "Is that correct?"

Members of the class assure him timidly that it is. His persona is overwhelming.

The Chairman now directs a question to the student next to Phaedrus. He is baiting him a little, provoking him to attack.

The student doesn't attack, and the Chairman with great disgust and frustration finally dismisses him with a rebuke that he should have read the material better.

Phaedrus' turn. He has calmed down tremendously. He must now explain the dialogue.

"If I may be permitted to begin again in my own way," he says, partly to conceal the fact that he didn't hear what the previous student said.

The Chairman, seeing this as a further rebuke to the student next to him, smiles and says contemptuously it is certainly a good idea.

Phaedrus proceeds. "I believe that in this dialogue the person of Phaedrus is characterized as a *wolf.*"

He has delivered this quite loudly, with a flash of anger, and the Chairman almost jumps. Score!

"Yes," the Chairman says, and a gleam in his eye shows he now recognizes who his bearded assailant is. "*Phaedrus* in Greek does mean 'wolf.' That's a very acute observation." He begins to recover his composure. "Proceed."

"Phaedrus meets Socrates, *who knows only the ways of the city,* and leads him into the country, whereupon he begins to recite a speech of the orator, Lysias, whom he admires. Socrates asks him to read it and Phaedrus does."

"Stop!" says the Chairman, who has now completely recovered his composure. "You are giving us the plot, not the dialogue." He calls on the next student.

None of the students seems to know to the Chairman's satisfaction what the dialogue is about. And so with mock sadness he says they must all read more thoroughly but this time he will help them by taking on the burden of explaining the dialogue himself. This provides an overwhelming relief to the tension he has so carefully built up and the entire class is in the palm of his hand [Pirsig, 1974, pp. 385-388].

A keen awareness of the interplay between content, process, and purpose is necessary in order to penetrate the meaning of Plato's dialogues, for the dramatic situations and the relationships among the speakers all bear on the issues at stake (Anderson, 1976). For example, in the *Lysias,* a dialogue about friendship, the speakers end the dialogue without a shared definition of friendship, yet the process of the dialogue itself has made them friendly (Brumbaugh, 1962). Thus, if we are attentive, we can learn more from these dialogues than what the speakers say. Ironically, the teacher in the foregoing situation is so dedicated to displaying his mastery that he utterly fails to generate an educational dialogue within the seminar itself wherein the purposes, the process, and the text become mutually illuminating. Thus, he offers the students no direct experience in cultivating the quality of attentiveness necessary to follow the interplay of purpose, process, and task. The narrator of this excerpt, however, shows considerable appreciation for this interplay by what he chooses to describe, and by his capacity in the seminar itself to enact the wolf's role even as he analyzes it.

Developing the capacity to carry on a public discussion that moves back and forth dialectically among purposes, processes, and tasks, sometimes explicitly and sometimes implicitly, clearly requires practice. To take one very specific, microscopic example: In groups where members operate according to the mystery-mastery interpersonal strategy, members interrupt one another far more frequently than they help others to express what they are trying to say (Argyris, 1969). This pattern contributes to a competitive, threatening atmosphere in which participants hesitate to express their perceptions about what is going on. Consequently, one important exercise for someone seeking to increase his or her interpersonal competence and to encourage social atmospheres of inquiry would be to practice helping others to express what they wish to say rather than interrupting them with one's own agenda. However, a person who *never* interrupts others is not necessarily more interpersonally competent than one who does. One aim of practicing not to interrupt is to learn how to interrupt justly. Indeed, both of the interventions in the first classroom scenario are, in a behavioral sense, interruptions. These interruptions, however, are not intended to replace one person's agenda by another person's agenda but rather to inquire whether the existing process is effectively achieving the purposes of the overall occasion.

Components of Interpersonal Competence

One can identify three general kinds of interpersonal behavior that promote the inquiring mode of interaction—namely, self-disclosure, supportiveness, and confrontation (Torbert, 1973). In *self-disclosure,* one expresses and questions one's own experiencing, treating any judgment or evaluation that is offered as part of one's own experience rather than as a universal truth (Culbert, 1968; Jourard, 1968). *Supportiveness* encourages another to express his or her experiencing, not necessarily by agreeing with what the other says but simply by expressing empathy for the other's experience, sharing and reflecting their feelings (Rogers, 1961; Truax and Carkhuff, 1967). *Confrontation* involves juxtaposing two aspects of experience that seem to be incongruous with one another, such as another person's behavior compared with his or her espoused strategy or a group's use of time compared with a deadline it has set itself. The apparent opposition is posed as a dilemma that may require further exploration by all parties concerned.

The fluid and timely interplay of these three kinds of inquiring behavior permits a group to gather the data and make the judgments necessary to control its destiny. Indeed, the inquiring interpersonal strategy gives a person or group access to information about, and judgments bearing on, not only the technical issues relevant to the accomplishment of some predefined task but also the political issues relevant to defining that task. Thus, the inquiring strategy increases the potential range of control of a group. But because these three inquiring kinds of verbal behavior are so different from the more familiar mystery-mastery behavior and because collaborative control is so different from attempts at unilateral control and the resulting competitive bargaining, attempts to learn the inquiring mode may often make people feel as if they are losing control altogether.

Instead of taking part in a social game that seems completely predefined because the rules and the incongruities remain largely implicit, persons may find themselves in a situation where the rules of the game and even the very name of the game may be explicitly questioned. How disorienting this experience can feel is suggested by the following comment of a T-group participant two hours after the beginning of the group. Having early on vigorously proposed a program for the evening that met with little enthusiasm and having then lapsed into silence, he was later asked why he had ceased participating:

> I'm trapped. I kind of see what you are doing, just discovering where your immediate feelings, responses, and changed feelings are leading you, what kind of pattern is growing. I can see that my proposal was really a game for structuring our time so I wouldn't have to worry about what we were doing. But that's how my mind works—in games, and I can't say anything now because saying a feeling seems so artificial to me—like a game [Torbert, 1970, p. 10].

Such ambivalent and often awkward attempts on the part of persons accustomed to the mystery-mastery mode to understand the inquiry mode can be called *exploration of structure* (Torbert, 1973). Each particular event that invites existential social exploration becomes a confrontation of the entire mystery-mastery structure of reality. Such exploration reveals vulnerability (anathema to the mystery-mastery strategy) and requires inquiring relationships of tested trust (impossible to develop through the mystery-mastery strategy). To help another pass through this difficult transitional process requires a most compassionate and intelligent interplay of supportiveness, self-disclosure, and confrontation.

The following scenario illustrates these three kinds of inquiring behavior. Many of the early comments in the conversation are parenthetically identified as self-disclosing, supportive, or confronting. The scenario portrays a meeting of the seven-member, interracial administrative staff of an educational project. This administrative staff has agreed to several such "research" meetings in order to plan a faculty recruitment process, develop sufficient interpersonal competence to be able to choose interpersonally competent faculty, and clarify tasks and relationships within the administrative staff itself.

> Each member of the staff filled out and shared a job application form being developed for potential new staff members. One of its questions asked the applicant to describe the strengths and weaknesses of his or her interpersonal style. This question led to a conversation about Valery's style, when Grace asked how the rest of the staff reacted to a phrase Valery had included in her application, to the effect that "in general I am silently agreeable."
>
> Tim responded, "My reaction was that I agreed she was silent, but I wondered whether she was agreeable. To mention something I feel guilty about: in the past most of her time has been spent with books, forms, etc., and my feeling was, how easy to let her do it." [self-disclosure]
>
> "I was comfortable on that point, Valery," continued Patricia, "because I thought you were hired to do all those things, to be a sort of secretary, and I couldn't understand why you were dissatisfied." [self-disclosure] [This latter point referred to a meeting the past week, when, in redividing jobs for the winter and spring, Valery had said she would prefer not to continue handling all the bookkeeping.]
>
> Valery laughed nervously, as Patricia finished, "So now, months later, I don't know what you were hired for."
>
> A pause yielded no further response from Valery, so Tim asked, "Do you expect to continue to be silent?"
>
> "No," she offered. Another pause. "You are being," from Tim. [confrontation] Another pause.
>
> "What I can't imagine now" [this from Jim] "is not so much your being silent as your being agreeable. That is, I hear a number of conflicting things being said about you. I don't see how you could agree with all." [confrontation]

"I thought I'd made that clear: I said in general I'm agreeable, but then there's this." [confrontation]

"Yes, that's a good point," Jim replied, somewhat uncomfortable because his rather patronizing attempt to help her see a pattern in her behavior had misfired. "I'd be interested in hearing what you saw yourself hired for, what you saw as our original agreement, and how you felt about me." [self-disclosure]

"When I was hired, it was really unclear," she replied immediately, as though liberated by the specificity of his questions. "You were out there, I was in here—it had to be done—there was no one else to do it. But I thought this was just a matter of beginning, as I think I told you. Then, partly because we had no secretary . . . and I had started it, and no one else really wanted to do it, and who *was* going to do it? Now I'm working with the students . . . How I feel about you? Well, I guess I answered that." [self-disclosure]

"No, I don't feel you did. I heard you say 'I was stuck with it' and I can infer 'I was stuck with it by Jim.' But that's not the way you put it. I wondered what your feeling was towards me." [confrontation]

"Well, initially yes, by you, but other people came in and could have done it—little things. . . ."

"Yes?" [supportive]

"Valery," began Grace.

"I'm sorry, I want to hear *this*," Jim cut in. [supportive interruption]

". . . it was so strong, and no one else would do it, and it was necessary to do it. There's some things that you just have to do."

Grace reentered: "I wanted to ask how did you feel when I came into the office and said could you teach me this stuff. You probably thought I was unteachable. I was anxious to take some of it off your shoulders."

"Well, at that point, well, it was about the same thing, Grace. There were some things you were less interested by, and you said let's do them together. Which is about the same thing as doing it by myself, because that's just how I see it."

Now Patricia: "I want to apologize first of all because I have certainly treated you as if you had this job. Specifically last week, for instance, I made a request of you about changing my check."

"Right."

"You know why I'm sorry, Valery? That you couldn't say to me, Patricia, that's not my job, but here's who you contact and you do it."

"That's because you needn't apologize," replied Valery, "because you're not the only one, and I didn't really correct that."

Then Tim: "What bothered me was that I just carved out my job as I wished it and I couldn't say I didn't know what Valery's job really was."

And Rob: "As a matter of fact, when Greg interviewed me for the job he asked could I type, and I said not well, and he said *would* I type, and I said I would, and he said because we don't have a secretary, and that's the basis on which I first came. I do remember that I did some typing, but you clearly were doing more work on the books."

And Jim: "Other members of the staff *have* carved out jobs for themselves, and I guess I feel more comfortable with that than I do about the situation with you because I feel that your attitude invites us to impose on you, when you say, 'Some things have to be done.' I don't regard the world that way. I don't think anything *has* to be done. I mean that in the broadest possible sense."

Reflectively, Valery concluded the meeting with, "I didn't set a path for myself when I came. It was there and I took it, and I guess it should have been my responsibility to say to Jim, 'I want to change it.' "

After this meeting, her job did change. During the spring and summer she coordinated work on the books rather than doing it all herself, and she took on primary responsibility for student admissions in the spring and for contact with parents during the summer [adapted from Torbert, 1976a, pp. 96-98].

In the foregoing excerpt, a number of purposes are being clarified and served simultaneously. The administrative staff is learning how to use the application forms to generate interview material with potential applicants. The staff is also clarifying and re-solving some of its own relational dilemmas. Moreover, the group is attentive to its own living process, finding examples of the issue at stake (Valery's "silent agreeableness") in the conversation itself. The modes of self-disclosure, confrontation, and supportiveness help the conversation to gain focus and to keep a space open for Valery to enter it more actively than she customarily has. Gradually, all the members, including Valery, come to see how they interact to reinforce Valery's sense of powerlessness. In the second half of the conversation, Valery ceases to be "silently agreeable" and comes to take responsibil-ity for the role she has played in structuring her job as it is. As a result of the meeting, she begins to redefine her job in collaboration with the rest of the staff; the staff as a whole gains experience in how to work with a job applicant in an interview; and the staff as a whole gains more control over the political process through which it works. It is worth noting that there is little discussion of abstract principles in this excerpt, yet members are obviously thinking abstractly about when to say what and how in a complex collaborative inquiry.

Compare the foregoing, relatively inquiring conversation with the following, much more dogmatic one, in which abstract principles are bandied about like weapons rather than used to discipline one's own behavior intelligently and to help others to learn. The following conversation is taken from a meeting among students and faculty at Black Mountain College in the 1930s. Two faculty members have just been fired, and a number of students and other faculty are arguing for a more democratic decision-making process against the founder of the school, named Rice:

> Rice's reply was curt—and revealing: "There are also some people who are incompetent to have opinions." He went on to make acid reference to "the sud-den rise of democrats" at Black Mountain and to state unequivocally that he didn't believe "democracy in the sense of counting noses is right." When he had referred earlier to a majority of the community agreeing with the recent decisions of the Board, he had meant, of course, a majority of the "intelligent."
>
> "*You* determine that?" George Alsberg, one of the dissident students, shot back.
>
> "I do," Rice answered. "I can only test intelligence by intelligence."
> Alsberg persisted: "How do you determine how a person is intelligent?"
> "I could not make you understand, George."
> "Do you understand?"
> "Yes."
>
> James Gore King, temperamentally unsuited to confrontation, tried to bring the meeting back to some neutral ground. "Ought we not," he asked bland-ly, "to find a criterion for gauging 'the majority of intelligence?' " Rice was short with him: "You're not going to get to it by any mechanical means."
>
> At this point George stepped in to say that he agreed "a vote does not necessarily represent the best solution" for establishing community opinion. But he then added—lest Rice think he had an ally from an unexpected quar-ter—that voting "had no more disadvantages . . . than the method of trying to sample intelligent opinion. If I sampled it, it would not agree with Mr. Rice's sam-pling."

"That is true," Rice acknowledged, the tongue just slightly noticeable in his cheek.

"So I think," George went on, "there are objections to both methods. But this group is one in which people have a certain amount of intelligence. I would be more willing to rely upon a majority decision of the group, after proper discussion, than this hit-or-miss sampling."

Rice picked up the last remark and turned it to his own purposes. The device of majority vote, he said, was in fact the embodiment of "mere chance." The two important functions which the Board performed—appointments to the faculty and college finances—could not be left to the judgments of those who might lack the capacity to make them. "In any kind of society you should try to get the best people to perform the jobs which they can perform. The matter of judgment of people is a very delicate thing and one which also requires experience, as a rule. Some people are born with a gift for it, others never acquire it."

"But I believe I've heard you say," George Alsberg answered, "that the students are very good judges of their teachers . . . that as a rule, the students, taken as a group, were usually right about a teacher."

"Yes, George, about his teaching ability," Rice replied. "But there are much more important things which enter into this question."

Alsberg had no trouble shifting gears: "Do you think that teachers are better able than students to judge people as personalities?"

"I have not said that," Rice answered. He had only meant, he explained, that he would want to know who the judges are. "If you want a specific instance, I would say that I am a better judge of who ought to teach on this faculty than you are."

All that Alsberg managed to get out was, "Well, I disagree" [Duberman, 1973, pp. 129-131].

Rice may be perfectly right, in a formal sense, in some or all of his pronouncements. He is also self-disclosing and confronting in a conventional sense (for example, "I would say that I am a better judge of who ought to teach on this faculty than you are."). But his behavior is profoundly unintelligent and ineffective from the point of view of encouraging inquiry into who is more or less intelligent or how decisions at the school are or ought to be made. Instead, he provokes a highly polarized and defensive debate, seeking, or so it would seem from his behavior, to win points rather than to create a mutually educative climate. His behavior is not at all self-disclosing and confronting as these terms have been defined above because he does not describe his own experiencing but only his evaluations (for example, "I am a better judge"). Nor does he describe others' behavior by comparison with any standards. It might be fair to infer from his behavior here that one way he measures intelligence is by "quickness and sharpness of verbal retort." If only someone present at the discussion had had the perceptiveness to make this inference, the courage to confront Rice with it, thus testing its validity, and the perspicacity to ask whether such a definition is really intelligent! From the point of view that sees the encouragement of inquiry as the most convincing expression of intelligence, the answer to such a question would clearly be no.

Developing Interpersonal Competence Through Living Inquiry

Whereas formal inquiry is for the most part concerned with theoretical and empirical knowledge about phenomena occurring outside of the present moment, living inquiry begins with attention to one's experiencing in the present moment. To be lost in thought, no matter how profound, is not to be engaged in living inquiry. Living inquiry requires an attention that includes simultaneously what one is focusing on in the outside world, one's own perceptions and actions, the conceptual-emotional-political patterns at play in the present situation (including memories of the past and projections into the future), and the movements of attention itself (Torbert, 1973).

Living inquiry includes theoretical and empirical inquiry, but it focuses on the participants' own actions and purposes. Only through an inquiry that includes one's own actions can one possibly learn how to act more effectively. Only through an inquiry that includes the very movements of one's own attention can one learn what one's purposes are. Only through an inquiry that includes one's wishes, strategies, actions, and effects can one possibly become interpersonally competent, according to the definition offered in this chapter. Only through an inquiry this broad and this immediate can one explore the relationship between purposes and outcomes.

Socially, living inquiry generates a community of inquiry, a community in which the reigning definition of any situation (the myth or purpose, for example), the social norms and practices of the participants, and the value of outcomes are all subject to question (Torbert, 1976b).

Epistemologically, living inquiry generates an action science that

- Includes the inquirer within the field of observation
- Creates a structure for inquiry into axioms, theories, research instruments, and data as the study progresses, rather than starting with a predetermined method whose axioms are taken for granted
- Treats interruptions and conflicts as opportunities to test the validity of existing structures and axioms of inquiry
- Is interested in general, universalizable knowledge only to the degree that such knowledge aids in the development of a personal, social, and ecological knowledge uniquely relevant to the time and place of the ongoing study and action (Torbert, 1977a)

These three aspects of living inquiry—the kind of personal attention necessary, the kind of social community necessary, and the kind of scientific inquiry necessary—each require and foster one another. Moreover, all three of these aspects of living inquiry both foster and require interpersonal competence, as it is defined in this chapter.

Although formal education at present occasionally permits students to develop beyond dichotomous ("right-wrong") thinking (see Perry's chapter in this book) and beyond equally dichotomous ("good-bad") conventional moral judgments (see Gilligan's chapter), it generally reinforces dichotomous thinking and judgment in students, faculty members, and administrators. Formal education has this effect because of its fundamental assumptions about individual intelligence and learning, its fundamental axioms of logic and scientific methodology, and its myths about what constitutes institutional effectiveness. Individual intelligence itself is defined, through IQ tests and most other classroom tests, in terms of a student's competence at instrumental reasoning. Students are given predefined, cognitive problems with right and wrong answers, not ambiguous, experiential dilemmas with a variety of unique solutions.

Institutionally, the vast preponderance of higher education is currently organized in the bureaucratic, predefined productivity mode (Torbert, 1974, 1976a), with dichotomous criteria of success and failure, symbolized in the everyday life of students by the omnipresent bivariate grading system (whether in numerical, alphabetical, or categorical terms). Epistemologically, formal reasoning in philosophy and the sciences tends still to be based, not on temporally dynamic, dialectical logics, but on Aristotle's explicitly static and dichotomous logic, with its Law of Contradiction and its Law of the Excluded Middle (Mitroff, 1974, 1978). Thus, in psychological and pedagogical terms, in sociological and institutional terms, and in logical and epistemological terms, formal education as we now know it tends to inhibit persons from developing beyond Piaget's "formal operations" stage—beyond dichotomous thinking to dialectical thinking in action (Arlin, 1975; Gilligan and Murphy, 1978; Perry, 1968; Riegel, 1973).

The development of interpersonal competence, as it is defined in this chapter, requires a dialectical transcendence of formal education, not its rejection. Interpersonal competence involves a continuing dialogue between theory and practice, between the objective and the subjective, between the personal and the political, between the eternal and the timely. Interpersonal competence requires a commitment to inquiry far beyond that involved in facing up to logical contradictions; it requires the commitment to face up to existential and political contradictions in one's own life with others and to work toward a methodology for resolving them, rather than beginning with a predetermined methodology. Higher education can aid in the development of such an interpersonal competence only to the degree that it transcends both the ideal and the practice of formal inquiry for the still higher ideal and the far subtler practice of living inquiry.

Conclusion

The application of the sciences and their various technologies to social life during the past two centuries has transformed civilization, arming humankind with awesome powers. We now recognize that knowledge itself is a source of wealth and power (Loebl, 1976). But we can also see that such knowledge, wealth, and power can be used for either good or evil. Now the question facing humankind is whether we can discover a kind of knowledge directly related to our own practices with others—not a disembodied, technical knowledge but a personal, political knowledge that can help us to act more responsibly and humanely. Both Marxian and Freudian analysis represent early attempts in Western social theory to move beyond formal inquiry to living inquiry, but each focuses more heavily on a particular theory of social process than on the path by which people can come to see social process for themselves. Whereas in earlier times humankind sought to domesticate nature through technology, today technology is itself part of the environment we seek to domesticate, and we recognize that we ourselves are the most dangerous and least appreciated members of the world we seek to know. Past social theories and practices have imprisoned humankind in too narrow arenas. Only living inquiry opens us to realms wide enough to encompass our higher education in the age we now face.

References

Alschuler, A., and others. "Collaborative Problem Solving as an Aim of Education in a Democracy: The Social Literary Project." *Journal of Applied Behavioral Science,* 1977, *13* (3), 315-327.

Anderson, R. "The Dramatic Unity of Plato's *Theaetetus.*" Unpublished doctoral dissertation, Yale University, 1976.

Argyris, C. *Interpersonal Competence and Organizational Effectiveness.* Homewood, Ill.: Dorsey, 1962.

Argyris, C. "The Incompleteness of Social-Psychological Theory." *American Psychologist,* 1969, *24,* 893-908.

Argyris, C. *Intervention Theory and Method.* Reading, Mass.: Addison-Wesley, 1971.

Argyris, C. "Personality and Organization Revisited." *Administrative Science Quarterly,* 1973, *18* (2), 141-167.

Argyris, C., and Schön, D. A. *Theory in Practice: Increasing Professional Effectiveness.* San Francisco: Jossey-Bass, 1974.

Arlin, P. K. "Cognitive Development in Adtulhood: A Fifth Stage?" *Developmental Psychology,* 1975, *11* (5), 602-606.

Bakan, D. *On Method: Toward a Reconstruction of Psychological Investigation.* San Francisco: Jossey-Bass, 1967.

Bateson, G. *Steps to an Ecology of Mind.* New York: Ballantine, 1972.

Beckhart, D. *Process Consultation.* Reading, Mass.: Addison-Wesley, 1969.

Bennis, W. "Patterns and Vicissitudes in Training Groups." In L. Bradford, K. Benne, and J. Gibb (Eds.), *T-Group Theory and Laboratory Methods.* New York: Wiley, 1964.

Bion, W. *Experience in Groups.* New York: Basic Books, 1961.

Bowles, S., and Gintis, H. *Schooling in Capitalist America.* New York: Harper & Row, 1975.

Brumbaugh, R. *Plato for the Modern Age.* New York: Collier, 1962.

Cohen, D., and Lindblom, C. *The Usable Knowledge.* New Haven, Conn.: Yale University Press, 1979.

Cohen, M., and March, J. *Leadership and Ambiguity: The American College President.* New York: McGraw-Hill, 1974.

Culbert, S. "Trainer Self-Disclosure and Member Growth in Two T-Groups." *Journal of Applied Behavioral Science,* 1968, *4,* 47-73.

Duberman, M. *Black Mountain: An Exploration in Community.* New York: Doubleday, 1973.

Dunphy, D. "Phases, Roles, and Myths in Self-Analytic Groups." *Journal of Applied Behavioral Science,* 1968, *4,* 195-225.

Gilligan, C., and Murphy, J. M. "The Philosopher and the 'Dilemma of the Fact': Moral Development in Late Adolescence and Adulthood." Unpublished manuscript, Harvard Graduate School of Education, 1978.

Goffman, E. *Frame Analysis: An Essay on the Organization of Experience.* New York: Harper & Row, 1974.

Jourard, S. *Disclosing Man to Himself.* New York: Van Nostrand, 1968.

Laing, R. *The Self and Others.* New York: Quandrangle Books, 1962.

Loebl, E. *Humanomics.* New York: Random House, 1976.

Mann, R. "The Development of the Member-Trainer Relationship in Self-Analytic Groups." *Human Relations,* 1966, *19,* 85-115.

Mills, T. *Group Transformation.* Englewood Cliffs, N.J.: Prentice-Hall, 1964.

Mitroff, I. *The Subjective Side of Science.* Amsterdam: Elsevier, 1974.

Mitroff, I. "The Varieties of Social Science Experience." Unpublished manuscript, University of Pittsburgh, 1978.

Perkins, J. *College and University Presidents: Recommendations and Report of a Survey.* New York State Regents Advisory Committee on Educational Leadership, Albany, 1967.

Perry, W. *Forms of Intellectual and Ethical Development in the College Years: A Scheme.* New York: Holt, Rinehart and Winston, 1968.

Pirsig, R. *Zen and the Art of Motorcycle Maintenance.* New York: Morrow, 1974.

Riegel, K. "Dialectical Operations: The Final Period of Cognitive Development." *Human Development,* 1973, *16,* 345-376.

Rogers, C. *On Becoming a Person.* Boston: Houghton Mifflin, 1961.

Schein, E. *Strategies of Organization Development.* Reading, Mass.: Addison-Wesley, 1969.

Torbert, W. "Dominant Rationality, Unobstructed Feeling, Genuine Inquiry." Working Paper Series, Southern Methodist University School of Business Administration, 1970.

Torbert, W. *Being for the Most Part Puppets.* Cambridge, Mass.: Schenkman, 1972.

Torbert, W. *Learning from Experience: Toward Consciousness.* New York: Columbia University Press, 1973.

Torbert, W. "Pre-Bureaucratic and Post-Bureaucratic Stages of Organization Development." *Interpersonal Development,* 1974, *5,* 1-25.

Torbert, W. *Creating a Community of Inquiry: Conflict, Collaboration, Transformation.* London: Wiley, 1976a.

Torbert, W. "On the Possibility of Revolution Within the Boundaries of Propriety." *Humanitas,* 1976b, *12,* 111-146.

Torbert, W. "Why Educational Research Has Been So Uneducational: The Case for a New Model of Social Science Based on Collaborative Inquiry." Paper presented at the annual meetings of the American Psychological Association, San Francisco, August 1977a.

Torbert, W. "Organizational Effectiveness: Five Universal Criteria." Unpublished paper, Boston College, 1977b.

Torbert, W. "Educating Toward Shared Purpose, Self-Direction, and Quality Work: The Theory and Practice of Liberating Structure." *Journal of Higher Education,* 1978, *49* (2), 109-135.

Truax, C., and Carkhuff, R. *Toward Effective Counseling and Psychotherapy.* Chicago: Aldine, 1967.

Warner, W., and Havens, A. "Goal Displacement and the Intangibility of Organizational Goals." *Administrative Science Quarterly,* 1968, *12* (4), 539-555.

Watzlawick, P., Beavin, J., and Jackson, D. *Pragmatics of Human Communication.* New York: Norton, 1967.

8

Elizabeth Douvan

Capacity for Intimacy

Interpersonal competence, as described by Torbert in the preceding chapter, implies the ability to make one's way in the world of social interactions—to work cooperatively with others, compete effectively, seek and offer help, influence others, and perform well in one's various social roles. Against this more instrumental ability to deal with people stands the capacity for intimacy—the willingness and ability to commit oneself to close affective relationships for their own sake.

Intimate relationships are distinguished from role relationships by their relative freedom from normative prescriptions. Roles consist of shared expectations for behavior attached to positions in a social structure; they are affectively neutral, partial, and normative. By contrast, intimate relationships are affectively intense and relatively free of normative prescriptions. In the virtual absence of norms, the partners in an intimate relationship are freed to respond to each other spontaneously, as whole persons. The boundaries of self are relaxed, permitting a flow of interaction that is relatively unpredictable, filled with surprise. Value is attached to the partner and to the relationship itself rather than to some task or goal for which the relationship is instrumental, as in role relationships. This means that the relationship is essentially self-affirming—that the individual so valued and regarded by another is freed to experiment with less known aspects of the self in the relationship. Since my friend appreciates me for myself and will be broadly tolerant, I am freed to explore in friendship potential selves and aspects of the self that are relatively unfamiliar to me. The intimate relationship is thus conducive to personality growth in a way that family relationships and other relationships heavily infused with normative expectations cannot be.

Higher education should encourage the capacity for intimacy for two reasons. The ability to enter into and sustain such relationships is a major vehicle for increased self-understanding, in terms of one's motives, values, future plans and aspirations, and interpersonal style. These self-understandings have instrumental value on the job and in the home and the community. More importantly, such relationships are themselves major sources of satisfaction and fulfillment. Without them one's life is empty; without the capacity to sustain them one's life is filled with pain, frustration, or loneliness.

Definition of Intimacy

The *intimate relationship* is one in which (a) two people relate as whole persons in an interaction that is (b) affectively loaded and (c) relatively free of normative prescriptions, in which (d) loyalty is the only critical norm. The intimate adult friendship is the model, although true intimacy is an ideal, which is never completely realized and rarely even approximated. Buber (1937) conceives a true relationship as a momentary process of transcendence—the I-Thou. It is a goal of virtually all the interpersonal therapies: nondefensive encounter between people as whole, authentic selves.

Given our definition of intimacy, it seems unlikely that the individual is capable of intimate relationships before late adolescence. Until the young person has developed at least a rudimentary identity, no whole self exists to be disclosed and to fully encounter another. Erikson (1950) recognizes this developmental necessity when he suggests that intimacy is the task of late adolescence, following the resolution of identity in adolescence proper. Until the young person has some sense of who he or she is and where the boundaries of self are, the relaxing of those boundaries, which is implied by and essential to an intimate relationship with another, seems too dangerous for the developing self to permit. The self is too fragile, too vulnerable to influence by another. The task of adolescence is to solidify the self, to acquire self-knowledge and establish the boundaries of self, and this task is realized in large measure by distinguishing the self from others—particularly those others crucial in childhood, the parents. Only after these issues have been tentatively resolved is the adolescent in a position to risk intimacy without being overwhelmed or losing track of the developing self.

In addition to this developmental requirement—that one must have a relatively secure sense of identity—what else is required for one to be capable of close interpersonal relationships? In another place, I have described the crucial requirements this way:

> Trilling (1953) focuses on the essential requirement when he speaks of the struggle between love and power. To love is to open yourself to risk—the risk of rejection, hurt, unsettling surprise, and so forth. When you involve yourself closely with any other human system, you are opening your own system to forces over which you have no direct or decisive control. If you are preeminently concerned with predictability, security, certainty, control, and power, then clearly you should not involve yourself in *any* human relationship. Love exposes you to unpredictability, uncertainty, and to the risk of loss. Even if you love a saint, you assume the ultimate risk of loss through death.
>
> Involving oneself with others, then, implies at least a willingness to forego some measure of security or power. And clearly one is willing because of the positive rewards of such involvement: rewards like self-affirmation, stimulation, variety, excitement. To make the choice one must prefer an open, exciting system to a closed, controlled, and narrow one.
>
> At a more concrete level, to be good at close interpersonal relationships requires many of the same qualities that are required for any creative enterprise.

Besides a pleasure in risk-taking, you need a measure of narcissism—an appreciation for this self that is to be disclosed and affirmed in interpersonal relationships, a self-awareness and a taste for life that are both intimately related to narcissism (see Erikson on trust in self and trust in the world). You need a certain level of energy and liveliness that may spring from narcissism but takes the form of—is organized into—personal expressiveness. You need a playful tolerance—a capacity to suspend judgment—in order to be engaged by and engaging to other people, and an investment in surprise, pleasure in the unexpected.

But interpersonal creativity has some special requirements that other forms of creativity do not demand. One of these is the ability to express dependency. All creativity probably requires an element of passivity—you have to be able to dream, to make contact with the unconscious or the infantile or primary process or whatever label we give that inner spring—and to do so requires a certain passivity or ability to disassociate from imposing, compelling externals at least fleetingly. But the gift for intimacy requires a more specific form of passivity—the willingness to hand over control by depending on another, however briefly [Douvan, 1977, pp. 22-23].

Additional requirements for intimacy are worth distinguishing, although they are in a sense elements of the developmental requirement. One of these is freedom from over-riding neurotic conflict. The intimate relationship is characterized by nondefensive interaction. This means that the individual cannot be so heavily defended against intrapsychic conflict that there is neither energy for engaging the other, nor freedom to disclose the self, nor freedom to risk uncertainty and surprise for fear that the surprise might be lethal. To an individual who is frightened of the self, nothing is more dangerous than self-disclosure; to the person who is essentially distrustful or paranoid, disclosure can only be seen as self-exposure and handing over dangerous power to another.

To respond to the other in the free and spontaneous process of intimate interaction, one must be able to perceive the individual *reality* of the other. Any neurotic remnant that causes one to respond to all people as mere representatives of a class or role disallows the development of intimacy. The man who sees all men as competitors in the scramble for survival or victory cannot have an intimate friendship with another man. The woman who is so narcissistic that she sees people simply as objects to be manipulated in the service of impulse gratification will not respond to the reality of the other and will therefore never really know the other. The man who sees all older men through a transfer screen of Oedipal conflict will respond to older men as the frightening father and will be unable to know a particular older man as he really is, or have a friendship with him. For to form a friendship with another is to know and trust the other for what he or she is in reality—to appreciate both those qualities one shares with the other and those that are unique to the other and thus bring variety and interest to the relationship.

In our developmental analysis of friendship in girls (Douvan and Adelson, 1966), we found that this appreciation for the special and unique characteristics of the friend was a relatively late development. In middle adolescence (14 to 16) the emphasis in girls' definitions of friendship is on similarity (even identity) and security. At this stage, girls want a friend to share their concerns and interests, and to be a trustworthy confidante. Only in later adolescence (16 to 18) do we find a new developing emphasis on unique qualities of the friend—individual characteristics, talents, and resources of the friend that add zest and interest to the friendship and are appreciated in their own right.

One other requirement for close interpersonal relationships is *empathy*—the ability to take the role of the other. A crucial aspect of intimacy or friendship is the ability to feel for the other, to anticipate the needs and tastes of the other, to know what will stimulate delight and surprise in the other. The individual who is too bound up in intra-psychic conflict or too narcissistic will not have the energy or capacity for empathic response to others (see White's chapter in this volume) and will therefore lack the capacity for intimacy.

The playfulness that is part of the capacity for intimacy requires fluid boundaries between aspects of the personality, allowing relatively free access to preconscious elements of the self—to the realm of metaphor, wit, or humor. This brings us back, then, to the requirements intimacy shares with other forms of creativity.

Relation of Higher Education to Intimacy

To assess the relevance of higher education for the individual's capacity for intimacy, we must consider the student's age and stage of development. For college will have quite different effects depending on the student's developmental status at the time of entry. I will consider, first, the effects of college on the standard 18-year-old college entrant. In this discussion I will consider briefly the special problems and needs of students from disadvantaged backgrounds, for whom college represents a particular discontinuity in the sense that it implies upward mobility and a departure from the family background. Following discussion of the 18- to 20-year-old, I will look briefly at the particular developmental problems at two later life stages: middle age, when the mature individual returns to school to effect some change in life course or in an already established identity, and later life, when the individual may return to school primarily for self-enrichment or for new institutional and interpersonal ties to supplant earlier roles and relationships.

After considering the interpersonal status and needs of students at the various life stages, I will consider the domains of the college experience in which interpersonal development occurs. Clearly, the impact of higher education will also vary for different kinds of institutions (for example, the residential college versus commuter city college), but I will not consider these variations systematically or in detail since such an institutional analysis would go well beyond the limits of a single chapter. I will use as my implicit model the high-quality residential liberal arts college and will note the differential effects of commuter schools or community colleges when these are germane to the discussion.

Traditional College Students

The young person of traditional college age (18- to 22-years-old) is precisely at the stage of development when, according to Erikson's theory, intimacy is the central developmental task. The issue of identity has at least been broached and rough outlines of the resolution established during adolescence proper. Now the individual is ready to explore styles of friendship and intimacy, ready to suspend self boundaries to merge at least briefly with a lover, a friend, a model. Through the process, the individual will test aspects of the self, discover new elements and possibilities in the self, and incorporate some characteristics of the other through identification.

Self-Exploration. Although the task of establishing identity has usually begun before the young person enters college, it is by no means completed. The move from home to college often facilitates identity resolution. For the adolescent struggling to disengage from the parents, to strike out for autonomy in feeling, values, and self-direction, the move away from home allows a much clearer assertion of independence and responsibility for the self. Since autonomy during adolescence (when the individual is still living at home) implies confrontation with parents, girls are particularly likely to postpone the issue until they enter college. But the freedom of college is also crucial to those adolescents (mostly boys) who have asserted their autonomy in open confrontation. Often, the only elements of the self they can trust as authentic are those that clearly differ from or cause conflict with their parents. (For an extended discussion of this hazard to identity, see Douvan, 1974.) The separation provided by college may allow them to reclaim elements of the self that in fact they share with their parents but could not accept so long as they seemed to imply compliance with parents' wishes or standards.

College offers rich opportunities for exploring the self and its possibilities. For the first time, in college, one can leave behind old myths of the self and roles assigned by membership in a particular family in a particular community (for example, the minister's daughter or the bank president's son) and try out new possibilities, new roles, and new ways of playing old roles like student, friend, son or daughter. While adolescence sees the beginning of identity formation, the college years provide for most middle-class youth the setting and opportunity for what Erikson (1950) has described as a *psychosocial moratorium*—a condition of role suspension in which the young person does much of the work of identity exploration and resolution. To the extent that identity is resolved and the self boundaries secured, the young person is free to enter intimate relationships without fear of being overwhelmed or of losing the self.

Interpersonal Exploration. For many young persons, the college experience significantly broadens the social world. Depending on the narrowness and protectiveness of the family background, college is likely to expose the young person to a much wider range of people than previously encountered. For those from rural areas and small towns, and for many of those from upper-middle-class homes, college brings contact with people from more varied socioeconomic, ethnic, and cultural backgrounds than they have known before. The experience is broadening, in that it enlarges their view of the possible life styles and personal identities available, but it can also be troublesome, as any encounter with difference can be. Somehow the college student must come to terms with difference and reconcile it with his or her ideas about friendship and interpersonal relationships. In the face of this challenge, a student may take refuge in a narrow social milieu that excludes friendship with all but those of similar background and orientation; or, alternatively, the student may be attracted to and stimulated by variety, with its potential for broadening the self and social experience. An example of the first response occurs in *Catcher in the Rye* when Holden Caulfield encounters a roommate at one of his several prep schools:

> For a while when I was at Elkton Hills, I roomed with this boy, Dick Slagle, that had these very inexpensive suitcases. He used to keep them under the bed, instead of on the rack, so that nobody'd see them standing next to mine. It depressed holy hell out of me, and I kept wanting to throw mine out or something, or even *trade* with him. Mine came from Mark Cross, and they cost quite a pretty penny. What I did, I finally put *my* suitcases under *my* bed, instead of on the rack, so that old Slagle wouldn't get a goddam inferiority complex about it. But here's what he did. The day after I put mine under my bed, he took them out and put them back on the rack. The reason he did it, it took me a while to find out, was because he wanted people to think my bags were his. He really did. He was a very funny guy, that way. He was always saying snotty things about them, my suitcases, for instance. He kept saying they were too new and bourgeois. . . . At first he only used to be kidding when he called my stuff bourgeois, and I didn't give a damn—it *was* sort of funny, in fact. Then, after a while, you could tell he wasn't kidding any more. The thing is, it's really hard to be roommates with people if your suitcases are much better than theirs—if yours are really good ones and

theirs aren't. You think if they're intelligent and all, the other person, and have a good sense of humor, that they don't give a damn whose suitcases are better, but they do. They really do. It's one of the reasons why I roomed with a stupid bastard like Stradlater. At least his suitcases were as good as mine [Salinger, 1951, pp. 108-109].

Holden's solution is restrictive and unsatisfying, but his insight goes to the heart of a critical issue: Differences in wealth and status are facts to be reckoned with in the formation of interpersonal relationships; if they are not overcome, they may limit the possibility of open, nondefensive interpersonal exchange because they inject envy, guilt, and status-consciousness into the relationship.

Many students assume an orientation quite different from Holden's, looking to college as the opening of new worlds, full of stimulating variety. This anticipation of a larger world was a common response of young women to the question: "What do you hope to get out of college?" (Douvan and Kaye, 1962). After self-growth and vocational goals, it was the next most frequent response.

The college experience provides stimulation for interpersonal growth and also *time* for interpersonal exploration. Removed from the demands of parents and not yet restricted by the heavy role requirements of adulthood—of earning a living, maintaining a marriage, raising children—college students have the license to place self-exploration and interpersonal experimentation at the center of existence. In a real sense, these related tasks represent the occupation of college youth. At no other stage in life is there the same concentration of resources and freedom for exploring friendship and interpersonal styles and values. College youth have time, energy, curiosity, and narcissism, which stimulate and facilitate rich interpersonal encounter. Heightened sexuality presses the young person to explore relationships, in some ways complicates relationships, and in most cases contributes energy, tension, and zest to interpersonal encounters.

In the previous discussion, I have assumed a traditional middle-class, 18-year-old student entering a high-quality residential college. In a few places, I have had to step back and qualify statements about the effect of college on students' interpersonal development, by alluding to variations in the developmental status, sophistication, and breadth of experience with which students enter college. Clearly, many upper-middle-class students now come to college with relatively well-formed identities, having resolved dependency and autonomy issues with the collaboration of educated and sophisticated parents, and having had quite broad experience with people of various social classes and cultural backgrounds. Egalitarian movements in our society and competitive pressures for higher education have operated to enlarge and enrich the social experiences of adolescents and have contributed to early disengagement from parents by young persons in our society. Entry into college does not represent a radical change for such students, and they do not suffer the homesickness and culture shock that were relatively common among freshmen twenty-five years ago. The model student in our more selective colleges and universities makes many descriptions of students written in the fifties sound quaint and dated.

Culture Shock. Yet for many students college still means a dramatic culture change. Those who come from rural areas meet a cosmopolitan culture, which they may have known about from television but not experienced themselves. And many young people for whom college represents mobility out of the working class, or the ranks of the poor, find the style and expectations of the academic culture quite alien. The egalitarian thrust of our society has resulted in opportunities for some young people from very poor and culturally deprived families to attend some of the most select colleges in the country. For these students, the college experience can bring both enrichment and severe conflict. However it is dealt with, the college culture represents a radical departure for such students. They enter a world of ideas, values, and styles that are disjunctive with their previous experiences. One highly mobile student, an artist whose talent had eased some of the problems of transition, looked at his working-class family with new awareness after several years in college. He loved them and remained close to them, but he rejected many of their attitudes and values. Further, he became aware of a critical difference in style:

> My mother was knitting and my father was waiting until the ball game started on television. I realized after a while that no one said anything unless I asked a question or started talking. So I decided at one point to see how much time would go by before they talked. *Two hours* went by like that, everyone sitting together saying not a word. I realized that that was the story of my life before coming to the University. I came from a verbally impoverished world. No one talked. I have moved into a world where people talk all the time, and that's why I can now see what my family is like. But all the time I was growing up, I didn't see it. I just never knew that talking was something that brought people pleasure until I left home.

Riesman, Gusfeld, and Gamson (1970) describe the tension that developed in an industrial area near Detroit when an experimental college launched a program to bring high-quality education to working-class youth in the area. The values of the faculty—with regard to questioning, judging, entertaining all theoretical possibilities, and cultivating the imagination, playfulness, and art—were difficult to convey to these pragmatic, vocationally oriented products of working-class high schools. The problem of cultural discontinuity was a tough one. But when faculty could manage to loosen the hold of convention on some of these youngsters, it was alarming to parents and reverberated through the community and back through the college administration; the community became suspicious of these "outside influences" and pressed administrators to restrain "faculty radicals." The problem for the responsive student in this situation is somehow to integrate the new self with the past social and family background. Of course, going away to school allows more room and more time for this integrative work. Commuter students must come to terms with their new experiences while at the same time living in their parents' homes, and the resultant conflicts and pressure are often more than they can manage easily or gracefully.

For many students, the social mobility implied by college creates serious problems around issues of loyalty and the integrity of their early lives. Socialization to middle-class values and styles of behavior, as well as the adoption of intellectual goals, distances them from their own culture of origin and creates conflicting loyalties. As they gain skills and become more middle-class, they feel their old ties slipping and fear that they are deserting people and a way of life that bred and nurtured them. Sensitive youth, in particular, suffer guilt and conflict about changing in ways that imply such an abandonment of the past. This makes their socialization in college difficult. Somehow they must find a way to learn new patterns while at the same time neither denigrating nor abandoning the old.

The final integration is, of course, worth the extra effort. An earlier model of social mobility in this country assumed that people would abandon the past in the interests of success and acceptance into a higher status group. But a maturing sense of the legitimacy and value of cultural diversity—the growing insistence of ethnic and racial minorities on the independent value of their unique histories, traditions, and heritages—has led to awareness of the terrible cost exacted by this earlier model. To say that one wants access to the advantages and perquisites traditionally reserved to a dominant group is not to say that one wishes to be identical to members of that group or to give up legitimate identification with one's own heritage.

The issue is perhaps clearest in the case of the artist. For the creative individual's originality depends on access to childhood and the relatively primitive aspects of the self. If the artist denies the validity of earlier experience, the creative process, whose fluidity depends on contact with other and earlier ways of constructing reality, will suffer. Integrating diverse experience and elements in the self is more demanding work, more taxing to ego resources and energy, than developing a self in a homogenous and continuous environment. But if it succeeds, it will also lead to a self that is rich, articulated, and flexible.

One final point should be made about the conflicts that socially mobile students face. Essentially, those students who fear abandoning their pasts are struggling with the issue of loyalty. Denying or denigrating their past would mean abandoning their families and cultural roots. Young people whose interpersonal development is strong and whose capacity for intimacy is large will choose, rather, to try to integrate their past with their present selves. To the extent that college can support such choices and help students with their integrative struggles—through counseling services, wise teaching, warmth, and appreciation—it will contribute to interpersonal development in those most capable of rich and generous interpersonal lives.

Mature Students (30 to 50 Years Old)

Mature students, returning to higher education after having learned and lived a variety of adult roles, face and present challenges different from those of traditional college students. Presumably, they have already established identities and formed intimate relationships before launching themselves on this new educational enterprise. What can we say of their development and the effects of higher education on their interpersonal lives?

Women. Recent research on women returning to school has revealed some interesting clues to the interpersonal implications of education for this important group of older students. It seems clear that returning to school often causes problems in the women's established relationships, even disrupting marriages in a significant proportion of cases. Conversely, for many the return to school is itself stimulated by some change in the interpersonal sphere—for example, a divorce or the departure of the last child from home. For almost all, it represents a return to the identity issues of adolescence—a search for autonomy and self-definition on the basis of internal and individual characteristics, in contrast to the interpersonal and often vicarious identity developed during the earlier period of family service. Many of the women consciously feel that they want some self-definition that is portable—that they can carry within themselves irrespective of external changes in their life situations or the choices of other people. As Wiersma (1977) has observed, identity formation for these women seems to be a two-stage process: (1) the development of an interpersonal identity in early adulthood in the family and (2) the resolution of achievement-autonomy issues in middle adulthood.

The pursuit of autonomy and a more independent self necessarily implies some dislocation in the woman's close relationships. In a purely practical sense, she is less available to serve the needs of her family to the extent that she assumes obligations at school or in her own work. But, what may be more important, she is psychologically less available to the degree that she invests herself in her work and her own development. Her emotional cathexis, like that of the adolescent, is redistributed, with a greater share centering on the self.

Such a shift of attention and emotional investment by one member of a social system necessarily reverberates throughout the system, affecting all the members and their interrelations. In the case of the woman returning to school, the husband and children are bound to chafe at the disruption of family patterns; they need time to adjust to the shift, to find other ways to meet some of the needs that were formerly satisfied by the wife-mother. Most women who return to school suffer role overload, too little time for themselves and their families, and guilt feelings about their home and family responsibilities (see Bernard's chapter in this volume). If they complete their educational programs, most of the women retrospectively feel that it was worth the struggle, but they are clear about the fact that it *was* a struggle, a time filled with tension, anxiety, and guilt (Center for Continuing Education of Women, 1977). The guilt that women report as they and their families juggle priorities and work toward adaptation is particularly germane to our present discussion because it points to a flaw in our cultural myths about work, autonomy, and interdependence. By analyzing this guilt, we can learn something relevant to higher education.

Women returning to school feel guilty because they do not have enough time for their children and housework. They feel guilty about asking their husbands and children to assume a greater share of household responsibilities. Sometimes they feel guilty for using family resources to pay tuition and other costs of schooling. Now guilt, so long as it does not cripple the person experiencing it, is a mark of a responsible person. And evidence indicates that women by and large report more guilt feelings than men whatever their life status and condition. I do not view the guilt experienced by women in school to be in any sense a sign of pathology or debility.

But the reasons these women give for their guilt reveal a distorted understanding of the social process. These women return to school seeking a new autonomy, and for the most part they find it—that is, they learn to test their own competence, to set their own intellectual and vocational goals, to pace their own efforts, and to take responsibility for their own individual work and products. They do these things, all in all, extraordinarily well. What they do not apparently grasp or learn nearly as well—judging from their guilt— is to make legitimate demands on others or to credit the interdependence of all human activity. And their failure to learn these lessons reflects directly on the educational system. We in higher education perpetuate the myth of total individual autonomy and rarely teach students the nature and significance of interdependence.

Here are women who have spent some ten or more years meeting the needs of other people, modifying or denying their own desires and programs to fit the needs of dependent children and the demands of a husband's work life. They can assert their own needs for autonomy and achievement comfortably only so long as such assertion makes no claims on the time or convenience of others. They feel guilty taking tuition money from the family bank account, as though they did not believe in their own contribution to that family resource, did not recognize that without their supportive services their husbands could not have earned or saved the money in the first place.

Men. While women comprise the majority of mature students, men may also return to school in middle age—frequently to effect a radical change in the direction of their lives. There are indications that this trend may grow over the next several decades. With increasing affluence and changes in retirement programs, it may become increasingly possible for men who have established themselves in one field or vocation during the years of major financial responsibilities and family obligations to then retool their skills and take on a new career that offers greater personal satisfaction. Union contracts that allow retirement at a relatively early middle age may free industrial workers to launch more gratifying careers by returning to college (or beginning college) when they have completed their twenty-five years on the line.

So far, major midlife changes have been rare among men, and largely restricted to highly successful men who have been able to accumulate financial resources sufficient to support themselves and their families during the transition and schooling required for a new career direction. We have virtually no research data on these cases and can at this point only speculate about the special problems they present. Presumably, men returning to school do not have the same problems that women have with regard to autonomy and independence. They have, after all, established their competence as independent workers (see Chapter One). They may, however, share with returning women a sense of guilt about their decision, a feeling that investment in their human capital is a luxury and an indulgence. And they may also share two other problems commonly reported by returning women: (1) anxiety about their competence as they face the challenge of acquiring new skills and testing themselves beyond the limits of their known competencies and proven skills and (2) an experience of the infantalizing aspects of the student role, of returning to a role that demands compliance and continual submission of the self to judgment and evaluation by others.

Older Students (50 to 80 Years Old)

Many institutions are creating programs to attract older students, those age 50 to 80. These schools have imaginatively seen that early retirement programs could create a new market for education and are already advertising and reaching out with innovative programs to attract potential students from much later age groups who have the leisure and security to return to school.

While students returning to school in middle age are often motivated primarily by vocational goals—either acquiring marketable skills after years spent out of the labor force or seeking a change in occupation that will provide greater self-realization—such goals are much less likely for those who return in late middle or old age. These persons are more likely to seek self-enrichment and intellectual stimulation of a less instrumental nature. And they are at a stage in life when broader perspectives concerning self and others may lead to new sets of social relationships that enrich their life and well-being. While the search for friendship and interpersonal ties in an organizational structure may not be central in the conscious motivation of these older students, it may in fact be the major benefit accruing from their educational venture.

Two crucial problems create stress during these later years. The end of active work life significantly reduces the organization of life by eliminating the individual's established roles and ties to a productive unit. Retirement—even when it is actively chosen—disconnects the individual from much that has previously structured and punctuated life and from the social and interpersonal supports that the work group and work functions have provided. And aging brings interpersonal losses through illness and death. Attrition in one's age group means that those who are left at each succeeding age are more and more likely to have lost at least some of the crucial people who provided them with love, support, and stimulation.

Recent data from national and regional samples of adults reveal the impact of both of these problems on the lives of older people. Studies of retirement have documented the stress that accompanies detachment from the work role and the loss of institutional connections. Recent data from a national study of mental health document both the decrease in informal social supports that occurs from middle age to old age and the increase in stress experienced by older people as they lose interpersonal relationships (Antonucci, Kulka, and Douvan, 1978). Lowenthal and her colleagues (1975) have documented the importance of interpersonal ties to the adjustment of older people. (See also Chapter One.) Among widows, it was found that having one close friend in whom to confide distinguished those who adapted from those who suffered serious maladaptation. Having informal social supports also differentiated old people who remained in the community from those who had to be institutionalized.

The role of college student could, then, serve to reconnect older people to a social system and provide a setting within which they could develop new friendships and informal networks as earlier relationships drop away. With their life experience and freedom from overriding vocational motivation, older people can also contribute in unique ways to the richness and complexity of the educational enterprise.

Peer Relationships

The peer group is usually the primary setting for interpersonal exploration and learning. And the college environment offers young persons interpersonal experience of greater breadth and diversity than they have previously encountered. This can be both stimulating and problematic for particular students. The provincial youth who has been a good pupil without in any way being contaminated by ideas or intellectuality (a common pattern among women of earlier generations and among vocationally oriented males of any generation) may be greatly stimulated and attracted by the questioning, intellectually committed, and excited style of more cosmopolitan students. Or this same youth may be intimidated by such apparent intellectual advantage, at least initially.

The University of Michigan, for example, draws a significant group of very bright "culturally disadvantaged" students from the rural upper peninsula and from culturally traditional towns like Grand Rapids. The encounter between these young people and the cosmopolitan culture of Ann Arbor can be electric with tension and possibility if the newcomer is not overwhelmed. I have very often heard such students bare their fears and sense of disadvantage ("the other students have read *everything*") and occasionally their resentment toward their parents ("How could they have stayed in a place where my sister and I would get such an inferior education?"). I try to reassure these youngsters that, while they have their whole lives ahead to read and fill in the gaps in their education, city youth can never retrieve the particular strengths and advantages of growing up in a small town—the sense of place, the experience of community, the density of interconnections, the chance to fill many roles in school, the closer contact with adults and the reality of adult life. Often the pointing out of these advantages comes as a gratifying insight to these students. Occasionally, a highly sophisticated youth from Ann Arbor, the child of intellectual parents with every possible advantage, will come home from a first semester at Harvard or Vassar railing against his or her family for failure to stimulate and discipline intellectual effort ("My roommate knows all of the Shakespeare sonnets and her family speaks French at the table"). Again, we are reminded that diversity is the crucial stimulus and that advantage is a relative matter.

Roommates and Classmates. For some students, the social diversity of college holds other lessons. Living with a roommate whose personal style and habits are at odds with one's own can be interesting but can also lead to conflict of a kind that has not previously been confronted because friendship has not involved living together. Many schools provide, in one form or another, mechanisms to facilitate congenial rooming arrangements. Most colleges and universities allow freshmen to room with a friend or hometown acquaintance when they ask to, and some schools allow freshmen to shift rooms and roommates during the first six weeks of the school year. In a kind of "musical rooms," freshmen sort out their relationships to minimize conflict and find their own most congenial arrangements. But differences cannot all be eliminated by such mechanisms, and roommates are still likely to have to work out solutions and compromises in interpersonal exchange. Behavior patterns and preferences about times for waking and sleeping, the amount of traffic and socializing in the room, the volume at which music can be played, temperature and fresh air, cleanliness and orderliness—all these areas of potential difference and conflict must somehow be worked through. Learning to face and resolve conflict with relative strangers is a new experience for many college freshmen, and many may have difficulty mustering the required assertiveness. Yet learning to deal with such differences is critical for interpersonal development. Failure to face differences or failure to assert the self will limit the possibility of forming friendships or of having friendships with any but those few individuals who are just like oneself.

Resolving conflict with one's roommate is critical because the relationship is inescapable. Undergraduate women often complain that they lack experience in facing open conflict, that their socialization has not prepared them to fight through differences, to assert their own preferences as a matter of right. They have been socialized to empathize with others' needs and desires, and to undervalue their own. If differences cannot be easily compromised or harmonized through subtle accommodation, charm, and mutual desires to please, they are at a loss for further instrumental acts. They complain that, unlike their brothers, they have not been taught to fight openly or to practice open confrontation. Nevertheless, young women may have learned a variety of subtle and sophisticated methods for averting conflict or resolving differences without open confrontation. The movement into the role of roommate has not been studied extensively, and it is a point of transition that could conceivably reveal a great deal about processes of interpersonal development.

Whatever mechanisms they use to resolve differences, roommates are likely to become friends. In all studies of college youth, proximity emerges as the major force determining friendship during the first year in college (Gurin, 1970; Katz, 1968; and Sanford, 1962). Friendships developed toward the end of the first year and in subsequent years tend to be based on common interests and values, but early friendships stem primarily from proximity. The need for interpersonal warmth and support in this first year away from home is great—prehaps greater at this stage of development than at any other life stage. It will find satisfaction even with the most unlikely candidates for friendship, who seem to serve until more substantially grounded friendships come along.

And they do, of course, come along. In academic courses and in extracurricular activities and groups, students will meet others with whom they share interests and value orientations. In many areas of the liberal arts curriculum, the exposure of values and dominating interests is stimulated in class discussion and in confrontation with teachers. The Socratic method and open confrontation are held by many academics to be among their most effective and treasured tools for educating the young—for engaging the deeply personal and so exposing it to the influence of argument, persuasion, and change.

In such classes and in extracurricular and informal groups that reveal particular values by the sheer act of joining—like religious and political associations, language and sports clubs, literary or arts circles—students discover like-minded people among whom they can find close friends. Newcomb's superb study of the acquaintance process (1961) demonstrates that these relationships—based on common values—are the ones most likely to persist and to develop into friendships.

Male Versus Female Friendships. Not all friendships are intimate friendships, but they offer at least the possibility that intimacy might develop. The realization of that possibility depends on numerous factors, among which gender must be counted one of the more crucial and clearly documented. Men are less likely to form intimate friendships than women are. And further, when a man does develop an intimate friendship, it is likely to be with a woman rather than with another man. In large studies of college youth, findings repeatedly demonstrate the force of sex role socialization: girls are bred to the interpersonal and the social, whereas boys' socialization focuses more exclusively on achievement and competitiveness. Women are allowed and encouraged to be expressive, open to the inner reality of fantasy and feeling, willing to express dependency and vulnerability. Men have been taught to be self-controlled, aggressive and competitive, fearful of exposing dependency and vulnerability. Men are socialized, in other words, to a rather specific incapacity for interpersonal intimacy, to an objective and impersonal style of exchange, to competition and power (see McArthur, 1955).

Except in heterosexual friendships, the male's competitive orientation tends to interfere with intimacy. Since all men are potential rivals, the exposure of vulnerability to another man carries the danger that that vulnerability will come back to haunt one—that the "friend" may in some future competitive situation call on and use it to his own advantage. Examples of the differences between men and women with respect to competitiveness are easy to cite. The traditional one is the difference between male and female sex talk. Young women learn about sex—and the nature of their own sexual responses—in their intimate friendships with other women. This is the stuff of college women's late night talk sessions: how did he act, what did you do, how did it feel, how did you handle it, and so on. The inexperienced learn from their more sophisticated sisters. But such talk involves a great deal of self-disclosure and expression of vulnerability. And the male cannot reveal his vulnerability. While young women share their sexual knowledge and experience, young men compete with theirs. Sex is a topic for asserting one's prowess, for boasting, not for candidly exploring feelings and experiences.

Sex is not the only area in which males assume this competitive stance. In discussions of academic work, some males may be unable to admit to any uncertainty or self-doubt. If a friend speaks of not understanding a particular concept or of being nervous about a particular examination, a highly competitive male may respond not with sensitivity and sympathy but with a litany of his own powers and successes—how unafraid he is, how complete his grasp of concepts, how original his ideas. Needless to say, such responses make intimacy impossible. The competitive success has been won at the cost of self-knowledge and friendship.

In addition to the obstacles of rivalry and competitiveness, closeness between males is discouraged by fear of homosexuality—a fear that runs deep in our culture. Psychic intimacy, particularly in adolescents and young adults, is likely to carry erotic overtones. And for males the implications of erotization are too specific and dangerous to be easily tolerated. The culture allows greater intimacy between women, and female sexuality is more diffuse and more capable of sublimated expression. The experience of closeness with another woman is less likely to create homosexual panic in a young female than a like-sexed intimate friendship is in a young male.

It seems possible that ideological movements of recent decades—in particular the women's movement and the gay activists' movement—will effect changes in the friendship patterns of males as well as females. Young men may come to value close like-sexed friendship and be more willing to express both tenderness and vulnerability in their friendships. Clinical reports and small studies (for example, Gutmann, 1970, and Keniston, 1970) suggest that such changes are occurring, but we have as yet no large-scale evidence of such change.

So the male college student—like the adolescent—forms like-sexed friendships based on shared interests and activities in which very little self-disclosure or intimate communication develops. The male companions enjoy doing things—like sports—together and like to be able to count on the friend's being there, but the emphasis is on parallel response to the activity rather than interactive and mutual exploration of the relationship itself or the feelings, ideas, and values of the partners.

Men experience a form of closeness and interdependence with other men in team sports and other group efforts—in some of which survival itself may depend on trustworthy bonds among teammates. This is an important experience in human interdependence and one that feminists want for young women as well as young men. But it is by no means as important in contemporary life as Lionel Tiger (1969) would have us believe, and it has much less to do with intimacy, the sharing of inner thoughts and feelings of tenderness and vulnerability, than womens' friendship forms have. It is also usually limited to men who are very much alike and is thus less important to interpersonal development than those friendships that accommodate wide differences between partners.

If a man shares his feelings with anyone, it is more likely to be a woman friend than another man (Gurin, 1970). Women, in contrast, form intimate friendships easily with other women. Women also have close friendships with men, but, if anything, these are more problematic than like-sexed friendships because of the ever-present possibility of erotization. A young woman can share an intimate friendship with her own boyfriend, lover, or fiancé, but the possibility of closeness with other men is complicated at this developmental stage by the preeminence of sexual concerns and the difference between male and female vocabularies for warmth, closeness, comfort, sharing, and love. Lillian Rubin (1976) has shown the disruptive force of this difference in working-class marriages, but it is probably ubiquitous in heterosexual relationships. Women have a more refined and differentiated vocabulary and can carry on relationships at various levels of intimacy with or without sexualization. But men tend to identify warmth and closeness with sex. This can cause confusion and misunderstanding in friendships between men and women, particularly in adolescence and early adulthood. The young woman responds warmly without meaning to signal sexual interest, and the young man receives the warmth as a sexual signal. Often attractive young women decide that the only men eligible for friendship (that is, nonromantic, nonsexual closeness) are childhood friends ("like a brother") and homosexual males (see Nin, 1966).

Despite this complication, the college years offer unusual opportunity for men and women to come to know each other and share nonsexual and nonsexist friendships. The college years may, in fact, be unique in this respect. Traditional college freshmen have recently negotiated adolescence, the period par excellence for resolution of sex role issues. During high school, sex role is at the center of youngsters' preoccupations and the core of the self-concept. Adolescent behavior is understandable only if one recognizes that, above all, youngsters at this age are trying to establish themselves as acceptable males and females, to prove their adequacy in their sex roles. Coleman's findings about the values of high school students demonstrate this preoccupation, as do analyses of adolescent self-concept (Coleman, 1961; Douvan and Adelson, 1966; Dunphy, 1963; Chilman, in press). In adolescence, therefore, heterosexual interaction is a test or proof of one's sex role adequacy. When adolescent boys and girls interact, the interaction almost always has a sexual agenda (Chilman, in press; Douvan and Adelson, 1966).

By the time they enter college, most young men and women have some experience and security in their sex roles. While it is not an unimportant issue for them, sex role adequacy is a less salient concern than in adolescence proper. And the college itself emphasizes and insistently demands attention to other issues. During the first year, most students are highly challenged by intensified academic demands. They have, in addition, the problems of adapting to a strange environment, to new people, making friends, and learning the role of college student. Furthermore, they are offered in college an unprecedented opportunity for autonomy, including the freedom to choose courses and activities on the basis of personal taste and passion. For many students, college represents the first opportunity to act through choice rather than in response to external demands and requirements. And this is often a heady, involving experience, releasing energy and intellectual verve the student has never known before.

The college also provides settings in which young men and women can work together and interact without domination by erotic and sex role considerations. Working together on a student newspaper or in student government, discussing intellectual issues in class or studying together for important exams—such interactions allow intense exchange around issues of importance, in which students reveal to each other much that is central to the self. They meet as equals in collegial exchange; they encounter each other as minds and persons. Nonsexualized colleague relationships are stimulated and situationally supported perhaps more than at any other time or place in the life cycle. Because of segregation in the occupational world, as well as the claims of marriage and family roles, adulthood closes off, for most individuals in our society, the opportunity for significant friendships with members of the other sex.

Sexual intimacy is also a crucial arena in which young adults explore the self, establish values, learn to commit themselves, and develop aspects of the self-concept. Fitting one's sexuality into the context of one's values and one's life is a critical task of the period. Although the age of marriage has increased in recent years, most young adults at least experience committed love relationships during the undergraduate years, and many first experience full sexual expression during this period. Sexual norms have changed dramatically since World War II, in the direction of greater sexual equality. Reiss (1967) and others who have monitored the change find that the dominant norm among college students is "sex with affection" for both sexes. In this normative view, sex is seen as legitimate and acceptable if the partners have a reasonably committed relationship and affection or love for each other. Sex is, in other words, integrated into the context of a relationship rather than considered in isolation as a mere physiological need or as a competitive achievement.

Although the college years provide for most young people uniquely rich and varied opportunities for interpersonal exploration and growth, it is clear from research and observation that some students do not take up the opportunities, but use a narrow group of like-minded peers from backgrounds similar to their own to insulate themselves against the ideological and interpersonal influence of the college. Newcomb (1943) found such groups at Bennington, isolated from the mainstream of the college culture and effectively cleaving to parental values and attitudes by defending members from the liberalizing influence of faculty, curriculum, and the dominant student culture. The Siegels' classic study (1957) of membership and reference groups demonstrates that sorority-like row houses at Stanford protect their members in much the same way. Girls who live in row houses show the least reduction in authoritarianism of any group on campus. The Greek societies on state university campuses traditionally operated under the severe eyes of alumni who intended to provide an environment as close as possible to those of the homes of members and to protect members from the cosmopolitanism, diversity, and liberalism of the large campus. In cases like these, then, peer groups are used quite consciously to consolidate the young person's identity as a member of a particular social class and to continue socialization in the manners, forms, and beliefs of that class. Although their influence has diminished on campuses since the fifties, such groups have by no means disappeared or abandoned their functions.

Mature Students. The peer interaction of mature students—those returning to college in midlife or later—have not been analyzed extensively, but from observation and the limited research that has been done we can at least speculate about the special forms and effects of such relationships.

The initial response of mature students to their nineteen-year-old compères in the classroom is often one of apprehension. Older adults, particularly women returning to school after a long educational hiatus, often feel anxious about their ability to measure up to the performance of the more practiced young students. If a woman still has heavy home responsibilities, she may also feel at a disadvantage vis-à-vis the students who are free to immerse themselves totally in their studies. In addition to these feelings of marginalism, insecurity, and disadvantage in the academic realm, most older students are probably also anxious about whether or not they will be accepted by their young colleagues. They want simply to be liked, respected, and listened to and are not at all certain they will be. As older students come to represent a significant proportion of the student body, they will presumably also feel less marginal and more able to take their mature colleagues as at least one important audience and reference group. At the moment, however, the older student has no choice in the matter; the young are often the only possible source of interpersonal and collegial satisfactions.

If mature students can master their anxieties and if they find at least some real response from their young colleagues, the friendships that develop can, of course, be unusually rewarding and stimulating for both the older and younger partners. The mature woman may develop friendships with colleagues who are in the same developmental stage as her own children. The nonfamilial cross-age friendship may give her a perspective on her own children and may also give her children a new sense of her as an attractive and valuable person.

The older male, having already established himself in competitive achievement, may now be less defensive and more open to interpersonal intimacy than he was at earlier stages in his life. He may find in friendships with young colleagues at school the chance to develop and enjoy relationships more nurturing and richer than he had either the time or openness for when his own children were growing up. The adult in later life may find among his young colleagues new and significant friendships to supplant lost relationships. And for the young, the opportunity for a significant relationship with a nonfamily member of an older generation offers a potential role model, perspective on parents, and other rewards.

Faculty-Student Relationships

The interaction between faculty and students can also have crucial effects on interpersonal development. Faculty influence the interpersonal development of students both explicitly and by representing particular values and styles in their own interactions. They affect students, that is, by teaching and relating to students and also by serving as models. Although individual faculty members vary in their capacities for intimacy and their styles of interaction with students, they all participate in the academic culture and share certain common beliefs and values, which traditionally differ from those of the larger society and the dominant business culture. Academics value the life of the mind, scholarship, the cultivation of the intellect and spirit. They are more or less self-consciously the conservators of culture and the transmitters of that culture to the younger generation. They value communication, intellectual analysis, clarity of expression and creativity. At least theoretically, intellectuals in academic institutions are the critics of society, testing existing institutions and social arrangements against ideal theoretical models. In the society yet not completely of it, the university community has the distance that allows critical evaluation of society and also, ideally, the development of innovative ideas for social change.

In all these respects, the university and individual faculty members represent values and styles of behavior different from those of the conventional business community and the home backgrounds of most students. And the dominant culture and parents are in many cases clearly aware of the difference. King and Bidwell (1958) noted the self-conscious choice of law and business school graduates as junior deans at Harvard College—a choice designed to counteract faculty hegemony and provide students with more conventional models of manly virtue and conduct to counterbalance the faculty's intellectuality and apparent disinterest in worldliness. Alumni, parents, regents, and dominant figures in the business community keep a wary eye on faculty for signs of radicalism or serious deviations from conventional morality; they are quick to exert pressure on college administrators when they sense that the faculty or the students are "going too far" or "getting out of hand."

The faculty, then, are likely to represent models of a particular life-style and a style of interpersonal behavior that vary from the received styles many students bring with them when they enter college. The academic style emphasizes self-awareness and verbal skill, critical analysis, iconoclasm, and originality. Humanist values, reflection, thought, and development of taste are its critical underpinnings. The integrity of these values and the conduct of faculty under stress—whether they adhere to humane values and the intellectual tradition or falter—can have crucial effects on students (Adelson, 1962; Douvan, 1976).

But faculty also influence students through their own interpersonal exchanges, and their individual styles differ vastly. Some college teachers never break the role set between themselves and students, maintaining throughout the formality and status disparity and limiting exchanges to those for which clear formal role expectations and prescriptions obtain. Other teachers, particularly in small schools, have a variety and range of role interactions with students—as teacher, colleague in college governance, fellow participant in dramatic productions, employer of the student's babysitting services, and personal adviser. This opportunity to see and experience faculty in various roles allows the student to apprehend the teacher's self at role intersections and even perhaps to form a friendship with the teacher. The potential for student growth in such friendship is very great at this stage of development when the young person is still disengaging from parents and developing a new style of relationship with adults who are older and authoritative but not implicated in family dynamics. The importance of friendship with some admired and loved teacher figures prominently in the biographies of most intellectuals and persons of achievement. Closer than a model, the inspiring teacher-friend has in recent discussion of career development been designated a *mentor* and recognized as a crucial force in the lives of those who achieve significantly (Sills, 1976; Sheehy, 1977; Levinson, 1974). Joseph Katz (1962) has described college teachers who represent this style. Tangri (1972) found a close relationship with a junior faculty member or graduate assistant to be one of the distinguishing experiences of college women who make an intellectual, nontraditional commitment to work.

Still other teachers think of themselves in one degree or another as missionaries whose charge is to convert the unwashed to the quest for self-discovery and commitment to the intellectual life, the humanistic enterprise. Such teachers do not see themselves as conservators and transmitters but rather as charismatic shamans who affect students through the force of their own personality and intellect. They set off in their students an excitement of spirit and a process of self-discovery that they assume will lead to originality of self-expression and insight. The primary tool for such faculty is the intimate personal relationship, a laying on of the hands (see Riesman, Gusfeld, and Gamson, 1970, in their analysis of Monteith College). So long as no challenge or conflict arises in their exchange, faculty and students can maintain an illusion of interpersonalism. When, however, a conflict arises over a critical academic value (for example, a question of plagiarism) the illusion quickly dissolves and everyone feels betrayed.

Older students may present challenges to faculty that they have not previously encountered in dealing with their conventional college-aged charges. I have alluded to the problems that older people may have in integrating with younger colleagues in the classroom, and it is clear that teachers can help or hinder the process. By responding sensitively to the older students, by treating their contributions and questions with respect, by assigning students to congenial work groups, and in many other ways a faculty member can facilitate the integration of nontraditional students and ensure them a respectful reception. As with any leadership role, the teacher has the power to decisively influence the interpersonal tone of the group.

Occasionally, an older student may present a threat to a faculty member. Twenty years ago, when the movement for continuing education had just begun and it was relatively rare to see older adults in college classrooms, a colleague of mine in another field was quite taken aback and unnerved when his chairman's wife—a very sophisticated woman who had excellent training in an allied field and had been thinking and reading about his specialty for years—signed up to take one of his courses. And well he might have been. He was relatively young and this situation was particularly heavy with status overtones. But some elements of the situation are quite common with older students and can represent a challenge to the security of young faculty. Often older students will come to the classroom with experience and knowledge, perhaps even outstanding success, in other fields. They may feel insecure about their abilities as students, but to a young and inexperienced faculty member they can seem imposing indeed in other ways. If, however, the older student and the faculty member can manage an accommodation, the class discussions and interpersonal milieu can be enriched and enlivened by the different experience and skills the older student brings to the classroom.

For the faculty member, interpersonal stimulation must be counted as one of the key side benefits of the academic vocation. The opportunity and setting it affords for refreshment and renewal in both the intellectual and emotional spheres cannot be overestimated. Contact and exchange with lively young minds and older students with different life experiences and perspectives nurtures and enriches the life and ideas of faculty who are open to receive their gifts.

Curriculum

Sanford (1962) has outlined clearly and forcefully the ways in which the liberal arts curriculum can affect interpersonal values and growth in students. The student coming upon *Madame Bovary* for the first time in a French literature class learns something about the latitude of possibilities in human behavior, interaction, and expression. In courses in literature and art history, students encounter varieties of human experience, action, relationships, and fate, which extend their concepts of the human condition. Such authors as Shelley, Lawrence, and Joyce provide insights concerning underlying motives and dynamics among friends and lovers; professors can help students discover the multiple levels of expression in poetry and fiction. While contemporary students are more sophisticated than the Vassar freshmen Sanford studied in the fifties, they are by no means immune to the broadening influence of such experiences at this critical developmental period when they are setting their own values, limits, and ideas of acceptable and possible behavior.

Courses in the social sciences can also reveal to students styles and substance of social interactions previously unimagined. They also introduce them to new ways of thinking about the meaning and function of relationships. The very idea that friendships, family relationships, or love relationships can be analyzed systematically is probably as alien to many freshmen as are concepts like the black hole or the quark.

Beyond these curricular contents, a wide variety of group processes and techniques for self-exploration have been introduced, over the last twenty years, into the curriculum in social science or into extracurricular activities and counseling services. Some of these take the form of community outreach programs in which students are apprenticed to schools, social agencies, hospitals, and clinics, and gain experience in help-giving roles. While they gain knowledge of the work world and socialization through particular paraprofessional roles, students also meet active adult professionals and often develop relationships with adults more various than they have known in their home communities or on the campus. They may also gain a first experience in meaningful giving of the self, of altruism, in these roles (see White's chapter on humanitarian concerns and Duley's chapter on experiential learning in this volume).

But the most common of the new forms of experiential learning is the group that focuses directly on personal self-expression or group process. Courses in small group theory turn into encounter groups and self-analysis. Counseling services offer therapy groups for every variety of student and even sometimes for parents and spouses. Dormitories form discussion groups for freshmen to air their problems and apprehensions. Graduate students form thesis support groups. The group is ubiquitous on many campuses.

The group encounter, like psychoanalysis twenty-five years ago, can be a heady experience for young people who have lived until recently in a world heavily conditioned by parental demands, teachers' expectations, and the obligations of conventional middle-class life. In some respects, group process and encounter are probably as heady for middle-aged returning students as they are for 18-year-olds. In fact, older students, raised in that earlier period when self-control and restraint were highly valued and self-expression seemed the province of artists rather than of Everyman, may be more attracted than the young to self-discovery through encounter. Middle-aged, middle-class adults have been the primary clientele of the self-discovery movements, and the return to college itself may be one other sign of a spirit seeking expression. For both young and mature students, the discovery of one's own feelings, taste, and judgment—as opposed to the received wisdom about how one should feel, what one should prefer, and how one should make judgments—can be both liberating and problematic. The outcome of the experience will depend on many factors, notable among them the skill and wisdom of the group leaders.

Mature students, particularly those in later middle age, are often less dominated than the young by vocational preoccupations and are freer to engage broad areas of the curriculum with zest and even passion. Educators continually remark on the intellectual breadth and verve of the mature woman student. It is as though the years away from school have stimulated intellectual appetites and the successful performance of major adult roles (for example, family roles) has established a basic sense of competence that allows these women to immerse themselves in the intellectual enterprise. Course content may be diverse and esoteric; these students do not constantly measure it against vocational goals or other practical criteria of relevance but respond to the intrinsic interest of the material itself. They can thus contribute a sense of excitement and commitment to the classroom. In addition, the adult student often has a world of practical experience to draw on and use to concretize and clarify abstract concepts.

Earlier I alluded to the problems many returning women have asserting claims on their families. In part, these problems stem from a limited understanding of social process and the interdependencies implied in all productive work. Social science courses may offer older students some insights into such issues, but by and large the academic world does not offer models or contexts for cooperative interdependent work.

The individualistic-competitive model is as dominant in the academic world as it is, say, in the business community. We teach students that ideas are individual creations and in the nature of personal property. We assign projects and papers individually and glorify the image of the isolated scholar or scientist digging through hillocks of material to unearth a nugget of understanding, pursuing a lonely voyage to discovery or clarification. In traditional fields, the practice of citation, which might be used to signal and demonstrate the interdependence of scholars, has become rather a ritual for crediting ownership of ideas. In fact we do not develop or train our students in the interactive, collaborative endeavor on which all original and creative work depends. To the extent that we emphasize isolated, individual, competitive work and products, we both mislead students about the nature of work and construct obstacles to their interpersonal development. It is in the area of the *interdependence* of all work that higher education has a largely uncharted world to explore. And in such exploration we will also find ways to help our students move toward increased capacity for intimacy.

References

Adelson, J. "The Teacher as Model." In N. Sanford (Ed.), *The American College*. New York: Wiley, 1962.

Antonucci, T., Kulka, R., and Douvan, E. "Informal Social Supports." Paper presented at the American Psychological Association, Toronto, August 1978.

Buber, M. *I and Thou.* (R. G. Smith, Trans.) New York: Scribner's, 1937.

Center for Continuing Education of Women. *Newsletter, X* (1). Ann Arbor: Center for Continuing Education of Women, University of Michigan, 1977.

Chickering, A. *Education and Identity.* San Francisco: Jossey-Bass, 1969.

Chilman, C. *Social and Psychological Aspects of Adolescent Sexuality.* Washington, D.C.: Center for Population Research, NICHHD, in press.

Coleman, J. *The Adolescent Society.* New York: Free Press, 1961.

Douvan, E. "Commitment and Social Contract in Adolescence." *Psychiatry,* 1974, *37* (1), 22-36.

Douvan, E. "The Role of Models in Women's Professional Development." *Psychology of Women Quarterly,* 1976, *1,* 5-20.

Douvan, E. "Interpersonal Relationships: Some Questions and Observations." In H. Raush and G. Levinger (Eds.), *Close Relationships.* Amherst: University of Massachusetts Press, 1977.

Douvan, E., and Adelson, J. *The Adolescent Experience.* New York: Wiley, 1966.

Douvan, E., and Kaye, C. "Motivational Factors in College Entrance." In N. Sanford (Ed.), *The American College.* New York: Wiley, 1962.

Dunphy, D. C. "The Social Structure of Urban Adolescent Peer Groups." *Sociometry,* 1963, *26,* 230-246.

Erikson, E. H. *Childhood and Society.* New York: Norton, 1950.

Feldman, K. A., and Newcomb, T. M. *The Impact of College on Students.* San Francisco: Jossey-Bass, 1969.

Gurin, G. *A Study of Students in a Multiversity.* Ann Arbor: Institute for Social Research, University of Michigan, 1970.

Gutmann, D. "Female Ego Styles and Generational Conflict." In J. Bardwick and others, *Feminine Personality and Conflict.* Monterey, Calif.: Brooks/Cole, 1970.

Katz, J. "Personality and Interpersonal Relations in the College Classroom." In N. Sanford (Ed.), *The American College.* New York: Wiley, 1962.

Katz, J., and Associates. *No Time for Youth: Growth and Constraint in College Students.* San Francisco: Jossey-Bass, 1968.

Keniston, K. *Youth and Dissent.* New York: Harcourt Brace Jovanovich, 1970.

King, S. F., and Bidwell, C. *Personal communication,* 1958.

Levinson, D. *The Psychological Development of Men in Early Adulthood and the Midlife Transition.* Minneapolis: University of Minnesota Press, 1974.

Lowenthal, M., and Haven, C. "Interaction and Adaptation: Intimacy as a Critical Variable." *American Sociological Review,* 1968, *33* (1), 20-30.

Lowenthal, M. F., Thurnher, M., Chiriboga, D., and Associates. *Four Stages of Life: A Comparative Study of Women and Men Facing Transitions.* San Francisco: Jossey-Bass, 1975.

McArthur, C. C. "Personality Differences Between Middle and Upper Classes." *Journal of Abnormal and Social Psychology,* 1955, *50,* 247-254.

Newcomb, T. M. *Personality and Social Change.* New York: Holt, Rinehart and Winston, 1943.

Newcomb, T. M. *The Acquaintance Process.* New York: Holt, Rinehart and Winston, 1961.

Newcomb, T. M., and others. *Persistence and Change: Bennington College and its Students after Twenty-Five Years.* New York: Wiley, 1967.

Newcomb, T. M., and Wilson, E. K. (Eds.). *College Peer Groups.* Chicago: Aldine, 1966.

Nin, A. *The Diary of Anais Nin.* New York: Swallow Press, 1966.

Reiss, I. *The Social Context of Sexual Permissiveness.* New York: Holt, Rinehart and Winston, 1967.

Riesman, D., Gusfeld, J., and Gamson, Z. *Academic Values and Mass Education.* New York: Doubleday, 1970.

Rubin, L. *Worlds of Pain.* New York: Basic Books, 1976.

Salinger, J. D. *The Catcher in the Rye.* Boston: Little, Brown, 1951.

Sanford, N. "Higher Education as a Field of Study." In N. Sanford (Ed.), *The American College.* New York: Wiley, 1962.

Sheehy, G. *Passages: Predictable Crises in Adult Life.* New York: Bantam, 1977.

Siegel, A. E., and Siegel, S. "Reference Groups, Membership Groups, and Attitude Change." *Journal of Abnormal and Social Psychology,* 1957, *55,* 360-364.

Sills, B. *Bubbles, An Autobiography.* Chicago: Bobbs-Merrill, 1976.

Tangri, S. "Determinants of Occupational Role Innovations Among College Women." *Journal of Social Issues,* 1972, *28* (2), 177-199.

Tiger, L. *Men in Groups.* New York: Random House, 1969.

Trilling, L. *The Liberal Imagination.* New York: Doubleday, 1953.

Wiersma, J. "Mid-Life Change in Women." *Newsletter, X* (1), 9-10. Ann Arbor: Center for Continuing Education of Women, University of Michigan, 1977.

9

Donald H. Blocher
Rita S. Rapoza

Professional and Vocational Preparation

Vocational development theory assumes that careers arise, not from a series of isolated and independent decisions, but rather from the complex interweaving of various psychological threads or themes. In other words, a distinct pattern of psychological realities gives order and predictability to the events of an individual's vocational life. Thus, vocational development is seen as part of patterned psychological growth and development, including concepts of self, attitudes, values, interests, and ways of thinking about work and workers. This overlap between personal and vocational growth forms a basis on which the general goals of higher education and vocational development can be seen to converge. Most students go to college to get a better job or prepare for a more challenging career. Despite the negative attitudes of many academics toward vocationalism, career preparation has been a recognized mission for higher education since the first university was established at Bologna; centuries later, Harvard University was established to train the clergy. Because professional and vocational preparation are primary motives for students and because such preparation will continue to be a major responsibility for higher education, we need to understand how this development occurs. The growth of awareness of self as worker and total person is a central energizing core around which the college experience can be organized.

These assumptions lead naturally to an ecological approach to vocational development—an approach that focuses on the quality of interaction between the developing student and his or her environment. A framework within which to assess this interaction is provided by the concepts of developmental tasks, social roles, and coping behaviors. Vocational development, like psychological development in general, is assumed to entail an orderly sequential progression of psychosocial tasks leading toward maturity. In vocational terms this means a reasonable fulfillment and investment of self in work. Essentially, the developmental tasks and behaviors are those required of the individual at each life stage to master the immediate demands of the present social environment and to be prepared to move on to the next higher stage of development.

A schema more fully elaborated elsewhere (Blocher, 1974) is given in Table 1. It describes key developmental tasks in various life stages and classifies the kinds of coping behaviors necessary for mastery of basic developmental tasks. This schema is more general but not unrelated to the cognitive developmental view described by Perry in this volume. The general schema is adapted from Erik Erikson's conception of the eight stages of life, but several of his stages are further subdivided. It may be noted that, although the stages and coping behaviors are stated in general terms rather than in vocationally oriented terms, the great overlap between concepts of personal and vocational development is quickly apparent.

From Early Childhood on, with the development of autonomy, the child is engaged in a set of developmental processes that are crucial to vocational as well as interpersonal functioning. In Later Childhood, the development of initiative and industry lay down major foundation stones for vocational functioning. From Later Adolescence on, vocational and personal development converge in ways that make them virtually inseparable. The Realization and Stabilization Stages are crucial vocational, as well as personal, phases of development. Much of the phenomenon of midlife career change, which we will discuss later in the chapter, centers around efforts to find more satisfying work and achieve some degree of mastery over one's vocational life. Studies in the liberal arts, relationships with faculty and fellow students, and participation in appropriate extracurricular activities, in addition to studies specifically focused on professional training, can all help students take charge of their own careers.

The adoption of an ecological view of vocational development calls for a careful examination of student population characteristics and needs. All too often, students have been stereotyped as adolescent, white, middle-class, and vocationally immature. They have been seen, at various times, as inexperienced fledglings moodily preoccupied with the mysteries of sex, sports, and social status, and as unthinking revolutionaries and skeptics. Such stereotypes are no longer tenable.

During the past decade, dramatic changes in the *composition* as well as the size of college populations have occurred. In October 1975, for example, 1.2 million college students, or more than 10 percent, were 35 years of age or older. More than a million were black. The percentage of black high school graduates entering college was about the same as for white graduates. The percentage increases in college entrance for women grew about twice as rapidly during the first half of the 1970s as the increases for men. Steady increases in the proportions of part-time students and students in two-year programs were also observed during this period (U.S. Bureau of the Census, 1976).

These data make clear the fact that in terms of vocational characteristics and needs the present population of college students is a very heterogeneous group. Many have already made firm vocational choices and are in special programs designed to implement them. Many more already have careers to which they have made major commitments and are attending college part-time to improve their situations. For example, many

Table 1. Developmental Tasks, Social Roles, and Coping Behaviors by Life Stages

Life Stages	Social Roles	Developmental Tasks	Coping
Infancy (Birth-3 years)	Love-object roles; receiving and pleasing	Trust: learning to eat solid food and feed self, control elimination, manipulate objects, walk, explore immediate environment, communicate, relate to family, accommodate to a daily life rhythm	Approaching, receiving, accepting
Early Childhood (3-6 years)	Sibling, playmate, sex-appropriate roles	Autonomy: developing sense of separate self, sense of mutuality, realistic concepts of world; learning to be a boy or girl, manage aggression and frustration, follow verbal instructions, pay attention, become independent	Controlling, discriminating, attending
Later Childhood (6-12 years)	Student, helper, big brother or big sister roles	Initiative-Industry: learning to read and calculate, value self and be valued, delay gratification, control emotional reactions, deal with abstract concepts, help others, formulate values	Mastering, valuing, working
Early Adolescence (12-14 years)	Peer roles, heterosexual roles	Identity development: learning to be masculine or feminine, participate in various relationships, control impulses, be positive toward work, study, organize time, develop relevant value hierarchy	Achieving, relating, organizing
Later Adolescence (15-19 years)	Peer roles, heterosexual roles	Identity as a potential worker: learning to move from group to individual relationship, achieve emotional autonomy, produce in work situations	Reciprocating, cooperating, separating
Exploration (20-30 years)	Marriage roles, career roles	Intimacy and commitment: developing generativity; learning to commit self to goals, career, partner; be adequate parent; give unilaterally	Sexual relating, risk taking, value clarifying
Realization (30-50 years)	Leadership, helping, creative, accomplishment roles	Ego integrity: learning to be inner-directed, be interdependent, handle cognitive dissonance, be flexible and effective emotionally, think creatively, develop effective problem-solving techniques	Objectifying, analyzing, concentrating, problem solving
Stabilization (50-65 years)	Leadership, helping, managing, creative, accomplishment, authority, prestige roles	Learning to recognize change; developing broad intellectual curiosity, mature idealism, realistic time perspective	Accepting change, empathizing, valuing differences
Examination (65+ years)	Retirement, nonworker, nonauthority roles	Learning to face death, cope with retirement, use leisure time, affiliate with peers, adjust to changed living conditions, adjust to reduced physical vigor, care for the aging body	Affiliating, recreating, personalizing self and past

hold positions for which an academic degree is deemed necessary for legitimacy. Many are battling the restrictions placed on them by racial and sexual biases. Many women are struggling to combine career and family life. Many mature students are preparing for mid-life career shifts, while others are pursuing straight-line upgrading of educational and career qualifications. To view all these people within traditional adolescent stereotypes would be a gross denial of their unique needs and problems. It may be helpful, then, to look at the vocational characteristics and needs of several major subgroups of college students before coming back to the question of positive interventions in the college environment.

Adolescents and Young Adults

A very large research literature exists regarding the vocational characteristics and needs of college students in the adolescent-young adult category. Most of these studies deal with males. When both males and females are studied and sex differences are analyzed, the differences very frequently are significant. College women will be discussed, therefore, in a separate section of this chapter.

More than two hundred empirical studies were identified dealing with the vocational development of college students in this category. Obviously, not all these studies can be discussed or even referenced, so instead the literature will be examined in terms of several general themes that emerge.

A number of large-scale systematic studies of the vocational goals and choices of college entrants are reported in the literature. Cooley and Lohnes (1968) conducted a five-year follow-up study in which they predicted the vocational development of young adults, utilizing data from Project Talent. Watley (1968) reported a somewhat similar study following up Merit Scholarship students seven to eight years after college entrance. Dole (1965) reported results of six individual studies, some of them longitudinal, that compared stated plans of students at different educational levels. The picture emerging from these studies is one of rather *superficial planning* at the college-entrance level, with very marked shifts *away* from those plans during college and after college graduation. Watley's (1968) study, for example, found only three broad college curriculum areas (medicine, law, and biological science) in which as many as 50 percent of the entering students persisted through graduation.

It appears that the vocational goals of entering college students are heavily influenced by family expectations (Venerable, 1974; Grandy and Stahmann, 1974). Factors mentioned by college freshmen in discussing their choices appear to be rational, conventional, and relatively superficial (Elkins, 1975). Some vocational theorists suggest that the complex cognitive task of making a realistic and individualized vocational choice is beyond the level of cognitive development of many entering college students (Bodden, 1970; Jepson, 1974; Knefelkamp and Slepitza, 1976). Experimental work by Bodden and James (1976) lends some support to this supposition.

At any rate, there is little evidence that most students enter college with relatively stable and well-formed vocational plans that are further crystallized and refined during an exploration process carried out over the college years. Rather, the research supports the view that most students enter college with pat, superficial "pseudo-plans" heavily influenced by the expectations of significant others, and that these "plans" are quickly abandoned.

The notion that students simply refine the vocational goals they bring with them to college is belied by several studies. Baumgardner (1976), for example, found that college sophomores were less analytic and more intuitive in their thinking about vocational choices than were college freshmen. Buck (1970) found increased crystallization of interest patterns to be unrelated to vocational exploration during college years. Scott, Fenske, and Maxey (1974) studied nearly three thousand students in two-year colleges, comparing changers and nonchangers of vocational goals in terms of ability, interests, and family backgrounds. Titley and others (1975), in a somewhat similar study in a four-year college, found that specificity in vocational choice actually declined with increase in number of years in college. Lunneborg (1976) studied vocational indecisiveness in college students and found only slight relationships between the degree of indecisiveness and interest and ability measures taken in high school. Present college grades were positively related to vocational decisiveness. *The research, then, suggests that the process of vocational development in the college years is more a function of the college experience than a function of antecedent conditions.*

The findings just reviewed give a picture of considerable indecision and absence of stable planning at college entrance, even though the students may verbalize considerable certainty. The college experience basically "shakes up" these pseudo-plans and decisions rather than confirming them or crystallizing their elements. Very basic shifts in goals, plans, and choices occur during college and are not confined to any single curricular area or personality type. Rather, changes in values, social perspective, intellectual interests and long-range purposes occurring normally in college students seem to result in marked changes in vocational plans. Thus, indecision or ambiguity in vocational plans is probably a normal and healthy aspect of the development of the adolescent college student.

What accounts for these changes in students' vocational plans? Hearn and Moos (1976) reported findings suggesting that such changes may be related to particular norms or expectations of college living units. Goodwin (1969) found changes in vocational goals and values of students to be related to the values held by their professors. DeVoge's study (1975) reported considerable change in personality needs between freshman and senior years. No relationship was found between these changes and freshman scores or intended college major. There were, however, significant positive relationships between achievement scores taken during the senior year and chosen college major. A positive relationship was also found between academic major and the nature of employment after graduation. Lucy (1976) observed considerable stability between vocational preferences and both college major and employment histories of 884 college alumni.

Again, this evidence shows that significant vocational reorientation occurs during the college years, followed by a period of greater stability at or shortly after college graduation or leaving. What emerges in study after study is the view of the college years as a time of crisis and revolution in vocational development. These studies are in effect a testimonial to the impact of college on the development of adolescent students.

This picture becomes clearer yet when viewed in the perspective of modern vocational theory. Holland and Lutz's (1967) theory of vocational choice was developed out of data obtained from two large, nationwide samples of college students. Basically, the theory categorizes occupations into six types: Realistic, Intellectual, Social, Conventional, Enterprising, and Artistic. Vocational preferences, choices, and aspirations are seen as expressions of basic personality traits.

A considerable body of research has pointed to the usefulness of the Holland schema in understanding the changes in vocational goals observed in adolescents and young adults (Holland and Gottfredson, 1974; Holland and Whitney, 1968; Morrow, 1971; Gross and Gaier, 1974; Krause, 1970). The college years can be seen as a developmental period during which students cast aside externally imposed plans and engage in the task of assessing their increasing knowledge of themselves against their widening and deepening perceptions of work and workers. As the body of knowledge about self and others is enriched, planning and decision making become much more complex. This kind of problem solving probably requires the kind of higher-order thinking described in Perry's chapter.

The evidence indicates that many students do accomplish this developmental task successfully during the college years and are able to move on to make significant vocational commitments. For others, the task presents greater difficulty and may be accompanied by severe stress and considerable wasted effort and frustration. Some evidence suggests that students with high self-esteem and clear, consistent self-concepts are able to make vocational choices with greater assurance than those with low self-esteem or confused self-concepts (Wigent, 1974; Resnick, Fauble, and Osipow, 1970; Korman, 1967; Isabelle and Dick, 1969). These findings seem to support the general view that the key vocational developmental tasks involve reconciling self-perceptions with perceptions of work and workers. It seems clear that this process is essential to the general educational and intellectual development that has traditionally been a goal of liberal education.

Generally, then, the research evidence supports the concept of college as a learning environment in which young adults struggle with self-awareness and awareness of others in order to form commitments to career and work that will sustain consistent and realistic plans and choices. This growth process is an aspect of overall personality development, and its crises are not easily separated from so-called personal adjustment problems (Osipow and Gold, 1968; Karr and Mahrer, 1972). Difficulties with key vocational development tasks may underlie dissatisfaction with college, poor achievement, and other problems (Waterman and Waterman, 1969; Walsh, 1974; Fullerton and Britton, 1976).

It may be concluded that for successful vocational development adolescents and young adults need a learning environment that (1) supports the development of self-awareness and self-esteem, (2) provides information about strengths and weaknesses, and (3) offers opportunities to experience a variety of significant relationships with people in a wide range of role situations. These needs are fairly well represented in the tasks specified for Later Adolescence and Young Adulthood in Table 1.

College Women

Any consideration of the vocational needs and characteristics of women college students must be approached cautiously. Much of the research evidence has been generated around variables and questions extrapolated from research on men. Some of the basic assumptions inherent in this research may be untrue or irrelevant in the study of career development of women.

Farmer (1978) lists six basic issues that are raised by studies of young women. These may be stated in the form of propositions or problems that must be addressed by those interested in facilitating the career development of women. They reveal the obstacles, both external and internal, that must be overcome if women are to achieve the same levels of self-fulfillment and social contribution through work as men do.

Proposition One: Women generally experience a decline in academic self-confidence during the college years. Tomlinson-Keasey (1974) and Farley (1974) found that, although college women as a group tend to report higher grade-point averages than comparable groups of men, women tend to describe themselves as less intelligent than do men. Homall, Juhasz, and Juhasz (1975) found that college women saw themselves as having low prestige and low aspirations. Epstein and Bronzaft (1974) found that college women generally desired fewer years of education than did men.

Proposition Two: College women actually fear success, or rather, the negative social consequences associated with high achievement. Horner and others (1973), Katz (1973), and Monahan, Kuhn, and Shaver (1974) have all demonstrated the existence of a "fear of success phenomenon." This phenomenon is apparently based on the assumption that high levels of achievement or success make a woman less acceptable socially, particularly in heterosexual relationships. While it is probable that males also experience similar fears to some degree, it seems from the research that fear of success may be a major inhibitor of women's aspirations. Alper (1974) suggests that more sophisticated research is needed to determine more precisely what situational variables interact with the fear of success.

Proposition Three: Vicarious achievement motivation—that is, satisfaction in the achievements of significant others rather than in one's own accomplishments—limits the aspirations of women and increases acceptance of traditional female vocational roles. Lipman-Blumen and Leavitt (1976) and Lipman-Blumen (1972) have studied this phenomenon and report that the motivational framework frequently adopted by women is one in which one's own success is defined by the accomplishments of husband or children. Getz and Herman (1974) reported that college women tend to judge other women as successful *only* if they are successful in marriage and family roles, regardless of personal career achievements.

Proposition Four: The inability to cope with conflict, both real and perceived, between the social role expectations regarding family and career inhibits the aspirations and achievements of many college women. Morgan (1962), Farmer and Bohn (1970), and Van Dusen and Sheldon (1976) have all studied this phenomenon. It seems clear that a myth exists regarding the categorization of women into "career" and "family" types. Actually, most college women report that they want to combine family and career activities (Hoffman and Hoeflin, 1972). Oliver (1974) found no differences between so-called "homemaking" and "career" types of college women on achievement and affiliation needs, but found that interactions between the two variables operated differently for the two groups. That is, individuals weighted the importance of the two roles differently rather than excluding either.

Steinmann's (1975) longitudinal and cross-cultural study found that communication problems between men and women over role problems are more acute when the woman's educational level is high. College women, then, especially need to be able to manage sex role conflicts in their marriage and family relationships.

Proposition Five: Sexist attitudes, real and perceived, about working women inhibit the career development of college women. Birk, Cooper, and Tanney (1973), Gump (1972), and Almquist (1974) have studied sex role attitudes and their effects on women's vocational development. No evidence was found that career-oriented women are less well adjusted, contrary to popular stereotypes. Some indications were found that ego strength was related to adoption of nontraditional sex role concepts. In a large-scale study of college women conducted by Karman (1973), the women reported that college had done little to expand traditional sex role concepts. Dodge (1974) found that college students in women's studies programs perceived the faculty, administration, and curriculum as being unresponsive to their interests and needs. Dickerson (1974) reported similar perceptions among women students generally. A study at Stanford University (Committee on the Education and Employment of Women, 1972) of 280 graduating women reported somewhat similar perceptions by women of the negative impact of the college environment.

Hawley (1972) found that the vocational attitudes of college women are heavily influenced by their perceptions of the attitudes held by men in the area of sex role behavior. Almquist and Angrist (1971) found that the career orientations of college women were affected by their perceptions of the attitudes of faculty. Clearly, women are sensitive to, aware of, and influenced by the attitudes and norms that exist in the college environment.

Angrist (1972) and Harmon (1971), in separate studies, reported that constricted and traditional early vocational choices made by women tend to be relatively unchanged by the college experience. These findings seem to present considerable contrast to those reported earlier for males.

Proposition Six: The career development of college women tends to be limited by lower risk-taking ability than is shown by men. Maccoby and Jacklin (1974), in a comprehensive review of the research literature, conclude that women are less likely than men to take risks in most situations. Gable and others (1976) found that a personal orientation reflecting "internal locus of control" or sense of personal agency and responsibility for outcomes in one's own life was associated with increased vocational maturity in college women. Bardwick and Douvan (1971) contend that the strong affiliation needs of adolescent and adult women make them more externally controlled and unwilling to risk social disapproval.

The research cited here very strongly suggests that a number of powerful negative influences inhibit the career development of women in the college years. Some of these negative factors are rooted in the college environment itself. Little evidence exists that the college experience on the whole works to expand the awareness or range of choices of college women, or that it greatly facilitates the growth of women in areas of planning, decision making, or conflict resolution, which are crucial elements of vocational maturity in women. The career needs of women seem to receive relatively little systematic support in the educational process. The college milieu apparently has considerably less impact in "unfreezing" the vocational thinking and behavior of women than it has for men. Generally, college women aspire to combine career and marriage roles, but their aspirations tend to be considerably lower and more tentative than men's in the face of inhibiting factors in the college environment and in the total society.

The relative neglect of the vocational needs of college women continues despite clear evidence of women's needs for careful vocational planning and decision making (Tyler, 1972; Rapoza and Blocher, 1978). Van Dusen and Sheldon (1976) document the trends, noted earlier, of increasing enrollment of women on both full-time and part-time bases in college programs. They point out that women tend to be marrying later, having fewer children, and spending less of their lives in childbearing and childrearing activities. Steady increases in the numbers of women functioning as heads of household are also evident.

Neugarten (1976) notes that contemporary life-styles and life cycles will lead to increasing participation in the labor market by women and that the patterns of this participation will be complex and related to the individual's age and family cycles. Successful management of these complex career patterns obviously requires even more careful planning and preparation than that required by men. Apparently, greater appreciation of the significance of work for women is needed in higher education, and in the greater society. So long as society and its educational institutions are unable to recognize that women work for a variety of economic and psychological reasons, little improvement is likely to be made in the kinds of services and experiences offered them.

A number of students of the psychology of women have forcefully pointed out that work is a major role and vehicle for self-expression, personal fulfillment, self-esteem, and self-discovery for women (Kievit, 1974; Schlossberg and Pietrofesa, 1973; Hedges and Bemis, 1974). Wolfson (1976) has studied the career patterns of women in a longitudinal design and has found that subsequent patterns are difficult to predict at the point of college entrance, thus indicating a need for continuous planning activities during college. Programs of continuing education and planning assistance are crucially important for women (Wells, 1974). Eyde (1968) found that women place higher values on work motivation and achievement mastery ten years after college than at graduation or even five years after. These findings again support the need for continuing education and counseling programs.

Minority Students

It is impossible to give any simple categorical description of the needs and characteristics of so-called "minority" groups, since these needs and characteristics vary widely both within and across groups. Most of the available research emphasizes the dangers of generalizing from data generated on predominantly white, middle-class samples, rather than giving definitive generalizations about minority groups themselves. Wakefield and others (1975), for example, found that the Holland typology fits somewhat less well for black undergraduate students than for white students. Borgen and Harper (1973) arrived at similar conclusions after examining predictions made from data from the Strong Vocational Interest Blank. Vander Well (1970) found that differences in financial need and the availability of financial aid strongly affected vocational-educational plans and aspirations. Schoenfeld (1972) found that students from lower-status families tended to crystallize vocational plans earlier than did those from higher-status families. Pressures apparently exist for the former group that may produce premature closure, bringing possible future dissatisfaction. Pfeifer (1976) found that correlations between college grades and probability of completing a degree were higher for black than for white students. The availability of academic counseling and help with study skills may be a crucial factor in the career development of these students (Jones, Harris, and Hauck, 1975).

A study by Littig (1975) indicates that black males attending colleges that attract primarily working-class students tend to aspire more frequently to occupations having a "power" or managerial orientation and that have been traditionally closed to blacks. Black males attending middle-class colleges tend to aspire more frequently to social service occupations and the professions.

A number of studies (Oman, 1971; Lewis and Sedlacek, 1971; Mortimer, 1975; Berman and Haug, 1975) all point up the strong relationship between family background, the experience of working, and occupational aspirations. Generally, these data suggest that students from families of lower socioeconomic status may possess lower aspirations, lower self-confidence, and less well-developed work habits than those from middle-class backgrounds. The implication seems clear that if the college experience is to facilitate the optimal career development of all students then special assistance in the form of counseling, study skills counseling, vocational exploration, financial aid, and extracurricular opportunities should be made available to students whose needs have been carefully assessed on an individual rather than a group membership basis.

Older Students

A number of special commission reports have been addressed to the needs and problems of older students and "midlife career changers" (Entine, 1974; National Advisory Council on Adult Education, 1972; National Council on the Aging, 1966). Most of these reports had available relatively little empirical data. Generally, they hypothesize a midlife identity crisis in which workers attempt to find more satisfying and meaningful work as they confront approaching retirement and death. Sarason, Sarason, and Cowden (1975) summarize this point of view and suggest the need for education and counseling across the life span. The problems faced by students in midlife transition seem akin to the tasks described in the Realization Stage of Table 1. At this point, the rather sketchy literature points to the existence of three major subgroups of mature students, each with rather distinct needs and characteristics.

The first group consists of *vertical changers*. These people seek lifelong educational opportunities to move ahead within a well-defined career pattern in which they have demonstrated considerable commitment and from which they have obtained some degree of satisfaction. They need information about and access to educational opportunities and programs related to their chosen career goals. They may also need renewal of learning skills and some support for risk-taking in pursuing higher-level programs and aspirations.

The second consists of *voluntary changers*. These people seek greater life satisfaction through midlife career changes. Their needs probably include clarification of goals and values and career exploration processes relating to newly discovered aspirations.

The third group consists of *involuntary changers*. These people are forced to change careers because of drastically altered social and economic circumstances. This group may include widowed or divorced men and women, economically displaced workers, or physically or emotionally handicapped workers. These people may need rather comprehensive psychological services and considerable emotional, financial, and practical assistance in utilizing appropriate educational opportunities.

The limited information available on the needs of mature students thus suggests that they are a heterogeneous group of people with a variety of needs but that they do constitute a population strikingly different from the traditional young adult group and should have services attuned to their special characteristics.

Implications for Higher Education

The struggle between vocationalism, in the form of students' desire for career preparation, and the loftier goals of the colleges and universities themselves has pervaded the history of higher education. Despite the protestations of the colleges to the contrary, it seems clear that most college students and their families continue to view college primarily as an avenue to financial security and status. The decision to attend college most often represents a desire to obtain the benefits of membership in the professional and managerial occupations of our industrial and technological society (Fenske and Scott, 1973). Part of the present crisis in higher education stems precisely from the narrow vocationalism represented by student motivations and expectations. Goals of personal and intellectual development, which most colleges view themselves as equipped to facilitate, are not foremost in many students' minds.

As Chickering and Havighurst point out in Chapter One, the economic realities of the present decade have cast grave doubt on the capacity of the economy to meet the vocational aspirations of most college students. In the eyes of many of these students, the society has promised that college would open the way to the Great American Dream. That dream is now turning into a nightmare for millions of college students. Zehring (1975) calls the reaction to the shattering of this dream "rejection shock" and characterizes it as the major psychological theme of contemporary college life. This shock wave of disillusionment seems to represent a primary force in reshaping the political, economic, and educational values of a whole generation of college students.

There is a certain irony in the fact that for millions of students despair over the collapse of cherished hopes is centered in the very place that has ostensibly been designed to expand their goals and to stimulate their motivations. Perhaps a genuine opportunity exists for colleges to move into the psychological vacuum created by "rejection shock" with a healthier, more realistic, and more intellectually honest approach to vocational development than the narrow one that brought so many students to the campus in the first place.

Taken in this broader context, then, vocational development is by no means antithetical to the traditional ideals of higher education.

Vocational development theory as a framework for conceptualizing student personnel services implies very strongly that such services should not be limited to a brief series of interviews immediately prior to graduation but instead should be addressed to the overall interaction between the student and the college learning environment. Thus, the formal curriculum, experiences in extracurricular activities, interactions in unions and residences, and part-time work experiences all represent potential opportunities for personal and vocational growth. All of these, therefore, are potential sites for positive interventions by student personnel services.

The review of research on the career development needs and characteristics of college students gives rise to a number of conclusions, which in turn yield clear implications for curriculum development, student services, and overall programs in American colleges. These conclusions can be summarized under the following generalizations:

1. American college students and their families tend to perceive college primarily as an avenue to vocational advancement and security.
2. Many college freshmen enter college with very superficial and externally influenced plans and aspirations, which (for men) quickly dissolve in the more intellectually complex and emotionally independent environment represented by college.
3. The reintegration of vocational plans and aspirations based upon increased self-awareness and deeper understanding of work and workers is a function of experience in the total college environment as well as of general intellectual and emotional development.
4. The vocational needs of women are poorly served in the contemporary college environment. Women obtain relatively little help in overcoming the problems imposed by constricting socialization processes, covert discrimination and conflicting social expectations. For many women college is simply another environment which mirrors the prejudices, unresponsiveness, and male domination of the larger society.
5. The racial and socioeconomic composition of the student population is becoming more heterogeneous. The resulting variability of backgrounds, needs, and cultural characteristics defies any neat categorization of subgroups. Wide ranges of approaches, programs, and services need to be available in the college community. Such services can be effectively utilized only when combined with a thoroughly individualized approach to students with special needs.
6. The age range represented in the college population is wider than seems to be generally appreciated. Many older college students have vocational needs quite different from those of adolescents and young adults. Such students may be part-time, off-campus, hard-to-contact individuals who are struggling to combine higher education with active family and vocational commitments. Such students may have a wide variety of motivations and aspirations and may require different delivery systems to meet their needs.

A review of the research and the conclusions that it supports suggests the need for sweeping changes in the nature, organization, and delivery of vocational development services. A number of studies over the past twenty years have documented the much-needed expansion of the goals of higher education (Katz, 1967; Lenning and others, 1974). If increased attention is to be given to the career development needs of students, this must occur as part of a vital and dynamic change in the mainstream of higher education.

The conceptual basis for this kind of change may well be found in the ecological approach mentioned earlier. New consideration will have to be given to the impact of the overall campus environment upon general personality development and career development (Chickering and McCormick, 1973). A number of recent approaches to and studies of college student personnel work have taken the ecological perspective (Miller and Prince, 1976; Corrazzini and Wilson, 1975; Banning and Kaiser, 1974). Future designs for intervention programs should be incorporated into comprehensive models. Such programs should be capable of providing a variety of services to different sectors of the college community. It seems apparent that the traditional counseling center model, even with the patchwork addition of outreach programs, is inadequate to meet the career development needs of the total college community.

Several basic flaws exist in the traditional student services and counseling center organizational structure. Typically, these services are housed administratively outside of the academic line of administration and tend to come under staff and supportive services. Efforts at addressing vital aspects of the development of students simply cannot be administered in the same way that lawn maintenance, cafeterias, and bowling alleys are operated.

Secondly, these services are generally grouped with and allied to clinical services designed to remedy sickness rather than help students with normal developmental tasks. The stigma associated with these services may even detract from the basic purposes of a service designed for forward-looking students. In many such agencies the interests, training, and skills of the staff are such that vocational development activities have low priority and are carried out poorly, if attempted at all.

Finally, such counseling and student personnel programs tend to have neither high visibility nor credibility with faculty and academic units. They are often perceived as peripheral and relatively ineffective bureaucratic agencies staffed by professionals who are unfamiliar with and unacceptable to the academic college community.

It seems vital that student development programs in the future be organized directly under the egis of the president or academic vice-president and articulated directly and clearly with academic departments and colleges. Prototypes of this kind of organizational model have been proposed by Miller and Prince (1976) and Hurst and others (1973). Obviously, great difficulties in reorienting contemporary views of college structure and administration attend the implementation of these kinds of models.

Ideally, however, leadership in career development activities should come from within some type of office of student development or environmental design and be related directly to academic units. Such leadership should consist largely of assistance to academic units in assessing needs of students, and consultation in the development of programs and services to be coordinated with the academic departments or colleges. The effort should not be to "reach out" from a separate structure but to "reach in" to the mainstream of campus activity—the academic department, school, or college. The chapter by Kolb in this volume helps to document the differential needs of students from different curriculums.

As these kinds of programs are developed with the combined resources of the academic units and the student development staff, a wide range of modes of intervention and points of delivery must be employed. The following suggest some of the directions these programs may take.

Organizational and Curriculum Development. Efforts at changing basic structures and philosophical commitments of academic units should be undertaken in order to improve the basic climate of the institution. Such efforts might well include inducing greater commitment to education as a lifelong process (Knowles, 1972); seeking to encourage greater participation and responsibility for students in policy making (El-Khawas, 1976; DeShong, 1976); obtaining more flexible programming, including the possibility of programs other than traditional four-year bachelor's programs (Haywood, 1974); introducing functional models of career development into the basic curricular and instructional activity (Luther and Smith, 1974; Conyne and Cochran, 1973).

Many of the basic institutional changes needed to improve the quality of the learning environment for women students could also be pursued through organizational development interventions. Some changes that would be particularly helpful to women, older, and part-time students are developing daycare centers; keeping major offices and facilities open during evening hours; allowing credit for community experiences and allowing credit by examination (see Keeton's chapter on assessing and crediting experiential learning); monitoring admissions requirements to ensure that there is no discrimination by age, race, or sex; encouraging community liaison activities to reach prospective students; and systematically utilizing campus and community employment opportunities to enhance the career development of students (Cook and Stone, 1973).

Consultation with Faculty and Administrators. A major mode of delivery for career development services is consultation with faculty and administrators. Conyne and Clark (1975) describe an intervention model based on faculty consultation and aimed at improving the quality of the campus learning environment. Hadley (1975) and Gelwick (1974) have outlined similar programs of consultation and training with faculty.

Direct Teaching and Training. A growing pattern of intervention is the development of credit courses or modules within credit courses aimed at direct facilitation of vocational and professional development. Such programs have been described and evaluated by Comas and Day (1975), Babcock and Kaufman (1976), and Hackney and Williams (1975). It seems likely that the greatest single resource to be mobilized is the individual professor in the classroom.

Group Vocational Counseling. Probably the most popular mode of intervention employed in career development on the campus is group counseling. "Career exploration" or "life planning" groups, as they are often called, are formed in a variety of ways and employ a number of formats and theoretical approaches. Among the more carefully described and evaluated procedures discussed in the recent literature are those reported by Healy (1974), Mencke and Cochran (1974), Westbrook (1973), and Smith and Evans (1973).

Informational and Self-Instructional Systems. A major innovation in the delivery of vocational development services is the use of automated data-processing facilities to retrieve information. These can be accessed directly by students in response to their immediate needs or in conjunction with conventional vocational counseling activities. Such programs are described by Zagorski and others (1973) and Sander and Wolff (1975). Less highly automated information systems are described by Reardon (1973). Holland's Self-Directed Search is a prototype of an integrated approach between assessment information and client informational needs. Other self-directed programs, which can also be used as modules within courses or vocational planning groups, are described by McAleer (1975) and Pappas and others (1972). Some such systems utilize simulations and videotape modeling of relevant behaviors (Fisher, Reardon, and Burck, 1976; Ryan, 1969; Little and Roach, 1974).

Traditional Vocational Counseling Services. While contemporary trends involve use of a wide variety of delivery systems other than one-to-one counseling, this approach is by no means outmoded and should not be discarded. Often it is used in conjunction with a number of supplementary approaches such as those described above. A major advantage of one-to-one counseling is that it can deal with vocational concerns and issues in direct conjunction with other kinds of problems that confront students at the same time. Since evidence exists that a variety of personal problems accompany transitions in vocational development, represented by events such as college graduation, this is a very significant advantange (Karr and Mahrer, 1972).

Conclusions

Our examination of vocational development issues in higher education can be summarized by a few basic conclusions. (1) The vocational needs of college students are many and diverse and must be met by coordinated efforts involving the whole college environment. Efforts must be made to address the unmet needs of the hitherto "invisible" students; minority, older, part-time, and commuting members of the college community. (2) Immediate and determined efforts must be made to improve the quality of the learning environment for women. (3) Responsibility for the coordination and evaluation of community-wide efforts must be centralized at very high levels in the academic administration. (4) Needs assessment and program development activities must pervade the college community, including primary involvement of academic departments as well as special resource agencies such as libraries, unions, and student services organizations. (5) A wide variety of approaches and delivery systems must be utilized in addition to traditional counseling and advising activities. These must include organizational development approaches that address basic problems of curriculum, organizational structures, educational philosophies, and social attitudes that bear directly on the quality of the learning environment and its impact on student development generally, and vocational and professional development specifically.

References

Almquist, E. M. "Sex Stereotypes in Occupational Choice: The Case for College Women." *Journal of Vocational Behavior,* 1974, *5,* 13-21.

Almquist, E. M., and Angrist, S. S. "Role Model Influences on College Women's Career Aspirations." *Merrill-Palmer Quarterly,* 1971, *17,* 263-279.

Alper, T. G. "Achievement Motivation in College Women: A Now-You-See-It-Now-You-Don't Phenomenon." *American Psychologist,* 1974, *29,* 194-203.

Angrist, S. S. "Counseling College Women About Careers." *Journal of College Student Personnel,* 1972, *13,* 494-498.

Babcock, R. J., and Kaufman, M. A. "Effectiveness of a Career Course." *Vocational Guidance Quarterly,* 1976, *24,* 261-265.

Banning, J., and Kaiser, L. "An Ecological Perspective and Model for Campus Design." *Personnel and Guidance Journal,* 1974, *52,* 370-375.

Bardwick, J. M., and Douvan, E. "Ambivalences: The Socialization of Women." In V. Gornick and B. K. Moran (Eds.), *Woman in Sexist Society.* New York: Basic Books, 1971.

Baumgardner, S. R. "The Impact of College Experiences on Conventional Career Logic." *Journal of Counseling Psychology,* 1976, *23,* 40-45.

Berman, G. S., and Haug, M. R. "Occupational and Educational Goals and Expectations: The Effects of Race and Sex." *Social Problems,* 1975, *23,* 166-181.

Birk, J., Cooper, J., and Tanney, M. "Racial and Sex-Role Stereotyping in Career Information Illustration." Paper presented at 81st annual meeting of the American Psychological Association, Montreal, Canada, August 1973.

Blocher, D. H. *Developmental Counseling.* (2nd ed.) New York: Ronald Press, 1974.

Bodden, J. L. "Cognitive Complexity as a Factor in Appropriate Vocational Choice." *Journal of Counseling Psychology,* 1970, *17,* 364-368.

Bodden, J. L., and James, L. E. "Influence of Occupational Information-Giving on Cognitive Complexity." *Journal of Counseling Psychology,* 1976, *23,* 280-282.

Borgen, F. H., and Harper, G. T. "Predictive Validity of Measured Vocational Interests with Black and White College Men." *Measurement and Evaluation in Guidance,* 1973, *6,* 19-26.

Buck, C. W. "Crystallization of Vocational Interests as a Function of Vocational Exploration in College." *Journal of Counseling Psychology,* 1970, *17,* 347-351.

Chickering, A. W., and McCormick, J. "Personality Development and the College Experience." *Research in Higher Education,* 1973, *1,* 43-70.

Clopton, W. "Personality and Career Change." *Industrial Gerontology,* 1973, *17,* 9-17.

Comas, R. E., and Day, R. W. "Career Exploration for College Students: A Report on a Program." Paper presented at the meeting of the Southern Association for Counselor Education and Supervision, Mobile, Ala., October 1975.

Committee on the Education and Employment of Women. *The Stanford Woman in 1972.* Stanford, Calif.: Stanford University, 1972.

Conyne, R. K., and Clark, R. J. "The Consultation Intervention Model: Directions for Action." *College Student Personnel,* 1975, *16,* 413-417.

Conyne, R. K., and Cochran, D. J. "Academic and Career Development: Toward Integration." *Personnel and Guidance Journal,* 1973, *52,* 217-223.

Cook, B., and Stone, B. "Counseling Women." *Guidance Monograph Series.* Series VII: Special Topics In Counseling. Boston: Houghton-Mifflin, 1973.

Cooley, W. W., and Lohnes, P. R. *Project Talent Five-Year Follow-Up Studies: Predicting Development of Young Adults.* Interim Report 5. Pittsburgh, Pa.: School of Education, 1968.

Corrazzini, J. G., and Wilson, S. E. "Students: The Environment and Their Interaction— Part II." Colorado State University Student Development Reports. Fort Collins: Colorado State University, 1975.

DeShong, B. P. "Student Involvement in University Policy Groups and Resultant Attitude Change." *Research in Higher Education,* 1976, *4,* 185-192.

DeVoge, S. D. "Personality Variables, Academic Major, and Vocational Choices: A Longitudinal Study of Holland's Theory." *Psychological Reports,* 1975, *37,* 1191-1195.

Dickerson, K. G. "Are Female College Students Influenced by the Expectations They Perceive Their Faculty and Administration Have for Them?" *Journal of the NAWDAC* [National Association of Women Deans, Administrators, and Counselors], 1974, *37,* 167-172.

Dodge, D. *Attitudes of Undergraduate Women Toward Careers.* Final Report. Washington, D.C.: Office of Education, Department of Health, Education, and Welfare, 1974.

Dole, A. A. *Follow-Up Studies of the Determinants of Educational-Vocational Choices.* Report No. CRP-2109. Honolulu: University of Hawaii, 1965.

El-Khawas, E. H. *New Expectations for Fair Practice: Suggestions for Institutional Review.* Washington, D.C.: Office of Academic Affairs, American Council on Education, 1976.

Elkins, J. K. "Factors in College Students' Career Planning." *Vocational Guidance Quarterly,* 1975, *23,* 354-357.

Entine, A. D. (Ed.). *Americans in Middle Years: Career Options and Educational Opportunities.* Los Angeles: Ethel Percy Andrus Gerontology Center, University of Southern California, 1974.

Epstein, G. F., and Bronzaft, A. L. "Female Modesty in Aspiration Level." *Journal of Counseling Psychology,* 1974, *21,* 57-60.

Eyde, L. D. "Work Motivation of Women College Graduates: Five-Year Follow-Up." *Journal of Counseling Psychology,* 1968, *15,* 199-202.

Farley, J. "Coeducation and College Women." *Cornell Journal of Social Relations,* 1974, *9,* 87-97.

Farmer, H. S. "Why Women Choose Careers Below Their Potential." In L. S. Hansen and R. S. Rapoza (Eds.), *Career Development and Counseling of Women.* Springfield, Ill.: Thomas, 1978.

Farmer, H., and Bohn, M. "Home-Career Conflict Reduction and the Level of Career Interest in Women." *Journal of Counseling Psychology,* 1970, *17,* 228-232.

Fenske, R. H., and Scott, C. S. "College Students' Goals, Plans, and Background Characteristics: A Synthesis of Three Empirical Studies." *Research in Higher Education,* 1973, *1,* 101-118.

Fisher, T. J., Reardon, R. C., and Burck, H. D. "Increasing Information-Seeking Behavior with a Model-Reinforced Videotape." *Journal of Counseling Psychology,* 1976, *23,* 234-238.

Fullerton, T. F., and Britton, J. O. "Collegiate Persistence of Vocationally Undecided Males." *Journal of Educational Research,* 1976, *69,* 300-304.

Gable, R. K., and others. "Perceptions of Personal Control and Conformity of Vocational Choice as Correlates of Vocational Development." *Journal of Vocational Behavior,* 1976, *8,* 259-266.

Gelwick, B. P. "Training Faculty to do Career Advising." *Personnel and Guidance Journal,* 1974, *53,* 214-217.

Getz, S. K., and Herman, J. B. *Sex Differences in Judgments of Male and Female Role Stereotypes.* Paper presented at 46th annual meeting of Midwestern Psychological Association, Chicago, May 1974.

Goodwin, L. "The Academic World and the Business World: A Comparison of Occupational Goals." *Sociology of Education,* 1969, *42,* 170-187.

Grandy, T. G., and Stahmann, R. F. "Family Influence on College Students' Vocational Choice: Predicting Holland's Personality Types." *Journal of College Student Personnel,* 1974, *15,* 404-409.

Gross, L. J., and Gaier, E. L. "College Major and Career Choice: A Retest of Holland's Theory." *Journal of Vocational Behavior,* 1974, *5,* 209-213.

Gump, J. P. "Sex-Role Attitudes and Psychological Well-Being." *Journal of Social Issues,* 1972, *28,* 79-92.

Hackney, L., and Williams, C. E. "Career Awareness Mini-Seminars." *Vocational Guidance Quarterly,* 1975, *23,* 365-366.

Hadley, E. E. "Helping Faculty Advisors Deal with Vocational Indecision." *Vocational Guidance Quarterly,* 1975, *23,* 232-236.

Harmon, L. W. "The Childhood and Adolescent Career Plans of College Women." *Journal of Vocational Behavior,* 1971, *1,* 45-56.

Hawley, P. "Perceptions of Male Models of Femininity Related to Career Choice." *Journal of Counseling Psychology*, 1972, *19*, 308-313.

Haywood, C. R. "Two By Four: Associate Programs in Traditionally Four-Year and Graduate Degree Granting Institutions." *Journal of Higher Education*, 1974, *45*, 682-690.

Healy, C. C. "Evaluation of a Replicable Group Career Counseling Procedure." *Vocational Guidance Quarterly*, 1974, *23*, 34-40.

Hearn, J. C., and Moos, R. H. "Social Climate and Major Choice: A Test of Holland's Theory in University Student Living Groups." *Journal of Vocational Behavior*, 1976, *8*, 293-300.

Hedges, J. N., and Bemis, S. E. "Sex Stereotyping: Its Decline in Skilled Trades." *Monthly Labor Review*, May 1974, pp. 14-22.

Hoffman, D. S., and Hoeflin, R. "Freshman and Sophomore Women: What Do They Want Most in the Future?" *Journal of College Student Personnel*, 1972, *13*, 490-493.

Holland, J. L., and Gottfredson, G. D. "Applying a Typology to Vocational Aspirations." Baltimore, Md.: Center for Social Organization of School Reports, Johns Hopkins University, 1974.

Holland, J. L., and Lutz, S. W. *Predicting a Student's Vocational Choice.* Iowa City, Iowa: American College Testing Program, 1967.

Holland, J. L., and Whitney, D. R. "Changes in the Vocational Plans of College Students: Orderly or Random?" ACT Research Report. Iowa City, Iowa: American College Testing Program, 1968.

Homall, G. M., Juhasz, S., and Juhasz, J. "Differences in Self-Perception and Vocational Aspirations of College Women." *California Journal of Educational Research*, 1975, *26*, 6-10.

Horner, M., and others. *Scoring Manual for an Empirically-Derived Scoring System for Motive to Avoid Success.* Unpublished monograph, Harvard University, 1973.

Hurst, J. C., and others. "Reorganizing for Human Development in Higher Education: Obstacles to Change." *Journal of College Student Personnel*, 1973, *14*, 10-15.

Isabelle, L. A., and Dick, W. "Clarity of Self-Concepts in the Vocational Development of Male Liberal Arts Students: An Abstract." *Canadian Psychologist*, 1969, *10*, 20-31.

Jepson, D. A. "The Stage Construct in Career Development." *Counseling and Values*, 1974, *18*, 24-31.

Jones, J. C., Harris, L. J., and Hauck, W. E. "Differences in Perceived Sources of Academic Difficulties: Black Students in Predominantly Black and Predominantly White Colleges." *Journal of Negro Education*, 1975, *44*, 519-529.

Karman, F. J. "Women: Personal and Environmental Factors in Career Choice." Paper presented at annual meeting of the American Educational Research Association, New Orleans, La., February 1973.

Karr, S. D., and Mahrer, A. R. "Transitional Problems Accompanying Vocational Development and College Graduation." *Journal of Vocational Behavior*, 1972, *2*, 283-289.

Katz, J. (Ed.). *Growth and Constraint in College Students: A Study of the Varieties of Psychological Development.* Stanford, Calif.: Institute for Study of Human Problems, Stanford University, 1967.

Katz, M. *Female Motive to Avoid Success: A Psychological Barrier or a Response to Deviancy?* Princeton, N.J.: Educational Testing Service, 1973.

Kelleher, C. H. "Second Careers: A Growing Trend." *Industrial Gerontology*, 1973, *17*, 1-8.

Kievit, M. B. "Will Jill Make Department Chairman?" *American Vocational Journal*, 1974, *49*, 40-43.

Knefelkamp, L. L., and Slepitza, R. A. "A Cognitive-Developmental Model of Career Development: An Adaptation of the Perry Scheme." *The Counseling Psychologist,* 1976, *6,* 53-58.

Knowles, M. S. *Toward a Model of Lifelong Education.* Working Paper for Consultative Groups on "Concept of Lifelong Education and Its Implications for School Curriculum." Hamburg: Institute for Education, UNESCO, 1972.

Korman, A. K. "Self-Esteem as a Moderator of the Relationship Between Self-Perceived Abilities and Vocational Choice." *Journal of Applied Psychology,* 1967, *51,* 65-67.

Krause, D. A. *A Study of Work Values as They Relate to Holland's Six Personal Orientations.* New York: Columbia Teachers College, 1970.

Landan, C. J., and Crooks, M. M. "Continuing Education for Men." *Canadian Counsellor,* 1976, *10,* 83-88.

Lenning, O. T., and others. *The Many Faces of College Success and Their Non-Intellective Correlates: The Published Literature Through the Decades of the Sixties.* Monograph No. 15. Iowa City, Iowa: American College Testing Program, 1974.

Lewis, A. H., and Sedlacek, W. E. *Socioeconomic Level Differences on Holland's Self-Directed Search.* College Park: University of Maryland, 1971.

Lipman-Blumen, J. "How Ideology Shapes Women's Lives." *Scientific American,* 1972, *226,* 34-42.

Lipman-Blumen, J., and Leavitt, H. J. "Vicarious and Direct Achievement Patterns in Adulthood." *The Counseling Psychologist,* 1976, *6,* 26-32.

Littig, L. W. "Personality, Race, and Social Class Determinants of Occupational Goals." *International Mental Health Research Newsletter,* 1975, *17,* 2-6, 13-16.

Little, D. M., and Roach, A. J. "Videotape Modeling of Interest in Non-Traditional Occupations for Women." *Journal of Vocational Behavior,* 1974, *5,* 133-138.

Lucy, W. T. "The Stability of Holland's Personality Types Over Time." *Journal of College Student Personnel,* 1976, *17,* 76-79.

Lunneborg, P. W. "Vocational Indecision in College Graduates." *Journal of Counseling Psychology,* 1976, *23,* 402-404.

Luther, R. K., and Smith, V. M. "A Functional Model for Career Development." [National Association of Student Personnel Administrators] *NASPA Journal,* 1974, *11,* 60-66.

McAlleer, C. A. "Life Planning: An Action-Oriented, Self-Directed Approach." Paper presented at 50th annual convention of American College Personnel Association, Atlanta, Ga., March 1975.

Maccoby, E., and Jacklin, C. *The Psychology of Sex Differences.* Stanford, Calif.: Stanford University Press, 1974.

Mencke, R. A., and Cochran, D. J. "Impact of a Counseling Outreach Workshop on Vocational Development." *Journal of Counseling Psychology,* 1974, *21,* 185-190.

Meyer, J. W. *The Effects of College Quality and Size on Student Occupational Choice.* Washington, D.C.: Office of Education, Department of Health, Education, and Welfare, 1970.

Miller, T. K. "A Student Development Model for Student Affairs in Tomorrow's Higher Education." *Journal of College Student Personnel,* 1975, *16,* 334-341.

Miller, T. K., and Prince, J. S. *The Future of Student Affairs: A Guide to Student Development for Tomorrow's Higher Education.* San Francisco: Jossey-Bass, 1976.

Monahan, L., Kuhn, D., and Shaver, P. "Intrapsychic Versus Cultural Explanations of the 'Fear of Success' Motive." *Journal of Personality and Social Psychology,* 1974, *29,* 60-64.

Morgan, D. "Perceptions of Role Conflicts and Self-Concepts Among Career and Non-Career College Educated Women." Unpublished doctoral dissertation, Columbia University, 1962.

Morrow, J. M. "A Test of Holland's Theory of Vocational Choice." *Journal of Counseling Psychology*, 1971, *18*, 422-425.

Mortimer, J. T. *Social Class, Work, and the Family: Some Implications of the Father's Occupation for Familial Relationships and Son's Career Decision.* Bethesda, Md.: National Institute of Mental Health, 1975.

National Advisory Council on Adult Education. *Career Renewal for Adults Through Education.* Washington, D.C.: National Advisory Council on Adult Education, 1972.

National Council on the Aging. *Staff Report on Conference Findings.* Appendix II. New York: National Council on the Aging, 1966.

Neugarten, B. L. "Adaptation and the Life Cycle." *The Counseling Psychologist*, 1976, *6*, 16-20.

Oliver, L. S. "Achievement and Affiliation Motivation in Career-Oriented and Homemaking-Oriented College Women." *Journal of Vocational Behavior*, 1974, *4*, 275-281.

Oman, R. N. "The Self-Concept of Occupational Ability and Related Characteristics in Community College Occupational and Academic Students." Unpublished doctoral dissertation, Michigan State University, 1971.

Osipow, S. H., and Gold, J. A. "Personal Adjustment and Career Development." *Journal of Counseling Psychology*, 1968, *15*, 439-443.

Pappas, J. P., and others. "Career Development Symposium." Paper presented at American Psychiatric Association Convention, Honolulu, September 1972.

Pfeifer, C. M. "Relationship Between Scholastic Aptitude, Perceptions of University Climate, and College Success for Black and White Students." *Journal of Applied Psychology*, 1976, *61*, 341-347.

Rapoza, R. S., and Blocher, D. H. "A Comparative Study of Academic Self-Estimates, Academic Values, and Academic Aspirations of Adolescent Males and Females." In L. S. Hansen and R. S. Rapoza (Eds.), *Career Development and Counseling of Women.* Springfield, Ill.: Thomas, 1978.

Reardon, R. C. "The Counselor and Career Information Services." *Journal of College Student Personnel*, 1973, *14*, 495-500.

Resnick, H., Fauble, M. L., and Osipow, S. H. "Vocational Crystallization and Self-Esteem in College Students." *Journal of Counseling Psychology*, 1970, *17*, 465-467.

Ryan, T. A. *Reinforcement Techniques and Simulation Materials for Counseling Clients with Decision-Making Problems.* Proceedings of 77th annual meeting of the American Psychological Association, Washington, D.C., August 1969.

Sander, D. L., and Wolff, W. W. "Computer-Assisted Career Development for College Students." *NASPA Journal*, 1975, *12*, 257-261.

Sarason, S. B., Sarason, E. K., and Cowden, P. "Aging and the Nature of Work." *American Psychologist*, 1975, *30*, 584-592.

Schlossberg, N. K., and Pietrofesa, J. J. "Perspectives on Counseling Bias: Implications for Counselor Education." *The Counseling Psychologist*, 1973, *4*, 44-54.

Schoenfeld, E. "Status and Career Decision: An Analysis of the Time Dimension." *Sociological Quarterly*, 1972, *13*, 496-507.

Scott, C. S., Fenske, R. H., and Maxey, E. J. "Change in Vocational Choice as a Function of Initial Career Choice, Interests, Abilities, and Sex." *Journal of Vocational Behavior*, 1974, *5*, 285-292.

Smith, R. D., and Evans, J. R. "Comparison of Experimental Group Guidance and Individual Counseling as Facilitators of Vocational Development." *Journal of Counseling Psychology*, 1973, *20*, 202-208.

Steinmann, A. "Female and Male Concepts of Sex Roles: An Overview of Twenty Years of Cross-Cultural Research." *International Mental Health Research Newsletter*, 1975, *17*, 2-11.

Titley, R. W., and others. "The Major Changers, Continuity or Discontinuity in the Career Decision Process." Colorado State University Student Development Reports. Fort Collins: Colorado State University, 1975.

Tomlinson-Keasey, C. "Role Variables: Their Influence on Female Motivational Constructs." *Journal of Counseling Psychology*, 1974, *21*, 232-237.

Tyler, L. E. "Counseling Girls and Women in the Year 2000." In E. Mathews (Ed.), *Counseling Girls and Women Over the Life Span*. Washington, D.C.: National Vocational Guidance Association, 1972.

U.S. Bureau of the Census. *School Enrollment—Social and Economic Characteristics of Students: October 1975*. Current Population Reports, Series P-2, No. 303. Washington, D.C.: U.S. Department of Commerce, 1976.

Vander Well, A. R. *Influence of Financial Need on the Vocational Development of College Students*. Iowa City, Iowa: American College Testing Program, Research and Development Division, 1970.

Van Dusen, R. A., and Sheldon, E. B. "The Changing Status of American Women: A Life Cycle Perspective." *American Psychologist*, 1976, *31*, 106-116.

Venerable, W. R. "Parental Influence on College and Vocational Decisions." *Journal of the National Association of College Admissions Counselors*, 1974, *19*, 9-12.

Wakefield, J. A., and others. "The Geometric Relationship Between Holland's Personality Typology and the Vocational Preference Inventory for Blacks." *Journal of Counseling Psychology*, 1975, *22*, 58-60.

Walsh, W. B. "Consistent Occupational Preference and Personality." *Journal of Vocational Behavior*, 1974, *4*, 145-152.

Waterman, A. S., and Waterman, C. K. *The Relationship Between Ego Identity Status and Satisfaction with College*. Troy, N.Y.: Rensselaer Polytechnic Institute, 1969.

Watley, D. J. *Stability of Career Choices of Talented Youth*. Evanston, Ill.: National Merit Scholarship Corporation, 1968.

Wells, J. A. *Continuing Education for Women: Current Developments*. Washington, D.C.: Employment Standards Administration, U.S. Women's Bureau, 1974.

Westbrook, F. P. *A Comparison of Three Methods of Group Vocational Counseling*. College Park: University of Maryland Counseling Center, 1973.

Wigent, P. A. "Personality Variables Related to Career Decision-Making Abilities of Community College Students." *Journal of College Student Personnel*, 1974, *15*, 105-108.

Wolfson, K. P. "Career Development Patterns of College Women." *Journal of Counseling Psychology*, 1976, *23*, 119-125.

Young, A. M. *Going Back to School at 35 or Over*. Special Labor Force Report 184. Washington, D.C.: Bureau of Labor Statistics, 1975.

Zagorski, H. G., and others. *Automatic Data Processing Systems and Procedures: Computerized Academic Counseling System*. Santa Monica, Calif.: Systems Development Corporation, 1973.

Zehring, J. W. "Rejection Shock." *Journal of College Placement*, 1975, *35*, 34-35.

10

David A. Kolb

Learning Styles and Disciplinary Differences

Along the Cleveland heights there is a vantage point where I can view the university spreading beneath me toward the horizon—in the foreground is the new medical complex of concrete and glass towers placed among older yellow brick hospitals and laboratories. To the left, stretched along the road that separates it from the medical buildings is the long, low, steel, glass and brick home of the natural science laboratories.

Nested against this brick and steel spine, lie vestiges of science past. On one side, the old physics building, large and austere with a red tile roof slowly turning black, and tall, narrow windows that belie the high-ceilinged dark rooms within. On the other side, two black stone fortress-like buildings, one capped by an observatory telescope. Paralleling these buildings around a mall punctuated at one end by a towering smokestack and at the other by a computer center office tower, lie the squat, functional ceramic brick and concrete buildings of the engineering and management schools, almost defiantly ugly, as though to emphasize that appearances are secondary to reality.

In the distance across Euclid Avenue, still another world—strong gothic stone

Note: I am indebted to David Brown, Arthur Chickering, and Suresh Srivastva for their comments and suggestions on this chapter.

buildings beside awkward Victorian red brick constructions, the old Western Reserve campus now home for the humanities and social sciences. Beyond is the flashy, contemporary law school building, its black one-way windows revealing as little inside as a state trooper's sunglasses. And finally, the serene, classic beauty of Severance Hall and the Museum of Art.

I have stopped here several times as I framed this essay. The diversity that lies below is staggering—not one university but many, each with its own language, norms, and values, its own ideas about the nature of truth and how it is to be sought. By crossing the street, or in some cases even the hallway, I can visit cultures that differ on nearly every dimension associated with the term. There are different languages (or at least dialects). There are strong boundaries defining membership and corresponding initiation rites. There are different norms and values about the nature of truth and how it is to be sought. There are different patterns of power and authority and differing criteria for attaining status. There are differing standards for intimacy and modes for its expression. Cultural variation is expressed in style of dress, furnishings, architecture, and use of space and time. Most important, these patterns of variation are not random but have a meaning and integrity for the members. There is in each department or profession a sense of historical continuity and in most cases historical mission.

While there are obviously points of interpenetration among these "cultures" and in some cases, true integration, I want here to emphasize the themes of differentiation and diversity.

In considering the student careers that are spawned and shaped in the university community and the university's responsibility for the intellectual, moral, and personal development of its members, we have often emphasized the unitary linear trend of human growth and development at the expense of acknowledging and managing the diverse developmental pathways that exist within different disciplines and professions. These paths foster some developmental achievements and, as we shall see, inhibit others. The channels of academic specialization are swift and deep, the way between them tortuous and winding. For example, these days the major career transitions in college are from science to the humanities (Davis, 1965). When I taught at M.I.T., I served for a while as a freshman adviser. Two or three of my students in each group faced the awkward realization near the end of their freshman year that a career in engineering was not quite what they had imagined it to be. What to do? Transfer to a liberal arts school and possibly lose the prestige of an M.I.T. education? Endure the institute's technological requirements and "bootleg" a humanities major? Switch to management? Most decided to wait and see but, in so doing, experienced a distinct loss of energy and increase in confusion. I felt powerless about what to advise or even how to advise.

It was only later that I was to discover that these shifts represented something more fundamental than changing interests—that they stemmed in many cases from fundamental mismatches between personal learning styles and the learning demands of different disciplines. That disciplines incline to different styles of learning is evident from the variations among their primary tasks, technologies and products, criteria for academic excellence and productivity, teaching methods, research methods, and methods for recording and portraying knowledge. Disciplines even show sociocultural variation—differences in faculty and student demographics, personality and aptitudes, as well as differences in values and group norms. For students, education in an academic field is a continuing process of selection and socialization to the pivotal norms of the field governing criteria for truth and how it is to be achieved, communicated, and used, and secondarily, to peripheral norms governing personal styles, attitudes, and social relationships.

Over time these selection and socialization pressures combine to produce an increasingly impermeable and homogeneous disciplinary culture and correspondingly specialized student orientations to learning. This, briefly, is the thesis I will attempt to articulate in this chapter.

In reviewing the research on differences among academic disciplines, I have been struck by the fact that relatively little comparative research has been done on academic disciplines and departments. In fact, Biglan (1973a) has stated:

> One of the most easily overlooked facts about university organization is that academic departments are organized according to subject matter. . . . While the organization of university departments has received increasing attention from social scientists . . . , the way in which subject matter characteristics may require particular forms of department organization has not been examined [p. 195].

The reason for this lies in the same difficulties that characterize all cross-cultural research —the problem of access and the problem of perspective. The relatively closed nature of academic subcultures makes access to data difficult, and it is equally difficult to choose a perspective for interpreting data that is unbiased. To analyze one system of inquiry according to the ground rules of another is to invite misunderstanding and conflict and further restrict access to data.

Studying disciplines from the perspective of learning and the learner offers some promise for overcoming these difficulties, particularly if learning is defined not in the narrow psychological sense of modification of behavior but in the broader sense of acquisition of knowledge. The access problem is eased because every discipline has a prime commitment to learning and inquiry and has developed a learning style that is at least moderately effective. Viewing the acquisition of knowledge in academic disciplines from the perspective of the learning process promises a dual reward—a more refined epistemology that defines the varieties of truth and their interrelationships and a greater psychological understanding of how individuals acquire knowledge in its different forms. Over fifteen years ago, in the distinguished predecessor to this volume, *The American College*, Carl Bereiter and Mervin Freedman envisioned these rewards:

> There is every reason to suppose that studies applying tests of these sorts to students in different fields could rapidly get beyond the point of demonstrating the obvious. We should, for instance, be able to find out empirically whether the biological taxonomist has special aptitudes similar to his logical counterpart in the field of linguistics. And there are many comparisons whose outcomes it would be hard to foresee. In what fields do the various memory abilities flourish? Is adaptive flexibility more common in some fields than in others? Because, on the psychological end, these ability measures are tied to theories of the structure or functioning of higher mental processes, and because, on the philosophical end, the academic disciplines are tied to theories of logic and cognition, empirical data linking the two should be in little danger of remaining for long in the limbo where so many correlational data stay [1962, pp. 567-68].

It is surprising that, with the significant exception of Piaget's pioneering work on genetic epistemology, few have sought to reap these rewards.

The research that has been done has focused primarily on what from the above perspective are the peripheral norms of academic disciplines rather than the pivotal norms governing learning and inquiry. Thus, studies have examined political and social attitudes and values (Bereiter and Freedman, 1962; Kirtz, 1966), personality patterns (Ral, 1956), aspirations and goals (Davis, 1964), sex distribution and other demographic variables

(Feldman, 1974), and social interactions (Biglan, 1973b; Hall, 1969). The bias of these studies is no doubt a reflection of the fact that psychological research has until quite recently been predominantly concerned with the social and emotional aspects of human behavior and development. Concern with cognitive or intellectual factors has been neatly wrapped into concepts of general intelligence. Thus, most early studies of intellectual differences among disciplines were only interested in which discipline had the smarter students (for example, Wolfle, 1954; Terman and Oden, 1947).

In the fifteen years since *The American College* was written, there has been a great burgeoning of research and theory focused on intellectual development and cognitive style—on how one comes to know his world and cope with it. The preceding chapters in this volume reflect this new focus of concern. As a result, we now have new tools and concepts available for the study of the learning process. My own research work during this time has focused on an approach to learning that seeks to integrate cognitive and socioemotional factors into an "experiential learning theory."

Experiential Learning Theory

The experiential learning model represents an integration of many of the intensive lines of research on cognitive development and cognitive style. The result is a model of the learning process that is consistent with the structure of human cognition and the stages of human growth and development. It conceptualizes the learning process in such a way that differences in individual learning styles and corresponding learning environments can be identified. The learning model is a dialectical one, similar to Jung's (1923) concept of personality types, according to which development is attained by higher-level integration and expression of nondominant modes of dealing with the world.

The theory is called *experiential learning* for two reasons. First, this term ties the theory historically to its intellectual origins in the social psychology of Kurt Lewin in the forties and the sensitivity training of the fifties and sixties. Second, it emphasizes the important role that experience plays in the learning process, an emphasis that differentiates this approach from other cognitive theories of the learning process. The core of the model is a simple description of the learning cycle—of how experience is translated into concepts, which, in turn, are used as guides in the choice of new experiences.

Learning is conceived as a four-stage cycle (see Figure 1). Immediate concrete experience is the basis for observation and reflection. An individual uses these observations to build an idea, generalization, or "theory" from which new implications for action can be deduced. These implications or hypotheses then serve as guides in acting to create new experiences. The learners, if they are to be effective, need four different kinds of

Figure 1. The Experiential Learning Model

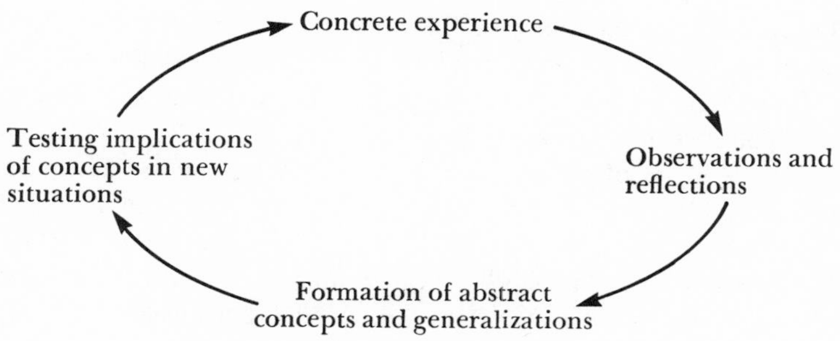

abilities: *Concrete Experience* abilities (CE), *Reflective Observation* abilities (RO), *Abstract Conceptualization* abilities (AC), and *Active Experimentation* (AE) abilities. That is, they must be able to involve themselves fully, openly, and without bias in new experiences (CE); they must be able to observe and reflect on these experiences from many perspectives (RO); they must be able to create concepts that integrate their observations into logically sound theories (AC); and they must be able to use these theories to make decisions and solve problems (AE). Yet this ideal is difficult to achieve. Can anyone become highly skilled in all these abilities, or are they necessarily in conflict? How can one be concrete and immediate and still be theoretical?

A closer examination of the four-stage learning model indicates that learning requires abilities that are polar opposites, and that the learner, as a result, must continually choose which set of learning abilities to bring to bear on various learning tasks. More specifically, there are two primary dimensions to the learning process. The first dimension represents the concrete experiencing of events, at one end, and abstract conceptualization at the other. The other dimension has active experimentation at one extreme and reflective observation at the other. Thus, in the process of learning, one moves in varying degrees from actor to observer, from specific involvement to general analytic detachment.

These two dimensions represent the major directions of cognitive development identified by Piaget. In his view, the course of individual cognitive development from birth to adolescence moves from a phenomenolistic (concrete) view of the world to a constructivist (abstract) view and from an egocentric (active) view to a reflective internalized mode of knowing. Piaget also maintains that these have also been the major directions of development in scientific knowledge (Piaget, 1970). Much other research has focused on one or the other of these two basic dimensions.

Many other cognitive psychologists (for example, Flavell, 1963; Bruner, 1960, 1966; Harvey, Hunt, and Schroeder, 1961) have identified the concrete-abstract dimension as a primary dimension on which cognitive growth and learning occur. Goldstein and Scheerer (1941, p. 4) suggest that greater abstractness results in the development of the following abilities:

1. To detach our ego from the outer world or from inner experience.
2. To assume a mental set.
3. To account for acts to oneself; to verbalize the account.
4. To shift reflectively from one aspect of the situation to another.
5. To hold in mind simultaneously various aspects.
6. To grasp the essential of a given whole; to break up a given into parts to isolate and to synthesize them.
7. To abstract common properties reflectively; to form hierarchic concepts.
8. To plan ahead ideationally, to assume an attitude toward the more possible, and to think or perform symbolically.

By contrast, concreteness, according to these theorists, represents the absence of these abilities, the immersion in and domination by one's immediate experiences. Yet the circular, dialectical model of the learning process would imply that abstractness is not exclusively good and concreteness exclusively bad. Witkin's (1962, 1976) extensive research on the related cognitive styles of global versus analytic functioning has shown that both extremes of functioning have their costs and benefits; the analytic style includes competence in analytical functioning combined with an impersonal orientation, while the global style reflects less competence in analytical functioning combined with greater social orientation and social skill. Similarly, when we consider the highest form of learning—

through creativity insights—we note a requirement that one be able to experience anew, freed somewhat from the constraints of previous abstract concepts. In psychoanalytic theory, this need for a concrete childlike perspective in the creative process is referred to as "regression in service of the ego" (Kris, 1952). Bruner (1966), in his essay on the conditions for creativity, emphasizes the dialectical tension between abstract and concrete involvement. For him, the creative act is a product of detachment and commitment, of passion and decorum, and of a freedom to be dominated by the object of one's inquiry.

The active-reflective dimension is the other major dimension of cognitive growth and learning that has received a great deal of attention from researchers. In the course of cognitive growth, thought becomes more reflective and internalized, based more on the manipulation of symbols and images than overt actions. The modes of active experimentation and reflection, like abstractness and concreteness, stand in opposition to one another. Kagan and Kogan's (1970) research on the cognitive-style dimension of reflection-impulsivity suggests that extremes of functioning on this continuum represent opposing definitions of competence and strategies for achieving. The impulsive strategy is based on seeking reward for active accomplishment, while the reflective strategy is based on seeking reward through the avoidance of error. Reflection tends to inhibit action and *vice versa*. For example, Singer (1968) has found that children who have active internal fantasy lives are more capable of inhibiting action for long periods of time than are children with little internal fantasy life. Kagan and others (1964) have found, however, that very active orientations toward learning situations inhibit reflection and thereby preclude the development of analytic concepts. Herein lies the second major dialectic in the learning process—the tension between actively testing the implications of one's hypotheses and reflectively interpreting data already collected.

Individual Learning Styles

As a result of our hereditary equipment, our particular past life experience, and the demands of our present environment, most of us develop learning styles that emphasize some learning abilities over others. Through socialization experiences in family, school, and work, we come to resolve the conflicts between action and reflection and between immediate experience and detached analysis in characteristic ways. Some people develop minds that excel at assimilating disparate facts into coherent theories, yet these same people may be incapable of, or uninterested in, deducing hypotheses from those theories. Others are logical geniuses but find it impossible to involve themselves in active experience. And so on. A mathematician may emphasize abstract concepts, while a poet may value concrete experience more highly. A manager may be primarily concerned with the active application of ideas, while a naturalist may concentrate on developing observational skills. Each of us develops a unique learning style, which has both strong and weak points. Evidence for the existence of consistent unique learning styles can be found in the research of both Kagan and Witkin, cited earlier (Kagan and Kogan, 1970). Their research, while supporting Piaget's view that there is a general tendency to become more analytic and reflective with age, indicates that individual rankings within the population tested remain highly stable from early years to adulthood. That is, individuals seem to develop consistent and distinctive cognitive styles.

We have developed a brief self-descriptive inventory called the Learning Style Inventory (LSI) to measure differences in learning styles along the two basic dimensions of abstract-concrete and active-reflective (Kolb, 1976a). Although the individuals tested on the LSI show many different patterns of scores, we have identified four statistically prevalent types of learning styles. We have called these four styles the Converger, the Diverger, the Assimilator, and the Accommodator. The characteristics of these types are based both on research and clinical observation of these patterns of LSI scores.

Convergers' dominant learning abilities are Abstract Conceptualization and Active Experimentation. Their greatest strength lies in the practical application of ideas. We have called this learning style the *Converger* because persons with this style seems to do best in those situations, like conventional intelligence tests, where there is a single correct answer or solution to a question or problem (Torrealba, 1972). These persons organize knowledge in such a way that, through hypothetical-deductive reasoning, they can focus it on specific problems. Liam Hudson's (1966) research in this style of learning (using different measures than the LSI) shows that convergers are relatively unemotional, preferring to deal with things rather than people. They tend to have narrow interests and often choose to specialize in the physical sciences. Our research shows that this learning style is characteristic of many engineers (Kolb, 1976a).

Divergers have the opposite learning strengths from those of the Convergers. They are best at Concrete Experience and Reflective Observation. Their greatest strength lies in imaginative ability. They excel in the ability to view concrete situations from many perspectives and to organize many relationships into a meaningful "gestalt." We have labeled this style *Diverger* because persons of this type perform better in situations that call for generation of ideas, such as "brainstorming" sessions. Divergers are interested in people and tend to be imaginative and emotional. They have broad cultural interests and tend to specialize in the arts. Our research shows that this style is characteristic of persons with humanities and liberal arts backgrounds. Counselors, organization development consultants, and personnel managers often have this learning style.

Assimilators' dominant learning abilities are Abstract Conceptualization and Reflective Observation. Their greatest strength lies in the ability to create theoretical models. They excel in inductive reasoning, in assimilating disparate observations into an integrated explanation (Grochow, 1973). They, like the convergers, are less interested in people and more concerned with abstract concepts, but less concerned with the practical use of theories. It is more important that the theory be logically sound and precise. As a result, this learning style is more characteristic of the basic sciences and mathematics than of the applied sciences. In organizations, this learning style is found most often in the research and planning departments (Kolb, 1976a; Strasmore, 1973).

Accommodators have the opposite strengths from those of the Assimilators. They are best at Concrete Experience and Active Experimentation. Their greatest strength lies in doing things, in carrying out plans and experiments and becoming involved in new experiences. They tend to be risk-takers more than persons with the other three learning styles. We have labeled this style *Accommodator* because persons with this style tend to excel in situations that call for adaptation to specific immediate circumstances. In situations where the theory or plan does not fit the facts they will most likely discard the plan or theory. (The opposite type, the Assimilator, would be more likely to disregard or re-examine the facts.) They tend to solve problems in an intuitive trial-and-error manner (Grochow, 1973), relying heavily on other people for information rather than their own analytical ability (Stabel, 1973). Accommodators are at ease with people but are sometimes seen as impatient and "pushy." Their educational backgrounds are often in technical or practical fields such as business. In organizations, people with this learning style are found in "action-oriented" jobs, often in marketing or sales.

It is important to stress that these types should not become stereotypes. Perhaps the greatest contribution of research on cognitive style has been the documentation of the diversity and complexity of cognitive processes and their manifestation in behavior. Three important dimensions of diversity have been identified:

1. Within any single theoretical dimension of cognitive functioning it is possible to identify consistent subtypes. For example, it appears that the dimension of cognitive complexity-simplicity can be further divided into at least three distinct subtypes: (1) the tendency to judge events with few variables versus many, (2) the tendency to make fine versus gross distinctions on a given dimension, and (3) the tendency to prefer order and structure versus tolerance of ambiguity (Vannoy, 1965).

2. Cognitive functioning in individuals will vary as a function of the area or content it is focused on—the so-called *cognitive domain*. Thus, an individual may be concrete in interactions with people and abstract in work (Stabel, 1973), and children will analyze and classify persons differently than nations (Signell, 1966).

3. Cultural experience plays a major role in the development and expression of cognitive functioning. Lessor (1976) has shown consistent differences in thinking style across different American ethnic groups; Witkin (1967) has shown differences in global and abstract functioning in different cultures; and Bruner and others (1966) have shown differences in the rate and direction of cognitive development across cultures. Though the evidence is not conclusive, it would appear that these cultural differences in cognition, in Michael Cole's words, "reside more in the situations to which cognitive processes are applied than in the existence of a process in one cultural group and its absence in another" (1971, p. 233). Thus, Cole found that African Kpelle tribesmen were skillful at measuring rice but not at measuring distance. Similarly, Wober (1967) found that Nigerians functioned more analytically than Americans when measured by a test that emphasized proprioceptive cues, whereas they were less skilled at visual analysis.

Inquiry Norms of Academic Disciplines

My first hint that experiential learning theory might provide a useful framework for describing variations in the inquiry norms of academic disciplines came when we examined the undergraduate majors of a large sample of 800 practicing managers and graduate students in management. We found that, although these individuals shared a common occupation, they showed variations in learning style that were strongly associated with their undergraduate educational experience (Kolb, 1976b). Figure 2 shows the average Learning Style Inventory scores for various undergraduate majors reported by the managers. (Only majors with more than ten respondents are included.) Undergraduate business majors tended to have accommodative learning styles, while engineers, on the average, fell into the convergent quadrant. History, English, political science, and psychology majors all had divergent learning styles. Mathematics and chemistry majors had assimilative learning styles, as did economics and sociology majors. Physics majors were very abstract, falling between the convergent and assimilative quadrants. These data suggested that undergraduate education was a major factor in shaping individual learning style, whether by the process of selection into a discipline, or by socialization in the course of learning in that discipline, or both.

Results from other studies are consistent with these findings. Anthony Biglan (1973a) used a method well suited to answering these questions in his studies of faculty members at the University of Illinois and at a small western college. Using the technique of multidimensional scaling, he analyzed the underlying structures of scholars' judgments

Figure 2. Learning Style Inventory Scores on Active-Reflective (AE-RO)
and Abstract-Concrete (AO-CE) Dimensions by College Major

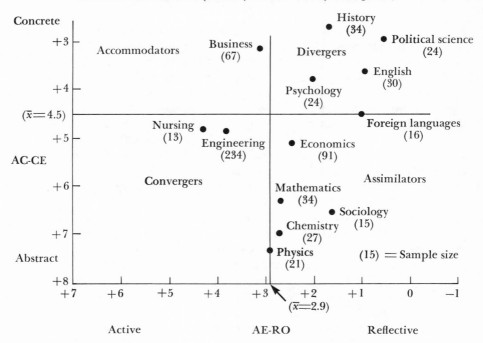

about the similarities of subject matter in different academic disciplines. The procedure
required faculty members to group subject areas on the basis of similarity, without any
labeling of the groupings. Through a kind of factor analysis, the similarity groupings were
then mapped onto an n-dimensional space, n being determined by closeness of fit and
interpretability of the dimensions. The two dimensions accounting for the most variance
in the University of Illinois data were identified by Biglan as *hard-soft* and *pure-applied.*
The mapping of the academic disciplines on this two-dimensional space (Figure 3), reveals
a great similarity between Biglan's data and the clustering of data on the learning style
dimensions of abstract-concrete and reflective-active. Of the twelve disciplines common
to the two studies, nine are in identical quadrants. Business (assumed equivalent to accounting and finance) is accommodative in learning style terms. Engineering is convergent, whereas physics, mathematics, and chemistry are assimilative. The humanistic fields
of history, political science, English, and psychology fall into the divergent quadrant.
Foreign languages, economics, and sociology were divergent in Biglan's study rather than
assimilative. Biglan reported that the pattern of relationships between disciplines shown
by the small college data was very similar to that shown by the Illinois data.

These two studies suggest that the abstract-concrete and active-reflective dimensions identified by experiential learning theory differentiate sharply among academic disciplines. A more extensive data base is needed, however. The learning style data came
from a single occupation, and in the case of some academic areas sample sizes were small.
Biglan's study was limited to two universities, and differences here could be attributed to
the specific characteristics of these academic departments.

In search of a more extensive and representative sample, I examined data collected
in the Carnegie Commission on Higher Education 1969 study of representative American

**Figure 3. Classification of Academic Disciplines at the University of Illinois
on Hard-Soft and Pure-Applied Dimensions**

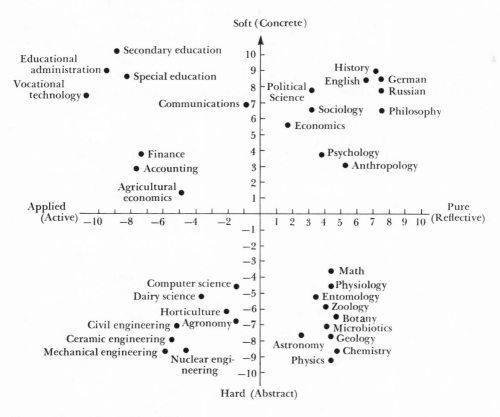

Source: Adopted from Biglan, 1973a.

colleges and universities. These data consisted of 32,963 questionnaires from graduate students in 158 institutions and 60,028 questionnaires from faculty in 303 institutions. Using tabulations of this data reported in Feldman (1974), I created ad hoc indexes of the abstract-concrete and active-reflective dimensions for the forty-five academic fields identified in the study. The abstract-concrete index was based on graduate students' responses to two questions asking how important undergraduate backgrounds in mathematics and humanities were for their fields. Mathematics is an abstract field, relying heavily on models, theories, and symbolic manipulation, whereas the humanities are concrete, involving human feelings, intuition, and metaphorical representation of knowledge. There was, as predicted, a strong negative correlation (−.78) between the answers to the mathematics and humanities questions. The index was computed using the percentage of graduate student respondents who strongly agreed that either humanities or mathematics was very important:

% Math important + (100−% Humanities important)
2

Thus, high index scores indicated an abstract field in which a mathematics background was important and humanities not important.

The active-reflective index used faculty data on the percentage of faculty in a given field who were engaged in paid consultation to business, government, or other organizations. This seemed to be the best indicator on the questionnaire of the active, applied orientation of the field. As Feldman (1974) observed, "Consulting may be looked upon not only as a source of added income but also as an indirect measure of the 'power' of a discipline, that is, as a chance to exert the influence and knowledge of a discipline outside the academic setting" (p. 52). The groupings of academic fields based on these indexes are shown in Figure 4.

Figure 4. Concrete-Abstract and Active-Reflective Orientations of Academic Fields Derived from the Carnegie Commission Study

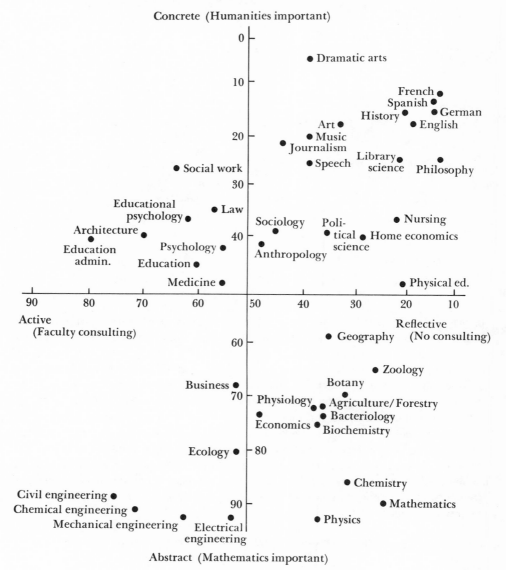

Concrete (Humanities important)

Active (Faculty consulting)

Reflective (No consulting)

Abstract (Mathematics important)

The indexes reveal a pattern of relationships among academic fields that is highly consistent with Biglan's study and the managerial learning style data. The results suggest that the commonly accepted division of academic fields into two camps, the scientific and the artistic, or abstract and concrete (for example, Snow, 1963; Hudson, 1966), might be usefully enriched by the addition of a second dimension, namely, active-reflective or applied-basic. When academic fields are mapped on this two-dimensional space, a fourfold typology of disciplines emerges. In the abstract-reflective quadrant are clustered the *natural sciences and mathematics,* while the abstract-active quadrant includes the *science-based professions,* most notably the engineering fields. The concrete-active quadrant encompasses what might be called the *social professions,* such as education, social work, and law. The concrete-reflective quadrant includes the *humanities and social sciences.* Further evidence for the validity of this typology can be seen in the different ways that knowledge is structured and created in these fields.

Knowledge Structures and Inquiry Processes

When one examines the four major groupings of disciplines just cited—the natural sciences and mathematics, the science-based professions, the social professions, and the humanities and social sciences—it becomes apparent that what constitutes valid knowledge differs widely from one to another. This is easily observed in differences in how knowledge is reported (for example, numerical or logical symbols, words or images), in inquiry methods (for example, case studies, experiments, logical analysis), and in criteria for evaluation (for example, practical versus statistical significance). Currently we are developing a typology that describes the basic structural dimensions of different knowledge systems (see Table 1). In this typology, the professions can be seen to employ predominantly discrete inquiry strategies, aimed at understanding particular events or phenomena,

Table 1. A Typology of Knowledge Structures and Inquiry Processes
in Four Types of Academic Disciplines

Discipline Type	Social Professions	Science-based Professions	Natural Science and Mathematics	Humanities and Social Science
Inquiry strategy	Discrete synthesis	Discrete analysis	Integrative analysis	Integrative synthesis
Dominant philosophy	Pragmatism	Empiricism	Structuralism	Organicism
Theory of truth	Workability	Correspondence	Correlation of structure with secondary qualities	Coherence
Basic inquiry question	How	When, Where	What	Why
Basic units of knowledge	Events	Natural laws, empirical uniformities	Structures	Processes
How knowledge is portrayed	Actions	Things	Symbols	Images
Typical inquiry method	Case study	Classical experiment	Model building	Historical analysis Field study Clinical observation

whereas the basic disciplines employ more integrated strategies, in their search for structures or processes that apply universally. The scientific professions and basic disciplines are predominantly analytical, seeking to understand wholes by identifying their component parts, whereas the social-humanistic fields tend to be synthetic, believing that the whole can never be explained solely by its component parts. The impact of a poem, play or painting, for example, cannot be understood by analytic dissection but only by grasping the totality. Human behavior and economic systems require similar synthetic approaches.

In the social professions the dominant philosophy is pragmatism, and truth as defined by workability. Inquiry centers around the question of how actions shape events. The case study is a common method of inquiry and analysis. In the science-based professions, empiricism is the dominant philosophy, and correspondence is the main criterion for truth. Thus, knowledge is created by locating phenomena in time (when) and space (where). Here the emphasis is on the analysis, measurement, and categorization of observable experience and the establishment of empirical uniformities defining relationships between observed categories (natural laws), with a minimum of reliance on inferred structures or processes that are not directly accessible to public experience. The classical experimental method is the typical inquiry method.

Mathematics and natural science are dominated by a structuralist philosophy, which seeks to distinguish the primary, essential elements and relationships in a phenomenon from the secondary, accidental relationships. Piaget (1968) defines these structures as follows:

> As a first approximation we may say that a structure is a system of transformations. Inasmuch as it is a system and not a mere collection of elements and their properties, these transformations involve laws: the structure is preserved or enriched by the interplay of its transformation laws, which never yield results external to the system nor employ elements that are external to it. In short, the notion of structure is comprised of three key ideas: the idea of wholeness, the idea of transformation, and the idea of self-regulation [p. 5].

Thus, quantitative model building is a typical inquiry method. The humanities and the social sciences share an organicist philosophy concerned with basic processes. The primary criterion for truth is coherence, a meaningful "gestalt" that integrates phenomena. Here there is a concern with ultimate values, with why things are as they are. The anthropological field study, historical analysis, and clinical observation are typical inquiry methods.

Some fields seem to include within their boundaries considerable variation in inquiry norms and knowledge structures. Several of the professions (particularly management, medicine, and architecture) are themselves multidisciplinary, including specialties that emphasize different learning styles. Medicine requires both a concern for human service and scientific knowledge. Architecture has requirements for artistic and engineering excellence. Management involves skill at both quantitative and qualitative analysis. Several of the social sciences, particularly psychology, sociology, and economics, can vary greatly in their basic inquiry paradigms. Clinical psychology emphasizes divergent learning skills, while experimental psychology emphasizes convergent skills; industrial and educational psychology emphasize practical, accommodative skills. Sociology can be highly abstract and theoretical (as in Parsonian structural functionalism) or concrete and active (as in phenomenology or ethnomethodology). Some economics departments may employ very convergent modes of inquiry, emphasizing the use of econometric models in public policy; others may employ divergent modes, emphasizing economic history and philosophy.

This brief description cannot do justice to the complexity and variation of inquiry processes and knowledge structures in various disciplines. Nevertheless, it may suggest how the forms of knowledge in different fields can be differentially attractive and meaningful to individuals with different learning styles. Indeed, every field will show variation on these dimensions within a given department, between departments, from undergraduate to graduate levels, and so on. The purpose of this analysis is not to pigeonhole fields but to identify useful dimensions for describing variations in individual learning styles and in the inquiry processes of different disciplines, in order to better understand and manage the educational process.

Impact of Disciplinary Norms on Student Learning

The selection of Charles Eliot as President of Harvard in 1869 marked the end of classical education in American colleges; no longer would all students take the same courses in Greek, Latin, and mathematics. By introducing electives and "majors" into the Harvard curriculum, Eliot began what, considering the rapid growth of knowledge, was the inevitable specialization and fragmentation that characterizes the modern university. In the system that has emerged in the last 100 years, students have been increasingly free to select their courses and to define a program suited to their needs, interests, and abilities. Academic disciplines have enjoyed a corresponding freedom to choose those students who best fit their requirements.

The result is an educational system that emphasizes specialized learning and development through the accentuation of the student's skills and interests. The student's developmental process is a product of the interaction between his or her choices and socialization experiences in academic disciplines. That is, the student's dispositions lead to the choice of educational experiences that match those dispositions, and the resulting experiences further reinforce the same choice dispositions for later experiences.

Witkin (1976) has shown, for example, that global (field-dependent) students choose specializations that favor involvement with people, such as teaching, sales, management, and the humanities, while analytical (field-independent) students choose areas that favor analysis, such as the physical sciences, engineering, and technical and mechanical activities. Clinical psychology graduate students tend to be global, whereas experimental psychology graduate students tend to be analytical. In addition, Witkin has found that when cognitive style matches the demands of a given career specialization, higher performance results.

It is important to note that cognitive style affects not only the content of choices but also the choice *process* itself. Thus, global students make choices preferred by their peer group, while analytical students are more likely to use systematic planning and goal setting. Plovnick (1974) found a similar pattern when he used the Learning Style Inventory (LSI) to study medical students' choice of medical specialty. There are significant relationships between the LSI scores and specific choices made—accommodators chose family medicine and family care; assimilators chose academic medicine; divergers chose psychiatry; and convergers chose medical specialties. In addition, LSI scores were related to the process of choosing—students who thought in concrete terms tended to base their choices on role models and acquaintances, while abstract thinkers relied on theoretical material and interest in subject matter.

Robert Altmeyer (1966) has dramatically illustrated the result of the accentuation process on cognitive abilities in his comparative study of engineering/science and fine arts students at Carnegie Tech. In a cross-sectional study, he administered two batteries of tests to students at all levels in the two schools—one battery measured analytical reasoning, the other creative thinking. As predicted, engineering and science students scored highest on analytical reasoning and fine arts students highest on creative thinking; over the college years these gaps widened; engineering and science students became more analytical and arts students more creative. The surprising finding was that engineering and science students decreased in creative thinking and fine art students decreased in analytical reasoning over the college years. Thus, educational processes that accentuated one set of cognitive skills also appeared to produce loss of ability in the contrasting set of skills.

We found further evidence for the accentuation process in a large survey of M.I.T. seniors (Kolb and Goldman, 1973). Results showed a correspondence between learning style and departmental major consistent with the findings reported earlier in this chapter. In most cases, students who planned graduate study in their major field had learning styles more strongly biased toward the inquiry norms of their field than those who did not; for example, management students pursuing graduate study were more accommodative, while potential mathematics graduate students were more assimilative. To examine the dynamics of the accentuation process in greater detail, four departments whose learning style demands matched the four dominant learning styles were selected for case study. The four departments chosen and their learning style demands were mechanical engineering = accommodation; humanities = divergent thinking; mathematics = assimilation; and economics = convergent thinking (see Kolb and Goldman, 1973, for details of this selection process). Students in these four departments who planned careers in their major field tended to have learning styles that matched the inquiry demands of the field. Those whose learning styles were not matched tended to choose careers outside of their field of study. In addition, matched students indicated greater commitment to their chosen career than mismatched students.

Learning Styles, Academic Performance, and Adaptation

To ascertain if students' learning styles were an important determinant of their social adaptation and performance in the university, we compared, on a number of variables, the students whose learning styles fit their disciplines' demands with the students whose learning styles did not fit in the four departments mentioned previously. To begin with, student cumulative grade averages were examined. The mechanical engineering and economics departments both showed results consistent with our prediction; accommodative students in mechanical engineering had higher grades ($p < .10$) than mechanical engineering students with other learning styles, while convergent students in economics had much higher grades ($p < .001$) than economics students with other learning styles. In the mathematics department, however, there was no difference between the two groups of students, and in humanities the six students whose learning style was not divergent had somewhat higher grades. While the humanities department results represent a reversal of our original prediction, the results offer evidence for the hypothesis that humanities and the divergent learning style associated with this academic area are incongruent with the convergent engineering norms of M.I.T. as a whole; thus, humanities students who are not divergers should perform better academically.

The same pattern of results was found when another aspect of academic performance, student perceptions of how heavy the academic workload is, was examined. In mechanical engineering, mathematics, and economics, those students whose learning styles were congruent with their discipline norms felt the workload to be lighter than those students whose learning styles did not "fit." (Statistical significance levels for mathematics and economics were $p < .05$ and $p < .10$, respectively.) Again, the humanities department showed a trend in the opposite direction.

We were also interested to see if mismatches between learning style and discipline demands had any effect on the student's social adaptation to the university. Incongruence between students' learning styles and the norms of their majors might well undermine their feelings of belonging to the university community and alienate them from the power structure (faculty and administration). To test these hypotheses we used a version of Olsen's political alienation scale (1969) and McCloskey and Schaar's anomie scale (1963), which were adapted to apply specifically to the M.I.T. environment (see Kolb, Rubin, and Schein, 1972, for complete details of these scales). These scales measure two uncorrelated aspects of alienation that influence student adaptation. Political alienation results from the failure of authorities, teachers, administrative officials, and the "system" as a whole to meet the student's needs. The politically alienated student feels that the authority structure of the university is not legitimate because it is unconcerned about students, because it does not involve them in its decision procedures, because it allows its priorities to be set by vested interests, and because it is incapable of solving the problems it faces. Anomie stems not from dissatisfaction with the formal authority system but from a lack of contact with the norms and values that determine and direct behavior of individuals in the university. These norms and values are communicated most directly through conflict with one's peers. We have found, for example, that feelings of anomie among M.I.T. students are strongly associated with lack of involvement in a personally important group of peers (Kolb, Rubin, and Schein, 1972). Anomic students feel lonely, isolated, and out of place at M.I.T. They have difficulty determining what is expected of them and what they themselves believe. Political alienation and anomie scores for matched and mismatched students were generally consistent with our prediction: more anomie and political alienation were found among those students whose learning styles were incongruent with their discipline norms. (None of the political alienation differences were significant statistically, however. Anomie significance levels for humanities and economics were $p < .10$ and $p < .01$, respectively). One interesting result was the very high political alienation scores of all students in the humanities department. Humanities, in fact, scored highest on this variable of all the departments in the institute. This further develops the pattern of humanities as a deviant learning environment at M.I.T.

Further insight into the impact of learning styles on social adaptation was gained by examining student involvement with an important peer group. As we have already noted, our previous research showed high involvement with peers to be associated with low anomie. In all four departments, students with learning styles matching departmental norms tended to be highly involved with their peers. This pattern was most pronounced in the humanities ($p < .05$) and economics ($p < .01$) departments. These results suggest that student peer groups may be an important vehicle for the communication of the learning style requirements of a department, although, as we already know from many studies of formal and informal organizations, peer group norms may sometimes run counter to the formal organizational requirements. Some evidence for this special role of the peer group can be seen in a comparison of the economics and humanities departments. In both of these departments, students whose learning styles matched the discipline demands were very involved with their peers; and both groups of students scored very low in anomie, as we predicted. Yet the convergent economics students scored very low in political alienation, while the divergent humanities students felt extremely politically alienated from the university. Thus, in humanities, student peer group solidarity among divergers was apparently based on norms of alienation and rebellion from the university, while in economics the convergent peer group norms supported the goals and procedures of the formal authorities. This may in part account for the fact that the grades of the divergent humanities students were lower than those of other humanities students, while the grades of the convergent economics students were far higher than those of other students in economics.

The M.I.T. study was undertaken to ascertain the usefulness of the experiential learning model and the typology of learning styles derived from it for describing variations in the ways individuals learn and variations in the learning demands of different academic disciplines. The results of the study show that, at least in this one institution, the learning style typology is useful for describing the learning demands of different academic departments and for predicting the direction of student career choices. Additionally, through examination of the matches and mismatches between student learning styles and departmental learning demands, the typology helps to explain variations in academic performance and adaptation to the university. These results suggest that the experiential learning model may well provide a useful framework for the design and management of learning experiences. As we have noted, the dominant trend in research on classroom and cut-of-class learning environments has been to focus on the impact on performance and adaptation, of such social-emotional variables as motivation, attitudes, participation, liking for the teacher, and social isolation. Many of these variables have been shown to be important. However, the results of the M.I.T. study suggest that learning environments might as productively be examined in terms of their impact on the learning process itself, and on the learning styles of students. Rather than being a cause of successful academic performance, motivation to learn may well be a result of learning climates that match learning styles and thereby produce successful learning experiences. Similarly, the sources of student alienation and protest may lie as much in failures to achieve the university's central mission—learning—as they do in its social milieu.

Experiential Learning Model of Personal Growth

In addition to providing a framework for conceptualizing individual differences in learning styles and social adaptation, the experiential learning model suggests more normative directions for human growth and development. As we have seen, individual learning styles affect not only academic learning but also broader aspects of adaptation to life, such as decision making, problem solving, and life-style in general. Experiential learning is not a molecular educational concept but rather a molar concept describing the central process of human adaptation to the social and physical environment. Like Jungian theory (Jung, 1923), it is a holistic concept that seeks to describe the emergence of basic life orientations as a function of dialectical tensions between basic modes of relating to the world. As such, it encompasses other more limited adaptive concepts, such as creativity, problem solving, decision making, and attitude change, which focus heavily on one or another of the basic aspects of adaptation. Thus, creativity research has tended to focus on the divergent (concrete and reflective) factors in adaptation, such as tolerance for ambiguity, metaphorical thinking, and flexibility, while research on decision making has emphasized more convergent (abstract and active) adaptive factors, such as the rational evaluation of solution alternatives.

From this broader perspective, learning becomes a central life task, and how one learns becomes a major determinant of the course of personal development. The experiential learning model provides a means of mapping the different developmental strategies and also a normative adaptive ideal—a learning process wherein the individual has highly developed abilities to experience, observe, conceptualize, and experiment.

The human growth process can be divided into three broad developmental stages (Kolb and Fry, 1975). The first stage, Acquisition, extends from birth to adolescence and marks the acquisition of basic learning abilities and cognitive structures. The second stage, Specialization, extends through formal education or career training and the early experiences of adulthood in work and personal life. In this stage, development primarily follows paths that accentuate a particular learning style. Individuals shaped by social, educational, and organizational socialization forces develop increased competence in a specialized mode of adaptation that enables them to master the particular life tasks they encounter in their chosen career path. This stage, in our thinking, terminates at mid career, although the specific chronology of the transition to the third stage will vary widely from person to person and from one career path to another. The third stage, Integration, is marked by the reassertion and expression of the nondominant adaptive modes or learning styles. Means of adapting to the world that have been suppressed or have lain fallow during development of the more highly rewarded dominant learning style now find expression in the form of new career interests, changes in life-styles, or new creativity in one's chosen career.

Through these three stages, development is marked by increasing complexity and relativism in dealing with the world and one's experiences, and by higher-level integrations of the dialectical conflicts between the four primary adaptive modes—Concrete Experience, Reflective Observation, Abstract Conceptualization, and Active Experimentation. With each of these four modes, a major dimension of personal growth is associated. Development in the Concrete Experience adaptive mode is characterized by increases in *affective complexity*. Development in the Reflective Observation mode is characterized by increases in *perceptual complexity*. Development in the Abstract Conceptualization and Active Experimentation modes is characterized, respectively, by increases in *symbolic complexity* and *behavioral complexity*.

In the early stages of development, progress along one of these four dimensions can occur with relative independence from the others. The child and young adult, for example, can develop highly sophisticated symbolic proficiencies and remain naive emotionally. At the highest stages of development, however, the adaptive commitment to learning and creativity produces a strong need for integration of the four adaptive modes. Development in one mode induces development in the others. Increases in symbolic complexity, for example, refine and sharpen both perceptual and behavioral capabilities. Thus, complexity and the integration of dialectical conflicts among the adaptive modes are the hallmarks of true creativity and growth.

Figure 5 graphically illustrates the experiential learning model of growth and development as it has been outlined thus far. The four dimensions of growth are depicted in the shape of a cone, whose tapering toward the apex represents the fact that the four dimensions become more highly integrated at higher stages of development. Any individual learning style would be represented on this cone by four data points on the four vertical dimensions of development. Thus, a converger in the second (Specialization) stage of development would be characterized by high complexity in the symbolic and behavioral modes and lower complexity in the affective and perceptual modes. As this person moved into the third stage of development, complexity scores in the affective and perceptual modes would increase.

While we have depicted the stages of the growth process in the form of a simple three-layer cone, the actual process of growth in any single individual life history probably proceeds through successive oscillations from one stage to another. Thus, a person may move from stage two to three in several separate subphases of integrative advances, followed by consolidation or regression into specialization. (For a more detailed description of this development model, see Kolb and Fry, 1975.)

Figure 5. The Experiential Learning Theory of Growth and Development

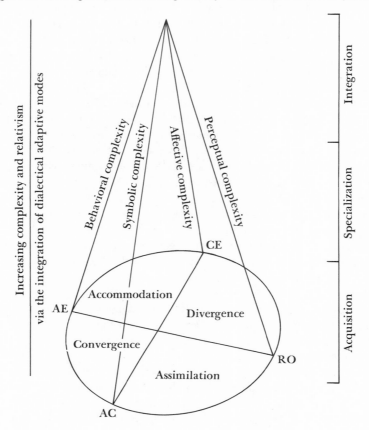

Specialization Versus Integration in Adult Development

As we have seen in previous chapters in this volume, there is considerable agreement among students of adult development that growth occurs through processes of differentiation and hierarchical integration and that the highest stages of development are
characterized by personal integrations of complex, highly articulated views of the world
and one's experience in it. From the perspective of experiential learning theory, this goal
is attained through a dialectical process of adaptation, achieved through the expression of
nondominant modes of dealing with the world and their higher-level integration with specialized functions. For many, however, the needs of modern society seem to be in direct
conflict with these individual developmental needs. Jung (1923) puts this case as follows:

> The favoritism of the superior function is just as serviceable to society as it
> is prejudicial to the individuality. This prejudicial effect has reached such a pitch
> that the great organizations of our present-day civilization actually strive for the
> complete disintegration of the individual, since their very existence depends upon
> a mechanical application of the preferred individual functions of men. It is not
> man that counts but his one differentiated function. Man no longer appears as
> man in collective civilization; he is merely represented by a function—nay, further,
> he is even exclusively identified with this function and denied any responsible
> membership to the other inferior functions. Thus, the modern individual sinks to

the level of a mere function because this it is that represents a collective value and alone affords a possibility of livelihood. But as Schiller clearly discerns, differentiation of function could have come about in no other way: "There was no other means to develop man's manifold capacities than to set them one against the other. This antagonism of human qualities is the great instrument of culture; it is only the instrument, however, for so long as it endures man is only upon the way to culture" [p. 94].

Yet the implication of Schiller's (1826) observation is that, although human beings are the instruments of culture in their specialized adaption, they are creators of culture through integrative fulfillment. This can be illustrated by comparing the development of scientific knowledge and the personal career paths of scientists. As Piaget (1970) and others (for example, Kuhn, 1962) have documented, the historical development of scientific knowledge has been increasingly specialized, moving from egocentricism to reflection and from phenomenalism to constructivism—in experiential learning terms, from active to reflective and concrete to abstract. Yet the careers of successful scientists follow a different path. These individuals usually make their specialized abstract-reflective contributions quite early in their careers. With recognition of their achievements comes a new set of tasks with active and concrete demands. Nobel Prize winners must help to shape social policy and to articulate the ethical and value implications of their discoveries. Researchers become department chairmen and concern themselves with nurturing the development of the younger generation. So in this career, and most others as well, the higher levels of responsibility require an integrative perspective that can help shape cultural responses to emergent issues. In fact, there are integrative developmental challenges at all occupational levels.

Implications for Higher Education

At present, higher education encourages early specialization, which necessarily accentuates particular interests and skills. Should we continue to follow the trend toward increasingly specialized education or should we be creating new educational programs that reassert the integrative emphasis lost in the demise of classical education? Coincidentally, as I write this conclusion, I have just received Derek Bok's 1976-77 President's report for Harvard University (Bok, 1978), outlining a revised undergraduate curriculum plan—a plan that some have characterized as a return to classical education, with its compulsory core courses in science and mathematics, literature and the arts, history, philosophy and social analysis, and foreign cultures. The pendulum swing toward specialization that Charles Eliot began in 1869 with the modest introduction of electives and the concept of a major may have reached its peak in the late 1960s in the course proliferation that came with student demands for relevance and participation in the educational decisions that affected their lives. The "back to basic skills" climate that seemed to permeate American education at all levels in the 1970s may among other things signal the reassertion of an integrative emphasis in the educational process.

There is little question that integrative development is important for both personal fulfillment and cultural development. It appears essential for growth and mastery of the period of adult development that Erikson has called the crisis of generativity versus stagnation. The educational issue is how and when to intervene in a way that facilitates this development. The "hows" are not easy. Bok compared the introduction of the new core curriculum to "reorganizing a graveyard." Specialization in the university is greatly reinforced by faculty reward systems, selection and evaluation criteria, and disciplinary values. The impact of these organizational processes is brought into sharp focus when we examine the difficulties and obstacles that attend the establishment of truly interdisciplinary programs of research or teaching, or when we examine the struggles for survival and viability that face "deviant" disciplines in an institution where attention, resources, and prestige are focused on the dominant academic culture. Even at a scientific institute like M.I.T. where the humanities are firmly established with a distinguished faculty, we see intense student alienation, departmental evaluation standards that appear more attuned to the inquiry norms of engineering than the humanities, and a subtle but powerful imperialism of the dominant scientific culture on research and teaching activities. However useful scientific analyses of the humanities (for example, computer models of Greek myths) may be in their own right, one must ask how well such activities serve to broaden the world view of the science or engineering specialist.

Thus, it would seem that a central function for the larger university organization is to provide the integrative structures and programs that counterbalance the tendencies toward specialization in student development and academic research. Continuous lifelong learning requires learning how to learn, and this involves appreciation of and competence in diverse approaches to creating, manipulating, and communicating knowledge.

To assume that this integrated appreciation and competence can be achieved solely by distribution requirements or other legislative approaches is highly questionable. As with racial integration, we must closely scrutinize any strategy that requires students to do what we ourselves cannot or will not do. To build integrative programs of teaching and research requires that reward systems, selection and evaluation criteria, and inquiry values be confronted and adjusted to sustain interdisciplinary activity. In addition, some kind of focal point may be required for successful integrative education. Successful interdisciplinary programs I have seen have had a common reference point for integrative activity. In the professions, this reference point is often the professional role itself, in which critical functions and tasks emphasize the need for specialized knowledge from various disciplines. In the "pure" academic disciplines, this focus can come through the broad application of a methodology such as systems analysis or through a research problem that requires multiple perspectives. Other practical approaches to the achievement of this integrative emphasis are explored in Parts Two and Three of this volume.

The "when" question may suggest even more fundamental changes. The continuing knowledge explosion and the corresponding rapid rate of change raise serious questions about the current strategy of "front-loading" educational experience in the individual's life cycle. When, as current labor statistics indicate, the average person will change jobs seven times and careers three times during his or her working life, it makes more sense to distribute educational experiences throughout adult life in order to assist in the preparation for and mastery of these changes. In this model, the university becomes a center for lifelong learning. Integrative learning experiences take on new meaning and vitality when they are directly connected with the integrative challenges of adult life. Discussions of human values and the quality of life are very different with high school graduates than they are with managers of an oil refinery. Quality patient care has one connotation to the idealistic pre-med student and quite another to the harried medical specialist. Perhaps the richest resources for integrative development lie in the dialogue across age levels that the university for lifelong learning can provide.

References

Altmeyer, R. "Education in the Arts and Sciences: Divergent Paths." Unpublished paper, Carnegie Institute of Technology, 1966.

Bereiter, C., and Freedman, M. "Fields of Study and the People in Them." In N. Sanford (Ed.), *The American College.* New York: Wiley, 1962.

Biglan, A. "The Characteristics of Subject Matter in Different Academic Areas." *Journal of Applied Psychology,* 1973a, *57,* 195-203.

Biglan, A. "Relationships Between Subject Matter Characteristics and the Structure and Output of University Departments." *Journal of Applied Psychology,* 1973b, *51,* 204-213.

Bok, D. "The President's Report." *Harvard Magazine,* May-June 1978.

Bruner, J. *The Process of Education.* New York: Vintage Books, 1960.

Bruner, J. *The Process of Education.* New York: Atheneum, 1966.

Bruner, J., and others. *Studies in Cognitive Growth.* New York: Wiley, 1966.

Cole, M. and others. *The Cultural Context of Learning and Thinking.* New York: Basic Books, 1971.

Davis, J. *Great Aspirations: The Graduate School Plans of American College Seniors.* Chicago: Aldine, 1964.

Davis, J. *Undergraduate Career Decisions.* Chicago: Aldine, 1965.

Feldman, S. *Escape from the Doll's House.* New York: McGraw-Hill, 1974.

Flavell, J. *The Developmental Psychology of Jean Piaget.* New York: Van Nostrand Reinhold, 1963.

Gerstein, M. "Why Do They Feel Awkward and Out of Place at M.I.T.: A Study of an Undergraduate Student Culture." Unpublished doctoral dissertation, Sloan School of Management, Massachusetts Institute of Technology, 1973.

Goldstein, K., and Scheerer, M. "Abstract and Concrete Behavior: An Experimental Study with Special Tests." *Psychological Monographs,* 1941, *53* (239).

Grochow, J. "Cognitive Style as a Factor in the Design of Interactive Decision-Support Systems." Unpublished doctoral dissertation, Sloan School of Management, Massachusetts Institute of Technology, 1973.

Hall, D. "The Impact of Peer Interaction During an Academic Role Transition." *Sociology of Education,* Spring 1969, *42,* 118-140.

Harvey, O. J., Hunt, D., and Schroeder, H. *Conceptual Systems and Personality Organization.* New York: Wiley, 1961.

Hudson, L. *Contrary Imaginations.* Middlesex, England: Penguin Books, 1966.

Jung, C. *Psychological Types.* London: Pantheon Books, 1923.

Kagan, J., and Kogan, N. "Individual Variation in Cognitive Processes." In P. H. Mussan (Ed.), *Carmichael's Manual of Child Psychology.* Vol. 1. New York: Wiley, 1970.

Kagan, J., and others. "Information Processing in the Child: Significance of Analytic and Reflective Attitudes." *Psychological Monographs,* 1964, *78* (1).

Kirtz, J. "Cultural Diversity and Character Change at Carnegie Tech." Unpublished doctoral dissertation, Johns Hopkins University, 1966.

Kolb, D. *The Learning Style Inventory: Technical Manual.* Boston: McBer, 1976a.

Kolb, D. "Management and Learning Processes." *California Management Review,* 1976b, *18* (3), 21-31.

Kolb, D., and Fry, R. "Toward an Applied Theory of Experiential Learning." In C. Cooper (Ed.), *Theories of Group Processes.* New York: Wiley, 1975.

Kolb, D., and Goldman, M. "Toward a Typology of Learning Styles and Learning Environments: An Investigation of the Impact of Learning Styles and Discipline Demands on the Academic Performance, Social Adaptation, and Career Choices of M.I.T. Seniors." M.I.T. Sloan School of Management Working Paper, 1973 (December), 688-773.

Kolb, D., Rubin, R., and Schein, E. "The M.I.T. Freshman Integration Research Project: A Summary Report." Unpublished report, Massachusetts Institute of Technology, 1972.

Kris, E. *Psychoanalytic Explorations in Art.* New York: International Universities Press, 1952.

Kuhn, T. *The Structure of Scientific Revolutions.* Chicago: University of Chicago Press, 1962.

Lessor, J. "Cultural Differences in Learning and Thinking." In S. Messick and Associates, *Individuality in Learning: Implications of Cognitive Styles and Creativity for Human Development.* San Francisco: Jossey-Bass, 1976.

McCloskey, H., and Schaar, J. "Psychological Dimensions of Anomie." *American Psychological Review,* 1963, *30* (1), 14-40.

Olsen, M. "Political Alienation." In J. Robinson and P. Shauer, *Measures of Social Psychological Attitudes.* Ann Arbor: Institute for Social Research, University of Michigan, August 1969.

Piaget, J. *Structuralism.* New York: Harper & Row, 1968.

Piaget, J. *The Place of the Sciences of Man in the System of Sciences.* New York: Harper & Row, 1970.

Plovnick, M. "Individual Learning Styles and the Process of Career Choice in Medical Students." Unpublished doctoral dissertation, Sloan School of Management, Massachusetts Institute of Technology, 1974.

Ral, A. *The Psychology of Occupations.* New York: Wiley, 1956.

Schiller, F. *Uber die ästhetische Enziehung des Menschen* [*On the Aesthetic Education of Men*]. Cotta'sche Ausgabe, 1826.

Signell, K. A. "Cognitive Complexity in Person Perception and Nation Perception: A Developmental Approach." *Journal of Personality,* 1966, *34,* 517-537.

Singer, J. "The Importance of Daydreaming." *Psychology Today,* 1968, *1* (11), 18-26.

Snow, C. *The Two Cultures: On a Second Look.* England: Cambridge University Press, 1963.

Stabel, C. "The Impact of a Conversational Computer System on Human Problem Solving Behavior." Unpublished Working Paper, Sloan School of Management, Massachusetts Institute of Technology, 1973.

Strasmore, M. "The Strategic Function Re-evaluated from the Organization Development Perspective." Unpublished master's thesis, Sloan School of Management, Massachusetts Institute of Technology, June 1973.

Terman, L., and Oden, M. *The Gifted Child Grows Up.* Stanford, Calif.: Stanford University Press, 1947.

Torrealba, D. "Convergent and Divergent Learning Styles." Unpublished master's thesis, Sloan School of Management, Massachusetts Institute of Technology, 1972.

Vannoy, J. "Generality of Cognitive Complexity-Simplicity as a Personality Construct." *Journal of Personality and Social Psychology,* 1965, *2* (3), 385-396.

Witkin, H. "A Cognitive Style Approach to Cross-Cultural Research." *International Journal of Psychology,* 1967, *2,* 233-250.

Witkin, H. "Cognitive Styles in Academic Performance and in Teacher-Student Relations." In S. Messick and Associates, *Individuality in Learning: Implications of Cognitive Styles and Creativity for Human Development.* San Francisco: Jossey-Bass, 1976.

Witkin, H., and others. *Psychological Differentiation.* New York: Wiley, 1962.

Witkin, H., and others. *Field-Dependence-Independence and Psychological Differentia-*

tion: A Bibliography Through 1972 with Index. ETSRB 73-62. Princeton, N.J.: Educational Testing Service, 1972.

Wober, M. "Adapting Witkin's Field Independence Theory to Accommodate New Information from Africa." *British Journal of Psychology,* 1967, *58,* 29-38.

Wolfle, D. *America's Resources of Specialized Talent.* New York: Harper & Row, 1954.

11

Jessie Bernard

Women's Educational Needs

It is difficult to discuss the situation of women students in academia without touching upon matters of curriculum and administration—the domains of Parts Two and Three of this book. Many women have commented on the sexist nature of the curriculum, the exclusively male criteria applied in evaluating and grading academic work, and the administrative machinery geared to the life patterns of male students. Not only has learning been by and large about men but it has often positively put women down. Thus, a chapter on women students must include some reference to the bias in the learning presented to them. It must also say something about the administrative innovations called for by the presence of new kinds of students. Thus, while considering the educational needs of women at different stages of their lives, we will also note some of the accommodations that colleges must make to meet them.

Women in the Academic Marketplace

One does not have to be a Marxist or an unregenerate cynic to note that the rise in women's college attendance from the 1960s—when the last comprehensive statement on American colleges was made (Sanford, 1962)—to the present time is not a result of changed ideology on the part of the colleges, nor legislation and affirmative action, nor even raised consciousness. The proportion of women in the college population has not been increasing because the old myths, logic, and arguments that buttressed discrimination have been discarded (Furniss, 1974). Far more mundane forces, including demographic ones, have been at work.

Daniel Patrick Moynihan has presented a vivid statement of the demographic situation then and now and in the probable future. He contrasts the rate of increase in the 14- to 24-year-old age bracket—which, of course, includes the traditional college-age population—in the succeeding decades of this century.

> If you go from 1890 to 1960, you find the size of this subgroup . . . growing a little bit each succeeding decade: 10 percent, 8 percent, sometimes not at all, but usually growing a little bit. In the whole of that 70 years, 1890 to 1960, the total increase of the "cohort," . . . was 12.5 million persons. Then in the 1960s it grew by 13.8 million persons, an increase of 52 percent in one decade, five times the average rate of the preceding 70 years. . . . During the 1970s this cohort (14-24) will grow only by 6 million persons—remember it grew by 13.8 million in the previous decade—and *next* decade it will *decline* [Moynihan, 1977].

Computations based on the civilian, noninstitutional population give somewhat different results since they exclude persons in the armed services and incarcerated persons, primarily males. These computations show an increase among the 14- to 24-year-olds of 10.3 million between 1960 and 1969 and 4.8 million between 1970 and 1975 (U.S. Department of Labor, 1977, Table B-6, p. 196).

The decline of the conventional college-age population of both sexes during the 1980s is now common knowledge. Already some of the smaller liberal arts colleges have had to close up shop. Today the doors of the universities are open wider to women, then, not because educational institutions have become convinced of the justice of admitting more women but because the "market" has changed. And market forces seem to have greater impact on women than on men, favorable or unfavorable. In 1950, women constituted 38 percent of all first-time entering degree students; in 1976, almost half—48 percent (Andersen, 1975b). The number of women 16 to 34 enrolled in college increased 216.7 percent between 1960 and 1974 (U.S. Bureau of Census, 1976, Table 6-12). In 1970, the college enrollment rate for women 20 to 24 was double that in 1960 (U.S. Bureau of Census, 1964, 1973). "Almost three times as many women were enrolled in college in 1972 as in 1960 and the college enrollment rate . . . more than doubled for women in their twenties during those twelve years" (Glick, 1975b, p. 17). The author of a Women's Bureau pamphlet saw a counterbalance for the expected decline or leveling-off of college-age student enrollments in the continuing education programs for women. The Carnegie Foundation for the Advancement of Teaching, however, exhibited more concern with declining enrollments. It looked to the increasing enrollment of older, part-time, and nondegree women students to at least partially compensate for the slower increase among undergraduates (Women's Bureau, 1975).

The concept of an academic marketplace is not a new one. Caplow and McGee (1958) saw it as applicable to faculty some twenty years ago. It is also applicable—figuratively speaking—to students. In the early 1960s, educational institutions were in a "seller's market." More students wanted to get into college than the colleges had places for. The problem was how to select rather than how to entice applicants (Chickering, 1976). There was no special invitation extended to women. Now many of these institutions are in a "buyer's market." There are more than enough places for those seeking admission. And women are being accepted to occupy them. Even the most traditionalist and elitist male institutions have now become coeducational—though the transition has not been easy, for either the men or the women (Schwartz and Lever, 1973).

Accepting women is not the same as warmly welcoming them. The disillusioning experiences of the first generation of women undergraduates at Yale, for example, have been documented in some detail (Lever and Schwartz, 1971; Getman, 1974; Deinhardt, 1974). Even in institutions with a long coeducational tradition, "in many quarters there are remnants of objectionable attitudes toward coeds" (Rodriguez, 1974, 70-71). The "objectionable remnants," many women feel, will have to disappear. For the women entering academia in the near future are going to be part of a cohort with large future responsibilities. American colleges cannot afford to shortchange them in any way.

Far from having to lower their academic standards to admit more women, colleges are finding women applicants better qualified than ever—in fact, frequently better qualified than men. The average high school grades of college-entering women in 1974 were higher than in both 1970 and 1966: 22.6 percent of women students in 1974—as compared with 17.9 percent in 1970 and with 20.2 percent in 1966—had average high school grades of A. And only 14.7 percent—as compared with 19.1 percent in 1970 and 19.9 percent in 1966—had average high school grades of C (Andersen, 1975a, Table 75.178). The women had higher averages than entering men in all three years. The disparity was especially marked in 1970, when the proportion of women with A grade averages (17.9 percent) was about 50 percent greater than the proportion of men (11.6 percent).

In the same period between 1966 and 1974, the proportion of college-entering women planning professional degrees, though still small, increased markedly (Andersen, 1975a, Table 75.179). The percentages of women working toward medical and law degrees increased from 1.9 to 5.3 percent and from .2 to 2.6 percent, respectively. Women students in the health professions, but not medical degree students, increased from 9.8 to 13.3 percent. The major fields of study showed increased numbers of women —though still only small proportions—entering traditionally male domains, including business (10.9 to 15.5 percent), engineering (.3 to 1.0 percent), and agriculture (.1 to 1.0 percent). And the proportion preparing for careers considered nontraditional for women (business, medicine, dentistry, engineering, farming or forestry, law, and scientific research), though still small in 1974, was greater than in 1970.

The increase in women studying mathematics or statistics is especially interesting. In the last few years there has been great concern expressed among academic women about what they call "math anxiety"—an avoidance of mathematics learned in the course of sex-role socialization, which has kept women from acquiring the mathematical basis required for scientific careers. Courses have now been devised to help women overcome their "math anxiety." Colleges have thus been dealing not only with a growing female population but also with one that has been perceptibly changing in both quality and aspirations.

A significant demographic factor in the current college population of women students is the increasing age range. Recent years have brought a population beyond the traditional college age. These women, like their college-age sisters or daughters, constitute a not inconsiderable proportion of the students colleges of the future will have to deal with. The age differences have implications for both curriculum and administration. To understand these implications it is necessary to know something about women's life cycles and developmental stages.

Women's Life Cycles and Developmental Stages

In their chapter, Chickering and Havighurst point out that educational needs are conditioned to a great extent by the characteristic psychosocial challenges at different stages of the life cycle. Later chapters also reveal the relationship between education and individuals' developmental stages. Hence we should consider how the research on the life cycle and developmental stages applies to women.

The concept of a *life cycle* as a series of stages is an old one (Cain, 1964, pp. 272-309). But the delineation of the actual stages has varied with changes in the culture in which the lives were lived. From time to time, it has been necessary to add new stages—adolescence, for example—and to break down former stages into substages. It has been difficult to keep up conceptually with the actual way lives are lived. The main problem, though, from our point of view, is that most of the thinking and research on the life cycle has dealt with men's lives, either explicitly or implicitly. Relatively little of it, therefore, is useful in helping us understand the lives of women (Bernard, 1975, p. 100).

In the past, women's lives, when or if anyone cared to examine them, could be reduced to three stages defined in terms of childbearing: (1) the premenarcheal years, (2) the childbearing years, and (3) the postmenopausal years. Childbearing is still a major factor in understanding the female life cycle, though it is no longer so preponderant. Gone is the day when one other event equalled childrearing as a life-stage marker, the loss of virginity. The importance placed on virginity as a first-line defense against irresponsible parenthood was not irrelevant for schools and colleges, as the whole issue of parietal rules indicates. The enforcement of such rules may no longer plague the staffs in colleges of the future, but health services still have to wrestle with problems related to childbearing.

The Family Life Cycle. It has become apparent that the traditional conception of the life cycle, based as it is on male life experiences, does not tell us much about women. So in recent years there have been attempts to view the life cycle of women in more appropriate terms. For insights here we have had to turn to research on the family life cycle. And we are fortunate to have at our disposal a considerable corpus of research to help. In 1957, for example, Paul Glick presented a picture of the family life cycle based on several major demographic events. This work has become a classic, which has enormously influenced our thinking about women ever since.

The demographic events Glick used to mark the stages in the family cycle were a woman's age at first marriage, age at birth of last child, age at marriage of last child, age at death of spouse, and age at death. He added to the value of his findings by comparing the age data for 1950 with those for 1890 and 1940 to show trends. The age of the mother at the birth and marriage of her last child had declined; the age at widowhood and death had gone up. The age at first marriage had remained fairly steady; it declined in the late 1960s but rose somewhat thereafter. In general, it has fluctuated around the age of 21 (Parke and Glick, 1967).

The Glick schema is quite general. There have been attempts to flesh it out with respect to special populations. Thus, Helena Lopata, for example, has delineated five adult female stages on the basis of successive roles as she has observed them in her study of housewives: (1) becoming a wife and housewife, (2) becoming a mother, (3) a full-house plateau with increasing community involvement, (4) a shrinking circle as children leave home, and (5) gradual disengagement (Lopata, 1971, p. 43). Another model, based on the lives of working-class women, has distinguished five stages also: (1) a premarital period of "dedicated man-hunting," (2) the "relatively trying stage" of early marriage, (3) the early stage of childrearing, in which women have "traditionally 'staid put,' emotionally bogged down . . . overly busy and tired, demanding and complaining," (4) a time of assertion or rediscovery that "they do not need or want to be perpetual mothers and housewives," and (5) the postfamily stage, which, especially among younger women, is "a focal point for much of the independence and flexibility, bounty and liberality which are beginning to appear in the modern working-class outlook" (Coup, Greene, and Gardner, 1973, pp. 133-135).

Interesting as these schemata may be, even they are too limited for the present time because they do not incorporate work outside the home. A second strand of research has to be incorporated into the thinking about women's lives—especially college women's lives—namely, the "natural history" of their work careers. Twenty years ago the National Manpower Council (1957) was among the first to call our attention to the spectacular changes taking place in our society:

> At the close of the last century, about half the adult women never entered paid employment. Now at least 9 out of every 10 women are likely to work outside the home in the course of their lives. Women who reached adulthood around the turn of the century participated in paid employment, on the average, for 11 years in the course of their lives. Those who reached adulthood just before World War II are likely, on the average, to work over 20 years. Today's school girls may spend 25 years or more in work outside the home [p. 10].

As of 1960, the young 20-year-old woman would spend 45.3 years in the labor force if she remained single, 34.9 years if she married but remained childless, 25.0 years if she had one child, and 22.0 years even if she had two children—the most probable number (Garfinkle, 1969). In 1967, among women 30 to 44 years of age with one or more years of college, almost two thirds (64 percent) would work half of their adult lives (U.S. Bureau of the Census, 1976, Table 9.5, p. 44). The proportion may be higher today.

Even more interesting than the mere growth in labor force participation by women has been the change in its timing in the life cycle. In the past, most paid work outside the home occurred before marriage. Now most of it occurs after marriage, even after motherhood. Later in the chapter we shall consider how "contingency scheduling" relates to women undergraduates and to women 35 years of age and over whose last child is at least of school age. But first let us glance at the second basic concept, developmental stages.

Women's Development and Socialization. Research on *developmental stages* has shown the same male bias as the conceptualization of the life cycle. In a recent book on adolescence, for example, an important paper on physical and sexual maturation notes that the major features of maturation differ somewhat in boys and girls. Still, all the discussion deals with males (Clausen, 1975). In the same book, another paper notes that "almost all of the studies /on attainment/ . . . have been restricted to males. . . . 'Status attainments' are often treated as synonymous with male attainments" (Alexander and Eckland, 1975, p. 179). This despite the finding that identical factors may lead to different effects in women and in men. For example: "our analysis of sex interactions with other background variables suggests a not inconsequential compounding of the liabilities of status ascription (the allocation of lower status as a function of sex biases); the educational attainments of women, already lower on the average than those of equally competent males, are themselves more responsive to the influence of social origins than of ability, while just the reverse applies to men. Thus, we find evidence of substantial sex and status ascription, with the latter being more pronounced for women" (Alexander and Eckland, 1975, p. 195).

Chickering has assembled the major schemata dealing with the various dimensions of psychological and social development—ego development, moral and ethical development, intellectual development, interpersonal style, and development of social interests (Chickering, 1976). They highlight the "counter-development" bred in women by their sex-role socialization. Women have been socialized to remain in the conformist stage of character development, conscious preoccupation, and cognitive style, and in the dependent stage of interpersonal style. The moral development of girls has tended to be arrested at the "be-good-so-people-will-love-you" stage. Women have been socialized to be defensive and immature—that is, to be passive and dependent, to have a limited behavioral repertoire and shallow interests, and to habitually assume a subordinate position (Safilios-Rothschild, 1979). Only in "development of social interest" are women socialized to reach the higher developmental levels. They do show commitments to deep and reciprocal intimate relationships and investment in community, religious, social, or global concerns. Girls are socialized to be humanitarian, and for many years college women have sought careers in humanitarian causes (Bernard, 1964).

The sex-role socialization of girls has been "counter-developmental" in the sense that, far from emphasizing autonomy and independence, it has emphasized the "achievement"—sometimes against odds—of dependency (Bernard, 1975). Thus, when Erikson (1968) turned his attention to the development of women, once his attention was called to his neglect of them, he saw their achievement of identity in terms of their dependency. True, he permitted a young woman a "moratorium" in college to develop her intellectual interests, to explore the "outer-space of the male world" during the hiatus between dependency on family and on husband, but the return to dependency after marriage was not challenged.

It would be diversionary to document in further detail how counter-developmental so much of the sex-role socialization of girls has been. Many of the early colleges attempted to maintain the immature level in their students, trying only to fit them into the dependent, subordinate niche they were to occupy in their later years. Some of the more radical colleges, however, tried to help their students overcome the socialization for dependency and achieve a higher level of maturity, even autonomy. But the college years have been and remain a time when the young woman must struggle to overcome the counter-developmental pressures that have been operating on her, to achieve autonomy. Joseph Katz (1976) suggests that "girls in late adolescence are troubled by questions about their own worth and about what others think of them, anxious about their physical appearance, guilty because they are hanging onto childhood and at the same time struggling against their dependencies" (p. 91). Even the women returning to college have much the same kind of struggle. The standards for adult women have permitted, even called for, developmental arrest (Broverman and others, 1970). Colleges have, at least nominally, attempted to help young women through this struggle against their dependencies. But even Erikson, who permitted them a wide intellectual tether, still saw this stage as merely an interim between one kind of dependency—on parental family—and another—on husband.

Undergraduate Women: Careers and Contingencies

One of the most insightful studies of the backing and filling, the advance and retreat that characterizes women undergraduates in this developmental stage of their lives—as they seek to balance their striving for autonomy with their socially instilled desire to remain dependent—is a longitudinal study of eighty-seven women in the cohort in college during the years 1964-1968 (Angrist and Almquist, 1975). It is based on a "life-style" index consisting of items that "reflect whether the woman wants to be employed under family conditions at various stages in the life cycle and without economic pressure to work, whether she values working in a self-directed occupation, and whether she plans to attend graduate school" (pp. 71-72).

Predictably, considerable heterogeneity was revealed in commitment to careers by five different types of students, namely: (1) careerists (18 percent), (2) noncareerists (33 percent), (3) converts to careerism (22 percent), (4) defectors from careerism (13 percent), and (5) shifters (14 percent). Several important themes relating to the developmental process stand out:

First, students' desires to work and even to pursue careers *do* increase somewhat during the college years, but many women rest firm in their original family-centered aspirations. The decision to work is virtually unanimous when there are no children or the children are at least school age and financial needs are compelling.

Second, the changes noted in these women's lives from year to year reveal that role development is far from consistent. There are both converts to career and defectors from it. Still, the net changes on most of the specific variables show an increased career orientation.

A third conclusion is that the students are highly changeable during college; they are uncertain or ambivalent about their choices, though they try to be pragmatic. The authors do not imply that indecision is characteristic only of women; men are subject to it as well. But it has a special cast among women:

> even among the most unbending careerists and noncareerists much vacillation, worry, and uncertainty prevail. These college women, despite their consistency, are inconsistent, groping for handles on the future they cannot predict, seeking sensible plans among hazardous contingencies. They exhibit the common ambivalence about a woman's life, whether to forge ahead or whether to hold back (Bardwick and Douvan, 1971). This struggle to complete the puzzle while the big pieces (husband, children) are missing haunts all the women [Angrist and Almquist, 1975, p. 81].

"Take a few education courses. Then if . . . God forbid . . . anything should happen, you can always take care of yourself" (Rabiner, 1976). This was the advice one young woman received from her parents. It conveyed the normal expectation that she would find someone to take care of her, while also stressing the importance of being prepared to take care of herself in case she did not find a husband or her husband died or left her.

In a sense, of course, everyone's future is contingent. It depends on remaining alive, on remaining well, on having a job, on the absence of war or a severe depression, on a host of "missing pieces." What makes the contingencies in the woman undergraduate's life unique is the peculiar combination of control and lack of control in dealing with them.

The major missing pieces in the young woman's planning for her future—marriage and children—are contingent in her life as an individual, but there are overall regularities revealed in demographic trends. Thus, we know, for example, that whether or not any specific woman aspires to a career, more than half of all women with college experience are going to be in the labor force. Among married women, 52.9 percent with one or more years of college were in the labor force in 1974 (Women's Bureau, 1975, p. 23). Whether or not she says she plans to marry, we know that more than nine out of ten will marry. And despite the increasing number of young women who say they do not want to have children, we know that most of them will have at least one child. The problem, thus, is not whether or not women are to combine marriage and motherhood with work or career but how they are to do so—concomitantly in a two-role continuous pattern or sequentially in a pattern involving job or career discontinuities. The planning has to do with the best way of combining the components of a satisfactory life-style.

The Angrist-Almquist data trace the developmental process in the college-age years, 18 to 22. To carry the story on from there, we now have a study that, though retrospective, tells us not only what the preferences were but how and when they changed later on. Phyllis Diness, in a follow-up study of 542 women who had received scholarships from the Business and Professional Women's Foundation, elicited data on career-versus-homemaking preferences at ages 25, 30, 35, and 40. She reported the following:

> The general career-orientation change pattern seen was that age 25 was the point of greatest preference for homemaking only (no career), and age 35 was the point of greatest preference for combining homemaking with a career. Age 40 was the point of greatest preference for having a career (with no mention of combining it with a homemaking role). The greatest increase in preference for some degree of career life (career alone or in combination with homemaking) was seen between age 25 and age 30 [Diness, in press].

The years between ages 25 and 30 are more critical than any other period for role change planning in women. It is relevant to insert at least parenthetically that Sandra Tangri found in a follow-up of college women three years after graduation that though they may have been full-time homemakers, their career aspirations remained high (Tangri, in press). The Diness data suggest that life-style preferences change sequentially over time: from a one-role (homemaking) pattern, to a two-role (career combined with homemaking) pattern, and again to a one-role (this time, career) pattern.

For most women, childbearing—if not marriage—will mean career discontinuities. Eli Ginzberg and associates (1966), on the basis of the career histories of 311 achieving women, distinguished four kinds of career discontinuities: (1) minor breaks or discontinuities, (2) intermittent breaks, (3) periodic breaks, and (4) terminal breaks. He later telescoped his categories of work histories into simply (1) continuous, (2) broken, and (3) terminated. About half of his distinguished women fell into the first category (continuous), a quarter into the second (broken), and a quarter into the third (terminated)—a distribution unlikely for a less achieving sample. The discontinuities in the career history of women may vary in length; they may be no longer than a short maternity leave of a week, at one extreme, or as long as it takes for a last child to reach college, at the other. Actually, it is not only the length of the interruption that is important but its timing as well, when it occurs in the career, early or late. Before considering life-style "scheduling," let us look at the major events on which the career is contingent—marriage and childbearing.

Marriage: Contingency 1. There was once a time when learning was such a jealous mistress that even male scholars were supposed to live celibate lives. Long after that requirement disappeared, it remained the case for women. For a long time, therefore, only maiden ladies were supposed to make a lifelong commitment to learning (Bernard, 1964). Young women argued among themselves the "marriage-*versus*-career" issue, taking it for granted that this was the only choice open to them since either precluded the other. Only recently have young women come to think not of marriage *versus* career but of marriage *and* career. For although there may have been a time when marriage and career were incompatible, no longer is marriage in and of itself a major obstacle to the pursuit of a career. True, in 1960 marriage might reduce overall female labor-force participation by about ten years (Garfinkle, 1969), but among career women Ginzberg found that marriage in and of itself did not seem to make much difference in achievement. His married subjects were as productive as his never-married subjects (Ginzberg and Associates, 1966). And we know that an increasing number of young women do not allow marriage to cut off their college education (Bernard, 1976). If there are no children, marriage need have relatively little impact on either the education or careers of women. With few home responsibilities, they can function in both areas without too much strain. Nevertheless,

Saul Feldman (1974) found that female married graduate students did less well than male married graduate students but that the reverse was true for divorced students. Apparently, the support of a wife helped the man's performance; supplying such support in addition to undertaking graduate work hurt the woman's.

Marriage is one contingency that young women have at least a modicum of control over. Not complete control, however. There is sometimes a fear expressed that if they do not marry in their early twenties all the desirable men will be spoken for by the time they decide to marry. It is even harder to control the contingency involved in mate selection, as contrasted with marriage itself. It is not only if or when the young woman marries that will determine her future, but who. Her future will be largely influenced by her husband's income, occupation, mobility, and attitudes. A supportive husband can greatly enhance career success; a hostile husband can render it all but impossible.

The salience of marriage in the life-style planning of college women is sometimes made the butt of disparaging remarks by the male academic establishment. They are above all that. Actually, marriage is important in the life-style and total career of men as well as of women. Robert Parke once commented that his male graduate students did not seem able to settle down in their careers until they were married. There is considerable evidence of the importance of marriage to men (Bernard, 1975). The difference is that the men have better control over the timing of their marriage.

The importance of marriage in the career plans of women lies not, then, so much in the event itself as in the consequence for the second major contingency, childbearing, which does have great impact on work histories and careers. It has been said that if a teen-age girl has a baby, almost 90 percent of the script of her future has already been written.

Childbearing: Contingency 2. Much depends on the amount of time devoted to childbearing—and this, of course, on the number of children. The trend seems to be in the direction of short rather than long career interruptions for childbearing. About a decade ago, Garfinkle (1969) noted "an astonishing change in the work lives of women"—namely, that childbirth was affecting work life continuity less and less. Some women were taking no more time off for having a baby than a man might take to recover from a minor illness. The lowered fertility rate today suggests fewer as well as shorter interruptions for childbearing.

Even so, the impact of childbearing on careers is powerful. For most women it takes a big bite out of career advancement. True, women have a modicum of control, first, in the decision to have children at all, second, in how many children to have, and third, in the timing of each birth. But basic life decisions are not necessarily rational or well thought out. Young women 18 to 22 do not usually plan their life courses as clearly as young men are required to do. In a vague and general way they know they will marry, bear children, and at least part of the time be in the labor force or pursue a career. But they are far from clear about the details. On the basis of their work, Angrist and Almquist (1975) urge college counselors to stress the total life view, to clarify for the student as much as possible what the options are, to help her examine and evaluate them, to judge the pros and cons of each. Not that all the contingencies can be transformed into certainties—but understanding them can help in dealing with them.

Contingency Scheduling. In the following schema, professional training, career initiation, and career resumption are shown in different combinations and permutations with marriage and childbearing, with approximate ages for each. College education is taken for granted since we are dealing with undergraduates and it is assumed that college must precede career initiation, just as marriage is assumed to precede childbearing. It is assumed that professional training involves three years beyond college and that career initiation involves three years beyond that. It is further assumed that the first child is born two years after marriage and the second, or last, child two years later. "Childbearing" covers the years from the birth of the first child to five years after the birth of the second child, or seven years. The ages at the several demographic events are not precisely correct for all women. Marriage and childbrearing tend to come somewhat later for college-educated women than for less educated women. They also vary historically.

The timing of childbearing is a source of concern to young women. Graduate students or women in professional schools in the early years of their careers who are happy in their work enter their thirties with a question. They have until now assumed that, yes, they would have children, but they have been putting off the actual date. They now begin to wonder about further delay. One says she plans to have her baby as soon as she receives tenure; another when she has completed her book; another when she gets her law degree. As they approach their goals, they may have second thoughts about the baby. They may worry about birth defects or mongolism, though many will be reassured by the availability of amniocentesis, which can detect many such defects. The major decision for them is not biological so much as psychological. Is motherhood what they really want? Or just the idea of motherhood? The biological calendar may be less constraining than before, but it remains a salient factor in most women's life scheduling. At the other end of the gamut, too-early childbearing may have seriously dysfunctional consequences for a woman's life course (Furstenberg, 1976).

The schedules shown here are, of course, far from exhaustive. They are meant to be suggestive only—to accustom the young woman to think beyond marriage, to take a total life view.

Contingency Schedules

A. Marriage, 22; childbearing, 23-29; professional training, 30-32; career, 33-
B. Marriage, 22; professional training, 22-24; career initiation, 25-27; childbearing, 28-35; career resumption, 36-
C. Professional training, 22-24; marriage, 25; childbearing, 26-33; career, 34-
D. Professional training, 22-24; career initiation, 25-27; marriage, 28; childbearing, 29-36; career resumption, 37-

Havelock Ellis, in his study of British genius, found that achieving women characteristically married either very early or fairly late. They thus "escaped from, or found a modus vivendi with, domestic and procreative claims" (Bernard, 1971, p. 182). If valid, this conclusion would tend to favor schedules A, B, and D, leaving C as least favorable. Any schedule that interposes childbearing between professional training and career initiation would seem to be counterproductive. The woman who has at least a toehold on her career is in a better position to pursue her career later on. In the absence of more empirical research, however, it is fruitless to attempt to evaluate the several schedules.

It should be noted that people are beginning to discuss changes that would simplify the contingency scheduling for women. Alan Pifer, President of the Carnegie Corporation, has this to say, for example, in his 1976 annual report:

> Many women leave the labor force for several years to have children, sometimes taking the time to engage in volunteer work and further education or training before re-entering paid employment. They can, however, pay heavily for this "irregularity" by having to start all over again at beginning entry levels, forfeiting seniority and hence opportunity for advancement both in position and in earn-

ings, and losing the chance to compete for more interesting jobs. One could imagine a new, flexible arrangement, however, in which it would be normal for most people—women and men—to alternate periods of study, employment, and *work in the home* and to plan their lives accordingly. While this would require major changes in present administrative structures and financial arrangements, the idea of making new life patterns possible for those who want them should not be out of the question. The gains to be expected from greater flexibility in life patterns are many. If, for example, it were to become normal practice for both men and women to withdraw temporarily from the labor force, for periods of study, to retrain for new careers, *to care for children,* or just to pursue special interests, intermittent employment would have to be accorded society's official sanction, and the special onus now placed on women would be removed [pp. 16-17, emphasis added].

Such "major alterations in the traditional stages of the life cycle" are indeed intriguing.

Impact of the Feminist Movement. Are college women any better off today? Has the feminist movement had any impact on their life plans? Are they any more autonomous than the 1964-1968 cohort studied by Angrist and Almquist? Are they more advanced intellectually than preceding classes, as their high school grade averages would suggest? There are differences of opinion. Some have cited favorable evidence (Bernard, 1975). But others are raising questions. They ask: Have we oversold careers for women? What about the women urged to pursue careers who will never find them in a declining labor market? (Oppenheimer, 1973; Bernard, 1976). And what about the young women who have not really assimilated the implications of the new options? Matina Horner (1974), for example, tells us of college seniors who are planning for neither marriage nor careers, who talk a good liberation line but have not yet really come to grips with it emotionally. She holds us educators partially to account, for "we haven't been fair with your young people about all the realities, the cost-benefits of the new kind of life-style they seek and value" (p. 5). As a result, they expect instant happiness. Not having been adequately warned about the trade-offs called for in nontraditional career orientations, they do not see the long-term implications of their choices. And, Horner reminds us, "in the long run that is what equality is all about: knowing what you are and being able to make a choice" (p. 5).

But what, the male academic establishment has asked, does any of all this have to do with us? Academia has, in fact, been somewhat embarrassed by the introduction of such personal matters into its thinking. Its members may have gossiped and joked about the personal lives of their colleagues, but officially they have maintained the facade of a strictly intellectual enterprise—one conceived and operated on a male design. If women chose a career option, they were expected to follow the male pattern, even if it so often meant a sacrifice of love, marriage, and family. Since academia had been a male preserve for so many centuries, it seemed only natural that if women wanted to enter it they had to make all the adjustments. Certainly, academia could not be expected to accommodate to women. And so it was for a long time. Even when women established their own colleges—or when others established them for women—the model was strictly a male one. The early women's colleges were glorious copies of the best the men had achieved. But now these automatic and unthinking reactions are being challenged. An attorney, in a suit against Yale University by four undergraduates and an assistant professor alleging sexual harassment, was quoted in the press as saying: "male-oriented institutions such as Yale are accustomed to thinking of such incidents as trivial, acceptable, and personal" (Mastro, 1977).

In the 1950s colleges began to make concessions to returning veterans. And in the 1960s they permitted young men who were restless and wanted experiences that engaged them more directly to take a year or more off from school—a Wanderjahr. The colleges came to accommodate them, as they had always had to accommodate students who dropped out to earn money. There may not have been many such cases of temporary dropping out, but they symbolized a recognition of a need for more flexibility than was standard in the past. A major question now for the colleges as well as for women is this: Should women be required to adjust their lives—the scheduling of marriage and childbearing—to the procrustean bed of academia, or should academia be asked to make provision for the different life calendars of women?

Angrist and Almquist (1975) grant that the feminist movement has exposed problems and highlighted dilemmas. But it has by no means moved mountains. Academia does not yet, as Angrist and Almquist recommend, create an enriched environment and welcome women into it or provide enough role models. It should throw overboard ossified notions and reliance on old myths. It should cultivate greater flexibility. When or if colleges decide to accommodate themselves to the needs of women, the range of students will increase the diversity of the student population. We will become accustomed to young mothers entering college at, let us say, ages 28 to 30 for the first time as freshmen —as we are now becoming accustomed to women returning to college to complete their degrees or even to begin new careers.

In this section we have been looking at young college women in their early twenties as they planned for their future. In the next section we look at a fairly new kind of college student after at least part of that future has taken place. Most have married, most have had children, and, in the case of most of them, the last child is now in school. So are they.

Returning Women

In 1977 adult education was news. The popular press was becoming aware of an important educational trend. Here is how *Time* was reporting this "news":

> There is a continuing increase in the demand for adult education, with the emphasis on practical skills and crafts rather than abstract knowledge. . . . Colleges and universities will have to adjust swiftly to this developing educational market— even if tenured professors of medieval English have to be retrained to teach economics and auto repair [Feb. 28, 1977, p. 74].

Lost in this overall—inaccurate—view is the almost spectacular increase in adult education for women. Especially notable was the increase—108 percent—in college enrollment among women 25 to 29 between 1970 and 1974, and the increase of 85 percent even among women 30 to 34. These women were among those who had opted for childbearing before they completed their college education or professional training. "Her children," *McCalls* discovered, "are grown and she finally has the time to attend college; she's one of a growing number of divorced women who must become family breadwinners; or she's a working woman who sees a better (or better-paying) job up the line or in a different field. Ninety-five percent are career-oriented" (Pascoe, 1977, p. 45).

Because the women returning to college are highly motivated, they perform most creditably. Pascoe (1977) quotes an unnamed college professor as saying, "there's no question about it—she (the returning student) works harder, digs deeper and gets more out of college than any other group of students" (p. 45). She quotes another, Deborah

Ray, of Norwalk, Connecticut, Community College, to the effect that "they're earnest, they study harder, they contribute more, their papers are better. They set the pace in the classroom." Pascoe reports that the college teachers she interviewed found "the middle-aged woman a more intellectually stimulating person to teach than the younger student," and she quotes Dean William Boast of the Community College of Denver as saying, "younger kids tend to sit there and just take in what they're told. Older women have more intellectual curiosity." Many do better than they did as undergraduates (Pascoe, 1977). Katz (1976) explains this interesting fact by noting that the inner turmoil of their undergraduate years may have interfered with their learning.

Fortunately, we have two large-sample studies that give us further insights into two contrasting populations of women students who are returning to college to continue their education—one by Helen S. Astin and her associates (1976) of over a thousand current (649) and recent (541) participants in continuing education courses and one by Phyllis Diness (in press) of 763 applicants for scholarships from the Business and Professional Women's Foundation. The first deals with a set of women who, on the whole, have a fairly wide gamut of options. Only 15 percent were separated or divorced; the others were married to men who had at least moderate incomes—in the $10,000 to $19,000 range—and who were supportive of their wives' wish to return to school. The other deals with a quite different population, more needy of support. Almost half of this sample, 41 percent, were divorced or separated—a contingency they had apparently not planned for.

The "typical participant in a continuing education program," as found in the Astin (1976) sample, was a 36-year-old white woman from a middle-class background. But the age range was from 18 to 75, and there were women from different backgrounds and socioeconomic status, some of whom were nonwhite. Most came from Protestant backgrounds, although an unusually large proportion were Jewish. They varied in prior educational attainment from less than high school graduation to doctorates. Consequently, they also varied in the degree they were seeking, from a certificate of some kind (about a fourth) to a simple bachelor's degree (about half), all the way up to professional degrees (about a fifth). Their fields of study ranged from the natural sciences and mathematics to the social sciences. Among the more than half who were employed, occupations ranged from clerical to professional.

The "typical participant" was "married to a 42-year-old business executive or professional with an income in the $10,000 to $19,000 range" (Astin and Associates, 1976, p. 61). She was fortunate in the support she received from him. Katz (1976) summarizes the marital factors in this sample: "emotionally and financially, husbands were strongly supportive of their wives' returning to school. . . . Many wives and husbands reported that their marriages had improved. . . . Many wives and husbands reported that the family had drawn closer together" (p. 103). Typically, these women had two or three school-age children, and a fourth of them had preschool children. Almost half had children eighteen or older.

There is almost unanimous assent to the rule that any kind of professional or career success among women calls for the support of husbands. The old adage that behind a successful man there is a woman applies in reverse to the successful career woman: behind her there is a supportive husband. Hanna Papanek (1973) introduced the concept of the "two-person career." Although she applied it to male careers, female careers also call for two persons if the woman is married. Jane V. Anderson, summarizing the stories of successful scientists, noted that "from what almost all these women have described, very significant figures in their adult years, who have provided ongoing facilitation, have been their husbands" (1973, p. 205). Millicent McIntosh was particularly insistent: "the basic factor in the success of married women in careers is the cooperation and support of their husbands" (1973, p. 51).

The average age may be significant in terms of the life cycle. Some years ago, without specific research backing, I identified age 35 as a critical point in the development of women (Bernard, 1956). It is the time when the last child is likely to be in school, no longer needing the mother's round-the-clock availability. Over half of these mothers of school-age children are in the labor force. A considerable proportion are, apparently, also back in school, either to prepare for entering the labor force or for improving their status in it. Overall, these returning women reportedly constitute some 6 percent of the student population (Pascoe, 1977).

The second major study of returning women (Diness, in press) is based on a follow-up of 542 among the 763 women who, over a period of four years (1970-1974), had received Career Advancement Scholarships from the Business and Professional Women's Foundation. Some indication of the rapid increase in returning women may be gleaned from the number of applicants for these scholarships. Between 1973-1974 and 1975-1976, the applications increased more than fivefold. These were, clearly, not average or run-of-the-mill women. Still, the sample was not obviously biased on all variables. Diness, who analyzed the data, tells us who these returning women were:

> [They ranged] in age: from 25 to 66 years old; in geographic location: throughout the United States, in rural to urban settings; in educational attainment and educational programs: the entire range from women not having a high-school diploma to those holding graduate degrees, enrolled in programs from six-week training courses in a job-related skill or refresher courses to long-term graduate or professional schools for Ph.D. or law or medical degrees. All marital statuses are represented, and while the majority of past scholarship recipients are mothers, the ages and numbers of their offspring vary widely, to include a number of women with from six to thirteen children, as well as a number who have the responsibilities of single parenthood. And even though all the recipients are characterized by financial need, their household incomes range from below subsistence level to middle-income which affords moderate comfort but not educational completion. Thus, the sample of women students comprising the scholarship recipient group appear to represent an important sector among the mature-aged women who go to school. They are representative of the women who, having but low to moderate income, have recently undertaken, resumed, or continued in some educational or training program for the purpose of starting, re-entering, changing, developing, or advancing in careers [in press].

These women necessarily reflect the criteria used in their selection—namely, financial need and potential for career advancement. They can thus be described as "characterized by high internal resources (motivation) and low external resources." Nevertheless, Diness believes that the results based on these women "can be generalized to serve as indicators of the experience of many other women who share their circumstances and educational patterns." And the picture they present is certainly relevant for colleges dealing with them. For, although the prime objective of the study was to help the foundation in the selection of future recipients of awards, the results also served to "broaden the whole informational base about nontraditional students in educational programs."

"Nontraditional" these women may have been as students in educational programs, but even among themselves they differed in degree of traditionalism in sex role and self-image. Diness classified the women into three self-labeled categories: (1) traditional, (2) nontraditional or "liberated," and (3) intermediate or transitional. Predictably, the women's self-categorizations varied by age: almost half (45 percent) of those under 35 were nontraditional or liberated; fewer than half that many (20 percent) were traditional; and just under a third (30 percent) were transitional. Among the women 55 and over, the reverse was found: almost half (44 percent) were traditional; about a fourth (26 percent) were nontraditional, and the same proportion (26 percent), transitional.

On the basis of career plans, Diness classified her informants into five categories: (1) steadily committed careerists (26 percent), who reported wanting a career at each age up to the present age, (2) semi-steadily committed careerists (10 percent), who could be inferred to be similar to the steadily committed careerists, though they had left unanswered critical questions on the questionnaire, (3) second chancers (35 percent), who were career-oriented at all age levels except age 25, (4) early bloomers (11 percent), who were not career-oriented at 17-18 but were so at age 25 and thereafter, and (5) late bloomers (18 percent), who became career-oriented only after age 25. Not surprisingly, more women under 40 than those 40 or over were committed careerists or early bloomers, and more women 40 or over than younger women were second chancers and late bloomers. Angrist-Almquist "noncareerists" and "career defectors" are, of course, missing from the Diness schema. Age of children as well as age of the women themselves influenced career-orientation.

On the basis of her analyses, Diness draws the following conclusions about the returning women students most in need of moral support:

> 1. Women in given age-life cycle-status sets—for example, "young mother of young children" or "older, divorced, low-income mother of postadolescent children"—who deviate from the traditional expectations for these sets must struggle against pressures to conform to them.
> 2. Struggling against such social expectations takes some emotional strength, which is sometimes conditioned by past experiences, especially by past personal failures and successes affecting self-confidence.
> 3. Past educational and occupational failures or successes are important factors shaping self-confidence for subsequently undertaking related goals.
> 4. The women who have had the fewest relevant successes in the past, and especially those who tend to see themselves personally as the basic source of past successes and failures, have the least basis for self-confidence in undertaking related endeavors. The more that the new endeavor is deviant from, and unsupported by, social expectations, the greater the need for self-confidence in undertaking it. Moreover, the weaker the basis for self-confidence, and the greater the degree of deviance of the undertaking, the greater the need for external social and relevant sources of moral support [in press].

Diness believes, therefore, that among those most in need of moral support will be "older married women in associate or bachelor's degree programs, especially in fields often considered 'less practical'; married and single women whose education had been interrupted for unspecified, personal reasons; and those in transition from traditional to nontraditional orientations. In brief, "the general profile of the scholarship recipients most needing and most amenable to a morale boost from a distant source is that of the later-blooming or re-blooming older married woman who senses a transition in her life and has begun to test her potential for achieving a new role" (in press).

It is clear that these returning students are well worth investing academic resources in. It is also clear that they need more than the refresher courses and counseling services—including workshops in assertiveness training, career and academic planning, and tactics for survival in graduate schools—now offered (Pascoe, 1977). Among the concessions such students have had to ask for from colleges have been structural changes that make it possible for them to accommodate both family and academic obligations, such as changes in course times or pace of programs, and provision of childcare services.

One drawback of providing these equalizing conditions is the fact that it has, in effect, created academic ghettoes in at least some of the noncredit programs of continuing education for women. In most of the courses scheduled at times and places suitable for these women, women have inevitably predominated. This has been both liberating and limiting. Association with other women has strengthened these women's self-confidence (Katz, 1976), but it has also tended to be segregative. This, it may be added parenthetically, is a policy issue that plagues other minorities also: how much separatism? how much assimilation? It is an old issue in the field of women's education (Howe, 1975). The answer seems to lie in finding the best "mix."

Flexibility, it has been pointed out, does not mean absence of structure. If traditional structures are too rigid, new patterns might not be structured enough. Perhaps one of the most valuable aspects of any serious educational program is precisely its discipline. Attempting to explain how some women have survived the grueling obstacle course toward successful careers, Dorthy Zinberg (1973) notes that "what seems to mark those who have overcome many of the vicissitudes . . . and who have climbed the next rungs of a successful career . . . is that their work was and is a relatively conflict-free sphere of their personalities" (pp. 134-135). This observation may have relevance for colleges dealing with returning women. The goal, Zinberg suggests, is not to do away with discipline but to create "an environment in which women are enabled to resolve their women-work conflict with more support from the system" (p. 135).

Implications of the Feminist Perspective

Curriculum. There is a growing belief among women that the knowledge embedded in the college curriculum does not take sufficient account of women's experience and hence does not prepare either women or men for current realities. In 1976, for example, Ruth Hubbard, one of only fourteen tenured faculty women at Harvard, called attention to the fact that "out of roughly 700 courses offered by the Arts and Sciences faculty, about half a dozen dealt explicitly with women's experiences and only one or two did so from a feminist perspective" (Hubbard, 1976). Wilma Scott Heidi comments that "since it can be demonstrated that those other some 694 courses are, in effect, limited men's studies, albeit by other names, a profound social illiteracy results from such continued miseducation" (Heidi, 1978).

Academia has had a hard time coming to terms with women. Learning has historically been a male preoccupation, and it bears a strong male stamp. It has been even harder for men to admit women to the world of learning than to the world of work or of social life. Learning was their prerogative. They had created it. It reflected their concerns, their interests. Women were not really capable of entering into that realm—at least not very far into it. They could imitate, but only at a fairly low level. They were not at home in that male world. There is, indeed, a great deal of truth in the statement that learning to date has been basically designed to meet male needs.

But we are coming now to see that academic learning is incomplete, biased, parochial. It has little to say about women or the world of women. Today, however, women—and some men—are busily engaged in correcting these defects and, in the process, creating whole areas of thought and research. In the last few years, a notable group of women scholars have been producing work in the arts, the humanities, the social and behavioral sciences, anthropology, and history that enormously enlarge our perspective on human life and culture, both past and present. Elise Boulding (1976) has put together a great deal of "the underside of history." Michelle Zimbalish Rosaldo and Louise Lamphere (1974) have supplied a critique of the sexual biases in anthropology. Rae Carlson (1972) has shown how a great deal of psychological research fails to deal adequately with women. Jessie Bernard (1976) has pointed out the sexist nature of sociology. In October 1977, a conference on "The Equitable Pursuit of Knowledge" was held at the University of Wisconsin to explore the implications and consequences of inequitable and biased pursuit of knowledge in such disciplines as history, philosophy, psychology, literature, theology, sociology, and political science. New interpretations of these areas of learning were presented by scholars of national note (Sherman, 1979). Colleges in the future will be remiss if they do not incorporate this body of learning into their curriculums.

To date, much of this research and scholarship has been presented in "women's studies" courses, so-called, rather than incorporated into the mainstream of academic learning. In 1975, Barnard College was offering a dozen such courses in eleven departments; some schools were offering majors and some even graduate degrees (*New York Times,* May 7, 1975). This despite the reluctance of some administrators to recognize them. One administrator questioned whether this body of scholarship really represented an academic or intellectual discipline. The new courses seemed too emotionally involving —not "cold" enough. Barnard's president, Mary Bunting (1974), attested to their gripping quality: "the study of women is, itself, an exciting focus. Those of us who have seen previously tepid students become self-directed historians, psychologists, or sociologists understand the stimuli and can only applaud" (p. 210). She maintained that the existence of such courses and "eventually the inclusion of appropriate material about women in regular courses in history, economics, literature, social studies, and the arts will help to change the climate of unexpectation that . . . undoubtedly discouraged many" in the past (p. 210).

The problem of how best to introduce this burgeoning corpus of scholarship and research has by no means been solved. Should the research on women be taught in separate courses or should it be incorporated into other courses where relevant? Some students of the problem prefer the model of separate courses, offered within the traditional departments if not in special departments. Others object to departmental courses, preferring interdisciplinary approaches. Still others believe that the scholarship dealing with women should be integrated into all the relevant courses. They fear that separating it into special courses, whether in traditional departments or in separate departments, will mean relegating it to an intellectual ghetto, into which few male students will venture. Kenneth Boulding (in Strober, 1976) sees a new interdisciplinary science emerging, which he labels *dimorphics.*

One solution to the problem of incorporating the new work—in this case, on sex roles—into the curriculum is exemplified by an experiment at M.I.T., which takes the form of "co-teaching." Mary Rowe (1977) describes it:

What Do We Teach?

Robert Fein and I have co-taught women's studies at M.I.T., in a seminar called Androgyny, since 1973. The seminar is open to students, employees, faculty, and spouses. It is an interdisciplinary, scholarly overview of sex roles. The goals are: to help students formulate a coherent, intellectual perspective on sex roles, to understand their own values in this arena, and to develop a basis for rational public policies affecting the lives of women and men. Seminar materials change every semester, as new research is published, and to reflect the changing public policy implications of sex role studies. Most materials are drawn from the fields of history, psychology, economics, management, political science, and law. The seminar can be taken as part of a "humanities concentration" in Wo/Men's Studies, but is ordinarily taken as an elective, by students in many disciplines. . . .

The Rationale for Wo/Men's Studies

Both of us have been profoundly influenced by women's materials and men's materials separately read and taught and discussed. Each of us has participated over time in a single-sex discussion group. Each of us has seen the past and continuing need for women and men sometimes to be able to meet and do sex-role research on their own. Why then do we teach (and co-teach) Women's Studies/Men's Studies?

As it happens, the Women's Studies/Men's Studies formulation is now a convenient one, from the legal point of view, since Title IX problems are being raised elsewhere around the country about teaching just Women's courses. This is, however, a serendipitous advantage for M.I.T., since we began to teach as we do for different reasons. I would like to begin by a comment on the nature of Men's Studies, for those to whom the concept is not familiar. Many feminists believe that most standard education and most traditional history are his-tory, the study of men. "All M.I.T. *is* men's studies!" people say. We intend the term Men's Studies to refer to the study of men's lives within a new paradigm, as feminism and Women's Studies represent a new paradigm for thinking about women. Men's Studies inquires into the counterpart issues for men: expressiveness, nurturance, the ways men relate to each other, occupational segregation for men, and so on.

Men's Studies is not a "Men's Auxiliary to the Women's Movement." Studies of male sex roles, and needed changes for men, are undertaken by many men on behalf of men. As many women have been interested in women's studies principally on their own behalf, many men are interested in men's lives principally for their own reasons. . . . Why do we co-teach? We have both come to believe that the experiences of men and women are so profoundly different from each other that it is very difficult to teach and learn about androgyny by oneself, let alone teach both sexes of students by oneself. Having a co-teacher, particularly in a frontier field, where teachers and students must both continually work to understand their own feelings about the subject matter, also provides relief and greater objectivity and perspective. It allows for greater individual support and guidance for students in need [pp. 10-11].

So much, then, for some of the implications of the feminist perspective for the contents and presentation of the curriculum. In addition, the feminist perspective also has implications for other aspects of the organization and governance of colleges. It raises the question with respect to the resolution of every policy issue: Is this decision fair to women?

Professional Development. In 1976, Helen Astin pointed to our lack of information on "how graduate and professional schools affect women's development" and asked "what experiences do women graduate students have?" and "how are they being socialized? who are their mentors and how do they treat them?" (p. 3). Some light has been shed on these questions in recent years. In the past, women graduate students accepted discrimination "as a normal state of affairs" (Weiner, 1973, p. 74). When several young women soon after World War II "wanted to go on to graduate school for master's or doctor's degrees in meteorology, our professors were considerably shocked. Some laughed, and a few in key positions were openly hostile" (Simpson, 1973, p. 65). Nor had blatant sexism markedly subsided in the late 1960s. But women graduate students were no longer accepting it as a normal state of affairs. They were protesting it vigorously

(Rossi and Calderwood, 1973). And they were being heard. The Women's Program of the Department of Health, Education, and Welfare sponsored a study of the way women in schools training students for the health professions were being dealt with. Not only the blatant forms of discrimination but also the more subtle ones—such as the put-down and the "stag effect" (Bernard, 1976)—were being called to our attention. Mary Rowe (1977) of M.I.T., in an unpublished paper—"Saturn's Rings"—which has now become a classic, described the small, subtle ways in which sexism reveals itself. Others have followed her example. By now, a fairly extensive research literature exists documenting the adverse conditions for the development of women in academia and the actual discrimination directed against them (Rossi and Calderwood, 1973; Furniss and Graham, 1974; Roberts, 1976).

Barriers to the professional achievement of women have traditionally been so high that only exceptional women have been able to surmount them. But Felice Schwartz (1973) now asks, why should women have to be so much more talented and motivated than men to reach the same level of achievement? By definition, the broad population of educated women does not possess extraordinary strengths. Therefore, to the extent that we wish to help women work at a level commensurate with their abilities, it is more productive to examine the life situations and needs of *most* women than it is to dwell on the special conditions that enhance the ability of extraordinary women to achieve great success but will not, in themselves, enable less-than-extraordinary women to pursue productive careers.

When Wellesley College was established, the president was so eager to have women on his faculty that he was willing to subsidize their training. But there has been relatively little emphasis placed on professional development of women faculty in recent years—despite the strong feeling among women that there should be more women on faculties of all kinds of colleges, not only for the contribution they can make intellectually but also for the example they can set for women students. Joseph Katz (1976) has commented on the camaraderie that can develop among women faculty and students:

> there is [among the women he studied] the shared sense of the community of scholars, an exchange of ideas, attitudes, perceptions, and feelings beyond what many undergraduate women can accomplish and beyond what many professorial scholars can achieve in their academic departments, separated as faculty are from each other by virtue of the divisions of rank, competition, and sheer lack of leisure [p. 93].

Colleges in the future may well find that investment in the professional development of their women faculty members is one that pays off well, not only in the correction of the almost exclusively male perspective embedded in their curriculums but also in the contribution their sheer presence may make to the development of students.

Administrative Style. The male style—competitive and hierarchical—still prevails in academia, with its almost compulsive ranking to see who or which school is tops, middle, low. Competition for research grant money, for research contracts, for foundation funding continues to characterize academic institutions now as in the past. But there is also a counter-culture developing that is more hospitable to the new kinds of students colleges now have to deal with—hospitable not only to women but also to members of lower-socioeconomic classes and ethnic minorities.

Thus, for example, there is a small social movement called Re-evaluation Counseling that is attempting to substitute a cooperative, loving relationship in the learning enterprise for a hostile, competitive one. Its newsletter, *Colleague,* reports on two College and University Faculty Workshops, at which such topics as these were discussed: ending teaching biased toward the middle and upper classes, becoming people's intellectuals, and counseling on racism. In contrast to the implicit snobbism of so much of academia, this counter-culture is strongly anti-elitist. According to Harvey Jackins (1977), in *Colleague,* "Elitism not only separates us from our allies, the other sections of society who do the work and produce the value upon which we live, but it has a damaging effect upon ourselves. The other side of the coin of elitism is loneliness and isolation. Elitism spoils every day of our lives to the extent that it gets into our practice and our feelings" (p. 9).

What would colleges be like if women were more involved in running them—if they had more to say about their policies, organization, and operation? Pamela Roby (1972) has summarized the answer of one young woman to this question:

> Academics would live and work in cooperation and love, as women, once jealous of one another, are learning to do in the women's movement. Faculty would be known by the quality of their teaching, community service, scholarship, and colleagueship with faculty and students, rather than judged on the number of their publications, consultationships, professional affiliations, and research grants. In listening to one another, academics would try to grasp the ideas each had to offer and help develop them, rather than search only for clues as to how they might be rejected. Their relationships would not be without differences of opinion, but the differences would be honestly aired rather than hidden under layers of subterfuge.
>
> In a cooperative setting, academics would trust one another with problems, both intellectual and personal, and grow through sharing them. They would support and help one another, freely exchanging, rather than guarding, information, ideas, and data. No longer having to guard their ideas, failures, and successes from other faculty, professors could more easily share them with students. Furthermore, with cooperation rather than competition characterizing relations among faculty, superfluous status distinctions between professors and students would disappear, for professors would not need the distinctions to reinforce their egos. Instead, students, knowing faculty as human beings, would admire their strengths and empathize with their weaknesses. Both would learn much personally as well as intellectually from one another, and their personal development would facilitate greater intellectual development.
>
> Surely, academics would find, as movement women are finding, that an atmosphere of love is more conducive to creativity and growth than one of self-seeking and adverse relations. This vision of interpersonal relations is not out of our reach. . . . Given society's norms for men and women, achieving this model of social relations is likely to require greater change in the socialization and culture of men than in that of women. But men as well as women have been victimized by the present system and oppressed by its norms. We all have our humanity to gain from change [pp. 119-120].

Whether or not this utopian view is the wave of the future, it is an essential ingredient in the thinking of some of the younger academicians of both sexes today about colleges in the future. It will take time before it infiltrates into the traditional college. But it is implicit in the orientation of this volume toward the future American colleges, which would serve nontraditional students of whatever age, background, and sex.

References

Alexander, K. L., and Eckland, B. K. "School Experience and Status Attainment." In S. E. Dragastin and G. H. Elder, Jr. (Eds.), *Adolescence in the Life Cycle, Psychological Change and Social Context.* Washington, D.C.: Hemisphere, 1975.

Andersen, C. (Ed.). *A Fact Book on Higher Education.* Second Issue. Washington, D.C.: American Council on Education, 1975a.

Andersen, C. (Ed.). *A Fact Book on Higher Education.* Third Issue. Washington, D.C.: American Council on Education, 1975b.

Anderson, J. V. "Psychological Determinants." In R. B. Kundsin (Ed.), *Women and Success: The Anatomy of Achievement.* New York: Morrow, 1973.

Angrist, S. S., and Almquist, E. M. *Careers and Contingencies: How College Women Juggle with Gender.* New York: Dunellen, 1975.

Aries, P. *Centuries of Childhood: A Social History of Family Life.* New York: Knopf, 1960.

Astin, H. S., and Associates. *Some Action of Her Own: The Adult Woman and Higher Education.* Lexington, Mass.: Heath, 1976.

Bernard, J. *Remarriage: A Study of Marriage.* New York: Dryden Press, 1956.

Bernard, J. *Academic Women.* University Park, Penn.: Pennsylvania State University Press, 1964.

Bernard, J. *Women and the Public Interest: An Essay on Policy and Protest.* Chicago: Aldine, 1971.

Bernard, J. *Women, Wives, Mothers: Values and Options.* Chicago: Aldine, 1975.

Bernard, J. "Women's Continuing Education: Whither Bound?" In H. S. Astin and Associates, *Some Action of Her Own: The Adult Woman and Higher Education.* Lexington, Mass.: Heath, 1976.

Boulding, E. *The Underside of History: A View of Women Through Time.* Boulder, Colo.: Westview Press, 1976.

Broverman, D., and others. "Sex-Role Stereotypes and Clinical Judgments of Mental Health." *Journal of Consulting and Clinical Psychology,* 1970, *34* (1), 1-7.

Bunting, M. I. "Education: A Nurturant if Not a Determinant of Professional Success." In R. B. Kundsin (Ed.), *Women and Success: The Anatomy of Achievement.* New York: Morrow, 1974.

Cain, L. D. "Life Course and Social Structure." In R. E. L. Faris (Ed.), *Handbook of Modern Sociology.* Chicago: Rand McNally, 1964.

Caplow, T., and McGee, R. *The Academic Market Place.* New York: Basic Books, 1958.

Carlson, R. "Understanding Women: Implications for Personality Theory and Research." *Journal of Social Issues,* 1972, *28,* 17-32.

Chickering, A. W. *A Conceptual Framework for Educational Alternatives at Empire State College.* Saratoga Springs, N.Y.: Empire State College, 1976.

Chickering, A. W. "Developmental Change as a Major Outcome." In M. T. Keeton and Associates, *Experiential Learning: Rationale, Characteristics, and Assessment.* San Francisco: Jossey-Bass, 1976.

Clausen, J. A. "The Social Meaning of Differential Physical and Sexual Maturation." In S. E. Dragastin and G. H. Elder, Jr. (Eds.), *Adolescence in the Life Cycle, Psychological Change and Social Context.* New York: Wiley, 1975.

Coup, R. F., Greene, S., and Gardner, B. B. *A Study of Working-Class Women in a Changing World.* Chicago: Social Research, 1973.

Deinhardt, B. " 'Mother of Men'?" In W. T. Furniss and P. A. Graham (Eds.), *Women in Higher Education.* Washington, D.C.: American Council on Education, 1974.

Diness, P. *Older Women Who Return to School: Follow-up of Recipients of Scholarships by Business and Professional Women's Foundation,* in press.

Erikson, E. *Identity: Youth and Crisis.* New York: Norton, 1968.

Feldman, S. D. *Escape from the Doll's House: Women in Graduate and Professional School Education.* New York: McGraw-Hill, 1974.

Furniss, W. T., and Graham, P. A. (Eds.). *Women in Higher Education.* Washington, D.C.: American Council on Education, 1974.

Furstenberg, F. F., Jr. "Prenatal Pregnancy and Marital Instability." *Journal of Social Issues,* 1976, *32,* 67-86.

Garfinkle, S. "Work in the Lives of Women." In *International Population Conference.* Vol. 3. Dorchester, England: Dorset Press, 1969.

Getman, L. "From Conestoga to Career." In W. T. Furniss and P. A. Graham (Eds.), *Women in Higher Education.* Washington, D.C.: American Council on Education, 1974.

Ginzberg, E., and Associates. *Life Styles of Educated Women.* New York: Columbia, 1966.

Glick, P. *American Families.* New York: Wiley, 1957.

Glick, P. "A Demographer Looks at American Families." *Journal of Marriage and the Family,* 1975a, *37,* 15-27.

Glick, P. *Some Recent Changes in American Families.* Current Population Reports: Special Studies, Series P-23, No. 52. Washington, D.C.: U.S. Government Printing Office, 1975b.

Heidi, W. "Feminism Making a Difference in Our Health." In M. Nottman and C. Haddson (Eds.), *Women in Context: Development and Stresses.* Vol. 2. New York: Plenum, 1978.

Horner, M. "Research Trends and Needs in Women's Education and Career Development." Occasional Paper No. 1 (H. Astin, Ed.) presented at a meeting of the National Coalition for Research on Women's Education and Development, sponsored by the Johnson Foundation at Wingspread, Racine, Wis., June 1974.

Howe, F. "Women and the Power to Change." In F. Howe (Ed.), *Women and the Power to Change.* New York: McGraw-Hill, 1975.

Hubbard, R. "With Will to Choose." *Harvard Crimson,* Oct. 19, 1976.

Jackins, H. "Becoming People's Intellectuals." *Colleague,* 1977, *2,* 9-12.

Katz, J. "Home Life of Women in Continuing Education." In H. S. Astin and Associates, *Some Action of Her Own: The Adult Woman and Higher Education.* Lexington, Mass.: Heath, 1976.

Lever, J., and Schwartz, P. *Women at Yale: Liberating a College Campus.* Indianapolis, Ind.: Bobbs-Merrill, 1971.

Lopata, H. *Occupation Housewife.* New York: Oxford University Press, 1971.

McIntosh, M. C. "Education." In R. B. Kundsin (Ed.), *Women and Success: The Anatomy of Achievement.* New York: Morrow, 1973.

Mastro, R. "Two Yale Faculty Accused of Sex Harassment." *Washington Post,* July 19, 1977.

Moynihan, D. P. Address at commencement exercises of Capitol Page School, June 6, 1977.

National Manpower Council. *Womanpower.* New York: Columbia University Press, 1957.

Norton, A. J., and P. C. Glick. "Marital Instability: Past, Present, and Future." *Journal of Social Issues,* 1976, *32,* 5-20.

Oppenheimer, V. K. "Demographic Influence on Female Employment and the Status of Women." In J. Huber (Ed.), *Changing Women in a Changing Society.* Chicago: University of Chicago Press, 1973.

Papanek, H. "Men, Women, and Work: Reflections on the Two-Person Career." In J. Huber (Ed.), *Changing Women in a Changing Society.* Chicago: University of Chicago Press, 1973.

Parke, R., Jr., and Glick, P. C. "Prospective Changes in Marriage and the Family." *Journal of Marriage and the Family,* 1967, *29,* 240-256.

Pascoe, E. J. "For Older College Women." *McCalls,* March 1977, p. 45.

Pifer, A. "Women Working: Toward a New Society." In *Annual Report of the Carnegie Corporation.* New York: Carnegie Corporation, 1976.

Rabiner, S. *The Village Voice,* May 24, 1976.

Rich, A. "Toward a Woman-Centered University." In F. Howe (Ed.), *Women and the Power to Change.* New York: McGraw-Hill, 1975.

Roberts, J. I. (Ed.). *Beyond Intellectual Sexism: A New Woman, A New Reality.* New York: McKay, 1976.

Roby, P. "Women and American Higher Education." *Annals of the American Academy of Political and Social Science,* 1972, *404,* 118-139.

Rodriguez, G. "Coeds View an Undergraduate Campus." In W. Furniss and P. A. Graham (Eds.), *Women in Higher Education.* Washington, D.C.: American Council on Education, 1974.

Rosaldo, M. Z., and Lamphere, L. (Eds.). *Woman, Culture and Society.* Stanford, Calif.: Stanford University Press, 1974.

Rossi, A. S., and Calderwood, A. (Eds.). *Academic Women on the Move.* New York: Russell Sage Foundation, 1973.

Rowe, M. "Co-Teaching Wo/Men's Studies at M.I.T." Unpublished paper, Massachusetts Institute of Technology, January 1977.

Safilios-Rothschild, C. *Sex Role Socialization and Sex Discrimination: A Syllabus and Critique of the Literature.* Washington, D.C.: National Institute of Education, 1979.

Sanford, N. *The American College.* New York: Wiley, 1962.

Schmidt, G. P. *The Liberal Arts College: A Chapter in American Cultural History.* New Brunswick, N.J.: Rutgers University Press, 1957.

Schwartz, F. N. "Women and Employers: Their Related Needs and Attitudes." In R. B. Kundsin (Ed.), *Women and Success: The Anatomy of Achievement.* New York: Morrow, 1973.

Schwartz, P., and Lever, J. "Women in the Male World of Higher Education." In A. S. Rossi and A. Calderwood (Eds.), *Academic Women on the Move.* New York: Russell Sage Foundation, 1973.

Sherman, J. (Ed.). *The Prism of Sex: Toward an Equitable Pursuit of Knowledge.* Madison: University of Wisconsin Press, 1979.

Simpson, J. "Meteorologist." In R. B. Kundsin (Ed.), *Women and Success: The Anatomy of Achievement.* New York: Morrow, 1973.

Strober, M. H. "Toward Dimorphics: A Summary Statement to the Conference on Occupational Segregation." In M. Blaxall and B. Reagan (Eds.), *Women and the Workplace: The Implications of Occupational Segregation.* Chicago: University of Chicago Press, 1976.

Tangri, S. *Effects of Background, Personality, College, and Post-College Education on Women's Post-Graduate Employment.* In press.

Weiner, R. "Chemist and 'Eco-Freak.' " In R. B. Kundsin (Ed.), *Women and Success: The Anatomy of Achievement.* New York: Morrow, 1973.

Women's Bureau. *1975 Handbook on Women Workers.* Washington, D.C.: U.S. Government Printing Office, 1975.

Zinberg, D. "College: When the Future Becomes the Present." In R. B. Kundsin (Ed.), *Women and Success: The Anatomy of Achievement.* New York: Morrow, 1973.

12

Jacqueline Fleming

Special Needs of Blacks and Other Minorities

Each year more black and other minority students are entering major American colleges and universities, and for the first time a majority of them are enrolled in predominantly white schools. These students face special adjustment problems, both social and academic, which colleges must recognize if they are committed to providing equal opportunities for minority students. Although most of our evidence comes from studies of black students, our daily experiences suggest that the same problems are encountered by other minorities as well.

Black students on white campuses are a relatively recent phenomenon. Less than thirty years ago, over 90 percent of black students (approximately 100,000 in 1950) were being educated in traditionally black schools—excluded from other institutions by law, custom, or financial barriers. In the South, segregation barriers made it impossible for blacks to attend white colleges. At the same time, few northern institutions were willing to enroll black students, partly because of stereotypical beliefs that blacks were unable to benefit from higher education and partly because of the social stigma attached to the black presence in white society (Gurin and Epps, 1975). Up until the Civil War, only about 28 blacks had graduated from American colleges (Gurin and Epps, 1975), and by 1936 only 143 blacks had earned B.A. degrees from northern white institutions (Johnson,

1938). Even by 1964, only about 20 percent of baccalaureate degrees awarded to blacks were earned at predominantly white colleges (Gurin and Epps, 1975).

According to some current estimates, about two thirds to three fourths of the black students now in college are in predominantly white educational settings (Boyd, 1974; Gurin and Epps, 1975). As of 1967, there were estimated to be 133,000 black students in white colleges and nearly 95,000 of them in colleges outside the South (Bowles and DeCosta, 1971). Gurin and Epps report that 278,000 students were in non-black institutions in 1968—representing a 144 percent increase from the 114,000 enrolled in 1964. In 1970, the U.S. Census Bureau reported that 378,000 black students were attending predominantly white colleges and universities. But, while the absolute numbers seem large, blacks are still underrepresented in college—particularly in private and four-year public institutions, since about one half of all black college students are enrolled in two-year colleges. Only about 25,000 black students were enrolled at selective white colleges by 1970 (Levitan, Johnston, and Taggart, 1975). In the last ten years or so, the percentage of black students has increased from less than 1 percent to more than 5 percent on many major college campuses (Gibbs, 1974), but on individual campuses the numbers of black students are actually quite small. In a study of four institutions, Willie and McCord (1972) point out that the 384 students on the combined campuses represented less than 2 percent of the combined student bodies of 26,750. Furthermore, in many private schools and in most southern schools the proportions are even lower (Winkler, 1974; Davis and Borders-Patterson, 1973).

Major American colleges have, to be sure, had very little contact with black students or other minority groups until recently and thus have had little experience in meeting their needs (Bowles and DeCosta, 1971). Many black students in these institutions are there by virtue of recruitment efforts that began on a large scale in the 1960s. During this same decade, the formerly segregated institutions of the South first opened their doors to black students. The prospects for these students must have seemed bright. The students were said to be motivated, and scholarships were available for the well-qualified. More important, they were taking advantage of opportunities denied blacks until this time. The numbers of black students enrolled suggested that these students would not suffer the isolation experienced by their counterparts just a decade before. Indeed, Davis and Borders-Patterson (1973, p. 8) reported that incoming black students (in North Carolina colleges) seemed to be "reasonably confident and unapprehensive, to be excited about their eventual opportunity to get a job, and to be open-minded to the prospect of a pleasant new experience."

However, while some researchers present a positive picture of black student adjustment in spite of racism and relative social isolation (Boyd, 1974), others point to notable academic failure, demonstrations, and revolts as indications of considerable dissatisfaction (Sowell, 1972). Furthermore, colleges have frequently been unable to retain blacks, especially in the advanced years of higher education, and to graduate them on time (Davis and Borders-Patterson, 1973). There are, then, indications that the simple enrollment of black and other minority students merely means the beginning of new adjustment problems. The fact that minority students promise to constitute a sizable population in American colleges requires that we take a close look at the colleges' responsiveness to their needs.

Developmental Issues

The preceding chapters in this volume have examined many aspects of the developmental process and their relationship to education. In essence, these chapters consider how (or how well) the current system facilitates or feeds into a series of theoretically optimal paths toward responsible self-actualization. From these inquiries, we learn that college education has the potential for facilitating and stimulating development but that it may also ignore some important aspects of development and therefore have no impact on them or even inhibit them. There is a critical interaction between what the individual brings to the educational setting and the opportunities for change offered within it. The final outcome depends on both sets of contingencies.

For example, the college experience has the potential for broadening students' social worlds by exposing them to a wide range of people, within the peer group as well as the faculty. However, as Douvan notes in this volume, membership in exclusive peer groups (such as fraternities and sororities) can insulate potentially stimulating social diversity. Likewise, as Weathersby points out in her chapter, the process of learning is accompanied by anxiety and by change in the self system that is capable of stimulating a developmental crisis from which the individual could emerge with new personality strengths. However, too much inner stress and disequilibrium could place some students—particularly minority students—"at risk" in the face of life changes. Perry's chapter demonstrates that the development of a cognitive style conducive to open-minded thinking can develop gradually throughout the educational process as an adaptation to learning tasks. Yet students may come to college with highly fixed cognitive styles that are unresponsive to the intellectual tasks at hand.

Beyond the broad social and intellectual influences of college on students' development are the more subtle influences, which are often either taken for granted as by-products of the formal agenda or left to other unspecified agents or institutions. Optimal moral development, which is related to intellectual development, is shown not to be a simple, natural outcome of education (see Gilligan's chapter). In the usual absence of a direct effort to build moral character, its enhancement depends upon transcending a rigid adherence to moral right and wrong and developing the capacity to shift perspective, comprehend relative truth and justice, and question what was formerly taken for granted. For example, the development of an empathic concern for others or for something beyond oneself would seem to be essential for the development of a more humanitarian society. Yet White, in his chapter, points out that while education may be humanitarian in intent, the creation of a humanitarian environment within which the appropriate social concern might be fostered has been far from a guiding principle in education. Indeed, the competitive atmosphere in educational environments, both among faculty and students, constitutes a block to the development of empathy for others.

In many respects, then, higher education offers the promise of facilitating intellectual and personality growth. But a number of pitfalls exist for any given student, depending on such factors as modes of instruction, nature of contact with faculty, and influences of the informal educational subculture. If college students in general face such developmental challenges, what outcomes can be expected for those who come to college with a special set of characteristics that they must somehow reconcile with existing educational environments? How important is it that the cultural experiences of black students are often vastly different from those of average American populations? To the extent that racial prejudice and the psychological sets associated with minority status affect development, important issues are raised for black college students. The concrete issues of academic preparedness and sophistication add to their problems of adjusting to the academic environment.

Of course, the task before black students is to gain as much as possible from major American colleges and universities. Having only recently been provided with the opportunity to do so, they, like others, must learn to function in a socially and ethnically diverse society. For many black students, the college experience will be the most significant exposure to an integrated social environment, while for others an integrated environment will not be new or unusual. The college experience extends beyond the academic world, and in that broader respect it will certainly constitute a critical experience. So it becomes necessary to examine the impact of college on the development of black students and, specifically, the extent to which the colleges' lack of experience with black students, the small numbers, and the apparent lack of commitment to them, affects their chances of optimal development.

The sharp increase in numbers of black students on predominantly white campuses, as well as the social protests of the 1960s, have called attention to the adjustment problems facing minorities. One consequence has been a series of studies focusing on the experiences of these students. It is worth noting that the adjustment problems voiced by black students and researchers investigating their plight seem not to have been anticipated by the colleges and universities in question. Perhaps, as Kysar (1966) suggests, educational institutions have a need to subscribe to democratic ideals of intracultural unity and to ignore the effects of sociocultural and other factors on performance. Gibbs (1973) has pointed out that many of the problems experienced by black students can be traced to the incongruity between expectations of university staff and students themselves. Perhaps because of their lack of experience with black students, administrators and faculty members seemed to expect that black students would be assimilated into the university community without modification of the curriculum, provision of support services for high-risk students, hiring of minority faculty or staff, or attention to the sociocultural issues of dormitory life, dating, and social relationships.

The university's attitude toward minority students seems to be in line with its perception of itself as primarily an educational institution with only limited responsibilities to provide for the nonacademic life of students. Apart from traditional obligations for the housing, care, and feeding of residents, many universities have assumed that it is beyond the scope of their responsibility to concern themselves with the socioemotional welfare of students. Indeed, a survey of major institutions by McDaniel and McKee (1971) found a substantial lack of commitment to mobilizing university energies toward providing a comfortable environment for populations with special needs. The lack of attention to the optimal development of minority students is much like the lack of attention to many other aspects of general human development under consideration in this volume, which are seen by some as tangential to the task of education per se.

While there are a number of factors impinging on the educational experiences of black students, they can broadly be considered under social and intellectual factors.

Social Adjustment

A number of studies have recently been published on the social adjustment problems of black students. Unfortunately, there seems to be a dearth of theories specifically concerning the social functioning of minorities. However, Eriksonian theorizing on the developmental stage of adolescence (see References) may provide an appropriate viewpoint from which to interpret the significance of the research evidence, inasmuch as it is primarily concerned with ego identity—a concept that pervades much of the research. Adolescence, the transitional period between childhood and adulthood, which is artificially extended in our technological society and thus given added importance, is a period in which uncertainty about adult roles, the search for a new sense of continuity, and the need for establishing identity pose problems that must somehow be resolved. Developing the capacity for intimacy becomes a central task in establishing a personal identity as well as maintaining a sense of social solidarity.

Doubts about one's ethnic or sexual identity can lead to serious identity confusion. While attempting to establish secure psychosocial identities, adolescents may engage in behaviors to protect themselves against identity loss, such as immersion in adolescent subcultures, clannish and exclusive behavior, and testing others' loyalties. Although minority group membership could certainly serve to facilitate identity resolution (Gurin and Epps, 1975), Kysar (1966) suggests that minority students are prone to identity disorders and that the social atmosphere, whether one of acceptance or rejection, thus plays an important part in the developmental process during this period.

Social Isolation. Ideally, the college experience should provide an entrée into a broader social arena with new opportunities for making friends, dating, and learning and displaying social talents. But in contrast to the general opportunity for social broadening, some black students may face a more constricted social life than ever before. According to Boyd (1974), 60 percent of his nationwide interview-survey sample of black students complained about the low proportion of black enrollment. Jones and others (1970) found that black students on four white campuses ranked inadequate social life as one of their two most serious problems and attributed academic difficulties to these psychosocial factors. In a study of black students admitted under a special program at the University of Michigan, Hedegard and Brown (1969) found that freshmen tended to feel intense loneliness and that black women had a more difficult time socially on white campuses than did black men. Hedegard also found evidence that middle-class students were better able to adjust to the relatively impersonal environment of a large college.

In a study conducted by the Southern Regional Educational Board (Institute for Higher Educational Opportunity, 1970), black students on the campuses of five predominantly white junior colleges reported feeling isolated and expressed the desire for more opportunities to become involved in the full range of campus life. Willie and McCord (1972), in their study of black students on four predominantly white college campuses, provide evidence from personal interviews of the impoverished social lives of many black students on white campuses and suggest that the social situation can be especially severe when the absolute number of blacks on campus falls below seventy-five, as it often does. The limited range of social contacts that can be made with other blacks and the correspondingly limited range of personalities among which to establish alliances create a special set of problems. Also problematic are the lack of privacy in such a small world, which may be exacerbated by segregated floors of dormitories, the boredom with seeing the same faces, and the frustration of being forced into social encounters by necessity rather than by choice. Willie and McCord point to the anxiety that can be created by "last-chance" dating fears or premature moves toward exclusivity. Thus, social isolation clearly seems to constitute a problem for many black students—one that must frustrate the natural developmental needs at this age for interpersonal sharing.

Racial Prejudice. Several studies report that blacks come to integrated college settings expecting to be accepted by both blacks and whites and to establish friendships across as well as within racial lines. Sylvester Monroe (1973), in a personal account of his experiences as a Harvard undergraduate, writes that "black students were coming to Harvard expecting to be accepted and absorbed into the mainstream of university life." According to Davis and Borders-Patterson (1973), few of their respondents in four-year institutions in North Carolina had experienced close personal relationships with white individuals or groups, but most reported having had high hopes that they would be less likely to experience racism and discrimination in a university setting. However, the sometimes harsh realities of interracial encounters seem to combine with initial expectations to produce a heightened sensitivity to racial rebuffs. Davis and Borders-Patterson (1973) report that many of the black students in their study had experienced instances of what they perceived as racial prejudice—experiences of traumatizing indignities, which created the sense of being in a hostile environment. These authors also point out the particular sensitivity of black students to any rebuff in encounters with white students and suggest that under other circumstances similar incidents might be interpreted differently. Nonetheless, the perception of racial prejudice appears to result in a growing dislike and distrust of white people as well as general feelings of alienation. Indeed, research reports of the black students' experience routinely point to deliberate insults by whites, condescending attitudes, and the use of race as a basis for many forms of rejection (Willie and McCord, 1972; Boyd, 1974; Sowell, 1972).

Monroe's (1973) account considers the experience of being assigned to live with white roommates and points out that such an encounter can constitute one's first real confrontation with the issue of blackness, especially if one hails from an all-black environment. Even if the previous learning environment has been integrated, the intimacy of living arrangements necessitates a different level of contact. Black students may become upset and angered by white students' ignorance of black people and black customs and their unrestrained curiosity about physical and cultural differences:

> I remember vividly the questions they would ask: Someone would want to know whether my parents grew up on a plantation or whether my grandmother was a slave. Or someone else might ask whether my family's diet consisted mainly of soul food or whether anyone in my family had ever won a dance contest because of natural rhythm. I recall a friend's telling me once that a white girl even wanted to touch her [Afro-styled] hair [p. 46].

To the overt racism and hostility that do inevitably occur, some students react with shock, despair, and bitterness. But even when interracial relationships are not fraught with identifiable tensions or white supremacist attitudes, the lack of common background interests or future goals can create amiable but empty gaps in communication. Although Douvan notes that roommates are likely to become friends despite the inevitable interpersonal conflict arising from differences in habits and personalities, for black students the roommate relationship is complicated by racial anxieties that undoubtedly reduce the potential for long-lasting friendships. Thus, the odds may be stacked against a constructive resolution of one of the first and most critical college relationships.

Black Separatism. Black students may react in different ways to their minority status on predominantly white campuses. Among students seeking counseling at Stanford, Gibbs (1975) describes four general modes of adaptation: (1) withdrawal, (2) separation, (3) assimilation, and (4) affirmation. All four modes appear to be responses that black students employ in coping with their identity conflicts. The mode of separation, in particular, seems to derive from sensitivity to racism or hostility to whites and constitutes an aggressive stance akin to Pettigrew's (1964) "movement-against-the-dominant-group" response to oppression or perceived oppression. This mode, which has been given a great deal of attention in the literature, is characterized by a withdrawal (provided the numbers of black students are sufficient) into an all-black subculture. The evidence from Boyd's (1974) survey sample suggested that separatism was a minority viewpoint among black students. Gibbs (1975), however, describes separation as a frequent mode of adaptation among students who seek counseling services. According to Gibbs, this mode is characterized by "anger, hostility, conflicts in interpersonal relationships which may be expressed as rejection of whites, contempt for middle-class white values and behavior patterns, and active protests against white institutions and customs" (p. 734). Davis and Borders-Patterson (1973) also link feelings of alienation resulting from racial prejudice to a need to take refuge in black separatism.

Willie and McCord (1972) note that the separatist movement of black students on many college campuses is more than a political fad stemming from the political activities of the 1960s. It appears to be a product of the racism encountered by individual students and is a phenomenon that increases rather than decreases with the degree of interracial contact. The movement toward separation may not occur until there is a critical mass of students providing sufficient numbers and diversity within which to meet common needs. Monroe (1973) recounts his Harvard years as a predominantly black experience and reveals the conscious effort by black students to avoid any unnecessary contact with whites. He emphasizes the psychological closeness and solidarity that resulted from being able to share similar daily experiences, as well as past life experiences in black communities, and develop black organizations serving unifying social and political purposes. Thus, Willie and McCord describe black student separatism as an indication of a failure in the relationship between the black individual and white society, and as an adaptation to stress due to rejection—that is, a form of self-protection.

In a review of the literature on black students in white colleges, Ramseur (1975) observes that attendance at predominantly white schools tends to lead to changes in blacks' racial attitudes and orientation toward whites, on two levels. The experience not only increases the personal saliency of "blackness" and the issues associated with it but also precipitates broader ideological changes involving the cultural, interpersonal, and political orientation of black students toward other Afro-Americans and their culture. Davis and Borders-Patterson (1973) also specifically stress their "significant and undeniable finding that experience in white senior colleges or universities in most cases seems to lead the student toward an increasing consciousness of his blackness, toward an identity not with all people but with black people" (p. 8). These authors further point out that the small numbers and common experiences of black students on these campuses work together to sharpen their previous perceptions of themselves as identifiable minorities and also help them to identify unique aspects of their own cultural heritage, which may not have come so clearly into focus in an all-black institution.

It would seem that immersion in a white educational environment could provide an impetus for crystallizing the more inclusive identity elements, including the positive recognition of African roots alluded to by Erikson (1968). Monroe's statement that "everything I have done since then has been guided by a conscious black perspective" captures on an individual level the identity-focusing impact of the experience. Erikson's characterization of identity as a subjective sense of an "invigorating sameness and continuity, . . . an element of active tension, of holding one's own" seems to be reflected in a statement by another Harvard undergraduate (Williams, 1973, p. 44):

> In spite of what declaimers on either side have said, the two cultures are not incompatible. We prove that every day. There should be no reason why blacks at Harvard, or anywhere else, should be made to negate those qualities in ourselves that render us distinct from the mass while, simultaneously, affirming its existence. Black people in this country have a certain important input, a certain significant perception; this input and perception cannot possibly be pathological, since they have provided us with the necessary prowess to survive within a hostile American environment for over four hundred years. And they have been an input and perception that have provided this nation with conscience, and humor, and rhythm, and beauty.

While all black students may not undergo identity transformations, there is evidence that the movement toward a black ideological perspective is not an idiosyncratic phenomenon. In Ramseur's (1975) study of Harvard undergraduates, most of the change in black ideology occurred during the freshman year, and among freshmen there was a decreasing concern over integration (that is, a movement away from whites) and an increasing concern for black group unity. Amount and nature of previous and current interracial contact as well as organizational activity were the major predictors of status on these ideological issues. Using Ramseur's black ideology scale, Fleming (1977) found that in a sample of black students from four predominantly white schools in the Southeast there was a significant rise in mean black ideology scores after the effects of social class and Scholastic Aptitude Test (SAT) scores were controlled. No such increase in salience could be observed among students in three predominantly black schools in the same area. So it seems that it is specifically the experience in a predominantly white learning environment, rather than college education per se, that precipitates a rise in pro-black consciousness.

Although black student separatism may be a way of escaping stress that the individual cannot comfortably handle, it may itself have adverse effects. For example, Monroe (1973), a willing member of the separatist subculture at Harvard who sought the protection of the "black shield of solidarity," also acknowledged that it isolated black students from all experiences and environments that were not appealing, including opportunities to grow socially and intellectually:

> In essence, too many blacks simply misuse the ideological strength of black solidarity as a kind of cover to dupe the white community into believing that behind their united front of blackness they are mature, self-confident, and functioning black individuals, who know exactly what they want and how they will get it. But what I see and hear instead are frightened and insecure young black men and women who—in the words of a James Brown song—are constantly "talking loud and saying nothing" in an attempt to persuade themselves, more than anybody else, that they have the right answers [p. 48].

Kilson (1973a, b) holds that the separatist movement constitutes a crisis for black students and elaborates on several potentially negative effects. First, black students may be cut off from the rest of the student body by membership in separatist groups marked by antiwhite militancy and powerful peer group pressures for conformity to black solidarity behavior. Such pressures can produce emotional ambivalence in black students, who must decide to whom they owe their loyalties. Thus, not sitting at black dining tables, not living on black floors or in black dormitories, and developing friendships with white students could become the basis for rejection by other blacks. Indeed, Gibbs' (1974) separatist mode of adaptation results from an inability to live up to ideal expectations due to conflicting sets of pressures from blacks and whites and a desire to merge those elements of black and white culture consistent with one's personality and goals. Second, separatism effectively limits the participation of blacks in other social, cultural, and academic activities of the university that might contribute to broader development. It is dynamically akin to the effect, described in Douvan's chapter, that peer groups such as fraternities and sororities can have in protecting students from diversity in order to preserve or continue a distinct but narrow socialization. Thus, the critical stimulus and developmental value of diversity may be minimized for some students. Although there may well be diversity within the black student body, it cannot offer the exposure needed to help develop a tolerance for the stress accompanying black-white interactions.

Preoccupation with Social Problems. To the extent that black-white interactions do occur, they seem to have a definable impact on black students. Davis and Borders-Patterson (1973) report the feeling of one black freshman that he had become "cold, hard, cruel, calculating, prejudiced, and unfeeling . . . just like the whites in order to survive." The capacity to survive in an integrated setting may well require new coping mechanisms and personality changes. Fleming (1977), for example, found a number of indications that black students in white schools become more socially assertive and manipulative. The students expressed subjective feelings of having learned to deal with people and to cope with their current situation, using newly acquired techniques for survival. A great deal of their energies appeared to be directed toward learning to assert themselves in the face of an unresponsive or hostile environment.

There were actually indications in the data that black students were spending more of their energies in learning interpersonal coping strategies than in pursuits conducive to intellectual growth. These findings seem consistent with the observation by Davis and Borders-Patterson that black students in their North Carolina schools showed no unusual concern about academic performance in spite of alleged lower academic averages and higher attrition rates. The responses from their subjects suggested, instead, a preoccupation with social and interpersonal problems as opposed to academic ones. Indeed, their recommendations for easing the adjustment of future generations of black students centered on the interpersonal elements of college life.

Kilson (1973b) has specifically linked a preoccupation with militant separatist ideology to the "academic disarray" found among significant numbers of black students in Ivy League schools. He cites as evidence (1) that bright students (that is, those with high SAT scores) are performing below capacity, (2) that larger proportions of black than white students were ranked as unsatisfactory in academic performance, and (3) that fewer of the black graduating seniors take honors. Ramseur's (1975) study of Harvard undergraduates confirms Kilson's observation in that he found higher militancy scores among dropouts during the freshman year. Clark and Plotkin (1963) further showed that failure to establish satisfactory dating patterns and sensitivity to racial pressures were negatively related to academic functioning. Thus, whatever the nature and interrelationship of the various social influences and responses to them may be, it seems clear that they are critical to both college adjustment and intellectual development.

From the available literature, then, a number of specifically social factors can be isolated that constitute potential problems for black students in predominantly white colleges and universities. While not all black students necessarily face such problems, the numbers who do are substantial enough to have attracted considerable attention. Gibbs (1975) observes that the frequent clinical symptoms of role confusion, anxiety, and depression displayed by black students appear to be symptoms of the classic identity crisis.

Intellectual Influences

In Erikson's treatment of adolescence, the issues of interpersonal relationships and task orientation, which are preparatory to intellectual performance in college, are intertwined. Precisely because of the uncertainty of future adult roles, attention and energy become diverted toward and preoccupied with the interpersonal. But during this time fragmentary attempts are nonetheless made to look for people and ideas to have faith in and to serve. The choice of an occupational goal assumes primary significance in college. The inability to settle on an occupational identity disturbs many youth and may lead to a series of ideological attachments to clique heroes. During the search, the adolescent is "eager to be affirmed by peers, to be confirmed by teachers, and to be inspired by worthwhile ways of life."

Performance in Biracial Settings. Research investigating the intellectual and task behavior of blacks in controlled biracial settings has demonstrated that the productivity of black males may be seriously disrupted in biracial work situations (Katz, Goldston, and Benjamin, 1958; Katz and Benjamin, 1960). Blacks became less active in participating in problem-solving tasks, even when matched with white subjects for aptitude. They had less influence on team decisions and made more errors in biracial work groups compared with individual performance. Furthermore, black subjects displayed a distinctly compliant orientation to whites even when matched for intelligence, as indicated by less active communication, directing communications mainly to whites, and ranking whites higher on task performance despite no real differences in performance. To explain this alteration of black intellectual and social behavior, the researchers proposed the hypothesis that the generalized inhibition was due to feelings of personal threat, which were traceable to the black subject's fear of arousing white hostility by being assertive or displaying intellectual competence. In later studies the degree of interaction required by the task was reduced, and white experimenters or reference groups were used in place of white environments. Even so, similar inhibitive effects were induced by the presence of a white experimenter (Katz, 1967; Katz, Roberts, and Robinson, 1965) and by anticipated comparison with white norm groups (Katz, Epps, and Axelson, 1964; Katz and others, 1970). By contrast, the use of black experimenters and reference groups generally improved black students' performance.

However, Katz and his coworkers reported studies showing that blacks' performance is not necessarily disrupted in white environments. Although the performance of seriously disadvantaged students was likely to be impaired in stressful white settings, particularly when the intellectual significance of the task was stressed, performance of black students was actually enhanced in white settings when (1) a relatively relaxed atmosphere was created, (2) motor tasks (versus IQ tasks) were used, and (3) subjects had a history of academic achievement (Katz and Greenbaum, 1963; Katz, Roberts, and Robinson, 1965; Katz, 1967). The appearance of these inconsistencies made it clear that white environments may disrupt blacks' performance but that not all black subjects will be so affected. It also became clear that there are important differences in the climate and social meaning of integrated situations, which differentially contribute to the arousal of intellectual anxieties in black students. Consequently, researchers attempted to enumerate the debilitating and facilitative factors that might account for the variation in results. Most of this research concerned group effects, but a few attempts were made to assess individual differences in response to interracial situations. Using black male children aged 7 to 10, Katz, Henchy, and Allen (1968) showed that boys with a high need for approval performed very poorly when a white experimenter expressed disapproval and that boys with a low need for approval were unmotivated except when a black experimenter gave positive feedback. Katz and Benjamin (1960) found that subjects who reported being nervous in a threatening white environment performed more poorly than other subjects.

A summary of these studies indicates the following about black students' performance in biracial settings: (1) A high degree of interaction with whites on work-related tasks is likely to be accompanied by anxiety over the consequences of displaying competence and assertiveness. As a result of such fears, black students are likely to avoid such highly interactive situations. (2) Performance in the presence of whites, without a high degree of interaction, can also generate anxiety when the climate is hostile or the students are disadvantaged and are aware of this fact. (3) There are individual differences in the responses of black students to white environments. Thus, although the evidence derives from controlled laboratory situations, it clearly suggests that the backgrounds and personalities of black students may interact with the climate of white educational environments to create intellectual anxieties for some students and, perhaps, interfere with the normal developmental quest for competence. The basic areas for which at least some evidence is available on the real experiences of black students are faculty-student interactions, academic preparation, and curriculum.

Faculty-Student Relations. It is obvious that faculty play a key role in the college experience. Blocher and Rapoza, in this volume, point to the influence of faculty on students' vocational development, and Gurin and Epps (1975) show that informal contact with faculty outside the classroom is a critical factor in fostering high aspirations among black students. In addition, off-the-record testimonies to the importance of good faculty-student relationships are frequent. For example, a gathering of "outstanding" seniors at a well-known women's college revealed that each student could point to a member of the faculty or staff as a mentor who had provided professional or emotional encouragement and support.

Yet, despite the importance of good faculty-student relations, black students frequently find it difficult to establish rapport with their teachers. Boyd (1974) reports that 60 percent of his nationwide interview-survey sample expressed dissatisfaction with the percentage of blacks on the faculty and in the administration. About half (49 percent) of the students had experienced racial discrimination, and the incidents most often involved treatment by faculty members. Major problems appeared to involve perceived assumptions by blacks that professors view them as incompetent and dishonest, and that professors question the validity of outstanding work, ignore blacks, and are accessible only to white students. While the specific incidents range from the overt to the covert, they appear to have similar effects on students.

Willie and McCord (1972) also devote considerable attention to the lack of trust between faculty and black students. Seventy-five percent of their sample reported feeling that they received little, if any, help from faculty or administrators. Actual contact with faculty outside class was low, in that 40 to 45 percent of the students never conferred with a teacher during the course of a semester. Black students were less likely than white students to seek faculty advice in choosing classes or instructors and felt reluctant to register academic complaints directly with teachers. Furthermore, they felt faculty ignored them, as well as the black experience in their subject matter. In a comparative study in which black and white students in an engineering school rated their satisfaction with various aspects of the college experience, white students' evaluations of faculty and administration became more positive from freshman to senior year, while those of black students became more negative (Fleming, 1977).

There is, apparently, a clash between the expectations of black students and those of college staff, which makes rapport difficult to establish. Gibbs (1973) points out that while college staff may expect black students to become assimilated into the university without any substantial adjustment of academic structure or programs and to compete academically with whites who have had superior high school preparation, many of the black students seem to expect the university to be more flexible in responding to their needs and to impose less stringent academic requirements. The black faculty adviser can play an important role in bridging this gap in expectations (Willie and McCord, 1972). The black adviser serves as someone to talk to and identify with, as well as a source of information and help with academic problems. Yet to the extent that the adviser is assumed by students to hold ultimate loyalties to race rather than to administrative obligations and pressures, the relationship harbors potential sources of stress.

In sum, the experience of overt and covert racism in faculty-student interactions, together with the gap between faculty and student expectations, may create a climate of rejection and hostility for some black students. The experimental research has shown that such a climate is hardly conducive to optimal intellectual performance and that it could even thwart some of the primary psychological needs of adolescents for adult confirmation. As the experimental results suggest, however, faculty-student tensions may be alleviated if black faculty and advisers are available and supportive.

Academic Preparation. The push to increase black undergraduate enrollment in the face of a small pool of highly qualified black high school graduates has meant active recruiting efforts, which have necessarily extended to some students who do not meet all traditional admissions criteria. Thus, in any given college there will be some students who do not have the skills or preparation that the majority of students bring to the learning situation.

In an examination of the factors related to successful matriculation of black students in white schools, Green (1969) reports evidence that SAT-type scores are equally good predictors of performance for black and white students but that attitudinal and personality factors play a more crucial role in black students' performance. Effective tutorial and counseling programs can address both the academic and psychosocial problems and thereby help high-risk students perform successfully. Unfortunately, the response by colleges and universities to these needs of some minority students has been mixed. Although McDaniel and McKee (1971) found that the vast majority of reporting institutions had adjusted admissions requirements in some way, only 50 percent reported any kind of academic help program. Further, special programs to meet the needs of blacks were supported with institutional funds at only one fifth of reporting colleges, and only a minority of the schools reported trustee or faculty and administration support for such programs. The survey results agree with Green's (1969) report that many universities disclaim any responsibility to help overcome or make up for prior (and known) deficiencies of the high-risk students admitted.

Many of the black students see preparation for college as a major problem. According to Boyd (1974), 71 percent of his sample reported that, given another chance, they would prepare differently to eliminate deficiencies in their high school course work, especially in math, science, and English. Fifty-two percent rated their preparation for college as fair or poor, and 50 percent felt that they were "special admits." Willie and McCord (1972) also found that black students tend to feel that they were admitted by virtue of race without regard to their actual qualifications.

What with feelings of academic underpreparedness and less than adequate remedial help, it is no surprise that many black students find academic competition difficult. In Boyd's sample, only 26 percent of the black students had B averages or better, indicating that many would be unable to fulfill their high occupational ambitions. According to the self-report data gathered by Willie and McCord, only 23 percent of the black sample, as opposed to 49 percent of the white sample, maintained B averages or better, but racial gaps in performance appeared to have been bridged by the senior year. (Fleming, 1977), however, found that black students in engineering tended to perform more poorly than white students (with SAT scores controlled) and that their relative efficiency actually suffered some deterioration by the senior year.

In addition to the academic factors already mentioned, lack of demands for achievement can undermine black students' performance. Gurin and Epps (1975) point out that one of the factors associated with aspiration and achievement is an institutional belief that every individual can and will succeed. The attention that small black schools give to each student and their refusal to accept excuses for failure seem to induce students to perform at the top of their capabilities. In contrast, many complaints of black students in predominantly white colleges revolve around being ignored academically, being given less attention than other students, and generally not being valued. Such a syndrome seems akin to the findings of Katz, Henchy, and Allen (1968) that, among students needing approval, positive reinforcement goes a long way toward improving performance, while the lack thereof may depress performance.

Although many black students may be able to perform well in college, the consequences of academic failure for the individual must be considered. One of the patterns observed by Gibbs (1975) in counseling black students was a withdrawal response associated with academic failure and feelings of inadequacy. While academic failure seems to be associated with background factors such as low socioeconomic status and segregated high schools which may reduce tolerance for academic or social stress, such failure nevertheless makes students susceptible to depression and dropping out entirely. Bowles and DeCosta (1971) also warn that, while in the long run adjusted admissions policies will increase educational opportunity, in the short run there is the risk of multiplying the personal tragedies of failure, which may lead to student discontent and protests. Indeed, Sowell (1972) explicitly links a series of academic injustices done to black students—including admitting practices that bypass or reject very capable black students in favor of less qualified students who fit a more fashionable stereotype—to the widespread protests of the 1960s. Fleming (1977) finds evidence to suggest that thwarted academic energies of black students may be redirected into extracurricular activities providing an opportunity for symbolic or actual protest.

Thus, the literature suggests that some black students may be less qualified than many of their peers or may harbor feelings of academic underpreparedness. This situation appears to create a serious potential for failure, withdrawal, or even protest, depending on the specific background factors and experiences encountered. The experimental literature shows that perceived intellectual inferiority is an important factor in depressing performance below expected levels, and Erikson's theory clearly suggests psychological disturbance as one consequence of task-related failures at this age.

Curriculum. To the surprise of many educators, black students at predominantly white colleges have expressed considerable discontent with the content of the curriculum. Willie and McCord (1972) suggest that many black students, either because of a strong vocational orientation or because of their immersion in community problems, may have expected the curriculum to deal with issues real and relevant to them and to help provide solutions to community problems. Instead, they encountered subject matter having only peripheral relevance to their lives. Black literature was rarely assigned, offerings in African civilizations and languages were absent, and the black contribution to American culture was ignored. Furthermore, the ethnocentric tone of many subjects was apparent, and, in the absence of formal knowledge of black issues or authorities to whom to turn, black students often felt unable to challenge obvious racism.

Although black and African studies emerged largely as a response to militant demands, there was and is a growing consensus that the need for such programs is legitimate. But in spite of growing opinion in favor of such curriculums, many institutions offer no such programs and are making no efforts to create them (McDaniel and McKee, 1971). Furthermore, many existing programs are engaged in financial and political battles for survival.

The need for curriculums that are relevant to minority students' concerns can be understood on several levels. The situation with respect to curriculum recalls the experimental findings on performance in threatening (IQ-type) tasks versus nonthreatening (motor-type) tasks, inasmuch as content areas removed from or excluding black experience may create psychological blocks in the context of a hostile environment. Also, as

Schaie and Parr note in this volume, optimal learning depends on optimal degrees of novelty and familiarity in the educational stimuli. In practical educational terms, this usually means optimal levels of challenge and preparedness. Relevance has not usually been an issue in considering education compatible with that of the dominant culture. Yet for blacks, among whom the series of aforementioned factors may combine to create motivational inertia, the ability to identify with some aspect of the learning process may provide the necessary degree of involvement.

It is also possible, however, that the availability of black-related subjects may offer a ready escape from other pressures—what Willie and McCord refer to as a protective armor insulating students from a hostile white environment in much the same way as the retreat into black separatism. While near-total immersion in Afro-American studies may satisfy a pressing psychological need, there remains the question whether black studies alone can provide the skills necessary to confront the existing social problems after college. This same concern led Monroe (1973) to ask, "if the future holds nothing more for the graduates of black studies departments than teaching jobs in the black community, then who will be the black doctors, the technicians, and the architects of the future black community?"

Despite the prevalence of influences that may be intellectually debilitating for black students, there is little convincing evidence of differential persistence or attrition for black and white students (Institute for the Study of Educational Policy, 1976). The impact of these factors seems as a rule to inhibit and redirect performance rather than to disrupt it. Thus, black students' grade-point averages may be depressed below expected levels, and their choice of career goals may be influenced more by the traditional openness of the fields to blacks than by their personal interests. It would seem that black students in general would have to be motivated by a strong sense of challenge or obligation in order to surmount the long list of potential obstacles. It may also be that many black students today do not, as Katz once suggested, suffer from strong internalized fears of asserting themselves in work-oriented situations.

Prospects for Minority Students

Although the research reviewed specifically addresses the adjustment problems of black students, similar concerns could be raised for other minorities, such as Spanish-speaking Americans. Theoretically, any minority group visible enough to be a target for prejudice and discrimination may face a similar series of social and intellectual experiences. Indeed, for Spanish Americans, whose numbers on major campuses are even smaller than those of black students, social strains, arising from an inadequate network of social contacts and the inability to take refuge in a supportive subculture, may be even greater.

From the foregoing, it would seem that the prospects for black and other minority students in American colleges are at best uncertain. Beyond the usual problems associated with college life, black students also face problems peculiar to their minority status. As if minority status were not challenge enough, the psychological needs and vulnerabilities characteristic of adolescence intensify these students' problems. The lack of expertise that white institutions display in providing appropriate support for minorities is matched only by the discontinuity in the experience of many blacks entering college. At best, predominantly white colleges provide a training ground that can prepare students for the real-life interactions to come. Those who respond well to this challenge gain certain skills and confidence in their ability to cope. However, those who cannot cope with the shock of minority status and discrimination may experience loss of motivation and seek various kinds of insulation against the psychic tensions. For some of these students, the withdrawal may constitute a psychological period of regrouping, which may ultimately result in new personality strengths. But there will be those who do not resolve the conflicts aroused and who may have to relive them at a later and less flexible stage in life. Given the number of negative influences latent in the educational environment, the overall adjustment of black students certainly seems satisfactory. Still, there is room for improvement if optimal human development is the goal.

Given the less than optimal prospects for black students in mainstream American colleges, what might their prospects be in the hundred or so predominantly black colleges and universities? Black schools have had a long and venerable history to which the black middle class and today's prominent black leaders trace their intellectual roots (see Willie and Edmonds, 1978). However, these schools are now engaged in a struggle for survival on a number of counts. Among the educational consequences of their limited financial resources are poorer physical facilities and low salaries for teaching faculties. Thus, a prevailing opinion is that predominantly white colleges are better able to assume the responsibility for educating black Americans, as well as preparing them for life in an integrated world (Sowell, 1972; Myers, 1978). It is often conceded that black colleges offer an environment in which learning can take place without a high level of conflict and social isolation (Gurin and Epps, 1975). Indeed, predominantly black colleges not only provide a wide range of social contacts and dating opportunities but also encourage students to assume leadership positions in academic as well as extracurricular activities. The possibilities for recognition become virtually limitless in such surroundings, whereas in white environments the pervasive mechanisms of exclusion place artificial boundaries on the opportunities for self-validation. While the merits of a relatively conflict-laden educational environment versus a relatively supportive one must be decided by individual students, there is preliminary evidence that for some students the reduction in racial tension on black college campuses may offset the better resources of major American colleges, producing greater cognitive gains in addition to a well-rounded social development (Fleming, 1977).

References

Bowles, F., and DeCosta, F. A. *Between Two Worlds.* New York: McGraw-Hill, 1971.

Boyd, W. M. *Desegregating America's Colleges.* New York: Praeger, 1974.

Clark, K., and Plotkin, L. *The Negro Student at Integrated Colleges.* New York: National Scholarship Service for Negro Students, 1963.

Davis, J. A., and Borders-Patterson, A. *Black Students in Predominantly White North Carolina Colleges and Universities.* Research Report 2. New York: College Entrance Examination Board, 1973.

Erikson, E. *Identity: Youth and Crisis.* New York: Norton, 1968.

Fleming, J. "The Impact of Predominately White and Predominately Black Environments on the Functioning of Black Students." *Second Annual Report to the Carnegie Corporation.* New York: Carnegie Corporation, 1977.

Gibbs, J. T. "Black Students/White University: Different Expectations." *Personnel and Guidance Journal,* 1973, *51* (7), 463-469.

Gibbs, J. T. "Patterns of Adaptation Among Black Students at a Predominately White University." *American Journal of Orthopsychiatry,* 1974, *44* (5), 728-740.

Gibbs, J. T. "Use of Mental Health Services by Black Students at a Predominately White University." *American Journal of Orthopsychiatry,* 1975, *45* (3), 430-445.

Green, R. "The Black Guest for Higher Education: An Admissions Dilemma." *The Personnel and Guidance Journal,* 1969, *47,* 905-911.

Gurin, P., and Epps, G. *Black Consciousness, Identity and Achievement.* New York: Wiley, 1975.

Hedegard, J., and Brown, D. "Encounters of Some Negro and White Freshmen with a Public Multi-University." *Journal of Social Issues,* 1969, *25* (3), 131-144.

Institute for Higher Educational Opportunity. *New Challenges to the Junior Colleges: Their Role in Expanding Opportunity for Negroes. A Progress Report.* Atlanta, Ga.: Southern Regional Education Board, April 1970.

Institute for the Study of Educational Policy. *Equal Educational Opportunity for Blacks in U.S. Higher Education.* Washington, D.C.: Howard University Press, 1976.

Johnson, C. S. *The Negro College Graduate.* Chapel Hill: University of North Carolina Press, 1938.

Jones, J. C., and others. "Differences in Perceived Sources of Academic Difficulties: Blacks in Predominately Black and Predominantly White Colleges." Unpublished paper, 1970.

Katz, I. "Motivational Determinants of Racial Differences in Intellectual Achievement." *International Journal of Psychology,* 1967, *2,* 1-12.

Katz, I., and Benjamin, L. "Effects of White Authoritarianism in Biracial Work Groups." *Journal of Abnormal and Social Psychology,* 1960, *61,* 448-456.

Katz, I., Epps, E. G., and Axelson, L. J. "Effects upon Negro Digit Symbol Performance of Anticipated Comparison with Whites and with Other Negroes." *Journal of Abnormal and Social Psychology,* 1974, *69,* 77-83.

Katz, I., Goldston, J., and Benjamin, L. "Behavior and Productivity in Biracial Work Groups." *Human Relations,* 1958, *11,* 123-141.

Katz, I., and Greenbaum, C. "Effects of Anxiety Threat and Racial Environment on Task Performance of Negro College Students." *Journal of Abnormal and Social Psychology,* 1963, *66,* 562-567.

Katz, I., Henchy, T., and Allen, H. "Effects of Race of Tester, Approval-Disapproval and Need on Negro Children's Learning." *Journal of Personality and Social Psychology,* 1968, *8,* 38-42.

Katz, I., and others. "Factors Affecting Response to White Intellectual Standards at Two Negro Colleges." *Psychological Reports,* 1970, *27,* 995-1003.

Katz, I., Roberts, S. O., and Robinson, J. M. "Effects of Task Difficulty, Race of Administrator, and Instructions on Negro Digit Symbol Performance." *Journal of Personality and Social Psychology,* 1965, *2,* 53-59.

Kilson, M. "Black Students at Harvard: Crisis and Change." *The Harvard Bulletin,* 1973a, *75* (8), 24-27.

Kilson, M. "Blacks at Harvard: Solutions and Prospects." *The Harvard Bulletin,* 1973b, *75* (10), 31-32, 41-42.

Kysar, J. "Social Class and Adaptation of College Students." *Mental Hygiene,* 1966, *50* (3), 398-405.

Levitan, S., Johnston, W., and Taggart, R. *Still a Dream—The Changing Status of Blacks Since 1960.* Cambridge, Mass.: Harvard University Press, 1975.

McDaniel, R., and McKee, J. "An Evaluation of Higher Education's Response to Black Students." Unpublished paper, Indiana University, 1971.

Monroe, S. "Guest in a Strange House." *Saturday Review of Education,* February 1973, *1,* 45-48.

Myers, M. "Black Colleges' Future: An NAACP Official Speaks." *Los Angeles Times,* December 26, 1978, p. 7.

Pettigrew, T. *A Profile of the Negro American.* Princeton, N.J.: Van Nostrand, 1964.

Ramseur, H. "Continuity and Change in Black Identity: A Study of Black Students at an Interracial College." Unpublished doctoral dissertation, Harvard University, 1975.

Sowell, J. *Black Education: Myth and Tragedies.* New York: McKay, 1972.

Williams, E. "Professor Kilson's Contentions: A Reply." *Harvard Bulletin,* 1973, *75* (10), 43-45.

Willie, C. V., and Edmonds, R. R. *Black Colleges in America.* New York: Teachers College Press, 1978.

Willie, C. V., and McCord, A. S. *Black Students at White Colleges.* New York: Praeger, 1972.

Winkler, K. *The Chronicle of Higher Education.* 1974, *9* (8).

13

Allen Tough

Interests of Adult Learners

A fresh and fascinating picture of lifelong learning has been emerging recently. A vigorous line of research has found that youth and adults of all ages carry out far more learning efforts than anyone realized. And they do so with competence and enjoyment. Many of their efforts to learn and grow are closely related to the dimensions of life described in the earlier chapters of this book. And the recent picture of lifelong learning certainly raises questions and implications for the remainder of the book.

The Concept of Lifelong Learning

By passing the Lifelong Learning Act in October 1976, Congress officially recognized the importance of lifelong learning throughout the United States. During 1977, the Lifelong Learning project prepared its major report on how to implement the Act: *Lifelong Learning and Public Policy* (Education Division, 1978). It defines *lifelong learning* as "the process by which individuals continue to develop their knowledge, skills, and attitudes over their lifetimes." The report emphasizes that "all deliberate learning activities are included, whether they occur in the workplace, the home, through formal or nonformal organizations, through traditional or nontraditional methods, or through the self-directed efforts of the individual himself or herself."

One line of research into this phenomenon has emphasized in-depth interviews with a wide range of adults and youth. They were asked about the entire range of their major learning efforts during the year before the interview. Only major, highly deliberate efforts to gain and retain some definite knowledge or skill were recorded by the interviewers. (Details of the definition and criteria are provided by Tough, 1971, Chapter 1 and Appendix A.)

The typical learning effort turned out to involve 100 hours of sessions or episodes in which the person's primary intention was to learn. To be counted in the survey, the learning effort had to include at least seven hours (the equivalent of a working day) of highly deliberate learning sessions within a period of six months.

The original in-depth survey was conducted in Toronto in 1970. The results and their implications are discussed in detail in a comprehensive report (Tough, 1971). That early research has sparked a great many further research studies: fourteen in the United States, ten in Canada, and one each in Ghana, Jamaica, and New Zealand. A wide variety of populations have been surveyed, including adult high school diploma students, clerks, college administrators, cooperative extension agents, factory workers, general populations in a geographical area (Tennessee, Nebraska, USA nationwide), library users, literacy class members, managers, ministers, mothers, older adults, pharmacists, politicians, professional men, salesmen (IBM), school teachers, unemployed persons, union members, university professors, and youth (ages 10 and 16). For a review of this research, see Tough (1978).

I have a very strong commitment to classroom teaching and earn my living as a university instructor. I decided, though, to study the entire range of learning efforts, not just learning in courses and at conferences. The reason? By understanding the *context* within which we, as educators, are operating—by studying the total range of learning efforts into which we fit—we may gain a better idea of learners' needs and the services that colleges might offer them.

Current Learning Efforts

Despite the diversity of regions and populations studied, a remarkably consistent picture of lifelong learning emerged, regardless of the population being interviewed. One surprising facet of this picture is the amount of learning. About 90 percent of all adults conduct at least one major learning effort each year. The average person conducts five distinct learning projects in one year—that is, in five distinct areas of knowledge, skill, or personal change. The person spends an average of 100 hours per learning effort in a year, which adds up to a total investment of 500 hours in all of his or her efforts in the year. That is almost 10 hours a week, on the average—a lot of time!

During the interviews, many unsolicited statements and actions conveying enthusiasm and commitment confirmed the quantitative data about the importance of lifelong learning. The strong determination to succeed and the perseverance despite difficulties evidenced by many of the subjects indicated how important their learning efforts were to them. People seem eager to talk about their learning efforts, partly because they rarely have a chance to describe them in detail to an interested listener. Although trying to improve oneself—to gain new knowledge or become a better person in some way—is certainly an exciting part of one's life, people do not usually discuss their learning adventures and process at parties or the dinner table. This is unfortunate, because such a discussion can reveal a very positive aspect of a person that is not evident during other conversations. Several times, during an exploratory interview with a family member or friend whom I thought I knew very well, I have discovered an attractive but unsuspected side of the person. Sometimes this impressive new aspect is a goal or an interest, sometimes an earnestness or thoughtfulness, and sometimes an intelligent, aggressive striving to become a better person.

Another surprising facet of the picture is the amount of learning that is self-planned. Adults (and youth, in their nonschool learning) tend to plan and manage their learning themselves, instead of turning this responsibility over to an instructor or institution. To be more specific, we asked who was responsible for the day-to-day *planning* of what and how to learn. We found that 20 percent of all learning efforts are planned by a professional (someone trained, paid, or institutionally designated to facilitate the learning). The professional operates in a group (10 percent), in a one-to-one situation (7 percent), or indirectly through completely preprogrammed nonhuman resources (3 percent). By contrast, 80 percent of all lifelong learning efforts are planned by an "amateur." This is usually the learner himself or herself (73 percent), but occasionally a friend (3 percent) or a democratic group of peers (4 percent).

These statistics suggest that formal learning—the learning that occurs in classrooms, courses, and conferences—is merely the tip of the iceberg. This is the portion we have talked about, financed, researched, and included in policy statements. And there is no doubt that this will continue to be a very significant form of learning. (I, for one, devote at least half of my professional time to facilitating learning in that format.) But it turns out that this group form of learning represents only about 10 percent of all learning. The bulk of adult learning is self-planned. The individual learner retains the responsibility for planning the learning from one learning session to the next. The individual obtains advice and suggestions from other sources, perhaps, but nonetheless makes the majority of the planning decisions himself or herself.

What People Learn and Why

Men and women of all ages set out to learn a wide range of knowledge and skill. Some of the subject matter is complex, advanced, or abstract; some is simple, routine, even trivial. Individuals may wish to effect changes in their feelings and interpersonal relationships, in their cognitive knowledge, or in their physical skills. These may be major, far-reaching changes, which will affect the learner's self-concept, confidence, or even mental health, or they may be relatively short-term changes related only to routine or external goals.

In certain learning efforts, the adult merely seeks some specific information that can be used as is. At other times, he or she must integrate or transform the information before applying it. Most learning projects seek established knowledge, which is gained directly or indirectly from other people who already possess it; a research scientist, though, may set out to gain some original knowledge or insight.

A great deal of lifelong learning is related to the person's *job* or *occupation.* Because performance and attitudes on the job are of great importance to the economy of any nation, this type of learning is very significant to society. Before entering a new occupation or job, an individual may have to take special courses or learn new skills. In order to obtain a promotion or major new responsibility, the person may need to undertake an intensive learning effort. Job-related learning will probably continue to be important after the person enters the occupation or obtains a new job. The range of trade, business, vocational, and professional subject matter is very wide. The fields of learning include electronics, tool design, blueprint reading, business administration, real estate, finance, salesmanship, accounting, law, agriculture, teaching methods, office management, typing, shorthand, bookkeeping, automobile and television repair, foreman training, practical nursing, welding, data processing, and countless others.

Attempts to update and upgrade one's knowledge and skill are only a part of job-related learning efforts. Many other learning projects are directed toward a particular problem, case, or task. The person's goal is to prepare a report, make a decision, solve a problem, handle a case, or complete a short-term project. In order to do so successfully, he or she may decide to spend a great deal of time learning about certain aspects first. In this situation, the knowledge and skill are acquired for some immediate and definite use or application. This sort of learning is often self-planned, either because the desired knowledge is rather unique or because the person wants it immediately.

A politician, senior government employee, or top executive, for example, may be faced with a decision that will have a great impact on many individuals, or on the future of the organization or country. Before making that decision, he or she may devote many hours to learning about it. Many teachers of youth and adults want to improve their performance. In order to do so, they might study the subject matter to be taught, the use of certain teaching methods, or the cultural and intellectual backgrounds of their students. In addition, they might seek feedback concerning weaknesses by asking students and others for their reactions or by watching videotape recordings of their actual teaching.

In much lifelong learning, the person expects to use the knowledge and skill in *managing the home and family* rather than on a job. In one year, for example, close to two million Americans made a sustained attempt (with or without an instructor) to learn about sewing or cooking (Johnstone and Rivera, 1965). Adults also learn about home decoration and consumer goods. Before buying a house, car, washing machine, tape recorder, or hobby equipment, they may learn about the cost and characteristics of various available items. Men and women also learn about budgets, insurance, the stock market, and investing. Other learning efforts may begin just before a wedding, childbirth, or move to a new neighborhood. Through reading, counseling, discussion, or encounter groups, adults may try to improve their relationships with their spouses or children. The welfare of children and youth is, of course, greatly influenced by the competence, attitudes, and goals of their parents. Fortunately, many parents make an effort to learn about caring not only for their children's health but also for their emotional and social development. Parents also learn about changes in schools and society that will affect their children, and later they learn how to set their adolescent children free.

Much lifelong learning is related to some *hobby* or other *leisure-time activity.* In one year, more than a million American adults took lessons in golf, swimming, bowling, tennis, skiing, sailing, scuba diving, surfing, curling, squash, or some other athletic activity (Johnstone and Rivera, 1965). Many learned some decorative art or craft, such as ceramics or flower arranging. Others tried to improve their painting, drawing, sketching, or photography. Each year, a large number of adults learn to play a musical instrument, to sing, or to dance. One of every 4.8 Americans plays a musical instrument, "making self-made music second only to reading as the nation's most popular leisure-time activity" (*Time,* January 14, 1966, p. 40). Other adults learn about stereo equipment, stamps, hiking, bridge, or pets. Some adults who plan a trip spend many hours gaining information about where to go and what to see.

Many learning efforts begin with a *question,* a feeling of *puzzlement* or *curiosity,* or just a general interest in a certain body of subject matter. Some people, for example, are concerned about political or social developments that they read about in the newspapers and embark on studies in political science or the social sciences in order to better understand them. Some people feel a need to work out their own set of religious beliefs or philosophy of life. They may learn about their own religion, other religions, or humanism. According to one estimate, approximately three and a half million people study the basic teachings of a particular religion, or some other religious or moral topic (Johnstone and Rivera, 1965). Other common areas of learning are literature, history, the physical and biological sciences, and financial matters.

Sometimes a puzzling or upsetting event will prompt a person to begin a major effort to understand what happened and why. A person who is suddenly asked for a divorce or separation, for example, may set out to understand the behavior and events that led to the other person's feelings. Similarly, important personal decisions may require a great deal of study. Examples are choosing a career, deciding which university and course to enter, considering whether or whom to marry, deciding whether to have an additional child, selecting a place to live, or planning for retirement.

To summarize, a number of studies in several Western countries have shown that some anticipated *use* or *application* of the knowledge or skill is the strongest motivation for the majority of learning efforts. Most adults, in most learning projects, are motivated by some fairly immediate problem, task, or decision that demands certain knowledge or skills. In relatively few learning efforts is the person interested in mastering an entire body of subject matter.

Just in passing, before we leave this section. I would like to suggest that we explore better ways of helping individuals see clearly what they already are learning and what else they should learn. Constantin Doxiadis raised this possibility in 1968. While writing his chapter for the book *What I Have Learned,* he realized that "we cannot make an inventory of our intellectual gains as easily as we can of our material ones—perhaps because there is no internal revenue department to keep track of them. Is it not time to think of an annual declaration of our gains in learning, not in order to pay tax on them but so that we may know how far behind we are and what we need to catch up?" (p. 36).

Learning for Credit

Most of the intensive studies on lifelong learning have adopted a broad definition of learning for credit. In my own studies, for example, I have included "credit toward some degree or certificate or diploma, . . . toward passing a test or examination, completing an assignment for a course, or producing a thesis, . . . toward some license, or a driving test—or toward some requirement or examination or upgrading related to a job." Despite the broad definition, studies of adults who are not full-time students have found that only about 5 percent of all learning projects are motivated by credit. The other 95 percent of adult learning is motivated by other considerations. At the same time, of course, the actual number of adults and youth taking courses for credit is rather impressive, even though the percentage is not. And studies that included young people and adults who are full-time students would produce a higher percentage.

Reacting to an early draft of this chapter, one university professor made an interesting observation: "Recently, it seems to me, most of the pressure for credit comes from students of traditional college age. Given this pattern, the question I would like to raise is this: How can we help young students to separate learning and studying from the formal reward of credit and grades? To do so would increase the likelihood of turning to self-study in later years."

Why People Choose Self-Planning

Over the years, educators have discussed various learning efforts that are somewhat similar to self-planned learning projects, though not identical. These learning efforts have been given various labels: *self-education, self-instruction, self-teaching, individual learning, independent study, self-directed learning,* and *self-study.* The learners engaged in such efforts have been called *autonomous learners, self-propelled learners, self-teachers,* and *autodidacts.* Self-planned learning has always been popular. Why do learners usually prefer to direct their own learning programs, instead of turning to someone else? Granted that they may go to various sources for suggestions on the details of what and how to learn, why do they choose to retain the primary responsibility? Several reasons may account for this.

McCatty (1973), who studied only men, found that in almost half of all self-planned learning efforts one major reason for self-planning is the desire for individualized subject matter. The learner does not need an entire body of knowledge provided by a class, course, or conference. Instead, he wants to select the subject matter relevant to his particular interests. An architect who wanted to learn about office landscaping, for example, employed self-planning in order to get the highlights without a lot of details. A professor who wanted to remain current in the behavioral sciences was aware of the gaps in his knowledge and wanted only to fill them. And a medical doctor who read about internal medicine in order to keep up-to-date knew where his knowledge was deficient and was able to select the relevant titles from the available literature.

Others have a very specific problem and need only the particular knowledge that bears on that problem. The available courses are too general to be applied to their particular problems. A lawyer who was incorporating a company, for example, wanted to obtain the information that was applicable specifically to that task. A physicist who was preparing for a new job had to learn about the federal government's science policy; since he was the only person doing that kind of job, his knowledge requirements were very specific. An architect who was acting as a consultant in a legal case had to learn the details of the case in order to make a judgment.

Physical availability of learning resources is also a common reason for choosing a self-planned approach. It is often easier and faster for persons to conduct their learning in locations that are especially convenient for them. One lawyer in McCatty's study who remained current by reading legal journals said that the fact that they were available right in the office was a factor in choosing the self-planned approach. Another lawyer, who wanted to study the Middle East crisis, said that it was much easier to study at home than to go out to a class. A medical doctor liked the time-saving feature of keeping physically fit at home rather than going to a gymnasium.

A few learners choose self-planning because it suits their own personalities. They may want to prove to themselves that they can work on their own—that they can be independent and self-reliant.

In a national survey of Americans, Penland (1977) asked which two reasons were most important for preferring to learn on your own, instead of in a class or course. From the ten items on the card, the ones most often chosen were "desire to set my own learning pace," "desire to use my own style of learning," "I wanted to keep the learning strategy flexible and easy to change," and "desire to put my own structure on the learning project." Difficulties with transportation or money were chosen least often.

David Kolb's chapter makes the important point that people have different preferred styles of learning. An awareness of this fact can make us more sensitive to differences among the learners with whom we work. I am impressed by the flexibility and diversity of learning styles exhibited by many individuals I have interviewed: each appears to be capable of altering his or her learning style to fit the requirements of each particular learning project. Indeed, the diversity of any one person's list of learning projects for a given year is quite remarkable. At the same time, Kolb is quite correct in pointing out that many individuals favor or lean toward one particular style.

Learning and the Life Cycle

As pointed out in earlier chapters of this book, the particular knowledge or skill sought by any individual will often be influenced by his or her stage in the life cycle, as well as vocational development, intellectual development, ego development, and moral development or level of humanitarian concern. Although the amount and methods of learning remain reasonably stable throughout the life span, the particular subject matter does vary somewhat from one stage to another. One clear example from research is the emphasis on job preparation in credit courses among adults under the age of 30, as compared with older adults.

Unmet Needs

We have seen that 80 percent of all highly deliberate learning is planned and managed by the learner or by a friend. In general, these "amateur" planners do a competent and efficient job. They perform many of the planning tasks that are otherwise performed by a teacher (Tough, 1967). At the same time, almost without exception, our interviewees tell us that their lifelong learning would have benefited from additional help. Here are the major unmet needs that emerge from intensive interviews:

1. Better help in choosing what and how to learn. This help could be received through a group, through individual counseling, or through printed resources.
2. Some means (again it could be through group programs, individual counseling, or printed materials) of developing greater competence at planning the learning and at learning through individual methods.
3. Individualized learning resources, such as tapes and correspondence courses, instead of only classroom-centered courses.
4. Help in finding a partner for learning or an expert who is interested in teaching the skill or subject matter for little or no fee.

Already there are signs that educational institutions will increasingly try to meet these needs, in addition to providing the courses and services that they already provide.

Implications for Colleges

As you reflect on this chapter, you may begin to wonder, "Well, this picture of lifelong learning is all very interesting, but what are the implications for me as a person concerned with the American college of the present and future? What can I *do*?" I hope you will think creatively about this question and experiment with some of your answers. To stimulate your thinking, here are some suggestions about what you can do.

1. Become committed to fostering the entire range of major learning efforts. Feel a kinship with the total helping enterprise devoted to facilitating persons' efforts to learn and grow. Feel part of an even wider enterprise: the movement to foster the humane, loving, liberating, growth-enhancing, creative elements in our society.
2. Through printed material, in one-to-one conversations, or in groups, experiment with helping learners to perform three functions:
   a. To thoughtfully choose their learning goals (after reflecting on their life goals, seeking feedback on their performance, clarifying needs and interests, and examining their current learning patterns).

   b. To become aware of the vast panorama of available opportunities and methods (including self-guided and peer-guided) and to choose the most appropriate strategies.

   c. To become competent at making choices and plans more effectively and independently next time.

3. In your entire program or institution, or at least in your own work with learners, be sure that the learners have plenty of freedom and options. Provide a variety of opportunities and resources for learning and personal growth, including cassettes and videotapes as well as books and courses. As much as possible, give the learners a wide choice of how and what to learn, but simultaneously be sure they can get enough help. Shift away from "we know best," from emphasis on credit or grades, from coercion or forced attendance, from a high degree of control by the instructor (Tough, 1971, Chapter 14 and Appendix C). Carl Rogers (1977) is very helpful in this regard. The chapter on individualized education by F. Thomas Clark in Part Three of this book describes effective approaches through learning contracts that can be used with individuals or with classes and other groups.

4. Be sure people can get plenty of information about the available opportunities and resources. In American learning today, the problem is not so much with resources as it is with *access* to resources. People simply do not know what is available, and, as Peterson's following chapter reveals, there is a wide range of alternatives.

5. Encourage autonomous groups of peers, or "self-help" groups, to form around a common interest or need. This can be done in a class by passing around a list for names and interests. For a more elaborate, far-reaching approach, see Knowles (1975). You might also be able to foster the formation of groups from persons throughout an entire dorm, campus, or town.

6. *The Lifelong Learner,* by Ronald Gross (1977), and the broad panorama of opportunities described by Matson (1977) are very useful in stimulating and helping people make choices for their own learning and growth. For many persons, the various available life-planning and career-planning guides are useful. For persons who are especially thoughtful about their own personal and spiritual growth, comprehensive frameworks such as those of Naranjo (1974) or Grof (1975) may be useful. Consider taking steps to have books such as these—books *about* learning and growth—mentioned in various courses and conspicuously displayed in campus libraries and bookstores. The chapter on educational advising and career planning by Shipton and Steltenpohl in Part Three of this book offers some very helpful and concrete suggestions, as well as leads to other pertinent literature.

7. Develop or integrate new knowledge about all this, or encourage others to do so. Eventually, this increased understanding will lead to better help and resources for the entire range of intentional human learning.

8. Try to improve as a learning consultant and helper. For example, you could read about lifelong learning, study your own learning, read about being an effective helper, seek constructive feedback, try to listen better, or attend a personal growth group.

9. Become familiar with what is happening in the parts of your college devoted to continuing education, community services, extension courses, experiential learning, and counseling and information.

    These specific suggestions illustrate the wide range of approaches that can be pursued by faculty members, department heads, and others in various disciplines and professional preparation areas throughout the college and university. Although not all adult learning efforts relate to curricular alternatives and courses currently offered by colleges and universities, many do. Once colleges recognize these learning efforts and develop flexible responses to them that take into account the important differences in individual purposes and background, the talents of college and university professionals can be employed to serve many of the needs for lifelong learning revealed by these studies. More important, the interaction between experienced professionals and adult learners can enhance the perspectives of both. The learners can be helped to see how particular knowledge, competence, or experience that is of immediate interest relates to other areas worth pursuing. The professionals can be helped to see how their own areas of expertise can contribute to meeting the developmental needs that arise for all of us as we cope with life cycle challenges and with the social changes affecting our work, families, and communities.

There, are also powerful implications here for the range of educational processes and environments discussed in Part Three of this volume. It seems clear that the diverse approaches and resources discussed in the chapters concerning individualized education, experiential learning, distance learning, and residential learning all can provide useful responses to adult learning needs. Increased investments in the kinds of educational advising and career counseling discussed by Shipton and Steltenpohl can help learners of all ages clarify their purposes, find and use the most pertinent resources, and evaluate their usefulness. The kinds of changes suggested in the chapter on "out-of-class activities" could create stimulating contexts for many adult learning efforts.

The ubiquitous and substantial nature of much of the learning revealed by these studies also lends urgency to the question of the assessment of experiential learning, discussed by Keeton. It seems both clear and appropriate that most learning will not be "for credit." But at the same time, adults are entering our colleges and universities to obtain credits and credentials required for occupational advancement, or enrichment, or other long-range purposes. We need to recognize the knowledge and competence they already have in order to avoid redundancy and to provide real service.

Finally, this wide-ranging adult learning has implications for college administration, governance, and professional development examined later in chapters by Benezet, Hodgkinson, and Lindquist. There are first the issues of mission and function. How should different types of two-year and four-year colleges and universities define themselves and their roles in relation to this impressive host of adult learning efforts? What kinds of efforts might be defined as "college-level learning?" Which are still best left to individual pursuit without formal assistance? Which are best assisted by other institutions and agencies: libraries, museums, high school and community adult education activities, in-service training activities by businesses, social agencies, civil service units, and the like? Once those questions of mission are settled by a particular college or university, the question of governance arises. To what extent will, or should, these adult students play more powerful roles in determining institutional priorities among research, service, and teaching? To what extent should, or could, these constituencies be mobilized as sources of political support backing budget requests? What role should, or will, they play in matters of curriculum planning and course content?

With these questions come complex issues concerning institutional change and the professional development of faculty members and administrators. What kinds of knowledge and competence will be called for if new institutional alternatives are to be designed, implemented, and evaluated? What will teachers need to know about these diverse students and their motives, and what will they need to understand about themselves and their disciplines, if teaching and learning, research and service are to respond to the pervasive drive for lifelong learning?

One thing seems certain. Those learning projects will be undertaken: those efforts will continue to be made. The learning society is well under way. It will continue its vigorous growth with or without the blessing of higher education institutions. It also seems clear that the nation's colleges and universities have much to offer. Whether or not that potential is realized depends upon how they respond to some of these concrete possibilities and fundamental issues.

If we, as individual professionals, can undertake some of these actions and help our own colleges or universities to make suitable changes, students' needs for lifelong learning will be better served. In so doing, we need not take over responsibility for all these diverse learning efforts. Such an aspiration is neither practical nor desirable. But we can help students become more effective independent learners and thus advance the learning society.

References

Doxiadis, C. A. "Learning How to Learn." In *What I Have Learned: A Collection of Twenty Autobiographical Essays by Great Contemporaries from the Saturday Review.* New York: Simon & Schuster, 1968.

Dumazedier, J. *Toward a Society of Leisure.* (S. E. McClure, Trans.) New York: Free Press, 1967.

Education Division, Department of Health, Education, and Welfare. *Lifelong Learning and Public Policy.* Washington, D.C.: U.S. Government Printing Office, 1978. (Stock No. 017-080-01847-1.)

Grof, S. *Realms of the Human Unconscious.* New York: Viking Press, 1975.

Gross, R. *The Lifelong Learner.* New York: Simon & Schuster, 1977.

Holt, J. *How Children Learn.* New York: Pitman, 1967.

Johnstone, J. W. C., and Rivera, R. J. *Volunteers for Learning: A Study of the Educational Pursuits of American Adults.* Chicago: Aldine, 1965.

Knowles, M. S. *Self-Directed Learning: A Guide for Learners and Teachers.* New York: Association Press, 1975.

McCatty, C. "Patterns of Learning Projects Among Professional Men." Unpublished doctoral dissertation, University of Toronto, 1973. *Dissertation Abstracts International,* 1974, *35,* 323A-324A. (Microfilm available from the National Library of Canada: Canadian Theses on Microfilm No. 16647.)

Matson, K. *The Psychology Today Omnibook of Personal Development.* New York: Morrow, 1977.

Naranjo, C. *The One Quest.* London: Wildwood, 1974.

Penland, P. R. *Individual Self-Planned Learning in America.* (Final report of project 475AH60058 under grant no. G007603327, U.S. Office of Education, Office of Libraries and Learning Resources.) Unpublished manuscript, Graduate School of Library and Information Sciences, University of Pittsburgh, 1977. May be purchased from the University of Pittsburgh Bookstore under the title *Self-Planned Learning in America.*

Rogers, C. R. *Carl Rogers on Personal Power: Inner Strength and its Revolutionary Impact.* New York: Delacorte, 1977.

Tough, A. *Learning Without a Teacher: A Study of Tasks and Assistance During Adult Self-Teaching Projects.* Toronto: Ontario Institute for Studies in Education, 1967.

Tough, A. *The Adult's Learning Projects: A Fresh Approach to Theory and Practice in Adult Learning.* (2nd ed.) Austin, Tex.: Learning Concepts, 1979; Toronto: Ontario Institute for Studies in Education, 1979.

Tough, A. "Major Learning Efforts: Recent Research and Future Directions." *Adult Education,* Summer 1978, *28* (4), 250-263.

14

Richard E. Peterson

Opportunities
for Adult Learners

This chapter describes the full spectrum of resources for education and learning that people in the United States may avail themselves of after leaving compulsory (usually secondary) schooling, and then comments on what colleges and universities, within this postsecondary complex, may need to do to realize their potential as society's key instruments for facilitating intellectual and human development.

Resources for Education and Learning

The range of providers or sources of education and learning available to Americans is wide indeed. In addition to the familiar types of programs offered by schools and colleges, numerous opportunities are provided by government, industry, and community organizations. Furthermore, as Allen Tough noted in the previous chapter, the majority of people also engage in systematic *independent,* or self-directed, learning. Finally, virtually everyone continues to learn *unintentionally,* simply by living.

The material in the first section of this chapter, dealing with the broad range of learning opportunities in America, was largely developed under a 1977 Exxon Education Foundation grant to the Educational Testing Service, which supported a comprehensive review of adult learning policies and practices in the United States. This review is contained in the book by Peterson and associates (1979).

The data in Table 1 indicate the magnitude of participation in these activities, or what Moses (1971) has termed the *learning force* in America. The estimated numbers of

Table 1. Sources of Education and Learning in the United States

	Approximate Number of Participants (in millions)
Deliberate Education and Learning	
I. In the Schools	
A. Preprimary education	10.0
B. Elementary and secondary education	42.0
C. College and university undergraduate education	9.5
D. Graduate and professional education	1.5
E. Public school adult education	1.8
F. Proprietary schools	1.2
G. College and university extension and continuing education	3.5
H. Community education	.5
II. In Nonschool Organizations	
A. Private industry	5.8
B. Professional associations	5.5
C. Trade unions	.6
D. Government service	3.0
E. Federal manpower programs	1.7
F. Military services	1.5
G. Agricultural extension	12.0
H. City recreation departments	5.0
I. Community organizations	7.4
J. Churches and synagogues	3.3
K. Free universities	.2
L. Parks and forests	no meaningful estimate
III. Individually Used Sources	
A. Personal—at hand	virtually everyone
B. Personal—at distance	virtually everyone
C. Travel	virtually everyone
D. Print media	virtually everyone
E. Electronic media	virtually everyone
Unintentional Learning	
I. In the home	virtually everyone
II. At work	virtually everyone
III. From friends	virtually everyone
IV. From the mass media	virtually everyone
V. Other sources	virtually everyone

participants were determined by various surveys, mostly governmental, conducted since 1972, and should be regarded as rough estimates, subject to all the shortcomings inherent in surveys. But mindful that these figures include double and even multiple counting, we estimate that each year, out of a total of some 116 million deliberate learners of all ages in organizational settings in the United States, some 10 million, or 9 percent, are in preprimary schooling; 42 million, or 36 percent, are in compulsory schooling; and an estimated 64 million, or all the rest, participate in postcompulsory learning. Of these 64 million adults, roughly 18 million (28 percent) are enrolled in schools and colleges, while 46 million (72 percent) learn through nonschool organizations. From these figures, it is clear that many more adults utilize nonschool sources of learning than attend schools and colleges. But because all these figures are "head-count" estimates, and because the participants in the nonschool sector typically are employed adults who are studying part-time, in terms of total "learning hours" or "learning effort" on the part of participants the school and nonschool sectors of noncompulsory education may be roughly comparable.

Larger by far, however, than either of these sectors is the extent of unintentional learning as a by-product of living, and of intentional but individual or "do-it-yourself" learning. To see the distinctive role of the American college in the context of all the various sources of education and learning listed in Table 1, let us consider first the extent of unintentional learning, then of self-directed intentional learning, nonschool sources of education, and noncollegiate schooling.

Unintentional Learning

Unintentional learning (or *incidental* learning, as academic psychologists call it) is virtually synonymous with living. Most people learn—that is, acquire new cognitive, affective, or motor responses—throughout their lives without intending to do so. Among the sources of this unplanned learning are home life, work life, friends, and the mass media.

In the Home. Few people live entirely solitary existences. Most individuals live out most of their lives in close association with one or more others—usually relatives—in a home. About the only period away from home, in fact, is between the years of going off to college or to work and of getting married or entering into some sort of family relationship. And people, without necessarily trying to, learn from family members. Parents may try to be, and often are, models for children, as are older siblings. Parents learn from their children—about the schools, the community, and the directions of cultural change—and children learn modern history and cultural continuity from grandparents. Families talk together, as at mealtime; they do things together; and all their members learn something, unintentionally, from each other's "learning projects." Ideally, the larger and more diverse families are, the greater are their learning sources and the more stimulating they are as learning environments.

At Work. On the order of three quarters of the nation's adult population have regular, paid jobs, and most of them spend one half of their waking hours at their workplace. Many young people spend ten to twenty hours per week at part-time jobs. Added up over a span of years, the impact of these work experiences on one's intellect and personality can be substantial. Without trying to, one may acquire new knowledge, skills, and feelings about one's self and self-worth simply through undertaking different activities on the job: the secretary does editorial work; the engineer, cost accounting; the teacher, some administration; and so forth. In addition, people typically work closely with a small number of associates. Some may even spend more time with such coworkers in a lifetime than with anyone else, including their spouse. They also may spend one to two hours per day commuting with colleagues. All these work-related associations become learning sources. From them, workers adopt interests and beliefs, acquire ways of thinking about things, and come to share values about what is important and right.

From Friends. Friends are a third major source of unintentional learning. As with the family and coworkers, the more time one spends with them, the more important they become as learning sources. Friends are particularly significant up until the time of marriage or entry into some form of family relationship, when their importance may decline somewhat. Later in life, they assume renewed importance, especially when spouses separate, divorce, or die. Experiences take on more meaning when they are shared and reflected upon with others. Through shared experiences with respected friends, one can sharpen skills, gain insights, and improve understandings.

From the Mass Media. Television, radio, newspapers, and magazines, in addition to being sources for deliberate learning and, all too often, as major distractions from serious learning activities, are also pervasive sources for unintentional learning. Unfortunately, what is unwittingly learned from commercial broadcasting, particularly by the young, is largely counterproductive from the perspectives of serious learning, personal development, and the good society—engendering as it does anti-intellectual values, psychological passivity, and insensitivity to violence and other inhumane actions, and displacing the practice of interactive communication skills. Commercial television and radio have shown remarkable capacities for capturing the attention of great numbers of the citizenry. They are immensely powerful unintentional learning sources—and that is why it is so disheartening that they are not in the service of more estimable goals.

Individually Used Sources of Deliberate Learning

Second in extent only to unintended learning is independent (self-planned and self-directed) study. Present interest among adult educators in this domain of learning can be traced to the seminal research of Allen Tough, who described his work in the previous chapter. More recently, a national survey by Penland (1977) found that 79 percent of American adults could be classified as "continuing learners": 60 percent engaged only in self-initiated learning projects, 16 percent engaged in *both* self-planned and course work, and 3 percent participated only in courses or "school-like activities." In sum, a great many people—perhaps three times as many as those who take a course at a school or college—engage in "do-it-yourself" learning from time to time during a given year.

Do-it-yourself learning by people wishing to set their own terms for their studies can, of course, make use of organization-based resources in schools, colleges, and other institutions, but by and large these learners find it appropriate to study in a wholly independent manner, with little or no recourse to group activities. We may divide such "individually used sources" of learning into five categories, as shown in Table 1.

Personal—At Hand. Among individuals who can be used as learning sources, Penland (1977) identified four major types as being highly regarded by independent learners:

Experts who are close friends were the single source in Penland's list judged to be most important. Such expert friends may be experienced in vocations, trades, crafts, or hobbies. Information or advice from them is ordinarily free.

Close friends or relatives were the second most highly regarded source in Penland's study. Clearly, people wishing to learn something rely most readily on friends or relatives, and, conversely, knowledgeable or talented people are most inclined to share their knowledge with friends and relatives.

Tutors, defined by Webster as those "employed to instruct another in some branch . . . of learning, especially a private instructor," are generally paid for their teaching, and their association with the learner commonly extends over a series of lessons or sessions. Tutors usually dictate the terms of each lesson, but they are employed at the pleasure of the learner.

Paid experts are professionals, such as doctors, nurses, lawyers, psychotherapists, architects, engineers, builders, and financial advisors, for whose services fees are charged. Their expertise is not extensively used in adults' learning projects; rather, their advice is used to identify other less expensive sources of learning.

Personal—At a Distance. This source of independent study may seem like a contradiction in terms, although correspondence school officials would be quick to deny any contradiction.

Correspondence study, the primary example, has been a familiar feature on the American educational landscape for over seventy years. It is the learning method of choice for solitary learners—solitary either by preference or by circumstance, such as military assignment. Currently there may be about five million correspondence students in the United States (Macken and others, 1976). A 1970 survey found 57 percent enrolled at federal and military schools, 24 percent at private schools, 10 percent at religious schools, and 7 percent at colleges and universities (usually their extension divisions). Correspondence courses have the advantage of allowing students to set their own pace; but this lack of structure leads many to fail to complete the course. And completion rates, as is well known, are indeed low: only about 61 percent in university extension divisions, and about 20 percent in private schools. (Non-prorated or no-refund policies for non-completers at many private home study schools are a major reason why these schools have been strongly criticized. New York is the first and so far the only state to require prorated refunds.)

Networking is a learning strategy, described by Gross (1977), whereby networks of people interested in sharing ideas correspond with and learn from each other. One way of joining such informal networks is by writing to, say, an author of a magazine article, who then adds the new person to a list of correspondents. Often the ideas shared are in the nature of frontier thinking in the field. Scholars of a subject scattered throughout the world may form an "invisible college" of learners.

Travel. That traveling is education is a truism. While travel is assuredly an occasion for much "unintentional learning," it can also be a means for deliberate learning. Two general approaches are apparent: (1) learning as much as possible from a trip taken for any reason, such as business or to visit relatives, and (2) planning a trip with the express purpose of learning something.

Regarding the first, all that is needed when one travels outside familiar environs is to consciously adopt a questioning stance. Spare time can be spent finding out about the nature of things in the new locale. As for the second, when one travels with the intention of learning, extensive preparation may be called for, including reading books on the history, economics, and geography of the area, interviewing recently returned travelers, and possibly even learning a new language.

Print Media. Of the major print media used in independent learning, *books* no doubt come to mind first for academic professionals and the relatively literate stratum of the population in general. If you want to learn something about a subject, you go out and get a book about it. A number of companies are now publishing books as "courses," some in the format of programmed texts, with the independent learner in mind. The range of types of available books—in libraries, bookstores, drug stores, and supermarkets—is truly remarkable.

Newspapers are read, according to surveys, by practically all adults capable of reading. The photographs they contain are presumably viewed by an even larger number. Hence newspapers are probably the chief source of information about current events. Beyond an overview of current events, locally and elsewhere, it is not clear what else is learned from "the paper." Certainly, over the years newspapers have taken to providing much more than news (and editorials, sports, and want ads). Newspapers may now have sections on business and finance, real estate, travel, weekend entertainment, home improvement, gardening, fashion, sewing, automobiles, cooking, books, hobbies (chess, bridge, coins, and so forth), art, music, theater, film, astrology, beauty, and wine. Sunday editions often compete in comprehensiveness with national news magazines.

Magazines, like newspapers, are also widely read—by almost four fifths of adults in the country, according to a 1966 survey. Many, like some newspapers, consist largely of pictures. Nevertheless, even skimming a national news magazine is likely to yield a modicum of learning. Many people are highly loyal to their favorite magazines, including "serious" ones. Probably just as important as the serious magazines as a learning source is the vast assortment of hobby magazines. People of different ages and interests devour the likes of *Outdoor Life, Road and Track, Camera, Butterick, Popular Mechanics, Tennis, Rock and Gem, Sail, Guitar Player,* and *Kilobaud.*

Electronic Media. From the perspective of deliberate learning, *television*—or at least commercial television—is largely a wasteland. There is, of course, the occasional documentary, public affairs program, or television play, as well as the regular news. Such programs may attract great numbers of viewers and have a tremendous impact (as did "Roots," for example). The educational potential of commercial television is staggering. The major networks' production capabilities are consummate. Almost every home has a television set. Yet commercial television, chiefly because of its capacity for distracting, may on balance do more harm than good for potential learners.

Public television, however, despite many difficulties, has expanded to become a significant source of learning for people of all ages. Its future seems even brighter in view of current Carter Administration plans for greatly expanded federal funding (Leubsdorf, 1977). As of late 1977, there were 271 public television stations—connected into the Public Broadcasting Service (PBS)—located in all the major population centers. Sixty-five percent of the population is reached (Carnegie Task Force on Public Broadcasting, 1977).

The advent in 1979 of the public broadcasting satellite is allowing local stations to broadcast simultaneously over three channels (rather than one), which has substantially increased the variety of programming and the viewer's choice of programs.

At present, *radio* ranks lower even than television as a source for deliberate learning, according to Penland's study. Commercial radio is a national cultural disaster, its mindlessness barely relieved by hourly news breaks. The alternating current of music and commercials numbs and distracts, especially teen-agers, from more profitable activities.

Public radio, like public television, is making progress, and promises even better performance with the aid of the proposed Carter appropriations and the use of the satellite, which will provide four new frequencies per station. As of December 1977, there were 203 public radio stations licensed to universities (65 percent), communities (20 percent), and public school systems, libraries, states, and local municipalities (15 percent). National Public Radio (NPR) was set up in 1971 by the Corporation for Public Broadcasting (CPB) to produce programs and to serve as an interconnection facility for public radio licencees. NPR produces and distributes approximately forty hours per week of programming (which may or may not be used by local stations). Perhaps NPR's best-known program is "All Things Considered," a very intelligent ninety-minute news magazine aired six days a week. Another good program from NPR is the weekly one-hour "Options in Education." Public radio is essentially a local service, with all but 15 percent of the programming, which is mostly recorded music, originated locally.

Tapes and records, while rated low in Penland's survey, are additional means of learning having considerable potential. The advantage of tapes and disks, compared with the other (mass) electronic media, is that they can be controlled by the individual; they can be repeated in part or in total according to the learner's interests and needs. They may be a boon especially to nonreaders and the blind.

Videotapes (combined with audio) are also becoming increasingly available. Equipment for playing videotapes on one's home television set is on the market, but it is prohibitively expensive for most people. The price is expected to come down. In the meantime, many libraries and other community organizations have videotape playback equipment. The cost of the tapes themselves—around $25 for a lecture or lesson—are such that most people will want to rent rather than purchase them. Video disks will be less expensive. In some quarters they are seen as the electronic innovation that will finally make a wide contribution to serious learning. Most libraries have a large stock of tapes to lend. Many publishing houses, especially publishers of specialized magazines, are now in the cassette business. Many professional associations supply tapes to their members to provide updating on current developments in the field.

Home computers—the last type of electronic media that we will consider here—are obviously not for everyone, even those able to afford them. The cost, however, is not as great as one might think, and it is expected to come down. About a third of all home computers are kits, bought and assembled by computer hobbyists. The cheapest cost about $250. The average hobbyist is said to begin with about a $1,000 investment, which is then augmented by another $1,000 worth of attachments—additional memory capacity, a typewriter-like keyboard, a television monitor, a tape deck, a printer. A wide variety of programs ("software") are becoming available on either tape cassettes or plastic (floppy) disks. Home computers have already been found useful in teaching math and spelling. Programs in elementary logic, algebra, Russian, and computer programming were used in a project described in Macken and others (1976). Numerous other subjects are likely to be amenable to home computer learning—advanced logic and math, English grammar, most foreign languages, and various elements of the natural sciences, for example.

We have discussed independent learning and individually used sources at some length both because this large and increasingly rich domain is probably not sufficiently appreciated by many educational professionals and because these individual sources will offer increased competition to academic institutions in the future.

Nonschool Organizations

Twelve types of nonschool sources of education and learning are arrayed in Table 1 roughly in order of their typical degree of organization or structure. The first six are generally large-scale, classroom-based programs; the latter six tend to be much smaller programs, with more varied settings and modes of instruction. The first seven generally provide education oriented toward external objectives, often those of the organization itself, or toward occupational advancement in some form for the student; the others enable learning that is more often motivated by personal, nonoccupational interests. The sources oriented toward occupational advancement are used almost entirely by people in the period between compulsory schooling and retirement—that is to say, by adults in the *work* stage of the life cycle (see Stern and Best, 1977); by contrast, the sources oriented toward personal development may be used—in different ways, to be sure—by adults of all ages.

Private Industry. Many analysts, perhaps in part because of the high estimates made by the Carnegie Commission on Higher Education (1973), regard private industry as the largest provider or sponsor of adult education in the country. They cite the huge training programs of such corporate giants as IBM, AT&T, and Xerox, some of which are now granting bachelor's degrees and at least one of which—Arthur D. Little—grants master's degrees. Fortunately, a report by the Conference Board (Lusterman, 1977) carefully lays out the nature and scope of education in American industry. It divides industry-sponsored education and training activities into four categories:

1. *In house—during hours*—by far the largest of the four, with 30 percent of all companies surveyed having at least one such course of at least thirty-hour duration, and with 3.7 million employees (11 percent of the total employee force) participating in the past year.
2. *In house—after hours,* offered by 39 percent of the firms, with an estimated total participation of .7 million.
3. *Outside the company—during hours,* typically taking the form of paid education leaves, provided by 9 percent of the firms surveyed for perhaps 100,000 employees.
4. *Outside the company—after hours,* typically consisting of tuition-aid programs, in effect at 89 percent of the companies surveyed, with an estimated 1.3 million (4 percent of the total employee force) participating.

The total level of participation, about 5.8 million, agrees closely with the 1972 figure of 5.9 million from the survey by the Commission on Nontraditional Study (Carp, Peterson, and Roelfs, 1974) but is much higher than the 1975 figure cited by the National Center for Education Statistics of 2.6 million (Boaz, 1978) and much lower than the Carnegie Commission estimate (1973) of about 16 million.

Professional Associations. Nearly all occupational groups have associations of member practitioners to advance the interests of the occupation as a whole and, often, the occupational or professional competence of individual members. They may be organized nationally, statewide or regionally, or locally (as in chapters). The nature and scope of education and training sponsored by professional associations have not been surveyed in any systematic way. Certainly there is variation. Some associations—for example, the California Bar Association—design and conduct extremely well-conceived programs for their members. Others, such as associations of health professionals, may rely on cooperation with colleges and universities. Still others, often groups of academic professionals, rely mainly on national meetings. Probably most active are associations for middle-level business managers; seminars, workshops and short courses in accounting, data processing, supervisory skills, and the like abound in hotels and conference centers around the country.

Trade Unions. As a source of continuing education, labor unions are something of an enigma. Unions are always listed among the major sponsors of learning, often linked with business. Yet most trade unions do not offer extensive educational opportunities, certainly not in comparison with the education and training sponsored by industry and government. There are some 20 million organized workers in the United States, with a little over two thirds in AFL/CIO-affiliated unions. On the order of .6 million, about 3 percent, are estimated to be involved in education and training through some four general types of programs.

Roughly 500,000 workers are in apprenticeship programs operated jointly, under contract, by management and labor, with close to 300,000 of them in federally funded programs registered with the Bureau of Apprenticeship and Training in the Department of Labor, according to a recent U.S. Department of Labor (1977) report. Apprenticeship training typically involves both on-the-job practice and classroom work (144 hours), which, in many localities, is conducted in cooperation with community colleges.

Many trade unionists, perhaps 75,000 in a given year, are involved in labor education sponsored by the education departments of individual unions. The emphasis tends to be on "tool" courses—shop steward training and grievance handling, for example.

A third type of program is what now is commonly called "labor studies," offered through colleges and universities. Forty-one universities (Turner, 1977) currently offer "labor studies" curriculums either through extension divisions or regular degree programs, and numerous community colleges, many at the urging of the United Auto Workers, offer the AA degree in labor studies. Some thirty-one institutions altogether reportedly have labor studies majors (Dwyer, 1977). In contrast to the earlier "labor education," which consisted mainly of "tool" courses, "labor studies" is more broadly conceived to include topics from all the social sciences that may be relevant to modern collective bargaining.

A fourth type of educational opportunity for trade union members takes the form of tuition assistance arrangements negotiated by a good number of unions, under which fees for college courses are defrayed, in part or totally, as a fringe benefit. Currently there are some 280 such contracts, up from only 29 in 1967 (National Manpower Institute, 1977). Many of these plans stipulate that courses be job-related, although increasingly there are no such strings. Somewhat surprisingly, only about one percent of the 2.5 million eligible workers take advantage of this opportunity.

Government Service. About one sixth of the national work force is in the employ of government at some level. Altogether there are some 15 million civilian government workers (U.S. Bureau of the Census, 1976); 60 percent are employed by local government, 22 percent by state government, and 18 percent by the federal government. Extensive training opportunities in a variety of formats are made available to government employees at all three levels.

Currently there are on the order of 3 million federal employees. According to the latest training effort report from the U.S. Civil Service Commission (1977), close to 600,000 individual employees (21 percent of the total) accounted for 958,297 "instances" of training during the 1976 fiscal year. ("Instances" are planned units of formal classroom instruction of at least eight hours duration; the average "instance" covered about 43 hours.) Two thirds of the training was provided internally by the employee's own agency or department; the balance was provided by interagency training groups, other departments, or by nongovernment organizations, such as colleges, commercial firms, or professional associations.

Few data are available on the nature and scope of employee education and training conducted by *state* governments. By contrast, there is reasonably good information about training of *local* government employees. In a 1975 national survey of cities of over 10,000 population conducted by the International City Management Association (Brown, 1976), two thirds of all the cities were found to operate training programs. Ninety percent have on-the-job and specific skill development programs; 79 percent have supervisory training; 40 percent and 31 percent have interpersonal relations and team-building programs, respectively.

Federal Manpower Training Programs. Work and training programs administered by the Department of Labor are an important and often overlooked source of education for both adult and youth. Altogether involving 3.3 million first-time enrollees in fiscal year 1976, they are in general designed to increase the employability of people who are out of work or underemployed. There are three separate programs that have education components: the Comprehensive Employment and Training Act (CETA) program, the Job Corps, and the Work Incentive (WIN) program.

CETA, enacted in 1973, consolidated a range of previously existing programs aimed chiefly at youths. Its basic policy premise is that every youth and adult should have an opportunity to work. Program planning and implementation are decentralized among some 450 local "prime sponsors" (for example, city or county governments). The Job Corps, a separate program (though Title IV of CETA), is a residential program for severely disadvantaged youths. It had some 44,000 new members in 1976. Education consists mainly of basic remedial work and skills training. The recently enacted Youth Employment and Demonstration Projects Act (YEDPA), Title VII of CETA, will provide funds for work experiences for unemployed youths (age 16 to 23) to aid in the transition from school to work. CETA prime sponsors are the administering agents and will enter into cooperative agreements with school districts. The WIN program (now, as modified, WIN-II) is operated in cooperation with local welfare agencies. Some 20,000 Aid to Families with Dependent Children (AFDC) recipients lacking marketable skills received job experience and limited amounts of classroom and on-the-job training during fiscal year 1976.

Military Services. Currently, over 2 million people—most of them relatively young, most of them men—serve in America's armed forces. Military requirements are said to call for recruiting almost one of every three qualified 18-year-old males. Fortunately, it is still an all-volunteer military service, education is used as the prime incentive in recruitment, and all the branches have acted to provide extensive educational opportunities for their members.

In general, education and training fall into two categories: (1) training directly related to performance as a member of the armed forces, most of which is transferable to civilian jobs and (2) voluntary education, which allows individuals to pursue personally determined educational goals. Some 575,000 service personnel, about one fourth of the total complement, are participating in what is called the Voluntary Education Program. They are part-time students during off-duty hours in some 1,000 colleges operating on or near military bases. Seventy-five percent of their tuition costs are ordinarily reimbursed. Each service operates its own programs.

Three major programs for voluntary learners apply across all military branches:

The Defense Activity for Non-Traditional Education Support (DANTES) administers several nationally recognized credit-by-examination programs—CLEP, GED (overseas only), ACT, SAT, and ACT/PEP as well as its own DANTES Subject Standardized Test in some seventy-five subjects, and facilitates use of independent study (correspondence) courses from regionally accredited civilian institutions.

The Servicemen's Opportunity College (SOC) is a network of over 360 colleges and universities (half two-year, half four-year) that have agreed to support education of service personnel chiefly through flexible residency and transfer policies. During the fall of 1977, an associate degree program was launched that involves thirty-one colleges and all major army bases. SOC is jointly funded by the Department of Defense and the Carnegie Corporation and is co-sponsored by twelve organizations, mostly associations of postsecondary institutions.

Finally, the American Council on Education's (ACE) Office on Educational Credit evaluates military courses and periodically publishes a *Guide to the Evaluation of Educational Experiences in the Military.* The current *Guide,* which contains degree credit recommendations for over 5,000 formal military courses, has been forwarded to virtually all postsecondary institutions to assist in assigning credit to veterans for their education in the military.

Education in the military, needless to say, is a significant part of the nation's total education panoply. For a great many youths it is an opportunity for basic education and skill training that would not otherwise have been available. Thirteen percent of enlisted men have not graduated from high school (and many more than that lack basic skills). Each of the services has high school equivalency programs, and in 1975 as many as 80,000 active-duty servicemen were granted diplomas.

Agricultural Extension. The Cooperative Extension system, as it is known, is indeed a cooperative, certainly a multi-constituency, enterprise. Overall guidance comes from the Extension Service of the U.S. Department of Agriculture. States, in consultation with county governments and other public and private interests, propose programs, which are then administered by the land-grant universities in the respective states. What is done each year in each state is an amalgam of all the interests and requirements of the parties involved (with the state extension director acting as the key administrator or mediator).

Cooperative Extension work nationally is divided into four categories: Agriculture and National Resources, Home Economics, 4-H Youth, and Community Resource Development. The percentage of resources (in terms of staff years) expended on each in 1975 was 39 percent, 21 percent, 32 percent, and 8 percent, respectively.

All this adds up to an impressive array of educational services, centering on farm operations and rural family living, for "farmers and ranchers, agricultural industries, rural families and youth, and rural communities." Especially impressive are the great number of volunteers. It is difficult to estimate the total number of people who learn through Cooperative (agricultural) Extension in a given year. Perhaps the figure is about 12 million. These people are of all ages, except perhaps the very young and the very old. Many, however, have only occasional and brief contacts with an "instructor," say, once a month with an extension agent.

City Recreation Departments. City parks and recreation departments have been an integral part of the educational complex in the great majority of American cities, including all the large ones. Their services, many of which enable deliberate learning, span a wide range—from A to Z, including aquariums, arboretums, archery ranges, arts and crafts centers, botanical gardens, camps, childcare centers, environmental education centers, golf courses, music shells, museums, nature centers, planetariums, swimming pools, tennis courts, theaters, and zoos. Such a list gives scant indication of the variety of specific activities, which are mostly in arts, crafts, athletics, and other vocational areas, and are often designed for special groups such as senior citizens, preschool children, and the physically handicapped and mentally retarded. Frequently, city recreation departments cooperate with city schools to provide after-school activities on school grounds.

Community Organizations. A great deal of education and learning takes place in so-called community organizations, as a 1972 survey by the National Center for Education Statistics (NCES) made clear (Kay, 1974). One perhaps thinks first of the YMCA and Red Cross, with their well-organized programs in swimming and first aid. But there are also the historical societies, the Jewish Community Center, senior citizens' groups, chess clubs, the Junior League, the Lions, and, in more recent years, the myriad small self-help groups. Some of these groups are highly organized; others are hardly organized at all. Membership in some is tightly controlled; others are open to all. Many are chapters of or otherwise affiliated with national or other multi-unit organizations; many others are strictly local. These community organizations are nongovernmental, with the possible exception of libraries, and nonprofit. The learning that takes place is seldom certified in any sense. And over three fourths of the teaching is done by volunteers (Kay, 1974).

Community organizations include the following general categories (the typology is elaborated in Peterson and Associates, 1979): multipurpose organizations (such as libraries and Y's), cultural/intellectual groups, personal improvement/awareness groups, church-sponsored organizations, senior adult groups, youth programs, recreation groups, political organizations, social service organizations (such as the Red Cross and various charitable organizations), civic/service clubs, and fraternal and social clubs.

It would be interesting to know what the trends are, if any, in community organization-based learning. We do know that the image and role of public libraries are changing markedly. Formerly seen as sources of books for the bookish, many libraries, especially metropolitan ones, are now actively involved in a wide range of adult (and childhood and youth) learning services—information and referral (I & R) concerning all locally available human services, General Education Development (GED) preparation, television and video-tape learning, and assistance with all sorts of independent or self-directed learning projects. The museums, too, are shedding their old image and have begun to offer—and market—educational programs with wide appeal.

The rise of the psychological self-help groups ("personal improvement/awareness groups" in the typology) is something of a social phenomenon in itself, so new as not to be recognized in any of the 1972 national surveys. Many of these groups are sponsored by churches and Y's; others are activities of various counter-culture and "personal development" organizations. Especially in metropolitan areas, there are groups for aiding just about every type of person who judges himself to be in some way marginal to the American mainstream (the physically handicapped, single fathers, gay couples, and so on). There are also the informal groups of "co-learners" and "self-formed groups of equals" mentioned in Gross (1977) and Penland (1977).

Churches and Synagogues. As a source of education and learning, churches might be discussed along with the other community organizations. For several reasons, however, it is useful to consider them separately. For one thing, they far outnumber all the other types of community organizations; they numbered more (172,000) than all the other types of organizations included in the 1972 NCES study combined (61,800). Second, in many small towns and rural areas the church is the only site for community or social life; thus, churches must be multipurpose organizations.

According to the 1972 NCES survey (Kay, 1974), 29 percent of all churches reportedly conducted adult education courses. Enrollment, which totaled 5.2 million registrations, divided into the following categories: religion, with 73.5 percent of the registrations; personal and family living, with 17.2 percent; community issues, 4.1 percent; general education, including adult basic education, Americanization, and GED work, 2.5 percent; and sports and recreation, 1.1 percent.

However, adult education programs (in the NCES sense of formally conducted classes) account for only a small part of church-sponsored learning. As a social institution, the modern church is truly multifaceted—serving a wide range of human needs with activities ranging from worship services and discussion groups to pastoral counseling, lectures, workshops, musical groups, drama, graphic arts, childcare, summer school, and charitable and social action projects of all kinds.

Free Universities. Free universities appear to be a genuine educational innovation —at least in the United States. They allow people to learn without the conventional academic trappings of grades, credits, and the like. Their basic premise is that people want to learn something for its own sake. Anyone with expertise in a particular area—whether accredited or not—may teach a course, and anyone may be a student, in keeping with the free university's philosophy that "anyone can teach and anyone can learn." About two thirds of the free universities are based at conventional colleges or universities; often they are given funds and space by the respective student governments, and many of their enrollees are students from the local campus. A few are located at a community center such as a library or church. The rest have their own offices somewhere in the community.

Free universities operate by recruiting teachers and publishing a bulletin containing course descriptions and meeting times and places. When students register, they may pay small fees, and later they may be asked to evaluate the courses they have taken. Classes are held in homes, community facilities, or college buildings. A wide range of courses is typically available; while unlimited in principle, topics tend to focus on crafts, performing arts, practical skills needed in everyday living, personal psychology, and political and social thought.

Parks and Forests. As any occasional domestic traveler knows, the federal government, the states, and other jurisdictions own and maintain vast park and forest preserves. There are also national and state monuments, memorials, historical sites, archeological sites, parkways, seashores, riverways, grasslands, and battlefields. The statistics of acreage and use (visits) are staggering. Usage trends are even more remarkable; as one example, visits to all areas of the National Park System numbered 33.3 million in 1950 and 238.8 million in 1975 (1976 Statistical Abstract)—a 700 percent increase.

A great deal can be learned while visiting the various parks and other sites, be it botany, geology, natural history, cultural change, or whatever. These visits can also be occasions for acquiring and strengthening attitudes about conservation and related national concerns.

Other types of nonschool organizations also serve as sources for education and learning. The nation's prisons, for example, reportedly provide educational services to between 200,000 and 300,000 inmates. Projects of the National Endowments for the Arts and Humanities provide numerous learning opportunities. All in all, at least twice as many adults are learning through this nonschool "periphery" as through the school-based "core," though usually not in as intensive a way.

Postsecondary Schooling

America's sources of postsecondary schooling include all the categories of school-based education listed in Table 1 except for preprimary and elementary and secondary education.

College and University Undergraduate Education. Approximately 50 percent of all high school graduates go on to college or university—a figure that has remained remarkably stable over the past decade. The figure, however, varies substantially from state to state (and region to region), depending in large part on the accessibility of colleges—for example, community colleges (Willingham, 1970). Some 80 percent of college students are enrolled in public institutions, where the tuition is much lower than at private colleges. In many community colleges (in California, for example) there is no tuition. The upshot is a national (and state) higher education system that is substantially stratified by social class (despite expanding financial aid programs nationally and in many states).

Of all the organization-based sources of education, the public community colleges have by far the best track record of serving older and other "new clientele," in both on- and off-campus settings. Community college enrollment increases have far outstripped those of all other types of schools in the past decade.

Attrition and retention rates vary by type of institution, with higher retention rates associated with institutional selectivity and prestige. Nationally, across all institutions, the attrition (or retention) rate is about 50 percent—about half of all students graduate within four years—a figure that has also changed very little over the years. (On the order of 70 percent of all four-year college students eventually receive their bachelor's degree.)

Graduate and Professional Education. Graduate enrollments dropped off slightly in the 1970s, in part in response to the economy's inability to suitably employ all the country's highly educated manpower. Certain subject fields, primarily in the arts and humanities, have been much harder hit than others. The result is an expanding force of the underemployed, many pessimistic predictions (for example, Freeman, 1976), and a host of difficult problems for educational and social policy.

So much for the standard sequence of higher education in the United States. Next we consider several alternative forms of education or sources of additional education—all designed mainly for adults.

Public School Adult Education. The great majority of school districts in the country operate adult education programs, or "adult schools." Taken together, they have several important functions. They enable people who dropped out of elementary or secondary school to come back and earn the equivalent of a high school diploma, usually by preparing for and then taking and passing the General Education Development (GED) tests. They are the chief operating arm of the federal government's campaign against illiteracy; under the Adult Education Act of 1966, funds are distributed to the states for adult basic education (ABE). (The Right to Read Effort, which is directed at adults as well as children, is the other major federal anti-illiteracy program.) Roughly one third of adult school enrollees are in ABE courses. Great numbers of so-called English-as-a-Second-Language courses are also conducted by school districts on the east, south, and west coasts of the country. In addition to their primary purpose, they serve a kind of socialization function for non-English-speaking immigrants. Adult school programs also typically provide an assortment of occupational or skill courses, though not usually complete programs leading to a credential. And finally, they offer a broad range of general academic as well as avocational courses, all pretty much in response to local community interests.

Proprietary Schools. An important alternative to conventional postsecondary education is provided by the for-profit (and some not-for-profit) proprietary schools. Some are owned by large corporations, such as Bell and Howell; most are owned by individual entrepreneurs. Altogether there are about 9,000 (Kay, 1976), more than three times the number of conventional colleges and universities. These schools provide "no nonsense" (read, no general education) training for specific occupations. There are seldom entrance requirements, and the schools usually promise job placement. As a type of postsecondary education, they are controversial. Numerous critics have judged many of the proprietaries to be fraudulent (for example, the Federal Trade Commission, 1976; Cowen, 1977). Other writers have been highly supportive (for example, Hebert and Coyne, 1976).

University Extension and Continuing Education. Yet another important school-based source for lifelong learning is extension and continuing education. An estimated 1,233 four-year colleges and universities operate extension, continuing education, correspondence, and various noncredit programs (Kemp, 1978). Historically, such programs often concentrated on the professional upgrading of elementary and secondary teachers. In 1975, there were some 3.3 million participants (Boaz, 1978), with more than four fifths enrolled at public institutions. While some courses may be taken for credit, typically most are noncredit courses. The range of course offerings can be astonishingly diverse. Courses are conducted in a variety of formats at many different types of locations.

Participants in extension or continuing education are typically well-educated and relatively affluent. Programs are commonly "self-supporting," meaning that they operate almost entirely on the revenues from student fees. Fees can be high, averaging at a public university around $75 for a course that meets three hours a week for a semester. Nonetheless, the number of four-year institutions with continuing education programs has more than doubled since 1967-68.

Community Education. Community education, the last of the school-based sources of education and learning to be considered, is also difficult to define precisely, chiefly because of the expansive rhetoric regarding its purposes. Its basic operating idea is that school buildings (and other community facilities) should be made available during nonschool hours to all members of the community for a wide assortment of educational and learning activities. The concerns of community education, however, are broader than merely instructional: they have been variously said to include using the school as a "focus of community life," mobilizing all available resources toward resolving community needs and problems, viewing the school as a "total opportunity center," and developing a "sense of community" among residents in a neighborhood or other locality.

The general idea probably originated with the Charles Stewart Mott Foundation of Flint, Michigan, which has generously supported community education in Flint and elsewhere for close to four decades. In 1974, the federal Community Schools Act was passed, under which grants are made to both states and local school districts. To its participants, who frequently are parents of school children, community education costs little if anything. Learning activities tend to be loosely organized and may range across a very broad range of topics—from effective parenting, to health matters, to community issues and problems, for example—in response to judged community needs. Adults of all ages participate.

The College's Role in Adult Learning

Of the roughly 64 million adults pursuing learning through some kind of organization, some 12 million—slightly less than one fifth—are enrolled in the nation's 3,000 regionally accredited, degree-granting colleges and universities. In gross numbers, the American college serves about the same number of people as the Cooperative Extension Service of the U.S. Department of Agriculture. But here most comparisons end. When learning is measured in terms of effort or time invested, college easily emerges as the largest source for adult learning. It is probably also the most diversified source. With the possible exception of community organizations in the largest cities, no other source provides as broad a range of educational philosophies and even social values. Certainly no other organization offers the range of subjects for study—the *curriculum* diversity, if you will—of the typical comprehensive college.

Are there certain subjects, certain areas of knowledge, that can be systematically studied only at a comprehensive college or university? Fewer and fewer, it seems. One can be trained in many trades and occupational skills at proprietary schools, through trade union apprentice programs, in the military services, and in government manpower training programs. One can learn farming through the Cooperative Extension Service. One can study management and various professional fields through programs sponsored by professional associations—the American Management Association, and so forth. Much in the arts—broadly defined—can be studied through public school adult schools, city recreation departments, and museums and other community agencies. Languages can be learned through adult schools. Indeed, one can dabble in—not systematically study—almost all the humanities and social sciences through the adult schools and various community organizations.

So what is unique about the role of the American college? Of course, it is a uniquely *academic* institution—an institution where for two, four, six, eight, or more years, one can systematically study one of the liberal arts or sciences. Beyond such in-depth study, the typical American college affords the opportunity for some acquaintance with the totality of human knowledge. And, of course, colleges provide certification for academic accomplishment and professional training in the form of degrees.

These academic studies can be expected to enhance undergraduates' commitment to intellectual values and instill in them a zest for critical thinking and enjoyment of ideas. They should also contribute to the cultivation of esthetic sensitivities, humane attitudes, and personality development along the lines set forth in earlier chapters in this book. It is to be hoped that the intellectual commitment engendered in college will be permament—that colleges will send forth graduates who are truly autonomous lifelong learners. For it is our contention that the capacity for continued learning is critical to adult development through the life cycle. Furthermore, for older adults college has a unique potential for fostering human development, precisely because it can represent both intellectual and more broadly human values. If the college is to remain the key element in the nation's postsecondary learning framework, it must adapt to the needs of adult learners. Several existing policies and practices limit colleges' abilities to meet adults' needs.

Youth Orientation. Most colleges and universities continue to serve mainly the traditional 18- to 21-year-old student population. Even at community colleges, older adults attend mainly in the evening and are taught mostly by part-time faculty with little allegiance to basic institutional goals. Likewise, at public four-year colleges the average age of students is increasing; yet professors are accustomed to teaching youths and are reluctant, often for career advancement reasons, to teach adult classes.

At most selective universities and independent colleges, the move to accommodate older students has been slow or nonexistent. This is unfortunate, from our viewpoint, since these institutions, with their liberal arts orientations, are in a particularly advantageous position to foster human development across the life span. However, as matters stand now, these colleges' contributions to development are pretty much limited to the young.

Vocationalism. As noted earlier, American colleges and universities vary substantially in their basic missions and, accordingly, in their curriculums. Vocationalism, including preparation for a profession, is probably now the top priority at a majority of institutions, particularly public ones. It is a priority that legislators and other politicians can identify with and support. As a basic curricular orientation, the new vocationalism of the 1970s appears to be largely a response to students' demands for marketable skills in a period of poor job prospects for college graduates in many fields.

Vocationalism—or at least narrow vocationalism—is generally at odds with human development objectives. Thus, community colleges and four-year state colleges, with their heavy emphasis on occupational training, can perforce give rather little attention to matters related to adult life stages—even though these are the institutions that have attracted disproportionate numbers of older students.

Public Control and Accountability. Some 80 percent of all students are enrolled in colleges and universities controlled and financed by state or local government. Throughout the 1970s, and now with Proposition 13-style fiscal conservatism taking hold, public institutions are being asked to budget stringently and to render careful account for expenditure of public funds. Government has commonly preferred occupational, service, and other objectives that are clearly in the public interest. It will be programs in these areas that public agencies will support, and results from them that they will demand. Allocation of resources for essentially personal (entirely noneconomic) and even purely intellectual (and liberal arts) goals will be increasingly problematic in an era of financial conservatism.

Retention and Attrition. The high college dropout rates—50 percent nationally over the four years and much higher at most community colleges, particularly urban ones —present a seemingly intractable problem. Some (not the colleges, certainly) say the phenomenon is not a problem, but more appropriately a kind of youth life-style or a subcultural mode of growth. However, to the extent that individuals drop out of college never to return, and to the extent that colleges are agents of commitment to continuous learning and human development, the high attrition must be viewed as a problem of major proportions. To be sure, many individuals leave college for strictly personal reasons, and dropping out temporarily may even be beneficial for their development, in some cases. However, many others leave because the institution, in some way, has proved unable to accommodate them. Where open admissions policies prevail, in particular at urban two-year colleges, the situation is especially serious. Students may find themselves in a revolving door: a semester of trying and failing; a probationary semester, also failed; dismissal; re-entry on probation one or two terms later; failure; dismissal. Hence a great many people, because of negative college experiences, are turned off from further college work; closed off are the opportunities both for further academic achievement and for any aid in personality development and life crisis resolution that colleges and universities may afford.

Academic Conservatism. One of the messages of this volume is that colleges will have to modify a number of their policies and practices—along some of the lines outlined in subsequent chapters—in order to become effective instruments for continuous individual development. Many forces, however, beyond the vocationalism and youth orientation already noted, will be operating to maintain the status quo.

In order for colleges to aid individuals moving through the various adult stages, they must obviously open up their admissions to adults of all ages. But academics may balk, for example, when older students look "substandard" on admissions criteria, such as standardized tests. It may be feared that "academic quality" will be jeopardized. Needed new courses, course sequences, and degree programs, as well as new psychological services —counseling and assessing, for example—could generate opposition from entrenched cliques operating under zero-sum assumptions. New scheduling patterns—for example, late afternoon and evening courses—will not be welcome by professors accustomed to familiar teaching routines. And colleges and universities are typically "tenured in." It would be a mistake to underestimate the internal forces militating against real institutional reform on behalf of objectives related to human growth throughout the life span.

Class Bias. Survey research clearly indicates that it is predominantly the already well-educated and high-income adults who avail themselves of the opportunities for development afforded by participation in continuing education (see, for example, the analysis by Cross, 1979). We have, in short, a massive problem of equity, with the problem more serious in the collegiate sector than elsewhere in the postsecondary complex. Government, particularly the federal government, with its clear commitment to equity as a policy goal, will be disinclined to allocate major funds to providers of adult learning services so long as the fact of differential participation by social class remains.

Needed College Reforms

Numerous reforms seem necessary for colleges effectively to facilitate lifelong learning and human development in a context of multiple resources for postsecondary learning. The following suggestions by no means exhaust the possibilities.

Age Neutralism. As we noted earlier, for colleges and universities to meet developmental needs through the life span, they must admit adults of all ages and be ready to accommodate their education and career needs. Preferably, there should be no discrimination by age whatsoever in the provision of educational services.

Fewer reforms are needed among the two-year community colleges—many of which have been extremely resourceful in devising programs for older students—than among most four-year institutions. While many, to be sure, have taken steps on behalf of older students—external degrees, special programs for returning women, fee reductions for senior citizens, and other measures as described by Atelsek and Gomberg (1977), Powell (1979), and Valley (1979)—by and large they are small steps, often taken mostly because of declining enrollments of "regular" students. Comprehensive institutional commitment to accommodating older students, as described, for example, by Bennis (1978), is extremely rare.

A host of new policies need to be implemented. New curriculums will be needed, informed when possible by theories of adult development. Courses will need to be offered in the evening, during the late afternoon, perhaps on weekends. Student services will need to be available during all those hours. Registration and various other administrative procedures affecting students should be simplified. Courses and other educational activities should be conducted at off-campus locations convenient for students to reach, as long as the quality of instruction is not affected. The broad goal is to achieve a genuine and pervasive commitment to age neutralism at the institution.

Collaboration with Local Organizations. In initiating new programs for nontraditional populations, educational institutions typically go it alone rather than collaborating with any of the other organizations in the area that provide educational services for adults. Especially as the numbers of traditional-age students decline, institutions tend to compete with each other for the adult market—to try to corner as much of the market as possible, to snare as many bodies as possible. Not only are the ethics and possibly the quality of such endeavors questionable, as the Carnegie Council (1979) has recently warned, but also it can be argued that aggressive recruiting of students is not in the best interests of individual learners. It would undoubtedly be better if individuals could first be helped to understand their learning needs and then directed to the organization—school or nonschool—that seems best able to meet those needs. This service should be provided by a neutral *educational broker* (Heffernan, Macy, and Vickers, 1976).

Most communities have no organizing body, such as an education council, for the cooperative planning and coordination of educational services. As the key institution for adult learning and development in any locality, the college should probably take the lead in forming such a council. Among other activities, the council could conduct comprehensive community needs assessments, inventory available resources, and negotiate which institutions will meet which unmet needs (see Peterson and Associates, 1979). Additionally, such a council could sponsor or operate an educational brokering agency to provide assessment, information, and counseling services to potential adult students.

This same spirit of cooperation should extend from the college to agencies in the community that provide psychological (rather than strictly educational) services. As college staff members become aware of individual students' developmental quandaries, they should be able to make referrals to appropriate public or private agencies.

Crediting Noncollegiate Learning. Another implication of the existence of multiple postsecondary learning resources is the fact that many adults who enroll in (or return to) college to earn a degree are likely in the meantime to have learned much in other settings. It seems only reasonable that students should not be required to study what they already know. Colleges should have procedures for assessing new students' skills and knowledge, for granting degree credit for prior learning, and for placing students appropriately in the curriculum.

Individualized Learning Programs. While it is probably not helpful to make glib generalizations about the differences between adult and "college-age" students, it should be kept in mind that most adults have more, and more varied, daily obligations than their younger compeers. Structured instruction, like classes that meet thrice weekly at the same time of day, may be inappropriate for many adults—traveling salespersons, shift workers, and flight attendants, for example. Ideally, an adult student should have the opportunity to work out an individualized program, tailored to his or her career goals and avoiding conflicts with work, family, and other obligations.

Colleges should also recognize that there are many sources in the community through which people can learn and should actively encourage and facilitate noncollegiate learning (for example, at the job site, at a museum, or via a television course) as part of individualized (degree) programs, perhaps formalized through learning contracts.

An additional benefit from most strategies for individualized learning is that the student meets frequently with a faculty member acting as a mentor or adviser. This person is in a particularly good position to act as a sounding board on developmental matters and to make referrals to campus or community agencies as deemed necessary.

Vocational Preparation and Human Development. The chapter by Blocher and Rapoza in this volume treats in detail issues related to professional or vocational education and adult development. But the problem of how to combine the two warrants comment here also. Research (for example, Cross, 1979) clearly shows that adults in their middle years who attend college do so overwhelmingly for occupational and economic reasons. Such students tend to be concentrated in public two- and four-year colleges. Most of their instructors are technical specialists, who are not likely to be familiar with, or even particularly interested in, conceptions of adult development. Therein lies a substantial problem—and a major challenge.

Curriculum planners will face the challenge of devising programs that supplement job training with education related to life cycle transitions, interpersonal competence, humanitarian concern, and the like. Faculty development specialists will be called upon to help professors whose lives have been spent in specialized fields assume a broader vision of what college can do and mean. Indeed, the entire institution's philosophy will be challenged to change—to expand.

Quality, Evaluation, Accountability. One uses the word *quality* with a measure of embarrassment; it is one of American education's most widely used yet most elusive terms. Perhaps, in the context of adult learning, *quality* might best be defined in terms of student satisfaction. In order to maximize student satisfaction, many of the traditional indexes of quality might indeed often be necessary: knowledgeable and experienced instructors or mentors, sensitive counselors, pleasant physical facilities, a general climate of congenial yet productive relations between staff and students, and so forth.

It is critical that college staff constantly evaluate programs for adults in light of their real worth to them. They must avoid charges of fraud, which have been leveled at many adult learning programs. For the protection of unsophisticated students who are poorly prepared to judge educational services for themselves, college staff must prevent inferior services from being offered in the first place. All program plans should include evaluation components. Continuous—institutionalized—evaluation serves the twin goals of (1) improving plans and programs and (2) implementing accountability. Just as important, institutionalized evaluation serves to prevent the complacency that leads to stagnation of programs and organizations and inhibits the advance of adult development efforts more broadly.

A case can be made on rather simple ethical grounds that human service agencies, including colleges, ought to be accountable in some meaningful way to the recipients of their services. College staff cannot simply give lip service to accountability and patronizingly assume that adult students, like most younger students, lack the sophistication and assertiveness to make it known when they believe they are receiving poor treatment. Unfortunately, we have seen few descriptions of methods by which adult learning programs have implemented accountability. No matter how they do so, future collegiate programs for adults will have to systematically render account to student-participants, as well as to legislatures and other funding sources.

The Promise

We opened this commentary by describing the wide range of sources through which adults may study and continue learning. We then observed that the American college, despite the expanding activities of other providers of education, still performs unique academic functions and, in an important sense, sustains the commitment to continuous learning, which is a key ingredient in adult development. Finally, we considered a number of factors that inhibit the capacity of colleges to serve adult development needs—and some general steps that might be taken to improve that capacity.

It seems well in concluding this analysis to be both realistic and idealistic. Beyond such problems as rampant vocationalism in higher education, the very high attrition rates at many institutions, class bias in participation, and government disinterest in collegiate programs lacking clear economic benefits, there is the new public mood of fiscal conservatism calling for reduced spending by government. It is possible, even probable, that educational services for adults—judged to be of low priority by legislators—will soon be curtailed in many states. This has already happened in California, for example, where, because of the reduction of course offerings necessitated by Proposition 13, enrollments in public adult school and community college evening programs dropped markedly in 1978 and 1979. Should the independent colleges and universities then expand their offerings? They no doubt should, but one result, unfortunately, will be a worsening of the equity problem mentioned earlier.

As we saw in the previous chapters, there is an expanding body of provocative theory about how adults develop and change. Much of its content is classically liberal. While its component conceptions are likely to be refined in the years just ahead, it does seem that we now understand some of the important dimensions of development, and also some of the problems encountered in the process of development.

Colleges and universities have unique potential for promoting adult development, largely because—at their best—of their commitment to intellectual values, including lifelong learning. Much needs to be done to realize this potential. As of now, it may be only the small, residential, liberal arts colleges that are actively committed to developmental goals of the kind set forth in this book; these efforts are largely restricted to affluent 18- to 21-year-old youth (accounting for perhaps 5 percent of the total college population). Such opportunities ideally should be available to all adults. Needless to say, the case for accessible adult learning and development services will need to be made with great resourcefulness in the current period of economic stringency and governmental cutbacks.

The challenges, in short, are formidable. Yet the benefits are conceivably great indeed. Current conceptions of adult development—of interpersonal, moral, and humanitarian growth, for example—can provide worthy visions for academic professionals. The promise is individual lives that are more meaningful, more useful, and more satisfying. The quality of the culture and the life of the society would be enhanced accordingly.

References

Atelsek, F. J., and Gomberg, I. L. *College and University Services for Older Adults.* Washington, D.C.: American Council on Education, 1977.

Bennis, W. "Toward a Learning Society: A Basic Challenge to Higher Education." Paper prepared for the HEW Lifelong Learning Project, Washington, D.C., 1978.

Boaz, R. L. *Participation in Adult Education: Final Report 1975.* Washington, D.C.: National Center for Education Statistics, 1978.

Brown, C. A. "Municipal Training Programs: 1975." In *Urban Data Service Reports No. 8.* Washington, D.C.: International City Management Association, 1976.

Carnegie Commission on Higher Education. *Toward a Learning Society.* New York: McGraw-Hill, 1973.

Carnegie Council on Policy Studies in Higher Education. *Fair Practices in Higher Education: Rights and Responsibilities of Students and Their Colleges in a Period of Intensified Competition for Enrollments.* San Francisco: Jossey-Bass, 1979.

Carnegie Task Force on Public Broadcasting. *Summary Report.* New York: Carnegie Corporation of New York, 1977.

Carp, A., Peterson, R. E., and Roelfs, P. J. "Adult Learning Interests and Experiences." In K. P. Cross, J. R. Valley, and Associates, *Planning Non-Traditional Programs: An Analysis of the Issues for Postsecondary Education.* San Francisco: Jossey-Bass, 1974.

Cowen, P. "Book Reviews." *Harvard Educational Review,* May 1977, *47,* 232-236. (See also "Correspondence" in November 1977 issue.)

Cross, K. P. "Adult Learners: Characteristics, Needs, and Interests." In R. E. Peterson and Associates, *Lifelong Learning in America: An Overview of Current Practices, Available Resources, and Future Prospects.* San Francisco: Jossey-Bass, 1979.

Dwyer, R. "Workers' Education, Labor Education, Labor Studies: An Historical Delineation." *Review of Educational Research,* 1977, *47*(1), 179-207.

Federal Trade Commission, Staff of the Bureau of Consumer Protection. *Proprietary Vocational and Home-Study Schools: Final Report to the Federal Trade Commission and Proposed Trade Regulation Rule.* Washington, D.C.: U.S. Government Printing Office, 1976.

Freeman, R. B. *The Overeducated American.* New York: Academic Press, 1976.

Gross, R. *The Lifelong Learner: A Guide to Self-Development.* New York: Simon & Schuster, 1977.

Hebert, T., and Coyne, J. *Getting Skilled: A Guide to Private Trade and Technical Schools.* New York: Dutton, 1976.

Heffernan, J. M., Macy, F. U., and Vickers, D. F. *Educational Brokering: A New Service for Adult Learners.* Washington, D.C.: National Center for Educational Brokering, 1976.

Kay, E. R. *Adult Education in Community Organizations, 1972.* Washington, D.C.: National Center for Education Statistics, 1974.

Kay, E. R. *Programs and Enrollments in Non-Collegiate Postsecondary School: 1973-74.* Washington, D.C.: National Center for Education Statistics, 1976.

Kemp, F. B. *Noncredit Activities in Institutions of Higher Education for the Year Ending June 30, 1976.* Washington, D.C.: National Center for Education Statistics, 1978.

Leubsdorf, D. P. "Carter Changes the Picture for Public TV." *Change,* October 1977, *9,* 46-57.

Lusterman, S. *Education in Industry.* New York: Conference Board, 1977.

Macken, E., and others. *Home-Based Education: Needs and Technological Opportunities.* Washington, D.C.: National Institute of Education, 1976.

Moses, S. *The Learning Force: A More Comprehensive Framework for Educational Policy.* Syracuse, N.Y.: Educational Policy Research Center, Syracuse University, 1971.

National Manpower Institute. *Negotiated Education: Tuition Assistance in Collective Bargaining Agreements.* Washington, D.C.: National Manpower Institute, 1977.

Penland, P. R. *Individual Self-Planned Learning in America.* Washington, D.C.: Office of Libraries and Learning Resources, U.S. Office of Education, Department of Health, Education, and Welfare, 1977.

Peterson, R. E., and Associates. *Lifelong Learning in America: An Overview of Current Practices, Available Resources, and Future Prospects.* San Francisco: Jossey-Bass, 1979.

Powell, S. "State Policies: Plans and Activities." In R. E. Peterson and Associates, *Lifelong Learning in America: An Overview of Current Practices, Available Resources, and Future Prospects.* San Francisco: Jossey-Bass, 1979.

Stern, B., and Best, F. "Cyclic Life Patterns." In D. W. Vermilye (Ed.), *Relating Work and Education: Current Issues in Higher Education 1977.* San Francisco: Jossey-Bass, 1977.

Tough, A. *The Adult's Learning Projects: A Fresh Approach to Theory and Practice in Adult Learning.* Toronto: Ontario Institute for Studies in Education, 1971.

Turner, J. C. "Labor and Continuing Education." In *Proceedings of the Invitational Conference on Continuing Education, Manpower Policy, and Lifelong Learning.* Washington, D.C.: National Advisory Council on Extension and Continuing Education, 1977.

U.S. Bureau of the Census. *Statistical Abstract of the United States.* Washington, D.C.: U.S. Department of Commerce, 1976.

U.S. Civil Service Commission. *Training Effort Government-Wide.* Washington, D.C.: U.S. Government Printing Office, 1977.

U.S. Department of Labor. *Employment and Training Report of the President.* Washington, D.C.: U.S. Department of Labor, 1977.

Valley, J. R. "Local Programs: Innovations and Problems." In R. E. Peterson and Associates, *Lifelong Learning in America: An Overview of Current Practices, Available Resources, and Future Prospects.* San Francisco: Jossey-Bass, 1979.

Willingham, W. *Free-Access Higher Education.* New York: College Entrance Examination Board, 1970.

Part Two

Implications for Curriculum

Part One presented key findings concerning student development and learning throughout the life cycle. In Part Two we ask, "What are the implications of those findings for teaching in particular disciplines and areas of professional preparation?" And conversely, "How can teaching in these different fields be managed so as to help students meet life cycle challenges and to encourage developmental change?" The first chapters deal with representative disciplines from the arts and sciences—namely, English, drama, philosophy, history, economics, psychology, anthropology, and biology. Then, after a chapter on interdisciplinary studies, we turn to four representative professional areas—business administration, engineering, education, and human services.

We begin with literature and drama because, as Lois Lamdin and Lois Fowler state in Chapter Fifteen, "in every age and country, literature has been the record of what it means to be human, to be alive, to love, to suffer, to face death, and to seek God. Before formal history, philosophy, science, or math, was the poem, the tale, and the counting rhyme." And, we might add, the play. Reading, writing, discussing literature, and performing plays can help students experience new relationships, ideas, and values with minimal risk. Such studies can help them observe and experience the play of life cycle dynamics, personal intimacies, and alienations. In Chapter Fifteen, Lamdin and Fowler remind us of the rich experiences and perceptions older students bring to the study of literature. They describe the applicability of Kolb's experiential learning theory for the active reading of literature and note how such literary classics as Shakespeare's *King Lear,* Dostoevski's *Crime and Punishment,* and Dickens' *Hard Times* illuminate issues related to the life cycle, intellectual and ethical development, and development of

humanitarian concern. They conclude by pointing out the necessary relationships between the teaching of literature and the development of improved reading and writing skills. In the richness of adult perspectives they see a potent opportunity for restoring English to its central place in the college curriculum.

In Chapter Sixteen, Larry Friedlander and Martin Esslin reveal the dramatic performance as "an integrated moral, emotional, intellectual, and sensual universe," which "demands of all those who work with it a concomitant integrity of body, mind, and soul." They remind us of the wide range of disciplines and theoretical studies that are involved in theater arts in addition to the crafts of acting and directing and the technical skills required for design and production. The maturity and diverse experiences of adult students help them to be empathetic and make them powerful contributors to dramatic productions. At the same time, dramatic productions provide a dual opportunity for adult development, first through analyzing and metabolizing the play itself and then through the expressive activities and working relationships required to make the play come alive. These actions encourage the living inquiry and interpersonal competence described by Torbert in Part One.

In Chapter Seventeen, William Bondeson reviews some current controversies concerning philosophy as a discipline and method, and recognizes the pertinence of Gilligan's discussion of moral development and Kolb's stages of cognitive development. In discussing the educational process and the teaching of philosophy, he notes that Torbert's emphasis on "living inquiry" suggests skills appropriate to philosophy's dialectical processes. He also notes how philosophical dialogue is encouraged by the type of intimacy described by Douvan. His final section concerning implications for adult development pursues in more detail the issues raised by Gilligan and Kolb and moves on to address broader implications of Weathersby's chapter concerning ego development and Chickering and Havighurst's chapter on the life cycle. He reminds us that older students, by virtue of the challenges they have met, are particularly well equipped to consider the existential issues basic to philosophy today.

Paul Ward, in Chapter Eighteen, is particularly interested in the implications of Gilligan's and Perry's chapters on moral and intellectual development for the teaching and learning of history. He notes that the moral and intellectual orientations associated with different levels of development have an influence on the analysis and interpretation of history. He also notes how history can promote empathy and objectivity, thus encouraging humanitarian concern. At the same time, of course, he is concerned about the "morality" of teaching morality at any level. After wrestling with these issues, he considers some concrete applications to curricular content and teaching practices, referring to Torbert's concept of living inquiry and the life cycle patterns described in Chapter One.

In Chapter Nineteen, George Dawson reminds us that every society must answer the same basic economic questions: What shall we produce? How much? For whom? How? Every individual is affected by these economic decisions and by the value judgments that underlie them. Thus, the primary mission of economic educators is to create better-informed citizens—to help students understand the economy and its institutions and develop the analytical skills necessary for that understanding. Dawson briefly reviews various priorities in relation to these broad goals and then turns to the implications of Weathersby's ideas concerning self-directed learning and stages of ego development. He recognizes the pertinence of Schaie and Parr's conceptions of intellectual development throughout the life cycle and the potential contribution of study in economics to the organizational, integrative, and interpretive skills they find essential. He finds Kolb's experiential learning cycle directly relevant to the study of economics, in which concrete experiences accumulated through daily living provide a rich basis for reflective observation and abstract conceptualization. He also recognizes the pertinence of Gilligan's chapter on moral development to an understanding of the value choices involved in economic goal-setting.

In Chapter Twenty, Richard Mann provides an integrating model for the diverse activities and goals that currently characterize "psychology." A triangle with Science, Healing, and Wisdom at its points provides a diagrammatic framework for six major orientations: psychology (1) as a science, (2) as an applied field, (3) as a helping profession, (4) as a facilitator of self-development, (5) as a source of human wisdom, and (6) as metaphysics. Mann finds the current fragmentation and competition among these orientations detrimental to the larger discipline and argues for curricular content and teaching practices that integrate these complementary orientations. After proposing more appropriate curricular goals and teaching practices, he describes three current working models that illustrate appropriate directions for future development. Throughout the chapter, the developmental concerns of the Part One chapters by Weathersby, Perry, Gilligan, Torbert, Douvan, White, and Kolb are addressed as they relate to the six major orientations of psychology and to psychology curriculums and teaching.

James Gibbs' chapter suggests powerful interactions among academic and field studies in anthropology and intellectual development, ego development, moral development, and life cycle perspectives. Used as a major teaching strategy, the comparative inductive method—combined with the student's confrontation with cultural relativity—creates requirements that challenge dualistic thinking and conformist, culturally bound concepts of human characteristics, social organization, values, and behavioral norms. The concept of metathought—thinking about how one thinks and where one's ideas come from—encourages a self-critical mind, which provides a basis for continued self-development. Field experiences in diverse cultures challenge specific attitudes and behaviors, values, life-styles, and assumptions about human requirements. As one stands back and views cultures through broader historical and economic perspectives, cultural domination becomes a moral issue. Finally, Gibbs proposes that anthropology can help us continually enrich our ideas of adult development and the life cycle as we look beyond the blinders of our own culturally bound paradigms and research findings.

Elof Carlson, in Chapter Twenty-Two, suggests how the large lecture class can be revitalized to introduce nonmajors to biological issues of critical concern to society. He sees an opportunity to appeal to students of all ages by connecting aspects of the "human condition" with students' life cycle experiences and concerns. Through concrete examples concerning population, birth control, prenatal diagnosis, sexuality, carcinogenesis, radiation hazards, mutagenesis, racism, the IQ controversy, eugenics, human aggression, and germ warfare, he indicates how issues of moral and intellectual development can be confronted in the course of learning about basic biological theory and research. He recognizes that this twofold outcome depends not only on reform of content but also on careful organization of large group activities, explicit attention to the teaching-learning environment, and intentional adoption of the scholar-teacher staffing model.

David Halliburton's chapter on interdisciplinary studies (Chapter Twenty-Three) begins by analyzing conceptions of the disciplines and the core curriculum, as a way of identifying the habits, assumptions about knowledge, and teaching traditions that have been built into our educational psyche and condition our educational reflexes. Against this background, Halliburton describes major approaches to interdisciplinarity, taking us through the cultural heritage, great books, and problem-centered orientations to thematic and future-oriented frameworks for organizing course content and activities. He finds these problem-centered and future orientations of interdisciplinary studies more suited to the pragmatic concerns of adults than traditional disciplinary approaches that emphasize theory without concern for application. Throughout this discussion he notes the pertinence of these various approaches to life cycle issues identified by Chickering and Havighurst, and to the conceptions of ego development, intellectual development, intimacy, humanitarian concern, and experiential learning discussed by other authors in Part One. Halliburton concludes the chapter with a list of propositions concerning the significance of interdisciplinary studies for adult learners—their learning styles, life cycles, ego development, intellectual and ethical development, and professional development. He addresses some of the critical developmental differences of men and women made by Bernard in her Part One chapter.

In Chapter Twenty-Four, Paul Grambsch describes the growing popularity of business administration for students throughout the life cycle. He also notes the influx of women into business schools and acknowledges that they probably encounter many of the same obstacles described by Blocher and Rapoza. He then examines the pros and cons of Bernard's various contingency schedules for women and points out how these schedules might conflict with the expectations of the business world. After tackling the issue of specialization versus liberal education, Grambsch examines the value of experiential learning and Kolb's theories as they apply to the case method and internship practices. He reminds us that night school and continuing education have long been traditional in business education and finds the intellectual orientations and motivations of older students described by Schaie and Parr accurate for business school students. Looking toward the future, he sees interpersonal competence and ego development as increasingly important concerns in business administration. These developments may be supported by a move toward more experience-based degree programs. He notes current lively interest in issues related to humanitarian concern but recognizes tough trade-offs as those values interact with the competitive and materialistic orientations of the larger society on which business depends. He finds Gilligan's chapter on moral development particularly relevant to individual-organization issues. Thus, Grambsch's realistic analyses make clear both the powerful potential in business education for helping students tackle life cycle concerns and developmental issues, and the powerful realities that may counter efforts in that direction.

Dean Griffith opens Chapter Twenty-Five by remarking upon some of the current ambiguities besetting engineering as a profession. He notes recurrent issues concerning technique versus theory, practical training versus scientific understanding, and the place of humanities and liberal arts. He then calls attention to some promising experiments such as the Worcester Polytechnic program, which addresses directly issues of leadership and social responsibility in addition to technical proficiency. He sees in this program direct applications of conceptions of ego development and humanitarian concern described by Weathersby and White. He then describes cooperative education as a promising means of promoting students' total development through experiential learning. Data from a recent survey concerning relationships between age differences and curricular preferences show a good fit with the life cycle patterns described in Chapter One and the stages of ethical and intellectual development addressed by Perry and Gilligan. A concluding section calls attention to the pertinence of Tough's chapter on adult learning and to the increasing significance of interpersonal competence for engineering professionals.

In Chapter Twenty-Six, Robert and Dorcas Saunders briefly recap the history of professional studies in education and then discuss current developments, which recognize the increasing range of educational activities carried on by government, business, and industry. They call attention to the need for curriculums and teaching practices that will help prepare persons for educational roles in these organizations and find Part One chapters concerning the life cycle, ego development, and adult learning especially pertinent to these new constituencies. They then turn attention to the developmental needs of four different client groups, defined in ways analogous to the Blocher and Rapoza categories: Initiates, Lateral Extenders, Vertical Changers, and Specialty Changers. Each of these groups requires curriculums that take into account life cycle stages as well as students' own objectives. The Saunders also recognize the importance of assessing prior learning as a basis for creating sound programs and cite Keeton's chapter on this topic in Part Three. They find Schaie and Parr's ideas concerning intellectual development, the role of the faculty member as facilitator, and the need for self-pacing by older students especially important to keep in mind in dealing with these different groups. Kolb's experiential learning cycle is particularly pertinent to the needs of Initiates; his ideas concerning the integrative stage and reassertion of nondominant learning styles offer important clues for program design with more mature Vertical Changers, who are accepting increasing responsibilities. The Saunders conclude their chapter by considering the implications of these findings for faculty development, referring, in this connection, to Lindquist's concepts in Part Three. They see a clear need to pay explicit attention to the life cycle and developmental needs of faculty members as professional development activities are made available.

Chapter Twenty-Seven, by Audrey Cohen, describes a model—the College for Human Services—for preparing practitioners for the new profession she calls "human service." The college provides a working example of a program that addresses many of the dimensions of adult development described in Part One: ego development, the development of humanitarian concern, interpersonal competence, capacity for intimacy, and intellectual and ethical development, with explicit attention to the area of values and moral choice. This model also recognizes the critical importance of linking theory with practice—of active application of abstract concepts—and thus operates in ways consistent with Kolb's concept of experiential learning and his broad stages of the human growth process: Acquisition, Specialization, and Integration.

Part Two concludes with a chapter by Rhoda Miller and Carol Wolff concerning education for all of the helping professions. The rapid expansion of these professions, the increased emphasis on employing indigenous and minority group persons, and the sharper attention to clients' rights have created pressures for curricular revision and new models to supply professionals prepared for more diverse roles. Such forces also imply a shift away from specialized training to a more generalist orientation. This shift, together with an increasing number of older, mature students, makes apparent the need for more sophisticated assessment of prior experiential learning, as discussed by Keeton in Part Three, and more systematic integration of field studies, internships, and practica based on experiential learning theories like those described by Kolb in Part One and by Duley in Part Three. Miller and Wolff note the need for changes in curriculum and teaching that will foster increased self-understanding and the kinds of intellectual competence described by Schaie and Parr. They also recognize the pervasive value questions confronted by human services workers and emphasize the importance of liberal arts studies that can promote the kinds of moral and ethical development described by Gilligan and Perry in Part One. They find especially pertinent Green's ideas concerning the disciplines, as articulated in his chapter on the acquisition of purpose in Part Three.

15

Lois Lamdin
Lois J. Fowler

English

Numerous journal articles as well as much public wringing of hands in the popular press attest to the confusion that besets the English profession today. The question of why students cannot read has been succeeded by the question of why they cannot write; and, thanks at least in part to open admissions policies, we are finding out that despite their having taken some form of English from grades K to 12 they still cannot read and write when they get to college.

Reactions to the "crisis" range from elaborately designed and funded remedial programs to a new elitism that would simply ignore the problem. Meanwhile, in college English departments in which the number of persons taking English electives is declining and the English major is becoming an endangered species, writing programs, after years of neglect, are at last becoming the focus of attention; the profession is re-entering into dialogue about student's language, the goals of teaching composition and literature, and the limits of departmental "territory."

What, in all this new uncertainty about ends and means, does the emergence of a new adult population in the colleges mean? Is it a blessing or a new burden? How can we cope with and what can we offer to the older student? Perhaps a better way to approach the problem is to ask the question in reverse—that is, not what can English offer to the new adult population but rather what will that population, more experienced and more concerned with learning that has immediate relevance for their lives, demand from teachers of English, and what changes might their presence bring about?

In an article on reform in the English curriculum, John Gerber (1977), long one of the most astute spokesmen for the profession, reminded us forcefully that, despite the rhetoric with which we cloak our purposes, "we are basically teachers of reading and writing" whose subject matter is simply everything that is "the product of the verbal imagination" (p. 313). As teachers of reading and writing, how do we prepare to meet the challenges of the coming decade, of new populations, new crises, and old unresolved problems? Since prophetic declarations must rest on what has been and what is, we begin with a short history of the past twenty years of the profession.

Emphases of the Sixties and Seventies

The uproar that followed Sputnik in the fifties and the resultant perception of the mediocrity of American education triggered the landmark 1959 Woods Hole Conference, in which scholars from many disciplines came together to clarify objectives and to propose approaches for improving teaching methods in the United States. The major ideas that emerged from the conference were synthesized by Jerome Bruner in *The Process of Education* (1962), which provided a theoretical base for curricular innovation and reform. Woods Hole sparked a revolution. There was agreement across the disciplines on the importance of teaching *conceptual structures* and confidence that a sequence or ordered structure could be developed in any discipline (Bruner's *spiral curriculum*). Specific examples of such discipline-oriented, teacher-centered curriculums emerged almost immediately in math and the natural sciences. But in the humanities, and especially in English, although the impact of the conceptual approach was great, it remained theoretical for a time as we struggled toward agreement about defining not only the concepts but also the relative importance of the elements of the discipline: literature, written and oral communication, and language.

Among the first attempts at structure and sequence in the English curriculum were the U.S. Office of Education's Project English grants, which emphasized teaching— that is, what should be taught and how rather than what should be learned and by whom. Materials, textbooks, and methodology flooded the market on all levels. In literature, the emphasis lay on close reading, detailed analyses, and objective interpretation of the work; in language, on descriptive rather than prescriptive grammar; and in writing, on critical analysis of literature within a structured step-by-step approach from the simple to the complex. The personal interaction between reader and text evaporated under too much close textual analysis, and writing, devoid of its experiential character, become for many students a meaningless academic chore. There were problems with language too. Despite general agreement about the advantages of the descriptive approach, conflicting linguistic theories eradicated any possibility of a sequenced curriculum unless a student were fortunate enough to have similarly trained teachers from grade school through college. By the mid sixties, students and some faculty had begun to reject what they felt was rigidity in humanities education.

At the Dartmouth Conference in 1966, which brought together leaders in the field of English and English education from both the United States and England, the romance with structure and sequence in the curriculum ended abruptly. The participants shifted the emphasis from teachers to students or "learners," put the study of language at the center of the discipline, and replaced the concentration on formal literary analysis with a renewed interest in reading literature for an understanding of values, of life, of what it has been like to be alive for other people in other times. Experience, empathy, personal reactions, and discussions of related experiences replaced the more formalistic goals in literature as well as in writing; students were encouraged to express themselves less formally about personally meaningful topics. The notion of the "teacher-proof" curriculum was discarded in favor of what has been seen in retrospect as the "cult of the individual." In an effort to respond to the "relevancy" cry of the sixties, English teachers designed thematic courses, offered electives of all sorts, brought film and drama and pop culture into the classroom, and tried desperately to bridge the gap between television and the printed word. Or at least in theory they did. In practice, many of them went on as though the revolution had never happened, continuing to subject the texts to painstaking formal analysis, to demand five-paragraph expository essays with topic and subtopic sentences, and to treat language as something God had handed down complete on the sixth day.

Present Trends

The preceding summary is, of course, an oversimplification of what happened in the sixties and seventies, but it suggests how the pendulum has swung between opposing philosophies and what different sorts of problems have followed. Today, complaints about lack of structure, goals or objectives, and attention to "basics" appear daily both in the media and in professional journals. English professors still struggle to reach consensus about their discipline—and to satisfy the demands for "literacy" in a literal sense. Or worse yet, they abandon the struggle. In far too many departments of English, the search for self-definition has been seen as a concern of the secondary schools. With a genius for self-destruction, we have set out to teach students whose acquaintance with literature has been minimal—for whom there exist great gaps between Dr. Seuss and James Joyce and in whose minds float vague memories of *The Scarlet Letter* and *Mill on the Floss,* with perhaps some shreds of Vonnegut or Tolkien—to trace the food imagery in *Antony and Cleopatra,* or to discuss James' use of the unreliable narrator, or to puzzle out the difference between metonymy and synecdoche (which we have of course looked up before class). We have talked about structuralism and diacritics and explored the piquant notion that ambiguity in *Moby Dick* is partially dependent on the negative affix. And we have assigned endless research papers, which are even drearier to read than to write and which would tempt a saint to resort to a commercial paper-writing service.

Traditionally, in American colleges and universities, English has been held to be at the heart of the humanities. We in English think of ourselves as more broadly educated, better attuned to the concerns of our students, more apt to deal holistically with human needs, aspirations, dreams—with the very stuff of life and death. But, in fact, we have grown narrower, not broader. We are increasingly specialists, confined to our own scholarly domains, madly trying to keep up with the floods of professional literature and to contribute our drops to the scholarly seas. And in our personal pursuit of the white whale of esoterica, we look with scorn at those who would "dilute" the elixir that is literature, agreeing implicitly with Joseph Epstein, who wrote in a *New York Times* article that courses in science fiction and film remain in the curriculum "like stains on the shirt front after a drunken night on the town" (1977, p. 88).

The problem was summed up recently by William D. Schaefer (1978), the retiring executive director of the Modern Language Association: "The basic problem is the failure of the humanistic disciplines to relate to the society that supports them, a failure to explain and to justify the humanities and to prove their value to society" (p. 1). It would seem an appropriate time to look at what it is English departments do in order to judge how the advent of a new and different student population might affect current practices. We begin with literature, and with a reminder that whatever other aims we may have, our basic aim should be to make literature accessible, to make it a source of enrichment and enjoyment to students.

Teaching Literature

In the study of literature, there is assumed to be a sort of progressive order of attention, calling upon increasingly sophisticated analytical abilities. Crudely stated, the successive levels are these: (1) the thematic content of the work, what it is about, the universal concerns it embodies; (2) the context out of which the work arises, the nature and intent of the artist, the intellectual climate of the times, the historical or socio-cultural milieu; and (3) the complex of esthetic concerns that not only further illuminate the content but also have to do with the nature of the specific genre and with art itself.

Each of these areas commands a number of critical schools devoted to exploring methodologies appropriate to their primary concerns, but for the past thirty or forty years, beginning with the so-called New Critics of the thirties, interest has increasingly centered on the third of these, the esthetic, while literary history and thematic criticism have tended to take a back seat. Currently, literary criticism is again in ferment. Critical approaches derived from anthropology, philosophy, psychology, and linguistics are multi-plying the perspectives from which we can approach a text; our journals are the arena for dazzling hermeneutical display as structuralists pit their insights against adherents of Lacan and Errida, the Buffalo school jousts with the Geneva critics, and reception esthetics strikes everyone as a promising approach if one could just understand it. All of this is great intellectual sport, and, indeed, literary criticism has become *the* arena for graduate students and their professors, but the importation of such abstruse concerns into the undergraduate classroom threatens to deepen further the students' alienation from the poem or the story. Much has been lost in the process that connects people with litera-ture in a vital, humanizing way.

The continuum from theme to context to esthetic concerns may need modifying for most students, but particularly for the new adult population. We may find that the initial point of entry, the theme or universal concerns embodied in the work, is also the culminating point, and that the study of literature should not be seen as a continuum but as circular, leading back always to universal concerns. Or better yet, Bruner's figure of the spiral may be the image of choice; the student, having gone from theme through context to esthetic concerns, can return to theme, reexperiencing it with an enriched awareness of how structure and texture have combined to shape his response to the work of art.

Many of the formulations of human development presented in Part One of this book suggest that for any student, but particularly for the older student, literature can play a crucial role in education. Chickering and Havighurst remind us that in the midlife transition major questions concerning priorities and values are examined, that students reevaluate old attitudes and forge for themselves new relationships to things, to people, and to self. We know that in our most successful work as teachers of literature we have eased postadolescents through earlier transitions and crises, helping them to discover new relationships, new ideas, and new values through literature at minimal risk. How much more that same literature can offer to the adult, whose experiential base is broader, who comes to it committed to the search for meaning, and who has already lived through many of the archetypal situations that are at its core!

On the basis of our experience thus far plus the new research that has appeared on adult cognitive and affective development, it would seem that the influx of adults into higher education offers an unparalleled opportunity for departments of English to restore their discipline to its central place in the curriculum. Anyone who has ever taught in a continuing education class can tell stories of the riches of experience and perception that older students bring to the study of literature, as well as of the riches they take away with them. For literature is and always has been the primary vehicle of ideas, emotions, and values. In every age, in every country, literature has been the record of what it means to be human, to be alive, to love, to triumph, to suffer, to endure loss, to face death, and to seek God. All the intellectual and spiritual strivings of the race are embodied in its stories and poetry; all that has been thought and learned and felt has been recorded for posterity. Long before there was formal history or philosophy or science or math, there was the poem, the tale, the counting rhyme. And before there were written records there was oral literature that recorded the onset of wars, the passing of kings, the best planting times, and the religious myths that sustained a people, all in words and rhythms whose beauty and power have endured over the centuries.

In a sense, David Kolb's model of experiential learning is an apt one for the active reading of literature. The initial reading constitutes a mediated but still concrete experience; this is followed by a period of reflection and observation (which may be nurtured by class discussion); and then, if the study has been well planned, abstract conceptualization takes place. The fourth stage, active experimentation, may in some situations be obviously difficult or even undesirable. One need not have an affair to test out one's conceptualizations of adultery. One might, however, be encouraged to write of experience in such a way as to relive it imaginatively or to make it real for someone else. Whether or not one applies Kolb's model, there is no question that the basic phenomenalistic/constructivist modes of knowing are implicit in literature, language, and writing. It is the tension between the concrete and the abstract that stimulates creativity and that makes the English classroom such a fertile ground for learning.

On its most basic level, the study of literature is the study of reading. Such study may, of course, be remedial in nature, but since remediation will, it is hoped, be addressed in the future by the high schools, we shall not consider it within the scope of this chapter. We merely note in passing that it would be well for some reading professionals to turn their attention from the cognitive abilities of 6-year-olds to those of mature adults so that the nature of adult reading might be better understood and appropriate strategies devised for teaching reading to older students.

The reading skills emphasized in the study of literature tend to be those hermeneutical skills required for literary analysis and interpretation of texts. However, we must be aware that for some returning older students, uncertain of their skills, reading comprehension means accruing data; for others, reading well means reading fast. They will find that much-vaunted ability to "skim," which they may have learned in speed reading courses, does not work when one is confronted with a literary work of art. To skim a poem or story is not to have read it at all. Similarly, if, as William Perry has indicated, many students have learned to concentrate on the text without really thinking about what the author is saying, if they are storing up facts rather than making an effort to empathize and understand, to imaginatively reconstruct the author's world, then the experience of that literature is passing them by. For such students, the literature classroom must truly be a reading class.

Perry's chapter on intellectual and ethical development is useful here as it reminds us not only of what we do in the classroom but of the meaning of what we do in a developmental context. His "positions," from the simplistic Right-Wrong of position 1 through the evolution of Commitments in a relativistic and self-contradictory world (positions 7-9), recapitulate what for teachers of literature and writing is a central concern: the developing complexity and relativism of thought in students' writing and responses to literature. What many students find unsettling in literature is that there is rarely a right or wrong interpretation of a given text, or a right or wrong answer to most of the questions posed for class discussion. Two critics looking at the same text can (and frequently do) offer quite different interpretations, each of which may be perfectly valid within the context of the critic's approach and argument from the work itself. At first, to students, particularly those in the conformist stage, this is unsettling, and for a while threatens to plunge them into nihilism. Perry's position 4a ("Anyone has a Right to His Own Opinion —No One's Opinion is Wrong or Better") is translated as "any interpretation is as good as any other interpretation, and my opinion is as good as T. S. Eliot's or I. A. Richards' or Edmund Wilson's."

Authority orientation is difficult to deal with at any age, but particularly with the older student for whom it may be engrained by habit and role. The person who has as parent or manager exercised considerable authority may have expectations that the professor will exercise comparable authority. Such a student may become impatient with the inductive method and wonder why the instructor cannot simply tell what the poem is *really* about. The question "What do *you* think?" may be perceived as weakness or lack of knowledge on the instructor's part. Some students may go through a semester or more of free-wheeling class discussion without ever truly understanding that "truth" lies not in one student's or one professor's or even one critic's interpretation of a text, but rather that the accretion of interpretations around a given text encompasses the resonances of that text. Henry James' novella *The Turn of the Screw* offers one opportunity to confront this problem head on. Gerald Willen's *Casebook* (1960) presents a number of essays by major critics on this most provocative of fictions. There is a Freudian interpretation of the story, an anti-Freudian interpretation, various Christian and mythological interpretations, and so on. Any one of them read alone is convincing; each is based on a close reading of the text and an understanding of the contexts, and each is written by an experienced and perceptive critic. At first, students confronted by the contradictions, paradoxes, and ambiguities of these critical analyses are bewildered, even angry, and feel that it is all a sort of game indulged in by intellectuals who have nothing better to do. They may pay grudging respect to the coherence of each of the various visions of the novella but still feel as though they have been "put on." Or they may wonder, if all interpretations are acceptable, whether the work of literature really matters or has any inherent meaning at all. All too frequently this is the situation at the end of a semester; literature has been relegated to the status of the crossword puzzle without the comfort of having the "right" answers available in tomorrow's paper. However, it is the task of the instructor *not* to let matters rest here but to go on to allow students to see that the multiplicity of interpretations is only possible when the text is sufficiently dense with meaning to support such analysis. Indeed, one must develop tolerance for ambiguity if one is truly to apprehend the multidimensioned richness of the major texts. Perhaps all the meanings are present and possible; perhaps some are more meaningful than others; perhaps the student may say something that uncovers still another possibility for interpretation. Some of the most exciting insights into literature come not from the instructor's reading or from the critics' but from one of those rare class discussions in which each student's piece of the "truth" serves to highlight or augment another student's insight, and the aggregate of these minor and major perceptions, intuitions, and variant readings shed new light on a text that until that moment we had thought we understood.

Once students have truly apprehended the multiplicity of possible points of view, it is crucial to make certain that they can take the next step, which is to be able to make value judgments with which they can feel secure. With skillful teaching and some luck, students may begin to exult in their growing ability to interpret literature for themselves, basing their interpretations on a close reading of the actual words on the page and trusting to their own empathic responses. The possibility that they may ultimately come to the same or similar conclusions as the critics or that they may also, without incurring the instructor's displeasure, disagree with the critics becomes exhilarating. They begin to see themselves as possessed of critical/analytical skills that they had heretofore considered the exclusive province of "professionals."

In his chapter, Robert White notes that the affective root of humanitarian concern is the experience of empathy—feeling the feelings that another person appears to be feeling. We may surmise that literature can play a crucial role in developing such concern by helping students go beyond their limited encounters with their family and local community to the broader human experiences so powerfully expressed in fiction, plays, and poetry. An extreme example of how literature may arouse our capacity for empathy occurs in Dostoevsky's *Crime and Punishment* in the scenes immediately following Raskolnikov's brutal murder of two women, an old pawnbroker and her daughter. The murders had been irrational; Raskolnikov had little to gain. And still, such is Dostoevsky's art that when Raskolnikov hears people on the stairs and hides behind the door, we as readers have entered his consciousness so totally that the tension is unbearable. All our sympathies and dormant guilt feelings are mobilized on behalf of this despicable hero. Our hearts beat faster, we feel his terror, hope fervently that he is not discovered, almost cease breathing until the danger is past. Moreover, that total empathy with a murderer is sustained throughout most of the rest of the novel as Raskolnikov and the police investigator play out their cat and mouse game. Despite our intellectual knowledge of right and wrong, our rational understanding of society's need for law and order, and our internalized adherence to the sixth commandment, our sympathies remain with Raskolnikov. Dostoevsky's genius in allowing us access to the disordered world of the murderer makes it impossible for us ever again to read the headlines that proclaim still more crimes of violence without partially entering into the horror and terror that lie behind the black ink.

Another kind of empathy may be experienced by the reader of *King Lear*. Although the powerful primary experience of the play is its depiction of the tragedy of age, and although we live through the pity and terror for the old king alone upon the barren heath, for some of us there has been at least a twinge of understanding for those arch-villains, the ungrateful daughters Goneril and Regan. As a student once remarked only half-facetiously, "I suppose it was hard to have all the old man's soldiers and horses hanging around the courtyard. Weren't there any old folks' castles in those days?" Although making a joke of it, he had also read past the conventional wisdom about the play to understand that the children of older people have problems too.

Literature can not only arouse our sympathies for the plight of the individual but convey that plight in a larger social context. Thus, the reader of Dickens' *Hard Times* not only empathizes with the victims of Gradgrind's factual theory of education and with the laborers in Bounderby's factories but also understands the soul-destroying qualities of a prototypical nineteenth-century mill town, is made aware of the early environmental pollution spewed upon the landscape by such Coketowns, and understands the ills of the novel to be a direct result of a dominant materialism, related to the hard-edged philosophy that rationalized the effects of the industrial revolution. Furthermore, the obvious parallels with the contemporary world are also perceived and internalized and must affect in some way the student's response to his own world.

Because of the personal nature of its substance, class discussion of literature becomes an important sharing experience between instructor and students and among students. The frequent intensity and intimacy of such interaction has implications for outside the classroom as well as within. Elizabeth Douvan's definition of intimacy as the ability to transcend social roles and meet as whole persons suggests that the capacity for intimacy may very well be nurtured in the English classroom. Any real experience of a literary text is a personal one; any real sharing implies intimacy, a mutual exploration of feelings and values. In the process of mining the text, students support and refute each other, argue, persuade, reach out, draw back, come to collective understandings, and, in Douvan's terms, "disclose the self to another." In these discussions faculty must transcend their own roles as dispensers of knowledge and become co-seekers after the truth. They must learn to be open to criticism from students who are their chronological peers or even elders, while still retaining the ability to criticize and evaluate those students' work. The interpersonal tasks are complex, but for adult students, particularly, such sharing may help individuals develop relationships and modes of relating beyond the boundaries of their prescribed family and career roles, to develop relationships less dependent on who they are than on what they think. They may indeed find in the classroom new friends with whom they can discuss the moral questions that confront them as well as the characters in the works they are reading. If literature provides the middle ground between the abstract and the personal, on which we may experience life without falling victim to its perils, its sharing through discussion may also influence the student's capacity for intimacy in the world outside the classroom.

Teaching Writing

Writing, like the study of literature, is connected to affective and cognitive learning in ways that have particular meaning for the adult student. However, if approaches to the teaching of literature have been eclectic, approaches to the teaching of writing have been chaotic. The connections between good reading and good writing have long been apparent, but research has yet to define their precise relationship; and while the diagnostic writing sample is currently ubiquitous for diagnosis and placement, few English departments routinely assess reading skills, which might be just as germane to the writing process.

Writing, despite its centrality in the English curriculum (and its bread-and-butter support of many English departments), has until recently received only minimal intellectual attention. Most people who taught writing really wanted to be teaching literature and were serving out their apprenticeships in English 101 only until tapped for higher things. Writing was taught indifferently by some, superbly by others, by a variety of means with a variety of results. Some discouraging research indicated that it did not make much difference in students' writing abilities whether they had taken a writing course or not, or if they had, what constituted the content or the methodology of the course.

Here in methodology lies the crux of the problem in the teaching of writing. As the research develops, the lag between research and practice seems to grow. Creating writing strategies for specific situations and student populations becomes too difficult for the teacher trained to teach literature, who in many cases retreats to techniques dimly remembered from undergraduate days. Articles in current journals describe worthy attempts to confront such challenges, but the variety of approaches tends to be confusing, and synthesis is lacking. In fact, they verify William F. Irmscher's (1977) point that "perhaps the biggest obstacle to an articulated writing program is getting teachers to agree upon and adopt a controlling philosophy or theory to understand what difference one concept or another makes" (p. 33). The approaches, well thought out but not applicable to specific situations, range from John Schultz's (1977) story workshop method, which constructs bridges between oral and written communication, to Linda Flower and John Hayes' (1977) problem-solving approach, which rests on formal research and describes "an alternative strategy for confronting the thinking process" (p. 451).

Given what we know about adult education, perhaps the key to thinking about a methodology for teaching writing lies in the importance adults give to understanding the "why" of learning or the use that learning serves for them. Elizabeth Haynes' (1978) synthesis of research on the teaching of writing demonstrates changes in writing skills in the regular classroom. What aspects of that research seem most applicable to an adult audience? Haynes cites four important factors that seem to effect change: (1) good readers, even if they are poor writers, learn to write more quickly; (2) the technique of sentence combining improves writing; (3) interpersonal feedback is important in changing poor writing habits; and (4), most important, students need to be involved in the writing process itself—that is, not simply receive a graded paper, a product, but rather discuss and understand the steps in the process of writing. The importance of interpersonal feedback as a critical tool in the teaching of writing corresponds to Douvan's notion of the importance of intimacy in adult classes. By *interpersonal feedback,* we do *not* mean the red marks that English teachers traditionally apply to students' papers, while complaining about the time involved in "marking" papers, but rather the supportive, useful exchange that can take place in the classroom, in which the teacher may act primarily as a facilitator of such exchanges among adult students. The question always remains the same: How well does the writer communicate? If the group's rapport is such that freedom to criticize is not perceived as threatening, a great deal of learning can take place.

Most important, adult students must become involved in the writing process itself. They must feel that their writing has a real purpose, which can be communicated, more or less effectively, to their audience. New writers, especially, need topics relevant to their own concerns, a responsive audience, and a chance to work through the various steps of the writing process. Writers need first to think, to invent, whether in the bathtub, the kitchen, or the subway. One does not just sit down and write, and teachers should be aware of that. They should encourage students to write down their ideas in any form as they come and to spend time developing them—not necessarily in linear, organized fashion. Editing can come later. And the editing process itself can be a satisfying experience once students begin to look more critically at their own work, organized from the material rather than from an artificially imposed outline. Students can learn to spot the rough spots and anticipate the reader's reaction, especially if audience is kept in mind. Peer evaluation of a final report can show students how effectively they have communicated their ideas and stimulate further reflection on the writing process.

Such questions as whether or not to teach grammar, and if so, which grammar—traditional, structural, or transformational—were once thought to be the province of high school teachers and professional linguists. In the colleges, it was assumed that only those hapless souls to whose lot fell the remedial sections faced the necessity for dealing directly with syntax. Most grammatical indiscretions were dealt with by means of red penciled marks in the margins, and classroom periods were spent on rhetorical matters of a higher order.

In the past decade, however, under the pressure of open admissions as well as in response to the perception of generally declining literacy among college freshmen, basic questions about the nature of language and the teaching of writing have been taken up not only by linguists and remedial writing instructors but by the profession at large. Our teaching of standard English, or what Mina Shaughnessey (1977) called "written English," has been significantly altered by linguistic theory that has thrown the old "correct" or "incorrect" judgments of an earlier generation of writing teachers into total disarray. Furthermore, as linguists have come to more sophisticated understandings of the structures of nonstandard dialects, some have made a strong case for including their study in the curriculum, or even for accepting dialectal variants as legitimate written expression in academic writing exercises. (See the National Council of Teachers of English statement on "Students' Right to Their Own Language," 1974.) Meanwhile, many English professors, trained in literature, for whom "correct" syntax is as normal as breathing and as unexamined, are making a valiant effort to distinguish between structural and generative grammars, to learn the intricacies of immediate constituent analysis, to try out sentence-combining techniques in the classroom, and to answer thoughtfully those students who accuse them of teaching a white imperialist language.

Despite the strains of the present, in which opposing ideologies and pedagogies frequently seem to have chosen the writing classroom as their battlefield, this is in fact a time of healthy ferment. Much creative research is currently being done in language, and we may be on the verge of synthesizing a workable theoretical structure on which we can build the teaching of composition. Such recent books as Shaughnessy's previously cited *Errors and Expectations* (1977) as well as E. D. Hirsch's *The Philosophy of Composition* (1977) indicate rational ways of formulating an approach to teaching writing. And such groups as those involved in the Bay Area Writing Project and the City University of New York Association of Writing Supervisors, among others, are devising innovative strategies to deal with current problems.

To date, however, there has been only minimal research on the development of language skills among adults. We cannot discuss with any authority the ways in which adults differ from traditional-age college students in learning grammar, in enriching their vocabularies, or in bending the structure of the sentence and the paragraph to their own uses. Nor can we suggest specific strategies for teaching writing to this new population. One suspects that there may be special problems in changing ingrained language patterns (as in speakers of nonstandard dialects), and that, in general, the developmental stage of easy acquisition of language skills is long past. (This is true, of course, for 18- to 22-year-olds as well.) However, it is also possible that the adult's strong motivation may be a compensating factor. Certainly it is true that if one can tap the accumulated wisdom of adults' life experience in their writing, the prose will be rich with meaning.

Sensitive teachers of writing will probably modify the writing topics they assign when adults are in the classroom. One instructor, whose favorite beginning topic was "What, in the best of all possible worlds, will I be doing twenty-five years from now?" was taken aback when an older student commented sadly, "I really don't think I'll get much out of writing about pushing up daisies." Instructors will also recognize the need to wean those older people (and younger as well) whom we can now recognize as being in the conformist stage of development, away from bland, safe topics, and help them to avoid the flavorless, pasteurized language they think is expected in English classes.

Older students, whose high school experience was somewhat different from that of the present college-age students (and many of whom grew up before the television era) are, in general, more competent in handling language than their younger confreres, but, having been schooled in prescriptive grammar, they frequently come armed with a series of "thou shalt nots," which they hold sacred and which may impede the flow and spontaneity of their writing. Such pronouncements as "never use the pronoun 'I' in formal writing" or "never begin a sentence with 'and' " have the force of scripture. To such students a split infinitive may seem a greater fault than murky diction or hazy logic, and the fear of being "incorrect" paralyzes their imagination. When it is pointed out that even the topic sentence, that mainstay of composition teachers for generations, is frequently not found in professional writing, the ground crumbles beneath their feet.

Adults tend to be somewhat more sensitive to criticism than younger students, particularly when, as in writing, the product being criticized is a direct expression of their thoughts and feelings. Moreover, the interactions of the English classroom tend to be conducted on a more personal level than is typical of other disciplines, and the topics written about may encompass everything from dope dealing to religious awakening to one's great aunt's lesbianism. Thus, the English instructor may find it difficult to treat in an impersonal manner writing that has been struggled over and that may be intimately revealing. But, just as we help our friends when they ask for an opinion by attempting to fuse kindness and honesty, so we must attempt to fuse sympathetic response to the content of the writing with more objective response to its form. Writing grows from experience, and that experience must not be questioned; however, the clear communication of that experience has to be questioned in ways that do not alienate the writer.

Even students with strong egos and a lively interest in writing may need to be steered gently toward the realization that the English professor is really interested in the merit of their ideas, the effectiveness of the language in which they are presented, and the clarity and coherence of what they say. Of course, writing instructors care—passionately, many of them—about spelling and punctuation and matching subjects and verbs and participles that do not dangle and phrases that march in parallel order and all the rest of it; but they care even more passionately for ideas of merit, for logically structured arguments, for economy and elegance of style.

Language and Literacy

The study of language itself is, or should be, closely connected to the study of literature and writing; and the relationships between language, culture, and individual psychology can hold particular interest for adult students, who tend to seek a holistic vision. When students are introduced to such matters as language as a reflection of sex (for example, the fact that there is a woman's language and a man's language in Western culture); when they recognize the ways in which language affects thinking (the literal translation of the English admonition to the child "be good" comes out in French "be wise"); when they study the power of connotation and semantic manipulation; when they explore the relationships between language and cognition, and ponder the question of whether it is possible to think without language, they will have to come to grips with primary ways of understanding what it is to be human.

Because of their broader experience, adults can better understand how misunderstandings can arise from language problems. Does "Whatever you say, darling" mean loving agreement or grudging acquiescence? Is language a horizontal activity, used in the same way for everyone, or a vertical one in which people speak appropriately for specific situations: one way at a ball game, another in a business meeting? Why are linguistic symbols so important, and how do those symbols influence the way we live and think? Why can one find so many words for *woman—chick, wench, babe, lady,* and so on—but no other words for *chemical*? A word can acquire connotations, just as *hydrogen,* although scientific, has in this age of atomic warfare. One cannot separate language from culture; once adults see this, they will discover and discuss numerous examples from their own experience.

With adult students, much that has been conceived of as disciplinary study be-comes—is stretched to—interdisciplinary because such students are not tabulae rasae. They bring their own perspectives, derived from family, career, wide reading, and the experiences of life, to bear on everything they read. They are not only more open to interdisciplinary studies, they tend naturally toward integration of knowledge, toward making connections between their studies, and between their studies and their lives. In fact, adults tend to be impatient with what they see as artificial separations: they will insist upon connecting the study of *Huckleberry Finn* with what they know about slav-ery, child psychology, the geography of the Mississippi River, and the economic impor-tance of the steamboat in nineteenth-century America. They question the family and social environment of Jane Austen's small country towns; they quote existentialist philos-ophers when reading French poets. The passion for integration informs their studies, and it is the joy of putting the disparate pieces together that they—and we—call education.

Although traditionally the English department is the place where such integration has been most possible, all too frequently these days we have taken a narrower view of our purview. Meanwhile, our colleagues in other disciplines are appropriating literature for their own purposes. Historians find in it a helpful record of the past; sociologists use it for the insights it provides into social structures and mores; philosophers turn to Kafka and Beckett, psychologists to Lawrence and Joyce. For an example close at hand, we find that Carol Gilligan, in discussing the moral relativism of late adolescence, refers to Ham-let, Raskolnikov, and Stephen Dedalus.

For older students seeking to synthesize what they know, what they are learning, and how they will live, the interdisciplinary mode satisfies both the short-range goals upon which they insist and the longer-range goals toward which we as educators strive. Increasingly, courses designed around issues like feminism, revolution, ethnic problems, and the like proliferate in departments other than English. If English departments are to continue to function as the heart of the humanities, English teachers may have to go beyond what we call esthetic literature to the literature of ideas. We may have to include Freud and Jung and Marx and Darwin, and possibly Marcuse and Bronowski and Hannah Arendt, in the pantheon of gods to whom we pay homage in our syllabi. Thus, Halli-burton's chapter on interdisciplinary studies is highly pertinent here.

To admit literature from other disciplines, to restore that much maligned word *relevance* to its rightful place in the curriculum, to offer broader, more flexible programs and less critical, more experiential approaches to literary study, to make writing assign-ments that expand students' skills and relate to their goals, to structure language study that has broader, perhaps more social implications, will be to make English the humanis-tic study we all imagine it to be. Given the economic and demographic realities of the foreseeable future, the number of English majors will probably continue to decline, but the study of English is open to the public and should require no union card for admission. Literature was written for human beings, not for literary critics. In our pursuit of mul-tiple layers of meaning, of ironies and image clusters, of the elusive paradox and the dominant metaphor, we must not forget the readers we all once were.

The best thing we can do for students—and for ourselves, if the profession is to survive—is to enable them to connect with the mobs at the Globe Theatre, with the masses awaiting each new installment of Dickens' novels, with the soldiers who went off to World War I with Trollope in their knapsacks, with the crowds in Red Square gathered to hear their poets' voices. Of course, we will continue to teach the budding scholars, but we must also reach that vaster audience that will ensure literature's survival. We must make literature available to the common reader.

References

Bruner, J. S. *The Process of Education.* Cambridge: Harvard University Press, 1962.

Cooper, C. R., and Odell, L. (Eds.). *Research on Composing: Points of Departure.* Urbana, Ill.: National Council of Teachers of English, 1978.

Epstein, J. "Bring Back Elitist Universities." *New York Times Magazine,* February 6, 1977, p. 88.

Fisher, D. (Ed.). *Minority Language and Literature: Retrospective and Perspective.* New York: Modern Language Association, 1977.

Flower, L., and Hayes, J. "Problem Solving Strategies and the Writing Process." *College English,* 1977, *39,* 449-461.

Gerber, J. C. "Suggestions for a Commonsense Reform of the English Curriculum." *College Composition and Communication,* December 1977, *25,* 313.

Haynes, E. "Using Research in Preparing to Teach Writing." *English Journal,* 1978, *67,* 82-87.

Hirsch, E. D. *The Philosophy of Composition.* Chicago: University of Chicago Press, 1977.

Irmscher, W. F. "The Teaching of Writing in Terms of Growth." *English Journal,* 1977, *66,* 33.

Josephs, L. S., and Steinberg, E. R. (Eds.). *English Education Today.* New York: Noble and Noble, 1970.

Labov, W. *The Study of Nonstandard English.* Urbana, Ill.: National Council of Teachers of English, 1969.

National Council of Teachers of English. "Students' Right to Their Own Language." *Conference on College Composition and Communication,* Spring 1974.

Ohmann, R. *English in America: A Radical View of the Profession.* New York: Oxford University Press, 1976.

Orange, L. *English: The Pre-Professional Major.* (2nd ed., rev.) New York: Modern Language Association, 1973.

Profession 77. New York: Modern Language Association, 1977.

Profession 78. New York: Modern Language Association, 1978.

Profession 79. New York: Modern Language Association, 1979.

"Report on Teaching: 2." *Change,* 1976, *8* (6), 28-49.

Schaefer, W. D. "Still Crazy After All These Years." In *Profession 78.* New York: Modern Language Association, 1978.

Schultz, J. "The Story Workshop Method: Writing from Start to Finish." *College English,* 1977, *39,* 411-436.

Shaughnessey, M. *Errors and Expectations: A Guide for the Teacher of Basic Writing.* New York: Oxford University Press, 1977.

Willen, G. (Ed.). *A Casebook on Henry James's The Turn of the Screw.* New York: Crowell, 1960.

16

Larry Friedlander
Martin Esslin

Theater Arts

Acting, and participation in theater, can foster the development of the whole personality, strengthening self-confidence and independent action in a setting that encourages communal relationships and sensitivity to others. Drama involves us with mankind, helps us escape from egocentricity, develops our capacity for intimacy. The anxiety that accompanies learning is handled within the work, as part of the problem of performing. Flexibility and openness to change are rewarded. Performing is a high-risk activity, but it brings both immediate and long-range rewards. The actor's ability to make choices and to act decisively is an essential ingredient of his success as a performer. The play is an integrated moral, emotional, intellectual, and sensual universe; it demands of all those who work with it a commensurate integrity of body, mind, and soul.

There are dangers in theater, of course. Performing can be selfish, analysis can be lifeless, competition can be fierce. However, the rewards of successful theater can contribute directly to the goals articulated in this book—the types of challenging, flexible, mature learning that are truly responsive to the varied needs of a changing society and its diverse members.

The wide range of disciplines represented in theatrical activity makes drama an ideal subject for imparting a general education, enhancing artistic sensibility, and fostering the capacity to work as a member of a team. However, in a society such as ours, in which theatrical activity is rather limited (compared, for example, with the theater in countries like Germany, the Scandinavian countries, France, or England), the practical applicability of theater studies is still somewhat questionable. There are, accordingly, considerable differences in the objectives and attitudes of different drama or theater departments—and not a little confusion about the definition of such objectives.

In some cases, theater studies are pursued as a vocational type of training and aim at producing professional directors, actors, designers, and theater technicians. In others, the objective is to produce theater scholars, highly versed in the analysis and interpretation of dramatic texts and in the history and sociology of the theater. Both lines of training can lead to posts in other theater departments teaching theater skills to further generations of students. But theater training can also be part of the training of elementary and high school teachers specializing in the use of drama as a teaching aid and educational method. In addition, theater departments regard their activity as simply part of a wider general humanistic education for undergraduates, who, by participating in productions and taking survey courses of theater history and dramatic literature, will be better able to enjoy drama as theatergoers. And, finally, theater departments also fulfill the function of supplying theater to their communities and therefore provide a vital cultural service to the colleges and universities of which they are a part. All these objectives are desirable and wholly legitimate, provided that theater departments design separate programs to fulfill each, rather than leaving the distinctions undefined and offering a compromise program that covers all the objectives only superficially.

Theater Studies

In order to evaluate the place of theater in the American college of the future, we should first consider the scope of theater studies and the skills that such studies are designed to develop. As suggested earlier, one of the special characteristics of theater or drama training is its interweaving of theoretical and practical knowledge from a variety of different fields.

Theoretical Studies. On the theoretical plane, the study of theater overlaps with the wider field of general *literary history*—the study of texts within their historical context. This includes textual criticism—for example, to establish a valid text for the plays of Shakespeare—and the study of the historical and social background of the great drama of the past, which in turn includes social, intellectual, and religious history. For example, to understand the masterpieces of Athenian tragedy of the fifth century B.C., one needs to understand the religious myths of the ancient Greeks and the organization of Greek city-states as well as the political history of the times—for instance, the relationship between certain thematic concerns in the plays of Aeschylus or Euripides and the events of the Persian and Peloponnesian wars of their time. As drama mirrors life, an understanding of the drama of any period requires familiarity with the social and political conditions of that time.

But the study of drama does not merely call for an understanding of the *content* of theatrical masterpieces; of equal importance is a grasp of the *formal* aspects—that is, the esthetics of drama as they have changed through the centuries. This implies a study of the general principles of literary form, the methodology of the analysis and interpretation of texts, and a knowledge of the development of the critical vocabulary of drama from Aristotle to the theorists of our own time. As drama is an eminently social form of art, this again leads toward social history and, as drama overlaps with so many of the other arts (architecture, painting, music), toward the history of art in general. For example, no understanding of drama is possible without a knowledge of the evolution of theater architecture or the development of the use of perspective in painting.

An awareness of the historical, literary, and social context of drama must, however, also be linked with the ability to analyze and discuss its technical and esthetic aspects. This leads to a study of the methodology of *criticism* and its vocabulary. The techniques of criticism are essential for all who work in the theater, not only for those who specialize in writing about the theater for newspapers, periodicals, or scholarly journals. The director will not be able to communicate with actors or designers, and the latter will not be able to understand the director, if they are not skilled in the techniques of discourse about drama. Hence drama is a field in which the methodology of criticism is of the utmost practical importance.

Another practical application of the skills just described is in the teaching of creative writing in the theater. It is from the analysis of great texts of the past and a comprehension of the esthetic theories on which they were based, as well as from the ability to think and talk about the principles of their own creative process, that budding playwrights can acquire those elements of their craft which *can* be taught, although it is clear that creative talent itself, the imaginative power of genius, lies outside the field of academic study.

Finally, there is the study of the performance aspects of theater—the history of theatrical performance and its techniques, as distinct from the literary history of drama. Theater history is a fascinating field, which straddles a great number of subjects: the social position of actors, their techniques of speaking and movement, the history of costume, the history of directing, and a multitude of others.

From the above it will be seen that the *theoretical* study of drama opens up access to what, if it is properly structured, would give the student a good general education in the humanities: the drama of the past cannot be understood without an awareness of history, philosophy, and sociology. Moreover, the study of drama also involves the development of *practical* skills, which are no less important and in many ways complement the theoretical side.

Acting. The art of acting is central to theater studies. Acting requires a unique combination of intellectual, emotional, and physical aptitudes. The actor uses his own body as his expressive instrument, and hence the training of the body—its movement and flexibility, the strength and modulational range of the voice, the expressiveness of the features—is of utmost importance. But these physical factors are at the service of a creative imagination and an analytical mind. The actor or actress has to understand the motivations of the character he or she portrays. He must develop an imaginative grasp of his character's psychology. And, to do so, he must also understand the character's social background, mode of dress, and the whole intellectual and social universe he inhabits. In addition, the actor, as an interpretative artist called upon to infuse life into the text provided by an author, must understand the structural principles upon which the play as a whole is built. He must grasp its rhythm, its inherent poetic pattern and style. There is also, of course, improvisational acting, in which the actor is, as it were, his own poet.

Acting is in fact the paradigmatic theatrical activity, for theater primarily exists in the performance of texts, and from the performers spring those qualities that are unique to theater. It is worth pausing to consider the kind of person an actor must be, what skills he needs to acquire, and how this actor "personality" fits into the university environment.

What does the actor do? While it is commonly assumed that the actor's central skill is the ability to imitate other people's actions, and to imaginatively enter their lives, actors in fact are good only insofar as they can find the character's emotions within themselves. If the actor is emotionally agile—"loose," in the terms of the profession—he can summon up almost any feeling at will from his own experience. Carefully assembling these feelings, he develops or suggests the "character" demanded by the text. Thus, the actor must confront, within himself, many feelings, impulses, and desires he may consciously dislike, find foreign or forbidden. In order to deal with such "taboo" experiences, he must free himself from prejudice and develop a certain playful and tentative relationship to his own feelings; he must be willing to dissolve the normal boundaries of his ego. The ability to take emotional risks, to delight in strange experiences, and to refrain from overcontrolling his reactions is the mark of a fine actor. It is clear from many statements in Part One of this book, such as Weathersby's chapter on ego development and Douvan's chapter on intimacy, that these qualities are important for learning and change in any area.

What further complicates the actor's task is the communal nature of theater. Unlike much of the learning in the academy, acting is done with other people, to other people, in front of other people. In fact, plays are primarily concerned with relationships. An actor's attention is centered on his fellow actors' feelings and gestures. His performance is dependent to a great extent on others: on the technical and artistic staff as well as on his fellow actors. If he is not a deeply "empathetic" personality, capable of swift and accurate responses to changes in other people's attitudes, he cannot perform. The actor works out of an intuitive sense of interpersonal demands. His very body must change, subtly but exactly, in response to the needs and pressures generated by others. Acting thus trains us to be responsive to others, and further, to accept the influence of others on our lives and thought. As such, it offers a way to lead all students, especially those who have withdrawn from the complexities of community, into an awareness of the fundamental interdependence of human beings.

Acting not only demands new kinds of empathy, interpersonal competence, and the capacity for intimacy. It asks the actor to think in special ways. In a play, thought is always concrete, embodied in an action or event, in a gesture, tone, or word. One cannot act a concept, one can only perform those actions which reveal or evoke thought. The actor is forced to connect the conceptual and physical realms, and find ways to move easily from one to the other. He learns the limitations of thought: he cannot perform everything he thinks or imagines. Indeed, the nature of the theatrical script reinforces this qualification and criticism of pure thought. Thus, Kolb's experiential learning cycle underlies the creation of every character.

In a play, no person knows or embodies the "truth" of the work. All characters live in a "contextual" and "relativistic" world such as that discussed by Gilligan in her chapter on moral development. Each character displays or encounters his versions of "truth" through his confrontation with other characters' assertions of their own truths. Ideologies grow out of human needs and feelings. The actor must discover the connections between what a character wants and how he thinks. Consider, for example, how the concept of action is presented in *Hamlet*; we understand the concept by watching very different people enact their own conceptions of action within the specific circumstances of their lives. For Claudius, action is plotting, for Laertes it is impulsiveness, for Ophelia it is a retreat from thought into unrestrained feeling, or madness. The play's "thought" arises from the confrontation of these concrete modes of behavior, from a rhythmic, dynamic, complex meeting and opposition of wills. Generally, the academy tends to suffer from an imperialism of the intellect, a one-sided evaluation of the nature and quality of thought-in-the-world. Theater can do much to humanize and refine our understanding of the place and power of ideas. For those students who come late to the academy, rich in experience but with little training in abstract thought, it can offer a bridge from the familiar flow of events they know to the abstract world of knowledge.

Finally, the actor must accept himself as a limited and conditioned being, tied through sympathy and need to other beings more or less like himself. He must not judge himself or others as he performs; he must accept his feelings and those of his fellow actors. He must forgo the temptation to control events, remembering that his first task is to make his character, as drawn in the script, come alive. True, for others his performance will have meaning and resonance, but if the actor attempts to predetermine this meaning and his effect on an audience, he destroys his character's believability.

To summarize: Acting introduces the student to modes of thought and feeling not common in the university. Above all, it asks from the student an organic, unified response to life. The performer's actions resonate through the three psychic tiers of his reason, will, and passion. He conspires with his opposites, he finds himself in self-forgetfulness and discipline, he achieves wholeness through conflict. Acting combines the traditional academic good of withdrawal, observation, and understanding with a passionate involvement in what is immediate, sensual, and changing.

Directing. The director, as the coordinator of the whole performance, must obviously be well versed and fully trained in the craft of acting. In addition he or she must possess the critical and analytical skill to grasp the meaning and structure of the play, as well as the expressive power and the vocabulary to communicate these insights to the actors and the other members of the company: the set designer, the costume designer, the lighting designer, the stage manager, and the other technicians. But these skills are only the technical basis for the director's work. In addition, she must possess—and training must try to impart—the full gamut of leadership qualities associated with the field of management. The director must be able to inspire confidence in her cast and crew; she must have the charisma that induces people to work hard and give of their best. And she must display the organizational capabilities needed to assure the smooth flow of the production process, which involves difficult problems of logistics and the accomplishment of an intricate structure of interdependent tasks within a narrowly defined time schedule. A successful director must thus possess a multitude of talents, some of which clearly are inherent in her given personality, but many of which can be greatly enhanced by a well-designed course of intellectual and practical training.

Technical Skills. The design functions (set, costumes, lighting) clearly derive from their own special fields: set design from painting and architecture, costume design from dress design and fashion, and lighting design from electrical engineering. But in order for these skills to be applied in the theater, the *designers* must be able to understand the nature and requirements of drama. They must be capable of reading a text with a clear understanding of how their contribution can enhance the totality of the dramatic experience. They must therefore be highly familiar with the techniques of acting: placing a door in the right area of the stage, for example, might greatly enhance the expressive power of an actor's entrance or exit; the cut of a costume might help an actor tremendously in giving effect to his gestures, and the details of the costume provide important clues to characterization; the lighting of the play might be important in enhancing mood and focusing attention on the aspects of the action the director wants to emphasize. The *theater technicians,* too—scene painters, carpenters, stagehands, and the rest—all contribute to a theatrical event and must be fully aware of the part their work plays in the total production. For example, a scene change that lasts only a few minutes longer than the rhythm of the play demands might destroy the effect of a whole act or even the entire play.

The coordination of the technical flow of the production is the task of the *stage manager.* Stage management is an important and highly specialized skill, which is also part of the training provided by theater and drama departments. This, too, demands complete familiarity with all processes involved, a grasp of the intellectual and artistic implications of the play as well as strong organizational and leadership abilities.

Some theater departments also provide courses in *theater administration,* an area where theater studies overlap with general management and business training. Here a thorough knowledge of the vast field of union rules and regulations, fund-raising techniques, publicity, and public relations is as essential as complete familiarity with techniques of selling tickets, accounting, and tax law.

What unites and integrates all these extremely diverse functions is the need, for every member of the highly diversified team, to be fully conversant with the dramatic and theatrical qualities of the end product of their efforts, the finished play. The box office manager as well as the stage carpenter and the musical director must be able to read and analyze a text and be aware of its potentialities and requirements. The box office manager must recognize its potential attractiveness to audiences; the carpenter must solve the technical problems required for optimum realization of the text's potential; the musical director must understand the type and amount of music the play will require—and so on through all the different functions involved in producing a play.

The Work of Drama Departments

There is, over and above these multiple specialized skills, a central core of purely theatrical, dramatic knowledge that everyone who works in theater must possess, or at least understand in its essentials. It is this general core of theatrical knowledge that integrates the work of theater or drama departments. And it is this central subject that must form the basis of all instruction. Essentially, this amounts to imparting the skills required to read a dramatic text in such a way that the performance can be fully and graphically imagined in all its aspects. This entails training in the analysis of texts, which, by their very nature, require careful decoding to determine the relationships of the characters, the style of performance required, and the theatrical effects envisioned by the author. To achieve mastery of this skill, *all* members of the theatrical team, the humblest as well as the most creative, must at one time or another have been involved in all aspects of the production process. The actors should have worked as stagehands or box office managers and the stagehands as actors.

If these considerations inform the educational practices of theater departments, theater training will become a veritable character training process. Each member of the theatrical team must learn the need for discipline, the virtues and necessity of cooperation, regard for the contributions of other members of the collective, and respect for the importance of each element and specialized skill that goes into creating the total effect. Training in the analysis of texts will sharpen the capacity to think clearly and logically, to analyze human character, and to understand the social conditions and manners of distant periods or different civilizations. Involvement in acting will strengthen powers of observation, concentration, body and voice control, and the art of being relaxed while being intensely self-aware. And this is all over and above the specialized technical requirements of each theatrical specialty.

In view of all this, there can be little doubt that well-conceived drama training has much to offer students, whether or not they aspire to careers in theater. Drama training can clearly promote general personality development as well as teach a number of skills that can be used outside the theatrical context. The analytical techniques learned in the process of reading and understanding complex texts will enhance the individual's ability to read and reason. The improvisational techniques and theater games used in the training of actors develop the imagination and sharpen the individual's ability to react quickly and effectively to unexpected situations. The development of voice and body control will inevitably enhance one's capacity to express oneself and to present oneself to one's best advantage in any life situation.

Drama Training in the Future

Drama training and theatrical activity would thus appear to be ideal educational instruments for the college populations of the next decades. Drama is the most accessible of all literary forms, particularly in a society that, through the mass medium of television, is exposed to enormous amounts of dramatic material, however inferior in artistic and intellectual quality it might be. The study of drama is particularly well suited to bringing middle-aged people who have hitherto not been exposed to high art and serious intellectual activity into contact with these fields. Drama opens a way into poetry, history, social problems, and philosophical speculation, and it does so in an amusing and exciting manner. At the same time, it provides a rich opportunity for human contact, as well as the opportunity to be noticed and admired, applauded and recognized. Nor does the fitting of older students into existing patterns of drama training present any difficulties. Indeed, drama and theater departments have tended to be hampered in their production activities by the absence of middle-aged and older students who could take on the parts of parents and character roles in plays requiring older persons. The professional skills that such older students would bring to the mounting of plays should be equally welcome and immediately appreciated, whether it is a housewife's skill in sewing, an electrician's ability to wire the lighting system, or a businessman's training in selling tickets or keeping the accounts. There is hardly one professional aptitude of this kind that could not be put to excellent use in the collective effort of theater production.

Depending upon the specific nature of student populations in different areas, special programs could be initiated to meet the needs of particular socioeconomic, ethnic, or age groups. Thus, for example, the production program could highlight certain types of drama whose subject matter would appeal to such groups: proletarian plays for people with a working-class background, plays from different ethnic cultures for Blacks, Armenians, Hungarians, Latvians, and so on. Plays could also be selected to deal with the problems of old age, the unemployed, or specific psychological problems of women at different life stages.

The therapeutic aspect of acting training and the socializing influence of teamwork could also be put to good use. A production team is, during the rehearsal process, a social unit of considerable cohesion and usually develops into a kind of ad hoc family group. Integration into such groups might well be of considerable benefit to people who feel lonely, isolated, or unfamiliar with the college and its mores. For such individuals, participation in the cooperative work of a drama project might well help to develop social allegiance and a sense of belonging. The therapeutic aspects of acting training have already been stressed. For elderly people or the middle-aged adjusting to a new environment, it could bring such benefits as enhanced emotional and physical flexibility, relaxation of body and mind, and increased concentration. Close physical and emotional contact with other people during the rehearsal process would also widen horizons, and participation in a variety of plays might well open up possibilities for new life-styles and broaden social horizons.

Theater is particularly useful in restructuring the university because it involves learning through clearly defined projects. These projects have clear goals (performances, for example), clear time limits, and precise conditions. Moreover, dramatic projects, as we have indicated, are extremely flexible in choice of materials, in emphasis and approach, and in levels of competence demanded of the participants. A play can be performed casually, script in hand, or in full production; by amateurs or by would-be professionals; in classrooms or in hospitals or on street corners. People of very differing abilities, backgrounds, and age can work together, contributing skills their varying backgrounds have supplied. For example, older people can contribute expertise in carpentry or sewing or management without ever having previously acted. Acting projects can be tailored to the needs of a group; one may choose to use the project to develop literary or philosophical skills, or to enhance bodily awareness, to free feelings, or to create community. As long as the leader and the group agree on the aim, any dramatic project can be a complete and valuable experience.

Drama and the Community

The increasing enrollment in drama and theater courses of older students from ethnically diverse backgrounds has significant implications for the community. In an age when the working week is likely to be progressively reduced, the increased leisure time at the disposal of the working population will present an ever more acute social problem. The training given by drama and theater departments to mature students who come directly from the working community will provide the expertise needed to organize community theater and amateur dramatic activities, which can provide valuable enrichment of leisure both for those who are active within them as performers and production auxiliaries and for the larger number who will attend as spectators. The college or university can thus become a focal point and powerhouse for the cultural life of the community.

Through this link with the community and amateur dramatic activities, the university or college can become more closely involved in local activities. The people trained in the college who have become active in such theatrical undertakings can always return to the college for advice and help in tackling difficult conceptual problems, choosing or interpreting plays, or solving practical problems. These activities can, in turn, be integrated with the wider study projects of the university or college. For example, the college's theater department could work with community theaters to mount a cycle of related plays illustrating a theme such as race relations, local history, or the work of a specific playwright, such as Shakespeare or O'Neill, or to mount a community arts festival.

With the increasing employment of married women in jobs outside the home, older relatives are increasingly called upon to provide supervision for children. Here theater training might also be of considerable value, as it imparts skills specifically designed to create entertainment of educational value in and out of the context of formal schooling. The growth of childrens' theater sections in university and college drama departments emphasizes this very important new application of theater studies. Training of both teachers and lay drama group leaders for children might therefore assume considerable social importance.

Another social development that may well call for drama training is the increasing use of drama as a method of communication, most obvious in the onslaught of television. A high proportion of television programming, from major drama productions to serials right down to television commercials (which are typically skillfully constructed mini-dramas), is in dramatic form. Hence an ability to criticize and evaluate this material and to recognize its formal esthetics and subliminal influences is vital if a responsible democracy is to be maintained in an age of manipulation of the masses through the media. The creation of a well-informed, critical public, able to judge the quality of the material as art and as social comment, is thus a pressing social need in our time. Training in the critical analysis of drama and in an evaluation of its practical aspects would go a long way toward meeting this need.

As a separate academic subject, the study of the theater arts—that is, dramatic art in theory and practice, including actual performance—is a relative newcomer to higher education in America. The variously named Theater Arts, Drama, or Speech and Drama Departments gradually evolved as extensions either of the study of rhetoric in speech departments or of English, when it was realized that at least some knowledge of the practice of performance might be helpful in the understanding of the texts of Shakespeare and other great playwrights. As theater and drama departments evolved between the wars, and especially after World War II, impressive theater complexes arose in many American colleges and universities. The regular performance of plays, ranging from the classics of Greek drama to modern musicals, became an important cultural asset to the colleges and universities themselves as well as to their surrounding communities in areas otherwise lacking professional theater.

Theater, as an activity that involves intricately structured teamwork and the cooperation of people versed in a multitude of skills, from scene painting and electrical engineering to the highest forms of scholarly analysis or creative talent, naturally straddles a large range of disciplines, not all of which at first sight might appear to be in themselves academic subjects—for example, voice training, fencing, ballroom dancing, carpentry, tailoring, millinery, or the construction of property swords. While this hybrid and somewhat amorphous nature of the subject has created a not inconsiderable number of problems and confusions in the definition of the purpose and methodology of drama and theater departments, it also presents tremendous advantages to any educational philosophy that stresses the need for development of the whole human personality. Theatrical activity can be seen as a microcosm of society itself, in which activities of the humblest physical kind are subtly orchestrated and blended with those of the highest intellectual and artistically creative nature to produce a harmoniously balanced whole, each part of which is interdependent with every other part of the final result, which is itself not a dead object but an ongoing, living process.

17

William B. Bondeson

Philosophy

The theme of this volume and of this chapter might well be found in Aristotle's *Nicomachean Ethics*:

> Now each man judges well the things he knows, and of these he is a good judge. And so the man who has been educated in a subject is a good judge of that subject, and a man who has received an all-round education is a good judge in general. Hence, a young man is not a proper hearer of lectures on political science; for he is inexperienced in the actions that occur in life, but its discussions start from these and are about these; and further, since he tends to follow his passions, his study will be vain and unprofitable because the end aimed at is not knowledge but action. And it makes no difference if he is young in years or youthful in character; the defect does not depend on time, but on his living   [Book 1, chap. 3, 1094B28-1095A-7].

This passage reflects Aristotle's belief that political and moral matters, and the entire range of topics in philosophy, are best discussed by those with many years of experience, who have achieved at least common-sense wisdom about the basic questions that philosophy pursues. Plato, too, in Book VII of *The Republic,* prescribes a long and arduous process of living and education as the necessary prerequisite for any kind of philosophical inquiry; one should begin to study philosophy at age 50 and only then with a great deal of previous training and education. These views of Plato and Aristotle are no reflection on the young; few philosophers have expressed as much concern as they for the development and education of young people. However, their comments on the study of philosophy suggest that older students, with their greater experience of life, may be best prepared to study philosophical issues, which deal with the most basic concerns of human life. The *method* of philosophical reflection need not be limited exclusively to the adult student; indeed, interesting experiments by Matthew Lippman and others give evidence that there are educational benefits in teaching philosophy even at the grammar school and high school levels. Philosophy, especially its methods, can probably be taught at almost any level of education. But the important point here is that it is best taught to students who have had time to learn lessons from life, experience conflicts in values and obligations, undergo personal and social tragedy, and begin a search for ideas and values that integrate conduct and thought.

Several of the authors in Part One have spoken to this point. For example, Schaie and Parr maintain that, although older adults may have difficulty sorting through large amounts of information, they may have a greater ability to consider the meaning and implications of focused problem areas in light of experience. The work of Schaie and Parr indicates that philosophy can be learned by adults even in old age. But there is a more important question: is there any evidence that adults really need the kinds of skills, methods, and content that philosophy can give them? Schaie and Parr's observation that new material must have some "egocentric meaning" for adults if they are to learn it well has implications for the teaching of philosophy. This chapter explores the "egocentric meaning" of philosophy for the older student. Research on adult development suggests that philosophy can be an important part of the older student's education. If this is true, it is indeed ironic that, in the history of American higher education in this century, the humanities in general, and philosophy in particular, have been taught almost exclusively to students under the age of 25. This is not to say that students between the ages of 17 and 25, and even younger students, derive no benefit from philosophy or the other humanistic disciplines, but students who could most profitably study these disciplines have been systematically neglected. Chickering, reviewing a wide span of research on adult development and its implications for higher education, notes:

> Such data show us the more fundamental purposes behind significant desires, from the desire to earn a degree or change careers to the desire to meet new persons, read more widely, and explore new ideas and interests. This research reminds us that the existential questions of meaning, vocation, social responsibility, and human relationships, which so many adolescents face with difficulty, are reconfronted by many when they are thirty or forty or sixty years old [Chickering, 1976, p. 88].

This chapter does three things. First, it characterizes the discipline of philosophy, its methods and its subject matter, referring, for examples, to some recent philosophical concerns and alternative philosophical methodologies. Second, it considers philosophy as an educational process. And finally, it discusses how philosophy can be applied to the specific developmental tasks of the older student, drawing upon the rich store of data supplied by other authors in this volume.

Philosophy as a Discipline and a Method

Probably the safest generalization about philosophy, covering both its history and current practice, is that agreement as to its precise definition, problems, and techniques is simply out of the question. The reason is that the definition of *philosophy* is itself a philosophical issue. In our day, many Anglo-American philosophers prefer to do something called *analytic* philosophy, and many Continental philosophers do something far more speculative and theoretical. Many followers of Bertrand Russell in England, for example, think that the followers of Martin Heidegger in Germany are simply spinning out schemes of words that have no meaning or supporting evidence. The latter, for their part, believe the former are engaging in an analysis of linguistic minutiae and neglecting basic and pressing human concerns. This is not to say that philosophers are hopelessly beyond any kind of agreement; nor is it to say that the house of philosophy has only one room. One problem in teaching philosophy to students of any age is the assumption, following what the public often perceives as the model of the natural sciences as applied to philosophy, that there should be some single, convincing, and "right" answer. Following are three characterizations of philosophical topics and methods that are not mutually exclusive but that emphasize different problems and approaches.

Basic Philosophical Problems. One of the most traditional ways of approaching philosophy is in terms of its basic topics or problems. This approach originated with Aristotle, and it has had wide acceptance ever since. In this approach, philosophy is viewed as a rational attempt to answer three basic questions: (1) What is real? (2) What is knowable? (3) What is valuable? Attempts to understand rationally what is fundamentally real are usually classified as *metaphysics.* Inquiries into the nature of knowledge and its objects are usually called *epistemology.* The study of values embodied in individual human practice is usually called *ethics*; the study of values involved in political and social enterprises, *political philosophy*; and the study of values in works of art, *esthetics.*

To talk about philosophy as rationally trying to say something about the nature of ultimate reality or rationally trying to say something about the nature of human knowledge raises another philosophical question. How are we to distinguish between "rational" attempts to answer these questions and other kinds of attempts? There is some general agreement that philosophy proceeds by arguments, theses, and counter-theses, that conclusions are derived from premises, and that there is an appeal to some kind of experience or evidence to make premises acceptable. But again, there is considerable disagreement as to what a rational procedure is precisely and what constitutes a rational methodology.

In *metaphysics,* some philosophers have attempted to develop arguments for the existence of God, and other philosophers have tried to show that those arguments are either invalid or misconceived. There has been discussion as to the nature of persons and the relation of persons to their bodies, often formulated as the problem of what constitutes the essential features of a person (or of a mind), what constitutes the essential features of a material body, and how these two concepts might be joined together. This kind of discussion often gives rise to questions about survival after death, or the immortality of the soul. Metaphysical reflections have led philosophers to views about very basic concepts concerning all of reality, such as being, power, change, and even appearance. Is there any general set of characteristics that can be used to describe all of reality? Does reality fall under some general ordering principle, whether that principle be a God or some system of general laws? Reflections on the orderliness of things have led some philosophers to make the claim that reality is a totally connected, causally determined series of events such that every event is totally predictable, at least from the point of view of an ideal observer. Other philosophers have maintained that some events, at least, do not fall within such a deterministic scheme and, consequently, that human beings are autonomous determiners of their own actions (at least in some cases) and thus human freedom is a reality.

As Immanuel Kant would put it, the basic metaphysical questions are those of

God, freedom, and immortality. Such metaphysical questions, although they are peren-
nially important, become particularly pressing to the older adult. If, as many authors in
this volume and elsewhere have claimed, old age can be a time of putting one's affairs in
order and reflecting on the significance of one's life and life in general, then metaphysical
questions have a special importance. It is not only looking back upon one's life that gives
rise to such questions but also concern about the end of life and what may or may not
follow this life. Whether there is any sort of existence after bodily death becomes an
increasingly pressing question in old age. Before he drank the hemlock on the last day of
his life, Socrates discussed the most important question for him, that of the immortality
of the soul (see Plato's *Phaedo*).

In *epistemology*, philosophers have discussed the nature of human knowledge,
arguing about the sources of our knowledge, the objects of that knowledge, and the extent of that knowledge—and skeptics both in epistemology and in metaphysics have
argued that such enterprises are not possible at all. Philosophers have claimed that our
knowledge must ultimately begin with some series of basic facts, propositions, or principles from which all other knowledge can be logically derived. Some philosophers have
taken those facts to be experientially ultimate; others have proposed that there are principles that are simply self-evident. Some philosophers have maintained that the ultimate
model for our knowledge is like that of mathematics, in which knowledge is deduced
from fundamental principles; others have argued that our knowledge is ultimately more
like the inductive models of the natural, and especially biological, sciences; and still
others have argued that all our knowledge is historically and culturally determined in such
a way that any "absolute" model is an impossibility.

Philosophers have worked with other epistemological problems, such as the role of
sensory experience in the development of knowledge as contrasted with, or complemented by, the role of rational analysis in interpreting sensory experience. Naturally, for
those philosophers who take the data of the senses as the source, and in some cases the
limiting condition, of our knowledge, there is a great reluctance to engage in any kind of
theoretical or abstract speculation. Philosophers of that kind tend to dismiss most metaphysical problems as beyond confirmation by sensory experience and thus not resolvable
by reason alone. By contrast, there have been philosophers who stressed the ability of
reason not only to interpret the data of the senses but to discover principles on which
more general theories and speculative enterprises could be carried out. These kinds of
epistemological considerations have an effect not only on the general area of metaphysics
but also on the nature of models and theories in the empirical sciences. In this way, epistemology can also deal with the extent and limits of human knowledge and the kind of
certainty we as knowers can attain.

How do these epistemological issues relate to the concerns and learning styles of
the adult student? The issues in epistemology are of two kinds, both of which relate to
the basic patterns of adult development. First, epistemological issues are *foundational;*
that is, they deal with the sources of our knowledge. Clearly, the integrative tasks of the
adult described in this volume are only possible on the grounds of a theory of knowledge.
When one develops one's religious beliefs, for example, the grounds and sources of those
beliefs need to be considered as well. But the argument for the importance of these issues
in adult development holds only if these issues are related to other issues, notably metaphysical ones, that are particularly important to the adult. But second, epistemological
issues are also *structural*; that is, they deal with the ordering and patterning of what we
claim to know. As Kolb's data concerning disciplinary inquiry norms suggest, academic
disciplines are characterized by a variety of knowledge structures, which may correlate

with various modes of inquiry. Whether or not Kolb's typology is correct, it does suggest that any disciplinary inquiry has an epistemology built into it and that such an epistemology may be more or less compatible with various learning styles. It is not clear that such differences in learning styles are age-related, but this question suggests a fruitful line of research for adult learning theorists.

Ethics, political philosophy, and esthetics are often grouped together under the *theory of value*. In its broadest sense, *ethics* deals with questions about the nature of goodness and the good life for individuals. Questions about the kind of life human beings ought to lead, the nature of goodness or rightness, and what human happiness consists in, have all been discussed by ethical or moral philosophers. Some have equated the good with pleasure, some have argued for the existence of general, but formal, moral rules, and others have invoked the criterion of the greatest good for the greatest number of people. Thus, ethics deals with the nature and derivation of moral principles, although the field, like the others, has not been without its skeptics and relativists. *Political philosophy* deals with the values expressed in social and political activities and organizations. Political philosophers have formulated views about the nature of the best form of human society, the nature and grounds of political obligation, the case to be made for civil disobedience, the distribution of social goods, and the nature of political rights, duties, and responsibilities. And finally, *esthetics* deals with values as embodied in works of art. Estheticians have discussed the problems of the nature of a work of art, what distinguishes a work of art from other kinds of objects, the ways, if any, in which works of art can be evaluated and compared, and the value of artistic products as compared with other kinds of human goods and activities.

Carol Gilligan, in her chapter on moral development, contends that the development of moral understanding depends on the integration of contextual relativism with experiences of moral responsibility. And she concludes that if the ability to relate to others as ends rather than means requires, beyond a formal construction of equity and reciprocity, a contextual understanding of actual differences in point of view, then the educational experiences likely to foster moral development will be those which enhance the capacity to shift perspectives. That there are value differences between human beings is a matter of simple fact; those differences, however, are also matters of differing valuational principles, more or less articulated. I would add to Gilligan's statement the claim that the capacity to understand and appreciate varying valuational *principles* is equally important in moral development. And this is surely one of the main purposes of teaching anyone about values.

Analysis of Concepts. The preceding sketches indicate the kinds of questions philosophers pursue. However, that is not the only way of characterizing the field. A second way is in terms of a basic set of philosophical concepts, which are used in many of the activities of daily life as well as in the various sciences. The following list is in no way complete. But if one maintains, as many contemporary philosophers do, that the activity of philosophy is basically the analysis of concepts, then the following are proper objects for philosophical consideration: truth, value, obligation, duty, right, goodness, God, freedom, rationality, beauty, community, and love. These concepts can be analyzed into more limited concepts, which could be considered the parts or aspects of larger ones. Such conceptual analyses illustrate at least one mode of philosophizing about the content and substance of what is discussed.

In a very general way, one might characterize philosophers as either *analytic* or *synthetic*. They either work on the details of some particular concept and try to get its logical workings in proper order or look for an overarching system of concepts by which the human enterprise and its relation to the totality of nature can be understood. The first kind of philosopher believes that the task is to carry out a detailed analysis of some particular form of human discourse or experience; the second believes that the task is to work with the most general and universal concepts in order to form a unified and systematic whole. It is fair to say that the major philosophical thinkers of the West have tried to do both, first working on some subset of concepts and then trying to find a single metaphysical, epistemological, and valuational framework in which they can be fit. The great philosophers have developed complex and comprehensive systems and have produced a vision of man in the universe that aspires, at least, to a degree of completeness. It seems to me that there are particular benefits to be gained from both the analytic and synthetic approaches to philosophy; each develops certain skills, which can be particularly useful to the adult student.

Although I am reluctant to push the point too far, there are some similarities between analysis and synthesis as philosophical methods and Kolb's comments on cognitive development. Philosophical analysis, as an attempt to deal with particular concepts by an analysis of their parts, has some parallels with the second developmental stage of Kolb's learning model, which he calls *specialization.* This might entail understanding the logic of one's area of special interest or skeptically examining the foundations of one's beliefs and practices. But the tasks of synthesis, or *integration,* Kolb assigns to higher levels of cognitive development. He notes that at the highest stages of development there is a strong need for integration of the four adaptive modes of learning. Development in one mode precipitates development in the others. Increases in symbolic complexity, for example, refine and sharpen both perceptual and behavioral possibilities. Thus complexity among the adaptive modes is the hallmark of true creativity and growth.

Philosophies of Different Fields. Philosophy can be categorized in yet a third way. Any given human enterprise or practice has its theoretical, methodological, and normative aspects. And, correspondingly, for almost any field or discipline there exists a set of views that might be called the philosophy *of* that enterprise. Thus, people have written about the philosophy of law, the philosophy of religion, the philosophy of science, the philosophy of history, the philosophy of technology, the philosophy of education, and most recently, the philosophy of medicine. Each of the preceding can be considered a field or an area of specialization in philosophy, not displacing the pursuits mentioned earlier but rather offering complementary ways of understanding the same problems or concepts. Take the philosophy of education, for example. Philosophers of education have discussed such topics as the difference between education and indoctrination, the assumptions behind various educational methodologies, the role of education in society, the nature and derivation of educational principles, the values embodied in educational practices, and the relation of education to other scientific and humanistic disciplines. A particular body of knowledge is examined for its principles, its guiding assumptions, its ways of knowing, and the values expressed in its practice. This is simply another way of saying that the practice of education may have a metaphysics, and epistemology, and a theory of values and that it is the task of the philosophy of education to critically analyze the process of education in order to make these all the more evident. This kind of activity has both its analytic and synthetic modes.

Philosophy has always been in danger of becoming too abstract, too removed from the actual practices of the sciences and the other modes of inquiry. First principles can become so abstract and general as to be without point or meaning. Hence the line between philosophy and other modes of inquiry cannot and never should be drawn sharply. It appears to me that philosophy in the last quarter of the twentieth century, especially in its Anglo-American modes, has been coming out of a period of highly abstract discussions, which became so removed from ordinary concerns and subjects as to provoke the disdain of other inquirers. Two pieces of evidence suggest that philosophy, in some areas at least, is headed in a more productive direction. First, several philosophers of science are returning to detailed studies of actual scientific practice and the production of scientific biographies. It seems reasonable that philosophers of science, while they need not be practicing scientists, should know the details and developments of that mode of inquiry. Second, within the last ten to fifteen years a rather new philosophical area has emerged, the philosophy of medicine. The practice of medicine raises many of the traditional philosophical questions, about knowledge, about values and conflicts between values, about the nature of a person, and about the criteria for determining when a person comes into existence and passes out of existence. Although the questions are as ancient as the practice of philosophy itself, discussing them from the point of view of medicine makes the answers to those questions richer, more informed, and closer to actual human experience and practice.

This requirement for genuinely experiential learning can make philosophy especially available for life cycle developmental tasks, including the analysis of particular problems as well as the synthesis of larger and more comprehensive principles. Philosophy can attempt to bridge the gaps between the ways we understand the world in the sciences and the ways we view it from the perspective of ordinary, everyday activities.

> The philosophical problems which seem more remote from the analysis of discussion are those which turn around what are often called the great issues— God, freedom, and immortality; mind and nature. But consider, for example, the difference between a neurophysiologist talking about mind and the body and a philosopher talking about the same topic. The neurophysiologist tries to find out which cells in the brain are involved in particular forms of mental activity. The philosopher is concerned with quite different questions, such as whether everyday explanations of human behavior in terms of reasons, motives, and intentions are not compatible with explanations of human behavior in physiological terms. It is the meshing of two different types of explanations that presents him with his problem [Passmore, 1967, p. 223].

It is these two complementary modes of philosophy that characterize its activities best. If philosophy is concerned with the details of particular human activities, it is also concerned with the big problems. Human beings will always want to know the answers to such general questions as the meaning of human life, the basic characteristics that distinguish human beings from all other forms of life, the general nature and purposes of the universe, and how a human life is best to be lived. These may be very difficult questions, but they are nevertheless questions to which all of us, whether implicitly or explicitly, provide an answer by the ways in which we act and live.

Philosophy as an Educational Process

Any educational process seems to have three principal features. First, there is usually some basic set of facts or items of knowledge that must be communicated and learned. To say that one must learn some basic facts to study the natural sciences is a truism. But even in the most abstract and theoretical subjects, such as philosophy, there is always a set of definitions and concepts that must be learned if any sort of discussion is to be fruitful. A student cannot do much chemistry without knowing the details of the table of chemical elements; a student cannot get very far in philosophy without knowing something about the definitions of its basic terms. Knowledge may be structured in a variety of ways. There may be alternative structures to be discussed. But the point remains that any discipline or mode of inquiry does have a factual base in terms of which its propositions and theories are made intelligible.

Second, the knowledge *that* such and such is the case must be supplemented by the knowledge of *how to do* certain kinds of things. Philosophers have long distinguished between two very general kinds of knowledge—knowing that something is the case versus knowing how to do something. The relations between these two kinds of knowledge have been much debated. But the point here is simply that once a student has learned the basic facts, concepts, definitions, and so forth, then he or she must be able to handle or manipulate those facts, analyze the concepts, and evaluate the hypotheses, theories, and models that are based on them. These are the skills of inquiry—knowing how to critically discuss the subject at hand.

Finally, in the process of coming to know what is the case and to know how to manipulate the relevant subject matter, a student also acquires a set of values, pertaining to the subject matter at hand as well as to the nature of inquiry itself. Education is fundamentally a normative activity; there is no such thing as simply transmitting whatever facts are supposed to be basic. The discussions of the last fifteen or twenty years, both within philosophy and outside it, have shown that the notion of "value-free" science is simply misguided. Any time we attempt to decide what needs to be known, implicit in that decision is also a judgment about what does not need to be known. Any collection of facts is of necessity selective; any educational process, insofar as some things are chosen to be learned over others, involves judgments about some things being more important or valuable to know than others. How one decides in the sciences which problems are more important and worthy of study and financial support is difficult to determine. Political, social, and other kinds of factors enter into the decision. Nevertheless, there are values implicit in the various sciences and the other modes of inquiry. The recognition of those values, contrary to the position of some philosophers, does not reduce those practices to simple subjectivity.

Philosophical Knowledge. If any educational process can be discussed in terms of the knowledge, skills, and values that are conveyed, then what are these elements in the teaching of philosophy? Many philosophers would argue that there is no basic knowledge in philosophy in the sense of some universal principles, kinds of experience, or other data to which all philosophers would inevitably appeal. Exactly what counts as data or evidence for any philosophical point of view is itself a philosophical question. However, philosophy does have a long and rich tradition. Knowledge of that tradition is fundamental for any genuinely productive work or study in the field. The major figures in the history of philosophy have not only raised the basic questions in interesting ways but also provided systematic and comprehensive answers to those questions. To do philosophy without a knowledge of Plato, Aristotle, Descartes, Hume, and Kant, to name only a few, would be to think in an intellectual vacuum. This is not to imply that the views of any of these thinkers are the last word. The history of philosophy is full of thinkers who have considered the basic questions in great detail, and their ideas, whether accepted, rejected, or modified, can be the basis of further philosophical reflection. Knowing what the major philosophers had to say is basic knowledge in the field.

There is, derivative from this, another kind of knowledge, namely that of basic terms and arguments. One can hardly do philosophy without knowing a rather substantial group of definitions. One can hardly expect a student to engage in philosophical reflection without knowing the meanings of terms like *metaphysics* and *epistemology*. One could hardly expect a student to think critically about moral problems without knowing that hedonism is the view that takes the good as pleasure, that the doctrine of the mean finds virtue in a middle ground between two extremes, and that utilitarianism is the view that happiness consists in the greatest good for the greatest number. My general point is this: Although philosophers have differed widely over solutions to various philosophical problems and have even differed as to the best way of posing those problems, the history of philosophy provides a large supply of statements of those problems, systematic solutions to them, terms in which those problems and solutions are expressed, and arguments in support of various solutions of those problems. All of these are basic to the study and teaching of philosophy. They are just as much a matter of fact as anything in the empirical sciences.

To say that such knowledge is the only information needed confines the discussion too narrowly. If philosophy is really a critical discussion of critical discussion, then the student of the philosophy of science, for example, must be well prepared with information about scientific theories, the actual practice of scientists, and the history of science. A student of the philosophy of medicine obviously needs to know a great deal about actual medical practice and the details of clinical situations that form the basis of a philosophical understanding of medicine. Or, to return to Aristotle, the student of morals and politics should have some knowledge of the culture and history of his society and have sufficient maturity to flesh out his reflections with the actual experiences of living. It is because of this demand for rich, complex, and detailed experience that the adult is in a good position to pursue philosophical reflection. Much of philosophy is done by the use of examples and counter-examples; in this sense, philosophical activity is based on experiential learning.

Philosophical Skills. What skills can be transmitted through philosophy? What does it mean to have a critical discussion of critical discussion? There seem to be two modes of philosophical activity, analysis and synthesis; the skills of analysis and synthesis are basic to any kind of philosophical activity. When students of philosophy examine a certain point of view, usually in some text, they need to do two things. First, they have to determine precisely what is being said, what terms are being used, and how those terms are defined. A great deal of work may be required to interpret statements and clarify the view under discussion. Once a view is clearly stated, the next task is to understand the data, arguments, and other kinds of supporting evidence. Thus, philosophy students can spend a great deal of time analyzing arguments, isolating individual premises, reconstructing premises in some kind of rational order, articulating assumptions or presuppositions of various premises, and analyzing how the premises fit together into a coherent whole or lead to a particular conclusion. Sometimes a concept can be best understood by analyzing its constituent parts to see whether those parts are consistent with one another. Sometimes, after the premises of an argument are isolated, it becomes clear that various premises are not compatible with one another or need to be supplemented with other kinds of premises. Knowing how to analyze concepts, views, and arguments is never simply a matter of knowing a certain group of facts; argumentation is far more a matter of skill, which is learned only by practice.

But the analytic mode, when limited to assessment of arguments, must be complemented by a synthetic mode. There is rarely a philosophical point of view that is supported by only a single and absolutely convincing argument. There is virtually no philosophical argument that does not have important connections with other concepts. The big questions about the existence of God, the meaning of life, and the nature of the universe are never matters of simple argumentation. The existence of God, for example, is affirmed or denied on the basis of many kinds of arguments and many kinds of evidence. In philosophical synthesis, arguments must be weighed and judged against other arguments. Some kinds of evidence are found more acceptable than other kinds. This weighing and balancing of views, of thesis and antithesis, is a matter of skill in judgment, being able to think through all the arguments, being able to analyze all the concepts, and then being able to put them together, after critical reflection, into a whole. In ethics, for example, most human beings operate according to a scheme of values, more or less articulated. Finding the support for those values and putting them together into a hierarchy, deciding which are more or less important, is essentially a synthetic activity.

There may be a relation between the analytic and synthetic modes of philosophy and Kolb's stages of cognitive development. But two further points need to be made. First, the activity of analysis is both a logical and temporal condition of synthesis. The activity of analysis, whether in terms of a philosophical method or in terms of a task of cognitive development, must chronologically precede the activity of synthesis. Although these may alternate in stages, the details of experience, the experience of individual cases, and the careful analysis of concepts and arguments are the materials out of which the larger syntheses are constructed. Second, analysis and synthesis are in a continual dialectic with one another, in continual tension with one another, throughout the stages of adult development.

Plato said that philosophy lives in the argument, that *dialectic,* to use his term, the interplay of argument against argument, of view against view, makes philosophy an interpersonal and conversational activity. It is one thing to read an argument, analyze its parts or premises, and be able to recite them. It is quite another thing—and this is really where philosophy lies—to be able to work through an argument, to retrace its steps, to see how the premises and conclusions fit together, and, most important, to decide which among many competing arguments is the best and most convincing. That cannot be handed over to anyone like a set of facts; it is a skill, a matter of knowing how, which is acquired only by working through arguments oneself. In this sense, dialectic is much like debate, although without the sophistry that can sometimes give debate a bad name. Torbert's emphasis on "living inquiry," in his discussion of interpersonal competence, suggests ways in which skills in managing these dialectical processes might contribute to that important area of human development.

In her chapter on the capacity for intimacy, Elizabeth Douvan laments the dominance of the individualistic-competitive model in the academic world—a model that glorifies individual achievements at the expense of collaboration. We teach students that ideas are individual creations and personal property. We assign papers and projects individually, and glorify the image of the lonely, isolated scholar or scientist digging through hillocks of material to unearth a nugget of understanding, pursuing a lonely trek to discovery or clarification. To the extent that we emphasize isolated, individual work and products, we mislead students about the nature of work and construct obstacles to their interpersonal development.

I submit that philosophy is built on a long tradition of views and arguments in which many individuals have participated and, more important, that the activity of assessing those arguments, synthesizing points of view, and developing a philosophy of one's own is essentially social and interactive. It is a matter of a continuing dialogue, a continuing evaluation of different points of view. Thus, the skills of philosophy are essentially those of analysis and synthesis; a student must learn how to carry out these activities, to formulate arguments and to respond to others. Such an interplay demands a respect for the integrity of the other person, and a willingness to examine and be examined. In this sense, philosophy can be both interactive and collaborative.

Given the dialectical character of philosophy, it is an open question whether philosophy can be taught successfully in noninteractive kinds of situations. Many educational theorists, cognizant of adult students' work and family obligations, have concluded that "learning at a distance" is the most viable mode of instruction for this population. This view has led to discussion about the various kinds of educational technologies that should be developed in order to reach adults. Whether philosophy can be taught through the use of educational radio or television is a matter for empirical investigation, and, as far as I know, no such study has been carried out. Apart from the usual range of correspondence courses, the only sustained attempt to teach philosophy using various educational media has been that of the British Open University. Much research needs to be done to ascertain the effectiveness of teaching philosophy through these technologies. (For further reflections on this topic, see Bondeson, 1979.)

Values Implicit in Philosophy. What values ought philosophy to teach? In one sense, philosophy articulates various schemes of values, which differ according to one's philosophical point of view. But are there any values that are implicit in the very activity of philosophy itself and that, even if only indirectly, are imparted to its students? Clearly, there are values that follow from the dialectical character of philosophical activity. If philosophy lives in the argument, then there must be a fundamental respect for argumentation and for those who are engaged in that process. There must be a willingness to follow, as Socrates exhorted, wherever the argument leads, however difficult that path may be and however great the challenge to one's previously held views. There must be respect for intellectual activity as such and for the variety of views that intellectual activity can generate. The genuine practice of philosophy should transmit the value of honestly forming one's own views while at the same time realizing that there can be equally honest contrary formulations. Philosophical practice seems to have two diseases: a tendency toward dogmatism, or "hardening of the categories," and a tendency toward excessive abstraction. Such tendencies are negative values in the pursuit of philosophy. The ideal is rather a balance between what William James called "tender-minded" and "tough-minded" philosophy.

Before turning to a discussion of how philosophy applies to the developmental tasks of the older student, let me add a serious note of caution. The preceding discussion of the knowledge, skills, and values that are part of the teaching of philosophy is essentially normative. It deals with those things which, in my view, ought to be part of the teaching of philosophy to students at any age or stage of development. However, and with all due apologies to David Kolb's chapter in this volume, there is precious little evidence, to my knowledge at least, concerning the actual effects that the teaching of philosophy has upon students. We know from many of the chapters in this volume that students, again at various ages, express an interest in the kinds of problems with which philosophy, religion, and politics deal, but there is much empirical research to be done on how students actually are affected by philosophy. Those of us who are in the profession can give anecdote upon anecdote. We can cite the student whose faith was visibly shaken and who had to be carefully led through a spiritual crisis; we can cite the student whose scattered and diverse views became strengthened and whose faith was deepened. We can cite students who became weary of playing one argument off against another and who came to hate the process of reasoning itself. We can also cite students who found an intellectual joy in thinking critically and who became active partners in the life of inquiry. But, at this stage, the evidence goes little beyond anecdote. In a day when the public is questioning more and more the value of a liberal education, we should be able to supply reliable data as to the kind of person such an education produces. Our collective faith is that we are making students more tolerant, more rational, more sympathetic to the needs and ideas of others, and more able to analyze critically the issues of the day. But that is still an act of faith.

Implications for Adult Development

One can speculate about the effects that the study of philosophy might have on students at various developmental stages. There are at least two kinds of variables to be taken into consideration: (1) the particular developmental stage of the student and (2) the kind of philosophy that is being taught. Loevinger's stages of ego development, cited in the chapter by Rita Preszler Weathersby, suggest some of the directions that students' philosophical thinking might take. If, for example, at the conformist stage thinking is conceptually simple and frequently relies upon stereotypes and clichés, a student at this stage might be attracted rather easily to some large and popular metaphysical or political view, such as existentialism or Marxism, provided that view is coherent with the view of whatever social group he or she identifies with. The adoption of such a philosophical view at this stage bespeaks the need for simple answers, obtainable without much reflection upon either the reasons for those answers or their consequences. (I do not intend the use of Marxism and existentialism as examples here to be construed as a comment on their validity as philosophies; they are both popular and more available to students in that they have literary as well as philosophical expressions.)

The student at the conformist stage may adopt a particular philosophical view as a response to peer group pressure or to the charismatic personality of a philosophy teacher. Similarly, one could infer from Carol Gilligan's discussion of Kohlberg's scheme that a student at a stage of moral development characterized by rebellion against parental or other kinds of authority might use a philosophical view as the means of that rebellion. Thus, one could well imagine a student raised in a politically conservative home adopting a socialist or Marxist point of view simply as a kind of protest, or a student from a religious background adopting some version of atheistic existentialism for the same reason. In terms of the distinction between philosophical analysis and philosophical synthesis mentioned earlier, this kind of thinking might be termed synthesis without the necessary analysis, a superficial synthesis at best. This early stage can have the dualism described by Perry as one of its basic features—a dualism in which the world is viewed in terms of "we-right-good" and "other-wrong-bad." Such an early stage of development, which may include the self-protective, conformist, and conscientious-conformist stages identified by Weathersby, can be characterized by the "ideological" character of the philosophical views adopted—that is, the enlistment of these views in shaping an emergent identity but without, and this seems to be the crucial point, the necessary reflection on either the foundations for the views or the consequences of those views. In philosophical terms, this is equivalent to having a metaphysics or an ethics without an epistemology.

There is another stage of development, described by Gilligan, that poses equally serious problems for the teaching of philosophy. Precisely how this stage relates to the various stages identified by Weathersby and Loevinger is not clear to me, but the stage is a genuine one nevertheless. Gilligan's description strikes a familiar chord (and an ancient one, recalling Thrasymachus in the *Republic*) for anyone who has taught philosophy. Gilligan reports Kohlberg's discovery of a strong strand of moral relativism in the students he was studying and Fishkin's finding that such relativism could undo even the most principled moral understanding. Studying honor students in Philosophy at Oxford whose capacity for mature moral judgments was readily apparent, Fishkin surprisingly found among such students a total repudiation of the validity of all moral judgments. To these students, moral questions were unanswerable because there was, in their judgment, no way of knowing the "right" thing to do. Note that the views of these students about morality are not so much based on the adoption of an ideology in the manner of a student at Loevinger's earlier stages, although there could be some grounds for maintaining that moral relativism was their conformist ideology; rather, this seems to be a more sophisticated point of view. The Oxford students seem to be saying that moral questions are unanswerable because moral knowledge is impossible; there is no epistemological foundation for morality, and therefore there are no moral principles. This kind of relativism may be the necessary prelude to genuine moral development such as that described by Gilligan and Perry, in which moral commitments are made with full awareness of contextual relativism, in which personal commitment and actions are taken.

Thus, there are several stages of relativism; the mature stage is overlaid with moral commitments and is earned after consideration and reflection. The earlier stage may have an epistemological skepticism as its source. "After all, how can we really be sure of anything?" the student may ask. That, to this writer at least, is a more sophisticated point of view than a simple conformist one. It shows some reflection, at least, on the sources and foundations of belief. Thus, relativism can be part of a conformist or rebellious ideology, but at the higher levels of development it can be part of genuine moral and intellectual maturity.

This raises an important matter for empirical investigation: What factors prompt movement from one developmental stage to another? And, especially, how does the study of philosophy contribute to that developmental process? I would argue that whether one uses the stages of ego development as described by Weathersby or the stages of cognitive and moral development as described by Perry and Gilligan, there seem to be three rather general changes that occur across those stages: (1) an increasing interest in the foundations or sources of the student's views, (2) an increasing interest in the consequences and implications of those views, and (3) an increase in the complexity of those views because of the realization of the multiplicity and diversity of alternative points of view. If these can be shown to be valid generalizations and if, more important, they can be shown to be causal factors, then the study of philosophy can have a very important role in a student's development. The development in terms of intellectual foundations or sources is, in philosophical terms, the consideration of theories of knowledge. The development in terms of consequences and implications is partly analytic and partly synthetic, implying, I would judge, a greater role for synthesis in the later stages. The development of complexity should occur because of the confrontation of alternative intellectual and moral points of view—precisely the kind of dialectical interaction that philosophy ought to produce.

Philosophy can have a significant effect on the education of any person at virtually any age. In Chapter One, Chickering and Havighurst observe that a person's values and ideals fall into a hierarchy—that a scale of values emerges as the child becomes an adolescent and the adolescent becomes an adult. Analysis of values becomes possible, though it is not undertaken explicitly by many people. Civilized life is full of unforeseen conflicts of value, in which the individual must make the choice on his own responsibility because no moral rules have been made to cover such cases. Members of our society are constantly faced with problems of this nature from the age of early adolescence. Those who go to high school and college show their concern about such problems by their readiness to engage in discussions of general moral questions, by their interest in the rational aspects of religion and ethics, and by their readiness to appeal to moral principles in deciding what practical courses to follow in the solution of social problems.

Chickering and Havighurst seem to be right that for certain segments of the population there is a perennial interest in philosophical, political, and religious questions, although there do not seem to be any data showing how widespread this kind of interest might be. But their comments also suggest an important teaching strategy for philosophy. It is the questions of value and value conflict that seem most likely to engage the interest of students at any age. The issues of fairness and justice, of right and wrong, of desirable and undesirable, and general principles derived from these kinds of reflection seem to have a basic hold on many students. Students in general are also interested in a wide range of problems in religion, such as the nature and existence of God, the immortality of the soul, and the relation between faith and knowledge. Teachers of philosophy are well advised to begin their introductory courses with discussions of these topics.

In my experience, students are not typically intrigued with epistemological problems, problems concerning the nature and structure of science, the mind-body problem, or the general run of metaphysical issues such as the nature of the person or the concept of freedom. But since the problems of philosophy are all interrelated in one way or another, a student may well begin with some moral or political problem such as the nature of justice and after reflection be led to consider how we come to know or derive the principles that best express that ideal. Students might also begin to discuss problems about the nature and existence of God but quickly be led to an equally important discussion about how we know or do not know that a being called God exists. In one sense, the problems of morals or religion are more concrete or down to earth, but intelligent reflection on them presupposes an understanding of many other topics in metaphysics and epistemology. In the last analysis, philosophy is always systematic. What differentiates students of philosophy from others is their appreciation of systematic philosophical reasoning and their ability to work with it.

For adolescents, it is important, as Chickering and Havighurst point out, to examine critically the reigning ideology of their parents and their teachers. The traditional ideology is no longer credible. At this stage of life, the analytic mode of philosophy may indeed be most appropriate, provided it is employed with sufficient care that it does not become destructive. The techniques that philosophers use to examine arguments, tease out their assumptions and presuppositions, and discover logical relations between statements can be an exciting enterprise for a young person, especially if the view under question is one held by his superiors or his culture.

Such a task, however, is hardly sufficient for the mature adult. In discussing the psychosocial tasks of adulthood, Chickering and Havighurst recall Erikson's last four stages: identity, intimacy, generativity, and integrity. Ego identity consists of developing a clear sense of one's own self, including a sense of continuity and self-assurance concerning a career, sex role, and a system of values. I would extend that notion of identity to include an understanding of one's place in society and in the world at large. Such a task, vague though it may be in its definition, is one of the essential tasks of becoming a fully developed human being. Insofar as philosophy can help the student put received and shared values together in a systematic hierarchy, it can help achieve this task of adulthood. But, a mere system of values, however it is articulated and organized internally, can never be truly satisfying to the individual without some commitment to a set of views about how those values come about and how they relate to society in general and the universe as a whole. Understanding one's own values is surely a stage in the development of an identity, but locating those values in a scheme of ideas that serves to place the individual in nature and the cosmos becomes an even more important kind of task.

The task of developing intimacy naturally focuses on intimacy with a partner of the opposite sex. However, the virtues of friendship should not be overlooked. If, as I have already argued, philosophy is of necessity dialectical and conversational, then such communication between human beings is a kind of intimacy as well. Both Plato and Aristotle wrote movingly of the relationship between philosophy and friendship. Indeed, the sharing of one's ideas and life commitments seems to be an important part of friendship.

The task of generativity includes the concept of the adult person as a productive and responsible citizen. Productive activity can only be carried out on the basis of moral and political principles arrived at through some process of discussion and justification. In order to talk about the obligations of citizenship with any degree of sophistication, it is first necessary to have some idea of what it means to be a citizen and what a good community would be like. And such judgments should never be made simply by taking accepted views and values and then trying to put them into practice. Social ideals always contain some idea of what constitutes a good or desirable human life, and of course it is precisely this kind of issue that philosophy can best articulate. The ideals of equality and social justice, for example, do not make much sense until one has a clear notion of what equality really is, what justice is, and what the criteria are for treating someone equally and justly.

Philosophy can play the same role in the development of integrity, a basic acceptance of one's life as having been inevitable, appropriate, and meaningful, versus a sense of despair and a fear of death. Discussions about the meaning of life are again appropriate philosophical concerns. It does not make sense to ask about the meaning of anything until some criteria for meaning are identified. Surely the old questions of God, freedom, and immortality come to the fore once again.

Philosophy can obviously have great practical value insofar as the skills of analytic and synthetic thinking can be applied in almost any situation. But it remains true that philosophy, when pursued with any degree of sophistication and completeness, requires leisure. The leisure that comes in later life with the freedom from having to earn a living permits work on what I consider to be the most important developmental task: making sense out of one's life and achieving some coherent point of view about oneself and the world in which one lives. For the person in the later stages of adulthood, philosophy can provide a kind of summing up and integration of ideas and attitudes. Chickering and Havighurst note that, although older persons may experience limitations in the physical, mental, and economic spheres, and often in the social sphere as well, the boundaries of the spiritual sphere need not necessarily shrink and may even expand. Philosophy can provide an important spiritual resource. It can provide answers to the big questions of life, the ones we all inevitably must answer. In later years, they are no longer simply a matter of theoretical speculation; they can become pressing and immediate problems as one tries to order the final stages of one's life.

References

Bondeson, W. B. "Philosophy and Open Learning." *Teaching Philosophy,* 1979, *6* (1).
Chickering, A. W. "Developmental Change as a Major Outcome." In M. T. Keeton and Associates, *Experiential Learning: Rationale, Characteristics, and Assessment.* San Francisco: Jossey-Bass, 1976.
Passmore, J. "Philosophy." In P. Edwards (Ed.), *Encyclopedia of Philosophy.* Vol. 6. New York: Macmillan, 1967.

18

Paul Ward

History

Can history play a strong role in the education of today's new kinds of students, particularly adult students? The latest statistical evidence makes this seem doubtful. The Center for the Study of Community Colleges' sample of two-year colleges, according to Friedlander (1978), shows a 9.4 percent decrease in history enrollments over the two years 1975-77, even though humanities enrollments as a whole experienced no more than a 2.6 percent decrease and total enrollments rose by 3.2 percent. Hammett's survey in 1976 of the place of history in continuing education found agreement among the department chairmen polled that interest in history was falling, with European history not surprisingly the big loser (Hammett, 1977).

Surely this state of affairs calls for thought and new efforts. Regrettably, evidence on successful new ways of teaching history to nontraditional students is still so scattered and insubstantial that for an index of the possible teaching approaches we must turn instead to the teaching of traditional college-age students, which is better reported. Judgments as to successes here, of course, are subtly governed by assumptions as to what the values of history for students really are; and the rhetoric of most history teachers about the value of their subject has tended to be all too like that of the first pages of college catalogues, rose-colored and vague. Moreover, what has customarily been emphasized is history's role in conserving and transmitting traditional liberal learning, and this, given the social history of our country, carries elitist overtones far from congenial to most elements of the new student clientele. For them, a revised definition of the value of studying history is needed. It must do justice to history's humanistic function of making past human experience more accessible, through helping students learn how to select and grasp more fully what can most profit them.

A useful perspective on what may be profitable for these students is provided by the recent findings summarized in Part One of this book regarding the typical stages of students' development. Thus far, admittedly, little of the literature on the teaching or learning of history at the college level has shown awareness of research of this sort. The gap between most current thinking about the values of history for its learners, on the one hand, and research findings as to the nature of such students, on the other, is unmanageably wide. Our first step, therefore, must be to give the former topic—what students get out of history—something of the specificity and realism that the chapters in Part One have given to the latter. A simple recourse is to look at the record. What, in broad terms, have been history's successes and failures in recent decades in appealing to college students?

The Appeal of History

The most obvious feature of the record at the moment is the boom and bust in history enrollments since the 1950s. The statistics on this are clearest for the number of B.A. majors nationwide, which in general has not been a constant percentage of the total number of undergraduate enrollments whenever these have been compared. In his *America's Resources of Specialized Talent,* in 1954, Dael Wolfle estimated that history had had almost exactly 3 percent of the total B.A. majors in each five-year period from 1905 to 1950, through all the monumental expansion and changes of higher education in those eventful years. Then—and we rely now on the figures compiled annually since 1948 by the Office of Education in its *Earned Degrees Conferred*—history's share of B.A. majors began in 1953 to increase, at first very gradually and then faster, reaching a high of 5.34 percent in 1967, when it leveled off and then dipped until in 1976 it was below 2.9 percent. Since the total college population was growing throughout this period, the actual numbers of history majors kept increasing for a while after 1967. The total increase thus was from 9,576 to 44,931 between 1953 and 1971, a doubling and a doubling again and then more in the eighteen boom years. History's appeal to students came in those years to seem in the nature of things, and the letdown since then has been distressing.

Yet, as all well-informed commentators now seem to agree, history's appeal during those boom years was largely vocational. Like English, history has in modern times been a field of study oriented toward teaching careers, whether in high school or college. By the mid fifties, the postwar baby boom had begun to evoke forecasts of an insatiable demand for teachers; in June 1954 the American Council on Education sounded the first alarm of what the (greatly underestimated) tide of students would mean at the college level. Students rushed to acquire liberal arts degrees. In the aftermath, in the early 1970s, news articles and personal protests testified bitterly to the belief of many history majors and new Ph.D.s that, having put in the required amount of work, they were entitled by right to a satisfactory teaching position. These all-too-human expectations could not last long, however, in a job market in which the supply of teachers had come to greatly exceed the demand.

What the whole painful episode has set in relief is the fact that part of the appeal of history to college students is inevitably vocational. Some of them cannot resist thinking of themselves as possibly one day in their teacher's position. Intensive recent studies of other career possibilities make it plain that the alternatives for history graduates, like the career sequels to liberal education generally, are diverse and so can give little direction to college curriculums. Teaching as a prospective career for history students means teaching history, and so the pointers it offers depend on the developing character of the field itself.

Vocational prospects aside, recruitment into the field probably owes the most to the introductory Western Civilization course, which has recently been revived after falling, along with other requirements, before the storm of student protests in the sixties. The heyday of Western Civilization was roughly from 1912 to World War II in the pace-setting institutions. If memory serves, a strong freshman course of this sort was before 1941 a feature of instruction in nearly all institutions where history stood high among student preferences. Giles Constable, in his talk at the American Historical Association meeting in December 1976 (Constable, 1977), suggested that the introduction of the course at Harvard was plainly inspired by the growing involvement of Americans in European affairs. This agrees with my personal memory that the deep appeal of the derivative freshman elective taught with great success at Amherst by Laurence Packard was the insight it gave into the humanly value-laden workings of the European state system. The principal alternative, the Contemporary Civilization course introduced at Columbia after World War I, was more of an introduction to the rich cultural traditions of Western Europe. In hardheaded terms, both were embodiments of the "finishing school" for upwardly mobile Americans that it had been history's function to provide since the discipline took shape around 1890.

After World War II, the no longer deferential posture of the United States in world affairs called for a more discriminating approach to European culture. Thus, while the Harvard survey course, slightly modified under the name of Social Sciences 1, continued with lessening popularity, a companion Social Sciences 2, with more of an interdisciplinary and analytical focus on the historical development of Western political institutions, took hold vigorously and is still popular. At Stanford, on the opposite coast, the most successful "Western Civ" course of all, to judge from the percentage year after year of history majors in the senior class, flourished and when the tempest finally came, bent but did not bow. Required of all students since 1929, Stanford's freshman survey was in fact abolished during the academic troubles of 1969. But the distress then voiced by faculty in other departments at what they could no longer count on their students to know led to polls first of upperclassmen and then of alumni, which showed it to be far and away their favorite or most valued course. Reinstatement in 1973 with again the best possible teaching staff has led to an impressively large elective enrollment in what was nicknamed "Son of Super Civ."

Two features of the Stanford experience deserve emphasis: (1) the freshman survey has consistently been taught by the best professors a first-rate university could hire, assisted (now) by teaching fellows recruited from elsewhere with unusual care, and (2) it has plainly enjoyed wide support as an important "service course," providing essential information and skills for subsequent on-campus learning as well as for later life. Much other evidence teaches that an academic service course can be a striking success among students *if* granted first-rate teaching staff and strong support from faculty colleagues generally. These two provisos are important. Any survey course in history inevitably covers much material that the student has no specific reason for wanting to know; interest in the past is not innate, however much academic historians may wish it were. Sensitive teaching and prestige can generate the long-range motivation for learning. Otherwise, such a course will need the thematic justification, which, to cite an example already mentioned, has been a feature of Harvard's Social Sciences 2.

The point here may be worth a moment's underlining. History learned as entertainment, out of a passing curiosity, or only dutifully, is especially apt to end up as the "inert ideas" that Alfred North Whitehead, at the opening of his *Aims of Education,* so sharply pointed to as the great danger in education (1929, p. 2). One is reminded of that humble rule for students of history: "Never memorize a date until you know why it is important for you." Historical data learned inertly, I would observe, are likely to prove no less inert when subsequently used, whether in later learning or in the course of later living. In other words, the long-term value of historical study depends greatly on mobilization of a variety of lively motivations from the very start.

The survey course as such is perhaps no longer a natural course to teach, as Giles Constable suggested in his 1976 talk. Over the past two generations, leadership in historical research has been passing from those who assume responsibility for mastery of broad fields to those who dedicate their efforts to exploring specific themes and issues. The contrast is instructive between the original *Cambridge Modern History* of around 1900, with its collection of survey chapters, and the *New Cambridge Modern History* of the late fifties, with its greater focus on issues.

We turn, then, to the new sorts of courses that have here and there been notably successful since World War II, though none has caught hold generally. One sort is the "how to" course, focused on the craft of the historian and his specific skills of inquiry. (For one compilation of such skills, see Ward, 1971.) Early influential examples were the Yale courses using the volumes of selected problems edited, beginning in 1945, by Thomas Mendenhall, David Potter, and others. Later came the programs of freshman seminars, just as strongly substantive in character but now turning away from attempts at survey. Interdisciplinary courses, on the model of Samuel Beer's Social Sciences 2 at Harvard, have also become popular, especially at the advanced level. As David Hollinger (1977) has noted in *The Chronicle of Higher Education,* the leadership of the discipline of history today with remarkable unanimity welcomes cooperative work with other social science disciplines as well as continued cooperation with a variety of humanities disciplines. If my impression is correct that thematic courses of all these sorts have until recently been largely limited to liberal arts colleges and the leading universities, one reason may be that the heavy enrollments of the recent boom years allowed history departments that were chiefly teaching future teachers to get by all too comfortably with the old formula of survey courses.

As a reflection of the postboom circumstances, the provisions for history in Harvard's 1978 core curriculum proposal, drawn up by a committee particularly strong in its membership of proficient historians, have amounted to a fresh assessment of the appeals of history to students today. Under the proposal, one required semester course was to be interdisciplinary and devoted to explaining historically some aspect of the modern world, presumably somewhat as Social Sciences 2 has successfully done for years. One other was to be devoted to some revealing controversy of the past, a dispute now dead and so readily judged with impartiality; this would correspond to the surprising popularity around the United States of medieval studies, with focus on such topics as witchcraft and monasticism. The two requirements together reflect the two faces of a fully developed interest in history; to quote what I myself have written in the American Historical Association's *Newsletter,* these two aspects are "(1) positive interest in the 'pastness' and peculiarities of past human experience, and (2) confidence in the past's yielding both expected and unexpected sidelights on the present, many of them truly and personally useful" (Ward, 1973, p. 25).

The Harvard committee also recognized the need for what history departments for generations have offered in service courses to other humanities majors. It proposed requiring within literature and the arts an interdisciplinary semester course illustrating the social and historical contexts of culture. I note that, in this as in the two other requirements, the committee seemed to be allowing for the fact that currently much of the best research and teaching on historical subjects is being done in academic departments other than history. And each requirement was explicitly intended to impart "a critical appreciation of and informed acquaintance with the major approaches to knowledge, not in abstract but in substantive terms," to help students understand what such knowledge may "mean to them personally"—which on a broader scale corresponds to the purposes of "how to" courses in history offerings.

Any such formulation of the best approaches to history for students today may be more understandable if we pause to look at three major works that helped bring the discipline out of a distinct crisis of confidence thirty years ago. Doubts as to the validity of historians' approaches to truth had come to a head in this country by 1946, and yet as John Higham's *History* (1965) points out, a renewal of history followed almost immediately. The upturn in history's enrollments became perceptible in the mid fifties before the prospective demand for teachers could make its impact.

All three books were by masters of the historian's craft. R. G. Collingwood's *The Idea of History* (1946) argued centrally against survey history, which Collingwood decried as scissors-and-paste history, and for understanding the historian's task as centrally to "re-enact the past in his own mind" (p. 282). This last was certainly too narrow a metaphor, but it helpfully directed attention to the difficulty and validity of the historian's search for the truth below the surfaces. If Collingwood's book seemed addressed more to philosophers than to historians, Herbert Butterfield's BBC lectures of 1949 on *Christianity and History* probably reached more college teachers than research professors in this church-going nation of ours; their message was that the self-critical probing by the historian into the ambiguities and tragedies of history is deeply in resonance with some religious perceptions of a thoughtful behavior. Finally, Marc Bloch's *The Historian's Craft* (translated in 1953) made the point that any historian's evidence is only as good as the questions he manages to ask of it; and it implicitly directed attention to the record of Bloch's previous work as showing that a widely interdisciplinary range of questions—from why the long persistence of belief in the king's power to heal scrofula, to the odd timing of the triumph of the water mill—could indeed pay rich dividends.

These three scholars, then, helped to firm up the standards of the discipline of history in relation to truth, to values, and to evidence. In the next years, the Scylla and Charybdis of antiquarianism and presentism lost most of their earlier terrors, freeing inquirers to pursue each inquiry in its own terms. As Carl Schorske (1967) has testified, special studies began to surpass the general surveys in value and meaningfulness, setting up new tensions between research and conventional teaching. Today, as vocational preparation and socialization to adult culture both take their places as merely parts of what students seek from studying history, the deeper appeals of history probably count for more, as the Harvard proposal plainly suggests.

Before turning to the next topic, let me emphasize that there have been successful reforms of history curriculums at many institutions other than those few mentioned thus far. The Harvard faculty itself, parenthetically, considered the proposed history requirements possibly excessive and, in approving in April 1978 the proposed core curriculum, reduced the first two to a one-semester requirement, the other semester course (either one) being replaced by an elective chosen from the entire core curriculum offering. At the University of Kansas, as Sidman (1975) has testified, the history department has since 1973 had in notably successful operation a program characterized by carefully designed course offerings for other departments and professional schools and by an array of special-topic courses in place of surveys. The many attempts around the country to focus history teaching specifically upon competencies that a student should acquire have not, on the whole, had anything like the success of the content-oriented programs in appealing to students. One interesting exception, Northeastern University's Western Civilization course reported by Herman (1977), which employs videotaped lectures, focuses on the specifically historical competencies that have characterized "how to" courses. While allowing its teachers to play up content-oriented interests, it reinterprets "coverage" as helping students to develop a set of contexts to connect parts of past and present for their lives.

Implications of Developmental Research

We turn now to the insights into student development presented in Part One of this book. The recent modifications of history courses to increase their appeal to students essentially amount to a shift away from emphasis on authoritative coverage to emphasis instead on themes and acts of judgment more flexibly connected with individual development. And the shifting between narrow themes and larger sets of contexts, the tension between the attractions of the past in its uniqueness and those of its potential for explaining the present, and even the persistent attention both to process (learning "how to") and to content, all suggest that the connection between the study of history and individual development is complex rather than straightforward. The effective connection seems indeed to be chiefly with the inner struggles over ideological issues, which characterize, as Gilligan points out, the adolescent's struggle over identity. Perry's report on *Forms of Intellectual and Ethical Development in the College Years* (1968), commented upon in his chapter in this book, is the most penetrating account of these inner ideological struggles. The confirmatory research since 1975 that he also summarizes makes clear that his findings are by no means limited in applicability to college scenes like the Harvard of their origin. Indeed, if we can allow for the specific differences between the adolescent's primary concern with identity and the older person's rather different concerns, as described in Chapter One, the general character of Perry's findings may point the way to successful modifications of history teaching for adults. Attention to the deeper level of student need and involvement, for ethnic and other new students as well as adults, may bypass the distracting issue of history's "elitist" attention to phenomena in the past that were in the nature of things limited to the social elites. Certainly this was borne out in my personal experiences of deeply responsive students in central China (in 1948-49), who were in fact awaiting Communist rule, and of equally responsive young engineers in Pittsburgh (in the 1950s), who had in mind futures with no place for the ornaments of traditional elitist culture.

A key feature of Perry's (1968) findings, as the title of his book itself indicates, is that what at bottom seemed to matter most to his students—working out a responsible personal stance toward doubt and diversity—made intellectual and ethical choices deeply akin. Success on either of these fronts meant courage for the other. It comes as no surprise to find in one of Perry's early footnotes (p. 48) that a student's attitudes toward academic work and religion were more in step than those toward any other pairing of the five content sectors distinguished—the other three sectors being the extracurricular, interpersonal, and vocational. Perry's pages finally cite Michael Polanyi's *Personal Knowledge* as treating "precisely what our students address: the ultimate welding of epistemological and moral issues in the act of Commitment" (p. 202).

In the relative privacy of the classroom, many effective history teachers are if anything all too free with interlarded obiter dicta on both these subjects. A significant amount of attention to both realms is surely called for by the considerations that we have been reviewing. The seriousness and respect with which any class approaches the underlying human issues in a past controversy, for example, can have much to do with what the individual student can get out of studying it and, indeed, with the degree to which he can throw his energies into that study. The practical question may only be to what extent, and in what ways, it is wise for teacher and learner to give open attention to moral issues and large intellectual issues. There is always the danger that such broad considerations may make it harder to see what the material at hand, properly questioned, itself has to say.

There are several relevant points to consider here. First, a central skill in historical work is the ability to discover how far the evidence, properly sought out and questioned, will bear out the argument that is under examination. Among habitual historians, so to speak, an issue may need only initial mention, and thereafter the demonstration or confutation by the evidence is understood and judged without difficulty. Students, of course, cannot be expected to follow such a "pantomime" without sooner or later losing track of the argument. Yet in good historical work the many asides that may be needed to keep them on track, like asides often needed to wake up older hands preoccupied with some other and older argument, are still secondary. Under these rules of the game, there is no impropriety in including in the evidence under the spotlight, along with unobtrusive asides, those pieces of evidence embodying argument pro and con on issues inherent in the subject that will engage the students at points of their deepest questionings and efforts.

Second, it is normal in historical practice, just as it is helpful for student development, for issues of such seriousness to be kept tentative and questioning when they are embodied in evidence and signaled by asides. Gilligan tells us that some students, ones who evidently have moved into Perry's stages of "commitment in relativism," show an advanced moral relativism by asking questions from quite new angles—that is, by a problem-finding (as Arlin reportedly terms it) that places the moral issue in a wider or different frame. This seems close in character to the sober rethinking of moral judgments that Butterfield (1949) argued was characteristic of history at its most serious, and also to the active question-asking that Bloch (1953) recommended.

Third, the tact with which different levels or separated sectors of value judgment are handled in the classroom matters a great deal. Probings into the value judgments of even advanced students may, if at all heavy-handed, provoke relativistic responses that are far from the whole story. By contrast, in the course of class discussion of some value-laden controversy, I myself have often found it easy to support unobtrusively the sophisticated questionings of an advanced student through asides, while directly pursuing the much simpler ones of the rest of the class. My feeling afterward was typically that the advanced student had been able to appreciate both levels of the discussion, as if at different levels within himself. When in Perry's (1968) book one of the students in Position 6 is quoted as saying of religion, "when I take it up again, I feel . . . I will meet it and develop it and really bring it into my life" (p. 144), one's impression is that the student was taking comfort from feeling that something in deeper levels of his personality was a resource for possible later times of need.

The direct teaching of morality at any level can, of course, meet with direct resistance. As Weathersby notes drily, there is no clear consensus in outside society that institutions of higher education should promote student development toward greater acceptance of complexity, flux, and uncertainty; and Douvan notes the tendency of some students to form like-minded enclaves to defend themselves against the liberalizing influences of faculty, curriculum, and peers. Perry speaks even more vividly of the mounting anxiety and anger shown by students who, lacking such defenses, felt besieged by liberal probings for which they were not ready. For this reason, a history teacher might do well not to allow the classroom's moral judgments, even implicitly, to seem to apply recognizably to any of those present—unless, that is, attention can be shifted to open and fruitful discussion of the issue in itself. As Butterfield (1949) says in his lectures, "all the moral verdicts that we may pass on human history are only valid in their application as self-judgments—only useful in so far as we bring them home to ourselves," and "our ultimate feelings . . . are hardly matter for common discourse" (p. 62).

Fourth, once students are playing the game of recognizing and following issues implicit in the inquiry, and important to them at different levels of meaningfulness, the teacher may be able to single out for concerted awareness on a particular day not just one but two issues, of quite different sorts, which both promise to be in some way satisfyingly illuminated by the inquiry. The presence of the two "in the wings," especially if they involve different attitudes toward life, gives the students freedom of choice, and freedom indeed to shift from one to the other in background preoccupation during the discussion, with none of the sense of constraint so characteristic of scenes of indoctrination. The result has often been a wholeheartedness of class agreement and a rush of energies into the factual inquiry, carrying it forward to its own natural resolution. There need be nothing concealed or manipulative about choosing the background issues. The students themselves come to share in this and in managing the discussion, and so learn in the process more about how to marshal and maximize their own deeper motivations for learning.

Last but not least in importance, skills of contextual thinking play a key role, on the evidence of Perry's findings, in the learning by which a student can move beyond the (finally frightening) irresponsibility of sheer "multiplicity" to the rational, fruitful uses of "relativism." The skills taught in the "how to" aspects of history courses are themselves largely skills of contextual judgment. As Butterfield (1949) observes early in his lectures, "in a great deal of historical work mere skepticism carries one nowhere and everything depends in the last resort on the very delicate balancing of the mind as it makes what we call an 'act of judgment' " (p. 17). It may be a positive disservice to students to let them think that the skills involved in such judgments are applicable only within professional history, or that the "how to" course exists solely to mold them into historians, since that tends to seal off the possible energizing connections with their own most serious concerns. When childhood authorities have proved inadequate and a student is seeking his footing in the quagmire of a complex and changing world, it may mean much to discover a constellation of skills of judgment that, applied with care, can wrest for him from a medley of indirect evidence a conclusion he finds is trustworthy.

The different academic disciplines rely on rather different sets of skills of judgment, of course, and practitioners within each differ in what they employ, just as purposes and problems also vary. Within history, to choose an example from my own somewhat limited 1959 summary of the necessary skills, one procedure often used to particularly good effect is to stand back and compare the situation under investigation with another similar to it and also close to it in space and time. Whereas in another academic discipline this might be done as an exercise in comparative studies, or even as a first step toward some relatively universal generalization, the historian more often counts on it simply to sharpen his eyes to things he has been missing, and to help firm up his sense of the order of importance of the factors in the situation of his primary interest. The neighboring situation is for him, that is, a revealing piece of context. Moreover, to use the language of maps, a shift from a small-scale treatment to a much larger scale, or vice versa, often provides valuable comparison in the same style. Skill in making just such diagnostic comparisons, and in combining their results with other contextual and internal evidence, is built up through practice on historical problems that command serious interest. Reliance on skills of this sort, I used to remark informally to students, comes to feel like sea legs: you come to feel able to trust your weight to the conclusions they yield, with a kind of flexible tentativeness quite different from the more unhesitating firmness with which you step forward on the firm pavement of reality as defined for you by unquestioned authority.

Intimacy and Empathy

Thus far, of all the Eriksonian stages of development reviewed in Chickering and Havighurst's chapter, we have confined our attention to issues connected with the stage of identity. These are the issues that have been central in motivating the fully engaged learning of history by undergraduates. Vocational and socialization concerns themselves fit well with them, of course. But the next stage in Erikson's scheme, intimacy, also often plays a part, as Gilligan illustrates toward the end of her chapter. Historical inquiry, confronting the complexity of past human situations, is indeed not likely to become self-motivating—that is, to be meaningful and rewarding to the student—until the unique qualities of that piece of the past and its special relationship to the present are recognized as personally relevant and appreciated in their own right. Douvan notes early in her chapter that the capacity for the corresponding feature of intimacy develops only in later adolescence (16 to 18) in girls, and it presumably develops at least equally late in boys. And yet, as White remarks in his chapter, the expansion of empathy is aided by a great variety of experiences in late adolescence.

The mature learning of history is well known to be at odds with the easy identification with a historical figure—one against all others—that is the charm of most fictional and popular history. Admittedly, even senior historians have now and then achieved distinction in their work without sufficiently distancing themselves from the figures to whom they first became attached. But the duty of the history teacher to disturb such attachments of students is fairly generally recognized as flowing from the need for a measure of objectivity in historical work. With a touch of considerateness and luck, the student's critical perspectives can be roused into common focus with empathy, yielding the enlightened understanding of more mature intimacy. For lack of this kind of help from teacher or fellow students, the self-planned learning discussed in Tough's chapter may often, in the case of history, be seriously defective. Where, however, history teachers themselves often fall short is in choosing enough personalities and situations for study on which the evidence permits arriving fairly quickly at both a warmth and a distancing of relationship, simultaneously.

Is this balance of warmth and distancing—required for historical work—consistent with the requirements of individual development? Erikson has proposed that failure to achieve an assured sense of identity can be a serious handicap to subsequent efforts to deal with intimacy. Confident identity, as we have been implying, normally involves some achieved stance on basic intellectual and ethical issues. So when Douvan initially defines the interpersonal relationship of intimacy as "relatively free of normative prescriptions," there may be reason to bear in mind that this is quite consistent with an awareness of normative differences. Similarly, the moral understanding of the students whom Gilligan describes as having in a sense gone "beyond good and evil" ideally may not so much replace as subsume the judgments they earlier reached out of an ideology of right and wrong. The commitment in Perry's "commitment in relativism" seems usually an affirmative choice of some particular truth or right, according to his examples, although the student now considers people of different beliefs in no way alien or unreal, no matter how different from him. Is this not in Erikson's terms a commitment (of identity) touched with a sense of, or at least a readiness for, intimacy?

These then, under the Eriksonian headings of identity and intimacy, are points at which findings on the development of students of college age relate to the learning of history. Before we turn to the teaching of other students, is it objected that all these are points relatively remote from the workaday choices of the college history teacher? One answer is that they bear directly on the obiter dicta and asides with which the teacher in the classroom guides the students' thinking about the historical topic at hand. The desired character of the classroom interaction must shape much of the teacher's preparatory work, from the choice of content for the course to the last decisions on sequence of details and on supporting documents or audiovisual aids. During the preparatory work, since there are no pat answers, what is likely to be of most value is a continuing discussion with colleagues, drawing on their experience of what issues have and have not struck home to students, and on their stories of deft ways of handling the issues. Since history, like other disciplines in the humanities, requires reaching students at several different levels simultaneously, the sheer diversity of suggestions picked up from colleagues is invaluable. One approach that verges on sheer entertainment may work well when paired with one that implicitly raises some troubling problem of "truth," of value judgments, or of the validity of evidence against ingrained skepticism. The pairing may bring about the sense of free choice of background issues mentioned earlier.

History for Adult Students

If our observations about the possibilities for more effective teaching of history to conventional undergraduates have been well taken, these observations should apply equally well—mutatis mutandis—to the teaching of adults and other nontraditional students. The shift we have observed in history teaching is in general from the "cultural tourism" of many past introductory courses to more thought-provoking and meaningful themes. Schaie and Parr, in their chapter, point out that according to the literature on the subject, while novelty seems to be an adequate learning stimulus for younger persons, meaning and some degree of familiarity are required for material to be assimilated by older learners. They also note that among the Primary Mental Abilities, in at least one sample, Verbal Meaning has shown a peak age of as late as 46 years of age. There is particular reason not to rely, in preparing history courses for adults, upon old formulas that trust to vocational aims and socialization as adequate sources of motivation. Hammett's (1977) report on continuing education explained the decline in European history enrollments as due, in his words, partly to "student reaction against the Western Civilization course, which was frequently required and resented" (p. 245).

It is particularly noteworthy that, according to Blocher and Rapoza, a study of adult students by Ladan and Crooks found that while the men were more concerned with specific career-related goals, the women were more concerned with personal growth. Joseph Katz has reported that women returning to school tended to put interest in learning and achievement of independence and identity ahead of getting a job. The excitement they expressed over their learning reminded Katz of "the dedication one observes in highly motivated scholars." I myself observed exactly such excitement and dedication in at least one continuing education class, in English literature, at Sarah Lawrence College in the early 1960s. Chickering and Havighurst note that the age period of 35-45 may be something of a second adolescence for many people, a period in which they have to rediscover or reconstitute an identity. It is plausible to suppose that women, more than men, have been able to turn to account, for the purpose of helping them rethink their identity, courses essentially designed for the adolescent identity crisis. May some minimal equivalent of the special psychosocial "role suspension" that society allows to those of college age, as Douvan notes, be somewhat easier for women than for men to exact from their associates around age 40? Such a difference between women and men in their motivations for study might help explain the contrast in the past few years between the rapid continuing increase in numbers of women students over 25, and the leveling off of the parallel numbers of men, according to the *Chronicle of Higher Education* in April 1978.

There appears to be a special opportunity here for history teaching. Although recent years have seen a modest increase in courses like the history of women or the family in a given period, historical curriculums still predominantly focus on subjects closer to men's careers and choices in public life. Levinson, as Chickering and Havighurst note, has found men at middle age working through a process of disillusionment and emotional turmoil that seems to be essentially identity crisis, though without the aid of role suspension. College years provide this suspension for most middle-class youth, as Douvan's chapter notes. Moreover, the issues that characterize Erikson's stages of generativity and integrity, in later adulthood, seem eminently open to illumination through the study of topics currently being explored by historical research. Choice of topics that both invite deep personal engagement and permit serious inquiry can be arrived at in dialogue with good students, supported by ongoing discussion with colleagues.

The narrower challenge here, then, is to develop for adult men courses in history that will supplement their vocational courses and bring about involvements that arise when study issues interact with the learner's struggles in the developmental stages of the sort identified by Perry. A handy model, among recent courses for conventional undergraduates, might be the course on "The History of American Presidential Assassinations," which drew 916 enrollees when first offered (by Hopkins) in 1976 at Western Illinois University. This course not only stressed the skills of historical inquiry but also cast a new and searching light on American social and political life. To speak more to the disillusionments of men at middle age, a course in American social history could choose to investigate the successive "earthquake" changes of national mood and assumptions precipitated by major historical events, starting perhaps with the advent of Jacksonian democracy and including the onset of the flapper age after World War I. The parallel with the changes that hit our society around 1970 would be obvious enough, and as adults the students would themselves recognize the contrast between what was socially acceptable before and after that watershed (to use the commoner metaphor among historians).

Topics of new sorts are likely to present substantial practical difficulties, of course. An example relevant to the issues of generativity and integrity might be a course exploring reactions within society to radical movements, perhaps dealing in turn with the pendulum swings after Cromwell's army rule in England, after the collapse of the ancien régime in France, after the abolitionist efforts in nineteenth-century America, and after the Spartacists and their predecessors in Germany early in our own century. Looking not so much at revolution as at the backlash to it, such a course might, for example, consider what was on Frederick Douglass' mind during his two days of discussion with John Brown in the Chambersburg stone quarry, or the despair of the poverty-fearing women of French cities after the closing down of all ancien régime charities, so as to estimate better the force and character of resistances that developed against change. A course of this sort presumably could deeply engage issues on the minds of serious adults, both men and women. Yet it would cut across quite separate historical specialties, and un-less—which is wholly unlikely—some publisher were willing to risk a purely experimental textbook, it would require an unusual amount of preparatory work by several different teachers.

Administrators should be aware that courses capable of making a real difference in the learning of adults or other special clientele can rarely be arranged without special funding for preparations, very much as in the commoner cases of interdisciplinary courses. In fact, as the record of Harvard's Social Sciences 2 amply indicates (in Richter's 1970 summary), even an interdisciplinary course on historical subjects, to be successful, must normally center around an integrated set of standards for thinking.

One final question related to adult learning requires particular attention. Is it possible to learn how to do good historical work except in and through a classroom course? One-to-one teaching in the Oxford and Cambridge tutorial tradition relies for its effectiveness, as Moore (1968) has pointed out, on the teacher's not posing, or even serving, as an authority. "The good teacher will thus help the student to refute or correct him, which is to say that he will teach method rather than hard and fast conclusions" (p. 19). But this is difficult for teachers in our country, who commonly can look to classmates to provide for each other the needed experience of refuting and correcting. The established professor, especially if he has something like Nobel laureate distinction, can be led by the rewards of effective teaching into habits of exposing his own doubts and encouraging well-considered student rebuttals. But junior teachers commonly find it hard to relinquish authority to that extent, given their primary duty of leading students up to and through unexpected difficulties of thinking.

Thus, as the Gaffs' chapter on student-faculty relations notes, students who live in dormitories benefit intellectually and personally much more from college life than commuter students. The implications of this for adult students are obvious. They seem even more serious for the self-planned learning discussed by Tough in his chapter. Countless books and museums on the Williamsburg model cater to individuals who are interested in learning history on their own. Yet to gain real competence in history, students need to experience a clash of well-grounded individual judgment. Unfortunately, the academic profession has too often limited its teaching of these to substantive courses, in strictly apprenticeship style; and its printed discussions of them are little more than rules for scrutinizing individual pieces of evidence and writing up results. For growth in historical understanding that can connect with the deeper springs of energy that Perry has identified, the student needs guidance in these skills, as well as experiences of the self-disclosure, supportiveness, and periodic confrontations emphasized in Torbert's discussion of ways to promote effective inquiry.

The research findings in Part One, taken as a whole, seem to bear out the proposition that there is a connection between what underlies and energizes good learning, and the arduous efforts of students to grow in independence and responsibility as persons. Perry's book earlier told us that much good teaching at the undergraduate level has in fact been tacitly speaking to the deepest concerns of students. Increasing numbers of practicing teachers have responded by saying that his tentative scheme gets to the heart of what they understand liberal education to be about. Tacit and tactful handling of the deeper dilemmas of morality and truth, of intimacy and generativity and integrity, seems to many historians built into the true study of history. More explicit attention to this dimension of history teaching may be able to yield in the near future some significant breakthroughs on the new frontiers of higher education.

References

Bloch, M. *The Historian's Craft.* (P. Putnam, Trans.) New York: Knopf, 1953.

Butterfield, H. *Christianity and History.* London: G. Bell and Sons, 1949.

Cole, C. W. "Introduction: Laurence Bradford Packard." In H. S. Hughes (Ed.), *Teachers of History.* Ithaca: Cornell University Press, 1954.

Collingwood, R. G. *The Idea of History.* Oxford: Oxford University Press, 1946.

Constable, G. "Beyond Western Civilization: Rebuilding the Survey." Society for History Education, *Network News Exchange,* 1977, *2* (3), 9-12.

Friedlander, J. "The Status of History in the Two-Year College." *AHA Newsletter,* 1978, *16* (4), 6-7.

Hammett, H. B. "The Future of History in Continuing Education." *The History Teacher,* 1977, *10* (2), 242-247.

"Harvard Weighs Plan to Reform College Curriculum." *The Chronicle of Higher Education,* 1978, *16* (2), 1, 15-18.

Herman, G. "An Integration of Teacher and Technology in a Western Civilization Program." Society for History Education, *Network News Exchange,* 1977, *3* (1), 14-16.

Higham, J., with Krieger, L., and Gilbert, F. *History.* Englewood Cliffs, N.J.: Prentice-Hall, 1965.

Hollinger, D. A. "History and the Social Sciences." *The Chronicle of Higher Education,* 1977, *15* (3), 15.

Hopkins, G. E. "Assassination As History." *AHA Newsletter,* 1976, *14* (8), 5-7.

Moore, W. G. *The Tutorial System and Its Future.* Oxford, England: Pergamon Press, 1968.

"More People Over 25 Are Going to College." *The Chronicle of Higher Education,* 1978, *16* (7), 2.

Perry, W. G., Jr. *Forms of Intellectual and Ethical Development in the College Years: A Scheme.* New York: Holt, Rinehart and Winston, 1968.

Real, J. " 'Son of Super Civ'." *Change: The Magazine of Higher Learning,* 1976, *8* (2), 30-32.

Richter, M. "Introduction." In M. Richter (Ed.), *Essays in Theory and History.* Cambridge, Mass.: Harvard University Press, 1970.

Schorske, C. E. "History's New Scholarship and the Education Gap." *Experiment and Innovation,* 1967, *1* (1), 1-9.

Sidman, C. F. "Report on Kansas Plan." *AHA Newsletter,* 1975, *13* (7), 5-7.

Ward, P. L. *Elements of Historical Thinking.* Washington, D.C.: American Historical Association, 1971. (Original edition, *A Style of History for Beginners,* 1959.)

Ward, P. L. "A Suggested Approach to Objectives for the Study of History." *AHA Newsletter,* 1973, *11* (2), 21-27.

Whitehead, A. N. *The Aims of Education and Other Essays.* New York: Macmillan, 1929.

19

George G. Dawson

Economics

  Economics is the study of how people allocate scarce resources in the effort to satisfy wants. The basic problem is *scarcity*—the fact that no society has enough resources to satisfy the wants of its members. Because we cannot have everything we want, we must choose from among alternatives. Every society must attempt to answer the same basic questions: What shall we produce? How much? For whom? How shall we produce?

  Every individual is affected by economics. We are all consumers. Our very lives depend upon how society organizes its productive resources to help meet our needs and wants. Most of us are also producers, providing goods or services not only in the marketplace where our output is sold at a price but also in various nonmarket situations such as the household. The person who washes dishes, cooks the family meals, and so forth is as much of a producer as the worker on a factory assembly line.

  While individuals must make economic choices that affect them personally and directly nearly every day, societies must also make choices that will affect every member. If a nation is fully and efficiently using its productive resources and decides to build more war planes, it must shift the factors of production—natural resources, human resources, and capital resources—away from something else. Thus, the *real* cost of the additional war planes might be automobiles, farm equipment, or other goods that could be produced with the same resources.

  In the private enterprise marketplace our "dollar votes" help determine what will be produced. If people want skateboards and are willing to pay enough to cover production costs plus a profit for the producer, then skateboards will be manufactured. If skateboards go out of fashion, and people want water skis instead, demand for the former will drop and demand for the latter will rise.

Some important decisions, of course, are left to the "experts." If inflation is seen as a serious problem, someone must decide whether to combat it by raising taxes, reducing the money supply, cutting government spending, controlling wages and prices, or some combination of these. The average person has little direct influence and probably lacks the knowledge of economic principles needed to make intelligent suggestions in such matters. Thus, the Congress, the President, and the Federal Reserve Board will try to decide what to do, and the citizen's influence will be indirect at best.

These are some of the economic issues that affect us all. The question confronting economic educators is: What should we teach? The decision on what to include in a course in the principles of economics is a most difficult one. Generally, the college teacher has avoided *personal* economics in favor of what we might call *social* economics. That is, little attention has been paid to the individual and the family. Overwhelmingly, the courses concentrate on national issues such as inflation, unemployment, stability, and economic growth, and on the theories needed for an understanding of the workings of the market, such as the laws of demand and supply, diminishing returns, and diminishing marginal utility.

Although there are some courses devoted to "consumer economics," and although teachers at the precollege levels often favor personalized approaches, the college instructor rarely makes an effort to deal with the personal needs and interests of the students. Indeed, even though only a small fraction of students in most introductory courses intend to major in economics, the professor often acts as if all will be going on to the intermediate or advanced courses and structures the introductory course accordingly. The student receives large doses of theory (often quite abstract) and is baffled about what to do with it. What the student does with it is not the professor's concern, many argue. "Economics is economics." There is no such thing as economics for nurses, economics for business executives, economics for black people, and so on. Now, to a certain extent this is true. The law of demand remains much the same regardless of who looks at it, although it does not always work quite the way the textbooks say it is supposed to work.

What, then, has been the economics professor's goal? Fortunately, there have been some formal attempts to find the answer. In a study conducted in 1973-74, Horton and Weidenaar found that the vast majority of economists and economic educators responding to their questionnaires rejected the idea that economic education is "to help us to be more capable as direct participants in the economy—that is, as consumers, workers, businessmen, or investors" (Horton and Weidenaar, 1974 and 1975). Instead, they favored the goal "to improve our understanding of the world in which we live." Similar results were obtained by Dopp as part of a doctoral study made in 1977. Dopp sent questionnaires to colleges to determine the content and structure of the principles of economics courses. The great majority considered the most important goals of an economics course to be to "prepare the student to become a better-informed citizen through an understanding of our economy and its institutions" and to "develop within the student the analytical thinking skills necessary for economic understanding." The objective considered *least* important by 93 percent of the respondents was to "prepare the student for a professional career" (Dopp, 1977). If these studies are correct, then most college economics teachers do not yet see economics as a practical instrument for helping the student make key personal decisions.

The goal of helping people to become better-informed citizens is one that some of the nation's leading economists have promoted. In 1960 a National Task Force on Economic Education was created by the American Economic Association and the Committee for Economic Development to set forth "the kind of economic understanding needed for responsible citizenship and effective participation in today's complex economy" (National Task Force on Economic Education, 1961). Students should be provided with an "analytical tool kit" for the "objective, reasoned consideration of economic issues." The Task Force was attempting to provide secondary school teachers with guidance on what to include in courses or units on economics, but the substance of its recommended outline could be found in any standard college textbook on the principles of economics. Its list of "essential" topics almost totally ignored the consumer's personal economic problems.

Nevertheless, the Task Force Report is a landmark in economic education and has had a profound impact. The authors of high school textbooks written after the publication of the report often claimed to have followed its recommendations, and courses and in-service workshops for teachers were also based upon those recommendations. Before publication of the report, the typical high school economics textbooks had been largely descriptive. After the distribution of the report, several new textbooks of a more analytical nature were published (Townshend-Zellner, 1970). Most economic educators applauded this, and rightly so.

Although it is probably safe to say that most professional economists give little thought to the problems of teaching their subject (and certainly care little about teaching it at the high school level), it is also clear that the Task Force Report did begin to arouse the interest of some college professors. Indeed, the number of college economists now actively involved in the economics education movement is far greater than it was in 1960.

Although there are some college economists who have a deep concern for the improvement of their teaching, most probably give little thought to the various aspects of human development, such as ego development, interpersonal competence, and the life cycle, discussed in Part One of this book. Indeed, if we pay careful attention to the subjects recommended by the Task Force and to the goals set forth by that group and by the economists polled by Dopp and others, we will probably conclude that the college teachers see little need to tailor their courses to fit the students' interests. Since the basic goal is decidedly *not* to help the student get a job, become more proficient as a consumer, or cope with personal economic problems, but to acquire that "analytical tool kit" that will enable the individual to understand national issues and world problems, the instructor need not be concerned about the student's age, sex, marital status, maturity, interpersonal competence, or what have you. In fact, the accepted goal and the standard content of the basic introductory economics course seem to have a comfortable universality that fits all people at all times and in all places! How nice—and how much easier it is to teach it that way!

Now, if the goal and the content apply equally to everyone, what about the method of instruction? Two recent studies (Dopp, 1977, and Monson, 1977) indicate that the lecture method still prevails. Lecture sections of over 200 students are not uncommon. Even though fewer than 10 percent of the students in the introductory course will be economics majors, all tend to get the same treatment as those going on to higher-level studies in the discipline. Dopp reported that only 20 percent of the colleges in his sample offer separate courses for students who are not majoring in economics or business.

This is not to say that nothing has changed during the past twenty years. Although the vast majority of college economists appear to be adhering to the traditional textbooks, course outlines, goals, and methods of teaching, there is clearly a growing interest in the newer developments. The next section will be devoted to the work of that small but growing band of college economists who are reexamining their time-honored conventions and beginning to seek new and better ways of teaching and of relating their discipline to the needs and interests of students.

Changes in the Teaching of College Economics

A search of the literature reveals that professional economists paid little systematic attention to the teaching of their subject before the decade of the 1960s. After 1960, however, a substantial number of college economics instructors began to raise questions about the teaching of their discipline. Some leading economists began to deplore the fact that instructors were making little effort to evaluate the effectiveness of their teaching. The eminent economist G. L. Bach of Stanford University wrote as follows:

> We economists like to consider ourselves scientists. Our journals bulge with econometric tests of elegance and statistical precision—carefully specified models and testable propositions, plus rigorous evaluation of the evidence to support or reject the hypotheses. . . . Yet in planning and judging our own major activity, teaching, we are not only unscientific, we are often openly aitiscientific [1967, p. 74].

Another luminary, George Stigler of the University of Chicago, made the following statement in his 1962 presidential address to the American Economic Association:

> I propose the following test: Select an adequate sample of seniors (I would prefer men five years out of college), equally divided between those who have never had a course in economics and those who have had a conventional one-year course. Give them an examination on current economic problems, not on textbook questions. I predict they will not differ in their performance [1963, p. 657].

These acerbic comments did not go unheeded. Bach practiced what he preached by engaging in research on the teaching of economics. Such well-known economists as Kenneth Boulding, Rendigs Fels, and Campbell McConnell developed new methods of teaching and subjected their experiments to rigorous controlled evaluations. New instructors as well as veteran professors joined in the search for better ways of presenting "the dismal science" to students. By 1969 the number of studies on the teaching of college economics had reached at least 240. By the late 1970s the total was well over 800 (Dawson, 1975 and 1976).

For many years, a major activity of the Joint Council on Economic Education and its affiliated centers and councils has been running workshops for elementary and high school teachers. It is not unusual to find nearly a hundred such programs operating in any given summer. The participants usually receive intensive instruction in basic economics in addition to information on how to teach it to their own students. It is unlikely that a decade ago anyone would have dared propose similar workshops for college teachers. "If you know your subject, you can teach it" was the common assertion of those who tended to look upon "educationists" as useless appendages. The Joint Council, however, felt that the new Ph.D. fresh from graduate school could benefit from instruction in how to teach economics. When a workshop for such persons was organized in 1973, the response was highly positive. Indeed, some of the most prestigious of institutions (such as Harvard) reacted with enthusiasm. By 1978, at least a dozen colleges had adopted the Joint Council's Teacher Training Program for economists.

The authors of the chapters in Part One of this book might not think these developments are very significant. To those of us who have been laboring in the economic education vineyards for a quarter of a century, however, they represent giant steps in the right direction. In the final section of this chapter I shall discuss ways in which economic education might change in the future in the light of the research and theory given in Part One.

Economic Education in the Future

Predictions are dangerous. Even the econometricians, with their highly complex mathematical models, seem to be wrong as often as they are right when they predict a future Gross National Product figure, unemployment rate, or whatever. Perhaps what I say in this section is more wishful thinking than serious prognostication. Nevertheless, there are a few signs suggesting that a substantial number of college economists will begin to see their discipline as an instrument for helping students deal with problems related to the life cycle or various dimensions of their personal development.

It is no longer unusual to find a college economics professor who has heard of Bloom's taxonomy or Mager's behavioral objectives. Indeed, some demonstrate a thorough knowledge of educational psychology, up-to-date learning theories, and psychometric methods. These are people who see their responsibility as something beyond merely presenting students with facts and concepts. A few universities have actually established separate graduate programs in economic education, and Ohio University at Athens has a Department of Economic Education that offers both masters and doctoral degrees (Dawson, 1971). The students in these programs usually get a heavy dose of economic theory so that their preparation in the discipline is as intensive as that of students with no interest in education. Then, they are also trained in educational theory and method. It is important to note, however, that a knowledge of learning theory and an interest in how the study of economics might relate to an individual's personal development are not confined to those who have been exposed to these formal programs.

One important breakthrough is the growing interest in personalized, individualized, or self-paced instruction. The recognition of the fact that not all students learn best in the same way, using the same materials, and for the same reasons may well lead to an acceptance of the notion that the content of the basic economics course itself can have different meanings and different utilities for different individuals. Over eighty colleges and universities have adopted some sort of self-pacing in their introductory economics course (Allison, 1975). At least sixty research projects have been conducted on some aspect of personalized, individualized, or self-paced instruction in college economics (Dawson, 1977). I shall return to the subject of personalized instruction later.

Some of the approaches to the teaching of economics that college economists and education specialists are recommending to high school teachers may conceivably come to be adopted at the college or adult level as well. For example, take the World of Work Economic Education Program initiated by the Joint Council on Economic Education a few years ago. Workshops for teachers were held and materials were produced to help the schools use economics as a vehicle for improving their career education programs. If there is nothing wrong in using economics to help high school youngsters prepare for the world of work (Calderwood, 1977), why should there be any objection to using it in the same way with college students and adults who are contemplating career changes? Economics can be taught in such a way that it not only meets the goals agreed upon by the economists surveyed in the Horton and Weidenaar study and the Dopp study cited earlier, but also helps the student in career planning. It is often taught this way by New York's Empire State College. For example, suppose that someone planning to enter the health care delivery field is studying basic economics. That student could use a conventional two-semester principles textbook and thus learn the basic theory needed as background for advanced study or for understanding current economic issues. At the same time, however, the student could be relating everything in that text to the health care delivery system by attempting to answer questions of the following type:

- How does the market allocate resources generally, and how are health care resources allocated?
- To what extent does the market model apply to health care delivery?
- How are costs determined in health care delivery?
- How are the factors of production used in health care delivery?
- What is the demand for health care, and how does it differ from the demand for other goods and services?
- What characterizes the supply side of the health care delivery "market"?
- How does the concept of elasticity apply?
- How are health care facilities organized in both the public and private sectors?
- How is the health care delivery system affected by the business cycle?
- How has inflation affected the system?
- What is the role of government in health care delivery?
- What labor problems exist in health care delivery?
- How is health care related to economic growth both here and in other parts of the world?
- How is the problem of inequality in the distribution of income related to the health care delivery system?
- How is health care provided in our economic system as compared with nations having different economic systems?

It does not require a great deal of imagination to see how the same sort of questions could be applied to any other occupational field, and thus how the study of economic principles could have real practical value to the student in career planning.

There is evidence that some leading college economists are ready to accept (albeit cautiously) changes in the goals of economics instruction in the direction of greater attention toward individual needs. The Task Force Report of 1961 ignored personal or consumer economics when it set forth the subject matter that ought to be included in high school economics programs. Feeling that the old Task Force Report needed to be revised and brought up to date, the Joint Council on Economic Education recently established a new group of college economists to develop a new master curriculum guide. Additional groups made up of economists and education specialists were formed to identify what could be taught at each grade level and to suggest methods and materials for teaching economics at every grade level.

S. Stowell Symmes, Director of Curriculum for the Joint Council, writes as follows in the "Foreword" to *A Framework for Teaching Economics: Basic Concepts* (Hansen and others, 1977):

> Everyone who moves symbolically into adulthood at age 18 is required to fulfill many roles, foremost among them the roles of consumer, worker, and voting citizen. Each role requires personal economic literacy: to achieve levels of consumer satisfaction from limited income; to make informed decisions about income-earning opportunities which require individuals to understand, improve, and maintain their human capabilities; and to participate effectively in public debate on crucial issues such as the best way to spend our national, state, or local tax dollars [p. iv].

And the authors themselves wrote:

> There are general concerns, such as the role of prices in a market economy, the impact of government, and the unemployment-inflation dilemma. But there is

also a need to teach students something about personal economic decision making —how to earn an income, invest their savings, budget personal expenditures, and the like. We believe that emphasis must be given to preparing young people to grapple with both social and personal issues and questions. To do so, they must, in each case, be familiar with the concepts and approach of economics, and they must be able to apply them in a reasoned way so as to come to informed decisions on specific issues. Although our report is cast largely in terms of the broader economic issues, we recognize that, when properly used, various teaching approaches —such as personal economics—can be useful vehicles for teaching students the basic concepts of economics and their applications [p. 22].

If the new framework is as influential as the old Task Force Report was, economics might eventually lose its reputation as "the dismal science" and become a fascinating and useful tool for helping people solve their personal problems as well as understand world and national issues.

But where might we go from here? It is to be hoped that economics teachers in the future will present their discipline not just as a set of facts, concepts, and principles but as a way of thinking—or, as the great economist A. C. Pigou once put it, as an instrument for the bettering of human life (Lekachman, 1976).

Relation of Economics to Human Development

At this point it might be appropriate to try to relate economic education to some of the theories presented in Part One. Weathersby stresses that learning how to learn is the hallmark of self-directed learners. According to economist John E. Maher (1969), what makes economics a distinctive science is how it organizes and analyzes its materials and how it views the world. The analytical tools of economics and the economic perspective can be applied to many of the problems with which individuals are commonly confronted. The individual who learns this "brand" of economics can be better prepared to rise to higher stages of ego development, including the Individualistic Level identified by Weathersby.

Incidentally, Weathersby notes that at the Self-Aware Transition stage of ego development adults see education as an investment and at the Conscientious Stage, as having significance for improving society. Economic educators should be aware of this, for economists often refer to education as "investment in human capital" and point out that education is instrumental in improving our national well-being—at least in terms of the increase in goods and services. (Indeed, several studies show that in recent decades investment in education has been the major factor in America's economic growth and development.)

In discussing intellectual development, Schaie and Parr note that both younger and older learners need skills in problem solving. Economics is ideally suited to supply such skills, for it has adapted the problem-solving approach of the physical sciences for use in dealing with practical individual and social problems. The specification of goals is one of the first steps in the process, and this clearly relates to the need to integrate long-range goals with the solution of current real-life problems, which, according to Schaie and Parr, is characteristic of middle adulthood. Furthermore, economics education stresses the organizational, integrative, and interpretive intellectual skills that these authors consider to be essential.

For the learner between young adulthood and middle age, there should be no difficulty in relating economics to personal and social goals, and in drawing upon life experiences to make the subject meaningful. For the older learner, Schaie and Parr recommend a variety of learning programs, and the research done by scores of economic educators indicates not only that such a variety exists in economics but that many teaching strategies can be effective. According to these authors, the successful older person is one who rather than having disengaged from society has become reengaged in a meaningful fashion. Economics can be a powerful force in bringing about this reengagement. For example, the retired executive can be "retooled" through a study of modern economics, and with his (or her) up-to-date knowledge of economic theories and problems can serve as a volunteer consultant to minority business firms. (Such a "volunteer executive corps" currently exists in New York.) Economics can indeed have the "egocentric meaning" that these authors consider necessary for the older learner and can be taught in a personalized and individualized manner.

Kolb's experiential learning model lends itself neatly to the learning of economics. We begin with a concrete experience. For example, a man in New York City during the night of the great power blackout goes to a nearby store to buy candles. He finds dozens of others there also trying to purchase the limited supply, and the price rises from a few cents to several dollars per candle. By contrast, during the great snow storm of February 6, 1978, the Metropolitan Opera offers tickets for only a fraction of their regular price. Now we move to "observations and reflections." Our hero notes that when the demand rose sharply in relation to the supply (of candles), the price rose; when the demand for seats at the opera suddenly plunged, the price dropped also. Reflecting upon these and similar observations, the man concludes that when the demand for something rises while the supply remains relatively fixed, the price goes up. When the demand for something drops while the supply is relatively fixed, the price drops. There is a direct relationship between changes in demand and changes in price, other things held equal. Finally, this generalization is put to the test in new situations. He buys Christmas cards on December 26 for half the price the vendor was charging on December 15 because demand has dropped. He goes to the movies during the day while most cinema lovers are at work and finds that tickets are cheaper than they are after six or seven o'clock in the evening. He takes his vacation at a popular resort shortly before or shortly after the regular tourist season and gets his motel room at a lower rate than those who travel in June, July, or August. This person has discovered the "law of demand," has internalized it, and uses it to good effect.

In regard to Kolb's learning styles, economists—in my judgment—ought to avoid concluding that there is *one* best style for the teaching of their discipline. Kolb notes that some economics departments are "very convergent" while others are "divergent," and asserts that several social sciences, including economics, can vary greatly in their basic inquiry paradigm. If we, as economics teachers, believe that our subject is worth teaching to everyone, then it is imperative that we recognize the fact that people do have different learning styles and vary our teaching techniques accordingly. Kolb asserts that motivation to learn may well be a result of learning climates that match learning styles and thereby produce successful learning experiences. A particular department or school, then, ought not to be receptive to only one type of student or one learning style. Let the mathematically oriented student play with curvilinear regressions and ponder the problem of multicollinearity, but do not reject the learner who wants to apply economic concepts to personal or social problems.

So far, so good. But what about moral development, as discussed by Gilligan? Many economists argue that economics is a "value-free science," and to a certain extent this is true. To insist that the price of a crop declined because farmers increased their output is not to say that the farmers were naughty or nice, or that the result is good or bad. After economic analysis, we have determined that the increase in production (relative to demand for the product) resulted in a drop in the market price. We are not "for" or "against" farmers in reporting this—we are just "telling it like it is." Our economic goals and values are determined by everyone, not just by economists. *As economists,* we can tell you that the goal you have set will probably involve such and such a cost, but we cannot—as pure economists—tell you that your goal is right or wrong.

Nevertheless, economic analysis can certainly have an effect on the economic goals that our society sets for itself. It can also help the individual to determine what economic goals he or she will support. Gilligan observes that in late adolescence individuals struggle with the problem of reconciling principles with experience, and through this struggle become aware of the relativism that makes moral judgments contextual. For example, many young people today idealistically (and properly, in my opinion) accept the goal of protecting the environment from pollution. At the same time, these young people (who suffer a higher unemployment rate than adults) also favor a full-employment policy. In many particular cases, however, the action taken to protect the environment results in the loss of jobs. One community forced a pollution-causing factory to close down, but several hundred workers lost their jobs in the process (Gordon and Dawson, 1980). In another area, the home-building industry declined sharply when requirements for cleaner home heating systems raised housing costs by 30 percent. A knowledge of economics can make people aware of these "trade-offs" and perhaps give them a more realistic picture of the feasibility of their goals. One of the great modern dilemmas is that of the Phillips curve (my secretary once erroneously but aptly called it the Phillips *curse*). It seems that the actions we take to end unemployment tend to create (or aggravate) inflation, and that actions taken to control inflation can cause (or aggravate) unemployment. Training in economics will not tell the student which problem is more serious—for a moral judgment is involved here—but it will show the trade-offs and give a fairly good picture of the real costs that will be incurred if one chooses to solve one of these problems at the expense of the other.

Indeed, Gilligan suggests that the questioning of knowledge formerly taken for granted is a part of the student's moral development. One who is well trained in economics is trained to raise intelligent and probing questions—not just to "make bullets" but to get at the heart of the matter or to show that things are not as simple as they seem. Learning to think for oneself, to cope with life's problems, to deal with increasingly complex situations, to avoid simple answers to complex questions, and to see things in a broader context are some of the goals of development noted by Weathersby and others. Economics can help students to analyze the "causes and consequences of human social interaction," as Weathersby puts it, and add a touch of realism to idealistic moral values by revealing the many and varied effects of any given course of action.

Applications of Economics

Let us turn now to some examples of the possible applications of economics to some imaginary (but realistic) problems that individuals are likely to face as members of a complex society.

Alicia Montez is 42 years old and works as an electronics engineer with a large manufacturing firm. Alicia is contemplating a career change of sorts. She would like to teach engineering at a university. How can Alicia use economic analysis in deciding whether or not to leave her current position and become a professor? First, she ought to identify and clarify her goals. For starters, let us suppose that Alicia's goal is to increase her money income and raise her standard of living. Assume that professors of engineering make higher salaries than engineers in private industry (I warned you that this was a fairy tale!). Alicia must employ cost-benefit analysis before she makes her decision. First she might identify and list all the costs of making the change, and then try to determine the benefits that will result therefrom. If the benefits outweigh the costs, then she will change jobs. If Alicia simply compares her current salary with the salary offered by the university, she is guilty of "bad economics."

A number of costs will be incurred in changing jobs, and Alicia should try to identify all of them. A few examples will suffice to make the point. Perhaps the university insists that Alicia take some formal courses to expand her competencies before she is appointed. Her tuition, the price of books and supplies, transportation to and from her classes, and other out-of-pocket expenses will be part of the cost. If Alicia could be earning money in some productive activity during the times she attends classes and engages in out-of-class study, she must also consider this forgone income as part of the cost. Because of the additional demands on her time as a result of her studies, Alicia has to eat more of her meals in restaurants (thus raising the cost of food), hire someone to clean her apartment, and send her clothes to the laundry instead of washing them herself. These are additional items she must build into her cost estimate. Of course, she also has to look beyond the salary differences and take into account fringe benefits. Some of these can be measured very precisely (such as the value of company-paid insurance), but others can only be estimated. She should also consider the time she will have to spend working. If she has been putting in forty hours per week at the industrial firm, but the university job will require fifty hours (including time spent at home in preparing lectures, grading papers, and so on), then perhaps the university salary is not higher after all, if one divides it by the hours worked. And what about transportation? Will Alicia have to drive farther to get to the university than she did to get to the plant? These are but a few of the factors that might be taken into account in a simple cost-benefit analysis, and some have been grossly oversimplified. The major point should be clear, however.

Now, it must be understood that economic analysis is not always confined to easily measurable dollars-and-cents questions. Some of the same principles can be brought to bear on less tangible factors in a decision like the one Alicia must make. Suppose, now, that Alicia's goal is not to make more money or to increase her material standard of living but to engage in work that she finds more satisfying. Let us be more realistic this time and say that the university position pays $3,000 less than the industrial firm is paying Alicia. It is not up to the economist to say that Alicia would be foolish to change jobs, even if we assume that all other measurable factors have been accounted for. That is, let us say that she has accurately measured all the dollar-and-cents costs of making the change and finds that—everything else being equal—she will suffer a loss of $3,000 per year in money income. The satisfaction that Alicia receives from teaching (her "psychic remuneration") may well outweigh the loss in money income and the drop in her material standard of living. The economist does not care which choice Alicia makes—the important thing is that she has considered all the costs and all the benefits and that she realizes what she is sacrificing when she chooses one alternative over the other.

If Alicia has learned her economics well, she will realize that the same kind of thinking that entered into her job-changing decision can also apply to broader social issues. For example, Alicia is a member of the city council. There is a large vacant lot near the central business district. The land belongs to the city, and the merchants in the center of town urge that it be developed as a public parking lot. This would enable more people to park near their stores, add to their revenues, and perhaps even put some more money into the city treasury. (The city might charge parking fees, for one thing, and the taxes paid to the city by the store owners might rise because of their added incomes.) However, many citizens are demanding that the lot be made into a small park that would help to beautify the city and provide a safe place for children to play. This would benefit everyone (at least potentially) and not just the merchants and their customers. It might even serve to attract more people to the town and benefit the merchants by providing them with more customers. Obviously, a trade-off will be involved. The *real* cost of using the lot for cars is the sacrifice of the park; the real cost of developing a park is the benefit that would have been derived from a parking area. What are the costs in each case? Who bears those costs? What would be the benefits in each case? Who derives those benefits? These are the questions the city council must try to answer.

The same kinds of decisions must be made on a national and even international scale. If our nation's resources are fully and efficiently employed and we want more housing, we can have it only by sacrificing something else that would be produced with the same resources. If we want to increase our domestic oil supply through offshore drilling, but we also want to avoid possible damage to the coastal environment, should we go ahead with the drilling or not? Should we have full employment and the high rate of inflation that seems to come with it? Or should we control inflation and bring about an increase in the unemployment rate? These and a thousand other questions must be decided by our society. Economic analysis cannot tell us what the answers should be, but it can tell us the relative costs and benefits of alternative courses of actions.

Now, if the economist's tool kit can be used in dealing with personal problems as well as with national issues, the college instructor ought to welcome the chance to teach the subject in a way that enables students to see the almost universal application that the discipline can have. Perhaps there is a massive "selling job" to be done to convince the economist that the principles of the discipline have potential application that he or she never dreamed of. As a beginning, the economics professors need to develop an awareness of other fields and what they contribute to an understanding of human society. They must realize that social problems do not exist in a vacuum—in real life there is probably no problem that is purely an economic problem, purely a political issue, or purely a sociological situation. And, since every current problem involves human beings, psychology must likewise be taken into account. This point has been made by one of the most honored members of the profession, Gunnar Myrdal, winner of the Nobel Memorial Prize in Economic Science. Myrdal recently stated that he was "distressed by the confusion among my colleagues." He criticized economists for keeping "together as a sect at the universities, making models built on assumptions they have not clarified and which have no relation at all with reality" (quoted in Gordon and Dawson, 1980, p. 4). Economics journalists have expressed similar concerns. Paul Lewis of the *New York Times* wrote: "The truth is that while economics textbooks may explain how individuals and countries ought to behave, they are a poor guide to how they will behave in practice. All sorts of other factors enter into the equation, on the natural (*sic*) level as well as the personal. The real springs of economic action often seemed buried in the mysteries of the psyche" (Lewis, 1976). (The word *natural* should probably be *national*.) Happily, the notion that marriage between economics and psychology—although still rare—can be successful is gaining acceptance, thanks to the pioneering work of George Katona, a scholar trained in both disciplines (Katona, 1975).

The economist who will take the time to become familiar with developments in other disciplines and to explore the relationships between those disciplines and economics will better serve the student and will create an exciting new image of the subject that has for so long been avoided by students who are aware of its dismal reputation. Economics instructors need to take note of changes that might be occurring in the student population, whether they be changes caused by the influx of older people, minorities, or whomever, and to ask themselves how the discipline of economics can be a practical instrument to help these students achieve their goals. This does not imply a sacrifice of the rigor that has characterized introductory economics in the colleges nor a departure from the goals that the majority of teaching economists have accepted as primary.

Finally, let us go one step further—a very long step. What is the goal of higher education and how can economics work with other disciplines to help meet that goal? We could fill this book with our attempts to determine *the* goal of higher education and how we might then achieve that goal. I shall be deliberately vague, then, and state that the goal is to produce educated people. It is unlikely that many would argue with that as a basic goal. We might argue endlessly, however, over what an "educated person" is. If I am not mistaken, the word *education* is related to or derived from the word *educe*—to draw out, or to evoke. It does not mean to cram in. It implies that teachers are supposed to help students to develop the potential that exists within them. Although some dictionaries state that to educate is to train, I should like to make a distinction between education and training. Rather than attempting to formulate precise definitions, let me illustrate with another hypothetical example.

Adam Maynard Smythe is a brilliant young man with a Ph.D. in agricultural economics. He is a competent econometrician. Adam has been hired by The Farmer's League to make a study of a sudden and unexpected rise in the price of corn. He designs a research project that thesis advisors would be proud of. He surveys the literature in the field and consults with colleagues. Considering every possible variable that he and his colleagues can think of, he gathers data with meticulous care. His sources are checked and rechecked for accuracy and reliability. The data are then subjected to highly sophisticated techniques of statistical analysis. Adam analyzes the results and concludes that there are several possible explanations for the rise in the price of corn, and he provides estimates of the relative importance of each. He carefully avoids asserting that there is *one* cause, and he makes sure to point out the probabilities of error in his own findings. The Farmers League gladly pays him his fee. The editor of an economics journal accepts his report for publication as an article. His colleagues praise him for a job well done and his college may even grant him a promotion.

But now Adam is at a dinner party with some friends. The conversation turns to the topic of crime, and someone cites the statistics regarding the increase in the crime rate in recent years. When someone wonders why this has occurred, Adam has *the* answer. Judges are too lenient, Adam insists. Now, Adam has done no research on the possible causes of the rise in crime rate. He is not a sociologist or criminologist. His assertion reflects only his own opinion, which is affected by his prejudices. In short, the scholarly attitude and techniques that Adam so carefully applied in his own discipline have been forgotten. Adam is not educated—he is trained. What can we do about this?

Although it will not be easy, we need to bring together representatives of all disciplines to attempt to identify the common elements and to develop an "intellectual tool kit" that has application to every discipline. Then, all students—as early in their college careers as possible—should be taught this tool kit. The kit might contain a survey of all the disciplines and how they relate to society as a whole and to one another. It should certainly include the scientific method and how that method can (or cannot) be applied to other subjects the student will confront both in school and beyond the college walls. Identifying and defining a problem, clearly defining key terms, objectively and thoroughly gathering data, formulating hypotheses, obtaining all points of view, recognizing assumptions, being able to distinguish between fact and opinion, understanding the concept "frame of reference"—these are but a few of the things all students should have in their intellectual tool kits. If well taught, the kit will apply not only to practically everything the student studies in the future—from biology to art history—but will serve that student for the rest of his or her life, as personal and social problems are confronted in the daily business of living.

Perhaps it is time for college teachers to learn from those at the precollege levels. "I'm not teaching history, I'm teaching children." "I'm concerned with the *whole* child." Hackneyed, but good. Some professors are not joking when they repeat that old witticism: "College would be great if it weren't for the students." Many are so microscopically committed to their disciplines that they lose sight of the fact that we are supposed to be serving human beings. Economics has much to offer in helping to develop the whole person, in aiding people to make life decisions, and in working cooperatively with other disciplines for the betterment of all people everywhere.

References

Allison, E. "Self-Paced Instruction: A Review." *The Journal of Economic Education,* 1975, *7* (1), 5-12.

Bach, G. L. "Student Learning in Basic Economics: An Evaluated Experimental Course." In K. G. Lumsden (Ed.), *New Developments in the Teaching of Economics.* Englewood Cliffs, N.J.: Prentice-Hall, 1967.

Becker, W. E., and others. "A Debate on Research Techniques in Economic Education." *The Journal of Economic Education,* 1976, *8* (1), 37-51.

Calderwood, J. D. "Career Education and Economic Awareness: The Interface." *Colorado Economic Issues,* August 1977, *1* (12), 1-2.

Center for Business and Economic Education, Empire State College. *Personalizing Instruction in Business and Economics.* Old Westbury, N.Y.: Long Island Regional Learning Center, Empire State College, 1976.

Dawson, G. G. *Research in Economic Education: A Bibliography.* New York: Center for Economic Education, New York University, 1969.

Dawson, G. G. "Pre-Service, In-Service, and Graduate Programs in Economic Education." *Review of Social Economy,* 1971, *24* (1), 63-78.

Dawson, G. G. "Research in the Teaching of College Economics: An Overview." *Eastern Economic Journal,* 1975, *2* (3), 185-191.

Dawson, G. G. "Special Report: An Overview of Research in the Teaching of College Economics." *The Journal of Economic Education,* 1976, *7* (2), 111-116.

Dawson, G. G. *A Summary of Research in Personalized, Individualized, and Self-Paced Instruction in College Economics.* Old Westbury, N.Y.: Center for Business and Economic Education, Empire State College, 1977.

Dawson, G. G., and Bernstein, I. *The Effectiveness of Introductory Economics Courses in High Schools and Colleges.* New York: Center for Economic Education, New York University, 1967.

Dopp, J. A. "A Survey of the Content and Structure of Principles of Economics Courses." Unpublished doctoral dissertation, Lehigh University, 1977.

Fels, R. *The Vanderbilt-JCEE Experimental Course in Elementary Economics.* Special Issue No. 2 of *The Journal of Economic Education,* Winter 1974.

Froman, L. A. "Graduate Students in Economics, 1904-1940." *American Economic Review,* December 1942.

Gordon, S. D., and Dawson, G. G. *Introductory Economics.* (4th ed.) Lexington, Mass.: Heath, 1980.

Hansen, W. L., and others. *A Framework for Teaching Economics: Basic Concepts.* New York: Joint Council on Economic Education, 1977.

Horton, R. V., and Weidenaar, D. J. *The Goals of Economics Education: A Delphi-Like Inquiry.* Paper No. 462C. West Lafayette, Ind.: Institute for Research in the Behavioral, Economic, and Management Sciences, Purdue University, 1974.

Horton, R. V., and Weidenaar, D. J. "Wherefore Economic Education?" *The Journal of Economic Education,* 1975, *7* (1), 40-44.

Katona, G. *Psychological Economics.* New York: Elsevier, 1975.

Leftwich, R. H., and Sharp, A. M. *Syllabus for an "Issues Approach" to Teaching Economic Principles.* Special Issue No. 1 of *The Journal of Economic Education,* Winter 1974.

Lekachman, R. *Economists at Bay: Why the Experts Will Never Solve Your Problems.* New York: McGraw-Hill, 1976.

Lewis, D. R., and others. *Educational Games and Simulations in Economics.* New York: Joint Council on Economic Education, 1974.

Lewis, P. "Keynes and Freud Meet In the Free Market." *The New York Times,* November 21, 1976.

Maher, J. E. *What is Economics?* New York: Wiley, 1969.

Monson, T. D. "Some Aspects of Undergraduate Economics Programs in Liberal Arts Colleges, Ph.D. Granting Universities, and Former State Colleges." Unpublished paper. Houghton: School of Business and Engineering Administration, Michigan Technological University, 1977.

National Task Force on Economic Education. *Economic Education in the Schools.* New York: Committee for Economic Development, 1961.

Rodin, M., and Rodin, B. "Student Evaluations of Teachers." *Science,* 1972, *177,* 1164-1166.

Saunders, P. "The Lasting Effectiveness of Introductory Economics Courses." Unpublished paper. Final Report, NSF Grant GY7208. Bloomington: Indiana University, 1973.

Saunders, P. "Experimental Course Development in Introductory Economics at Indiana University." Special Issue No. 4 of *The Journal of Economic Education,* Fall 1977.

Saunders, P., and Welsh, A. L. "The Hybrid TUCE: Origin, Data, and Limitations." *The Journal of Economic Education,* 1975, *7* (1), 13-19.

Soper, J. C. "Soft Research on a Hard Subject: Student Evaluations Reconsidered." *The Journal of Economic Education,* 1973, *5* (1), 22-26.

Stigler, G. J. "Elementary Economic Education." *American Economic Review,* 1963, *53,* 653-659.

Stigler, G. J. "The Case, if Any, for Economic Education." *The Journal of Economic Education,* 1970, *1* (2), 77-84.

Townshend-Zellner, N. "A New Look at the High School Economics Texts." *The Journal of Economic Education,* 1970, *2* (1), 63-68.

Tuckman, B., and Tuckman, H. "Toward a More Effective Economic Principles Class: The Florida State University Experience." Special Issue No. 3 of *The Journal of Economic Education,* Spring 1975.

Welsh, A. L. (Ed.). *Research Papers in Economic Education.* New York: Joint Council on Economic Education, 1972.

Whitney, S. N. "Measuring the Success of the Elementary Course." *American Economic Review,* March 1960, pp. 159-169.

Wolfe, A. B. "Undergraduate Teaching of Economics." *American Economic Review: Supplement,* May 1946, pp. 848-852.

20

Richard D. Mann

Psychology

In this essay I hope to offer an encompassing vision of psychology and its curriculum. And, in so doing, I hope not only to validate our teaching as it stands today but to challenge us all to reach toward a much needed synthesis of the field, one that will guide our work in the classroom and on the curriculum committee. I share with many of my fellow psychologists moments of feeling that the field is just too big, too heterogeneous, but I always end up sensing that my task as a teacher is made richer and more rewarding by the field's enormous range. Certainly, the benefits for students and the larger society that flow from this complex enterprise need to be explored. It seems to me that the challenge we face in constructing an adequate set of goals and procedures for our teaching is essentially the challenge of placing our work in an appropriately large and meaningful context. This leads me to the four basic, orienting theses of this chapter:

1. We should take as large and complex a view of psychology as possible, creating as we do a paradigm for understanding the diverse elements of the field and how they fit together to make one loosely integrated domain. Psychology's origins and essential goals reflect not only the quest for knowledge through scientific inquiry but also the urge to heal and be of service, to become more self-aware, and to grow in wisdom and understanding.
2. It is important to keep in mind that psychology shares its goals with many neighboring fields and many age-old traditions. Hence the broadest view of psychology would emphasize not only its unique methods, findings, and concepts but also its similarities and indebtedness to a wide range of human efforts.
3. We should be aware that students differ greatly as to why they approach the field,

how they learn best, and what they intend to do with what they learn. If, as seems to be the case, it is increasingly inappropriate to view our students only or even primarily as potential graduate students or psychologists in our own mold, the task of finding appropriately diverse goals and strategies becomes particularly urgent.

4. Finally, we should not overlook the teacher's own development as a scientist-scholar, as an educator, and, especially, as a total human being. That teaching which facilitates the teacher's own maturation across a wide range of dimensions profits the teacher and the students and the field.

The Domain of Psychology

To develop the four theses just cited, it is necessary first to bring some order to the multiplicity of psychology's activities and underlying goals. The schema in Figure 1

Figure 1. Three Basic Aspects of Psychology

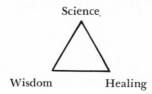

Science

Wisdom   Healing

has helped me to define three basic aspects of this complex field—namely, psychology as a science, psychology as a healing profession, and psychology as one of the liberal arts, a contemporary form of the ancient search for wisdom, meaning, and beauty. I see no necessary hierarchy among them, but at the risk of suggesting one I have placed science at the vertex of the triangle. We can acknowledge that what differentiates psychology from its predecessors and neighboring fields is its distinctive emphasis on the scientific study of human behavior and experience. But to know and teach a field one needs to grasp more than what makes it distinctive. The insidious notion that fields are in competition with one another for funds, students, and so on leads more to narrow self-advertising than to self-portraits that reveal how much the various fields have in common.

The three aspects of psychology represented in the diagram do not reduce into each other. One can know and live by more than can be attested by the science of one's time; one can serve and heal persons in need by means of human resources not as yet captured by the methods of research; and one can scrutinize through the methods of science the apparent truths and cures of the centuries and find compelling reason to modify one's views or one's healing technique in the light of the evidence. The paths of intuition, rational inquiry, and effective and selfless service all yield their distinctive gains, and if the gains cannot be reconciled, there seems to be no *a priori* reason for not pursuing each path to its unique end.

It is important to recognize that these three aspects of psychology are not mutually exclusive. In fact, three of psychology's most interesting missions lie somewhere between the points of the triangle in Figure 1. Figure 2 amends the diagram to include these intermediate orientations. Somewhere between psychology as a pure science and psychology as a healing profession exists the burgeoning domain of applied psychology, where the interplay of scientific method and client- or patient-defined problems has led to a host of new techniques, findings, and occupational roles. Psychology shares with a number of other disciplines and traditions the goal of facilitating human growth, and this

Figure 2. The Six Orientations of Psychology

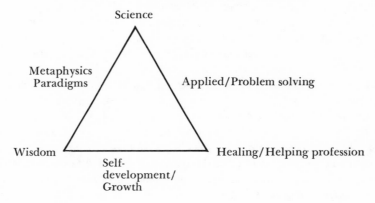

process of facilitating self-awareness and self-actualization seems to engage the techniques and insights of healers, priests, artists, seers, and helpful relatives, to name but a few. The human growth movement is certainly not the exclusive domain of psychology. Through participation in it, however, psychology now seems more open to the teachings of philosophical, artistic, and religious traditions. Some of these teachings concerning how to live a more satisfying, effective life are derived from centuries of trial and error. But other teachings and insights merge back into science. All form part of the evolving metaphysics of our age. New paradigms, new efforts to rethink how we know and what we must assume if we are not to gloss over the challenging new findings of science itself—these are also part of psychology's mission.

Nowhere is there more intense pressure to pursue and to coordinate the various aspects of psychology than in the college classroom. The students, both in their collective diversity and in their individual complexity, press upon the teacher to help them make gains with respect to virtually every aspect of psychology. The teacher must both teach and learn whatever will be useful to the students and to his or her own development. One operating assumption of this chapter is that the complexity of this task will mount as psychology's identity comes to rest less upon its status as science and more equally upon its status as a helping profession and as a liberal art and carrier of human wisdom. A second assumption is that the shifting nature of students' expectations and needs will contribute to the process of diversification. It is time now to attempt a more systematic inquiry into how the teaching of psychology can best proceed for each of the six unique aspects of the field just outlined.

Teaching the Six Orientations

The six orientations shown in Figure 2—psychology as (1) a science, (2) an applied, problem-solving field, (3) a helping profession, (4) a part of the human potential movement, (5) a liberal art and repository of wisdom, and (6) a branch of metaphysics, epistemology, and ontology—manifest themselves in the various motives that impel students toward psychology in the first place. But what do the students find when they arrive? How does each aspect of psychology fit into the field's overall curriculum? And where are the tensions and opportunities for curricular change?

Psychology as a Science. The allure of psychology as a science for prospective students derives in part from the intrinsic interest aroused by the thought of studying people and in part from the prestige and appeal of science itself. To the beginner, the scientific approach holds out the possibility of dealing rationally with subjects that are often clouded by prejudice, dogma, and unfounded opinion. One might actually discover something new about matters ordinarily taken for granted. The prospects of a stable body of empirical knowledge and increased control over human behavior stir the interest of many students.

Psychology has tended to link its teaching, especially its undergraduate teaching, to its mission as a science. Its vigorous programs of research and theory-building have shaped the curriculum. The core courses have been designed (1) to prepare some students, preferably the best ones, to go on in the field and (2) to educate the future citizenry to be intelligent consumers and firm supporters of psychology's scientific activities. The theories, the methods, and the findings of the field are contrasted favorably with the "armchair," nonempirical, nonreplicable, and value-laden contributions of psychology's predecessors and neighboring fields of inquiry. In terms of Kolb's analysis of learning styles (see Kolb's chapter in Part One of this volume), the undergraduate curriculum seems best suited to faculty and students with the abilities of the assimilator and the converger. These two share a preference for an abstract, depersonalized approach to psychology and a tendency to prefer dealing with concepts and things to dealing with people. One cumulative effect of the past decades of teaching has been the creation of a large, committed, and competent cadre of psychologist-scientists who continue to do a very effective job of conveying the rationale and substance of all this research activity to successive waves of students.

Many of the new influences on the teaching of psychology can only be made clear after we have finished reviewing the other aspects of psychology. But three points can be made before we move on. One concerns the degree of success, in its own terms, of psychology as a science; the second concerns the national climate of support for basic research; and the third concerns the diminishing viability of students' aspirations to pursue a purely academic, research-oriented career.

Much of the charm and forgivable excess of psychology as a young science derived from the heady optimism about science itself. The successes in the older sciences seemed to offer models for psychology's eventual achievement: rigor of method, parsimony of theory, prediction, control, and all the rest. So much that seemed vague or entanglingly complex in prior commentary on the human condition could now be cut loose as untestable or nonoperational.

The era of the Big Theory came and went. The rush of enthusiasm that in the near future it could all be boiled down to a few explanatory concepts or a few functional relationships was deflated as the theories became more cumbersome than elegant and the findings more special than general. The big theories were followed by the hot topics and the latest key independent variables, and they too seem to have lost their appeal. Psychology has settled in for the long haul, and middle-range theories and slowly expanding research programs now appear more appropriate.

The climate of support for pure, theory-oriented research has diminished. The granting agencies need to show results and hence expect results, and the promising young field has found, not unlike any promising young individual, that when it is time to "go out and find some work" the needs and problems of those controlling the funds tend to replace the dreams and programs of the one who is seeking to be funded. At the same time, and for related reasons, the field is becoming less open to new, would-be researchers and academics. The clogged-up tenure ranks and the changing patterns of support make "going on in the field" a less compelling option.

One important repercussion of these changes is that it is becoming increasingly inappropriate for the teacher to design the curriculum and the evaluative procedures as if their major function were preparation and gate-keeping for a career in psychology as a science. Put more positively, the challenge exists to frame a new curriculum for a broad student constituency, a curriculum that presents in their most general framework both the substance and the procedures of this crucial aspect of the field.

Psychology as an Applied Field. There was a time, not long ago either, when psychology shared the older sciences' internal boundary dividing theoretical work or theory-testing research from applied work, the task of technology or engineering. Thus, researchers might well spurn a project that seemed too applied. But the times have changed. Now, and increasingly, major segments of the field find their research originating in and aimed toward a particular set of questions, problems, or concerns determined by the client or consumer of the research activity.

The game of creating an applied cover story for carrying out basic research is being foiled more and more by the granting agencies in Washington and the various client systems. Those dispensers of scarce research funds are learning how to recognize a real willingness to take the problem as given and solve it as best one can. The field of applied psychology is thus an increasingly explicit accommodation to the field's continuing need for work. The great skill of this breed of psychologists lies in overcoming the split between psychology as a growing young science and the "real-world" concerns of those who turn to psychology for useful answers.

The applied psychologists have always been there, working away in industry, school systems, the military, and so forth. What is changing is the impact these psychologists are having on the teaching of psychology in undergraduate programs, schools of education and business, and the health fields. They are able to show the students how psychology can be useful, how it turns the most appropriate (but not necessarily the most elegant) research design to the tasks of problem solving and solution evaluation. For some, this news comes as a great surprise, a pleasant alternative to the clever but dubiously relevant studies that tend to proliferate shortly before a hot topic cools to the point where everyone abandons it altogether. There seem to be real skills and, connected to them, real jobs associated with psychology as an applied, problem-solving science. Guided, but only when helpfully so, by the concepts and techniques of the purer wing of the field, the applied psychologist or "human engineer" serves as a model for the students who wonder whether their college work has any practical import.

The content of the courses, from sensory perception to organizational psychology, from human performance to experimental clinical and community psychology, all reveal this new center of gravity—psychology as an applied field. In Kolb's terms, the deductive skills and the associated style of active experimentation are more and more reflected in the curriculum of psychology.

Psychology as a Helping Profession. Helping and healing people are activities that are far more on students' minds as they approach psychology than studying people or predicting and controlling their behavior. In fact, only the complex layering of course prerequisites, the pressure of internal distribution requirements, and the use of Graduate Record Examinations as screening devices prevent an awkward oversubscription in clinically oriented psychology courses. How has this disjunction between the students' interests and the departments' offerings come about?

We live not so many decades removed from the era when the great internal debate of one department after another was over whether or not to include the material of clinical psychology in the teaching, especially the undergraduate teaching, of psychology.

These great, rancorous struggles hinged partly on the then current view of psychology's sole mission as pure science. But other factors were, and still are, at play. There has always been considerable suspicion about why students wanted to know about all this. Were students really only interested in learning about themselves? If so, did they have the proper academic interest in the material? And in any case, what would prevent the worst nightmare—an army of young would-be helpers going around without guidance, damaging themselves and others with their newfound insights and therapeutic formulas? It has often been concluded that it would be better to reserve this material for graduate training. But this cautious view fails to recognize students' intense desire to use their undergraduate education to explore their future roles in the adult, occupational world. The appeal of all the clinical and applied courses is testimony, I would argue, to the students' desire to explore the possibility of "working with people" in some capacity. The humanitarian urge of which White writes so understandingly in his chapter flows directly into fantasies of helping to relieve some part of the world's pain, disability, or need. The prospect of neither exploiting people nor "merely" studying them has great appeal. One can imagine doing something useful, something concrete and immediate.

This ground swell of student motivation creates more than a few difficulties for the teaching of psychology. We may note, in passing, that it might necessitate the addition of clinically trained faculty to departments with a primary interest in graduate teaching and research productivity. But this is a minor concern compared with the inherent difficulty of creating an effective teaching and learning situation in this area. Quite simply, clinical psychology cannot be learned from books. Recognition of the human reality behind the diagnostic, psychopathological terminology and knowledge of what would help transfer very inefficiently from the textbook to the student's deepest layers of empathy and instinct. We are confronted with a breakdown in the expert model. The teacher's assignment extends beyond the task of transferring information to helping students become aware of the skills and insights required for helping others.

Two kinds of classroom situations, each with its own special sort of teacher, have emerged as responses to this problem. In one the teacher emerges as the hero, as the exemplar, and in the other the teacher becomes the facilitator of the student's own process of gaining experience, finding inner resources, and surviving the inevitable moments of confusion and inadequacy. The first, when effective, permits the students to learn by identifying with the teacher's experience. The stream of anecdotes, the evidence of mastery via humor and compassion, merge with documented moments of clinical effectiveness. The task slowly comes within range. The student's admiration of the teacher's insightfulness or effectiveness becomes one vehicle for imagining what it would be like to become a healer. Students learn far more than the gradable course material, and, in fact, some students are left with a great bitterness over the disparity between what they feel they learned and what they "got" in terms of grades. Be that as it may, this first sort of classroom brings to the surface a truth that is less readily appreciated in classrooms focusing on psychology as a science, namely this: What is at stake is far more than the knowledge of the teacher. The teacher's usefulness in the construction of an ego ideal is at stake, and each student's prior development will give this process a unique quality. One will seek and find an exemplar of intelligence in the service of truth, one an exemplar of enthusiasm and buoyancy, and another an exemplar of the tender-but-tough-enough healer found in their dreams of one possible occupational life.

The second sort of classroom, the one that finds the teacher functioning primarily as facilitator, responds to the students' felt and actual need for direct experience. The students want to see for themselves, to put the concepts they have learned to the test.

The challenge for the teacher is how to find situations in which students can learn but not get in over their heads, or do more harm than good. Fortunately for both teachers and students, there are many institutions, agencies, and projects for which the major need, as they perceive it, is precisely the kind of direct, "human" contacts one might expect of novice students under proper supervision. One such structure, Project Outreach at the University of Michigan, was born when a former Brandeis student reminisced that she had learned more from her experience of working one-to-one with "her" patient for a year than in all her other courses. Project Outreach has created a diverse assembly of projects, some in mental hospitals, some in the community agencies, and some within the university setting. But common to them all is a commitment to what has come to be called *experiential education.* We will return to this course in our later discussion.

   Psychology as a Facilitator of Self-Development. Some students arrive at the classroom sensing that acquiring more knowledge or mastering yet another elaborate conceptual scheme may prepare them for the exam but not even begin to bring about the deeper changes that they know they need to become more effective, mature, and content. They arrive wanting to change, and fearing it; courting change, and resisting it. And what do they find?

   They find, typically, a curriculum that values and promotes certain kinds of change but ignores or decries certain others. Changes in the direction of a rational, abstract, depersonalized style of thinking about human affairs are fine. What is not so fine is the effort to make explicit, and even deliberate, changes in personal maturity, self-esteem, self-control, risk-taking, and the like. As Torbert's commentary in this volume makes clear, it is one of the supreme ironies of academic life, no less than of the larger culture that it reflects, that there is so much mystification and so little inquiry when it comes to the participants themselves and their relations with one another.

   Why should this be so? Many answers suggest themselves. There is in academia a deep tradition of what Adorno and his colleagues (1950) called *anti-introception,* which emerges to defend a largely externalized model of how and what to learn. Studying oneself, in this view, seems to run counter to the goals of objectivity, of seemliness, and of privacy. It seems to open the way for narcissism, for incomparability of performances, and for subjective and incontrovertible assessments of a student's success. There are important issues of authority and expertise raised here and, I suspect, a not unrealistic fear that the demands of teaching will overrun the time and psychic energy alloted to it by most faculty.

   Teaching and learning are difficult enough when confined to the realm of abilities and mastery, performance and evaluation. But education for actual, personal change necessarily raises the even more difficult issue of integration, of synthesis. The capacity to connect the outer learning with the inner process of maturation is at the heart of what Kolb calls *experiential education.* All the elements can be mastered, and students (or teachers) can demonstrate that mastery in such discrete forms as exams or lectures, but does their experience change? Is there any greater capacity for new perceptions and thoughts outside the training and testing situation?

   One interesting implication of Weathersby's study, reported in this book, of how differently students use their education is that apparently any curriculum can be used as the medium for growth. There is no need to have a course called Growth. The crux of the matter is how the student and the institution conspire to define what is happening. But can more than the most highly developed students be assisted to see the growth issues so easily submerged in education and work? Many of the people who have answered yes to this have developed explicit programs and training contexts. Some are located inside the usual course structure; more are at the periphery, in dormitories, counseling centers, and campus ministries; and still more are outside traditional academia altogether, in the world of adult education and the movement for human potential. The list of innovative efforts, mainly developed outside the academic perimeter, is very long: T-groups, personal growth labs, body awareness labs, and topical seminars on racism, sexism, and assertiveness, to name but a few.

It may be useful to place the various efforts to facilitate personal development in a context both wide and deep enough to suggest the magnitude of the teaching task. Each effort tends to combine (1) a form, a technique, or a discipline, (2) an underlying vision of human or transhuman potentiality, and (3) an awareness of how one's own development affects others. This latter appeal to experience for testing and expanding what one has learned provides a check to the much-feared drift into narcissistic self-absorption. Whether one returns as healer or teacher more centered in oneself, and thus more able to hear and serve others, or whether one returns to the flow of everyday life with kin, friends, colleagues, and strangers, the results of personal growth are realized in the larger context of one's life.

At the level of technique, it is clear that psychology's efforts to develop human potential draw upon rich traditions. Every practical philosophy, every religious, artistic, and martial tradition, has evolved a set of forms that are directed toward personal transformation. Prayer, fasting, meditation, contemplation; cultivation of the rational, logical mind and curbing the mind's emotional sense-bound ways; expressiveness, spontaneity, vigor—what has not been tried in the world's long history? Each form is a tribute to the appeal, for some, of lifelong learning, the drive to become consciously aware of what one seeks and what works best, at least for oneself. Any technique, however, even the traditional academic technique, can gradually lose its connection with the vision of human potential that originally suggested that experience as a key element in human development. And thus techniques change. Free association, mandala drawing, "hot seat" work—all the major therapeutic innovations of this century are expressions of what Freud, Jung, Perls, and others sensed to be reachable by means of the technique. Similarly, the gradual broadening of technique to include such traditional forms as meditation, martial arts, dancing, and chanting betokens a parallel broadening of the goals of education among teachers and students alike.

Psychology as Human Wisdom. What, then, is the irreducible core of human motive, human potential, or human nature? Psychology may affect a hurried indifference to such basic questions, but willy-nilly its answers to these and other such enduring questions are an essential element of what the field teaches its students. The issues here concern metaphor and vision, assumptions and values. Psychology has become one of our culture's oracles. It functions within the liberal arts mandate of the university to collect, sustain, and enliven the vast diversity of basic questions and basic answers that constitute the culture's source of wisdom.

Perhaps what human life boils down to is seeking pleasure and avoiding pain. Some schools of philosophy, and later, schools of psychology, have found this to be the core. Other schools avow that, yes, this may be how it is in ordinary life, but there is more. What more? Some psychologists, but more philosophers, artists, or monks, find the essence of human nature in some higher, even nonmaterial domain. For Aristotle this was the intellect, for poets like Rabindranath Tagore and St. John of the Cross, the human yearning for merger with the Absolute or the Beloved, and for Meister Eckhart and Jung after him, the Self. Still others find the core of human nature in drives, instinctual tendencies of eros and thanatos, and dramas of survival and competition.

We have entered the domain where proof yields to predilection. It is an act of will to choose an assumption system, and how shall one choose, among what alternatives? The world of science, at least psychology as science, is largely the domain of analysis, especially analysis of the relationships between various causes and effects. It asks how we can measure better, predict better. But the domain of wisdom is far more that of synthesis. It inquires into the ground or basis of all this diversity. This apprehension of an overarching reality takes two forms. One form, the unprovable intuition, the "self-evident truth" says, for example: "The deepest human fear is anxiety over one's existence" or "All human beings contain a spark of the divine flame." The other form, the statement that assigns value, says: "This is a possibility," this life, this moment, the sum of all manifest possibilities or actualities, is worth contemplating. Existence itself, in all its profusion, is worth contemplating, appreciating, opening oneself to. Why? Because in that way one can have an experience of ordered aliveness, an intuitive appreciation of beauty and of purpose, which are the bases of real wisdom.

It may be useful to recall various familiar forms of teaching in this domain. There is a form of teaching that approaches the communication of wisdom through the exchange of summary formulations, as in philosophy or humanistic psychology, or through the more oblique means of sharing works of art and literature. William James' writing on the value of saints was in part a tribute to the importance of teaching by example. And there is another tradition in which the highest form of teaching is silence. What unites all such forms is a sense that this sort of teaching would be better described as the awakening of inner understanding and acknowledgment of what one already knows than as the acquisition of new ideas. Teaching, as Socrates, the Buddha, and saints and monks all around the globe have demonstrated, can assume a prior fullness, even an essential divinity, on the part of both teacher and student. The metaphors that try, in vain, to capture this aspect of teaching reflect the effort of preparation for the ultimately effortless experience of receiving inner illumination or grace.

Our recurrent theme in all such commentaries on wisdom is captured by the phrase "going beyond the mind." Another sort of knowing is being hinted at here, not sense experience and not mere rationality. As Thomas Aquinas and Aristotle saw it, and as much of Buddhist and Hindu psychology has always seen it, beyond the senses and the mind lies the intellect, the *buddhi,* the source of intuition and of what Meister Eckhart called divine knowledge. And over and over again the fruit of this form of insight centers around being or pure consciousness, which is itself formless and yet everything. The esthetic experience, the sudden moment of compassion and love, the inescapable sense of the sacred, in this view, are all indirect but crucial avenues by which we can come to affirm the basic wisdom that we already knew but had forgotten.

The recognition that psychology is inevitably part of this culture's storehouse of wisdom would be reflected not necessarily in some new and separate addition to the curriculum, such as "The Wisdom of Psychology," but in an appreciation of psychology's power to enhance or diminish our view of human existence, and especially our own part in this totality. Students, in this era of alertness to unannounced side effects, not only need to learn the explicit facts, theories, and techniques of the field but also need to be aware of what is gained and what is lost as one enters any system of metaphor, any vision of human life. If humans are consistently viewed through mechanistic metaphors, whether computers, automatons, or black boxes, how will they view employees, their children, and themselves? If a tragic view of human potential, rooted in a persistent assumption about the inevitability of human misery, replaces other assumptions about human fate, how will this affect, for example, the conduct of therapy or the agenda of personal development?

What is needed, for many reasons, is a clearer, franker, and more dialogue-inviting presentation of psychology's many key metaphors and assumptions. (See, for example, Tart, 1975.) This takes us back to our original concern with psychology as a science. Even beyond the possibility that psychology at times entertains impoverished images of human life, there is a strong possibility that even its scientific mission is entangled in its commitment to a particular paradigm of reality. To explore the adequacy of that paradigm is the constant task of the aspect of psychology closest to the traditional domains of metaphysics and epistemology.

Psychology as Metaphysics. The place where the enduring but shifting currents of human understanding most powerfully affect, and are affected by, the evolving science of the age is the realm of paradigm. There was a time when the best minds knew there were no such things as meteors falling from the sky simply because in the scheme of things they held dear such things just could not happen. The fundamental perspective of one age can seem increasingly to be a hindrance, rather than a help, in forming a coherent picture from the available knowledge. There are those who argue that now is such a time, and from several quarters it appears that the paradigm that has sustained most of psychology for most of its history is becoming just such a hindrance.

Key tenets of the classical paradigm in physical science have been revised in the light of evidence suggesting relative rather than absolute status for space and time and quantum field theory's radical revision of the subject-object relationship. The limits within which the intertwined assumptions of the entire Newtonian, Cartesian picture of reality seem to work well are becoming more and more evident. As physicist David Bohm has pointed out, the assumptions of atomism or even of field theory presume distinct and separate points and moments whose interrelations must be local—that is, between contiguous elements. This ascription of fundamental reality either to the particle moving across space or to the field transmitting force through space underlies a theory that fits the data in many areas but is distinctly inappropriate in the area of quantum physics. Only by changing one's assumption system, Bohm (1976) argues, and by ascribing fundamental reality to the whole can a more adequate picture be formed. It is the part, from this view, that is the abstraction, a particularization of the totality by means of specifiable conditions of observations. All parts interpenetrate each other, and each part contains information about the whole.

In philosophy, this search for a new, more adequate paradigm has addressed the very same assumptions of the Cartesian order. The monadic, self-enclosed atom of society, the person, uncontactable and isolated within an individualistic perspective, split irrevocably into mind and body—this Cartesian construct has seemed less and less satisfactory as the basis for a scientific study of human beings. As Schroeder (1979) points out, the writings of Husserl, Hegel, Heidegger, and Sartre are all part of the search for a new paradigm, one that makes room for larger structures within which individuals and relations emerge. And, as well, the new paradigm would join quantum field theory in no longer ascribing to the subject-object distinction its familiar, central place in the process of knowing. Rather, acting, disturbing the total field, and a constant process of self-expression become central to viewing the full transaction of self and other.

These and similar revisions of the paradigms of physics and philosophy offer psychology a chance to see the limits of its own paradigms. What questions have remained closed because they seemed to stray from the only viable paradigm of the time, and what questions would emerge (or re-emerge) if the paradigm shifted? If it were not necessary to view the individual as the atomic building block, would exploration of such seemingly impossible phenomena as intuitive, direct knowledge by one person of another's experience, not mediated by known sensory channels, emerge from the realm of unaskable questions? If physicists can speculate about time flowing both forward and back, could psychology begin to explore precognitive phenomena again?

One psychologist who is exploring such questions, in the light of these new paradigms and data, is Carl Pribram (1978), neurophysiologist and student of brain and behavior for four decades. The fact that he and David Bohm have focused upon the mathematics as well as the instrumentation of holography in their effort to capture the necessary new vision of part-whole relations is instructive. The hologram, a distinctly un-Cartesian prototype for reality, focuses our attention on how the totality of things informs each part, and we find ourselves in the realm of infinite series, not finite, and continuous processes, not discrete. Before long, the emergent paradigm begins to cast doubt on the whole effort of analyzing particles, tracing effect back to cause, and generally creating the fragmented world so inherent in our system of basic assumptions.

William Perry's subtle and convincing narrative, in this volume, of the student's journey into adulthood is no less apt as an account of psychology's own development. How do we know what we say we know? Does the whole edifice crumble, as so many young students fear about their own belief structure, if it turns out that we are forever rediscovering our own selves when we thought we were discovering something Out There? The delicate balance of commitment and tentativeness, the spirit of openness, and the search for an inclusive but manageable identity all play a part in the development of the field, the teacher, and the student of psychology. If all these evolving identities are not to be foreclosed and rigidified, the classroom must be an arena where all the basic assumptions by which we live find respect. And, as Perry notes, to honor one's own as well as each other person's assumptions and wisdom it is necessary to grasp the paradox of sustaining a commitment to absolutes by means of symbols that are necessarily incomplete, relativistic, and open to change.

Curricular Goals and Obstacles to Their Attainment

We are now in a position to formulate a few basic goals for the psychology curriculum and to explore some problems and potential solutions that might be expected should these goals be pursued. One primary goal, I would argue, is to maximize the mutual understanding and interaction between the various aspects of the field—for the sake of the field, its practitioners, and the whole body of students coming through its classrooms. A corollary goal, which alerts us to slightly different indexes of success or failure, would be to seek to facilitate maximum convergence of interest between students and faculty. It would be useful to go on to include even larger possibilities of convergence, extending out into the society at large, but I will not pursue this point.

The vision I embrace is of a field that, rather than rejecting or ignoring elements that do not fit one or another definition of the field, encompasses instead all the elements needed for the next surge of educational creativity. Our review of the six aspects of psychology suggests that the field falls short of this vision. We find not synthesis but boundaries, splits among psychologists that effectively keep the curriculum from fostering this search for unity across the whole field. Why is this so?

Several factors underlying the field's disunity can be discussed in terms of the sixfold scheme of psychology's complex identity. We can recognize a series of either-or's, a series of fractures that cause psychologists to feel they have to choose sides, preserve the purity of their side, and drive the other version from the fold. We can find evidence of a distinctly uncomfortable relationship between neighboring aspects, a tension caused by the inclination to say "This far and no farther" with respect to one's own area of psychology. And we may find that some difficulties in teaching across the entire range of psychology derive from difficulties in incorporating into one's teaching style all the diverse demands on the teacher's identity that are entailed by the diverse aspects of the field.

The triangular diagram of psychology's six aspects (see Figure 2) provides one potentially useful way to capture the major schisms within the field. The approaches closest to psychology as a science tend to value rationality over intuition, and objectivity over personal engagement and self-awareness. The approaches closest to psychology as a healing profession tend to define the work of the field in terms of concrete problem solving involving sequences of deductive reasoning and trial-and-error risk-taking, as opposed to the more abstract, inductive, and theory-building agenda of both psychology as a pure science and psychology as facilitator of human wisdom. Finally, the approaches closest to psychology's function of conveying and furthering wisdom all strike a unique stance with respect to the self. Unlike the scientific and healing orientations, which focus upon people as objects of study or treatment, the orientations of growth, wisdom, and epistemology give far greater attention to the self, to paradoxical issues of will and receptivity, to participation in a context of self-awareness and reflection. It is this last split that most clearly differentiates between those activities valued or tolerated within the academic context and those ignored or excluded. The tilt toward the externalizing, objectifying, and distancing modes of work in psychology is such that those on the other side seem to be something else, some other category of inquiry. Moreover, each of the three splits is potentially the occasion for two truly unhelpful dynamisms within the field: (1) narrow specialization and self-isolation within an aspect of the field and (2) intrusion across boundaries to disrupt other styles of work by imposing standards of competence and importance that are appropriate only within one's own perspective.

Ignorance of each others' work or unhelpful intrusions are understandable enough when the two aspects are far apart from each other, when the psychologists differ on just about every issue of style and agenda, but what about relations between neighboring aspects of the field? It is here, I would argue, that the current reality is often most troubled and yet the most ready for curricular change. Specialists in each aspect of the field, for reasons found in similar sectarian struggles in politics and religion, tend to be more preoccupied with their immediate boundaries than with distant ones. Before elaborating on this situation, I should emphasize that I am depicting the obstacles to integration here, not drawing a full picture of how each aspect invariably impinges on each other. There are many specialists whose relations with other parts of the field, near and far, are inclusive, respectful, and collaborative. Our present focus is on the disunifying trends within the field.

Psychology as a pure science has certainly had its day of disdaining to admit applied psychology into the inner sanctum of the field, but today this boundary seems relatively peaceful. The constant interplay of abstract or inductive with concrete or deductive approaches, assuming an unwavering preference for impersonal and rational modes of inquiry, is now a central feature of psychology's scientific strategy. The boundary between applied and clinical or helping aspects of the field raises the crucial issue of intuitive, personal engagement. Here we begin to pick up the first inkling of the "This-far-and-no-farther" dynamism. Applied psychology is still scientific, still objective, but to move beyond is to jeopardize one's inclusion in the field, at least in the high-status wing of the field. The price of inclusion for the helping profession is reflected in the demand for a research-oriented doctoral dissertation, for a highly conceptual approach to psychopathology and therapy, and for evidence of a "cognitive component" (by which is meant a scientific component) to experiential education. The intuitive, relationship-developing mode of learning is always on the verge of being defined as extracurricular.

Psychology as a helping profession has been struggling over its place in the curriculum for quite a while, and perhaps this accounts for its relations with its neighbor on the other flank, psychology as self-development. Clinical psychologists are notoriously wary of offering a curriculum with which students may address their own needs to resolve personal problems and explore methods aimed at their personal growth. "This far and no farther" is the understandable dictum of a subfield caught between two powerful but seemingly divergent pressures, one for scientific inquiry and the other for self-awareness.

For self-development approaches, the price of even provisional inclusion is that they focus intently on the *method* of whatever change they generate, on descriptions and analyses of the process of change, but leave as extracurricular concerns the goals of change or the personal content of any heightened self-awareness. The struggle to keep even personal growth objectified, quantified, and noncommittal on controversial issues of values underlying change is a struggle to keep intact what I have called the major boundary of academic psychology. It is all right to discuss experience and the processes of change, but value issues and insights into the goals that integrate and give meaning to these processes are defined as being beyond the purpose of the curriculum. No one wants to get into "trips," pressure, or dogma, but, in avoiding these obviously disagreeable possibilities, all too often the path to wisdom is blocked by precisely the naive relativism or multiplicity of which Perry writes in this volume. It is a relativism designed to avoid controversy and commitment.

The boundary between psychology as a liberal art and carrier of wisdom and the realm of metaphysics and paradigm is another boundary full of tension. Breaking these boundaries involves moving beyond knowing "because I just know," beyond the reliance on authority and aphorism, and back to tentativeness and finally, at science, back to evidence. It involves trying one's best to find models and conceptual schemes with which to meet the results of empirical operations halfway. And it also involves a return to the world of successful or unsuccessful predictions, interventions, and applications.

I would argue that the boundaries drawn between the various aspects of psychology block the way to a fully integrated field. There are differences among aspects of the field, and undoubtedly people will find their most comfortable and creative niches. But when it comes to teaching, to conveying the value and the content of areas outside one's special niche, many difficulties do arise. In an earlier study of the teacher's several self-definitions (Mann and others, 1970) it was found, for example, that some teachers are strongly attached to functioning as expert in the classroom, while others chafe at this role ascription and work best as facilitator. The main point here is twofold. Those who specialize in one aspect of psychology are not always aware of the existence of other forms of expertise than their own and of the need to broaden their own competency accordingly. But even more acute at times is the teacher's uneasiness at finding that other aspects of the field generate pressures to function as exemplary model, as facilitator, or as fellow learner in the face of a particular pedagogical situation. For example, when growth in self-awareness is the goal, the effective teacher is often the one who is as subject to the discipline or technique as the student; the student can observe that the teacher is open to change and growth and not merely administering a technique for others' benefit. The dawning of understanding and the surge of creativity in a student are often contingent on a degree of disinterest on the teacher's part, a patience and a realization that such things cannot be forced or hurried. Thus, in many ways the challenge of creating an integrated curriculum challenges the teacher to discover inner resources, innovative forms, and the courage to endure the moments of failure.

Examples of Curricular Integration

Before the apparent difficulties inherent in creating a more unified curriculum stir up a general pessimism over prospects for change, let me turn to three quite different efforts to solve some of the problems we have been discussing.

The first is a course at the University of Michigan, Introduction to Behavior Modification, which has evolved over the past ten years or so under the direction of James McConnell and James Papsdorf. Each instructor, in somewhat different ways, has managed to engage students in either a direct intervention project or a self-change project. The students not only read a standard text on the theories and techniques of behavior modification, they design and administer a small experiment, find out for themselves how the technique works, and, in the case of self-change projects, measure the effect in terms of their own altered behavior. They take smoking, weight control, study habits, or whatever behavior they choose to work on as their "problem."

The course demonstrates the potency of one of psychology's new applied fields. It does not matter that the projects the students propose have been done before by others; it matters only that they gain direct experience on both ends of the intervention process. Thus, for some students the great opportunity is to see how they would like to do such work, to design such projects and help people with their problems in this way. For others, the payoff is more personal. They can continue to adopt the behaviorist stance toward their problems and design appropriate self-change projects in one area of their life after another.

The capacity of the behavior modification course to traverse the pure science-applied science boundary leads to two very important outcomes. The students read widely in the experimental and theoretical literature, and thus the course is solid, substantial, and rigorous, while at the same time it is practical, relevant, and immediate. This dual outcome explains the course's stable place in the department and also the students' enthusiastic response to it. Not many courses can manage both halves of this outcome. But even more difficult boundaries are traversed by this course. Behaviorism's familiar diffidence about postulating inner states is overwhelmed by the necessity to capture one central aspect of the students' direct experience: their own desire for and increased capacity for self-control. Their heightened sense of mastery over the urgency of their inner pulses is achieved via a piece of practical wisdom that goes back to the beginning of moral education. Attention to stimuli, to environment, was at the heart of the ancient proscription to avoid bad company. And the central wisdom of this teaching, in traditional or modern garb, is that we choose our environment. We choose that which provokes, seduces, and strengthens us, and our choices can be made more conscious and more in our own best interest. Another admirable feature of such a course is that its limits are also specifiable. Not everyone wants to help or be helped in this way, nor would such efforts succeed in numerous possible areas of application. Some are drawn to areas where personal contact, depth of understanding, and the unplanned, spontaneous intervention are still the methods of choice and necessity.

A second curricular innovation, one that has evolved over the past fifteen years at the University of Michigan, is Project Outreach. (See Cytrynbaum and Mann, 1969, for an early account of the course.) This course engages the would-be helper in ways that lead to both challenges and crucial learning. The demands of the field setting do not provide the student with predictable interactions; rather, the wide range of face-to-face interactions calls for spontaneity, adaptiveness, and fundamental human qualities that everyone is still developing. Thus, the student must decide when to hold in mind theories and techniques learned in the classroom and when to jettison them as excess baggage in situations not treated by their academic preparation. The ancient initiatory rite, wherein one plunges into largely unknown territory, finds its echo in just such educational structures. The hallmark of this course is direct experience, engagement in a field setting that can make room for and find some benefit from students with no special skills or training. The students are there to observe, to be of assistance, and inevitably to learn both about others and about themselves. Within an increasingly elaborate structure of supervision and peer teaching, Project Outreach introduces nearly one thousand students per term to the first level of psychology as a helping profession. The students, to an impressive degree, testify that they learn invaluable lessons about life, about the strengths and difficulties that people have, and about themselves as agents for care and change in such settings. We need to pause for a moment to explore some of the implications of such courses for the field, the university, and the teacher in the classroom.

The great potential of courses such as Project Outreach lies in their capacity to bridge the various schisms that divide the psychology curriculum. There is opportunity for testing out in a specific setting the concepts learned in lecture and text, and the shifting situation inevitably calls for some synthesis of rationality and intuition, attention to ideas and attention to people. There is time for planning and reflection, time for being abstract or deductive, but there is also more than ample occasion for risk-taking and creative adaptation. Finally, the student may become aware that increased effectiveness with others hinges on increased self-awareness, maturity, and wisdom, and suddenly a course's boundaries dissolve into life's fuller agenda. White's observation, in this volume, that education can foster opportunities for developing empathy and humanitarian concern are borne out by this course. And so is Douvan's sense that some courses may lead to the kind of mutuality and personal engagement that in turn contribute to the evolution of mature intimacy in the classroom and beyond.

How has the actuality of Project Outreach matched its potential? Very well, I would say. But, like any innovation, it has had mixed results, which illumine certain difficulties other such courses might well encounter. What started out as an integral part of the introductory course soon broke off to become the "Experiential Learning Component of the Department of Psychology." The student was left with the greater part of the difficult task of integrating the experience gained with the remaining or "academic" part of the department. Thus cut off, the course came under attack for lack of substance or "content," as such criticism is usually encoded. One recent response to this criticism was to beef up the academic component of the course by having more "cognitive input" from those who manage the field settings and from some relevant faculty, while an earlier response was to give only Credit-No Credit evaluations and to not have the course count for concentration in the department.

Clearly, it is no easy matter to achieve real integration across such a range of teaching goals and educational settings, but still we must ask how we can do this better. How can the full process of experiential education, as described by Kolb in this volume, be enclosed within one educational adventure without constantly falling into isolated components or becoming the captive of a narrow, pre-occupational definition of its mission? The helping professions are as prone to locking in on limited paradigms as any science, and they can be as constricting and growth-inhibiting in their training of neophytes as any other line of work. How can students preserve the liberating potentiality of the liberal arts tradition in the face of so many trends toward fragmentation and premature specialization?

We need to stand back and see all the helping professions as oriented both toward their scientific context, pure and applied, and toward the older humane traditions on which they draw when they seek to explore (1) the nature and causes of human suffering, (2) the process of cure or growth, (3) the highest realms of human potential, and (4) the training and frame of mind necessary for one who would heal others. Only by broadening their frame of reference can such professions see beyond their frustration with the scientific experts of their tradition. If all the young student or teacher can sense is the disjunction between the practiced realities of the particular setting and the formalisms of the scientific corpus closest at hand, it would be tempting to develop an anti-expert, even anti-intellectual, stance and espouse some form of "We're all experts" egalitarianism. Nothing rattles the academic assumption system more than such assertions.

Finding one's field's scientific mentors less than helpful in one's search for ways to become a healer does not necessarily imply that one is all alone in the enterprise. What it might imply is that one is being distracted from seeing the centuries and infinite varieties of healing for the reference domain that they could become. Psychology is not alone in suspecting, although it may be somewhat alone in preferring to ignore, that to help or even to observe another person entails a risky form of self-engagement. To sense the risk, and to overcome one's avoidance of such risk, is part of becoming a healer. What literature, what sort of self-expressive work, what sorts of self-disciplining activities might assist the would-be helper of others to achieve significant internal changes to that end?

Empathy, self-awareness, and a feeling for the many layers of simultaneous meanings—how can these be taught? That *is* a hard question, but not really much harder than its opposite—how can they be ignored? These subtle learnings are achieved in many instances, but what is lacking is the rationale, the sanction, for such activities. The internal debate within psychology would be intense if proposals were made suggesting that its healing and experiential aspects develop stronger links to the humanities and even beyond the traditional academic perimeter. But some such reorientation seems only sensible if practicum-oriented teaching projects are to have properly rich and envigorating intellectual grounding. New perspectives, new appreciations of hidden meaning and possibility, these are the express aims of much of the world's literature and scripture. But best of all would be to combine this material with the kind of supportive, close teaching that students receive in field settings and discussion groups within courses such as Project Outreach.

The process of learning from one's experience is, as Kolb points out in this volume, a much-neglected aspect of higher education. But what Kolb seems to play down is the potential of learning from other people's experience. He seems to focus more on "abilities," more on the heroic process of abstracting it for yourself, and less on the opportunities afforded by hearing some great truth that serves to crystallize one's experience in ways only few could ever do for themselves. We not only "create concepts"; we receive them and we are transformed by them. However, I fully agree with Kolb that these moments of insight, self-created or received, need the full context of experience and experimentation in order to become integral to the person's life. Project Outreach has gone a long way toward bringing these contexts into the arena of academic life.

The fullest example of what I am suggesting is needed, by the field, the educator, and the student, is found in the dream reflection seminar at Evergreen College. Richard Jones has long been a pioneer in experiential education, at Brandeis and at Santa Cruz. The seminar he and his colleagues in many fields have evolved strikes me as a marvelous synthesis in one educational format of all the aspects of psychology we have been review-ing. Too cryptic a summary of what the seminar entails would do it a great disservice, so permit me to quote Jones directly:

> The dream reflection seminar was a popular success and in the following four years evolved into this more elaborate format:
>
> 1. We first read a work of literature and discuss it in a seminar, from the points of view of the meanings possibly intended by the author, the meanings suggested by the text, and our personal responses to the work.
>
> 2. On a subsequent morning someone brings to the seminar a dream and his or her written reflections on it—typed and dittoed, so that everyone has a copy.
>
> 3. The dreamer reads the dream and the reflections.
>
> 4. As we close our eyes and try to visualize our own versions of the dream's imagery, the dreamer reads the dream again. This has the effect of calm-ing inevitable personal jitters and getting us into a studious frame of mind.
>
> 5. For approximately the next two hours we discuss the dream from two points of view: what it may be saying to us and what we may be prompted to say back to it. Thus, our objectives are to understand the dream *and* to enjoy it. In this latter venture we learn to respond to the dream's play on words and images, its sound symbolisms and flourishes of synesthesia, its visually alliterative se-quences, its deployments of the figurative and literal, its double entendres, stag-ings, artifices, puns, and jokes. The discussion is guided by the rule that we are free to advance any hunch, speculation, or intuition, ask any question, offer any interpretation or outright guess which may help us to achieve the two objectives: understanding and enjoyment. This freedom is limited only by the common acknowledgment that the dreamer will be the ultimate judge as to the correctness of the understanding and as to the tastefulness of the enjoyment.
>
> 6. We then go off individually and write for two hours. The dreamer's writing usually consists of summarizing the highlights of the discussion and ex-tending his reflections on the dream. The rest of us write something—a poem, an essay, a letter, a story, some dialogue—which links our reflections on the dream to our understandings of the week's common reading assignment. This is the most challenging step in the sequence, and, when successful, the most rewarding.
>
> 7. We then re-convene as a seminar and read to each other what we wrote. The writings tend to be of such startling liberated quality as to generate a mood of uncommon mutual respect—sometimes falling not far short of shock.
>
> 8. The writings are then typed and printed, so that each week everyone receives copies of the previous week's writings.
>
> The tone of the seminar tends to be one of scholarly good humor. Ther-apeutic gains in self-knowledge are expected and accepted, but the prevailing expectation is that personal insights will be extended to grace some aspect of our academic commitments with personal meaning [Jones, 1980, p. 15].

It is certainly not the special content of this seminar that makes it so useful as a model. Numerous other topics in psychology could generate this much interaction and be equally relevant to the student and the instructor. What makes it so useful is the way the boundaries that crisscross the field are treated not as obstacles but rather as helpful indi-cators of what else might be included in the total design of the course. The personal act of creativity, the scholar's attention to text, the perilous process of active listening and response, the immediate necessity to review one's assumptions about human potential and our ways of knowing anything—all this and more swirl through the days' discussions. As one student, Lloyd Houston, put it, "Everyone becomes more sensitive to everyone, more civil, more thoughtful, more human. And, as is true of a good play, the sign of a good dream reflection seminar is always lots of hearty laughter." The task has become large enough to remind everyone that there is work to be done, that one takes one's help in such work from the whole of human understanding. Yet never lost is the realization that it is the learner's own experience that makes such education self-validating.

Adult Development and Curricular Planning

How does the diverse array of psychology's subidentities and curricular possibilities mesh with the most important variations among students? I am forcibly reminded by the early chapters of this volume that students vary in age and life stage, in intellectual, moral, interpersonal, and ego development, and I cannot but wonder how such different students can and should be served by their educators. I begin to respond to this question by rejecting a few straw answers that emerge rather quickly in my mind. I reject the notion of designing quite different packages for different sorts of students. I resist starting with the assumption that students are enduringly different and prefer instead the more tractable possibility that some students put only a small fraction of their current potential into the educational arena, and thus that they may only appear constricted, conformist, achievement-oriented, or cynically resistant to commitment and choice. The best route for curricular design is not to "place" students or to "tailor-make" a program for each apparent variation but to pursue the implications of each student's great potential for growth. I sense that this is the main import of the early chapters on adult development. The central goals of education are depicted recurrently by such words as *holistic, integration, autonomy, dialectics,* and *achievement of meaning,* to name but a few.

It would follow, then, that the curriculum itself needs to be whole, fully integrated, and the very exemplification of the ongoing quest for meaning and commitment. In the light of student variability, it would seem that the proper mixture of what is familiar and what is challenging, what draws out competent performance and what spurs on needed development, can only be provided by the most wide-ranging array of psychology's many aspects. Let us consider briefly several of the important variations within the student body of tomorrow.

From the work of Weathersby, Gilligan, and Perry reported in this volume comes a rather coherent picture of the major student orientations to college education. We find, first, an early and probably never completely extinguished complex of conformity, absolutism, and vigilance. The whole business of education seems remote to these students. It is not their territory at all. Somebody else is in charge. What do they need from a curriculum? How can the door be left open for them to explore the possibility of dropping this excessive concern over getting things right without propelling them into an environment unmanageably devoid of familiar points of orientation? It seems to me that many paths have been and can be developed. For some of these students, what is needed is the opportunity to discover the pleasure of pulling the learning process into their own territory, as in a self-change project or an Outreach field setting. For some, it is a painful but extraordinarily powerful experience to find the opportunity, in an educational setting of all places, to see themselves with an increasing clarity. A curriculum that excludes such opportunities for getting outside the relentless pressure of abstraction, performance, and evaluation seems likely to lock students into this stage of adaptation for at least that part of their existence when they are "in school." For those who left school not having moved beyond this orientation to education, and who now return, it is particularly important that the curriculum not plunge them back into the world of alien knowledge, to the exclusion of those capacities for service and reflection that they have developed outside academia.

The great gain in relativistic sophistication and perspective, also known as the *sophomore regression,* raises quite different questions for curricular planning. Gone are the right answers, gone is the sense of being the stranger in a foreign territory, but suddenly words like *adrift, solipsism,* and *futility* come to the fore. There are no more right answers, but they (the faculty) are still trying to change us (the students), and this new orientation seems well designed to prevent exactly that. As Gilligan's framing and resolving of this developmental puzzle reveals, the sophomore's discovery of multiplicity serves a necessary function in maturation, but the perils of stagnation and despair are considerable. How can we trace out the curricular implications of this crisis?

I take the evidence Gilligan and Perry offer to suggest that the antidote to stagnation lies in the gradual accumulation of experience with others that admits mutual vulnerability, that moves one from abstraction to full and affectionate engagement, and that is fundamentally self-enhancing and conducive to self-trust. The source of this experience seems often, even usually, to be relations with peers. The prospect of remaining detached and cynical in the educational arena, self-protectively immune to new ideas, is thus heightened by a curriculum that seems to know nothing of how open, committed, intuitive, and self-trusting one has become elsewhere in life. This is hardly a problem confined to sophomores. In fact, it seems to me that we all recycle continually through the freshman and sophomore stages until we can find some quite specific solution and move on.

I sense that there are quite a few ways around this impasse. Some teachers, without ever seeming to waver from the scientific and didactic modes of approaching their task, can demonstrate how much commitment and wisdom are possible, even necessary, in pursuing psychological issues. Without themselves becoming particularly personal, they nonetheless reveal their own beliefs and behaviors in ways that seem strikingly more interesting than any nay-saying, uncommitted posture. But for many students the turning point seems to depend on encountering their own creativity in an academic setting, in conjunction with seeing a teacher confront quite similar tasks. To see the teacher try and only partially succeed, to see the teacher's own continuing self-discipline and commitment to form, and to share with the teacher both form and product, these seem crucial in many cases of close teaching, such as Richard Jones' dream reflection seminar. A curriculum closed to the resonance of inner wisdom and to the paradoxical fruits of an evolving epistemology seems particularly likely to block students, young or old, from using education to develop their deepest and most personal agendas.

Finally, what can be said about the students who develop into, or return to school having developed into, mature, autonomous individuals? I imagine a few arrive and find the classroom quite trying, the whole approach rather unreal and bland in contrast to the vividness of a rich personal life. But I think this is not the major outcome and not the major challenge for curricular planning. I suspect that at the urging of such students, and with their help, teachers may find ways to open up the entire curriculum to its fullest potential. Such students reveal a great readiness to learn the material of this field, since the problem of relevance is often solved by their greater pool of experience and questions. More important, however, their maturity is reflected in an awareness that the external forms of science, scholarship, and professional training both reflect and impart the deepest wisdom of the field. These forms can, and often do, provide avenues for achieving that ephemeral right relation to things, the path by which the experience of education is not far from the experience of awe or the esthetic pleasure of creating and discovering at the same time. And this is not a path that skirts the difficult, dry stretches of practice and preparatory labor. Thus, a curriculum that did not open up the long march of gradual mastery would block off the opportunities to make a real contribution and to achieve the heights of intellectual development.

A curriculum that can address the developmental needs of these conformist, cynical, autonomous, mature and all the remaining sorts of students could seem almost beyond the realm of possibility unless one looked again at the great teachers of the field. Unless one noticed with what grace the writing and teaching of such as Robert MacLoud, Rollo May, Gardner Murphy, and Robert White move among all the aspects and demands of the field, it would all seem quite impossible. Their use of the research literature, their creativity and their wisdom, are woven into their acute sense of audience and self, and what might seem impossible emerges as the worthiest, but still reachable, goal for any teacher in the field.

How will the curriculum and mode of psychology's teaching efforts change in the next few years? The answer seems to be a compound of many answers, many trends. Psychology as science and scholarship will evolve and dictate the answer in part. But so too will the students, as they vote with their registration forms and their enthusiasm, determine the next phase of the field's educational efforts. They, and our colleagues from other fields, and the deans as well, may save us from our own momentum and help us expand our self-definition and our own enthusiasm for our work. The final common path seems to be faculty innovation, the sometimes collective but more usually solitary effort to take the next step. Through an increasingly explicit and collaborative effort to consider these next steps and their implications for psychology's full identity, the curriculum may come to serve the interests of all who teach, all who learn, and all whose lives depend upon the outcome of this encounter.

References

Adorno, T. W., and others. *The Authoritarian Personality.* New York: Harper & Row, 1950.

Bohm, D. "Quantum Theory as an Indication of a New Order in Physics. Part A: The Development of New Orders as Shown Through the History of Physics." *Foundations of Physics,* 1971, *1,* 350-381.

Bohm, D. *Fragmentation and Wholeness.* Jerusalem: Van Leer, 1976.

Cytrynbaum, S., and Mann, R. D. "Community as Campus—Project Outreach." In P. Runkel, R. Harrison, and M. Runkel (Eds.), *The Changing College Classroom.* San Francisco: Jossey-Bass, 1969.

Jones, R. M. *The Dream Poet.* Cambridge, Mass.: Schenkman, 1980.

Kelley, C. F. *Meister Eckhart on Divine Knowledge.* New Haven, Conn.: Yale University Press, 1977.

Mann, R. D., and others. *The College Classroom: Conflict, Change, and Learning.* New York: Wiley, 1970.

Pribram, K. H. "What the Fuss Is All About." *Re-vision,* 1978, *1* (3/4), 13-18.

Schroeder, W. "Others: An Examination of Sartre and His Predecessors." Unpublished doctoral dissertation, University of Michigan, 1979.

Tart, C. *Transpersonal Psychologies.* New York: Harper & Row, 1975.

21

James Lowell Gibbs, Jr.

Anthropology

Anthropology contributes to developmental education for adult development by—to paraphrase Kluckhohn's (1949) classic image—serving as a mirror for humankind in which it can see itself in its infinite variety. But that mirror also shows us certain patterns of uniformity. Are there implications here for developmentally oriented higher education such as that proposed in Part One?

As a discipline, anthropology is holistic—seeing humankind in both its biological and cultural dimensions, and studying cultures in their totality. It is also comparative, relativistic, eclectic, and strongly rooted in intensive fieldwork. In the United States, anthropology traditionally includes four subdisciplines: (1) physical anthropology, (2) archaeology, (3) cultural and social anthropology, and (4) anthropological linguistics. This makes anthropology the only discipline that is simultaneously a science, a social science, and a member of the humanities, giving it extraordinary potential as a tool for developmental education.

Within the academy, anthropology often has served as a gadfly. When other disciplines have constructed generalizations based on their research, we often have pointed out that the "generalizations" were based on observations made only in one culture or in one

Note: I would like to thank Jerry N. Boone and William Torbert for their comments on an earlier version of this paper, and Arthur W. Chickering for his comments and criticisms and for his neverending patience as an editor. My wife, Jewelle Taylor Gibbs, also was particularly supportive when conflict between time and intentions seemed to forestall progress.

kind of culture, usually a European or European-derived culture or a modern, industrial culture. "It may be true in Switzerland," we are fond of saying, "but not among the Puka Bora." We can assume this familiar stance regarding the findings of developmental education. Many of the generalizations about the nature of intellectual, personal, and moral development are based on studies limited to a very small range of the earth's peoples. We cannot yet be at all sure that the developmental "steps" and "stages" hypothesized by such writers as Piaget (1928), Erikson (1950), or Perry (1970) are universal or nearly so. One of our tasks as anthropologists is to help subject such schemes to further cross-cultural testing and verification.

After further cross-cultural testing, the findings and implications of education for adult development undoubtedly will be revised and modified. As they stand, however, they have implications for the teaching and learning of anthropology. This is true for the teaching and learning of anthropology at every level. However, in this chapter I will draw examples from the teaching of introductory college-level anthropology.

Most anthropologists feel that anthropology has an important place in the liberal arts curriculum and that underclass students should be exposed to the introductory course because it is "good for them." We rarely spell out how and why, preferring to view that as somehow self-evident. Even the classic work in the field, *The Teaching of Anthropology* (Mandelbaum, Lasker, and Albert, 1963), left many of these assumptions largely implicit. A partial exception was the paper by Bennett, "A Course in Comparative Civilizations," which listed some of the traits of freshmen thinking that his course was designed to correct or, at least, adapt itself to: concreteness, bipolar thinking, pragmatic bias, limited time perspective, ethnocentric attitudes, confusion, hesitance, and basic seriousness (Bennett, 1963). Most anthropologists who teach an introductory course in general anthropology or one of the four subfields have in their heads some such template characterizing their students, notions of changes they would like the course to make on that template, and some conception of the process by which those changes can be made to occur. In this chapter I try to make some of those assumptions explicit and relate them to the material in Part One of this volume.

Anthropology and Intellectual Development: Toward Relativistic Thinking

Intellectual development of traditional-age students is an important instructional goal in undergraduate anthropology courses. But, particularly in introductory courses, instructors have given equal weight to the humanistic concern of developing tolerance of other cultures. Sometimes the intellectual anthropological skills developed by the student are seen as a *means* to this humanistic end (see Bruner and Spindler, 1963). Under this model, anthropological study involves increasing one's tolerance of other cultures by learning about the cultural context of behavior and the relativity of culture. However, following these steps usually brings about simultaneous achievement of another intellectual goal—shifting from absolutistic thinking to relativistic thinking (see Perry, 1970 and in this volume). The paradigms of intellectual and ethical development (Perry, 1970) show that this is the key intellectual task in undergraduate education. Implicitly or explicitly, we anthropologists recognize this as an outcome of effective teaching in our discipline. However, the attainment of parallel outcomes in moral and personal development is seen by many anthropologists as our discipline's unique mission in liberal education. I will say more about this later.

The Comparative Inductive Method. How do undergraduate anthropology courses facilitate the shift from absolutistic to relativistic thought? Introductory courses in general anthropology or in cultural and social anthropology always include some exposure to ethnographic descriptions of a sample of the varying forms of social and cultural institutions. The traditional-age beginning student thus learns of the existence of variation in patterns of basic aspects of culture that, up to now, he or she had taken for granted. The lesson is not completely a new one for most beginning students today. But even television exposure to other cultures and knowledge of self-conscious alternative "counter-culture" variants in our society do not prepare them for everything they will learn in an introductory course.

For reasons that Part One of this volume makes clear, the inductive method of teaching is particularly appropriate for presenting comparative material from other cultures in an introductory course. By immersing their students in materials about a *few*, carefully selected cultures, anthropology instructors strengthen the possibility that the student will reason from the particular to the general, inferring regularities for himself or herself. This helps to reinforce the shift in student perception of the locus of intellectual authority from external to internal (see Weathersby, this volume). However, this method requires exceptionally careful planning on the part of the instructor and considerable tolerance for ambiguity on his or her part. In the inductive method, outcomes do not follow a script.

The immersion-in-few-cultures method requires heavy use of discussion and dialogue, not all of which need be oral. The assignment of frequent papers is a way of enhancing the dialogue for those students whose learning styles are more oriented to written expression. Skillful instructors steer the dialogue to discussion of students' direct experience of their own culture or of cultures in which they have traveled in order to bring this dimension into the learning equation. Heavy use of written and oral dialogue with the students enables the instructor to shape the learning experience more to the varying cognitive styles that characterize different adult age groups (see Schaie and Parr, this volume). Then too, students learn in various ways from the discussion contributions of persons in different phases of life experience or with different cognitive styles (see Schaie and Parr, this volume).

Depending on the problem at hand, the learning environment in which this comparative and inductive approach is employed is perceptually complex or symbolically complex or both as Kolb reminds us in Part One.

It is for both intellectual and developmental reasons that the exotic and therefore engaging inventory of humankind's cultural variations are an attractive starting point for students *and* instructors in anthropology courses. For example, traditional-age undergraduates are particularly captivated by puberty rites and varied customs of betrothal and marriage such as infant betrothal and polygyny. Not surprisingly, older students are intrigued more by parent-in-law/child-in-law relations in unilineal extended families or by culturally institutionalized senilicide. And all students are fascinated by cultural institutions like ritualized warfare, blood brotherhood, or trial by ordeal. Harris' (1974, 1977) best-selling writings have demonstrated anew the appeal of such hoary exotica as potlatches and sacred cows.

Of course, understanding of adult development informs us of some of the reasons for the appeal to students of a given age of studying particular exotic cultural institutions: the participants in those institutions are of the same age or stage as the students and face similar personal questions and dilemmas. By studying institutions of other cultures and their impact on individuals of their own age, students can gain help in comprehending the changes in their own behavior that reflect maturation and aging (see Schaie and Parr, this volume). As for the instructors, some of the exotic material is relevant to *their* own present or past (not to mention future) age and stage. Then, too, what instructor would not prefer to teach with pedagogically engaging and relevant material?

The shift away from absolutistic thinking that can occur in undergraduate introductory courses in cultural and social anthropology results not from mere exposure to descriptions of a range of cultures, cultural institutions, and cultural practices, such as those just mentioned, but from the understanding of the *meaning* of those cultural forms as revealed in the ethnological explanations and analyses that usually are a part of those descriptions. Most of those explanations center on the concept of function and related concepts such as adaptation.

Students are introduced first to the apparent function of cultural forms. For example, they readily grasp the fact that the levirate, a form of marriage in which a deceased husband is replaced as a marriage partner by a kinsman culturally defined as a brother, is a way of providing for the care of the widow and her children. They learn that assumption of this responsibility can be critical in a society whose habitat and state of technology dictate a strong division of labor by sex, which makes economic contributions by adults of both sexes essential. Next, students are introduced to the idea that the levirate as a "secondary" or "continuation" marriage is a way of giving expression to the notion of marriage as linking two groups of kin and to the idea of the conceptual equivalence of siblings, or both. They learn, too, that conceptions like the continuity of marriage beyond the biological life of a partner and the equivalence of siblings may be given symbolic expression in a culture. They will be taught that an anthropologist may check his or her hypothesis that such conceptions underlie the levirate by looking for their reflection in symbolic beliefs and behavior.

The instructor, sometimes prodded by students' observations and comments, must move to the observation that "function" is not always *eu*function and may include *dys*function. He or she must raise the question of how one properly defines the consequences by which one attempts to determine function and deal with the pitfalls of circular reasoning and teleology.

Thus, in an introductory anthropology course the student learns something of the context of behavior, especially of how behavior is rooted in cultural norms. He or she comes to see how these norms reflect cultural values and adaptation to the possibilities (and more often the limitations) of habitat. Finally, the student learns that each culture has its own explanation of the reasons for cultural practices and of their meaning and that these stated reasons may or may not coincide with the reasons or consequences posited by the anthropologist. Before long, the student discovers that a custom abhorrent to one society may be not only highly valued in another society but eufunctional in that society —in short, he or she is introduced to the concept of cultural relativity.

Introduction to Cultural Relativity. Mere exposure to the fact of significant variation in basic aspects of culture such as forms of marriage will shake the hold of absolutistic thinking on the student (see Perry, 1970, and in this volume). But introduction to the concept of cultural relativity and repeated examples of it speed the shift to relativistic thinking. This has long been understood as a major contribution of anthropology to liberal education. Time and time again, the student learns that what at first blush seemed superstitious and primitive has a logic of its own and consequences that are understandable. For example, not to have a completely free choice of spouse may not be inherently bad. Once the student recognizes that fact, the existence of so-called "freedom of choice" of spouse in our own society may be more closely examined and seen to be limited in highly patterned ways. Thus, old "truths" dissolve or are transformed into new ones.

Disengaging from the truths that one has been handed by Authority (including one's culture) may be very difficult for the student. Anthropologists ease this disengagement and facilitate the shift to relativistic thinking by use of the comparative method and the inductive approach, both of which have been partially implicit in the discussion so far.

Let me make this classical pedagogical strategy of anthropology explicit. The basic idea is to have the student study an institution or problem first in the literature about another culture. Reading about, say, infant betrothal, secondary marriage, or culturally permitted killing in another culture, the student is more likely to be able to be "objective," or, more precisely, to have less interference from early traumas, current intergenerational conflicts, community prejudices, religious training, and so on. Then, under the rubric of the comparative method, the instructor moves closer and closer to the student's own culture and subculture. For example, one moves from consideration of infant betrothal in premodern Nigeria to arranged marriages of young adults in traditional China and then to arranged marriages in some American subcultures. The pattern of limited freedom of choice of spouse in American culture that our exemplary student discovered earlier under his or her nose can now be examined more dispassionately than it otherwise would have been—in terms of functional pros and cons, like the more explicitly limited choices he or she examined in other cultures. It is to be hoped that the student will draw the inference that arranged marriages function to promote marital stability partly because physical attraction and romantic love are played down in favor of other attributes that may be more important over the life of the marriage. Attention then can be turned from benefits of arranged marriages to the matter of the correlated "costs" of both arranged marriages and those of "free choice" and to an assessment of the circumstances under which either form of marriage choice may be advantageous.

This pedagogical method capitalizes on both the exotic and comparative aspects of anthropology. First the institution in question is examined in another, distant culture to which the students bring little or no cultural "baggage." With the knowledge and relatively objective stance gained through that distantiation, the students can then be brought to examine the same institution or its functional equivalent in our own culture. The aim is for the students to see our own cultural institution in perspective. Often, they will perceive something about that institution that they had not noticed before approaching it with a comparative perspective. In performing this kind of exercise, the instructor tries to help the students to examine the role of an institution from the perspective of various actors and groups and from the point of view of "society" or "culture," while avoiding the twin pitfalls of reification and teleology.

The attempt to assay the net worth or effectiveness of a cultural institution can boomerang. Asked to attempt such an assessment, the student may raise the question of relativity and ask how such a judgment can be anything other than ethnocentric. In short, while the concept of the relativity of culture can help to speed the shift from absolutistic thinking, it can also reinforce the student in moral relativism, thereby slowing or blurring his or her moral development (Perry, 1970). I will return to this point in a later section of the chapter. For now, however, let me return to the issue of how the study of anthropology reinforces the conception that truth is not absolute.

Linguistics and Value Studies. The study of anthropological linguistics can reinforce the notion of relative truth. One of the most important concepts of linguistics is the Sapir-Whorf hypothesis, the view that the grammatical categories of a language have some effect on the perceptions and characteristic ways of thinking of the speakers of that language. Linguists, psychologists, and psycholinguists agree that grammar does not *determine* perception or thought, and the extent to which it shapes or guides them is a matter of contention. Understanding of this hypothesis is more profound for the student who has studied a foreign language long enough to see the applicability of the hypothesis to the speakers of that language and their behavior.

I have found that a particularly compelling way to present the Sapir-Whorf concept is to screen the Navajo-made films produced as part of a study by Sol Worth and John Adair (1972) aimed at understanding Navajo thought from an "inside" view, what anthropologists have come to call an "emic" view. More precisely, the goal of the Worth and Adair research was to determine the degree to which motion picture film as a medium of communication would be shaped by the categories of Navajo language and by other aspects of the Navajo world view. I have the students read Worth and Adair's lively yet germinal monograph documenting how the format and visual language of the films reflect grammatical categories of Navajo language as well as Navajo conventions of myth telling. The monograph is a fine supplement to another assigned reading that is part of the unit, Dorothy Lee's well-known paper "Lineal and Non-lineal Codifications of Reality" (1950), which traces out some contrasts between the basic world views of the Trobrianders and of the West. The Navajo, like the Trobriand Islanders, have a nonlineal view of reality. The West, of course, has a rather pervasive lineal view of action and causality.

The students (sometimes with some guidance from the instructor) should come away asking: "To what extent are Anglo and other Western-made ethnographic films shaped by a basic world view about causality and connectedness between events and by the linguistic patterns of the filmmakers?" At a more personal level they should ask themselves: "To what extent are *my* thoughts or assumptions about the world shaped by the fact that I am a native speaker of English (or whatever)?" And so, the student is introduced to another dimension of relativity, of meaning varying with context.

Another perspective on the relativity of truth can be gained through the study of values as an underlying and determinative attribute of culture. A now classic example is the Harvard Values Study, which researched values in five American subcultures all occupying the same southwestern habitat: the Navajo, Zuni, Mormons, Texans, and Spanish-Americans (Vogt and Albert, 1966). The basic hypothesis of the study was that since habitat was a constant, intercultural variation in adaptation to the ecological setting would not be due to ecology but to differences in values and the resulting cultural traditions. A piece of research that makes a similar point is the UCLA study of four East African societies, each of which has both an agricultural and a pastoral component. The research notes the role of values in shaping the differential adaptation to the same habitat by pastoralists, on the one hand, and agriculturalists, on the other (Edgerton, 1971). Because they use the method of controlled comparison (Eggan, 1954), utilizing habitat as a constant, these studies highlight sharply the role of values as a significant determinant of thoughts, attitudes, and actions. Again, students should ask themselves: "How much are my thoughts and those of others determined by the handed-down values of our culture?"

Meta-Thought. Discussion of the role of values is a good place for the anthropology instructor to stress the role of meta-thought, thought about thought. Traditional-aged college students should be particularly receptive to learning about meta-thought, for, as Gilligan notes in this volume, it is in adolescence that one acquires the capacity for reflective thought, the ability to think about thought itself. But training in meta-thought should be equally relevant for the middle adult stage of cognitive functions, which, according to Schaie and Parr, is characterized by the importance of organizational, integrative, and interpretive intellectual skills.

A major joy in teaching introductory cultural anthropology is seeing the sense of discovery that even many contemporary students have when they are exposed to the concept of ethnocentrism, a concept and label based on meta-thought. Research in anthropological linguistics and on values shows how world view and values (as cultural conceptions of the desirable) shape behavior and morality (of which more later). The Harvard Values Study and the Edgerton study mentioned earlier are but two among many studies that can be used effectively to introduce the notion of ethnocentrism and make students aware that their values, like those of the Zuni, the Kamba, or the whomever, are strongly shaped by culture. The label *ethnocentrism* makes it easier for students to perceive that fact and to see that they are likely to judge the institutions and behavior of other cultures by the values of their own. Ethnographic examples can be used to show how values vary not only with culture or ethnicity but with caste, class, age, sex, and so on.

Once introduced to the question of ethnocentrism, students who are more mature intellectually raise the question of whether the assumptions and methodology of anthropology itself are not ethnocentric—one more product of the anthropologist's culture. They are in good company. As Cora DuBois notes, "the prime importance of relativism in the perspective of the undergraduate student is that it places Western thought within rather than above the rest of the human scene . . . [for it] can raise the question of the degree to which our Western scientific treatment of sociocultural data is itself a patterned and partial phenomenon" (DuBois, 1963, p. 33). Since DuBois' comment, the whole question of the ethnocentrism and intellectual imperialism of anthropology has become a more conscious and widespread concern within our discipline, especially among the proponents of "radical anthropology." There is a rich and growing literature in this area about which to center class discussion (see Hymes, 1969).

Discussion about meta-thought is most likely to occur in the context of discussion about anthropological methods of analysis, including making inferences from data and constructing and testing hypotheses. Case studies that one can use as a basis for such discussion abound in anthropology, two such being Obeyesekere's study of pregnancy cravings among Sri Lankan women and my own study of a therapeutic dispute settlement process among the Kpelle of Liberia (Gibbs, 1963). The Sri Lankan research suggests questions like "How do you differentiate a manifest function from a latent one?" and "How do you verify a latent function?" My own paper suggests the question "When are two therapeutic processes—in this case, a Western and an African one—enough alike to be called 'similar'?" This approach is usually thought of as training the student in "critical analysis" and has been touted as an important benefit of undergraduate training in anthropology. But the recent critiques of anthropology I mentioned earlier (for example, Hymes, 1969) suggest that we might move closer to the approach of philosophy by making our fundamental assumptions and biases more explicit.

The Archaeological Perspective. Exposure to some of the anthropological subdiscipline of archaeology is still another way in which anthropology can assist a student's development of relativistic thinking. Because archaeological study of the past includes prehistory, it treats larger time periods than does history. Archaeology shows how over very long periods of time human knowledge and actions were shaped by many forces— with human intelligence and purpose being only one among them. Especially in the archaeological record of early times, whose material nature necessarily emphasizes technology and economic patterns more than, say, religion and kinship, we can see the role of shifting climates, resulting migration, diffusion, and technological change. These processes, in turn, over time changed and still change humankind's biological makeup. Through archaeology, students are introduced to more than historical reconstruction. They become aware of cultural evolution. With some data from physical anthropology they can also perceive biological evolution and the relationship between it and cultural evolution. From archaeology comes the humbling view that early human culture every-where developed in broadly similar ways, following the laws of cultural evolution. The role of individuals stressed so much by history as a discipline (see Chickering, 1976) is muted in the prehistoric records. Archaeology puts individual choice and individual will in perspective as subject to the limitations of biology, habitat, and pre-existing cultural technology.

Anthropological study of the past also facilitates students' development of toler-ance for intellectual ambiguity, a concept closely linked to developing relativistic think-ing. Tolerance for intellectual ambiguity refers to the fact that there are some areas of knowledge where one can never "know" the "truth" or even delude oneself into thinking that one does (Perry, 1970). A case in point would be "knowing" what primate form was the first "human." Even an introductory course in physical anthropology will teach stu-dents that that particular "truth" changes quite regularly. (Older students whose knowl-edge of early human evolution comes primarily from the popular press will realize that they have read press releases about the "first human" with increasing frequency over the years.) More important, it will teach them that what form one counts even temporarily as the first human depends on how one defines *human* and on the phenomenal chanciness of which few individuals survived in fossil form and which (probably very few) of those have been discovered. Some instructors have brought the point home in a compelling way by assigning a science fiction novel that turns on the question of whether or not a particular primate individual can be classed as human.

The Self-Skeptical Mind. The culmination of the several kinds of exposure to anthropology that I have mentioned should be the self-critical mind. As I have said else-where (Gibbs, 1976), the mind that has been exposed to anthropology—that has learned something of other cultures and of cultural relativity, of the role of values, of the influ-ence of language, and of evolutionary processes—should begin to understand better how to evaluate knowledge itself. That mind will begin to understand how it—and all minds—are shaped by the structure of language, values, and historical circumstances—including the state of knowledge of its own times. As a result, one should become capable of in-formed skepticism about one's own thinking and pronouncements as well as those of other individuals. One will have learned that knowledge is not absolute but relative, that knowledge is both complex and limited.

In working to bring this about, the anthropology instructor must bear one caution in mind. Changes in cognitive development bring personality changes in their wake (see Weathersby, this volume), and the instructor must be prepared to cope with these ego changes in the role of mentor and advisor.

Anthropology, Ego Development, and Stages of Life

The study of anthropology can enhance the adult's ego development as well as his or her intellect. *Ego,* in much of the literature on ego development (see the chapter by Weathersby in this volume), is used in the Adlerian sense of "style of life." It refers to the unity of personality, its "individuality, method of facing problems, opinion about oneself and the problems of life, one's whole attitude to life and the schema of life" (Loevinger, 1976, p. 9). It is, then, a global term, encompassing much that characterizes the indi-vidual, including the structural notion of "stages" that flow in a logical sequence, each of which is marked by characteristic dilemmas and concerns. The study of anthropology can help the student to work through and solve some of the dilemmas and conflicts that char-acterize particular stages of ego development.

Let us turn first to the stage of adolescence. Erikson (1950) has noted that the development of identity is a major psychosexual or developmental task of adolescence. Helping the adolescent define his or her identity has traditionally been recognized as a goal of liberal education, although most often it has been considered an intellectual goal rather than a developmental one. Thus, Lyman (1971) observes: "a principal objective of education [is] to find out, to the limits of one's ability, where one stands in relation to the rest of the human race, the long sweep of human history, and—for that matter—the universe." Anthropology strives to achieve this end in ways I described earlier, by first helping individual students to understand something of the institutions and conventions that have shaped their own characters and values, to see how and to what extent they are creatures of culture. This is one function of the study of dominant American culture and of our subcultures, including—but not exclusively—one's own.

But in order to provide students with perspectives that will help them define their own identities, we must go beyond exposing them to variants of American culture. Reading an ethnography or monograph about an exotic culture inevitably leads to implicit, and often explicit, comparison with one's own culture. Each such cross-cultural exposure provides another point of triangulation from which the nature of one's own culture and hence one's self can be plotted. For example, a traditionally reared, somewhat sheltered young woman from a small town in Utah and a peer from Manhattan who read an ethnography on village life in Pakistan both gain perspective on the "restrictions" of their society and on themselves on a continuum of compliance versus assertiveness. Of course, such perspective does not convey automatic insights; the guidance of a developmentally oriented instructor is helpful.

Study of cultures contrasting with one's own can help one to see those features that distinguish one's own culture and shape some of one's life tasks. Thus, through exposure to even a small range of other cultures the American student becomes aware of the relative distinctiveness and pervasiveness of the rapid technological and culture change characteristic of contemporary societies (see Schaie and Parr, this volume).

One reason why skillful ethnographic studies of other cultures sharpens awareness of one's own identity is that a sensitive ethnographer builds his or her writing around the questions that the reader from an outside culture will bring to the material. Fifty years ago, in writing her classic study *Coming of Age in Samoa* (1928), Margaret Mead asked, in effect, "What makes a Samoan a Samoan?" She hoped that her readers would ask "How would I feel to be a Samoan? How would a Samoan feel to be me? Do the same factors that operate on a Samoan to make him or her a Samoan operate on me to make me an American, or a particular type of hyphenated American? Or are there different factors that operate in American culture? Both similar and different factors? Or similar factors operating in *different* ways?" Mead would also want her readers to ask if there are circumstances unique to individual Samoans or Americans that shape them, for she did not really see culture as the only force that molds individual character. By working through these questions first for a Samoan or a member of another culture and then for himself or herself, a student sharpens his or her sense of identity, of—if you will—roots.

Developing or strengthening a sense of being rooted in a culture—an identity—usually is particularly important for minority group students because their cultures so often are viewed as "*sub*cultures" in the pejorative sense. As the various ethnic pride movements of the 1960s and 1970s have stressed, study of the culture of one's homeland and full treatment of the American variant of that culture enhance a sense of identity and self-esteem.

For older students of either majority or minority background, immersion in knowledge of other cultures usually does not develop a sense of identity, but it may crystallize, affirm, or enlarge the sense of identity.

Chickering and Havighurst, citing Levinson, note that a developmental task of the middle-aged is to reduce some of the illusions or assumptions and beliefs about oneself and the world that are not true. But some illusions serve a purpose, and distinguishing between the helpful ones and the harmful ones is not always easy. The anthropological study of myth and symbolism, following the classic approach of beginning with distant cultures and then moving closer to one's own, would help adult students to externalize and intellectualize this task. Here the writings of Lévi-Strauss and Victor Turner would be relevant (for example, Lévi-Strauss, 1969, and Turner, 1969, 1977).

As I have observed elsewhere (Gibbs, 1976) and others have noted too (for example, Chickering, 1976), the study of literature can help foster personal awareness by enabling the student to try on other identities and live them vicariously. Reading autobiographies of persons from other cultures or their life histories as written by anthropologists can have the same result. In contrast to these other vividly experienced lives and identities, one's own may come into sharper focus. One can ask of anthropological life histories the same questions that Chickering (1977) sets for literature: What are the pressures which force those persons (characters) toward one level of development or another? What internal strengths, from what sources, provide leverage against those external forces? The popularity of Oscar Lewis' (1959, 1961, 1964, 1965, 1966) documentary life histories of Latino individuals and families shows that many readers undoubtedly recognize—at least subconsciously—their usefulness in fostering self-awareness.

Developing a capacity for empathy and intimacy is one aspect of ego development (see Douvan, this volume). In late adolescence this is connected with acquiring friends and relating to them. This developmental task can be related to intellectual ones, although this may not be obvious to students. As Douvan notes in this volume, the idea that friendship or family relationships or love relationships can be thought about and analyzed systematically is probably as alien to many freshmen as are concepts like the black hole or the quark. But anthropological study of friendship can move the traditional-age student beyond the ethnocentric, idealistic view that friendship is solely affective or that it is exploitative or manipulative to value the pragmatic, instrumental aspects of friendship.

Let me flesh out this suggestion with an example. Studying the anthropological literature on blood brotherhood, the student might see aspects of ordinary friendship projected in bold relief in this ritualized form of friendship. In most cultures blood brotherhood places very high value on both intimacy *and* utility (see Gibbs, 1962). Here, again, we see the heuristic value of our pedagogical paradigm that compares the far with the near. Armed with this insight from the anthropological literature, the student might reexamine friendship in our culture and see more clearly that instrumentality is a significant part of it. The student might now see that the strong normative primacy that our society gives to the dimension of intimacy in characterizing friendship reflects more the values and ideals of our society than the actuality of friendship. The payoff for ego development would come when the student could acknowledge that admitting the coexistence of instrumentality and intimacy in friendship is neither cynical or manipulative. In the student's own friendship, he or she would be more able to accept less than complete intimacy and to view instrumentality in friendship as a legitimate goal rather than as an intrusion or subversion. The student would have moved closer to achieving realistic intimacy in friendship. Again, the developmentally related insights do not emerge spontaneously. Skillful Socratic questioning by an instructor helps to elicit them.

For the traditional-age student, the developmental issues concerning empathy and intimacy are linked to the task of resolving the tension between autonomy and interdependence. Douvan, in this volume, notes that the latter issue is a developmental task for older women students, too. They may be helped in resolving the tension between autonomy and interdependence by intellectualizing it and externalizing it. Following reasoning parallel to that I have used earlier in this chapter, she observes that by formal study of social systems they can learn of the inevitability of interdependence and, thus, to accept it in their own lives. Of course, the same strategy is applicable to traditional-age students, whose problems with autonomy versus interdependence come at an earlier developmental stage.

Older students, having lived longer and encountered a greater variety of people—and, perhaps, cultures—than traditional-age students, seem to find much of the excitement and applicability of anthropology in exploring the universals or similarities of cultures. Because of their life experience, they tend to take the differences among cultures more for granted. More than with younger students, there is an understanding and appreciation of, say, what is universal in fatherhood—or grandmotherhood. This makes possible another developmental application of the study of anthropology. Again, by externalization and intellectualization, the study of other cultures can help these students to accept their need for generativity, to be nurturant and supportive of oncoming generations—not just of their own children and kinsmen but of other persons as well (Erikson, 1959, and Chickering and Havighurst, this volume).

A good case in point is Guttmann's (1974) research on passivity in older men. Guttman's paper uses the Druze of Syria and Israel to show that the disengagement that is reported as characteristic of old age in many societies is not true of old men in that society. Using comparative data, Guttmann suggests that passivity is characteristic of old age, but that it need not take the form of disengagement.

The literature on both cognitive and ego development shows that formal study may have the effect of shifting a student to the next cognitive or ego stage (see Perry and Weathersby, this volume). Careful research probably would demonstrate that exposing older students to the notion of generativity as it is expressed in the allocation of roles in differing social structures and kinship systems may prompt individuals poised on the edge of accepting their generative needs to cross the boundary to this next ego stage.

Let me conclude this section with a caution. In using anthropology for strengthening ego development, we must beware of unwittingly encouraging students' acquiescence to the *status quo* (see the criticism of pre-1970s anthropology in Hymes, 1969). As in my example of the young women from Utah and Manhattan, cross-cultural exposure may be used to provide persons with "realistic" perspective on their current situation. But sometimes the change must be made "out there" rather than inside the person. At times cross-cultural exposure suggests that a situational change is necessary and appropriate to handle the developmental issue of a particular life stage. Cross-cultural exposure may even suggest what form that situational change might take. As Weathersby notes in her chapter, individuals at the higher stages of ego development are able not only to cope with the complexities of society but also to view society's rules with a critical eye.

Anthropology and Moral Development

Discussing moral development during the college years, Gilligan notes in this volume that the educational experiences that foster moral development will be those which enhance the capacity to shift perspectives. She observes that history and literature can make important contributions to moral development by extending students' experience through the study of other lives, both past and present. Chapters Fifteen and Eighteen develop Gilligan's point well. Obviously, the same claim can be made for anthropology. However, anthropology fosters moral development not only through the study of individual *lives* of other times and places but also through the experience of other *cultures* via the writings of anthropologists and the direct experience of fieldwork.

The same material that anthropologists use to foster the student's intellectual development—by speeding and guiding the shift from absolutistic thinking—and ego developent also can be used to foster the student's moral development. Here, again, we see the possibility of promoting several developmental objectives simultaneously. This, of course, is one of the most important implications of Part One of this volume. For example, in attempting to stimulate moral development, the anthropology instructor can return students to Obeyesekere's study of pregnancy carvings among Sri Lankan women cited earlier, keeping in mind Gilligan's suggestion that knowledge of the causes and consequences of human suffering is a source of the moral capacity to respond actively to social experience. With their initial naiveté and particular cultural set, most tradition-age American students exposed to the description of the Sri Lankan institutionalized practice would probably see the young married women suffering at the hands of their in-laws, especially the husband and his mother. The young wife would be seen as giving up her "autonomy" to move into the joint family household of her husband—partly because autonomy versus dependence is a salient life stage issue for most tradition-age students. (Older students would be more apt to identify with the joint family upon which she is "intruding.") But Obeyesekere's analysis helps the student to see that the "cause" of the suffering is equally the woman's natal family, specifically the way in which they reared her. In short, the contrast between her childhood life and her married life creates a situation of relative deprivation. The pregnancy cravings and the household's response to them function partly to alleviate the sense of deprivation. Obeyesekere's analysis also suggests other factors that can be labeled "causes."

The point to be emphasized is that Obeyesekere's paper, which ostensibly does not focus primarily on moral issues, *can* be used to show a class not only that determining cause and consequence is not easy but that judging the morality of an act is equally difficult because ascribing "blame" requires prior ascertainment of cause. Determining cause and blame or moral fault is certainly risky if the observer brings to the situation simply his or her own unexamined perspective.

Other examples can be cited to show the complexity of the causes of human suffering and the related moral and ethical issues. Thus, drought is the result of complex interaction between people and habitat. High value placed on the use of cattle for bride-wealth may lead to overgrazing, which results in erosion, exacerbated by shifts in the pattern of the rains. Of course, the ethical consequences of interrupting this cycle at any point also are very complicated.

I use the Sri Lankan example to show how the same ethnographic description and analysis can be used to stimulate both intellectual and moral development. However, for fostering moral development, more apt examples would involve cultural patterns in which moral issues are more explicit and more central. The classic example, and one that is relevant to older students even more than traditional-age ones, is the conventional Eskimo practice of senilicide. In this custom, elderly persons whose feeble condition endangered the mobility and, hence, the lives of the nomadic group, would commit suicide or be killed by a designated member of the group. A vigorous discussion can be stimulated by questions such as: "Is it moral?" "By what standards?" "Suppose a particular old person protested, should he or she have the right to live?" and so on.

In discussing the role of anthropology in nurturing intellectual development, I observed that introducing the students to the concept of cultural relativity has implications for their moral development. Let me return to that issue. Gilligan, in reviewing the literature on moral development, cites the work of Kohlberg on the phenomenon of moral relativism—notably, the claim made by students that, in the face of individual difference and cultural heterogeneity, moral judgment was impossible and therefore that one "should" do what one wanted to do. Not surprisingly, students' familiarity with the concept of cultural relativity and with data from other cultures tends to reinforce this tendency. After all, from anthropology one learns to take the perspective of the other cultures. One's own moral standards are revealed to be largely an artifact of one's culture—a culture shaped by many forces, of which the conception of morality is only one. So how can there be a way of making absolute moral judgments except possibly within a single culture? Even anthropology itself has no easy answer to that question. This leaves the anthropology instructor interested in education for adult development with a moral obligation of his or her own to help the student move beyond the moral relativism that his instruction may have aggravated. But how? One way is to link the issue of the relativity or absoluteness of morality to field experience.

Fieldwork and Moral Development. Doing fieldwork often pushes anthropologists themselves beyond absolute relativism. Participation in fieldwork can have the same effect on students. Even hearing of or reading about field experiences and subjective responses to them may achieve this result. I can make my point best by recounting some relevant personal experiences.

At the end of my senior year in college, when I was completing my major in sociology and anthropology, I was a finalist for a national Woodrow Wilson Fellowship, which, subsequently, I was awarded. As part of the selection procedure I was interviewed by two professors at Princeton. The conversation turned to the topic of cultural relativity. One of them, a historian, probed to see if I was as committed to the concept as I seemed to be. "Suppose," he said, "you were an anthropologist doing fieldwork in India and you saw a widow about to be thrown on her husband's funeral pyre in the custom of *suttee.* What would you do?" Hesitating only briefly, I said that I would not do anything "because anthropologists could not interfere with the customs of the people we study, nor pass judgment on them." I knew that my response seemed callous, but saw no way out of the dilemma. The professor smiled slightly (with hindsight I suspect it was indulgently) and said that in time I might arrive at a different point of view. Gilligan's label of *moral relativism* would surely have applied to my stage of moral development at the time.

Five years later, the same issue arose during my doctoral fieldwork, this time in still more dramatic form. The powerful paramount chief in the town where I was doing my fieldwork, my "father of the stranger," suspected some of his many wives of adultery. He had administered to them a "medicine" that would cause any of them who had committed unconfessed adultery to become ill and, perhaps, to die. One of them, a young woman whom I shall call Nowai, became ill. The mother of three very young children, she was not an informant for me or my wife, but she was a frequent casual visitor at our house. She lay on a mat in front of her house in the paramount chief's compound, shunned by most of her co-wives, berated by the chief, and becoming progressively weaker and losing weight. Two weeks went by and she was so sick that she could no longer nurse her youngest child. The illness, with symptoms of dysentery and malaria, was attributed to the effect of the "medicine," which "caught" her for unconfessed adultery. Her husband, the chief, declined to call the medicine man to counter the effect of the combined pharmaceutical and fetish.

My wife and I both called on Nowai as we made our daily rounds of the town, and my wife, who became increasingly concerned about her, asked me if I would give Nowai some Western medicine for her symptoms. We discussed the pros and cons heatedly and at length. In contrast to five years before, I could see more shades of gray, including contextual complications. But I thought we should not risk treating her and incurring the chief's wrath. "After all," I argued, "*he's* her husband. Even her co-wives won't help her. If we interfere, the chief could force us to leave the village. And Nowai has refused to give you any interviews about childrearing, something she could easily have done." The continuation of the fieldwork deserved the highest priority in determining the course of action, I thought, even though I felt great anger at the chief for the way in which he was treating his wife. I did go so far as to ask him if he did not think it was time to relent. Had not Nowai been punished enough? His answer was "no."

Nowai's condition worsened and, unbeknown to me, my wife gave her medicine for dysentery and malaria from our kit, reasoning that either or both would do some good. In a very few days, Nowai was better and soon was walking about town. My wife revealed to me her hand in the dramatic recovery. It was, of course, already known to Nowai's co-wives and to the chief. I waited for the chief's reaction. Much to my surprise, he commended my wife for her actions. "That's how women are," he confided to me, "they stand together against us men." I should be proud, he observed, that my wife had reached out to help another person in distress.

I had learned a valuable lesson. The townspeople were not going to judge us morally or ethically by the canons of anthropological works on methodology or field methods that stress "objectivity," "noninterference," and preserving access to the data for the enlightment of future generations and the enrichment of anthropological knowledge. No, they judged us as human beings in the broadest sense. The standard of humanitarian concern (see White in this volume) was to be the prevailing one. I could have done what seemed right and natural to me personally and not only been understood but even admired. I had assumed far too little transmutability between our culture and morality and that of the Kpelle.

Eleven years later, on a third field trip to the same town, the issue of the ethics of intervention arose again. By now I was in my late thirties and was armed not only with still vivid memories of Nowai's illness but with a few years of parenthood and other life experiences that fall under Gilligan's rubric of "experiences of irreversible choice and of sustained responsibility for the welfare of others." This time I was in the field for a short summer period of eleven weeks and was accompanied by two students. One was a senior and the other a graduate student who was carrying out a study of the Kpelle treatment of illnesses. The latter, whom I shall call Ted, had as an undergraduate premedical student had some experience working in a hospital emergency room and would thus give townsmen medicine for the more common ailments, especially when the dispensary operator was not in town.

One night after midnight, in the midst of a tropical downpour, Ted was sent for by the head official of the men's secret society, a medicine man who was one of his major informants. The old man's daughter, a young woman in her twenties, was seriously ill. Ted had seen her earlier in the day because she was quite nauseous and not responding to the local healers. Now, the vomiting had become worse and everyone was worried. Ted went to see the woman and came back to our house. His best judgment was that she was indeed seriously ill and needed to go to the hospital, thirty-five miles away, as soon as possible. Our vehicle was awaiting the arrival of a replacement spare tire. The only transportation available was a Volkswagen bug, a "taxi" that had arrived too late to make the return trip to the county seat. We could charter it. The woman's father reluctantly agreed to the hospitalization and to the charter. But he had nowhere near enough money. Who would pay? I would pay for the charter and the hospitalization, I said, casting my money where my feelings were, on the side of intervention. In consideration of the old man's dignity, I said that I would "loan" him the money. In the context of local custom and the immediate situation it was understood but unstated that he would repay the loan if he could, but that he might not be able to.

The sick woman, her father, Ted, and the taxi owner squeezed into the Volkswagen for the trip to the hospital. It was midafternoon the next day before the old man and Ted returned with the story of what had happened. By the time they had traversed the thirty-five miles of dirt roads, the young woman was in a state of shock. The doctor, who was roused from his bed at 3:00 A.M., had examined her and determined that she had an ectopic pregnancy, one in which the fetus is carried outside of the uterus, in the abdominal cavity. It was necessary to operate right away. The operation was successful. But, the doctor said, if another four hours had passed, the woman would have died.

Ted's initial feeling was one of elation. He had played a major role in saving a life, largely because he was right as to the seriousness of her condition, even though he could not have known the actual diagnosis. Moreover, he was a hero in the eyes of the woman's father, the most important medicine man in town. The implications for his self-esteem and for the success of his research and his personal standing in the community were obvious.

But by the next night Ted was troubled by consideration of alternative consequences that might have followed our intervention. "How could you let me do it?" he asked. "Suppose she had died? I don't know enough medicine to have assumed so much responsibility." We sat up half the night talking through the pros and cons and the ins and outs of the situation. Space precludes repeating all that was said. Among other things, I pointed out that he knew more about medicine than anyone else in the town, including me, so his expertise was the best we had available. I recounted the story of Nowai and assured him that if the young woman had died, people would not have blamed him but noted that he had tried to help. Moreover, the responsibility was shared since I had supported the decision and backed it with the "loan." Nor should he underestimate the role of the woman's father. Perhaps we were being arrogant in assuming that it was "our" decision. Perhaps the real decision was the old man's and his daughter's.

Being supportive and avuncular during our talk into the wee hours of the morning enabled me to make explicit to Ted what I saw as the critical dimensions in the moral and ethical crisis in which we jointly had participated. The most important of these was commitment in the face of uncertainty (see Perry, 1970, and this volume). Being supportive and avuncular also met my own developmental needs—generative needs characteristic of my own life stage.

In the field situation it becomes clear later if not sooner that humanitarian concern (see White, this volume) is a moral value that prevails over moral relativity. And it may be that, in one form or another, this is a universal or quasi-universal human value.

As a result of the educational changes of the 1960s, many instructors now deem it appropriate to let students become aware of our nonclassroom professional activities and concerns. If we also reveal our personal encounters with ethical and moral issues in the course of those activities and the consequences for our own development, we can advance the moral development of our students (see Kolb's concept, in this volume, of the teacher as "mirror" or facilitator).

The three instances I have recited are among the most instructive experiences of my professional life, and I have recounted them in detail because they can also be instructive for anthropology students. I find it hard to be as self-revelatory as recounting these instances demands. But the gain in doing so is that the chronology of the three events shows so clearly how particular circumstances can wean one away from absolute moral relativity. Because the events are "real," involving the instructor they see three times a week, students to whom they are told can empathize with the dilemma and the pain of the anthropologist's moral growing up and learn vicariously from his experience.

Since I have introduced fieldwork in such graphic terms, let me say something about its place in developmentally oriented teaching of anthropology. Direct experience of culture is the core of fieldwork, the most critical and distinctive part of the anthropological method. Anthropologists take great pride in the fact that they personally immerse themselves in the cultures that they study. Fieldwork is a kind of experiential learning, obviously, and anthropologists feel that through it they learn something that other social scientists do not. What is that? Chickering's (1976) definition of experiential learning helps us to see what that something is: He defines *experiential learning* as "the learning that occurs when changes in judgments, feelings, knowledge, or skills result for a particular person from living through an event or events" (p. 16). In carrying out fieldwork one acquires knowledge about another culture. But one also enhances one's anthropological empathy and insight. Every anthropologist knows that his or her insight into all cultures is enhanced by the fieldwork he or she has done in one or a few of them. In the field it readily becomes apparent that one's own prior personal history and cultural upbringing influence what one perceives and what one understands. Thus, the fieldworker comes to understand at a visceral level the shaping influence of culture and the relativity of truth, to know them in a way that one cannot understand them from textbook knowledge alone. And as the experiences I recounted suggest, one learns not only of the differences among cultures but of the universals.

Obviously, such benefits from fieldwork are not simply cognitive and professional in the intellectual sense. Repeatedly, anthropologists have commented on the fact that fieldwork increased their personal awareness and insight. More than one fieldworker has compared fieldwork to undergoing psychoanalysis. This is partly because fieldwork is like drama. It requires that one play a role and also observe. And like performing in a play, fieldwork "creates an experiential context that supplies rich capital for postplay self-confrontation and self-examination" (Chickering, 1977, p. 70). As my field examples indicate, the postevent self-confrontation may take place while one is still in the field.

Although fieldwork for introductory students is difficult to arrange for logistical, financial, and ethical reasons, it is an extremely valuable experience for developmental education. For the student, as for the professional anthropologist, it can sharpen both anthropological insight *and* personal awareness. But to be effective, fieldwork requires carefully selected supplemental reading, self-observation, and "working through" by reflection and dialogue with a more experienced person. When all these conditions obtain, fieldwork, more than most learning experiences, can be tailored to the motives, learning style, and developmental stage of the student.

One of the reasons fieldwork is such a good vehicle for developmental education is that as a learning environment it combines attributes of all four "pure" types of learning environment: (1) affective complexity, (2) perceptual complexity, (3) symbolic complexity, and (4) behavioral complexity (see Kolb, this volume). This is one reason why the summer in which I did the fieldwork with two students mentioned earlier turned out to be one of the most satisfying teaching experiences I have had. As the incident recounted earlier indicates, fieldwork provides a setting in which the intellectual and developmental relevance of tasks at hand is apparent. And the instructor can capitalize on this in guiding the experience.

Traditionally, developmentally oriented anthropologists have encouraged their students to do minor fieldwork in American ethnic communities or subcultures. This has taken the form of small-scale observation or interviewing or both. It was felt that a class, by learning about minority communities, would become more tolerant of them and minority individuals. The goal was to enhance both ego development and moral development and only secondarily to strengthen intellectual development through some acquisition of field skills. Douvan, in this volume, notes that one goal in developing a capacity for intimacy is avoiding responding to people as members of classes or representatives of roles. First-hand study of one's own group helps the student to see persons more as individuals. Additional first-hand study of another group helps even more.

But student intracommunity studies have become a touchy matter, and for good reason. Anthropology has come more and more to recognize that the peoples traditionally studied by anthropologists are also the peoples who, by and large, are powerless and that interviewing them to help develop the interviewers' sense of identity treats them as objects. It is one more form of exploitation or oppression. Hence this form of field experience is no longer utilized except under carefully prescribed conditions.

Students' ethical and moral development is enhanced when fieldwork has a civic orientation, as when students are apprenticed to community agencies in help-giving roles (see Douvan, this volume) or carry out actual volunteer research that otherwise would not be possible for the agencies. This enhances the student's ability to make choices and commitments, which Perry (1970) notes to be the most important outcome of ethical development. Since the 1960s, many anthropologists have increased their students' opportunities to work in this kind of applied setting. At Stanford University this is done through the Action Research Liaison Office (ARLO), which enables students, under faculty supervision, to do research that is useful to community agencies, yet linked to the students' formal course work.

Because it is so difficult to take significant numbers of students to the field, anthropologists increasingly are simulating some aspects of the field experience through the use of ethnographic films. Improved portability of 16mm cameras and synchronous sound recording equipment and changing conceptions of filming have resulted in films that do less processing of the culture being filmed, making it possible for the student to learn more directly about the culture. A noteworthy film of this sort is Rouch and Morin's (1961) *Chronicle of a Summer*. Other examples include the *Faces of Change* series (Miller, 1978) produced by the American Universities Field Staff. Each of these films makes use of the device of interviewing a respondent on camera with synchronous sound, using subtitles (rather than a narrator's voice) for translation of the foreign language. Obviously, this increases the sense of reality, or at least versimilitude, and enlarges the opportunity for the student to learn inductively. Again, the effective use of ethnographic films requires very careful planning and use of supplementary readings as well as written and oral dialogue. With all this in place, the student is drawn into the material in a particularly compelling way, virtually seduced into the experiencing of other cultures and their analysis. Needless to say, learning via the visual mode is particularly compatible with the learning styles of the current generation of tradition-age students and, increasingly, of older students, who have also logged many hours in front of television screens.

Let me return to the matter of how the study of anthropology can enhance a student's moral development. At an early stage of moral development, a student will tend to see the world in terms of moral absolutes, believing that cultures should be consistent in their ideals—for example, not claiming justice for all while treating highly placed persons differently from others in the criminal justice system. Again, externalization and intellectualization may help the student to achieve a more relativistic and realistic moral position. He or she can study another culture in which conflicting polarities are present—equality and inequality, good and evil, cooperation and competition, ascription and achievement, and so on. Consequently, the student may come to accept the inevitability of conflicting tendencies in his or her own culture and no longer perceive their presence as necessarily indicating moral weakness or hypocrisy. Eventually, this should help the student to see the necessity for making moral and ethical choices even in the face of conflicting interpretations (see Perry, 1970). In this effort the student may be aided by exposure to treatises on the question of the universality of values and morals, such as those by Kluckhohn (1952, 1953, 1955), or on the universality of laws (Hoebel, 1954).

Cultural Domination as a Moral Issue. The fact that Western culture, including the American variant, is culturally imperialistic and dominates most cultures with which it comes in contact raises a moral issue of concern to both anthropologists and their students. They may ask questions such as these: What are the sources of cultural domination, cultural imperialism, and oppression of one culture by another? Are there sets of conditions that spawn these phenomena? From the comparative approach of anthropology (and history), students will learn that cultural imperialism has occurred in other times and places, as with the impact of Hindu India on Indonesia centuries ago, that it is not limited to the postexploration West.

The traditional anthropological literature on culture change provides a partial framework for understanding cultural dominance. But the contemporary literature of radical anthropology (see Hymes, 1969) and interdisciplinary dependency theory (for example, Arrighi and Saul, 1973) goes far beyond it in explaining the post-industrial revolution dominance attained by Western capitalistic societies and, less completely, the attempted domination by socialistic societies. These two sets of literature explain phenomena that are salient to socially concerned students of all ages, such as economies dominated by commodity production and extremely sensitive to fluctuating world commodity prices, plantation economies, migrant labor, and the resulting destabilization of family life. The frame of reference of dependency theory provides a means for understanding the mechanisms of oppression and their functions for both the oppressors *and* the oppressed. The empirical portion of the literature permits students to see the consequences of cultural domination from the point of view of the culture dominated.

Only after grounding in this kind of factual background and analytical frameworks are the students and the instructor ready to tackle the moral issues involved. Is it ever moral for one culture knowingly to dominate another? More narrowly, is it "oppression" when employment on plantations or as migrant miners produces income that can be taxed to build social welfare facilities such as clinics? What does one have to know or take account of to answer the question? Suppose it is elected leaders of the dominated country that arrange for the labor contracts for the miners? Does this make a difference in how we judge the situation? Where multinational corporations are involved, what responsibility do consumers of the corporations' products have for corporate actions in developing countries?

Questions like these speak to the ethical and moral concerns of middle-aged students and call upon their ability to assume a stance of moral relativity (see Gilligan, this volume). The multifold analyses required to answer them demand the integrative and interpretive intellectual skills that characterize the middle stage of life (see Schaie and Parr, this volume). Answering such questions perceptively also requires empathizing with the other, and this ability is more characteristic of the older student (Douvan, this volume). And much of the motivation for making the attempt may be rooted in humanitarian concern (White, this volume). This area is one in which anthropology and our sister social sciences can contribute much to the developmental training of adult students.

Study of the anthropology of cultural domination can play another role in developmental education apart from enhancing the moral development and, simultaneously, ego development of older students. It can help minority students to develop a sense of identity and enhance their self-esteem. Many aspects of ego development of minority persons (for example, capacity for empathy and intimacy) may be impaired by the consequences of racism, such as discrimination. Some coping responses such as self-hate, attempted assimilation, or self-segregation and compartmentalization can cause further complications for ego development, particularly for identity. The literature on the anthropology of cultural domination referred to earlier can be supplemented by the literature on the psychology of oppression (see Fanon, 1965) to help minority students and other students understand the personal consequences for the minority individual of the oppression of a subculture by a dominant culture. Once the minority person understands intellectually the subtle ways in which the dominant culture seduces emulation and rewards it, it may be possible for him or her to assume a stance of principled independence and to be less ambivalent about identifying with his or her own culture. In achieving this goal, the study of other pluralistic societies also is of value.

Minority students and majority group students can benefit from discussing the moral issues implicit in the structure of cultural domination and its psychology—for example, how can one justify either assimilation or pluralism in a society that has a "melting pot" image as part of its ideology? But such discussions are more fruitful when most of the students involved have resolved the more directly personal issue for ego development of the inequality of cultures in a pluralistic society. When successful, moral training of this sort enhances competence as "capacity for action" (see Schaie and Parr, this volume).

Anthropology and Developmental Education

Anthropology has much to contribute to the development of the conceptions that underlie developmental education as well as to the delivery of education in the developmental mode. In recent years cognitive anthropology, psychological anthropology, and cross-cultural psychology all have added to our understanding of cognitive development and problem-solving abilities in other cultures. Especially notable in this regard are the studies of Gay and Cole (1967), Cole and others (1971), Cole and Scribner (1974), Lave (1944), and Bruner, Olver, and Greenfield (1966). Gradually we are increasing our understanding of the cultural factors that influence problem-solving abilities. There are suggestions that the unfolding of the Piagetian stages of cognitive development (Piaget, 1928) are not everywhere the same.

In the literature of psychology there is a significant body of material on individual differences in learning styles (see Kolb, this volume). And there have been several attempts to determine the cross-cultural distribution of learning styles (for example, Witkin, 1967; Wober, 1967). Lesser's (1976) paper summarizing the patterned differences in learning styles that characterize American ethnic groups (and the commentaries on it by Cole and Gordon) certainly should be of interest to anyone who proposes to teach the more heterogeneous students of the 1980s. Most of the studies of cultural differences in learning styles have focused on American populations. Work among unspecified "Southern Nigerians" (Wober, 1967), Eskimo, and Temne (Berry, 1966) are notable exceptions. We should sample a larger portion of the world's peoples in testing the validity of our conceptualization of learning styles. Given the anthropological penchant for fieldwork, anthropologists can be expected to do some of this research. And we certainly can assist with the conceptualization.

How universal are the stages of ego development or their progression as traced by theorists like Buehler (1962), Erikson (1950), Levinson and others (1977), and Loevinger (1976)? How about the "developmental tasks" of Chickering and Havighurst (this volume), who are no strangers to anthropology? Mead's (1928) pioneering work on Samoa taught us that adolescence is not necessarily a period of *Sturm und Drang* even though it is in the United States. And even a cursory knowledge of traditional China informs one that old age need not be a period of low community regard. So we have every reason to suspect that all of the proposed stages of ego development may not be universal. And those that are probably unfold in rather different ways in divers cultures. Once again, we can ask: Is the midlife crisis posited for American adults universal? And even among Americans, does it vary in its manifestations across ethnic groups? If we are to design education to promote ego development, we need a much better understanding of cross-cultural and subcultural variations in ego development.

A number of questions relevant to the study of ego development in other cultures are suggested by the cross-cultural frame of reference of anthropology. For example, we know that the life tasks of some periods of adult life are sex-linked (see Chickering and Havighurst, this volume). Under what cultural conditions is the content of the ego stages and their developmental tasks sex-linked? Are the conditions found in some American subcultures? Does the presence of rapid culture change have implications for ego development and therefore for developmental education? One consequence of rapid culture change seems to be conflict between the generations. What implications does this have for ego development and for education? Does the presence of cultural heterogeneity have implications for ego development, especially for the tasks that characterize the various ego stages?

Obviously, the list of questions could be extended. Suffice it to say that we should make sure that our conceptions of stages of ego development as an aspect of "human nature" are based on a sufficiently full sampling of the human population. Otherwise, we may overlook some important dimension of the phenomenon. Cross-cultural research can help to resolve the conflict between the approaches of Piaget and Inhelder and Loevinger as to whether ego development involves discrete sequential stages or gradations along a quantitative continuum (see Weathersby, this volume).

The third area where anthropology can make a contribution to the conceptual underpinnings of developmental education is in the study of the culture of education (see Spindler, 1974). The "ethnography of education" is a relatively new subfield within the subdiscipline of anthropology of education. It asks questions such as these: What are the operating assumptions in an educational institution or portion of it about the role of the student, the teacher, and the nature and purposes of education? Are there latent assumptions as well as manifest ones? How do they affect the operation of the system? Ethnographers of education already are working on issues such as the differential nonverbal treatment by teachers of minority students or students defined as "slow" (McDermott, 1974). We need to know more about every aspect of the culture of educational institutions. For example, in the mode of Lévi-Strauss, what are the myths of an institution, and how do they convey important truths about the institution? Are there other truths that are conveyed via other modes of communication, and how do they affect the performance of the various actors in the system? In my view, an important task of the ethnography of education is to inform us as to what really happens in the culture of the educational institution so we can begin to judge the extent to which that conforms to what we believe *should* happen in a developmentally oriented educational setting.

In sum, anthropological contributions to the conceptual armory of developmental education can address themselves to the questions: Do we know enough about cultural variations in human cognitive, ego, and moral development? And do we know enough about the actual culture of institutions of higher learning? But even as we address these questions, it is clear that the study of anthropology can facilitate the shift from absolute to relative thinking, enhance ego development, and facilitate moral development. Most importantly, perhaps, anthropology can strengthen the concepts underlying education for adult development.

References

Arrighi, G., and Saul, J. S. *Essays on the Political Economy of Africa.* New York: Monthly Review Press, 1973.

Bennett, J. W. "A Course in Comparative Civilization." In D. G. Mandelbaum, G. Lasker, and E. M. Albert (Eds.), *The Teaching of Anthropology.* Berkeley: University of California Press, 1963.

Berry, J. W. "Temne and Eskimo Perceptual Skills." *International Journal of Psychology,* 1966, *1,* 207-229.

Bruner, E. M., and Spindler, G. D. "The Introductory Course in Cultural Anthropology." In D. G. Mandelbaum, G. Lasker, and E. M. Albert (Eds.), *The Teaching of Anthropology.* Berkeley: University of California Press, 1963.

Bruner, J. S., Olver, R. R., and Greenfield, P. M. *Studies in Cognitive Growth.* New York: Wiley, 1966.

Buehler, C. "Genetic Aspects of the Self." *Annals of the New York Academy of Sciences,* 1962, *96,* 730-764.

Chickering, A. W. "Developmental Change as a Major Outcome." In M. T. Keeton and Associates, *Experiential Learning: Rationale, Characteristics, and Assessment.* San Francisco: Jossey-Bass, 1976.

Cole, M. "Cultural Differences in the Context of Learning." In S. Messick and Associates, *Individuality in Learning: Implications of Cognitive Styles and Creativity for Human Development.* San Francisco: Jossey-Bass, 1976.

Cole, M., and others. *The Cultural Context of Learning and Thinking.* New York: Basic Books, 1971.

Cole, M., and Scribner, S. *Culture and Perception: A Psychological Introduction.* New York: Wiley, 1974.

DuBois, C. "The Curriculum in Cultural Anthropology." In D. G. Mandelbaum, G. Lasker, and E. M. Albert (Eds.), *The Teaching of Anthropology.* Berkeley: University of California Press, 1963.

Edgerton, R. J. *The Individual in Cultural Adaptation: A Study of Four East African Peoples.* Berkeley: University of California Press, 1971.

Eggan, F. "Social Anthropology and the Method of Controlled Comparison." *American Anthropologist,* 1954, *56,* 743-763.

Erikson, E. H. *Childhood and Society.* New York: Norton, 1950.

Erikson, E. H. *Identity and the Life Cycle.* Psychological Issues Monograph 1. New York: International Universities Press, 1959.

Fanon, F. *The Wretched of the Earth.* London: MacGibbon and Kee, 1965.

Gay, J., and Cole, M. *The New Mathematics and an Old Culture.* New York: Holt, Rinehart and Winston, 1967.

Gibbs, J. L., Jr. "Compensatory Blood-Brotherhood: A Comparative Analysis of Institutionalized Friendship in Two African Societies." *Minnesota Academy of Science Proceedings,* 1962, *31,* 67-74.

Gibbs, J. L., Jr. "The Kpelle Moot: A Therapeutic Model for the Informal Settlement of Disputes." *Africa*, 1963, *33*, 1-11.

Gibbs, J. L., Jr. "Stanford Education in the 1970's: A Call for Educating the Whole Person." [Stanford University] *Campus Report*, 1976, *8* (21), 232-245.

Gordon, E. W. "Group Differences Versus Individual Development in Educational Design." In S. Messick and Associates, *Individuality in Learning: Implications of Cognitive Styles and Creativity for Human Development.* San Francisco: Jossey-Bass, 1976.

Guttmann, D. L. "Alternatives to Disengagement: The Old Men of the Highland Druze." In R. A. Levine (Ed.), *Culture and Personality: Contemporary Readings.* Chicago: Aldine, 1974.

Harris, M. *Cows, Pigs, Wars, and Witches: The Riddles of Culture.* New York: Random House, 1974.

Harris, M. *Cannibals and Kings: The Origins of Cultures.* New York: Random House, 1977.

Hoebel, E. A. *The Law of Primitive Man: A Study in Comparative Legal Dynamics.* Cambridge, Mass.: Harvard University Press, 1954.

Hymes, D. *Reinventing Anthropology.* New York: Random House, 1969.

Kluckhohn, C. *Mirror for Man.* New York: McGraw-Hill, 1949.

Kluckhohn, C. "Universal Values and Cultural Relativism." In *Modern Education and Human Values.* Pittsburgh: University of Pittsburgh Press, 1952.

Kluckhohn, C. "Universal Categories of Culture." In A. L. Kroeber (Ed.), *Anthropology Today.* Chicago: University of Chicago Press, 1953.

Kluckhohn, C. "Ethical Relativity: *Sic et Non.*" *Journal of Philosophy,* 1955, *52*, 663-677.

Lave, J. "Cognitive Consequences of Traditional Apprenticeship Training in West Africa." *Anthropology and Education Quarterly,* 1944, *8*, 177-180.

Lee, D. "Lineal and Non-lineal Codifications of Reality." *Psychosomatic Medicine,* 1950, *12*, 89-97.

Lesser, G. S. "Cultural Differences in Learning and Thinking Styles." In S. Messick and Associates, *Individuality in Learning: Implications of Cognitive Styles and Creativity for Human Development.* San Francisco: Jossey-Bass, 1976.

Lévi-Strauss, C. *The Raw and the Cooked.* New York: Harper & Row, 1969.

Levinson, D. J., and others. *Seasons in a Man's Life.* New York: Knopf, 1977.

Lewis, O. *Five Families: Mexican Case Studies in the Culture of Poverty.* New York: Basic Books, 1959.

Lewis, O. *The Children of Sanchez.* New York: Random House, 1961.

Lewis, O. *Pedro Martinez.* New York: Random House, 1964.

Lewis, O. *La Vida: A Puerto Rican Family in the Culture of Poverty. San Juan and New York.* New York: Random House, 1965.

Lewis, O. *A Death in the Sanchez Family.* New York: Random House, 1966.

Loevinger, J. *Ego Development: Conceptions and Theories.* San Francisco: Jossey-Bass, 1976.

Lyman, R. W. Speech before Stanford University alumni in Chicago, February 3, 1971. Mimeographed.

McDermott, R. P. "Achieving School Failure: An Anthropological Approach to Illiteracy and Social Stratification." In G. D. Spindler (Ed.), *Education and Cultural Process: Toward an Anthropology of Education.* New York: Holt, Rinehart and Winston, 1974.

Mandelbaum, D. G., Lasker, G., and Albert, E. M. (Eds.). *The Teaching of Anthropology.* Berkeley: University of California Press, 1963.

Mead, M. *Coming of Age in Samoa.* New York: William Morrow, 1928.

Miller, N. (Ed.). *Faces of Change, Five Rural Societies in Transition: Bolivia, Kenya, Afghanistan, Taiwan, China Coast.* Lebannon, N.H.: Wheelock Educational Resources for American Universities Field Staff, 1978.

Perry, W. G., Jr. *Forms of Intellectual and Ethical Development in the College Years: A Scheme.* New York: Holt, Rinehart and Winston, 1970.

Piaget, J. *Judgment and Reasoning in the Child.* London: Routledge & Kegan Paul, 1928.

Rouch, J., and Morin, E. *Chronicle of a Summer.* New York: Corinth Films, 1961.

Spindler, G. D. *Education and Cultural Process: Toward an Anthropology of Education.* New York: Holt, Rinehart and Winston, 1974.

Turner, V. W. *The Ritual Process: Structure and Anti-Structure.* Chicago: Aldine, 1969.

Turner, V. "Process, System, and Symbol: A New Anthropological Synthesis." *Daedalus,* 1977, *196,* 61-80.

Vogt, E. Z., and Albert, E. M. (Eds.). *People of Rimrock: A Study of Values in Five Cultures.* Cambridge, Mass.: Harvard University Press, 1966.

Witkin, H. A. "A Cognitive-Style Approach to Cross-Cultural Research." *International Journal of Psychology,* 1967, *2,* 233-250.

Wober, M. "Adapting Witkin's Field Independence Theory to Accommodate New Information from Africa." *The British Journal of Psychology,* 1967, *58,* 29-38.

Worth, S., and Adair, J. *Through Navajo Eyes: An Expression in Film Communication and Anthropology.* Bloomington: Indiana University Press, 1972.

22

Elof Axel Carlson

Biology for Nonmajors

Many issues in biology have vital significance for society as a whole—for example, the genetics of newly arising mutations, both induced and spontaneous; the relation of carcinogens to induced cancers, especially from cigarette smoking, industrial pollution, and occupational hazards; the use of defoliants, first in the Vietnam war and now in national forests; and the evidence regarding biological determinism of human intelligence and social behavior.

All too often, however, the decision makers who set policy on issues related to the life sciences are biologically illiterate, hostile to the sciences, or willing to follow the advice of a few "expert" witnesses who may not be representative of their scientific disciplines. So far during this century, as a result, biological illiteracy has allowed misguided officers of the Eugenics Record Office to convince Congress of the alleged inferiority of European immigrants, leading to the restrictive immigration laws of the early 1920s. And shoddy research has been used to support compulsory sterilization laws for various categories of the "unfit," including the insane, the chronic pauper, the retarded, and the "habitual" criminal.

As we look at how biological knowledge and principles are applied or ignored by society, it becomes clear that biological education has failed to meet the general public's need for knowledge. Potential leaders benefit little from the standard course for nonscience majors, which skeptical professors have dubbed a "tiptoe through the phyla." And the abstract principles of nucleic acid chemistry, Mendelian laws, mitotic divisions, and developmental processes are remote and quickly forgotten by students if they are not directly tied to students' own experience.

How can colleges and universities cure biological illiteracy and make biology a valuable liberal arts experience, satisfying students' need for knowledge that can be applied to their personal and public life? It is my belief that this much needed reform of biological education involves two aspects of introductory nonmajors courses—their content and their presentation. Failure to consider both may prevent the successful education of liberal arts students, including those among them who will be tomorrow's leaders.

Content of Introductory Courses for Nonmajors

Small colleges often offer a single introductory course in biology, but larger colleges and universities offer at least two—one for students planning to major in biology and another for nonscience majors. At these institutions, the content of the course for biology majors is usually departmentally mandated, whereas the content of the course for nonscience majors may be of little concern to the biology department. Moreover, the faculty members who teach the nonmajors course may receive the assignment as a punishment for poor scholarly productivity. The course is usually out of favor with the rest of the faculty, who perceive nonmajors as lacking the capabilities and enthusiasm that biology majors frequently bring to their courses. Yet few biology majors will be among the lawyers, business executives, legislators, ministers, consumer activists, and journalists who will shape and decide the values and laws that govern the applications of biology to the individual and society.

Today many students—both biology majors and nonmajors—enter the college or university with uneven academic skills. Some cannot write effective prose. A considerable number have no idea how to take effective notes during a lecture. Many do not have experience with relational thinking and tend to identify memorization of terms with learning. But despite these shortcomings, most nonmajors who take introductory biology want to learn. They not only want a solid introduction to facts and principles, they want to relate them to an overall view of the world. For them, knowledge of biology is most stimulating when it can be related to other fields such as history, literature, and psychology, to current events, or to different philosophical world views. The degree to which we are aware of that need and the skill with which we can make such connections will often determine the success of our courses.

Basic Principles of Human Biology. Consider five major principles of biology—the cell, the gene, development, molecular biology, and evolution. Taught as abstract principles, they are indistinguishable from those found in any university introductory biology course, and students in their later life are likely to forget the connection between such principles and the reality of their daily existence. But consider how these principles relate to the human condition, and we suddenly see that we and our families are part of this biology:

1. We begin our biological existence as a fertilized egg. But fertility cannot be taken for granted; 20 percent of all married couples fail in their attempts to achieve a pregnancy for a full year. Sooner or later half of these infertile couples will achieve a pregnancy, but 10 percent of all marriages will remain sterile.
2. If the fertilized egg begins to develop and an implantation occurs, we expect, some nine months later, to be parents. But one fifth of all pregnant women experience a spontaneous abortion. Nearly 40 percent of these aborted fetuses contain abnormal chromosome numbers.

3. Even if the fetus does make it to delivery, there is a 5 percent chance that the baby will have a serious birth defect requiring major medical attention.
4. Some 30 percent of all pediatric admissions to our municipal hospitals involve genetic disorders and birth defects.
5. The divorce and separation rate of parents who have a child with a serious and long-lasting birth defect or genetic disorder (for example, spina bifida, muscular dystrophy, cystic fibrosis) exceeds 75 percent.
6. About 20 percent of adults will die ten years or more before their mean life expectancy because they harbor a higher than average genetic load, which they received at fertilization.

Note that to understand why things go wrong the student needs to know the normal processes by which sperm and eggs are formed. This includes the processes of mitosis, meiosis, and fertilization. It requires a knowledge of nondisjunction and of embryogenesis. To understand birth defects the student needs to know Mendelism, X-linked inheritance, and polygenic inheritance. These, in turn, have to be related to meiosis. But when all this is learned in the context of the student's life and related to the experiences of friends and relatives, the scientific terminology becomes a way of grasping the causes of those age-old human tragedies.

The principles are reinforced in new contexts. Cell division is given new meaning when it is followed after radiation breaks a chromosome. Understanding the cycle of abnormally fused chromosomes and how this prevents normal cell division, eventually killing the dividing cell, provides the basis for understanding radiation sickness and rendering the victims of Hiroshima and Nagasaki as victims of a chromosomal breakage-fusion-bridge cycle. This historical reality and the threat of atomic warfare are thus woven into biology through a simple principle first discovered in corn in the 1930s.

It is precisely this relational aspect of teaching that is usually missing in the nonmajors course. We delude ourselves if we simply teach the principles of mitosis and meiosis and consider that our obligations as teachers end there. Far from it! Unless the nonmajor sees mitosis as part of the human condition and learns why that process is essential for an understanding of certain public controversies, then we have forfeited a basic function of democratic society. We must relate our principles to those realms of life in which they are critical to responsible decision making. How can legislators decide on regulating nuclear industries if they do not know how to distinguish chromosome breakage from gene mutation? How can good judgment develop from an overreactive fear or a naive denial of any risks from low levels of radiation? Do we not, as citizens, need to know the biology that determines our own health? Why then do we present those principles separated from our human experience? If mitosis is presented in an abstract fashion, with illustrations from the sea urchin or onion root tip, then, of course, neither the nonmajor nor the professional who emerges from our courses will have the vaguest idea of what genetics and biology have to do with human life.

I list below a roster of further topics that lend themselves to the nonmajors course. Not only do they demand the courage to present controversial issues in class, they also demand skill in relating them to the principles of biology and to those biological facts best suited to clarifying and possibly resolving controversies about them. In some debates on these issues, the biology is ignored; in others it is misused. The function of the scholar-teacher in teaching biology to nonmajors is one of clarification—helping students see what biological principles are actually involved, what we really do and do not know, and how the values of contending groups are applied to different aspects of these principles. These dozen topics are only a sample of the current issues related to biology. It would require a textbook to present an analysis of even these twelve issues, and, unfortunately, no such text presently exists for those who wish to teach a biology of the human condition.

Population. The Malthusian doctrine, according to which population growth tends to outstrip the food supply, has been invoked as an argument for population control. But people have values and a technology that affect both sides of the Malthusian equation: reproductive rates and food resources. Is it valid, then, to apply an animal model to humans? Students should be exposed to the values of those advocating zero population growth (ZPG), those advocating no artificial birth control, and those who believe that the problem is self-correcting without misery and catastrophe. Note that evolutionary theory, population ecology, and comparative, reproductive biology are involved in this issue.

Birth Control. There are several reasons why people elect birth control. They may want a small family; they may wish to avoid transmitting hereditary defects; they may be protecting the health of the woman; or they may be concerned about economic, social, or political factors that would influence their ability to be effective parents. The biology involved in this question includes spermatogenesis, oogenesis, fertilization, implantation, hormonal regulation of gametogenesis, anatomy of the reproductive system, and the physiology of spermicides (are they mutagenic? do they break chromosomes?).

Prenatal Diagnosis. Amniocentesis is a diagnostic procedure that can reveal the existence of certain genetic and chromosomal defects in the 14- to 16-week-old fetus. It is used by women who are at risk for birth defects. Involved in the biology of this issue are genetic laws (Mendelian ratios), chromosome karyotyping and banding, and biochemical processes (enzyme assays; how mutant genes work). The election of the procedure involves human values: Should a parent have the right to request a termination of pregnancy for a severely malformed or disordered fetus? Is it psychologically sound for a parent to know in advance that a child will have a birth defect, whether that parent elects to terminate the pregnancy or not? In any such discussion it is important to know the status of the nervous system in the 20- to 24-week-old fetus and also how we relate actual and potential capacity for human functions.

Sexuality. Humans actually have seven sexes: genetic, chromosomal, gonadal, internal genital, external genital, secondary, and psychological. When these come together, a normal male or female exists. But gene mutations, chromosomal defects, hormone therapy during pregnancy, tumors of the pregnant mother or individual, and behavioral models can all alter that congruence. Pseudohermaphroditism, homosexuality, and transvestism are various departures from the anatomical or psychologically traditional identifications of sex gender and function. Our values enter into this when we define what is normal and when we assign social functions (intelligence, talent, occupation, behavior) to sexual gender. Much needed is a clarification of what we know to be a consequence of our chromosomal composition and what we infer, by analogy or by tradition, to be typically male or female traits. Note that the biology includes developmental biology (differentiation of the gonads, wolffian ducts, müllerian ducts, and so on) as well as physiology and genetics.

Carcinogenesis. Why are cancer frequencies ethnically and geographically so variable? Cancers may be induced by habits of food preparation, tobacco smoking, radiation exposure, chemical pollutants from industry, and a variety of additives to our foods. To understand the nature of cancer, we need to know the biology of the cancer cell, the mutational and viral theories of cancer, lysogenic viral life cycles, regulatory genetics, and the developmental differences between cancer cells and normal tissues. To apply this knowledge to social concerns, we need to know the history and economics of industrial waste disposal and the tobacco industry, and the defined role and limitations of the Food and Drug Administration. We also need to know the dietary habits of different societies (for example, the amount of animal fats in the diet; whether food is boiled, fried, or broiled; the temperature of foods when swallowed; the spices and additives used in preparing, storing, or flavoring foods; and so on).

Radiation Hazards. Medicine, industry, and the military are the major sources of radiation hazards. To understand the debates (fallout, nuclear reactor construction, test ban treaties, lead shielding for routine dental and medical examinations) several aspects must be discussed. The distinction must be made between chromosome breakage (which kills dividing cells) and gene mutations, both of which are radiation-induced. Students must learn the breakage-fusion-bridge cycle and its relation to radiation sickness. This includes knowledge of which tissues divide in the adult. It also involves analysis of the risk-benefit assessments by those on both sides of the debate—those focusing on individual risk (which is usually insignificant) and those emphasizing the absolute number affected in a population (which may involve thousands of anonymous victims). Additionally, aspects like biological amplification of trace elements must be understood for participation in debate or arriving at a position.

Mutagenesis. Chemical agents as well as radiation result in gene mutations. Students should learn how chemicals alter purines and pyrimidines. They should identify those products known to be mutagens that are used in households or major industries (for example, formaldehyde, nitrous acid, nitrosoamine, hydrogen peroxide, alkylating agents, and so on). Somatic and germinal mutation should be distinguished. Gene function after mutation can also be discussed (why losses of function are more apt to occur than the very rare changes to new or improved functions).

Racism. Surprisingly, few biology texts cover the genetics and biology of human skin color inheritance. There are several models that give reasonably good analyses of the various miscegenations between whites and blacks and their descendants. Mendel's principle of independent assortment, quantitative inheritance, and the distinctions between dominance, codominance, and intermediate inheritance are applicable. So, too, are the adaptive theories of skin color (for example, the vitamin D theory, protective coloration, ultraviolet filtration and skin cancer, body heat loss, and so on), all of which invoke biological principles. The values involved in racism include notions of inherent superiority, spurious assumptions about the segregation of traits from miscegenation hybrids, and various religious and social attitudes about human potentials and functions.

The IQ Controversy. The measurement of human talent and mental potential for abstract, verbal, or mathematical skills is difficult and flawed with cultural bias. To understand the biology, students need to know the genetics of polygenic and multifactorial traits, the biology of one-egg twins (including the consequences of the MZ fetal-diffusion syndrome on IQ), the environmental and biological factors of mental retardation, and the various models of genius and eminence. The value issues include class prejudice, racism, xenophobia, various types of elitism, and the relation between IQ scores and educational practice.

Eugenics. If gene mutation occurs spontaneously and represents the raw material for evolutionary change, what are its consequences in human populations living in affluent societies where natural selective forces (malnutrition, disease, environmental hazards) are inhibited? Some geneticists claim that an increasing quantity of mutations will gradually occur, resulting in more medical problems for each family. Others claim that other forms of selection (especially assortative mating) will compensate. Those who express concern about the greater number of mutations in the human population often suggest compensatory selection to minimize the number of children born with this risk. Besides the various values (and *Brave New World* fears) students must know the frequency and nature of spontaneous mutation and its consequences in populations (Hardy-Weinberg law, impairment, detrimental genes, and so on) to assess these viewpoints.

Human Aggression. Sociobiologists argue that mammals have innate aggressive instincts, which are released by ritualized displays, fighting, or snarling. Such aggression is associated with sexual selection and territoriality. Some biologists extend these animal models to humans. The genetics of behavior is still at an early stage of scientific development. Few Mendelian traits are behavioral, and little is known about the distinction between polygenic and environmental components of such traits. Even less is known about their heritability in humans. Yet many popular books advocate a genetic determinism of behavior, which would have far-reaching implications for criminal justice, warfare, housing, and social justice. Both animal behavior and the genetic analysis of quantitative traits are important for evaluating this controversy.

Germ Warfare. It is now possible to create microbes that are resistant to most antibiotics and novel microbes that combine rapid spread with pathogenicity. If the genes for the toxic effects of diphtheria were inserted deliberately into a bacterium that makes cheese or into a virus that makes cold sores, serious public health problems would result. The techniques of recombinant DNA and many other molecular approaches to microbial and cell biology might be discussed. Such social values as those of terrorists could be included in the discussion of how abuses of biology can be prevented. Also needed are realistic appraisals of microbial functions brought about without planning (alleged "superbugs" and other runaway epidemics from naive accidents). Much sensationalism exists, along with complacency among scientists who believe that research per se justifies any risks of abuse.

I have not included in this list the more obvious and much discussed ecological aspects of pollution (DDT, other pesticides, polluted streams and lakes, smog, automobile emissions, industrial smoke) because these have been well documented and brought to public attention. Our internal biology and the hazards of the human condition just identified have not received such public attention, and for this reason I have listed these twelve areas of public debate for those who might wish to construct a biology course that is not limited to ecology.

Students who listen to these controversial topics—racism, the IQ controversy, carcinogenesis from environmental pollutants and additives, mutagenesis from radiation and chemicals, eugenics, human sexuality, birth defects and prenatal diagnosis, elective abortion, contraception, human evolution, cloning, and recombinant DNA—soon learn that they cannot escape making decisions on incomplete knowledge. They learn that science does not know all the answers, yet what it does know is an important component for arriving at their own values and decisions.

Concerns of Different Students. Many of the principles of biology developed in this biology course are useful in debating national and international issues. Of course, the response to these issues will reflect the student's age and experience. The chapters in Part One of this volume devote considerable attention to intellectual development, moral judgment, and the life cycle. In all likelihood, younger students (17 to 22 years old) will be particularly interested in population, birth control, prenatal diagnosis, sexuality, and mutagenesis, especially as they approach their personal life decisions to marry and raise a family. Students in middle and late adulthood will be more interested in the problems of carcinogenesis, racism, and radiation hazards. Although their emphases will vary, the concerns of both younger and older students will benefit from the development of humanitarian concern, described by White.

Younger students are more likely to exhibit dualistic thinking and come up with dramatic or radical approaches to solving problems. Older students are more likely to hold opinions that have been shaped by the press, television, and community standards. In both these constituencies, however, there will be conscientious and independent thinkers who will approach these controversies in constructive ways. The reader of the chapters by Weathersby, Perry, and Gilligan will not be surprised to find, in both the essays of a large lecture class and in smaller discussion groups, such differing viewpoints. These will reflect not only genuine beliefs but also developmental stages, with their characteristic moral, ethical, and cognitive strengths and weaknesses.

The application of biological principles to issues of personal and public concern should stimulate the kinds of intellectual development described by Schaie and Parr, turning students from memorization of facts to the integrative use of them in their own living concerns. An example from my own acquaintance was a student at UCLA who had been a theater arts major before he enlisted in the Peace Corps. He was sent to the rural Phillipines to teach English. After a few weeks he complained to his supervisor, "How can I teach English literature to my students when they're dying?" He was taken out of the classroom and sent to a field hospital to learn parasitology. When the student returned to college, his career goals had changed: He wanted to learn tropical medicine so he could help the underdeveloped countries overcome their handicaps of malnutrition, inadequate public health services, and ignorance about waste disposal.

Presentation of Biology to Nonmajors

It would be an error, I believe, to predicate the teaching of biology to nonmajors on an individualized or even small-group instruction model. Rather, I feel confident that most institutions, and particularly the large state universities and colleges, will require large lecture classes of several hundred students to accommodate the enrollments in lower-division introductory biology courses. The formal lecture has been a college institution for more than 800 years, and it is unlikely to be replaced entirely by tutorials, field projects, independent study, audiovisual self-study, or other modes of instruction. The reason is simple fiscal reality: beginning courses usually enroll the largest number of students, can be taught economically in a large lecture room, and often have the lowest ratio of support in the department's allocation of funds for teaching. The irony, of course, is that the most heterogeneous students, in terms of background and skills, and those at a stage of intellectual development at which they are most in need of individual attention, are likely to experience personal neglect, ineffective teaching, compartmentalized content, and Spartan austerity for much of their first two years of college.

Economical, low-budget lecture courses are often unpopular and are properly criticized by students because they are poorly taught. There is no intrinsic reason, however, why they should be so ineffective in most universities. They can be revitalized, and technology is not the answer. Ideally, the large lecture should be supplemented with special review sessions, a place for optional audio-tutorial cassettes and film loops, and Xerox facilities for copying the instructor's lecture notes. Such aids would not replace a lecture format because a good lecture course serves many purposes that audio-tutorial programs cannot. Lectures can be intellectually exciting and communicate both enthusiasm and the model of a scholarly mind at work. They can provide spontaneity and immediacy through references to current events or sudden flashes of wit or inspiration. They can tie together many ideas and topics that might not come together for students lacking the necessary experience, critical judgment, or mastery of the subject. And they permit hundreds of students to be influenced by the scholar-teacher's values.

Problems must be overcome, however, in large lecture classes—for majors as well as nonmajors. Contrary to general academic belief, majors are not necessarily self-paced and motivated scholars. They are undergraduates, not fantasized images of ourselves as neophyte graduate students. They have considerable difficulty with abstract problem solving and relational thinking. They tend to be more competitive and aggressive than nonmajors and will take up more time arguing over examinations and final grades. They may even panic and resort to theft and vandalism of library reserve materials if they do not have adequate opportunity to learn effectively in class or through properly supervised and helpful supplementary programs of audio-tutorial or other materials.

From every perspective, whether in the actual delivery of lectures or in the administration of courses, large classes are demanding of time, talent, and commitment. Unless department heads, deans, provosts, and college presidents recognize these special needs, both the student and the reputation of the school are likely to suffer. Even some of my faculty colleagues believe that a large class consists of 50 students or that there is little difference in the preparation required for a class of 50 or 500 students. They are wrong.

Consider this analogy. Imagine that you are in a concert hall and a violin soloist comes out with an armful of music, sets up the stand, and announces, "Today, I'll try to cover some Romantic music, starting with Brahms, and if time permits, we'll end the concert with Mendelssohn." After this announcement, the violinist selects some music and begins to play, backtracking if an error is made, pausing to turn the pages, and occasionally sounding as if the passages were stitched together rather than part of a continuum. The result would be an outrage. You paid for excellence, mastery, control, preparation, and the unique excitement that a skilled performer can convey to a receptive audience. Instead you got a typical lecture—casual, disorganized, indifferently presented, and lacking in the fire which can ignite receptive minds.

In a room of 15 or 30 or even 50 students, that erratic, informal, somewhat sloppy presentation need not be disturbing. It might even be effective if the teacher knows how to provoke questions and discussions in class. There is an intimacy between teacher and student that is not even disturbed by the invisible line that separates the students' seats from the instructor's desk. But in an auditorium with 500 seats, most of them occupied, that intimacy disappears and a new psychological expectation arises—the teacher is now a performer and the class is an audience. Casual, unrehearsed lecturing will not do in this situation. Rather, the students expect a highly organized, well-delivered, and well-prepared lecture. When they do not get this, they feel cheated.

To be effective in a large class, the instructor must convey a mastery of subject matter, a near flawless delivery in a voice that projects throughout the auditorium, an intensity and enthusiasm that reflect a love for learning, and those special skills that are necessary for reaching large numbers of people. The teacher must be alert to the sounds in the room. Any rustling or murmuring indicates the need for a change of pace or a repetition. But the teacher cannot repeat without using a new context or some of the class will be bored because they did grasp the concept. Thus, when I reach mitosis, I give the chromosomal events first. I repeat the process by showing these events in the entire cell. Then I repeat them a third time by following a broken chromosome in its cycle leading to cell death. The effective teacher learns to organize a lecture as a story. It has a beginning that provides an overview of what the lecture will discuss. It uses extensive relational thinking to bring in history, controversy, the human condition, or current events to enrich the meaning of the subject. It concludes with a summary of the major points and implications of the principles discussed. Throughout the lecture the teacher must be guided by the sounds of silence. Are the students stunned by too complex a presentation, or are they on the edges of their seats with anticipation? The former response is often accompanied by a bewildered look and the movement of heads to a neighbors' notebooks; the communion of an enraptured audience is immediately apparent from the presence of a thousand eyes looking at the teacher.

Achieving mastery of subject matter is easier than achieving mastery of presentation. A scholar may be a master of a body of knowledge but still be unable to share the joy of knowledge with an audience. Stage fright, inexperience, an untrained voice, lack of eye contact, irritating mannerisms, insecurity, and a failure to explore the broader implications of the subject will all defeat the efforts of the ineffective teacher. When students express their boredom or confusion, such a teacher may blame the students' intellectual shortcomings for their failure to grasp the ideas presented.

Lecturing is only part of the organization of a large course. There are problems of testing, grading, and, most important, providing an opportunity for students to discuss the material they are trying to learn. Thus, the large lecture course needs a budget adequate for its functions. It should include provision for a course coordinator, a permanent employee at the B.A. level, who can carry out most of the administrative functions (typing, mimeographing, Xeroxing, filing, recording grades, arranging schedules for discussion sections, calling students or teaching assistants, assigning tutors, scheduling audio-tutorial sessions, and so on). And it should include a modest investment in film loops and supplementary audio-tutorial equipment. If students' study habits or writing skills are to be diagnosed effectively, a special staff should be provided for this purpose.

Over the years I have worked out solutions to some of these problems. First, I recognized that it is both unfair and undesirable to rely on graduate teaching assistants for such a course. There are too many majors courses that have higher priority for these teaching assistants. Furthermore, many graduate students emulate their sponsors' negative attitudes toward the teaching of lower-division courses. So instead, I designed an undergraduate course in college teaching. Students receive credit for being an undergraduate teaching assistant. They apply for the course and look upon their selection as an honor. They are familiar with the students, the instructor, and the institutional facilities. I spend one hour a week with them evaluating teaching by having them prepare ten-minute lectures. They deliver these talks and learn eye contact, blackboard presentation, pacing, elimination of intrusive mannerisms, voice projection, and how to tie points together. By criticizing each other, they learn how to improve their own habits as a student as well as a teaching assistant.

The undergraduate teaching assistants have a one-hour discussion section with twenty or fewer students. They tutor those who receive D or F on the first examination, and they go over the students' notebooks to correct errors. They then invite the students to sit with them to observe an actual model of note-taking. The teaching assistants also grade homework or examination questions. To make sure the teaching assistants are grading properly, I alphabetize the examinations after a test and thus know which teaching assistant is grading any given student. I then provide the students with the same answer keys used by the teaching assistants, and if there is a request for a regrading the student fills out a mimeographed form attached to the examination. I do all such regrading and note what errors the teaching assistant is making. I then call in the teaching assistant and discuss effective ways to improve grading (for example, more marginalia on the students' essays or more careful reading of the students' factual statements). The goal, in working with teaching assistants, is not to exploit cheap labor but to help these students develop effective teaching skills, whether good discussion habits, effective tutoring, accurate and informative grading, or lecturing. Also, the student learns to effectively marshal the facts and arguments in a written request for a regrade. Whether the regrade is granted or not, the student benefits because the error (by the teaching assistant or the student) will be made as clear as possible. My major point in introducing undergraduate teaching assistants to teaching is quite specific: Every function of a course should, as much as possible, be a learning process for the persons participating in it.

Having given both essay examinations and computer-graded examinations in large courses, I have been able to analyze the problems students have in minimizing the gap between what they know and what they actually answer on the test. The computer-graded examinations permit an item analysis that ranks the questions according to their difficulty and shows how the upper, middle, and lower thirds of the class fared on each item. For a majors course in genetics (sophomore-junior level) given to 400 students, I found that almost all students do well on memory questions but about half of the students have difficulty with problem solving or relational thinking (drawing implications or applications from a principle, such as mitosis, Mendelism, or X-linked inheritance). When I have held review sessions or talked with students during office hours, I have learned that students are not given sufficient instruction in problem-solving skills. Most of the students have been called upon to use these skills only in large classes. If they do not grasp the skills, they have few resources available to improve their understanding.

Part of the students' difficulty is developmental and part is just a result of neglect. According to Piagetian learning theory, the capacity for abstract reasoning develops in adolescence. Those students who have not yet developed a facility for problem solving are apt to have difficulties, particularly in their lower-division courses. Regrettably, few colleges and universities attempt to identify those students in need of special instruction to remedy this weakness. Since the students in a biology major's genetics class are a self-selected group of motivated students (mostly pre-med students concerned about their grades), the fact that half of them are in need of such instruction indicates that they are being neglected. It is, I believe, more likely that their interest in the sciences reflects a potential for abstract work that suffers from neglect than that they lack this potential and are in the wrong field. If Piagetian analysis is essentially valid, that abstract skill will be attained by most of them by their senior year.

The nonmajors course, however, most likely has a much higher percentage of students who will be lost if problem-solving skills are demanded of them—for example, mapping genes, computing risk ratios for genetic disorders, or applying the genetic code. For this reason, it is important, in designing the introductory courses, to distinguish between a nonmajors learning environment and that of the majors. The nonmajors would clearly suffer in a course that attempts to reach both majors and nonmajors or that places a heavy emphasis on problem-solving activities.

Staffing the Introductory Course

Staffing the large introductory course is a major problem, which many universities have handled ineffectively. Preferably, the instructor should be tenured because both experience and a major commitment of time are needed for a successful course. One's obligations do not end with lecturing. In a large class there are always special problems that need attention. In a class of 400 to 600 students there are bound to be three or four cases of mononucleosis, a student in a wheelchair, a blind student, two or three foreign students with less than perfect facility for writing essay questions, two or three students with deaths in the family, several instances of missed classes or examinations involving car trouble (if commuters form a significant segment of the student body), and a variety of other unusual situations (for example, suicide attempts, arrests for drug dealing, and students with severe emotional crises) that prevent them from attending lectures or taking an examination. In a class of 30 or 40 students such events are rare and do not require a major amount of time for make-up examinations, assigning tutors, rescheduling appointments, or locating resource persons to help the troubled student. Also, in a large class there will be more A students requesting letters of recommendation for various professional schools.

The problems of examinations are also multiplied for the large class. Alternate seating is impossible in a large lecture room filled to capacity (and that may be the only large room on campus). Thus, duplicate examinations, color coded or numbered, must be used to prevent cheating, and this involves a considerable amount of time for typing and mimeographing. It is much easier for the determined cheater to succeed in such a situation than in a small class where all the students are known by the teacher. This increases the time and energy devoted to prevention of such abuses.

All these activities could easily overwhelm and discourage a young faculty member. But if the course is assigned to an older faculty member who has no real interest in it, many of these factors will be ignored or poorly handled, either because teaching is not that person's forte or because that instructor foresees no personal reward from the job. If effective teaching in such courses has little influence on merit raises, colleague recognition, or further promotion, the person taking on that assignment is not likely to do a good job with it.

What is needed for the reform of introductory courses is an acceptance of the model of the scholar-teacher. Virtually all universities respect the scholar. This has been the prevailing model since Daniel Coit Gilman set up Johns Hopkins University as a graduate, Ph.D.-granting institution over a hundred years ago. But the scholar-teacher is virtually unknown. Instead, a false dichotomy exists: Scholars are intrinsically valuable because they create new knowledge, and teachers are useful to a university only if they remain productive in the creation of new knowledge. The scholar-teacher restores a neglected aspect of Gilman's credo. He sought not only an institution where scholars generated new knowledge but also the dissemination of that knowledge. That transmission has been too narrowly interpreted as technical publications in journals or monographs.

The scholar-teacher publishes reviews, innovative textbooks, and trade book popularizations. The books and essays of T. H. Huxley, Julian Huxley, and such recent scholars as Stephen Gould (1977) and Carl Sagan (1977) are examples of the type of work that scholar-teachers can produce. All these essayists have made their primary contributions not through laboratory research and highly technical journals but through their outstanding ability to think relationally and make apparent to their colleagues and the lay reader the implications of new knowledge. The scholar-teachers know research well but elect not to make it their primary academic activity. They are generalists, not dilettantes, who find pleasure in viewing facts from many perspectives and communicating the excitement of new ideas to numerous audiences, both skilled and uninformed.

If scholar-teachers are as valuable to a university as research scholars, colleges and universities should try to recruit them. They may be identified through carefully screened programs, such as the E. Harris Harbison awards of the Danforth Foundation or the Distinguished Teaching Professorships of the New York State University System. Most universities have faculty-student committees (often from the Academic Senate) that make annual awards for gifted or distinguished teaching.

Annual awards for teaching, however, are not as effective as lifelong recognition. Productive research scholars receive merit raises and promotions, not annual awards. If high-quality teaching is to be encouraged, it must be rewarded by both promotion and merit raises. Scholar-teachers also need grant agency funds for using their summers productively, either for writing or research. Various federal agencies—National Institutes of Health, National Science Foundation (NSF) and others—can provide leadership by mandating a special subvention fund for those universities receiving research grants. The money would be earmarked for the development of improved undergraduate courses and the provision of summer salaries for scholar-teachers. Increased funding to the Fund for the Improvement of Postsecondary Education (FIPSE) would also help scholar-teachers who attempt to make their contributions known to a wider audience.

A major contribution to educational reform could be accomplished by bringing together scholar-teachers at an annual meeting so that they could exchange ideas, techniques, and resources. Funding for such a meeting might be obtained from FIPSE and the NSF, both of which are concerned with science education.

Conclusion

Effective undergraduate teaching offers many benefits to a college or university. It stimulates intellect and creates respect for rational approaches to the social applications of knowledge. It makes students aware that knowledge does not exist independently of human values, that the misapplication or failure to apply new knowledge will have serious effects on human life. The well-taught courses attract future majors to the field. They also help students appreciate the relationships between apparently unrelated areas (the arts, sciences, humanities).

The effective teacher also serves those whose work is translated from the technical journals to the working language of the undergraduate. We publish not just for our fellow professionals but for a wider audience because most new knowledge has implications for other areas. Scholar-teachers, who base their lectures and courses on a critical survey of journal articles and reviews, must keep up to date on developments in their own fields and outside them. In all the years that I have taught, I have never used the same set of lecture notes twice. I rewrite an outline for each lecture, adding new material and discarding older, less useful information.

The well-taught course attracts more students. This can be valuable to those departments whose budgets are based on the number of students enrolled in the department's courses. Often the teacher of that course generates additional faculty positions, and thus a department can expand its upper-division and graduate offerings by investing in a first-rate teacher for its introductory course.

The university benefits, too. Students tell their friends and relatives about their pleasures and frustrations with their school experiences. If the quality of instruction is excellent, the brighter students in secondary schools will want to apply. If they hear that the school ignores undergraduates or that its courses are poorly taught, those students in a position to choose will elect to go elsewhere.

Finally, the reforms suggested here for the nonmajors biology course are consistent with the aims of liberal arts education. We want our students to mature intellectually, but we also want them to develop moral and ethical judgment, humanitarian concern, and responsible citizenship. By addressing the principles of biology to the human condition, in a course such as that described in this chapter, we can help achieve these academic and social goals.

References

Chase, A. *The Legacy of Malthus.* New York: Knopf, 1977.

Gould, S. J. *Ever Since Darwin.* New York: Norton, 1977.

Lawson, A. E. "Developing Formal Thought Through Biology Teaching." *American Biology Teacher,* 1975, *37,* 336-429.

Milunsky, A. *Know Your Genes.* Boston: Houghton Mifflin, 1977.

Sagan, C. *The Dragons of Eden.* New York: Random House, 1977.

23

David Halliburton

Interdisciplinary Studies

Over the years, academic disciplines have built up a massive body of research habits, assumptions about knowledge, teaching traditions, means of self-justification and, ultimately, strategies for survival (McHenry, 1977). But the same is not true of interdisciplinary studies. Since these studies are comparatively new, their habits, assumptions, traditions, and strategies are in flux—indeed, they are often in the very process of formation. That is one reason why discussions of interdisciplinary studies tend to take place in a vacuum. A second reason—and one that bears more directly on the concerns of this book —is the lack of recent theory and research on how students, especially those beyond the traditional college age, develop and learn, and how social changes are pressing educators to improve their ways of dealing with these students. The present volume, by addressing these problems from a variety of perspectives, helps to fill the vacuum to which I have just referred. The present chapter draws upon the relevant theory and research of the preceding chapters for background, reinforcement, points of departure, and general guidelines for the future.

Disciplinary Versus Interdisciplinary Approaches

"Discipline," Green reminds us, "is always connected to some practice," the practice of the academic disciplines generally being "the exercise of theoretical reason, the practice of inquiry." A *discipline* may be defined—going a step further—as a set of scholarly, pedagogical, social, and political practices carried out by an epistemic community. The term *epistemic,* from the Greek *episteme,* designates a body of shared assumptions, usually very few in number and very deep-seated, about reality in general, and the nature of knowledge in particular (Foucault, 1970). These assumptions constitute the grounds of inquiry, debate, and dissemination on which like-minded academic practitioners operate in their professional lives.

The concept of an epistemic basis for disciplinary practice immediately invites comparison with the role of paradigms in the history of academic revolutions (Kuhn, 1962). Both of these concepts, the epistemic and the paradigmatic, attempt to articulate underlying educational "positions," which often go unrecognized precisely because, to those who use them, they appear to be the very stuff of reality. What Kuhn says about scientists applies to persons in all disciplines: "scientists work from models acquired through education and through subsequent exposure to the literature often without quite knowing or needing to know what characteristics have given these models the status of community paradigms. And because they do so, they need no full set of rules. The coherence displayed by the research tradition in which they participate may not imply even the existence of an underlying body of rules and assumptions that additional historical or philosophical investment might uncover" (Kuhn, 1962, p. 46).

Departments may draw their power from paradigms that are unexamined and from rules that have less to do with any public reality than with a discipline's internal history, as Kolb points out in Chapter Ten. To put it another way, a given discipline predicts the phenomena it intends to handle. The methodologies it employs, the language it speaks, the traditions it accepts as legitimate—all these largely predetermine the very reality it sees. The situation is analogous to the use of "terministic screens" (Burke, 1966). "When I speak of 'terministic screens,' I have particularly in mind some photographs I once saw. They were *different* photographs of the *same* objects, the difference being that they were made with different color filters. Here something so 'factual' as a photograph revealed notable distinctions in texture, and even in form, depending upon which color filter was used for the documentary description of the event being recorded" (p. 45). To expand on the point: Paradigms, rules, and terminologies combine to produce their own view of the way things are. A discipline held together by these paradigms, rules, and terminologies can be seen as a reflection of reality. But precisely because it is something made up—an invented set of assumptions and practices—it selects reality; and selecting means leaving things out—perhaps a lot of things. Thus, while the discipline *re*flects reality, it also *de*flects reality (Burke, 1966). That is why no single discipline can claim to be equal to all tasks.

The interdisciplinary orientations in this chapter point up some of the limitations of fixed disciplines by focusing on problems, specifically, problems regarding the future, the environment, and cultural heritage. Similarly, to the extent that the great writers, thinkers and doers achieve a high degree of integration, it is at least in part because they take problems, themes, or issues as their point of departure. That is why it is so difficult to put them into pigeonholes. The only way to classify a Pascal is to say "Pascal"—he is his own classification. But bring Pascal into a modern college and he would quickly be channeled into one department—mathematics or philosophy or religious studies or literature—unless, of course, he were fortunate enough to be invited to participate in a program of interdisciplinary studies!

The existence of rigidly defined disciplines, as embodied in academic departments, clearly forms one of the obstacles to interdisciplinary innovation, just as it clearly forms an obstacle to the revitalization of liberal education in general. Whether the topic is interdisciplinary or liberal education, those who identify exclusively with one discipline see or imagine threats to their "territory." The more the topic is aired, the more each epistemic community feels called upon to defend its position. Some academics defend the liberal arts curriculum by arguing for the primacy of certain disciplines, or more recently for the primacy of certain competencies. This leads to the question of the core curriculum—and more specifically, the role of the disciplines and their justifications for their respective shares of the curriculum.

The Core Curriculum. When we speak of a core curriculum, we mean that selected courses are judged to be central from some educational point of view. But what do we mean by central? Three answers suggest themselves, in ascending order of validity, as follows. One answer is that centrality implies centralizing; that is, the core acts centripetally as a focus for other disciplines. An area of study such as social psychology would fit this model if we could show, first, that it arose from a convergence of sociology and psychology, and second, that it then moved toward the center of the curriculum, finally taking its place in the core. In fact, it is more accurately regarded as a subdiscipline of psychology, or at least as functionally subordinate to the latter in most organizational structures. In any case, it does not figure in most examples of core curriculums. Thus, although it is attractive to imagine a variety of disciplines flowing to a core, that does not seem to happen in practice.

A second model depicts flow in the other direction—from the core disciplines out to the others. Such movement could be called centrifugal; or, to adopt a more organic metaphor, the central curriculum could be likened to the core of a fruit. This would make the core "generative," and would indeed more accurately reflect some actual developments. Departments of English, for example, are noted for generating offerings, such as comparative literature and media studies, that themselves may come to constitute disciplines or subdisciplines. Much the same applies to mathematics, which has played a role in generating statistics, computer science, information theory, and mathematical logic. The superiority of this model to the previous one is that, although the relation it shows is not a necessary one, it is one that can sometimes be observed. Moreover, it sharpens our sense of the manner in which the core curriculum can display, for lack of a better term, its power.

A third and better model portrays core disciplines as foundational. While not excluding the many other senses of the term *foundational,* I draw here on a modern concept in logic (Husserl, 1970), adapting it to a particular use. On an abstract level, something can be said to be founded in something else if the latter makes its existence possible—that is, constitutes a necessary condition for its existence. Translated into disciplinary terms, a foundational discipline is one that makes it possible to carry out certain activities on higher and higher levels. The justification of disciplines in a core curriculum rests on an agreement about the activities that learners should be able to carry out and the belief that certain disciplines, because they are foundational in the sense described, are "what you cannot do without." Training in mathematics, for example, provides the tools for the natural sciences as well as for daily tasks (balancing the household books and the like) or occupations such as accounting or computer operations. Training in English provides reading and writing skills that can be put to use in many other courses in a curriculum and in any daily pursuits that are verbally oriented. Additionally, the methods employed in the study of literary texts provide useful analytical tools, while enriching the quality of one's intellectual and esthetic life. There appears to be all but universal agreement among educators that these two capacities—*numeracy* and *literacy,* as they are often called these days—are essential to any core curriculum. There is also substantial agreement, it would appear, about the importance of studying history as a way to understand the formation of the contemporary world and thereby to prepare for the future, as a way of learning to appreciate the past, and as a way of developing, from these foundations, habits of thought and action conducive to informed decision making and value judgments.

If there is also substantial agreement about two other areas of study—the natural sciences and the social sciences—there are differences of opinion concerning which disciplines best represent them. The result is that one selects from what amounts to "clusters" of disciplines. Through the disciplines in one cluster, the natural sciences, learners come to know more about the material world. Through the disciplines in another cluster, the social sciences, they come to know more about society and the individual. Psychology, a representative discipline from the social science cluster, investigates, among other things, attitudes and life strategies that can help learners reach a better understanding of themselves and of others. A representative discipline from the natural sciences cluster—such as biology—illuminates the structures and processes of organic being and increases the learner's comprehension of life systems.

Interdisciplinary Challenges. Current reexaminations of the core curriculum have frequently pointed toward enlargement and diversification. Thus, more and more colleges are deciding that students should be more fully exposed to a culture other than their own. This is true both of competency-based curriculums (for example, Mars Hill) and of curriculums at more traditional institutions (for example, Harvard). And such a requirement goes beyond the normal core curriculum. I believe that a curriculum that claims to be central to the educational process should also take fuller account of the need for flexibility created by the increasing presence of adult learners. Our academic disciplines developed in a time—and a very long time it was—when learners were typically in a late or postadolescent phase. Significantly, increasing interest in nondisciplinary approaches coincides with rising enrollments of older students. In effect, the changing composition of the student population, combined with our changing perceptions of students' capacities and needs, is pressuring academic programs to become more flexible, more problem-oriented, and more creative. As Schaie and Parr point out in this volume, projections of future societal needs suggest that creative problem solving and behavioral flexibility may be as important—for all students—in predicting success as the more conventional diagnostic and predictive measures of performance.

New approaches to learning can stimulate creativity in both students and educators. In Chapter Eight, Douvan reminds us that the creative person depends on access to childhood and to primitive, or early, aspects of the self for life and originality. If the artist denies his or her past or cuts himself or herself loose from the experiences and anchorings of childhood, there can be none of the fluidity of vision, no contact with other and earlier ways of constructing reality, on which the creative process draws and depends. Integrating diverse experience and elements in the self is a more demanding work, more taxing to ego resources and energy than developing a self in a homogeneous and continuous environment, but if it succeeds it will also eventuate in a self that is rich, articulated, and flexible. In a highly organized, highly technological society in which learning is predominantly of one type (cognitive) and for one type of student (the 18- to 22-year-old), it can be useful, and freeing, to let minds discover and invent through the mode of play. One of the greatest of modern historians has shown the crucial role of play in all major civilizations (Huizinga, 1955). It has also been shown to perform a crucial role in the formation of strong interpersonal relationships; in her chapter on the capacity for intimacy, Douvan remarks that the playfulness that is part of the capacity for friendship is based on fluid boundaries between aspects of the personality, allowing relatively free access to preconscious elements of the self—to the realm of metaphor, wit, humor. This brings us back, then, to the requirements friendship shares with other forms of creativity.

In theory, creativity and play can be built into a conventional disciplinary curriculum. But, with rare exceptions, this simply does not happen. One means of increasing the likelihood that students' creative potentialities will be realized is to encourage some participation in the arts; and careful consideration should be given to that remedy. But the same goal can be attained through interdisciplinary approaches such as those discussed in later pages, which break down barriers in liberating ways.

It is noteworthy that the progression from a stage of development at which an individual is ego-centered to a more advanced stage in which he or she becomes outward-looking resembles the progression from a stage at which an educational practice is dictated by a discipline's own interests and a more advanced, outward-looking stage. The attainment of the latter—which interdisciplinary strategies can do much to promote—does not, to be sure, compel disciplines to abandon their own interests; but it does press them to look beyond themselves to an unusual degree. An attitude that can foster such change is exemplified by the movement, described by Jessie Bernard in her chapter, to replace competitive, individualistic models of educational practice with more cooperative models. Development in that direction clearly parallels the development of humanitarian concern, the focus of White's chapter, as well as the capacity for intimacy and interdependence discussed by Douvan. Moreover, it accords with the more advanced types of cognitive style described by Loevinger, such as conceptual complexity, patterning, and broad scope.

The development of such capacities does not mean that learning will henceforth proceed blissfully. On the contrary, as Loevinger points out and Weathersby reminds us, the attainment of higher stages of development cannot be equated with greater happiness or adjustment to life's problems; rather, it represents an ability to conceptualize and cope with increasingly deeper and more complex problems. The psychological or social cost of learning to conceptualize and cope in this way can mean much the same for an adult learner and for an interdisciplinary program. Both may undergo "a developmental crisis" in which they are "at risk" in the midst of change (see Weathersby's chapter). If anything, it is even likelier that a program will be at risk for this reason, for while individuals may experience different degrees of crisis (some may undergo no significant disruption at all), interdisciplinary initiatives are risk-taking by definition. They spring up in hostile environments, and their high visibility makes them easy targets. Insofar as disciplines stand for academic order, nondisciplinary approaches are often seen as standing for academic *dis*order, which means that innovators must struggle against sometimes heavy odds to prove their very right to exist.

Defining Interdisciplinary

The prefix of our term, from the Latin *inter,* means "between, among, amid, in between, in the midst." Thus, the compound term *interdisciplinary* indicates an approach that may or may not take its departure from disciplines but that operates, in any event, in spheres not specifically claimed by those disciplines. Competing terms, according to recent analyses (Jantsch, 1972b; Humphreys, 1976), are *multi, pluri, cross-,* and *transdisciplinary* (see Table 1). A *multidisciplinary* approach, in this taxonomy, draws simultaneously on two or more disciplines without establishing relationships between them. Thus, the disciplines are brought into play together, but there is no cooperation. In the *pluridisciplinary* approach, the relationships between disciplines are emphasized and there is an effort at cooperation. Coordination is introduced in the *cross-disciplinary* approach,

Table 1. Steps for Increasing Cooperation and Coordination Between Disciplines

	General Concept	Type of System	System Configuration
Multidisciplinarity	A variety of disciplines are offered simultaneously, but without making explicit possible relationships between them.	One-level, multi-goal; no cooperation	
Pluridisciplinarity	Various disciplines are juxtaposed, usually at the same hierarchical level, in such a way as to enhance the relationships between them.	One-level, multi-goal; cooperation (but no coordination)	
Cross-disciplinarity	The axiomatics of one discipline is imposed upon other disciplines at the same hierarchical level.	One-level, one-goal; rigid control from one disciplinary goal	
Interdisciplinarity	A common axiomatics for a group of related disciplines is defined at the next higher hierarchical level or sublevel; thereby introducing a sense of purpose; *teleological* interdisciplinarity acts between the empirical and pragmatic levels, *normative* interdisciplinarity between the pragmatic and normative levels, *purposive* interdisciplinarity between the normative and purposive levels.	Two-level, multi-goal; coordination from higher level	
Transdisciplinarity	All disciplines and interdisciplines in the education/innovation system are coordinated on the basis of a generalized axiomatics (introduced from the purposive level down) and an emerging epistemological ("Synapistemic") pattern.	Multi-level, multi-goal; coordination toward a common system purpose	

Source: E. Jantsch, 1972b, pp. 106-107.

but through the dominance of one discipline's purposes or assumptions. In an offering in "human life systems," for example, the efforts of teachers from philosophy, religion, and biology might be coordinated by shared assumptions about genetic predispositions, indicating that the field of biology is determining the course's direction more than the other two fields.

The *interdisciplinary* approach has been defined as follows: "A common axiomatic for a group of related disciplines is defined at the next higher hierarchical level or sublevel, thereby introducing a sense of purpose" (Jantsch, 1972a). Although other practitioners use different terms, this is a serviceable definition of *interdisciplinary* as that term is often understood. Animated by a sense of purpose, different disciplines adopt an overarching concept that coordinates their respective approaches. Whereas a cross-disciplinary approach adheres to a norm determined by one of the disciplines, the norm adopted in an interdisciplinary approach is determined collectively.

A fifth term, *transdisciplinary*, refers to the coordination of all disciplines and "interdisciplines" in a manner that, though not lacking in theoretical interest, is overly utopian for the purpose of the present essay.

The problem with all these definitions is not that they put the cart before the horse but that they are, so to speak, all cart. That is to say, they all employ disciplines as touchstones for determining a type of activity not necessarily based on disciplines. As Green observes in his chapter, academic disciplines and the intersections of disciplines are considered in those settings where our consciousness is focused either upon what happens in the *process* of inquiry—whether the methods are sound, for example—or upon the *content* of the inquiry—whether our questions are like those of physics, history, or economics. When such questions of practice are considered seriously, our consciousness is focused on "the problem" or "the need"—better housing, more beauty, better treatment of our friends—and *academic* disciplines are not considered. "Problem" may be read as shorthand for a number of things that others call by different names—issues, topics, challenges, themes, and so on. It will be argued in this chapter that learning can be more effectively achieved by reversing the standard procedure of working from the discipline toward the problem; for why should we not begin with a problem, then find a suitable solution? It is tempting, therefore, to regard the problem as the horse that can pull the disciplinary cart. But again that leaves us with too much cart—too much of that disciplinary deadweight that we persist in dragging along.

The goal should be to develop whatever investigatory modes are appropriate to the problems, issues, topics, challenges, or themes we are trying to address. *Interdisciplinary* suggests, first of all, the study of a problem in its totality—an effort that, by its very nature, can never be completed. In this sense, interdisciplinary investigation is always an interim investigation, is always subject to revision and revitalization. And even in the process of moving forward one is faced with the paradoxical necessity of looking backward. For despite the reservations just expressed, one does not dispense with disciplines all that easily. It is as dangerous to be facile about the disciplinary as it is to be facile about the interdisciplinary. The relation between the two "poles"—between approaches defined mainly by disciplinary assumptions and those defined by problems—is, at least at this point in history, dialectical. It remains difficult to state what the one is, or is becoming, without some reference to the other.

Types of Interdisciplinary Curriculums

It will be helpful at this point to look at a few major types of curriculums, emphasizing those aspects which are especially significant from an interdisciplinary point of view. We use the taxonomy developed by Bergquist (Chickering and others, 1977).

Heritage-Based Curriculums. One long-standing type of curriculum is based on cultural heritage, with a Western European emphasis. The rationale for this type of curriculum, which is showing new signs of life, is spelled out by Boyer and Kaplan (1977): "Colleges have an obligation to help the human race remember where it has been and how, for better or worse, it got where it is. All students must be introduced to the events, individuals, ideas, texts, and value systems that have contributed consequentially to human gains and losses. . . . The successful approach will always ask of the past what it has to do with us, how we are shaped by it, in what ways our notions of where we are and what we may become are controlled by our senses of where we were and how we got here" (p. 62). This recalls Schaie and Parr's suggestion that the quality of life in any society can be measured by that society's success in maintaining cultural continuity in a rapidly changing world.

This type of curriculum exists in an unusually pure form at St. John's College, where students discuss great books on a well-established reading list, and at Columbia University, where the problem of "general education" is consciously linked to "the reintegration of the university" (Belknap and Kuhns, 1977). Numerous institutions (for example, Occidental, Eckerd, and Reed) have offered versions of this approach in the form of survey courses or course series. Brown University offers a wide variety of perspectives on the Western cultural heritage through extradepartmental offerings (for example, Faustian Man and Voices of Romanticism), and Stanford is moving toward a broadly based required course series in Western Culture. At Austin College the study of cultural heritage has been linked with instructional innovation, while Alverno and Sterling Colleges have largely merged the heritage approach with their competency-based curriculum.

It has been argued that a great-books approach is in itself interdisciplinary because the writers of those books, transcending disciplinary limits, integrate modes of thinking and experiencing that the modern educational system has chopped up into pieces. In practice, heritage-based curriculums tend to be modeled, however, on the history of ideas (Foucault, 1972), which is itself a kind of floating subdiscipline, now housed in departments of literature, now in departments of history or philosophy. Thus, this type of curriculum has its own limits. Its real advantage is that the richness of the heritage poses challenges that no single discipline can meet, and therefore invites interdisciplinary approaches. Within the heritage can be found any number of unique and recurring problems, concepts, or issues that can help to form an overarching purpose for an interdisciplinary curricular design.

The nature of such a design depends upon which cultural "moments" one decides are the most important. The criteria would surely include the density of the moment (the way it serves as a magnet for social, economic, political, and intellectual forces); the degree to which it represents the crystallization of a historic characteristic (for example, the neoclassic) or a historic transition (for example, Newtonian physics); and the way in which that moment radiates out to include ourselves (Boyer and Kaplan, 1977). History is full of critical incidents, such as the trial of Galileo, which open up learning possibilities on numerous fronts. The Galilean crisis, which illustrates a paradigm shift requiring the definition of new domains of inquiry or knowledge, can be viewed prismatically through religion, physics, philosophy, and the history of ideas. No single discipline can handle this type of task. Nor is it feasible to speak in terms of "coverage," which usually means little more than the loose connecting of bits and pieces in the hope that synthesis will at some point burst forth, by a kind of spontaneous generation, from mere sequence. "Perhaps it is more fruitful to sacrifice the traditional survey material of colonial history in order to include a three-week case study of the Salem witch trials. To choose a few things carefully; to study them intensively and across disciplinary lines; and through them to see our own times—these goals may be adequate for the new [curricular] core" (Boyer and Kaplan, p. 64).

This is done but rarely. Even rarer are attempts to take advantage of the fact that cultures and individuals both go through stages, with certain crucial thresholds of change and consolidation—historical crises, revolutions, or paradigm shifts, on the one hand, and critical incidents, personal crises, milestone sequences, or midlife transitions, on the other (see the chapters by Chickering and Havighurst, Weathersby, and Schaie and Parr in this volume). But through interdisciplinary approaches one can make the connections relating the learner's own experiential processes with the experiential processes of a society or a culture. In this regard, it is worth noting that, as Duley's chapter in Part Three makes clear, the experiential education movement is not dominated by a disciplinary point of view because educators must work from the starting point of experience toward the suitable approach.

One reason why an interdisciplinary, problem-oriented approach has been slow in gaining ground is that the disciplines themselves are so complex, and their subspecialties so divergent, that it is not always easy to get a "fit" between a given discipline and a given problem or theme. Classics, for example, is not so much a single field as a gathering of fields, including philosophy, philology, archeology, literary criticism, art and architecture, epigraphy, religion, geography, and history. A classicist may in some instances already be more interdisciplinary than some of his or her colleagues, especially if he or she draws together, for example, philology, history, and philosophy. In the same vein, Kolb, in his chapter, observes that several of the professions (particularly management, medicine, and architecture) as well as several of the social sciences (particularly psychology, sociology, and economics) are themselves multidisciplinary, including specialties that emphasize different learning styles and vary greatly in their basic inquiry paradigms. Architecture has requirements for artistic and engineering excellence while management involves skill at both quantitative and qualitative analysis. Sociology can be highly abstract and theoretical (as in Parsonian structural functionalism) or concrete and active (as in phenomenology or ethnomethodology).

Thematic Curriculums. A second type of curriculum is based on themes or specifically targeted problems. Several colleges in the Southeast (such as Alice Lloyd) frame their curriculums in part around the study of Appalachia, while schools in or near cities offer courses dealing with urban problems (for example, the Third College at the University of California, San Diego). Both of these curricular strategies take advantage of the surrounding environment. In the cases just mentioned, that environment is largely a cultural one. However, the College of the Atlantic emphasizes the natural, in particular the marine, environment, featuring in its ecologically oriented curriculum a course on the whale as a living theme in which many environmental issues come together. At the University of Wisconsin, Green Bay, a set of problems is the focus of the entire institution, each college having its own emphasis. The institutional master plan called for the College of Creative Communication to house two "problem-based departments," one concentrating on esthetic awareness and environmental design (Communication Action) and the other on Humanism and Cultural Change. The College of Community Sciences had three divisions: the first took the problem of modernity as its organizing concept (Modernization Processes); the second and third focused on regional problems (Regional Analysis) and urban problems (Urban Analysis), respectively (Weidner, 1977).

Even this small sample of organizational structures makes it clear that learning, under such an arrangement, could not be approached through a single discipline or even through a combination of closely related disciplines. "Thus, every department would have to be authorized to hire biological and physical scientists, social scientists, and humanists, as its members thought best. . . . Obviously, the course structure of the concentration needed to be interdisciplinary, too. Clusters of courses in a series of disciplines would not do. The department would have to give more attention to the future than to the past, except to the extent that the past presented a series of signposts for the future. The curriculum clearly would be highly relevant. Students would be given opportunities to engage in many kinds of experiential or project learning. Getting off the campus and participating in community projects or problems and analyses would be a basic part of their education" (Weidner, 1977, pp. 65-67).

A thematic curriculum tends to "force the issue" as far as the disciplines are concerned, since the very nature of the theme calls for multifaceted concepts and strategies. There is, however, a tendency to slide back into disciplinary attitudes, so that new organizational arrangements begin to look like modified versions of earlier arrangements. Nonetheless, in principle themes lend themselves to interdisciplinary modeling because they demonstrably transcend the reach of any single discipline.

Future-Oriented Curriculums. A third type of curriculum takes the future for its theme in the attempt to prepare learners for "future shock," both in the immediate and distant future. A 1974 survey discovered that more than 500 future-oriented courses were being offered throughout the country, and in view of the increasing attention given to futuristics in education circles and the media, it is likely that the number has grown. At Davis-Elkins, a course called The Future provides the capstone to a four-year sequence called The Liberated Life. At Pacific Lutheran University, participants in Integrated Program Studies, which has recently focused on The Dynamics of Change, may take as one of their main "tracks" a future-oriented two-course sequence. The first course is The Technological Society and Thrust for Growth, and the second is The Technological Society and Limits to Growth. All these courses take a team-taught, interdisciplinary approach. An entire curriculum based on the future remains the exception, although Whitworth College is reported to be developing one.

An advantage of a future-oriented design is that the future matters mightily to everyone, yet no one knows what it will be. The shape of the future depends upon what teachers and students (both in their scholarly capacities and as citizens) decide, with other members of a society, to make it. Studying future possibilities, analyzing choices, and conceiving scenarios bring learning to bear on, among other things, the process of decision making, requiring the exercise of "practical reason" (see Green's chapter). And, while every discipline has some decision-making process of its own, none has a process adequate to the major problems that the world faces.

Decision making, in this broad sense, is an exercise capable of fostering learning in students of all ages, especially when it is related to their own processes of development. The fact that different types of problems require different types of resolution is more easily demonstrated when problems are approached in an interdisciplinary way that does justice to their dynamic, matrix-like, "transdisciplinary" complexity. Such a learning strategy may have special appeal for those adult learners at the "executive" and "responsible" or "reintegrative" stages (see Schaie and Parr).

Finally, this orientation increases the contact between students and their heritage and provides a basis for establishing a greater sense of continuity. In this regard, generativity—defined by Erikson as "the concern in establishing and guidance of the next generation—goes beyond caring for one's own young to caring for all of mankind.

Justification for Interdisciplinary Curriculums. As we have observed, the future, the environment, and our cultural heritage all challenge the narrow disciplinary approach. Let the burden of proof rest therefore upon the opponents of interdisciplinary studies; let them show that these topics can be treated adequately with conventional strategies. It may, of course, be argued that students need not deal with such matters at all. But the challenge applies equally to all educational matters. For, once the burden of proof is shifted to the disciplines, any curricular focus can become a challenge. That this is not readily apparent can be explained by the fact that, at least for the moment, the burden of proof rests upon the interdisciplinary side. It is the interdisciplinary studies that are called upon to justify themselves; thus, stricter standards of performance are often imposed on interdisciplinary studies than anyone would dream of imposing on the disciplines.

At this point we have come far enough in our consideration of interdisciplinary studies to see what justifications of a discipline-based core curriculum have in common with justifications of an interdisciplinary curriculum. Each says: "If we want to accomplish such and such agreed-upon goals, here are the things we cannot do without." The things in the first case are the single academic disciplines; in the second case they are approaches that move away from those disciplines. The goals in the first case are those specified by the requirements of expertise in a field; the goals in the second case arise from the set of phenomena in question. Because these phenomena vary, teachers and curriculum designers must get together in different ways under different headings and along different organizational lines. Both disciplinary and interdisciplinary approaches depend upon a working consensus about goals and about ways of achieving those goals. The practical difference is that the interdisciplinary approaches are still struggling to achieve consensus while the disciplines are simply maintaining consensus.

Value of Interdisciplinary Approaches

A changing world puts pressure on academic disciplines. Foreign language departments are threatened by slackening requirements in the recent "climate of choice," and by the fact that, in a job-conscious era, the study of a foreign tongue seems less practical than some other kinds of study, such as chemistry. Meanwhile, certain disciplines put pressure on themselves by examining their own objectives, or develop schisms that eventually lead some practitioners to branch out into a "new field" or set up special outposts within the original disciplinary territory. Interdisciplinary approaches can serve as a way of breaking out, if only part way, from a disciplinary structure that has thus begun to bulge, sometimes embarrassingly. They are a way of coping with paradigm shifts, when familiar grounds of inquiry, debate, and dissemination begin, in a kind of seismic manner, to tremble. The change from a Ptolemaic, earth-centered cosmology to a Copernican, sun-centered model is a prime example of such a shift. On a smaller scale, there are signs that the discipline of history is undergoing a shift, as a more socially oriented, demographic, statistically minded "anonymous" historiography begins to displace a more settled positivistic and individualistic tradition. A comparable shift may be under way in anthropology. If we follow experts into this terrain, we can learn something about a concept that is crucial to an appreciation of interdisciplinary studies.

In his studies of rites of passage, Van Gennep distinguished three crucial stages (Turner, 1977). In the first, the individual or group making a passage between sociocultural states undergoes separation. The second stage transpires on a "threshold," from the Latin *limen*: in rites of initiation, in particular, this "liminal" stage is often very extended. In the third stage, the individual or group is assimilated into the social fabric. (Subsequent researchers further distinguished a stage of intensification, in which the rites reinforce a group's basic social unity.) Of Van Gennep's original three stages—the pre-liminal, liminal, and postliminal—our immediate concern is the second. University of Chicago anthropologist Victor Turner discovered that he was himself undergoing a liminal process as he awaited a visa to the United States, and did some "adult learning" of his own. A native-born Scot at the threshold of an American academic career, he began to reflect on the experiences of "liminars" like himself. "Liminars," he learned, are "neither here nor there: they are betwixt and between the positions assigned and arrayed by law, custom, convention, and ceremonial." The liminal process corresponds with the *ludic,* to use a generic term for activities resembling play. Breaking down conventional barriers, the ludic process invents alternative modes of social and individual behavior, providing the zest of variety. At the same time, by this very process of release and experimentation, it functions as a collective safety valve that contributes to long-range cultural continuity, providing on a collective level much the same opportunity for reintegration that is to be found on the individual level in the later stages of personal development.

All this leads me to the proposition that interdisciplinary studies provide a means of getting more healthy play, more creative liminality, into our curriculum. Such a proposition sees in the college experience a broad analogy with the rites of passage in less indus-trialized societies. Erikson refers to a phase of preadult life as a "moratorium" phase, in which the individual is held out of society for a time. College is one such phase. We know now that many older persons use college similarly, as a special context outside their daily rounds. They use this context to get perspective on their current condition, chart plans for the future, and learn skills. The challenge is to get more life into that phase by making it possible for learners of all ages to do a little less marching and a little more dancing, as it were. The college years, at whatever stage one enters or re-enters them, form a con-spicuously liminal time. That is one reason why curriculum designers have given attention to entry-level courses, and why surveys, especially of the Western Civilization type, have tended to cluster in the freshman year. But the first year is only a more visible demonstra-tion of the liminal quality, or at the very least of the liminal possibilities, of the entire college experience. The crucial process during that time is the process of passage—every bit as much for the adult learner as for the younger learner. In this process, learning "how" vies in importance with learning "what." Hence a further advantage of an inter-disciplinary approach is its greater willingness to explore *modes* of learning—to concern itself with developing ways of learning that suit whatever problems or themes present themselves. This view recalls the emphasis on learning styles and modes in Weathersby's and Kolb's chapters.

If the present chapter tilts in the direction of play, it is to compensate for recent emphasis upon work—which has itself been a useful compensation for earlier discussions that altogether neglected the relation of study to work. I do not want to overcompensate, since this would contradict my own past efforts to strengthen the connections between the academic process and the everyday world. I mean simply to point out the value of play—to suggest that in fact "play works." That is, a more flexible mode of course and curriculum building—a more modal, problem-oriented interdisciplinary approach—can lead to better ways of learning about the world. Victor Turner calls in effect for a more dynamic, interdependent relationship between academic work and play: "My suggestion is that, instead of working in blinkers, anthropologists and scholars in adjacent disciplines interested in cross-cultural problems should make an earnest (and 'ludic') attempt at mutual empathy—earnest in the sense that various anthropological perspectives, hybrids such as ethnography, and fields such as the sociology of knowledge, and significant others, might be treated at least as a unified field whose unity might have something to do with the systems theory view that there are systems and systemic relations so fundamental that they occur in many different living and even inorganic phenomena" (Turner, 1977, p. 75).

That is no small thing to achieve. But other things can be achieved as well. For once a curriculum is opened up to this kind of innovation, it is easier to open it up to other, related possibilities. An interdisciplinary orientation, for example, tends to favor team-teaching approaches, which range all the way from mere "serial" arrangements, in which instructors from different fields follow each other on stage; to more thoroughly planned pairings, with two or more teachers working together in the same setting; to still more elaborate structures in which small-unit teams are articulated into larger units as components of a large-scale curricular strategy. Further, the processes required for successful team building and team performance converge with and reinforce other processes of constructive institutional change, such as faculty development.

One of the first steps is one of the most important—the breaking down of longstanding barriers. A report by the Group for Research and Innovation in Higher Education (Nuffield Foundation) comments: "The pervasiveness of the craft model in academic teaching is of central importance here, because it is a model which is challenged by interdisciplinary work. Once one moves out of the shared domain of the single discipline, one is forced to communicate in a new way: forced to develop a 'mediating language' in which to discuss the relationship between disciplines" (Squires and others, 1975, pp. 24-25).

Significance for Adult Learners

The significance of interdisciplinary studies for adult learners is something about which, at present, we can theorize and speculate; it is not something about which we have a great deal of knowledge. I would therefore like to put the following propositions in a hypothetical mode, recognizing that they constitute a series of educated guesses and that they need to be tested—as, in time, they almost certainly will be.

First, there is the question of learning styles. My own experience in working with adults, confirmed by colleagues, is that older learners are not always as ready as their younger counterparts to master the protocols and niceties of disciplinary distinctions, which strike them as hermetic. To put the matter more affirmatively, they seem frequently willing to look beyond the trees of an academic specialty to the forest of general implications. As the Gaffs observe in their chapter, older learners expect faculty not to teach isolated "subjects" but rather to relate the many facets of knowledge in any area to each other and to the larger society.

A second and related point is that adult learning styles are intimately connected with adult life-styles, which tend to show a greater degree of integration than that normally achieved by undergraduates (see Kolb, Perry, Gilligan, and Weathersby). Interdisciplinary approaches may thus hold out unusual appeal for adult learners. As Robert and Dorcas Saunders point out in their chapter, adult learners will have made some of the connections between various disciplines as we now teach them in higher education and will, in fact, find interdisciplinary approaches to learning much more compatible with their own stylistic preferences.

A third consideration, to which I have already alluded, is that some adult students will be "at risk" in the face of life changes. They will experience heightened anxiety and disequilibrium in the course of their studies, yet also have a greater opportunity to develop new personality strengths (see Weathersby). For this reason, care should be taken, as Weathersby implies, to ensure that interdisciplinary programs are coordinated with the planning and delivery of support services, including counseling services by persons with special training in the problems of adult development.

Fourth, because adult learners have survived some of life's more difficult crises, and have coped with the pressures of work assignments and the vicissitudes of parenthood, they can adapt more readily to the kind of task-oriented teamwork often required for interdisciplinary studies. Interdisciplinary studies frequently call upon those interpersonal skills which enable one to relate constructively to others in problem solving, decision making, and management of conflict. The inquiry processes described by Torbert in his chapter on interpersonal competence, are precisely what interdisciplinary studies consistently require. But it would be a mistake, of course, to suppose that interdisciplinary goals can be met only by team learning or team teaching, and this leads me to my next point.

Fifth, the integrating "unit" in the learning process may not be a pair of teachers, for example, or a group of students; it may be the individual. For there is no guarantee that bringing teachers and students together from different fields will result in significant new learning, any more than there is a guarantee that one can accomplish this by oneself. Yet there are individuals on many college campuses who can make that claim, for they have worked their way through one field, then another, learning from each, combining new knowledge with old, adapting themselves to novel modes of inquiry, and building up a competence to treat problems they were previously unable to attack or perhaps even to recognize. Pascal, again, is a paradigmatic instance of such a process; the contemporary anthropologist Victor Turner and the contemporary literary historian Leo Marx (referred to later) are others.

Sixth, the adult learner is a problem-solver: to get by in the world, he or she has *had* to be. Furthermore, the adult learner has long been living in the "real world" (to use a term that is not completely satisfactory), in contrast to the relatively enclosed world of a younger age cohort; and that real world, it should be added, is not a world of scholarly debates over departmental territoriality—it is a world of problems. It therefore seems likely that orientation toward problems—which, as I have said, characterizes interdisciplinary approaches to an exceptional degree—is inherently appealing to adult learners and, further, that their lives have supplied them with a foundation of experience on which to develop appropriate strategies for addressing the problem in question.

Seventh, recent research, discussed in this volume, reveals a further aspect of problem orientation, namely, problem-*finding*: "A similar notion of an advanced stage appeared in the subsequent work of Arlin (1975), who claimed to have found a 'fifth Piagetian cognitive stage,' which she called *problem finding* to distinguish it from the *problem-solving* orientation of formal thought. Arlin's interest lay in the creative capacity of adult intelligence, and her research therefore was focused on the kinds of questions people generated when shown an array of disparate items. She distinguished questions concerning the operation of variables within a formal system from questions of implication and transformation pertaining to the operation and the system itself. Her results suggested that formal operations were a necessary though not sufficient condition from the problem-finding capacity to raise generic or higher-order questions—a precondition for creative intelligence" (Gilligan, Chapter Five). Adult learners may then be expected to work with teachers of interdisciplinary studies toward the very definition of the tasks to be addressed. In other words, where adult learners are concerned, interdisciplinary studies assumes as one of its goals the creative formulation of *questions* as a complement to the creative formulation of *answers*.

An eighth hypothesis is that older students, precisely because they are older, and therefore in many cases nearer the age of their instructors, can more easily work with instructors in peer relationships—something it is difficult for adolescents to do. Without waxing utopian, I would suggest that it becomes possible to take real steps toward the creation of a community of learners in which collective inquiry can become a reality.

Ninth, teachers, as members of such a community, can themselves experience significant intellectual, social, and personal change. In our legitimate and necessary concern for serving students, we sometimes forget that professors undergo challenges in life, too, and, more specifically, that the challenge of devising interdisciplinary approaches, and of fitting these to the needs of learners nearer their own age, can contribute much to their own development. Indeed, it has been apparent that interdisciplinary studies, while not being necessarily linked to what we have come to call *faculty development,* do tend to foster development of various sorts. The teacher who designs a course that reaches out beyond the usual confines (however those confines are defined in a particular case) becomes to some extent a new teacher. In short, interdisciplinary studies *for* adult learners *by* adult teachers may be described as co-developmental. Lindquist's chapter in Part III pursues this point in some detail.

A tenth consideration is that a large number of our "new" adult learners are women. Significantly, Women's Studies has become one of the most vital areas of interdisciplinary activity. Bernard, in her chapter, notes the important recent contributions of women scholars to the arts, the humanities, the social and behavioral sciences, anthropology, and history. She then raises the question whether the research on women should be taught in separate courses or incorporated into other courses where relevant. Some argue for separate courses, while others fear that these might create an intellectual ghetto. However this issue is resolved, I would suggest that interdisciplinary approaches to, for example, the history and culture of women, or to the role of women in science, derive much of their vitality from the participation of the older, "returning" female student; from the capacity she typically demonstrates for working from problems toward suitable approaches; and from her capacity to help in forming, with relative dispatch, a community of learners dedicated to collective inquiry. (It is meanwhile to be hoped that those who undertake such endeavors will glance back at previous interdisciplinary, programmatic initiatives—as in various types of minority ethnic studies—in order to avoid the difficulties the latter have sometimes encountered.)

What of older students who happen to be men? Assuming that they find interdisciplinary approaches congenial, where precisely should they turn? Bernard provides at least a partial answer in her account of recent developments that join women's studies to "men's studies": While noting that many feminists believe that most standard education and traditional history *are* men's studies, she proposes that special Men's Studies programs be developed to study men's lives within a new paradigm, as feminism and Women's Studies offer a new paradigm for thinking about women. Men's Studies would inquire into the counterpart issues for men: expressiveness, nurturance, the ways men relate to each other, occupation segregation for men, and so on.

Organizational Issues

The trends just discussed have broad organizational implications, some of which have been noted by Toulmin (1977):

> The current shift in academic preoccupations . . . is bringing about changes not just in the orientation of research but in institutional organization also.

(Prototypically, one might consider the discussions at M.I.T. over the question whether the institute's work might not be structured in part around, for example, problems of transportation, communication, etc., rather than entirely around, for example, the techniques of electrical engineering, civil engineering, etc.) So understood, the alternative codeword with which the critics of the sixties countered the advocates of academic "excellence"—namely, "relevance"—can at any rate be given some content. For, indeed, the academic preoccupations of the seventies are not merely interdisciplinary in a way they could not have been twenty years ago: they are also focused on problems and issues that are relevant to specific human applications. The general academic skills built up with such pain and care over the previous forty or fifty years are now being put to work in dealing with problems that require us to mobilize the resources of several disciplines to serve specific human needs [p. 158].

There are problems, too, of course; and they are much the same for students as for teachers: the problem of developing trust (along the lines of Douvan's creative intimacy); the problem of adapting to differences in styles of teaching; a frequent lack of suitable materials; and finally, to quote Squires and others (1975), the problem of "overloading and the lack of an institutional base. Overloading can result from the unwillingness of staff to leave out what they consider essential to each discipline: sins of omission are rare in interdisciplinary course planning.... Lack of an institutional home can affect students in both obvious and subtle ways. If their course straddles two or three departments, they literally have no home, no coffee-room of their own.... Paradoxically, these very conditions sometimes force the student group to develop a distant identity and cohesion of its own" (pp. 28-29).

The creation of an interdisciplinary course, program, or core curriculum is, of course, a political as well as an academic issue; and, though space does not allow us to explore the political considerations here, it may be worthwhile to point out how interdisciplinary innovation can become mired in them. For example, interdisciplinary offerings, may, as Bernard reminds us, become "ghettoized." Because they differ in so many respects from other kinds of offerings, because they can be perceived as unsettling and even dangerous to the status quo, persons or groups not involved in such offerings may treat them with everything from benign neglect to the cold shoulder. An interdisciplinary proposal can also be used as a wedge to break open existing power structures, especially at the departmental level. A shift from a departmental to a divisional organization can do the same thing. Both efforts can have the effect of weakening the department's role as a leverage point, leading to the possibility that the administration will become more "managerial" in its strategies. To put it another way: the ghettoization of the innovative sector, combined with the breakdown of disciplinary structures, invites more managerial control —or, more precisely, it makes it more likely that more attention will be given to "cost efficiency" than to what I call "cost appropriateness." It is for these reasons that I have stressed the merit of seeing the relation between the interdisciplinary and the disciplinary as dialectical. The point of innovation is not simply change but constructive change, which means, in the present case, that interdisciplinary approaches can strengthen a curriculum without necessarily undermining the role of the disciplines.

The Promise of Interdisciplinary Studies

The effect of interdisciplinary studies on learners has not been systematically studied, as shown by a preliminary report on research needs in curriculum and learning sponsored by the Policy Analysis Service of the American Council of Education. One turns, in the meantime, to summaries of outcomes such as those furnished by Leo Marx, who headed the well-known Kenan Colloquium at Amherst College from 1972 to 1974.

> Turning now to the actual conduct of the colloquium, let me describe some of the distinctive, largely positive results of teaching and learning within this novel interdisciplinary context. The first was a not unconventional effort to place works of literature historically in relation to a surrounding culture. The ruling assumption is that we can apprehend the full power of a literary work only when we recognize how it illuminates and is illuminated by that culture. . . .
>
> Perhaps the most significant difference derived from the concept of the three environments—biophysical, socioeconomic, and cultural—and the overarching questions set by the colloquium. . . . The format of the colloquium gave an unusual edge to classroom discussion, for the students in each seminar were particularly sensitive to the adequacy with which each writer conceived the influence of a particular environment. Thus, the tendency of American writers to underestimate the significance of social structure seemed more obvious to our students than it would have in a conventional literature course in which primary emphasis is placed on esthetic categories [Marx, 1975, pp. 34-35].

While there is no strong evidence that environmentally oriented approaches are "catching on" around the country, the experience of University of Wisconsin at Green Bay has been deemed successful: "When the University of Wisconsin began its planning in 1966, many persons suggested that the development of a problem-based and interdisciplinary academic plan was an exercise in futility. Even the most sympathetic observers believed that the experiment might last as long as three or four years, but that the university would then be forced to go back to the traditional departments. Yet if anything, the dynamics at Green Bay currently are in the opposite direction" (Weidner, 1977, p. 85). This success must be attributed in a large measure to the fact that an interdisciplinary orientation was conceptualized for the institution from the beginning and built into its curriculum "from the ground up." This is also true for Evergreen State College and helps to explain the latter's comparative success as well.

Most interdisciplinary programs, obviously, must be undertaken in existing, conventionally oriented institutions. Yet in principle they can pursue a very similar if not identical goal—to provide "a desirable alternative for students who want an instrumental real-world education as a step to their future employment experiences and life satisfaction" (Weidner, 1977). It is not that this approach or any of the others—such as the cultural heritage approach—leads directly to employment opportunities. With virtually all predictors agreeing that most people will change jobs much more frequently in the future than in the past, and with our classrooms increasingly occupied by adult learners who have already changed jobs and may be in the process of changing again, a good argument can be made for general education, planned along interdisciplinary lines. The Nuffield report notes with considerable approval the argument that

> interdisciplinarity provides a good *general* education; the student is confronted with a relativity of approaches and problems which he may well miss in a specialized degree. As such, interdisciplinarity inherits some of the impetus toward a more general curriculum and the emphasis on the development of general skills.
>
> The "applied" argument for interdisciplinary work is the one we have come across most frequently, and it may reflect an increasingly nonspecific relationship between higher education and employment. The less predictable students' career choices and patterns become, the more it seems sensible to give them

a broad or multipurpose education. In this sense, interdisciplinarity can be seen as a reaction against overspecialisation [Squires and others, 1975, pp. 49-50].

On such a basis one can argue that such an applied, interdisciplinary, general-education approach can develop in learners a flexibility and a depth that finally do more real human good than the narrower education toward which we have been drifting. Learners of all ages need a variety of shared experiences, organized according to the demands of actual problems and not according to mere disciplinary habit; and interdisciplinary studies provide a means to this end. It is not a question of a guarantee but of an opportunity—an opportunity for learners to engage, in creative ways, their own individual and collective futures.

An approach that can help to bring all this about can properly be called foundational. What is built on it may be different from what is built on more familiar foundations. But the structures that rise from this newer foundation can be, in their own right, tall and strong.

References

Belknap, R., and Kuhns, R. *Tradition and Innovation: General Education and the Reintegration of the University.* New York: Columbia University Press, 1977.

Boyer, E. L., and Kaplan, M. *Educating for Survival.* New York: Change Magazine Press, 1977.

Burke, K. *Language as Symbolic Action: Essays on Life, Literature, and Method.* Berkeley: University of California Press, 1966.

Chickering, A. W., and others. *Developing the College Curriculum.* Washington, D.C.: Council for the Advancement of Small Colleges, 1977.

Foucault, M. *The Order of Things: An Archaeology of the Human Sciences.* New York: Pantheon, 1970.

Foucault, M. *The Archaeology of Knowledge and the Discourse on Language.* (A. M. Sheridan Smith, Trans.) New York: Pantheon, 1972.

Huizinga, J. *Homo Ludens: A Study of the Play Element in Culture.* Boston: Beacon, 1955.

Humphreys, L. *Interdisciplinarity: A Selected Bibliography for Users.* Change in Liberal Education Resource Directory, Number 1, 1976.

Husserl, E. *Logical Investigations.* (J. N. Findlay, Trans.) 2 vols. London: Routledge & Kegan Paul, 1970.

Jantsch, E. "Inter- and Transdisciplinary University: A Systems Approach to Education and Innovation." *Higher Education,* 1972a, *1* (February), 7-27.

Jantsch, E. "Towards Interdisciplinarity and Transdisciplinarity in Education and Innovation." In L. Apostel and others, *Interdisciplinarity: Problems of Teaching and Research in Universities.* Paris, France: Center for Educational Research and Innovation, Organization for Economic Cooperation and Development, 1972b.

Kuhn, T. *The Structure of Scientific Revolutions.* (2nd ed.) Chicago: University of Chicago Press, 1962, 1970.

McHenry, D. E., and Associates. *Academic Departments: Problems, Variations, and Alternatives.* San Francisco: Jossey-Bass, 1977.

Marx, L. "Can We Create Together What We Can't Create Alone?" *Change,* 1975, *7,* No. 6 (Summer), 30-38.

Squires, G., and others. *Interdisciplinarity.* A Report by the Group for Research and Innovation in Higher Education. London: Nuffield Foundation, 1975.

Toulmin, S. "From Form to Function." *Daedalus,* 1977, *106* (3), 143-162.

Turner, V. "Process, System, and Symbol: A New Anthropological Synthesis." *Daedalus,* 1977, *196* (3), 61-80.

Weidner, E. W. "Problem-Based Departments at the University of Wisconsin—Green Bay." In D. E. McHenry and Associates, *Academic Departments: Problems, Variations, and Alternatives.* San Francisco: Jossey-Bass, 1977.

24

Paul V. Grambsch

Business
Administration

"The worst handicap this school faces is the ignorance of you gentlemen as to what a business school is all about," a business school dean told the president and academic vice-president of his university in leaving the school for a prestigious, lucrative job in industry. His leaving may have emboldened him, but his complaint was justified: business schools are among the least understood institutions of American higher education. All many administrators know about them is that they are high-volume, low-cost schools with docile students and faculty who generally support the administration and the establishment.

Business schools are twentieth-century institutions, having risen to prominence only after World War II. They have no direct European antecedents as such, although there are scattered references throughout European history to schools that have dealt with business subjects. In the United States they have had three principal origins: (1) traditional college departments of economics, (2) so-called commercial schools of typing and shorthand that were merged into traditional college or university settings, and (3) new schools created by faculty members dissatisfied with the standard academic approaches of the day.

Although the business community provided some financial support for the establishment of business schools on campus, the dominant force in their founding was a small band of faculty within each institution. Their task was no easy one. There was considerable resistance from other members of the faculty, particularly to programs with a commercial school orientation, which offered such courses as business mathematics, business English, and secretarial science. Because of this internal university resistance, plus the natural bias of the business faculty, business schools tended to isolate themselves from the rest of the university. This isolation contributed to some of the misunderstandings that exist even to this day. Not until after World War II did business administration become a more or less accepted discipline or attract much attention. The GI Bill, which did so much to make the United States a college-attending society, was a great boon to business schools. Along with the increase in student population, new institutions were created in droves. Overnight small two-person departments became full-fledged schools with sizable faculties and even more sizable student bodies. By the early 1950s, the educational world suddenly realized that an important newcomer had arrived on the scene.

The newly emerging Ford Foundation had found in a 1947 study that one out of every seven students enrolled in college was studying in a business administration program, and that if only male students were counted (business schools at that time being almost exclusively male institutions—with the exception of some secretarial programs), the ratio was one in six. The foundation concluded that much of business education was of a low intellectual caliber, consisting of a collection of descriptive courses and "how to do it" techniques without any basic discipline underpinning. Thus, over the period of 1952 to 1964, the foundation spent 28 million dollars in upgrading business schools through programs ranging from the retreading of faculty in basic disciplines to assisting doctoral candidates with generous fellowships. With the ready cooperation of the American Assembly of Collegiate Schools of Business—their principal professional organization and accrediting agency—the schools of business were essentially remade into schools with intellectual substance. Seldom today is the business school the "dumping ground" of the university.

Since the ending of the Ford Foundation's largess, business schools have been solidifying their position as a discipline. A number of research journals have been launched as well as new fields of study. Business schools have attracted a larger and larger share of students, especially women, into their programs. Furthermore, a large number of students in other university programs have started taking elective courses in business. In some of the other professional programs such as forestry, home economics, and some of the health sciences, courses in business subjects are actually required. In sum, while many parts of universities are scrambling for students, business schools are filled to overflowing.

The Expansion of Business Administration

The lure of business administration education to current students is probably best explained by a quotation from Alfred North Whitehead's *Aims of Education* (New York: New American Library, 1976): "When classics was the road to advancement, classics was the popular subject for study. Opportunity has now shifted its location, and classics is in danger. Was it not Aristotle who said that a good income was a desirable adjunct to an intellectual life?" (pp. 69-70). Whitehead was addressing classicists in this essay at a time when the president of the United States, Calvin Coolidge, was uttering the famous remark that the business of America was business. Whitehead's phrase "road to achievement" applies aptly to business administration these days. Ours is a society in which organizations play a major role. Business schools concentrate on the study of organizational activities, stressing the goals of efficiency and effectiveness—the two criteria by which organizations are judged. Further, almost all the business curriculum is studied in an organizational setting. In preparing for advancement, therefore, the student is preparing to make a maximum contribution to the operation of the business organization—in minor positions at first and then increasingly responsible ones. It is not only in business that success is measured by advancement in the organization. Oftentimes we find that business students are planning to tread the road to advancement in nonbusiness organizations. The same criteria of efficiency and effectiveness apply, and, although the techniques may be different, the basic operations are not.

The stages of the life cycle as listed in Chapter One describe the business administration student population fairly well. The late adolescent and early adult stage is where we find the student in junior college and regular four-year college programs. The business administration majors are characterized as being more vocationally oriented. Their learning style probably makes them less imaginative but more diligent in their studies than liberal arts students. However, because they take many courses in common with liberal arts students, some of these differences disappear. They are considered to be more grade-conscious and competitive. Right or wrong, they believe that recruiters and employers make decisions about them on the basis of their grades. They tend to be well informed about the grade requirements for admission to graduate programs, especially the M.B.A. degree. The undergraduate business student is about on a par with the liberal arts student (other than pre-med or pre-engineering) on standardized tests.

For the most part, undergraduate business students are required to select an area of business (marketing, finance, personnel, or some other area) during their junior year. Junior college students, of course, choose business courses earlier, especially those who are not going on. Later on, as graduation approaches, the major subject tends to govern the recruiters they interview and the entry-level jobs they obtain.

Accounting students follow a somewhat different path. Accounting is a recognized profession with state-regulated credentials, namely, the C.P.A. Not all accounting students are headed for the C.P.A. examination, but those who are immerse themselves in accounting courses. While the collegiate program cannot fully prepare one for the C.P.A. examination, it comes reasonably close. The accounting profession is moving to require more education. New York State now requires five years of education in order to sit for the C.P.A. examination. Nevertheless, accounting students are not significantly different from regular business administration undergraduates.

The M.B.A. student population is considerably different—at least in today's world. Twenty-five years ago, when the number of M.B.A. students was relatively small, the extra year or two tended to be an extension of the basic college preparation. But M.B.A. degree programs have grown tremendously in recent years (some estimates run as high as 100,000 degrees a year throughout the eighties), and the path to the M.B.A. has changed. More and more, students are going out into the working world for a few years after graduating from college and then returning for professional education such as the M.B.A. degree. As a matter of fact, many schools are now requiring several years of experience before a student is admitted to the M.B.A. program. This pattern obviously diverges from the life cycle described in Chapter One, which assumes that one must complete one's education before tackling other developmental tasks, such as those of raising a family and becoming a responsible citizen.

The regular full-time M.B.A. student body comes from a diverse background. First of all, business schools pride themselves on holding the door open to all students regardless of undergraduate major. The business undergraduate degree is not considered to be the favored preparation. Hence it is hard to classify these students. Like all business students, however, they are interested in "practical matters" as opposed to theoretical ones. By the time of graduation, they are a homogeneous group with much the same outlook. This is due in large measure to the standardized curriculum. The M.B.A. curriculum in most schools is at least 50 percent required courses, to be taken in sequence starting with a fall admission.

Another factor that contributes to homogeneity is the admission process. The Graduate Management Admissions Test (GMAT) is required of virtually all M.B.A. admissions across the country regardless of sex, race, or age of the student. The accrediting standards specify a minimum score. The test, prepared and administered by Educational Testing Service (ETS), is a paper-and-pencil test of aptitude. In addition to the test, undergraduate grade performance is used as a criterion for admission by most schools. Because most schools have tried to make M.B.A. admissions compare favorably with other graduate admissions in the university, the traditional "B" average is usually required and is actually written into accrediting standards. Of course, the well-documented "grade inflation" of many undergraduate programs has made admissions to many M.B.A. programs easier than it was in the early days.

Women in Business Administration

The most noteworthy change in business enrollment over the last fifteen years has been the great influx of women. A handful of women have always enrolled in the regular business school programs, both at the undergraduate and master's degree levels, and occasionally women have found their way into the faculty ranks, but the only business schools that enrolled large numbers of women were those which had a program in secretarial studies. Even in these schools, women usually found it advantageous to take courses in education colleges and prepare for teaching in business education. In the business schools that did not offer programs in secretarial studies, virtually 100 percent of the student body and the faculty were male.

Over the last decade, the situation has changed drastically, and if present trends continue there is every reason to expect that women business students will approach parity in numbers with men in the near future. The reasons for the increasing numbers lie beyond the business schools and probably beyond education altogether. A pure economic reason is the fact that there were not enough interested and qualified males to satisfy the need for executive and managerial talent. Women were needed, therefore, to enable the economy to prosper.

Other important reasons are the changing status of women, the changing nature of the family, and the rise of the women's liberation movement. All these factors have contributed to a changing status of women and a changing outlook on the part of women themselves toward the work force and, in particular, toward managerial positions in business organizations.

The entry of the federal government into the battle against employment discrimination, heralded by the Civil Rights Act of 1965, has not only opened more managerial positions in business organizations to women but also mandated employers to actively seek and recruit women for the positions. Therefore, in increasing numbers women are entering the predominantly male world of business management at all levels, and to prepare for managerial positions they are enrolling in the business schools as a part of their college education.

It is entirely possible that the negative influences identified by Blocher and Rapoza in their chapter are still inhibiting women in their career development. The factors that they describe as major career obstacles—sexist attitudes, role conflicts, and uncertainty—no doubt affect women students in business programs as in other college programs. However, the fact that they have chosen to major in business subjects is an indication that at least some of the negative factors have been overcome. Further research, possibly of a longitudinal nature, following students from the freshman year through the senior year and into the M.B.A. level, is needed to either confirm or temper the Blocher and Rapoza propositions.

One further observation with respect to the Blocher-Rapoza thesis is worthy of attention. It is easy today to document individual cases where women are paid considerably more than their male counterparts upon being hired for their first job after graduation. What impact does the higher salary have on inhibitions and self-confidence? Nothing of their performance in business school would seem to indicate any more or less inhibition than in an equal population of male students. It must be kept in mind, however, that a generalized career decision has already been made and that family life will somehow be fitted around the career, rather than vice versa. All indications point to the fact that women business students visualize home and career as acceptable dual goals.

Looking at the matter from a different perspective, we might ask what impact the presence of large numbers of women students has upon the American school of business administration. The traditional view of the professional curriculum is that the subject matter, rather than the characteristics of the students (male or female, black or white, adolescent or middle-aged), governs the nature of the course, the way it is taught, and the expected outcomes. The practice of management, however, is a skill, and, while the knowledge base may remain the same for both sexes, it is doubtful whether the practice by men and women is similar. In those cases where the problem is factual in nature, involving numerical or financial data, the gender of the problem-solver matters little. However, if the problem involves a human relations decision, for example, is the gender of the problem-solver unimportant? Will males and females weigh the variables in reaching the solution to the problem quite differently? Much of business management is concerned with behavioral or human relations problems. If there are characteristic male and female solutions, then the presence of a large number of women would seem to augur a change in both the business school curriculum and in the business firm itself.

There are, of course, a number of stereotypes, but most of them have to do with decisions affecting the so-called "bottom line"—for example, "women are not competitive," "they will not drive hard for making budget or profit goals." As generalizations, these are demonstratively false. However, the expression "she thinks like a man" (usually voiced by a man) is considered to be an expression of respect and admiration. Whether it should be is open to question.

For whatever reasons, the business school courses, textbooks, and programs are cast in a male mode. The texts center on men, the cases almost always involve male managers (but female subordinates), and the courses are generally taught by men. While large numbers of women are enrolling in business school programs, the numbers entering Ph.D. programs and hence the academic profession are relatively few. This may change, however, as the job market for women M.B.A.s becomes saturated. At the present time women M.B.A.s are in such demand and can command such high salaries that the academic profession offers virtually no competition. As a result business schools are turning more to women doctoral candidates in other disciplines in order to fill their ranks. For example, students with Ph.D.s in education, psychology, and sociology are being recruited for teaching positions in business schools.

Whether because of the paucity of women faculty members or the general acceptance of the male view of business management, women business school students have resisted efforts to establish courses for women only. There are short courses dealing with subjects such as assertiveness training, but in all other respects the education program in the business schools is approached from the view that men and women need to learn the same body of knowledge and to practice the same skills. They rise or fall on the basis of the same grade comparisons.

Jessie Bernard, in her chapter on women, lays out some possible chronological timetables for various kinds of "contingency scheduling." The relationship of marriage, childbearing, and career are set forth as being a series of discrete steps. For women in the business world, however, where there are laws concerning pregnancy benefits and in many cases programs for assisting both mother and child, family and career are less sharply separated. Women choosing business careers find that it is difficult to maintain a position in an organization if one is away from the scene for an extended period of time (one to two years, for example). While the old job might be waiting and in some cases mandated by law, the nature of the work and the change in technology and organization may be such as to render an individual obsolete.

It is difficult to construct a scheduling model, however, and undoubtedly as more women enter the business world from schools and colleges, "contingency scheduling" will give way to a new model. That new model might easily be described as continuous career development. Given the pace of the modern organizational world, women achievers will find it more and more difficult to divide their lives into discrete time periods, say at five-year intervals, alternating between marriage and family periods and career periods. Instead, the two scheduling functions might be split horizontally, with varying amounts of time given to career and to home throughout an entire career. Thus, a woman might start out in her career with a standard eight-hour day, with home life occupying the off hours. At some later date, with the arrival of children, the career time might shrink to four hours a day, the additional hours being given over to home and family. As children grow older, the amount of career time might become larger once again. This pattern is not unlike that followed by many people in the performing arts world, where a singer does not completely drop her career because of the arrival of children. Undoubtedly, an organization design of this kind will require some major adjustments in business organizations, but it could be done if the advantages of lifelong careers for women are perceived. Changes of this magnitude might bring about the need for a rather major shift in the perspective of the feminist movement as described by Bernard.

Undoubtedly, one of the major changes that will take place in the business schools in the near future will be the development of curriculums for those women who want to enter the business world at the age of 40 or over. The continuing education program for women as described by Bernard tends to focus on the issues of women's roles, rather than upon marketable skills. That there is a mission for the business schools to provide the so-called marketable skills is quite evident, but there is little research on the kind of program that would be most beneficial. All that most schools can offer is a package of traditional courses gleaned from the regular degree programs.

The Study of Business

Business firms are organized on the principle of specialized tasks or functions. As a firm grows, these tasks or functions are further subdivided, thereby creating more specialized functions in what appears to be a never-ending process. Each of these specializations accumulates a body of knowledge and a set of techniques. These various functions and subfunctions provide the basis for many of the courses in the business administration curriculum. Graduate programs have increasingly produced specialists in different business functions, and their recruitment into the teaching force has led to the organization of business schools around the concept of business functions. Over time, specialized courses have proliferated, giving rise to the charge that many are narrow, or even trivial, courses without intellectual content or educational value. This has prompted some business schools to reevaluate their course offerings; the specialization issue is still being debated at many places.

While this issue is by no means unique to the business school (it appears to be endemic to all higher education), there is one interesting difference. Business students have virtually demanded specialized courses. They look upon specialization as an important part of their credentials to be presented to a potential employer. Whether specialization works to the students' benefit is difficult to ascertain. Top business management officials, in general, sing the praises of the liberal arts, but the fact remains that college recruiters tend to put emphasis on what are considered to be "relevant" courses. The combination of student interests plus faculty orientations make conditions ripe for divisional or specialized thinking, especially when there is controversy over goals and objectives. Nevertheless, the very controversy about goals has enabled the "generalists" to prevail in many instances.

The accrediting standards, largely the product of the deans of the business schools acting as a body, have moderated some of the extremes of specialization. Also, the rapid rise in the number of business students has kept the available faculty busy with the basic courses rather than elective specialties. Finally, most business faculty themselves come from academic backgrounds where they had considerable exposure to liberal studies and consequently recognize the value of general education.

The boundaries of the overall field of business administration are getting harder to define with each passing year. This is due in part to the dynamic nature of the business firm in today's society and in part to the advancing scholarship of business faculty members. Another consideration—although less important than the other two—has been the gradual realization, by other disciplines as well as business, that the business institution can be a fruitful area of research and observation. Thus it is that sociologists interested in role and status or in conflict resolution can find the business firm a useful place to study. Likewise, psychologists are using the firm for the study of behavior. Modern mathematics textbooks draw on business problems in areas such as probability and modern algebra. Still, it would be incorrect to say that the rest of the American education establishment has given anything other than a cursory glance to the business firm as an institution worthy of study.

Business firms are among our most dynamic institutions. The discipline of the "bottom line" forces management to be receptive to new technology as well as new methods and procedures. The image of business managers, including bankers, as conservative refers to their political philosophy rather than their philosophy of operating a business. There is always concern that competitors are forging ahead and that sooner or later this will have an adverse effect upon one's bottom line. Businessmen support organizations such as the American Management Associations plus a host of more specialized institutions, all of which are designed to impart the best of current practice or the latest technique in all functions of the business enterprise. While not all change is for the good, even for the bottom line, nevertheless, the pressures of competition and the availability of new technology are ever-present forces for dynamism in the business institution.

Business schools, by contrast, do not and cannot change at anywhere near the rapid pace of business management. Faculty members have not always had entree to the inner circle of the business institution; therefore, they are often ignorant of the changes that have been taking place until well after they have been consummated. Worst of all, in too many instances by the time the concept or practice is codified and placed in the appropriate slots in our knowledge base, the idea is obsolete and the firm has gone on to something else. As an example of this process, accounting data in all but the very small firms has for a number of years been printed mechanically and, in many cases, fully analyzed by computer. Some accounting textbooks, however, still show examples in which the records are copied by hand. While this is the extreme, there are hundreds of other examples in which the business organization is considerably out in front of the school.

Whether the impetus came from business, the faculty, or the students, the emphasis of many of the courses in business administration curriculums was initially on "how" rather than "why" and upon technique rather than concept or principle. Gradually over time, however, the situation has changed, and in recent years the gap between the schools and the business firm has narrowed considerably. Businessmen have discovered that, while they still want new employees who understand the terminology and know how the various component parts of the organization work, they also want people who can think and who have some management skills. Business schools, for their part, have been sorting out the items in their curriculums with the view to providing a better intellectual base as well as more up-to-date and realistic applications of theory and principle. The computer has served as a catalyst for bringing the schools and the business firms closer together. In the need for better understanding of the computer as substantially more than a fast calculator, businessmen have increasingly turned to knowledgeable people in colleges and universities, and a large number of these people are affiliated with business administration programs. The new knowledge in all fields has given rise to new study programs requiring more demanding backgrounds of students and faculty alike.

A major problem facing business schools is the integration of subject matter in the curriculum into a cohesive whole. The schools have followed a building-block philosophy starting with foundation subjects and working up to specialized applied areas. Courses tend to be compartmentalized, and there is little attempt to integrate them. Although some reports of integration experiments have appeared in the journals, such reports are still so rare as to be newsworthy.

Despite the specialization of courses, the business administration student is expected to be a generalist in the true sense of the word. He or she is expected to apply knowledge from other academic disciplines to a large number of problem areas in business management. How to focus this knowledge in such a way as to avoid mere superficiality is the challenge facing all business administration faculty. The criticism of the past was that the business schools deliberately avoided intellectual rigor in their programs. A common complaint today is that they are now trying to apply too much. Whatever their faults, they are trying to bring both academic integrity and professional competence to their educational delivery system. To quote one business school dean, "Our new program may be the last great hope for a truly general education."

Teaching Methodology

In business administration, as in other areas of the college or university, faculty have depended heavily upon textbooks as the principal teaching vehicle. In recent years textbook writers (usually academics in the field rather than business managers) have provided considerable case study material in the textbook itself as well as companion workbooks for students. The fierce competition among texts has prompted authors to provide teachers' guides to their books, which include examination questions as well as helpful hints on discussing each chapter with the students. In due time, audio- and videotapes will come along to enrich the course even more. These resources have made it possible to bring to the classroom a wide variety of teaching methods. The abundance of books of readings on almost all subjects in business administration has made more knowledge available to students than they could get from their library research or professors' lectures.

Probably the most important instructional approach in business administration is the *case method*. The business case method was pioneered by the Harvard Graduate School of Business Administration in the early twenties, and that school is still its principal exponent. The business case is an adaptation of the law case but with one important distinction. The decision in the law case is known, and the study of the cases revolves around the legal reasoning of the jurist who decided the case and commentaries on that reasoning. The business case as used for teaching purposes is quite different. Although the case is real, as is the law case, the actual decision is not known to the student and often not to the professor either. Students must decide what they themselves would do and subject their reasoning to the scrutiny of peers and the professor. The emphasis is upon gaining skills in analysis and interpretation along with a method for making decisions. Such knowledge of business functions as are needed the student will acquire on a "need to know" basis. The professor's role is much more indirect in that his job is to guide students in their development as analyzers, interpreters, and decision makers. This not only requires a great amount of skill on the professor's part but also a great deal of patience. Because there is no "school solution" that can be advanced as the right answer, the professor has to be alert to see that solutions advanced by students are well developed and show careful thought and analysis.

Is the case method a form of experiential learning as described by Chickering and Kolb elsewhere in this volume? In the sense that it forces the student to actually make decisions, it might be thought of as "learning by doing." It is not, however, comparable to learning by doing. No amount of case description, no matter how carefully drawn by an experienced case writer, is free from the communication problems of encoding, transmission, receiving, and decoding. More important, the case is dealt with in a classroom in which the stresses, human factors, and other dynamic aspects of the real world are not present, or are present in a different form. Even the most realistic of training operations are still simulated and do not evoke the same emotions as the real thing. David Kolb, in his very thoughtful chapter, indicates that students of management or business administration tend to be Accommodators—that is, those who learn best from concrete experiences and from active experimentation rather than from reflective observation or abstract conceptualization. Whether the case method serves this learning style well is difficult to say at this time because studies have not been reported by the Harvard Business School or any of the other of the handful of schools that use the case method as extensively. One might speculate that because business management is perceived as being a hardheaded, no-nonsense type of operation, only those kinds of students are attracted to it (even though their backgrounds may be liberal arts or science). Whether they are especially attracted to the case method programs, however, is difficult to say.

Under the auspices of the Ford Foundation in 1955, Harvard embarked on a substantial program to educate the faculties of other business schools in the case method. First, they conducted a summer seminar for faculty in which each person selected a company, investigated and wrote a case, and then proceeded to "teach" it to the other seminar participants. Then the Harvard Business School established the Intercollegiate Case Clearinghouse as a vehicle for collecting and disseminating cases written by business faculty over the entire country, and indeed, around the world. Any faculty member at any school can order cases from the catalogue, not only single copies on approval but also in quantity for class use. Undoubtedly, these educational efforts have had a great deal to do with popularizing the case method. At the present time, cases are used in some courses of almost every school. It must be noted that the Clearinghouse is not the only disseminator of cases. There are a number of case collections bound together with text material offered on the market. For example, one group of the Harvard Seminar participants from the southern part of the country banded together under the name of The Southern Case Writers and have produced several volumes of cases.

Despite the best efforts of the Ford Foundation, scarcely any schools have made the commitment to the case method as a primary method of instruction. This is due in part to the lack of resources and, probably in many cases, sheer inertia. At a more fundamental level, however, there have been questions raised about the efficacy of the case method as a method of teaching decision making. Some scholars believe that a more rigorous disciplinary approach is needed. Granted, great strides have been made in the field of management science. However, management is a human activity, subject to all the variability of human thought and behavior. Therefore, judgment of the sort that the case study method is designed to develop is still a valued commodity. As time goes on, both points of view and both methodologies will be recognized as important.

An interesting variation on the case method is the *management game,* which has come into prominence in recent years with the advent of the computer. The ability to simulate an entire business or an entire industry, for that matter, has opened up an entirely new field of study. The game differs from the business case in that students' decisions are tested in the "real world" of the industry being simulated. The feedback carries the learning process forward another step. Management games have proved to be a useful educational device, and with more time and attention, as well as resources, they could serve in an even greater capacity. The way management games are conducted offers the opportunity for research on a wide variety of human behavior problems. For example, some schools have facilities for observing and listening to students' discussions in the management game situation, making it possible to observe motivational factors at work. Many students involved in the game realize, for example, that they need to review the course work they have had in economics, accounting, or finance, and this time they really learn the material. While the game, or simulation, is not the same as the real world, it identifies the dynamics of the business system. Decisions have to be made for a hypothetical period of time, and the consequences of those decisions are eagerly awaited by the various teams (companies) involved in the simulated industry. The process is then repeated for the next time period. It may take only an hour to simulate the events of three months.

For all their emphasis on practical problems and the value of experience, the business schools have been very slow to adopt experiential methodology. Southern Methodist University has experimented with an alternative form of a master's degree using experiential methodology, and several other schools are following suit. However, experimentation with this methodology has been limited for a number of reasons, not the least of which is the vested interest in the status quo. It is widely assumed that there is so much fundamental knowledge to be learned that the most efficient educational approach is to have the instructor teach it to the students. Experiential learning is looked upon as relatively expensive and time-consuming. Also, it creates problems of measurement and evaluation. Although the case method may be considered a form of experiential leaning, it is conducted within the classroom framework.

Field research, of course, is nothing new in business administration, but recently students have been getting more exposure to it. Many schools now have formal programs in which the students work on a real problem in a business firm. There are two factors that are making field research programs more feasible. First, educational institutions are a great deal more flexible today as to what constitutes academic credit. Up until recently, the idea of giving academic credit for other than the standard academic activities was frowned upon. Even internship programs, except in medicine, were looked at somewhat askance. However, new institutions and programs such as the University Without Walls have changed attitudes about academic credit: now experience of all kinds is evaluated. Eventually, business schools, which have long dealt with "nontraditional students," will probably adopt experiential programs of a nontraditional nature.

A second factor is the growing appreciation by business management of the fact that a group of able, young, fresh minds, albeit without experience, can come up with eminently practical solutions to problems. The age-old complaint that all the young people learn in college is theory, which must be knocked out of them before they can be useful to the business firm, is seldom heard. Thus, there is increasing receptivity on the part of business management to working with schools in providing field opportunities for students, either singly or in small groups. There are an increasing number of success stories from firms that credit single field research projects with saving them substantial amounts of money. The essence of the field research project as an academic learning vehicle is that it enables the student to gain insight into the linkage between theory and practice.

It is quite evident that from these nonclassroom learning experiences that the business schools are entering a new era. We may expect many new ideas to emerge. In particular, competency-based education, which focuses on outcomes rather than upon input, is being explored.

Continuing Education

Business administration has always been involved in continuing education. The American Management Associations, for example, which started in 1924, have built a tremendous empire concentrating on continuing education. Their work has been so all-pervasive that, as might be expected, a number of other organizations have been spawned in their likeness. Indeed, the amount of money spent on continuing education in business dwarfs the amount spent on the standard collegiate fare, whether it be at the undergraduate or master's level. As a matter of fact, a large share of the continuing education movement has grown up outside of the colleges and universities. It is entirely likely that in the years to come some of the more ambitious and innovative programs outside of the collegiate sphere will become the major delivery systems for education in this field.

There has always been a demand for "night school" in the major urban areas, and most colleges have responded with special programs. While it is true that schools such as Harvard have not looked upon night school as part of their mission, Northeastern University, Boston University, and a number of other schools in the Boston area have pursued work in this field with a great deal of success. The same thing can be said for almost every metropolitan area. The American Assembly of Collegiate Schools of Business (AACSB) has tried very hard to maintain the standards for evening school work as well as for day school work on the grounds that business administration education should be identical for both. For many years, it tried to avoid accrediting schools whose courses were given primarily at night on a part-time basis, taught by part-time faculty. This is because the

AACSB has thought it more important to be "respectable" in the eyes of the liberal arts college than in the eyes of the business community. We are now seeing changes in this attitude, although the business schools still like to think of themselves as being predominantly day school operations with the majority of the classes being given from nine in the morning until noon, preferably on Monday and Wednesday.

What of the students in evening and continuing education programs? Are they "losers" as alleged by many members of the day school faculty? Are they interested in moving up the managerial ladder? Or are they merely individuals who are trying to keep abreast of technology by acquiring new vocational skills, as suggested by Schaie and Parr? There are some students who have been passed over on the promotion ladder and who will undoubtedly never reach the organizational goals they have set for themselves, but such students are not necessarily failures. Many students in business administration have entered an organization on a very low rung of the ladder but, after they have worked there for a while, have come to realize that the people in positions above them are not supermen and women as they once appeared to be.

Then too, as Schaie and Parr suggest, continuing education students are often motivated by the simple desire to understand the world about them. They find that courses in night school help them to cope with a difficult supervisor or to understand the statements about their company that they read in the paper or the memos from the top administration. These are people who seek knowledge largely to help them understand their work environment rather than to be more proficient in their positions. It is often remarked by teachers in this field that their students seem to apply the "aha method," in which suddenly an expression in the classroom clarifies something that they have known all along about their work experience.

Every faculty member who teaches in evening programs understands full well the problems of fatigue, which are the greatest barriers to learning in evening programs. Fatigue affects both the students and faculty alike, and it is only overcome through skillful and diligent work on the part of both parties. Physiologically, it is known that most people cannot be at their best at 8:00 in the evening if they have been working all day on a job starting at 7:00 in the morning. Probably the greatest injustice in education is done to those students whose teachers believe that as much can be accomplished in the evening hours as in the day program. Yet evening school students may bring so much to the course in the form of experience that the slightest adjustment in curriculum could open up an enriched educational experience for both students and faculty. Instructors in evening programs still tend to use course materials geared to students of full-time day programs. But as they gain more experience with evening programs, this deficiency will no doubt be remedied.

A large percentage of night school and continuing education courses in business are taken by women. Many of these women are in relatively low-ranking positions and are striving for advancement. Often they have college degrees but have found that they need courses in business administration to advance in their work. Still others are housewives who are entering the labor market for the first time and have decided that a degree in home economics, fine arts, humanities, or even education does not appear to be particularly impressive to prospective employers. These are women who are driven by the "need to know" and who quite often are unusually fine students in their various subjects. They are the people who benefit from courses designed with full-time, inexperienced students in mind.

To conclude, continuing education represents a considerable dilemma for business schools. Try as they might, they cannot ignore the continuing education field. Yet if they devote their principal resources to continuing education, they tend to move out of the mainstream of college education in general. While the schools know very little about their full-time traditional students, they know even less about the evening students because the evening students represent such a diverse student body. The part-time student has not exercised political power in the university in the past, but this day may be coming to an end. Evening students are beginning to assert their rights much as other students have done over the last two decades. Instead of sitting by docilely and taking whatever course the professor decides to give, evening students may soon make their feelings known through course evaluation processes similar to those now used in day programs.

It is entirely likely that we will find more continuing education in business administration rather than less in the future. The field is still a new one, technology in business has expanded its horizons, and many organizations are just beginning to discover the management function. As a result, more courses are offered and more students are enrolled in evening courses than in regular day programs. This is true for graduate work leading to an M.B.A. degree as well as undergraduate work. The evening or extension part of the program adds a dimension to the field of business administration that is not found in any of the more traditional forms.

Future Prospects

One of the notable changes manifesting itself in business administration programs is the increasing emphasis upon human behavior in all its aspects. Thus, in subjects such as management information systems (MIS), research studies, term papers, and indeed even entire courses are given over to human problems. Although consumer behavior is still a relatively new subject, marketing and advertising have, of course, always had as their goal the understanding of human behavior. Management courses have shifted their emphasis from the technical aspects of management functions, such as planning, organizing, and controlling, to human behavior in the widest possible context. Even subjects such as accounting, statistics, and economics are not adverse to discussing human behavior problems.

The aims of business administration's increased emphasis upon human behavior are many. Certainly an important one is increasing interpersonal competence, both on a one-to-one basis and in small groups. Since much of business activity is group activity, competence in working with groups is often an important factor in success in business organizations. Such competence, of course, ultimately depends on personality development. If, as suggested in this volume by Chickering, Havighurst, Weathersby, and others, personality development can be promoted in educational settings, then the business schools and education programs in industry take on added significance. Unfortunately, the college programs in business administration have seldom concerned themselves with personality development. The movement of students through developmental stages from "impulse" to "integration" will require that the faculty make a concerted effort to develop new programs and reform existing ones. The pressure of time itself and the continuous stream of students make it difficult to carry out such a project. There must be, of course, a willingness on the part of everyone concerned. Possibly the only way a major change of this kind can be accomplished is to create a new environment—for example, in a branch situation or even a new school. It is significant that the new experiential programs have usually been developed in new institutions rather than existing ones.

There is no indication that radical changes are imminent in the business schools (why should they be when the schools are enjoying record enrollment and faculty are getting more involved in research and consultation?), but there are some indications of changes in the wind. The American Assembly of Collegiate Schools of Business has a committee that has been focusing its attention on trying to identify desirable outcomes of the collegiate education process. Eventually the AACSB may create some new standards of accreditation making students' demonstrated competence the criterion by which the school is evaluated rather than the admission standards expressed in terms of grades and test scores or the academic degree qualifications of the faculty or a "lock step" type of curriculum. As the AACSB committee completes its task and develops a model, the challenges for the schools will become clear. Recent reports on trying to promote radical change in other professional fields, such as law, medicine, and engineering, indicate some of the difficulties the business schools will face.

The growing interest in experience-based education in business may stem from a somewhat different model than the AACSB is contemplating. The most intriguing program is the new master's degree proposal of the American Management Associations. This is to be a completely experience-based degree program based upon management competencies as identified by McBer and Company of Cambridge, Massachusetts. The program consists of an assessment center approach, in which the assessment of a student's competencies leads to an individual learning plan designed by the student to remedy his or her deficiencies. In addition there is to be an on-the-job series of events designed for reality testing and further demonstration of competency. As this program develops, it will undoubtedly spark the imagination of other people in the field, and it is possible that the evolutionary process may turn into a revolutionary movement. There are underneath the surface some widespread feelings that the traditional course approach, which emphasizes imparting knowledge, does not serve the true mission of the business school.

Finally, business administration is showing a new concern with values. Specifically, the role of the corporation in today's society is a topic of lively interest. Unfortunately, many business administration students are more interested in business as a technical subject, and courses that deal with philosophical problems are usually ranked far down the list by students in assessing the school's curriculum. Still, humanitarian concern is a live issue. White, in his chapter, condemns the competitive and materialistic nature of current society, but the fact is that materialism is a part not only of our culture but of cultures throughout the world. Humanitarianism, like the basic precepts of the great religions, does not appear to be universally embraced. It is a fact that business administration cannot afford to ignore. Nevertheless, the business schools do believe that it is possible to serve the needs of the whole person as well as the firm and that business administrators require a high degree of empathy, not only for successful living but for successful business.

Closely allied to the question of humanitarian concern is the issue of moral development. Gilligan's work, as reported in this volume, may be quite useful to the business schools, especially as it concerns the relationship of the individual to the organization. The moral dilemma created by this relationship from time to time can be very significant. Unfortunately, her work does not deal with the dilemma in which the individual finds himself faced with mutually exclusive alternatives. Understanding what the alternatives are does not make the decision easier. As a matter of fact, in some cases it is even harder. The Eichmann case is the extreme, but there are hundreds of lesser cases faced by individuals on almost a continuous basis. The aim of any teacher of organization is to teach the students the difference in degree. Teachers of future managers have the added burden of teaching their charges the importance of minimizing these conflicts for their subordinates as well as coping with their own.

Alfred North Whitehead, one of the most eminent scholars of the first part of this century, addressed the Annual Meeting of the American Assembly of Collegiate Schools of Business in 1927. In beginning his remarks he made the following observation: "Universities have trained clergy, medical men, lawyers, engineers. Business is now a highly intellectualized vocation, so it fits well into the series. There is, however, this novelty: the curriculum suitable for a business school, and the various modes of activity for such a school, are still in the experimental stage. Hence the peculiar importance of recurrence to general principles in connection with the moulding of these schools" (1976, pp. 96-97). During the fifty-odd years since Professor Whitehead made these remarks, the study of business administration has come of age. Its role in the university or college is no longer questioned. However, once again the business curriculum in an experimental stage, and the various modes of activity are in a state of flux. Probably the greatest change that Whitehead might find if he were to examine business administration today is that the field is poised on the threshhold of a new era of institutional development, which will enable it to deal more satisfactorily with the development of students as outlined in much of this volume. Undoubtedly, he would applaud such a move as a worthy endeavor.

25

Dean E. Griffith

Engineering

Colleagues in higher education and laymen will be surprised to find engineering educators debating the meaning of this chapter's title. Why? Do not all engineers receive the same professional training? Our current engineering population is over 1.2 million (Alden, 1976). Approximately 300 engineering schools produce bachelor's level graduates in over fifty curriculums (Engineers' Council for Professional Development, 1977). There is even greater variety at the graduate level. There are no uniform state laws governing registration for practice in engineering, and not all states subscribe to reciprocity. Engineers, and engineering educators themselves, do not even agree as to whether or not engineering, as it is known today, is a profession. And therefore no agreement exists among these same groups as to what constitutes adequate preparation for engineering practice.

At this writing there is a heated debate about whether or not the Engineers' Council for Professional Development should continue to accredit engineering curriculums on two levels: the basic level typical of four-year programs, and an advanced level typical of master's programs, or a so-called "first professional degree." Institutions with accredited curriculums at the advanced level increased from 25 in the fall of 1976 to 41 in the fall of 1977, out of approximately 300 engineering schools. This trend, while still emerging, is expected to continue since it is supported strongly by engineers in practice. The details of this debate are given in the proceedings of the annual meeting of the Engineers' Council for Professional Development (1977). The proceedings of the annual Deans' Institute of the American Society for Engineering Education frequently carry additional new viewpoints on this matter (O'Brien, 1978).

Engineering educators at all levels are concerned about the engineering curriculums as preparation for engineering practice. Quite possibly no other professional group has studied its own curriculums in greater detail and with more enthusiastic criticism than have the engineers. Major national engineering curriculum studies have been reported by Fletcher in 1896; Magruder in 1906; Mann in 1918; Wickenden in 1930; Hammond in 1933, 1940, and 1944; Grinter and others in 1955; Walker in 1968; Holloman and others in 1975; Corcoran and others in 1977; and Grayson in 1977. Each of these studies and reports has had significant impact on engineering curriculums. Engineering curriculums are constantly being influenced by new technological knowledge, new legislation, new general academic requirements by their parent institutions, and pressing social issues such as equal opportunities, occupational health and safety, and especially the growing diversity of students served. Of all the factors influencing the current engineering curriculum, accreditation standards of the Engineers' Council for Professional Development (1977) dominate. Engineers, cautious and conservative by nature and training, want to know the rules of any game they play. Engineers plan and operate by those rules, whether the rules be physical laws of the universe, man-made laws, or curriculum criteria set by an accreditation standards committee.

Engineers are also, in general, oriented to inanimate objects—that is, hardware, software, processes that operate under close control, and the like. Engineering curriculums since the mid 1940s have been technology-oriented and dominated by topics from the physical sciences. For many years the humanities and social sciences were considered to be important but peripheral curriculum components. It is not too surprising, then, to find the vast majority of engineering faculty, themselves educated to a hardware-software curriculum emphasis, in turn emphasizing technical aspects of a professional career at the expense of personal development or growth as described by Weathersby, White, and others in Part One of this book.

Changes in Engineering Education

During most of the period since World War II—that is, for the past thirty plus years, engineering has been a curriculum in great demand by a significant segment (8-10 percent) of college students because of the high employment opportunities. With a few exceptions, during periods of economic downturn, engineering faculty have instructed large classes. In fact, the senior course sizes in many colleges have increased from 15-25 in the mid 1950s to around 45-60 in the early 1970s and may be even larger in the early 1980s when the current underclass enrollments reach professional levels. The pressures on engineering faculty to increase their production of graduates are significant.

During World War II, the scientific weakness in the engineering curriculum was pointed up when the government turned to many physical scientists, mostly physicists and metallurgists, to manage the Manhattan (atomic bomb) Project. The postwar recovery and the advanced technology demands of the military during the Korean War eventually led to a comprehensive study of the engineering curriculum (Grinter, 1955). The Grinter Committee recommended significant changes in engineering education, including the replacement of descriptive courses with courses of greater scientific depth—in essence, a scientific core of engineering mechanics, solid mechanics, fluid mechanics, thermodynamics, heat transfer, electronics, and higher mathematics.

Between 1954 and the late 1960s, essentially all accredited engineering schools accommodated these curriculum recommendations. The resultant curriculum burgeoned with semester credit hours totaling between 140 and 160. The flood of new technologies (especially computers, avionics, and new materials designs) during the 1950s was interpreted by engineering faculty as requiring more technology exposure in the under-graduate curriculum. Five-year programs were designed to meet this need, with most of the fifth year devoted to newer, analytic engineering approaches (Walker, 1968). Engineering faculty fought desperately to accommodate each new technological advance as well as many of the more traditional courses: surveying, drafting, algebra, trigonometry, analytic geometry, introductory chemistry, remedial English, and so forth.

After the removal of draft deferments for engineering and science students, many scientifically oriented students began selecting less demanding curriculums. Students not interested in pursuing careers involving extensive engineering analysis often enrolled in other scientific fields that required only four years of study. In addition, many more career path options were opened on most campuses. Curriculums expanded from the more traditional disciplines of the liberal arts, the natural sciences, business administration, education, and engineering to include architecture, law, nursing, communications, public administration, international (area) studies, and other new curriculums. The student Free Speech movement of 1964 culminated in student demands for social relevancy in the curriculum of the 1970s. Many of the new curriculums—for example, social work and urban studies—provided relevant educational opportunities, and the students enrolled. The engineering faculty reduced the credit hour requirements, cutting out the "weakest" descriptive courses, attempting to maintain balance, and striving to attain a level that would ensure that the graduates more than satisfied the minimum technical standards for entry into engineering practice.

Humanities requirements proved something of an enigma. The Engineers' Council for Professional Development maintained accreditation criteria requiring at least one half year of humanities. But often faculty attempts to appropriately address this humanities minimum were hampered by legislative or institutional requirements that precluded the liberal arts courses necessary to meet individual student needs. The net result was that engineering curriculums became primarily focused on developing a student's technical problem-solving abilities. Other aspects of human development were neglected or abandoned to the liberal arts and communication school faculties, whose own courses were being increasingly designed for the preparation of professionals in their respective fields. Engineering became known as a very "challenging" curriculum, and engineering students, because of their problem-solving work load, became known as "grinds."

Industrial recruiters, while recognizing the excellent technical preparation given to engineering students, deplore the students' inability to "get the job done"—that is, to be effective in implementing real-world solutions. The recurrent weaknesses in engineering education are in communication skills and skills in working with others. The academic solution of adding yet another course to the already full curriculum has not proven satisfactory. Through the late 1950s, engineering students were involved in group activities, were required to prepare laboratory and other reports and to present talks. Students learned, by doing, the art of technical communication and cooperation. In recent years, however, the demands of technical problem solving have left less time for such activities. As a result, in the late 1960s and early 1970s many students who were previously interested in the engineering route to management decided to enroll directly in business or the liberal arts.

For close to a century, the engineer has held the key to applied technology. True, a few early chemists controlled the chemical industry and a few early physicists led the solid-state electronics industry, each for a short period. But, in general, engineering has been the route to industrial management.

In recent years Bachelor of Technology Program enrollments have grown substantially. The new engineering technology graduates now often fill positions previously requiring engineering degrees. Rapid growth of engineering technology is causing much concern on the part of engineering educators (Dalton and Thompson, 1971). At first many engineering faculty and administrators tried to ignore the engineering technologists and later tried to fight them. But by now many engineering educators have joined with engineering technology faculty and others, such as engineering registration boards, to articulate the differences between engineering curriculums and engineering technology curriculums as well as the differences between their respective graduates.

This identity crisis in engineering is now forcing each school to reexamine what happens to its graduates. Longitudinal studies of graduates now are included in the reaccreditation data requirements of the Engineers' Council for Professional Development (1977). Faculty involved in these longitudinal studies will begin to see the outcomes of their educational processes. They will begin to find out, as did the Worcester Polytechnic Institute planning faculty, that the evolving traditional engineering curriculum does a marvelous job of preparing graduates to handle "given" technical problems. But the traditional engineering curriculum does not well equip the young graduate to assert the new leadership our pluralistic society requires. The Worcester faculty totally redesigned their undergraduate curriculum to prepare the new engineers so required by our society.

> [It is the goal of the Worcester Plan] by means of coordinated programs tailored to the needs of the individual students, to impart to students an understanding of a sector of science and technology and a mature understanding of themselves and the needs of the people around them. WPI students, from the beginning of their undergraduate education, should demonstrate that they can learn on their own, that they can translate their learning into worthwhile action, and that they are thoroughly aware of the interrelationships among basic knowledge, technological advances, and human need. A WPI education should develop in students a strong degree of self-confidence, an awareness of the community beyond themselves, and an intellectual restlessness that spurs them to continual learnings" [Grogan and others, 1977b, p. 1].

Loevinger's concept of ego development as described by Weathersby and White's model of the development of humanitarian concern through empathy, social participation, and humanitarian environments could be instrumental in implementing this plan.

Cooperative engineering education, in which engineering students alternate course work with practical experience in corporations, has recently emerged as a dynamic force in the shaping of the engineering curriculum (Moore, 1978). Student cooperative engineering enrollment is growing significantly as corporations recognize and employ student coop graduates. Cooperative education periods, when carefully planned to provide progressive experiences, can contribute significantly to students' personal growth as described by Moore (1978). There is growing controversy among engineering educators whether or not to award credit for cooperative periods in industry. Many engineering faculty have little or no experience in evaluating this form of experiential learning. Again, Kolb's circular model of cognitive development could prove useful in the development of progressive coop experiences.

During coop periods in practice, the engineering student has excellent opportunities to observe the general human development cycle in the population at large and in the practicing engineers with whom he works. These latter serve as important role models for the student. Coop students are, albeit without much needed observational training, thus exposed to a much wider cross-section of adults than they would encounter in traditional college classes. In addition, the cooperative education setting is a less sterile, idealized format for learning about professional life than is the campus, where students are normally isolated from the routine cares of family, job, or community. In the future, cooperative education periods may be used as opportunities to explore personal development styles and purposes (Moore, 1978). Cooperative education may hold the key to life education, just as classroom and laboratory activities now hold the keys to preparation for problem solving.

Engineering Students

Since World War II engineering enrollments have been on a continual roller coaster. Freshmen enrollments went through a minimum in 1957, a peak (of 79,500) in 1965, and another minimum (of 51,925) in 1973 (see Alden, 1976). From this recent relative minimum, the number of students in each successive freshman engineering class has increased significantly: 63,444 in 1974; 75,343 in 1975; 82,250 in 1976; to an estimated 87,300 in 1977. The fall 1978 freshman engineering enrollment is expected to increase to over 90,000. This surge in engineering enrollment was unexpected and unpredicted in the early 1970s. The early 1970s aerospace recession and the general industrial recession following the removal of wage and price controls caused major industries to curtail their capital expansion plans. Engineering manpower demand is closely tied to capital expansion planning and expenditures in the United States ("An Engineer Shortage . . . ," 1978). The 1973 oil embargo merely aggravated an already uncertain future for capital expansion in the United States. The net effect of these economic fluctuations was to build up a backlog in engineering manpower demand. Ultimately this demand had to be satisfied by increasing the starting salaries of new engineering graduates. Engineering technologists and others have also been hired to perform the engineering jobs that could otherwise not be filled by engineering graduates.

The engineering curriculum of the mid 1970s has provided a route to immediate employment not found in any other curriculum with the exception of accounting. The forecast is for the strong enrollment in engineering to continue until around 1982, when much of the pent-up demand for engineers should be satisfied and the demand will begin to slacken. If the 1982 graduates enter a marketplace already saturated with engineers, the mid 1980s could be a disaster for higher engineering education. In the mid 1980s the absolute enrollment in colleges of the 17- to 22-year-old group is expected to fall approximately 20 percent from its 1970s-1980s high.

Possibly no other college curriculum, with the exception of nursing, has been as traditionally dominated by one sex as has engineering. Until 1970 women represented less than 1 percent of engineering population. Although small numbers (and very small percentages) of minorities have been present in the engineering profession for most of the century, until the 1970s engineering had not attracted significant numbers of minorities. Engineering has also traditionally been a young person's curriculum. Very rarely did adults return to college to pursue an entry-level engineering degree. Engineering curriculums were primarily constructed to serve the full-time student living on or near the campus. The daytime scheduling of laboratories and classes made part-time education very difficult.

Large urban universities have broadened their class schedules to accommodate the employed adult returning to school after hours. A number of major innovations have been attempted in the engineering curriculum to better serve the special needs of adults. For the most part, these innovations embody new educational technology—instructional television, videocassettes, electrowriters, and teleconferencing, for improved off-campus delivery, and on-site lectures—rather than modification of the subject content taught or of the course or curriculum objectives. Even the modifications implemented to meet the special needs of minorities or women have been supplementary in nature without really changing significantly the basic engineering curriculum.

These new populations are considered as engineering students first and only secondarily as individuals representing new groups with special needs to be addressed. The engineering curriculum is thus still designed to make the student "fit the model" rather than to enhance special individual talents.

Women and Minorities. Engineering has been, and is, a male-dominated curriculum. Traditionally, the engineering student body has been composed of lower-middle-class white males. From World War II to the late 1960s, there was a gradual influx of Orientals, East Indians, and Mideastern Arabs, essentially all male. In the 1970s this picture began to change. Women now compose up to 5 percent of the entering freshmen engineering class; minorities compose about an equal percentage. Many new national organizations have been formed to support individuals in these two groups while they attend college. Most significant, however, are the actions that have been taken by engineering employers. Whether as a result of enlightenment or of equal opportunity regulation, most employers provide excellent job opportunities for the young woman or minority engineering graduate. The wide availability of these successful role models will go far toward assuring steady attraction of women and minorities into engineering (Griffith, 1978).

The curricular consequences of these changes in student body composition are just now being felt. Many engineering faculty are having to surrender their male chauvinism and their racial prejudice. Faculty are having to modify male-oriented teaching techniques. Women and minorities are questioning subject relevance and traditional faculty attitudes. These questions force faculty reexamination of course and curriculum objectives. Some women and minorities are out-performing their more traditional colleagues in the classroom and laboratory. These realities significantly increase the social awareness of white male engineering students. No longer can engineering students hide from the realities of our societal problems by totally immersing themselves in the engineering curriculum; the same interpersonal problems they will confront in practice now confront them in the classroom.

During the 1980s the effects of women and minorities on engineering curriculums will be seen most clearly as curriculum decisions are made by faculties who better understand the needs of these special populations and who in fact have moved toward greater sexual and ethnic balance by hiring women and minority faculty members.

Older Students. For the most part, the engineering student body is composed of fresh high school graduates with strong aptitudes for mathematics and the physical sciences. Since 1957, because of significant scholarship funding, most high school graduates with high aptitude for engineering have had opportunities to attend college directly out of high school. But now there is a growing new trend changing, or threatening to change, this absolute dominance of youth in the undergraduate engineering curriculum. Many high school graduates are electing to pursue technology and industrial education degrees at technical institutes or community colleges. After graduation with associate or bachelor of technology degrees, many of these students find their upward progress constrained by their lack of advanced-level technical knowledge. They then frequently apply to enter engineering programs. In addition, many practicing engineers want, and need, courses in subjects that are new to the engineering curriculum since they graduated. This growing trend of adults in the classroom is especially marked in those communities attractive to industrial expansion. Such communities often were former home locations of rural universities that have become urbanized through the development of industrial parks.

This early exposure of fresh high school graduates to the spectrum of ages with which they will later be working will have a salutary effect on life cycle education as described by Havighurst and Chickering in Chapter One. It is expected, and to be hoped, that this process of a more heterogeneous and representative learning environment at colleges and universities will broaden both the fresh high school graduate and the older engineer.

While the engineering student body is becoming more diverse, the absolute number of engineering students is rising to a new high. Higher education administrators with fresh mental scars from the early 1970s' plunging engineering enrollments are resisting engineering faculty expansion. Engineering faculty are again having to cope with burgeoning enrollments and mass education techniques—for example, large lecture sections and the use of graduate laboratory and teaching assistants to help with large classes. The faculty are often too busy "teaching" to attend to individual student needs.

Most students are primarily interested in completing the engineering curriculum and graduating so that they can accept one of many phenomenal job offers typically made to new graduates. These students may resent being treated as "one of many," but they are far more interested in getting their education over with and entering the world of work and high salaries than they are in setting their lifetime developmental base. Only when students face the prospects of the real world of work and life do they realize that their engineering education was too narrow. In a recent survey I made of practicing engineers (average age 33.8) enrolled in Clemson's rigorous externally delivered Master of Engineering Program, the students indicated "broadening of technical knowledge" to be a priority motivation for return to school. Establishing lifelong learning skills was among the least frequently mentioned motivations for enrolling.

When do most engineers become concerned about the life cycle development tasks discussed in Part One of this book? A number of years ago a cross-sectional survey of engineering graduates from Purdue University, conducted by Dean George Hawkins, followed these graduates' continuing education interests at various life stages (LeBold, 1978). The results of this study were as follows:

Age	Time Since Degree	Continuing Education Interest
21-26	0-5 years	Greater technical depth
26-31	5-10 years	Greater technical breadth and supervisory skills
31-46	10-25 years	Management knowledge and skills
46-60	25-39 years	Appreciation of the arts
60-	40- years	Retirement activities

Detailed refinement is greatly needed if these results are to be applied.

After ten years out of school, many engineers normally *begin* to question the life goal values resulting from their narrow education. Successful engineers, as indicated by their regular, almost linear, progression in occupations and salary, seldom question seriously their personal concepts of life cycle. But at the first sign of business recession or depression, or during transition periods of mass "transployment," engineers begin to seriously question their life goals, which often are confused with their current concepts of job perpetuation. Frequent traumatic shifts in high-technology industries have created a serious need for career and life counseling for middle-aged engineers and scientists. Much of this trauma could be reduced if undergraduates were exposed, through work-study or internship programs, to a realistic appraisal of the engineering life cycle—demythed of the Thomas Alva Edison and Alexander Graham Bell role models.

The principal engineering programs that have faced this problem squarely are the Worcester Polytechnic Institute Plan (de Rhoda, 1976; Grogan, 1977; Hazzard, 1975; Roard, 1977), where students learn very early, through intern project experience, what constitutes engineering practice, and the Education and Experience in Engineering (E^3) Program (Torda, 1973) of Illinois Institute of Technology. The latter is an interdisciplinary approach to integration of liberal arts into the technical curriculum. It uses the problem-solving approach to develop creative attitudes and to increase and integrate knowledge supplemented by lectures, directed individual study, and seminars. The relative context in which the broad residual virtues of life are taught is critically important to pragmatic engineering students. The approaches advocated by Gilligan and Perry in this book could be very helpful to faculty incorporating moral and ethical development into the engineering curriculum.

Engineering and Adult Development

Engineering faculty seldom incorporate new concepts permanently into the curriculum that have not been thoroughly tested and evaluated first as educational experiments. This is characteristic of the scientific approach instilled in engineers through their undergraduate and graduate studies. Findings on life cycle development, ego development, intellectual development, development of the capacity for intimacy, and the like do not usually appear explicitly in the reports of educational innovations in engineering. The context of engineering curriculum changes is usually much more pragmatic.

For example, engineers perceive that they have been poorly received in congressional and state legislative hearings on legal matters that greatly influence engineering practice. This perception has led to a new concern in engineering education for the development of legislative process skills. In the early 1970s several technical societies, most notably the American Society of Mechanical Engineers and the Institute for Electrical and Electronic Engineers, with a few academic institutions, created Washington internships for selected students to spend an academic period learning about the processes of government as they affect engineers or engineering. This experiment is now being considered for adoption as part of public policy curriculums, which will have a significant influence on engineering students' development of humanitarian concern. The full effect of this curriculum reform will not be known until the early 1980s. However, results to date promise a significant broadening in the political sophistication and social concern of students who participate (Hyman, 1978).

Engineers have long prided themselves on their problem-solving abilities. In the late 1960s, however, the engineering profession began to realize that in solving some problems, such as clogged highways and urban decay, engineered projects were causing other, often more severe, problems such as freeway anxieties and industrial air, water, solid waste, and noise pollution. The national impact was evidenced by congressional legislation in the form of the Environmental Protection Agency and Environmental Impact Statements. The continued stream of congressionally legislated engineering practice has in turn caused engineering faculty to include broader coverage of societal need issues in their courses as well as to accept more related courses in sociology, geography, and demography as electives. A broader problem-solving context, such as advocated by Schaie and Parr in this book, is now needed to match these broader problems.

Project and Andragogy Models. A few other experimental engineering education programs in progress today will have significant potential impact on adult development, learning styles, and the developmental challenges of the life cycle. One key learning technique is the project. Almost all adults learn efficiently when the learning is embedded in a project of great personal importance, as Tough notes in his chapter on lifelong learning. Adults so involved are often described as highly motivated. The importance of the project approach is to focus attention on priority learning requirements. The Worcester Polytechnic Institute Plan (Grogan and others, 1977) and the Education and Experience in Engineering Program (Torda, 1973) organize essentially all learning around major student projects. The results to date have been quite gratifying. The experiential learning model described by Kolb in his chapter on learning styles has great apparent application in engineering. Knowles (1976) and Doigan (1977) have proposed an andragogical model alternative of equal value.

Interpersonal Relations. Many engineering graduates have a difficult time in dealing with their fellow employees, or their clients, or others. Interpersonal relations may be known by faculty to be a problem in the engineering curriculum, but to date very little has been done nationally to include this topic in engineering curriculum accreditation criteria (Engineers' Council for Professional Development, 1977).

Cooperative education and group or team student projects have given students opportunities for developing interpersonal skills but generally without specific guidance. Interpersonal relations skills are an area of great future potential. But the leadership in engineering reform will come from industry rather than from academia unless significant external support is obtained for special faculty development activities in interpersonal relations.

Moral and Ethical Development. As has already been indicated, engineering curriculums have been greatly shaped by the technological thrusts of our society. Until the late 1940s many engineering faculty had extensive engineering experience either in industry or as consultants. Faculty were aware of the ethical dilemmas (conflicts of interest, kickbacks, and so on) often posed for the young engineer fresh out of school. During these early years professionalism and ethical concerns were often discussed in the classroom along with other important but qualitative factors of engineering (Grinter and others, 1955). This attention to the moral and ethical development of students was relaxed during the 1950s and the 1960s. New technologies were quickly wedged into an already bulging curriculum. In this squeezing, the "soft sciences" and humanities usually paid the greatest price. Increasing attention was devoted to qualifying graduates for positions in high technology; decreasing attention was devoted to the nontechnical problems engineers might face in practice.

Over this same period, managers from major industries revealed their growing cynicism about what was required to "win" in the industrial world. Probably the biggest shock to hit the engineering profession was Vice-President Agnew's indictment for accepting payments from engineers who had received contracts to do work for the state (Ross, 1974). This single incident drove home the complex ethical and moral problems not addressed as the curriculum drifted away from the applied humanities (Rosenstein, 1973).

Recent investigations into offshore construction practices, a highly capital-intensive activity, have indicated sizable special payments (kickbacks) from construction companies to high officials of several client energy companies. Comments from industry observers included the typical justification of accepted practice. How do young engineers gradually succumb to such warped ethics that they eventually accept obvious conflict-of-interest dealings as "common practice"? This is an area of concern among sensitive engineering educators.

In another famous case, that of the Bay Area Rapid Transit System (BART) and its myriad problems in becoming operational, Robert Anderson (1978) of Purdue University has documented the many questionable practices by which BART officials attempted to fend off the ethical concerns of several developmental engineers working on the BART project. These engineers suffered considerably in the process but cut a path through the maze of professional society inaction, bureaucracy, and legal maneuvering that will be invaluable to future engineers and engineering faculty interested in the ethical and moral instruction of engineers.

To help address the reintroduction of ethical concerns into the engineering curriculum, the National Endowment for the Humanities has funded a three-year (1978-1980) National Project on Philosophy and Engineering Ethics under the direction of Robert J. Baum, Director of the Center for the Study of the Human Dimensions of Science and Technology, Rensselaer Polytechnic Institute (Baum, 1977). The studies reported by Perry in Part One of this book will be very helpful to faculty involved in this new ethics project—a greatly needed activity long overdue.

Career Planning. Considerable engineering career development research has been conducted and reported by G. W. Dalton and P. H. Thompson (1971); Samuel S. Dubin (1974); J. Peter Graves (1977); Harold G. Kaufman (1974a, 1974b, 1975, 1978); Richard Kopelman (1974); Donald B. Miller (1974, 1977a, 1977b, 1977c); R. Renck (1969); and Walter D. Storey (1974). The emphasis of their works has been on policies and procedures to assist engineers after they graduate from the academy. Very little of this research has yet been applied to the redesign of engineering curriculums at the undergraduate or graduate levels. However, some career-planning factors are beginning to be included in programs planned for continuing engineering education. Organizations are beginning to offer special career-planning courses (Miller, 1978a and 1978b).

For the better part of the past decade, major corporations have recognized the paramount importance of career planning for individual and corporate growth. Many universities now conduct career-planning sessions as part of their continuing engineering education offerings for practicing professionals. In a few organizations, such as General Electric, International Business Machines, Celanese Chemical Corporation, and Phillips Petroleum Company, members of the technical staff have been delegated responsibility for perfecting the career- and life-planning process for in-house use. Growing numbers of corporations, agencies, and universities have monitored these developments and have adopted the workshop and counseling approaches of these leaders. Wide-scale adoption and adaptation of these techniques are the *sine qua non* of lifelong career planning.

A new thrust by universities has taken the form of career guidance centers and career orientations. As universities become familiar with industrial success in career- and life-planning activities, they will follow suit by adopting and adapting these important techniques to integrate university career planning into lifelong planning, not merely discipline career paths, which usually last less than ten years. Versatility is important!

What is now crucial, however, is for universities to develop cadres of faculty and staff with the career planning and counseling skills needed to help students resolve uncertainties. The importance of this activity has not yet been recognized by engineering faculty at large. Young engineering faculty, usually more receptive to educational innovation, could well provide the impetus for quick adaptation of experimental career and life-planning programs as part of the regular engineering curriculum. The perspectives supplied by Blocher and Rapoza in their chapter on vocational development will be extremely useful to these faculty members.

Psychological Type and Preferred Learning Styles. Recent educational research involving significant numbers of engineering students is just now being applied at a handful of engineering colleges throughout the United States. Mary McCaulley (1976) at the Center for Applications of Psychological Type, University of Florida, has been accumulating a data bank on the psychological types of engineering students attending numerous cooperating institutions. The Myers-Briggs Type Indicator used by McCaullay includes the dimensions of extraversion-introversion, sensing-intuition, thinking-feeling, and judgment-perception. McCaullay has collected more than 80,000 cases during the 1970s. One of McCaullay's cooperating correspondents, Lee Harrisberger, at the University of Alabama (Tuscaloosa), has demonstrated the application of the Myers-Briggs Type Indicator to student learning in undergraduate design engineering courses involving business simulations. These data and the Myers-Briggs Type Indicator will be used more often in the future to help categorize student learning styles and to help faculty members select appropriate learning mechanisms for each student. We are on the threshold of tailoring education to individual needs and individual differences—an exciting challenge for all of engineering education.

As engineering matures into a full-fledged profession, will it recognize the significance of life cycle differences and the ways in which curricular requirements and teaching methods must respond if students and their employers are to be well served? Will it help its professionals develop the interpersonal competence to work effectively with others as they move into supervisory and executive positions, as they work with legislative bodies, planning commissions, and representatives of public interest groups? Will it take seriously the shifting requirements of multiple careers and vertical and lateral changes, and help its students—young and older—think through alternative plans and design their education accordingly? And where will engineering stand on those fundamental issues of moral and ethical development, of interdependence and humanitarian concern? Will it encourage graduates to satisfy uncritically any corporate request for assistance, respond reflexively to any political call for technological assistance, no matter what the product or potential outcome? Today's heated debates concerning the profession, its mission, and education processes need to seriously consider such issues. If they do not, professional identity and integrity will be hard to come by. We will more likely continue simply as a handy set of tools, grasped by social architects when useful but otherwise tossed aside and ignored.

References

Alden, J. H. *Engineering and Technology Enrollments.* Fall 1976 Edition. New York: Engineering Manpower Commission, Engineers' Joint Council, 1976.

Anderson, R. M., Jr. Personal communication, June 1978.

Baum, R. J. *National Project on Philosophy and Engineering Ethics.* Troy, N.Y.: Rensselaer Polytechnic Institute, 1977.

Corcoran, W. H., and others. "Engineering and Engineering Technology Education—A Reassessment." Report of the Ad Hoc ASEE Committee for Review of Engineering and Engineering Technology Studies. *Engineering Education,* May 1977, pp. 765-776.

Dalton, G. W., and Thompson, P. H. "Accelerating Obsolescence of Older Engineers." *Harvard Business Review,* 1971, *49,* 57-67.

de Rhoda, A. "The Making of a Technological Humanist." *American Education,* January-February 1976, *12* (1), 11-15.

Doigan, P. "Andragogy: A New Technology." *Engineering Education,* May 1977, p. 752.

Dubin, S. S., and others. "Defining Obsolescence and Updating." In *Maintaining Professional and Technical Competence of the Older Engineer—Engineering and Psychologi-*

cal Aspects. Washington, D.C.: American Society for Engineering Education, 1974.

Ebaugh, P. "The Engineering Research Council: Its History, Present Status, and Possible Future Role." *Engineering Education,* March 1978, pp. 452-455.

"An Engineer Shortage Hits Industry Again." *Business Week,* July 3, 1978, pp. 18-19.

Engineers' Council for Professional Development. *45th Annual Report.* Vol. 1. New York: Engineers' Council for Professional Development, 1977.

Fletcher, R. "A Quarter Century of Progress in Engineering Education." *Proceedings of the Society for the Promotion of Engineering Education,* 1896, *4,* 31-50.

Graves, J. P. "Now Even Obsolescence May Be Obsolete: A New Look at Careers and Their Development." *Proceedings, 1977 College Industry Education Conference.* San Antonio, Texas: American Society for Engineering Education, 1977.

Grayson, L. P. "A Brief History of Engineering Education in the United States." *Engineering Education,* December 1977, *68* (3), 246-264.

Griffith, D. E. Report to the Long-Range Planning Committee on "Reassessing the Problems of Engineering Education for Minorities and Women," San Diego, Calif., January 1978.

Grinter, L. E., and others. *Report on Evaluation of Engineering Education (1952-1955).* Washington, D.C.: American Society for Engineering Education, 1955.

Grogan, W. R. "Continuous Education: Time for Wash and Wear Fundamentals." *Engineering Education,* May 1977, pp. 751-752.

Grogan, W. R., and others. *The WPI Plan: A New Approach to Education.* Worcester, Mass.: Worcester Polytechnic Institute, 1977.

Hammond, H. P. "Promotion of Engineering Education in the Past Forty Years." *Proceedings of the Society for the Promotion of Engineering Education,* 1933, *41,* 44-66.

Hammond, H. P. "Aims and Scope of Engineering Curricula." *The Journal of Engineering Education,* March 1940, *30* (7), 555-556.

Hammond, H. P., and others. "Report of the Committee on Engineering Education After the War." *The Journal of Engineering Education,* May 1944, *34* (9), 589-614.

Hazzard, G. W. "For the Technological Humanist: The WPI Plan." *The American Biology Teacher,* January 1975, pp. 19-20.

Holloman, J. H., and others. *Future Directions for Engineering Education—System Response to a Changing World.* Washington, D.C.: American Society for Engineering Education, 1975.

Hyman, B. "Educating Prospective Engineers for Public Policy." *Engineering Education,* April 1978, pp. 730-734.

Kaufman, H. G. "A Comparative Analysis of University versus In-company Continuing Education for Engineers." In *Maintaining Professional and Technical Competence of the Older Engineer—Engineering and Psychological Aspects.* Washington, D C.: American Society for Engineering Education, 1974a.

Kaufman, H. G. *Obsolescence and Professional Career Development.* Washington, D.C.: AMACON, 1974b.

Kaufman, H. G. *Career Management: A Guide to Combating Obsolescence.* Institute for Electrical and Electronic Engineers Press/Wiley, 1975.

Kaufman, H. G. "Technical Obsolescence: An Empirical Analysis of Its Cause and How Engineers Cope with It." *Proceedings, Annual Meeting of the American Society for Engineering Education.* Vancouver, British Columbia: American Society for Engineering Education, 1978.

Knowles, M. S. "Adult Learning: New Strategies Needed." *Engineering Education,* May 1976, pp. 823-825.

Kopelman, R., Thompson, P., and Dalton, G. "Factors Contributing to the Effectiveness of the Older Engineer." In *Maintaining Professional and Technical Competence of the Older Engineer–Engineering and Psychological Aspects.* Washington, D.C.: American Society for Engineering Education, 1974.

LeBold, W. K. Personal communication, 1978.

McCaulley, M. H. "Psychological Types of Engineering Students: Implications for Teaching." *Proceedings, 1976 College Industry Education Conference.* Washington, D.C.: American Society for Engineering Education, 1976.

Magruder, W. T. "Report of the Committee on Statistics of Engineering Education." *Proceedings of the Society for the Promotion of Engineering Education,* 1906, *14,* 94-96.

Mann, C. R. *A Study of Engineering Education.* Bulletin No. 11. New York: Carnegie Foundation for the Advancement of Teaching, 1918.

Miller, D. B. "Technical Vitality of the Older Engineer in Industry." In *Maintaining Professional and Technical Competence of the Older Engineer–Engineering and Psychological Aspects.* American Society for Engineering Education, 1974.

Miller, D. B. *Personal Vitality.* Reading, Mass.: Addison-Wesley, 1977a.

Miller, D. B. *Personal Vitality Workbook: A Personal Inventory and Planning Guide.* Reading, Mass.: Addison-Wesley, 1977b.

Miller, D. B. *Career Management: An Annotated Bibliography for Those Who Want to Improve Career Success.* San Jose, Calif.: IBM General Products Division, 1977c.

Miller, D. B. "Counteracting Obsolescence in Employees and Organizations." Paper presented at 49th Human Resources Conference, American Management Association, Chicago, Ill., February 9, 1978a.

Miller, D. B. "Work, Learning, and Vitality." Paper presented at Conference on Education in Business and Industry, University of Vermont, 1978b.

Moore, J. "How Do Co-op Experiences Complement Academic Studies?" *Proceedings of the 1978 College Industry Education Conference.* San Diego: American Society for Engineering Education, 1978.

O'Brien, J. F., Jr. (Ed.). "Speakers Papers." 15th Annual Institute for Engineering Deans, Point Clear, Ala., March 5-8, 1978.

Renck, R. *Continuing Education for R and D Careers.* Washington, D.C.: National Science Foundation, 1969.

Roard, A. C. "A New Curriculum Is Engineered for Technological Humanists." *The Chronicle of Higher Education,* January 10, 1977, p. 8.

Rosenstein, A. B. "The Applied Humanities and the Institutionalizing of Change in Higher Education." Pts. 1 and 2. *Engineering Education,* 1973, *63* (7), 523-527; (8), 599-602.

Ross, S. B. "Engineers Can Govern Themselves." *New Engineer,* April 1974, *3* (4), 9.

Storey, W. D. "An Introduction to Self-directed Career Planning." In *Maintaining Professional and Technical Competence of the Older Engineer–Engineering and Psychological Aspects.* Washington, D.C.: American Society for Engineering Education, 1974.

Terman, F. E. "A Brief History of Engineering Education." *Proceedings of the Institute for Electrical and Electronic Engineers,* September 1976, pp. 1399-1402.

Torda, T. P. "E³=Education and Experience in Engineering." *Engineering Education,* October 1973, pp. 23-75.

Tribus, M. "The Challenge of Continuous Education–Will Universities Be Part of the Problem or Part of the Solution?" *Engineering Education,* May 1977, pp. 744-750.

Walker, E. A. *Final Report: Goals of Engineering Education.* Washington, D.C.: American Society for Engineering Education, 1968.

Wickenden, W. E. *Report of the Investigation of Engineering Education 1923-1929.* Vol. 1. Lancaster, Pa.: Society for the Promotion of Engineering Education, 1930.

26

Robert L. Saunders
Dorcas S. Saunders

Education

A review of the history of teacher training in the United States leads to several rather clear conclusions. (1) To supply enough teachers for the public schools, it has been necessary to sacrifice quality for quantity. No other alternative seemed consistent with a democratic school system. In virtually every instance when it has had to be decided whether to employ an unqualified teacher or not to have the class at all, the decision has been to employ the unqualified teacher. This situation is not unknown in the education profession today. The continuing shortage of teachers up until this decade has, without doubt, retarded the elevation of teacher training standards in this country. (2) As Lawrence Cremin noted in his paper "The Education of the Educating Professions" (presented February 21, 1978, in Chicago at the annual meeting of the American Association of Colleges for Teacher Education), the training of teachers as an organized, systematic effort is a relatively young movement in America, really less than a century old. During this period, the preparation of teachers has been basically a process of exploration, experimentation, and change. Institutes have come and gone; the reading circle has flourished and died; normal schools have been transformed into teachers' colleges; and schools and departments of education in colleges and universities have enjoyed unprecedented prosperity and growth, which threatened at times to overshadow the academic divisions of higher education. Teacher education has undergone continuous change. No clearly conceived theory of teacher training has evolved in this country, although curriculum patterns over the country are relatively uniform, or more alike than different. (3) Limited by the factors just mentioned, the information base regarding the learning process, pedagogy itself, and the effective ways of teaching people have been handled essentially as a series of loosely conceived efforts with only partial evaluation. Only in isolated instances can the profession consider itself to have a solid base of proven factual information upon which to build its practice. However, this shortcoming may be a blessing in disguise, for, as we shall see later, vast changes will be needed in professional studies in education to accommodate large numbers of significantly different students—adult learners. Necessary changes might be made more readily—and with less attachment to traditional practices—than they could be in the context of a highly structured, well-developed, and strongly defended model.

Too little attention has been given to developing curriculums that retain an emphasis on teaching or learning concepts but enable institutions to prepare persons for teaching in the broader sense. Some movement in this direction within the past five years is discernible; it is wise and overdue. Reflecting this change, several schools and colleges of education have adopted new names to better describe their extended mission. Such titles as School of Education and Allied Professions, College of Education and Human Development, and College of Education and Human Services are illustrative of these changes.

Given well-developed programs in learning theory, educational psychology, measurement, growth and development, and so on, teacher education can move into a variety of closely related program areas with good prospects for success. Some of these areas are in fact being occupied by education graduates who until recently were regarded as having been unsuccessful in their efforts to secure appropriate placement. Several institutions, for example, have expanded counselor education programs to include preparation for careers in various community agencies, such as halfway houses, correctional agencies, recreation centers, and religious organizations.

The developing national policy to educate all handicapped citizens to their maximum potential offers great opportunities for initiating new programs and for modifying recently developed ones. Rehabilitation services of various kinds are already in operation and need additional personnel appropriately trained. As greater numbers of handicapped citizens pursue higher education, increasingly being made available to them, new preparation programs should emerge for persons to provide instruction and related services. In some instances new personnel will be called for; in other instances existing personnel will need new training. For example, higher education has had little experience in instructing students with seeing and hearing impairments. Citizens with these and other handicaps have attended higher education in numbers proportionately less than their overall ratio in society. Many faculty and administrators must have additional training if they are to give leadership and direction to this "new" client group. Additional personnel will be required as well, some at professional levels for which preparation already exists (such as rehabilitation counselors employed by universities) and others at paraprofessional levels (such as readers, interpreters, listeners, and various other types of support personnel).

Good potential exists also for moving into virgin educational territory within the fields of government, business, and industry. As Harold Hodgkinson pointed out in his paper "The Postsecondary Learning Arena: Who Are the Players?" (presented April 6, 1978, at Memphis State University), tremendous amounts of adult learning are already taking place in these arenas and others not connected with schools and colleges. Collectively, such organizations teach more adults than do colleges and universities. Higher education may not be able to recapture these client groups. It may not wish to do so. In any event, the preparation of educators to work in these nonuniversity adult learning centers is an appropriate and attainable goal for professional education. Curriculums can and should be established for this purpose. Persons who seek or are already in educational training programs in business can be prepared for such work through professional studies in education. Courses in the curriculum designed specifically to prepare classroom teachers for public schools (such as history of American education, child development, and children's literature) could be replaced with courses and other experiences in business, adult psychology, and some of the theory now emerging in the general field of adult learning, lifelong learning, life cycles, and ego development.

Much of the theory presented in Part One of this book can be useful in preparing persons to work in adult learning settings. It can be useful for educational occupations and roles in the Department of Defense and in other governmentally sponsored learning programs, in local and state programs in the general area of human development, and in business, industrial, and professional organizations. The potential role of professional studies in education in the continuing education of persons already engaged in educating other adults is great, as those educators seek to develop additional competencies needed for effective teaching of the large, diverse client groups who are adult learners.

Students in Education

As noted earlier, professional studies in education are both evolutionary in nature and reactive to external societal changes. One of the forces most likely to influence the future American college is the changing nature of the students themselves. Four client groups can be identified: (1) persons who are preparing for initial entry into the field as a first career, (2) persons who are already employed in some area of education but are extending their preparation, (3) persons who are seeking higher levels of responsibility, and (4) persons who are changing their specialties. These groupings are not unlike those described in the chapter by Blocher and Rapoza.

Initiates. Because it has mistakenly been assumed that undergraduate education students are a fairly homogeneous group of 18- to 22-year-olds, the curriculum has tended to emphasize the cognitive domain at the expense of developmental issues, and content has been aimed at the traditional chronological norm. Women students, especially, have too often been victims of the traditional role expectation that they will aspire to fill a classroom teacher or librarian position—and that only until marriage or motherhood demands their attention. When serious consideration is given to the changing nature of undergraduate students, however, it will be seen that this group needs a vastly different and more individualized approach. In the future, professional studies in education will be serving students with a greater diversity in developmental stages. Factors that must be considered include the disappearance of the age norm, the influence of the changing experiential background, and the social-cultural developmental stages of the new clientele. Changing role expectations for women will undoubtedly prompt many to climb the career ladder toward top administrative positions.

Lateral Extenders. John Doe has a baccalaureate degree plus certification and experience in elementary education. However, the job market favors specialists, such as in reading. John returns to college to extend his preparation in order to take advantage of the new job opportunities or because he has shifted interests. Jane Doe has discovered that her field, social science, in which she has credentials, is flooded, but there are many openings in mathematics. She thus returns to college to acquire the credentials to teach mathematics. When these two persons and hundreds of others like them appear in education courses, what special needs will they have that demand a different approach to their academic preparation?

These students have already reached a level of competence in teaching techniques; their personal styles of learning are set and difficult to change; they are masters of disguising their real academic needs, having developed an effective set of coping skills; attaining their immediate goal of recertification is so important that they do not easily risk the perils of behavior modification. Although the professionals in teacher education programs have recognized the diversity of the client group in both age and developmental stages, still too little attention is given to assessment of prior competence, either in program design or teaching practice.

Vertical Changers. With a wealth of experience to draw upon, strong economic motivation, and a well-defined purpose for engaging in further professional study, vertical changers present both a challenge and an opportunity to their mentors. Given the current reward system in education, these students will most likely be seeking credentials for supervisory or administrative positions. Having already earned the baccalaureate and probably the master's degrees and logged several years of experience, they will usually be in their early thirties or approaching middle age.

Traditional approaches in professional education have largely ignored the personal development needs of this client group, focusing instead on certification requirements. In reality, the developmental tasks of this client group place them in a high-risk, success-driven relationship with their professional studies activities. These students cannot divorce themselves from the demands of family, community, and work, as perhaps they could in preparing for their initial careers. In addition, their intellectual development might even be hampered by their strong experiential background. Certainly, these and other experienced students will demand more accountability. And persons in this group will be better able to evaluate instruction since they too have been practitioners for some time.

Specialty Changers. This group of clients is composed mostly of persons trained in an academic discipline who are moving from a "pure" discipline or a profession to teaching. Admittedly, very few of this group (proportionately) enter formal teacher preparation programs. For a vast majority, training in the intricacies of teaching has taken place on an informal trial-and-error, on-the-job basis. This will no doubt continue as long as universities emphasize research over teaching in the reward system. However, this in no way negates the necessity for concern about this group's professional growth and development.

A basic question that must be addressed with this group of clients relates to purpose. Why are they changing their career emphases? For most, this change represents a second career and will probably occur as they are going through other midlife transitions. Especially for older persons entering the education profession after a first career in another dimension of the discipline, it will be quite difficult for them to recognize their own developmental needs, much less those of their students. They will continue to maintain close ties with their first academic discipline or professional field and view themselves as transmitters of knowledge rather than as facilitators of learning. At the elementary level in education, the "readiness" level of students is recognized as promoting success in coping with developmental tasks. That same factor is just as important for adults. Earlier, the question of purpose was raised. As Blocher and Rapoza pointed out in their chapter, the "voluntary changers" are the people whose needs probably include clarification of goals and values and career exploration processes. The "involuntary changers," as characterized by Blocher and Rapoza, are persons forced to change careers because of external circumstances. Whether their career changes are voluntary or involuntary, persons in this group will not respond readily to an academic environment that is structured for the novice.

Teaching Practices

In broad, general terms, instruction has four components: (1) goals and objectives, (2) teaching, (3) materials and other supporting resources, and (4) evaluation. The adult development theory presented in Part One of this book is pertinent in varying degrees to all four components of instruction, for all four client groups described earlier.

Goals and Objectives. The diversity of the four client groups involved in professional studies in education dictates a far-ranging, open-ended set of goals and objectives for instruction. "Meeting the needs of students" becomes more than a professional cliché when these needs are observed closely. Chickering and Havighurst, in Chapter One, underscore the importance of designing the curriculum to meet the needs of students at various stages of the life cycle. The most obvious requirement for such a curriculum is greater participation by the students themselves in setting goals and objectives. The goals that students cite will be better understood if they can be related to life cycle changes and developmental tasks.

It should go without saying, of course, that the integrity of certification standards must be maintained. However, extending more options in programs of study need not create conflicts with the standards set by external agencies. For instance, the variable of time has traditionally been used rather inflexibly to accommodate the institutions' accounting systems. If, as many educators propose, curriculum designers embrace the concept of individualized education, then time allowed for meeting the course goals must be flexible and adjustable to the individual student's ability to progress. Of particular concern, in this regard, are the needs of women with family responsibilities. Not only must the time component be flexible in terms of days but there must also be some reconsideration of what constitutes "prime time" for scheduling formal class work. The latter consideration is just as important for clients who remain active in a position while simultaneously attending school, such as the "extenders" or "changers."

With all the difficulties inherent in individual goal-setting, it is even more difficult to determine the starting point for an individual student. From the previous discussion of the variations in experience and knowledge that students bring to the academy, it logically follows that a single beginning level in a given course cannot be suitable for all. Imagine, for a moment, the student in a graduate course on teaching methods who must wade through the whole gamut of basics even though he or she has already had both prior preparation and several years of teaching experience. Yet, without some recognition of prior learning, that is exactly what happens. Just as the education professor cannot assume that all students have or should have identical goals, neither can he or she impose on the student unneeded, extraneous, or already learned content. One way to determine the beginning point would be to administer the final exam on the first day of class.

Along the higher education frontier, the concept of credit for prior learning, discussed by Keeton in Part Three, is gaining in both acceptance and practice. This concept has special relevance for professional studies in education. When goals and objectives are individualized to respond to the particular needs of the four client groups, diagnostic techniques will certainly include, and to some extent be based upon the student's background. This seems especially important in determining criteria for admission to graduate programs. A woman who has maintained a home (management), reared one or several children (child care and development), or managed the family budget (bookkeeping) is not by any stretch of the imagination starting at the same point as an 18-year-old on her own for the first time. With adequate assessment and broad involvement of the student herself, goals and objectives can be established that use these prior experiences as building blocks.

Conversely, the older "new" student may be intimidated by the tremendous advances that have taken place in educational technology. As Schaie and Parr pointed out, many older learners face an immediate and critical need to overcome obsolescence suffered from these technological changes. Mini-courses designed to help students update their knowledge can help remove this particular barrier. For example, computer-assisted instruction is rapidly becoming a fundamental instrument in individualized education. Professionals who have remained active in the field might use computer terminals with ease, but to the uninitiated they can be terrifying. Remember, the "experts" themselves at one time were not so adept.

A common fear among adult learners is that they will be unable to compete on an equal basis with younger students or with those professionals who have remained active and current. Before they can focus on the future, returning students must feel comfortable with the present. Professional jargon is a case in point. It is easy to fall into using special professional language and, by doing so, completely sever communication. Those experienced "changers" may have a special problem with the language, since they probably will continue using that of their own discipline. Thus, there are now two foreign languages spoken.

Competency-Based Teacher Education (CBTE) is not without merit. However, the profession must resist the temptation to state competencies only in cognitive terms or to ignore the specific purpose to which the student will apply his or her knowledge. It is to be hoped that most teacher-training institutions will use their sets of competencies as guidelines, not as iron-clad and all-encompassing goals and objectives. Green raises the question of integrating institutional and individual goals and points out that the problem is how to allow for pursuit of conflicting purposes. The simplest answer, of course, is for the institution to identify its role and scope and let the clients fit in wherever they can. However, that stance ignores the fact that "consumerism" is reaching the point where the *why* as well as the *what* and *how much* are seen as negotiable components of college degrees.

Facilitation. In modern lingo, the connotative term *facilitator* is often substituted for the traditional label *teacher,* implying a changed role for the leader of a learning experience. According to Schaie and Parr, the facilitator role of professors of adult students must be the rule rather than the exception. That is, adult students should be able to determine the content and method of their own learning. This implies a different but exciting student-teacher relationship on the adult-adult plane.

By changing the role of the instructor from the traditional "fountainhead of all wisdom" to that of facilitator of learning, the professor can encourage the development of the student's capacity for intimacy, as pointed out by Douvan. Although Douvan was referring specifically to young persons in a stage of disengagement from parents, the same need could be found in women who are searching for new friendships separate from their husbands and children. These new relationships between students and teachers strengthen professional learning and encourage more general developmental change (as discussed in Part One).

In addition to the new adult relationship between student and professor, the facilitating role will also incorporate other responsibilities such as counseling. Unfortunately, counseling, whether personal or career, traditionally has been viewed as a separate and distinct function from teaching. In light of the theories of adult development presented in Part One, supportive counseling must become an integral part of the teaching process rather than an adjunct function. According to Schaie and Parr, this broadened role of the teacher is a legitimate expectation of the adult educator.

Materials and Support Resources. There is no gainsaying the fact that Americans have rapidly become extensive users of, and even addicted to, audiovisual communication devices. Rather than bemoaning this phenomenon, the wise teacher will capitalize upon it in the teaching-learning process. The use of videotapes is already widespread in the field of education. Through the utilization of an unobtrusive but objective camera in micro-teaching exercises, students can be given the chance to see themselves as others see them and thereby analyze their own strengths and weaknesses.

Reference was made earlier to the problem of obsolescence of knowledge in older students returning to college after a prolonged absence. One way of closing this gap is through recorded information that can be retrieved at the convenience of the student—in the car going back and forth to work or school, after the children have been put to bed at night, while preparing the family meal, or during a lunch break at the office.

The endless possibilities of computer-assisted instruction are especially promising for the adult student who is at a developmental stage where immediate reinforcement of learning is of paramount importance. Another distinct advantage of computer-assisted instruction is its capacity to permit reasonable increments in the mastery of subject matter. The fragile nature of the self-concept often demands a protection from failure to reach broad goals. In the open-admission community college, where the "new" student, as defined by Patricia Cross in her book *Accent on Learning* (Jossey-Bass, 1976), is the rule rather than the exception, the most effective teaching strategies incorporate some means of sequencing learning in small segments.

Of course, the broader use of technology demands a concomitant ability of the professor to handle the machinery and tools of technology. In a later section of this chapter, the developmental needs of professors will be addressed.

Evaluation. Many implications have already been noted for the evaluation component of instruction. There are, however, some rather specific principles of evaluation that can be enumerated in the context of adult development theory as presented in Part One.

1. Criterion-referenced rather than norm-referenced evaluation: The most important message for the future American college is the diversity of the student population. There simply will not be a normative reference point for the "bell-shaped curve." Lock-step, preordained units of learning will be replaced by assessments that validate the individual's progress toward tailor-made goals. Criteria for awarding credit will be geared more to the career goals of the individual than to the hypothetical norm of all professionals in a given category. As was pointed out earlier, there are many differences in needs between the four client groups and among the individuals within these groups.

2. Varying increments of achievement: Schaie and Parr commented on the need for self-pacing for older adults. One of the authors of this chapter personally experienced the need to regulate learning tasks according to the student's ability level. In one community college where the mathematics program is designed for mastery learning, a separate testing center has been established. Students go to the center to take tests when the student and teacher *together* determine that the student is "ready." An application of this concept in professional studies in education would allow the practicing professional to plan his or her program around the demands of the career itself.

3. Prescriptive as well as descriptive evaluation: A new and exciting dimension of evaluation is finding out what one needs to learn as well as how much one already knows about a certain subject or unit of knowledge. Prescriptive evaluation in the medical model is used to determine what "treatment" is indicated. In professional studies in education, the information could also be used as the client plans his or her career path. As Tough pointed out, the bulk of adult learning is self-planned, with the person planning the learn-

ing from one learning session to the next. Prescriptive evaluation can contribute greatly as it becomes part of the learning process rather than merely a sorting device.

4. Assessment of affective as well as cognitive development: In the context of the holistic approach to human growth and development, a wide range of abilities will be assessed, including, but not only, the cognitive skills. Ability to relate new information to old, processing skills, interpersonal competence, creativity, and other dimensions of learning are all important facets of evaluation. This approach to evaluation will depend less on pencil-and-paper assessment strategies and more on student-teacher interaction.

It should go without saying that all the evaluation principles outlined here will not necessarily be used in every situation. It should be obvious, also, that incorporation of these techniques will demand a different distribution of both students' and teachers' time.

Curriculum

The rationale for a general studies curriculum has always included the need for interrelationship of the academic disciplines. This need is no less pressing in education curriculums. However, integration of knowledge assumes a different configuration in the professional training of educators for our four client groups.

Traditional programs in education have sorted students both vertically (preschool, kindergarten, lower elementary, higher elementary, middle school, and so on) and horizontally ("majors" in music, history, mathematics, ad infinitum). We now know that such a fragmented approach to teacher training puts unnecessary restrictions on career opportunities too early in the training program. By isolating students through compartmentalized programming, we deprive them not only of flexibility in their career planning but also of interaction with a variety of other students. Education simply does not occur in tight compartments—it is part of, and reactive to, the whole social system. White, in his chapter, is especially concerned about the separatist approach to education. He emphasizes the need for developing what he calls "social conscience" through the influence of interaction with diverse realities. Blocher and Rapoza express the belief that the present crisis in higher education stems precisely from the narrow vocational thrust of the college curriculum. It seems especially pertinent to programs in professional studies in education to take a more integrative approach to program design, both within the professional schools themselves and between them and the other academic components on campus. A closer look at the four client groups will give us more insight on this particular aspect of teaching practices and curriculum design.

Initial Entry. Even the most rudimentary knowledge about human development should lead program planners to delay or at least deemphasize specialization at the entry point of career development. (Lest it be objected that certification requirements demand specialization, we might note that we are looking at the *future* American college. It is to be hoped that the professional schools and departments will have some positive influence on credentialing agencies.) The focal point of professional study in education should be the professional role in its broader sense, as described in Kolb's chapter. The fact that an entering student declares an intention to prepare to teach American history in a senior high school does not free the profession from its obligation also to promote that student's ability to function within an organization, to be a part of the more inclusive community, or to develop a sense of responsibility for the total impact of the profession itself. To narrow the student's preparation program to a single area of specialization at the entry point would certainly make it difficult, if not impossible, to reach the integrative level.

Extending Preparation in the Same Field. This client group may be the most difficult of all to reach. As was noted earlier, they have well-defined goals, most of which are
stated in terms of specific career aspirations. It is for this precise reason, however, that
greater attention must be given to including activities designed to encourage an interdisciplinary approach to learning. Team teaching, for instance, with the team members coming
from both the "pure" disciplines and education, could be used to great advantage in demonstrating the interrelationship of knowledge. Such an organization will require scrutiny
of the university bookkeeping system in credit-hour production. A positive side effect of
such an arrangement, however, will be the contribution made to the development of the
professors' own integrative skills.

Changing Level of Responsibility. With the vast wealth of experiences that adult
students in this group have to draw upon, the instructor who can comfortably assume the
facilitator role and who can embrace the concept of individualized learning will probably
enjoy a most rewarding and challenging experience. Kolb, in his chapter, characterizes the
integrative stage as marked by reassertion and expression of the nondominant adaptive
modes or learning styles. For the professional educator, this will probably mean moving
from active to reflective and from concrete to abstract. At the point of re-entry into
professional studies, the student is, or will soon become, the mentor or nurturer of
younger colleagues.

Changing Specialty. It is often with fear and trembling, yet with a strong sense of
purpose, that persons in this client group enter professional studies in education. Beginning a new career after an earlier one in another profession, especially if the student is
simultaneously going through a difficult personal life crisis, can be either traumatic or
fulfilling. Much depends on the mentors with whom the student studies. As increasing
numbers of these "voluntary" changers choose to enter professional studies in education,
the challenge is to capitalize on the strengths of the students while introducing them into
the profession. In essence, these individuals have completed their personal and social
developmental tasks in one career and now face these same developmental stages in another profession. Like the 18-year-old high school graduate, they must start at the beginning; yet there are striking differences, which must be recognized. Time is limited, and
progress toward the desired credentials must be realized as soon as possible. The most
efficient way to acquire knowledge is through its relationship to other knowledge. Rather
than denying the existence of and stifling the use of expertise from a first career or a
lifetime of experience, the instructor in professional education courses might better help
students integrate their existing knowledge with the new competencies to be developed.

Faculty for Professional Studies

Any attempt to envision what professional studies in education will be like in the
future would be incomplete without taking into account the faculty. For our purposes,
professional faculty may be defined broadly to include both those directly involved in the
instructional process and other professional personnel whose roles support the instructional process—administrators, counselors, research specialists, and evaluators.

Enrollments in higher education are not expected to increase significantly in the
foreseeable future. Consequently, many observers predict that there will continue to be
an overall surplus of professional personnel in professional studies in higher education.
And no doubt faculty mobility, which has been reduced drastically in recent years, will
remain low. These combined factors suggest that efforts to shape professional studies in
education in the future American college should assume that the professors of this pro-

gram are already on the job. This is to say that faculty currently employed are expected to be the predominant group for at least the next two decades. Proportionately small numbers of new faculty will be employed as replacements for those who will retire, die, or otherwise leave the profession. Limited numbers of new faculty will be needed also to staff new programs, as discussed earlier. The growing demands for community college and technical institute staff, where teaching is the primary purpose, will possibly increase the need for preparation programs for teachers. But the number of new faculty needed is expected to be relatively small, given the expected economic constraints on program expansion. Thus, it is very likely that a child born this year who enters college eighteen years hence to engage in professional studies in education will be taught by faculty who are already there. What, then, should be expected in regard to the professional faculty?

Lindquist points out in Part Three that in recent years a significant number of colleges have initiated professional development programs. Operating under different taxonomies and with varying purposes, they all recognize the need for professional personnel to enrich themselves, develop new competencies, and otherwise "tool up" to meet both programmatic and student needs of tomorrow. Lindquist and other major contributors to this movement (Gaff, Phillips, Bergquist, and a few others) have documented several compelling reasons why faculty renewal and development are essential.

The developmental needs cited by Schaie and Parr for faculty in the future American college are certainly applicable to professional studies. In fact, it can safely be said that faculty in professional studies in education will have developmental needs not wholly different from those of their students. Though it might be expected to be otherwise, it is erroneous to assume that faculty in schools and departments of education have significantly less need than other units within colleges for professional developmental programs. It seems to be true, however, that education schools and departments have been among the first to recognize the need for professional development and to initiate programs toward that end.

Broad categories of need that new students—particularly, adult learners—will bring to programs in professional studies in education were described in the preceding section. Why professors, administrators, and other support personnel need to develop new competencies in order to be effective in their work with these new students is discussed in an earlier section also. In addition, Lindquist addresses the question of need as a part of his overall treatment of professional development. Thus, no attempt is made here to extend the earlier sections of this chapter or to repeat the points made by Lindquist. The point here is to emphasize the fact that professional development is needed for professional studies in education and that programs for that purpose should accommodate the kinds of new competencies and abilities implicit in the previous sections on students and curriculum.

In addressing the matter of faculty for professional studies in education in the future American college, one additional point must be made. The single model that now exists in higher education and that dominates the way instructional faculty are recruited, employed, and deployed is not likely to serve tomorrow's college very well. Probably 90 percent of all college instructional personnel have basically the same role expectation. Faculty are typically classified as instructors, assistant professors, associate professors, and full professors, but with few exceptions their role assignments are very much the same. Almost all are expected to perform the tripartite functions of teaching (generally in the traditional definition of that term), engaging in research and scholarly writing, and providing professional service. Moreover, faculty are expected to be at least minimally effective and productive in each. Rank differentiation reflects experience and presumed

degrees of competence or effectiveness rather than role expectation. Only rarely are variations found in the degree to which a professor may elect to emphasize only one of the
three roles—although in large, prestigious universities some exception to this is seen in
regard to research specialization.

Whereas the vast majority of instructional faculty have a single role assignment
and at most only four or five classifications, a wide range of classifications exists for nonacademic personnel—as many as forty to fifty in moderate-sized colleges, including elec-
tricians, plumbers, data processors, internal auditors, and so on. A correspondingly wide
range is found in the nature of performance expected. It is our contention that this kind
of differentiated model is needed for academic instructional personnel as well. Staffing
patterns should also enable some instructional personnel to emphasize teaching with relatively little emphasis being required on research or service. The converse is true as well.
Professors who are permitted to be instructors will also need additional flexibility in being
permitted to emphasize a particular type of teaching. Some may serve as expert lecturers,
engaging primarily in group instruction. Other instructors may become specialists in
"nontraditional teaching," managing the development and use of learning contracts, out-
of-school learning experiences, or independent study. Still others may specialize in program development, curriculum design, and student and program evaluation.

The point has been made several times that the students who are expected to
populate tomorrow's colleges will differ from each other in many important ways. We
need to remember that faculty members are likewise heterogeneous. They also have different instructional values, preferences, proclivities, and styles. Forcing them into a single
work style is as dysfunctional as doing the same to students.

Summary

Professional studies in education, like other major program areas within colleges
and universities, will be challenged in significant ways by the growing numbers of adult
learners expected in the years ahead. These students will possess characteristics strikingly
different from their counterparts in years past. Their needs and desires, perhaps even their
demands, will tax faculty and administrators to organize, program, and teach in different
ways.

This chapter has described the new student clientele in terms of four major groupings: (1) initiates, (2) lateral extenders, (3) vertical changers, and (4) specialty changers.
While these groups have some things in common with each other and also with traditional
students, each group has unique characteristics that influence the nature, purpose, and
kind of instruction desired and needed. The diversity of the four client groups suggests far-ranging and open-ended goals and objectives. Curriculum patterns and content
will probably be quite different from those developed in years past. Change is likely to be
seen, also, in teaching methodologies, class scheduling, and systems of delivery. Most of
the changes expected to take place will be toward flexibility, openness, and instructional
systems that recognize students' individuality and uniqueness, in contrast to the emphases
on standardization and group-centered activities that have predominated in most colleges
and universities up to now. The changes are timely and will probably be well received by
traditional students as well as the new adult learners.

Similar need for change will be placed on the shoulders of faculty and administrators. New and different kinds of competencies will be required of both groups. Programs
of professional development designed to help develop those competencies should be expected to receive higher priority. But the development of new competencies per se is

likely to be inadequate without corresponding changes in recruitment and employment procedures along with plans for differentiating the roles of professional personnel. Faculty roles and assignment patterns now in existence offer little hope for the kinds of institutional responses demanded by the changing needs of future students. Thus, role differentiation and associated professional development activities will need substantially increased time and attention.

27

Audrey C. Cohen

Human Service

The emergence of human service as a field of study is a recent phenomenon that grew out of social, economic, and educational trends of the 1950s and 1960s. Foremost among these trends was a decline in the number of jobs in business and industry and an increase in service jobs of all kinds. The shift to a service-oriented society that began after World War II continued apace as more and more people found employment in the service sector, both public and private. Demand was greater than the supply of available qualified personnel. As a result, nonprofessionals were employed. Certain groups, especially in mental health and in community action programs, were willing to hire people regardless of their educational background. They experimented with self-help programs, in which people with the same problems helped each other. The people participating in these programs represented many groups—white as well as black, middle-income as well as low-income, paid as well as unpaid (Sobey, 1970). Through anti-poverty programs administered by such agencies as the Department of Labor, the Office of Education, and the National Institute of Mental Health, the federal government actively supported local initiatives that employed community people in new areas and sometimes in areas traditionally reserved for credentialed professionals. Federally financed community action programs created new roles, new tasks, and new fields of employment for people regardless of credential. The mental health field was especially active in realizing the importance of breaking old patterns. Mental health professionals redefined their work on the basis of experience, rejecting the medical model in which the patient defers to the authority of the doctor. They adopted an approach that was client-centered, holistic and pragmatic (Fisher, 1974).

What began to emerge was the clear need for a new professional who could solve

512

multiple problems and who had a strong theoretical base from many disciplines. Higher education was ill-suited in content and structure to educating such generalists. The whole apparatus of higher education was geared for specialization. The usual practice was to meet a new demand—such as that for training in human services—by developing a new specialty, breaking down knowledge and skills within an established field into further discrete parts. The result was not only fragmentation of the subject matter but overly specialized professionals who knew how to deal with only certain client needs, not the whole person or the whole problem. Traditional institutions could not simply reverse gears. Only a new educational initiative free of the constraints of tradition and specialization would be able to provide transdisciplinary education for client-centered, performance-based, holistic service.

Complicating the matter further was the problem of credentials. Society demanded that professionals be credentialed in recognized areas, most of which were highly specialized, and educational institutions were under pressure from employers, professional associations, and students themselves to provide a traditional credential. In such an atmosphere, colleges and graduate schools were therefore reluctant to create a new kind of human service program even though the demand for a different kind of service was coming from many directions.

The Paraprofessional Movement

A number of movements beginning in the 1950s and 1960s underscored and indirectly supported the need for a new human service education. These included the civil rights movement, the community action movement, the welfare rights movement, the women's movement, and the paraprofessional movement. Since World War I, helping persons had worked with or "alongside" professionals in a lay capacity, holding no more than a high school diploma or perhaps a certificate. These helpers included paramedics, nurses aides, lay clergy, and other nonprofessionals or subprofessionals. By 1965 between 25,000 and 40,000 were serving as school aides, most of them white, middle-class women who volunteered or worked for the minimum wage (R. Cohen, 1976).

With the rise of community action programs, the paraprofessional movement exploded in several directions, one of which would ultimately lead to the professionalization of the whole field of human service. Many "indigenous" workers had not had access to higher education, and it gradually became clear that they would be unable to advance in their careers unless formal training opportunities at a higher level were available (Houston, 1970). Even though the untrained workers understood the needs of their communities and might be successful in agencies they created or helped to create, the transferability of this competence was limited. If they were to move into traditional agencies, where their special kind of know-how and dedication were particularly needed, they would require educational credentials and permanent job opportunities.

The first organization to conceptualize this dual need and to set up a program that would provide both education and job opportunity was the Women's Talent Corps. Founded in 1964 and funded as a demonstration project by the Office of Economic Opportunity, it proposed to train neighborhood women committed to improving their communities, using as their teachers educated women with a similar commitment. Trainees were placed in jobs created especially for them in clinics, hospitals, daycare centers, housing developments, and legal services. This cooperative venture with the agency provided the women with "practical on-the-job training that will serve as a basis and motivation for careers in community service" (Women's Talent Corps, 1965).

At about the same time, an influential book by Pearl and Riessman (1965), *New*

Careers for the Poor, appeared. Then in 1967, Congressman James Scheuer introduced the New Careers Amendment to the Economic Opportunity Act of 1964, which spawned demonstration projects all over the country to train and employ low-income adults. Their emphasis was on creating jobs and opportunities for a career, not simply providing temporary relief from financial need. "By 1970, an estimated 20,000 persons had enrolled in the Scheuer New Careers program and 250,000 to 400,000 paraprofessionals were employed with federal support in a variety of human service agencies" (R. Cohen, 1976).

The original paraprofessional movement was rapidly becoming the new profession of human service, attracting middle-income as well as low-income people. New agencies and new jobs were created with federal, state, and local support to handle mental health, alcoholism, drug abuse, child development, retardation, youth, geriatrics, criminal justice, and rehabilitation. They employed a vast new population of workers with an identity of its own, cutting across traditional professions and disciplines. Human service workers began to call themselves "new professionals" to distinguish themselves from paraprofessionals (Gross and Sterman, 1972), despite the argument that paraprofessionals were "equal to but different from existing professionals" (James, 1980). They felt they were not "para" anything but professionals in their own right.

In 1967, the Women's Talent Corps became the College for Human Services, training men and women to form the vanguard of the new profession. In 1970, the *New Careers Newsletter* became the *New Human Services Newsletter* and then the *New Human Services Review.* In 1974, a conference was held at Columbia University, sponsored by the Fund for the Improvement of Postsecondary Education and the College for Human Services, for the specific purpose of officially founding the new profession (Cohen, 1974). At the conference, the American Council for Human Service was started. And recently the federal government gave the human services nationwide recognition by creating the Department of Health and Human Services.

Human Service as a Professional Field

Human service is now a profession, albeit a very new one. It has a scientific knowledge base drawn from the social sciences (especially psychology and sociology) and the humanities. It demands from practitioners a high level of commitment to the enhancement of individual and societal well-being. It is not simply social work given a new name or self-help on a large scale. It is not simply mental health practiced in a caring way, nor is it solely a matter of human relations skill. It is all this and more. It is not "a" helping profession, it is *the* helping profession. It has the all-encompassing quality that social philosophers have long sought, by providing a holistic approach to people and society. In it, academic disciplines at last merge with professional competence, theory blends with practice, and philosophy is integrated with social sciences.

Empowerment. The principles underlying the new profession represent a departure from those of traditional social service. Central to this new field is *citizen empowerment,* a basic concept that distinguishes it from other service approaches. Empowerment is the ability of people to manage their lives, to recognize and meet their needs, and to fulfill their potential as creative, responsible, and productive members of society (Cohen, 1978). Emphasis on empowerment reflects the conviction that all citizens have the capacity as well as the right to manage their own lives. This underlying ethic is expressed in the society in many ways—in court decisions establishing the right of such special groups as the physically handicapped, bilingual children, and the retarded to the normal privileges of citizenship, in demands for the accountability of the professions, and in the effort to reorganize fractured and ineffectual services.

Human service professionals have selected empowerment as their ultimate service goal. In all their work, their aim is not simply to help people through an immediate crisis but to teach them the skills they need to manage their own lives and improve their own communities. This goal is accomplished by personal contact in working closely with clients to help them clarify their feelings, their values, their goals; assisting citizens to become aware of conflicts and ambiguities; and by helping them learn how to make difficult personal decisions. The human service profession has promoted the concept of empowerment from the level of mere rhetoric to that of actual practice in specific ways that will be discussed later in this chapter.

Generic and Holistic Service. A second principle is that of generic or holistic service, essential both to improve quality and to reduce costs in a time of fiscal contraction. Professionals who are *generic* in their approach to human service practice can solve a wide range of human problems. Training such a qualitatively different worker requires that professional education focus directly on practice. Increasing concern for the individual has placed citizen participation and control of services at the forefront of the new profession. Citizens demand that they be considered "complete individuals" and be treated *holistically.* Specific needs are no longer regarded as separate and unrelated. The interrelatedness of problems requires that the professional discontinue responding to the individual through fragmented, isolated services.

Treating the citizen holistically has implications both for service delivery and for the education that human service professionals receive. It requires a general outlook and training for professionals and a broad service perspective. Knowledge of the interdependencies and interconnections within which social service systems operate has become an integral part of a human service worker's expertise.

This approach also synthesizes elements of traditional academic disciplines—anthropology, sociology, psychology, philosophy, the natural sciences, and the humanities. The result is more integrated service delivery systems as in referral networks. The emergence of comprehensive human service agencies reflects an effort toward economy and efficiency. However, this reorganization also indicates a new-found respect for citizens and acknowledges a mounting awareness that they cannot be factored into a series of discrete problems to be handled through separate offices and agencies; they must be dealt with as whole people with integrated needs. In such interdisciplinary multiservice agencies, citizens, aided by professionals, act ultimately as integrators of their own services.

Productivity and Accountability. With empowerment as the focus, and with professionals who perform direct service and have an integrating role within comprehensive delivery systems, it may finally be possible to measure human service delivery against standards of productivity. These standards concentrate on citizen outcomes and on their movement toward empowerment.

The orientation of human service calls for increased accountability and productivity in service delivery—an area not traditionally known for either. Despite popular belief to the contrary, productivity in human service is measureable; we can develop criteria against which this measurement can be made. Productivity must focus on both results and quality of service. The current system of evaluating productivity by caseload and number of papers processed does not measure either. More promising is a system that assesses performance and competency by using empowerment as the assessment criterion. Educational institutions and agencies must look at actual performance and evaluate and promote professionals on the basis of the level of empowerment achieved by the citizens with whom they work. Assessing performance through an identifiable objective is essential in all aspects of human service. This relatively recent thrust to measure and reward performance accordingly promises a radical departure from the previous methods of career advancement based on years of service, academic degrees, and other criteria un-related to actual job competence and performance. The social services will become more effective and productive as human service workers are held directly accountable for their actions.

The American Council for Human Service recognizes the importance of the fol-lowing principles:

- The purpose of the human service profession is to empower citizens and communities so that they achieve greater self-reliance.
- Human service professionals should be measured on the basis of evidence that citizens and communities have achieved a higher level of empowerment.
- A career continuum for human service practitioners should be based on this demon-stration of increased empowerment in citizens.
- Competency as well as academic degrees should be recognized in human service.
- Service to citizens should be generic, reflecting knowledge and skills derived from many different disciplines.
- Service should be humanistically oriented, reflecting caring as well as competence.

A coalition of nine mental health organizations—the National Alliance for Mental Health Workers, which represents thousands of mental health workers around the United States—labeled themselves human service professionals at their second major meeting, held in the summer of 1980. At this meeting they also adopted a set of principles that mirror those of the American Council for Human Service.

Educational Programs

With this new profession emerging, colleges and universities all over the country have begun to offer courses to meet the demand. By 1975, some 950 were offering degree-granting programs in the human services (New Human Services Institute, 1975). Most of the first were community colleges and small four-year institutions serving a local student population, but a growing number of large four-year colleges and universities took up the idea, and by 1977 Johns Hopkins, Cornell, New York University, the Univer-sity of Minnesota, Michigan State, and the University of Southern California among others were offering human service programs (Burnford and Chenault, 1978).

Most institutions have created their human service programs primarily by re-shuffling existing courses and adding a few new ones. Some of the programs found a home in schools of adult or continuing education, which was logical since so many stu-dents aged twenty-one and older were seeking human service training. Many were attached to special centers or institutes, the traditional way to accommodate interdisci-plinary programs. Some were housed in graduate schools of education, social work, public health, or public administration, which emphasized administration, planning, and evalua-tion. Recently several of these programs have dropped their heavy emphasis on adminis-tration and broadened the scope of their programs, while others have begun to break away from identification with any one professional field and establish a conventional interdisciplinary curriculum—among them, the College of Community Service at the Uni-versity of Cincinnati, the School of Human Research and Education at the University of West Virginia, and the College of Human Ecology at Cornell. At the University of Minne-sota, the new field of Community Mental Health has been established through a coopera-tive arrangement between the School of Public Health and the Department of Psychiatry of the School of Medicine.

Only one traditional university attempted to drop its course structure altogether. Southern Illinois University at Edwardsville set up an "organic," or process, curriculum in 1972, which reorganized course content in novel ways, combining elements of preservice, inservice, and continuing education for personnel in virtually all human service systems and for multiple roles. Work experience and the curriculum were integrated and student groups initiated and implemented activities for community change. This program was discontinued in 1975, however, due to lack of support from the university as a whole. A more successful effort has been that of Lincoln University in Pennsylvania. Using a model provided by the College for Human Services, it set up a graduate level human service program in 1977, joining with Eagleville Hospital and nine other agencies to offer workers (some of whom were not high school graduates) a chance to earn a professional degree without giving up their jobs. This program is now a permanent part of the Lincoln curriculum.

The College for Human Services represents a totally new approach to professional education. As an independent program from the beginning, with no history to live up to or break away from, it had a clean slate on which to write new ideas and to test them in practice. There are some who consider it a model of "telic reform" (Grant and Riesman, 1978) and believe that its value orientation, its performance base, and its emphasis on the full empowerment of citizens represent a major innovation in American higher education. The College holds that if one of the purposes of education is to prepare people to function effectively within the society in which they live, then education in general, and human service education in particular, must be restructured to reflect the ethos of contemporary America. Educational institutions must build learning models that are compatible with the demands of a technically advanced service society. An appropriate model of professional education for this society is one that purposefully applies knowledge to the improvement of human existence. Students who are to become professionals should examine new insights into human development and stages of learning, such as those described in Part One of this book, in a context that allows them to understand the implications of new theories. If these students are to develop both analytical ability and responsible judgment, they must see the situations and needs of other human beings from a holistic perspective. And if they are to be capable not only of generating new knowledge but also of solving—with others—major human problems and instituting basic changes to improve service delivery, their education must be restructured.

For example, today's world requires professionals who understand what Carol Gilligan, in Chapter Five, has termed the "connection between morality and thought." Their education must prepare them to make choices and solve problems within a moral framework, a framework of universal principles. Gilligan observes that the widely accepted principles of respect for persons and of equality and reciprocity in social interaction would seem a natural basis for rational agreement, but this "utopian conception" is difficult to apply to the facts of daily life, "the dilemma of the fact," as one student has called it. College and postgraduate study years provide an unparalleled opportunity for young adults to raise such value questions. These years usually coincide with a period of youthful idealism, sometimes expressed in a wish to help humanity. If there is no way to harness this idealism, if the opportunity for testing ideals is not part of the educational experience during these years—separating intellectual growth from idealism as irrelevant to actions—this concern for others remains at best undeveloped and at worst may disappear altogether. As White makes clear in Chapter Six, these linkages are essential.

In current educational practice, young adults are encouraged to remain in school too long without facing the complex reality of the human condition. They have little or no opportunity to experience the confusing variety of facts and choices that will confront them in later life or to learn the skills needed to deal with them. When they emerge from the educational cocoon with degrees that signify professional status, they often cannot deal effectively with the complex service needs of those they are presumably trained to assist. Instead of our present fragmented, ivory-tower education centered around narrow academic disciplines, educational institutions should permit students to learn through the experiential learning cycle described by Kolb.

If, as Erikson tells us, "caring" represents the highest stage in human development, we need an education that will teach us to be caring—especially in human service. To ensure that this becomes a reality, human service education must show how value clarification or moral development—the ability to make choices based on principle and understand the consequences—is related to serving society. It must enable the student to gain this value awareness outside of the classroom. Exposing students to real-life situations is the ultimate professional education; in the field, value issues become life-and-death matters. When a service agency is seen and used as an educational environment, would-be professionals can struggle with values, clarify their relationships to such issues, and test service theories in practice. In this way, moral issues, which are so critical to sensitive, effective service, are not separated from the rest of the educational experience.

The value-oriented and performance-based program of the College for Human Services seeks to train professionals who understand the holistic nature of service delivery, who can design services in a caring, humane, and collaborative way with clients, who keep the search for knowledge alive, and who take advantage of this knowledge to improve service. At the College, theory plays an important, but untraditional, part in the curriculum. Theoretical material is chosen for study because it illuminates real-life problems or issues. In this sense, the College represents a radical break with the past, as did the land-grant and community college movements. It assumes that the "event" comes before the idea, reversing the order described in Plato's parable of the cave and challenging a basic assumption of classical education.

The curriculum design also includes a paradigm for competent, humane services delivery as well as for assessment and evaluation of services. It is client-centered, insisting on a collaborative role for the citizen receiving the service. (The College uses the word "citizen" rather than "client" to emphasize the new model's goal of empowering a person to assume control of his or her own life.) Furthermore, its philosophy of service stresses the generic nature of the professional role, which requires the professional to move to different settings with citizens as necessary. Of course, this does not include specialization; indeed, this model enables the professional with special expertise to be used to the fullest extent. With a view toward making human service education and practice more holistic—that is, more effective in dealing with the whole person and the full complexity of human problems—and more productive in terms of quality of service, the College has formulated the following eight principles:

1. In education, it is necessary to combine theory with practice and to provide the framework that makes this possible. Students must have the opportunity to work in the field while learning theory, or they will not know what it really means to work with different human problems. They must learn to listen to what people are really saying (not what one would like them to say) and experience the "pain" inherent in complex learning, especially when part of that learning involves challenging deep-seated assumptions of human services practice or personal assumptions reflected in the lives of individuals and their families.

2. In a service-oriented society, it is important that education at all levels reinforce a positive self-image, which includes a caring attitude toward others.

3. For the practitioner, human service based on moral and ethical principles represents, in a very real sense, a striving to reach the highest stages of human development. In fact, it is doubtful that one could make the commitment to service as we define it without having attained a high stage of human development.

4. The ideal of a human service model is to produce practitioners with a "Renaissance" breadth of humanistic competence for the service age.

5. To generate new knowledge that will improve the quality of human service, we must move away from study organized around narrow, fragmented disciplines. These must be replaced with major areas of performance so that knowledge may be explored from service perspectives and applied to real problems.

6. There is a need to conjoin institutional goals and student goals. We must foster institutions that do care about preparing persons for work in service and that demonstrate that concern in their programs.

7. Education must be part of the total environment of one's life rather than a set of experiences isolated in classrooms. Only through immersion in a total environment can changes occur that will improve our lives and the lives of others.

8. An education that is concerned with human qualities must acknowledge its debt to those patterns of behavior that have traditionally been part of women's socialization. The nurturing qualities, heretofore associated almost exclusively with women and often denigrated, are essential in a society where service to others is paramount. These are learned qualities, and they must be part of a humanistic education for both men and women.

College for Human Services Performance Areas and Dimensions of Practice

Testing the principles just enumerated has led to two important discoveries. First, we were able to define the elements of effective human service practice and develop a comprehensive picture of what a human service practitioner does in a broad range of service agencies. Eight *performance areas,* which the College labels *crystals,* define this comprehensive practice and are currently being taught and tested in actual field practice: (1) assuming responsibility for lifelong learning, (2) developing professional relationships with coworkers and citizens, (3) working with others in groups, (4) teaching, (5) counseling, (6) serving as a community liaison, (7) supervising, and (8) acting as an agent for change.

Second, we concluded from our research and from other research on human development that citizen empowerment was the ultimate and achievable goal of human service practice. Empowerment has five steps: (1) establishing and achieving appropriate purposes, (2) clarifying one's values and dealing with value issues, (3) understanding self and others, (4) understanding and working effectively with systems, and (5) developing and using needed skills. These five dimensions provide guidelines for the professional to use in exploring the multiple needs of particular citizens or citizen groups and in defining appropriate outcomes. Successful empowerment involves all five areas.

Students must master the eight areas of human service performance before graduating; these areas allow the human service professional to work as a generalist. This generic practice, this synergism, distinguishes the human service profession from such professions as social work, psychology, education, and counseling, all of which contribute elements to human service practice. These eight major areas are consciously integrated into agency practice over time and with the cooperation of agency supervisors. Students may, for example, spend two days in the classroom and three days in agency practice for a total of at least thirty-five hours per week. Thus the student practitioner has immediate opportunities to test theories and concepts learned in the classroom.

Students must also articulate the five dimensions of practice with all of the eight areas of learning and practice. The intersection of performance areas and dimensions of practice illustrates the general concept of the human service profession and of human service practice. Whether one is working in a hospital, a daycare center, a drug rehabilitation clinic, or a mental retardation facility, this concept facilitates total, holistic service rather than a fragmented approach. Human service professionals must strive to meet the immediate needs of the citizen and help the citizen become empowered.

The educational model of the College for Human Services is interdisciplinary, or more accurately, transdisciplinary, since it extracts relevant learning and knowledge from a wide range of sources. It represents a new way of organizing knowledge around service needs. The student focuses on one major performance area at a time. As students move to each new area, earlier performance areas are integrated into the new area being studied, thus reinforcing the generic emphasis of the curriculum.

The five dimensions provide the frame of reference for the total educational and practice experience. In the counseling segment of the curriculum, for example, students attend classes dealing with values in counseling, systems in counseling, and so on; they are also assessed from these perspectives. Work areas may shift, but the dimensions are constant and they guide the choice of theory. Major bodies of knowledge are extracted from the social sciences, the humanities, and the natural sciences as they relate to work in the human services. For example, in the purpose dimension, faculty members identify relevant aspects of logic and philosophy. In the values dimensions, concepts from ethics and philosophy are brought to bear on human services problems, and the self and others dimension includes psychology, sociology, and anthropology.

Over five academic years, students read, analyze, and absorb a tremendous amount of material covering, I believe, far more than is offered in traditional professional programs. More important, their practical experience in service agencies requires that they constantly examine this knowledge in the light of what will be useful to them as professionals attempting to empower citizens to solve life's problems. The educational experience confronts the real issues of service delivery. Table 1 indicates the bodies of knowledge and some of the readings focused on in the performance area of teaching, which looks at cognitive development.

The curriculum emphasizes the context within which service needs are met. In each of the eight performance areas, the relevant issues are identified and students are expected to learn how to resolve these issues. The resolution depends on the context of the situation, which is analyzed through the dimensions, to help ensure that students look carefully at every aspect of an issue. Determining purpose, for example, means identifying the problem and establishing what one is going to do. Clarifying values requires analyzing the particular issues involved and assuring that this analysis is in keeping with the underlying principle of human service—empowerment based on respect for individuals, a belief that everyone has both strong points and potential for growth, and a sense of the fundamental equality of human beings. Analyzing issues from the perspective of self and others means trying to understand the people involved in each situation. Understanding systems involves not only knowing how systems affect a particular situation but foreseeing what the effect of alternative courses of action will be. And making good use of skills requires choosing those skills that will contribute to the contextual resolution of problems, as well as using them effectively.

Constructive Action

A "constructive action" experience—a major service project in which the student works with one or more clients—is required for each of the eight performance areas. Not

Table 1. Model of a Performance Area's Five Dimensions

Dimension 1 Establishing and achieving appropriate purposes	Function as a teacher, helping people to define and achieve appropriate learning goals.
Dimension 2 Clarifying one's values and dealing with value issues	Philosophies of education: Plato, *The Republic*; Dewey, *Democracy and Education*; Bird, *Born Female*; Freire, *Cultural Action for Freedom*; Rousseau, *Emile*; Rawls, *A Theory of Justice*; DuBois, *The Souls of Black Folk.*
Dimension 3 Understanding self and others	Cognitive development: Erikson, *Childhood and Society*; Piaget, *The Origins of Intelligence in Children*; Rose, *The Conscious Brain*; Bruner, *Studies in Cognitive Growth.* Learning theories: Bruner, *Toward a Theory of Instruction*; Keller, *Learning Reinforcement Theory*; Piaget, *The Language and Thought of the Child*; Thorndike, *Educational Measurement*; Rogers, *Freedom to Learn.* Factors that affect learning: Rosenthal and Jacobson, *Pygmalion in the Classroom*; Clark, *Prejudice and Your Child*; Weber, *Handbook on Learning Disabilities*; Perry, *Teaching the Mentally Retarded.*
Dimension 4 Understanding and working effectively with systems	Educational reform: Rippa, *Education in a Free Society*; Fantini and Gittell, *Decentralization: Achieving Reform*; Clark, *A Possible Reality*; Toffler, *Learning for Tomorrow*; Dewey, *School and Society*; *Plessy* v. *Ferguson*; *Brown* v. *Board of Education.*
Dimension 5 Developing and using needed skills	Building the learning environment; designing curriculum and instruction; methods and materials for teaching: McKeachie, *Teaching Tips*; Ashton-Warner, *Teacher*; Gordon, *Teacher Effectiveness Training*; Bernathy, *Instructional Systems*; Taba, *Curriculum Development: Theory and Practice.*

only must it involve actual performance, including practice in clarifying goals, but it must contribute directly to citizen empowerment. It is the mechanism through which practitioners demonstrate that they can integrate theory with practice for the direct benefit of the citizen. It brings together what is covered in seminars with what students encounter in their agencies. A constructive action is a three-stage process. First, a plan is worked out answering the goals and needs of a citizen (or several citizens); the planners are the citizen concerned, the student, or professional-in-training, the faculty member, and the agency supervisor. Next, the plan is carried out with appropriate modifications. Finally, the action is evaluated by comparing its actual results with the goals proposed at the outset. Movement toward empowerment is the ultimate test of a constructive action, which is assessed at each stage by the four participants.

The purpose of the constructive action is to give the student an opportunity to test his or her ability to use the skills and theory learned in a particular performance area to plan and carry out a service activity with the client. It requires that service designs recognize and deal with the total, interrelated needs of a citizen and calls on the practitioner to respond to these needs with the full range of his or her knowledge. With a concern for purpose and values, constructive action fosters a new relationship of mutual respect between the client and professional. Through the constructive action, a student learns in a contextual framework how to work on life's problems. A potential vehicle for ensuring accountability, it assesses not only students' knowledge but their performance in actual service encounters.

The five dimensions of human service practice—purpose, values, self and others, systems, and skills—can be used to establish progressive criteria for empowerment—from immediate to long-range goals—within the constructive action process. It measures results of service; if some goals are poorly met, then those particular goals or the service delivery system affecting them can be examined and modified. The constructive action process also shows the degree of success or failure in any attempt to empower citizens. It provides data indicating what must be done to help citizens set appropriate goals and determine appropriate strategies to meet these goals. This assessment of outcomes sets up a rational basis for credentialing professionals; it is also a sounder basis for determining promotion procedures than the standardized measures and civil service type of examinations now in general use.

Faculty and Agency Roles in Improving Performance

Jointly, faculty members plan the curriculum for each performance area—identifying major bodies of knowledge, organizing material from those bodies around performance issues, and specifying the elements that should be stressed and looked for in agency performance. They not only teach seminars but work with students in field agencies on a regular basis. In this way, they can see if theory and practice are coming together. Is practice improving? Are students integrating earlier performance areas into ongoing practice? Faculty members, along with agency representatives and citizens, also have assessment responsibility. The instructor is challenged to move beyond a discipline, beyond the classroom, and into the service area to see if the curriculum is supporting students as they work with clients.

Agencies are recognized and supported as educational institutions. Where else can students face situations as complex and diverse as those they will find in their work? In agencies students are constantly exposed to complex problems related to addiction, juvenile justice, child care, and care for the aged. The alliance of educational institution, agency, and citizen allows continuing concentration on the development of effective, humane services approaches. This, in turn, may lead to service improvement.

Agencies committed to the human service model are involved deeply in the educational process. Supervisors are trained in the new design and in the implementation of the constructive action process as the framework for professional practice. Together, the College for Human Services and the agency work to build a program around a body of knowledge and a body of values. When students are introduced to the agency to begin their field internship in the second performance area (developing professional relationships), for example, two major questions are explored: (1) What is the role of the learner in the agency? This question leads to an examination of attitudes toward professionalism, the value of experience, the notion of the expert, attitudes toward authority, formal, experimental, and empirical knowledge, and inductive and deductive reasoning. (2) How does the practitioner weigh conflicting responsibilities to the agency, its constituency, society, and self? This question leads to an examination of role behavior and expectations; the nature and obligations of personal and professional relationships; obedience; responsibility; attitudes toward change; and approaches to coping with and resolving value conflicts.

The following value statements constitute a part of the basis for reading and discussion in this performance area:

- Each person has a unique capacity to understand his or her needs and to determine the best way of meeting them; each person has strengths to build on and a potential for growth.
- At various times, in various degrees, it is to be expected that people will require assistance in achieving the growth of which they are capable, meeting their needs, or solving particular problems.
- The most effective professional relationships are built on a mutual perception of equality and respect.
- Systems and institutions have a major influence on the extent to which people are able to achieve their potential for growth; it is appropriate for those people whose lives and work are affected by these institutions and systems to work to make them responsive to their needs.

Materials for the values dimension under this performance area include analysis of professional, union, and civil service standards and regulations as well as such texts as Abraham Maslow's *Toward a Psychology of Being,* Jean Paul Sartre's *Intimacy,* Carl Rogers' *On Becoming a Person,* and *Introduction to Social Research* by Doby and others (1967). The total reading list consists of thirty-five to forty sources.

To cite another example of how both knowledge and values are dealt with, here are some of the topics of discussion for the values dimension of the counseling area:

- To what extent is it possible or desirable for the counselor to remain neutral in assisting people to recognize their feelings and make decisions about their lives?
- To what extent can people's behavior be attributed to environmental factors, and what does this imply about their responsibility for their behavior?
- Under what circumstances—if any—is it appropriate to abridge a person's right to manage his or her affairs?

The following value statements constitute part of the basis for reading and discussion:

- By recognizing and dealing with their feelings, people enhance their ability to lead rewarding and productive lives.
- Every person has both the capacity and the right to understand his or her own feelings and needs and to find ways of dealing with them that contribute to personal growth and satisfaction without impinging on the rights of others.
- A continuing effort to identify and deal with their own feelings and needs is essential to the effectiveness of human service counselors.

In dealing with the values dimension in this performance area, students look at the laws and customs relating to mental and emotional competence. They review major counseling constructs, their aims, assumptions, and value implications: existentialist, client centered, psychosocial, psychoanalytical, functional, problem solving, behavior modification, and others. They consider the implications of cultural and role differences for counseling processes and examine arguments for and against the thesis that counseling is most effective when carried out in a compatible cultural milieu. An extensive reading list includes Lillian Hellman's *Pentimento,* Erich Fromm's *Man for Himself,* James Baldwin's *Sonny's Blues, O'Connor* v. *Donaldson* (a 1975 U.S. Supreme Court case), William James' *The Dilemma of Determination,* and Andre Schwarz-Bart's *Woman Named Solitude.*

Table 2 outlines a plan for one performance area. The top section indicates the kinds of activities that occur in agencies and how they are treated in field focus classes at the College. It also shows the activities that go into beginning a constructive action—for example, keeping logs and writing a proposal for the field supervisor, as well as the client and College faculty adviser, to approve. After the proposal is approved, the student continues to maintain logs and to be observed by faculty members and supervised in agencies while carrying out the constructive action. When a student is ready for assessment, he or she writes an analysis of the work done for the performance area. This does not mean the end of service with the client; it simply marks the completion of the constructive action for the purposes of assessment.

Empowerment and Education

At the center of the conceptual and curricular framework for the human service model is the concept of empowerment. Each of the performance areas and the dimensions that cut across them is focused on teaching the professional-in-training to facilitate the citizen's movement toward self-sufficiency. This concept, in turn, controls the formation of the body of knowledge that provides the theoretical underpinnings of human service.

Citizen empowerment, like all concepts, is more easily defined in theory than in practice. Part of the difficulty stems from traditional models of human services education that assume the omnipotence of the professional; part stems from the citizen's acceptance of this definition of the professional's role. Traditional practice rests on the notion that the citizen is helpless and needs the professional's expertise. In contrast, a professional trained under the new human service model attempts to create a service relation based on mutual respect, a commitment to empowerment, and collaboration with the citizen in need.

As stated earlier, the other major philosophical difference between the traditional model of professional education and the model proposed here is the latter's underlying assumption that real-life problems must be brought into every class, dissected, and subjected to critical analysis using any relevant theory as a tool but not as an end in itself. While many professional schools use a clinical approach or internship as part of the curriculum in an effort to introduce the student to real life, in the new model the reality test pervades the entire curriculum. Every "subject" or performance area is studied at all times from the perspectives of psychology (self and others), philosophy (values), and sociology, economics, and political science (systems). I believe these perspectives should be introduced at all stages of the educational process.

Human Services Education and Adult Development

The theoretical and philosophic perspective of the College of Human Services is appropriate for all levels of education—elementary through graduate—including professional education in such areas as law or medicine. For education in general, this perspec-

Table 2. Model of a Performance Area's Weekly Integration of Classroom Studies and Field Experience

	Week 1	Week 3	Week 5	Week 8	Week 10	Week 12
Practice as carried out in the field and discussed in field focus group	Review agency as an environment for learning; the resources it provides, the constraints it imposes. Analyze your teaching functions in agency. Make final decision as to learners you will work with on your constructive action.	Work with learners toward a mutual understanding of their learning needs. Explore values you and they bring to the teaching-learning situation. Explore your and their experience as teachers and learners.	Develop with citizens a plan to meet their learning needs. Identify long-term goals, objectives for the constructive action, teaching strategies, value issues, systems resources and constraints, teaching resources, research areas, needed skills.	Work with citizens toward achievement of agreed-upon goals. Test strategies, modify as necessary. Develop weekly lesson plans. Investigate teaching resources. Explore literature related to specific field situation.	Work with citizens to assess outcome of constructive action, their performance, your performance. Discuss objectives and strategies for the future.	Meet with supervisor and coordinator teacher to discuss your and their assessment of the constructive action. Begin to prepare for Crystal V: Review counseling roles in the agency. Assess opportunities for counseling constructive action.

Begin logs ———— Continue logs ———— Write plan-of-action ———— Continue logs ———— Write analysis of constructive action

Revise or edit constructive action

action ———— Schedule field observations ———— Record as required

	Week 1	Week 3	Week 5	Week 8	Week 10	Week 12
Values seminar	Teaching and learning roles and their value implications.	Purposes of education: Finding the truth (Socrates, Plato, Dewey, Sartre, James).	Purposes of education: Socialization (Illich, Goodman, Curtis, Freire).	Purposes of education: Education for work (B. T. Washington, Ginsberg, Berg, Levitan, DuBois).	Equal opportunity (DuBois, Clark, Jencks, Rawls).	Current issues in education: strategies for integration; public versus private education.
Self and others seminar	Cognitive processes. The elements of thought and language (Bruner, Rose).	Stages of cognitive development (Piaget, Rose, Bruner, Isaacs, Erikson).		Theories of learning (Bruner, Thorndike, Skinner, Rogers, Piaget, Tyler).	Factors affecting individual learning: physical, social, emotional (Rosenthal, Bettelheim, Clark, Perry, Weber).	

(continued on next page)

Table 2 *(Continued)*

	Week 1	Week 3	Week 5	Week 8	Week 10	Week 12
Systems seminar	Educational reform: the democratic and egalitarian heritage of the United States as a context for education.	Historical perspectives on education in the United States (D. Bell, S. Alexander, Rippa, N. Sanford, Bailyn, Dewey, *Plessy v. Ferguson, Brown v. Board of Education*).		The federal role in public schools (*Plessy v. Ferguson, Brown v. Board of Education*).	The legal rights of children: handicapped children (Riley Reid decision, Education of All Handicapped Children Act of 1975).	
Skills laboratory	Identifying teaching and learning functions in Human Service settings.	Building the learning environment (Knowles, Gordon, Ashton-Warner, McKeachie, Moustakas).	Designing curriculum and instruction (Bernathy, Taba, Tyler, Schmuck). Lesson plans.	Assessing learning outcomes. Methods and materials for teaching (Hoover, Griffith, Medley, Boston, Cytrynbaum).	Exploring resources for ongoing teaching.	
Crystal group	Analysis of model constructive actions _____	Discussion of student teaching demonstrations.	Assignment of student teaching demonstrations.	Presentation and assessment of student teaching demonstrations		
				Analysis of model constructive actions _____		

tive means supporting the development of, and building on, moral and ethical values. For individuals, it means consciously designing experiences that encourage personal growth and a sense of competence against a background of their values and those of others as well as against a view of life that recognizes its complex, multidimensional nature.

This model, developed independently at the College for Human Services, incorporates the work of many colleagues who, during the same time, were concurrently examining the theoretical aspects of growth and development—that is, ego development, intimacy, interpersonal competency, and learning styles—as they relate to education. The typologies that have emerged from the work of these individuals are being applied to an extent not readily visible elsewhere in education today.

Take the example of caring as an essential aspect of competence. If we believe that caring is critical for a person who works with others, or if we believe—as Green indicates in Chapter Twenty-Nine—that competence emerges through "confirming the worth of the individual and by making the self specific," then we must give all learners an opportunity to experience competence beyond what transpires in a classroom. The human service model does this consistently, purposefully, and from a value base that says that we learn to be competent and caring through practice.

In Chapter Eight, Douvan directly addresses another anomaly between traditional education and life: In a world where interdependence is increasingly important, our education continues to foster the cult of the individual. She cites the need to develop intimacy and to form interpersonal relationships, characterized by willingness to disclose the self to another. Among educational models only the human service model directly fosters interdependence rather than traditional individual competition.

Kolb outlines three broad developmental stages in the human growth process—acquisition, specialization, and integration—in Chapter Ten. He tells us that throughout these stages, development is marked by increasing complexity in dealing with the world and one's experiences, and by higher levels of integration. Traditional education does not readily adjust to different learning styles and makes little attempt to actively integrate each stage of development. By contrast, the human service model consciously does this through its continuing blend of theory and practice, which encourages different kinds of learning styles, and by evaluating constructive action projects in terms of effective performance.

In discussing the purpose of teaching, Perry cites the need for a teacher to confirm an offering of community. At the highest reaches of development where "both formal logic and even reflective probabilistic judgment fail to support the tensions of life's paradoxical polarities," students risk their continued growth, Perry says in Chapter Three. The faculty role, as defined in the human service model, is a direct response to this need to confront the uncertainties and pain that occur when previous certainties are challenged. The supportive element included in the faculty role in the new model is built directly on this concern.

The structure of the human service model makes possible a high level of individual development for those who successfully experience it, especially when one's goal is to serve others. In the model, the complex thinking and analysis in which the effective human service professional is expected to engage is analogous to the higher milestones cited by Weathersby in Chapter Two. At the highest level of development is toleration for ambiguity and a broad sense of objectivity.

A human service perspective, so critical to effective human service delivery—which, in turn, ought to be the hallmark of a service society—has been neglected in American education. The abilities to view situations in all their complexities, to develop moral commitment in the context of these situations, to harness theoretical learning so that it helps students gain this holistic view of life and enables professionals and citizens to operate from a base of mutual respect in making decisions have not been addressed by higher education. It is time to reexamine our standards of professional education and professional performance. It is time to incorporate realistic human service education into American life.

References

Bell, D. *The Coming of Post-Industrial Society: A Venture in Social Forecasting.* New York: Basic Books, 1973.

Burnford, F., and Chenault, J. *The Current State of Human Services Professional Education.* Human services monograph series, no. 7. Washington, D.C.: Project Share, Department of Health, Education, and Welfare, 1978.

Cohen, A. C. *The Founding of a New Profession: The Human Service Professional.* New York: College for Human Services, 1974.

Cohen, A. C. *The Service Society and a Theory of Learning That Relates Education, Work, and Life.* New York: College for Human Services, 1976.

Cohen, A. C. *The Citizen as the Integrating Agent: Productivity in the Human Services.* Human services monograph series, no. 9. Washington, D.C.: Project Share, Department of Health, Education, and Welfare, 1978.

Cohen, R. " 'New Careers' a Decade Later." *New York University Education Quarterly,* Fall 1976.

Doby, J. T., and others. *Introduction to Social Research.* (2nd ed.) New York: Irvington, 1967.

Fisher, W., and others. *Human Service: The Third Revolution in Mental Health.* New York: Knopf, 1974.

Grant, G., and Riesman, D. *The Perceptual Dream: Reform and Experiment in the American College.* Chicago: University of Chicago Press, 1978.

Gross, R., and Sterman, P. O. *The New Professionals.* New York: Simon & Schuster, 1972.

Houston, L. P. "Developing New Careers in the Public Sector: Experience and Findings." In L. Feinberg and W. English (Eds.), *Rehabilitation in the Inner City.* Syracuse, N.Y.: Syracuse University Press, 1970.

James, V. R. *Paraprofessionals and the Mental Health Service System.* Washington, D.C.: National Institute for Mental Health, 1980.

New Human Services Institute, Queens College. *College Programs for Paraprofessionals: A Directory of Degree-Granting Programs in the Human Services.* New York: Human Services Press, 1975.

Pearl, A., and Riessman, F. *New Careers for the Poor.* New York: Free Press, 1965.

Sobey, F. *The Nonprofessional Revolution in Mental Health.* New York: Columbia University Press, 1970.

Women's Talent Corps. *Proposal to Office of Economic Opportunity for Training Community Women.* New York: Women's Talent Corps, 1965.

28

Rhoda Miller
Carol Wolff

The Helping
Professions

The helping professions have undergone radical changes in the past twenty years. The civil rights' movement, the women's movement, and the poverty programs of the 1960s and early 1970s all contributed to a variety of major changes within the social welfare system. During this period social welfare institutions and programs came under close scrutiny and attack. There was enormous and rapid growth of services. Agencies experimented with new programs, reconstructed old ones, and generally became more consumer oriented. This caused much turmoil, fragmentation of services, and reexamination of priorities. New jobs and accelerated career opportunities were created by the growth of services, and it became necessary to look at the role and function of the human services worker in a new way. Workers were needed in such diverse fields as child care, corrections, health care, mental health, and services for the aged and mentally retarded. As the kinds of services increased, so did the kinds and levels of job functions. There were more job openings for people from the client groups themselves, including such jobs as community worker, teacher aide, patient assistant, social worker, and home health care aide.

Trends in Helping Professions Education

The expansion of services and jobs directly influenced helping professions education. Before the 1960s, formal undergraduate human service education was practically nonexistent, and the profession resisted any move in this direction. In the 1960s emphasis was placed on employing more indigenous and minority people in the service delivery system. Training programs for paraprofessionals were developed. Educational programs, both at the associate and bachelor levels, sprang up to train and credential workers. Fisher, Mehr, and Truckenbrod (1974) and Gilbert and Specht (1976) discuss the new prominence of the human services.

The education of workers for the helping professions in the 1980s will have to take into account the changes that began in the 1960s. There has been a shift in philosophy concerning the relationship between the individual and society. There is less emphasis now on the purely psychological approach of helping individuals to adapt to society and more emphasis on the sociological perspective of restructuring society to meet the needs of the individuals. Thus, human services workers must now understand and concern themselves with the tensions between the needs of society and the needs of the client. The rights of the client, including the right to be directly involved in the decision-making process, have become a critical issue. This concern for client rights has led to the development of self-help groups, movements toward a new system of health care, the regular practice of advocacy, and a reexamination of the general quality of client life. All these changes involve complex economic, political, and social dimensions.

These changes imply a new role for workers in the helping professions. They must now have the ability to work with groups as well as individuals, the capacity to establish collaborative relationships with other professionals, the skills to act as an advocate for the client, and the knowledge of the broad array of human services delivery systems and their interrelationships. The nature of this role requires that the worker function more as a generalist than as a specialist.

The shift toward a generalist approach has important implications for education. Traditionally, baccalaureate programs have provided the broad theoretical underpinnings for more specialized graduate training. In addition, the generalist approach, tied closely to a liberal arts education, prepares the human services practitioner to grapple with the social problems of the future. Curriculum designs with this in mind are based on a core concept of skills and knowledge. This common core is needed for effective practice, regardless of the worker's particular role in the field. This curricular approach also assumes that the generalist may need to develop some specialized abilities. However, the important point is that the generalist approach and the core of common knowledge increase the human services worker's ability to meet the client's needs in this complex, changing society.

Students in the Helping Professions

With the changes in the role of people in the helping professions have come changes in the kinds of students entering human services programs. Undergraduate enrollees in human services programs now come from diverse backgrounds. Although there are still conventional-age students, their percentages have been declining in the past few years. The civil rights' and women's movements have had a direct impact on the number of women and minority students. Women, especially, are returning to school in record numbers, prompted by both internal factors and external ones, such as the inflation rate. Bernard's chapter on women notes that mature adult women are enrolling in college to prepare for entering the labor force or to improve their status in it. Women have traditionally selected careers that are service-oriented. They still do. Many of these women are paraprofessionals from community agencies who feel the pressure of licensing and credentialing requirements. Many volunteered in human services organizations during the 1960s and have now decided to pursue a career. Others have worked at the lower levels of the civil service system and wish to climb the career ladder. In addition, we see a number of women who enter college seeking a career in human services because they see this as an extension of their role as a homemaker.

These older students more often than not have relevant experience and are seeking a program that takes into consideration the knowledge and skills they already have. A program that capitalizes on this prior knowledge will reflect this in a curriculum design similar to Kolb's experiential learning model. In this model, Kolb describes four learning modes—concrete experience, reflective observation, abstract conceptualization, and active experimentation—which are distinct but linked to each other. Most adults view their life experiences from a concrete perspective. The very nature of their learning, since it has not been in a formal, structured learning situation, has involved active experimentation in problem solving and testing new ideas. Our experience has indicated that the modes of learning encompassed by reflective observation and abstract conceptualization have not been an integral part of the learning styles of most adults. If educators are aware of this, they can build into programs appropriate activities to strengthen these learning modes. The use of the journal can provide students with one tool to begin this process.

Assessment of the students' experiential learning, as described by Keeton, is important for two reasons. First, it provides a process for meeting individual needs. Take, for example, a student with extensive experience who can demonstrate high-level skills in interviewing. This student's experience could be used as a starting point for studying another part of the interviewing process. This would involve an examination of interviewing principles, which could then be used to assess practice. Second, assessment can provide a way of looking at curriculum development. For example, working with the student who demonstrated competency in interviewing, one could develop further studies in this area dealing with such matters as interviewing principles, the philosophy of helping, and theories and approaches to counseling.

Providing an opportunity for adult learners to reflect upon and to analyze their learning will foster the setting of individual goals. Students who recognize their strengths and weaknesses are in a better position to effectively utilize the resources of the college setting. This process also frees students and faculty to interpret curriculum in a meaningful manner. Thus, the assessment of learning from work and life experience may not only affect teaching methods but also influence accessibility, resources, support systems, and, most important, the commitment of faculty and institution to adult learners (see Tough's chapter on lifelong learning).

The Helping Professions Curriculum

Our purpose here is not to define the curriculum but simply to suggest ways to enhance learning for diverse adult students. (See Dolgoff and Lowenberg, 1971, on undergraduate helping services programs.) We have chosen the three major aspects of human services education: (1) knowledge and understanding of self, (2) liberal arts education, and (3) professional development.

Knowledge and Understanding of Self. It is critically important for people in the helping professions to have an understanding of self in order to help others. Self-awareness is a continual process and an integral part of the development and training of human services workers. Each of us has developed his or her own system of values and attitudes based on life experiences. Understanding of self involves looking at one's motivation, values, and beliefs. The complexity of motives, as discussed by White in his chapter on the development of humanitarian concern, bears close examination by students in the helping professions. Understanding of self also includes looking at questions of identity and searching for the meaning of one's life experiences, as Weathersby discusses in her chapter on ego development. To achieve this level of self-understanding, workers in the helping professions need to engage in a systematic self-assessment to identify strengths, weaknesses, and areas for improvement. Recent research into adult development provides a number of frameworks for helping students do this self-assessment.

The human services worker is faced with helping others in different situations. Helping is done in many ways, but one of the worker's main tools is the use of self. The worker is there to help clients identify their own values and to make their own decisions. During this process, the worker must be careful not to impose personal values and beliefs on the client. Conflicting problems that encompass different values bombard the worker daily. Therefore, it is important to have the ability to recognize one's own values and to differentiate them from those of the client. In addition, the worker needs to communicate with a number of different individuals and groups to be effective in the field. This requires strong interpersonal competence as described by Torbert. For these reasons then, it is important that the worker be aware of self, personal needs, and the patterns of his or her own behavior.

Students should be encouraged to examine self from different psychological, sociological, cultural, and economic perspectives. The following questions can be used as an organizing framework:

1. Why do I want to help people?
2. How do I see myself in relationship to others?
3. How do I relate to the society in which I live and work?
4. What is my own philosophy?

There are many ways in which students and instructors can begin to address these questions.

- One approach is to have students write their own autobiographies focusing on their development. They should take into account both the inner and outer forces that shaped their development. The autobiography can be related to life stages of adult development as described by Chickering and Havighurst in Chapter One.
- As part of a classroom activity, students can pair up with others of different cultural or ethnic backgrounds to compare and contrast the influences of family on self-development. Specific activities may include interviews with family members, oral histories, and readings. In addition, students can compare and contrast the popular cultural representations of families (for example, television families or prominently noted families) with their own families.
- A class can be divided into groups to devise incidents that represent conflicts in values such as these:
    A welfare worker complains that her clients are making more money than she is.
    A worker is confronted by a woman who has six children and is six weeks into her seventh pregnancy.
    A client uses drugs in front of the worker, and the worker knows the client will be sent to jail if she reports this.
These dilemmas can help students clarify and look at their own values in a safe way.

- Students can explore the changing roles of women in American society by comparing and contrasting the role expectations of their grandmothers, mothers, and sisters (or other contemporary women). They can interview these women to discover how they made decisions about careers and motherhood and what they think about such issues as divorce and women's rights.
- Students can keep a journal over a school year recording situations in which personal conflicts arise. The journal can include a description of the situation, the student's reactions and feelings, the way in which the conflict was resolved, and its meaning for the future. These journals can be shared with other class members.

As Schaie and Parr point out in their chapter, adult students find real value in reflecting on their life experiences as they confront questions about life's meaning. Adults are keenly aware of societal pressures and their own internal struggle to maintain a sense of control over their lives. For human services students awareness of these pressures and realistic assessment of their own life situations are essential if they are to work effectively with clients whose lives are chaotic. (See Avila, 1971, and Combs and others, 1971.)

Liberal Arts Education. The liberal arts studied at the bachelor's level serve as a foundation for greater understanding of self and the world. Inasmuch as liberal arts studies encourage individuals to think critically about values, issues, and problems in our society, these studies quite naturally support the education of human services workers. Gilligan, in her chapter on moral development, emphasizes the importance of an educational process that fosters the capacity to question what was formerly taken for granted. In Part Three, Green maintains that the principal value of liberal arts studies lies in the way in which they help us to understand our lives and our society, and ultimately, to make judgments. Since, in the professions, these judgments must often be made within ambiguous contexts, it is all the more important that the helping professional have the ability to conceptualize and think about problems from a number of perspectives.

There are issues that are particularly important to the human services student. The following questions can stimulate examination of these issues from a liberal arts perspective:

1. What is the purpose of education? Is it to promote social harmony? build character? prepare one for a vocation or profession?
2. What are the means by which social control is exercised in different societies?
3. How has modern society affected the structure of family life?
4. What is normal and what is deviant behavior? Who defines normality? For whom? What are the various areas (law, mental health, education) in which behaviors are defined? How have these concepts and definitions of normality changed over time?

There are several activities that can suggest the connections between the liberal arts, professional development, and knowledge of self.

- Students studying psychological and physiological growth processes can recall their concepts of "right" and "wrong" behavior as a child, adolescent, and adult. Analyzing the changing references for their judgments at each stage would be useful in discussing the psycho-social-moral development process.
- Students can choose a national or local political issue such as the busing controversy for a debate. In researching the issue, the participants in the debate might develop a bibliography and interview students, residents, legislators, and educators. The following steps could serve as a guide.

Identify the leaders and key participants or organizations.

Describe their political values or ideology.

Identify their short- and long-term goals and objectives.

Analyze how the goals are shaped or influenced by political values, economics, and public opinion.

Describe the basis of their power.

Analyze the strategies they use to achieve their goals.

- To increase their understanding of social attitudes in today's society, students might read such sources as Gordon Allport's *The Nature of Prejudice,* William Ryan's *Blaming the Victim,* and Kenneth Clark's *Prejudice and Your Child.* Before reading these books, they could write a paper discussing their own views of prejudice and discrimination, and afterward prepare a report on how the readings compared with their initial views or how they influenced their thinking.

The traditional dichotomy between the liberal arts and professional education is easily bridged by the need for the helping professional to view social problems from a number of perspectives. The liberal arts provide a framework for careful examination of the economic, political, historical, and sociological factors in working with individuals and service delivery systems. Dressel (1978) and Klemp (1977) address the role of curriculum in career development.

Professional Development. As Kolb suggests in his chapter on learning styles and disciplinary inquiry norms, professionals in the human services and other applied sciences must be able to integrate knowledge from a number of disciplines in order to help people with their problems. Adult students in the human services field can use their diverse life experiences to make connections between their professional work and the liberal arts.

Since the human services include a myriad of occupations in the helping field, the development of general skills and knowledge is critical. The general consensus seems to be that at the undergraduate level the generic approach—that is, the development of intervention, group, and advocacy techniques—provides the best foundation for the helping professional. The professional development of people in the helping professions also includes examination of the ethical and ideological concerns as well as the current issues in the field. The problems presented to the helping professional are complex and require that the worker's role change according to the specific problem. Thus, the worker must be a generalist.

The key questions that students should ask themselves regarding professional development are these:

1. What does it mean to be a professional?
2. What is the role of the helping professional? advocate? enabler? supporter? broker? facilitator?
3. How can I personally develop useful skills for my work?
4. Should social welfare be a right or a privilege of every individual in our society?
5. How does the worker continue his or her professional development?

Professional development can be examined through a variety of learning approaches.

- As an individual or group project, students can construct a model of an effective helping professional, describing the personal qualities, skills, and knowledge required. The model can be developed through the use of literature, analysis of personal experience, and interviews with professionals in the field. This project, carried out over at least a semester, can provide students with a framework for self-assessment as well as further knowledge of the field.

- Students can be divided into groups to explore some of the ethical issues that commonly confront human services practitioners. Such issues might include the following:

  Confidentiality: the collection, maintenance, and dissemination of records with special reference to issues of privacy and the client's right to know.

  Advocacy: the risks faced by the helping professional in advocating social change.

  Client's rights: informed consent, right to treatment, charity versus rights.

As John Duley observes in his chapter on field experience learning, field placements provide an excellent means for developing professional skills and knowledge. Students can systematically examine their own agency settings, focusing on such areas as the origin and goals of the program, organizational structure, funding, staffing, and the relationships of these areas to delivery of services.

- A helpful approach to understanding group process is to record verbatim a number of brief interaction sequences. The next step is to analyze these segments and compare them with principles, methods, and ideas found in the readings. Examples of things to look for may include empathy, feeling versus intellectualization, pacing, and problems of clarity.
- A group of students working as a team can select a current community problem and develop and implement a plan for dealing with it, for example, a group home for the mentally retarded or an alcohol and drug abuse treatment center. The following action steps can be used as a guide to exploring the problem:

  Gather data through literature and interviews with the community.

  Assess the needs and attitudes of the community.

  Develop and implement an action plan.

  Evaluate the process.

  Keep a journal documenting the process, including factual as well as personal observations.
- Students can investigate a social problem such as the rights of children by simulating a court case. Investigation should include a close examination of the laws governing the case and their implications. Students should look at the roles of parents, children, legal representatives for both, judge, social worker, school psychologist, and juvenile officer. The simulation should represent all the views of the various parties. Feedback should follow the simulation.
- As a final project, students can design and organize a conference on the problems of professional development in the field. Students should be encouraged to ask for the participation of clients, professionals, and educators.

The Future of Helping Professions Education

Human services education has concentrated on preparing students to enter the helping professions. But learning is a lifelong process and we live in a constantly changing society. Therefore curriculum design must move beyond the limited concept of providing students with solid foundation for practice, and begin to reflect the relationships between the academic, professional, and political worlds. As educators we need to take a closer look at the needs of adult learners and the use of experiential learning.

Experiential learning can serve as a link between theory and practice. Many adults bring with them to higher education a great deal of practical experience without the theoretical component. For example, students with grass-roots experience in community work know how to organize a community and can discuss the rationale for their actions. However, they probably have not had the opportunity to study the underlying principles, to examine alternative strategies, and to look at the broader political and economic influences. It is incumbent upon academic institutions to provide learning opportunities that mesh students' needs and capabilities with the goals of the institution. The student with a background in community organizing might study the relationship between economics and social problems and simultaneously have an internship as a legislative aide. This dual approach of study and internship can foster a student's ability to link theory and practice, to critically analyze social problems and to think independently.

An institution can also strengthen the curriculum through the use of individualized learning. Individualized approaches to learning, examples of which have been discussed earlier in this chapter, can help students identify their own goals, learning styles, and the resources needed. This individualized approach allows the institution to be more flexible in responding to diverse student needs and levels. It also expands the curriculum and facilitates faculty development. In addition, faculty, with institutional support, will develop new teaching styles to meet the demands of this new approach. The individualized approaches to learning tend to promote collaborative student-faculty relationships, which break down the authoritarian educational roles and place more responsibility on the student for developing learning opportunities. Faculty have the opportunity to see the adult student as a unique individual with extensive experience that can be a resource for learning. Students for their part can perceive faculty as facilitators of learning rather than merely providers of information. Ideally, this relationship is characterized by mutuality, collaborative decision making and planning, and a respect for each other's competence. Such a relationship can serve as a model for the helping professional's practitioner-client relationship.

Helping professions faculty are uniquely able to provide a useful service to the community, the profession, and themselves. Institutional policies should provide faculty with an ongoing opportunity to work in the field. Faculty can bring an expertise to the identification and solution of agency and community problems. For example, faculty from a number of different disciplines can provide staff development or in-service training to health-care agencies; topics might include health care in other cultures, counseling principles and techniques, and behavior modification. Ongoing, hands-on work in the field keeps faculty in touch with new and emerging problems in the field. At the same time, agencies and communities can use human services educational programs as a source of renewal for their staff. Professionals from the field can be instructional resources; they can help to design courses and provide input on current problems and issues in human services. This represents a reciprocal process of community and institutional involvement.

Human services educators can provide a leadership role by actively helping to set priorities in the field. This requires appropriate and realistic research, attention to the political process, and active involvement in the community. The academic community can serve as a neutral forum for discussion and formulation of public policy. This could result in community participation in the decision-making process, more effective service delivery, and an education for human services workers that responds to the needs of a changing society.

Human services educators must be aware of and responsive to the developmental needs of their adult students, particularly women. Adult students are proving that they are competent and resourceful, that they have the capacity to deal with life situations in a creative way. Institutions must be ready to meet these students' special needs. Scheduling, childcare, and accessibility are only a few of the needs. For example, students should be allowed to engage in learning at their own pace. This may mean educational leaves for personal and professional reasons. Students should be involved in their own degree program planning and the institutional policies that affect them. This process, which recognizes the individual's right and responsibility to be involved in the decisions that affect his or her life, provides a model for effective work in the helping professions.

References

Avila, D. L. (Ed.). *The Helping Relationship Sourcebook.* Boston: Allyn & Bacon, 1971.

Combs, A. W., and others. *Helping Relationships: Basic Concepts for the Helping Profession.* Boston: Allyn & Bacon, 1971.

Dolgoff, R., and Lowenberg, F. *Teaching of Practice Skills in Undergraduate Programs in Social Welfare and Other Helping Services.* New York: Council on Social Work Education, 1971.

Dressel, P. L. "Liberal Education and Career Development." Paper presented at the National Conference on Higher Education, Chicago, March 20, 1978.

Fisher, W., Mehr, J., and Truckenbrod, P. *Human Services: The Third Revolution in Mental Health.* New York: Knopf, 1974.

Gilbert, N., and Specht, H. *The Emergence of Social Welfare and Social Work.* Itasca, Ill.: Peacock, 1976.

Klemp, G. O. "Three Factors of Success in the World of Work: Implications for Curriculum in Higher Education." Paper presented at the National Conference on Higher Education, Chicago, March 21, 1977.

Part Three

Consequences for Teaching, Student Services, and Administration

Part One presented major concepts concerning adult development and learning throughout life. Part Two considered (1) how recognition of those concepts might enhance learning in several disciplines and professions and (2) how disciplinary and professional studies might help students cope more effectively with challenges and encourages more generic aspects of adult development. Part Three also addresses two complementary questions: What are the implications of the concepts concerning adult development and the life cycle for particular educational practices, extracurricular programs, or administrative activities? and What contributions might these various institutional processes and characteristics make to adult development?

Part Three begins with two chapters that speak to some fundamental concerns: the problem of articulation among students' purposes, institutional goals, and social needs; and the relationships between our traditional instructional methods and student outcomes. Then we look at four areas that are particularly important for diverse adult learners: individualized education, field experience learning, mediated instruction, and the assessment of experiential learning. Chapters Thirty-Five through Thirty-Eight examine student-faculty relationships, student life and out-of-class activities, residential learning, and educational advising and career planning. Part Three concludes with four chapters concerning governance, administration, professional development, research, and assessment.

In Chapter Twenty-Nine, Thomas Green first posits the characteristics of a person with purpose: competence, discipline, practice, service, and the exercise of judgment. He then defines these elements more precisely and considers how higher education, in its purposes and practices, strengthens them. In his view, "service" and "judgment" are the missing elements; he argues that in the American college of the future these two elements will underlie most of the fundamental issues concerning curriculum, instruction, college organization, and higher education's contribution to society. And indeed, these issues underlie most of the other chapters in Part Three that deal with more specific institutional practices.

Robert Menges, in Chapter Thirty, covers relationships among outcomes, learner and teacher characteristics, and instructional methods; he brings us sharply against the interacting variables that determine the success of our efforts to encourage complex learning. He begins by proposing a comprehensive scheme for classifying learning outcomes in postsecondary education: psychomotor, memory, complex "linear" and "nonlinear" cognitive, and emotional outcomes. He then discusses learner and teacher characteristics as they relate to these outcomes. Here he builds on Green's discussion of purpose and notes the significance of several conceptual frameworks discussed in Part One: Torbert's distinction between "formal inquiry" and "living inquiry," Chickering and Havighurst's life cycle developmental tasks, Schaie and Parr's conceptions concerning intellectual competence, Weathersby's stage differences in ego development, and Kolb's learning style model. Then Menges considers the strengths and weaknesses of various instructional methods.

Chapter Thirty-One, by Thomas Clark, tackles the problem of responding to a wide range of diverse students. With a case history of a woman returning to higher education, Clark takes us through orientation, program planning, and assessment, which culminate in a degree program and an individualized first learning contract. But Clark recognizes that most teaching and learning will take place in groups and not through individually designed learning contracts. In the second half of his chapter, he turns to the problem of recognizing individual differences within groups. He then describes a four-step process for identifying and responding to individual needs and illustrates how this approach works for a large class in a fifteen-week course.

John Duley looks closely in Chapter Thirty-Two at field experience education within the general perspective of experiential learning programs that directly engage the student. He begins with a typology concerning objectives that include work experiences, institutional analyses, preprofessional training, service learning, field research and participation in the arts, social and political action, and career exploration. He describes pedagogical styles in experiential learning and variation in faculty and student roles along a continuum where the learner's role shifts from dependence and passivity to independence and activity. These program objectives, pedagogical styles, and shifting learner roles are then examined in relation to concepts concerning life cycle developmental tasks and ego, moral, and intellectual development, as discussed in Part One. Duley then turns to the particular contributions field experience learning can make to the development of humanitarian concern, learning style development, and self-directed learning as articulated by White, Kolb, and Tough.

Chapter Thirty-Three first identifies considerations for estimating the future of educational technology—television, film, radio, computers, microfiche, xerography—and print. Francis Keppel and Arthur Chickering caution against massive investment of funds at the expense of other policies and ask if the learner can be persuaded that technology is an effective substitute in his or her own interest for a human intermediary. They consider the relationship between the quality of mediated instruction and the kinds of learning desired, as well as matters of teacher readiness, competence, and the substantial capital and recurrent costs. Keppel and Chickering also look at Blocher and Rapoza's discussion of professional and vocational development, Loevinger's stages of ego development, and Kohlberg's stages of cognitive and moral development. The problems of fit between student purposes and institutional objectives and differences in intellectual development are reviewed. The authors conclude by proposing two approaches that combine the use of low cost, locally produced combinations of print, radio, television, and field experience with nationally or regionally produced public television and radio series.

Morris Keeton addresses three questions in Chapter Thirty-Four: What functions do assessment and credentialing now best serve? What difficulties will have to be met in performing these functions? What contributions can assessment services make to adult development in the future? In speaking to the first question he recognizes the radical change in functions, timing, and content of assessment needed for a curriculum explicitly designed to foster ego development, intellectual and ethical development, the development of humanitarian concern, the capacity for intimacy, and student learning styles. Keeton then turns to problems of managing assessment and credentialing processes and establishing sound criteria. In considering the contributions of assessment to adult development, he notes the increased self-esteem, sense of options, and clarity of purpose that often result from assessment.

The first part of Chapter Thirty-Five, by Jerry and Sally Gaff, examines the complexities raised by differences that characterize diverse students throughout the life cycle and the implications of these differences for their relationships with faculty members. The Gaffs review the research on student-faculty interaction and suggest the changes in practice necessary to promote productive relationships. They then describe the kinds of faculty development needed if such changes are to occur. The broad experience, knowledge, and competence of older students is sometimes beyond that of the younger teacher; role reversals may occur. The Gaffs recognize the differences in the developmental tasks of various age groups, their pragmatic goals, and the varying demands on their time and energy. They recommend changes in educational practices, such as concentrating on fewer subjects and developing residential learning opportunities to create periods when faculty and students can have sustained contact that allows them to go beyond superficial issues and relationships.

Theodore Miller and John Jones begin Chapter Thirty-Six by calling attention to the substantial research documenting the contributions of extracurricular activities to student development. They focus on the implications of social and cultural activities for adult development and give particular attention to interpersonal competence, the capacity for intimacy, and the development of humanitarian concern. They next turn to service and leadership activities and their potentials for intellectual and ethical development. Miller and Jones also examine educational and vocational activities and recreational and athletic activities; they emphasize the emerging concerns regarding women's athletics. The chapter ends with a list of twenty-seven specific recommendations for helping out-of-class activities become a more salient part of the educational experience of all students.

Harold Riker reviews trends in the uses of student residences since the early 1960s—noting the shifts in parietal rules and increased efforts to link classroom and residential learning—in Chapter Thirty-Seven. Despite substantial evidence, few board members, administrators, faculty members, parents, and students recognize the developmental impact of residential experiences. Riker examines the potential values of residential experiences and the consequences for ego development and cognitive skills. He presents a series of concrete illustrations drawn from institutions around the country, including the student development program for freshmen at the University of Wisconsin, Stevens Point, the variable length residency programs that are part of Empire State College's individualized contract learning approach, and the elderhostel movement. Riker concludes with concrete suggestions about implementing residential learning programs, such as the needs to strengthen organizational relationships and to integrate residential activities with academic studies.

Jane Shipton and Elizabeth Steltenpohl open Chapter Thirty-Eight by discussing the critical role a college education plays in clarifying the interrelated issues of identity and work as they intersect with life cycle challenges. They describe such parts of the life planning process as decision making, task definition, and implementing decisions. Their chapter concludes with specific recommendations concerning resource materials, organizational structures and personnel, and the sequence of activities for a sound and financially feasible program.

The last five chapters of Part Three turn to more general issues concerning governance, administration, professional development, research, and public policy. Louis Benezet, in Chapter Thirty-Nine, provides a tough-minded perspective concerning interactions among governance, the realities of power, and human development. Benezet identifies some theoretical and practical bridges between college governance and college education and wrestles with the difficulties of recognizing the needs of administrators and faculty members while serving students. He addresses the implications for students' moral development and recognizes the problems that result when the authority of the disciplines is confronted by the reality of diverse adult experiences. Student participation in decision making based on broad experience and competence are different grounds from the participatory democracy issues raised in the 1960s. The chapter closes with consideration of various types of governance mechanisms and their implications for education and student development.

In the first part of Chapter Forty, Harold Hodgkinson addresses a number of management issues: defining more clearly the management task, understanding what characterizes good managers, increasing the sophistication of evaluating administrative performance, and improving understanding about the fit between different administrative styles and different institutional conditions. He then focuses on adult development, concentrating on the midlife crisis, dubbed "middlescence," and the years beyond that until retirement. He reminds us that college administrators, like other people, need to cope with readjustments in marriage, family life, and professional expectations.

In Chapter Forty-One, Jack Lindquist begins with four highly recognizable archetypes; the rest of the chapter follows these persons—three professors and one administrator. He examines four major areas for professional development: continuing knowledge and sophistication of one's field, increased teaching effectiveness, more general dimensions of personal development, and organizational development. In each of these areas he describes the range of activities and resources required and the current state of the art. He then offers a series of particular challenges for professional development and closes with an argument for a holistic approach to professional development that recognizes the needs for lifelong learning and adult development among all those who staff our colleges and universities.

Chapter Forty-Two, by Timothy Lehmann, on assessing program effectiveness and costs for adult learners, starts by calling our attention to the endemic resistance to program evaluation despite our cries for accountability. Lehmann then takes us through a model program evaluation process with an institutional planning cycle. Having set this basic conceptual stage, he then summarizes several different research programs and their associated instruments for assessing various dimensions of adult development. His detailed discussion of the Program Effectiveness and Related Costs (PERC) model developed at Empire State College illustrates how cost analyses can be linked to the evaluation of developmental outcomes. The chapter concludes with a set of basic program evaluation principles.

29

Thomas F. Green

Acquisition of Purpose

Although there seems to be no invariable sequence that describes how a sense of purpose develops in human beings, we can nevertheless describe what is meant by having purpose. That is, we can describe what it consists of, what it presupposes, and what social conditions its possession requires. Such an approach is nondevelopmental in its logic. It can provide guidance for educational thought and practice, but it will do so from a perspective that views things as "parts and wholes" rather than as "means and ends." The educational process must contain certain elements and provide for certain experiences not because they are means to the development of human purpose but because they are parts of what enters into its possession.

Aimlessness Versus Purpose

In opposition to a sense of purpose, there is such a thing as aimlessness in human life. If extended very far, it becomes an enervating, pathological condition, it issues not only in a kind of indolence or idleness but also in a loss of self-respect, of confidence and hope. "I don't know where I'm going," "I seem to be getting nowhere"—are the voices of aimlessness. Purpose dispels aimlessness. It represents confidence, hope, energy, and the capacity to discriminate between what matters and what does not. When we talk of the acquisition of purpose in the context of education, we have in mind the development of an orientation that we contrast with aimlessness—an orientation that we recognize as the formation or adoption of a life plan or a plan for a significant part of one's life.

To ask, then, how academic institutions can aid the acquisition of purpose is to ask how they can contribute to the formation, adoption, and pursuit of a life plan—and not merely the pursuit of *any* life plan but of a worthy and workable one. The answer involves the development of characteristics or elements that are present in a person possessed of purpose. I shall consider five of these elements, grouped in three categories: (1) competence, (2) discipline and practice, and (3) service and the exercise of judgment.

Competence is essential to the possession of purpose, both because competence defines the individual's potential and because it is experienced as self-worth—a salient characteristic of all who are purposeful.

Discipline and practice are essential because competence is always expressed through some practice, to which discipline gives order or structure. The value of the *academic* disciplines for the acquisition of purpose is not to be found in the knowledge they contain but in the *virtues* that they develop for their corresponding practices. And this is true whether the disciplines in question are the disciplines of inquiry, piety, carpentry, or homemaking. To acquire the virtues of a discipline is to assume the required habits and rules of some practice through which purpose can be given expression.

Finally, service and judgment are essential because those human purposes that we tend to regard as highest are those that serve society through practices that require the exercise of judgment. Accordingly, as we shall see, the ultimate purpose of an academic institution is service.

These five elements are the parts that enter into the whole that we describe as the possession of human purpose. No doubt there are others, but these, it seems to me, are central, and central as well to the educational responsibility of academic institutions.

Competence

What is the importance of competence in the formation of human purpose? How does it enter into the conquest of aimlessness and the pursuit of life plans?

Being competent means being good at doing something. Although being competent in one's job does not necessarily imply being well educated, one who is not competent at *anything* is badly educated or uneducated. The absence of all competence is the mark of a faulty education. It is, indeed, more than that. It is also the sign of a certain kind of *moral* fault, a defect of character. Surely, one cannot be a good person and yet not good *at* anything or good *for* anyone—that is to say, good for nothing. Competence of *some* kind is required not only by our conception of what it means to be well educated but also by our conception of what it means to be a good person. Competence is, in both connections, a necessary but not sufficient condition.

It is difficult for us to imagine an individual with a healthy self-respect who honestly, and accurately, confesses to not being good at anything. The two self-conceptions are inconsistent. When a child can point to something that he has done and say, "See that! I did that. Isn't that good?" and others respond, "Yes, it is good," then the child can conclude that *he* is good. Indeed, viewed phenomenologically, the experience of *being competent* at doing something and the experience of *being good* or of having worth are one and the same, though described in two quite different ways. That is why we sense a contradiction in the supposition that a person may have a realistically favorable opinion of self and at the same time deny being good at anything.

The statement "I am good at *X*ing" entails the statement "I am good." And conversely, the statement "I am good" entails the statement "There is some kind of *X*ing at which I am good." The point I wish to stress here is not the logical point that there is a relation between "being competent" and "being good" but the phenomenological point that the experience of the one is the experience of the other. (Of course, the logical point is also important. It suggests, for example, that much of the research on the relation of self-concept to learning is fatuous, inasmuch as becoming competent *at learning* is the same thing as coming to have a favorable self-concept *as learner*.)

Being competent, which is to say, being good at doing something, especially when confirmed by others, is simply one of the ways that self-respect and worth are experienced. However, competence—being good at doing something—aids not only in confirming one's worth but also in making the self specific. It helps to tell us what kinds of things we are good at, which is one way of determining the kinds of persons we are and, therefore, the kinds of purposes we may adopt.

Essentials for Developing Competence. The development of competence in human beings requires a certain kind of world. It requires, first of all, the presence of a public within which it is possible to receive confirmation of one's competence and thus validation of one's worth. It goes without saying that such a public must be the kind that pays attention to one's activities and efforts.

Small organizational settings are often preferred, in education as well as elsewhere, for this very reason. Within small settings, an individual can receive signals indicating that his actions "make a difference," whether his efforts have succeeded or failed. In education, class size is probably less important in itself than whether the setting is one in which one's competence and, therefore, one's worth can be confirmed. No doubt the use of interactive programming permits machines to provide some feedback for students. Yet do they also provide confirmation of the student's self worth? If not, then they are not providing the conditions for the cultivation of competence.

It is worth noting here that organizational size—or more accurately, the degree of anonymity it allows—also has a bearing on moral behavior. Why is it, for example, that so many, who would not think of cheating ordinarily, think nonetheless that, without any moral consequences at all, they can cheat "Ma Bell" on long distance calls by asking for the wrong person at the other end and thus conveying a prearranged message? I suspect that the answer lies partly in the enormous scale of AT&T. No signals are returned to show that such actions have consequences. In such a large system, one's action goes unnoticed.

Beyond the requirements of attention and response to one's actions, there must be a means by which one's competence can be recognized by a public that values it. One can be competent, of course, in doing almost anything. One can be a competent liar and cheat, and I suppose there is even such a thing as being competent in the exercise of venality. I recall the keen disappointment voiced by an adolescent of my acquaintance who was arrested for breaking and entering when what he was really good at was swindling and stealing cars, acts requiring a higher order of skill and intelligence. The public had no way of recognizing his competence in areas of action where he was really good, since being good in such things means not being caught. His situation was like that of anyone who performs some great feat under conditions prohibiting its public exposure. He could not be noticed for his own peculiar excellence. Hence, he felt insulted. That one's excellence remains unnoticed is always an insult to the human spirit.

This example calls to mind the fact that the competence sought in the context of education is not just being good at doing any sort of thing but being good at doing things that some public values. If the exercise of competence is to contribute to the acquisition of purpose, then the world in which we seek the development of competence must include a public that will confirm one's worth, respond to one's actions, and permit the possibility of doing *good* things well. When any of these conditions are absent, the development of human purpose is likely to be aborted.

Competence and Education. The development of competence in individuals leads to certain consequences, including social consequences. But we cannot seek to develop competence merely by securing those consequences. We must not suppose, for example, that simply because competence produces good feelings of self-worth, we may therefore concentrate on the production of such feelings. Let us suppose that we could (although clearly we cannot) institute the practice of praising people for what they do even when they do bad things well and good things badly. We would not thus secure the phenomenological and social accompaniments of competence. For even if we succeeded, we would have done so without securing competence itself. Instead, we would have perpetrated a massive fraud, a fraud that would inevitably surface with devastating consequences to individuals and to society.

Competence has its own peculiar logical and phenomenological form. It is part of what we see displayed in a person who is purposeful. Its cultivation is essential for escape from aimlessness. Yet it is not related to the development of human purpose as means are related to ends but as a part is related to the whole. Having purpose in life requires having competence, but competence is not the *means* to the development of purpose. It is rather a part of having purpose at any stage of human development.

Discipline and Practice

Competence requires the development of discipline. The root meaning of *discipline* is "form," "rule," "order," or "structure." The disciplines of everyday life are those demands like getting to work on time, meeting deadlines, keeping appointments, and the like, which, imposed upon the conduct of day to day affairs, give them form, order, or structure. Submission to those disciplines cultivates the virtues of punctuality, craft, responsibility, and so forth.

This meaning of *discipline* is best displayed, perhaps, in liturgy, which consists always of an established outline, form, or sequence in which symbols are ordered, meaning is voiced, and a certain *practice* is given structure. When one enters an *order* in the Church, one enters a life that is arranged by an established sequence and by accepted standards for doing things. The discipline of the order is the rule that orders life. The same is true in the acquisition of any high skill—whether cabinet making, statesmanship, or inquiry. Each practice has its corresponding discipline. *Discipline,* then, is the rule, order, form, or structure by which any *practice* is conducted. It is essential to the acquisition of competence in that practice. Indeed, it defines that competence. Being good at the conduct of any practice implies the acquisition and exercise of its corresponding discipline and therefore the acquisition of the virtues that that discipline produces. Thus, discipline is always connected to some practice. Whenever we speak of a discipline, we must ask "What is the practice for which the discipline provides the form and structure?"

Practice and the Academic Disciplines. What, then, is the practice that is given form and structure by the academic disciplines? It is the exercise of theoretical reason, the practice of inquiry. Theoretical reason is that exercise of reason answering to the human need to know. Yet most of life is concerned with a different human interest, namely, the interest in deciding what to do. It answers not to the human need to know but to the human need to choose and to decide. Theoretical reason asks "What can I know?" Its disciplines are those most purely exemplified in the disciplines of the academy. Practical reason asks "What should I do?" Its disciplines are those most perfectly displayed in the disciplines of ordinary life.

The apparent disjuncture between the disciplines of the academy and those of ordinary life arises not because the academic disciplines lack some utility for practical affairs. It arises rather because these different disciplines correspond to different practices. They are aimed at the cultivation of different virtues. In the practice of inquiry, for example, we are disciplined to withhold judgment until the data are in. That is a virtue in inquiry. But if carried too far it will produce an incapacity to act, and that is a vice in the practices of ordinary life. We are permitted no such luxury in deciding what to do. The data are never in. The disciplines of knowing and deciding offer form and structure to different practices. Since the apparent breach between them does not arise from any lack of utility of the academic disciplines, it should be no surprise to discover that such a breach is not repaired by restoring some lost utility or by introducing some imagined new utility.

We in the academy often agree that the disciplines of knowing, taken singly or in series, do not sufficiently inform us of the practices of life. Problems do not present themselves in academic departmental capsules. And so we are apt, especially nowadays, to suppose that the remedy is found in something interdisciplinary, or multidisciplinary, or transdisciplinary. But there are two difficulties in this approach. It is true, of course, that life is not arranged to accord with the divisions of the academic disciplines. But, by the same token, neither should we expect the problems of life to appear in interdisciplinary forms. The practices of ordinary life and their related disciplines are neither disciplinary nor interdisciplinary. When we ask—and ask with the serious intention of acting—such questions as "How can we provide better housing in our community?" or "How can I compensate my friends for my failings?" or "What can I do to make my surroundings more beautiful?" we may ask questions that are asked also by psychologists, planners, economists, and philosophers, but we are not *doing* psychology, economics, or philosophy. Neither are we "applying" the academic disciplines on such occasions. Nor does it make sense, in such contexts, to speak of interdisciplinary approaches. Interdisciplinary talk makes sense only in a setting where academic disciplinary talk also makes sense—that is to say, in the academy and not in the affairs of life outside.

This point, again, is not merely logical; it is also phenomenological. We speak of the academic disciplines and their intersections when our attention is focused either on the *process* of inquiry—whether the methods are sound, for example—or on the *content* of the inquiry—whether our questions are like those of physics, or history, or economics. But if we are serious about questions of practice, we focus on "the problem" or "the need"—better housing, more beauty, better treatment of our friends—and we do not speak of the academic disciplines at all.

There is a big difference between *studying* the reallocation of the public budget and actually reallocating it. They are different practices requiring different disciplines. There is, to be sure, an academic discipline of economics, and especially public finance. But actually reallocating public funds requires more than the mere study of public finance. Its discipline is not the academic discipline of finance. But we are no better off in supposing that the practice is interdisciplinary. It is neither. It is not an academic discipline at all. In such matters, our practice is simply the effective and therefore disciplined expression of our concern for neighbor and community—that is, as exercise of certain virtues of action and choice, not inquiry.

The academic disciplines will be revealed in the form they impose upon our approach to the problems of ordinary life—the ways we attend to fact, for example, our capacity to draw on the experience of others, the quest for principle, the concern for truth, and the myriad other ways that the virtues of those disciplines are evident in our action. They will be present as style is present in a work of art, namely, as something that is displayed, but not paraded, something that is present, but not the point.

The Practice of Inquiry. To many persons it may seem transparent that the academic disciplines are described by their content. Even in other chapters of this volume, the assumption often voiced is that the academic disciplines are the various fields of knowledge or the various fields of study defined by their respective subject matter and methods. Mastery of an academic discipline is, therefore, often taken to consist simply of mastery of a certain body of knowledge. I have been concerned to pose a counter-view, one that seems to me more fruitful if our concern is to understand how the academic institution can contribute to the formation of human purpose.

The educational value of the academic disciplines does not lie in mastery of their subject matter, even though it is true that those disciplines will never be advanced unless there is such mastery. Rather, the educational value of the academic disciplines, like the value of *any* disciplines, lies essentially in their capacity to cultivate the virtues peculiarly associated with their corresponding practices—in this case, inquiry. The academic disciplines do not lack utility. They have the same utility that all disciplines have, namely, the capacity to nurture those virtues that are essential to the competent or excellent conduct of a certain practice. That the practice of inquiry does not exhaust the disciplines of life is, of course, true. But it is also true that the virtues cultivated by the practices of inquiry are important in *every* activity of life.

From this view, the disciplines of the academy are not the various bodies of knowledge. To suppose otherwise would be like supposing that the discipline of cabinet making consists of all the cabinets made or that the discipline of playing baseball consists of the records of all the games that have been played. The disciplines of the academy, like all others, are related to a practice. Their related practice is inquiry. Like all other disciplines, their cultivation is required for competence or excellence in that practice. Knowledge is the result of that practice; it is one of the consequences, just as cabinets are the result of the practice of the discipline of cabinet making. Thus, the academic disciplines are not the various fields of human knowledge. Rather, the academic disciplines are the rules, order, and structure that are, as it were, stamped upon the conduct of human beings as they inquire. Such disciplines specify a set of virtues required for excellence at a particular practice.

Thus, to ask the purpose of the academic disciplines is like asking the purpose of friendship. The purpose of friendship is friends. In the academy, the purpose of the academic disciplines is inquiry. The disciplines of friendship exercised in practice lead to good friends, just as the academic disciplines exercised in practice lead to good inquiry. If we suppose that the mastery of the academic disciplines is the mastery of what is known, then cultivating the virtues of inquiry will be displaced by the mere piling on of knowledge. Teaching then becomes concerned not with cultivating the virtues of the academic disciplines—not with courageous argument, acuity of thought, and richness of imagination —but with merely transmitting the results of inquiry. We have a word to describe that effort. The word is *pedantry*.

On this inherent relation between competence, discipline, and practice, one further point needs elaboration. In saying that every discipline is related to a practice, I have been using the word *practice* as we use it in speaking of "the practice of medicine" or "the practice of law," or "the practice of inquiry." But we also use the word in another way, as when we speak of "practicing the piano" or "practicing French pronunciation" or "practicing for the game on Saturday." The latter sense of *practice* has the meaning of "preparation." The former has the meaning of "performance."

The meaning of *practice* as preparation may carry with it a certain lack of seriousness. I have a friend who sometimes chides her lawyer husband with the question "When are you going to stop *practicing* the law and start *doing* it?" The humor draws upon our consciousness that there is something "unreal" and purely preparatory about practicing *at* an art or craft as opposed to actually performing it or engaging in it. The whole point of practicing as preparation is to provide a context in which errors and mistakes may occur without serious consequences. In football practice a missed block will not change Saturday's score. In the actual game, it may.

Within the academy, there is a great deal that lacks seriousness in exactly this way. Much is preparation. Little is performance. No property is exchanged, no duties are shaped, nor are any rights defended by the classroom study of the law. Moot court is a good exercise, but everyone who participates knows it is "made up." The outcome is "moot" indeed. It does not count in the way that the practice *of* the law counts in the affairs of human beings.

The fact is that the competent exercise of any art or craft requires the acquisition of its disciplines. And, moreover, it requires their acquisition as *virtues*—that is, as the settled dispositions by which the standards, rules, and structure of that art become stamped upon the conduct of the artisan. That requires a setting in which errors of judgment, skill, and inference are without serious social consequences, a setting in which the virtues, imperfectly acquired, can be exercised without causing harm to other people—a setting, in other words, in which practice in the sense of preparation is permitted to exist alongside practice in the sense of performance. The academic institution is just that kind of setting.

Therefore, there will inevitably exist within the academic institution a certain kind of irrelevance, a certain lack of seriousness, a certain kind of detachment. What kind? The kind that makes it possible to study the public budget without actually affecting it, to plead a case in moot court without actually changing anyone's life, to argue the merits of different social arrangements without actually trying them out. The presence of that kind of detachment, irrelevance, or lack of seriousness is viewed by many as a defect of the academic institution. I would argue, on the contrary, that it is both essential to its function and the foundation of its freedom. We can be certain that if the academic study of the public budget had consequences more than merely academic, then the role of such study as preparation would be aborted and the freedom to engage in it would be severely and quickly limited.

This distinction between practice as preparation and practice as performance is not an artificial one that might simply be dispensed with. It should not be viewed as a kind of failing into which the academic institution is prone to lapse. Rather, it marks an essential tension that must always exist within the college, stemming from the intractable fact that competence in any practice requires the acquisition of its corresponding discipline and the further fact that that requires, especially for the so-called higher arts, a context within which activities are predominantly preparation. This is an essential constraint upon the activities of the academic institution.

Service and Judgment

It is a peculiarity of the academic institution that, although for many it is the setting for practice in the sense of preparation, it is for some the setting also for practice in the sense of performance. It is a proper institution for the conduct of scholarship in philosophy, history, sociology, mathematics, government, and the natural sciences, and in that sense it is the setting for the practice of inquiry as performance. But it is also the setting in which one develops the virtues essential for the conduct of such activities. It is the institution in which those academic disciplines are practiced both as preparation and performance. Thus, students typically write for their professors, but professors typically write for others in their academic or professional guild. The students' work is preparation. The professor's is performance. And both kinds of practice are contained within a single institution.

But that fact presents dilemmas—for the student, the teacher, and the academy. There are those who come to higher learning with the purpose of actually entering into the practice of the arts of inquiry. For them, the academy is a suitable place both for preparation and for actually engaging in those arts. They are those for whom it is suitable to contemplate a life or a brief sabbatical of scholarship within the academy itself. They are few, however, and they ought to be few. Still, they are the ones that the academy is likely to identify as the "best" students, those whose purposes are captured and nurtured by submission to the academic disciplines as defined by the respective guilds of the academic institution. They are those who contemplate becoming historians, philosophers, artists, physicists, and the like—for a while, at least. Their essential purpose is to pursue the intense and durable pleasures of learning. The academic institution is for them the setting both for preparation and for practice of the disciplines that give order to their lives.

But there are others, by far more numerous, for whom the virtues to be gained by submission to the disciplines of inquiry are only prelude to some other practice. Their purposes point far beyond the purview of the academy. They are those whose sights are set on the exercise of competence in the professions, the crafts, the arts, and business. They are the prospective engineers, lawyers, physicians, craftsmen, and public servants of many kinds. The college or university is not the place for the actual practice of law, engineering, social work, or the professions generally. For the group mentioned earlier, submission to the academic disciplines means actually entering upon the practice that they intend to pursue. But for this latter group, submission to the academic disciplines is merely prelude to some other practice not contained by the academy.

How can the academy foster the acquisition of human purpose in the face of such a fundamental difference? The quick and easy answer is that the academic institution must be pluralistic. It must include liberal arts colleges as well as professional schools. It must support research and graduate education as well as provide instruction in the most basic practices of life. It must include four-year colleges as well as two-year programs of instruction. It must serve the midlife inquirer as well as the professional. All this is true, as far as it goes. But it does not cut very far into the harder problems of curriculum, instruction, and the relation of the college to the public.

A deeper and more satisfactory answer will be found in the exploration of two extremely fundamental propositions. The first is that, though the standards of the academy in all its efforts are intellectual, nevertheless, its presiding purpose is service. Service is the fundamental purpose of the academy whether the purposes of students are aimed at the practices contained within the academy or aimed at those beyond it. The second proposition is that in all the higher practices in which the academic disciplines play a role, their indispensable contribution is not the advancement of knowledge but the cultivation of human judgment.

Service and judgment are the missing elements in our account of that whole we recognize as the possession of purpose. I would argue that in the American college of the future, these two propositions, together with our analysis of competence, discipline, and practice, will go far toward setting the terms of debate on the most fundamental issues of curriculum, the management of instruction, the organization of the college, and its relation to the public.

The Purpose of Service. Consider the first of these propositions—the claim that the essential purpose of the academy is service. The problem posed by this proposition is as follows: If we distinguish, as I think we must, between two senses of *practice,* the one as *preparation* and the other as *performance,* then the problem for the academy is to create opportunities for both in appropriate sequences and combinations. Can we accomplish preparation in the context of practice? How often? Can preparation be improved by the addition of practice? When? The *educational* difficulty with moot court, as I said before, is that it is all "made up." It lacks the seriousness of actual practice. But its virtue is that it provides a setting in which students in preparation are subjected to the standards of judgment employed by distinguished practitioners. The difficulty is that it is all preparation. The virtue is that it comes about as close as one can to actually engaging the disciplines the student seeks to cultivate. Preparation and performance are brought closer together by such a pedagogical invention than would be possible without it.

For the student of history or philosophy, the problem is to enter as quickly as possible into a relation of colleagueship with historians or philosophers. This may mean publishing a piece of scholarship, since that is the essential practice of academics. For the student of public affairs or planning, it may mean creating settings within which the virtues of scholarship are exercised in the service of some public problem on which there are persons prepared to act.

In these examples, and in all others like them, there are three components: (1) a discipline to be acquired, (2) a problem that is "real" and not merely "made up," and finally, (3) some audience beyond the student's immediate academic community, a public prepared to take notice of the work undertaken and to act upon it. For the student of history, it is the exciting possibility of contributing to that public that consists of historians. For the student of public affairs, it is the possibility of actually contributing to a decision. It is a sobering thought to any student that there is somebody other than his teachers who may take notice of his work, act upon it, and judge its intellectual qualities, its conformity to the standards of reason, argument, and practicality, and its capacity to suit their needs. In such circumstances, it is not merely probable but practically certain that the student's own standards of work will be raised. His capacity to acquire the virtues of the academic disciplines will be enhanced by their placement in the context of service. What is otherwise "unreal" becomes serious.

But this claim should be no surprise. It is precisely where our analysis of competence, discipline, and practice was bound to lead in our quest for a satisfactory portrayal of human purpose. We cannot imagine anyone developing a realistic life plan without developing some competence, nor can we imagine that competence developing except within a public that takes notice and finds one's effort to be of service. Indeed, what else can we mean by a "life plan" except a plan for the exercise of one's competence? That is what purposefulness is. Yet, as we have seen already, we are not satisfied with any purpose. We require a purpose that is good for others; that is, we expect a purpose that includes service, one that makes sense within the context of a public. It is partly that addition of service that, when understood, unites the purposes of students to the purposes of those already within the academy, and the purposes that the society, any society, seeks to advance in supporting the academy.

The standards of the academy are intellectual because those are the peculiar virtues of its disciplines. But its purpose is service. The two should be considered together. And when they are, then the curricular, instructional, and organizational problems of the college will be resolved partly in the effort to join the practice of those disciplines as preparation to their practice as public service. In that context, not only will the virtues of the academic disciplines be more efficiently acquired but the intentions of the social order will be more visibly served.

Sometimes, in contrast to the ideal of service, the function of the university is claimed to consist of nothing more—and nothing less—than the pursuit of truth. But the pursuit of truth is here construed as a proper kind of service. The essential point may be revealed by analogy. I believe it is a common misunderstanding that the monastic ideal of the Middle Ages *aimed* simply at a withdrawal from the world and therefore was of no public service at all. Such was, in some respects, the view of Luther. And indeed, there was that *consequence* of the monastic movement, especially in its more degenerate forms. Yet the truth, thus stated, is at best a partial truth. When the perfection of the prayerful life of work and study is denied to most people by the need to earn their daily bread, then it may be construed as a service that some withdraw under different arrangements to perfect, on behalf of others, the life that is otherwise denied them. The monastic ideal was not, therefore, aimed at a mere withdrawal from the world for the sake of those who submitted to the disciplines of the different orders. It was aimed, rather, at a withdrawal and submission of some as a proper service to all others.

The standards of the monastic life were the standards imposed in the different orders by their respective disciplines—a situation not entirely unlike the modern college or university. But the life lived in submission to those disciplines was construed to be lived not merely for the salvation of the monk but on behalf of all. In short, its purpose was service, and its standards were the standards of the various disciplines. That is the meaning that I wish to convey in the claim that, though the standards of the academy are intellectual, its purpose is service. Its standards are those imposed by the disciplines, the various ways that we pursue the truth. But the purpose of that pursuit is nothing less than service. Truth is always needed and always in contention, even when we do not know its use.

It would be a grave mistake for the academy to sacrifice its undoubted monastic tendencies in the effort to realize its purpose of service. But it would be an equally great mistake to suppose that the monastic expression of that ideal is sufficient. In that case, we would probably forget that the virtues of the academic disciplines are often best acquired when they are sought in the context of service to a public beyond the walls of the academy. Indeed, it may remain an open question whether the virtues of the academic disciplines are best acquired in the context of service outside the academy. In the present volume, Cohen's description of the College for Human Services may be viewed as a paradigm of that alternative. It is clear that the college aims to cultivate the virtues central to the academic disciplines even though their cultivation arises in the context of actual employment in a human service setting. That account may serve as an exemplar of the effort to draw together the functions of preparation and performance in the interests of service.

The view I have been exploring is rich in other implications for the future American college. I have been scrupulous in adhering to the distinction between the academic disciplines and the fields of academic study. The disciplines, I have argued, are distinguished by the virtues they aim to inculcate in those engaged in the conduct of inquiry. They structure, order, and control the conduct of those possessed of them. It therefore becomes an open question of the most radical kind whether the *educational* value of the academic disciplines is cultivated best in classes and courses defined by the limits of the subject matter described by the academic departments of the college. Does one best acquire the virtues needed for historical study through courses entitled History? Are we to suppose that it is only through courses in philosophy that one can acquire the virtues of the philosophical discipline—those peculiar capacities to attend to argument, to assess assumptions, to muster the courage to doubt, and to follow the argument wherever inference may lead?

The answers to these questions, and a thousand like them, are by no means obvious. It is probably true that no great advances in philosophical, mathematical, or historical research will be produced by those who have only casually pursued the practices of those disciplines. Yet I believe that nobody can say with any confidence that the peculiar virtues that are the fruits of philosophical study cannot be acquired through the study of history, economics, or sociology. A student of my acquaintance in environmental sciences sought to understand more thoroughly the principles and problems of public choice. She was urged by her advisers to enroll in a course in ethics within the philosophy department, apparently on the assumption that choice and values are the subject matter of philosophy. She found much that was interesting and a bit that was useful. But it was only later, after a course in public finance, that the hard realities of conflicting social values and the disciplines of choosing were made apparent to her. One might attribute that outcome to the bad teaching of philosophy, but I rather suspect the accurate answer is a different one. Nobody can claim with certainty that the virtues gained through the study of economics cannot be acquired in philosophy, or vice versa, that the virtues of philosophical study cannot be acquired in economics.

Courses limited by the boundaries of disciplinary subjects give us some assurance that certain topics will be covered by the student. But they give us no guarantee that the virtues of the disciplines will be acquired. These can be gained in the most improbable settings. By the same token, neither can we be sure that the disciplines of some relevant practice will be acquired by the creation of new disciplines or by the establishment of "interdisciplinary" arrangements. Both arrangements will be defective as long as we persist in seeing the academic disciplines as consisting, not in the ways they order, constrain, and shape the character of thinking and action, not in the ways they inculcate the virtues of the academic disciplines, but in the subject matter of departmental divisions in the college. If the academy is to contribute to the formation of human purpose, then we shall have to understand that the academic disciplines are not defined by their subject fields but by the virtues that submission to such disciplines can lend to the practices of life.

The Cultivation of Judgment. Consider now the second proposition: the claim that in all the higher practices in which the academic disciplines can play a role their indispensable contribution is not the advancement of knowledge but the cultivation of human judgment. Knowledge displaces judgment; that is to say, on all matters where we have knowledge, we have no need for judgment. If the banker knows that the prospective borrower will repay, he does not need to make judgments of character. If we know the exact distance from one point to another on the highway, then we do not need to make a judgment. We make judgments always and only in the absence of knowledge. Of course, a judgment cannot be made without any information or method; a judgment is not simply a guess. The banker does not make loans on the basis of mere conjecture. He seeks to accumulate whatever information he believes will assist in estimating their soundness. Judgment, in short, is the capacity to make reliable estimates on the basis of some method but in the absence of decisive information.

Let us imagine a matrix in which we array various occupations along two dimensions (see Figure 1). On the X axis we array occupations according to the predictability, from high to low, of the behavior of the materials with which they deal. For example, the behavior of lead, jute, plastic, copper, solder, and fluids is highly predictable. And so a plumber deals with materials that are highly predictable in their behavior. A carpenter or

Figure 1. Predictability of Materials and Results in Different Occupations

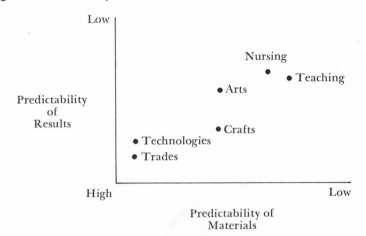

cabinet maker, however, works with somewhat less predictable material; each piece of wood is in some respect unlike any other. On the Y axis let us similarly array occupations according to the predictability of the results they produce. The plumber knows with high reliability what will result from one course of action as opposed to another. A worker in the silver crafts may have less certainty. A nurse has still less.

In a space defined by these parameters, we may locate a wide variety of occupations, ranging from the trades, crafts, and technologies to the professions. The distribution of these occupations will tend to cluster around the diagonal since unpredictability in the behavior of materials will tend to be associated with unpredictability of results. The essential point to note, however, is that as we extend farther into the range where judgment is required, we approach more closely the conditions for the practice of the professions. The education of professionals is essentially an education in the capacity to make sound judgments and to act in the midst of larger and more serious uncertainties than most of us have to deal with in most aspects of our lives.

I do not advance this observation to define what we mean by *profession*. The professions are usually defined not by the conditions of judgment but by the possession of a body of knowledge that is supposed to provide the basis for the professional's special expertise. I do not wish to question that point. It is true that professionals are usually in possession of some special, even arcane, body of knowledge on which their practice is based. But it is based upon that body of knowledge not because its possession provides certainty in professional practice but because it provides a basis for managing more subtle and more complex judgments in the midst of uncertainty.

Truly professional teachers are not distinguished by the certainty with which they approach their tasks so much as by their ability to understand the behavior, reasoning, and responses of students, on the basis of which they are able to shape their own action. Unpredictability is endemic to the teaching profession. It stems, moreover, not merely from the human material with which teachers, like nurses, work but also from the fact that the teachers' own actions are a part of the data they must take into account. They must have the capacity to observe their own practice. The discipline of those who are most professional in their practice consists not merely in mastery of a body of knowledge but in self-understanding and judgment. Thus, professional education, at its reaches, is education in self-knowledge.

We have now come full circle. Competence is an essential part of the development of purpose. It is one part of what is required if anyone is to have a life plan or a workable and good plan for a significant part of life. Competence—that is to say, being good at something—is essential partly because it helps to make the self specific. Knowing what we are good at, we know better who we are, what kinds of purposes or plans may be workable, what our limits are. But now we can see also that that kind of self-knowledge is a component in the development of human judgment. And the exercise of judgment in large measure defines the "higher" disciplines of life—that is, those disciplines most clearly devoted to public service. They are the "higher" disciplines because they deal most explicitly with the fundamental requirements of life outside the academy. Competence, discipline, practice, service, and judgment—these are the parts of that whole we call "being possessed of purpose."

30

Robert J. Menges

Instructional Methods

If *teaching* is defined as the intentional arrangement of situations in which appropriate learning will occur (Menges, 1977), it follows from this definition that teachers must decide what the outcomes of learning should be—that is, how learners should be different after their teaching—and then select the instructional methods most likely to promote these intended outcomes in the particular learners. Thus, their choice of instructional method should be governed by two factors: First, the method must require learners to perform tasks that promote the intended outcomes, and second, the method must be congenial to the instructor and appropriate for the learners' intellectual and motivation levels.

Accordingly, this chapter is organized around these factors. The first section offers a classification of learning outcomes that postsecondary teachers may intend for their students. The second section relates the characteristics of teachers and students to particular outcomes. And the third section discusses several teaching methods in light of their appropriateness for particular learning outcomes and the numbers of students they can accommodate.

There would be no need for this chapter if we, as teachers, consistently based our choice of instructional methods on the intended outcomes of learning and on our own characteristics and those of our students. Unfortunately, however, all too often we fail to select appropriate methods; instead, we adopt methods because of their familiarity to us from the days when we were students or because of our unexamined beliefs and the traditions of our institutions, or simply because of circumstances, such as the number of students enrolled or the assigned location and length of our teaching sessions.

This chapter is therefore itself meant to be a teaching tool. As an author and teacher, I have in mind the following four learning outcomes for anyone reading the chapter: (1) The reader will acquire concepts for classifying learning outcomes and for analyzing instructional methods. (2) The reader will be able to specify learning outcomes for a specific teaching assignment that illustrate the variety of outcomes discussed in the chapter. (3) The reader will identify his or her own characteristics as a teacher and those of students that are most relevant to the choice of outcomes and methods. (4) The reader will subsequently select instructional methods that are feasible, that adequately serve the desired outcomes, and that are appropriate to the learners.

Intended Learning Outcomes

The major learning outcomes intended by most postsecondary teachers can be categorized as psychomotor, memory, complex cognitive, nonlinear cognitive, and emotional. The following paragraphs discuss each of these categories primarily in relation to content, whether that content is cognitive or affective, and readers can easily relate outcomes in each of these categories to the discipline-defined content of their own fields or those discussed in Part Two of this volume. The relation of these outcome categories to the discussion of student development in Part One of the book is more complex. Developmental change, such as movement from one of Perry's or Kohlberg's stages to the next, is not treated here as an outcome of instruction (although, of course, it could be). Instead, the learner's developmental stage is seen as one of several characteristics that should affect the teacher's choice of instructional method.

Psychomotor Outcomes. Psychomotor learning involves skeletal-muscular reactions mediated by cognitive knowledge. Although most closely related to instruction in the studio, laboratory, or gymnasium, such outcomes can be identified in all fields. For example, skill in oral or written communication has a large psychomotor component. Unfortunately, however, in most "academic" areas, psychomotor learning is more often assumed than taught.

Psychomotor learning is typically denoted by goal statements or expressions such as "the learner executes . . . ," "the learner can perform . . . ," or "the learner accomplishes. . . ." Such learning obviously requires rehearsal and is demonstrated by overt performance. Learning begins with individual movements such as grasping the tennis racket or sounding a specified note on the string bass. Movements are then linked into chains: Grasping the racket is integrated into a backhand stroke; the note is played as part of a melody. Finally, a well-practiced chain becomes part of the psychomotor (or kinesthetic) repertoire: the backhand is executed under the pressure of match point; the melody is improvised in four-bar exchanges with another musician.

Conditions that promote psychomotor learning include the following:

- The learner imitates the movements of a model who has already mastered the skill.
- Feedback from the teacher gradually shapes more adequate movements by reinforcing closer and closer approximations to perfect performance.
- Self-observation is used to improve performance.
- During practice of movement chains, feedback from the teacher is gradually reduced.
- The learner executes movements and chains in situations that are less structured and more like the real performance situation.
- The learner reflects on judgments by which particular movements and chains are chosen in performance situations.

Readers who wish to formulate objectives keyed to psychomotor outcomes can find examples of objectives and of more elaborate classification schemes in Harrow (1972) and Simpson (1966).

Memory Outcomes. Memory, the first of three cognitive categories, deals with verbal learning of minimal complexity. Illustrations of simple cognitive memory include pairing an English word with its counterpart in another language, memorizing a poem, and mastering the steps in a routine procedure, such as long division. To denote cognitive memory outcomes, we might say "the learner recalls. . . ." Memory learning is thus shown by reproducing associations, repeating verbal chains, and paraphrasing or summarizing verbal material.

Acquiring verbal associations, such as terminology in a particular field, requires extensive repetition. Speed of learning and retention increase when the material to be learned is related to learners' previous experience or when appropriate mnemonic devices are used. Chains of verbal material such as lists of instructions can also be acquired more effectively with the help of mnemonics. However, verbal units and chains are not of much value (except for memory-based examinations) unless they can be retrieved in new situations. When information can be recalled to answer questions that are not identical to those encountered during learning, it has become part of the learner's verbal repertoire.

Useful discussions about memory and its improvement range from the popular (Lorayne and Lucas, 1974) to the scholarly (Norman, 1976; Morris, 1977). Conditions known to promote memory learning include the following:

- Highly repetitive practice is essential even though unpleasant; understanding *why* practice is effective can reduce its unpleasantness.
- Mnemonic devices, such as vivid images linking words to be paired, increase retention.
- Retention is enhanced when new information is in a form easily integrated with the learner's previous experience.
- Discussing what one recalls and how it is recalled can improve memory by making the process more explicit.

Complex Cognitive Outcomes. Complex cognitive learning requires that the learner operate upon recalled information by classifying, analyzing, or synthesizing it in a new context. Memorized knowledge is a necessary but not sufficient component of complex cognitive learning. Because the learner is responding to an instance or to a problem never before encountered, previously memorized associations or chains are inadequate. Complex cognitive outcomes are denoted by such statements as "the learner can classify . . . ." or "the learner is able to apply. . . ."

Concepts are the basic units of complex cognitive learning. Children acquire *concrete* (picturable) concepts such as "dog" and "house." Most college instruction is concerned with *defined* concepts such as "energy" or "style" or "demand," which are at a higher level of abstraction. The learner may master a verbal definition of the concept, but recalling a definition denotes memory rather than complex cognition. Complex cognition requires assimilation of knowledge such that the learner can recognize the concept in new contexts.

Sequences of concepts, when linked together into verbal propositions, are termed *principles.* Principles define the relationships among constituent concepts: "Acceleration times mass equals force" or "A behavior's resistance to extinction increases as a result of intermittent reinforcement." Principles are often taught only as rules to be memorized, but in fact they require both mastery of constituent concepts and also correct application to new situations.

At the most complex level, concepts and principles serve the learner's mastery of *intellectual strategies.* From experience with a large number of problems, learners discover strategies that apply across the whole class of problems. Or they may develop strategies for dealing with the process of learning itself. One difference between effective and ineffective learners is that effective learners generate their own strategies for coding, retrieving, and manipulating knowledge; they are in control of their learning processes.

Conditions that promote complex cognitive outcomes include the following:

- The learner demonstrates prerequisite knowledge (memory).
- The learner discriminates correct and incorrect examples of concepts or concept chains. Educational problems should include correct and incorrect examples of increasing subtlety and variety.
- The learner applies principles to new problems. These problems should require the learner to modify previously used principles—dealing both with subject matter content and with the process of learning—or generate new ones.
- The learner practices problems from which cognitive strategies can be generated and receives feedback on the adequacy of responses.

Discussions of planning and evaluating complex cognitive learning can be found in Payne (1974) and Hannah and Michaels (1977). Several chapters in the handbook by Bloom, Hastings, and Madaus (1971) deal with these issues in specific academic subject areas, and Merrill and Tennyson (1977) provide a detailed guide for teaching concepts.

Nonlinear Cognitive Outcomes. Not all cognitive processes are as systematic as the previous two categories imply. Readers of this chapter, for example, may experience insight, may grasp wholes rather than parts, and may find that the literal is enhanced or supplanted by the metaphoric. Such cognitive processes are holistic rather than analytical and expansive rather than reductive. To suggest their character, I have called them *nonlinear processes.* A careful reading of the following pairs of words, the first column referring to linear cognition and the second to nonlinear cognition, may evoke the concept:

analytic	holistic
objective	subjective
static	dynamic
literal	metaphoric
history	myth
replicate	create
converge	diverge
segment	cycle
linear time	cyclical time
narrate	free associate
reduce	expand
specificity	ambiguity
perform	imagine
work	play
system	person
rational logic	psycho-logic

deductive	intuitive
manifest content	latent content
secondary process	primary process
left hemisphere	right hemisphere
sequential	simultaneous
linear	nonlinear

Nonlinear cognitive outcomes are described in such terms as "the learner creates. . . ."

Nonlinear cognition begins with the recognition of discrete states of consciousness. These states are conventionally said to be five: waking, dreamless sleep, dreaming, meditation, and hypnosis. But the list could easily be extended to include daydreaming, ecstasy, trance, intuition, and mystical states. (States induced artificially by drugs could be added, but they are not our concern here.) Most persons in Western cultures are inexperienced at sensing cues associated with these states; even asking a class how they know whether the present is or is not a dream produces provocative discussion. However, Eastern psychologies have terms for scores of states of consciousness.

Such states are productive rather than reductive, increasing data with which the mind can work. Dreams, fantasies, images, and self-hypnosis are all methods that serve nonlinear cognition. A dream diary may serve as an aid to self-understanding, not only providing the material for later dream analysis (linear) but perhaps also prompting a return to sleep in order to redream the ending of a dream (nonlinear). Sensory receptiveness to a work of art (nonlinear) provides gratification beyond that which comes from examining it intellectually (linear). Contemplation of a teaching story from the Sufi or Zen tradition may illuminate incidents of daily life that bear no logical relationship to events in the story.

The accomplished nonlinear learner is fluent in a variety of states of consciousness and also has the ability to choose a state appropriate to the circumstances and to move in and out of that state at will. In the concert hall, this individual will be esthetically receptive; at prayer, open to divinity; in a marathon race, able to tap personal depths otherwise unavailable; and in the science laboratory, capable of generating hypotheses in ways that defy logical analysis.

The study of problem formulation rather than of problem solving is consistent with the distinction between nonlinearity and linearity and suggests tasks that might be used with students. For example, students might be provided with raw materials—laboratory equipment or census data or personality profiles or artist's materials—and challenged to list as many problems as they can that the materials could illuminate. The problems listed might be evaluated both quantitatively and qualitatively.

Conditions that foster nonlinear cognitive outcomes include the following:

• The learner engages in meditation, guided imagery, and other supervised exposures to altered states of consciousness.
• The learner experiences carefully structured environments—for example, esthetic and religious—both sensing and analyzing their differences.
• The learner practices identifying and formulating problems regardless of intent to solve them.
• The learner uses modes of expression other than logical, verbal narrations to convey personal experience and subject matter content. These modes might include pictures, maps, sounds, and collages.

Several approaches to what I term nonlinear cognition are provided by Houston (1975), Miller (1976), Ornstein (1976), and Samples (1976). Smith's (1976) best-seller treats several of the same topics in a broader cultural context. Applications to education are made by Hendricks and Fadiman (1976).

Emotions as Learning Outcomes. For emotions to be treated as learning outcomes, learners must show facility in verbalizing and otherwise expressing both their own feelings and their awareness of others'. Interpersonal learning settings tend to be most conducive to learning involving emotions. Such learning is denoted by statements such as "the learner perceives . . . ," "the learner feels . . . ," and "the learner communicates. . . ." Emotions as learning outcomes require the learner to experience and reflect upon a variety of feeling states. Attaining such outcomes facilitates an increase in self-determined emotional maturity.

Some teachers, learners, and institutions may deny the importance or appropriateness of emotion as subject matter. Others may prefer highly structured or analytical exercises (Egan, 1976; Kagan, 1978). Still others may want to plunge into experience first and cognitively reconstruct that experience later—at which time they may conclude that such reconstruction is unnecessary or impossible. It seems to me that educational programs have a responsibility to help persons develop as emotionally expressive individuals, however this is accomplished. The capacity for intimacy, as described by Douvan, and interpersonal competence, as described by Torbert, are central to our interaction with others. While an institution should not attempt to produce persons with identical emotional profiles, any more than to graduate people with identical cognitive views, it is obliged to assist learners toward emotional fluency as well as toward ideational fluency.

The units of emotional learning are discrete emotional states. The first steps toward emotional literacy require identifying one's own emotional state and naming it appropriately. The learner's vocabulary for this purpose may be inadequate, but, if necessary, instruction can enlarge that vocabulary.

Sending and receiving feeling-laden communications is a higher level of emotional learning. Assuming that I am in touch with my emotional state, can I communicate it accurately to another? Does my anger look like anger, or do I distort it? Are affectionate feelings shown as affection, or do they appear to be something else? Likewise, do I accurately perceive emotions expressed by others when they communicate with me?

Possessing a repertoire of emotional states permits one to better discriminate and control one's emotions. In one situation, a person may "let it all hang out." In a second situation, the person will be able to empathize fully with the feelings expressed by another—entering into a friend's grief, for example. In a third situation, on the basis of physiological cues, the person may be able to differentiate potentially confusing states—for example, to distinguish felt depression from felt hostility, and respond appropriately.

In addition to enabling emotional communication appropriate to the context, this repertoire also permits deliberate distortion of messages sent to others. The distortion may be for questionable purposes, such as closing a sale not really in the buyer's interest, or for laudable purposes, such as entering fully into a characterization during a dramatic performance. This repertoire also permits learners to be more objective as they deal with emotionally provocative learning materials. Kagerer (1974) found that as college students progressed through their four years they were able to deal more objectively with highly controversial material encountered in their courses. The ability to distinguish fact from opinion is required if learners are to reach Perry's stage of Multiplicity in intellectual and ethical development. The empathy required for the development of humanitarian concern, as described by White, requires that education make room for emotional learning.

Conditions fostering emotions as learning outcomes include the following:

- The learner acquires vocabulary adequate to describe each emotion in a wide range of experience.
- The learner receives physiological feedback for comparison with felt emotions.
- The learner receives interpersonal feedback against which to compare the emotion intended for communication.
- The learner practices sending and receiving emotion-laden messages.
- The learner experiences and analyzes feeling content in more and less structured groups.

Emotional and interpersonal functioning are discussed by Cross (1976) and by Menges (1977). Gazda and others (1977) provide exercises dealing with communication skills. Johnson and Johnson (1974) suggest ways of structuring learning environments to promote cooperation, and Ringness (1975) discusses the assessment of affective learning.

The Learning Outcomes Matrix. In Table 1 the five major categories of learning outcomes form the columns of a learning matrix. (The first three columns of this matrix follow closely Tiemann and Markle, 1973, which in turn draws from Merrill, 1971.) The three rows within each category represent levels of complexity. These levels refer to the *basic elements* of the category (Units), *connections* between these Units (Linkages), and the *transfer* of Units and Linkages to new situations (Repertoires). Each cell contains an illustration; the illustrations are drawn from a variety of disciplines and activities. (Students in several of my classes provided helpful critiques as the matrix was being developed.)

When the matrix is viewed as a whole, the interdependence of the cells becomes clear. Some cells represent prerequisites to other cells. One must have psychomotor competence before one can express complex ideas in writing. One must possess a verbal repertoire before one can describe the levels of emotion being communicated in a group. Using images as a mnemonic device to improve memory first requires facility with nonlinear cognition. Any strategy for self-management of the verbal learning process is itself an example of complex cognition.

Columns as well as rows of the matrix suggest the level of complexity of outcomes. In general, complexity increases not only as one moves upward from one row to the next but also as one moves to the right across the columns. A developmental sequence is also implied; to cite the extremes, psychomotor fluency is likely to develop first and emotional fluency is likely to develop last. When a particular outcome is sought, the following question is pertinent: Has appropriate learning occurred in each cell below and to the left? The matrix is useful for identifying prerequisites to complex learning and for diagnosing difficulties learners may have in acquiring complex outcomes.

The matrix can also assist in specifying goals for instructional programs. Most of us are familiar with stated goals for higher education that are so general as to ensure endorsement. The catalogue of my own institution states the following as its educational aim: "To be a community of scholars in which faculty and students can acquire the knowledge, competence, and wisdom to live full lives and to contribute to the well-being of their fellow men" (Northwestern University, 1977-78, p. 7). Aims of such generality are unlikely to inform instruction until they are translated into more specific outcomes, and the matrix categories may serve as guides to such translation.

Table 1. The Learning Outcomes Matrix

	Psychomotor Learning	Memory	Complex Cognition	Nonlinear Cognition	Emotions
Repertoires	*Kinesthetic repertoire*: Dives at a new height from a new board	*Verbal repertoire*: Narrates a play-off basketball game	*Repertoire of cognitive strategies*: Generates new categories for comparing pairs of novels	*Repertoire of conscious states*: After taking a fantasy journey, generates novel ideas for a course project	*Repertoire of emotional states*: During emotional class discussion, differentiates reactions to content from reactions to people
Linkages	*Movement chain*: Takes own blood pressure	*Verbal chain*: Locates a specified entry in *Dissertation Abstracts*	*Principle*: Describes use and consequences of Boyle's Law in given situations	*Consciousness expansion*: Reports a new experience in terms of all five senses	*Communicating feelings*: Identifies emotions expressed by other group members
Units	*Movements* (the brush for-ward of the foot in ballet)	*Verbal associations*: Names the five last winners of the Nobel Peace Prize	*Concepts*: Identifies examples of "melody"	*Conscious states*: Identifies differences between waking and daydreaming	*Feelings*: Reports visceral cues associated with particular feeling states

Note: Complexity increases from left to right and from middle (linkages) to top (repertoires).

Goal identification may occur on a systemwide basis, as illustrated by the Tennessee Higher Education Commission's (1977) specification of some of the skills and basic understandings that college graduates should have mastered.

- Describing concisely and clearly a witnessed event, such as an accident.
- Knowledge about the growing interdependence of nations, especially regarding natural resources and economic development.
- Knowledge of the development and the importance of accurate measurement and observation for scientific conclusions.
- Presenting literature as a form of valuable vicarious experience relevant to everyday life.
- The ability to distinguish between first- and second-hand information and between hypotheses and verified conclusions.

These items can be matched with particular cells in the matrix. They communicate much more than the university's single broad goal cited earlier.

Once an array of outcomes has been derived for a course or a curriculum, the matrix can also serve as a corrective. Are all cells that the instructor deems important for that course represented in its objectives? Are some cells given undue weight? Is appropriate lower-level learning (prerequisite learning) provided for? And so on.

The greatest inadequacy of the matrix is in dealing with holistic outcomes of education. As an analytical tool, the matrix seems not to comprehend qualities such as the acquisition of purpose, described by Green in this volume. Further, because of its emphasis on identified outcomes, the matrix is easily distorted for "training" individuals in the "skills" of intimacy or interpersonal competence or creativity. Such attempts are reductionist. They fail to do justice to the richness of the concepts with which they purport to deal. Goal-direction may even be self-defeating in the areas just mentioned. As Douvan points out in Part One, intimacy is not an instrument for some goal; intimacy requires openness, playfulness, unpredictability. The capacity of the matrix for dealing with holistic concerns deserves special attention.

Purpose illustrates the strengths as well as the potential weaknesses of the matrix scheme. Purpose, as portrayed by Green, is integrative, representing more than the total of the matrix cells. But purpose is not incompatible with the matrix. The cognitive outcome categories are relevant for mastering fields of knowledge and for mastering the rules, order, and structure governing the conduct of inquiry. Mastery of inquiry itself, as Green describes it, relates primarily to the cognitive outcome categories; indeed, practice —that is, the learning that occurs in the academy—seems to be primarily intellectual. We must ask what happens when the learner leaves the academy, when practice is to become performance, when intellectual inquiry is to be transformed into service. The matrix helps us see that transformation into service is unlikely unless the learner has emotional mastery as well as intellectual mastery and nonlinear competence as well as linear competence. (Torbert's discussion of "living inquiry" and "formal inquiry" in his chapter on interpersonal competence pursues this critical issue in more detail.) Thus, the matrix adds an imperative to Green's views on purpose. If learning is to lead to service, the academy must deal with emotional and nonlinear, as well as cognitive, learning. In that way the matrix scheme can correct for instruction that fails to match the breadth and richness of the concepts that are supposed to govern it.

Other influential work in taxonomies of learning includes several editions of a book by Gagné (most recently 1977) and a number of the chapters in the handbook edited by Bloom, Hastings, and Madaus (1971).

Learner and Teacher Characteristics

The choice of instructional strategies should be determined according to the characteristics of students and of teachers as well as according to intended learning outcomes. Salient characteristics of learners, many of which are identified in Part One of this book, can be determined by the teacher for students in a course or retrieved for all students at a college from institutional data banks. Quantified aptitude scores, high school grades, family income, age, sex, and scores on a variety of other tests are not only useful for describing learner populations: They also permit inferences about other learner characteristics. Age, for instance, permits inferences about the interests and experience of learners. Differences between adult and adolescent learners that can be inferred include these three from a research review by Cross (1978): First, adults have very different self-concepts from adolescents. They experience themselves as decision makers and in fact are more likely than adolescents to have consciously and freely decided to undertake further education. Second, they are pragmatic in their approach to learning. They wish to apply knowledge now rather than to assimilate it for later use. Third, their life experiences are many. They have had extensive prior learning to which new learning may be related. Thus, the digits denoting age merely suggest the richness of such details.

Four types of learner characteristics seem particularly important for discussion here: (1) the life situation in which learners find themselves, (2) the goals and needs that seem to motivate their behavior, (3) the learners' ego and intellectual stages, and (4) the dispositions that underlie learning styles.

Life Situation. Consider two learners enrolled in the same college. The first is a 19-year-old woman living in a campus dorm and beginning pre-medical studies. Her grades are good, but she sometimes feels depressed by a series of unsatisfactory love affairs. Her family pays most of her bills, and, except when her mind wanders during long evenings of study, she acknowledges that she is pretty lucky. The second is a 35-year-old woman who is widowed and caring for three children. Completion of several courses will qualify her for promotion to a higher executive assistant position. She is intimidated by her instructors and texts and feels she never has time for adequate preparation, especially in the liberal arts courses required of her. Nevertheless, she feels fortunate to have this opportunity to improve her situation.

Persons whose life situations are so different may turn up in the same course or workshop. Because of differences in available time and energy and facilities, their subjective experience of instruction will be far less similar than the objective characteristics of the learning setting might suggest. Only by providing considerable flexibility in instructional activities and assignments can teachers accommodate learners whose situations are so different.

Goals and Needs. In Part One, Schaie and Parr discuss the differences between younger and older learners' educational goals. Adults' goals follow from the changes that occur with the passage of years, including physical changes in the aging body, occupational changes, which may result from evolving personal goals, and exploration of alternative roles during retirement. These life cycle changes create needs quite different from those of younger people.

The distinction, made by Chickering and Havighurst, between instrumental and expressive aspects of education also implies that learners respond differently to instructional procedures depending on their goals and needs. Those making instrumental use of education experience present learning as leading them toward future goals. By contrast, those using education expressively find immediate satisfaction in the experience of education itself. For them, the goal of learning sometimes is the act of learning.

Even from these limited illustrations, it is not difficult to speculate about the dimensions of instructional strategies that most relate to learners' need and goals. Some learners prefer and profit from a social learning setting, others from a personal setting, and still others from an impersonal setting. For some the context for subject matter should be abstract and theoretical, while for others the context should be applied.

Ego and Intellectual Stages. Of the many schemes for viewing stages of development, I shall refer briefly to two: stages of ego development and stages of intellectual and ethical development. The stages of ego development proposed by Loevinger are described by Weathersby in Part One of this book. Students who view education as something you get in school (stage I-2) would probably find most appropriate a combination of lecture and text with a discussion group where questions can be answered. Those who think of education as an experience that affects one's inner life (stage I-4) probably require occasions where they can discuss learning experiences with others.

The stages of intellectual and ethical development proposed by Perry have equally direct implications. Students who see the world dualistically want authoritative teachers who can provide answers. Those with pluralistic orientations gain from instruction that presents competing alternatives and suggests ways for choosing among them. Those making commitments need opportunities to apply and test ideas in a variety of real settings. Teachers' and students' increased sophistication about stages of intellectual and ethical development can also help create teaching and learning activities that encourage movement from one level to the next. Developmental change can become an explicit objective intentionally addressed by students and faculty while more immediate instrumental purposes are also achieved.

Learning Styles. Research has identified a number of cognitive styles. These styles of perceiving and processing information greatly influence what is learned and how learning occurs. That learners with different cognitive styles will prefer different instructional styles is obvious. We may expect that tools for reliably diagnosing cognitive style will someday be available.

One of the most frequently studied cognitive style dimensions is called *field-dependence versus field-independence.* Those who are field-dependent rely heavily on context. Those who are field-independent rely less on context and more on stimuli isolated from their backgrounds. Research suggests that this cognitive style dimension is related to learning style, teaching style, and vocational choice and performance (Witkin and others, 1977). Persons who are field-independent, for example, are more successful in traditionally taught science courses than those who are field-dependent. Several other cognitive style dimensions are described by Messick and Associates (1976). Particularly provocative are the *conceptualizing style* dimension, which refers to the ways in which differences and similarities among stimuli are perceived during concept learning, and the *reflectiveness versus impulsivity* dimension, which refers to speed of information processing and hypothesis selection.

A second approach to learning style is represented by Kolb's model, described in Part One of this book. Kolb's brief forced-choice inventory provides scores on four dimensions: concrete experience, reflective observation, abstract conceptualization, and active experimentation. These are four steps in the learning cycle as well as four dimensions of style on which learners differ. Those whose style is predominantly abstract conceptualization, for example, are more likely to benefit from lectures, while those whose predominant style is concrete experiencing are more likely to benefit from projects and discussion.

Turning from student characteristics to those of teachers, we note first that most instructors develop a sense of self-as-teacher that reflects both their objective teaching skills and their subjective preferences for particular learning outcomes and particular instructional methods. Thus, less experienced teachers often prefer either a great deal of structure and control or the appearance of no structure at all. (At both extremes, it might be noted, the rules are unambiguous because the unequivocal absence of structure can be as unambiguous as the presence of rigid structure.) Voice quality, verbal facility, and physical appearance, as well as other objective characteristics, may lead to a preference for one method over another. A preference for particular learning outcomes can also be influenced by such characteristics. For instance, a teacher adept at establishing verbal chains may not be effective with emotional communication, while another who has been in therapy may comfortably employ fantasy journeys in teaching but be impatient with the repetition required by exercises that promote concept acquisition.

Unfortunately, teaching assignments are usually determined by instructors' personal preferences rather than by thoughtful matching of teaching skills and subject matter. Teachers' preferences are based in part on information about their own performance, but more significantly, on their beliefs and values regarding teaching and the learning process. Surveys show high faculty agreement throughout higher education on such goals as "mastery and appreciation of the subject or discipline," "clear thinking," "scholarly thinking," "reasoning," "interest and desire for self-directed learning," and "developing creative capacities"—a cluster of values described by Platt, Parsons, and Kirshstein (1976, p. 305) as "an orientation stressing the development of intellectual, autonomous, and cognitively competent students." Other beliefs deal with subject matter and how it is organized. Kolb's research concerning disciplinary inquiry norms and learning styles, reported in Part One, shows that most academics, for example, subscribe to a particular paradigm governing their academic field. Each paradigm reflects a particular set of beliefs and particular ways of thinking about the content of a field, and these beliefs affect instructors' preferences for instructional methods and intended learning outcomes.

If teachers are to reduce incongruities between espoused learning outcomes and the instructional methods employed, they must have opportunities to air and examine their beliefs. An apparent incongruity (a teacher espousing creativity as an outcome but relying on lectures that require information to be memorized, for example) is explained when we learn that the professor believes that students learn primarily by listening to knowledgeable people talk about their knowledge. Opportunities for examining beliefs range from formally structured curriculum review committees to informal discussions of videotapes showing teachers in action. To be most effective, such occasions should enable the teacher to confront beliefs, intended outcomes, and an array of possible instructional methods. Only by making beliefs explicit will dissonances between them and outcomes or methods be revealed.

Instructional Methods

Because the number of students enrolled in a course is such an important factor in the choice of instructional methods, these methods are discussed here first with regard to their suitability for large groups, small groups, and individuals. Then their appropriateness for each of the intended outcomes discussed earlier in this chapter is examined. These three class size categories are meant to convey not only enrollment but also the situation in which students learn—whether with many other students, with a few other students, or alone—and the dominant communication pattern—whether lecturing by the teacher, class discussion guided by the teacher, or a mutual exchange between teacher and student. Table 2 summarizes the relationships among instructional method, group size, and desired outcomes elaborated in this section.

The most comprehensive recent review of research on instructional methods is the book edited by Gage and Berliner (1979). Practical advice on methods for college teaching is provided by Eble (1976), Hyman (1970), and McKeachie (1978). The text by Gage and Berliner (1979), although not specific to college teaching, gives useful hints on a variety of classroom procedures, including chapters on lecturing, on the discussion method, and on individual instruction.

Large Group Instruction. The defining characteristic of the large group, for our purposes, is its communication pattern. Communication in large groups flows primarily from teacher to learner, there is more teacher talk than student talk, most student talk is in response to the teacher's questions, and most student comments are directed to the teacher. This communication pattern may, of course, occur in small groups as well; I have stood outside college classrooms with as few as five or six students that might as well have been classes of two hundred since none of the advantages of a small group were being exploited.

In the large group, size itself constrains the communication pattern so that it is predominantly teacher to student. A class of six is not constrained in this way. A class of twenty-five probably is, since during a fifty-minute meeting, even if the teacher were silent, each member could average no more than two minutes of speaking time. Of course, groups of several hundred can be subdivided into threes or fours for perhaps a third of the meeting, and then each member may have five or six minutes of floor time.

Yet research has documented few strengths of lecturing. Studies have failed to find sufficient attention by students during lectures, or high retention of information after lectures, or effective stimulation of higher cognitive capacities such as analysis and synthesis (McLeish, 1976). It seems unlikely that this situation will change. Improving retention of content would require carefully sequenced presentations with built-in redundancy, review, and self-testing by the audience, and those very procedures might produce more tedium than retention. Improving attention would require oratorical skills. Yet how many academics are capable of such skilled performances? How many even wish to become capable? And to what extent are such skills effective when many in the audience are present involuntarily rather than voluntarily?

Under some conditions, it makes sense for people to gather voluntarily to hear a lecture. Inspiration is one reason. The lecture also is a convenient mechanism for disseminating information and ideas that are not otherwise available, so long as it does not merely duplicate what students could read in a transcript of the lecture. It may be that content is illustrated in ways that print cannot capture. Or the presence of the lecturer may vitalize the material, especially if the audience feels it is witnessing the workings of a great mind. The lecturer may also elicit comments and questions from the audience and integrate and respond to them in a way that increases involvement.

Without doubt, lectures *can* be effective. But the likelihood that any particular lecture will be effective is low. For promoting analysis and synthesis, lectures are inferior to methods requiring more student involvement, such as group discussion. For conveying information and promoting retention, lectures are more efficient than discussion but are inferior to the printed word. To successfully inspire their hearers, lecturers must possess qualities that are quite uncommon among academics. And so the lecture receives little endorsement here among methods for large group instruction.

The heterogeneity of students is another problem of large classes and, according

Table 2. Instructional Methods Related to Desired Learning Outcomes and Group Size

Group Size	Desired Learning Outcomes					
	Psychomotor Learning	Memory	Complex Cognition	Nonlinear Cognition	Emotions
Large group	Demonstrations	Lecture Quiz	Lecturer as model thinker Task groups	Evocative media Guided imagery Lecture alternating linear and nonlinear modes	Evocative media Field trip
Small group	Practice with feedback Discussion with critique	Recitation Quiz by peers Discussion about process	Democratic discussion Peer tutors Case study Simulations	Problem formulation Brainstorming Games	Encounter/sensitivity Role playing Leaderless discussion
Individual	Practice with mediated feedback Laboratory	Mediated drill Mnemonics PSI	Interactive computer PSI Retired/adjunct tutors	Meditation Diary Interactive computer	Internship Diary

to Brock (1976), ranks next to the problem of student anonymity for teachers of large introductory courses. The range in class standing, ability, experience, interests, and motivation may be quite large. A questionnaire given at the start of a course will reveal to the instructor the variability among students, and class activities and assignments might be adjusted to accommodate students' interests and abilities.

Testing and grading in large classes arouse special complaints among students and faculty. Testing procedures that are efficient for the teacher may be resented by students as being impersonal. Special care must be taken to inform students, preferably in writing, what is to be tested and how grades are to be determined. Students also deserve personal comments on their work whenever possible. Several of these practical considerations in running large classes are discussed in Part Two by Carlson, who has given careful thought to the design of a large biology course for nonmajors.

In a large class, what instructional methods are conducive to the five types of learning outcomes described earlier in this chapter? The suggestions that follow are keyed to the outline in Table 2.

Little *psychomotor learning* occurs when students are spectators, as members of most large classes are. Nevertheless, large audiences sometimes profit from witnessing a performance of the skills they are to acquire. A live or recorded demonstration with commentary can inform as well as inspire. Although seeing such a performance is not sufficient for learning, images of the performance can be recalled during subsequent practice.

For *memory outcomes* students are expected to recognize, recall, or paraphrase information. When memory is the goal, the best medium of instruction for a large class is undoubtedly the textbook. Lectures can be an efficient way of conveying information, too, although retention may not be as great. Learning in lectures is enhanced by distributing full or partial texts of the lectures. Complex diagrams, in particular, should be distributed, although key portions might be omitted to ensure that students must complete them during class. Slides, transparencies, posters, and other devices are effective because of the stimulus variation they provide, but they can be dulling when used continuously. The expectation of a quiz also enhances attention.

Cognitive involvement of students is promoted by oral or written questions. The teacher might take a poll in the form of a multiple-choice question on either the factual substance of the lecture or on students' opinion about the topic of the day. Only when students employ the information is it possible to determine whether learning, even rote learning, has occurred. Feedback from such questions reveals to students the extent of their mastery. Nevertheless, the large group cannot accommodate the individually paced drill that effective memorization requires.

Organizing the content of large group presentations requires special care. When memory is the desired outcome, clarity is especially important. Learners should know at all times where the presentation is going, as well as where it has been. The teacher should emphasize connections with material previously learned in the course and exploit categories that are already part of the learner's cognitive structure.

To attain *complex cognitive outcomes,* such as classifying concepts, generating examples, and originating cognitive strategies, the learner must be actively engaged with subject matter. In large groups, such involvement is infrequent but not impossible. The necessary teaching skills are, however, quite different from those appropriate for memory outcomes. To stimulate higher-order cognitive involvement, the instructor must exploit curiosity, dissonance, the need for closure, and so on. The lecturer might recount the development of work on a problem, thus modeling the thinking process of persons in the field. Or, to engage the learner more directly, the lecturer might pose a paradox or a problem for the learner to resolve—perhaps even a problem that bears upon circumstances in his or her own life.

Another way to ensure that learners respond to higher-order questions is to form temporary task groups. These groups of three or four students work on a given problem for a few minutes. Each member has opportunity to tackle the problem directly, and groups might be surveyed for their solutions when the class reassembles.

Nonlinear cognitive outcomes require an alteration in the learner's conscious processes. The large group setting is not necessarily uncongenial to that experience, but its tone must be informal and relaxed. There must be at least a moderate level of trust among participants, including the perception that it is not necessary to participate. Learners must also accept problem-finding as at least as important as problem-solving.

Given these circumstances, conscious states may be altered by relaxation exercises, guided imagery, fantasy journeys, and so on. Skillful use of projected visuals, amplified sounds, aromas, and tactile stimuli facilitate disassociation from ordinary consciousness. Even without such special procedures, a lecturer may evoke and enlarge nonlinear processes. The key is to appeal alternately to different modes of understanding. For example, a section of linear exposition might be followed by an anecdote that illuminates that information. McConnell (1978) tells how he dreamed of the perfect textbook in which definitions and step-by-step logical presentations alternated with exciting anecdotes and provocative analogies. The lecture can similarly shift between linear and nonlinear modes. Reconsider some of the word pairs in the list presented earlier in the chapter. How might a presentation shift from specificity to ambiguity? From segments to cycles? From history to myth? From the literal to the metaphoric? And then how might it shift back again? Nonlinear devices are used not merely to change the pace and wake up drowsy audiences but to engage quite different mental processes.

Large groups are inhospitable settings for *emotions as outcomes*. The large group is probably as appropriate for learning about emotions as for learning about any other subject. But the large group is inappropriate for experiencing, analyzing, and practicing emotional expression. Large group audiovisual presentations can evoke powerful emotional responses, but the large group provides no way to deal with the emotional energy thus released. It is uncertain how much learning can result if there is no small group experience.

Learners' emotions can be deeply affected by field trips, which frequently are large group activities. Such trips expose learners to strange environments, to unfamiliar customs, and to stressful or shocking situations. They engage emotions in ways impossible with other methods and may facilitate subsequent cognitive learning. Emotional arousal does not, however, ensure that emotional learning has taken place. Emotional learning is unlikely apart from the kind of feedback available in a small group.

Small Group Instruction. Much of postsecondary education takes place in relatively small classes of from four or five to twenty or thirty students, which are variously called discussion sections or seminars or lecture-discussion. The major problem in the small instructional group is the tendency for both students and teacher to behave in the same way as they would in a large, teacher-dominated group. The difficulty of maintaining democratic discussion is a common professorial complaint. In visits to discussion sections of large courses, I have seen teachers struggle to initiate and maintain discussion. In my own classes, I have often worked hard to increase student talk and to decrease my own teacher talk. The teacher's (or students') failures turn discussion classes into recitations, in which the instructor conducts what is virtually an oral quiz, or the discussion becomes a lecture in which the teacher explains to students what they might have discussed.

Research evidence documents the paucity of highly interactive discussions. For example, studying ten university classes ranging in enrollment from twelve to sixty-five, Karp and Yoels (1976) found that in classes under forty, about half of the students present participated; in classes over forty, about a fourth of those present participated. In other words, their striking finding is that about ten students participated per session regardless of class size. Further, only a few of those students who do participate account for most of the interactions. In classes with under forty students, three quarters of the interactions involved the same four or five students. In classes of more than forty, about half of the interactions were initiated by two or three students.

Students come to small classes expecting to participate, although they adjust that expectation according to whether the behavior of the instructor indicates that discussion really is desired in that class. In a highly participative class, students often gain satisfaction from the social context and from the emotional exchanges that occur during class sessions and outside of class. But effort by the teacher is required to bring about those socio-emotional consequences.

Clarity is as important for effective small group work as it is for large group work, but in the small group clarity of organization and communication is less important than clarity of expectation. Students often express confusion about the purposes of a discussion. The instructor is responsible for making discussion goals clear. Do we recite information? Do we express opinions? Are we looking for imaginative ideas? Is it okay to disagree with other students? With the instructor? Can the professor be distracted? Does the teacher set the agenda or do the students set the agenda? Each of these norms is settled early in the term. Even if the professor talks about some of these issues directly, students are more alert to what is *done* in class than to what is said. A norm for low or high participation can be established during the first class session depending upon the students' responses to the instructor's cues. Students, too, work at setting the norms they prefer, as many instructors discover too late.

Small instructional groups are good settings for cooperative learning. A cooperative goal structure requires that for one student to attain a goal, other students must attain it as well. Students who cooperate on tasks usually produce higher-quality work on those tasks than students under individual reward conditions, but that advantage does not necessarily extend to the course as a whole (see, for example, McClintock and Sonquist, 1976). One way to formalize cooperative goal structures is to create "peer-monitoring groups" of two, three, or four students. In a series of studies, students in such groups, when informed that their grade would be the average of their individual performance, achieved at a higher level even though they reported no greater studying time than did students under an individual condition (Fraser and others, 1977; Beaman and others, 1977).

The small instructional group can promote learning outcomes in each of the categories discussed in this chapter. Small groups can be very effective for promoting *psychomotor outcomes.* Students who wish to acquire skilled movements, movement chains, and movement repertoires find that the small group meets two essential conditions: (1) it provides feedback from the teacher and other students and (2) it permits discussion of the decisions that learners make while performing.

As learners practice movements and chains of movements, group members who are not participating in the drill may provide structured feedback. Each observer can concentrate on a different aspect of the performance—for example, a different skill or a different part of the performer's body. Feedback must be specific and immediate and must include suggestions for improvement. If another practice session quickly follows, performance should improve.

Acquisition of movement repertoires requires attention to the "psycho" component of psychomotor outcomes. In the press of playing a game, why does a player decide to do this rather than that? A postgame discussion provides helpful critiques of performance. The focus of discussion is not on improving movements or chains but on determining what options are available at particular points and how one chooses among them.

When *memory* is the desired outcome and the learner is to recall, to recognize, or to restate information, recitation is the traditional small group method. If used as an oral quiz, recitation reveals learners' deficiencies and may suggest their cause. Students may learn not only by answering questions themselves but also vicariously by putting themselves into the place of the student being questioned. Although students do not consider such interrogation particularly pleasant, it is excellent preparation if course examinations require recall of information. The combination of a grading scheme that is weighted toward such examinations and the discussion of specific course materials in a small group usually stimulates high attendance. Students are likely to report that such teaching is effective and that they feel they are learning a great deal.

Quizzes conducted by fellow students are similarly useful. Mutual study sessions aimed at reviewing and answering hypothetical examination questions help students focus their attention. In addition, they learn from what other students say. Although this technique works most effectively when goals are cooperative, even competitive groups can enhance memory outcomes.

Students engaged in memory learning also profit from small group discussion about their learning processes. Such discussion provides students with insights and strategies to improve their study effectiveness. By discussing their learning processes and by listening to others describe how they study, students may evolve more useful procedures for themselves, even while they engage in complex cognitive discussion.

When the aim of a small group is to foster *complex cognitive outcomes,* students must be helped to understand that aim and must become aware of the processes and the procedures that will be used to attain it. If democratic discussion is the vehicle, it is especially important for the leader to clarify the extent of authority he or she will retain. Democratic discussion can foster complex cognitive outcomes such as critical thinking. In a study of twelve college classes in different disciplines, it was found that classes with students who scored higher on critical thinking were also characterized by more student participation, encouragement, and peer-to-peer interaction (Smith, 1977).

Other devices besides democratic discussion may be appropriate for fostering complex cognitive outcomes in the small group. Peer tutoring for group discussion is sometimes helpful, providing that appropriate questions have been formulated. Case studies as springboards for discussion may give the discussion a measure of reality. Games and simulations provide immediate, common experience for the class and then inform subsequent discussion. Discussions based on simulations are often more lively and such classes are more memorable than those in which discussion is based solely on readings (Seidner, 1976).

Greater facility in problem formulation is the *nonlinear outcome* most relevant to academic learning. A variety of consciousness-altering devices such as those mentioned earlier in this chapter are useful for developing this facility. For fruitful nonlinear learning, both learners and teachers must be open to alternatives, must become more flexible, nonstereotypical, and holistic. Techniques such as brainstorming and synectics (see Joyce and Weil, 1972) can be used in problem formulation as well as in problem solving. Using varied media to represent how phenomena are patterned may be helpful. Games and simulations provide a new perspective from which experience may be viewed.

Small groups provide an environment in which *emotions as outcomes* are naturally fostered. In conventional classes, considerable energy is devoted to dealing with emotional matters, often indirectly. A skilled leader who seeks to stimulate emotional experience and growth in a group has a vast literature upon which to draw. Nondirective groups, awareness groups, and more structured training groups (see Joyce and Weil, 1972) are approaches that provide opportunities to generate and analyze emotion-laden behavior and to experiment with new behaviors.

Of the many exercises used in those approaches, role playing nicely illustrates the potential of creating for the group an emotion-laden situation in which students can identify others whose views and feelings are different from their own. Subsequent discussion of the exercise permits analysis of emotional responses and identification of more congruent or constructive response patterns.

When groups are structured without a leader, socio-emotional issues quickly come to the fore. This technique is commonly used in nondirective teaching and effectively raises questions about personal issues ("Why don't I take more initiative in this discussion?"), interpersonal issues ("Why does she keep arguing with him?"), and subject matter issues ("What connection does this stuff we're reading have with me?"). Leaderless discussions are least likely to serve cognitive outcomes effectively, but they are likely to evoke incidents useful for dealing with emotions in the group.

Individual Instruction. Individual instruction requires only one student, one teacher, and the subject matter. It is distinguished by the fact that a student works alone; even though other students may be studying the same material, there are no group discussions of the subject matter. Individual instruction need not imply instruction that is individualized, as we shall see later when we look at programmed and computer-assisted instruction. Individualization of instruction requires custom design (see Clark's chapter): Each student is given a unique diagnosis and prescription (Gage and Berliner, 1979). At its best, individualized instruction assesses the cognitive and affective stage of the learner, takes account of the learner's life circumstances, and on that basis devises learning experiences. Such content and procedural variations may be part of individual instruction, but not necessarily.

The communication pattern in individual instruction is far less complex than in larger group settings, since it theoretically consists only of interchanges between student and instructor. Those interchanges have many levels and nuances, of course. They are often frank and sometimes highly personal, carrying emotional as well as cognitive content. They also imply more commitment than do typical classroom exchanges.

The tutorial, associated with the Cambridge-Oxford tradition, holds a nostalgic appeal for many. In current American usage, however, tutoring often means remedial instruction, in which a teacher helps students with deficiencies rather than enriching those who are already well grounded in the fundamentals. The connotation of private attention from a faculty member is now carried by such terms as *independent study*.

Independent study should include a series of experiences requiring increasingly greater self-direction, according to Dressel and Thompson (1973). Every student, they argue, should have some such experiences during college, beginning perhaps with a modest project done as part of course work and culminating perhaps with one so ambitious that several months of concentrated effort are devoted to it. Such a process would help students *acquire* the skills of self-direction rather than merely exercise the skills they already possess.

Two serious problems beset individual instruction. One is the obvious problem of cost. The second problem is the tendency for individual instruction to become unnecessarily teacher-dominated. All too easily, an individual tutorial session becomes a recitation in which the professor conducts an oral quiz of a single student. Or the session becomes a monologue in which the professor lectures the student on the fine points of the subject at hand. My experience is that neither party is truly satisfied when events take such a turn and both welcome the end of the tutorial hour. But when tutorial conversation becomes real dialogue, the experience is memorable. In the meeting of minds and personalities around a topic, both student and teacher grow. Teachers have a different experience with every student even when the topics are the same.

The freedom possible in individual instruction depends upon mutual trust between teacher and student. The student trusts that meaningful choices are available. The teacher trusts that the student can make meaningful choices and will do so responsibly. Both exploit the particular strengths of the teacher and the particular resources of the student. A useful technique that prevents misunderstandings is a written contract in which services and obligations of both parties are specified (Berte, 1975).

The Personalized System of Instruction (PSI) is pertinent here because of its attention to individuals, even though it may be used in courses that enroll hundreds of students. Features of the Personalized System of Instruction (see Keller, 1968) and of mastery learning (see Block, 1971) are combined in the following brief description:

> A teacher planning instruction first carefully defines the subject matter that students are to master and specifies questions that they should answer or skills that they should demonstrate as evidence of learning. Subject matter is then divided into small sequential units and a criterion test constructed for each unit. When a student feels adequately familiar with a unit, the criterion test is available. It requires a score of 80 percent or 90 percent correct for a "pass." Failure on the test requires the student to do some remedial study and then return to take a parallel form of the test. Passing the test is the ticket to the next unit. Lectures, demonstrations, and discussions are used primarily as reinforcers. For example, permission to attend the class of a popular teacher or to see a film is granted only when the student has completed certain unit tests. Alternatively, classes may be used as review sessions (punishment) for those having difficulty with unit tests.

> Mastery learning uses tutoring in an important way. Each unit test is immediately graded by a proctor, who may be the teacher or a more advanced student. Immediate grading provides feedback and an opportunity for brief tutoring. When a student has completed the series of unit tests, the course is over and the grade is A. Lower grades come only as a consequence of failure to complete all units. The student is then eligible to start another course or perhaps an independent project, and such eligibility can in itself be highly reinforcing [Menges, 1977, p. 35].

To the extent that PSI minimizes group activities—and they are not central to the method —and maximizes self-pacing and individual quizzing by a tutor, the method satisfies the requirements of individual instruction.

Computer-assisted instruction similarly engages individual learners and provides them considerable control over the rate, often over the sequencing, and sometimes over the evaluation of their learning. Computer-assisted instruction has been praised as a breakthrough equivalent in significance to printing. The computer's storage capacities, capability for displaying dynamic graphics and generating sound, and immense memory, all of which can respond to each key press by the learner, have been explored in extensive research (Bunderson and Faust, 1976), but its potential has not yet been realized. No description of computer hardware or software is given here (see Rockart and Morton,

1975), but illustrations of its use for particular cognitive outcomes are given in the following sections.

Individual instruction may produce outcomes in each of the categories presented in this chapter. Several appropriate methods for each category are described below.

For *psychomotor outcomes,* solitary practice of single movements or of movement chains provides feedback sufficient for improvement only when the learner is highly sensitive to kinesthetic cues. Beginning learners require feedback from an external source. Electronic media may serve this purpose. Audio or visual recordings carry sufficient information for self-diagnosis, especially if the learner is familiar with examples of skilled performance. Convenience and flexibility in scheduling may well offset equipment costs.

Laboratory learning is often a solitary experience, even when other students are present, and so I discuss it as an instance of individual instruction. Psychomotor learning is probably the most frequent outcome of laboratory instruction, even though cognitive learning is usually its stated aim. Most cognitive learning is at a level so abstract that reading and discussion, perhaps supplemented by demonstrations and computer simulations, will promote more efficient learning than does laboratory experience. As McKeachie concludes after reviewing the little research on laboratory teaching he could find: "one would not expect laboratory teaching to have an advantage over other teaching methods in amount of information learned. Rather, one might expect the differences to be revealed in retention, in ability to apply learning, or in actual skill in observation or manipulation of materials" (McKeachie, 1978, p. 84). Skills of observing and manipulating materials and, I might add, of operating equipment are largely psychomotor. Psychomotor outcomes are probably the primary justification for laboratory teaching, whether the lab has six students at a table or each student alone in a carrel.

When instruction aims at *memory outcomes,* no tutor is more patient and accurate than a mechanical one. The computer, programmed test, or, more primitively, flash cards, provide practice and feedback more efficiently than any human teacher can. Such drill, unpleasant as it may be, is necessary. Unpleasantness decreases when the start and duration of practice are under the control of the learner. Mnemonic learning aids, provided in printed form or in person by the teacher, can enhance learning, retention, and satisfaction.

The Personalized System of Instruction (PSI) has been shown to be as effective as more traditional instructional methods for mastery of knowledge (Johnson and Ruskin, 1977). PSI illustrates individual instruction primarily because quizzes are frequent and scored immediately, and the results are discussed with a tutor. This tutorial session occurs just after a quiz, when student motivation is high, and therefore probably enhances retention. Under PSI, students usually study alone, are tested individually, and may receive individualized assignments based on results of the quiz. Such quizzes economically and comprehensively test the student's memory for course content.

The tutorial conversation is without doubt the most flexible and powerful tool for helping students to perform the *complex cognitive* operations of analysis, synthesis, and generalization based on memorized information. Unfortunately, in practice such conversations often concentrate on identifying and locating resources rather than on complexities of subject content. Such conversations are also likely to be expensive in terms of personnel time. Emeritus professors or professionals from the community may be available at lower cost and may be eager to take on limited tutoring roles. Their experience equips them especially well for helping students integrate knowledge at higher cognitive levels and for testing abstract knowledge against experience.

The computer can substitute admirably for the human tutor. Suppose the student is working on a complex interdisciplinary problem such as population growth. The computer's memory contains information about population statistics for several countries in relation to other variables. Its output consists of graphs showing population trends over time. Students can manipulate one variable—for example, Pakistan's birth rate or death rate—and observe the effect upon another variable, such as food consumption. Or changes in population growth as a function of a natural disaster such as drought may be examined from the graphic display. The student is spared calculations necessary for extrapolating future demographic trends but gains knowledge of significant principles. Such learning remains vivid partly because data appear as a result of particular questions posed by the student.

The Personalized System of Instruction will bring about complex cognitive learning to the extent that PSI quizzes contain questions calling for higher-order cognitive processes. Because quizzes are graded by a tutor, they can include questions that require comparing or contrasting, generating examples, originating principles, and producing multiple solutions to problems. The session with a tutor that immediately follows the quiz enables students to receive a critique of their efforts and to discuss additional ideas and hypotheses.

The alteration in mental processes needed for *nonlinear cognitive outcomes* can be brought about by a number of individual techniques. The regular practice of meditation is probably the most common, and learners may be able to integrate meditation into their general study program. Experiences gained while in altered states of consciousness should be recorded and available for subsequent analysis. A diary can provide a record of these private, personal events. Regular diary entries comprise a record from which trends over time may be identified and comparisons may be made.

The computer, as substitute for other students or for a live teacher, may stimulate novelty, metaphor, analogy, and other nonlinear processes. Computer programs for this purpose must be highly sophisticated in order to elicit responses from the learner and then provide appropriate further stimulation. The record of one student's interaction with a program for teaching writing designed by Ellen Nold and Sallie Cannom of Stanford, appears below. (Each line that the student, Chris, typed is set in italic.)

> Hi. What's your name?
> *Chris*
> O.K., Chris, let's talk about breaking out of the stereotypical perception that results in dull thinking and dull writing.
> Find pencil and paper and draw a hand.
> When you're finished, press the RETURN key.
>
> O.K. Now you've drawn a hand. How detailed is it?
> *Not very*
> Is it an evocative, thought-provoking representation?
> *Hardly!*
> Why?
> *Too little detail, too little attention paid to its creation.*
> Most hands have four fingers and a thumb, so that's a basic representation—a kind of stereotype. But past that, it's the differences rather than the similarities that make your picture interesting.
> Look at your own left hand as if for the first time. What do you see?
> *Softness, hardness, hills and valleys, wrinkles*
> All right. What else?
> *colors—gold, rosy flesh tones, the blue of veins*
> And?
> *nails—long, short, chipped, many shapes*
> You could write a lot more just about your left hand—not counting inferences or

speculations about the kind of person you are, or how your particular hand came to be.

Here's a poem:

                    Hands
              Hands can work
              Hands can play
              Hands are used
              Every day.
Not exactly spellbinding is it? But why?
Very pedestrian information put into dull phrases
Chris, using the details:
Softness, hardness, hills and valleys, wrinkles
colors—good, rosy flesh tones, the blue of veins
nails—long, short, chipped, many shapes,
you could write a much more interesting poem about hands. Want to?
OK
O.K. Here are five blank lines for you to use.

                    Hands
                  by Chris
          Soft flesh climbs bony ridges
          Rosy hued ridges, golden valleys
          Tipped by brittle jagged ovals
          The winding blue rivers
          Bring life to all
Was that fun? Maybe you'd like to do more with that poem later or perhaps write another one.
Practice in avoiding stereotypical thinking will increase your poetic perception and expression.
To write perceptively means to see perceptively.
For an exercise in seeing, try SAGE.
Bye for now, Chris [Nold and Cannom, 1977].

Students react favorably to such programs, although the program may strike readers of the printed page as too clever. The experience is solitary and to an extent is individualized. Carefully designed programs certainly have the potential to stimulate nonlinear processes.

Individual study lacks sources of feedback necessary for *emotions as outcomes.* Activities carried out individually are quite capable of arousing emotions, but in themselves they provide no way for students to deal with the emotions that have been aroused. Internships provide a setting in which students have to face emotional issues. If prior group experiences have given students the necessary resources, the internship is a kind of individual laboratory in which they may test out behaviors in new situations. The diary is a potentially useful device for keeping a record of emotional experiences and reactions. Nevertheless, apart from interaction with others, significant emotional learning is unlikely from this source alone. In short, the individual setting is less likely to produce significant emotional learning than to produce outcomes in the other categories.

Conclusion: Change Within Constraints

Choice of instructional method should be a function of both intended learning outcomes and the setting in which learning occurs (conveniently represented by group size), with due regard for learner and teacher characteristics.

The major criterion for assessing appropriateness of method is the extent to which the method ensures that learners pursue tasks essential to the desired outcome. To achieve memory outcomes, the learner must rehearse verbal associations and verbal chains. Listening to a lecture is passive, but recitation or computer-assisted drill ensures rehearsal. To achieve the mastery of emotions necessary for accurately perceiving emotional messages from others, learners must receive real messages from other persons. A book of case studies is not sufficient for such learning, but group exercises may be. The cells in Table 2 suggest other methods for promoting desired learning outcomes.

Faculty can cite circumstances that seemingly prevent them from adopting the method or methods logically derived by this analysis, yet many of those constraints turn out to be self-imposed. The severe limitations of the lecture method are clear from this chapter, for example, yet lecturing fills nearly all contact hours in many courses. Why does a professor lecture to a class of twenty-five when that method is counter to desired learning outcomes? Perhaps lecturing seems dictated by tradition. Perhaps the teacher has had no practice with alternative methods. Perhaps he or she fears that a less-structured situation will reveal teaching weaknesses. Whatever the reason, it is theoretically within the power of that instructor to overcome these constraints.

What factors make it more likely that professors will choose instructional methods according to the deliberate process I have described? Faculty members must be motivated to increase the effectiveness of their teaching. They must have knowledge of alternatives and should be able to observe models who have undertaken the changes being considered. Professional assistance from faculty development colleagues is also a great help (Lindquist, 1978). Most important is an institutional policy that regards changes in students as the primary mission of the institution and that rewards those faculty members who plan and conduct instruction in ways that bring about desired changes. (For more detailed discussion of professional development see Lindquist's chapter in Part Three of this book.) If such factors are not present—particularly if the institution's reward structure is not reinforcing—the choice of instructional methods will continue to be determined by tradition, a disquietingly irrational influence for an institution dedicated to rational inquiry.

References

Beaman, A., and others. "Effects of Voluntary and Semivoluntary Peer-Monitoring Programs on Academic Performance." *Journal of Educational Psychology*, 1977, *69*, 109-114.

Berte, N. R. (Ed.). *New Directions for Higher Education: Individualizing Education by Learning Contracts*, no. 10. San Francisco: Jossey-Bass, 1975.

Block, J. H. (Ed.). *Mastery Learning: Theory and Practice*. New York: Holt, Rinehart and Winston, 1971.

Bloom, B. S., Hastings, J. T., and Madaus, G. F. *Handbook on Formative and Summative Evaluation of Student Learning*. New York: McGraw-Hill, 1971.

Brock, S. C. *Practitioners' Views on Teaching the Large Introductory College Course*. Manhattan, Kans.: Center for Faculty Evaluation and Development, 1976.

Bunderson, C. V., and Faust, G. W. "Programmed and Computer-Assisted Instruction." In N. L. Gage (Ed.), *The Psychology of Teaching Methods* (75th NSSE Yearbook). Chicago: University of Chicago Press, 1976.

Cross, K. P. *Accent on Learning: Improving Instruction and Reshaping the Curriculum*. San Francisco: Jossey-Bass, 1976.

Cross, K. P. "The Adult Learner." Paper presented at meeting of the American Association for Higher Education, Chicago, 1978.

Dressel, P. L., and Thompson, M. M. *Independent Study: A New Interpretation of Concepts, Practices, and Problems.* San Francisco: Jossey-Bass, 1973.

Eble, K. E. *The Craft of Teaching: A Guide to Mastering the Professor's Art.* San Francisco: Jossey-Bass, 1976.

Egan, G. *Interpersonal Living: A Skills/Contract Approach to Human-Relations Training in Groups.* Monterey, Calif.: Brooks/Cole, 1976.

Fraser, S., and others. "Two, Three, or Four Heads Are Better Than One: Modification of College Performance by Peer-Monitoring." *Journal of Educational Psychology,* 1977, *69,* 101-108.

Gage, N. L., and Berliner, D. C. *Educational Psychology.* (2nd ed.) Chicago, Ill.: Rand McNally, 1979.

Gagné, R. M. *The Conditions of Learning.* (3rd ed.) New York: Holt, Rinehart and Winston, 1977.

Gazda, G. M., and others. *Human Relations Development: A Manual for Educators.* (2nd ed.) Boston: Allyn & Bacon, 1977.

Hannah, L. S., and Michaels, J. U. *A Comprehensive Framework for Instructional Objectives: A Guide to Systematic Planning and Evaluation.* Reading, Mass.: Addison-Wesley, 1977.

Harrow, A. J. *A Taxonomy of the Psychomotor Domain.* New York: McKay, 1972.

Hendricks, G., and Fadiman, J. (Eds.). *Transpersonal Education.* Englewood Cliffs, N.J.: Prentice-Hall, 1976.

Houston, J. "Putting the First Man on Earth." *Saturday Review,* February 22, 1975, pp. 28-33.

Hyman, R. T. *Ways of Teaching.* Philadelphia: Lippincott, 1970.

Johnson, D. W., and Johnson, R. T. *Learning Together and Alone: Cooperation, Competition, and Individualization.* Englewood Cliffs, N.J.: Prentice-Hall, 1974.

Johnson, K. R., and Ruskin, R. S. *Behavioral Instruction: An Evaluative Review.* Washington, D.C.: American Psychological Association, 1977.

Joyce, B., and Weil, M. *Models of Teaching.* Englewood Cliffs, N.J.: Prentice-Hall, 1972.

Kagan, N. "Influencing Human Interaction: Fifteen Years with IPR." Unpublished paper, Michigan State University, 1978.

Kagerer, R. "Toward an Affective Outcome of Higher Education." *Journal of Educational Measurement,* 1974, *11,* 203-208.

Karp, D. A., and Yoels, W. C. "The College Classroom: Some Observations on the Meaning of Student Participation." *Sociology and Social Research,* 1976, *60,* 421-439.

Keller, F. S. "Good-Bye Teacher...." *Journal of Applied Behavior Analysis,* 1968, *1,* 79-89.

Lindquist, J. (Ed.). *Designing Teacher Improvement Programs.* Berkeley, Calif.: Pacific Soundings, 1978.

Lorayne, H., and Lucas, J. *The Memory Book.* New York: Ballantine, 1974.

McClintock, E., and Sonquist, J. A. "Cooperative Task-Oriented Groups in a College Classroom: A Field Application." *Journal of Educational Psychology,* 1976, *68,* 588-596.

McConnell, J. V. "Confessions of a Textbook Writer." *American Psychologist,* 1978, *33,* 159-169.

McKeachie, W. J. *Teaching Tips: A Guidebook for the Beginning College Teacher.* (7th ed.) Lexington, Mass.: Heath, 1978.

McLeish, J. "The Lecture Method." In N. L. Gage (Ed.), *The Psychology of Teaching Methods* (75th NSSE Yearbook). Chicago: University of Chicago Press, 1976.

Menges, R. J. *The Intentional Teacher: Controller, Manager, Helper.* Monterey, Calif.: Brooks/Cole, 1977.

Merrill, M. D. "Classes of Instructional Outcomes." In M. D. Merrill (Ed.), *Instructional Design: Readings.* Englewood Cliffs, N.J.: Prentice-Hall, 1971.

Merrill, M. D., and Tennyson, R. D. *Teaching Concepts: An Instructional Design Guide.* Englewood Cliffs, N.J.: Educational Technology, 1977.

Messick, S., and Associates. *Individuality in Learning: Implications of Cognitive Styles and Creativity for Human Development.* San Francisco: Jossey-Bass, 1976.

Miller, J. P. *Humanizing the Classroom: Models of Teaching in Affective Education.* New York: Praeger, 1976.

Morris, P. "Practical Strategies for Human Learning and Remembering." In M. J. A. Howe (Ed.), *Adult Learning: Psychological Research and Applications.* New York: Wiley, 1977.

Nold, E., and Cannom, S. "A Program Named 'Mustard'." *People's Computers,* 1977, *6,* 28.

Norman, D. A. *Memory and Attention.* New York: Wiley, 1976.

Northwestern University. *Undergraduate Catalogue.* Evanston, Ill.: Northwestern University, 1977-78.

Ornstein, R. E. *The Psychology of Consciousness.* (2nd ed.) San Francisco: W. H. Freeman, 1976.

Payne, D. A. *The Assessment of Learning: Cognitive and Affective.* Lexington, Mass.: Heath, 1974.

Platt, G., Parsons, T., and Kirshstein, R. "Faculty Teaching Goals, 1968-1973." *Social Problems,* 1976, *24,* 298-307.

Ringness, T. A. *The Affective Domain in Education.* Boston: Little, Brown, 1975.

Rockart, J. F., and Morton, M. S. S. *Computers and the Learning Process in Higher Education.* New York: McGraw-Hill, 1975.

Samples, B. *The Metaphoric Mind.* Reading, Mass.: Addison-Wesley, 1976.

Seidner, C. J. "Teaching with Simulation and Games." In N. L. Gage (Ed.), *The Psychology of Teaching Methods* (75th NSSE Yearbook). Chicago: University of Chicago Press, 1976.

Simpson, E. J. "The Classification of Educational Objectives: Psychomotor Domain." *Illinois Teacher of Home Economics,* 1966, *10,* 110-144.

Smith, A. *Powers of Mind.* New York: Ballantine, 1976.

Smith, D. G. "College Classroom Interactions and Critical Thinking." *Journal of Educational Psychology,* 1977, *69,* 180-190.

Tennessee Higher Education Commission. *The Competent College Student.* Nashville: Tennessee Higher Education Commission, 1977.

Tiemann, P. W., and Markle, S. M. "Remodeling a Model: An Elaborated Hierarchy of Types of Learning." *Educational Psychologist,* 1973, *10,* 147-158.

Witkin, H. A., and others. "Field-Dependent and Field-Independent Cognitive Styles and Their Educational Implications." *Review of Educational Research,* 1977, *47,* 1-64.

31

Thomas F. Clark

Individualized
Education

Individualized education is the teaching-learning process that responds to the widest range of individual differences. It is often confused with independent study, since the student may work alone on parts of the program. But whereas *independent study* is defined by the fact of working alone and may actually utilize standardized study materials, *individualized programs* are intentionally flexible and multifaceted and may involve lectures or group activities if these suit the needs of the individual student. Individualized education has been implemented most widely in those institutions that have been specifically designed to serve "nontraditional" students; however, it is increasingly used with "traditional" students in "traditional" institutions because of its adaptability and positive results.

This chapter begins with a case study illustrating the principles of individualized education. (The case is drawn from the files of an actual program, with only the names of the student and the program changed.) The case also illustrates one model for student orientation and advising in individualized programs that addresses the developmental issues discussed in Part One of this book by Havighurst and Chickering. Gilligan, and Perry. The chapter then describes how a traditional course can be designed to recognize a variety of individual differences among students. It next discusses the different roles that faculty members must play in individualizing instruction. And finally, it speaks to practical administrative and faculty concerns about costs, time and work load commitments, and the effectiveness of individualized education.

An Illustrative Student and Program

Margaret Snow is 51 years of age. During the time she and her husband were raising their two boys, she worked with him in his hardware store as well as managing the family's household affairs. When both boys were in high school, she began taking courses in secretarial studies, accounting, and business mathematics—first in the local high school's adult evening education program and then at the community college in a nearby town. These educational experiences prepared her to take on greater responsibility in the family's expanding business. But when her younger son graduated from high school and entered the family business, Margaret, freed now to do other things, took a position as secretary to the chief psychiatrist at the state mental hospital in the area. At about the same time, she joined a community theater company and soon was asked to assume primary responsibility for its advertising, ticket sales, and fiscal management.

By the end of her second year at the state hospital, Margaret was promoted to administrative assistant to the chief psychiatrist. This position gave her the opportunity to attend staff meetings with psychiatrists, clinical psychologists, social workers, rehabilitation specialists, occupational therapists, and nurse supervisors. She asked and was permitted to observe intake, diagnostic, and therapy sessions with patients. She began attending state conferences and training workshops on new treatment methods, and she also enrolled in three community college courses: Introduction to Psychology, Introduction to Sociology, and Personality Theory (admission to this latter class was difficult because it was listed as an advanced course). On her own initiative she began reading about personality disorders, consulting her boss about titles and borrowing books from the hospital's staff library. This whole broad area of intellectual inquiry was new for Margaret. Although the reading was difficult, she knew the terminology from her work and therefore found the experience useful and rewarding. During this same period, she continued her work in community theater, serving as the company's official business manager. Asked to read for a part in Giraudoux's *The Madwoman of Chaillot,* she discovered that with hard work and good direction she could act—she even got a favorable review from the critic of the local paper.

While Margaret was having these new and rewarding professional and personal experiences, other aspects of her personal life presented difficulties. The family business was a continuing success—mainly through the energetic efforts of her son but her husband, who had had an alcohol problem for many years, had become a chronic drinker. Moreover, he resented her successes and let her know in no uncertain terms that he thought her place was at home. Despite her repeated requests that he seek professional assistance or join Alcoholics Anonymous, he denied that he had an alcohol problem. This problem and his attitude toward her work had created significant tension in their relationship and caused her a great deal of anxiety.

All Margaret's personal and professional experiences led her now to want a college degree. Exploration of admissions requirements, degree program requirements, and class schedules at a number of institutions in her locale revealed that if she wanted to continue working her only option was a continuing education program at a state university. An appointment with an official at the university convinced her that this option was not feasible because it was estimated that if she took courses in the evening—the only time available—it would take her approximately six years to complete a B.S. degree.

The Lifelong Learning Program. Still intent on pursuing her education, Margaret heard of an experimental Lifelong Learning Program sponsored by a university located eighty-five miles from her home. The program offered individualized learning through a teaching-learning mode called *contract learning.* Furthermore, the catalogue indicated that learning from work and life experience that could be articulated and documented could be evaluated for possible college credit. If assessed by a faculty committee as appropriate to the student's degree program, it could provide advanced standing—much like course credit transferred from another institution. Margaret studied the catalogue and decided that this program well suited her needs. She found out when information sessions were scheduled and went to one on a Saturday morning. At first she did not understand all the terms the program's representative used in describing the program, but later he answered a wide variety of questions, which clarified things considerably. The session was all the more useful because Margaret had an opportunity to review several sample student learning contracts and several illustrative portfolios containing descriptions, documentation, and expert evaluations of the students' learning from work and life experience. By the end of the session, she decided that she would apply for admission to the program.

Margaret was admitted to the Lifelong Learning Program. At the weekend orientation required for new students, the processes integral to the program were discussed. The first session was devoted to a discussion of the concept of individualized education. The faculty member who directed the program explained that individualized education was a way the university tried to respond to individual differences in students, that an individualized program of study *started* with the student. He further stated that individualized education assumes that people are different. They differ in a number of ways that affect learning but are frequently overlooked by educational practice, including chronological age, sex, race, socioeconomic class, stage of ego development, learning objectives, motivation for learning, the nature of past experience with formal education, level of basic skill development, and preferred learning style. All of these characteristics help define the learner; they helped Margaret clarify her needs and interests as she confronted the learning experience.

The faculty member then outlined several components of the educational process that can be individualized through a learning contract:

The first component is the student's objectives. Margaret's articulation of her own educational goals and purposes would be a critical factor in determining the other aspects of her learning contract. Of course, there might also be areas to be negotiated between her objectives and those of the faculty member or institution.

The second component concerns the places where learning is to be pursued. The contract process encourages the use of field placements and internships; sometimes travel may be employed. These settings are frequently the focus of learning when institutional policy recognizes and accepts the fact that learning can occur in a variety of settings other than a classroom.

The third component to be individually structured is time. The pace at which the learning is pursued as well as the length of time allotted for completion of a single learning activity or series of learning activities can be negotiated according to the individual's personal and professional commitments and subsequently recorded in the contract. In a completely flexible program, one can study full- or half-time, in blocks of one to six months, and thus work out an individual schedule. However, many institutions offer the contract option within a traditional semester, trimester, or 4-1-4 academic calendar. The Lifelong Learning Program operated on a schedule of four twelve-week quarters, so students were encouraged to conceive of learning contracts that were twelve weeks in duration, although it was explained that the contract could be extended or amended to suit specific needs.

The fourth component to be individualized is the content. The orientation workshop leader explained that some institutions use the learning contract to individualize a specific course, while others use it to provide each student with an opportunity to approach the content in whatever way makes most sense to that individual and his or her faculty instructor or mentor. Frequently, contracts call for learning within disciplinary frameworks. However, learning activities may also be interdisciplinary, thematic, or problem-oriented. Or they may be professional or vocational, planned specifically to integrate practice with theory. The learning contract has repeatedly demonstrated its usefulness in accommodating these new content configurations negotiated by faculty member and student. In the Lifelong Learning Program's orientation workshop, Margaret learned that with the contract approach she could work in a disciplinary area or pursue her study using any of the aforementioned organizing frameworks.

Learning activities and learning resources are the fifth and sixth components of the individualized process. The opportunity to pursue the study of a subject area in a variety of different ways normally follows the recognition by faculty that effective mastery of a subject can occur in places and ways other than solely in the classroom. Thus, a student could work toward understanding a topic by reading books and attending lectures, by using self-directed programmed materials, by using media-based materials such as films, audio-tutorial aids, or television programs, or by pursuing a field experience or internship in combination with appropriate readings. Margaret discovered that this wide range of available learning activities offered her a good opportunity to match her learning program to her needs.

The director of the Lifelong Learning Program explained that the faculty member and student must confront several questions:

1. What do I (the student) want to learn and why?
2. How do I (the student) learn best?
3. What learning activities are the most appropriate for the area of study that is to be engaged?
4. What are the most appropriate learning resources for the agreed-upon learning activities?
5. Do I (the faculty member) have the advising skills necessary to assist the student in assessing his or her objectives, and am I aware of the variety of available resources and appropriate kinds of learning activities?

The seventh component of the individualized process is the evaluation of the student's work and the effectiveness of the faculty member. The learning contract makes evaluation an explicit part of the learning process. Most faculty believe that evaluation is an integral and ongoing part of learning; therefore, evaluation is usually both formative and summative and is a process in which both the faculty member and the student participate. Margaret noted that a carefully constructed learning contract has a section specifying the methods to be used in evaluating the student's work, the criteria for evaluation, and the evidence or indicators that will show whether the work has been completed and what level of proficiency has been achieved. The speaker pointed out that active participation by the student in the evaluation process is a goal for which many faculty strive. Some faculty members ask the student to present, either orally or in writing, an evaluation of his or her own work and of the faculty member's work as well. Some contracts are very specific in citing the qualitative and quantitative criteria that a student's work must meet in order to receive a specific grade.

The eighth and final component of the process of individualized contract learning is *shared* authority and responsibility. A learning contract results from a negotiation, or series of negotiations, between a faculty member and a student. At this point, one new student asked how realistic this concept was in practice—citing several examples of situations in which he believed he had been penalized for disagreeing with a professor. The speaker reviewed several sample contracts to draw attention to the fact that the learning contract reflects the reality of shared authority and has proven itself effective in helping students become increasingly self-directed. The process is no way seeks to diminish the authority of the faculty member as expert educator-evaluator, but it does draw a sharp distinction between *authoritative* and *authoritarian.* At the same time, it seeks to help the student take primary responsibility for his or her learning.

    Assessing Individual Interests and Goals. The second session of the orientation was devoted to exploring individual differences and their implications for the student's teaching-learning experience. Prior to the orientation, Margaret, like other participants, had received a packet containing detailed information about the Lifelong Learning Program and a number of tasks to complete. She was asked to do the following:

1. Read Gail Sheehy's *Passages* and
2. Write a self-profile addressing the following points:
    a. Reason(s) for seeking admission to the Lifelong Learning Program;
    b. Projected concentration in the proposed individual degree program;
    c. Current point in Erikson's Life Cycle (as defined by Sheehy);
    d. Description of current career goals and how the B.A. or B.S. degree will enable the attainment of these goals.

Each new student was asked to make the profile available to the Lifelong Learning Program director one week prior to the orientation so that the document could be copied and shared with an appropriate faculty mentor. Each profile provided valuable information for the faculty member to use in helping the student construct an individual degree program and first learning contract.

    In this second session, Margaret first was asked to complete Kolb and Frye's Learning Style Inventory. She discovered that according to this instrument she was an "Accommodator." The description of this learning style read as follows:

> The Accommodator has the opposite learning strengths of the Assimilator. This person is best at Concrete Experience (CE) and Active Experimentation (AE). This person's greatest strength lies in doing things—in carrying out plans and experiments—and involving oneself in new experiences. This person tends to be more of a risk-taker than people with the other three learning styles. We have labeled this person "Accommodator" because this person tends to excel in those situations where one must adapt oneself to specific immediate circumstances. In situations where a theory or plan does not fit the "facts," this person will most likely discard the plan or theory. This person tends to solve problems in an intuitive trial-and-error manner, relying heavily on other people for information rather than on one's own analytic ability. The Accommodator is at ease with people but is sometimes seen as impatient and "pushy." This person's educational background is often in technical or practical fields such as business. In organizations people with this learning style are found in "action-oriented" jobs, often in marketing or sales [D. A. Kolb, *Learning Style Inventory Technical Manual* (Boston: McBer, 1976), p. 6].

Margaret found the activity helpful, since she had never given much thought to the fact that individuals learn in different ways and that they have preferred learning styles.

Following a discussion of learning style differences, a new speaker delivered what Margaret found to be a stimulating presentation regarding ego development—referring frequently to the work of Jane Loevinger. (See Chapter Two.) After this presentation, each student was given a chart and asked to think about his or her own ego development. Margaret studied the descriptions on the chart and ranked herself as both Conformist and Conscientious in the areas of Character Development, Interpersonal Style, Conscious Preoccupations, and Cognitive Style. She noted, however, that she believed herself to be moving to the Autonomous stage in the areas of Character Development and Interpersonal Style.

The faculty member leading the session then asked participants to re-read the essays they had written, prior to the orientation, on their places in the life cycle. Next he asked them to think about issues contained in the essay and to try to relate those issues to the characteristics identified on the ego development chart and the Learning Style Inventory. The group leader explained that each of these sets of descriptive characteristics could help one to think more comprehensively about himself or herself and, therefore, more realistically about his or her learning. The speaker also emphasized that these exercises should not be thought of as comprehensive diagnoses but rather as catalysts for thinking about one's development and learning.

The participants were then asked to form five-person groups—each of which was joined by a faculty member present at the session. Each individual in the group—including the faculty member who served as the group's facilitator—shared with others a sense of what characterized his or her development in terms of life cycle, ego development, and learning style. Margaret, reluctant, like the others, to be the first to speak, finally volunteered some of the characteristics that she believed typified her development. She indicated that she was wrestling with a number of "midlife" issues and explained why she thought of herself in particular ways in regard to the several aspects of her ego development. The individuals in her group were quite diverse in terms of life cycle issues and preferred learning style, but all had rated themselves as somewhere between Conformist and Conscientious in terms of various stages of ego development.

Following this activity, there was a period of unscheduled time. Participants were told that they would think about their degree plan since this was to be the focus of the activity scheduled after dinner.

After dinner, participants organized themselves into small groups on the basis of their academic interests. Margaret joined others whose primary interest was the social sciences. Each person indicated what he or she wanted or thought should be included as component parts of a degree program in the social sciences. Each was asked to refer to the *Lifelong Learning Program Guide,* which contained clear statements regarding the university's requirements for particular degrees. When it was Margaret's turn to speak, she summarized her background, her reasons for deciding to return to college, her career goals, and the fact that she wanted a degree program with a concentration in social psychology—with an emphasis on counseling theory and practice. Margaret indicated that she had learned a lot about how a state mental hospital operates and was learning more about psychotherapy, but had not formally studied the different theories of counseling. She had a specific interest in working with individuals who were experiencing "normal" problems, as opposed to those who required hospitalization. The faculty member working with this group drew attention to the fact that the university's degree programs had specific area or distribution requirements and asked the students in turn if they had considered how they intended to meet these requirements. Margaret explained that the only problem she foresaw was that of having to commute a long distance to attend the courses that she wanted to take in several subjects, particularly literature and biology. The faculty member explained that these courses could be taken at the community college near her home as learning activities in several of her future learning contracts.

By the end of the first day of the orientation, Margaret felt very positive about her decision to enroll in the Lifelong Learning Program. She had gained insight into her own development, begun to understand individualized education, become acquainted with several students in the program and faculty associated with it, and received some useful information and criticism regarding her proposed degree program.

Planning Learning Contracts. The next morning was devoted to the formulation of each student's first learning contract. It was explained that the learning contract represents the written record of the student's negotiation with a faculty member about the purpose and plan of study. The process begins with a discussion of who the student is, what the student's goals and objectives are, why the student wants to study particular content and skill areas, how the learning will be accomplished, what resources will be employed, how the learning will be evaluated, and how much credit will be awarded. Similarly, the faculty member indicates what expertise he or she possesses, the alternative ways in which the learning can be accomplished, alternative resources that may be employed, and what is expected in terms of the student's performance. The process assumes that there are two active participants—not an active teacher and a passive student. This transaction between student and faculty member is the essential component of the contract learning process.

Although institutional practices vary somewhat, most learning contracts have four parts: (1) a statement describing the student's long-range purposes, goals, or objectives; (2) a statement describing the student's specific objectives for the period of time in which the particular contract is in effect; (3) a statement specifying the learning activities in which the student will engage—including the content areas and skills to be mastered, the mode of study to be employed, the learning resources to be used, the length of time allotted, and the amount of credit the institution will award upon satisfactory completion of the learning activities; and (4) a statement of the methods and criteria or standards that will be used to evaluate the student's performance. Depending on institutional practice, the section describing the methods and criteria for evaluation may not include specific grades. This was an option in the Lifelong Learning Program. The speaker pointed out that it was important to note that as complete and precise as the written contract may be, it is at best only a limited representation of the teaching-learning process.

Following this explanation, the large group again broke into the small academic interest groups. The faculty mentor who met with Margaret's group was a psychologist. He first asked members of the group to think about their objectives and to write a brief statement of their long-range objectives. The faculty member asked each individual to refer to the statements written as part of the pre-orientation assignment. The next task was to write a statement describing specific objectives for the first learning contract. A number of illustrative samples for each task were provided by the faculty mentor. After these two tasks had been completed, each student was asked to share his or her statement with the group.

Following a discussion of each person's general and specific purposes, which generated ideas and criticism from the faculty member and other members of the group, each person was asked to think about the learning activities that could achieve the objectives that had been articulated. The students were asked to think about the profile that each had generated with the Learning Style Inventory. After an initial sharing of ideas for learning activities and a group discussion of each person's ideas, the faculty mentor arranged thirty-minute appointments with each student. It was suggested that students use the two and a half hours outside the appointment to examine sample portfolios that other students had submitted to document their learning from work and life experience. Further, it was suggested that, if time permitted, each student might begin the process of outlining his or her own portfolio. If no portfolio was to be submitted, the time was free for further thought about the degree program and first contract.

Margaret observed that her faculty mentor asked good questions about her learning from the courses she had taken in psychology and sociology as well as her learning from experience at the hospital. He also probed her understanding of theories and methods of counseling and therapy. She told him that she had read a lot about Freud and psychoanalysis as well as a great deal about behavior modification. He listened carefully to her responses. He then suggested that she combine her objective of learning about theories and methods of counseling and therapy with the observation and practice that her work setting provided. These learning activities seemed to meet her personal needs and professional responsibilities perfectly. The learning activities were well suited to her preferred learning style because they involved concrete experience. They were also intended to extend her repertoire of learning styles by engaging her in the study of theory, which involved a great deal of abstract conceptualization. As her ideas began to take the shape of specific learning activities, she became eager to get started.

The discussion turned next to the methods, criteria or standards, and products or evidence that would be used to evaluate the learning activities. Margaret was somewhat concerned about the amount of reading the faculty member recommended and the number of papers he thought she should write, but the faculty member convinced her that these were important activities and should be attempted. He also cautioned her that she should let him know immediately if she could not locate specific readings, or if she were experiencing difficulty in understanding concepts, or in writing her first paper. Before Margaret completed the interview, she discussed a topic that she had dealt with in her essay regarding life cycle issues—her husband's alcohol addiction. She told the mentor that this was an area that she wanted to study in a future contract. She had enjoyed the time with the mentor and felt that their discussion had produced a series of learning activities germane to her general and specific purposes.

Following the individual appointments with the faculty mentor and the negotiation and drafting of the learning contracts, the small group was reconvened for the purpose of discussing the Learning Activities and Evaluation sections of the contracts. Margaret Snow's first learning contract is shown in Figure 1.

Margaret found the two-day orientation to the university's Lifelong Learning Program extremely informative and productive. She had learned a great deal about herself and had developed several tangible "products"—a draft of her degree program, an outline of the portfolio documenting learning from work and life experience, and an individual learning contract, which she had actively helped create.

As the development of Margaret's individualized learning contract demonstrates, she and the faculty mentor negotiated a learning experience that started with her own interests and needs, utilized her work setting as an integral component of the learning, used a supervisor from the work setting (the head of the "rehabilitation team") as a resource for purposes of evaluation, employed disciplinary as well as problem-oriented modes of study, and used community resources (the "Dialogue on Drugs") as a central learning activity. While the process of negotiating an individual contract such as hers is relatively standardized, in terms of questions asked, the outcome is unique. The learning activities that could be used to meet particular student objectives are myriad. When effec-

Figure 1. A Learning Contract

Student's Name (Type Last Name First) Snow, Margaret	Social Security Number		Contract # 1
Address	Contract begins on 11/15/76	Contract ends on 2/15/77	Final Contract?
	Credit: 12		Full-Time ☒ Half-Time ☐
Telephone: Home Work	Check Type External Resource Used		
Mentor's Name (Type Last Name First)	Adjunct Faculty ☐ Internship ☐ Overseas ☐ Tutor ☒	Course Elsewhere ☒ ISP ☐ Residency ☐ Other ☐	Field Study ☒ Modules ☐ TV Course ☐

Give detailed description of (a) student's general purposes, plans, or aspirations; (b) specific purposes of this contract; (c) learning activities to be undertaken and schedule by which they will be pursued; and (d) methods and criteria for evaluation. Use the underlined as headings for the four sections of the contract, and attach additional pages as necessary.

A. Student's General Purposes:

The student's general purpose is to complete the work necessary to attain the bachelor's degree with a concentration in the areas of social psychology and counseling theory and practice.

B. Specific Purposes:

The specific purposes of this contract are as follows:
1. To engage in a comprehensive study of several major counseling theories and methods;
2. To integrate this study with her casework and the observation of patients at Middletown State Hospital;
3. To describe and analyze the treatment methodology which is being employed with the patients with whom she is working;
4. To describe and analyze her own theory of individual counseling and to describe her own method or style of counseling;
5. To gain greater understanding of drug dependence as a human problem.

C. Learning Activities:

The student's study of counseling theory and practice will include reading and study of the following:

Theories of Counseling, B. Steffire

Techniques of Counseling, J. Warters

These readings will provide an overview of this area of study. More specific readings will be completed in the following three specific areas:

Nondirective or Client-Centered Therapy:
  Client-Centered Therapy, Carl Rogers
Gestalt Therapy:
  Gestalt Therapy Verbatim, Frederick S. Perls
  In and Out of the Garbage Pail, Frederick S. Perls
Transactional Analysis:
  Transactional Analysis and Psychotherapy: A Systematic Individual and Social Psychiatry, Eric Berne
  I'm Okay–You're Okay: A Practical Guide to Transactional Analysis, Thomas A. Harris

A brief paper which describes the important aspects of each theory will be prepared by the student as she proceeds with the reading. In order to integrate this theoretical study with her ongoing work with schizophrenic patients as a member of a "rehabilitation team" at Middletown State Hospital, she will do the following with active tutorial assistance by the supervising psychiatrist:

1. Read *Asylums* by Irving Goffman and write a critique of Middletown State Hospital in light of Goffman's critical criteria;
2. Write four case studies which describe and analyze the treatment methodology which is being employed at the hospital with these patients.

Upon the completion of these assignments and through bi-weekly discussions with the mentor, the student should be prepared to present orally or in writing a description and analysis of her own theory and method of counseling. This presentation regarding theory should be comprehensive in nature and contain a well-developed rationale which explains her methodology.

In order to attain greater understanding of drug dependence as a human problem, the student will attend a seminar titled "Dialogue on Drugs" – a series of six workshops sponsored jointly by Orange County Community College and the New York State Drug Addiction Control Commission. After completing the seminar, the student will present a paper detailing her learnings from this experience.

D. Evaluation

Methods of Evaluation
1. Bi-weekly discussions of readings and case studies with the mentor;
2. The position papers on the theories and methodologies which are under study;
3. The paper analyzing the organizational dynamics of Middletown State Hospital;
4. The four (4) written case studies which are descriptive and analytic in nature;
5. The oral or written presentation of the student's own theory and method of individual counseling;
6. The paper on learning gained from participation in the seminar "Dialogue on Drugs."
7. An evaluation of her work with schizophrenic patients from Dr. _____, the field supervisor.

Criteria for Evaluation:
The student should demonstrate, through written and oral presentations, an understanding of the information, theories, and methodologies studied in the readings.

The student should demonstrate the ability to apply theory to practical situations through the case study presentations and the descriptive analysis of the hospital as a rehabilitation setting.

(continued on next page)

Figure 1 *(Continued)*

The student should be able to identify, describe, and evaluate her own theory of individual counseling.

The student should be able to demonstrate her learning regarding the current status of drug dependence and the success of different treatment methodologies.

The student should be able to demonstrate an understanding of schizophrenia as a phenomenon and an understanding of current rehabilitation practices to the satisfaction of her tutor, Dr. _____ .

Signature   *Date*

Student _____   _____

Mentor _____   _____

tively carried out, the contract process is characterized by sensitivity to individual differences, candor, intentionality, accountability, and closure. It should be pointed out that the contract development process can be a valuable learning experience for the faculty member as well as for the student.

Individualized Education in the Context of Groups

When a faculty member decides to individualize the educational experience for members of a class or seminar, a process similar in dynamics to the one just described for the individual student can be used. This process, sometimes called *contract teaching,* has a number of characteristics that should be noted.

Let us first spend a moment thinking about the group. The individuals who enroll in a particular class, seminar, or residency normally share a common interest in the subject under consideration. However, their levels of interest may differ, depending on their individual needs or reasons for engaging in the experience. The individuals who make up the group also bring diverse perspectives, values, and experience. This diversity is particularly apparent when the group is made up of older, "nontraditional" college students. When carefully orchestrated, this diversity can enliven and enrich the learning process for all. Furthermore, members of the group, when properly motivated, can offer psychological support to each other, engage in mutual criticism, and participate in both formative and summative evaluation of each other's work. Thus, the group can in many ways make the individual's educational experience more comprehensive than that obtained in the one-to-one encounter. The qualifier "properly motivated" is worth noting. If the group is not properly motivated or structured, few, if any, of the aforementioned benefits of the group learning experience will occur. In fact, in the typical class grouping, little attention is paid to individual differences; everyone hears the same lectures, reads the same books, takes the same examinations, and so on; perhaps the only element in the course that is individualized is the choice of topic for a final paper.

Now let us consider the individual and his or her needs. With regard to the learning experience, each individual in the group may have different objectives, need an individual pace or timing for the learning, desire different content emphases, or want to produce a unique outcome or product. Furthermore, students may have different learning styles and be at different stages of ego development. These individual needs are present in most groups, whether they are heeded or not.

The following diagram illustrates the two sets of interactive characteristics just described.

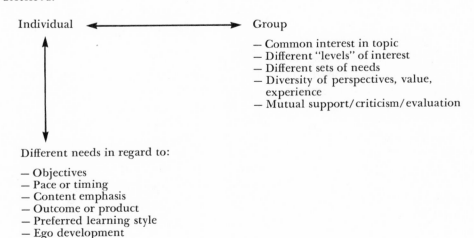

Individual ↔ Group
— Common interest in topic
— Different "levels" of interest
— Different sets of needs
— Diversity of perspectives, value, experience
— Mutual support/criticism/evaluation

Different needs in regard to:

— Objectives
— Pace or timing
— Content emphasis
— Outcome or product
— Preferred learning style
— Ego development

There are many ways in which a faculty member can facilitate individualized learning in the context of a group. However, certain basic steps are ordinarily followed in the individualization process.

The first step is an individual needs analysis or inventory. The questions included in such an exercise vary, but normally they address the following basic aspects of learning: (1) "Why are you taking this course?" is a typical question used to ascertain the individual student's purposes. (2) "What do you want to learn as a result of taking the course?" addresses the anticipated outcomes. (3) "What is your preferred learning style?" or "How do you learn best?" causes the student to think about differences in individual learning style and the matter of individual preference. (4) "How will you fulfill your purposes and achieve the stated outcomes?" directs attention toward the activities the student will pursue; a faculty member or other students can assist in answering this question by reviewing a series of alternative activities or strategies. (5) "How will you demonstrate that you have met your objective(s)?" concerns itself with the evidence as well as the methods to be used in evaluating the learning. (6) "How will the work or product(s) be evaluated?" raises related questions about the standards and evidence that will be utilized in the evaluation process. These sample questions are examples of those which can be used in conducting a needs analysis or inventory. The inventory can take the form of an interview, a preliminary assignment, or a brief paper and pencil exercise. Answers can be shared with only the faculty member, one other student, or the whole group.

The information generated from the individual needs analysis or inventory is useful in implementing the second step in the individualization process. Step 2 is the setting forth of an individual contract or plan that addresses each of the concerns queried in Step 1: (1) purposes, (2) outcomes, (3) preferred learning style or level of cognitive development, (4) learning activities, (5) demonstration of learning, and (6) methods, evidence, and standards to be employed in evaluation. The plan need not be lengthy, but it is important to go through the planning process, both because it brings intentionality to the learning process and because it identifies distinctive segments or parts of the whole.

Step 3 involves discussing the individual plans. From this, a decision as to the extent of individualization can be made. A faculty member with a group may decide that only some of the learning activities will be individualized. Or the decision may be made that the individual objectives are so unique that only a few group meetings will be held for the faculty member to present the theoretical information and data necessary to provide a common base for each member of the group. Step 3 can be accomplished efficiently if Steps 1 and 2 have been completed. The decisions made after the discussion of individual plans form the plan for the group. This group plan spells out not only what individual and shared activities will be pursued but also what is expected of each participant in the group—including the faculty member. This set of decisions regarding individual activities becomes a blueprint for the course.

The model described in the following paragraphs illustrates how the process of individualization can be implemented in the context of a group. This model is based on the experience of a faculty member who has been experimenting with ways of individualizing education for students in large class groups. His original motivation for experimenting was the continuing frustration he experienced when he was trying to "teach to the middle"; he kept discovering that the "middle" had disappeared and that what he confronted was in reality a collection of individuals—with a great array of differences that had significant impact on the teaching-learning process. This model is based on a fifteen-week semester. The following outline describes the process used in a course in Environmental Studies.

Pre-course Preparation: Individual Needs Analyses and Learning Plans. At the time of preregistration in the spring for the fall semester and in the fall for the spring semester, this faculty member schedules an organization meeting for students who intend to take this upper-division course in Environmental Studies. During the meeting, he explains briefly the range of content alternatives that the course might encompass and answers specific questions raised by individuals in the group. He distributes the Kolb and Frye Learning Style Inventory and also an inventory with clusters of descriptors that characterize different stages of ego development (this is based on Loevinger's work). He then distributes a questionnaire containing many of the questions noted above. The students are asked to complete the questionnaire and return it in one week if they intend to register for the course. The answers to these questions form the basis of the individual learning plan that each student is asked to propose—according to a sample format. The teacher asks the students to integrate the information gained from the Learning Style Inventory and ego development exercise with their responses to items on the questionnaire when drafting the individual learning plan. After he receives the questionnaires and the individual plans proposed by the students, he creates affinity groups around content areas reflecting students' interests. Students whose interests do not fit with any group will work independently. Next, he begins organizing appropriate learning resources—books, laboratory experiments, field placements, and internships.

Week 1: Review of Course Structure, Interests, and Resources. The first session is spent explaining the objectives of the course, the way the small groups will work, and the available learning resources. The teacher announces that during the week he will meet with each content affinity group to finalize learning plans. He then outlines how the course will work and how its general objectives will be met even though students are involved in a wide variety of learning activities. In this sample class, there are sixty individuals and seven content affinity groups of varying size. An eighth "group" is formed of individuals who have each elected an independent focus. The meeting with each group is about one hour in duration, so an equivalent of eight hours of group meetings is required for this part of the process.

Weeks 2-5: Information Core. In this four-week period, twelve lecture-discussion sessions are held to provide an overview of the topics included in the course and a common core of information for each student. The organization of the text is followed—the text for this class being *Living In The Environment: Concepts, Problems, and Alternatives* by G. Tyler Miller, Jr. Hence the information core is structured thus:

- Lesson 1: Man and Nature, An Overview (Population, Pollution, and Resources; Human Impact on the Earth).
- Lesson 2: Concepts of Ecology (Energy and the Environment; Ecosystem Structure, Function, and Changes).
- Lesson 3: Human Population Dynamics.
- Lesson 4: Population, Resources, and Pollution.
- Lesson 5: Urban Land Use.
- Lesson 6: Air Pollution.
- Lesson 7: Energy Resources and Nonrenewable Metal and Mineral Resources.
- Lesson 8: Water Resources.
- Lesson 9: Forest and Wilderness Land Use.
- Lesson 10: Pollution and Pollution Control.
- Lesson 11: Economics and Environment.
- Lesson 12: Politics and Environment; Environmental Ethics and Hope.

During this period, each student writes one short paper per week on an issue of his or her interest within the range of the topic(s) discussed during that week.

Weeks 6-13: Independent and Affinity Group Work. During this eight-week period, students work on the independent and small-group projects that were described in the individual learning plans. Since this course emphasizes the application of theory to practice and calls for student projects as the major outcome or "product," independent and small-group work is most appropriate. During this time the faculty member meets with the content affinity groups either once a week or every other week to discuss the progress of their work. Topics selected by the students for the content affinity groups included Population Control Methods and Birth Control Methods in the Future; The Automobile and Mass Transportation: An Evaluation of Alternatives; Energy Alternatives: Solar, Fusion, Geothermal, Wind, and Conservation; Economics and Pollution: A Study of the Connecticut River; Food Additives: An Evaluation; Endangered Wildlife Species; and The Problem of Feeding the World's Population: Evaluating Alternatives. Each topic in this list involves a number of moral and ethical choices. Implicit in each topic are questions of right and wrong, good and evil; thus an exploration of one's own values can become a significant aspect of each small-group study. This faculty member believes that the ongoing confrontation of these value questions and the activity of analyzing alternatives, making a choice, and writing a justification for the position are critical elements in the education of his students.

Weeks 14 and 15: Review. During this period the faculty member meets with each group to review the completed work of the group: lab reports, the results of field experiments, and the other "products" that individuals and small groups have produced. This faculty member calls the entire class together for one final meeting to provide a summary and synthesis of the accomplishments of the individual students and small content groups.

A number of models such as this can be used to achieve the objective of individualizing the student's educational experience and fostering self-directed learning in the context of a group. Most models require that the faculty member and the students perform a variety of roles and accept a variety of responsibilities.

Faculty Roles in Individualized Education

The implementation of individualized programs by an increasing number of colleges and universities has necessitated the development of new faculty roles and new educational functions. These new roles and functions require that faculty members develop new skills. For example, in order to negotiate a learning contract with an individual or group of individuals in an effective manner, a faculty member must demonstrate the ability to ask provocative questions; listen to what students are really saying; provide appropriate information regarding the institution; help the student structure an individualized set of learning activities; suggest a number of alternative approaches to the content to be studied; and specify the methods, criteria or standards, and types of evidence or indicators to be employed in the evaluation of the student's performance.

In the spring of 1975, faculty members from eight colleges and universities that use individualized contract learning convened in a workshop to discuss issues related to this and other nontraditional academic processes. They identified eight different roles they perform in the implementation of contract learning:

Facilitator/Counselor. These faculty pointed out that it is difficult, and in fact inappropriate, to lecture to students when working with them individually or in small groups. In these situations the faculty member is instead called upon to assume the role of facilitator. Similarly, it is almost impossible to avoid the counselor role when negotiating a learning contract because the student's educational interests and needs are only one aspect of his or her life—and these other responsibilities and needs inevitably enter into the discussion of learning activities. Clearly, this role of facilitator/counselor is essential to the contract learning process. Yet few faculty members have had formal training in graduate school to perform the role.

Broker/Negotiator. Faculty commented that the contract learning process causes them to become involved in negotiation. The contract process is rarely prescriptive, except when a course is included as a learning activity. Since the learning activities contained in a contract represent a balance between student needs and institutional requirements, each learning contract is a negotiated agreement unique to that individual. The role of negotiator is combined with that of broker because frequently the learning contract that is negotiated requires the faculty member to arrange a tutorial, internship, or field placement for the student with the institution or another agency.

Instructor/Tutor. This traditional faculty role is often performed in the individualized contract situation, specifically in cases in which the faculty member who negotiates the learning contract also serves as the primary source of instruction. Faculty often discover that they teach in new ways, however, particularly when the student is studying content that is interdisciplinary, multidisciplinary, problem-centered, thematic, or otherwise different from the course content they are currently teaching. Many faculty thus indicate that involvement in contract learning causes them to work as both subject matter specialists and as generalists in their field.

Evaluator. Faculty often report that the role of evaluator is more difficult in contract learning than in traditional programs. One reason is that the learning contract spells out so precisely the methods, criteria or standards, and evaluative indicators or evidence that must be followed. Beyond that, it requires a new orientation to have students actively involved in the evaluation of their own work and to hold evaluation conferences with students.

Administrator. When the student's contract contains learning activities overseen by tutors, field experience supervisors, and others, the faculty mentor must often assume an administrative role.

Developer of Learning Resources. The activities involved in this role include the location of field placements in a variety of settings including business and industry, the location of internships in social and environmental agencies, and the development of linkages with libraries, museums, radio and television stations, newspapers, theater groups, and other resources in the community that may provide important learning opportunities for the student.

Creator of Instructional Materials. This role is required when available materials are inappropriate for students' needs and new materials, such as annotated bibliographies or a set of readings in an interdisciplinary area, are unavailable elsewhere.

Planner of Individualized Degree Programs. This role emerges in many academic programs that use learning contracts because the student's entire degree program is individualized in the same way as a single learning contract. This role is similar to that of facilitator/counselor in terms of the skills required to perform it, but different in terms of the information about the institution with which the faculty adviser must be familiar in order to do an effective job. When it is adult students who are being advised, this role may become more comprehensive since educational planning often involves career planning as well. The process is thus more complex than helping the student plan the learning activities specified in a single contract.

Except for the roles of instructor and evaluator, this set of roles is new to most of faculty involved in individualized programs. Most of them have had to develop the skills required for these roles through intuition and "trial and error." Assistance in improving these skills—particularly those involved in advising students, evaluating learning activities, managing time and resources, and supervising field-based internships—can be provided by a faculty development program aimed at effective teaching and program operation.

Issues and Questions

The first question normally asked during a discussion of individualized education is whether this process is for everyone. The answer is yes, *if* one believes that the best learning starts with a student's goals and objectives and if students, faculty members, administrators, and thus institutions are committed to self-directed learning. Programs that seek to individualize the teaching-learning process exist from elementary school through graduate school.

A related question is "Do most adult as well as younger students welcome this learning approach?" The answer to this question is a qualified no. Many students have never been exposed to the approach. Others shy away from it because it seems more difficult than the traditional programs. Most teaching at all levels remains content-centered and teacher-directed, placing the learner in a passive role that often fosters a dependency relationship between teacher and student. Consequently, it may be difficult for some students to make the transition from passive to active participants in their own education—though several studies report that once the transition is made, students like and appreciate the individualized approach. It should also be noted that students who are by nature independent and highly motivated are initially more comfortable with the process than those who are not. Students who are highly dependent and conformist may take more time to become successful self-directed learners. This is why carefully planned and implemented orientation sessions and effective academic advising are so important to the success of the process.

The next question that faculty and administrators normally ask is "Do the students cannibalize the faculty?" Or, in other words, "How does individualized education affect the faculty's work load?" It is difficult to give a general answer since institutional practices and instructional costs per full-time-equivalent student vary so greatly. However, several observations can be made. First, faculty who have implemented individualized programs report that the total time involved in teaching the program is often no more than that involved in teaching regular lecture courses, and in those cases where the program does take more time, they report it seems worth the additional effort because they sense their students are more involved in learning. Second, the time involved in program planning is substantial, although less time is required later as students work independently on their projects. Thus, more time should be budgeted at the beginning for preparing materials and helping students with their plans. Rather than being expected to initiate a new program on an overload basis, faculty members should be allotted a load reduction, perhaps by one course, to organize the program and learn or sharpen needed skills through faculty development activities. Third, a number of individualized programs have been designed to be simultaneously more cost-effective and equal or higher in quality than "traditional" education. With too great an emphasis on cost-effectiveness, however, many of these programs have used highly unrealistic faculty-student ratios. In these programs, faculty have reported that the work load is greater and the job more demanding than a traditional teaching position. However, a number of institutions that have had approximately a decade of experience with individualized programs report that the increased use of groups to impart information, the increased effectiveness of orientation processes, the design of self-explanatory illustrative materials for use by students, and the refinement of administrative processes have all reduced the work load for faculty. Without such improvements, however, and without clearly stated expectations at the beginning of the process, the potential for "burn-out" is great.

Another question frequently asked is "Do individualized programs cost more or less than traditional ones, or are their costs about the same?" The answer is all of the above, since there are so many institutional variations in methods of calculating cost per full-time-equivalent student. Some institutions report that individualized education programs are less expensive than their traditional programs. Others report the programs require more faculty time and are therefore more expensive than conventional programs. Still others indicate the programs cost about the same as a traditional program. It is probably safe to say that the cost of instruction per full-time-equivalent student can be the same or less depending on how the program is structured. An unfortunately large number of institutions have initiated hastily instituted individualized contract learning for adults because they thought it was a more efficient or cheaper form of education and a way to stem the tide of decreasing enrollments. The question needs further study and more data before definitive answers can be given. The Program Effectiveness and Related Costs (PERC) Study offers an excellent research design and expertly analyzed data for individuals interested in such further study. The real question, however, is not simply "How much does it cost?" but "How much does it cost and how does it benefit the students involved?" The cost-benefit question is one to which continuing study must be directed. It is a critical question because simple assertions based on simplistic research designs will serve no one.

The last question—alluded to earlier in the chapter—is "How realistic is it for faculty to try to perform all eight of the roles described?" The answer is that a number of institutions differentiate functions so that a number of these roles are performed by specialists—particularly the roles of developer of learning resources, creator of instructional materials, and planner of individualized degree programs. In other institutions, all the roles described earlier are performed by faculty. In either case, it is important to point out the need for ongoing faculty and staff development activities. Lindquist's chapter later in this volume discusses these activities in detail, but it should be emphasized that faculty and staff development activities that are associated with individualized programs must focus not only on professional skill development but on the developmental issues discussed in Part One of this volume. With such activities, individualized programs can fulfill their common objectives—increased institutional responsiveness to individual differences, a more holistic approach to the educational process, increased integration of individual development with the teaching-learning process, and achievement of self-directed learning.

32

John S. Duley

Field Experience
Education

Like experiential learning of all kinds, field experience education engages students directly with the realities they are studying. Specifically, field experience education refers to the out-of-classroom and typically off-campus learning activities sponsored by educational institutions. In field experience education, the learner generally has greater responsibility for the management of the educational endeavor than is the case in the classroom, and usually has a specific task or work assignment as the major learning vehicle. Otherwise, field experience education may exhibit great diversity, ranging from a small project assigned within a classroom course to a full-time, year-long internship; from discipline-oriented field research to participation in the performing or graphic arts; and from preprofessional work experiences to general education programs of cross-cultural learning, career exploration, or service projects. One typology of field experience programs (Duley and Gordon, 1977, pp. v-vii) identifies eleven major categories of program:

Work Experience (Cooperative Education). The National Commission for Cooperative Education has defined cooperative education as "that education plan which integrates classroom experience and practical work experience in industrial, business, government, or service-type work situations in the community. The work experience constitutes a regular and essential element in the educative process, and some minimum amount of work experience and minimum standard of successful performance on the job are included in the requirements of the institution for a degree" (The National Commission for Cooperative Education, 1971, p. 3).

Career or Occupational Development. A student is assisted in finding a series of two or more placements which are chosen, in consultation with an advisor, to provide the opportunity for advancement in skills and experience related to a specific career. This is particularly useful in technological programs when classroom and on-the-job learning are closely integrated.

Institutional Analysis. "A student has a temporary period of supervised work that provides opportunities to develop skills, to test abilities and career interests, and to systematically examine institutional cultures in light of the central theoretical notions in a chosen academic field of study" (Zauderer, 1973, p. 1).

Preprofessional Training. A student serves in assigned responsibilities under the supervision of a professional in the field of education, medicine, law, social work, nursing, or ministry, putting the theory learned into practice, gaining skills in the profession, and being evaluated by his or her supervisor.

Service-Learning Internship. "Service-learning has been defined as: the integration of the accomplishment of a task which meets human need with conscious educational growth. A service-learning internship is designed to provide students responsibility to meet a public need and a significant learning experience within a public or private institution for a specified period of time, usually ten to fifteen weeks" (Sigmon, 1972, p. 2).

Academic Discipline/Career Integration. "A student is employed in a business, government, industry, service organization, or profession prior to entry into the educational institution. The faculty members and the educational institution provide the means of structured analysis and evaluation based on the academic discipline involved, integrating theory and practice and heightening the student's awareness and understanding of the world and his/her career in a conscious systematic fashion" (Cummins, 1975, p. 5).

Field Research/Participation in the Arts. A student undertakes an independent or group research project in the field under the supervision of a faculty member, applying the concepts and methods of an academic discipline such as geology, archaeology, geography, or sociology. Participating in the performing or graphic arts under the guidance of a qualified professional is similar for a student of the arts to field research for students in the sciences.

Social/Political Action. A student secures a placement, under faculty sponsorship, which provides an opportunity to be directly engaged in working for social change either through community organizing, political activity, research/action projects, or work with organizations seeking to bring about changes in the social order. A learning contract is usually made with a faculty sponsor to be fulfilled by the student in this type of experience.

Career Exploration. A student secures a supervised placement in business, government, industry, a service organization, or a profession in order to perform a useful service, to analyze the career possibilities of that placement, and to develop employment-related skills. The educational institution provides the means of structured reflection, analysis, and self-evaluation, the agency supervisor provides an evaluation of the student's work and career potential.

Personal Growth and Development. A student undertakes a program in an off-campus setting that is designed to further his or her personal growth and development, such as the wilderness survival programs of the Outward Bound Schools, an apprenticeship to an artist or a craftsman, residence in a house of a religious order for the development of his or her spiritual life, or participation in an established group psychological or human relations program.

Cross-Cultural Experiences. A student involves himself or herself in another culture or subculture of his or her own society in a deep and significant way, either as a temporary member of a family, a worker in that society, or a volunteer in a social agency, with the intention, as a participant observer, of learning as much as possible about that culture and his or her own.

Several educational goals are particularly appropriate to such programs, one or more of which will usually be found in most program descriptions. Among them are those of helping students achieve the following:

- Put theory into practice or develop the higher cognitive skills: learn how to apply, integrate, and evaluate knowledge or the methodology of a discipline or field of study.
- Acquire knowledge: engage in research, analyze the organizational structure of a firm or an agency.
- Acquire and develop specific skills: practice problem solving, interpersonal or group process skills, or psychomotor skills.
- Make progress in personal development: clarify values and increase self-understanding, self-confidence, and self-reliance.
- Learn how to learn independently: develop the ability to use experiential learning theory or engage in cross-cultural learning.
- Explore careers: develop self-understanding and acquire and use career exploration skills.
- Become responsible citizens: develop a firsthand understanding of the political and social action skills required for active citizenship.

It will be noted that many of the goals identified in the field experience education typology are consistent with the needs of adult learners.

A range of pedagogical and learning styles can be used in these programs. Table 1 describes a continuum of faculty roles from lecturer to resource person and evaluator, and of student roles from passive assimilator of information to independent learner. Pedagogical styles can be chosen to suit students' stages of development. This may mean either matching content and learning methods to their current needs and stage of development or allowing them to experiment with functioning at the next higher stage under conditions of low risk. This opportunity to experiment may facilitate the transition to the next stage of development. For example, by assuming more responsibility for their own learning projects, students may become more autonomous.

How does field experience education relate to the various stages and dimensions of adult development discussed in Part One of this book? The rest of the chapter seeks to illustrate potential relationships by describing different types of programs and pedagogical styles as they apply first to life cycle concerns, then to ego, moral, and intellectual development, interpersonal relationships, humanitarian concern, and finally, differences in learning style.

Relation to Life Cycle Concerns

Traditional College-Age Students. For late adolescents, 18 to 22 years old, the question of appropriate pedagogical styles and types of field experience programs is an individual one. What is the student ready to handle? It is clear from the numerous incomplete grades given for independent study that very few students at this stage, particularly as freshmen or sophomores, are ready for the use of a consultant pedagogical style (model

Table 1. Continuum of Pedagogical Styles in Experiential Learning

Models of Faculty and Student Roles and Sample Learning Experiences, from Most Dependent and Passive Student Role (1) to Most Independent and Active (9)

	1	2	3	4	5	6	7	8	9
Faculty Role	Disseminates information and evaluates learning	Acts as mentor and evaluator	Supervises and evaluates learning	Participates in learning project as colleague and evaluator	Designs or identifies learning environment and evaluates learning	Acts as consultant, adviser, and evaluator	Acts as facilitator, trainer, and evaluator	Acts as resource person and evaluator	Evaluates learning
Student Role	Assimilates information	Applies knowledge and skill under supervision	Receives instruction, observes demonstration, practices under close supervision at worksite	Participates jointly with faculty in research, study, or action projects	Applies knowledge and skill in simulations, role playing, or field placement and analyzes experience	Designs and carries out learning plan for research, independent study, or action projects	Develops self-understanding and interpersonal competence or other transferable skills	Makes conscious effort to apply experiential learning theory	Carries out a learning project and identifies and documents learning
Sample Learning Experience	Classroom instructions	Geology field trip	Cooperative education	Group research project	Service-learning internship	Career exploration	Environmental impact study	Cross-cultural learning experience	Portfolio method of claiming credit for prior learning

6 in Table 1). But it is difficult to predict students' ability to do independent work. Unfortunately, we do not yet have any simple method of determining the readiness of students to utilize the various pedagogical styles. Kolb's Learning Style Inventory can tell us how a person tends to approach a learning task, whether by direct experience, observation, and practice or by reading about and understanding the theory and applying the principles. But the pedagogical styles that I have identified for field experience education correspond not so much to learning styles as to degrees of maturity or independence. Since most faculty will not have the skill or testing resources available to determine these factors, the best solution may be to devise programs flexible enough to permit students to exercise as much independence as they are capable of.

Because 18- to 22-year-olds still have most of their lives ahead of them, any and all of the pedagogical styles may be useful to them at some time. Of particular value to students at this point in their life cycle will be those pedagogical styles and program types which assist in the developmental tasks of late adolescence. Three of these tasks are addressed directly by experiential education: (1) the need to achieve emotional independence of parents and other adults, (2) preparation for being on one's own, and (3) preparation for a career. A number of the program types and pedagogical styles offer opportunities to meet all three of these needs, while others address only one of them directly. Thus, Antioch's Cooperative Education Program on the Yellow Springs (Ohio) campus serves all three, since very few Antioch students live at home or on campus during their work terms. This is less true of cooperative education programs in large metropolitan areas where students are commuters and their jobs are in the same metropolitan area as at LaGuardia Community College in Long Island City, New York. Commuter students still learn the coping skills necessary to function effectively in the workplace and are prepared for a career, but they are helped less to achieve emotional independence and to learn to be self-sufficient than the students who leave home for job placements.

Early Adulthood. The period of early adulthood, from about age 22 to 35, is often described as the period fullest of opportunities for learning and emptiest of efforts to teach. The new responsibilities of this period, which provide so many occasions for learning, leave little time for formal learning. The important events of this age period are selecting a mate, starting a family, rearing children, managing a home, getting started in an occupation, and taking on civic responsibility. The types of experiential education programs that best serve these needs are personal growth and development programs, such as Parent Effectiveness Training and marital relations seminars, and on-the-job training programs offered by employers. As their children reach school age, young adults may develop interest in social or political action or in volunteer work, and find that a service-learning internship or a project in social or political action offered by a college or university is a good way to explore this interest. Such a learning experience is much more appropriate for this age person than a traditional classroom introductory course in social work or political science: Both its content and pedagogical style fit this stage of development better. At this age also the woman who quit school to marry and have.a family may become interested in completing her degree and may wish to explore career options or claim credit for learning acquired through her community activities. In both the career exploration and service-learning interests, depending on her experience and maturity, she could make good use of either the supervisor (3), designer (5), or consultant (6) pedagogical style. For personal growth and development seminars in parenting and marital adjustment, she and her husband could use a facilitator (7). In claiming credit for prior learning, she would simply need an evaluator (9).

Midlife Transition. The decade between 35 and 45 is an especially opportune time for people to turn to colleges and universities for assistance. It is a time of rediscovery and the re-establishment of identity. It may be a time to consider career changes. Such decisions are aided by realistic appraisals of one's skills as well as recognition of the direction in which one's career and avocational interests have developed. Personal growth and development programs concerned with identifying and evaluating skills, clarifying values, and enhancing interpersonal and other skills are all of interest at this time. Representative of such programs are the Centering and Venturing program at Davidson College, the programs of the Career Development Office at the College of Charleston, and the program offered through the Tucker Foundation at Dartmouth College. If, in addition to acquiring skills, students get an opportunity to investigate career possibilities through community surveys or supervised volunteer work, they will learn career exploration skills that will be useful throughout a lifetime.

There may also be interest in learning how a particular academic discipline, such as sociology or political science, is related to and might be useful in one's work. El Centro Community College in Dallas, Texas, offers such a course for law enforcement officers in which sociological concepts, principles, theories, and methods are taught using the daily work of the officers as the source of the illustrations. The officers themselves identify and present illustrations and applications of sociological principles, concepts, and methods and discuss them in class with the designer-instructor (5).

Both men and women in this age period may wish to complete unfinished undergraduate work as a way to begin their new careers or advance in their present ones. They may wish to claim college credit for learning they have acquired through their work and community leadership activities. In seeking college credit for that learning, they would depend on a faculty member-evaluator (9) to assist them in securing the credit. Those with work-related research experience or special interests or needs may find that some of their college work can best be done through independent study projects or field research. The experiential programs they would benefit from would depend on the nature of their previous experience, degree programs, and career interests. If they are concerned with social or political issues and their work is in the social sciences, institutional analysis, field research, social/political action or study, and service-learning might suit their interests and needs. They might also wish to gain some cross-cultural experience if they are preparing to work with minority persons. Depending on the career they select in the social sciences, preprofessional training might be necessary, as in social work or psychological counseling. If their interests are in the humanities, in literature or language or history, their learning would be enhanced by cross-cultural experience or by participation in the performing or graphic arts. At this age level some people will be able to develop their own learning plans and utilize a faculty member as a consultant (6) or as a resource person (8).

Middle Adulthood. The years between 45 and 60 are for many the fullest and most creative season of the life cycle. People begin to see their lives as time left to live, which requires them to develop priorities and make choices. With their broad experience and ability to handle complex environments, people at this stage may find that the best way to pursue their learning is by working with a consultant (6) who can help in the design of individualized learning plans and in the monitoring of them or a resource person (8) who can assist in the application of learning theory in a program of lifelong education. An increased sense of social responsibility may lead to special projects in community development or social and political action or a service-learning experience, or involvement in field research or the performing arts. This may also be a time of broadening horizons through travel and cross-cultural experience. The development of adult leisure time activities may lead to a collegial (4) relationship with people in the field or the utilization of a consultant (6) in an independent study program or a designer (5) in a programmed course in an applied subject such as photography, electronics, or carpentry.

Late Adult Life. The period from 60 years of age on is one in which the developmental tasks are usually related to retirement and reduced family responsibilities as well as to the acceptance of limitations of strength, health, and income and the loss of spouses and friends. Increasingly, people in this age group are beginning to organize for political and social change, putting their developed knowledge and skill to use for themselves and society. Educational activities related to specific issues, such as the management of limited income, legislation affecting housing for the elderly, and health care delivery services will attract some. Field research and social/political action projects will provide needed knowledge, political expertise, and power. The pedagogical styles appropriate for these will include collegial work (4) with a faculty member who shares students' interests and concerns, and the use of a consultant (6) or a resource person (8) who can assist in these learning endeavors. There will still be much interest in travel and other cultures, so programs offering cross-cultural experiences will be valued. Some will engage in service-learning projects such as the Foster Grandparent Program or in leadership roles in such organizations as the American Association of Retired Persons. Others may rely on experiential learning opportunities provided by colleges and universities for leadership training and personal development.

Ego, Moral, and Intellectual Development

The concept of ego development includes impulse control and character development, interpersonal relations, cognitive functioning, conscious preoccupations, and self-concept. Some of these dimensions of development have been treated separately in Part One of this book. But in discussing the uses of experiential learning in relation to these dimensions, I will deal with ego development, moral development, and intellectual development together in terms of the stages identified by Loevinger as Self-Protective or Opportunistic, Conformist, Conscientious, and Autonomous. As will be seen in the following paragraphs, the ordering of pedagogical styles in Table 1 corresponds in a general way to the stages of adult development and thus suggests which pedagogical styles will be most effective at each stage. (See Chickering, 1976, pp. 90-91.)

Self-Protective or Opportunistic Stage. The pedagogical style of disseminator of information, instructor in skills, and evaluator of performance (1), in which the student passively assimilates the instructor's teaching, is most congenial to the self-protective, opportunistic stage of ego development and the obedience-punishment stage of moral development. The corresponding level of intellectual development is that of memorization and practical application. The motive for education is to satisfy immediate needs; knowledge is seen as coming from external authorities; and learning is basically acquired from authorities by imitation.

Conformist Stage. At the next level, the conformist stage of ego development, students respond well to two pedagogical styles of experiential learning. In one the instructor serves as a mentor (2) or model as well as a provider of information and skill instruction. The student's role is to apply the knowledge and skills acquired under supervision, as, for example, in a chemistry laboratory. This fits both the moral development stage of approval orientation and the intellectual stage of comprehension and application. The second style is one in which the principal role of the instructor is that of supervisor (3) and model of appropriate professional or occupational behavior. This role is often played by the field placement supervisor rather than by the faculty sponsor. The student brings knowledge to the field placement, receives instruction about the relevance of the acquired knowledge to the work being done, observes demonstrations of application, and utilizes the knowledge and skills under supervision, as in many cooperative education placements. These models are particularly appropriate at the conformist stage of development since the student's dominant educational motive is to impress significant others, gain social acceptance, and obtain credentials and recognition. Knowledge, at this stage, comes primarily from external authorities and from asking what others expect and how to do it.

Conscientious Stage. It will be recalled that the conscientious stage appears to be modal for college students of traditional age during the first two years of college. "Rules are seen to have exceptions or to hold only in certain contingencies. . . . Motives and consequences are more important than rules per se. Long-term goals and ideals are characteristic, ought is clearly different from is. . . . Achievement is important, and it is measured by one's own inner standards rather than being primarily a matter of competition or social approval" (Loevinger, Wessler, and Redmore, 1970, p. 5). In the cognitive domain, analysis and formal operations of increasing complexity are possible at this stage.

There are three appropriate pedagogical styles for this stage. The college (4) or mutual involvement model utilizes projects in which faculty and students are involved together in carrying out a study or research project. In this style the responsibility for the conduct of the project and for the end product is a shared one, as in the group research projects of the College of the Atlantic. The role model of the faculty member in this style is that of senior colleague, as in research projects involving graduate student research associates.

The second model is one in which the faculty member is the designer (5) or identifier of the learning environment, monitor of the learning process, and resource person for the student during the learning experience. The student applies skills and knowledge previously acquired, secures new knowledge and skill as needed in the learning environment, becomes aware of values, both his own and those of the people with whom he is working, and uses these values in making important decisions pertinent to his learning and work responsibilities. The student also analyzes and synthesizes knowledge, skills, and values. An example of this type of program is an internship in which the student serves as an intake interviewer in a community mental health agency and, in so doing, develops empathy and interviewing skills and applies knowledge and methods from psychology, sociology, and political science. The learner also may acquire knowledge of the agency's power structure, its relationships with other agencies in the community, and its methods of making referrals. The student may become aware of personal values as well as the values of the client, staff, and agency, and the conflicts among them.

The third model pertains to another dimension of this stage. Loevinger points out that the conscientious stage is marked by heightened consciousness of self and inner feelings and the perception of multiple possibilities in situations. This, therefore, is an appropriate stage for the use of the faculty facilitator and trainer model (7). This model provides a structured, supportive learning environment in which the student may, with minimal psychological risk, develop self-understanding, interpersonal skills, and knowledge of transferable skills useful in career pursuits. Encounter groups and career exploration programs are examples of this model. These models are consistent with the student's motivation for achieving competence as measured by competitive or normative standards and the concern for increasing one's ability to meet social responsibilities. At this stage, education is often viewed as being for the purpose of developing competence in work and social roles.

Autonomous Stage. Individuals at the autonomous stage are characterized by their independence and initiative in learning, as well as by a deepened understanding of self and the world, an increasing capacity to manage their own destiny, and a heightened concern about social problems beyond their immediate experience. They are inclined to evaluate performance by internalized standards and principles rather than by comparison with others or reference to what others might think. People at this stage are capable of increasing conceptual complexity: not only can they deal with information objectively, they can also synthesize and evaluate knowledge and, with their high tolerance for ambiguity, wrestle with complex patterns of thought. The pedagogical models appropriate to this stage of development all shift the major educational responsibility to the student.

In the first model, the faculty member is consultant (6), adviser, and co-evaluator. The student designs, with the faculty member's advice, the learning and evaluation plans for a research study or action project, formulating the objectives, identifying the learning resources, developing the plan of action, and identifying the assessment techniques. Examples of this model are off-campus independent study projects in consumer protection or environmental impact studies done to protect an endangered wildlife area. The extent to which the positions taken are argued rationally and backed by moral principles and a real understanding of the dilemmas confronted in the situation will be a measure of the student's autonomy.

A second model appropriate to this stage of development is one in which the faculty member serves as a resource person (8) for the student, identifying the skills necessary for self-guided learning and developing or finding some structured means of reflection and self-evaluation so that the student may consciously apply experiential learning theory or cross-cultural learning skills in a pursuit of lifelong education. The student's role in this model is to consciously apply the learning theory or the cross-cultural learning skills and assess his own progress through self-evaluation methods. Personal experience and reflections, combined with personally generated paradigms, insights, and judgments, become the source of knowledge. This model will be discussed more fully in the last section of the chapter.

In the third and most passive type of faculty resource model, the faculty member simply acts as an evaluator (9), reviewing students' applications for academic credit for learning acquired in work or community activities. Using the college's curriculum as a guide, the faculty member assists students in identifying and articulating the learning acquired and in evaluating and certifying the learning. The students, through reflection and a study of the college's curriculum and courses, identify learning they think may be college creditable and then document it.

Interpersonal Competence

Interpersonal competence is one of the most complex aspects of adult development. It involves both style and skill—that is, both a responsive attitude toward others, including sensitivity to their feelings and flexibility in dealing with them, and the ability to initiate and maintain productive relationships. Attaining competence in interpersonal relationships involves unlearning, or controlling the use of, ways of relating to people deeply imprinted in our habits in childhood and adolescence which are inappropriate for adult relations in the family, at work, and in the community. In interpersonal relationships, most people's knowledge outstrips their practice. There are a number of reasons for this. Most of our interpersonal interactions involve some degree of psychological threat or emotional risk. Most of the time we are not functioning on a completely rational basis.

We are trying to look good, defend ourselves from attack, justify our behavior, hide our ignorance, or engage in any number of other psychological self-preservation ploys. Besides operating at this nonrational level, we are also concentrating our attention on the subject, problem, or issue being dealt with at the moment and may thus find it difficult to devote our attention to the practice of principles of good interpersonal relationships. Part of the problem may also be that we have learned these principles in the abstract but never really learned, through practice, how to apply them. Such experiential education activities as human relations workshops, gestalt and encounter groups, sensitivity training, and parent effectiveness training help people unlearn old habits and acquire more effective inter-personal skills. Needed in addition to these learning opportunities are means for transfer-ring that new knowledge and skill to our everyday activities. This requires the assumption of initiative and responsibility for self-directed and self-evaluative learning. The develop-ment and use of some structured means of observation, reflection, analysis, and evalua-tion could facilitate this.

Many people are unwilling to take initiative under new and challenging circum-stances because of a sense of incompetence or a generally passive, wait and see, attitude developed through long years of living as a dependent person in an environment that rewards passivity and dependence and inhibits assertive action. Personal growth and devel-opment learning involving the facilitator-trainer (7) pedagogical style can help overcome this sense of helplessness. An illustration of this is the Day-in-the-Field exercise of Justin Morrill College's Field Study program. In preparing students for cross-cultural learning experiences, it was found that most students were not taking much initiative in learning about the new culture; they just waited to see what would happen, and thus let the con-trol of the use of the learning environment slip out of their hands. In order to counteract this tendency, students, during the preparation seminar, are now dropped off individually in small communities of 500 to 5,000 people on a Saturday morning and told to learn as much about the community as they can in a day's time. This experience is followed by a group debriefing in which people recount their experiences and a seminar session in which the methods used in learning about the community are listed and compared with the methods of sociologists and anthropologists. The students reveal considerable apprehen-sion prior to the experience, relief and pride in their accomplishment when it is over, and new confidence in their ability to cope with interpersonal relations in a strange social environment. They are also pleasantly surprised to learn that, left to their own devices, they discover and use many of the same methods that professionals use in studying com-munities.

Development of Humanitarian Concern

Experiential learning has a similar contribution to make to the development of humanitarian concern. Humanitarian concern is essentially an extension of one's concern for the welfare of one's own family and social group to the welfare of others in the soci-ety. An important component, as White points out in his chapter, is the empathy that derives from a knowledge of others' needs. Information about these needs is disseminated widely by the media, but firsthand experience of the plight of others is a much more powerful teacher. Service-learning programs, human service experiences (as described by Cohen in Part Two), and cross-cultural experiences as well as field research are excellent opportunities for learning about the needs of others. But, as White reminds us, direct experience of the needs of others and the resistance of institutions and people to change may also put a severe strain on the humanitarian impulse. He rightly suggests involvement in the problems of people close at hand, wherein the individual's contribution makes an observable difference. This will strengthen the humanitarian impulse more than tackling global issues that the individual can affect minimally. Social and political action groups are valuable educational experiences in the application and further development of humanitarian concern.

One aspect of developing humanitarian concern is the process of becoming aware of your own and others' values and of the values of differing cultures. Facing situations where people of another culture value time, money, family, or work differently broadens one's perception of reality as well as tolerance of differences. Before you can act to meet the needs of other people, you have to know what is important to you and why. Experiential learning programs in cooperative education, preprofessional training, service-learning internships, field research, social/political action, and cross-cultural experience all provide occasions for value clarification. White gives two examples, one of a girl who volunteered as a nurse's aide in an understaffed hospital and one of a young man from a comfortable middle-class home whose summer work on a construction job prompted him to re-examine his values and those of his family in the light of his experience with men on the job. This kind of self-understanding as an outcome of experiential learning is confirmed by recent research (Quinn, 1972; Kiel, 1972; Nosow, 1975; Hoose, 1974; Wilson, 1974; Purnick, 1976).

Learning How to Learn

Tough, in his chapter on lifelong learning, indicates that the average adult conducts seven distinct learning projects a year, devoting 100 hours to each effort to learn a new skill, require new knowledge, or work at personal development. Only 20 percent of these projects are planned by a professional; 73 percent are planned by the learner; and 7 percent are planned with a friend or a peer group. Only 10 percent of all adult learning occurs in classrooms, courses, or conferences; all the rest is field experience. Thus, a high-priority task of educators working with adults ought to be to increase their proficiency in designing and executing self-directed learning projects.

The process of experiential learning as described by Kolb begins with concrete experience followed by observation, reflection, abstract conceptualization, and actual experimentation. Most learners need to improve all these skills, but two—observation and reflection—deserve special mention here.

I have discovered in preparing traditional undergraduates for cross-cultural learning that they are inexperienced in the skills of accurate observation and unable to record with clarity and precision what they have observed. They find it difficult to write a descriptive paragraph about a small town or a social agency they have visited. The students tend to summarize the impressions the town or buildings made on them with such statements as "It was a quiet and pretty town. The people were very friendly." Instead of providing a description of the town, the people, and their behavior and allowing the readers to draw their own conclusions, the students skip the detail work and give their impressions. Most of us do not do much better in reporting orally on what we have seen or experienced. We are inclined to pay attention to impressions and our feelings about things, persons, and events but allow the details that evoked those impressions to escape us. In short, we are not very good at either observing or recording experience. And these skills are important for all types of experiential learning.

One tool of observation that students need to acquire is skill in asking questions of others. Much work has been done on perfecting the interviewing skills of students preparing for the helping professions. We ought to use the results of that work in preparing people to learn on their own. Kagan's (1967) work on Interpersonal Process Recall (IPR) and his training film "Elements of Facilitating Communication" are very useful for teaching the use of different types of questions. Lifelong learning will be enhanced, as will any experiential learning endeavor, by helping students formulate questions and interact in ways that encourage the free exchange of information and clarify intent.

The skill of experiential learning in which people tend to be most deficient is reflection. One reason for this is that in our production-oriented society not much value is placed on reflection; indeed, it is often seen as nonproductive daydreaming, a waste of time. Yet when you try to make sense out of your experience, to put it in some perspective, to see what it is related to in the past and what it has to say about the present and future, you are doing the necessary background work for the development of theories, hypotheses, generalizations, principles, and explanations.

To help students engaged in cross-cultural learning develop the ability to reflect on their experience, a structured means of reflection called a Performance Analysis Report (PAR) was developed (see Duley and Gordon, 1977). This device was developed out of Flannagan's Critical Incident Technique as a means of self-evaluation rather than a report on the performance of another person under crisis conditions. A PAR is a report of a student's attempt to use a specific set of skills like information source development or interpersonal communication. In the report the student is asked to identify the set of skills being used; to describe what was being attempted, the context of the effort, and what the person actually did in using the skills; and to analyze the effort and evaluate what was learned. The PAR helps students reflect on and consciously work at improving their ability to function effectively in a different cultural environment. It gives them a framework within which to record their observations and describe their own behavior and that of other principal actors. It requires reflection through analysis and evaluation. A similar method would help people apply the principles of experiential learning—observing, reflecting, conceptualizing, and active experimenting—in their self-directed learning projects.

Kolb's discussion of experiential learning theory has a number of potential applications for field experience education. A study of placement sites in experiential learning programs might identify the learning styles they emphasize, and students might then be placed in them not only to gain experience but to increase their skill in a particular learning style. In career exploration, students' dominant learning styles could be determined and they could be placed in occupational settings that utilize those styles in order to test the occupations as career possibilities. With adults seeking career change, educators could determine which learning style they wish to try in a new career and having identified the direction in which they wish to move, find a part-time service-learning internship or similar opportunity for the individual to try before making a permanent shift.

Conclusion

The range of pedagogical styles and the diversity of program offerings in field experience learning can meet many of the developmental needs of adults at various stages of the life cycle. But this range of learning options, while available in the curriculum of many institutions, is not taken advantage of by most students. Even nontraditional students returning for additional undergraduate work, many of whom have been granted college credit for learning acquired on the job or in community leadership activities, are expected to utilize the dominant pedagogical style of traditional undergraduate programs

—the classroom-lecture model. The option of individualizing a degree program to take full advantage of the experiential learning activities offered in a college or university is not widely available, and it may be unrealistic to expect many students of any age to use such an option. A more realistic goal might be to work for the incorporation of more field experience learning opportunities within already established courses. Rather than seeing field activities as a substitute for classroom activities, we ought to see them as supplementary. We ought to encourage the incorporation of independent study projects, service-learning internships, group survey projects, empathy training weekends, and cross-cultural learning experiences into classroom-based courses. They might be optional assignments selected by students on the basis of their learning styles or a required outside assignment designed to permit supervised application of principles learned in the classroom. A course at Michigan State University entitled The Helping Professions and Community Service exemplifies this integration of classroom and field work. It has weekly lectures and assigned readings but also incorporates the case study method, a survey conducted by the class, and a field assignment: to find out what social service clients go through, each student must locate an agency, get there by means of public transportation, and seek aid.

The diversity of the student population in the modern American college—with respect to age, levels of development, learning styles, and motivation—makes it imperative that we overcome the separation of classroom learning and field experience learning. We need to find ways to mix pedagogical styles and incorporate experiential learning into all our courses.

References

Chickering, A. "Developmental Change as a Major Outcome." In M. T. Keeton and Associates, *Experiential Learning: Rationale, Characteristics, and Assessment.* San Francisco: Jossey-Bass, 1976.

Coleman, J. S. "Differences Between Experiential and Classroom Learning." In M. T. Keeton and Associates, *Experiential Learning: Rationale, Characteristics, and Assessment.* San Francisco: Jossey-Bass, 1976.

Duley, J., and Gordon, S. *College-Sponsored Experiential Learning—A CAEL Handbook.* Princeton, N.J.: Educational Testing Service, 1977.

Hoose, H. *Service Learning Internships: A Look at the Influences of Service Learning Internships on Fifty-six Students.* Raleigh, N.C.: The North Carolina Internship Office, 1974.

Kagan, N., and others. *Studies in Human Interaction: Interpersonal Process Recall Stimulated by Videotape.* East Lansing: Educational Publication Services, Michigan State University, 1967.

Keeton, M. T., and Associates. *Experiential Learning: Rationale, Characteristics, and Assessment.* San Francisco: Jossey-Bass, 1976.

Kiel, D. *Student Learning Through Community Involvement: A Report of Three Studies of the Service Learning Model.* Atlanta: Southern Regional Education Board, 1972.

Loevinger, J., Wessler, R., and Redmore, C. *Measuring Ego Development.* Vol. 1: *Construction and Use of a Sentence Completion Test.* San Francisco: Jossey-Bass, 1970.

Nosow, S. "Student Perceptions of Field Experience Education." *Journal of College Student Personnel,* 1975, *16*, 508-513.

Purnick, S. P. "Personal Growth and Attitude Change in a Field Study Program." Unpublished doctoral dissertation, Northwestern University, 1976.

Quinn, M. E. "An Investigation of Undergraduate Field Study at Michigan State University." Unpublished doctoral dissertation, Michigan State University, 1972.

Schneier, C. E. "For Whom Are Experiential Learning Techniques Effective?" Paper presented at the 37th annual meeting of the Academy of Management, Kissimmee, Fla., August 1977.

Tumin, M. "Valid and Invalid Rationales." In M. T. Keeton and Associates, *Experiential Learning: Rationale, Characteristics, and Assessment.* San Francisco: Jossey-Bass, 1976.

Wilson, J. W. *Impact of Cooperative Education upon Personal Development and Growth of Values.* Boston: Cooperative Education Research Center, Northeastern University, 1974.

33

Francis Keppel
Arthur W. Chickering

Mediated Instruction

Resources for mediated instruction—that is, education by means other than face-to-face communication—cover a wide range: correspondence, print, xerography, microfiche, telephone, radio, film, television, and the computer. We have become so accustomed to print and to its cousins, xerography and microfiche, that their listing here with new forms of communication technology may evoke surprise. Yet of all the results of technology, the printed word or picture is surely the most widely used technique of mediated instruction in higher education.

Until recently, interest in the new electronic technologies has tended to make us lose sight of the role of print and its related technologies. For a time, indeed, electronics seemed to offer the potential for replacing not only books but teachers. In 1972, for example, at the height of enthusiasm for mediated instruction, the Carnegie Commission on Higher Education (p. 1) forecast that "by the year 2000 it now appears that a significant proportion of instruction in higher education on campus may be carried on through informational technology." It hailed the new technology as "The Fourth Revolution," and offered such visions as these: "Higher education (and education generally) now faces the first great technological revolution in five centuries in the potential impact of the new electronics. . . . New technology has already transformed (a) research techniques in many fields and (b) administrative methods on many campuses. It is now (c) affecting large libraries and (d) is entering into the instructional process. . . . The new technology may provide the single greatest opportunity for academic change on and off campus."

As early as 1975, however, two authors of a study sponsored by the Carnegie Commission on the potential of computers in the learning process (Rockart and Scott Morton, 1975) were tempering the enthusiasm of this and similar reports:

> Somehow, the optimism expressed in these reports is not yet wholly shared by the people who will have to implement the computer's role in higher education. As we shall note in some detail later, professors and other educators tend to be somewhat cautious in their beliefs as to the "widespread use" of computer-based education. They are clearly less optimistic than their computer-technologist counterparts. In part, this may be because they lack a clear understanding as to just *what* the computer *should* do in the future of higher education, because a variety of forces are unfavorable to the spread of computer technology, and because many educators/faculty feel that the uses to which the technology has been put thus far touch only one relatively poorly matched aspect of the educational task. We suspect that the truth about the use of computers in higher education lies nearer the pessimism of the educators than the optimism of the technologists. In particular, we shall argue that any given technology is appropriate for certain types of material and quite inappropriate for others—being clear on where computer technology fits the material contributes to an understanding of where its ultimate impact will be [p. 203].
>
> It follows from the above that the real impact of the new technology will for the most part be adding to, rather than replacing, current learning mechanisms. Some current mechanisms will be displaced, but the new technology will allow two major improvements. First, it will provide opportunities for increased enrichment as noted above. Second, it will provide increased access by university faculty to students formerly outside the geographic limits of the regular educational system [p. 276].

The lowered expectations illustrated by these statements do not result from lack of imagination or from cynicism. A half century ago, the senior author's father devoted personal energy and funds to encourage the use of radio for education. He found but little reward. In the late 1960s and early 1970s, the senior author was chairman of a corporation that saw dreams of imaginary markets for sophisticated hardware turn into annual losses, which were recouped only by more profitable sales in cheaper print and low-cost visual products. During the sixties and seventies, communications technology for education attracted venture capital from public as well as private sources, but by 1976 reductions in public funding led *The Chronicle of Higher Education* to headline its article on the change in optimism, "Computerized Education: Time to Sink or Swim." Today, in the United States it is a safe estimate that less than one fifth of 1 percent of school expenditures goes for the purchase of sophisticated communications technology; and, if one leaves out the use of such technology for scientific research, this figure is not much more for higher education. The time has come to test the results of this technology in the marketplace of higher education—and no one is confident of the results. Perhaps the most balanced judgment is that of George Bonham, the editor of *Change,* "The Magazine of Higher Learning." In the April 1976 issue, under the title "Educational Media: A Mixed Bag," Bonham wrote:

> Whatever the technological inroads in American pedagogy, the products have been, by any measure, a mixed bag. On the whole, the past few decades have remained for academics an Age of Tinkering. . . One remembers, of course, the earlier enthusiasm: For much of the expansive postwar period, academics and communications technologists have glowered at each other across an intellectual

void, with only an occasional nod toward a more permanent alliance—which most thought a misalliance at best. The fuller consummation never took place, of course, and no one breathed easier than the professional academic. Indeed, it has turned out to be a multi-million-dollar misunderstanding, since the learning technologies thrown at the colleges and universities have been of monumental proportions. But the difficulties were—and are—more psychological than technological [p. 32].

Present Status of Mediated Instruction

From all the results of recent experiments and studies, several tentative conclusions are possible regarding the use of educational technologies in higher education in the next few years:

1. Print remains the most cost-effective of all media.
2. Sophisticated technologies using computers may be most adaptable and useful in libraries and administration.
3. Radio and television will have particular value in educational centers because of low cost (see Ginzberg, 1974).
4. But on balance, higher education institutions should be careful in making major investments of personnel or funds in modern educational technology. No one study is sufficient by itself to discourage adoption of any of the technologies, but together the studies argue for cautious experimentation and against both premature promises of dramatic educational or social results and massive investment of funds at the expense of other approaches that may have a better basis in social science or human experience.

Consider each of the conclusions in turn.

Print. At all levels of education in all countries, planners are returning to the topic of the role of print and its related technologies, xerography and microfiche. The World Bank, for example, which might reasonably be expected to view the benefits of technology independently of the predispositions of educators, has taken a cautious position on the use of sophisticated technology and, in its 1974 Sector Working Paper, pointed out that at the school level high priority should be given to the production of textbooks. It also questioned whether the present allocation of resources for textbooks and other learning aids is adequate, suggesting that the present percentage of the budget devoted for these purposes might have to be tripled in order to meet minimum standards for learning and to adjust educational programs to national needs. While this argument was made in the context of elementary and secondary education, it is surely worth consideration by higher education. The investment involved for such an increase in the print and print-related areas, though substantial, would be very much less than for sophisticated technologies and computer-related instruction.

It seems clear that print and electronic technologies should be considered together rather than viewed as mutually exclusive competitors for available funds. In any decisions on allocating scarce resources, the choice is typically not *which* technology to invest in but rather *how much* to allocate to each. Given the present state of development of all technologies, it seems more prudent for the next decade to increase rather than reduce allocations for print and related technologies.

Computers. No one questions that the computer is an essential instrument of research in both the physical and social sciences in modern universities. Computer costs have become a major issue in financing universities with strong research capabilities. Indeed, their budgetary impact often raises difficult questions about funding sources. Should the costs be borne solely by the universities' own budgets, or, as in most of technology and science, should they be supported at least in part by the agencies of government that have the greatest interest in the research itself, whether it be in medicine, energy, or some other critical area? Regardless of the decisions on these issues, one conclusion is certain: the modern university will have to calculate on the use of the most sophisticated technologies as essential ingredients in their research programs. The revolution of information technologies, which has made so profound an impact on other sectors of the society, has unquestionably entered the bloodstream of this aspect of the university as well.

More than a quarter of a century of intensive research and development has been devoted to the use of communications technologies in libraries. The use of microfiche is spreading rapidly. Computer terminals are increasingly present in libraries. The skyrocketing number of intellectual, scholarly, and scientific reports seems to be forcing a fundamental reconsideration of methods for information storage and retrieval. Nor is the problem only how to manage growth. It is also a problem of escalating costs, which the computer offers a means for controlling, if not reducing. The National Library of Medicine in Washington, D.C., is an admirable example of the application of computer technology in this area. Its development, which is still going on, required substantial start-up capital investments as well as current operating expenditures. Furthermore, decades of the most intensive and often frustrating professional and technical work have been required. It is, therefore, another example of the need for caution in predicting either quick or cheap results from the application of sophisticated communications technologies to higher education.

The computer network happily named PLATO offers another example. In 1976, the director of the University of Illinois laboratory working on computer-based education predicted that PLATO would reach more than a million people. He noted that there were PLATO terminals in twenty-two states within the United States and in Europe, all connected to a central computer. Fifteen thousand hours of prepared lessons were instantly available to users, including job training programs. He admitted that the present costs are high, $1.50 an hour, but predicted that technological progress by 1981 will cut terminal costs to only $1,000 each and the rate per hour to 10¢ (*Education Daily,* 1976, p. 3). These developments have been made possible by a decade of substantial grants from the national government. An observer can only admire the determination, hard work, and courage of those who are taking part in the effort. But we also are forced to point out that the capital costs are still way beyond the reach of any single institution, and the information on recurrent costs is still not firm enough to provide a safe basis for budget making in the near future. Nor is there sufficient evidence that students will devote more than a fraction of their time to using this sophisticated technology for their own learning purposes. If not, investment of resources in computer-based education may have to be counted as added expenditures rather than as replacements for existing expenditures.

Radio and Television. After print, radio and television, particularly radio, have the longest record of use by higher education. As yet neither of them has been absorbed fully into the regular operation of colleges and universities. Like films, they have been used in a variety of ways, and their use has gradually increased over the years. It is fair, however, to say that predictions in the 1920s for radio and in the 1950s for television, which projected an immense influence on all levels of education, have simply not been borne out. The exception seems to be where there are not sufficient numbers of students to justify the establishment of a school or college. Rural areas are the most obvious example. Radio will probably be particularly useful for such settings.

The current interest in "universities without walls" throughout the world suggests that higher education may well be entering an era when far more flexible methods of instruction will be used. Note that these methods do not necessarily rely primarily on audiovisual aids but rather use of them as an ancillary means of transmitting information, as a pacing device, and as a stimulus to motivation. Print media and the human tutor continue to play the central roles in instruction. The future of such "new" institutions surely depends on the demand for their offerings by the society they serve. Can they provide both the flexibility and the type of instruction that learners of varied ages and interests will find valuable? Can more traditional institutions also adjust their methods to meet the needs of this new clientele?

There is already evidence that the answer to both questions can be a tentative "yes." The well-known record of the British Open University heartens both those whose primary interest is to spread the benefits of higher education to persons who miss the opportunities afforded by traditional institutions and those who wish to increase use of educational technologies. The backbone of the program is the fine print materials. These are supplemented by television. In addition, there is a national back-up system of human resources: regional and local centers that offer tutoring and counseling on both individual and group bases. It also includes residential summer institutes, which give large numbers of students a chance for sustained study and long conversations with fellow students and faculty members.

Adaptations of this model are gradually being undertaken elsewhere in the world. Judgments about its applicability to the United States must recognize that the network of two- and four-year colleges and universities in this country substantially exceeds that in Great Britain and that the proportions of persons going on to some form of postsecondary education are also much higher. It is important to remember that, in one stroke, the British Open University's first 25,000 enrollees doubled the number of students pursuing higher education in that country. It obviously has become Britain's most significant agency for mass higher education. But here in the United States there are many other alternatives available at relatively convenient locations and at fairly low cost. The presence of these other alternatives probably accounts, at least in part, for the limited success of efforts to transplant the British Open University to Maryland, Texas, and elsewhere. Though enrollments have been sufficient to maintain the efforts and though evaluation shows adequate completion rates for reasonably well-prepared students, it is fair to say that so far there has been no spectacular or widespread adoption of those initial models. A slow process of adaptation to the needs of older than normal age groups is taking place throughout our institutions. Many changes—in course offerings, in their timing, and in their method of instruction—are in the process of experimentation. Radio and television programing is gradually becoming part of these new alternatives.

One particular approach to televised instruction deserves special attention. Although educational television has offered courses since the early 1950s, enrollments have been scattered and relatively small. Budgets for such courses usually have been limited, and there has been widespread criticism, in and out of educational circles, of the "poor quality" of the offerings. But in the fall of 1974 almost 200 colleges and universities joined a venture to offer "The Ascent of Man," along with its companion text and instructional materials, as a course of study. Over 12,000 students were enrolled by the time of the first broadcast on January 7, 1975. During the repeat broadcast in the fall of 1975, the number of schools is reported to have increased to 500 and the total number of students to almost 25,000. In summarizing her evaluative study, Marjorie Hochlander (1977) says:

> There appears to have been no precedent for this range of collaboration. Nonetheless, information gathered from this study indicates that there was no logistical plan commonly shared by the producer/publisher of the Bronowski content, the schools that prepared the adjunct materials, the public television stations that broadcast the programs, the schools that accepted these components as a basis for academic study, or the faculty members responsible for presenting "The Ascent of Man" to their students. Events took place in an atmosphere of excitement, speculation, last-minute decision, and brief acquaintance. The entire process, except for local evaluations after course offerings, lacked an integral research program to assist in predicting, guiding, or measuring the outcomes.
>
> Yet, underneath its trial-and-error entrepreneurial surface, what was done with "The Ascent of Man" represents an energetic and long overdue thrust toward providing, through the interactive use of television and text, an interdisciplinary course of high quality that could not have been easily duplicated in other ways.
>
> Although a few schools bought the series on film and showed them as they wished, the majority responding to this study turned to the broadcast mode for the relative economy it provided them, for the convenience of viewing that it afforded many of the students. Some also acknowledged that the regular television schedule served as a secondary discipline upon students in keeping up with the work.
>
> It appears that, in adopting "The Ascent of Man" for academic study, the emphasis among schools shifted strongly from concerns of past years about the instructional power of television to more definite exploration of how exemplary program content could be presented in a variety of learning situations [p. 17].

The first paragraphs of this quotation suggest the difficulties in such a complex effort. But the later paragraphs recognize the significance of this first major attempt and the potentials for its use in other areas.

That potential was soon tested again. In 1976, a thirteen-week, expensively produced television course built around "The Adams Chronicles," part of the U.S. Bicentennial series, was widely used for educational purposes. Of the more than four million estimated viewers of the series on the Public Broadcasting System, about 45,000 were students enrolled in postsecondary-level courses offered by 305 institutions around the nation. This was one of the most successful efforts to use sophisticated television programming for direct instruction, and it is causing a number of institutions to consider similar possibilities in the future.

Three aspects of the course based on "The Adams Chronicles" seemed to account for its success. First, there was the sheer professional and technical quality of the program's presentation. Second, there were available *at the time of presentation* readily accessible printed materials on which the program was based—materials that could be used by those enrolled in formal courses of instruction. This second key factor involved collaboration between the publishers of the printed materials and the producers of the television program at an early stage of development. Third, there was time to develop joint planning with educational institutions and teaching staffs interested in adapting their academic programs to use the television series. It is doubtful that the series would have succeeded if any one of these conditions had been absent. Together they provided motivation, continuity, the essential print materials for study and reference, and the human interaction with the teacher.

Factors to Consider in Adopting Mediated Instruction

The adoption of educational technology by an institution should be based on the findings of social science and educational research as well as on the political and financial realities of the institution. Four factors, in particular, must be considered: (1) student motivation, (2) instructional effectiveness, (3) staff preparation, and (4) cost. Those who have to make the final decision on a particular technology will have to face one troublesome but inescapable reality: Knowledge in the social and educational sciences lags far behind knowledge in the physical sciences and their related technologies; thus, knowledge about educational technology (in the sense of the capacity to distribute and to store information) is far more predictable than knowledge about the human capacity to absorb and make use of this technology in learning or to apply the results of such learning. Nonetheless, evidence about adult development and learning such as that from Part One can help in making better decisions about using distance learning, mediated instruction, and educational technologies most effectively.

Student Motivation. The first consideration is the most important of all. Human learning depends above all on whether individuals—of whatever age—want to learn. Under certain circumstances of fear and compulsion, they can be forced to learn some behaviors. But in general, and especially in higher education, individuals will learn far more effectively if they want to learn and understand what the personal results of such learning may be. Because of the extraordinary variety of adult learners' needs, as attested by the research and theory on the life cycle, adult development, and learning styles, the motivation to learn often depends on the mediation of some agent, whether human or not, that understands both the individual learner's reasons for wanting to learn and the level of his or her ability. It is reasonable to ask whether educational technology at its present stage of sophistication is able to undertake this task of mediation and motivation for such a diverse range of students.

The key to effective use of communications technology, in other words, is the motivation of the learner rather than the technology itself. There is, it seems to us, an important lesson here for educational policy makers. In the long run, even the best arguments for efficiency of instruction and economy of educational management will have to take into account whether the individual learners are willing to use such means and believe that they effectively serve their own interests. Students, especially older, self-supporting adults, vote with their feet and their dollars. Future development of educational technologies in higher education must therefore be based on realistic estimates of the attitudes of learners toward the technologies as well as on the attitudes of teachers.

It should be noted that the issue is not whether the technology is capable of asking the right questions of the learner and assigning the most efficient means of instructing him. The issue is subtler than just the cognitive relation between them. The deeper question is that of trust. Can the learner be persuaded that technology is an effective substitute, *in his or her own interest,* for a human intermediary?

Children who grow up learning through television at home may wonder why they cannot do likewise in school. But when they reach college age they may become more skeptical of whose motives are being served. Howard Bowen's (1977) observation about consumer sophistication as an outcome of college education is pertinent here. As we become sensitive to the ways in which commercials and other television programming attempt to influence attitudes and behaviors, we also become aware of the same potentials in educational media. So the issue of trust is complex. Of course that issue arises as well when the mediator is another person rather than print or pictures. But somehow most of us think we have learned how to read teachers to understand them and their motives and know whether they can be trusted. We may not be so confident about instructional technology.

In the transmission of news and entertainment, modern communications technology has won its spurs. The stimulation of interest and the general distribution of simplified facts and interpretation are clearly within the capacity of such technology, as is the presentation of readily understandable sequenced instruction. The question is whether educational technology can engage the learner at a deeper level.

Although research and theory concerning the developmental characteristics of our students will not provide any final answers, they do suggest some leads we might pursue. The developmental tasks of the life cycle suggest some of the ways in which motivation will vary for persons of different ages or for the same person at different times. The young adult man or woman coping with the first job as well as the responsibilities of parenthood will want content different from that sought by the person tackling the tough issues of the midlife transition or the older adult managing problems of retirement and seeking to develop new interests. Equally important, these persons will experience the same content quite differently. A work of literature or art, a history text or philosophical tract, will mean quite different things and serve quite different educational purposes depending upon the range of prior experiences, the particular motives brought to it, and the developmental tasks most salient at the time. Economic, political, and social theories will be received quite differently by persons who have lived through depressions and wars, and who have watched the ups and downs of nations and cultures, than by less experienced 18- to 22-year-olds. The effectiveness and contribution of distance learning, mediated instruction, and educational technologies will increase sharply if alternatives can be created that respond to the shifting requirements of persons throughout the life cycle. Until more is known about their motivation, however, caution seems called for in making major investments without solid justification from experiment and experience.

Instructional Effectiveness. The second general consideration is the extent to which mediated instruction (leaving out the use of print, for the moment) is more effective than the traditional means of instruction, however inefficient, of the human teacher and a classroom of students. In the opinion of the authors, who have spent long careers investigating educational methods in hopes of finding more effective methods than the traditional ones, the evidence is not persuasive enough to justify a massive change in public policy. On specific types of training for particular skills, often in military or industrial settings, the record is favorable for the less expensive types of audiovisual and "hands on" instruction. But even in these circumstances, the human intermediary seems to be necessary. The technology is a useful aid—but it has to be managed. There seems little evidence that it is more effective entirely to replace the human teacher by communications technology, if one measures the results in terms of actual learning. The issue seems rather to be that of deciding the most effective and cost-efficient mix of the two—and the data available for making the decision are far from adequate.

Educational effectiveness depends first and foremost on creating a sound match between (1) the student's motives, abilities, and background and (2) the nature of the content and the intellectual and emotional demands of the assignments. Piaget uses the concept of *optimal distance* to describe a good fit. Others have used terms like *readiness* and *preparation*. A magnet and iron filings can supply a fair metaphor. If the distance between the magnet and the filings is too great, nothing happens; if the filings are close, they jump quickly but not far. But there is an optimal gap that allows maximum travel and maximum acceleration as they cross the span. This optimum is a function of the strength of the magnet, the weight of the filings, and the amount of friction. Experienced teachers know the pulling power of various books, writing assignments, discussion questions, and examination tasks, especially when they are dealing with familiar students. They know how to make early judgments about which students may be too far away and which are on top of the subject matter. They know how to vary the distance, supply a nudge, or provide a little lubrication.

But most of us have little experience using the tools supplied by various educational technologies. And we are doubly handicapped when faced with unfamiliar students whose ages, backgrounds, motives, learning styles, and orientations toward knowledge are extremely diverse. We may recognize that if each person is to be effectively matched with educational alternatives relevant to his or her interests and aspirations, abilities, and learning styles, a wide range of resources and teaching methods must be used. We may be highly motivated to extend our teaching repertoires to include use of audiovisual materials, computers, programmed learning materials, radio, porta-pack television cameras, and televised instruction. But learning what works best, for what kinds of content and competence, with what kinds of students, is something else again.

Staff Preparation. The third consideration concerns the ability of teaching staff to use educational technologies effectively. So far, most college professors have been not only unprepared to use the new technologies but also somewhat suspicious of them. Despite the availability of sophisticated technologies—television, computers, and audiovisual media—for a generation or more, teachers have put them to use in only specialized and limited ways. It is not hard to guess at the reasons for such limited use: job protection, lack of training, and conservatism are only a few possibilities. Whatever the reason, the facts are indisputable: the mere availability of modern educational technology is not by itself sufficient to change educational habits. The record of the limited use of radio, film, television, and computer in colleges and universities over the last half century is written plainly for all save the enthusiasts to read. And at least one major reason for this record is the attitudes and habits of the teachers. The 1974 Sector Working Paper of the World Bank, referred to earlier, offers advice regarding educational broadcasting that applies to teacher acceptance of all instructional technologies:

> Preparing teachers to perform a new role in a changing educational technology is of crucial importance. Teachers are now expected to accept educational broadcasting not merely as a substitute for the blackboard but as a vehicle to introduce improved curricula and new subject matter into the classroom. The best way to secure the cooperation of teachers is to involve them with the work of broadcasting teachers in all phases of the program. Such cooperation will help secure a better product as well [p. 40].

Cost. The fourth consideration may seem crass to those educators who would prefer to limit their calculations to purely scientific or educational considerations. It is the question of finances: of capital and recurrent costs. The cheapest of all the educational technologies is print, including both production and distribution. Of course, the real costs of producing printed materials are hard to nail down. Such materials have often been heavily subsidized by faculty time and energy. Lecture notes and manuscripts for articles and books all provide ready materials for revision. Departmental and college-wide committee meetings devoted to course content and curricular issues, and their resulting reports, provide additional sources of background materials. But even if such hidden costs as these were taken into account, the costs of printed materials would still fall well below the current costs for preparing and distributing televised or computer-assisted instructional materials.

Other communications technologies escalate at dizzying rates in both capital investment and maintenance costs. The Swedish experience of the 1960s suggests that the investments of capital in technology, at least in part because of maintenance costs, did not result in any savings in recurrent expenditures for educational programs. In the United States, substantial capital expenditures since the late 1950s for hardware to help to teach foreign languages, plus substantial expenditures for teacher training, have not noticeably improved learners' performance or attracted more learners to the language programs. Our schools and colleges are filled with unused language laboratories gathering dust. The blunt fact is that this capital investment, in economic terms, has not paid off in recent decades. This fact suggests that those in charge of deciding on capital expenditures in the decades to come will probably be more cautious. Return on investment is a consideration in any area of society. As the 1974 World Bank report noted,

> Programs involving the use of such mass media as educational radio and television should be designed on the basis of careful analysis of costs and the capacity for the production of educational material. Emphasis should be placed on logistical problems, such as the distribution and maintenance of receivers, spare parts, and other materials. The unit cost of radio or televised instruction can be very high for small numbers of students but declines sharply as the numbers increase. In the Ivory Coast's televised project, for example, the estimated annual recurrent cost per student was $115 for 21,000 students and $6 for 700,000 students. It should also be remembered that where technical problems or costs make television prohibitive, radio may be a useful and cheaper substitute [p. 40].

These complexities concerning cost effectiveness argue powerfully for a deliberate step-by-step approach. Grand designs backed by massive investments are unlikely to work well given the pluralism and heterogeneity of higher education in the United States.

Implications of Adult Development Research

Several of the conceptual frameworks for understanding adult development outlined in Part One can also suggest the potential and the limitations of distance learning, mediated instruction, and educational technologies in helping students cope more effectively with their life cycle challenges and their developmental needs. In particular, Loevinger's classification of stages of ego development (self-protective or opportunistic, conformist, conscientious, autonomous, and integrated) as discussed by Weathersby, and Kohlberg's stages of moral development (obedience-punishment orientation; approval orientation; authority, rule, and social-order orientation; social contract orientation; legalistic orientation; and moral principle orientation) as discussed by Gilligan, offer clues to the role mediated instruction and technology can play during adult development.

Any institution serving a large number of adults will have students at different developmental stages ranging from opportunistic to autonomous levels of ego development and from obedience-punishment orientation to moral principle orientation in moral development. Because of this diversity an institution cannot simply pitch its educational program at a particular stage. It must develop the capacity to serve a full range of student needs.

The problem is that most institutions only focus on one or two developmental levels. Educational practices at many institutions are oriented toward the opportunistic or conformist levels of ego development and the obedience-punishment or approval-oriented levels of moral development. They treat education as though it were a commodity, a collection of discrete items, packaged in a few standard-sized boxes, sold by the Carnegie credit. It is not by chance that the supermarket has been an appealing metaphor for some educators and that curriculum committees and academic departments, like merchandisers, talk primarily about this or next year's *offerings* in the light of shifting student interests.

Few curriculums, courses, classes, seminars, or examinations help students build knowledge from personal experiences and personally generated syntheses and paradigms. Many teachers help students *acquire* basic competence and knowledge, but few help students *use* that learning to make some sense of life or to generate personal insights through subjective and dialectical processes. Certainly many students are not prepared or motivated for that level of work. But those who are need appropriate opportunities.

Many institutions treat truth as objectively real, modeled, given by authority, or "discovered" by logical or scientific analyses. Conceptions concerning the nature of knowledge, where it comes from, and how it is to be used emphasize acquiring information or competence in order to satisfy immediate needs, to obtain immediate benefits, to do a particular job, or to fill a particular role.

The relationship between developmental stages and educational activities becomes more apparent when explicit teaching practices, student-faculty relationships, and orientations toward evaluation are addressed. The lecture-examination system as often practiced is responsive to the fearful-dependent, opportunistic, and conforming-to-persons levels of ego development and to the obedience-punishment, instrumental egoism and exchange, and approval orientations of moral development. The key dynamic here is the comfortable fit between (1) the student's disposition to identify with persons in authority, to accept their definitions of right and wrong, and to avoid punishment by deferring to their power, and (2) the teacher's assertion of authority, an emphasis on dispensing information for students to memorize, and use of exams to punish wrong answers and reward right ones. When the lecture-examination approach goes beyond the personal authority of the teacher and makes use of more abstract authority, as often is the case, then the approach moves to an authority-, rule-, and social-order-oriented level.

Socratic dialogues, or teacher-led discussions, respond to the opportunistic and instrumental egoism and exchange orientations. They provide rich information about the teacher's views and permit students to shape their own responses accordingly and receive immediate rewards through the satisfying exchanges that result. Open, "leaderless," "learner-centered" discussions often suit the conforming-to-persons and approval orientations, inasmuch as they call for sensitivity, pleasing and helping others, and acceptance of group decisions.

Programmed learning, correspondence study, televised instruction, and most other forms of mediated instruction currently used fit well the conscientious stage and the authority, rule, and social-order moral orientation. In these instructional systems the teacher is a more distant authority: a talking head on the screen, a faceless individual who designs a correspondence course, a computer program, a radio series, a nameless member of a committee that decides on a course of study, reading assignments, experiential exercises, examination questions, and the like. The objectives of such instruction typically specify clearly defined areas of competence and knowledge. Students are judged against normative standards set by authorities based on pretesting or prior experiences with known student populations. The evaluation itself may be by machine or by trained professionals following agreed-upon guidelines. Students pursue course objectives by following structured sets of activities that call for memorization, rational analysis, synthesis, and evaluation. We would hope that mediated instruction and educational technology can serve students spanning the full range of ego and moral development rather than just those who are conscientiously oriented to such generalized authority. Reaching this wide range will call for the kinds of effective integration of educational technology with other human and experiential resources suggested earlier.

Many of the difficulties encountered by mediated instruction and educational technologies arise from unresolved conflicts of purpose. The success of new instructional materials hinges ultimately on questions of compatibility. Is there a reasonable fit between the purposes of the institution, the faculty members creating the materials, and the students for whom they are intended? For how many students of what kinds does that fit apply? How stable is that complex of purposes? Will there be significant shifts in the institution's requirements or the students' motives? Will the painstaking, expensive, and time-consuming investments required for high-quality materials ever be recovered? Or will these materials soon go out of date and be left on the shelf? So far our track record in answering those questions has not been outstanding.

Some other reasons for our limited success may stem from individual differences in intellectual development. Schaie and Parr bring us up to date on ways in which intellectual functioning changes with age. The learning and cognitive needs of different age groups—from the "acquisitive" and "achieving" stages of childhood, adolescence, and young adulthood, through the "executive" and "responsible" stages of middle age, to the "reintegrative" stage of late adults—have implications not simply for instructional content but for the cognitive processes called for by varied instructional methods, learning tasks, examination questions, and the like. So also do some of the sensory and perceptual changes that affect adult performance—particularly, declining visual and auditory acuity and speed of perceiving and responding.

Schaie and Parr also note the shift in adult learners' goals from the acquisition of the intellectual and social skills needed for adequate functioning in a certain society toward the maintenance and renewal of such skills. With advancing age, learners may look to education, first, for help in understanding the physical and psychological changes they are experiencing. Next, they may need help in understanding the rapid technological and cultural changes of contemporary society and, in addition, help in developing new skills to combat obsolescence. They may also seek to acquire new vocational skills to enable them to enter into a second career or satisfy changing personal goals. And finally, education may be seen as a means of developing satisfying retirement roles. If these major shifts in goals as well as in intellectual functioning were taken into account in the design of instructional materials, mediated instruction would serve adult learners better.

Perhaps some of the greatest potential for improvement of mediated instruction is suggested by Kolb's conceptions concerning experiential learning. The four-part cycle he proposes—concrete experience, observation and reflection, abstract conceptualization, and active experimentation or application—has its recognized counterparts in folklore and other conceptual frameworks. It deserves serious attention by anyone concerned with designing an effective educational program. Instructional packages can be created that build in all four elements of that cycle, and some of the best materials developed recently do just that. The home experiment kits and exercises integrated with the British Open University science courses are one example. In addition, assignments that ask students to make field observations, carry out interviews, or visit various community organizations can combine concrete experience, observation, and active application with memorization, analysis, and synthesis. But most correspondence and computer courses, television and radio programs, still ignore three fourths of the cycle and leave students almost entirely in the abstract conceptualization phase.

Potential Contributions to Adult Development

At first glance it might seem naive, or at least utopian, to think that educational technologies and varied forms of mediated instruction could contribute significantly to life cycle developmental tasks and to major dimensions of adult development. Many of us have come to have fairly limited expectations concerning the contributions these new resources might make. We concede that such vehicles may do a reasonably good job in imparting knowledge, communicating concepts, and helping students learn the language, methods of inquiry, and modes of thought of various disciplines or vocations. We recognize that such media may, when properly developed, achieve a wide range of training outcomes, especially if they can respond effectively to individual differences of the type mentioned in the preceding sections, as well as to the more familiar considerations of academic preparation, reading skills, and the like. But most of us would view skeptically the suggestion that such vehicles could aid students in more general areas of human development. Nevertheless, the possibilities are not so far-fetched that we should dismiss them entirely.

We need to recognize that educational technology, mediated instruction, and distance learning are still in their infancy. It is hard to remember that the computer, now as common as the horse and buggy a hundred years ago, essentially began with the Mark 1 built at Harvard in 1944. And plenty of us remember when there was no television. It is not surprising that we still have a long way to go in mastering the complex possibilities of these new technologies. The same thing can be said for correspondence study, xerography, microfiche, and the like. Although correspondence courses have been with us for some time, they have been treated like second class citizens, receiving little time, attention, or sustained support. As demands for off-campus learning increase, suddenly we may begin to recognize the possibilities of this Cinderella of the educational world.

Undoubtedly we can expect continued, if not accelerating, developmental efforts across the full range of educational technologies and resources for distance learning. It is entirely conceivable that such resources could be designed in ways that help students cope with life cycle developmental tasks; facilitate ego development, intellectual development, and moral development, contribute to professional or vocational development; and foster humanitarian concern. Some of the seeds are already well started in the simulation approaches being used in computer-assisted instruction.

The necessary changes are already well under way, as instructional materials, computer programs, and the like are becoming more varied in format, complexity, and comprehensiveness. Most distance learning materials aim at fairly narrowly defined objectives, achieved through a limited array of reading and writing assignments. Even when the programs are relatively broad-gauged, everyone is supposed to start at about the same point and end with roughly the same level of competence or knowledge. This traditional approach can serve specific education and training purposes well. But it needs to be complemented by another approach. There should be programs that give students the opportunity not just to pursue a single line of study to greater heights of complexity and perspective but also to explore various related areas of knowledge and expertise. These programs need not be conceived as courses. They could be larger units incorporating a variety of alternatives organized around a common method, theme, or particular student interest or purpose.

Nor must the resources and tasks be limited to reading and writing assignments. Resource persons in the community might also be called on for instructional assistance, field supervision, evaluation, and counsel. Community agencies and organizations can provide locations for field study, volunteer activities, part-time employment, and other experiential learning opportunities. Instructional units can provide information and advice about how to approach and use such resource persons and agencies, how to create mutually beneficial arrangements, and how to clarify mutual expectations. We are used to thinking of the local library, interlibrary loan, and librarians as useful resources for learning. Some creative thought, tested through experience, should permit us to extend that principle to numerous other locations and sources of professional assistance.

Nor need we assume that each student must inevitably work alone. There is no reason why interest groups similar to those organized for noncredit adult education activities could not be created to permit several persons to pursue together systematically designed studies for credit. Nor is there any reason why materials developed for mediated instruction and distance learning should not suggest such groups when they would strongly enhance the particular kinds of learning desired—and, having specified the size and composition of such learning groups, go on to suggest kinds of interactions among students conducive to the attainment of specified objectives.

Two Suggested Approaches

What kinds of activities might profitably be adopted by an institution or a department interested in distance learning or mediated instruction? And what strategies might best encourage lifelong learning and adult development and at the same time speak to local constituencies and institutional objectives? Perhaps two complementary approaches make most sense at this point: (1) developing cheap, flexible materials that capitalize on local resources and respond to particularly salient student motives and backgrounds and (2) taking advantage of major productions of commercial networks, educational television, and national public radio.

The first approach would use a combination of printed materials, low-cost cassette recordings, and inexpensive porta-pack television or tape-slide presentations. These productions would meet minimum standards of aural and visual clarity and solid educational substance, but would trade off technical elegance and fancy packaging for low costs, easy use, and transportability. The assumed life expectancy for each production would be short—perhaps three to five years at most. To the extent possible, materials would be modularized to permit easy revision, substitution, and updating by different teachers with different emphases or in response to changes in the field or in student interests. Such materials could capitalize on local opportunities for field observations, volunteer activities, internships, and the like. They could incorporate local festivals or historical celebrations; community development activities; local or regional conflicts or debates concerning resource management and environmental protection; education, health, and welfare services; strikes; political battles—the rich range of concerns that fill our daily papers and that occupy the attention of many of our adult students. Instructional materials could simulate local cases, suggest potential interview subjects, prescribe role-playing activities and their analyses, and supply tapes to trigger discussions. Thus, materials for distance learning and mediated instruction can provide information and abstract concepts as well as introduce students to the full experiential learning cycle described by Kolb, including concrete experiences, observation and reflection, application and active experimentation. And they can encourage stimulating social interactions. If the materials are kept cheap and simple, they can also be kept timely and responsive. And the costs and technical expertise required would be within the reach of most institutions or departments of reasonable size.

This orientation toward cheap local materials could be complemented by more intentional use of the increasing number of nationally marketed commercial and educational series, which may provide the basis for additional study. We have already noted the successful use of "The Ascent of Man" and "The Adams Chronicles." And we have recent examples of other series that could lend themselves to diverse educational uses: "I, Claudius," "Up the Down Staircase," "Poldark," and "Roots." All these and many others can provide frameworks for conceptual analyses and theoretical studies. Related literature in the humanities and social and behavioral sciences can enrich understanding of human dynamics, historical contexts, cultural norms, value conflicts, and a wide range of issues pertinent to life cycle challenges and adult development. Some of these series extend through time appropriate for traditional academic calendars; others are short and intense. For the latter, similarly short supplemental courses for limited credit can be designed, making studies more accessible to students whose schedules make greater time commitments difficult.

To exploit these nationally available educational resources requires some advance notice and a capacity for quick release of faculty time for preparation. But by monitoring reports of upcoming series and especially by capitalizing on reruns, necessary lead time can be found even when explicit working relationships with local network representatives do not permit inside information.

Both of these approaches require some back-up services if teachers and departments are to move beyond the classroom to distance learning and mediated instruction. There will need to be a commitment to faculty development and instructional services to address both psychological and professional concerns. Interested faculty members will need help in using equipment and in producing materials. They will need suggestions concerning ways print can be usefully supplemented by audio and video materials, and help in recognizing when such materials are redundant or irrelevant. They will also need help in doing the substantial legwork required for making community contacts, tracking down relevant opportunities for experiential elements, and evaluating the results of various modules.

This is the kind of service being offered by the instructional services and professional development units springing up around the country. These units also can take responsibility for monitoring and anticipating the nationally marketed commercial and educational television productions. They can identify local faculty members interested in developing supplementary readings, writings, examinations, field observations, discussion groups, and the like. And, if properly budgeted, they can provide seed grants to support release time for the faculty members who develop the initial resources to make use of such opportunities. That seed grant money can also be very productive in helping departments or individuals develop locally oriented materials.

Of course, the balance between the two approaches will need to vary from institution to institution. The basic point here is simply that our aspirations concerning educational technologies, mediated instruction, and distance learning need to move beyond the fairly limited conceptions that guide current practice. There will be continued need for diverse materials with sharply defined objectives and clearly articulated routes to those objectives, and for materials that rely heavily on verbal resources and verbal performance. But there is also a great need for a more open-ended and experiential approach that will give students diverse suggestions for learning and evaluation and include not only readings, films, and audio materials but also field work and observations, consultation with resource persons, and student interactions. With such materials as these increasingly available, our optimism concerning contributions to life cycle developmental tasks and significant dimensions of adult development might also gradually grow.

Conclusion

The use of mediated instruction and educational technology in higher education depends primarily, of course, on the role that such education plays in society. If, as seems likely, our society continues to place more and more responsibility on educational institutions for advancing knowledge, furthering the personal development of the individuals who make up the student body, training professionals, and instructing ever larger numbers, higher education will probably be called upon to use every aspect of communications technology to carry out these responsibilities. The question is not whether but how, and to what extent.

We have approached this topic with caution. Twenty-five years of experience with the predictions of specialists in both technology and audiovisual education have perhaps made us unduly skeptical of any claim that radical change is or should be in the offing. But we are not skeptical about the need for research, development, and experimentation. The lessons of recent decades may warn against relying on the claims and predictions made by advocates of a particular new technology, but they should not discourage us from trying out new ideas. Government authorities responsible for allocating funds for research in educational technology should be warned against exaggerated hopes and too rapid despair if results are not achieved. Of all the factors to be taken into account, therefore, time may be the most important: time to plan; time to develop courses of instruction incorporating diverse resources; time to preparing teaching staff; time to try out the technology itself; time to assess the results. To date, too much has been expected too soon, with the result that disillusion has followed closely upon original optimism.

With time, of course, goes money. The more sophisticated the technology, the higher the capital cost. As long as we lack satisfactory evidence that the use of sophisticated technologies actually improves performance, it seems foolhardy to throw out educational methods tested by experience. Nor is it reasonable to ask colleges and universities to experiment on their own with new methods, using funds from existing resources. The implication is clear: a policy decision to establish a long-term program of research and development has to be made. This has taken place in many nations already, and the accumulated results of these efforts can be expected, in the next decade, to have an impact on postsecondary educational institutions. If the past decades are any guide, however, the result will be a series of small advances rather than a great leap through any single technology, however sophisticated. In other words, change is likely to be incremental.

We need to remember that any given technology will be appropriate for certain types of students and subject matter and not for others. For this reason a program of research and development in mediated instruction should include *all* the purposes and *all* the technologies, and not be devoted to any one of them. To be helpful to those responsible for making policy and financial decisions in higher education, conclusions about the relative advantages of the technologies for particular purposes must be made as clear as possible. To concentrate on any one is to lose perspective.

It is this loss of perspective that may account for the relatively slow adoption of sophisticated technology in contemporary higher education. Too many new ideas may have arrived in too short a time, each with its band of enthusiastic supporters, for us to absorb them wisely and economically. There seems to be a general tendency to overstate the probable results of new ideas in education—whatever the modality—in order to gain the attention of those in charge. This process in recent decades has had several unfortunate results.

Exaggerated claims about the new technology have tended to make teaching personnel feel relatively less effective and important at a time when their responsibilities are growing. This leads to defensiveness, which impedes incorporation of the new proposal into educational practice. Concentration on a particular technology may result in neglect of the far greater potentials of combined technologies for certain purposes. And perhaps most important of all, perspective is lost if society is led to believe that higher education is ineffective in carrying out its duties and even reactionary in its response to suggested reforms.

To restore perspective is therefore a first responsibility, which has to be assumed not only by higher education professionals but also by the specialists in each of the educational technologies. As allies they can make progress. As adversaries, they can only weaken each other's position. As George Bonham (1976) put it, "the difficulties were—and are—more psychological than technological."

References

Bonham, G. "Educational Media: A Mixed Bag." *Change,* April 1976, p. 32.

Bowen, H. *Investment in Learning: The Individual and Social Value of American Higher Education.* San Francisco: Jossey-Bass, 1977.

Carnegie Commission on Higher Education. *The Fourth Revolution: Instructional Technology in Higher Education.* New York: McGraw-Hill, 1972.

Chickering, A. W. *Education and Identity.* San Francisco: Jossey-Bass, 1969.

Chickering, A. W., and McCormick, J. "Personality Development and the College Experience." *Research in Higher Education,* 1973, *1* (1), 43-70.

Education Daily, July 26, 1976, *9* (144), 3.

Feldman, K. A., and Newcomb, T. M. *The Impact of College on Students.* San Francisco: Jossey-Bass, 1969.

Ginzberg, E. "Educational Realism in Less Developed Countries." *Teachers College Record,* February 1974, *75* (3), 322-325.

Heath, D. H. *Growing Up in College.* San Francisco: Jossey-Bass, 1968.

Hochlander, M. E. "The Ascent of Man: A Multiple of Uses." Unpublished report, Corporation for Public Broadcasting and the Center for Advanced Study in Education of the City University of New York, in collaboration with Miami-Dade Community College and the University of California, San Diego, 1977.

Katz, J., and Associates. *No Time for Youth: Growth and Constraint in College Students.* San Francisco: Jossey-Bass, 1968.

Magarrell, J. "Computerized Education: Time to Sink or Swim." *Chronicle of Higher Education,* April 26, 1976, *12* (9), 1-9.

Rockart, J. F., and Scott Morton, M. S. *Computers and the Learning Process in Higher Education.* A report prepared for the Carnegie Commission on Higher Education. New York: McGraw-Hill, 1975.

World Bank. "Education." Sector Working Paper, Washington, D.C.: World Bank Headquarters, 1974.

34

Morris Keeton

Assessing
and Credentialing
Prior Experience

A number of factors, many of which are discussed in this book, are converging to change the aims of education, and with them, the functions of assessment and credentialing. This chapter addresses two major questions about the assessment and credentialing of learning that has taken place prior to the student's enrollment in a post-secondary education program: (1) In light of the findings reported in Part One, what functions can such assessment and credentialing best serve—in particular, what contribution can they make to adult development and effective adult functioning? And (2), what changes will be necessary if assessment and credentialing are to serve these functions well for modern students?

Functions of Assessing Prior Learning

Good teachers have always been aware that they need to know what knowledge and competence their students have brought with them in order to tailor their instruction to the capabilities and the interests of the students. Similarly, in assessing later what students have learned under their tutelage, they have borne in mind what the students already knew at the outset of instruction. From the perspective of society, an array of appropriate assessment and credentialing services can be a force for equity (fostering proper recognition and reward for individuals), for improved educational services (permitting programs to be adapted to student and societal needs), and for efficiency (facilitating sound placement in the work force).

A close reading of Part One of this book, however, makes it clear that the context within which assessments of prior learning were conducted in the past was vastly different from today's. In the first place, learners were much less diverse, and less was known about their developmental differences. Although teachers might try to vary their methods in order to achieve such goals as "enabling the student to become a mature person," "preparing the student for responsible citizenship," and even "fostering the student's moral development," their attempts were unlikely to rest upon such knowledge of human development as that delineated in the essays by Weathersby, Gilligan, Perry, White, and others in Part One. Those chapters suggest that the counseling of prospective students in the past may have overlooked some critical individual differences. For example, Bernard's summary of women's educational needs notes that different women respond quite differently to certain traditionally male-oriented, and hence often uncongenial, aspects of the academic environment. Whether by informal and individualized assessment or by other means, counselors of women students should probably sound students' feelings in this area to help them decide what they can do and what conditions best suit their learning needs.

Secondly, much less was known in the past than today about the relevant dimensions of prior learning and of readiness and capability for new learning tasks. For example, assessments of intellectual capability reflected little of the rich variety of distinguishable aspects of intelligence that Schaie and Parr review in their chapter. Their summary of the state of knowledge about changes in the intellectual functioning of older adults suggests that the assessment of older students should include data on their intellectual functioning. This might well affect the ways they are mixed with younger adults in study groups, the supports they receive for their learning efforts, and the policy of their instructors and graders about the timing of tasks for them. Similarly, knowledge about learning styles, as described, for example, by Kolb, was not developed sufficiently to permit systematic assessment of individuals' learning styles or to design instructional programs to accommodate different styles. Accordingly, the choices today as to what to assess are much wider than before.

Thirdly, the variety of educational options open to learners was not nearly as great even two decades ago as today. Our society, as depicted by Peterson and Tough, has become in a unique sense a learning society. It is a society in which schooling accounts for only a minor proportion of learning activities and in which the bulk of learning occurs after adults have reached the traditional years of maturity. Thus, Peterson estimates that some 116 million Americans are "deliberate learners in organizational settings" in a given year, as many as 40 percent of them pursuing studies outside the school and college sector. In addition, as Tough reports, about 80 percent of all adults engage in self-directed or "do-it-yourself" learning, relying upon "individually used sources." Clearly the greatest amount of all this learning occurs outside the context of traditional academic curriculums and assessments. Indeed, most of it occurs outside the context of any assessment system whatsoever. As a consequence, efforts at its measurement must occur after the fact, and often without documentary or other evidence that would facilitate understanding of its objectives and actual outcomes.

Today, what should be assessed is in part determined by the content and processes of the program under consideration by the learner. Thus, the functions of assessment may be (1) to test the learner's qualifications to enter the program, (2) to earn the learner an appropriate placement in the program, such as advanced standing, (3) to help learner and teacher fit the program to the learner's readiness and needs, (4) to exempt the learner altogether from the program and possibly award a license or some other credential, or (5) to guide educational planning to serve a whole class of students of whom the learner is an example.

The functions that assessment serves are also affected by institutional purposes and policies. For example, if a university prescribes a particular curriculum for its students and restricts its concern in assessment to their proper placement in the curriculum, then the sole agenda of the assessment might be that of comparing the learner's verified claims to knowledge and competence with a map of the knowledge and competencies required for courses making up the degree program. However, if the university makes human development its agenda, then assessment can be designed to diagnose as fully as means permit the characteristics of the learner that will aid in choosing the study options to pursue, the encounters to be arranged or permitted, the supports to be provided, and the schedule or sequence to be followed. For a university that gives priority to the development of its students, the relevant data for assessment will include not only the disciplinary content already mastered and the intelligence and competence of students but also their stages of ego development, cognitive development, and moral development, the "cultural myths" (as conceived by Douvan) previously absorbed by students about work, autonomy, and interdependence, and the aims of the students in enrolling. In such an assessment program, the incentive of academic credit for some of these developmental "achievements" could well be a part of the agenda of assessment. Progress on other dimensions might be assessed strictly for the purpose of aiding the process of educational planning.

Sometimes assessments, and the information sharing that results from them, can themselves be educational. Thus, in the *Validation Study* that Warren Willingham and his colleagues at Educational Testing Service did for the Cooperative Assessment of Experiential Learning Project from 1974 to 1977, it was found that as students are "debriefed" about their earlier learning experiences during the assessment process, they achieve measurably more learning than students in a different kind of assessment (Willingham, 1977). Informal inquiries among counselors and teachers with extensive experience assessing the prior learning of older adults indicate that a variety of new learning occurs during assessment. Some universities are thus encouraging students to use the assessment experience to search out intellectual activities related to the critical problems in their lives and thereby link their studies and their problem solving more meaningfully.

Numerous assessors report a highly charged discovery experience in which students, through the process of developing a portfolio on their achievements and receiving feedback on it, achieve new self-esteem, a vision of new potential in themselves and of more rewarding options for their future lives, and moral support for pursuing their choice among those options. In addition, it may come as a revelation to many adults that university authorities recognize the value of learning achieved outside of academia. It shows them that learning opportunities are all around them and, perhaps most important, that learning need not be purely career-oriented but may have to do with who they are and can become. The assessment process itself ensures that their new, more positive self-images are well-founded and not mere cosmetic repackaging of images. If these first intimations of greater possibilities in life can be strengthened by assessment and counseling processes that provide a grasp of the concepts discussed in Part One, the contributions to individuals' development will be that much greater.

Suppose in this regard, that an older adult holding a responsible job in management needs a college degree to qualify for advancement. He will want his assessment to establish what he already knows and is competent to do, both to avoid the boredom and expense of repeating the study of what he knows and to save time in getting on with his agenda of career advancement. But he will most likely be unaware of current ideas about the stages of human development. If apprised of them, assessed on various aspects of development, and counseled effectively about them, he may decide to incorporate developmental objectives into his educational program, in the interests of both greater effectiveness as a manager and better functioning in his family. To do so, he will need to find a program in which his priorities will be not just tolerated but actively fostered.

Similarly, suppose that a woman wishes to be assessed on her cognitive development, her learning styles (as defined, say, by Kolb), her baggage of cultural myths (as conceived by Douvan), her readiness to break with old roles and family or community norms, her new career potentials, and whatever else is needed to enable her to reshape her life in such a way as to make it more rewarding. In the course of helping the woman gather this information, interpreting it to her, and responding to her questions about its implications for alternative courses of action, the counselor is likely to set in motion some of the processes of developmental change described by Perry, which will lead to further ego, moral, and cognitive development.

A final important by-product of assessing one's prior learning is the contribution it can make to one's capability for self-assessment and taking charge of one's own learning. The capacity to obtain this benefit is related to stage of ego development (see Weathersby's chapter), but the stimulus to carry out self-assessment and to act may also contribute to ego development. Similarly, self-assessment may not only reveal one's dominant learning style but also encourage the development of alternative modes of learning, which, as Kolb points out, gives the learner further control over his or her learning and personal development. Assessments that are both illuminating and fun to do—as are simulations that take the form of games—can do a lot to stimulate learners' interest in self-assessment.

To sum up, the functions and contributions of assessment of prior learning today do not differ in principle from those of long-established tradition; but today's learners are more diverse, their options are more numerous and more varied, research concerning their modes of learning is more extensive and sophisticated, and the use of assessment services for personal, institutional, and societal purposes has grown more complex.

Needed Improvements in Assessment and Credentialing

Even learners who see themselves and their own aims in clear focus may have difficulty effectively relating their plans to the purposes and processes of their institution, their occupation, or the overall social context in which they must function. A well-developed assessment and credentialing program will address their needs and provide technical assistance in meeting them. If assessment and credentialing of prior learning are to promote human development, however, a variety of changes in attitudes, procedures, and institutional and public policies will be needed.

Changes in Attitude. Much of the literature on the assessment of prior learning seems to assume that assessment should occur at the beginning of a learner's re-entry into schooling and never again. In fact, for best learning, assessment should be conducted whenever a learner's objectives change, reasons arise for reconsidering the significance of an earlier experience, or evidence of error in earlier assessment is found. Periodic reassessment should be expected and provided for in programs extending beyond a year.

Another frequent tendency in assessing prior learning is for assessors to compare the claimed learning with the outcomes sought in particular courses already offered by their institution and listed in its catalog. Such assessors are oriented to the institution's management concerns primarily, not to the learner's goals. Rarely were those courses designed with the same purposes, the same starting points, or the same resources for learning that the independent adult will have had in his learning. There is, as a consequence, a need for a "bank" of assessment materials that can be drawn upon to tailor assessments better to the particular learner's claims and objectives. But this technical aid will not by itself effect the needed reorientation of the assessor and the assessment processes to the learner's situation and learning priorities. That change can come only from a reshaping of attitudes and the applied (not merely espoused) policies of the assessor and the sponsoring institution.

In reflecting upon and providing for the various uses of assessment, we should resist the tendency to link assessment programs and services always with credentials. Earlier we mentioned the contributions assessment can make to further learning and personal growth. The potential benefits of increased self-understanding and personal growth may greatly outweigh the importance of credentials for many individuals, especially those who are facing life cycle crises. As the knowledge of human development grows, advisers and assessors will need to exercise great care to avoid casting all assessment services in forms that make them merely tools of credentialing.

Changes in Procedure. Various procedural changes will be required to make assessment and credentialing serve the needs of modern students. One is greater individualization. We have already seen the need for individualization of learning programs to accommodate students' diverse learning styles, needs, interests, aptitudes, and prior achievements. Though economy of effort may call for standardizing some components of instruction, the ideal program for a given person is one tailored to that particular individual. Chickering and Havighurst's overview of the life cycle, Bernard's chapter on women, and the other chapters on various aspects of human development illustrate the wealth and welter of individual differences. These differences must be taken into account in assessment and credentialing as well as instruction. In effect, *mass* delivery of *individualized* learning and assessment services will be required for sound counseling and instructional planning. Much effort will have to be invested to find feasible ways to meet this need.

A major problem in assessing and credentialing prior learning arises from the fact that many, perhaps most, college credentials are based not upon direct assessment of the actual learning outcomes people have achieved but upon measurement of the inputs to the learning process. This measurement approach assumes that if these inputs are comparable to those used in traditional courses, they will have similar learning outcomes. For example, to get a degree in counseling, a student may have to "sit through" a specified number of hours in class for a particular number of courses at three levels of difficulty. However, there may be no minimum level of proficiency in that field required for a degree. Frequently, however, the input variables used for measurement do not correlate well with the desired outputs; and where they do, the predictability has to do not with the performance of the individual student but with a predictable average performance of the group tested. It thus appears that if society is to have the quality of assessment information that it needs for educational placement, job placement, and career advancement, there should be a shift away from input-oriented assessments of learning toward more direct measurement of what people actually know and can do.

This issue is sometimes seen as a controversy as to the relative merits of input measures versus output measures. However, this way of looking at the issue misconceives it. A measure of inputs that reliably predicts outcomes is an essential tool for planning educational services. One can never know in advance precisely what those educational services will yield; nevertheless, decisions must be made before the learning can get under way. The issue is not whether one should make such decisions about inputs but what kinds of decisions can appropriately be made on the basis of input measures and what inputs are best correlated with the learning outcomes sought. As knowledge grows concerning the factors that create a potent educational experience, educators will begin to develop alternative designs of educational experiences that accentuate those factors most likely to produce a substantial learning effect. Using measures of such factors in the forecast of learning outcomes will provide more reliable predictions of what will be learned in the future. These measures, however, will be much more reliable as measures of the aggregate or average outcomes of learning than as measures of learning by particular individuals.

For example, in the fellowship programs of the Ford Foundation and The Danforth Foundation for ethnic minority students, 58 percent of those who succeeded to the doctorate would have been ruled out if a cut-off score of 500 on the Graduate Record Examination verbal test had been used (Hartnett and Payton, 1977). This shows that individual scores may mislead educators both about the individual's capability and about the relationship between that capability and later performance. And the individual's stage of intellectual development and type of learning style are not the only factors that affect performance in assessment; stage of ego development and ethical development may cause a learner to respond to particular questions and tasks in ways that were not anticipated by those designing the assessment devices and the protocol for their interpretation. Therefore, while it seems likely that assessment practice will evolve in the direction of basing credentials upon direct measurements of the individuals' learning and competence, or upon the use of proxy measures highly correlated with direct outcome measures, greater precautions will have to be taken in the future in interpreting even these results.

Whether input measures or output measures of prior learning are used, there is a common technical difficulty in communicating assessment findings to third parties. To begin with, in what terms should such findings be expressed? Should a specific learner's achievement in computer programming be expressed in terms of his rank among 2,000 persons whose proficiency has been tested, or should the assessor rather report the proficiency in reference to a criterion that has been determined to define the needed competence for a particular job? The former, norm-referenced, measure is particularly useful for the employer or selector who is seeking, say, the best three candidates out of a pool of a hundred, regardless of how high or low the levels of proficiency represented in the pool may be. But for the agency wanting to assure itself of a minimum level of proficiency and desiring to avoid placing people in a task who are "overqualified" for it, the criterion-referenced measurement may be more serviceable. Arthur Chickering has suggested a third kind of standard that he calls *learner-referenced*. If the learner is simply engaged in self-improvement and does not need to attain some prescribed level of proficiency (as defined by a criterion-referenced standard) or wish to compete with others (thus in effect using a norm-referenced assessment), then an assessment that informs the learner as to his starting achievements and capabilities and registers his gains will be the most useful.

Traditional standardized tests are provided by their makers with a manual in which the meaning of the reported scores is defined and interpreted. No such aid typically accompanies a college transcript, though a key to symbols and some notes on credit policies may be provided. One suggestion that I have made in another context might aid in understanding college credit and degree awards, whether they were norm-referenced, criterion-referenced, or learner-referenced (Keeton, 1976). The suggestion is that a "standards file" be established, possibly using microfiche storage to minimize costs, in which for a unit of study (or an individual's process of growth) there would be retained three kinds of information: (1) the abstract statement of standards and criteria for performance in the unit, (2) a selection of performance samples (essays, tests, or products of other kinds) representing specified levels of adequacy of performance, and (3) the assessor's brief statement of the reasons for the rating of the performance sample with respect to the criteria applied. Where standardized measures are available, the manual for them would serve as the standards file. While concise symbols for performance level or brief summaries of standards could still be used, the standards file would now provide a ready means of translating the assessment language.

A critical technical question underlying those of score interpretation and utilization just discussed is this: Can individualized assessment of prior learning achieved under uncontrolled conditions be reliable and valid? The answer to this question is a qualified yes. The qualifications that need to be made are of two kinds: (1) Certain strictures must be observed if the *measurement* of what was learned is to be accurate and if the specification of those outcomes is to be communicable and understandable. And (2) the conventions of *converting* the information about what was learned into a *credential* must be understood and the nomenclature of the credential must be used in a consistent and meaningful way.

Historically, the most reliable assessment of learning outcomes has been made with mechanically scorable paper-and-pencil tests. These measurement vehicles obtained their reliability from the fact that they tested well-defined and highly limited (thus carefully selected) outcomes. Generally the testing was done for groups of people who for the most part shared the same language, a similar culture, similar learning experiences, and typically participation in similar types of classes in school or college. For learners who have not tried to learn the same things, who have not had the same kind of learning experiences, and who are seeking assessment of highly diverse kinds of learning, such instruments do cover the appropriate range of outcomes. In other words, they lack validity for the purpose at hand. Frequently, as noted earlier, what these instruments have predicted with reliability has been the distribution of performance within relatively large groups rather than individual performance in the future. But the kinds of assessment and credentials needed for the future will also emphasize reliability of prediction with respect to past and future performance of the individual.

The most extensive study thus far made of the feasibility of valid and reliable assessment of individual learning without the aid of machine-scorable tests is that conducted by Willingham (1977), referred to earlier in this chapter. It showed that psychometrically acceptable levels of reliability were achieved on a number of different assessment tasks. At the same time, however, it identified a variety of difficulties with such assessment and developed some sixty-six "Principles of Good Practice in Assessing Experiential Learning" to overcome such problems as clarifying the learning objectives with reference to which the assessment should be done, adopting and adhering to conventions of translating assessment results into credits or other credentials, and providing sufficient assessors and instances of assessment of the same learning to assure that measurement will be reasonably accurate and consistent. These conditions are sufficiently difficult to make the expense of such assessment activity prohibitive unless it can be carried out as an integral part of activity that is funded for other purposes. For example, if the assessment occurs as an activity of a course to develop a learning portfolio and to plan a degree completion program of, say, two or more further years, the expense becomes quite modest relative to the benefit.

In response to the growing recognition of learning that has occurred outside the classroom and the increasingly large numbers of requests by adults that they be permitted to continue learning without repetition of what they already can do, the Council for the Advancement of Experiential Learning (CAEL) has disseminated information as to how individuals can assemble, organize, and present evidence about their prior learning so it can be assessed in a reasonably cost-effective way by institutions of higher education. CAEL has also trained professionals to do valid and reliable assessment of such presentations. The effectiveness of this effort, however, continues to be limited by lack of economical measurement aids for the widening array of learning outcomes of interest to learners and to those who award the credentials. For example, in an increasingly complex society involving more and more interpersonal transactions with a growing diversity of people, effective functioning is increasingly a matter of interpersonal competence. Where, however, are the measures for assessing such competence? Or, to take a different example, the knowledge needed to address problems of energy shortage, environmental protection, the resolution of intergroup conflict, and so on, is not expressable as a given level of competence in a traditional academic discipline or even an interdisciplinary body of knowledge. Rather, this knowledge is an amalgam of information and concepts integrated by frames of reference different from those which govern the organization of traditional disciplines. Where, then, are the means for defining this knowledge clearly enough to test whether a given adult has mastered it? Even if such measurement aids were available, where are the people qualified to make the assessments? In asking these somewhat rhetorical questions, I do not mean to suggest that attempting such assessment is fruitless. The point is rather that the state of the art is relatively crude and its development will require a greater investment than many may be willing to make. Nevertheless, information about the qualifications of individuals to perform needed tasks becomes increasingly critical as those tasks become critical to the quality of life or the survival of society. In the course of time, therefore, it seems that equipping society for valid and reliable assessment of highly individualized learning outcomes of noncollegiate learning will become more and more pressing.

Changes in Institutional and Public Policy. The extension of crediting to learning that occurs outside of schools raises another controversial issue involving both policy and technical questions. Those opposed to the trend state the issue this way: "If everything and anything that adults learn is to be creditable, what will be the meaning or value of credit?" Implicit in this concern is an awareness that credits and degrees are a form of social currency; traditionally, they have not simply conveyed information about what the learner knew and could do but also conferred status and opened doors of opportunity. Frequently the measures on which the credentials were based did not correlate at all well with the tasks for which opportunity was opened—nevertheless, they effectively opened the doors. When people ask, uneasily, whether we should credit all manner of learnings by adults outside of the university context, they are concerned partly, though not always consciously, about the undermining of the traditional system of access to opportunity.

American society is moving increasingly toward equal access to opportunity. Of course, there is still resistance from the sectors of entrenched advantage, but the movement has a certain moral momentum that is very difficult to resist. How the issue will be resolved is impossible to say. It would seem, though, that any sensible resolution must begin with making the meaning of all credentials clearer so that they can be used more appropriately. Already the once clear meaning of college degrees has been so blurred that the courts are beginning to insist that they may not be used as the sole basis for selection of candidates for employment where their use has the effect of implementing racial bias, sex bias, or other constitutionally prohibited discrimination. (See Jessie Bernard's discussion of ways this discrimination affects women, for example.) The courts have begun to insist that better bases for selection and advancement be employed. If this trend continues, and if the technology of measurement keeps pace with it, credentials will begin to reflect more clearly what people really know and can do—though, granted, they may not have the same kind of clout or significance as the traditional baccalaureate or doctorate.

Quite apart from the effort to expand the domain of measured and recognized learning, there is an increasingly vocal demand for clarification of academic credentials. Wide discrepancies in the achievement certified exist among different colleges and even from teacher to teacher at the same college. A transcript showing "Introduction to Philosophy, 101, 5 credits" indicates little about actual achievement. I applaud this demand. The question of how much effort should go into such an endeavor and where the effort should be concentrated depends on societal priorities. The potential scope of this task and the sophisticated assessment required for it defy any overall management. But with appropriate attention to social priorities, educators and assessors can surely identify particular areas of learning and competence in which it is especially urgent to have better measurement and also to recognize relevant learning however it has been acquired.

With regard to the coinage into which assessment findings are translated, surely better alternatives exist than to express all learning outcomes in terms of Carnegie units of credit and collegiate degrees, or the recently coined continuing education units. An element hindering the adoption of such alternatives is the irrational assignment of advantage to the holders of college degrees and credits. As this advantage is whittled away by increasing public consciousness of the limitations of such credentials and by legal developments that undermine their advantage, it will become easier to give an appropriate place to alternative forms of credentials. However, academic credentials are not the only problem. We already have a vast array of licenses and certificates in our society. Trade associations and professional associations are highly prone to use these credentials and the systems through which they are obtained to limit access to opportunity in those callings. Here again advantage is accorded to the holders of credentials disproportionately to their qualifications for these opportunities.

Two things will be necessary for a more rational and fair use of credentials: (1) more exact definitions of the meaning and appropriate uses of the credential must be provided with the credential, and (2) the holders and users of such credentials will need to be educated about appropriate interpretations and warranted uses of the information. The credits and degrees currently awarded by colleges and universities are a crude form of shorthand. Society needs less crude credentials. When social and economic circumstances warrant the necessary expenditure of resources, measurement instruments and procedures will no doubt be developed to provide appropriate and reliable assessment of the types of learning relevant to society's needs.

Sometimes the kind of educational credential needed is not so much a precise measure of what people know and can do as a practical measure of their potential for doing the next task. For such purposes, a less sophisticated assessment may suffice; for example, for older adults claiming to know introductory-level materials in a discipline such as history or a profession such as business management, it may be easier to estimate whether the person can successfully perform intermediate-level work than to identify precisely what the person knows at the introductory level. In academic circles, the kind of judgment involved in such an estimate is expressed in a grant of "advanced standing" or "waiver of prerequisites." The learner is then allowed to enter upon intermediate-level studies. Frequently the learner does not in fact have the same skills and knowledge as a student fresh from a beginning-level course but is able to catch up quickly. This is more efficient for both the institution and the learner than starting at the beginning.

A further problem with prior learning credentials concerns their usefulness to graduate schools and employers. Even learners with traditional academic credentials have difficulty obtaining nondiscriminatory consideration for admission to graduate schools and to employment. The typical college transcript is oriented strictly to the way in which the student acquired the learning. It does not provide evidence targeted to the various intended audiences. Consider, for example, an undergraduate with a major in philosophy who upon graduation decides to pursue a doctoral degree in anthropology. He receives a transcript oriented to his qualifications as a potential philosopher, not to the requirements for being an anthropologist. Although many distinguished graduate schools regard a philosophy credential as an excellent background for doctoral study in anthropology, the data are at best a proxy measure of probable potential. The criteria for doctoral studies in anthropology and for the careers that follow would call for a different array of evidence. As consumer protection laws become stronger and more strictly interpreted, pressures for specifying such criteria and using them appropriately in selecting and admitting students will increase.

Since the future use of present transcripts is highly unpredictable, the ideal information on learners' qualifications would be arrayed and retrieved as in a library system. Access would be made possible by a complex system of defining and recording what is known and later recovering that information in accordance with quite sharply defined questions relevant to the next intended usage. Although such systems of information storage and retrieval of learning outcomes may sound impractical at present, they will no doubt be developed, on however modest a scale, as society's needs require them. Granted, a comprehensive information storage and retrieval system will probably be a late arrival on the scene. Instead, early efforts will be made to store information for specific anticipated uses. For example, if a college senior is unsure of her career interests but has narrowed them to three or four major possibilities, she may seek to have the information about her knowledge and competence recorded in a way that permits retrieval of the information for any one of these purposes. If her knowledge and competence in each of these fields have been assessed systematically, she could have a well-defined documentation of her knowledge and competence for each of those alternatives. This kind of information storage and retrieval will probably be developed first in the area of vocational competence, especially in fields in which licensing is prevalent or is developing.

In summary, there are better alternatives than our present system of tying so much educational assessment and credentialing to the prestigious current forms of credential. There is a need for a greater recognition of the variety of credentials already available and of their differential utilities for different purposes. In addition, efforts to create the next most urgently needed measurement processes and credentials need to be increased.

The difficulties in providing assessment and credentialing services, then, will range from those of purpose and priority on the part of different users to those of manageability of the attempted service systems, those of technical feasibility, and those in which purpose, method, and technique interact. Overall, however, the most beneficial approach to advancing the art of assessing and credentialing prior learning requires that the direction and philosophy governing the effort give priority to the emerging knowledge of human development described in Part One of this book.

References

Forrest, A. *Assessing Prior Learning—A CAEL Student Guide.* Princeton, N.J.: Cooperative Assessment of Experiential Learning (CAEL), 1977.

Hartnett, R., and Payton, B. F. "Minority Admissions and Performance in Graduate Study: A Preliminary Study of Fellowship Programs of the Ford Foundation and the Danforth Foundation." Paper presented at Aspen Institute Conference in Harrison House, Glen Cove, N.Y., August 2, 1977.

Keeton, M. T. "Credentials for the Learning Society." In M. T. Keeton and Associates, *Experiential Learning: Rationale, Characteristics, and Assessment.* San Francisco: Jossey-Bass, 1976.

Knapp, J. *Assessing Prior Learning—A CAEL Handbook.* Princeton, N.J.: Cooperative Assessment of Experiential Learning (CAEL), 1977.

Peterson, R. E., and others. *Lifelong Learning in America: A Sourcebook for Planners.* Berkeley, Calif.: Educational Testing Service, 1978.

Stutz, J. P., and Knapp, J. (Eds.). *Experiential Learning: An Annotated Literature Guide.* Princeton, N.J.: Cooperative Assessment of Experiential Learning (CAEL), 1977.

Trivett, D. A. *Academic Credit for Prior Off-Campus Learning.* Washington, D.C.: American Association of Higher Education, 1975.

Willingham, W. W. *Principles of Good Practice in Assessing Experiential Learning.* Princeton, N.J.: Cooperative Assessment of Experiential Learning (CAEL), 1977.

35

Jerry G. Gaff
Sally Shake Gaff

Student-Faculty
Relationships

The nature and dynamics of student-faculty interaction, always complex and subtle, are likely to be further complicated by the expanded age range of students. Although the relationships between the key actors in any educational drama are fixed to some extent by the traditional nature of that process and by the institutional context in which it occurs, certain changes can be expected as faculty increasingly find themselves dealing with older students, who differ in important ways from traditional college-age students. A summary of these differences and their relevance to student-faculty relationships constitutes the first portion of this chapter. Subsequent sections review the research on student-faculty interaction, suggest changes in practice necessary to promote productive relationships, and call for faculty development to bring about such changes.

Characteristics of Older Students

Anecdotes abound that illustrate the special character of relationships between faculty and older students. At a cocktail party recently, we found ourselves talking with a woman, the mother of three teen-agers, who has returned to college to acquire training as a nurse practitioner. Mindful of the task facing us, we tried to draw her out on the subject of student-faculty relationships. But she demurred, finally confessing that her experience

642

is atypical (since, as the wife of a physician in the community, she knows personally or at least socially many of the faculty members who are now her instructors. While not all mature students may enjoy such a special relationship with their instructors, many will have had life experiences that add new dimensions to the student-faculty relationship.

Extensive Life Experience. Most older learners simply have a greater fund of life experiences than traditional college-age students. They have traveled more extensively, worked in more varied settings, dealt with more personal crises, and perhaps even reached more advanced levels of development in some areas than their teachers. These students also have a longer history of independent thought and action, of responsibility for themselves and others, and of playing a variety of roles. Such a wide range of life experiences may be viewed as a challenge to the basic authority of a teacher. But if the teacher knows how to make use of it, the rich experiential mix can produce a broader and deeper understanding of the subject matter. Many of the chapters in Part Two of this volume illustrate this point in some detail, not only for such clearly pertinent areas as literature, history, and anthropology but for other less obvious areas such as economics, engineering, and biology.

Role reversals, in which the teacher becomes a learner and the learner a teacher, can be expected, given the broad experiential base of more mature students. Their greater experience tends to make these students both more independent as learners and more vocal. Professors may find their receptiveness sorely taxed by older learners who feel compelled to set them straight on every point. However, a young Ph.D. teaching a course such as Marriage and the Family for the first time may be forever in the debt of students who actually have lived the marriage and family stages about which he or she can only theorize, and who can flesh out the conceptual framework with personal testimony of what has and has not worked. In tapping students' experiences, teachers get a chance to see their ideas challenged, confirmed, or broadened. Both parties may find themselves playing unfamiliar roles, with all the attendant uncertainties. A genuine attitude of sharing truths learned over a period of years can help both students and teachers grow and develop beyond the limits of their own lives and can enrich their relationships immeasurably.

The "living inquiry" strategy described by Torbert in his chapter on interpersonal competence might be employed effectively in developing more satisfying student-faculty relationships. The currently prevalent "mystery-mastery" strategy, as Torbert points out, is not conducive to the enhancement of relationships between teachers and older students. The more open mode of communication represented by "living inquiry" might well help to maximize positive interaction and minimize role conflicts.

Different Interests. Adults face developmental tasks different from those of younger students. Chickering and Havighurst remind us, for example, that during the middle years adults are concerned with assuming mature social responsibility, helping teen-age children become responsible and happy adults, attaining satisfactory performance in their careers, developing leisure-time activities, adjusting to the physiological changes of middle age, and adapting to the needs of aging parents. These tasks may give adult students interests, concerns, and values different from those of their younger classmates. The resulting diversity of interests poses a challenge for any teacher concerned with individualizing methods of instruction. A continuing problem is how to permit exploration of issues related to a wide array of developmental interests and needs, while at the same time maintaining common grounds for discussion.

As students' experience repertoires become more rich and diverse and their developmental patterns more complex, student-faculty relationships also become more complex and varied. Given the numerous dimensions of human development described in this volume alone, it becomes apparent that the scope and depth of learner-teacher relationships must increase to accommodate them. Since development on all tasks or in all areas of life does not occur evenly, teachers may find themselves involved in many different types of relationships simultaneously. They may be friends, counselors, mentors, advisors, guides, and fellow citizens for various students in addition to continuing in more traditional teaching relationships.

Competing Demands. Adults may also have less time and energy to invest in education at any one time than younger students. The other demands placed on them by family, job, and community may deny them the "moratorium" available to many, though certainly not all, young persons. Education must be pursued alongside these other obligations. Hence adults may have less time and energy for learning and for developing educationally valuable relationships with teachers. Efficiency requires that ways be found to relate studies to other areas of their lives. But the relative lack of time or energy does not necessarily mean that older students want to settle for the easy or expedient in either educational programs or relationships. Adults seek meaningful and challenging learning opportunities, tasks, and relationships; it is simply that they must juggle these with more responsibilities and conflicting demands than most younger students have.

The formation of a personal identity is a major developmental task for an adolescent student, but identity issues are of importance to mature students too, especially since a return to college may alter established orientations and self-conceptions. There are complicating factors, however. Some may have to maintain a sufficiently fixed sense of identity in other areas of life to function satisfactorily in parental and worker roles, for instance. The persons with whom they have established relationships may insist on dealing with the "old self." While these other relationships may provide stability for the pursuit of education, they also may be barriers to growth and change. Nevertheless, it may be easier for some older persons, having accomplished the developmental tasks of younger adulthood and experienced personal changes previously, to cope with identity reformation.

Pragmatism. Adults tend to be more goal-oriented, pragmatic, and demanding as learners than younger students. If they have only a limited amount of time or must make real sacrifices to pursue an education, they may be more insistent that they learn something of value to them. Ordinarily, they are interested less in doctrines or theories than in concrete problems, as White points out in his chapter on humanitarian concern. Hence they expect faculty not to teach specific "subjects" in scholarly isolation but rather to identify, interweave, and relate the many facets of knowledge to each other and to the fabric of the larger society. As Schaie and Parr observe in discussing intellectual development, mature students have more situation-specific goals and hence need a greater variety of opportunities to enable them to meet their goals satisfactorily.

Older learners are thus likely to be more demanding consumers of education. Like consumers of any other service, they will insist on their rights and on consumer protection services. And these demands from tax-paying citizens can have a pervasive effect on student-faculty relationships. Faculty will be expected to perform their services with reasonable consideration for the needs and goals of their students, at reasonable costs—both financial and psychological—and to deliver what is advertised. Faculty may sometimes be forced into defensive, even combative relationships with their students. However, if faculty are attuned to this situation and are able to merge their own knowledge and interests with those of the students, both should profit from the exchange.

Career Orientation. Adult students frequently enroll for degree programs or specific courses as an aid to their career advancement. In years past, large numbers of public school teachers took work toward graduate degrees in response to a system of monetary incentives for additional schooling. Often, however, students are interested not so much in degree credit as in a concrete understanding of particular new concepts, techniques, or skills necessary for dealing effectively with aspects of a job. Such practical expectations may put students at odds with faculty members who are concerned with more abstract explanations of phenomena. However, given the right conditions, the tension between the abstract and concrete or theoretical and applied cognitive styles may be productive and may lead to a richer understanding than either approach would alone. Kolb's chapter is helpful here. The four learning styles described by Kolb—Converger, Diverger, Assimilator, and Accommodator—as well as his four categories of abilities—Concrete Experience, Reflective Observation, Abstract Conceptualization, and Active Experimentation—can help teachers and students cope with these complementary needs and expectations.

Job advancement is not the only career-related reason for further education. Many people find that they want to begin new careers or modify or completely change old career patterns, especially in midlife. Women whose major energies have been devoted to fulfilling the role of mother may seek ways to combine that role successfully with a career role. The contingency schedules discussed by Bernard in her chapter on the educational needs of women outline the pros and cons of various alternatives. Others, having experienced the relative neglect of their career needs and goals at an earlier stage in their education or having discovered new or more satisfying career interests, seek as adults to remedy the situation. For some the changes are voluntary, and for others, due to unforeseen life circumstances to which they must adapt, they are involuntary. Blocher and Rapoza examine some of these complexities in their chapter concerning professional and vocational development.

Need to Combat Obsolescence. Often older learners are prompted to return to school by the realization that their knowledge and skills have become obsolete. As Schaie and Parr point out in their chapter on intellectual development, many older learners are vitally concerned with overcoming the obsolescence they have suffered from the vast technological changes that have occurred since their early educational experience. The need to update their information and to learn modern skills, techniques, and strategies—including how to use the systems and services available in present-day society—is a recurrent theme among these students.

Adults may thus be rather impatient with the "container approach" to education, in which facts, figures, and theories—many of which will in time become obsolete—are poured into the minds of students. Insult is added to injury if, as occasionally happens, such supposed "truths" are being read from yellowed pages retrieved from a file folder year after year. At the very least, students may expect faculty and counselors to help them identify the areas in which their knowledge is obsolete, or likely to become so in light of current trends, and to master, insofar as possible, that knowledge which reasonably can be expected to endure longest. Some students may even conclude that, since what they will need to know will continue to change, they might better learn how to learn—how to analyze, synthesize, and acquire other learning skills—rather than simply learn the latest recognized set of "truths," which start to depreciate in value the next day.

Other adults want to revitalize areas of knowledge that they had to set aside at an earlier time in their lives or pursue a newly developed interest. This may mean acquiring information and skills to enrich avocational or cultural interests, or learning more about themselves. They may approach education with the intention of enhancing their esthetic or personal sensitivities or skills rather than with any work-related motive. Such students may object to education based on strictly interpreted principles of the Protestant work ethic. That may be the very reason they have moved back into an educational atmosphere. Hence they may look for relationships and approaches that permit more enjoyment of the learning process itself.

Implications for Teaching. Teachers frequently report that they learn from their students and that this is a major source of satisfaction in their work. Adult students, although complicating their lives and making their work more difficult, can add to the enjoyment of teaching. Faculty can learn more from adults not just because they have a broader range of life experiences but also because they are closer in age and share more of the same concerns. This type of stimulation can occur, however, only if faculty find ways to teach that permit two-way learning. This means using methods that not only help students learn the course material but also help the teacher understand how persons with quite different perspectives and backgrounds relate to it. Some of these methods will be discussed later in the chapter.

The general characteristics of older students just outlined raise various educational issues and questions about student-faculty relationships. There are limitations to the developmental model. One may agree with Blocher and Rapoza that mature students are a heterogeneous group with a variety of needs that require a multiplicity of delivery systems, or with Schaie and Parr that there is a greater range of individual differences in adulthood. But, much as teachers might like to work with students within a developmental context, it is obviously not possible for a teacher to respond to each and every student in terms of his or her precise stage of development on each of the dimensions described in this book. How, then, can developmental differences be accommodated?

Some will argue that the crux of student-faculty relationships is not age or stage of development but rather the type and quality of the educational process adhered to. It may be argued that "ageism" is as destructive of effective learning and teaching as is "sexism" or any other "ism" that seeks to isolate and set apart a group. A philosophical commitment to identify and emphasize goals and needs of individuals may serve as a fruitful stratagem for teaching students of all ages.

An axiom of the authors of this volume is that education can and should assist the development of adults, and a corollary is that faculty ought to modify the content of their courses and their teaching styles to facilitate such growth. But some faculty will hold other views. They might argue that the atom does not split differently no matter what the age of the physicist, student of physics, or science instructor. Nor does the course of history change. For those who hold to this belief, developmental needs and stages are at best peripheral to the basic student-faculty relationships centered on a given body of knowledge.

Others may observe that older learners, whatever the differences in their own learning styles and interests, often have firm ideas about educational propriety. For example, the memories and prior educational experiences of older learners may have led them to expect that teachers function as dispensers of knowledge and that students simply absorb as much as possible. But then this characterization may well apply to faculty also. To what extent ought a teacher-student relationship be one in which both feel most comfortable in their traditional roles, and to what extent ought both parties to the learning process be nudged into new patterns that research suggests promise greater rewards for both? Is a self-directed or actively learner-centered endeavor qualitatively better than a teacher or content-oriented enterprise in allowing satisfactory adult student-faculty relationships to flourish? Clearly, a basic problem is explaining the alternative roles and performance expectations in any given learning context so that all understand them.

The character of a faculty-student relationship will depend on the amount of time and energy both parties are willing to devote to it as well as on the model followed. For instance, if older learners and teachers have the time and interest to establish close interpersonal relationships of the type that Douvan discusses, that would seem to be worthwhile. But if students' purposes are more instrumental and vocational than are those of academics, as Green suggests, then perhaps relationships centered on achieving agreed-upon tasks and goals would be more appropriate. For adults who have faced restrictions on career attainment, such as women and members of minority groups, the major aims of student-faculty relationships might profitably be overcoming remaining obstacles and sharing knowledge of career alternatives that might best suit their personal and cognitive styles. (See Kolb's chapter on student learning styles.)

Research on Student-Faculty Relationships

What can individuals or institutions do to improve the quality of relationships between faculty and students, particularly older students? The emphasis of research on adults (as presented in the first part of this volume) has been on individual development rather than on relationships or educational practices. We might therefore begin by reviewing the research available on traditional-age students and their relationships with faculty to determine what characterizes productive interactions. From this research, it may be possible to extrapolate some general conclusions applicable to students of all ages.

Student Change. The study of student development flourished during the 1960s. Stimulated by Philip Jacob's *Changing Values in College* (1957), researchers focused on several clusters of student characteristics, particularly those regarded as marks of an educated person, such as intellectual ability, psychological and social maturity, and value systems. They sought to determine how these characteristics of students were distributed among various types of institutions as well as among various divisions within a single institution, such as places of residence or major fields of study. Eventually, studies also examined the ways in which various parts of the college environment, including student-faculty relationships, facilitated or inhibited growth during the college years.

One of the most thorough recent syntheses of the research literature dealing with the ways students change while in college has been done by Howard Bowen (1977). His conclusions are instructive.

> The evidence points to the conclusion that, on the average, higher education significantly raises the level of knowledge, the intellectual disposition, and the cognitive powers of students [p. 98].

> The structure of values, that is, the relative strength of different values, appears to shift during college, with substantial increases in theoretical and esthetic values, substantial decreases in religious values, minor increases in social values, and minor decreases in economic and political values.

> Colleges and universities appear to be effective in helping students to achieve personal identity—that is, to discover their talents, interests, values, and aspirations—and to assist them in making lifetime choices congruent with personal identity.

> In its impact on the psychological well-being of students, college appears to strengthen autonomy, nonauthoritarianism, and social maturity; to increase self-assurance and confidence; to enhance spontaneity and freedom; to lessen anxiety and alienation; and to increase the sense of self-esteem and control over one's destiny [p. 132].

These are generalized changes; not all students are affected in these ways nor to the same extent. Similarly, some institutions are more effective in producing these changes than others. Still, these results document that, by and large, students do tend to develop intellectually and personally.

Influence of Teachers. The effect of faculty on student development has been a topic of interest for some time. Jacob (1957, p. 7) cited evidence that "the quality of teaching has relatively little effect upon the value-outcomes of general education . . . so far as the great mass of students is concerned." His added proviso that "*some* teachers do exert profound influence on some students" did little to modify the thrust of his conclusions. Feldman and Newcomb (1969), in their review of a far more recent and extensive body of research literature, reached a similar conclusion:

> Though faculty members are often individually influential, particularly in respect to career decisions, college faculties do not appear to be responsible for campuswide impact except in settings where the influence of student peers and of faculty complement and reinforce one another [p. 330].

The experience of going away to college, the peer group, and the general atmosphere of the campus were found to be far more powerful in shaping the development of traditional-age students than were their teachers, the curriculum, or their more academic experiences.

Evidence emerged also about where faculty members do have the greatest influence on the lives of students. Jacob (1957) reported that:

> Faculty influence appears more pronounced at institutions where association between faculty and students is normal and frequent, and students find teachers receptive to unhurried and relaxed conversations out of class [p. 8].

Feldman and Newcomb (1969) put it this way:

> The conditions for campuswide impacts appear to have been most frequently provided in small, residential, four-year colleges. These conditions probably include relative homogeneity of both faculty and student body together with opportunity for continuing interaction, not exclusively formal, among students and between students and faculty [p. 331].

Another study of student-faculty relationships and their influence on the course of student development was conducted by Wilson, Gaff, and their colleagues (1975). Relating information obtained from students in their freshman year in 1966 and again in their senior year in 1970 to information gathered from faculty at the same institutions, they investigated aspects of the student-faculty relationship associated with the intellectual and personal growth of students.

Faculty members who had the greatest impact on undergraduate students, whether defined by the testimony of seniors or nomination of colleagues, differed from other faculty in several ways. First, they were more interested in teaching than in research and in teaching undergraduates than graduate students. Second, they reported they were more likely to strive to make their classes interesting by using anecdotes, telling humorous stories, or sharing their own experiences or research. Influential teachers were much more likely to talk with students about a variety of issues of importance to young adults of that day, such as drugs, sex, alternative life-styles, the draft, and student protest. It is important to note that these faculty did not differ significantly from their colleagues, however, in position or age; what mattered was only their willingness to explore these topics with students. The single biggest difference between the influential faculty and their colleagues was the extent to which they interacted with students beyond the classroom.

Some students developed more on the various measures of intellectual and personal development than others. Students who showed most development appeared to have made special efforts to expand their self-awareness. To a greater extent than other students, they became involved in a range of intellectual, artistic, and political activities, often of an unconventional nature, and they sought out faculty members for discussions of intellectual, social, and campus problems. They tended to study disproportionately in the humanities and to be influenced by literature reflecting strong personal and social values. In addition, they held an ideal of a college that involved working closely with teachers, provision for independent study, emphasis on broad, general education rather than narrowly specialized studies, and a rigorous set of academic standards. In short, their ideal—and to some extent their own actual experiences—could be characterized as an *intellectual community.*

Significant Interaction. The kinds of teaching and learning that are effective in promoting student development depend not solely upon the personal qualities of teachers and students but also upon the relationships by which they are joined. In the study by Wilson, Gaff, and others (1975), each student described a relationship with the faculty member who had contributed the most to his or her educational or personal development, and each faculty member described a relationship with a student to whose educational or personal development he or she had contributed a great deal. Although they were not necessarily looking at the same relationships, both faculty and students described particularly beneficial relationships as continuous (having been initiated early in the student's college career), casual, and personally engaging. Such relationships were unlikely to occur unless faculty and students were brought together in at least one course, and they were more commonly the result of being associated in two or more courses. Yet, in most cases, the relationships that made the greatest difference in the lives of students extended beyond the classroom. Furthermore, both faculty and students reported that such relationships were characterized by a good deal of intellectual excitement, and conversations usually ranged beyond the narrow bounds of course work. The implications are that conditions that increase the frequency, closeness, breadth, and duration of student-faculty relationships enhance the development of traditional-age students.

Pascarella and Terenzini (1977) investigated the patterns of student-faculty interaction and related them to college persistence and voluntary attrition among freshmen. Their results support the idea that student-faculty contact is a significant factor in predicting college persistence, but certain types of informal interaction, they found, are more significant than others.

> not all types of student-faculty interaction are of equal importance in fostering academic and social integration, and thereby, college persistence. Contacts focusing on intellectual or course-related matters clearly contributed most to the discrimination between persisters and voluntary leavers. . . . The second most effective discriminatory variable . . . involved discussions related to students' career concerns. . . .
>
> Perhaps it is in helping the student develop an interest in ideas and intellectual concerns which extends beyond the classroom into more leisurely interpersonal settings that student-faculty informal relationships have their most significant impact on students' social and academic integration [pp. 550-551].

In this study, while they did control for sex, academic aptitude, and personality needs, they did not control for age. Hence it is not known whether the same results apply to freshmen who were older than the conventional eighteen- or nineteen-year-old. In a more recent study, Pascarella and Terenzini (1980) replicate and extend their work. They say that their results "underscore the potential importance of faculty, in both their formal teaching and informal nonteaching roles, as an influence on freshman students' decisions to persist or withdraw from a particular institution. Indeed, . . . the quality and impact of student-faculty relationships made greater estimated contributions to the prediction of subsequent decisions to persist or withdraw than did scores on the scale concerned with students' peer relationships" (p. 72).

A recent large-scale survey (Astin, 1977) yielded results consistent with these earlier studies and also found that students' satisfaction with their education was importantly related to their relationships with faculty.

> Students who interact frequently with faculty are more satisfied with all aspects of their institutional experience, including student friendships, variety of courses, intellectual environment, and even administration of the institution. Finding ways to encourage greater personal contact between faculty and students might increase students' satisfaction with their college experiences [p. 223].

Two institutional characteristics that encourage such interaction were found by Astin to be size (total student enrollment, but not necessarily student-faculty ratio) and residential living. The importance of residential life has been thoroughly studied by Chickering (1974), who showed that students who lived in college dormitories derived far more intellectual and personal benefits from college life—including closer and more frequent interaction with faculty—than did commuter students. He offered a number of valuable suggestions for creating short-term, special residential experiences such as retreats, workshops, and short courses as ways to approximate residential experiences for students who cannot live in dormitories.

Other scholars have concentrated their attention on student-faculty interaction in subunits of the institution—a consideration that is especially important in large and comprehensive universities. Hartnett and Centra (1977), like Vreeland and Bidwell (1966) and Gamson (1967) before them, noted significant differences in the ways different departments shaped student-faculty interaction, and thus influenced the development of students. The differences in disciplinary inquiry norms described by Kolb in Part One are consistent with these results. Different residential halls or other living units also have normative structures that affect the quality and quantity of student-faculty relationships. And cluster colleges have distinctive environments that may make for radically different patterns of student-faculty interaction on even the same campus (Gaff, 1970).

Still others have focused upon more particularized and shorter-term types of interaction in a course or classroom. Mann and others (1970) have analyzed the dynamics of a college classroom; Thielens (1971) examined a number of factors that affect the quality of student-faculty relationships, including the interpersonal styles of faculty and students, communication patterns, and the social setting of the classroom. Ericksen (1974) has made an effort to translate the principles of learning that have been developed by psychologists in the laboratory into practical classroom strategies of teaching. He stresses making the student—not the class—the unit of instruction, building bases for the student to transfer what is learned in a classroom to the realities outside it, positively reinforcing the efforts of students rather than criticizing their failures, and helping students learn how to learn.

Although these studies have been conducted with traditional-age students, it is likely that the thrust of their conclusions can be generalized to adult students. That is, the quality of relationships with faculty is likely to be related to the satisfaction adults have with the college as a whole and to the intellectual and personal development they experience. It is quite likely that the value of quasi-residential experiences that permit students to interact with their teachers informally will be as important for adults as for younger students.

Needed Changes in Educational Practice

The growing research on student development and student-faculty relationships indicates a need for certain basic changes in educational practice.

Greater Flexibility. First, the traditional pattern of full-time enrollment in four or five fifty-minute, classroom-based, teacher-dominated courses will have to give way to more flexible alternatives. Critics have pointed out that students may indeed learn more by concentrating on fewer topics at a time or for different lengths of time than in the traditional educational regime. Adoption of a course system in which students take four four-hour courses rather than five three- or four-unit courses, has allowed more concentrated study. A few institutions have tried a three-course system or even an "intensive course" calendar in which students study one course at a time by taking courses sequentially rather than concurrently. Because of the constraints of time and energy on adults with a variety of responsibilities, the weekend college, the more established evening school, and short courses are promising variations.

These alternatives have potential not only because they are convenient for working adults but because they are more suited to some styles of learning. They allow individuals to become more immersed in the subject matter so that it may have greater influence upon their thinking. However, a shortened period of time means that interpersonal relationships will have to be formed more quickly and goals stated more clearly and explicitly. The more intensive schedule will obviously suit some types of learners better than others. It may not maximize learning in those individuals for whom the learning process takes a longer time.

The classroom as a setting for learning has many advantages. It provides an environment in which several persons can consider a given topic together away from the distractions of everyday life. It allows student peers and faculty to engage in dialogue, which may stimulate and develop ideas, define areas of disagreement or speculation, or point out gaps in existing knowledge. Attitudes, opinions, and ideas may emerge that would not surface in a program of independent learning. However, the overuse of this context does much to constrain the kinds of teaching and learning that may occur. It may exaggerate the authority of the teacher, predispose the teacher to lecture to the least informed, limit the degree of active involvement of the students, and isolate education from the larger world. When the students are the more independent, pragmatic, and experienced adults described earlier, such limits are all the more disturbing. True, there are teachers who can overcome these constraints. And there are instructional methods specifically designed to do so. But the existence of alternative settings does much to expand the character of learning. Independent study, tutorials, experiential learning, travel studies, internships, and the like illustrate approaches beyond the classroom that may be more effective for many kinds of adult learners. Such alternative settings enhance opportunities for more diverse relationships among students and between students and teachers.

Revised Content and Methods. In most educational systems the teacher is the main actor, who typically holds forth from center stage. Adults may well be less interested in what the teacher knows, however, than in what use that knowledge is to them. The interests and needs of the adult learner may become more central than the interests and competencies of the teacher; rather than being the principal actor, the teacher might better play the role of stage manager, arranging the conditions in which the learners can best perform. This need not mean that the teacher loses authority or control or that he or she is unimportant in the learning process; rather, it redefines the teacher's role as a facilitating one. This obviously changes traditional faculty-student relationships, making them closer and more collegial.

The content of courses may also have to be revised to make it more relevant to the developmental tasks students face in their work, family, or community. Faculty may have to adopt an open-ended approach that allows students to select what fits their particular interests from a body of knowledge. Hence adults will have to be encouraged to tap a broader range of learning resources than is customary—for instance, to consult experts in the local community, to draw upon the perspectives of various academic disciplines, and even to devise their own courses of study. Whatever educational content is selected, it must be related to other aspects of the students' lives if it is to engage them fully and meet their developmental needs. Granted, it is a difficult business to maintain a balance between what students think they need to know and what faculty, from a broader perspective, see that they ought to learn given their stated long-range goals and the character of the subject matter. Sometimes learners, including adults, may not see the relevance of learning some specific information or methods that faculty or practitioners in the field see as essential. Attempting to improve educational experiences for older learners need not mean giving absolute license to either faculty or students solely to determine those experiences.

More fully developed instructional alternatives will be essential if formal education is to be effective in aiding adults in their development. Given the wide, diverse dimensions of adult development, the many arenas in which that development is played out, and the various learning styles people manifest, more attention no doubt will be given to individualizing education. Otherwise, many individuals will be learning something they do not care to know, in ways they find uncongenial or difficult, at times when they are not really ready. Individual curricular contracts, self-paced instructional materials, and opportunities to pursue interests within more structured courses are devices that are now being used to individualize the educational process and that can enhance the learning process of those beyond the traditional age range. (See Clark's chapter on individualized education.)

A greater emphasis on experiential learning may be expected from adult students, who bring more personal experience to the learning endeavor than students in the 18-21 age bracket. Faculty theoreticians in any field will find themselves engaged in more vociferous dialogue about the applicability of general perspectives to the "real life" settings that adults have experienced and can describe in graphic detail. As some adult learners insist on "reality testing" of the material they are learning in the classroom, faculty members who have had little experience beyond the university may find themselves hard pressed to justify the relevance of their specializations to the larger world of work and citizenship. Other students will argue effectively and rightly for credit that recognizes knowledge and competence gained from life and work experiences. More and more faculty will be placed in the role of evaluators of "experiential learning." And university policies dealing with credit for such learning will need to be shaped, as will those providing for experiential learning directly sponsored and supervised by the institution.

More Faculty-Student Contact. The research on student development suggests that it may be necessary to find more arenas for faculty-student interaction, beyond the traditional arenas of the classroom and professor's office. Contact in these settings has a purposeful, task-oriented quality that formalizes the interaction and precludes much of the human drama that can stimulate growth. Additional opportunities for exploring ideas and values important to students' development are needed. If the development of younger students is aided by casual and frequent interaction with faculty and peers, it would seem that such interaction would facilitate personal growth for older students as well.

Most mature learners are not free to move into student residences, whatever educational benefits they might derive from them. But, as Chickering (1974) points out, residential periods need not be continuous, frequent, nor scheduled on a regular basis in order to produce the special relationships between students and with faculty members that are conducive to human development. Retreats, special trips, workshops, and extended seminars are illustrative of flexible, ad hoc arrangements that can be devised to bring groups of students and faculty together to eat, drink, talk, read, report, and write uninterruptedly for several days about any number of topics. There is evidence that, whatever the subject matter, it is likely to have greater impact on the development of students—young and old—if it is studied at least partly within a residential context.

Avoidance of Regimentation. Students' experience with institutional policies or procedures or with administrative staff can affect their attitudes toward the total learning endeavor. If they receive support and encouragement in the admissions, registration, and counseling offices, their resulting positive attitudes may carry over to relationships with faculty. If not, the faculty may serve as lightning rods for the frustration and anger caused by others. Adults who have continuing responsibilities at work and at home cannot be expected to be the only ones in the university system to bend their schedules. Faculty and staff may also need to offer evening or weekend hours so that students may tend to matters in the business office, avail themselves of counseling services, or develop new schedules of classes. In other words, the pressures for accessibility to faculty, staff, and services are likely to increase. Several two-hour blocks of time per week will no longer suffice as office hours if teachers are to serve these students adequately.

Mature learners, accustomed to serving others in their work, will certainly expect to receive service when they are paying for it. Faculty and staff may have to serve at other than their own or their department heads' convenience. "Branch" information, counseling, and business offices could be grouped together in a library or student union, or other location that is traditionally kept open during evenings and on weekends, so that busy adults could obtain needed services. No doubt many adults, especially the elderly, would find it both more convenient and safer to have a centralized service center.

Fred Harvey Harrington, in *The Future of Adult Education* (1977), comments that:

> With the rising interest in helping adults, the higher education establishment is giving way a little. There is talk about the value of adding mature men and women to the campus mix, about obligation to the disadvantaged, and about possible quotas for older degree candidates. But before much can be accomplished, educators must be prepared to (1) view the transcripts of adult applicants' academic records sympathetically; (2) accept part-time enrollment; and (3) provide financial assistance to adults, even if they are part-time students [p. 47].

Provision for generous transfer of credit between institutions, availability of credit for learning through life and work experiences, acceptance of part-time study, more appropriate admissions and residency requirements, and availability of supportive services such as counseling, daycare, and women's centers would help to alleviate some of the burdens on adult students.

Faculty Development

Whatever educational and procedural changes are adopted, effective education requires that faculty members relate to students effectively as persons as well as teachers. Faculty need to acquire sensitivity to students, awareness of the complexities of their lives, tolerance for alternative views of knowledge and education, willingness to grow themselves by entering into new kinds of relationships, and ability to master new instructional styles and skills and to relate all to their more pragmatic and concrete goals. In short, faculty development may be a necessary step in providing effective education for older learners.

Many institutions in recent years have established programs to help their faculty develop, not just in terms of understanding their subject matter but in many other aspects of their work, particularly their teaching roles. Through a variety of activities, such as seminars, workshops, conferences, teaching improvement grants, and use of videotapes, faculty members can learn more about the teaching-learning process and how to improve the effectiveness of their teaching. Since working effectively with adult students will require a number of changes in traditional approaches to teaching, it would be useful for institutions that enroll significant numbers of mature learners to offer special programs to help faculty learn about how best to teach them.

What might such a program consist of? First, it might include reading, seminars, lectures, and conferences designed to acquaint faculty members with the needs and special problems of adults. Second, it might include exploration of attitudes, values, anxieties, and other affective factors in teaching, along with various teaching styles that take these factors into account. (Menges considers some of these possibilities in his chapter on selecting appropriate instructional methods.) Third, a faculty development program could have workshops for faculty to learn alternative instructional skills and methods appropriate for adult students. Such workshops would go beyond talking and allow participants to get some hands-on experience with skills that are unfamiliar to them, such as devising curricular contracts or evaluating experiential learning. A close analysis of teaching acts, perhaps with the use of videotapes, might be useful in helping teachers become sensitive to their classroom performance or interaction with adult students. In addition, individuals or groups of faculty might be supported while they develop new courses or modify existing ones to respond more adequately to the needs of adult students.

An illustration of one particularly promising activity to promote good relationships between faculty and students is an adaptation of the student-faculty workshop devised at Loyola University, Chicago (Barry, 1977). Designed to free participants from the trappings of traditional student and faculty roles, the process begins as each faculty member tells a student partner what life was like when he or she attended college—for example, where she lived, what she majored in, how she financed her education, and so on. Following this, the student describes what his college experience currently is like. Individuals then tell each other what they like and dislike about students and faculty today. Eventually faculty are asked, "What is there about you that, if the students knew, they would be able to learn better from you?" For students, the parallel question is, "What is there about you that, if the teachers knew, they would be able to teach you better?" After this exercise identifies many issues and concerns, small groups can be formed to discuss specific problems and to consider ways to solve each of them. Plans for concrete follow-up action and reports can be made before the group disbands.

A different approach is being taken by a project directed by Mildred Henry and Joseph Katz with support from the Fund for the Improvement of Postsecondary Education; it aims to help faculty members work with students to facilitate their advancement to higher levels of development. Groups of faculty members in several different institutions work intensively with groups of students in their own classes to become better acquainted with their various learning styles. Faculty are trained to enhance their interviewing and observation skills and to study stages of development and their measurement. This in-depth exploration of student learning and development serves as the basis for redesigning the classroom activities and relationships that support and guide learning. At the University of Maryland, Lee Knefelkamp also is developing techniques to help faculty members in different academic specialties discover how they can consciously help students of all ages advance to higher stages of development using the Perry scheme.

By assuming that mature as well as young learners will continue to populate the nation's colleges and universities in the years ahead, those involved in higher education will face a continuing challenge to make those institutions hospitable to students of all ages. In doing so, they must become sensitive to the similarities and differences among learners of varying ages and knowledgeable about the research on effective educational relationships. Armed with such information, they can then fashion policies and practices, utilizing recent advances in faculty development, that will promote effective relationships among learners and teachers and thereby promote the full development of students of all ages.

References

Astin, A. W. *Four Critical Years: Effects of College on Beliefs, Attitudes, and Knowledge.* San Francisco: Jossey-Bass, 1977.

Barry, R. M. "Faculty-Student Workshop at Loyola University of Chicago." *PIRIT Newsletter,* No. 3, Project on Institutional Renewal Through the Improvement of Teaching, 1818 R Street, N.W., Washington, D.C., June 1977.

Bowen, H. R. *Investment in Learning: The Individual and Social Value of American Higher Education.* San Francisco: Jossey-Bass, 1977.

Chickering, A. W. *Commuting Versus Resident Students: Overcoming Educational Inequities of Living Off Campus.* San Francisco: Jossey-Bass, 1974.

Ericksen, S. C. *Motivation for Learning.* Ann Arbor, Mich.: University of Michigan Press, 1974.

Feldman, K. A., and Newcomb, T. M. *The Impact of College on Students.* San Francisco: Jossey-Bass, 1969.

Gaff, J. G. *The Cluster College.* San Francisco: Jossey-Bass, 1970.

Gamson, Z. F. "Performance and Personalism in Student-Faculty Relations." *Sociology of Education,* 1967, *40,* 279-301.

Harrington, F. H. *The Future of Adult Education: New Responsibilities of Colleges and Universities.* San Francisco: Jossey-Bass, 1977.

Hartnett, R. T., and Centra, J. A. "The Effects of Academic Departments on Student Learning." *Journal of Higher Education,* 1977, *48,* 491-507.

Jacob, P. E. *Changing Values in College.* New York: Harper & Row, 1957.

Knox, A. W. *Adult Development and Learning: A Handbook on Individual Growth and Competence in the Adult Years for Education and the Helping Professions.* San Francisco: Jossey-Bass, 1977.

Mann, R. W., and others. *The College Classroom.* New York: Wiley, 1970.

Pascarella, E. T., and Terenzini, P. T. "Patterns of Student-Faculty Informal Interaction Beyond the Classroom and Voluntary Freshman Attrition." *Journal of Higher Education,* 1977, *48,* 540-552.

Pascarella, E. T., and Terenzini, P. T. "Predicting Freshman Persistence and Voluntary

Dropout Decisions from a Theoretical Model." *Journal of Higher Education,* 1980, *51,* 60-75.

Thielens, W., Jr. "The Teacher-Student Interaction, Higher Education." In L. Deighton (Ed.), *Encyclopedia of Education.* Vol. 9. New York: Crowell, Collier, and Macmillan, 1971.

Vreeland, R. S., and Bidwell, C. E. "Classifying University Departments: An Approach to the Analysis of their Effects Upon Undergraduates' Values and Attitudes." *Sociology of Education,* 1966, *39,* 237-254.

Wilson, R. C., Gaff, J. G., and others. *College Professors and Their Impact on Students.* New York: Wiley, 1975.

36

Theodore K. Miller
John D. Jones

Out-of-Class Activities

From its earliest beginnings, American higher education has been concerned with more than intellectual development. College has been more than merely the curriculum; the mission of college has been education, and education has come in many forms—outside of class as well as inside. Since the early 1800s, when students created literary societies to supplement the prescribed classical curriculum of the period, they have participated in organized out-of-class education. Today this education is exemplified by a myriad of extracurricular interest groups, publications, teams, and residential societies that together make up the co-curriculum—that is, all the educational offerings of the institution that do not receive credit in the curriculum or are not required for graduation. Most institutions, in fact, have established a student services or student development division to focus attention on guiding students in using this co-curriculum as part of their education.

Research has repeatedly shown that out-of-class experience has a major impact on college students—emotionally, socially, morally, and physically, as well as mentally (Newcomb, 1943; Feldman and Newcomb, 1969; Jones and Finnell, 1972; Chickering, 1974a, 1974b; Astin, 1977; Bowen, 1977). It is relatively easy to see why this is true: Even students who are enrolled full-time spend only a few hours a week in the classroom, while spending the majority of their time in other pursuits. As James Coles, the former president of Bowdoin, has remarked, "It is not reasonable to expect that what the best professors can do in fifteen hours in the classroom can be fully effective if the remaining hours of the student's week are spent in an environment unsympathetic to what the professor would accomplish" (1963, p. 7).

Institutions have created their extracurricular programs both to reinforce their professors' aims with sympathetic resources—including study facilities, academic support services, course-related clubs, and dining and residential accommodations—and to promote student development as fully as possible by means other than those available in the classroom—ranging from the informal conversation of teacher and students over coffee or during lunch to recreational activities and cultural productions. As most educators know, the best teaching can often occur outside of class in such informal situations. One common characteristic of effective teachers, in fact, according to the research of Robert Wilson, Jerry Gaff, and their colleagues, is their accessibility to students outside the classroom: "The attempts of effective teachers to stimulate, to relate, and to educate are not limited to their classroom activities; they more frequently interact with students beyond the classroom as well, discussing careers and educational plans, course-related ideas, campus issues, and problems of immediate personal concern to individual students . . . by keeping office hours and frequenting student gathering places, lounges, or cafeterias" (Wilson and others, 1975, pp. 192-193).

For such reasons, out-of-class education cannot be viewed merely as supplementary to the curriculum in carrying out the educational mission of the American college but rather must be seen as an integral part of its educational program. More and better linkages are needed between the formal and the informal portions of this total program— between the credit curriculum and noncredit extracurricular activities. Only as such linkages are created will we be able to offer students a comprehensive educational environment designed to be responsive to all their educational and developmental needs as identified in Part One of this volume.

To this end, we must assure that our out-of-class educational offerings, as well as the curriculum, reflect changes in the student population, such as the increase of part-time, older, and commuting students. Such students have less opportunity to participate in traditional extracurricular activities than do full-time, younger, and residential students. They often have family obligations or career responsibilities that limit their interaction with teachers and fellow students outside the classroom. The 40-year-old businessman may be unable to meet a professor's morning office hours, attend a noon concert, or participate in afternoon intramurals, and may feel unwelcome or ill at ease in the campus "hangout" where other students and professors get together for coffee. The middle-aged housewife with three teen-agers, a busy husband, and a hiatus of twenty years away from the campus not only will have counseling and advising needs different from those of young adults but may be interested in different out-of-class activities, such as self-help groups for women re-entering the job force, or in campus activities that would allow her entire family to participate. Will campus facilities, resources, and programs conducive to total student development be accessible to them?

This chapter identifies ways in which colleges can become increasingly responsive to students' differing needs through their educational offerings above and beyond the curriculum. It illustrates how institutional sponsorship of out-of-class activities can aid student development in eight areas of student life—self-direction, career planning, social relations, leadership, volunteer service, cultural participation, recreation, and athletics.

Self-Direction

One of the primary purposes of higher education is to help students become more self-directed in their learning and other behavior. Self-direction implies the capacity to manage one's own life. It does not mean that one is totally independent, without regard to relationships with others or responsibility toward others; rather it means that one takes responsibility for one's own actions and development.

Self-direction requires both clarity of purpose and the competencies or skills essential to achieving desired goals. Younger and less mature students often need guidance in understanding their own development and encouragement to become more self-reliant in making choices, planning their time, organizing their priorities, and taking advantage of resources available to them. As they develop greater self-direction, the role of the teacher, and indeed that of the institution, can change from that of director of learning to that of facilitator and supplier of resources.

Four components seem essential to this process of developing self-direction (Miller and Prince, 1976). The first is *goal setting,* whereby students learn to clarify their values, set priorities among their interests, and determine their short-range and long-range goals. A second is *assessment,* since if one wishes to achieve a goal, it is essential to understand where one currently is in relation to it. Assessment involves collecting information about one's skills and needs as related to one's goals. Once the goal is clear and this assessment in accomplished, *change strategies* must be implemented to achieve the goal. This third step involves determining a plan for attaining one's goal and intelligently seeking out and using resources, such as courses, consultation, books, and informal instruction, to increase one's skills or overcome problems interfering with goal attainment. The fourth and final component is *evaluation,* by which one appraises the success of these efforts at accomplishing one's ends and adjusts one's efforts accordingly.

The educational climate of an institution is extremely important in fostering self-directed learning and other self-directed behavior. Obviously, opportunities for choice and experimentation, for testing oneself, experiencing failure, and overcoming setbacks are essential: We seldom learn how to learn and how to function in self-regulating ways by being required to follow others' rules. But other elements are also important in fostering self-direction, according to Knowles (1975). The educational environment must be one in which students feel that others care about them and their welfare, one that encourages mutual trust, respect, and open dialogue between students and instructors, and one in which students and instructors are secure in—and clear about—their respective roles.

Many institutions now offer courses in self-development as part of their curriculum, although the typical instructional techniques of some professors in these courses offer little opportunity for students to practice self-direction or learn how to learn. Informal out-of-class programs can offer these opportunities as well. A number of institutions are using freshman orientation sessions, special noncredit freshman seminars, faculty and peer advising programs, and residence hall programs together with courses in systematic efforts toward this end (see illustrative examples in Miller and Prince, 1976). Traditional student services and academic support services that readily lend themselves to these programs include advising and counseling services, admissions testing and diagnostic and placement testing programs, career planning programs, student activities and student union programs, living group programs, and developmental skills programs, including reading and writing skills, study skills, library use and class participation skills, time management and concentration skills, test anxiety-reduction skills, and other skills essential to being a successful student.

Some institutions have sought to coordinate these varied programs through establishing a student development center to enhance self-development of all students. Brown and Citrin (1977) have even advocated use of a "developmental transcript," complementing the traditional academic transcript, to record evidence of students' personal growth beyond that noted in course achievement. What is essential is to bring the resources of all campus services to bear upon the development of all students, young and old, residential or commuter. A joint effort of faculty members, administrators, student affairs staff, and students themselves is the key to making these services useful to all students. Systematic approaches offer greater likelihood of facilitating self-directed development of students than the traditional uncoordinated cafeteria of services so often offered in the past.

Career Planning

Both Blocher and Rapoza, in their chapter in Part One of this volume, and Shipton and Steltenpohl, later in this part, have dealt with career planning and placement services as an integral part of college responsibilities. They have advocated, for example, the integration of educational and vocational advising as well as bringing this advising into the mainstream of the educational process; and they have noted increased use of off-campus career exploration and experience as part of the curriculum, arranged through cooperative education, internships, and practica. Out-of-class activities offer extensive opportunities for students to explore career possibilities and test their career interests.

Far too often, students have nearly completed their degree requirements before they confront the issues of life work and employment skills. Integrating academic and career counseling is one way that institutions can strengthen career preparation. They also can improve their students' job-seeking skills by noncredit workshops or courses on resume writing, interviewing techniques, and sources of information about job opportunities. They can use their part-time employment opportunities and work-study programs both on campus and off campus to help students test particular career possibilities. They can develop volunteer service opportunities with local institutions such as the schools, hospitals, nursing homes, senior citizens' centers, mental health facilities, rehabilitation programs, and similar community agencies so that students can explore their humanitarian interests and enhance their empathetic understanding of what it means to be dependent or handicapped or old or unwanted. They can sponsor day-long, weekend, or even week-long teach-ins and career fairs, bringing representatives of the professions, of business and industry, and of other employers to campus for demonstrations and discussion. They can invite such representatives to campus at other times for meetings with interested students and faculty. They can bring in recent retirees as informal advisors and consultants to students. But most immediately, they can involve their older adult students—those already experienced in the marketplace and on the career ladder—in informing younger students about the world of work and the skills needed for successful progress in it. These adult students, whether enrolled for further advancement in their field, for avocational pursuits, or for midlife career changes, can show how education relates to one's work. But it is the faculty and staff of the institution who should take the initiative for such interaction, by creating opportunities for cross-generational dialogue through the co-curriculum as well as through course work.

Social Relations

Social competence has long been one of the implicit, if not explicit, goals of American colleges. To be effective in society requires social skills; and today's goals of "interpersonal competence," "capacity for intimacy," "humanitarian concern," and moral and ethical development continue a three-century concern of college faculty for effective social conduct and desirable social behavior.

The social arts of rhetoric and written communication have long been part of the core collegiate curriculum, and the debating clubs, the literary societies, and the Greek letter fraternities have a two-hundred year history, having been pioneered by the creation of Phi Beta Kappa at the College of William and Mary in 1776. "The literary society filled a curricular vacuum," John Robsen has noted (1976, p. 26); "the fraternity a social and emotional one. The former could offer no escape from the monotony, dreariness, and unpleasantness of the collegiate regime, which began with prayers before dawn and ended with prayers after dark. By providing an escape into a brotherhood of devoted men, the fraternity brought new meaning to campus life." Even today, the out-of-class educational program offers far more preparation in adult social behavior than can the classroom. The late-night bull session in the dormitory, the informal banter of professor and young colleagues over supper, the friendly advice of the drama coach or the athletic director for a cast or team member, the "rap session" between the president or dean or counselor and a group of concerned students—all illustrate situations in which human relations education takes place. Opportunities to learn from one another in such unstructured and unprogrammed ways should be a fundamental part of the educational environment on all campuses.

Interpersonal and social effectiveness involves not only communication skills such as attentive listening and clear spoken and written expression but also the demonstration of tolerance, trust, and acceptance of others. Such human relations skills can be taught in the classroom, but the behavior must be practiced outside. Avocational and vocational interest groups offer excellent opportunities for students to do so. Ornithologists, antique automobile buffs, classicists, and amateur archaeologists, whether faculty or student, may well appreciate the opportunity to form an interest group for mutual support and interaction.

As more adults enroll in college to enhance their continued development, such interest groups can offer opportunities for increased communication between young and old. Some institutions can establish relationships with existing adult social organizations in their community and offer campus facilities or resources for their use; and as the concept of lifelong learning gathers steam, community-based organizations may wish to establish institutionally recognized chapters or groups on campus. Interested older students or faculty can also create their own social organizations with little institutional assistance. In such ways, members of the institution can interact informally, regardless of age or status, by focusing on shared interests as a normal part of campus life, rather than relating to each other in formal or ceremonial settings. Expecting a freshman to learn much social competence by balancing a teacup on one knee while trying to make conversation during afternoon tea with the college dean and his wife may result in nothing more than the freshman's deciding never to attend another tea; while sharing supper over a campfire with the dean during a camping expedition to local historic and geological sites may encourage the freshman socially as well as intellectually. The mature adult can represent a potential role model and mentor for the young, while interaction with the young can in turn stimulate the adult's generativity. Regardless of the content of the dialogue that ensues, the very process of interacting is likely to be developmentally beneficial for all concerned. As Douvan notes in her chapter on the achievement of intimacy, it is in the area of interdependence as the context for all work and creativity that we in academe have a largely uncharted world to explore.

While we continue the college's traditional role of providing planned social activities for students as a part of its educational program, programming such activities *for* students and for students *alone* will need increasingly to give way to involving students directly in their planning and implementation and to making these activities available to others besides students. The fact that increasing numbers of married students and students with families will seek these activities for their spouses and families is one reason for this change of orientation, but not necessarily the most important one. A more significant one is students' need for interaction and involvement with other members of the campus community and with members of the larger community as a normal part of their higher education experience. This interaction can broaden students' social development while assisting them in intellectualizing the experience and incorporating in it their areas of academic interest. How better to extend the opportunities of the extracurricular program for social development beyond homecoming celebrations and beer blasts than to involve a variety of significant others as participants?

Leadership

Education for leadership has been an educational mission of American colleges since the American revolution, if not before, and most colleges would contend that they help students to develop strong democratic leadership skills. Many educators would most likely agree with Arthur E. Morgan (1960, pp. 116-117) that "the degree of democracy existing in college will largely influence the amount exercised by the graduate later in his community, and if anything like democracy is to survive in America it must have a school for training." Certainly colleges and universities have, for many years, offered students ample opportunity to get involved and take leadership in student activities programs and student government. Over the past decade, some students have been permitted to become involved in the actual governance of their institutions, through membership on governing boards, institutional senates, or policy-making committees. But the question remains whether these efforts have resulted in widespread participation of students in managing their own affairs and in widespread development of leadership skills.

Research on the outcomes of college does not tell us how effective our efforts have been in this area of student development. For instance, Bowen (1977) has noted his inability to find evidence in the research literature that leadership is, in fact, a product of college opportunities and incentives for students to develop their leadership potential. And Astin (1977) has found what seems to be a great deal of self-selection involved in students becoming student-body leaders. He reports that 43 percent of the students who predict as freshmen that their chances of being elected to student office during college are very good do, in fact, eventually become elected—in contrast to only 7 percent of those who predict that they have no chance of being elected. Thus, our efforts to promote student involvement in leadership activities may be resulting only in those with "natural" leadership abilities and interests taking advantage of the available opportunities, while many other students—perhaps the majority—do not become involved. This strongly suggests that colleges are doing little to *promote* leadership development among their students; instead, they are merely giving some students the means to *evidence* their existing abilities. This is not good enough. Williamson and Biggs (1975, p. 119) argue that only "continued participation of *all* students in some form of institutional management (and of student life itself) will significantly contribute maturity of skills and dedicated motivation to students in their roles as effective citizens in our democratic society."

Equally important, participation in student leadership activities may be only the foundation for leadership development. Most writers on leadership today define it as the process of influencing the activities of an individual or a group in efforts toward goal achievement in a given situation (Hersey and Blanchard, 1977, p. 84), but "situational" leadership theory calls for different leadership styles and behaviors for different situations and for dealing with different types of followers (Guest, Hersey, and Blanchard, 1977). What is needed beyond participation, therefore, is some type of leadership training that does away with much of the trial-and-error learning so common in student leadership activities. Systematic training, supervision, and consultation are necessary components to be added to student leadership programs if effective leadership development is to result. It is fine to give students the opportunity to become involved, but it is essential to aid them in developing the skills and competencies necessary to become socially responsible leaders.

A two-pronged effort is thus required. First, the opportunities for students to become meaningfully involved in managing student life activities on campus and in participating in campus governance along with faculty members and administrators must be increased. And second, new methods and modes of leadership training must be systematically built into out-of-class student leadership activities. These workshops, retreats, and even simple "postmortem" analyses of student meetings or decisions must be available not only to elected leaders and candidates for office but to any student wishing to increase his or her leadership potential.

In this connection, it goes without saying that the leadership behavior of institutional administrators and faculty will serve as an object lesson in such training. If institutional leaders employ a "mystery-mastery" strategy of leadership, in Torbert's phrase from his chapter on interpersonal competence, rather than the "inquiring" strategy that he advocates, students will most likely attempt to emulate it. Only as they experience interactions with administrators and faculty members who demonstrate an inquiring strategy of interpersonal relations can they be expected to acquire this type of leadership competence. Similarly, they cannot be expected to demonstrate the advanced ethical and moral qualities in their leadership actions that Perry and Gilligan have described in their chapters if such qualities are lacking in institutional leadership. Leaders in the making need constructive models as well as participation, training, and feedback on leadership behavior and strategies.

Volunteer Service

Almost everyone would agree that contributing to the welfare of others is a responsibility of enlightened citizenship in our society and that such service warrants inclusion in the out-of-class activities of students. The development of humanitarian concern is not achieved automatically. Sanford (1967, p. 78) has noted that the acquisition of full social responsibility requires experience in social action or in activities helpful to other people: "A young person needs this experience in order to test the adequacy of his judgment, to familiarize himself with the limits of what he can do, and, above all, to learn about the self-fulfillment that comes from being of service to others." It is via voluntary community and social service that some students enter human service as a profession. Such social action tends to sensitize all students to the real-world needs of human beings in distress as well as prompt them to continue volunteer work throughout the remainder of their lives.

Earlier in this volume, Green suggested that the very purpose of the academy is service and that the most effective learning may be acquired in the context of human service beyond the confines of the classroom. Still earlier, Chickering and Havighurst identified the "assumption of civic responsibility" as an important developmental task for adulthood. Colleges might do well to use their out-of-class co-curriculum to foster this important developmental learning. As White notes in his chapter, volunteer service can be instrumental in developing the empathy that is the affective root of humanitarian concern.

During the 1960s, college students were increasingly involved in community service activities on a voluntary basis. In state mental hospitals alone, during 1968, nearly 8,000 students from over 300 colleges spent two or more hours each week with mental patients in both formal and informal interaction (U.S. Public Health Service, 1968). Other students have been involved in community projects ranging from tutoring children and caring for the elderly to fund-raising and clean-up campaigns. A number of institutions have granted academic credit to students for such work, as advocated by the National Student Association in its Community Action Project (Duncan, 1968). Others have sought to involve more students in more ways with systematic noncredit programs, under such labels as the "Communiversity" program of one large southeastern university, involving continued community relations rather than off-again, on-again temporary projects. Big brother and big sister programs, school tutoring, home-bound invalid companionship, hospital volunteer work, correctional institution visitation, senior citizen assistance, and neighborhood rehabilitation are only some of the service activities that have real social impact and educational benefit as well.

Besides these off-campus service opportunities, another important type of service program has been growing in size and scope on many American campuses: peer or paraprofessional counseling, tutorials, and assistanceships, whereby students help other students in many ways, from new student orientation and residence hall organization to crisis intervention and "hot-line" referral.

The importance of peer influence on college students is well documented (Sanford, 1967; Chickering, 1969; Feldman and Newcomb, 1969; Brown, 1972), and that influence can sometimes be restrictive. As Charles Orth noted from his research, "Many students feel that rewards from their peers are at least as valuable as those offered by the faculty. They therefore limit their class performance to a point between the minimum acceptable level set by the faculty and the maximum acceptable level set by their peers" (1963, p. 18). Thus, the more institutions seek to involve students of all ages in service-related activities, the more this peer influence will be brought into harmony with institutional goals.

Peer helper services are not likely to be organized solely by students, even if there is ample evidence that students need such help. Rather, they are the result of coordinated efforts by administrators, faculty, student service staff, and student leaders in response to student needs. They involve student volunteers who are specifically selected, trained, and supervised to perform designated tasks designed to help other students. Naturally, all students help each other in their studies and their personal lives on a completely informal basis, and valuable learning can and does result from this informal assistance. But planned peer service programs offer more assistance in the long run, for they involve not only the opportunity to help but training and supervision in helping as well. Without this training and supervision, peers must rely on their own personal expertise in their attempts to serve others.

Many of the values of peer helper service programs are obvious. For instance, they give students additional resources to aid them in their education and personal development. Also, many students can learn specified skills better from their peers than they can from the faculty. Students often have a unique capacity to help other students to understand, perhaps because of their less formal relationships and more equal status. In many ways this allows for more effective presentation of student services. Another advantage is that the institution can make better use of its resources through such programs, inasmuch as trained students can free professional staff for more comprehensive efforts. Similarly, the students involved as peer helpers have a unique opportunity to become important liaisons between the students and the administration. Peer helpers are constantly in contact with other students as well as with supervisors and other institutional representatives associated with their area of student service. In this position they have great potential for informing the institutional leadership about the needs, concerns, attitudes, and desires of students in general. This allows the institution a unique opportunity to receive direct feedback and recommendations from members of the population served.

Of equal importance, however, are the benefits to students of serving as peer helpers. Delworth, Sherwood, and Casaburri (1974) have identified eight such benefits to the peer helper:

- Satisfaction and self-esteem obtained from "getting involved."
- Increased feelings of self-worth and confidence.
- Increased confidence in specific skill areas.
- Increased interest in their own educational experience.
- Increased contacts with key members of the college community.
- New work experiences providing increased understanding of particular careers.
- Skills and references of general value for future work or education.
- Advanced skills that may be directly applicable to employment after college.

For further information on students as peer helpers, see Delworth and Aulepp (1976) and Ender, McCaffrey, and Miller (1979).

There is little doubt that one's experiences as a student have the potential for influencing one's life thereafter. The more we can involve students directly in the process of assisting their peers as well as other members of the community, the more all students and the community at large will benefit. Whether recipients of peer helper services or helpers, students involved in these programs will come to view their institution as valuing, encouraging, and demonstrating interdependence, humanitarianism, and civic responsibility.

Cultural Participation

In the formative days of higher education in America, most colleges were intentionally located away from urban centers, with their notorious temptations. Their location made it necessary, however, for the colleges to provide their charges with institutionally sponsored cultural activities because they were not readily available in the surrounding community. To the extent that cultural sophistication was deemed desirable by the college for scholars and gentlemen, cultural exposure became part and parcel of the curriculum. Today, with no campus capable of being isolated from modern culture, whether electronic, printed, or pharmacological, the rationale for college sponsorship of cultural activities has at least two dimensions. One is that students, as in the past, do grow in cultural awareness and sophistication when exposed, as a normal part of their environment, to the best that has been written or created. The second is that the direct participation of students in planning and implementing creative cultural and artistic activities aids this assimilation process as well as enhancing their own creativity.

With advanced modes of transportation and larger populations situated near most American colleges, most students are within an hour or so of a multiplicity of cultural activities conceived and promoted by local communities—theater, symphonies, galleries, traveling exhibits. To this extent, the first half of this rationale for campus cultural programming is undercut. Already, many institutions work cooperatively with local community sponsors of cultural activities to accommodate student needs. Local sponsors provide tickets for students at a reduced price, while the institution's cultural programming budget makes up the difference between the reduced price and the regular price of admission. But as this trend develops and as institutions bring more and more professional artists and ensembles on campus to perform, there may be less opportunity for students to benefit from actively participating in the planning, creation, and implementation of cultural events. If such opportunities are diminished, the important learning that derives from direct participatory experience will likewise diminish. Clearly, a combination of opportunities for students as spectators and performers is desirable. Visiting professionals can offer master classes for students, coach them in their own work, and critique their efforts. At the same time, college administrators and student organizations can develop opportunities for students to participate actively not only in campus programs but in community-based programs—in local theater productions, symphonies, choral groups, art shows, and other events.

These links with other cultural organizations can better integrate the campus community with the larger community in several ways, not only providing ways for students to interact with professionals on and off campus but drawing potential students from the community to the campus. The cultural activities program has the potential for showing many adults that college is not only for the young and that they can fulfill many of their own developmental needs through its offerings. In this way, the college can become a community resource for intentional lifelong development of all who seek renewal. Granted, this is a giant step from the traditional student activities function of the past, which assumed that all students were in need of the same cultural exposure, but can it seriously be denied in the future?

Recreation

Recreational activities include informal leisure time relaxation, games, hobbies, and sports and can be separated for discussion purposes from the more organized activities of intramural, club, and intercollegiate athletics, to be described later. Recreational activities have had a somewhat spotty history in higher education. Physically oriented recreation, for instance, was not encouraged in many early American colleges. Thus, Princeton in the late eighteenth century forbade its students to play strenuous games deemed unbecoming to gentlemen and scholars (Rudolph, 1962); and even less physically active recreation, whether "light" reading, popular music, card games, dancing, or raucous conviviality, has in the past been suspect if not proscribed. More recently, however, calisthenics, swimming, tennis, jogging, and other forms of exercise not only have become popular among students but have been endorsed by institutions for their value in helping students maintain good physical health, enhancing their mental health by providing a respite from rigorous academic work, and teaching recreational skills with "carry-over" for leisure time exercise throughout life.

As more married students and adults with grown families attend college, there is more interest in family participation in recreational activities and thus greater demand for family use of campus recreation facilities. Colleges will be called on to open their facilities for family use. And as outdoor recreation, such as camping, canoeing, and backpacking, appeal to more and more families, colleges may well become central clearinghouses for scheduling if not sponsoring off-campus recreation.

In addition, colleges may make their recreational and sports facilities ever more available for community recreation programs, as illustrated by summer sports programs designed to involve local youngsters in college-sponsored gymnastics, swimming, track and field events, and team sports. Since campus facilities are often not fully utilized by regular college students during the summer months, these programs allow the college to serve the local community in a unique way. By offering such opportunities for local youth to become familiar with and comfortable on campus, the institution increases the likelihood that they and their families will eventually seek out its academic resources as well. Moreover, such programs allow college students majoring in recreation or child development to increase their career skills through summer employment.

Finally, through out-of-class programs, colleges can help all their students improve their health and their consciousness about health. Health education can take many more forms outside the curriculum than it can in the constraints of traditional courses and credit hours. Systematic weight loss, exercise, and body-building programs can be organized to help students develop better physical health and mental hygiene. Important health issues such as drug use, human sexuality, birth control education, alcoholism, and even accident and injury prevention in sports such as tennis and running, can be presented in informal sessions or workshops. Self-help techniques such as relaxation, meditation, and yoga can be demonstrated and discussed. Too often health education remains a specialty for students majoring in health, physical education, and recreation. Through out-of-class programming it can become available to every student.

Athletics

Organized athletic programs, in which competition is encouraged and rewarded to a greater degree than in recreation programs, operate at three different levels on many campuses: intramural, club, and intercollegiate.

Intramural programs are conducted to enable wide student participation in competitive activities between groups on campus, and large numbers of students are usually attracted to these programs. In these programs, greater emphasis is placed on participation than on developing expert skills, as in club and intercollegiate programs. But intramural programs differ from recreation activities in that they are organized around team competition rather than around individual activity or "pick-up" team games, and offer formalized rewards for winning.

Club sports are competitive athletic activities between institutions that are conducted on a much smaller scale and with far smaller budgets than intercollegiate athletics and that, in some instances, involve not only students but faculty and staff members of the institutions. Many of the less "traditional" American sports, such as soccer, rugby, and shooting are operated in this manner. For example, at one small private liberal arts college in New England that has no intercollegiate athletic programs as such, clubs are created each year by the students in response to student demands and may range from frisbee competition to martial arts. The teams are organized by sign-up sheets; anyone from a secretary to a friend's friend can play; practice sessions are held by mutual agreement; no coaches are provided, although instructors are available if technical assistance is needed; and the teams meet in competition against an assortment of colleges, junior colleges, schools, and other clubs throughout New England.

Intercollegiate athletics involve nationally and regionally regulated competition among institutional teams. The first American intercollegiate contest of any sort was a boat race between Harvard and Yale in 1852; the first game of intercollegiate baseball, between Amherst and Williams, followed seven years later; and intercollegiate football arrived ten years later with the Princeton-Rutgers game of 1869. By the time of America's centennial seven years after that, students representing their institutions on the playing fields in direct physical combat with those from other institutions was becoming accepted both by students and the public, if not by most faculty and administrators, as a way of college life. By the beginning of the twentieth century, minor as well as major sports were growing. Within another fifty years they were booming. Today many faculty members and administrators see them as serving important institutional public relations and fund-raising purposes, if not an educational function.

There is no doubt that organized athletics have the capacity to create a developmental milieu beneficial to all who participate in them (Sanford, Borgstrom, and Lozoff, 1973). They can advance students' levels of moral and ethical development, their willingness to accept responsibility, their critical thinking, and their acquisition of purpose—if the institution's athletic programs bear in these directions. However, if an institution's athletic philosophy agrees less with Grantland Rice that "it matters not whether you win or lose, but how you play the game" than with Vince Lombardi that "winning isn't everything, it's the only thing," students are faced with both moral and intellectual dilemmas. The athletic department's methods of recruiting and subsidizing athletes, for example, influence the moral tone of the campus at large. And insistence on victory at any cost and tight control over athletes may encourage dualistic thinking and limit students' moral development to preconventional levels. Paraphrasing Perry, "Our team is Right; others are different and Wrong. If we follow authority (the coach), all will be well." And paraphrasing Gilligan, "If we follow the rules (and the referee's interpretation of them), we'll stay out of trouble and avoid retribution."

In recent years, concern has grown regarding the role of athletics in higher education and in student development, and it is likely that athletic programs on many campuses—if not those with high-powered teams preparing stars for careers in professional sports—will undergo major changes in the not too distant future. (See Sarajian, 1976, for examples of such changes at a variety of institutions already.) Students interested in intramural and club sports may champion reallocation of athletic funds to their programs from intercollegiate teams. Financial support will need to be increased for women's teams, in compliance with federal guidelines. Many noncontact sports, such as swimming, tennis, golf, gymnastics, and track and field, may be organized on a coeducational basis, with men and women competing together on teams, although not necessarily against one another. And provisions will need to be made for allowing handicapped students to participate in athletics, as in wheelchair basketball. Despite these changes, athletic programs will be less affected by increases in the proportion of older students than will recreation programs, since more adult students are likely to be spectators at athletic events rather than participants.

A diversity of athletic programming may be called for on additional grounds, however: Students are likely to be interested in different forms of athletics depending on differences in their psychological as well as their physical development. For example, physical contact sports that provide students with an acceptable outlet for aggressive feelings may be useful for those at an impulsive or self-protective stage of ego development, as outlined by Weathersby. Team sports involving cooperation and less physical contact may be most applicable to those at conscientious-conformist levels. And more individualized activities such as golf, bowling, or track may hold most appeal for those at individualistic or autonomous levels. Ideally, athletic opportunities should be available to allow students appropriate challenge whatever their development, skill, or needs. These opportunities can bring out the best in students, enhancing their desire to overcome personal limitations and to better themselves; they can learn to compete, cooperate, and act as team members. Mature mentors can teach them skills and guide their development.

Conclusion

The rationale for out-of-class activities in college has traditionally been that these activities complement the students' educational development. More recent thinking, as illustrated in this book, holds that out-of-class activities form an essential part of this development. Today's efforts aim at designing these activities deliberately to facilitate the total development of all students. Campus student development or student affairs staff members are essential to these institutional development programs, but all the campus community must become involved if total student development is to be achieved.

This chapter has suggested a variety of ways that out-of-class programs can serve this purpose—for example, by promoting self-direction through helping students set goals, assess their needs, and utilize resources, by offering leadership training as well as leadership opportunities, and by encouraging volunteer service both in the community and on campus, where students can use their own knowledge and skills as peer helpers to facilitate the development of others.

Several steps seem essential if out-of-class programs are to play this role. First, institutions should systematically assess their students' interests and developmental needs so that they can devise appropriate out-of-class activities for them, rather than assuming that all students need or will benefit from the same activities.

Second, existing out-of-class programs should be reexamined and revised, if necessary, in light of their impact on the total development of all students. Similarly, specific skills and competencies essential to successful practice must be identified and developed.

Third, these programs should include participants from outside the student body, such as faculty and staff, spouses and children, and community members, to broaden students' contacts and assist in their development.

Fourth, the programs should cooperate with local agencies and organizations to involve students in active participation with members of the larger community off campus.

And fifth, to involve new and nontraditional student populations, such as part-time and older students, new types of programs such as those organized around vocational, avocational, disciplinary, or departmental interests should be launched.

Out-of-class programs can be more quickly created and changed to meet new needs than can the formal academic program. The major question is whether we who are responsible for them will be both sensitive to the developmental needs of students and responsive to them.

References

Astin, A. W. *Four Critical Years: Effects of College on Beliefs, Attitudes, and Knowledge.* San Francisco: Jossey-Bass, 1977.

Bowen, H. R. *Investment in Learning: The Individual and Social Value of American Higher Education.* San Francisco: Jossey-Bass, 1977.

Brown, R. D. *Student Development in Tomorrow's Higher Education: A Return to the Academy.* Student Personnel Series No. 16. Washington, D.C.: American College Personnel Association, 1972.

Brown, R. D., and Citrin, R. S. "A Student Development Transcript: Assumptions, Purposes, and Formats." *Journal of College Student Personnel,* 1977, *18,* 163-168.

Chickering, A. W. *Education and Identity.* San Francisco: Jossey-Bass, 1969.

Chickering, A. W. *Commuting Versus Resident Students: Overcoming Educational Inequities of Living Off Campus.* San Francisco: Jossey-Bass, 1974a.

Chickering, A. W. "The Impact of Various College Environments on Personality Development." *Journal of the American College Health Association,* 1974b, *23,* 82-93.

Coles, J. S. "Introductory Remarks." *Proceedings of the Symposium on Undergraduate Environment, October 18-19, 1962.* Brunswick, Maine: Bowdoin College, 1963.

Delworth, U., and Aulepp, L. *Training Manual for Paraprofessional and Allied Professional Programs.* Boulder, Colo.: Western Interstate Commission for Higher Education, 1976.

Delworth, U., Sherwood, G., and Casaburri, N. *Student Paraprofessionals: A Working Model for Higher Education.* Student Personnel Series No. 17. Washington, D.C.: American College Personnel Association, 1974.

Duncan, K. *Community Action Curriculum Compendium.* Washington, D.C.: U.S. National Student Association, 1968.

Ender, S., McCaffrey, S. S., and Miller, T. K. *Students Helping Students: A Training Program for Peer Helpers on the College Campus.* Athens, Ga.: Student Development Associates, 1979.

Feldman, K. A., and Newcomb, T. M. *The Impact of College on Students.* San Francisco: Jossey-Bass, 1969.

Guest, R. H., Hersey, P., and Blanchard, K. H. *Organizational Change Through Effective Leadership.* Englewood Cliffs, N.J.: Prentice-Hall, 1977.

Hersey, P., and Blanchard, K. H. *Management of Organizational Behavior: Utilizing Human Resources.* Englewood Cliffs, N.J.: Prentice-Hall, 1977.

Jones, J. D., and Finnell, W. "Relationships Between College Experiences and Attitudes of Students from Economically Deprived Backgrounds." *Journal of College Student Personnel,* 1972, *13* (4), 314-318.

Knowles, M. *Self-Directed Learning.* Chicago: Association Press/Follett Publishing, 1975.

Miller, T. K., and Prince, J. S. *The Future of Student Affairs: A Guide to Student Development for Tomorrow's Higher Education.* San Francisco: Jossey-Bass, 1976.

Morgan, A. E. "Developing Community Responsibility." In W. D. Weatherford, Jr. (Ed.), *The Goals of Higher Education.* Cambridge, Mass.: Harvard University Press, 1960.

Newcomb, T. M. *Personality and Social Change: Attitude Formation in a Student Community.* New York: Holt, Rinehart and Winston, 1943.

Orth, C. D., III. *Social Structure and Learning Climate: The First Year at the Harvard Business School.* Boston: Division of Research, Graduate School of Business Administration, Harvard University, 1963.

Robsen, J. "The College Fraternity: Two Hundred Years of Service." In T. Schreck (Ed.), *Fraternity for the Year 2000.* Commission for the American College Fraternity. Terre Haute: Indiana University Press, 1976.

Rudolph, F. *The American College and University.* New York: Vintage Books, 1962.

Sanford, N. *Where Colleges Fail: A Study of the Student as a Person.* San Francisco: Jossey-Bass, 1967.

Sanford, N., Borgstrom, K., and Lozoff, M. "The Role of Athletics in Student Development." In J. Katz (Ed.), *New Directions for Higher Education: Services for Students,* no. 3. San Francisco: Jossey-Bass, 1973.

Sarajian, K. "Alternative Athletics." *College and University Bulletin,* 1976, *29* (4), 1.

U.S. Public Health Service. *College Student Volunteers in State Mental Hospitals.* U.S. Public Health Service Publication No. 1752. Washington, D.C.: U.S. Government Printing Office, 1968.

Williamson, E. G., and Biggs, D. A. *Student Personnel Work: A Program of Developmental Relationships.* New York: Wiley, 1975.

Wilson, R. C., and others. *College Professors and Their Impact on Students.* New York: Wiley, 1975.

37

Harold C. Riker

Residential Learning

Residential learning refers to the learning that takes place as a result of group living. The experience of living closely with others in a student residence can facilitate change along all the dimensions of development described in Part One—particularly ego development, the capacity for intimacy, interpersonal competence, and humanitarian concern. When unplanned, this learning may be either positive or negative. In the past, it has been largely uncoordinated with other learning occurring elsewhere on campus. Yet residential learning may decisively influence students' attitudes and behavior and condition them for success or failure elsewhere. The impact of residential learning stems from two conditions. First, in residential living, the "teachers" are primarily fellow students. Second, the informal environment and rich range of problems and relationships offer many opportunities for learning.

Uses of Student Residences

In past years, student residences were simply that—residences; they generally had little or no connection with the institution's academic program. Until the early 1960s, their major purpose apart from simple housing was supervision of student conduct. Acting *in loco parentis,* residence staff kept a close watch over the social activities of the students in their charge, particularly the women students. During the late 1950s and early 1960s, many institutions increased their bed spaces by six to seven hundred percent. The emphasis on maximum numbers of beds and minimum construction costs per bed led to the construction of institutional living environments that bore little resemblance to aca-

672

demic communities. In fact, these environments had the unanticipated effect of increasing student feelings of impersonality and anonymity and contributing to attitudes of anti-intellectualism. With their noise and confusion, and inadequate study space, they proved unconducive to learning. Facilities that included lounges, recreation rooms, and food services served a major purpose as activity centers, but the frequent contrast between their attractiveness as places to play and the unattractiveness of classrooms as places to learn contributed to an overemphasis on extracurricular interests for many students.

Partly as a reaction against this role of residences as social activity centers, some college administrators, during the 1960s, began to conceive of residences as "living-learning centers" and to include in them classrooms, laboratories, and faculty offices. Since then successful efforts have been made at many institutions to link classroom and residential learning. Such efforts have often been traceable to the enthusiastic commitment of several faculty members and residence staff who saw the potential of residential learning as a means for supporting the academic development of students. Nonetheless, the planned utilization of the residential experience for learning really represents a break from the American tradition. Life in today's campus residences is vastly different than it was as late as the mid-sixties. Conduct regulations tend to be minimal and much more attention is paid to student preferences in equipping and decorating their rooms. The greatest single change has been in the designation of living areas where men and women may live in reasonable proximity with considerable freedom in room visitation.

Some administrators continue to view student residences as business enterprises that must be financially self-supporting; they focus their attention on budgets to the exclusion of the educational purposes behind those budgets. Parents often continue to expect college residences to control students' conduct. Students often tend to see these residences as separate from the educational endeavor and as centers for fun, games, and independence from authority. And many faculty remain indifferent, continuing to assume that classroom learning in the major disciplines is the only learning of consequence for students. They may recognize that friendships and training in citizenship are outcomes of the residence experience, but their view that academic life is strictly an intellectual activity leaves little room for attention to the emotional, spiritual, social, or physical development of students. Evidence that these elements do, in fact, have an important impact on the intellectual life should over time create more favorable faculty attitudes toward group living as a support of both personal and academic development.

Research in adult development, such as that reported in Part One of this volume, indicates that progress in one area of life affects and is affected by that in other areas. And a critical factor in several areas of development, including cognitive, ethical, moral, and ego as well as interpersonal development, seems to be a growing awareness of self in relation to others. Important learning about oneself—about one's identity, interests, hopes, and self-worth—can occur in conversation between roommates or within the context of a congenial group. Within such a group, students can clarify their values, identify their strengths and limitations, test new ideas, try new roles, and, on the basis of these experiences, review and perhaps refocus their goals.

In the process of learning about themselves, residents inevitably learn about others, enlarging their understanding of others and of the fact that others have rights, problems, needs, and values that may differ considerably from their own. For late adolescents and young adults, it can come as a surprise, if not a shock, that they must take others into consideration when making plans and reaching decisions that may impinge upon the feelings or activities of others. Even some older adults with well-established patterns of behavior may find that such patterns are not shared by those around them. In group living, students of all ages have an opportunity to develop their capacities for empathy, patience, and tolerance—critical ingredients for the development of humanitarian concern, according to White in Part One. When one student is able to say of another, "I was wrong in my first impression," real progress is being made; after this point is reached, the student will be more ready to analyze other stereotypes or assumptions and to consider their consequences.

One hoped-for outcome of learning about others is the development or strengthening of trust. Children tend to have this quality, but it is often lost or stifled by adolescence. The residence experience has the potential for building trust through the development of friendships and through satisfying group activities. When individuals discover that fellow group members can be both honest and considerate in their responses, they are likely to talk more openly about themselves and their problems, accept themselves more fully, and take more risks in trying out new behaviors. A new level of development is reached when they can rely on the integrity of others, confident that others will react as expected under a given set of circumstances. These conditions provide fertile soil for the development of interpersonal competence and the capacity for intimacy, as described by Torbert and Douvan in Part One.

Three types of interpersonal relationships merit special attention: relationships between the generations, between the races, and between the sexes. Regarding age or generation differences, an intergenerational residence can help students relate to people of different ages on bases other than parent-child or authority relationships and also help them appreciate the nature of the life cycle and its various stages. Interracial understanding can be increased by active interaction between students of different ethnic backgrounds, as opposed to the frequent isolation or segregation of minority students discussed in Fleming's chapter. One-to-one and small group discussion may be highly productive in developing respect for ethnic differences. Coeducational residences, by encouraging more informal relations between the sexes, can have the effect of helping men and women students see each other as human beings and individuals and relate to each other as partners in study, recreation, cultural activities, and personal and social development.

Learning about oneself and about others thus prepares the way for cooperative interaction—getting along with others, acting as a responsible group member, and carrying out the roles of leader, follower, and partner. Practical, firsthand experience in group formation and management is a major benefit of residential learning, sharpening both consensus-building and decision-making skills. Consensus building requires participants to consider the relative merits of the goals held by each person and to reach agreement based on careful, thoughtful evaluation of the views of all members. Decision making involves consideration of an objective and alternative courses of action, the establishment of priorities, and choices among competing options. Both skills are essential to the development of interpersonal and professional competence.

Finally, residential learning can support academic learning directly by increasing students' readiness to learn and effectiveness at learning. Not only does it help students focus their studies by helping them clarify their personal and professional goals; it offers the opportunity for like-minded students to study together and continue their discussion of classroom topics over the dining table and throughout the day and evening. It even encourages students to stay in college, as Astin (1975) and Chickering (1974) have shown. Using data from the Cooperative Institutional Research Project of the American Council on Education and UCLA, Astin showed that living on campus as a freshman tends to decrease the chances of students' dropping out by approximately 10 percent, compared with other living alternatives. Both Astin and Chickering have concluded that the values of residential living might well encourage colleges and universities to strengthen their residential programs even more than they have. Mood (1971) has gone so far as to advocate public support for one year's residence on campus for each student enrolling in higher education, to assure personal and interpersonal development.

Much learning of this type naturally occurs whenever students live in groups, but students stand to gain more when residential learning has the advantage of professional assistance. The direct involvement of teaching faculty in residential life, whether it takes the form of conducting tutorials or class meetings in residence halls, speaking to residence groups, or periodically dining with students, is most likely to strengthen the relationships between residential learning and academic study. Educational programs that make joint use of residential and classroom experiences also represent a means for attracting new student groups to the campus and stimulating new academic activities. But, in addition, specialists in personal and interpersonal development can serve as professional or para-professional group leaders for informal residence group learning sessions—not only facilitating discussion on topics from study skills and learning styles to values clarification and career goals, but also administering interest inventories or other personality instruments to help students understand themselves better and to provide faculty members with information about students' attitudes and needs in order to help them improve the effectiveness of instruction.

A few colleges and universities in the United States provide excellent educational programs in residences that both offer special opportunities for students' personal growth and enhance some element of academic learning. The six programs described here illustrate creative use of college residences for these ends.

Freshman Development Programs, University of Wisconsin, Stevens Point

Professional staff in the university residence halls at Stevens Point initiated a residential learning program for freshmen in the summer of 1978. This program is based on the Miller-Prince definition of student development as "the application of human development concepts in postsecondary settings so that everyone involved can master increasingly complex developmental tasks, achieve self-direction, and become interdependent" (Miller and Prince, 1976, p. 3). These authors identify nine subtasks under three major task categories: developing autonomy, which includes emotional autonomy, instrumental autonomy, and interdependence; developing mature interpersonal relations, which includes tolerance, mature interpersonal relationships with peers, and intimate relationships with the opposite sex; and developing purpose, which includes appropriate educational plans, mature career plans, and mature life-style plans. Table 1 provides additional descriptive details.

During the summer orientation program at Stevens Point, freshmen complete the *Student Developmental Task Inventory* (1978) and the *Lifestyle Assessment Questionnaire* (1978). The inventory is based on the major tasks and subtasks described in Table 1 and is designed to measure student progress toward achieving these tasks. The questionnaire, developed at Stevens Point, is designed to help students "assess their current level of wellness and the potential risks or hazards that they choose to face at this point in their lives," as the introduction to the questionnaire states. The four sections of this questionnaire are the "Wellness Inventory Section," based on Don Ardell's 1977 book *High-Level Wellness*; the "Topics for Personal Growth Section," which provides a resource list for further information on the topics checked; the "Risk of Death Section," based on current mortality data, which identifies conditions and behaviors likely to limit the life

Table 1. Student Developmental Task Inventory

Task 1. Developing Autonomy

Emotional Autonomy (EA). Students who have accomplished this subtask are free from the need for continuous reassurance and approval from others, especially from their parents, and have a reduced dependency upon family, peers, and social agencies (such as a need for grades as a study motivator, or the need to be policed concerning out-of-class assignments, etc.). Evidence of maturity on this subtask includes changes in one's relationship with parents, moving increasingly from that of child-to-parent towards adult-to-adult relationships (that is, relationships of reciprocal respect). Students see their parents more realistically as persons with their own needs, virtues, and shortcomings. *Descriptive characteristics:* self-confident, assertive, self-directed, self-motivated, self-reliant, manages emotions in appropriate ways.

Instrumental Autonomy (IA). Two major characteristics describe students who have accomplished this subtask. These are (1) the ability to carry on activities and cope with problems without undue help from others, yet also knowing when and how to seek help, and (2) possessing the ability to be mobile in relation to personal needs and desires. Students advanced in this area feel able to make their own livings and plan their activities and time in ways to maximize the outcomes. *Descriptive characteristics:* self-sufficient, self-supporting, problem solver, geographically mobile, manages time, money and other resources well, brings about desired changes when needed.

Interdependence (ID). Students who have accomplished this subtask can be described as having developed "mature dependence." They realize that they cannot dispense with their parents, that they cannot receive the benefits from others and society in general without contributing in return, and that they cannot feel comfortable accepting continuing support without working for it. Recognizing that loving and being loved are complementary and that there is a direct relationship between one's own behavior and community welfare in general are basic attitudes of students who have accomplished this subtask. *Descriptive characteristics:* supportive, good citizen, cooperative, does own share, helper, responsible, collaborates effectively with others.

Task 2: Developing Purpose

Appropriate Educational Plans (EP). Students who have accomplished this subtask have formulated well-defined educational goals for themselves and are able to see the relationship between academic study and the other aspects of their lives. They are aware of the educational setting (both resources and limitations), have made accurate assessment of their academic abilities, know the requirements for graduation, and are generally able to cope with the demands of the higher education environment. They are either personally satisfied with their educational experiences or are taking steps to meet their goals in other ways. *Descriptive characteristics:* goal-oriented, self-directed learner, educationally motivated, seeks indepth educational experiences, enjoys college, takes advantage of all available resources to enhance learning.

Mature Career Plans (CP). An awareness of the world of work, an accurate understanding of one's abilities and limitations, a knowledge of requirements for various occupations, and an understanding of the emotional and educational demands of different kinds of jobs are evidence of accomplishment of this subtask. Students who have high achievement on this subtask have been able to synthesize their knowledge about themselves and the world of work into a rational order which enables them to formulate vocational plans and which allows them to make at least a tentative commitment to a chosen career field. They will have taken at least the first steps necessary to prepare themselves through both educational and work experiences for eventual employment. *Descriptive characteristics:* tentatively committed to a career field, knowledgeable about self as a worker, seeks experiences related to chosen field, knows how to utilize available career information.

Mature Lifestyle Plans (LP). Achievement of mature lifestyle plans includes establishing a personal direction and orientation in one's life which balances vocational interests, per-

Table 1 *(Continued)*

sonal values, learned skills, hobbies, and future family plans. Plans need not be highly specific nor committed to an absolute, but must be of sufficient clarity to permit identification of appropriate present steps and reflect thoughtful long range goals. Students who have accomplished this subtask will have a general orientation that leaves open a wide range of future choices, but which provides a sense of direction and meaning to present activities. *Descriptive characteristics:* self-aware, purposeful, committed, thoughtful, future-focused orientation.

Task 3: Developing Mature Interpersonal Relationships

Intimate Relationships with Opposite Sex (IRS). Students having accomplished this subtask will have developed the sensitivity and awareness of feelings necessary for establishing close, meaningful relationships with members of the opposite sex. Mature intimate relationships reflect mutual support and commitment. They represent less a means for self-discovery and self-enhancement and more a means to achieve unity with another human being. Hopes, fears, aspirations, doubts, feelings, and thoughts are shared through frequent private conversations and other shared experiences. Involved in this subtask is the ability to love as well as to be loved and the testing of the ability to make long-term commitments. Differences of opinion and beliefs do not weaken the integrity of the relationship or the individuals. *Descriptive characteristics:* honest, caring, concerned about partner, supportive, aware of and expressive of feelings, sensitive to the needs and well being of the relationship.

Mature Relationships with Peers (MRP). Having accomplished this subtask, students will describe their relationships with peers as shifting toward greater trust, independence, and individuality. Their friendships survive the development of differences and episodes of disagreement; these friendships persist through times of separation and noncommunication. The need for many casual friends decreases in favor of spending more time with a few good friends. *Descriptive characteristics:* trusting, dependable, supporting, accepting of differences, warm, open, aware of the needs of others.

Tolerance (TOL). Respect for those of different backgrounds, habits, beliefs, faiths, values, and appearances describe students who have high achievement in the tolerance area. They respond to people in their own right rather than as stereotypes calling for conventional responses. There is an increasing openness and acceptance among students who have accomplished this subtask, which enables them to be flexible when interacting with others. It should be kept in mind, however, that tolerance does not mean either an improved capacity for teeth gritting and tongue biting or the development of screening devices to shield one from the values and behaviors of others. *Descriptive characteristics:* respectful, understanding, flexible, accepting of diversity, able to effectively and objectively interact with many different kinds of people.

Source: Used by permission of Winston, Miller, and Prince (1979). © Copyright 1979 by Student Development Associates.

span; and the "Medical Alert Section," which lists physical and psychological conditions that could be the basis for a health care system (*Lifestyle Assessment Questionnaire,* 1978).

After the fall period begins, residence staff members arrange to meet with students in small groups to review and interpret the computer printouts from these questionnaires. The purposes of these meetings, and of the overall program, are to encourage students to assess their developmental status in physical, emotional, vocational, and sociological terms; to develop positive plans for action; to evaluate alternative courses of action affecting their quality of life; and, finally, to initiate positive action.

Available for voluntary participation by student residents during the academic year are nine seminar series, each of which focuses on one of the subtasks of the major developmental task categories described by Miller and Prince. Each seminar series is organized around from five to eleven programs, which vary in format from two-hour evening meetings to one- or two-day weekend workshops. The principal teaching method is experiential, with program activities centered on simulations and a variety of group exercises. Group member participation is an essential program component. Content material is also presented as a part of each program. Although most of the seminars are intended for beginning students, any resident is welcome; several programs are planned to include upperclass students.

Programs may be led not only by professional or paraprofessional staff members but also by students (after special training), so detailed are the printed descriptions of subject matter content, group exercises, and simulations. Program objectives are stated in behavioral terms, which then serve as bases for evaluation. Student evaluations are expected as part of each seminar.

Professional residence staff members are responsible for initiating the various seminar series. The intent has been to schedule one series for each of the nine months of the academic year, so that students may have exposure during one year to materials and activities pertaining to each of the nine developmental subtasks. At the same time, scheduling depends on the needs of students in particular residences. The staff expectation has been that different seminars in the series would be offered concurrently in adjacent residences so that students would be able to attend the seminar most relevant to their concerns at a given time.

Student interest and response have been positive during the first year of this program. Particularly favorable reactions have been reported to the printouts from the Lifestyle Assessment Questionnaire relating to current conditions affecting physical wellbeing. More time is obviously needed for evaluation of this residence program. However, it is unique in its total approach to the developmental needs of college students at the early adult stage. Its use of computer printouts to suggest to students where they may be in their developmental process as they begin their college experience seems to be a particularly effective way to involve students in charting growth programs for themselves. These printouts should help to focus residence staff program efforts on current student needs. Such information might also prove useful to faculty members in their selection of teaching methods for courses enrolling primarily freshmen.

Cooperative Outdoor Program, University of California, Irvine

Organized in 1972, the Cooperative Outdoor Program (COP) emphasizes environmental awareness and individual responsibility. An early project of COP was the Outdoors Hall, which was designated for men and women students interested in outdoor or wilderness activities and life-styles. This hall actually includes two residences, Playa and Nubes, which provide living space for forty and sixty students, respectively. These residences are part of the large undergraduate housing complex located on the UCI campus. Student interest is the primary qualification for assignment. Residents represent the full range of undergraduate academic classifications and may have majors or minors in the Ecology and Evolutionary Biology Department or be taking courses in this area as electives.

Three credit courses are taught as a three-quarter sequence in the living room of Outdoors Hall: Coastal Ecology, which focuses on problems of coastal marine biology and adjacent terrestrial ecosystems; Desert Ecology, which introduces students to physiological, morphological, behavioral, and life history adaptations to desert environments;

and Mountain Ecology, which emphasizes ecological relationships within mountain environments, as well as game management and mountain survival. COP has sponsored a number of environmental lectures and films in Outdoors Hall, principally during evening hours. Speakers have included faculty, faculty visitors, and graduate students.

Two outdoor activities are arranged during each of the three quarters of the academic year for Outdoors Hall residents. Illustrative of these activities are a two-day backpack hike in the San Gabriel Mountains, a weekend camping retreat at Catalina Island, and a five-day Colorado River canoe trip.

One of the COP services is a Rental Center where students, faculty, and staff may rent high-quality equipment for the varied activities planned as part of both credit and noncredit programs. An environmental library, located in Outdoors Hall, has been developed by COP in cooperation with student residents in the Outdoors Hall and in other residences of the undergraduate housing complex. This library maintains a number of current and relevant journals.

The Outdoors Hall staff includes two resident assistants and two program coordinators, all of whom are students who live in the hall. Successful applicants for the program coordinator positions are selected before the spring quarter preceding their employment year. A major requirement is attendance during the summer at the Colorado Outward Bound School near Denver, with all expenses paid. The objectives of this school are to heighten in students a sense of confidence in self, compassion for others, and responsibility to society.

Although no formal evaluations of the Outdoors Hall Program are available, reactions of students and faculty are reported to be highly positive. An indication of student interest is that there is always a waiting list for assignment to the Playa-Nubes residences. Student staff positions are also highly competitive. Some financial support for this program comes from the university's Committee for Instructional Development, which has a special interest in innovative educational projects.

Residency Within an External Degree Program, Empire State College

Empire State College, a division of the State University of New York, has the special mission of providing alternative means of access to higher education for individuals with special needs, such as those who are employed, have family responsibilities, or need retraining. Empire State College's program is flexible and adaptable to the requirements of its students. They may initiate their work at any one of more than thirty centers located in various parts of New York State.

Students' academic programs are developed through learning contracts jointly prepared by the students and their mentors—that is, the faculty members overseeing their programs and work. These contracts describe the program, goals, study methods, time constraints, credits to be granted, and bases for evaluation. Goals may be pursued through independent study under a mentor's direction, tutoring, formal courses on a college campus, self-study, a short-term residency, or a combination of these approaches.

The residency approach is illustrated by a weekend workshop that was held at Saratoga Springs by the Learning Resources Faculty. The theme was "Knowledge for What?—The Social Uses of Knowledge"; the goal, to link several fields of knowledge. The teaching methods included a lecture series, social hours, and five seminars on a variety of topics. Students were asked to read in advance the book *Knowledge for What?* (Lynd, 1939) and to select the particular seminar that most nearly met their individual interests. Students attending the workshop for credit were expected to complete a project related to the seminar they selected. The residency itself met only part of the learning contract requirements. The 126 participants were asked to complete and return a form for use in evaluating the residency experience; 73 (58 percent) did so.

Of interest is the background of .the participants. Seventy-three percent of the respondents were women. The average age of participants was 37 years; 67 percent were married. One quarter of the group listed principal occupation as semiskilled, unskilled, clerical, or sales worker. Twenty percent reported their work as supervisory, such as plant superintendent, postal supervisor, or police captain. Twelve percent described themselves as occupational therapists, youth counselors, teachers, or practical nurses. The remainder were students, housewives, professionals, or individuals working in such fields as art, medical technology, and skilled trades. About half of the respondents were full-time students and half, part-time. These students are different from the typical undergraduate and are an example of the extension of residential learning experiences to a heterogeneous adult population.

General reactions to the residency experience were positive, with 26 percent reporting that they were very satisfied; 47 percent, generally satisfied; 20 percent, partially satisfied; and only 3 percent, not satisfied. Positive comments referred to the excellent presentations and opportunities to meet and talk with college personnel and fellow students from varied backgrounds. Of the residency activities, lectures and seminars ranked about equally as sources of new ideas and concepts. The social hours made it easier to meet others, and informal discussions were useful sources for learning. The major advantage of the residency, in the opinion of most respondents, was facilitation of their studies. Additional advantages were mutual stimulation through the sharing of ideas, opinions, and experiences; increased knowledge; and a heightened feeling of belonging to an academic community. Some felt that the residency plus a project was an easy contract requirement.

On the negative side, some felt that the seminar groups were too large, and that less time should be allotted to lectures and more to the seminars. Inadequate advance preparation by some students was noted, and better organization of the residency was suggested. When asked about problems encountered in attending the residency, about one third of the students mentioned arrangements for travel; 18 percent had to plan in advance for childcare, and another 15 percent, for time off from their jobs. However, childcare facilities at the residence were not considered important. One of the workshop evaluators recommended that greater effort be made by mentors to clarify residency goals and students' expectations prior to attendance.

The consensus of faculty at Empire State College seems to be that bringing students together for short-term residencies is both feasible and desirable from an educational point of view. Operationally, short-term uses of college residences require a conference center type of management. Once appropriate adaptations are made in operating procedures, residences provide a kind of setting that can facilitate student group interaction and learning.

Experiment in Intergenerational Living, Syracuse University

Syracuse University's Experiment in Intergenerational Living was developed in the 1960s around a public housing project for older persons located on the edge of the university's campus. The intergenerational housing complex consists of the twenty-four story Toomey-Abbott Towers project, housing 400 older persons, a university residence for

300 undergraduate women and another residence for 450 undergraduate men, and a three-story services center where all project residents may use such facilities as the cafeteria, snack bar, library, and meeting rooms. The All-University Gerontology Center and School of Social Work are located here.

Towers residents range in age from the fifties and sixties, in the case of dependents and spouses, to the eighties and nineties. Age 62 is the minimum age for eligible applicants, and the average age is 75 years. Considerable differences can be found in socioeconomic, ethnic, and educational backgrounds; some residents have less than a high school education, whereas others have graduate degrees and some have even been experts in various fields. Such differences accentuate problems in programming. It should also be noted that when this project was planned the primary concern was housing space rather than supporting services.

As it has developed, the program for this project has emphasized the learning needs of university students and research on aging processes and problems. Thus, the older residents have seemed to be more the subjects of research and advisers for educational programs than equal beneficiaries. However, some educational programs for both older and younger residents have been developed. Tower Topics, for example, is a series of seminars and lectures on such subjects as music, home economics, English, social work, environmental sanitation, and psychology. No fees are required; university faculty and graduate students serve as teachers on a voluntary basis, and leadership for the series is provided by graduate students assigned to the Towers for internship experiences. A good attendance record results in the award of a certificate from the university's chancellor.

Program diversity has been found to be an important factor in the success of these educational programs. The varied type of program presented in the fall met the needs of greater numbers of older residents; the unified type planned for the spring produced more consistent attendance. It has been suggested that several undergraduate survey courses, scheduled in the housing complex, might draw a better response from both older and younger students. Attending such university courses could give the older residents a more satisfying sense of participation in an educational community. And mixed age cohorts in courses treating common interests could provide opportunities for mutually rewarding interaction.

A second type of intergenerational program is more informal. Each year committees of student residents work with a Towers residents' organization to foster personal relationships between members of the two age groups. The result of this joint effort is the MATCHES Program in which individual students and older residents are paired on the basis of similar interests. Group activities for program participants are arranged both by the students and by the older residents.

The reactions of younger residents to living in an intergenerational housing complex and to the programs planned for them vary widely. At one extreme, some students keep very much to themselves and want no part of any programming or relationships with older persons. At another extreme are students majoring in gerontology or social work who find the experiences with older persons to be most stimulating. In between these extremes are students who welcome opportunities to be of service to older persons.

The older residents also exhibit a wide range of attitudes toward intergenerational living. Some do not want to be involved in any activities with anyone, younger or older. Some enjoy greatly their associations with younger student residents and have developed lasting friendships. A number feel that they are living in a fishbowl, having participated in many research projects and special programs on aging, and would prefer to be left alone.

The Bridge Project, Fairhaven College, Western Washington University

Fairhaven College was developed as a semiautonomous cluster campus of Western Washington University in Bellingham. With an enrollment of some 400 to 500 students, Fairhaven has been able to create a feeling of community and experiment with alternatives in liberal arts education. A decline in the number of younger students living on campus inspired the college administrators to implement a program of intergenerational living and learning.

Original plans called for adding to the Fairhaven community of 18- to 22-year-old students three additional age groups: (1) children, ages two to five, of students, faculty, and staff, (2) re-entry students, in the 25 to 60 age range, who wanted to prepare for or change careers, and (3) older adults, age 60 and over, interested in association with an educational community. The general purposes were to eliminate age segregation on the campus and to reinforce the concept of the extended family.

HEW's Fund for the Improvement of Secondary Education provided the resources that enabled the college to initiate its Bridge Project for the 1973-74 academic year. The first year's grant made possible a daycare program for about twenty-five young students, two half-time academic advisers for approximately a hundred re-entry students, the renovation of two adjacent residences for older students, and room and board subsidies for this latter group. Reduced grants for the second and third years necessitated reductions in personnel and services when sufficient substitute funds could not be obtained. For the older students, generally known as the "Bridgers," paraprofessional jobs have been made available within the college. Some state support has helped to stabilize the project.

Since the beginning, the number of Bridgers has remained each year at about thirty, which is the capacity of Bridgehouse, the residence for older students. An evaluation questionnaire, described by the project director, provides information regarding these older students (Douglas Rich, "An Evaluation of the Fairhaven College Bridge Project," December 1976, mimeographed). If anything can be said to characterize these students, it is their diversity; each differs from the others in motivation, objectives, and reactions. Why did these older adults come to Fairhaven? Primarily, they came for one or more of three reasons: general intellectual stimulation, social relationships with people of all ages, and a relatively inexpensive place to live. Some believed that Fairhaven would ease the transition from work to retirement; others hoped to find a reason for living. Some wanted to work on projects for which time had not been available before; others hoped to enjoy a new life-style.

Reactions to the Fairhaven experience have varied widely. Some residents were enthusiastic; others were withdrawn and unsure of themselves. Those whose primary interest was in a place to stay had the greatest adjustments to make. Relationships of older adults to their peers, to younger students, or to faculty were reported as occasional problems. In commenting on relationships with faculty, one older person felt that some instructors were uneasy with older students in their classes, especially those who were former educators. Another "found professors a bit snobbish and uninterested" (Rich, 1976).

Although the responses of faculty and younger students to the evaluation questionnaire were few in number, they tended to be positive. From the faculty standpoint, the older students were representative of middle-class America and prepared to contribute to college-level work. They provided a sense of perspective and a realistic view of the past. Problems in class were few; however, some were not motivated to undertake difficult intellectual activity, others needed to be at the front of the classroom to see, and still others indicated they had trouble hearing. Instructors discovered that older students greatly preferred group discussions and did not want to write papers or take examinations. The younger students felt that older adults were a valuable asset to their classes, in several ways. They provided a rich variety of experience, were intelligent, and did not hesitate to disagree with the instructor. They studied hard and remained active in class; they added wisdom, depth, and variety.

The older adults have made a number of recommendations regarding the project. Future adult participants are urged to be themselves, to learn to enjoy others of all ages, to participate, to make the effort to initiate personal contact with others, and—above all—to understand and accept younger students on their own terms. Project procedures could be improved by expanding the orientation program, providing a workshop on communal living, and adding social activities as a means for encouraging sociability and bringing older and younger students together informally. In terms of the academic program, older students suggested a greater variety of courses and more assistance with planning their course programs. They expressed a strong preference for instructors rather than students to provide class leadership.

In commenting on the re-entry students, the director reports that this project component has stabilized at 100 to 150 persons, with an average age of 26. His recommendation for this re-entry group is that its members be integrated into the social and educational life of the college; these students do not want to be identified as a separate age group. An academic adviser on the staff of the Student Services Office assists the re-entry group, the Bridgers, and the younger students. Special services to the re-entry group include supplemental academic and financial advising; vocational counseling; individualized consideration of exceptions to admissions criteria; information concerning family housing, schools, and daycare; and academic tutoring, as appropriate. Small, informal classes, the option of an interdisciplinary concentration, and credit for practical experience all represent attractive features of Fairhaven for re-entry students.

Since June of 1976, the Bridge Project has offered a successful, six-week summer program, primarily for older students. On-campus residences have been available, and classes have provided a useful introduction to academic work. Class topics have included the Arts, History, and Religions of Egypt, the History of Washington State (which involves travel in the state), and Summerstock Theater. Some participants report that this experience has produced the best summer they have ever spent. Some have used the summer session as a basis for considering enrollment for the academic year.

The Bridge Project, according to observers, has great potential, for a number of reasons: Its objectives focus on intergenerational living and learning, it provides members of different age groups with special opportunities for learning from each other, and it challenges faculty to work with individuals of older generations. Younger students can see aging as a natural part of living, while older students can better appreciate both the attitudes of younger generations and their own continuing value to society.

The Elderhostel Movement

In 1974 two men at the University of New Hampshire decided to apply the well-known concept of European youth hostels and folk schools to a college program for retired persons 60 years of age and over. David Bianco and Martin P. Knowlton speculated that the college environment could be used to renew older persons' belief in themselves and in their potential for continued growth and enjoyment of living. The declining activity of older persons, so often resulting not only from age but from "ageism," was to be replaced by action—intellectual, social, and physical—on the campus.

Participants in the Elderhostel program are expected to (1) live in a college residence for one week during the summer months and eat in the college cafeteria, (2) attend a maximum of three noncredit courses for five days during the week, and (3) take part in campus activities occurring that week. Cost is kept to a minimum, with facilities and services provided on a nonprofit basis. High-quality academic courses, with effective instructors, are essential to this program. To ensure an informal atmosphere, a maximum of thirty to forty persons may attend the week-long program.

The objectives of the Elderhostel program are "to demonstrate to elders that they are persons of worth and potential, and that they can act . . . as their own agents of change" ("Elderhostel Manual," 1976). Contributing to these objectives are a stimulating academic experience that proves to them that they can continue to learn, a residential experience that helps them to reexamine their lives, and, overall, an experience of self-renewal.

The subject matter of the noncredit courses ranges widely over the social sciences, literature, philosophy, natural sciences, arts, crafts, physical education, and technical areas. The most popular courses are reported to be those concerned with philosophy, history, writing, and art. The Oral History seminar is a particularly effective vehicle for building in older students a sense of self-worth and intellectual capacity. A balance in course offerings is recommended, such as (1) oral history seminar, charcoal drawing, and physical fitness, (2) local early American history, poetry of Robert Frost, and folk dancing, or (3) economic theories, philosophy of religion, and yoga. Variety and change of pace are strongly encouraged. To be avoided are such condescending courses as household repairs, cooking, and how-to-grow-old.

As a matter of policy, academic activities exclude testing, grades, and homework. Instructors may suggest readings, but they should be aware that reading assignments may be perceived as threatening by some people in the course. Encouragement and the experience of success have been shown to be most important to older students, as well as to younger ones. Classes that meet daily rather than two or three times a week seem to engender greater intimacy. Preferred time periods per class are an hour and a half to two hours, with twenty minutes between classes.

Instructors are highly positive about their Elderhostel courses. The older students bring to class discussions rich backgrounds of experience; they are enthusiastic, well motivated, full of questions, and hard-working. As a consequence, instructors say that they work hard themselves but feel amply rewarded, especially when they have been able to encourage favorable change in people's lives.

Complementing the course work are extracurricular activities that foster the informal exchange of ideas and promote interpersonal relationships. An orientation meeting the first evening is intended to provide information and help the new arrivals feel at home. A wine and cheese party the second evening facilitates the acquaintance process. Coffee breaks and film festivals with younger students on campus, theater trips, cookouts, concerts, group singing led by younger students, and discussion evenings with faculty members are other types of activities that have proved successful.

Typical residence accommodations are usually acceptable to these summertime students. However, certain planning precautions are necessary. For example, the residence must be located within a convenient distance of the dining room and classrooms, or transportation provided; a refrigerator should be available for storing medications; and rooms should have light switches within reaching distance of the bed. Few complaints about food are likely, but food servers should expect questions about ingredients from individuals on restricted diets.

The response to the Elderhostel program has been phenomenal. In 1975, five New Hampshire colleges made available 450 residential accommodations and 15 weeks of noncredit course work, and 220 persons took advantage of the program. During the summer of 1977, 4,800 accommodations and 156 weeks of course work were scheduled by sixty-one colleges in twelve states. A national board of directors and national office were organized to handle inquiries from older persons, offer advice to interested colleges, and develop a quality control procedure. By the summer of 1978, more than 120 colleges and universities in twenty states were participating. Projections for growth of this program anticipate as many as 25,000 spaces and 700 weeks of course work offered by 350 institutions in forty-eight states by 1980.

So far, the Elderhostel programs have been attracting a particular segment of the retired population, which seems to be above average in income, education, and activity level. However, the overwhelming response indicates that some important needs of older persons are being met. An important ingredient for success seems to be the combination of academic and residential learning. To be sought now are means for developing similar types of programs that will reach additional numbers of those who are 60 years of age and over.

Implementing Residential Learning Programs

The programs just described all underscore two basic requirements that must be met before residential learning programs can be undertaken. The first is understanding by appropriate faculty members and administrators of the program's objectives, procedures, and implications. Since these programs all recognize individual differences among students and the necessity for attention to differing stages of development, the clear implication is that institutional objectives and procedures will do likewise.

The second requirement is charting the elements needed for project support, together with the responsibilities and authority to be delegated to each. Very much a part of this requirement are organizational relationships, personnel qualifications, integration of learning activities, and physical facilities.

Strengthening Organizational Relationships. At most colleges and universities, student residences are an administrative responsibility of the chief student personnel officer. In some cases, the chief business officer has primary administrative jurisdiction. Specific academic programs are, by tradition, the responsibility of particular academic departments. When a community agency contributes in some way to a residential program, a distinctly separate authority becomes involved. Solving the resulting administrative problems in this situation becomes a matter of opening new avenues for organizational relationships.

Motivation for faculty members, administrators, and student personnel officers to find new organizational avenues for cooperative efforts should be generated by accumulating evidence that the impact on students of both academic and residential learning programs is increased when these programs are closely coordinated. Some coordination of learning and living experiences on campus may be especially important for the modern university's increasingly diverse student clientele. Important economic factors are also involved. Since higher education is entering a buyer's market, more attention will be given by both prospective students and institutions to the total educational package that is most likely to produce the best results for students.

The particular organizational relationships developed among the various institutional units concerned with a residential learning program will vary from campus to campus. One form of organizational structure is the institute, which focuses on a particular project or topic area, draws upon the expertise of a variety of departments, and is headed by a director with the authority and the budget to administer the project. Logically, such an institute for administering a coordinated academic-residential program should be a part of the overall academic administration. Another possible organizational structure is the committee, which includes representatives of the departments and organizations concerned with the residence project, approves policy decisions, and supervises the work of a director who is operationally responsible for the project.

The important point is, of course, that the organizational structure must facilitate project operations and make readily available the necessary institutional resources. To be overcome on some campuses are the more traditional patterns that separate and insulate organizational units from one another. To be encouraged everywhere is the realization on the part of all units that coordination of efforts provides the best assurance of institutional success in promoting learning in a diverse population of students.

Integrating Learning Activities. One effective way to begin is to develop an academic course for credit in student growth and development and schedule it within residence buildings. Student residents could be assigned to course sections in their particular residence. This procedure enables instructors to use group living experiences of their students as part of the course. In addition, students learn in class with those with whom they live. Advanced students, preferably from the graduate or upperclass levels, can be trained as course instructors, and supervised by a faculty panel.

Such a course should preferably be planned for an academic year of two semesters or three quarters, with first-time entering students given priority for enrollment. Major topics might include learning about oneself and others, improving interpersonal competence, organizing a community, leadership, problem solving, and understanding others who differ from oneself in age, race, and sex. Other important topics that might be dealt with in this course are career planning, planning for leisure time, and developing individual academic programs. Such a course could help to resolve common problems associated with academic advising.

A surprising number of credit courses are already being given in college residences around the country. Content tends to focus on training for particular student groups, such as resident assistants who serve as student staff members. A desirable objective is that a course covering topics such as those listed above be taken by all entering students. This procedure would bring commuting students into college residences where they might share vicariously in the residential experience.

At the University of Vermont, an Integrated Humanities Program is one of a number of credit courses offered in the Living-Learning Residence Center. This program consists of three coordinated courses drawn from the history, English, and philosophy departments; its goal is cultural awareness through a review of major achievements of Western civilization. The American Cluster Experience utilizes English and history to study American culture and values. Both courses take advantage of the interaction of residents with each other and with faculty outside of class to enrich the total learning experience.

A variety of academic disciplines could use the college residence as the setting for special projects intended to give realistic application to subject matter studied in class. Through appropriate organization and operating procedures, residential and academic learning could be mutually reinforcing.

Strengthening the Residence Staff. Key figures in implementing residential learning programs are the professional residence staff. In the past, these staff members have often been assigned routine administrative duties that have prevented consistent attention to student learning activities. In the future, such duties should be delegated to less highly trained personnel within the residence unit.

In the past, graduate training programs for professional residence staff have placed considerable emphasis on counseling and administrative duties. These qualifications are important. In the future, however, additional knowledge and skills will be necessary as residential programs become more closely related to academic programs and the types of student residents become more varied, as discussed in Part One.

In the first place, residence staff members should be familiar with the stages of adult development and the tasks typically associated with these stages. Staff should be aware of the processes involved in ego development, moral development, and the acquisition of new meanings and new learning styles. Such knowledge is essential for enlarging the capacity of staff members not only to better interpret student behavior but also to organize learning activities that will more nearly meet students' developmental needs.

In the second place, residence staff should be qualified to serve as discussion leaders and to facilitate group processes that contribute to the personal growth and self-discovery of group members. They must learn how to provide experiences that will be helpful in developing interpersonal competence through collaborative inquiry, such as that described by Torbert. In short, residence staff must be capable of serving as effective teachers, helping students to develop skills in understanding self and others and in relating easily to others.

A third qualification for residence staff is that they have enough understanding of both institutional and student purposes to recognize conflicts between them and be able to suggest approaches to resolving these conflicts. Some knowledge of institutional organization should make it easier to initiate cooperative action with various academic units. Such action may include consulting with appropriate faculty members about developmental needs of particular students and possible ways to meet these needs, using both academic and residential programs. Opening avenues of communication can prove useful for both staff and faculty, but especially for students. In some situations, academic faculty and residence staff may be the same persons.

If residential programs are to be organized primarily on a small group basis, it is obvious that professional staff must be augmented by paraprofessionals whose training becomes a responsibility of the professionals. Paraprofessionals have proved to be highly desirable as staff members when they are student peers and have been properly trained.

Adapting Physical Facilities. Too many existing residential facilities were not planned to accommodate the diversity of students and variety of programs anticipated in the years immediately ahead. Plans should be initiated to modify these facilities over a reasonable period of time to meet changed requirements. Maximum flexibility in use of these facilities is, of course, highly desirable.

Current residence construction is of apartment-type facilities, which are most likely to be adaptable to changing needs and types of students. Federal requirements that all campus residences be accessible to handicapped persons are revealing many deficiencies, which must be corrected. Modest improvements are presently being made in room equipment and safety features to accommodate older adults. As elements of academic programs are brought into residences to strengthen student learning, appropriate spaces for seminars, classes, and group activities must be created, if they do not already exist.

Conclusions

The indications clearly are that residential learning programs hold great potential for helping colleges and universities to meet the developmental needs of a diverse student population in the years ahead. Realizing this potential depends largely on focusing institutional goals on students as individuals, closely coordinating academic and residential activities, and enlisting residential staff prepared to serve as teachers of human relations and facilitators of student development.

Residential learning can aid development through increasing students' self-knowledge, self-confidence, sense of self-worth, clarification of goals, interpersonal competence, and regard for others and the community as a whole. As a consequence, students will be better able to take full advantage of their academic programs. With these objectives, residential programs are an indispensable part of the higher education enterprise.

References

Ardell, D. B. (Ed.). *High-Level Wellness.* Emmaus, Pa.: Rodale Press, 1977.

Astin, A. W. *Preventing Students from Dropping Out.* San Francisco: Jossey-Bass, 1975.

Chickering, A. W. *Commuting Versus Resident Students: Overcoming Educational Inequities of Living Off Campus.* San Francisco: Jossey-Bass, 1974.

"Elderhostel Manual." A special preliminary edition prepared for the National Elderhostel Evaluation and Developmental Seminar, August 27-29, 1976, Durham, N.H. (Mimeograph.)

Knox, A. B. *Adult Development and Learning: A Handbook on Individual Growth and Competence in the Adult Years for Education and the Helping Professions.* San Francisco: Jossey-Bass, 1977.

Lifestyle Assessment Questionnaire. Stevens Point: University of Wisconsin—Stevens Point Foundation, 1978.

Lynd, R. S. *Knowledge for What?* Princeton, N.J.: Princeton University Press, 1939.

Miller, T. K., and Prince, J. S. *The Future of Student Affairs: A Guide to Student Development for Tomorrow's Higher Education.* San Francisco: Jossey-Bass, 1976.

Mood, A. M. "Another Approach to Higher Education." In *Universal Higher Education, Costs and Benefits.* Washington, D.C.: American Council on Education, 1971.

Rich, D. "An Evaluation of the Fairhaven College Bridge Project." Bellingham: Western Washington University, 1976. (Mimeograph.)

Student Developmental Task Inventory. Stevens Point: University of Wisconsin—Stevens Point Foundation, 1978.

Winston, R. B., Jr., Miller, T. K., and Prince, J. S. *Student Developmental Task Inventory.* (Rev. 2nd ed.) Athens, Ga.: Student Development Associates, 1979.

38

Jane Shipton
Elizabeth H. Steltenpohl

Educational Advising and Career Planning: A Life-Cycle Perspective

Work is a major area of life in which persons define their identity—a recurring task of development that assumes different forms in different life periods. School has been called children's work. A college education can also be viewed as work. In college, choices are made to pursue a particular educational program or occupation or to change direction and pursue a new one. These choices set limits and create opportunities for one's whole life course and development. If a college is to support wise choices of goals and purposes among students, educational advising and career planning will need to play a much more central and unifying role in the future.

Since most colleges register a large number of students in a short period of time, educational advising—and hence career planning—is usually limited to a few brief encounters between student and faculty adviser. The faculty adviser is expected to give the student correct information about programs, majors, prerequisites, course sequences, course content, and availability. The outcome is a program held together largely by the major and distribution requirements of the curriculum. If questions about goals arise, the student may be sent to the counseling center to undertake career exploration. Otherwise, the student's only experience with career advising may be a visit to the placement office in the senior year.

Such a system does not address any of the developmental needs of college students raised in Part One of this book, nor does it take into account the accelerating social change in recent decades and its impact on individual lives. To be effective, educational advising must help students make the best decisions in light of both their own needs and the changing social and economic realities.

Educational, Career, and Life Planning

To contribute to the total development of students, educational advising and vocational counseling must be seen as elements of life planning. Today's students cannot expect outside factors to give their lives security and direction. It is no longer certain that one will live in the same community throughout one's life, work for the same organization for an entire career, or even stay married to the same partner for many years (Toffler, 1970). Stability will need to come from within, and one way to assure stability is by taking responsibility for planning one's own life. Although this would seem to be obvious, more often than not people tend to react to the conditions of their lives rather than act on the basis of long-term plans. Those who set life goals thoughtfully and develop well-considered strategies for attaining them are much more the exception than the rule.

In life planning, career decisions are critical elements. As Chickering and Havighurst point out in Chapter One, the career has become the organizing center for the lives of most men and women in democratic societies where choice and entrance to occupations are relatively free and open. Vocational theorists agree. Leona Tyler (1969, p. 132) sees career development as "an organizing focus for one's identity"; Abraham Maslow (1968, p. 95) observes that work "organizes life in psychologically meaningful, need-fulfilling ways"; Anne Roe (1956, p. 80) views career development as "satisfying psychological needs"; Donald Super (1957, p. 186) considers career development "a continuous process of developing and implementing a self-concept with satisfaction to self and benefit to society." And the investigations cited by Blocher and Rapoza in their chapter earlier in this book on professional and vocational development lead to the conclusion that work is a major vehicle for self-expression, personal fulfillment, self-esteem, and self-discovery.

All persons need to define the meaning of work for themselves in terms of its importance in their lives, the satisfaction or dissatisfaction it brings them, and its relationship to their leisure interests. Students need to become informed about developments in the work world that can affect the fulfillment of their purposes—especially the decline in employment opportunities in certain fields and the development of new opportunities in others. Women students, in particular, need information on the variety of opportunities available to them in business and the professions, the life-styles open to them, and the consequences for their career advancement of their own educational decisions and value systems. They need to be aware of possible options for the redesign of jobs, including part-time partnership employment in professional occupations, four-day work weeks, and flexible work schedules. Both men and women need to learn that the choice of an occupation is no longer a once-in-a-lifetime decision made during adolescence. Current labor statistics indicate that a traditional-age college student will change jobs seven times and careers three times over the life course. The choice of an occupation and the preparation that will genuinely contribute to development require career and educational planning within a life planning context.

In keeping with this concept, vocational counselors have abandoned the "test and tell" approach in working with clients on occupational choice. As Gysbers says (1974, p. 16), "*career development* is now seen as part of human development. It describes the interaction of psychological, sociological, economic, physical, and chance factors that shape the career or sequence of occupations, jobs, and positions an individual holds during the course of life." Indeed, Gysbers and Moore (1972) recommend using the phrase *life career development* to emphasize the relationship of career choice and career roles to other aspects of personal growth over the life span. Increasingly, American colleges should be prepared to help students of all ages define their career and life goals and plan their college programs accordingly.

Only a limited number of students come to college with their educational goals and purposes clearly defined. Some students know they want to get a degree but are not clear about the opportunities available to them or the educational outcomes they seek. Others come with some ideas about their goals but recognize the importance of assessing and clarifying them before choosing among educational options. Most students have difficulty relating study in particular disciplines to their personal goals, and few understand the relationships between traditional academic disciplines and occupations.

For some students, ambivalence about goals and purposes is anxiety-producing. It is all too tempting for them to select a course of study as quickly as possible simply to eliminate the stress of uncertainty. This premature closure cuts short the exploration of alternatives. Such a choice often forces the individual into a narrow vocational or professional focus on instrumental learning, ignoring needs for what Chickering and Havighurst have called "expressive" learning and thus limiting the possibility of achieving more complex stages of development.

Above and beyond these problems affecting students of all ages, some career and educational planning needs are specific to particular life stages, as Blocher and Rapoza and Chickering and Havighurst have discussed in detail in Part One of this book. Traditional-age college students need opportunities to develop their identities and self-confidence, as well as exposure to a variety of significant other people and a wide range of role situations. They need to identify the skills that will be most useful to them and explore possible alternatives before making a commitment. Midlife career changers need opportunities for rediscovery and re-establishment of identity. Persons contemplating retirement need to develop new interests and activities that can be sustained as they grow older. And at every age women need opportunities to expand self-awareness, consider a wider range of alternatives, and increase their competence in planning, decision making, and risk-taking.

If colleges are to truly enhance individual development and prepare students to cope with succeeding stages of development, faculty and staff advisers and counselors need to be prepared to assist students of all ages in clarifying their life, career, and academic purposes. This process of clarification can be cyclical, used again and again as developmental needs demand over the life course. Just as a plan devised at freshman orientation, for example, will need to be reviewed at the end of the freshman year, so the initial plans outlined by adult students who have returned to college after a number of years may need to be revised after they have had a chance to experience courses that open up new dimensions of growth. But this process of classification must focus on enabling students, no matter what their age, to take increasing responsibility for their own decisions —and thus move in the direction of the autonomous and integrated stages of ego development described in Weathersby's chapter in Part One.

Educational advising and career planning services of this kind will require a greater allocation of resources by the institution and a greater investment of time and energy by the faculty and student development specialists as well as students. However, there is much to be gained by encouraging students' educational and career planning. Not only will more effective learning take place because students will be motivated by their career plans and better fitted to their studies, but institutional efficiency will be increased as well because the amount of trial-and-error wandering among courses, majors, and colleges will be reduced.

In order to accomplish these goals, academic advising and career planning need to be brought into the mainstream of academic life, as Blocher and Rapoza have suggested earlier in this book, where they can become the concern of both faculty and student development specialists and, ultimately, a dynamic and vital part of the total educational process. To help faculty and staff implement these services as a central part of the educational process in college, the next section of this chapter discusses the elements of decision making with respect to life, career, and educational plans that we believe are highly congruent with the aims of a general and liberal arts education and in keeping with the purposes and goals of higher education as it seeks ways of helping individuals over the life course achieve further growth and development. The final section will discuss materials that students and facilitators can use in the planning process and will suggest the adaptability of the planning elements to a variety of educational settings utilizing students, faculty, and specialists as guides, counselors, and teachers.

Elements of the Planning Process

Successful outcomes of educational, career, and life planning can never be guaranteed, but the individual with the best control of the planning process has the best chance of achieving a good outcome. Educational and career goals cannot be clarified nor productive courses of action undertaken on the basis of hasty or ill-conceived choices.

Skill in decision making is integral to the process of development as Perry, Gilligan, and other authors describe it in Part One of this book. Perry discusses the place of commitment in going beyond the stage of relativism in thought. Gilligan speaks about the relation between assuming responsibility for others in the real world and the stages of development in moral judgment. Allen Tough reports the expressed desire of adults for help in planning their learning projects, and Blocher and Rapoza note the special needs of women in vocational planning. Traditional college-age students have reason to expect recurring use for decision-making skills as they progress through the life cycle or stages of adult development. And adult students, although they have already decided to return to school, may need to clarify their decision if their program is to contribute to their personal or career development and give them more control over their lives.

Students vary in their decision-making skills, and psychologists differ in explaining and identifying these variations. Some use a model of developmental stages to identify a student's level of sophistication in planning. Thus, Vincent Harren (1976) has been assessing the development of educational and career decision-making skills among traditional-age college students, using an instrument based on David Tiedeman's model (1961) of vocational development. Central to Tiedeman's work is the notion of steps in vocational development within the two major periods of anticipation and implementation of decisions. During the period of anticipation, an individual progresses through the steps of (1) exploration of career alternatives, (2) crystallization, in which patterns emerge among these alternatives, (3) choice, and (4) specification creating the potential for action. The subsequent period of implementation involves the steps of (5) induction, (6) transition, and (7) maintenance—that is, entry into, establishment of, and pursuit of a career choice. In his chapter, Green says that the ability to develop a life plan can be viewed as one aspect of the development of purpose. Weathersby speaks of the relationship between formation of educational/career purpose and stage of ego development. These notions and others suggest that "stages" in career planning are the manifestation of a complex interplay of numerous aspects of development.

The possibility of identifying the status of individual students with respect to such career planning stages is appealing, but not all psychologists working in the area of vocational development agree with the stage model of vocational decision making. For example, D. A. Jepsen (1974) bases his thinking on "decision" theory rather than "developmental" theory. He speaks of various "strategy types," or characteristic ways in which students organize information about themselves and vocational options. His research suggests that certain characteristics in planning may persist over the life span of individuals. He has tentatively identified more and less active planners based on the degree of richness and scope in their information-gathering behavior. Active planners, for example, tend to identify many more alternative occupations and possible outcomes than do less active planners. But whether strategy-type represents a consistent approach to coping with life generally or a characteristic that changes over time cannot be determined without further longitudinal research.

Other models of vocational planning based either on decision or developmental theory have been advanced in recent years (see Jepsen and Dilley, 1974; Gelatt and Varenhorst, 1968; and Katz, 1966, for example). Certain elements are common to most of these models. At heart, the decision-making process can be described as a strategy for processing three kinds or systems of data: (1) an information system, (2) a values system, and (3) a prediction system. And decision making is viewed as cyclical in nature, suggesting, for example, that career and program decisions are not made once and for all but may be revised over time.

In life-career-educational planning by college students, the decision-making process can be viewed as embracing the series of steps identified in the arrow-shaped Figure 1 (adapted from Walworth and Goodman, 1975, p. 47). These steps include (1) defining the task, (2) gathering information, (3) establishing a values hierarchy, (4) making a choice, and (5) taking action. The following descriptions and brief case examples suggest the implications of these steps for educational advising and career counseling.

Defining the Task. The planning process begins with the awareness of a decision situation. A student's recognition of a decision situation may be prompted by extrinsic factors, such as an institutional requirement that students select a major or family pressure for the student to select a career, or by intrinsic factors, such as a student's social service aspirations or need to become independent.

Once students recognize specific decision situations such as these, they need to be able to confront them by defining the task to be accomplished. Some students may be ready to plan a complete degree program to achieve clearly perceived goals; others may need to clarify their purposes through exploratory activities or the examination of their own past experiences in school, at work, or elsewhere. At this point, the student needs to define the task as sharply as possible to give direction to the subsequent stages of the planning process, while at the same time realizing that the task can be redefined as planning progresses. The process should not be allowed to stall for lack of complete clarity at this first stage.

To illustrate, Denise S., a student returning to college for a bachelor's degree,

Figure 1. Steps in the Decision-Making Process

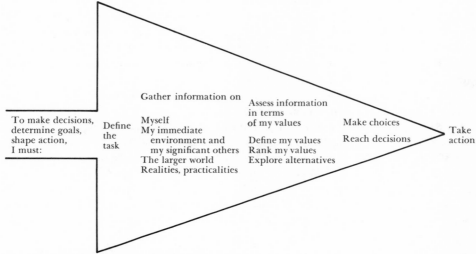

Source: Adapted from Walworth and Goodman, 1975.

described her decision situation and her approach to planning her program in this way:

> I have been an instructional aide in a rehabilitation center for the deaf and blind for seven years. I want to design a degree program that will best utilize my previous college experience and my work experience and fulfill my desire to up-grade my professional level in rehabilitation teaching. The program will also need to prepare me for possible future entrance into a master's-level program in special education or rehabilitation of the multihandicapped.
>
> I need to gather information about various agencies dealing with the handi-capped, the types of professional service positions available, and the specific edu-cational backgrounds needed. I also need to investigate a number of graduate pro-grams in departments offering preparation for work with the handicapped. From this I should be able to determine the requirements for entrance to several grad-uate-level programs in special education.
>
> Next I will begin a card catalogue of library resources with a focus on reha-bilitation and special education for use in my college studies and to be expanded upon as my schooling continues.
>
> I will determine the liberal arts credits I completed previously at the com-munity-college level and identify the components of my life learning in my area of concentration. From here I will be ready to plan appropriate studies to fulfill the requirements of a bachelor of science degree.

Gathering Information. The second phase of the planning process is gathering in-formation for the purpose of identifying the options available to the individual. Denise S., in the example just cited, gathered information about both employment opportunities and educational requirements and programs in the area of her career interest.

In life-career-educational planning at its best, information is collected both about oneself and the external world. *Information about oneself* involves at least four types: interests, skills (including abilities and aptitudes), values, and life-style preferences.

Psychometrists, psychologists, counselors, educators, and personnel and management specialists have devised a formidable array of tests, questionnaires, checklists, inventories, and workbooks designed to assist individuals in such self-exploration.

For many years, individuals engaged in career planning depended upon professional interpretation of tests to inform them about their own interests, skills, and values. But recently emphasis has shifted to materials that can be used independently by the planner, as illustrated in the section on these materials later in this chapter. Although controversy continues among counselors about the most effective approach to career and life planning, the research of Holland, Tiedeman, and others, the development of computer-assisted counseling, and the experience of efforts like the Career Education Project in Providence, Rhode Island, and the Career Education for Non-Traditional Students Project (CENTS) at Northern Virginia Community College all suggest that the individual is capable of self-directed exploration, assessment, and planning.

This change of locus of responsibility from the professional to the individual involved has important developmental and educational advantages. It enables the individual to take responsibility for his or her own planning. It provides tools for self-evaluation that can be reused when needed. It enables the individual to gain a personal grasp of the information instead of taking another's word for it. And it exemplifies the kind of self-directed inquiry or investigation that all college students need to master.

Some of the current literature on the life cycle can add an important dimension to this self-exploration. Locating oneself on the human development continuum, gaining an understanding of tasks already accomplished and those yet to be achieved, realizing that one's interests and preferences change over time, understanding the crises and strains of transition periods, and visualizing what is yet to come give students of all ages a broader perspective on future possibilities as well as deeper insight into present needs. For instance, it is reassuring to a homemaker emerging from the empty nest with the determination to gain competence and *do* something in the world, in spite of her husband's complaints, to know that she is not uniquely selfish or uncaring but shares these goals with others at the same stage in life. It is equally reassuring to a businessman in his late forties who is interested in developing a new career in social service to realize he has not taken leave of his senses but shares with others of his age this desire to change priorities. Young women may find a study of the life cycle particularly important in their career planning, as Bernard suggests in Part One of this book, since the insights gained from such a study can frequently enhance their self-confidence and make them more open to new alternatives.

For example, Pat S., 38, an accomplished registered nurse and mother of three children, discovered in the course of her study of the life cycle Bernice Neugarten's concept of "time left to live." Pat recognized that in her own life she was ready to shift gears from "achievement to self-satisfaction." In a paper defining her goals she wrote, "Perhaps it is not as important to have read all of Shakespeare's sonnets as it is to have read one and really understood it, have an opinion on its style, and be able to compare it to other sonnets or even create one of your own! Therefore, while I'm in college I would like to strengthen my writing skills. I have the ability to communicate ideas, feelings, and experience orally, but I've never had the opportunity to practice putting them down in an organized form of effective communication." Instead of planning a program to enhance her achievement in nursing, she planned one in the humanities and in writing for self-satisfaction.

Acquaintance with developmental literature makes clear that decisions about college courses or curriculums, occupations, and life-style preferences are subject to change.

This knowledge heightens interest in acquiring the tools for self-exploration, decision making and planning, and it frequently sets in motion a clarification that becomes the keystone of a student's plan. For example, Raymond D.'s initial experience in college left him with a sense of failure, and a series of clerical jobs in different cities did not contribute to his self-confidence. He had been married briefly to a young woman who was alcoholic. His major interest in returning to college was to learn to work with alcoholics, but this goal seemed a long way off and he desperately needed additional income to sustain his studies. As he reflected on his work experiences, it was clear that he had felt most challenged and satisfied when he had a large amount of disorganized data that needed organizing and processing. This suggested designing a program of studies to upgrade his skill in data processing as a short-range goal in order to increase his income potential, while he tested his interest in human services by doing volunteer work with alcoholics and drug addicts in the local probation department.

In Raymond's case, as in those of so many other adult students, his analysis of his work experiences, whereby he identified competencies and skills that he had employed with great satisfaction, provided the insight necessary for successful planning. This self-exploration gave him a sense of direction and purpose for the first time in many years. His discovery of a skill and an interest on which he could base a hopeful future would not have occurred without a systematic investigation of skills and interests.

Planning also requires gathering *information about the external world,* and in particular, facts about careers and educational opportunities. These facts are critical for informed decisions, particularly as new opportunities are emerging within various fields of work, lifelong learning is becoming a reality, and changes in occupation are becoming increasingly common over the life span.

To learn about careers, firsthand experience is naturally the best way. Taking a course or serving as a volunteer in a potential field of work would constitute direct experience and information gathering of this kind. In internships for college credit, education and work experience are truly joined. Such activities have much more developmental value than information gathering of a more vicarious sort, as Duley notes in his chapter on field experience education. Career testing through internship or volunteer work experience is an excellent means of forming the commitment that Gilligan discusses in her chapter on moral development, as well as a means of acquainting oneself with the vocational subgroups of particular fields, referred to by Kolb in his chapter on learning styles.

After experience, on the hierarchy of information-gathering activities, come observation, consultation, and the reading of printed materials about occupations. Printed materials are often not developmentally oriented and tend to be stereotypical, dated, or highly conventional descriptions of earnings, job duties, and the like. Needed are materials addressed to the potential of different occupations to satisfy the needs of men and women in various stages of the life cycle, to provide for the expression of humanitarian concern that White discusses, to contribute to the development of interpersonal competence as described by Tolbert, and to satisfy particular cognitive styles as Kolb defines them. Good case histories would be very helpful, particularly in conducting simulation activities in career planning. Literature in the form of biographies, autobiographies, and novels can also add a rich human dimension to the study of occupations providing illustrations of careers in true-to-life narratives.

Occupations can be approached for study singly or in clusters within vertical or horizontal career patterns. Clusters can be skill- or function-based or organized around personality types as in Holland's schema (1973). Thinking in terms of career clusters offers more options for expansion of opportunities and suggests the notion of occupational growth for persons already employed in a field they enjoy. Through this means students can be led to think developmentally about their choice of careers. Careers can also be viewed as being sequential or serial—an approach that may suit women who want to combine family and work over the life span or men who choose second or even third careers over the course of their lives.

The notion of sequential careers is illustrated in the experience of Martin H. As a young boy, he was intensely interested in "how things work," and he consequently followed an industrial arts course in high school. He then joined the Navy and was trained for electronics work. Upon discharge he went into an appliance business with his brother. He liked the repair end of the business best, not only because of the challenge of the work but because of the customer relations the job entailed. He enjoyed the contacts with people, but in time he found them superficial and insufficiently rewarding. This led him to recognize that he wanted to teach electronics, and he has taught technical classes successfully for ten years. In the course of his teaching, however, he has found students inappropriately placed in his classes and has had gratifying experiences informally counseling some of them into other curriculums. Now he is again rethinking his career plans. Looking at the sequence of his own career to date, he sees the pattern of his own development leading to a deepening interest in more intense relationships with people. He is now investigating the field of vocational guidance and is planning preliminary study in this field and some career-testing through volunteer work in a community agency. This will help him determine if a move into the guidance field will afford an opportunity for greater impact on the lives of others than teaching now affords him and with what age group he would be most satisfied working.

An individual not strongly attracted to one specific field of work would do well to select two or three fields to explore, thereby generating a broad base of information against which to test personal interests and ability. For example, having worked as a secretary for several years after high school graduation, and being married to a businessman, Cynthia M. knew when she started college that she liked the business world. But she also loved books. Her study of occupations centered on business management and library science. She investigated them both extensively and recognized in doing so that the library research gave her great satisfaction but also that she knew very little about actual library work. A career-testing experience as an unpaid assistant in the reference room of her local library was subsequently arranged. A year later Cynthia had combined her earlier alternatives into the occupational goal of library management.

Beyond information about self and occupations, facts about educational opportunities are essential. The immediate need of college students is to make decisions about their educational program. After the question "Why am I going to college?" has been addressed in relation to life and career plans, the more specific implications for education can be considered. In other words, after it has been determined whether college is a means of becoming credentialed, a means of becoming an "educated" person, a means for personal growth, or all three, more specific questions must be answered. Information must be collected on a range of topics as a basis for educational decision making. What kinds of intellectual and personal skills are going to be demanded for survival in our rapidly changing society? What do the traditions of liberal arts education mean for careers today? How can college study contribute to rewarding use of leisure time? What studies contribute to personal growth? What educational competencies do specific occupations require? What kinds of educational backgrounds do graduate or professional schools require for admission?

The modern college must offer a variety of resources, including consultation, written materials, and field experience, to meet individual student needs for information. If the full-time faculty of a college is limited to the traditional liberal arts disciplines and perhaps one or two human service professions such as teaching or nursing, students should be encouraged to contact experts outside the college in other fields or professions to obtain information for program planning and career choices. Likewise, with respect to modes of study, students will benefit not only from formal courses but also from less structured learning, such as through independent study and direct experience.

The importance of information gathering on educational options is exemplified by the experience of Marilyn S., a widow in her mid forties. Marilyn entered college with the intent of making a career change from secretary to travel agent after completing the associate degree in liberal arts through the New York State Regents' External Degree Program. Extensive consultation with college faculty and with personnel in the travel field, however, led her to aspire to the more ambitious goal of travel agency management or ownership within the context of a bachelor's degree program. Her next task was to identify the best means to prepare for her goal. Through library research on education in retail travel, investigation of local college programs, and further consultation with her college adviser, she identified several alternative educational opportunities. One option was a college-level independent study program in travel management sponsored by a professional organization; another was a sequence of traditional courses in retail travel at a nearby college that could be taken through cross-registration; still another was a concentration in business studies at Empire State College with an emphasis on her interest in travel. Among the options, the independent study program in travel management clearly offered the best specific preparation for her career goal and offered a mode of study in which she had worked successfully for her associate degree, but it did not meet the breadth and depth requirements of a concentration in a bachelor's degree program. Further reflection and consultation led her finally to develop a concentration in cultural studies with a focus on European history, art, and literature—fields of study that she enjoyed and that could provide deeper cultural understanding for her later work in the travel field. The independent study program in travel management then became part of the general learning in her degree program. In this way her degree program simultaneously fulfilled her personal goals, her preferred learning style, the expectations of the college for the components of a bachelor's degree, and the broad purposes of a liberal arts education. Through self-assessment coupled with information gathering about the travel field, she had come to set her own goals higher than before, leading to a more rigorous educational program but one fully within her own capabilities and opening the potential for greater liberal education, personal growth, and a fuller life. The need for women students whether of traditional college age or older to challenge themselves educationally and to discard the stereotypes relating to fields such as mathematics and science is very real. This is best done, it would seem, not as an end in itself, although that could be justified, but as a response to individual student recognition of the potential such studies offer for their future years.

Establishing a Values Hierarchy. Clarifying values and establishing a values hierarchy constitute the third phase of the decision-making process. Money, power, security, adventure, autonomy, and service are examples of values that the individual must weigh in order to formulate a value system or set of priorities. Students must decide what is really of worth to them in the spheres of education and career. Today, more than ever before, values seem subject to considerable fluctuation among individuals or over the life span. Witness the shift in student values from the rejection of "middle-class" values and the commitment to social reform in the late 1960s to the emphasis on personal, self-

fulfillment goals in the mid 1970s. The adult woman with grown children who is returning to college may find "family" taking a different place on her value scale than it would
have ten years earlier in her life. A number of the writers in Part One of this volume,
including Gilligan, Weathersby, Douvan, Perry, and White, suggest that changes in values
accompany the behavioral developments they describe. A common theme is the effect of
the development of personal autonomy on life values and decisions. Weathersby points
out, for example, that at an earlier stage of ego development individuals may select
careers that conform to external expectations, while at a later stage they are more likely
to choose careers that meet the demands of personal autonomy. Helping students find the
occupations in which they will best be able to realize their own potential and that are
suited to their stage of development as described by Weathersby, Perry, Gilligan, Schaie,
and Parr is highly relevant to the purposes of higher education.

   Dorothea J., 42, the mother of four children, illustrates a response to personal
values in career choice. She has worked in the employment placement field, most recently
as a placement officer in a rehabilitation center. On entering college, she planned to become a rehabilitation counselor, but her self-exploration revealed that her greatest satisfactions came from her ability to persuade personnel managers to hire her clients. At the
rehabilitation center, she had enjoyed selling or promoting the concept of the employment of the handicapped as skilled, productive, and low-risk employees. As a counselor,
she would have less opportunity to persuade and educate the world outside her agency. In
analyzing her values and rating them—that is, establishing a hierarchy of values—she
became aware that the role of rehabilitation counselor eliminated what, to her, was an
important value. She thus began to broaden her perspective. If she could persuade others
to employ the handicapped, why not minorities, women, or the aged? As a result, she
changed her goal to that of becoming an affirmative action officer in a large corporation
—a role that would give larger scope to her humanitarian concern.

   Making a Choice and Taking Action. Choosing among alternative courses of action
on the basis of values and the probability of various outcomes on risks associated with
them represents a critical summary stage in decision making. For example, the risk of
preparing for a profession with limited employment opportunities, such as teaching,
counseling, or library work, or preparing to start one's own business, given the high rate
of failures for such ventures, must be carefully weighed against an individual's values.
College students frequently demonstrate a fatalistic attitude toward finding a job in their
field of interest rather than confronting and assessing specific risks. But if they have carried out the earlier steps in the planning process, this stage becomes one of rather straightforward judgments. Charting the prospects of alternative courses of action on paper can
be helpful in making a decision. In Dorothea's case (just described), she eliminated the
rehabilitation counselor choice because it did not provide an opportunity for her to
utilize her persuasive and educational skills outside her agency. In spite of the risks involved, her choice to become an affirmative action officer was possible because of the
values she placed on using her persuasive skills on behalf of others.

   The case of Janice B. further illustrates the choice stage in decision making. Janice
was employed in selling advertising at the time she entered college. Her initial idea of her
educational and career goal was a degree in business that would qualify her for an administrative position in advertising. Through her self-assessment activities, she became aware
that she was not expressing her human services values and interests in her work. She identified three areas for consideration—religious education, business, and career counseling.
She found that most opportunities in the religious education field involved programming
for children, and she eliminated this option because she was weary of the child's world.

The two remaining options were both attractive. Business, particularly the sales field, offered both employment opportunities and financial rewards, since she had enjoyed and had been successful at selling advertising. Career counseling for the returning woman offered fewer opportunities and rewards but would allow her to express the human services values and interests she had discovered in her self-assessment. Before making her decision, Janice interviewed a number of career counseling professionals who worked with returning women and participated in a career development workshop for women as a participant observer. At the conclusion of the workshop, she carefully weighed the values and risks associated with each choice. Ultimately, she chose to take the higher risk of preparing for the counseling field where employment opportunities would be uncertain and her own skills untested rather than pursuing a business career because she felt it would stifle her values and interests. In describing how she weighed the alternatives, she said, "one of my high priorities in my values hierarchy was money. With six children to support you always worry about that. But we always managed to get along, and I'm sure we still will. Other priorities were personal satisfaction in my work and helping people. While I always got a lift out of making a good sale, it just couldn't compare with the way I felt in that workshop when I saw the way those women began to bloom as they became more self-confident about their own abilities. To think that I can learn to help other women to gain the courage to live new lives is so exciting I can't wait to begin. No amount of money could buy that feeling!" Janice has completed her education, quit her advertising job, and is not yet employed full-time as a career counselor, but she does freelance work in her new field and is confident she will find the full-time job she seeks.

The decision-making process is not complete until the decision has been implemented—for example, by signing up for courses in a college program or seeking experience in a possible career field. Thus, at the continuing education center of Oakland University in Michigan, adults who complete its program in career development are each asked at their final session to articulate a "commitment" to fellow group members on their next steps in education or their vocational search. The commitment may be to file a college or job application or it may be to undertake further inquiry, in which case extending the decision-making process becomes the plan of action that is implemented.

In sum, life planning can be raised to an art through the decision-making process just described. Helping students look critically at themselves, at the fields in which they can pursue their interests, and at program options during college will surely increase their control of their lives and the likelihood of their more complete development as persons.

Implementing Life Planning in College

Planning Materials. Because of our conviction that the individual must take personal responsibility for the planning process, we have been investigating and experimenting with materials that help individuals understand the decision-making process, explore their own interests, skills, abilities, and values, gather educational and occupational information and formulate personal educational and career plans. Although materials for students at the secondary level are quite abundant, they are totally inappropriate for mature adults. In identifying materials appropriate for varying age levels, we find that the common denominator of all the materials is their ability to be controlled and interpreted by the user. Two comprehensive sets of materials especially prepared for use with adults are the Career Emphasis Series produced by the Career Education for Non-Traditional Students Project at Northern Virginia Community College and the Career Opportunity Series and Education Opportunity Series published by Catalyst. We will refer to some specific titles in these series.

Guides designed to help students understand the entire decision-making process and to help them become independent· decision makers include *Emphasis: Decisions* (Epperley, 1977), *The Art of Developing a Career: A Student's Guide* (Carkhuff and Friel, 1974), *Directions for Change: A Career Development Workbook* (Walworth and Goodman, 1975), *Career Development for the College Student* (Dunphy, 1973), and *Guide to Resources for Life/Career/Educational Planning for Adults* (Steltenpohl and Shipton, 1976). This latter *Guide*, developed at Empire State College for use by faculty and students in the decision-making process, is divided into sections entitled "Decision-Making," "Adult Developmental Stages and Crises," "Self-Exploration and Assessment," "Work," and "Education" and contains an introductory statement on each topic with annotated references on a range of printed materials for each topic.

The most effective resources for students to use in self-exploration of their values, interests, skills, and life-style preferences are *Emphasis: Self* (Cooper, 1977), *Planning for Career Options* (Catalyst, 1975), *How to Decide* (Scholz, Prince, and Miller, 1975), and *PATH: A Career Workbook for Liberal Arts Students* (Figler, 1975). Suggesting that students review a variety of self-exploration resources such as these is sound practice. It places the responsibility in their hands and involves them more deeply in the process of self-exploration. Younger and less experienced students as well as women returning to college are likely to select one of the comprehensive workbooks that provide logical, sequential procedures for analyzing interests, skills, and values, while older and more self-confident students often select a variety of materials—interest identification exercises from one place, for example, and skills identification questionnaires from another.

Although there is a wide body of literature available on occupations and career planning, only recently has any of this literature been addressed to adults. Several of the most helpful references for use by adult students and their advisers are *Emphasis: Work* (Trabandt, 1977), *Career Opportunities Series* (Catalyst, 1973), *Non-Traditional Careers for Women* (Splaver, 1973), *New Work/New Life: Help Yourself to Tomorrow* (Bartlett, 1976), and *Where Do I Go from Here with My Life?* (Crystal and Bolles, 1974).

In addition to encouraging students engaged in the planning process to use published materials such as these, institutions can produce their own materials, which can have special value. For example, follow-up studies on an institution's graduates relating the career paths pursued by alumni to their college majors would be helpful. In light of the limited employment opportunities in fields such as teaching and the limited professional school openings in fields such as medicine, information on alternative careers pursued by graduates who could not enter the fields for which they prepared would be particularly useful. Another local publication might be a guide by faculty members and staff for colleagues and students to use in the planning process.

The Career Emphasis Series of Northern Virginia Community College, the Learning Style Interview and other diagnostic instruments of the Campus Free College, the Decision Making seminar guide of Northern Illinois University, and the *Guide to Resources for Life/Career/Educational Planning for Adults* that we developed at Empire State College are illustrations of this type of material. Ultimately, the more immediacy and reality that can be introduced into such materials, the more beneficial and compelling the entire planning experience should prove to students.

Organizational Structure and Personnel. The organizational structures and program arrangements for incorporating the life planning process into the college setting can be varied to fit both student and institutional needs. Basically, we support the recommendation of Blocher and Rapoza earlier in this volume that colleges integrate their academic and vocational development programs, thereby placing the student in the center of the educational process.

In order to do this, faculty members and student development specialists must agree on a comprehensive approach to helping students undertake the steps of the planning process. Each must become skilled in working with students on certain steps, and all efforts must be closely coordinated. If faculty and student development specialists are willing to work together and learn from each other, it should not be necessary to call in expensive outside experts. Faculty members can use their expertise in their discipline to enrich the student development specialists' base of knowledge, while the student development specialists can impart to faculty their skills of counseling, referral, and facilitating development over the life course.

We know that students are most responsive to planning experiences at points of transition in their lives. Thus, the life planning process might seem to be most reasonably initiated when students enter an institution as freshmen or as returning students. The process may ultimately prove to have greatest impact, however, when students choose a major field of study, such as during the latter part of the sophomore year. Keeping the process open and flexible once initiated is critical for its success. In the future, the use of a diagnostic tool such as Harren's experimental instrument, referred to earlier in this chapter, may help students and faculty members or counselors determine individual readiness for planning.

One scenario for organizing the life planning process might begin with student development specialists leading special orientation activities that introduce elements of the planning process. Follow-up activities might grow out of collaboration between faculty or staff specialists and student leaders in residence halls, student unions, or student organizations on ways to foster self-exploration. The psychology department might join in these endeavors by providing resources and by training students as group facilitators. Using students as facilitators not only helps to sell the planning process to other students; it also provides experiential learning opportunities for the facilitators themselves.

Group experiences in life-career-educational planning enable students to see that they are not alone in their concerns and uncertainties, many of which are common at their stage of the life cycle; they provide a forum in which students can test their thinking about themselves and their plans on a group of sympathetic peers and benefit from others' insights and reactions; they can lead students to take initiative for their lives, in contrast to the dependent role they assume in many traditional classrooms and even in some one-to-one experiences with faculty or counselors; and they can be highly motivating in encouraging information gathering and in establishing plans of action through individual accountability to the group. The Discovery Workshop offered to students at De Paul University in Chicago and the Life/Career Planning Seminar at Washington International College in Washington, D.C., are examples of such group approaches to the life planning process.

At the same time, for some students and for certain institutions an individualized approach to the process is more appropriate. A highly diverse student body, commitment to an individualized mode of education, or the impracticality for working students of group activities might be some of the reasons for choosing one-to-one conferences between faculty members or counselors and students. In many instances, a combination of individual and group experiences will make the most sense.

The academic departments, in concert with the placement office, library, and alumni, can play a major role in providing educational and occupational information.

Introductory courses in every discipline might devote one or two sessions to the contribution of that discipline to a host of occupations. Selected faculty members in each department might be designated as information specialists in the field, given release time for advising, meeting with student groups, fulfilling speaking engagements, developing and supervising field experiences such as internships, and identifying professionals in the community who would be willing to share their knowledge with students.

In order to assist students in integrating knowledge about themselves with information about educational and occupational alternatives, counselors and teachers must work together closely. Student service staff can offer small-group or one-to-one counseling for students who are ready to move from information gathering to making choices. Faculty can also counsel students making either long-range career plans or more immediate educational decisions.

Student participation in the life planning process can be made an expectation or even requirement for graduation. The full integration of academic and support programs can even lead to the award of college credit to students for learning achieved through this process. Significant opportunities for cognitive learning exist, for example, in understanding and applying steps in the decision-making process, in studying theories of adult development, in probing the meaning and future of work in our society, and in exploring the goals and meaning of higher education, including the relation of work and the liberal arts.

Conclusion

All American colleges currently offer at least some educational advising and career counseling to their students, but at many these services are not carefully organized or structured, and at only a few are they integrated systematically. As a result, the likelihood of student benefit is low.

Just as students need a plan, so do colleges. In our judgment, educational and vocational advising will be most effective if colleges conceive of it as part of life planning in general, organize it to encourage student planning and decision making, base it on the steps of the decision-making process, incorporate self-directed information gathering about oneself and about occupational and educational options as one of these steps, and involve faculty and student service staff jointly in the program. Such a program, which puts the student at the center of the educational process, can be infinitely varied with respect to setting, timing, and personnel responsible for implementing it. Each institution's administrators, faculty, and staff will doubtless see new possibilities for their own resources. But helping students become more self-directed by helping them to apply the planning process to their educational decisions and career choices should be the goal of every adviser or counselor, whether administrator, faculty member, or staff.

Only educational programs capable of responding to a range of student needs and interests will be able to succeed in the future. The economics of education as well as the developmental theory expounded throughout this book dictate that students assume greater responsibility for their own education. Only as opportunities are offered and expectations set for students to undertake life-career-educational planning will their developmental needs and individual differences be adequately served by the modern college.

References

Bartlett, L. *New Work/New Life: Help Yourself to Tomorrow—A Report from People Already There.* New York: Harper & Row, 1976.

Carkhuff, R. R. *The Art of Problem Solving.* Amherst, Mass.: Human Resource Development Press, 1973.

Carkhuff, R. R., and Friel, T. W. *The Art of Developing a Career: A Student's Guide.* Amherst, Mass.: Human Resource Development Press, 1974.

Catalyst. *Career Opportunities Series.* New York: Catalyst, 1973.

Catalyst. *Planning for Career Options.* New York: Catalyst, 1975.

Clifton, S., and Nejedlo, B. *Decision-Making.* DeKalb: Counseling and Student Development Center, Northern Illinois University, 1976.

Cooper, J. *Emphasis: Self.* Salt Lake City, Utah: Olympus, 1977.

Crystal, J. C., and Bolles, R. M. *Where Do I Go from Here with My Life?* New York: Seabury Press, 1974.

Dunphy, P. W. *Career Development for the College Student.* Cranston, R.I.: Carroll Press, 1973.

Epperley, J. R. *Emphasis: Decisions.* Salt Lake City, Utah: Olympus, 1977.

Figler, H. E. *PATH: A Career Workbook for Liberal Arts Students.* Cranston, R.I.: Carroll Press, 1975.

Gelatt, H. B., and Varenhorst, B. "A Decision-Making Approach to Guidance." *National Association of Secondary School Principals Bulletin,* 1968, *52,* 88-98.

Goodman, J., and others. "Down with the Maintenance Stage, Career Development for Adults." *Impact,* 1974, *3* (6), 44-51.

Gysbers, N. C. "A Comprehensive Approach to Career Development and Guidance." In G. Walz and others, *A Comprehensive View of Career Development.* Washington, D.C.: American Personnel and Guidance Association Press, 1974.

Gysbers, N. C., and Moore, E. J. "Career Guidance: Program Content and Staff Responsibilities." *American Vocational Journal,* 1972, *47,* 60-62.

Harren, V. A. *Assessment of Career Decision Making.* Progress Report, May 1976. Available from author, Southern Illinois University, Carbondale, Ill. 62901.

Holland, J. L. *Making Vocational Choices: A Theory of Careers.* Englewood Cliffs, N.J.: Prentice-Hall, 1973.

Jepsen, D. A. "Vocational Decision-Making Strategy Types: An Exploratory Study." *Vocational Guidance Quarterly,* 1974, *23,* 17-23.

Jepsen, D. A., and Dilley, J. S. "Vocational Decision-Making Models: A Review and Comparative Analysis." *Review of Educational Research,* 1974, *44,* 331-349.

Katz, M. "A Model of Guidance for Career Decision Making." *Vocational Guidance Quarterly,* 1966, *15,* 2-10.

Khosh, M. N. *A Career Planning Program for Women: The Experience Cue.* Washington, D.C.: National Association for Women Deans, Administrators, and Counselors, 1977.

Maslow, A. *Toward a Psychology of Being.* New York: D. Van Nostrand, 1968.

Roe, A. *The Psychology of Occupations.* New York: Wiley, 1956.

Scholz, N. T., Prince, J., and Miller, G. *How to Decide.* New York: College Entrance Examination Board, 1975.

Splaver, S. *Non-Traditional Careers for Women.* New York: Julian Messner, 1973.

Steltenpohl, E., and Shipton, J. *Guide to Resources for Life/Career/Educational Planning for Adults.* Saratoga Springs, N.Y.: Empire State College, 1976.

Super, D. E. *Vocational Development: A Framework for Research.* New York: Teachers College Press, 1957.

Tiedeman, D. V. "Decision and Vocational Development: A Paradigm and Its Implications." *Personnel and Guidance Journal,* 1961, *40,* 15-21.

Toffler, A. *Future Shock.* New York: Random House, 1970.

Trabandt, J. S. *Emphasis: Work.* Salt Lake City, Utah: Olympus, 1977.

Tyler, L. *The Work of the Counselor.* (2nd ed.) New York: Appleton-Century-Crofts, 1969.

Walworth, S., and Goodman, J. *Directions for Change: A Career Development Workbook.* (2nd ed.) Rochester, Mich.: Continuum Center for Adult Counseling and Leadership Training, Division of Continuing Education, Oakland University, 1975.

39

Louis T. Benezet

Governance

College and university governance, which we shall define—with appreciation to a long-time student of this topic, John D. Millett, and others—as the structure and practice of academic decision making, is a complex topic even for professional administrators, given the conceptual, organizational, and political problems it involves.

Conceptually, governance has protean meanings for colleges and universities, covering issues ranging from line-and-staff administrative organization and the development of curriculums to the question of how to bring students and staff into more active participation in campus affairs without bringing the house down upon the hard-pressed chief executive. One common source of confusion is the tendency to equate governance with administration. Early writers treated academic governance as the study of how the heads of institutions ran their enterprises, and the persistence of this view of governance —as something done *to* people rather than *with* people—was aided by such books as David Riesman's *Constraint and Variety in Higher Education* (1956) and John J. Corson's *Governance of Colleges and Universities* (1960, revised 1975). Granted, administration or management—the latter is a word that was earlier avoided in academic circles—has become the dominant element in governance on most campuses during the past two decades, as accelerating fiscal problems have led to the entry *en bloc* of management information systems; management by objectives; planning, programming, and budgeting systems; and other management "tools," such as those produced by the National Center for Higher Education Management Systems in Boulder, Colorado; and as the managerial functions of college administrators have been emphasized by the rise of faculty unionism and student self-interest organizations. Today, whether administrators like it or not, they must sit on the other side of the bargaining table from institutional staff; they must keep the institution intact and on target despite conflicting pressures; and they must account to the governing board or to state system officers for the financial management and planning of the institution. Yet they are only some of the participants in the decision-making process, just as management is only part of governance. In this chapter we will refer to *administration* as the total structure and set of operations by which the organization is led and to *governance* as the decision-making apparatus in which various members and constituencies participate with administrators to guide the organization along its way, especially at key junctures for policy.

The organizational difficulties inherent in academic governance have been pointed out with a vengeance by social scientists such as Cohen and March (1974) in their study, *Leadership and Ambiguity: The American College President,* a title in the Carnegie Commission's series of sponsored research. Cohen and March concluded that a college, and especially a university, is "organized anarchy"—a phrase taken up with delight by many and by now conventional wisdom. An example of its acceptance is a paragraph in a recent textbook on academic management by Baldridge and others (1978):

> To summarize Cohen and March, the image of organized anarchy differs radically from the well-organized bureaucracy. It is an organization in which people talk past each other, in which generous resources allow people to go in different directions without coordination, in which leaders are relatively weak and decisions are arrived at through the noncoordinated action of individuals. Since goals are ambiguous, nobody is quite sure where the organization is going or how it will get there. The situation is fluid. Decisions are often by-products of activity that is unintended and unplanned [p. 26].

The analyst of academic governance must face not only such disenchantment as this currently evident among organization analysts but also a fundamentally opposite view advanced by other social scientists. These writers assume that governance is part of teaching in a directive sense—that students come to college to absorb whatever their betters have to present, under terms printed in the catalogue and repeated by the president at convocation in the fall. Thus, to Parsons and Platt (1973) and Handlin and Handlin (1970), campus traditions and rules are important elements of student socialization. In the Parsons model, the student follows a prescribed hierarchical process toward "cognitive rationality"—the basis for habits of thought and action after college—when he or she joins the "fiduciary trust" of educated persons. (Parsons' prose has always presented a certain challenge to his readers.) Yet if academic governance follows the trend of decision making elsewhere, American colleges may find themselves relying less upon rules and regulations set by faculty and administrators than upon mutually acceptable relationships worked out by faculty and administrators with modern students who come to college more self-determined than their predecessors and who expect their education to be continuous with their experience in the world off campus.

Finally, academic governance deals with the issue of political power. It is attractive to think of college as a place where sensitive teachers and venturesome students come together spontaneously to promote learning and human development. It may be hard for members of former college generations to reconcile that idyllic image of academic life with the contemporary power struggles and tough decision making that go on in the board room, the president's office, or the departmental meeting. In reality, for example, students tend to lose power to faculty because of the wording of faculty union contracts (Kemerer and Baldridge, 1975; Boyd, 1973). Students view "the administration" (which may mean the president, the board of trustees, or the clerk in the bursar's office who has just declined to release a student payroll check because of a missing validation) as neutral toward their own purposes, if not at odds with them, and as useful largely as a counter-balance to organized faculty self-interest (Benezet, 1976). Some campuses have become inured to continual confrontations among contesting groups, each representing some constituency or subconstituency on or off campus—including associations and unions of professors; unions of classified employees; student lobbies and unions, both undergraduate, graduate, and teaching assistant; alumni councils; citizen groups; and sometimes powerful nearby news media as well as representatives of the lay public on the governing board. Students of the modern era are inclined to accept this as normal human interchange; campus newspaper editors have at last something interesting to report.

Yet unless connections can be found between governance as the exercise of power in decision making and education for human development, we face a block to accomplishing what earlier chapters of this book have advocated. The location of centers of power is the key question in the search for institutional change, and the exercise of arbitrary power—in saying who gets how much in order to do what—can keep a campus from becoming the collegial, adaptive, and participatory community for education that it ought to be. Most administrators carry out adequately their responsibilities for upward accountability to boards of control or to state system headquarters. They are not functionaries eager, as Machiavelli and others have warned rulers about administrators, to seize interests and authority of their own "with growing disregard for the formal rules and even in defiance of them" (Sills, 1968). And administrators are prone to mention their responsibilities of accountability when students or faculty claim that college governance should be as flexible and sensitive as learning itself. But governance models are needed that reflect accountability downward and sideward as well as upward. Between the extremes of the administrative satrapy, on the one hand, and the circle of adversary groups, on the other, forms of academic decision making exist that permit democratic governance, such as that advocated in Morris Keeton's book on college organization, *Shared Authority on Campus* (1971), and that offer a bridge between academic power and the type of education that has been proposed in this book. They will not automatically appear. Each campus, led by its most discerning (and patient) administrators, will have to discover the forms that work best in its own setting.

Coordinating Three College Constituencies

If college governance is to be recast in the mold of a process that facilitates education as individual development, there must be cooperation and coordination rather than adversarial contention between the main constituencies of the college: the senior administration, the corporate faculty, and the students. These separate constituencies give the modern college its best chance to maintain a balance between the needs of an outer society to be served, the needs of the college professionals (administrators and faculty members) to feel more than materially rewarded in their missions, and the dual needs of the students to find in the college (1) a vehicle for cognitive development in the broadest sense and (2) a model of social interaction that will hearten them for the lifetime of organizations ahead.

These three constituencies are often viewed with misgiving, as if their separate interests must inevitably result in destructive conflicts. Viewed differently, however, the motives of administrators, teachers, and students create a dynamic tension out of which may arise a decision-making process consistent with the broader aims of human development. Without those differing bodies of interest, decision making is easily downgraded to panels of consultants whose advice the chief executive will either accept or ignore.

It would be unrealistic to assume that administrators will sit back passively as the other constituencies move into decision making on the campus. The three major constituencies will continue to challenge one another. They need to learn to talk together in terms not bound by the bargaining table about what makes education meaningful and how it can best be brought to life for each student—and indeed, for each professor—given the limits of the resources that any college has to offer. And they will recognize the alignments among the respective purposes of (1) the administration, speaking for the institution as a whole, (2) the faculty, speaking for themselves and their disciplines, and (3) the students, speaking both as a group and as individuals.

Colleges' experiments with community governance over the past decade have with few exceptions been bold ventures into democracy that gradually became formalized as college senates or community councils. These tended to become sounding boards for the administration, so that decision making became more centralized as time went on. Yet the nation did not pass through the decade of the seventies without some important changes in the campus climate of governance. Thus, despite the public presumption that students are again apathetic and interested only in preparing for jobs, a growing convention now assumes that students belong on a wide range of governance committees, some at a high policy level. When an institution has voting students as well as faculty members on a University Priorities Committee, as at Princeton, the change must be considered real. Especially during periods of program retrenchment, it becomes quite a practical matter for professors and students to be represented among the decision makers.

The chief advance of the sixties and seventies over earlier attempts at shared governance has been that the constituencies no longer assume that some utopian identity of purpose can be expected among the three groups. Rather, presentation of each group's interests can lead to accommodation without adversary procedures.

Areas for Shared Governance

Thus far, student participation in academic governance has focused mainly on securing personal autonomy for students living on or near campus, control over organized student affairs, and a voice in central campus decisions affecting student interests, such as parking. Continuous student activity in these matters may reflect the impact of the youth culture, which James Coleman, Robert Coles, Kenneth Keniston, and others believe to be a major force in this country. The demand for freedom of social conduct actually was greeted with relief by administrators, who quickly ceased trying to police conduct in the dormitories and proclaimed that they could no longer act *in loco parentis*. Even many denominational colleges have conceded the point.

Three other areas of college life illustrate the need for meshing the purposes of students, curriculum construction, and institutional planning.

Academic Honor. The issue of academic honor has been distorted in recent years by widely publicized cheating scandals at the U.S. military academies, where reportedly archaic honor systems prevailed. Hence the public has missed the fact that student-controlled academic honor systems exist on civilian campuses throughout the country—they may not be numerous, but in several places they are operating strongly. They have been strongest in Virginia, where they are part of the tradition of the Southern gentleman. Colorado College has for twenty-five years had a Student Academic Honor Court, which hears cases of alleged cheating and plagiarism and may reach judgments as severe as suspension or even expulsion. This writer can testify that the situations and their resolution often dramatically illustrated what student decision making can do when called upon. The faculty adviser played a role no more than that title implies; yet in the twenty-five years I know of no instance in which the student court process and findings have been invalidated, much less revoked, by the president of the college.

Students' moral development, as Carol Gilligan has noted, is a topic that faculty tend to shy away from. The success of the Student Academic Honor Court is one happy example of concurrence on the good effects of making decisions about the integrity of an educational system and the consequences of its having been breached. It seems strange, therefore, that we have developed a callous disregard for the moral implications of the nationwide treatment of intercollegiate athletics, particularly in the top classes of competition governed by the National Collegiate Athletic Association. (See Howe, 1977.) The latest national survey, undertaken in this case by the American Council on Education, offers no more likelihood of promoting reform than have its predecessors. Since the takeover of intercollegiate athletics by the television industry, it has been conceded that bigtime athletics—mainly football, followed by basketball—is big business and that the coach and players are employees. (College history has perhaps forgotten the incident of the football player at the University of Denver who lost his scholarship when he was disabled from play, made a claim for restitution under the Workmen's Compenation Act, and won it.) The financial sums involved are so large that no board, president, or faculty group has dared to inquire what it really means for its university to be represented in a first-class league. More than twenty years ago the late John Dale Russell, then chancellor for finance for higher education in New Mexico, became so outraged by the size of the burden of intercollegiate football on universities with modest educational resources that he brought the figures to the attention of the state legislature. Its response was that the burden should be carried and the matter not made a public issue. The impact of athletic costs and pressures on institutionals integrity has yet to be examined in this country.

The challenge of athletic recruitment systems to moral development on campus was brought home by a controversy over the recruitment of hockey players at a northeastern college in 1976-77. Students and faculty charged that during the buildup of the school's hockey program the admissions dossiers of highly promising hockey-playing applicants were given special treatment. In the smaller colleges where students live closer together it is less easy to shrug aside the professional athletic cadre as an admitted sub-operation of the institution for the purpose of entertaining the public, gaining support from alumni as well as the legislature, and paying the bills of nonspectator sports. Yet the moral questions ought to remain on the overall agenda. If we are to accept football, basketball, and, gradually, other competing athletes and even band musicians as paid performers, what shall the dividing line be between college admission as a matter of a player's contract and college admission as a privilege for which persons who happen only to be good students and not entertainers are expected to pay? How shall it be decided when any extracurricular activities have become important enough to the popularity and revenues of the college to treat the student as an employee rather than as a participant in a community devoted to higher learning?

Curriculum Construction and Operation. Whatever gains have been made in student participation in academic governance, one suspects that the real test will not come until two inner walls of the academic corporation have been breached: (1) the construction and operation of the college curriculum, traditionally the province of the faculty alone; and (2) the making of major decisions about the institution's purpose and future as an educational corporation—decisions traditionally made by the board of control.

Let us begin with the question of participation in governance affecting the academic program. What students take away from college has been variously described as a combination of what they brought in from individual nature and nurture plus what the institution by its tradition and current policy contributed to their development (Astin, 1970). As Robert Pace (1975) has pointed out in an informal series of discussions and more recently in *Measuring Outcomes of College* (1979), this is not a complete picture of what happens to people as they go through college. The students themselves, as their levels of aspiration rise with learning experience, become dynamic factors in that experience, both in its input and its outcomes. The students' own contributions to the timing, the presentation, and even the content of learning are elements that cognitive psychologists might accept without question but a majority of academicians most likely will not –"not in *my* discipline, anyway."

Analyses such as Pace's suggest that responsible student entry into governance via the academic program can contribute to education and also strengthen the college community, once the rules of the game have been agreed on. However, the transformation of academic governance into a system that will serve a universe of personal and cognitive development needs will require more than a resolution of the administration or even of the corporate faculty. It will not proceed from the composing of new flow and feedback charts or the creation of extra committees on curricular reform. What it requires is a review of the philosophy of governance as far as content and process of classroom learning are concerned. These matters are normally held to be sacrosanct to the individual professor. Yet the advance of students' appraisals of their professors' effectiveness is on many campuses a continuing holdover from the unrest of the 1960s. If the student buyer's market in the 1980s puts them in closer access to academic decision making, we may again witness changes in curriculum emerging from student as well as faculty initiative. One can hardly imagine a university faculty embracing new theories of learning and student motivation as a result of the introduction of shared decision making in the classroom. We can anticipate the replies of professors, particularly those who during the 1960s made ad hoc concessions to students, buying peace in their time in order to introduce what was called "relevant" subject matter and then later blaming the administration for having been the cause of the knuckling under to student demands.

But student participation in decision making, as an increasing number of colleges are discovering, need not plunge us back into 1968 with its incidents of capitulation by faculty or administrators on points where professional expertise, values, and hard-won knowledge were held in check or even compromised. The more flexible student participation envisioned here, in which students have more say in the planning of their own curriculums, bears little resemblance to the billboard-style changes in course content and programming of the Vietnam and civil rights days. (Admittedly, quite a few solid new course sequences and materials did come out of that hectic era: environmental sciences, black and other ethnic cultural history, inner-city economics and politics, women's studies, and courses on world energy and hunger problems.)

Probably the greatest amount of change in undergraduate programs is occurring now as colleges and universities, under pressure of enrollment needs, are introducing professional and even vocational sequences to attract clientele from among populations not inclined to be drawn by liberal arts studies. Allied health and business courses of every description are being added.

The authority of knowledge is not one to be questioned lightly, as Walter Metzger (1970) makes clear in an article in *Daedalus*:

> Here again is the ultimate problem faced in professional terms. In these terms the complexities of the problem can be resolved to this: how can authority be removed as an issue and yet retained as a resource? Removing authority as an

issue would require yielding certain shibboleths about the learning. One of these is the assumption, which many academic teachers seem to harbor, that the only constructive forces in the classroom are their own benevolence and each student's appetite [1970, p. 606].

Metzger goes on to discuss the spiral of dilemmas that would result in the classroom from attempts to harness the group power of students to "didactic ends." He finds it inconsistent with the spirit of higher learning that a meaningful curriculum treating things that scholars know to be true could ever arise from a collaboration of student requests for contemporary subject matter with a professor's willingness to rearrange his or her priorities of what to teach. Metzger was one of the senior faculty who represented Columbia University during student riots of April 1968. The passage just quoted was written a year and a half later. Ten years since that time we find less disposition of student bodies to demand certain kinds of subject matter or certain methods of teaching. Nevertheless, decision making—the governance of learning, if you please—does not seem complete when it occurs at the professor's desk alone. The heritage of Herbert, Froebel, Pestolozzi, and indeed Dewey stays with us.

If a student is lucky enough to find a resourceful resident adviser in the dorm or perhaps even a freshman teacher with unusual empathy for adolescent problems, accommodations to personal need in the learning process can sometimes be found. Otherwise, it ends up with a Cronkite conclusion: "And that's the way it is." In this case, "the way it is" means that you study what you are given to study, work for grades high enough to get you to the next point, and have as good a time as possible in the meantime. The concrete result of college is that a majority—about 60 percent—of entering students sooner or later obtain at least a bachelor's degree and continue on in the world with fair to brilliant records of success. What remains undeveloped in very many cases is the feeling of having participated as a contributor to the process of making the educational experience a genuine adventure in finding one's self somewhere in the cosmos of knowledge, skills, beauty, danger, and human values.

Institutional Planning. Beyond the curriculum lies a final major area for student involvement in academic governance—the hallowed area of institutional planning, or decision making about the institution's purpose and future. The experiences of the 1960s left the public nervous about what can happen on any campus when students become excited enough about something to challenge existing authority. And subsequent experience with modern college students has led professors to a growing awareness that today's students, if no longer in an insurrectionary mood, can no longer be considered passive adolescents sitting before the master, pencils at the ready. Public Law 346, the G.I. Bill of Rights, was a breakthrough. Since then there has been a large admixture of older students in college classes, both in the evening and during the daytime. War veterans have brought in their experiences, both good and bad. James Coleman, Kenneth Keniston, Erik Erikson, and others have popularized the notion of a new "youth culture"—that widening stratum of young people who now not only vote at eighteen but who have traveled considerably, earned money through a variety of jobs, and already seen, heard, and sensed things beyond what most among the older generations experienced even in their early years after college. It is a truism to add that television, for all of its sins of omission and commission, has brought to almost the entire population vicarious experiences that were not available to any of us thirty years ago.

A generation going to college with such a background enters an institution organized and operated much in the style of the paternalistic academy of fifty to a hundred years ago. The freshman is greeted by piles of directives, a regimen of courses to sign up for, and a batch of diagnostic tests. The remainder of the college year follows varying patterns of freedom and constraint according to the institution. The general experience is one of sharp contrast with the considerable freedom typically enjoyed in the last two years of high school. On entering the classroom in the fall, the freshman encounters a new brand of authority in the figure of the college professor, and gradually becomes aware of a whole power structure—the department heads, assistant deans, and deans, who in varying degree really decide things. The professor, feeling the pressure of administrative actions, may tend to step up his or her academic authority within the classroom, proclaiming it to be the real discipline of the college. It is small wonder that students fall victim to confusion, anomie, and the kindred ailments of someone cast suddenly into "a world I never made." Students have been accustomed in the past two to four years before college to sharing in many, if not most, of the decisions of life. They now find (unless they come from private preparatory schools where arbitrary central authority is still in force) that students have little if anything to say about decisions that may vitally affect their education.

A modern college campus represents a microcosm of decision making concerning life's problems. It is time to increase student membership on policy committees from tokenism to fair proportions. Colleges that have experimented with this, including some of our strongest ones, have found the results to be good in the main.

There are numerous areas of a college operation that are vital to learning yet that have been all but inaccessible to student input: for example, the process of library acquisitions, including decisions about resources that serve no purpose except to boost the number of volumes. Another area is one where administrators for decades have persistently failed: the encouragement of faculty to try instructional aids, beyond the medium of chalkboard, microphone, and their vocal charisma, to enrich teaching. Professors are notoriously stubborn about this; students, however, are in many cases experts on electronic and other technical aids, which, far from mechanizing the learning process, can help bring it to life. Even computer-aided instruction is making slow progress in many departments and none at all in some (Dartmouth, which for a decade has been under the tutelage of mathematician-president John Kemeny, is still the promising exception).

At least until recently, the European university pattern has offered few examples of student involvement comparable to that advocated here. Thus, in *The Open University* (1977), Walter Perry gives a lucid account of what he calls "an ingenious, serviceable institution," which produced in Great Britain out of a void of degree holders with no chance to attend the conventional universities some 15,000 B.A. s five years after its inception. In fact, the notable success of Great Britain's Open University, whose organization, operation, and curriculum planning have been carried out without student participation, might seem to argue against the thesis of this chapter (see Perry, 1977). However, in Europe degrees tend to have a traditional and standardized value (as national education ministries insist they must). The United States, for good or ill, has chosen a different course. A college degree in itself does not determine one's station in life (though some nongraduates may flatly disagree). We have taken it for granted that with reasonable persistence and scholarship or loan money a student can earn his bachelor's degree, even though this will not necessarily be followed soon by a suitable job. American college students seem to be looking beyond career channeling and status to the quality of the experience. For them, the criterion of educational success is whether college has helped them to cope with the problems and pressures of American society. For this reason the British Open University, brilliant though its success in turning out degrees and expanding its list of applicants has been, is a model that does not answer our own questions of governance as a handmaiden of education. As Walter Perry might be the first to say, the two questions are of quite a different order.

In America, the campus revolutionary spirit of the 1960s has moved to a more reflective phase. Faculty no longer view students' requests to fashion their own courses of study as lapses into anti-intellectualism or defiance of academic authority. Their willingness to offer students more choice stems in part, no doubt, from their awareness that enrollment may drop by as much as 22 percent by the end of the 1980s. But the issue of student participation in planning goes beyond consumer choice of study. And such academic merchandising is already part of the current scene.

Experiments are going on now in this country that entail student participation in decision making over a broad front. Hodgkinson (1971) lists in his ERIC pamphlet on college governance eleven subtopics. Some of these bear directly on student participation in college planning. It should not be concluded that these represent attempts on the part of the colleges to attract enrollments through concessions to the student-consumer. The Colorado College academic plan, which has arranged for blocks of concentrated time on one subject for either three and one half or seven weeks, has existed for a dozen years and the reports remain good. It was originally planned not by the administration but by a small group of professors with active student participation. Teaching authority has not been sacrificed; students complain, in fact, that the faculty load on the work more heavily. Yet the arrangement seems to them more contractually fair since students participate in the initial planning of what the block course will cover. More of this should be looked for as a product of future college governance.

If governance, seen as the structure and practice of decision making, is to relate to the essential business of higher learning, then it is likely that American college administrators and faculty will be pressed to work out ways by which students can join with those faculty members and administrators not only in evaluating but in projecting the operation of the institution. This in turn may allow a college decision making that helps to shape the student's cognitive development.

A Model for Academic Decision Making

What would be the key elements of a college governance model in which decision making is shared over a broad front by students, faculty, and administrators? What would it have to say about traditional patterns of responsibility, accountability, and academic authority?

Consistent with the precedent established by earlier chapters, the discussion will avoid attempts to present a governance instruction book complete with a handy kit to be taken on to any campus for retooling administrative mechanisms into models of shared authority. Rather, it will outline the principal issues, which resemble the classic questions raised by any functioning democracy. The questions might include these: How can the student's interests be represented without a committee of the whole (a little difficult in universities with thirty to forty thousand students on one campus)? How can representatives of each constituency serve the interests of the whole while being faithful to their constituency's views? How can the individual have reasonable hope that his or her personal needs for development will be served by even the best-functioning system of democratic governance in which students have a significant voice? With regard to faculty concerns, how can scholars and teachers be assured that intellectual development, knowledge, and skills will remain the college's highest priority? (A declaration to that effect should probably be the first work of the united governance.)

Any model of governance for shared decision making in the academic community must recognize the built-in hierarchy that exists in that artificially created society between experienced and knowledgeable scholars and young and less-experienced learners. An umbrella philosophy is called for under which there can be accommodation between these two levels of knowledge without sacrificing either the authority of scholarship or the personal development of individual learners.

Beyond that, decisions reached in a shared manner must be carefully and wisely enough made that the president is able to join and support them in accounting to the board of control. Toward that end, the best insurance may be for colleges to do what few have remembered to do—bring in trustees as active members of the college community while it is about the business of learning, rather than as occasional visitors or even vague personified threats of authority. In its early years Pitzer College at Claremont held a long parley among the constituencies to thrash out a governance of the kind we have been describing. The trustees, a typically conservative group of business and professional persons with a few educators sprinkled in, were resistant to much of the proposition making until one of them observed aloud that they alone of all the constituencies had been excluded in the naming of members of the college community. The paradox appealed to everyone; it was promptly written into the by-laws that trustees are full-fledged members of the Pitzer community. From then on the conferences made markedly better progress.

To stand by decisions made in group fashion takes not a weak but a strong chief executive. The tactics and strategy have formed the contents of many a volume on administration, and no attempt even to summarize any of it will be made here. Suffice it to say that with the present constituency of more critically minded, self-assured, and experienced students and with the present status of faculty unionism (uncertain though that may be since the *Yeshiva University* decision), it becomes imperative that the president make explicit to the rest of the college community his or her definition of "consultation." If it means communication to the campus of administrative decisions before their release to the public, there might as well be no attempt at shared governance. If it means that the president and his or her associates will stay with the governance body until agreements can be worked through that will stand up under the inspection of each constituent group (no group perhaps getting all it wanted), then the president's backing of decisions made will need to be firm. If it means that the president restricts his or her role to taking the votes, the board of control probably ought to start looking for a more forceful executive. Otherwise, they may be expected to lose interest in the process altogether.

The problem of the student on the large campus is, and probably always has been, the feeling of alienation from what is going on or what is being planned. Governance involves large-scale decision making, which often comes to regard students, staff, and even faculty as masses to be moved here and there. Unless public funding authorities can be convinced to create large institutions on the plan of relatively small units with faculties and communities of their own—a plan long advocated by social psychologists and just as long disregarded by budgeteers—we shall always have with us the problem of depersonalization in higher education. One way to attack the problem might be to increase regular access for students to meetings of boards of trustees, senior administrative staff conferences, and even legislative committees in state capitals. The students might succeed in underscoring the excellence that comes from campuses that are decentralized into collegiate units small enough to develop personalities of their own, like Kresge at the University of Santa Cruz. Granted decentralization cannot by itself defeat university impersonality, as the University of California at San Diego has demonstrated. Here is an important area in which the president and his or her board might work with professors and students to keep the large college or university from becoming an educational factory unconcerned with students' developmental needs.

A problematic governance issue for some universities ambitious for prestige is the place of research. Not long ago I spoke with a professor from an institute of theoretical science whose activity is supported well, though by no means exclusively, from funds outside the university. To him the university existed solely for the purpose of discovering pure knowledge. Such attitudes do not stay hidden. While anyone who has administered a university will grant that the development of basic research is one primary reason for its being, most universities, even research universities, lack the luxury of a Rockefeller University, an All Soul's College of Oxford, or a Cal Tech, where enrollments are kept very small, faculty emphasis is placed on research, and teaching (at least at the undergraduate level) is minimized. In the typical large school, especially the state university, the instruction of thousands of undergraduates goes on willy-nilly because that function is the largest service to the state. Graduate assistants are assigned to teach as many of the large introductory classes as possible. The dissatisfaction of undergraduates with the situation reflects their awareness that from the university's point of view they are there in large measure to build up full-time equivalent enrollments whose tally directly helps support the research going on upstairs in small laboratories.

Governance concerning the place of university research can be and typically is entrusted to directors of research and their scholar-peers. An alternative might be to include a few representatives who balance research interests with a belief in improving undergraduate instruction. Reports of undergraduates' disenchantment with their experience in large state universities have already brought these institutions into disfavor with state legislators. Princeton and Dartmouth are examples of the strong alumni loyalty that results from an insistence on making the undergraduate experience the center of attention, never overshadowed by graduate or research activity.

The discussion of governance thus far may have given the impression that most of the work of college leadership is confined to decisions about educational policy, content, and method. In fact, however, today's administrators must deal with a host of other problems, ranging from the management of investment portfolios to the building of productive relations between the college and the community. Their managerial functions have so enlarged under present financial, personnel, and political complications that one might well consider the educational function to have been delegated to the provost or academic vice president.

It would likewise be wrong to assume in questions involving material assets and the handling of public relations or accountability to federal regulations that the constituted administrative officers will be bound hand and foot until the governance board, with its shared decision making, can sit down with the problem. If that impression has been left by this chapter, it is time for a note of realism regarding administrative necessity. Such realism need not discourage the spirit of shared decision making, since students and faculty, if they catch the spirit of how the material relates to the intellectual in a college, will have reason to give their attention to the most practical problems with which the administration decides to confront them.

The making of decisions affecting the planning, construction, and operation of institutions such as Penn State with annual budgets of nearly a half billion dollars, and nearly twice that when all of SUNY's budgets are brought together, is not soon going to be turned over to a democratized council of persons who teach, study, or perform other academic duties there. Higher education is either a 60 or an 80 billion dollar business according to how widely one wishes to connect it with the knowledge industry. If universities are considered integral parts of governmental research and of publicly sponsored communication, there is scarcely an end to the financial involvement. A $400 million annual budget enterprise will not be governed like a Vermont town meeting; legal requirements alone would preclude it.

Representation in Governance

This chapter contends that decision making in institutions of higher education will be better integrated in its purpose as it becomes a multisided process with broad participation under careful monitoring for effective action. The process should be controlled so as to serve the development of individuals of all ages, preparation, cultural description, and personal traits. Since no college system can teach by a one-to-one ratio, however, the process will continue to be organized with large groups in mind. The question of representation in governance thus comes to the fore.

Some system of representation recognizing the three separate campus constituencies is essential, I have argued, given the existential fact of differing purposes and values among administrators, faculty, and students. The recognition of different constituencies, however, need not consign decision making to adversarial procedures in the style of formal contracting or labor-management negotiations. The kind of governance that comes out of a union contract framework, is one viable method of getting the college's business done, as studies by Boyd (1973), Kemerer and Baldridge (1975), Angell (1977), Epstein (1974), and others are showing. But it does not give us the bridge between governance and education—unless we choose to believe that adversary relations are realistic preparation for interpersonal relations in modern society.

It may be useful to review some of the models between the autocratic and adversarial in order to speculate about which model offers the best basis for governance consistent with a climate of education that preserves the caring, individualizing activities of professors with students no matter how large the campus may be.

In a style more formal than, yet similar to, that of Morris Keeton, John Millett, in *New Structures of Campus Power* (1978), has proposed the community council as a model of academic governance that gives students a say in the form and content of the educational process. His community council aims to provide students with a "shared authority" and to merge administrative with academic affairs. Among the questions not answered by the community council are the differentiation between debate on policy questions and the council's power to make specific decisions; uncertainty concerning the residual powers of the central administration or the board to make a range of final decisions; and the consequences for organizational effectiveness of a wholesale redistribution of powers. Perhaps the most troubling problem in the community council format is once again the protective attitude of individual faculty members and departments toward their retained power to teach and plan programs of study. According to Cohen and March (1974), the faculty remain unregenerate in their preference for academic anarchy. Whether or not that be true, any governance system that attempts to temporize that preference with the idea of a central representative decision-making body, especially one with active student participation, will remain a prickly issue among most professors. At the State University at Albany from 1969 on, when students were first included in the University Senate, it became an annual procedure to decide whether or not student membership (one third of the 100 members) would be continued the next year. During the time that the writer was in office, efforts to make student membership in the Senate permanent were annually promoted by students and by some of the faculty. Still, when the votes were cast each spring, only a year-by-year membership plan was granted.

Morris Keeton's *Shared Authority on Campus* (1971), already referred to, might seem to rest on Keeton's long experience at Antioch, since for many decades that College has had a community council including students, which has taken a full range of questions of policy important to the institution, including academic subject matter and even decisions on individual faculty appointments. Nevertheless, Keeton's study, proceeding from a survey of thirty-five campuses, stops short of the conclusion that decision making of all kinds must involve faculty and students. The line is still drawn before the question of ultimate college policies, which are left to the trustees. The theme of Keeton's book indicates that disagreements among groups will continue to run deep but that constituencies can be brought together in nonadversary fashion so that normal differences can be dealt with without tearing the campus apart.

Our arguments for holding on somehow to a spirit of collegiality in decision making, as opposed to the adversary model required by unionism, may have a sound base of pragmatic sense. However, they are harder to defend than they used to be before the present era of faculty competition for tenure, for department growth, and for students. In regard to the onset of unions or something approaching them (if the *Yeshiva* decision should prevail—see Kaplin, 1980), friends in business corporations smile tolerantly when it is suggested that collegiality on campus, especially involving student participation, can survive a union contract. "Move over and join the crowd" is the common attitude of the corporation executive whose company long ago gave up all pretense to a communal attitude of the company in its organizational relations.

Some administrators at schools where unions have been voted in report that the faculty attitude becomes progressively less collegial and, as one president told me sadly and even bitterly, less professional even toward the teaching and scholarship. In the main, however, I am optimistic that the college and the university in America, being less political than their counterparts in Europe and certainly South America, can continue to preserve collegiality of a sort, whether or not faculty unionism expands in higher education —or, indeed, fades away, as the *Yeshiva* decision mentioned earlier may suggest. Something persistent in the attitude of the sincere academic professional resents the thought of surrendering to the bargaining table his own or his department's prerogatives regarding certain basic educational decisions.

About these matters nothing more should be ventured since they represent an involved, technical, and litigious complex of issues. We are here concerned with the spirit of an organization that can lend itself, despite the constraints of constituent interests, to an educational philosophy of broad participation in decisions affecting the lives of those who make the college their home. Nor does it seem too idealistic a position when compared to the writings of organization analysts in the business world. The tradition of studies by Mayo, Likert, MacGregor, Roethlisberger, Argyris, and others has earned a permanent place—not without challenge by other analysts—in what some call the human relations approach to industrial organization. The main issue seems to be whether a business organization can permit the participation of employees in company policy deliberations without violating its responsibility to its ownership.

Obviously, the issue is somewhat different in higher education, since students are not in the same position as employees. The student is in the unique position of being both client and product of the organization. Unlike cans of beans on an assembly line, students need to be consulted about the process that shapes them. Some students, particularly those in public universities during the years of the late 1960s, took the position that they were taxpayer clients of the institution and therefore in some real sense its employers. While we have passed beyond that period of earnest confusion over relationships, the accountability of the institution has been seen as downward as well as upward.

One of the larger contributions of higher education to governance in not-for-profit agencies is the connection between accountability of the members to each other and the achievement of a campus where education becomes a common endeavor rather than something dispensed as a series of company policy statements.

Conclusion

Whichever approaches to governance offer the best means for encouraging human development, a college remains a publicly accountable corporation whose rules are set by legally constituted governors, generally called trustees. What can be hoped is that these rules may become fewer as we learn how to bring the student more actively into his or her own education. The aim of the college will then be to delegate to students as much decision making as will benefit their development. Higher learning depends upon human exchange, even when one side of the exchange is literature of the distant past or an unarguable laboratory demonstration. Learning remains individual and defies collectivization. Nor can one truthfully speak of academic excellence as something inhering in the college. It depends on what happens within each student.

In his book *Self-Renewal* (1963) John Gardner reminds us that "we think of the mind as a storehouse to be filled when we should be thinking of it as an instrument to be used." Gardner thus neatly summarized the first chapter of Alfred North Whitehead's *The Aims of Education* ([1929] 1963). One of our colleges' low grades year after year on their own report cards is the level of accomplishment in inspiring creativity, which makes a more enduring impact on a student's education than does much of his course experience. Many students active in campus governance have said that it was the heart of their college education. Participation in governance can be a stimulus to learning and creativity.

The present volume offers hope that college governance will in time stand less for the making of rules than for collaborative—and creative—decision making that is itself part of the educative process.

References

Angell, G. W., Kelly, E. P., Jr., and Associates. *Handbook of Faculty Bargaining: Asserting Administrative Leadership for Institutional Progress by Preparing for Bargaining, Negotiating and Administering Contracts, and Improving the Bargaining Process.* San Francisco: Jossey-Bass, 1977.

Astin, A. W. "Measuring Student Outcomes in Higher Education." In B. Lawrence, G. Weathersby, and V. W. Patterson (Eds.), *The Outputs of Higher Education: Their Identification, Measurement, and Evaluation.* Boulder, Colo.: Western Interstate Commission for Higher Education, 1970.

Balderston, F. E. *Varieties of Financial Crisis.* Ford Foundation Program for Research in University Administration, Paper P-29. Berkeley, Calif.: Ford Foundation, March 1972.

Baldridge, J. V., and others. *Policy Making and Effective Leadership: A National Study of Academic Management.* San Francisco: Jossey-Bass, 1978.

Benezet, L. T. *College Organization and Student Impact.* Washington, D.C.: Association of American Colleges, 1976.

Boyd, W. B. "The Impact of Collective Bargaining on University Governance." Paper presented at the annual meeting of the National Association of College and University Business Officers, Chicago, July 1973.

Capen, S. P. *The Management of Universities.* Buffalo, N.Y.: Foster and Steward, 1953.

Cohen, M. D., and March, J. G. *Leadership and Ambiguity: The American College President.* New York: McGraw-Hill, 1974.

Corson, J. J. *Governance of Colleges and Universities.* New York: McGraw-Hill, 1975.

Epstein, L. D. *Governing the University: The Campus and the Public Interest.* San Francisco: Jossey-Bass, 1974.

Feldman, K. A., and Newcomb, T. M. *The Impact of College on Students.* Vol. 1: *An Analysis of Four Decades of Research.* San Francisco: Jossey-Bass, 1969.

Gardner, J. *Excellence.* New York: Harper & Row, 1961.

Gardner, J. *Self-Renewal: The Individual and the Innovative Society.* New York: Harper & Row, 1963.

Handlin, O., and Handlin, M. F. *The American College and American Culture.* New York: McGraw-Hill, 1970.

Hodgkinson, H. L. *College Governance: The Amazing Thing Is That It Works at All.* Report 11. Washington, D.C.: ERIC Clearinghouse on Higher Education, July 1971.

Howe, H. "Commentary on Sports." *Educational Record,* Spring 1977, *58,* 218-221.

Jencks, C., and Riesman, D. *The Academic Revolution.* New York: Doubleday, 1968.

Kaplin, W. A. *The Law of Higher Education 1980.* San Francisco: Jossey-Bass, 1980.

Keeton, M. *Shared Authority on Campus.* Washington, D.C.: American Association for Higher Education, 1971.

Kemerer, F. R., and Baldridge, J. V. *Unions on Campus: A National Study of the Consequences of Faculty Bargaining.* San Francisco: Jossey-Bass, 1975.

Metzger, W. P. "The Crisis of Academic Authority." *Daedalus,* Summer 1970, p. 606.

Millett, J. D. *New Structures of Campus Power: Success and Failures of Emerging Forms of Institutional Governance.* San Francisco: Jossey-Bass, 1978.

Mortimer, K. P., and McConnell, T. R. *Sharing Authority Effectively: Participation, Interaction, and Discretion.* San Francisco: Jossey-Bass, 1978.

Pace, C. R. "A Contextual Model for Evaluating the Impress of College on Students." Unpublished report prepared for the Spencer Foundation Research Committee, Graduate School of Education, University of California, Los Angeles, October 1975.

Pace, C. R. *Measuring Outcomes of College: Fifty Years of Findings and Recommendations for Future Assessment.* San Francisco: Jossey-Bass, 1979.

Parsons, T., and Platt, G. M. *The American University.* Cambridge, Mass.: Harvard University Press, 1973.

Perry, W. *The Open University: History and Evaluation of a Dynamic Innovation in Higher Education.* San Francisco: Jossey-Bass, 1977.

Riesman, D. *Constraint and Variety in Higher Education.* Lincoln: University of Nebraska Press, 1956.

Semas, P. W. "How Influential Is Sociology?" *Chronicle of Higher Education,* September 26, 1977, p. 4.

Sills, D. L. (Ed.). *International Encyclopedia of the Social Sciences.* New York: Macmillan, 1968.

Whitehead, A. N. *The Aims of Education.* New York: New American Library, 1963.

40

Harold L. Hodgkinson

Administrative Development

During the early 1970s, higher education paid increasing attention to faculty development, from in-service training to improvements in faculty evaluation. Little conscious attention, however, was given to administrative development—the training, selection, evaluation, and assessment of institutional managers. Since about 1975, the financial pinch in higher education, on top of the projected decline in students after 1980, has focused more attention on educational management—a trend that has produced major benefits for American colleges and universities. As a result, most institutions are much better managed than they were a decade ago, in terms of planning, budgeting, admissions, and record keeping. However, the in-service development of administrators has not kept pace with these initial increases in educational efficiency.

Problems of Administrative Development

One reason for this gap between the progress in educational efficiency and the development of administrators is the great difficulty in conceptualizing the field of educational management. (Indeed, referring to administrators in higher education as *managers*

Note: Some material in this chapter was developed from Hodgkinson, 1974a and 1978.

is still likely to raise some eyebrows, though not as many as in 1970.) An industrial middle manager in production can be transferred to packaging or transportation with little difficulty, while switching a bursar to the student personnel office might be a disaster, both for the money and for the students. There are, of course, a variety of functions in industrial management as well, but there is more overlap; more managers can do the same things and have the same skills.

Deans and department chairs do not generate credit hours as a part of their job; what then *do* they produce? How do they produce it? And, for that matter, what makes them tick: what are their aspirations and satisfactions, and why did they become administrators in the first place? How can we tell the difference between a good one and a bad one? How many administrators do we need, relative to students and faculty? None of these questions is currently answerable, given the very small body of knowledge that we have to work with.

There are few if any useful guidelines for assessing the quality of administrative performance. The problems are less severe as one moves toward output-oriented functions such as admissions and development, and more severe as one moves toward the academic core of faculty values, including the right of the individual faculty member to be supervised by virtually no one. The department chair is the key role in this puzzle, as this individual is from the faculty and yet must deal with the more bureaucratic values used in running an institution. Does a department chair *manage* the department? The answer is mixed. Budgets emerge from the departmental black box, as do tenure recommendations, requirements for the major, and so forth. But what goes on inside the box?

Fortunately, we are now seeing the beginnings of a professional literature on educational management. Most such literature is still inspirational, subjective, and hortatory, but changes are occurring. There have been several careful studies of the college and university president, including selection and evaluation (see Cohen and March, 1974; Hayes, 1977; Hodgkinson, 1971; Kauffman, 1977; and Munitz, 1976). Most professional associations of educational administrators, whether registrars, admissions officers, student personnel administrators, or financial officers, have now established some standards for their profession, and the search for better selection and performance indicators is clearly on. In addition, the processes and procedures whereby academic decisions are made by boards and faculty or campuswide senates have been the object of careful and useful study (Baldridge, 1971; Hodgkinson, 1974b; Paltridge, 1973; and Pray, 1964). Some administrators have subjected themselves to evaluation by the many constituencies they serve, in order to improve their own performance. Others are using professional growth contracts in order to achieve the same objective.

On the training and development side, a number of institutions and associations now offer workshops and institutes for college and university managers, including the member service-oriented associations like the American Council on Education, Council for the Advancement of Small Colleges, National Association of College and University Business Officers, and probably fifty more. Individual institutions are becoming popular as workshop sites, including Harvard, Stanford, and Claremont. State government agencies, interstate associations like the Education Commission of the States, professional agencies like the American College Testing Program and the Academy for Educational Development, and a number of foundations, particularly Lilly and Kellogg, are sponsoring workshops and institutes for managers of higher education. Probably the major investment, however, has been made by the federal government through Title III of the Higher Education Act of 1965, the Developing Institutions program. There is little doubt that Title III has significantly improved the quality of management in most of the 500 plus institutions that have been associated with the program, both through direct grants to institutions and through the support of consortia like the ACCTION consortium (Hodgkinson, 1974c). If higher education is better managed today, as I believe it is, these are the organizations that should share the credit.

Oddly enough, it is the vaunted pluralism of American colleges and universities that makes these programs difficult to assess. Institutions vary so widely by size, highest degree conferred, comprehensiveness, and clientele that few if any training programs work equally well for administrators of all colleges and universities. People should not yet expect *specific* gains from administrative training programs in higher education. Even in industry, it is difficult to relate a given management training course to an increase in production.

Changes Affecting Administrative Development

What changes are likely in the roles of educational managers? It would seem that in virtually every administrative area the push will be toward clarity of outcome. One of the major problems with outcomes is our tendency to be overly impressed with outcomes we can count. In many cases, clarification can be achieved without heavy reliance on quantitative information, particularly in curriculum and faculty development. It would be interesting if some states could base their institutional support systems on some unit other than the credit hour, but such a change seems highly unlikely. The credit hour is so countable and understandable that most state legislatures will continue with it even though credit hours would seem to have a very tenuous relationship to the knowledge in peoples' heads. Credit hour production data are not very analytical; they tell you little about what is really going on. This overuse of a "black box" educational performance indicator undoubtedly impedes the development of more useful conceptions of educational management. Some changes in the state formulas for credit hour reimbursement, however, will improve the lot of increasing numbers of part-time students, who are now not considered overly desirable because they cost as much to administer as full-time students yet generate only a fraction of the income.

Another major trend will involve greater interaction of college and university administrators with those who run educational programs in industry, the military, museums, health care institutions, and the like. Educators now attend the conference of the American Society for Training and Development (the major professional association for training directors of industry), and some educational administrators from industry and the military attend assemblies of the Council for the Advancement of Experiential Learning (CAEL) and other meetings. The American Council on Education has initiated talks between leaders in college and university systems and their counterparts in industry. For those who feel that industrial education programs are unworthy, consider AT&T's $750 million per year investment and the company's employment of over 2,000 Ph.D.s (Luxenberg, 1979). In addition, many of the larger firms are practicing internal promotion—a worker who has successfully completed a training program given by the company is automatically eligible for salary increases and promotions without translating these attainments into a college or university degree. The consequences of this trend for higher education could be painful indeed.

The potential benefits of increased contact between college and university administrators and those who administer educational programs in the military and industrial sectors are considerable. Management tasks in the latter systems are somewhat more comprehensible, as these systems produce concrete skills knowledge, and competence rather than degrees or credit hours. Much can be learned by trading ideas on the management of curriculum, teaching methods, instructional sequencing, and the like. For example, academic freedom is seen as a relatively unimportant issue in industrial and military educational systems, in which educational outcomes are more clear-cut. If an instructor's teaching is guided not by those outcomes but by some personal whim, that might well be considered not academic freedom but educational irresponsibility. Programs stressing clarified education outcomes, long a hallmark of military programs, are being adopted in medical and dental schools, as well as in some liberal arts undergraduate programs. These curriculum changes in specificity will have major impact on educational management and decision making.

Another question that managers might address jointly is whether there are generic managerial skills—that is, certain competencies that all good managers possess. Evidence from industrial sources is clear on a *knowledge* base required for all managers, but relatively vague on "people skills." It would appear that good managers, like good teachers, can have different types of personalities and still be effective. This issue of general management competencies could be the source of much helpful discussion, as could exchanges of techniques for planning, budgeting, performance assessment, and the like. Other research in general competencies, particularly the outstanding work of Gary Woditsch (1977), supports the notion that there are indeed general competencies in problem solving, that the liberal arts can develop these competencies, and that managers with high scores on these general competencies are superior performers on their jobs in a wide array of occupations. This work could be a start in eliminating the large and unproductive gap between the liberal arts and "real world" knowledge, skills, and competencies. The concept of competence, especially as implemented by colleges like Alverno and College III of the University of Massachusetts, Boston, offers a potentially useful base for collaboration between higher education and other social institutions, particularly on management issues.

Administrative Evaluation

Administration in higher education, along with most other institutional services or functions, suffers from a "snapshot" view of performance evaluation. That is, the techniques used in appraising administrative performance emphasize data taken at a single point in time and do not provide for measures of growth or change. Given what is known about adult development, it may make less sense to use psychometric tools—stressing as they do the performance of a person at one moment in time measured against an equally fixed criterion measure—than to use more clinical techniques rooted in sociology, anthropology and psychology. When the Supreme Court said in *Griggs* v. *Duke Power* that "devices and degrees must be demonstrably related to job success," they clearly were not thinking of statistics as the only way of making the demonstration. It is also vital to note that measures of *judging* performance (especially norm-referenced ones) will be of little help in *improving* performance (especially means of assessing improvement). People have been saying this for years, but when the chips are down we cling to the quantitative-judgmental and ignore the qualitative-diagnostic.

It seems likely that administrative styles vary as much as faculty styles do, and that the evaluation of administrators across campuses would also result in some major discrepancies. (The registrarial functions may be more common across institutions, but certainly admissions, dean of students, academic deans, presidents, and department chairs would show these differences in environmental conditions and pressures.) Those who spend time on many different campuses can also detect systematic differences in campus cultures depending upon public or private affiliation, state and region, size, highest degree granted, and so on. Any system of evaluation and assessment should take into account variations in institutional milieux that reward certain personal styles and talents and play down others.

It should be noted, too, that institutions at different times in their histories are "ready" for different administrative styles and strategies. For example, when the public schools of Berkeley, California, were to be integrated, the situation required a tough, rather thick-skinned individual with superb political skill in getting votes passed. After the laws were on the books, an implementer was needed who could work with the various groups in the community in a close and supportive way, promoting mutual trust and cooperation. As luck would have it, the community got exactly the right man for the first job, who did his work and moved on, leaving the field for a second superintendent with all the community consensus abilities we have mentioned. But it is worth noting that each would have been a near disaster in the other's role, even though both were "able administrators." Many administrators are simply in the right institution at the wrong time.

These qualifications are important in thinking about evaluating administrative performance and making suggestions for improvement. No one is saying that the job of each administrator is unique and cannot be analyzed systematically. But the analysis must be made for a particular role (for example, dean or admissions officer) within a particular institutional context.

Administration and Adult Development

In a previous paper (1974a) I have outlined the major stages in a model of adult development based on the work of Sheehy, Levinson, Gould, and others, and applied the model in a general way to faculty and administrators in colleges and universities. I would like to concentrate, in the remainder of this chapter, on the implications of but two stages of adult development—midlife crisis, or "middlescence" as I like to call it (see Brim and Abeles, 1975), and finishing up, or life after fifty—for administrators.

Middlescence. Administrators usually make a smooth transition into administration from faculty or other relevant backgrounds. However, most administrators come to the role considerably later than do faculty, who receive direct training in graduate school for what they will do as professionals. (To be a TA is to *teach,* but to be an RA in a dormitory is *not* to be a dean of students.) One gets one's first administrative title some years after faculty members have gotten theirs; in addition, one often has to muck around in the role for a while to find out whether or not it is compatible. While the faculty member may have had a decade of teaching experience before middlescence hits (at about 39), the administrator may well have to deal with this difficult challenge with only a few years of genuine performance in the major occupational role.

The normal range of marital difficulties experienced during middlescence may be accentuated for many administrators by the fact that their marriages are on public exhibition three days (and even more nights) a week. For some presidents, vice-presidents, and deans, the ceremonial feeding of large numbers and compulsory attendance of the administrator's family at any number of social functions may simply increase the marital stresses characteristic of this developmental period. It is my impression that women administrators with families have as many problems of this sort as do male administrators.

Levinson and others state that one of the major tasks during this period is the downward revision of the dream that was created during the late twenties. Most of us do not accomplish the romantic and unrealistic goals we set for ourselves in the late twenties; therefore, we must redefine ourselves to square with new realities. These new realities should be based on actual performance (for example, for faculty, "I got tenure but am not chair of my department," or "I'm secretary of the faculty but couldn't get elected AAUP president"). For many administrators, the performance cues are much more diffuse ("I've been a dean for five years and no one's fired me," or "I wasn't sure that I could do a registrar's job, but now after three years I know I can do it"). A frequent assumption of many presidents is that administrators can be ignored until something goes wrong—a strategy that guarantees that something will.

During the midlife crisis, ambiguity has a strong tendency to become paranoia. Strong and specific cues from people who matter are vital for the tasks of this period. It is frequently helpful for administrators at this stage to work out a professional growth contract that will provide these cues and arrange for a system of reinforcement based on the administrator's own goals and geared to specific rewards for achievements.

The midlife crisis may be particularly stormy for the department chairperson, as this is one of the most ambiguous roles in academe. For some, this is an administrator with faculty aspirations; for others, it is basically a faculty role (head teacher) with a few administrative busywork jobs to do, but not requiring any special skill or training. For most of the department chairpersons I have worked with over the last ten or so years, the title and function of department chair do not accord enough professional status or recognition, largely because the job is so diffuse. Like the art historian, rewarded by neither the artists nor the historians, the position is schizophrenic by definition. Rating forms are available for department chairperson evaluation, but these are mostly opinion surveys and do not represent consensus on the specific behaviors associated with excellent performance. For the overworked and underloved faculty member who is elected by colleagues to the chair of the department, the rewards are at best a mixed blessing. To have these "rewards" descend during the years in which marriage, personal credibility, and career aspirations are all under major stress is especially difficult. And in certain research-oriented universities, to do *overly* well as department chair is to lose status as an intellectual with colleagues. The administrative reward system for department heads is frequently such that if you do well your faculty friends will despise you.

Another problem that may make the midlife crisis period more difficult for administrators of all titles is the problem inherent in the management of stasis or decline. Administrators have typically gotten their personal and economic rewards from growth-oriented activities. During my first year as admissions director, the entering class increased by 150 students with higher SAT averages; while I was director of development, gifts and grants increased by 250 percent; while I was academic dean, we added two new majors and developed graduate programs in five new areas. Given the lay of the land for the next decade, few administrators will be able to enjoy that sort of reward. Typical of that problem is the college president who opened his speech to the alumni association with the words, "We're still in business!" He was expecting loud cheers, for this was indeed a major effort to keep the ship afloat, but no one applauded. Everyone's ego needs some public support now and then, but in the next decade administrators who work from intrinsic drives are more likely to thrive than those who work for extrinsic rewards. Again, the strategy of setting specific goals, both in terms of performance and improved human development, with a clear set of evaluative criteria, tailor-made to that administrator in that setting, seems to be the best way to gird administrators in midlife for the tough times ahead.

Finishing Up, or Is There Life After 50? The second period I would like to concentrate on is what I have called "finishing up"—the rather extended period of adult development after 50. There is now good evidence that neither physical nor mental powers inevitably decline drastically upon the fiftieth birthday; indeed, life apparently can be interesting and vigorous for at least twenty years after that date.

Retirement for a faculty member could easily be a rather benign change. At least half of his or her professional activity—keeping up with one's field and colleagues, writing for professional journals—can continue after retirement. For the administrator, however, the story is considerably different. Obviously, few administrative activities can be carried on after retirement, and if there are no other satisfying activities to take their place, retirement is likely to be stressful. One can always say, "Now I'll finally have time to write that book," but writing skills that have only been honed through interoffice memos for twenty years are not likely to be easily polished, or acquired.

However, retirement is not, as I see it, the major problem of these years for the administrator. Having spoken with a large number of administrators aged 55 to 60 during the last three years, it is my contention that "hanging on" is a very pervasive fact of administrative life in colleges and universities. "Hanging on" refers to the fact that there is a hiatus near the time of retirement when most administrators have completed what they wanted to do, may be suffering some decline in physical energy, and would like to leave the position to a younger person for the good of the institution, but find that there is nothing else for them to do. Thus, for either economic reasons or out of Calvinistic habit, administrators hang on, finishing their formal careers often with a diminished sense of their own worth as well as a sense of guilt for not fully serving the institution well.

What could be done about "hanging on"? Strategies will have to be highly individualized. However, there are several that have worked well for many people and institutions. One is the assignment of an administrative intern for the retiree's last two years in office, either under the assumption that the intern may take over the job if things work out, or simply as general training for the intern. This plan allows for a slight decline in the administrator's responsibilities with no loss to the institution if the intern handles the job well. In addition, it allows the administrator to begin the development of alternative activities so that retirement can be phased in. There is also time to begin a process of career assessment, which most people do at three or more times during their working lives. Some unfinished agenda items from one's career can easily be fit into a retirement agenda. For an academic dean, the working out of the ideal freshman general education sequence, a better way of figuring faculty workload, and all the administrative issues that could never be dealt with systematically could frame a very useful agenda for the first three or so years of retirement. The intern could be useful in gathering background data on these issues for the retiring administrator to deal with substantively during retirement.

Some institutions have made very good use of certain administrators as consultants for a few years after retirement, and the first few years of retirement are unquestionably the roughest. A recently retired academic dean, for example, can be very useful as a consultant for department chairpeople at his or her home campus without getting in the way of the new dean, as long as the activity is seen as technical assistance and training and not the development of academic policy. This strategy obviously shares the dean's knowledge and expertise, and may prepare the retired dean for some new and exciting work as a consultant. Development and admissions officers can provide excellent technical services on a minor scale during the first years of retirement for their, and other, institutions.

Several examples exist of an industry "trade," in which the newly retired administrator offers technical services to an industry—counseling employees with children of college age, serving as a consultant for in-company training activity, analyzing specialized library services within the industry, and so forth. Because so many businesses are now engaged in their own educational enterprises, with their own professional education and training staff, this area could offer increasing opportunities for recently retired academic administrators. (Registrars and deans of students could be very useful in some of these areas as well as academic deans.)

Conclusion

In this chapter, I have briefly reviewed the field of educational management—what is known about the tasks to be accomplished and the roles to be played, what college administrators have in common with managers in settings outside of higher education, what the trends are in the developing field of educational management, and finally, how some of the adult development literature might be applied to administrative development.

It seems clear that higher education, like banks and hospitals, will have to continue to clarify what it is doing. Much of this burden will fall on board members and on administrators. The institutional changes needed to accommodate to a declining youth cohort will be a problem for all managers, from department stores to bowling alleys to colleges. And most important, higher education administrators will have to become more aware of what they themselves are doing and why. In this era of change, management is likely to become one of the major agents of cohesion for educational institutions, and a conceptual and operational linkage with other societal institutions. As such, it should be clear that one of the major functions of an administrator or educational manager is to communicate, in clear and understandable terms, what the nature of the enterprise is, to the various interested publics. There is no more important agenda item today for higher education managers, from department heads to presidents. The public must come to understand what we are about. In this sense, tomorrow's administrator of higher education *must* be a teacher.

References

Baldridge, J. V. *Academic Governance*. Berkeley, Calif.: McCutchan, 1971.

Brim, O., and Abeles, R. "Work and Personality in the Middle Years." Social Science Research Council, *Items,* 1975, *29* (3).

Cohen, M. D., and March, J. G. *Leadership and Ambiguity: The American College President*. New York: McGraw-Hill, 1974.

Hayes, G. D. "Evaluating a President: The Minnesota Plan." *Association of Governing Boards Reports,* 1977, *18* (5), 5-9.

Hodgkinson, H. L. *Institutions in Transition: A Study of Change in Higher Education*. New York: McGraw-Hill, 1971.

Hodgkinson, H. L. "Adult Development: Implications for Faculty and Administrators." *Educational Record,* 1974a, *55*, 263-274.

Hodgkinson, H. L. *The Campus Senate*. Berkeley: Center for Research and Development in Higher Education, University of California, 1974b.

Hodgkinson, H. L. *How Much Change For a Dollar? A Look at Title III*. ERIC Higher Education Series, Research Report No. 3. Washington, D.C.: American Association for Higher Education, 1974c.

Hodgkinson, H. L. "Administrators, Evaluation, and the Stream of Time." In C. F. Fisher (Ed.), *New Directions for Higher Education: Developing and Evaluating Administrative Leadership,* no. 22. San Francisco: Jossey-Bass, 1978.

Kauffman, J. F. "The New College President." *Educational Record,* 1977, *58* (2), 146-168.

Luxenberg, S. "Education at AT&T." *Change,* January 1979, pp. 26-35.

Munitz, B. "Measuring a President's Performance." *Association of Governing Boards Reports,* 1976, *18* (1), 36-40.

Paltridge, G. *Patterns of Trustee Decision-Making.* Berkeley: Center for Research and Development in Higher Education, University of California, Berkeley, 1973.

Pray, F. C. "A Report Card for Trustees." *Educational Record,* 1964, *45* (3), 251-254.

Socolow, D. J. "How Administrators Get Their Jobs." *Change,* 1978, *10* (50), 42-54.

Woditsch, G. *Developing Generic Skills.* Competency-Based Undergraduate Education (CUE) Project No. 3. Bowling Green, Ohio: Bowling Green State University, 1977.

41

Jack Lindquist

Professional Development

Eric French is a 46-year-old full professor of English, more precisely of English Romantic Poetry. And he is in a midlife quandary. He has thirty articles and a textbook behind him, but no new topic catches his fancy. Indeed, he is wondering whether it was all worth the effort. He sees little more career climbing to do. He has been active in the Modern Language Association and in the Faculty Senate and is glad to be free of those political hassles. He has no interest in chairing the department or becoming a dean. Most of his teaching consists of upper-division and graduate courses in his specialty, but he has been doing those courses for years and is weary of the same material, the same student essays, the same class discussions. That weariness shows in declining student ratings. There are no great traumas at home, but even there the routine is getting pretty dull. Now what? Another nineteen years of grinding out Romantic scholars and scholarship? The same office, the same chitchat, the same house, the same daily search for parking, the same petty squabbles and budget threats in the department, the same social circuit, the same lousy weather? Is that all there is?

Meanwhile, over in Biology, Geneva Westgate stews over an impending tenure decision. Now 34, she went straight into teaching from graduate school. The university is her life. She has completed her dissertation and has published four well-received articles, but she has not published in the last two years. Instead, she has discovered undergraduate students and has found introductory biology and bioethics exciting vehicles for aiding their intellectual and ethical development. To become more skilled in teaching, she has attended faculty development workshops, and she is now serving on a team that is trying to get a formal faculty development program going. Yet there have been two troubling consequences of her new enthusiasm. One is that her growing assertiveness, born of her own developmental need for self-esteem and autonomy, seems to be making her husband and colleagues uncomfortable. The other problem is that her colleagues in the biology department have intimated, though not directly said, that all this attention to undergraduate student development, while laudable, is not helping the department build a reputation for graduate education and research. What if she fails to get tenure? What if her marriage breaks up? How can she pursue her own development and that of her students in a system that appears bent on thwarting both?

Down the hall, Dean Elinor Jackson finds her mind wandering from the curriculum committee discussion. How these committees can drone on! She sits on six different standing committees, *ex officio,* and has another four special task forces going, and none of them seem to get anywhere. Costs continue to spiral, educational problems mount, and the faculty union gets more obstreperous by the day. There must be a better way to run this college, but nothing in Elinor's background as a professor of political science has prepared her for this mess. Worse, the job demands sixty hours a week reacting to everyone else's agendas, she seems to have become the enemy of her faculty colleagues, and she is beginning to lose her patience in the office and at home. What is she doing in this impossible job? Is there a way to become more effective in administrative leadership and even to enjoy it? Is she ready to give up the status, the salary, the perquisites, the aspiration to a college presidency?

Sitting in the faculty lounge is George Miller, who likes to think of himself as a professor of nineteenth-century American history, with a special interest in Emerson and Thoreau. He calls himself a "humanist." But the administration seems to think of him as a teacher of remedial reading and writing. The few students who enroll in his classes seem to think of George as a foggy and irrelevant white male chauvinist. To his colleagues in the faculty lounge he rails against administration and students alike. "Philistines all! Disco dancers on the grave of Western civilization!" But left to himself, he worries that he is not able to teach reading and writing; that he may be prejudiced against women and minority races; that he cannot present his subject in ways that excite today's students; that his position will be cut if he cannot attract more students.

Eric, Geneva, Elinor, and George may be composite characters, but they are very real. I meet them every time I interview college professors and administrators, every time I lead a professional development workshop. In their experiences, I see the developmental issues of Part One of this book come to life. And I see the challenges for professional development in the modern American college.

For Eric French and other members of the tenured faculty majority, who are threatened with stagnation as colleges and universities get more and more "tenured in," professional development must bring renewal. It must help them out of the ruts into which they have fallen in their teaching and suggest new directions for growth in midlife.

For Geneva Westgate and other beginning teachers, it will need to provide aid and support in confronting the increasingly difficult question of tenure, for there will be few tenure slots and few alternative jobs in the immediate future of American higher education. It must also influence personnel systems so that eager teachers such as Geneva are rewarded rather than punished for pursuing teaching improvement, if colleges are to become institutions that effectively aid student development. And it must confront the prejudice that makes Geneva's own personal development a problem for her and her male associates.

For administrators such as Dean Jackson, professional development must aid in efforts to make academic committees work and to get faculty to join administrators in resolving serious financial, educational, and political problems. It will thereby make administration a more rewarding job.

And for the George Millers among our colleagues—learned people wedded to traditions that deserve preservation but need to be adapted to modern college students—professional development must open nonthreatening avenues to change. By reinforcing their strengths, it can permit them to admit underlying worries about teaching ability, personal prejudice, and threats to security and reexamine their approaches to teaching without compromising their academic values.

The first lesson, then, of these profiles is that professional development is in essence adult development. Part One of this book is about college staff as well as students. As staff members, we confront in our own professional growth and in our working relationships Erikson's life stages: basic trust, autonomy, initiative, industry, identity, intimacy, generativity, and integrity. We like to think we behave in an "integrated," fully developed fashion, but we suspect some other staff of being trapped in self-protective or conformist ways. Muckrakers could even cite evidence that aimlessness, lack of interpersonal competence, prejudice, and ignorance of one's own or one's students' learning styles—the negative side of the dimensions of development discussed in Part One—mark more than a few professors and administrators.

The second major lesson for professional development is that professors and administrators not only *are* developing adults but *aid* in the development of other adults—their students. They face the student counterparts of Eric French, bored by routine and in search of fresh breezes. They teach student Geneva Westgates, anxious about job and personal security yet growing into an ill fit with their current situations. And they advise Elinor Jacksons and George Millers and an infinite variety of other adults who hope that college can expand their narrowing options. In short, Eric, Geneva, Elinor, and George now sit on both sides of the professor's desk.

If academics are seen as developing adults who aid the development of other adults, it becomes clear that professional development is critical to the renewal of the American college. Recent trends in faculty, administrative, and organizational development suggest a new appreciation of this fact. This chapter briefly reviews these trends and then proposes a working model to facilitate the development of college staff as persons and as academic professionals.

Our Training as Students

In another volume (Lindquist, 1978a) I have described collegiate professional development as a deep-rooted, thick-trunked tree that lately has sprouted new branches. Beneath the ground spread the roots—our undergraduate and graduate student experiences. We learn what professors and administrators do, what constitutes college teaching and learning, by experiencing higher education for a good eight to ten years as students. As David Kolb points out in his chapter, we get channeled quickly into a major field consistent, usually, with our habits of mind. Our professors drill us in their subjects and instill in us the norms and values of the academic profession. Most of us have experienced the same basic system of instruction: formal courses of three to four months' duration, organized by academic subject, designed and monitored by professors specializing in those subjects, conducted in college classrooms by means of lectures, discussions, and labs, aimed at covering the subject, supplemented by reading assignments, graded on a

Figure 1. Professional Development Tree

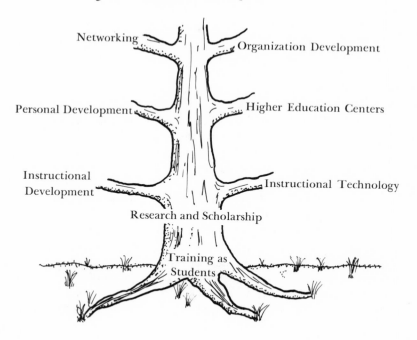

normal curve on the basis of essays and multiple-choice examinations, and continuing until 120 "credit hours," organized in a curricular menu of required and elective courses, are passed. All these hoops should be jumped between the ages of 18 and 22. This formula for higher learning is ingrained in faculty well before they ever step to the head of the classroom. Higher learning becomes synonymous with this pervasive set of practices.

A central feature of this system is the future professor's becoming an increasingly specialized scholar and researcher. Our higher learning begins broadly enough but then funnels us so that by the time we receive our ill-named "terminal degree" we know more than almost every undergraduate student needs or wants to know about very little. Then, even though we academics were a small minority in our own undergraduate class, we set out to replicate our student experience in the next generation.

I do not mean to belittle the strengths of this tradition. It has produced crackerjack scholars, researchers, and teachers. And although it is not organized to teach for adult development, except development of specialized expertise, it does influence intellectual and ethical development, as William Perry shows us. On the "affective" side, college experience, especially if residential, does appear to broaden students' sensitivities, strengthen interpersonal relationships, and promote autonomy (Feldman and Newcomb, 1969; Astin, 1977).

What I am suggesting is that most of today's professors and administrators have acquired, from their own experience as students, deeply rooted ideas about higher learning that may hinder their ability to respond to new circumstances. How can persons steeped in this tradition respond to 40- and 60-year-old students, to poor, minority adults well schooled in ghetto survival but not in the white middle class's approach to learning, to adult demands for assessment of college-level learning that did not take place in college classrooms? How can they open themselves to "universities without walls," to competency education and evaluation, to the use of mediated instructional resources? Higher education is becoming a strange new world to us faculty, and yet we are the tenured people who must cope with this world during the next fifteen years. Then, as we retire, students socialized in these new circumstances can replace us (only, I suspect, to find that their experience is behind the times too).

Perhaps the greatest challenge to collegiate professional development is to educate and socialize faculty and administration for tomorrow's postsecondary education. What are the aspirations and learning needs of today's and tomorrow's students? What are the advances in developmental theory and educational practice that can help us respond to those needs? How can we gain the skill needed to teach in ways foreign to our experience? More fundamentally, how can we open our minds to the potential worthiness of new students and new ways? Current answers to these questions are woefully inadequate in most American colleges.

Particular professional development programs to meet this continuing orientation objective will take various forms. But core ingredients suggest themselves. One is study of human development theory and research, the stuff of Part One of this book. Indeed, this might be the initial resource. A second ingredient is study of alternative curriculum, teaching, and evaluation practices, the stuff of Parts Two and Three. A third part of this core orientation should be study of *our* students, *our* educational mission, *our* curricular and teaching practices and outcomes, *our* organizational supports for staff and students. And a fourth core component should be study of the ways we do work, and might work, as an organization to regularly assess and improve our efforts. A staff continuously renewing its grounding in human development theory and educational practice, its understanding of the local educational situation, and its knowledge of how to go about academic improvement would be ready to tackle the future.

Research and Scholarship

The trunk of our tree is continuing advancement in one's field through new contributions to knowledge—the traditional meaning of professional development prior to 1960. Outside the local institution is a disciplinary association, replete with annual conventions, placement services, publications, and an "invisible college" of like-minded specialists. One's career advancement is often influenced more by this external peer network than by local authorities. A professor gets ahead by publishing in the association's journals and presenting papers at its conferences. New jobs are found not through local placement but through professional contacts in the field. In many ways, this system of peer influence has enabled American higher education to stimulate constant advancement in specialized fields—at the expense, undoubtedly, of teaching and other local services. In the near future, as career advancement depends on holding the job one gets, local and state pressures to produce student credit hours rather than scholarship and research may threaten to weaken our system for advancing specialized knowledge. The new influences seem to be state bureaucracies and legislatures, on one side, and faculty unions, on the other.

A major professional development challenge for our near future is to preserve this trunk of research and scholarship. Unless professors are encouraged, supported, and rewarded for pressing forward the frontiers of knowledge, few will. The academic tree as we know it will suffer rot. Although many recent faculty development programs concentrate heavily on teaching improvement, future programs also must reassert and protect the advancement of knowledge.

Each professional development program will find its own way to support research and scholarship. Old reliables such as research grants, personnel policies favoring publication, sabbaticals, course load reductions, travel moneys for professional meetings, visiting scholars programs, and special research projects all can help professionals keep abreast and contribute to the latest advances in their fields. And all provide the break from routine needed to breathe new life into Eric French, help Geneva Westgate meet tenure expectations, and permit Elinor Jackson to learn what is new in the field of higher education administration.

Assistance in Teaching and Administration

Prior to 1955, collegiate professional development consisted almost exclusively of one's experiential roots as a student plus that broad trunk, continuing support for advancement in a specialty. It neglected the tasks of teaching and administrating. And it neglected adult development.

Then three branches sprouted. One was the instructional resource center to which a faculty member could go to get help in using instructional television, the computer as a teaching aid, films, slides, and videotape. Few professors were appreciative of such resources or comfortable using them at first. The hardware and software were pretty primitive. But as technology has improved and faculty have grown accustomed to it, the professor and book have become supplemented by sophisticated media resources for learning. Certainly the professor of the eighties and nineties must learn to live with, develop, and use such technology. It is up to professional development to help reduce faculty resistance to mediated instruction, to help develop high-quality resources, and to assist professors and students in learning how to use the equipment and programs. As technology frees professors from information dispensing, drill, and elementary problem solving, they will have more time to devote to the subtler aspects of student development.

A second new branch that emerged in the sixties was "instructional development." At universities such as Stanford, Northwestern, and Michigan State, instructional development offices were established in which educational specialists helped voluntary faculty clients diagnose teaching problems, design new approaches, learn the new methods, and evaluate the results. Often, development grants were included to provide the time and materials needed for improving a teaching method. Student rating forms were developed by these centers as one way to diagnose teaching problems. On occasion, whole departments rather than individual professors have become the "clients."

Instructional development has expanded and merged with newer approaches such as faculty and organizational development, but its essential core remains the learning specialist, an expert in facilitating the solution of teaching problems. Centra's recent survey of the field revealed that those in charge of faculty development programs put this technical assistance at the top of their lists of effective services (Centra, 1976). Such assistance, grounded in recent theory of human development and learning, can be highly flexible and responsive to specific situations or needs perceived by faculty. It can assist the professor over time as well as with particular problems.

The administrative development analogue to instructional development is technical assistance in the methodology of administration: collecting and using management information, personnel selection and review, efficient office administration, budgeting, and the interpersonal side of management. Local administrative development staff, external consultants, and training workshops can be employed to help administrators increase their management skills. As with instructional development, skill development facilitated in the context of solving real and immediate administrative problems is a stronger approach than training out of context (Lindquist, 1978b).

Higher Education Research and Development Centers

The third limb of professional development that grew in the sixties was the study of learning, teaching, and administration, together with systematic dissemination of findings. Centers for the study of higher education sprouted in many education schools. A few universities established what the University of Michigan calls a Center for Research on Learning and Teaching. Publications on higher education rapidly proliferated. Administrators and, less frequently, faculty could come to higher education centers to learn about the subject through in-service seminars or doctoral programs.

Such study centers constitute vital resources for professional development in the modern American college. They supply theory and a data base. They provide a place where faculty and administrators can go to educate themselves about curriculum, teaching, student development, organizational dynamics, finance, innovation, and leadership. If they add action to study, such centers can facilitate faculty, administrative, and organizational development for their own universities and for colleges in their region. This last "if" is a big one, for it requires retooling of higher education professors to enable them to shift from information collecting and dispensing to problem-solving facilitation. But resources for professional development are there if nowhere else in many financially pressed institutions.

Memphis State University's own Center for the Study of Higher Education and its allied Institute for Academic Improvement illustrate how a study center can aid professional development in the modern American college. On a foundation of academic change and adult learning theory, the Center and Institute offer field-based doctoral and postdoctoral study, team workshops, an extensive summer institute, and multi-institutional development projects, all intended to assist postsecondary professionals as they attempt to improve academic practices. Through affiliation with the Institute, staffs of member colleges and universities enjoy a rich network of colleagues and activities through which to pursue their efforts to improve education for adult development.

Personal Development

Three new branches grew on our professional development tree in the seventies. All were around earlier, but you would not have wanted to swing on them. One was explicit attention to the personal development needs of the professional. Another was the introduction into higher education of principles and practices of organizational development. The third was the proliferation of professional networks, not just for one's discipline but for educational innovation.

During the sixties, so-called "radical" students and "humanistic" psychologists made the surprising contention that students were developing persons, not cranial cavities or engines needing tuning. *The American College,* Nevitt Sanford's predecessor to this book, sounded the alarm, along with the Hazen Foundation statement by the Committee on the Student in Higher Education (1968). Authors such as Joseph Katz and Arthur Chickering made eloquent cases for colleges attending to the developmental concerns of their young adult students. Cluster colleges or "living-learning" programs, popularized in prose by Jerry Gaff and founded through the work of social psychologists such as Theodore Newcomb, became practical attempts to apply developmental lessons. A major argument in all this work was that the personal life of the student is inextricably tied to his or her academic life. It can reinforce or thwart academic achievement. More important, such personal development goals as achieving a sense of identity, becoming autonomous in thought and deed, broadening one's sensitivities and awareness, and developing effective interpersonal relationships and social responsibility are the outcomes envisaged by liberal arts goal statements. Personal development is the mission of liberal education.

In the early seventies, attention shifted from the person of the student to the person of the professor. Here was a man, and occasionally a woman, who had just weathered the civil rights movement, the student movement, and the war protests. Now he faced sudden constriction in opportunities because inflation, recession, and the aging population combined to depress the academic job market. He faced public loss of confidence in the academic profession. He faced a new student demand for education that would lead to a job. He faced continuing pressure to equalize opportunities for racial minorities and women. He faced classes overflowing with students lacking basic reading, writing, and computational skills, often students with cultural backgrounds very different from his own. He faced a bewildering array of new teaching methods and technology. He faced funders who demanded more credit-hour production at less cost. If he was in the humanities or education, he faced declining enrollments as students gravitated toward the fields where the jobs still were. The fun was rapidly going out of college teaching.

Enter the same developmentalists. In 1973, Mervin Freedman and Nevitt Sanford authored an article on the personal development of faculty (Freedman, 1973), and the next year The Group for Human Development in Higher Education argued for attention to the personal needs of faculty in their widely read *Change* white paper *Faculty Development in a Time of Retrenchment* (1974). William Bergquist and Stephen Phillips created a faculty development model that added personal development to instructional development (Bergquist and Phillips, 1975), and, through their consultation across the country and their two volumes of the *Handbook for Faculty Development,* helped many institutions, especially liberal arts colleges, to implement personal development services for faculty (Bergquist, Phillips, and Quehl, 1975, 1977). Jerry Gaff came along, as he had in the sixties, to popularize a developmental model for faculty development in his *Toward Faculty Renewal* (Gaff, 1975). Arthur Chickering contributed a conceptual framework, as he had for student development in the sixties, with several articles synthesizing adult development theory (Chickering, 1976). Harold Hodgkinson, another educator active in the cause of student development in the sixties, adapted Levinson's stages of adult life to faculty and administrative career stages (Hodgkinson, 1974). Some faculty development programs, most notably ones at Illinois State University and the Kansas City Regional Council for Higher Education, made personal and career assistance to faculty central functions (Lindquist, 1978a).

The characterizations at the start of this chapter make clear that there usually is an important personal dimension to professional development. Persons faced with transitions in their adult lives often need colleague support and assistance, commodities hard to come by in the privatist world of higher education. They often need help in reducing their anxieties about whether change in teaching methods or subject will jeopardize their security, their professional stature, their chances for advancement, or their own self-esteem. They may need to find ways to bring enjoyment back into what has become a tedious, beleaguered, and increasingly difficult job. I should not belabor this point. Professors and administrators are developing adults, and any college that hopes to have a highly effective and satisfied staff will need to attend to the staff's personal needs and concerns.

A professional development program attentive to the personal side of teaching, administrating, and student learning would have several recognizable components. It would build professional development on the expressed personal and career development interests of staff and students. Included would be activities designed to help staff assess their own and their students' concerns as well as activities designed to advise staff and to help them advise students on these issues. Included would be personal support groups for staff plus training of staff in the creation of student support groups. Included would be brokering services to help staff and students find opportunities to pursue their own personal and career development. Included would be counseling, workshops, data feedback, and other means for helping staff members such as George Miller come to grips with personal attitudes that may stand between themselves and greater professional effectiveness.

Organization Development

Also in the seventies, organization development began to be applied to higher education institutions by such persons as Ronald Boyer and Anthony Grasha at the University of Cincinnati (Boyer and Crockett, 1973), Walter Sikes in an applied behavioral science project called "Training Teams for Campus Change" (Sikes, Schlesinger, and Seashore, 1974), and myself in a strategies for change project (Lindquist, 1978b). The major shift in thinking represented by these efforts was that enhancement of educational and scholarly effectiveness is not just a matter of individual assistance or administrative planning and participative governance; also needed are an organizational climate of openness and trust, an organizational ability to collaboratively identify and solve problems, an organizational respect and support for the persons of its members, and a system of organizational structures and rewards that encourages rather than inhibits attempts to improve learning and teaching, scholarship, and research.

Both personal development and organization development introduce the "process facilitator" to professional development. Rather than providing solutions, this person tries to help institutional members see themselves more clearly and solve their own problems. The process facilitator may use survey research or nondirective questioning, a highly sociological or a highly psychological approach. But the purpose in either case is to facilitate the client's development rather than to instruct.

Professional development programs with an organization development component would include systematic diagnosis of the organizational supports for staff and student development. Action-research teams would gather and feed back these data to institutional leaders in order to facilitate their identification of needed improvements in the organization. The team then would work with these leaders to design, implement, and evaluate changes in working relationships, organizational structures and policies, formal incentives for improvement, or whatever needs reform in the organizational system. In all this activity, as in teaching students how to learn while teaching them an academic subject, a major objective would be to strengthen the institution's ability to conduct regular self-assessment and problem solving.

Educational Networks

Until the late sixties, there were few opportunities for professors concerned about educational issues to meet and learn from each other. Then, within a short period of time, many budding networks bloomed (see Lindquist, 1980, for examples). A particularly useful network for small college educators is the Council for the Advancement of Small

Colleges, with its own annual institute, training programs, publications series, consulting network, experimental college, and affiliated technical assistance program. More recent is the Council for the Advancement of Experiential Learning, which also features national and regional assemblies, consulting services, training programs, publications, and local clusters of innovators. The American Association for State Colleges and Universities, through its Center for Planned Change in Higher Education, is also becoming a complex network for educational improvement. Less elaborate but representative of this boom in networking for postsecondary innovation are the Society for Field Experience Education, the Bachelor of General Studies group, the Association for Innovation in Higher Education, and the Center for Personalized Systems of Instruction, with its publications and workshops. The Union for Experimenting Colleges and Universities, although preoccupied for a time with development of the University Without Walls system (itself a network), and the Union Graduate School show promise of becoming another strong network for innovation. The Postsecondary Education Convening Authority is yet another seventies invention that provides an invaluable service by bringing together postsecondary educators and government to consider timely issues. The consortium movement itself represents an additional extra-institutional network by which new ideas can be shared. The Institute for Academic Improvement, as part of the Center for the Study of Higher Education at Memphis State University, is taking networking as one of its major tasks.

A professional development service that incorporates networking into its functions would seek to create a pattern of interaction among professionals such that information, personal support, and influence readily flow to those who need such resources. Cross-departmental and cross-institutional workshops would be held to share information and ideas. Persons or groups interested in professional development would be helped to locate the support needed to carry out that development. Information-linking services would be established so that clients could quickly be put in touch with resource literature, practices, or persons potentially useful to them. Local networks of interaction would be intentionally interwoven with external networks. Of particular concern might be involving faculty members in higher education associations such as the American Council on Education and the American Association for Higher Education, whose participants are mainly administrators despite the key role that faculty play in developing—or resisting—academic innovation.

The Current State of the Art

Collegiate professional development is not yet the full tree I have outlined. Faculty members' experience as students in traditional higher education systems remains a strong influence on their educational approaches. Support for disciplinary advancement remains the primary institutional investment in continuing education of faculty, with higher education associations and centers serving a comparable function for administrators. Networks for the improvement of student learning are much less developed but are under way. Instructional resource and instructional development centers have been instituted in many universities but not in many community or liberal arts colleges. Personal development, rather than being addressed by formal programs, has tended to be incorporated into faculty development activities in liberal arts colleges. Likewise, few programs have been devoted to organization development, though it too can be found as one ingredient in several faculty development programs. Administrative development is just beginning to receive attention in ongoing local programs that supplement higher education associations and centers.

A merger of these complementary approaches is easier said than done. Advocates of one thrust, say the advancement of knowledge, view other thrusts, say instructional or administrative development, as lesser in importance and unwanted competition for scarce resources. Practitioners of instructional development often are schooled in a behaviorist rather than developmental view of education, and quarrels erupt over who is hard or soft, cold or warm, right or wrong. Development leaders immersed in traditional networks often are unfamiliar with nontraditional practices and practitioners, and suspicious of their standards and motives. The distrust is mutual. One of the exciting features but also one of the problems of the new Professional and Organization Development Network in Higher Education is that it contains members with widely varying backgrounds, assumptions, styles, and approaches.

Certainly, an immediate need in this field is for a dialogue to begin. Professional development, like student development, must often treat person, task, and situation. Task itself includes the content and process of teaching and advising, the content and process of research, the content and process of service, and both sides of administration. These various approaches can complement each other. Thus, it is as important to integrate professional development approaches as it is to integrate approaches to student development.

Challenges for Professional Development

What are likely to be focal topics for integrated professional development programs of the eighties? Several need no crystal ball to be seen.

Facilitating Lifelong Learning. Postsecondary education is moving with the population curve toward a lifelong learning model. However, it is not there yet. Most college offerings are still one-shot degree programs, whether one takes that shot at 18 or 48. But there are signs all around that "the learning society" can become a reality and that colleges can play an important role.

College professors will need to learn how to assess learning derived from extensive adult experience, then design educational programs to build on that learning. Faculty will need to learn how to relate to students at all stages of the life cycle. They will need to learn how to facilitate individualized learning projects of the kind Allen Tough describes in his chapter—projects quite different in scope, pace, location, use of learning resources, and professor's role from traditional classes. Professors will need to learn how to tap community resources rather than relying almost exclusively on campus resources, which many adult learners will find intimidating and inaccessible. They will need to learn how to help adults plan learning projects, and they will need to learn how to act as educational brokers between learners and learning resources. Thomas Clark delineates many of these new professional roles in his study "Faculty Development for Non-Traditional Programs" (Lindquist, 1978a). Perhaps most important, professors will need to develop a new appreciation of lifelong learners and learning. All these changes in professorial knowledge, attitudes, and skills are best accomplished through professional development. Indeed, professional development *is* lifelong (at least career-long) learning for college staff; it can model the approach it seeks to develop.

For all these changes, administrators and other college staff will need their own professional development. They must learn what lifelong learning is (for themselves as well as in others), what types of educational services adult learners need, how to administer and finance such services, and especially how to work with faculty to develop and implement new learning programs. Student services staff members can play a particularly important role in assisting lifelong learners, once they learn how to work with this older age group. They especially will need the aid of professional development. Bringing student services and academic professionals together remains a vital objective if development in all its aspects is to occur.

Undergirding this area should be continuing research into life cycle stages and the potential of college-level learning for aiding adult development. The theory presented in Part One, rich as it is, only begins to give us an idea of the ways in which colleges can facilitate lifelong learning. Certainly one function of professional development programs should be to advance this research on adult learning.

Facilitating Education for Human Development. The adult development movement of the seventies has joined the student development movement of the sixties in turning attention from subject mastery as the essence of higher learning to human development, especially intellectual and ethical development. Mastery through development rather than development through mastery becomes the key to continuing effectiveness in a rapidly changing world.

Part One reflects this slow, but steady, shift. It certainly does not deny the importance of subject mastery, for adult work requires an increasing depth and range of knowledge. But placing the learner at the center of attention represents a recognition that subjects are taught to individuals, each with his or her own background, learning style and pace, aspirations, level of ego and intellectual development, and current life situation. These developmental differences not only must be taken into account in college teaching; they become a subject of teaching itself. Assessing prior learning, clarifying future learning objectives, and determining the most appropriate way to meet those objectives are diagnostic skills required by both teachers and the learners themselves. Knowing how to teach a "fearful dependent" or an "integrated" student, one who thinks in simple dualistic terms or one who is a contextual relativist, is a skill professors need in order to teach almost any academic subject; but aiding a student's own growth toward more complex, integrated thinking and valuing is itself an essential subject.

How can we take developmental ages and stages, learning styles, and life situations into account when designing and implementing college education? How can we enhance the intellectual, ethical, and ego development of students? And how can we enable students to take their development into their own hands? These questions should guide professional development programs in the modern American college.

Facilitating Career and Life Transitions. We can be fairly sure that the economically hard times ahead will force many college staff members into early retirement, into searching for jobs after being denied tenure or being cut because of enrollment declines, into teaching new subjects in new ways, and into nonacademic careers. Such transitions will be traumatic. Shifting to the student side of the ledger, we can be fairly sure that rapid social change in America's near future will catch learners up in stressful passages from adolescent to adult, from singleness to marriage to divorce and back, from career path to new career path, and from dream-like aspirations to hard realities.

Many college staff and students will manage life's transitions without help; but many will need support, guidance, and training for new roles. Personal counseling, support groups, placement services, postdegree retooling for new fields, exchange programs designed to provide experience in alternative careers, and a whole battery of continuing education opportunities will be needed both to facilitate transitions in the lives of college professionals and to enable them to facilitate similar passages in the lives of other adults (whether colleagues and administrative subordinates or students). A start has been made on professional development for career and life transitions by Illinois State University, The Kansas City Regional Council for Higher Education, and Loyola University. This is now a minor theme in professional development, but it must become a major one.

Facilitating Acquisition of Basic Skills. It is generally recognized that colleges will have to recruit less-prepared as well as older students not only to make ends meet but also to help our society live up to its democratic ideals. They already are doing both. Most faculty members, however, do not know how to facilitate the learning of persons who lack basic academic knowledge, skills, habits, and attitudes. Faculty cannot send back to high school a police chief who cannot do square roots or a math professor who cannot write in complete sentences. Furthermore, as such examples suggest, people lacking basic academic skills may have highly developed skills of other kinds. Part of the challenge is to recognize and build on the skills and motivations students do have.

Professional development programs might offer training to faculty in teaching basic skills, as Spelman College's Institute for Teaching and Learning does. They might, as Northwestern's Center for the Teaching Professions does, incorporate a basic skills center for students within a professional development program. Whatever the approach, the need is apparent.

Professional development programs also will need to help academics strengthen their basic skills in listening, speaking, writing, using the computer or other technology, and working in groups. Improbable as it may sound to suggest that professors may be unable to listen to their students or talk to them in ways that make meanings clear, we all know such professors. And the problem does not pertain merely to communication with inexperienced undergraduates. Often, professionals returning to the university for continuing education find their professors so unskilled in communicating with practitioners in their same field that whole articles or institutes are wasted. This kind of basic skills development may not be popular with many professors, but it should be no more a "put-down" to suggest to a sociologist that his technical jargon fails to communicate his meaning to lay people than to suggest to a student that his ghetto jargon fails to communicate to academic people. Both failures to convey meaning constitute professional development challenges.

Improving Conditions for Teaching. At present, many institutional and external reward systems for faculty encourage publication over teaching and graduate teaching over lower-division teaching. Such systems do not reward advising or committee effectiveness at all. As financial pressures increase, some institutions and states will reward grinding out credit hours over producing real learning, scholarship, or service. Compounding these pressures are college structure and governance practices that vivisect campuses into isolated and competing subgroups more concerned with protecting their own interests than improving teaching.

Most professional development programs of the past assumed that systematic intervention to improve institutional and external conditions for teaching was none of their business. That was a governance issue best left to the president, the senate, or the union. Lately, leaders such as Lance Buhl have argued that professional development facilitators are inhumane if they encourage professors to devote time to teaching improvement without also working to get the system to grant that time and reward that effort. (Lindquist, 1978a). Education of authorities to the need for improved conditions for teaching, projects to alter personnel policies and evaluation systems, activities that bring together people from diverse campus subgroups, and especially organizational development services are all strategies needed in the modern American college.

Managing Multiple Learning Resources. Until recently, a professor, a textbook, and a classroom were the basic learning resources of higher learning. In the near future, these basic resources will be supplemented by a wide range of alternative "teachers." Public television, and even commercial television in its finer moments, can be expected to play a large role in lifelong learning. In the home next to the television set will be low-cost computers accompanied by sophisticated educational software. QUBE (the interactive cable television station in Columbus, Ohio) already combines television and computer so that viewers and telecasters can interact during programs. Suddenly the television lecture becomes a discussion, and quizzes can be given to students at home with immediate feedback of student scores. Computer-assisted instruction systems such as IDEA are already attaining high levels of sophistication. Less complex but valuable in relieving professors of introductory information dispensing are slide-tape or videotape programs to explain how to conjugate a verb or how to use a spectrometer. Individual students can stop and replay such tapes at their leisure until the information is mastered. Self-instructional kits and learning guides are also proliferating.

Modern America is full of human resources for higher learning. Communities will have increasing numbers of college-educated retirees as our society grows older, and many of them, including retired professionals, will have both time and expertise to give younger learners. Student peers themselves, whether 20 or 70 years old, have been found to be excellent learning resources for one another and are too seldom used, despite the fact that teaching is an excellent way to learn. Nonteaching college staff members are other important human resources. Learning resource center staff and librarians, student services and dormitory counselors, secretaries and maintenance workers, and administrators all interact with students and can augment the professor's contributions to intellectual and ethical development. If we are ever to bring all our campus resources to bear on learning, the gap between academic and nonacademic staff must be closed. Professional development activities can pull campus staff together and facilitate their joining forces to aid learning.

As the costs of full-time college faculties climb beyond almost anyone's ability to pay, formulas will be contrived to augment a core full-time professoriate with other learning resources that, after initial development costs, are less expensive. That is an unnerving prospect for an already threatened academic community, but it may mean only that current faculty size will stabilize or slightly decline while other resources expand.

Professional development has many tasks related to this diversification of higher learning resources. One is to help professors learn how to use teaching technology. Another task is to help faculty learn how to incorporate educational television, computer-assisted instruction, slide-tape and videotape, independent learning guides, and other "mediated instruction" resources into their work with students. Chapter Thirty-Three on mediated instruction suggests ways in which these varied resources relate to student differences in orientation toward knowledge as well as different teaching practices. Professors will also need to learn how to use adjunct professors, tutors, and peers. Each such development may require faculty changes in attitude as well as ability, for traditional professors have little prior experience with such resources and tend to think college-level learning only occurs by direct contact with professors and texts. A large professional development task is to help faculty prepare all these resources. They, of course, provide the subject expertise, but they may be unfamiliar with the technology. They may need institutional grants of time and money in order to prepare that physics or language learning guide.

Another major professional development task in this area is to help those retirees, those working professionals, those student peers, to become skillful facilitators of college learning. Intensive orientation and regular developmental events can be an immense help to part-time faculty or peer teachers and advisers. Full-time faculty can be excellent resources for these part-timers and thereby can help strengthen links between "regular" and "irregular" staff. Certainly one objective of this kind of faculty development is to make nonprofessors feel part of the college and to make professors feel they are being augmented, not threatened, by these lower-cost staff.

The availability of diverse learning resources also challenges professional development to help professors and field supervisors make experiential learning effective. Traditional classroom teachers often do not know how to design field experiences, obtain cooperation in the field, train field supervisors, prepare students for the experience, and then help them reflect on what they have learned. They often are inexperienced in teaching for application of knowledge. Evaluation of nonclassroom learning, especially that which took place prior to the student's enrollment, can be very trying for professors unaccustomed to it. As the Council for the Advancement of Experiential Learning quickly discovered, faculty development must play a central role in making faculty willing and able to facilitate and evaluate nonclassroom learning.

In all this work to help professors supplement themselves, their books, and their classrooms, professional development facilitators will also have to show professors how to use these basic resources in new ways. If professors are freed from many routine teaching chores by other resources, they can then concentrate on the ones that most need their talents, say developing those resources in the first place or conducting the most difficult kinds of teaching, advising, and evaluating. Much of what is in textbooks may be conveyed more effectively by programmed learning guides, computers, television, or peer teaching. But the book remains a highly versatile and sophisticated medium. Reading remains a major aid to lifelong learning. And classrooms have the obvious advantage over other learning resources that a group of persons with like learning interests can be assembled and benefit from the rich learning resources there, including blackboards and professors and other students. Many professors do not use the full range of classroom learning resources very well; this traditional target of instructional development will continue to need attention in the modern American college.

Holistic Professional Development

Professional development has come to mean graduate training for teaching as well as research, extensive orientation and reorientation to one's institution, support for advancement in one's field of study, technical assistance in teaching or administrative methods and technology, aid in personal and career development, systematic organizational development, and elaborate professional networks. In the near future, it will need to deal particularly with issues such as facilitating lifelong learning, supporting the adult transitions of staff and students, strengthening basic learning and teaching skills, creating supportive conditions for teaching, and using a great diversity of learning resources. The kinds of collegiate professional development and the emerging topics are apparent. But how should such work be carried out?

I argue in another paper (Lindquist, 1980) that what is needed is a "social learning and problem-solving" strategy for professional development. It should attend to the person, the various tasks, and the situation of all college staff members and, through them, all students. It is an ambitious strategy, admittedly; but the challenges are too great and the parts of development too interrelated to be affected much by disconnected tinkering.

By *social learning* I mean an educational program by which staff learn from and with one another subjects not taught them in traditional graduate schools:

1. Adult developmental and learning theories and their implications for staff as well as student development.
2. The nature of their institution's mission, history, curriculum, teaching, research, and committee and administrative practices.
3. The backgrounds, interests, learning styles, learning needs, and situations of local students.

4. Political, economic, and cultural trends relevant to the college's future.
5. Alternative educational practices and research findings throughout postsecondary education.
6. The "press" of the institution and community on staff and students and the supportiveness and challenge surrounding their work.
7. The career prospects for staff and students, and the contacts and preparations needed to get ahead.

Continuing education on at least these subjects will be needed to create and sustain an informed college staff. Most colleges provide little information or opportunity to study such topics. What is available often is obscured by jargon or unread among the drifts of paper that inundate college staffs daily.

Professional development facilitators find that staff gain much more from interactions with colleagues or students than they do simply from words on paper. Centra (1976) finds that such interactions, which he calls "high faculty involvement" activities, are highly rated by practitioners. College staff members have much expertise to share with one another. Workshops, retreats, colloquia, bag lunch seminars, faculty meetings given over to learning instead of governance, study groups, and support groups or triads of staff members are some of the kinds of interaction that can foster professional development. Some colleges have a coordinated "curriculum," which a few "fellows" each year study through seminars, field trips, and individual projects so that sustained study and a supportive colleague group can be effected.

Attention in this interaction should be given to the establishment of a social network that brings innovators and opinion leaders together, that connects local staff to colleagues and resource persons elsewhere. As they identify needed changes, they perhaps first should attempt to adopt those changes themselves in their own professional work before seeking to persuade colleagues. But then facilitators will need to help these "early adopters" approach their more cautious or skeptical colleagues.

Attention also should be given in this social learning to individual and group differences. As Kolb reminds us, some will like debating abstract concepts, while others want the practical implications. Some will want research evidence, while others will want insights from persons involved in the programs. Also, some will be quite open to a certain topic or knowledgeable in it, while others will be initially closed or ignorant. Some will have time to learn in two months what others, deluged by other demands, will take a year to learn. A learning process for staff that respects such differences can model ways to respond to individual and group differences among students.

College staff, again like students, are not merely preparing for some future life; they are engaged in that life and want professional development to help them solve immediate problems. The second general developmental activity, therefore, should be assistance in current problem solving by individual staff, departments, and the institution as a whole. That assistance involves diagnosis of teaching, advising, financial, and governance problems. Professional development can help in gathering and interpreting diagnostic data. Facilitators will also need to help individuals and teams as they search for and formulate solutions, as they gain support and reduce resistance to solutions, as they acquire the knowledge and skill needed to implement changes, and finally as staff evaluate those changes. In all these services, facilitators will need to bring both technical expertise and process skills to bear.

I need not itemize the components of this problem-solving facilitation here. They are detailed in expositions of instructional and organizational development. It is worth stressing, however, that this approach mirrors a facilitative and developmental approach to working with students. Faculty members who complain about faculty development activities that are not relevant to their immediate problems are, of course, sounding like students. If professional development is done in ways effective for academicians, those adults will experience firsthand the kind of assistance in development their adult students deserve.

A final word about costs. Professional development does take time, expertise, and some material resources. If not built into the workload, it will be seen as an extra burden. If done without knowledgeable and skillful facilitation, it will quickly get a bad name. If not provided with some workshop, travel, secretarial, and supplies funds, it will not accomplish much. But a college need not go broke trying to help its staff become more effective. College calendars and individual schedules can be adjusted to provide professional development time without cheating educational quality. Staff can be trained as peer facilitators and given time for that vital function by temporary professional reassignment so that the cost of full-time professional development specialists can be minimized, though at least one will still be needed to ensure depth and continuity of service. Support budgets need not be lavish to make a difference, and much of that material support can be found by squeezing existing budgets a bit. The holistic approach I have described may seem prohibitive in cost at first glance, and it would be if each kind of professional development had its own staff and budget. But if *holistic* is taken to refer to the range of responsiveness of even the smallest team or staff, it need not cost more to respond to person, task, and situation than it might to concentrate on any one approach. A more widely expert and flexible staff, not more staff, is needed.

Too many colleges in financial straits use costs as an excuse to do nothing for their staffs. If the commitment to continuous professional growth is there, enough money can be found to provide at least a bare bones program. Perhaps the ultimate message of this book is that college leaders and faculty members must invest in systematic professional development. Unless they do, the modern American college is unlikely to meet the developmental needs of either staff or students.

References

Astin, A. W. *Four Critical Years: Effects of College on Beliefs, Attitudes, and Knowledge.* San Francisco: Jossey-Bass, 1977.

Bergquist, W. H., and Phillips, S. R. "Components of an Effective Faculty Development Program." *Journal of Higher Education,* 1975, *46,* 177-211.

Bergquist, W. H., Phillips, S. R., and Quehl, G. *A Handbook for Faculty Development.* Vol. 1. Washington, D.C.: Council for the Advancement of Small Colleges, 1975.

Bergquist, W. H., Phillips, S. R., and Quehl, G. *A Handbook for Faculty Development.* Vol. 2. Berkeley, Calif.: Pacific Soundings Press, 1977.

Boyer, R. K., and Crockett, C. (Eds.). "Organizational Development in Higher Education." *Journal of Higher Education,* 1973, *44.*

Centra, J. A. *Faculty Development Practices in U.S. Colleges and Universities.* Project Report 76-30. Princeton, N.J.: Educational Testing Service, 1976.

Chickering, A. W. "Developmental Change as a Major Outcome." In M. T. Keeton and Associates, *Experiential Learning: Rationale, Characteristics, and Assessment.* San Francisco: Jossey-Bass, 1976.

Committee on the Student in Higher Education. *The Student in Higher Education.* New Haven, Conn.: Hazen Foundation, 1968.

Feldman, K. A., and Newcomb, T. M. *The Impact of College on Students.* San Francisco: Jossey-Bass, 1969.

Freedman, M. (Ed.). *New Directions for Higher Education: Facilitating Faculty Development,* no. 1. San Francisco: Jossey-Bass, 1973.

Gaff, J. G. *Toward Faculty Renewal: Advances in Faculty, Instructional, and Organizational Development.* San Francisco: Jossey-Bass, 1975.

Group for Human Development in Higher Education. *Faculty Development in a Time of Retrenchment.* New Rochelle, N.Y.: Change Magazine Press, 1974.

Hodgkinson, H. L. "Adult Development: Implications for Faculty and Administrators." *Educational Record,* 1974, *55,* 263-274.

Lindquist, J. (Ed.). *Designing Teaching Improvement Programs.* Washington, D.C.: Council for the Advancement of Small Colleges, 1978a.

Lindquist, J. *Strategies for Change.* Washington, D.C.: Council for the Advancement of Small Colleges, 1978b.

Lindquist, J. "Improving the Teaching-Learning Environment." In P. Jedamus, M. W. Peterson, and Associates, *Improving Academic Management: A Handbook of Planning and Institutional Research.* San Francisco: Jossey-Bass, 1980.

Lindquist, J. (Ed.). *Increasing The Impact.* Battle Creek, Mich.: W. K. Kellogg Foundation, 1980.

Sikes, W. W., Schlesinger, L. E., and Seashore, C. N. *Renewing Higher Education from Within: A Guide for Campus Change Teams.* San Francisco: Jossey-Bass, 1974.

42

Timothy Lehmann

Evaluating
Adult Learning
and Program Costs

Regarding the perils of empirical research, John Van Maanen has written, "Those who refused to look through Galileo's telescope knew what they were about; if they did see the moons of Jupiter, then they would be forced to believe what they did not wish to believe. Therefore, it was wiser not to look" (1979, p. 29). Similarly, program evaluation on most campuses is still very much a question of what we are willing to look at with our twentieth-century telescopes. Are we willing to examine carefully our academic programs and assess what our students are actually learning? Are we willing to disturb our beliefs about what we think we are doing—change our behavior, if necessary?

In one sense, we spend a great deal of our time and energy in ongoing evaluation of our own and our colleagues' work: setting standards for teaching performance, assessing student performance, judging publications and papers, making personnel decisions, weighing the achievements and reputations of departments and colleges. But more often than we wish to acknowledge, these evaluation activities are incomplete, unsystematic, ad hoc, political, subjective, and based at least in part on unreliable information.

In another sense, educational evaluation is a demanding technical specialty, which has only recently been applied to college and university operations (Campbell, 1969; Weiss, 1972; Caro, 1977; Suchman, 1967; and Hodgkinson, 1975). Sophisticated evaluation strategies have been designed by experts in the field—including some of the authors in Part One—to assess educational experiences, learning styles, and students' intellectual, moral, and ego development program effectiveness in relation to educational objectives. As a consequence, we now have the capacity to focus our new assessment instruments on our academic activities.

This increased capacity comes at a time when pressures are mounting for colleges and universities to review and evaluate their programs, objectives, and expenditures. Federal, state, and local governmental agencies are monitoring institutional activities more closely and conducting far-reaching program audits to see if the taxpayers' dollars are being properly spent and the public interest served. Students, parents, taxpayer groups, and many other interested parties are asking serious questions about the educational and financial worth of a college degree. Accrediting agencies are seeking more information about what students learn and how students change. The costs of academic programs are spiraling; the pool of traditional-age students is shrinking; and the market for adult learners is becoming more competitive. It is no wonder that these pressures are forcing decision makers to evaluate the quality and costs of programs and to demonstrate their educational effectiveness and service to society. Program evaluation can be a good way to reaffirm the value of higher education.

This chapter describes the evaluation process, compares six different approaches to program evaluation, examines one of these approaches in detail in light of the ideas about adult development and the life cycle presented in Part One, and then offers some advice on program evaluation for institutions interested in starting their own evaluation efforts.

The Evaluation Process

Basically, program evaluation aims to provide accurate, timely, reliable, and valid information to decision makers about whether a given program is operating in such a way as to achieve its objectives at a reasonable cost. This definition suggests four key features of the evaluation process. (1) The providing of "accurate, timely, reliable, and valid information" assumes some sort of research strategy and evaluation framework. (2) Determining that a given program is "operating in such a way as to achieve its objectives" implies the use of certain standards for assessing the success of the program. (3) It is understood here, too, that the information must be useful to administrative and faculty decision makers if the results of the evaluation are to make meaningful contributions to improving the program and the institution. (4) Finally, "achieving objectives at a reasonable cost" means that program outcomes must be related to costs. Thus, cost data are an integral part of the evaluation effort, though they are considered after the program objectives and outcomes have been determined.

The evaluation process is inextricably tied to the program planning cycle depicted in Figure 1. That is, faculty members or administrators interested in conducting an evaluation of a particular program do so as part of the cycle of planning the program's objectives and operation, implementing the program, assessing its outcomes and costs, and deciding whether to continue the present operations or develop a new plan. To assess a program's outcomes, we must measure the degree to which its objectives are met and compare these outcomes with standards for success. This leads to a continuous evaluation cycle as shown in Figure 2.

Within the evaluation cycle, the specification phase requires developing realistic and clearly understood definitions of program purposes. For example, one program objec-

Figure 1. The Planning Cycle

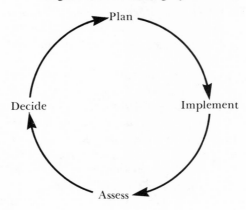

Figure 2. The Evaluation Cycle

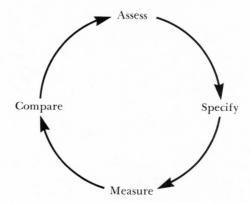

tive might be the development in students of the learning styles most conducive to success in their majors. Once program objectives have been specified, the question of measurement arises. How do we determine what has happened? The evaluator must find a research methodology that answers this question in terms of program activities, program outcomes, and program costs. Thus, for example, to measure learning styles, one might use Kolb's Learning Styles Inventory, a measurement instrument that yields scores on four learning styles: abstract-conceptual, reflective-observational, concrete-experiential, and active-experimental.

Next, the evaluation cycle brings us to the comparison component. Evaluation requires comparing the present state of affairs with some explicit standard in order to judge the relative success or current status of the program. The most frequently used standard is simply the conditions existing prior to the implementation of the program, but other types of comparisons can also be made, such as comparison of one program with another or comparison of a program against an abstract ideal.

Regardless of how sophisticated or elaborate the evaluation plan, these three processes—specifying, measuring, and comparing—determine the scope, depth, and eventual worth of the resulting assessment.

The interaction of the planning and evaluation cycles is illustrated in Figure 3. These cycles suggest that the evaluation process is a set of related activities occurring over

Figure 3. Interlocking Planning and Evaluation Cycles

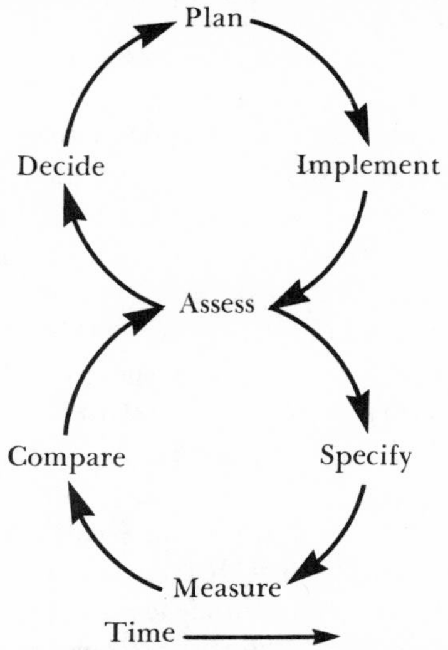

Source: Van Maanen, 1979, for figures 1, 2, and 3.

and over throughout the duration of any program. Evaluation begins during the program planning phase and does not end until all activities have ceased. Evaluation is thus an integral part of any program.

Approaches to Program Evaluation

In the past fifteen years, colleges and universities have become more aware of the need to carefully specify the general knowledge, skills, and attitudes that students must acquire to function effectively as adults (Bowen, 1977). The specification of educational objectives has in turn led to the need for evaluating educational outcomes. Do our students actually reach the educational goals considered important? What student needs and expectations are served? What are the program costs? What are the standards for judging program success? And what strategy and techniques will provide the needed data?

Six different approaches to program evaluation warrant description in terms of their answers to these questions. These approaches are the Institutional Research Program for Higher Education of Educational Testing Service; the College Outcomes Measures Project (COMP) developed by American College Testing Program; the Student Outcomes Information Services (SOIS) developed by the National Center for Higher Education Management Systems (NCHEMS); the Outcomes of Undergraduate Education Project developed at Harvard University; the Cooperative Institutional Research Program (CIRP) developed by Alexander Astin; and the Program Effectiveness and Related Costs (PERC) model developed at Empire State College. Each of these six approaches has special features and directs our attention to certain aspects of a given campus program or operation, but all produce valid and reliable information about the students entering a given college and their learning.

Institutional Research Program, Educational Testing Service. Educational Testing Service (ETS) has developed the Institutional Research Program for Higher Education (IRPHE) to assist colleges and universities in self-study, evaluation, and planning. It has produced a series of standardized research instruments and nationally normed achievement tests for use by students, faculty, administrators, alumni, and trustees in evaluating the effectiveness of a campus or program.[1]

The major instruments available are the following:

Student Instructional Report (SIR)
Student Reactions to College (SRC)
    (2- and 4-year versions—19 areas)
Institutional Goals Inventory (IGI)
    (20 goal areas)
Institutional Functioning Inventory
    (IFI) (11 scales)
Small College Goals Inventory
    (SCGI)

Community College Goals Inventory
    (CCGI)
Questionnaire Analysis Service
Undergraduate Assessment Program
    (UAP) (tests in 26 major fields and
    3 areas)
College Level Examination Program
    (CLEP)
Graduate Record Examinations (GRE)

One of these instruments—the Institutional Goals Inventory (IGI)—illustrates their applicability for program evaluation. The IGI consists of ninety statements of possible institutional goals covering many aspects of higher education. The IGI is designed to help colleges and universities define their educational goals, establish priorities among those goals, and give direction to present and future planning. Faculty, students, and administrators indicate their opinions about the importance of each goal statement—both as the goal exists on the campus ("is") and as the respondents would like it to exist ("ought"). Twenty different goal areas are covered, such as Academic Development, Individual Personal Development, Intellectual Orientation, Innovation, Off-Campus Learning, Vocational Preparation, and Culture-Aesthetic Awareness. In addition, colleges may add up to twenty goal statements locally and have the results tabulated and reported with the basic data.

Many of the goal areas on the IGI can easily be used to examine campus orientations to the ideas put forth in Part One of this volume. For example, the IGI contains four or five specific goal statements linking students' personal interests and abilities to the skills required in various vocational areas or careers. These goal statements provide a ready means of examining individual and group developmental patterns. Furthermore, the salience of vocational goals relative to other types of goals on campus can be noted. All such results, when further analyzed by sex and age group, can prove useful for curriculum planning, academic advising, career counseling, improving teaching strategies, and determining new support services for adult learners.

Other ETS instruments that may be useful to those interested in adult development issues are the Institutional Functioning Inventory and Student Reactions to College. At least five scales on the Institutional Functioning Inventory seem especially pertinent to life cycle concerns: the Intellectual-Aesthetic; Extracurricular; Human Diversity; Concern for Improvement of Society; Concern for Undergraduate Learning; and Meeting Local Needs. A careful examination of the specific questions in each scale will determine the appropriateness of a given scale for campus use.

Perhaps ETS is best known for its tests designed to measure academic ability and achievement. The Undergraduate Assessment Program (UAP) offers forty-eight exams including the Graduate Record Examinations. The UAP provides a wide range of tests covering most academic disciplines, along with a scoring service that allows a given college

---

[1]For further information, write the Institutional Research Program for Higher Education, Educational Testing Service, Princeton, N.J. 08541.

to measure the performance of individuals and groups against the norms of comparable institutions across the country. Those colleges desiring nationally normed standardized tests to measure and compare their students' performance in academic areas should carefully consider the ETS services.

College Outcome Measures Project, American College Testing Program. In 1976, the American College Testing Program sponsored the College Outcome Measures Project (COMP) as its response to the growing need of evaluating student learning. COMP has created assessment instruments and procedures to measure general education knowledge and skills believed necessary for successful functioning in adult society in six areas: Communicating; Solving Problems; Clarifying Values; Functioning Within Social Institutions; Using Science and Technology; and Using the Arts (*College Outcome Measures Project Annual Reports 1977, 1978*).[2]

Three assessment instruments—the Composite Examination, the Objective Test, and the Activity Inventory—have been developed and field tested over three years at some seventy institutions. The COMP instruments are designed for wide use by colleges and universities with students of all ages. In fact, COMP carried out three studies during 1977-78 on adults in Milwaukee and Miami as well as five participating colleges (*COMP Annual Report 1978*). Inventory results to date show adults scoring highest in the areas of the inventory that correspond to their community roles and strongest interests.

In terms of adult development and life cycle issues, the COMP instruments promise direct applicability to the lives and experiences of working adults. So far, the data have not been analyzed within an explicit adult development framework, but the questions used and the outcome areas identified apply to many of the developmental concerns discussed in Part One. The COMP battery contains four general education outcome areas that are particularly relevant to adult development issues: Clarifying Values, Functioning Within Social Institutions, Using Science and Technology, and Solving Problems. To illustrate, let us look at Clarifying Values. Clarifying Values involves the student's ability to identify the major value choices adults face in daily life in his own and other cultures, to analyze rationales for value choices, and to infer personal values from behavior. Such abilities tie in nicely with Torbert's ideas concerning interpersonal competence. His distinction between formal inquiry and living inquiry illuminates value clarification in the context of personal action and relations with others.

Another area of concern for adults is Functioning Within Social Institutions. Adult students are asked to identify the activities and institutions that constitute the social aspects of a culture, describe the structures and functions that underlie social institutions, explain the reciprocal relationship between social institutions and individuals, and explain the principles of development and change of social institutions (*COMP Annual Report 1977*). The COMP questions, for example, may ask the student to respond to a governmental memo that involves a basic constitutional rights issue and calls for an analysis of the relationship between an individual and a public agency. Adult students vary considerably in their work histories, practical experiences with governmental agencies, and general levels of knowledge about constitutional rights. Some adults have had considerable experience in dealing with governmental agencies; they are likely to score well on questions reflecting the development of analytical and applied skills and an approach to organizational life that is active, assertive, and open. Other adults, such as those re-entering the occupational world, may lack basic knowledge of governmental agencies

---

[2] For further information, write COMP, American Testing Program, P.O. Box 168, Iowa City, Iowa 52243.

and constitutional rights; they are thus likely to score low on the aforementioned questions. These adults represent a group of students in strong need of developing their abilities to function in a complex, interdependent organizational society. The adult development challenge, then, is to identify through such COMP questions particular knowledge and skill deficiencies of adult students that are relevant to their stage of the life cycle and to design appropriate educational programs and advising systems to alleviate those deficiencies.

Student Outcomes Information Services, National Center for Higher Education Management Systems. The National Center for Higher Education Management Systems (NCHEMS) has developed a comprehensive, computerized cost system to assist colleges in conducting cost studies. This system, the Student Outcomes Information Services (SOIS), includes a Costing and Data Management System, an Information Exchange Procedure, and a Resources Requirements Prediction Model (Collard and others, 1975). Both historical and predictive approaches are used. Historical studies require the identification and aggregation of cost-related data in terms of actual units (such as costs per credit hour). Predictive studies utilize selected parameters of operation (for example, average class size, faculty-student ratios, and faculty rank mix) as the basis for forecasting costs (Collier, 1978). Over the years, NCHEMS has applied and refined its costing strategy with hundreds of colleges using the system.[3]

Along with the cost system, NCHEMS has generated several taxonomies of outcome measures that focus on student growth and development, development of new knowledge and art forms, and community development and service (Micek and Wallhaus, 1973; Micek and Arney, 1973; Lenning, 1977). The outcome category of Student Growth and Development, for example, has six subcategories—Student Knowledge and Skills Development, Student Educational Career Development, Student Educational Satisfaction Outcomes, Student Occupational Career Development, Student Personal Development, and Student Social/Cultural Development. All of these subcategories are pertinent to various adult development frameworks. Each subcategory specifies a large number of measures that can be used to extract appropriate information (Micek and Wallhaus, 1973).

In 1979, NCHEMS put together a Student Outcomes Implementation Handbook containing five different questionnaires—Entering-Student, Continuing-Student, Former-Student, Program-Completion, and Recent-Alumni—and an analysis service for users (Gray and others, 1979). The handbook provides computer-ready questionnaires including a section wherein a college can add its own local questions. The actual integration of outcomes and cost data has not yet been discussed in the handbook, but clearly the cost system and recent outcomes approach can be brought together with the sophisticated computer packages NCHEMS possesses.

Let us examine one questionnaire from the SOIS package with regard to its implications for adult development. The Former-Student Questionnaire asks nineteen questions (with room for fourteen local questions to be added) concerning background characteristics; the student's academic, career, social, and personal goals; area of study; reasons for leaving the college; and evaluation of college services offered to the student. In analyzing data from former students according to age, sex, and possibly developmental stage, it may be possible to interpret both the students' goals and their reasons for leaving college in terms of particular life cycle demands. For example, for students in the midlife

[3]For further information about SOIS, directed by Aubrey Forrest, write to NCHEMS, Post Office Drawer P, Boulder, Colo. 80302.

transition period (ages 35-45), the pressures of work, family, and personal crises may make it difficult to pursue important personal development goals in a college setting (see Chickering and Havighurst's chapter on the life cycle). Thus, attrition rates may be considerably higher during this time than at preceding or succeeding life stages. The differential attrition rates over the life cycle for men and women suggest that faculty advising, campus support services, and educational program design should be carefully reconsidered. Adult students have different educational needs over the life cycle, and these needs must be met by different faculty and program responses if attrition rates are to be kept low.

Outcomes of Undergraduate Education Project, Harvard University. In 1975, Harvard University received a grant from the Fund for the Improvement of Postsecondary Education to initiate a study of student intellectual growth during the college years and to develop a set of instruments that measure the value added by college experience.[4] Following discussions of the essential dimensions of what constitutes a liberal education, ten instruments were developed or tested: the Test of Logic and Rhetoric, Analysis of Argument, Test of Thematic Analysis, Learning New Material, Cognitive Styles, Test of Moral Development, Profile of Non-Verbal Sensitivity, Undergraduate Questionnaire, Thematic Apperception Test, and Alumni Questionnaire. These instruments were applied at three different institutions—a private college, a state college, and a junior college. The results show that seniors scored significantly higher than freshmen at all three colleges (Whitla, 1975, 1978). Seniors' scores thus reflect important value-added contributions by the colleges and show significant gains in liberal education goals over time.

Focusing, as they do, on dimensions of intellectual growth, the Harvard instruments might conceivably be used to shed light upon different stages of adult learning. For example, Schaie and Parr, in their chapter on intellectual development, identify three broad stages of adult development, each of which emphasizes different kinds of intellectual processes. (1) The achieving stage finds the young adult striving toward a goal-directed, entrepreneurial style of achievement, which requires an efficient task-related, and sometimes competitive, cognitive style. (2) The responsible stage of middle adulthood finds the adult integrating long-range goals and improving problem-solving, organizational, and interpretive intellectual skills. And (3) the reintegrative stage of late adulthood reveals the adult relinquishing various occupational and family responsibilities but developing the ability to retrieve and act selectively upon the wealth of information and experience accumulated over a lifetime to bring meaning and order to the later years. The Harvard instruments could be used to see if young adults at the achieving stage score higher than adults at the responsible or reintegrative stages on the Test of Logic and Rhetoric, Analysis of Arguments, and Learning New Material, which measure the kinds of intellectual skills required for the goals and activities of this stage, and if, by contrast, adults at the two later stages score higher on the Thematic Apperception Test and the Profile of Non-Verbal Sensitivity. If so, these findings might indicate the need to consider variation in intellectual skills over the life span in the planning and evaluation of educational programs for adults.

If the aim of higher education is to stimulate the mind and develop its capacity for reflection and judgment, then education becomes embedded in the process of moral development. Gilligan, in her chapter on moral development, notes that adolescence is a

---

[4]The Harvard Project was under the direction of Dean Whitla. Further information about the project can be obtained from him at the Office of Instructional Research and Evaluation, 11 University Hall, Harvard University, Cambridge, Mass. 02138.

critical period for moral development and identifies moral relativism as the specific issue at this stage. Building upon Kohlberg's theory of moral develoment, she concludes that development may continue beyond the six stages Kohlberg has identified and that education is critical to this development. The Harvard study drew upon Kohlberg's work and used interviews to obtain moral judgment scores for students in their freshman and senior years. In general, seniors' scores were higher than freshmen's and men's scores higher than women's. This work should be extended to adult populations in order to build up a set of empirical studies on adult moral development parallel to those already conducted on college adolescents.

Cooperative Institutional Research Program, American Council on Education and University of California, Los Angeles. In 1966, the Cooperative Institutional Research Program (CIRP) was started under the auspices of the American Council on Education to study the effects of college on students. The program is now cosponsored by UCLA. CIRP is a national longitudinal study of American higher education, which has over the years involved more than 1,000 institutions, 100,000 faculty, and four million students—the largest ongoing empirical study of its kind (Astin and others, 1976; Astin, 1977). The program consists of an annual survey of entering freshmen and periodic follow-up surveys of graduates (Astin, 1977); dropouts (Astin, 1975); campus protests (Astin and others, 1975); education and work (Bisconti and Solomon, 1976); and campus change (Astin, 1978). Each annual survey provides a normative picture of the college freshman population for persons engaged in policy analysis, administration, educational research and planning, and guidance and counseling, as well as the general community of students and parents (Astin, 1978).[5]

The overall design of the CIRP effort (its longitudinal nature and multi-institutional features) makes possible more sensitive assessments of whether and how different kinds of colleges affect students. Astin has employed an "input-environment-outcome" model that allows him to predict outcomes on the basis of his input variables. That is, student change is assessed by comparing follow-up scores *not* with pretest scores but with scores predicted on the basis of student responses to the entering freshmen survey. Thus, comparisons of different colleges yield a measure of change attributable to the influence of a given college environment. Outcome variables are divided by type (cognitive and affective) and by type of data (psychological states and behavioral expressions) to generate a taxonomy of outcomes for presenting major findings (Astin, 1977). All the data used in these studies are derived from student self-reports.

Each year the CIRP program samples entering full-time students from at least 300 different colleges. Data are tabulated, and weighted national norms are reported each year. Each participating college receives a report on its students' profile. The national norms are reported separately by sex, race, type of college (two-year, four-year, university), control (public or private), geographic region, and selectivity level. Thus, any participating institution can not only compare its own results from one year to another but can also compare its results with those of other similar colleges. Such data can be useful to admissions and financial aid programs, short- and long-range administrative planning, and support services, including extracurricular activities and counseling, as well as academic planning for growth or stability of various departments, majors, and other educational programs.

[5]Further information about CIRP, directed by Alexander W. Astin, may be obtained from the Graduate School of Education, University of California, Los Angeles, Calif. 90024.

The CIRP studies provide a valuable data bank of longitudinal multi-institutional information about full-time entering freshmen across the country. As the student population shifts to large proportions of part-time adult students, this data bank will provide important normative benchmarks for each college or academic program.

The Student Information Form of CIRP contains a number of questions that can be interpreted in an adult development context, including areas likely to reveal important life cycle variations: students' reasons for attending college; students' expected undergraduate majors and probable career choices; and the importance they ascribe to specific personal goals. Each college anticipating use of the questionnaire for adult development purposes may want to examine some of the CIRP data to determine the practical significance of these questions for older students.

Program Effectiveness and Related Costs, Empire State College. The previous five approaches to program evaluation differ in their scope, purpose, complexity, and applicability to adult development. These approaches show that a range of instruments and testing and analysis services are already available for use at reasonable cost. The Program Effectiveness and Related Costs (PERC) approach of Empire State College, under development since 1973 by Empire State's Office of Research and Evaluation, specifically confronts the evaluation issues raised by an individualized educational program for adults.

Empire State's program provides for an individually designed degree plan (or major) and learning contracts. It also includes procedures for assessing and crediting learning from life and work experiences and makes substantial use of field experience learning as described in earlier chapters by John Duley and Morris Keeton. In a fundamental sense, an individualized educational program requires an individualized evaluation strategy. However, until recently, individualized evaluation seemed prohibitively difficult and expensive for most colleges (Hodgkinson, 1975). PERC seeks to match the evaluation challenges posed by an individualized education program and to combine several features of the different approaches reviewed earlier into a single unique approach that can be applied at more traditional colleges as well.[6]

The PERC strategy has four unique features: (1) it focuses on assessing educational outcomes first and then relates costs to those outcomes; (2) it relies upon a multiple perspectives strategy; (3) it calls for conducting studies within a longitudinal design; and (4) it emphasizes the practical utility of these results for academic decision makers.

Regarding educational outcomes and costs, the basic evaluation question is this: *What kinds of students working with what kinds of faculty in what kinds of learning programs change in what ways at what costs?* Embedded in this master question are the five core components of PERC—outcomes, costs, students, faculty, and programs. Among these five components, the primary relationship is the relationship between outcomes and costs. In contrast to much of the previous evaluation work that stressed cost-effectiveness or cost-benefit approaches, PERC places primary emphasis upon student learning and educational effectiveness and later introduces the costs associated with a given student's learning or educational program. All too often a primary focus on costs leads to a "lowest common denominator" style of decision making, which may shortchange programs that are genuinely effective.

Each college must identify the educational outcomes appropriate for its own stu-

[6]This research-evaluation project, supported by the Fund for the Improvement of Postsecondary Education, was directed by Ernest G. Palola. For further information write the Office of Research and Evaluation, Empire State College, Saratoga Springs, N.Y. 12866.

dents and academic programs. Thus, a college or its evaluation team must specify what its students seek to learn, what the program tries to achieve, and what kinds of learning activities and learning resources will produce the desired results.

Empire State College starts by defining outcomes based on student needs and objectives. With the help of a faculty mentor, each student designs an individual degree program that serves as the basic plan for the student's work at the college and provides the basis for evaluation of outcomes. The PERC framework classifies an individual student's objectives into eight outcome categories: (1) Substantive Knowledge, (2) Communication Skills, (3) Cognitive Outcomes, (4) Developmental Outcomes, (5) Personal Outcomes, (6) Occupational Skills, (7) Public Service, and (8) Unanticipated Outcomes. For example, Substantive Knowledge refers to the level of competence achieved within the context of the student's own goals and the college's minimum standards of performance; Cognitive Outcomes include comprehension, analysis, evaluation, synthesis, and application; and Developmental Outcomes cover interpersonal competence, awareness, clarification of purposes, self-understanding, and self-consistency.

The PERC model addresses this broad range of educational outcomes by means of a multiple perspectives evaluation strategy featuring five components: (1) multiple observers of student learning; (2) multiple methods of assessing student learning; (3) multiple decision makers using data relevant to policy questions they face; (4) multiple time periods for measuring change in student learning; and (5) multiple standards (Palola and others, 1977, 1978; Palola and Lehmann, 1976). This strategy assumes that student learning is a complex, dynamic, multifaceted, and ongoing process that no single observer, method, or instrument can fully capture. Therefore several observers are required to make judgments of student learning using various methods of evaluation. For example, the student at the center of Figure 4 is the central participant in the educational process and as such is in an especially advantageous position to evaluate certain aspects of his or her own learning in terms of his or her own objectives for learning. Thus, students may evaluate their own learning on such outcomes as subject matter knowledge, occupational skills, or interpersonal competence. Faculty can then evaluate students on the same outcomes and provide another perspective on what they have or have not learned. We expect to find general agreement on these outcome judgments, especially in the developmental domain. (For other studies that have applied a multiple perspectives strategy wherein several observers provide independent evaluations of a given student's learning and growth see Wilson and others, 1975; Sagen, 1974; and Blackburn and Clark, 1975.)

Other observers of learning outcomes shown in Figure 4 are the researcher, the administrator, and outside evaluators such as accreditors. The research staff using PERC may conduct its own evaluation of student learning, using, for example, standardized tests to measure student mastery of subject matter knowledge, as well as provide the focal point for carrying out the PERC evaluation. In this capacity, the research staff has the responsibility to bring together data provided by several observers, analyze the data, and prepare reports that can be used by different decision makers.

PERC's longitudinal design calls for a variety of surveys and case study techniques used in concert throughout the evaluation process (see Figure 5). This strategy provides the necessary multiple measures at each stage to create *chains of evidence* showing where a college or program is having effects and where it is not (Campbell and Fiske, 1959; Sieber, 1973; Hartnett, 1974; Peterson and Vale, 1973).

Implications of Evaluation Data

How can the seemingly complex, comprehensive, and abstract research approach just outlined help a faculty member, administrator, or external evaluator not only under-

Figure 4. PERC's Multiple Perspectives Strategy

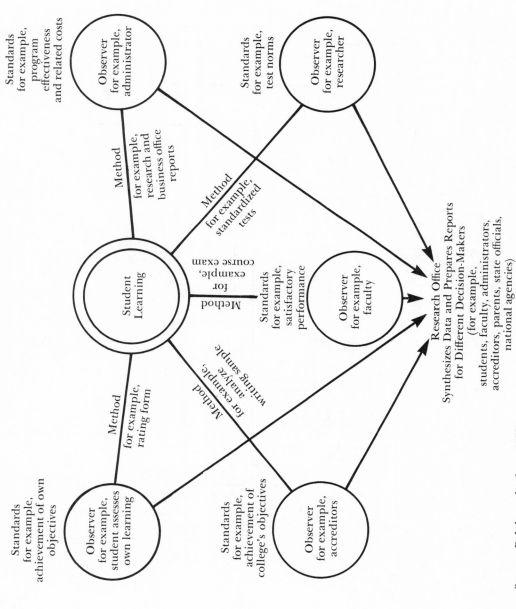

Source: Palola and others, 1977.

Figure 5. PERC Longitudinal Design

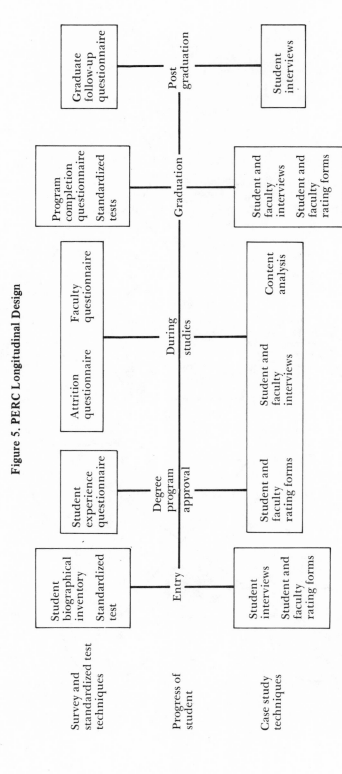

Source: Palola and others, 1977.

stand the learning process of adults but evaluate an academic program? Let us consider two items from PERC's Student Biographical Inventory (Figure 5) and their implications for adult development and program planning.

Using the adult development framework developed by Daniel Levinson and Roger Gould (described briefly in Chapter One on the life cycle), we analyzed the data collected from entering Empire State College students during 1974-75 on selected traits. Over 2,700 students (62 percent) responded to the PERC questionnaire (Lehmann and Lester, 1978).

Self-Perceptions of Success Orientation. Drive to Achieve, Leadership Ability, Ability to Handle Stress, and Independence are four traits analyzed under Success Orientation. These traits were selected and grouped together because they closely resemble the concepts Levinson and Gould used to describe the male path of career ambition and achievement over the life cycle. Success Orientation traits, then, were expected to reveal certain patterns that would confirm or disconfirm the life cycle framework set forth by Levinson and Gould.

Figure 6 presents the four Success Orientation traits in such a way that several types of comparisons can be made. First let us examine the patterns of men across the developmental stages. On the trait Leadership Ability, 60 percent of the men at the Pulling Up Roots Stage (the below-21 age group) rated themselves above average or higher. At the Putting Down Roots Stage, 78 percent of the men in that age group perceived themselves above average—the highest percentage of any group. At the Midlife Transition Stage, the percentage was somewhat lower—72 percent. And at the Early Retirement Stage, it was lower still—58 percent. The changes across these life stages show a steady rise during the first three stages, a decline at midlife, and a stabilization during the next two stages. Such a profile confirms rather nicely the patterns predicted by Levinson and Gould. Of course, it should be emphasized that the profiles shown here are derived from the responses of different age cohorts, not the same individuals across all stages.

On the other three traits, similar increases in percentages of men who perceived themselves to be above average on the traits were found up to the Midlife Transition Stage, with decreases thereafter. One exception to this general pattern is the marked decline in the Ability to Handle Stress during the Midlife Transition, followed by a rise to the highest level (82 percent) during Middle Adulthood. We interpret this pattern as congruent with Levinson's observation of the difficulties that men face during the Midlife Transition. Levinson makes the point that men during Middle Adulthood reach their peak ability to handle stress in the occupational world and in other areas as well.

The patterns for women are roughly similar. Young women at the Pulling Up Roots Stage show fairly high levels (55-75 percent) of self-perceived strength on all four traits. But two traits (Leadership and Drive to Achieve) decline sharply for the women in the next life stage, though they rise steadily among older women. Three traits—Ability to Handle Stress, Drive to Achieve, and Independence—reach very high levels by Early Retirement. Women at the Getting Into Adult World Stage are apparently less interested in competing with men or in establishing a career than in getting married and setting up a home. It is significant that women's self-ratings on all four traits show consistent increases from their low points at the Getting Into Adult World Stage through the Midlife Transition Stage and on three of the four traits surpass men's levels by Middle or Late Adulthood (Stewart, 1976).

Figure 6. Student Self-Perceptions of Success Orientation

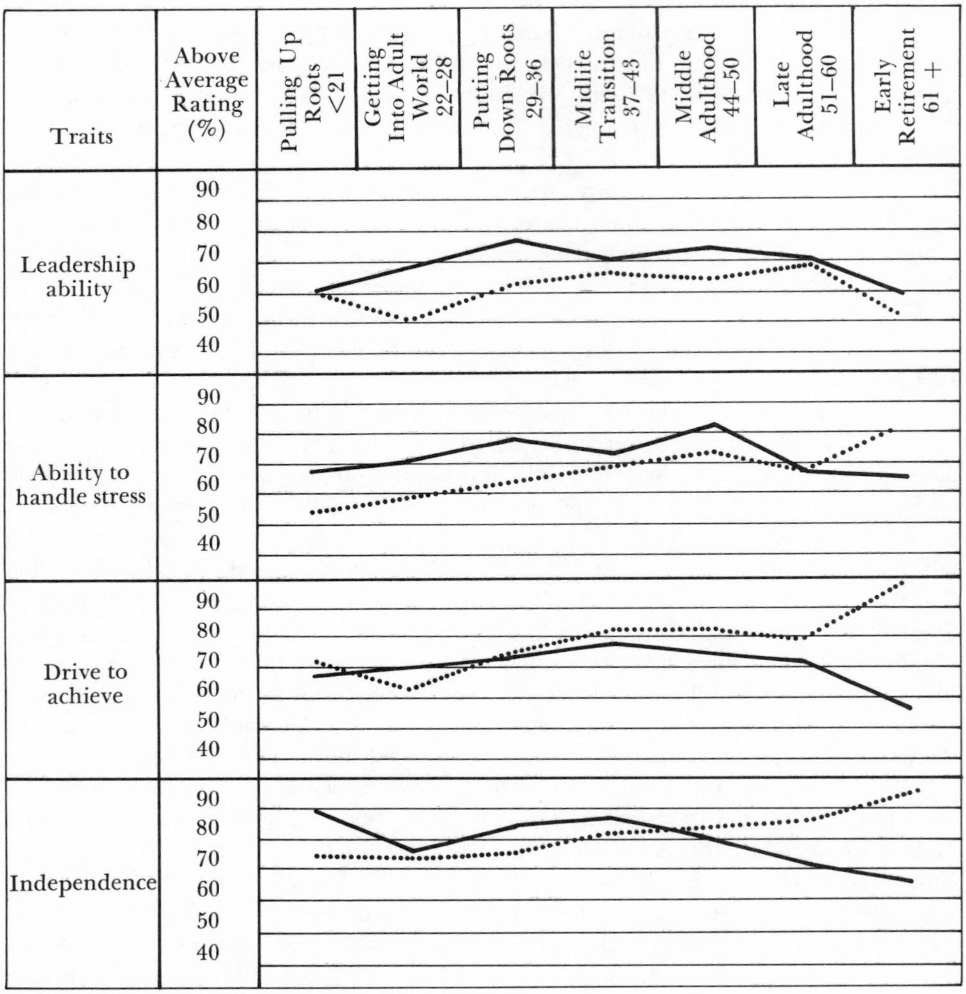

Traits	Above Average Rating (%)	Pulling Up Roots <21	Getting Into Adult World 22–28	Putting Down Roots 29–36	Midlife Transition 37–43	Middle Adulthood 44–50	Late Adulthood 51–60	Early Retirement 61 +
Leadership ability	90 80 70 60 50 40							
Ability to handle stress	90 80 70 60 50 40							
Drive to achieve	90 80 70 60 50 40							
Independence	90 80 70 60 50 40							

Note: The solid line represents male responses; the dotted line, female. All percentage differences greater than ten between men and women at a given stage are significant at the .05 level using the chi square test.

Source: Lehmann and Lester, 1978.

Finally, let us briefly compare men's and women's perceptions of their success orientations. On three of four traits, men start out slightly higher or at the same point as women during the Pulling Up Roots Stage. By Midlife, men still exceed women on the same three traits, but the gap has narrowed considerably. And by Late Adulthood, women exceed men on three traits. Women exceed men on Drive to Achieve during six of the seven stages. One possible interpretation for the steady and consistent increase in women's self-perceptions on these traits across the stages is this: Women are returning to college and to the work world after age 35 with strong commitments to achieve, establish independence, and seek new personal goals at precisely the time when men have reached their career peaks and are beginning to shift their aspirations and interests to noncareer activities.

Overall, we find that the Levinson and Gould arguments fit rather well the general pattern of men and women across the life cycle and account in part for some of the noteworthy differences between men and women in particular stages. Some implications of these findings for program planning will be discussed shortly.

Self-Perceptions of Academic Competence. Five different traits were grouped under the category Academic Competence: Academic Ability, Writing Ability, Reading Ability, Artistic Ability, and Intellectual Self-Confidence (Figure 7). On Academic Ability, men and women rate themselves about the same at the initial Pulling Up Roots Stage, but men's self-ratings decline dramatically during the next three stages, reaching a low point at Midlife, whereas women's tend to remain at the 50-50 percent level across the remaining six stages. The gap between men and women at Midlife is substantial (almost twenty percentage points).

On all five traits, the percentages of men who rate themselves as above average decline with successive age groups until the Midlife Transition, where the trend reverses. Thus, the Midlife Transition period is not only a low point (in all cases below the 50 percent level rating) but also a turning point in male student perceptions. Women see themselves declining on all four traits during the Getting Into Adult World Stage, but during the later Putting Down Roots Stage women show slight gains on Academic and Writing Abilities. Women also show a drop during the Midlife Transition Stage and a "flowering" during Middle and Late Adulthood.

On Intellectual Self-Confidence, a reverse pattern occurs. Men see themselves as more intellectually self-confident than do women across almost all developmental periods, although men show a 25 percent decline at the Midlife Transition Stage. According to the Levinson and Gould frameworks, we would expect women not only to start out lower than men on Intellectual Self-Confidence but also to hit their lowest points during the Getting Into Adult World and Putting Down Roots Stages, when they are occupied with family responsibilities. The data in Figure 7 essentially confirm that expectation. Women tend to gain on academic competencies during the Midlife Transition Stage and continue to gain Intellectual Self-Confidence during the succeeding three periods.

Comparisons of Success Orientation and Academic Competence Self-Perceptions. A comparison of Figures 6 and 7 reveals some striking differences in students' self-perceptions of Success Orientation and Academic Competence. In Figure 6, 60-70 percent of men and women perceive themselves to be above average in Success Orientation traits at the initial Pulling Up Roots Stage. Self-ratings rise to 70-85 percent at the Midlife Transition Stage and remain at the same level or decline slightly over the next three stages. In Figure 7, 50-60 percent of men and women rate themselves above average in Academic Competence at the Pulling Up Roots Stage. However, the proportion is only 35-45 percent at the Midlife Transition, and only slightly higher over the next three stages. These general patterns reflect a diamond-shaped set of self-perceptions. At midlife, both men and women rate their success-oriented abilities highly but return to college with low estimations of their academic competencies. For example, 70 percent of men at midlife rate

Figure 7. Student Self-Perceptions of Academic Competence

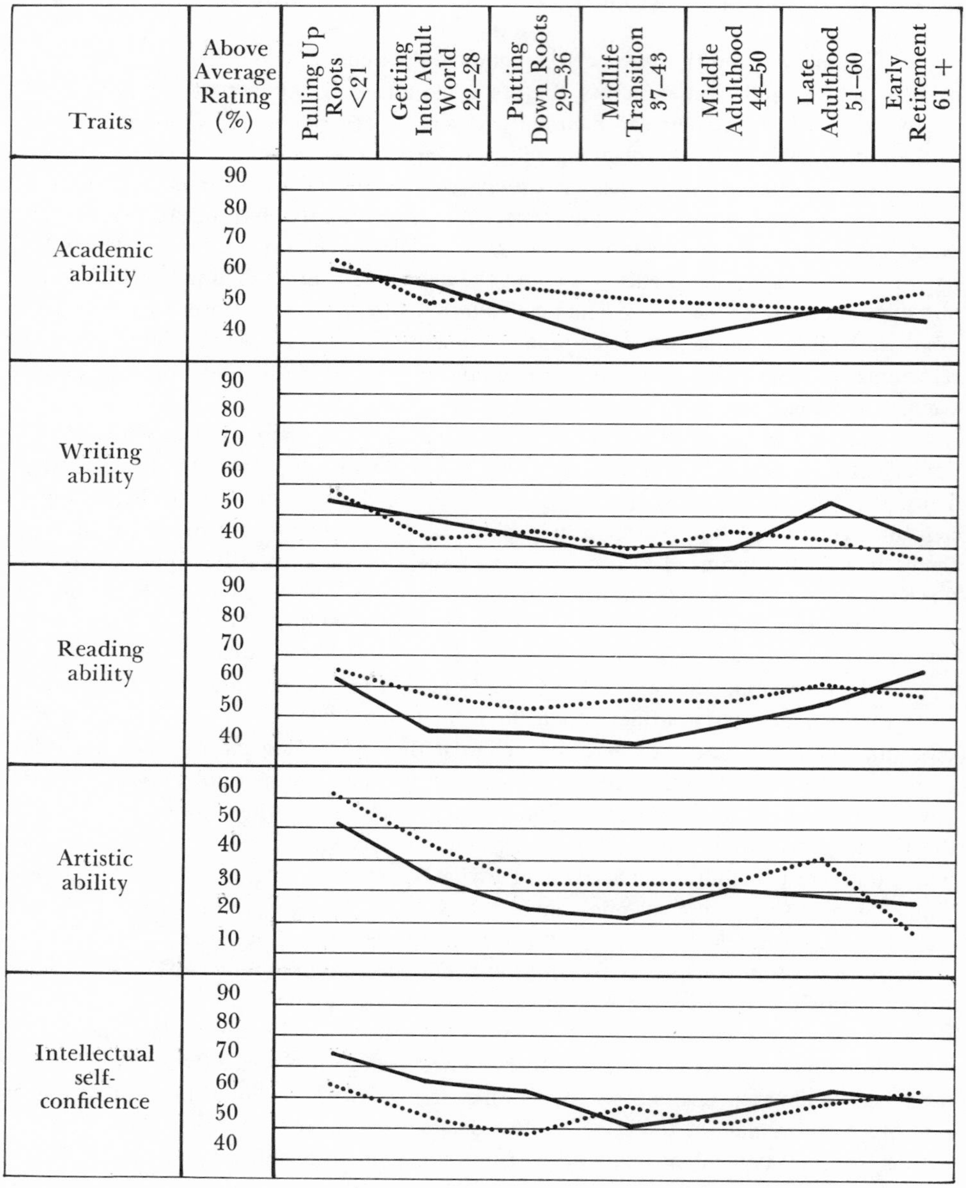

Note: The solid line represents male responses; the dotted line, female.

Source: Lehmann and Lester, 1978.

themselves above average on Leadership Ability, but only 35 percent see themselves as above average on Writing Ability. Such a diamond-shaped set of perceptions raises important educational questions for these students as they enter college. Because the gap is so large between students' views of their success in the work world and other settings and their academic competence, faculty may need to recognize this gap in early discussions about learning plans, offer support and counsel to sustain these students as they encounter college requirements, and take other steps as necessary to bolster limited self-confidence.

Implications for Program Planning. For illustrative purposes, let us explore the implications of the characteristic self-perceptions of academic competence at one stage. Male students who enroll in college during the Midlife Transition period have the lowest self-ratings on all six Academic Competence traits of all the male age groups. Such low intellectual self-confidence may represent serious academic problems for this group. The faculty member, through course advising and degree program planning, must offer strong academic support, personal encouragement, and patience if the student is to proceed satisfactorily. Special learning resources or tutorial supports may also be necessary to rebuild this student's academic abilities and confidence.

Women at this same stage, however, have different expectations. They tend to see themselves at a new juncture in life, having raised their academic expectations from preceding lower levels, and are ready and eager for an academic challenge and new academic directions. Often, what these women need most are career guidance, challenging learning activities that build on their academic skills, and a practical setting in which to test their vocational interests. For women who have been home-bound for a decade, this may be a time of intense personal searching for a new identity, a time for seeking a college degree and career commitments that will lead to a different life during the next thirty years (Knox, 1979). Such an interpretation is supported by Bernard's chapter on the educational needs of women, which points up the importance of the family life cycle in women's educational planning and suggests the need for "contingency scheduling."

Sensitive counseling and academic planning can have numerous beneficial effects upon the operation of the college. If faculty and other college personnel involved in orientations, assessment work, and advising clearly recognize students' situations at entry (using self-concept data as one indicator), they will be able to give those students the appropriate kinds of support and educational environment, which will undoubtedly reduce the attrition rate. And to the extent that the college improves retention, it can reduce recruitment efforts and expense, better manage the flow of students through the academic program, and reduce paperwork. Processing and paperwork costs are considerable when the ramifications of attrition-retention for admissions office, financial aids office, records office, billing, academic affairs, and computer services are recognized. Thus, for every adult student whose developmental needs are understood at entry and acted upon by the faculty and staff, so that a suitable educational program is constructed, the likelihood of attrition is reduced, educational effectiveness is enhanced, and overall program costs are cut.

This analysis of one item on an entry questionnaire in terms of adult development suggests that very different approaches may need to be taken to counseling and academic advising depending on the age and sex of the adult involved. It also suggests some of the implications of evaluation data for attrition and retention rates, which ultimately affect educational effectiveness and program costs.

The Outcomes-Cost Relationship. The PERC model works on the premise that the diversity of adult students' backgrounds, educational goals, personal interests, and levels of motivation will call for equally diverse educational plans, learning activities, learning resources, and evaluation strategies. As a result, the outcomes component is founded upon a careful assessment of an individual's program. Likewise, the cost component must be individualized since different students will use different faculty, tutors, courses, or other learning resources—all with different costs attached. Thus, the PERC cost framework has been developed to supplement the educational effectiveness framework: cost data are developed around and reported in relation to measures of effectiveness.

The PERC framework differs from other cost systems in that it is geared to the individual student's learning experiences rather than to some budgetary formula (for example, full-time equivalent students, or credit hours). The model also includes certain costs optional or omitted in other cost systems (for example, in-kind contributions—those without direct cost—of services, facilities, materials, and programs). PERC treats the cost of the development of learning sites, learning resources, and new programs as deferred assets. To locate learning facilities where adults are is an important part of delivering educational services to adult learners who may not be able to take advantage of on-campus learning. Finally, the PERC model assigns those parts of faculty time (and corresponding salary costs) devoted to administrative tasks to an overhead charge rather than calling those costs instructional.

Although the PERC cost model differs from other cost systems in these ways, the framework has been constructed so that we can compare its reports with those of most other cost frameworks, including the major efforts of the National Center for Higher Education Management Systems. By summing the appropriate individual student costs developed through PERC, reports can depict more conventional cost-analysis units: full-time equivalent, credit hours, major, and so on. Readers interested in more detail on the cost model may consult Palola and others (1977) and Debus (1974).

The PERC cost model is shown graphically in Figure 8. In Stage 1, all those learning activities and learning resources that a given student uses in a learning contract are identified and the appropriate costs calculated. All costs involved in the contract—faculty, location, and overhead costs—arc included. Stage 1 thus gives us a picture of the costs of each contract. Stage 2 combines the costs of all contracts for a given student. Stage 3 combines all contracts for all students in a given program of study A, B, or C. By moving through all three stages, the analyst can aggregate individual student costs into costs for all similar students in a program of study or at a particular location or in other categories that may be of interest in comparing this program with more conventional ones.

Program Evaluation Principles

The following principles may help colleges interested in beginning evaluation studies introduce the evaluation process successfully into the planning cycle.

Start Out Simply. Several of the program evaluation approaches mentioned earlier in this chapter may initially be too complex, comprehensive, and costly for colleges only now launching systematic evaluation of their programs. A fundamental principle for a new evaluation effort is to start out simply with a few objectives and later develop a more comprehensive strategy. If attrition, for example, is a major problem, a brief telephone survey of former students may suffice to find out why they left college, what their views of the college are, and what would induce them to return. Empire State's very first study was strategically focused on ten of the first thirty graduates to find out their reactions to the program and what happened to them after they received their degrees (Palola and Bradley, 1973). If colleges selectively channel energies and resources into evaluation

Figure 8. Empire State College Program Cost Analysis Model

Stage 1
(Each Contract)

Student Social Security No._____

Credit_____

Beg. Date_____

End. Date_____

Location_____

Level_____

Stage 2
(All Contracts of Single Student)

Student Social Security No._____

Total credit_____

Program of study_____

Level_____

Stage 3
(All Contracts—All Students)

Period:_____

Program of Study

Costs	A
Mentor's salary	
Mentor's fringe benefits	
Location overhead	
General overhead	
Auxiliary enterprises	
Debt service interest	
Capital outlay	
Endowment costs	
Fieldwork	
Tuition cost	
Independent study cost	
Module cost	
Student aid	
Tutor's salary	
Total	

Contract

	1	2	3	Total

Program of Study

	A	B	C	Total
Total number full-time equivalent				
Total per full-time equivalent				

Source: Adapted from Palola and others, 1977.

projects that are urgent and manageable within a reasonable period of time, they are more likely to obtain useful results.

Use a Grab Bag Evaluation Strategy. Every college or program exists in a unique environment and necessarily differs in certain ways from similar kinds of institutions or programs. The grab bag evaluation principle asserts that each evaluation project should borrow or adapt whatever seems useful from the existing instruments or strategies. Several handbooks have already been mentioned as guides to promoting sound evaluation practice. There are numerous other handbooks, self-assessment kits, and other instruments available today that can be consulted and used, including *Self-Assessment for Colleges and Universities* (1979), Bowen (1977), and Pace (Pace and others, 1975). A new evaluation team need not reinvent instruments; instead it can use existing materials and refashion them to fit the particular needs of the evaluation project.

Employ Informal Indicators Widely. Project teams should draw upon existing informal indicators of program operation and student learning to complement more formal assessment instruments. Talking and listening to students after class, in hallways, at counseling centers and in extracurricular settings can furnish a wealth of anecdotal materials about what students are thinking and doing and how the program is working. Keeping a program journal, a learning journal, or team journal of what transpires on an informal but regular basis can often show what directions new programs are taking and suggest the reasons why. Further, collecting and analyzing program documents, memos, and other record-keeping materials can greatly improve the overall nature of the evaluation efforts (Webb and others, 1966; O'Toole, 1971; Berelson, 1954; and Holsti, 1968). All too frequently, program documents are overlooked as a key source of information. The use of informal indicators can be an important addition to the more formal evaluation efforts in program assessment.

Move in From the Edge. Very few academics are opposed in principle to innovation or experimentation with new ideas and new programs. But in order to win their support for a new program, it is often necessary to keep the program small, test it on a pilot basis, and see what happens over a trial time period. Such a strategy requires that the program be protected from the usual curricular committee review and governance processes. Thus, such programs are at the edge of the academic environment.

Sound program development and dissemination require that successful programs, once they have gone through the development phase and initial evaluation, should move in from the edge of the academic curriculum and face the usual committee and governance reviews. Such programs, however, will be in a stronger position to gain acceptance if the evaluation effort has shown meaningful results. Most ongoing programs have not been subjected to evaluation study; thus, a new program, which usually must produce evaluation results to justify its continued support, is in a position to take its place alongside other programs if it has evidence of its effectiveness. Dissemination of program evaluation results requires astute use of the informal networks of influence so that faculty and administrators who will review the program are receptive to its merits (Lindquist, 1978).

Separate Program Evaluation From Personnel Evaluation. This principle is crucial if program evaluation is to be carried on effectively. The staff running a particular program will cooperate more fully and be more interested in the results if it is clear from the outset that the program itself is the target of evaluation—that is, that the object of evaluation is to identify the program's strengths and correct its weaknesses. Program evaluation can be threatening to staff. If staff evaluation is mixed with program evaluation, the staff's natural inclination to emphasize the positive may seriously distort the evaluation.

Personnel evaluation of program staff should either follow the regular personnel practices of the campus or be conducted, separately from any program evaluation effort, according to procedures established at the start of the new program.

One aspect of program evaluation does tie directly to professional development but still remains outside the arena of personnel evaluation. There is an important potential link between (1) program evaluation and program renewal and (2) professional development and professional renewal. Lindquist argues, in his chapter, that professional development in college is in fact adult development and thus should be at the heart of any college's renewal efforts. Those individuals who take on leadership in launching new programs or revitalizing old ones, or who become members of evaluation teams, are engaged in more than program development and program evaluation activities. In a very real sense, they are renewing themselves professionally, learning new skills, and encountering significant on-the-job experiences that may enrich their own perspectives and lives. Intensive learning experiences and professional development activities are implicit in most program evaluation efforts. More explicit recognition of this dimension along the lines suggested by Lindquist can be an important addition to most ongoing evaluation efforts.

Treat Program Evaluation as a Collaborative Enterprise. Finally, sound program evaluation cannot be carried out as an isolated activity. There are many parties to any evaluation effort: students in the program, program administrators, teaching staff, the evaluation team, higher-level administrators, business office staff, funding sources, and so on. Because the parties have different interests and expectations of the evaluation project, the evaluation team has the responsibility to plan carefully, keep the parties informed of evaluation activities, share results, and discuss the project frequently with the groups directly involved. Persistent follow-up activities are needed to cement the evaluation effort among these parties and tie the evaluation cycle (Figure 2) directly to the planning cycle (Figure 3).

The first step in this collaborative effort is to build an effective evaluation team. This team, whose members should be drawn from the parties involved in the evaluation, should meet often enough to ensure a concerted evaluation effort (Sikes, Schlesinger, and Seashore, 1974). Once the team has initiated the evaluation, it should expand its program evaluation activities along the lines suggested by the evaluation cycle and the previous principles. Treating program evaluation as a collaborative enterprise increases the chances that evaluation results will be useful to a program and that decision makers will respond to the reports and recommendations prepared. The principle does not guarantee the use of evaluation results, but the likelihood of their use is improved if constituent groups have been involved throughout the evaluation process. In the final analysis, evaluation is just that—an evaluation process, not a change process. There will always be a gap between assessment results and action, since assessment is only one phase of the planning cycle. Sound evaluation can point out the merits of new programs, the necessity of change, and the failures of existing programs; but by itself it can never provide all the answers decision makers need to choose among alternatives.

In summary, we are well beyond Galileo's days in terms of empirical research instruments but not necessarily beyond Galileo's problem regarding the acceptance of research evidence. Nevertheless, the potential exists for evaluation to substantially improve academic decision making. Our modern evaluation instruments now permit sophisticated assessments of program effectiveness and costs. If faculty and administrators are willing to accept the challenge of evaluation, they will be able to develop educational programs that better serve not only departmental, program, and professional objectives but also the developmental needs of diverse students. In the preceding chapter, Lindquist discussed this dual responsibility as it affects the professional development of faculty, administrators, and staff—the vital human resources of academic institutions. This chapter touches upon another part of this responsibility. Existing program evaluation strategies can inform us about how our programs work, what our students learn, and how much the learning costs. These strategies are needed now more than ever if American colleges are to plan realistically, bring costs into line with program needs, and serve students of all ages effectively. Looking through the evaluation telescope into the 1980s, we have an obligation to improve our educational programs by recognizing that the moons of Jupiter do in fact exist.

References

American College Testing Program. *Annual Report 1978.* Iowa City, Iowa: American College Testing Program, 1978.

Astin, A. *Preventing Students from Dropping Out.* San Francisco: Jossey-Bass, 1975.

Astin, A. *Four Critical Years: Effects of College on Beliefs, Attitudes, and Knowledge.* San Francisco: Jossey-Bass, 1977.

Astin, A. "Student-Oriented Management: A Modest Proposal for Radical Change in College Administration." Paper presented at the Summer Invitational Conference on Accreditation of the Commission on Postsecondary Accreditation, Pomona, Calif., 1978.

Astin, A., and others. *A Program of Longitudinal Research on the Higher Education System.* Washington, D.C.: American Council on Education, 1966.

Astin, A., and others. *The Power of Protest: A National Study of Student and Faculty Disruptions with Implications for the Future.* San Francisco: Jossey-Bass, 1975.

Astin, A., and others. *The American Freshman: National Norms for Fall 1978.* Los Angeles: Cooperative Institutional Research Program, University of California at Los Angeles and American Council on Education, 1978.

Berelson, B. "Content Analysis." In G. Lindzey (Ed.), *Handbook of Social Psychology.* Vol. 1. Reading, Mass.: Addison-Wesley, 1954.

Bess, J. "Classroom and Management Decisions Using Student Data." *Journal of Higher Education,* May/June 1979, *50,* 256-279.

Bisconti, A., and Solomon, L. *College Education on the Job—The Graduate's Viewpoint.* Bethlehem, Pa.: College Placement Council Foundation, 1976.

Blackburn, R., and Clark, M. "An Assessment of Faculty Performance: Some Correlates Between Administrator, Colleague, Student, and Self-Ratings." *Sociology of Education,* Spring 1975, *48,* 242-256.

Bowen, H. *Investment in Learning: The Individual and Social Value of American Higher Education.* San Francisco: Jossey-Bass, 1977.

Campbell, D. T. "Reforms as Experiments." *American Psychologist,* 1969, *24,* 409-429.

Campbell, D. T., and Fiske, D. "Convergent and Discriminant Validation by the Multitrait-Multimethod Matrix." *Psychological Bulletin,* 1959, *5,* 81-105.

Caro, F. (Ed.). *Readings in Evaluation Research.* (2nd ed.) New York: Russell Sage Foundation, 1977.

Collard, B., and others. *National Center for Higher Education Management Systems Costing and Data Management System.* Boulder, Colo.: National Center for Higher Education Management Systems, 1975.

College Outcome Measures Project Annual Report 1977. Iowa City, Iowa: College Outcome Measures Project, American College Testing Program, 1977.

College Outcome Measures Project Annual Report 1978. Iowa City, Iowa: College Outcome Measures Project, American College Testing Program, 1978.

Collier, D. *Program Classification Structure.* Boulder, Colo.: National Center for Higher Education Management Systems, 1978.

Debus, R. *Detailed Analysis of Empire State College Effectiveness Program and Relationship to NCHEMS Program.* Saratoga Springs, N.Y.: Office of Research and Evaluation, Empire State College, 1974.

Feldman, K. A., and Newcomb, T. M. *The Impact of College on Students.* San Francisco: Jossey-Bass, 1969.

Gould, R. "The Phases of Adult Life: A Study in Developmental Psychology." *American Journal of Psychiatry,* 1972, *129* (5), 521-531.

Gould, R. *Transformations: Growth and Change in Adult Life.* New York: Simon & Schuster, 1978.

Gray, R. G., and others. *Student Outcomes Questionnaires: An Implementation Handbook.* Boulder, Colo.: National Center for Higher Education Management Systems, 1979.

Hartnett, R. *Problems with the Comparative Assessment of Student Outcomes in Higher Education.* Princeton, N.J.: Educational Testing Service, 1974.

Hodgkinson, H. "Evaluating Individualized Learning." In N. Berte (Ed.), *New Directions for Higher Education: Individualizing Education by Learning Contracts,* no. 10. San Francisco: Jossey-Bass, 1975.

Hodgkinson, H., Hurst, J., and Levine, H. *Improving and Assessing Performance: Evaluation in Higher Education.* Berkeley, Calif.: Center for Research and Development in Higher Education, University of California, 1975.

Holsti, O. "Content Analysis." In G. Lindzey and E. Aronson (Eds.), *Handbook of Social Psychology.* Vol. 2 (2nd ed.) Reading, Mass.: Addison-Wesley, 1968.

Knox, A. B. (Ed.). *New Directions for Continuing Education: Programming for Adults Facing Mid-Life Change,* no. 2. San Francisco: Jossey-Bass, 1979.

Lehmann, T., and Lester, V. *Adult Learning in the Context of Adult Development.* Saratoga Springs, N.Y.: Office of Research and Evaluation, Empire State College, 1978.

Lenning, O. *The Outcomes Structure: An Overview and Procedures for Applying It in Postsecondary Education Institutions.* Boulder, Colo.: National Center for Higher Education Management Systems, 1977.

Levinson, D., and others. "The Psychosocial Development of Men in Early Adulthood and the Mid-Life Transition." In D. F. Ricks (Ed.), *Life History Research in Psychopathology.* Minneapolis: University of Minnesota Press, 1974.

Levinson, D., and others. *The Seasons of a Man's Life.* New York: Knopf, 1978.

Lindquist, J. *Strategies for Change.* Berkeley, Calif.: Pacific Soundings Press, 1978.

Micek, S., and Arney, W. *Outcome-Oriented Planning in Higher Education: An Approach or an Impossibility?* Boulder, Colo.: National Center for Higher Education Management Systems, 1973.

Micek, S., and Wallhaus, R. *An Introduction to the Identification and Uses of Higher Education Outcome Information.* Boulder, Colo.: National Center for Higher Education Management Systems, 1973.

O'Toole, R. (Ed.). *The Organization, Management, and Tactics of Social Research.* Cambridge, Mass.: Schenkman, 1971.

Pace, R., and others. *Higher Education Measurement and Evaluation Kit.* Los Angeles: Laboratory for Research on Higher Education, Graduate School of Education, University of California, 1975.

Palola, E., and Bradley, P. *Ten Out of Thirty*. Saratoga Springs, N.Y.: Office of Research and Evaluation, Empire State College, 1973.

Palola, E. G., and Lehmann, T. "Improving Student Outcomes and Institutional Decision-Making with PERC." In O. Lenning (Ed.), *New Directions for Higher Education: Improving Educational Outcomes,* no. 16. San Francisco: Jossey-Bass, 1976.

Palola, E., and Lehmann, T. "Evaluating External Degree Programs." *Peabody Journal of Education,* April 1979, *56,* 174-186.

Palola, E., and others. *The PERC Handbook.* Saratoga Springs, N.Y.: Office of Research and Evaluation, Empire State College, 1977.

Palola, E., and others. *The Uses of PERC.* Saratoga Springs, N.Y.: Office of Research and Evaluation, Empire State College, 1978.

Peterson, R., and Vale, C. *Strategies for Assessing Differential Institutional Effectiveness in Multi-Campus Systems.* Berkeley, Calif.: Educational Testing Service, 1973.

Sagen, H. B. "Student, Faculty, and Department Chairmen Ratings of Instructors: Who Agrees with Whom?" *Research in Higher Education,* 1974, *2,* 265-272.

Self-Assessment for Colleges and Universities: A Handbook for Self-Assessment. Albany, N.Y.: Office of Self-Assessment for Colleges and Universities, University of the State of New York, 1979.

Sieber, S. "The Integration of Fieldwork and Survey Methods." *American Journal of Sociology,* May 1973, *78,* 335-359.

Sikes, W. W., Schlesinger, L. E., and Seashore, C. N. *Renewing Higher Education from Within: A Guide for Campus Change Teams.* San Francisco: Jossey-Bass, 1974.

Solomon, L., and Ochsner, N. *New Findings on the Effects of College.* Washington, D.C.: American Association for Higher Education, 1978.

Stewart, W. "The Formation of the Early Adult Life Structure in Women." Unpublished doctoral dissertation, Teachers College, Columbia University, 1976.

Suchman, E. *Evaluative Research.* New York: Russell Sage Foundation, 1967.

Van Maanen, J. "The Process of Program Evaluation." *The Grantsmanship Center News,* January/February 1979, pp. 29-74.

Webb, E., and others. *Unobtrusive Measures: Nonreactive Research in the Social Sciences.* Chicago: Rand McNally, 1966.

Weiss, C. *Evaluation Research: Methods of Assessing Program Effectiveness.* Englewood Cliffs, N.J.: Prentice-Hall, 1972.

Whitla, D. "Progress Report on Value-Added Project." Unpublished paper, Office of Instructional Research and Evaluation, Harvard University, 1975.

Whitla, D. *Value Added: Measuring the Outcomes of Undergraduate Education.* Cambridge: Office of Instructional Research and Evaluation, Harvard University, 1977.

Whitla, D. "Student Growth During the College Years Can Be Measured." Unpublished paper, Office of Instructional Research and Evaluation, Harvard University, 1978.

Wilson, R., and others. *College Professors and Their Impact on Students.* New York: Wiley, 1975.

Conclusion

In introducing this volume, we argued that research and theory concerning human development and the life cycle can provide a unifying vision for higher education and lifelong learning. We proposed that colleges and universities intentionally encourage developmental change throughout the life cycle as their basic purpose. We noted that such an orientation is consistent with the traditional goals of higher education, can help address the major social challenges likely in the 1980s and beyond, can strengthen our capacity to achieve both immediate and long-range educational objectives, and can provide increased coherence and an enhanced sense of community, as well as shared effort on campus in achieving them.

In the preceding chapters, forty-six authors experienced in various aspects of higher education have considered the implications of human development as the overarching goal of higher education, discussing major facets of adult development in Part One, major disciplines and fields of professional preparation in Part Two, and major elements of the educational process in Part Three. Their conclusions suggest that such an overarching vision is workable, for their findings have significant implications for both the content and process of higher education. Applying what is known about human development to education will not only strengthen teaching and learning in the disciplines and professions but assure that other institutional services—from academic advising and career counseling to housing and program evaluation—contribute fully to learning and development.

Consensus on Development

To illustrate the importance of this knowledge about human development for education, Table 1 assembles in rough juxtaposition the major conceptual frameworks set

Table 1. Major Dimensions of Adult Development

Loevinger/ Weathersby — Ego Development	Perry — Intellectual and Ethical Development	Kohlberg/ Gilligan — Cognitive and Moral Development	Schaie/Parr — Development of Intelligence	Kolb — Learning Styles	Blocher/Rapoza — Professional/ Vocational Development	Torbert — Interpersonal Competence	Douvan — Capacity for Intimacy	White — Humanitarian Concern
Presocial/ symbiotic			Acquisitive	Acquisition	Approaching, receiving, accepting			
Impulsive	Position 1: dualism	Stage 1: fear of punishment by authority						
Self-protective	Position 2: dualism	Stage 2: bargaining with authority to gain reward, avoid punishment			Controlling, discriminating, attending	Mystery/ mastery: goal achievement, maximize winning, repress feeling		
Conformist	Position 3: multiplicity, prelegitimate	Stage 3: seeking good relations and approval of family group			Mastering, valuing, working			
Self-aware	Position 4: multiplicity	Stage 4: obedience to law and order in society		Specialization			Intimacy/self-exploration	

Conscientious	Positions 5 and 6: relativism	Stage 5: concern with individual rights and legal contract	Achieving role independence	Achieving, relating, organizing	Be rational	Empathy/interpersonal exploration	Empathy
Individualistic		Stage 6: concern with consistent, comprehensive ethical principles		Sexual relating, risk taking, value clarifying, objectifying, analyzing, concentrating, problem solving		Pursuit of autonomy	
Autonomous	Positions 7, 8, and 9: commitments in relativism		Responsible, executive	Accepting change, empathizing, valuing differences	Living inquiry: maximize information, free and informed choice, internal commitment	Nondefensive interaction	Principled humanitarian concern
Integrated			Reintegrative	Affiliating, recreating, personalizing self and past		Accept interdependence	

forth in Part One: the levels of ego development as conceptualized by Loevinger and interpreted by Weathersby, the stages of intellectual and ethical development as revealed by Perry, those of cognitive and moral development as conceived by Kohlberg and Gilligan, of intelligence as studied by Schaie and Parr, of learning styles as studied by Kolb, of professional and vocational development as examined by Blocher and Rapoza, of interpersonal competence as described by Torbert, of the capacity for intimacy as explained by Douvan, and of humanitarian concern as envisioned by White.

Of course, any attempt to convert the rich sets of ideas from these theories into specific positions on a two-dimensional grid runs the risk of implying an entirely unwarranted oversimplification. To combine these conceptual frameworks adequately would most likely require a complex, multisurfaced prism rather than a matrix, since the angles and planes of some theorists' ideas are more aligned than others. Nonetheless, their ideas all bear a relation to one another. Those of Loevinger and Weathersby, Perry, and Kohlberg and Gilligan, although different in significant ways, supply mutually reinforcing views of ego development, intellectual and cognitive development, and ethical or moral development. Similarly, Schaie and Parr, Kolb, and Blocher and Rapoza, while differing substantially in their substantive foci, posit similar developmental tasks. Torbert's conceptions of interpersonal competence are synergistic with Douvan's ideas about the capacity for intimacy and interdependence, and their views are consistent with White's ideas of empathy and self-extension as requirements for developing humanitarian concern.

Table 1, in short, demonstrates a great deal of internal consistency among these different theorists, each writing independently out of his or her own experience and research. Each has taken a different angle on adult development, each has sought to understand that development from a particular orientation, and each has looked at the phenomena through his or her own special theoretical lenses. Yet the combined result is a set of concepts with strong internal coherence and complementarity.

This complementarity raises a major possibility regarding adult development as the unifying purpose of higher education. It suggests that activities or experiences that encourage development in one area are likely to provoke or strengthen development in another. It points to the probability that whatever our particular tasks within our institutions, or the particular mission of our institutions, our efforts to aid one aspect of adult development can give us leverage on the whole. For example, if as teachers we address our task of developing intellectual competence—certainly fundamental to the role of higher education—in ways that help students move along the developmental continuum as set forth by Perry, we are likely to make a critical contribution to their ego development and to their moral and ethical development as set forth by Loevinger, Weathersby, Kohlberg, and Gilligan. If as counselors, professors, housing directors, or coordinators of off-campus learning we help students address the career development tasks posited by Blocher and Rapoza or the life cycle tasks summarized by Chickering and Havighurst, we tap sources of motivation that can stimulate the increased intellectual competence and more diverse orientations toward learning suggested by Schaie and Parr or Kolb. Thus, by seriously addressing one or two key dimensions we will not only serve their ego and moral or ethical development, we are likely to increase their intellectual development, their interpersonal competence, their capacity for intimacy, and the development of their humanitarian concerns. And whether in a community college, technical institute, field study station, or research university, if we intentionally create conditions where issues of humanitarian concern, interpersonal relationships, and interdependence are confronted, then we will be helping students move toward principled autonomy, integrity, and personal commitment—those higher stages of ego and moral development—and we will be enhancing their ability to cope with life cycle issues, including choosing a career, assuming civic responsibilities, and building sustaining relationships. Most importantly, all parts of our educational enterprise, all aspects of our college and university environments, can contribute to adult development.

Assuring Development

How can we assure this contribution to adult development? Table 2 suggests some answers. It builds on some ideas concerning orientations toward knowledge and institutional function developed by Harry Lasker and Cynthia De Windt at the Harvard Graduate School of Education and rests on a broad-based accumulation of research concerning college influences on student development. It posits relationships between the major dimensions of adult development outlined in Table 1 (represented here by only three columns—ego development, moral development, and the development of intelligence) and students' orientations toward knowledge, their learning processes, institutional teaching practices, student-teacher relationships, sources of evaluation, and overall institutional functions.

As with Table 1, the relationships between psychological characteristics and institutional practices that are suggested in Table 2 necessarily simplify and capsulize the substantial bodies of research evidence about institutional impacts that now exists, but they are consistent with this research as set forth in earlier chapters, both in Part One and by such authors in Part Three as Green, Menges, Clark, Duley, and the Gaffs. And just as each developmental stage listed in Table 1 incorporates and transforms earlier stages, so does each subsequent view of knowledge and institutional practice noted in Table 2.

The basic point made by Table 2 is that students' motives for learning, their orientations toward knowledge, and the educational practices of our institutions differ systematically in ways related to different levels of ego, moral, and intellectual development. As it illustrates, our motivation for education can expand as we develop psychologically from a concern for satisfying our immediate needs through that of gaining social acceptance, obtaining credentials and recognition, and meeting social responsibilities to deepening our understanding of ourselves and the world and developing increased ability to shape our own futures. Furthermore, this expanding motivation parallels other aspects of our psychological development. Similarly, our view of knowledge can increase from that of the possession of facts and objective truths to "know how" about problem solving and then to personally generated insights about ourselves and life, including the enjoyment rather than the fear of paradoxes. The value that we place on knowledge can expand from seeing it as a means to concrete ends and for social approval to a means for achieving our own standards of excellence and for our own self-development and self-transformation. Our sources of knowledge can expand from the precepts of external authority to conclusions based on rational inquiry and finally to personally generated insights and judgments. And our learning processes can increase from imitation to the discovery of correct answers through scientific methods and logical analysis and finally to seeking new experiences, developing new paradigms, and creating new dialectics of thought and vision.

The major failure of most colleges and universities is their orientation toward only one or two of these developmental and learning levels—primarily the simpler levels—although their students span the full range of development. That is, the educational practices and resources at most institutions are almost exclusively oriented toward the self-protective, opportunistic, and conformist levels of ego development, the obedience-punishment-oriented and approval-oriented levels of moral development, the acquisitive

Table 2. Adult Development and Higher Education

Ego Development	Moral Development	Intellectual Development	Motive for Education	View of Knowledge	Uses of Knowledge
Self-protective/opportunistic	Obedience-punishment oriented; dualism	Acquisitive	Instrumental; satisfy immediate needs	A possession that helps one get desired ends; ritualistic actions that yield solutions	Education to get: means to concrete ends; used by self to obtain effects in the world
Conformist	Instrumental egoism, exchange, and approval ("good boy") oriented; multiplicity		Impress significant others; gain social acceptance; obtain credentials and recognition	Objective truth given by authority; general information required for social roles	Education to be: social approval, appearance, status used by self to achieve according to expectations and standards of significant others
Conscientious	Authority, rule, and social-order oriented; relativism	Achieving role independence	Achieve competence re competitive or normative standards; increase capacity to meet social responsibilities	"Know how": personal skills in problem solving; divergent views resolved by rational processes	Education to do: competence in work and social role; used to achieve internalized standards of excellence and to serve society
Autonomous	Social contract and legalistic oriented	Responsible, executive	Deepen understanding of self, world, and life cycle; develop increasing capacity to manage own destiny	Personally generated insight about self and nature of life; subjective and dialectical; paradox appreciated	Education to become: self-knowledge; self-development; used to transform self and the world
Integrated	Moral principle oriented; commitments in relativism	Reintegrative			

Sources of Knowledge	Learning Processes	Teaching Practices	Student-Faculty Relationships	Source of Evaluation	Institutional Function
From external authority; from asking how to get things	Imitation; acquire information, competence, as given by authority	Lecture-examination system	Teacher is authority, transmitter, judge; student is receiver, judged	By teacher only	Arouse attention and maintain interest; show how things should be done
From external authority; from asking what others expect and how to do it		Teacher-led dialogue or discussion		By teacher only	Provide predetermined information and training programs; certify skills and knowledge
		Open, "leaderless," "learner-centered" discussion	Teacher is a "model" for student identification	By teacher and peers	
Personal integration of information based on rational inquiry; from setting goals; from asking what is needed, how things work, and why	Discover correct answers through scientific method and logical analyses; multiple views recognized but congruence and simplicity sought	Programmed learning; correspondence study; televised instruction	"Teacher" is abstraction behind system; student is recipient	By system	Provide structured programs that offer concrete skills and information, opportunities for rational analysis, and practice, all of which can be evaluated and certified
Personal experience and reflection; personally generated paradigms, insights, judgments	Seek new experiences; reorganize past conceptions on the basis of new experiences; develop new paradigms; create new dialectics	Contract learning with objectives, time, activities, and evaluation negotiated between student and teacher at the outset and held throughout	Teacher is resource contributing to planning and evaluation; student defines purposes	By teacher, peers, system, and self, with teacher the final judge	Ask key questions; pose key dilemmas; confront significant discontinuities and paradoxes; foster personal experience and personally generated insights
		Contract learning with objectives, time, activities, and evaluation defined generally by the student and modified with experience	Teacher has colleagial relationship with student; student defines purposes and criteria for evaluation	By teacher, peers, system, and self, with self the final judge	

level of intellectual development, the elementary conceptions of knowledge, and preadult learning processes. They put a premium on memorization and on getting right words in the right order. They treat knowledge and learning as though they were commodities—collections of discrete, fragmented items, packaged in standard-sized boxes, and sold by the Carnegie unit. The supermarket is their dominant metaphor; marketing experts discuss next year's "offerings" in the light of shifting student interests and academic styles; and students accumulate credits to exchange at commencement for the receipt of a degree.

Consider any ten institutions at random. How many curriculums, courses, classes, and examinations help students build knowledge from personal experiences and personally generated syntheses and paradigms, rather than treating truth as objectively real, given by authority or "discovered" by logical or scientific analyses? How many teachers not only help students acquire basic concepts, competence, and knowledge but also help them apply this learning through responsible action or use these ideas to make better sense of life and of themselves and generate their own personal insights through subjective and dialectical processes? And how many students, as a result, conceive of the nature of knowledge—where it comes from and how it can be used—as acquiring information or competence in order to satisfy immediate needs, obtain recognition, do a job, or fill a role, rather than as the process of becoming and transforming themselves? Consider, in contrast, the range of options open to institutions in encouraging further development by means of all their policies and procedures, as illustrated by the four examples in Table 2: teaching practices, student-faculty relationships, sources of evaluation, and basic institutional functions.

Teaching Practices. As typically conducted, the lecture-examination system best suits the opportunistic and conformist levels of students' ego development, the obedience-punishment and dualistic levels of their moral development, and the acquisitive stage of their intellectual development. The key dynamic is the comfortable fit between, on the one hand, the students' disposition to identify with persons in authority, to accept their definitions of right and wrong, and to avoid punishment by deferring to their power, and, on the other hand, the teachers' easy assertion of authority, emphasis on dispensing information for students to memorize, and use of examinations to punish wrong answers and reward right ones.

Most Socratic dialogue or teacher-led discussions best fit the conformist and approval-oriented levels of ego and moral development. They provide rich information about the teacher's views, and they permit students to shape their own responses accordingly, receiving immediate rewards through the satisfying exchanges that result. "Leaderless," learner-centered discussions usually fit best the more group-approval-oriented level, where openness, helping others, and acceptance of group decisions are called for. And when the lecture-examination system goes beyond the personal authority of the teacher and makes use of the more abstract authorities of textbooks or programmed learning materials, the teaching approach moves toward the conscientious, authority-, rule-, and social-order-oriented levels of development, where the "system" in general defines right and wrong.

Contract learning, in contrast, unless it is teacher-dominated, seems applicable to the advanced levels of development, but in two different forms. In one form, both the student and the teacher negotiate and agree on the objectives, the timing, and the activities of learning as well as the criteria for evaluating the learning; and their contract is a commitment to this plan, which is followed unless major events call for its renegotiation. This approach to contract learning best fits the autonomous stage of ego development, the social contract and legalistic stage of moral development, and the responsible, executive stage of intellectual development. In the second form, the student, with or without help from the teacher and others, defines the learning objectives, timing, and activities, and the criteria for evaluation. The contract may be quite specific or very general, but it is treated flexibly and modified in the light of experience. This approach best fits the integrated and moral principle levels of ego and moral development and the reintegrative stage of intellectual development, where the student is virtually if not completely self-sufficient and relies on a mentor more for colleagueship than for assistance and assessment.

Of course, contract learning can be highly teacher-controlled and authoritarian, not only in terms of learning activities and evaluation, but also in terms of the purposes judged acceptable. Furthermore, skilled teachers can use lectures and exams, seminars, and group discussions in ways that challenge autonomous students and also serve opportunistic, conformist, and conscientious ones. The assertions just made rest on studies of student responses to typical teaching practices. There are exceptional teachers, courses, classes, seminars, and discussion groups. Most of us have experienced them, but they are exceptions to the general fare.

Student-Faculty Relationships. The different teaching practices described previously typically define different patterns of student-faculty interaction. The teacher as authority, transmitter of information, and judge, carrying sole responsibility for evaluation, best fits the self-protective and opportunistic stage of ego development and the obedience-punishment level of moral development. The teacher as a model who is known well enough to permit student identification and who includes a student's peers in evaluation fits the approval-oriented stage. The teacher as mentor and resource, who helps students clarify objectives, identify appropriate materials and educational experiences, plan a course of action, and evaluate progress, as in the first form of contract learning, best fits the autonomous and social contract levels, while a collegial relation, wherein the student carries the primary responsibility for defining the contract and for evaluation, exemplifies the integrated and moral principle stages.

Source of Evaluation. In assessing student achievement, the judgments move from external to internal: first, from the teacher alone as the parental authority figure; later from the teacher and fellow students; from the teaching system at large, as in standardized norm-referenced or criterion-referenced tests; from all sources including the student; and ultimately from the student, based on all other sources of evidence. In this process, assessments tend to become more differentiated and focused. At the early levels, they often involve a simple "yes-no" judgment—true-false, pass-fail, or credit-flunk. Subsequently, the assessment is more specific: B+, 82 percent correct, 74th percentile. And ultimately it is detailed and qualified, as in narrative transcripts, written comments on papers, and conversation.

Institutional Function. All elements of institutional life, from freshman orientation to out-of-class activities, governance structures, and administrative styles communicate educational messages to students—messages about themselves, about what is expected of them and what they are to expect of themselves, and about life and the role of learning in it. These messages form the "hidden curriculum" that underlies the academic curriculum and, even though unrecognized and undiscussed, supports or negates its efforts. Together they distinguish the ethos of one institution from another as clearly as course offerings or campus architecture. At an elemental level, they convey the institution's basic function as that of arousing students' attention and maintaining their interest in education—but not much more. At a higher level, the institution functions as an information-processing, certifying, and credentialing agency. But above that, it can open opportunities for analysis and practice both on campus and off; and ultimately it can challenge students to confront dilemmas and paradoxes themselves and rely on their total experience and their own abilities for continued self-development.

The relationships that Table 2 posits between adult development and these institutional functions and procedures suggest a way of thinking about educational processes that will strengthen our capacity to enhance students' development throughout the life cycle: We can modify our typical institutional practices in directions that recognize developmental diversity and help students at each stage move toward higher levels. Every institution will enroll students at all of these developmental levels. Because of this diversity, it cannot simply pitch its educational program at any one particular stage. Many opportunistic and conformist students come to higher education with important, immediate, and instrumental purposes that deserve to be met, and these purposes should not be ignored. These students should not be turned away or turned off. But their needs will not be fully served if they are not helped to see more clearly the dynamics of the developmental stages that affect them or if they are not aided in growing more autonomous and principled. Alternatives need to be created that serve students at all levels. Institutions must be responsive to the full range of developmental stages and learning styles brought to them by the students they aim to serve.

For example, few institutions can or should operate exclusively through contract learning aimed at students already functioning at complex levels of development. But at the same time, other institutions need not restrict their lectures and examination, seminars, and group discussions to perpetuating less complex ways of thinking and behaving. These teaching methods can be used far more than they have been to raise powerful questions; expose unfettered relativism; challenge dualistic thinking; and foster principled autonomy, commitments in relativism, and responsible, executive, and reintegrative levels of intellectual development. To do so, however, faculty members must learn to be authoritative without being authoritarian, and teachers and staff members must enter upon collegial relationships with students as resource persons while at the same time remaining originators of critical appraisal and thoughtful evaluation. Assessment practices can increasingly involve student self-evaluation and detailed, specific, external evaluation. And throughout all their activities, institutions can challenge students to discover more ways of learning rather than merely demanding and certifying their learning.

Cool Passion

As college administrators and policy makers, we can examine Tables 1 and 2 in light of the earlier chapters from which they are drawn, and we can ask ourselves how our current students are distributed across these various stages of development and approaches to learning. We can ask how our current educational practices and procedures serve all these stages, as well as what changes of practice and procedure are needed to serve them better. As faculty members, we can ask how our own teaching methods, our reading and writing assignments, our field study experiences, our examination questions, and, indeed, our basic expectations for student performance relate to the current developmental stages and life cycle tasks of our students, as well as to those stages we seek to encourage. And as department members and curriculum planners, we can ask how our degree programs, course offerings, extracurricular opportunities, and even our criteria for student honors and achievement are appropriate to students' needed development. And then we must have the passion or the will to make the necessary changes.

Hegel, in his *Philosophy of Universal History,* asserts that passion is responsible for all significant historical accomplishments. But he emphasizes cool passion. Frenzied, unbridled passion, whether in love or work, seldom serves us well. Indeed, it often harms more than helps. To be enflamed, carried away, by an affection, ideology, or cause is easy, but such a state shrinks from reflective thought, public scrutiny, and tough-minded testing. Maintaining a steady fire that is critical as well as creative is more difficult, especially when it suffers frequent doses of icy logic and frigid resistance. Cool passion seeks fulfillment by joining the forces of heart and mind, commitment and critical analysis. Such passion pursues its purposes with "tenuous tenacity," as Tom Yakhub, a wise Indian teacher of mine, used to say.

It is this tone and orientation of cool passion that we need in reforming our policies and procedures to support adult development more fully, and it is this tone and orientation that my coauthors and I have sought to achieve in this volume. All of us share a passionate concern for higher education; yet we must seek to modernize our institutions by underpinning our passion with theory and analysis. By building on advances in knowledge about adult development, we can apply cool passion to reform and, in so doing, expand the civilizing role of the American college of the future.

Name Index

Subject Index